Symbol of tradition and progress

in directory publishing

DIRECTORIES of ORGANISATIONS

* Centres, Bureaux and Research Institutes — since 1987
* Councils, Committees and Boards — since 1970
* Directory of British Associations & Associations in Ireland — since 1965
  (also available on CD-Rom)
* Directory of European Industrial and Trade Associations — since 1971
* Directory of European Medical Organisations — since 1993
* Directory of European Professional and Learned Societies — since 1975
* Pan-European Associations — since 1983

GUIDES to COMPANY INFORMATION

* African Companies: Guide to Sources — since 1997
* Asian & Australian Companies: Guide to sources — since 1993
* European Companies: Guide to sources — since 1961

DIRECTORIES of DIRECTORIES

* Current British Directories — since 1953
* Current European Directories — since 1969

GUIDE to SOURCES of STATISTICS

* Statistics Africa — since 1970
* Statistics America — since 1973
* Statistics Asia & Australasia — since 1974
* Statistics Europe — since 1968

We welcome your enquiries

CBD Research Ltd

15 Wickham Road, Beckenham, Kent, BR3 5JS

Tel: 020 8650 7745 **Fax:** 020 8650 0768

E-mail: cbd@cbdresearch.com

www.cbdresearch.com

Centres, Bureaux & Research Institutes

the directory of UK concentrations
of effort, information and expertise

Edition 5

CBD Research Ltd

15 Wickham Rd, Beckenham, Kent BR3 5JS, England
Tel: 020 8650 7745   Fax: 020 8650 0768
Email: cbd@cbdresearch.com www.cbdresearch.com

062
CON

First Published	1987
Edition 5	2008
Copyright ©	2008 CBD Research Ltd
Published by	CBD Research Ltd

15 Wickham Road, Beckenham, Kent, BR3 5JS, England

Telephone: 020 8650 7745   E-mail: cbd@cbdresearch.com
Fax: 020 8650 0768   Internet: www.cbdresearch.com
UK Registered Company No. 700855

ISBN	0 900246 98 7
Price	£167.50 US$340.00

No payment is either solicited or accepted for the inclusion of entries in this publication. Every possible precaution has been taken to ensure that the information it contains is accurate at the time of going to press and the publishers cannot accept any liability for errors or omissions however caused.

CBD Research Ltd   are founder members of the Data Publishers Association (DPA) and the European Association of Directory Publishers, and are pledged to a strict code of professional practice designed to protect against fraudulent directory publishing and dubious selling methods.

Our membership of the DPA is your guarantee that this publication is comprehensive, authentic and reliable.

Printing and binding: Polestar Wheatons Ltd.

CONTENTS

*NOTE: the explanations of abbreviations are repeated inside
the front and back covers.

© CBD Research Ltd · Beckenham · BR3 5JS · Tel 020 8650 7745 · Fax 020 8650 0768 · E-mail cbd@cbdresearch.com · www.cbdresearch.com   iii

INTRODUCTION

1. 'Centres, Bureaux & Research Institutes' contains information on major organisations, most of which include 'Centre' or 'Bureau' or 'Institute' in their names.
    Some, such as WRc (formerly the Water Research Centre) or RAB Services (formerly the Radio Advertising Bureau) are now known purely by their initials, but continue to perform their former functions and so are still included.

2. This Directory answers such questions as:
    – What is the function of BIRTHA?
    – How can I contact the Centre for Tourism and Cultural Change?
    – Which organisations are conducting research into climate change?

3. Questionnaires were sent to the organisations listed, via post, fax and electronic mail, and the courtesy of those who responded is acknowledged by the symbol ■ preceding their addresses. In the cases of multiple organisations, information was obtained from or checked with the co-ordinating body (see paragraph 7).

4. For those that did not reply, various techniques were used to check details. Most were contacted directly, either by telephone or electronic mail. The Editor would particularly like to acknowledge the helpfulness and patience of the university switchboard operators who confirmed or updated the contact details for centres within their institutions.

5. 'Centres, Bureaux & Research Institutes' lists bodies which are concentrations of effort or expertise, or which provide information to the general public. Many of those listed conduct commissioned research for relevant industries, or provide services for specific customers.
    The Directory does not list concert, conference or exhibition centres, unless they are nationally known.
    It also excludes the many shopping centres, community centres and other local organisations and retail outlets throughout the country.

6. CBRI is arranged in the following sections:
    i) The Main Entries, which disregard alphabetisation of prepositions, articles and conjunctions, i.e.:
    Institute [of] Community Cohesion
    Institute [for] Community and Primary Care Research
    ii) Abbreviations Index - a list of generally used initials, acronyms or other short forms of the official names of organisations.
    iii) Index of sponsors and host / participating bodies - an alphabetical index of universities, colleges and other bodies listing the Centres, Bureaux and Institutes which they host or support.
    iv) Subject index - an index to the fields of interest of the organisations listed. Some scientific bodies, e.g. the Centre for Science and Technology in Medicine, conduct such a wide range of research that it is impractical to include them under every relevant subject heading; therefore they are just listed under their principal areas of interest.

7. Form of Entry
   Ideally, we include the following information for each entry in the Directory:
       Name of organisation.
       Abbreviation (in parentheses) by which the organisation is generally known.
       Year of establishment.
   ■ Validity indicator showing that either a completed questionnaire or current brochure was returned.
       Address, telephone and facsimile numbers.
       Website addresses.
       (Please note that not all website addresses begin with 'www'. If this prefix does not appear in an address, this is an intentional exclusion, not a typing error.)
       Names and designations of senior staff.
   E Establishment details including names of organisations or individual(s) responsible, where given; membership information is also given where appropriate.
   O Objectives for which the Centre, Bureau or Institute was established.
   ● Activities and services indicating the methods by which these objectives are achieved, and including other relevant data such as opening hours, facilities available to visitors, etc.
   ¶ Publications - including both regular publications and one-off titles.
   X Previous name(s); names of organisations which have been absorbed or have changed their names.
   Notes containing items not appropriate to the above fields.

8. Composite entries
   Certain categories, such as Buddhist Centres and Citizens' Advice Bureaux, are described in general terms which indicate their functions, who is responsible for them, etc.
   Either a list follows this description, or reference is made to a readily available source of information, often the Yellow Pages directories.

9. Enquiries and Suggestions
   The publishers welcome suggestions for inclusion in future editions of the Directory.
   Our records are constantly reviewed and updated, and we are glad to answer enquiries (preferably via post, fax or electronic mail) from anyone seeking relevant information which is not listed in this book.

10. Other sources of information
    Many of the organisations listed in this Directory are sponsored by associations and councils. Details of these are available in the CBD companion volumes 'Directory of British Associations and Associations in Ireland' and 'Councils, Committees and Boards'.
    Institutes which are primarily membership bodies (e.g. the Chartered Institute of Marketing) are listed in the 'Directory of British Associations'.

11. Acknowledgements
    The Editor acknowledges, with thanks, the assistance of all those who returned up-to-date information.

Beckenham
October 2007

SYMBOLS and ABBREVIATIONS

■   Validity indicator – shows that a completed questionnaire or brochure was returned

Br   Branch(es)

E   Establishment details

○   Objects of Centre, Bureau or Institute

●   Activities, facilities, services, availability

¶   Publications

X   Former name

q.v.   quod vide – which see

Degrees etc., after personal names are given in the form in which they were communicated to us.

Aber BioCentre
  see **Aberystwyth BioCentre.**

Aberdeen Centre for Energy Regulation and Obesity   (ACERO)
■   Robert Gordon University, Schoolhill, Aberdeen, AB10 1FR.
       01224 262000; 262728
       http://www.rgu.ac.uk/acero/
E   A research centre at Robert Gordon University.
○   To promote collaboration between scientists who have interests in the study of energy balance and regulation in the context of the
       development of obesity

Aberdeen Centre for Environmental Sustainability   (ACES)
■   King's College, University of Aberdeen, Aberdeen, AB24 3FX.
       01224 273978
       http://www.aces.ac.uk/
E   A research centre at the University of Aberdeen.
○   To carry out research to tackle the problem of environmental conflict where too much demand is placed on resources by
       consumers
Note: A collaborative venture with the Macaulay Institute.

Aberdeen Centre for Trauma Research   (ACTR)
■   Faculty of Health and Social Care, Robert Gordon University, Garthdee Road, Garthdee, Aberdeen, AB10 7QG.
       01224 263080   fax 01224 263053
       http://www.rgu.ac.uk/fhsc/
E   A research centre at Robert Gordon University.

Aberdeen Institute for Coastal Science and Management   (AICSM)   2002
■   College of Physical Sciences, Fraser Noble Building, King's College, University of Aberdeen, Old Aberdeen, AB24 3UE.
       01224 273856; 274474   fax 01224 272331
       http://www.abdn.ac.uk/aicsm/
       Director: Prof W Ritchie.
E   A research institute at the University of Aberdeen.
○   To conduct multidisciplinary research, training and consultancy with a clear focus on the coastal zone, broadly defined
●   Education and training

Abertay Centre for the Environment   (ACE)
■   Kydd Building, University of Abertay Dundee, Bell Street, Dundee, DD1 1HG.
       01382 308170
       http://www.ace.abertay.ac.uk/
       Director: Mary Cowie.
E   A research centre at the University of Abertay, Dundee.
○   To facilitate free environmental knowledge transfer and business support to small and medium-sized enterprises in Eastern
       Scotland
●   Consultancy

Aberystwyth BioCentre   (ABC)   1998
■   Edward Llwyd Building, Institute of Biological Sciences, University of Wales Aberystwyth, Aberystwyth, Ceredigion, SY23 3DA.
       01970 622316   fax 01970 622350
       http://www.aber.ac.uk/biology/
       Executive Officer: Mrs Jane Watts.
E   A research centre within the Institute of Biological Sciences (qv) at the University of Wales, Aberystwyth.
○   To conduct both leading edge and near market research to meet the economic and social needs of Wales, the UK and the rest of
       the world, by bringing together its three constituent Institutes - the BBSRC Institute of Grassland and Environmental Research, the
       Institute of Biological Sciences, and the Institute of Rural Sciences, (qqv)
Note: Often referred to as the Aber BioCentre.

Ability Net
■   PO Box 94, Warwick, CV34 5WS.
       01926 312847   fax 01926 407425
       http://www.abilitynet.org.uk/
E   A registered charity.
○   To provide advice and information on adaptive computer technology for people with disabilities
¶   Series of Factsheets and Skillsheets.

Able Children's Education Centre
see **Brunel Able Children's Education Centre.**

Academic Centre for Clinical Orthopaedics
see **Centre for Academic Clinical Orthopaedics.**

Academic Centre for Defence Mental Health   (ACDMH)   2004
■   King's College London, Strand, London, WC2R 2LS.
020 7848 5257
http://www.kcl.ac.uk/projects/acdmh/
Director: Prof Simon Wessely. Administrator: Randalle Roberts.
E   A research centre and part of the King's Centre for Military Health Research (qv) at King's College, London.
O   To be a resource of research excellence and expertise within Defence Medical Services (DMS) Mental Health Services (MHS) and to act as a catalyst for the promotion of a strong research-based culture within DMSMHS

Academic Centre for Travel Medicine and Vaccines
■   Department of Infection, Windeyer Building, University College London, 46 Cleveland Street, London, W1T 4JF.
020 7679 9153
http://www.ucl.ac.uk/medicalschool/
E   A research centre within the Centre for Medical Microbiology (qv) at University College London.
Note: The Centre is a World Health Organisation **WHO Collaborating Centre** for Reference, Research and Training in Travel Medicine.

Academic Development Institute   (ADI)
■   3 Winton Square, Staffordshire University, College Road, Stoke-on-Trent, ST4 2DF.
01782 294752
http://www.staffs.ac.uk/uniservices/adi/index.php
Head: Steve Wyn Williams.
E   A department of Staffordshire University.

Accelerator Science and Technology Centre   (ASTeC)   2001
■   Daresbury Laboratory, Daresbury, Warrington, Cheshire, WA4 4AD.
01925 603000   fax 01925 603192
http://www.astec.ac.uk/
Director: Mike Poole.
E   A research centre within the Council for the Central Laboratory of the Research Councils (CCLRC).
O   To carry out a variety of programmes of research and design in the field of accelerator science and technology

Access Grid Support Centre   (AGSC)
■   Kilburn Building, University of Manchester, Oxford Road, Manchester, M13 9PL.
0161-275 5997
http://www.agsc.ja.net/
E   A centre at the University of Manchester.
O   To improve the user experience of Access Grid through enhanced quality and robust, resilience services where people in different places can meet in a 'virtual venue' using audio and video tools, and other shared applications, such as presentations
Note: See **e-Science Centres** for further information.

Accounting Centre Ltd
Note: is a payroll service provider called Payplus and is therefore outside the scope of this Directory.

Acoustics Research Centre   (ARC)
■   Faculty of Business, Law and the Built Environment, Maxwell Building, University of Salford, Salford, Manchester, M5 4WT.
0161-295 5684   fax 0161-295 4442
http://www.buhu.salford.ac.uk/research_centres/acoustics/
Director: Prof Yiu Wai Lam.
E   A research centre within the Research Institute for the Built and Human Environment (qv) at the University of Salford.
O   To conduct research into various fields of acoustics including building and architectural acoustics, environmental acoustics, outdoor sound propagation, remote acoustic sensing of meteorological conditions, subjective response, especially for room acoustics and audio systems

Active Birth Centre   (ABC)   1985
■   25 Bickerton Road, London, N19 5JT.
020 7281 6760   fax 020 7263 8098
http://www.activebirthcentre.com/
Director: Janet Balaskas.
E   An independent non-profit-distributing organisation.
O   To provide a context in which parents-to-be can explore alternatives, increase self-awareness and understanding in order to have the best possible experience of pregnancy, labour and birth; to promote understanding of the normal physiology of labour, birth and breastfeeding; to encourage women to discover their instinctive potential for giving birth and to develop ease in the upright and supported postures natural to labour and birth
●   Active birth teachers' training course - Water-birth pool hire and sales service - Active birth comfort kit, books, tapes, videos and aromatherapy products - Consulting and meeting rooms Seminars and workshops - Information service

Active Learning in Computing: Centre for Excellence in Teaching and Learning   (ALiC)   2005
NR   Department of Computer Science, Science Laboratories, University of Durham, South Road, Durham, DH1 3LE.
         0191-334 1708   fax 0191-334 1701
         http://www.dur.ac.uk/alic/
E   A Centre for Excellence in Teaching and Learning (CETL) at the University of Durham.
○   To increase levels of students' engagement in the curriculum through the delivery of effective approaches, assessments and tools
         supporting active learning techniques
Note: A co-operative venture with the Universities of Leeds, Leeds Metropolitan and Newcastle upon Tyne.

Actors Centre   1980
■   1A Tower Street, London, WC2H 9NP.
         020 7240 3940
         http://www.actorscentre.co.uk/
         Artistic Director: Matthew Lloyd. General Manager: Tamsin Stanley.
E   A registered charity and association with c 2,500 individual members
○   To provide continuing professional development training for actors; to enable the pursuit of excellence by promoting high artistic
         standards across the profession
●   Education and training - Studio theatre
¶   Class Brochure.

Actuarial Research Centre   (ARC)
■   Cass Business School, City University, 106 Bunhill Row, London, EC1Y 8TZ.
         020 7040 8470   fax 020 7040 8572
         http://www.cass.city.ac.uk/arc/index.html
         Programme Manager: Ernest Eng.
E   A centre at City University.
○   To conduct theoretical and applied research in risk for actuarial science and insurance in the fields of health and care, life
         insurance, mortality, non-life insurance, and pensions

Acumedic Centre for Chinese Medicine   1972
■   101-105 Camden High Street, London, NW1 7JN.
         020 7388 5783   fax 020 7387 5766
         http://www.acumedic.com/
E   A profit-making business.
○   To integrate Eastern and Western medical knowledge with Chinese medicine under a system of preventive health care, aiming to
         help the body to reach its optimum state
●   Education and training - Exhibitions

Acupuncture Research Resource Centre   (ARRC)   1994
■   Faculty of Health and Human Sciences, Walpole House, Thames Valley University, 18-22 Bond Street, London, W5 5AA.
         020 8280 5123; 5176   fax 020 8280 5308
         http://www.cchim.com/chi/cam/index.htm
         Director: Prof Nicola Robinson.
E   A research centre within the Centre for Complementary Healthcare and Integrated Medicine (qv) at Thames Valley University.
○   To provide good quality research and information on acupuncture; to promote research amongst practitioners; to increase
         awareness of the role and effectiveness of acupuncture
●   Information service

Adam Smith Institute   (ASI)   1977
■   23 Great Smith Street, London, SW1P 3BL.
         020 7222 4995   fax 020 7222 7544
         http://www.adamsmith.org
         President: Dr Madsen Pirie. Director: Dr Eamonn Butler
E   An independent non-profit-distributing organisation.
○   To promote research into market economies and to develop viable market-based policies for Government; to explore new ways of
         extending choice, opportunity and competition into public services, and produce practical policy strategies; to introduce
         innovative ideas into public policy debate
●   Conference facilities
¶   Road Map to Reform [series of 4 on Deregulation, Education, Health, and Tax]. Flat Tax.

Address Management Centre   (AMC)
■   Royal Mail, Freepost SCO 5731, Edinburgh, EH12 9PG.
         http://www.royalmail.com/portal/rm/
E   A Government owned organisation and part of the Royal Mail.
○   To manage and develop the Postcode Address File (PAF), the Royal Mail database of all known addresses in the UK; to promote
         correct addressing and postcode use; to ensure that both business and social customers receive address management
         information

Adelphi Research Institute for Creative Arts and Sciences (ARICAS)
- Faculty of Arts, Media and Social Sciences, Peru Street, University of Salford, Salford, Manchester, M3 6EQ.
  0161-295 2801
  http://www.adelphi.salford.ac.uk/
  Director: Prof Rachel Cooper.
- E   A department of the University of Salford.
- O   To bring together academics who work in arts and humanities, social science and science

Aditya V Birla India Centre
- London Business School, Sussex Place, Regent's Park, London, NW1 4SA.
  020 7000 7000   fax 020 7000 7001
  http://www.london.edu/birlaindiacentre.html
- E   A research centre at the London Business School.
- O   To investigate India's role in the global economy

Adjudication Reporting Centre
- School of the Built and Natural Environment, Glasgow Caledonian University, Cowcaddens Road, Glasgow, G4 0BA.
  0141-273 1366
  http://www.adjudication.gcal.ac.uk/
  Director: Peter Kennedy.
- E   A research centre at Glasgow Caledonian University.
- O   To monitor the use of adjudication by the construction industry

ADULT EDUCATION CENTRES
Note: Adult Education Centres are provided by most local authorities and offer a wide range of daytime, evening and weekend courses covering vocational and leisure activities.

Advanced Biotechnology Centre (ABC)
- Faculty of Life Sciences, Sir Alexander Fleming Building (2nd Floor), Imperial College London, Exhibition Road, London, SW7 2AZ.
  020 7594 3000   fax 020 7594 3123
  http://www.imperial.ac.uk/advancedbiotechnologycentre/
  Chairman: Prof Tony Magee.
- E   A research centre at Imperial College London.
- O   To provide DNA sequencing and genotyping services, peptide synthesis and conjugation services

Advanced Centre for Biochemical Engineering (ACBE)
- Department of Biochemical Engineering, University College London, Torrington Place, London, WC1E 7JE.
  020 7679 7031   fax 020 7209 0703
  http://www.ucl.ac.uk/biochemeng/
- E   A research centre at University College London.

Advanced Centre in Drawing (ACID) 2002
- Bristol School of Art, Media and Design, Bower Ashton Campus, University of the West of England, Kennel Lodge Road, Bristol, BS3 2JT.
  0117-328 4716   fax 0117-328 4745
  http://www.acid.uwe.ac.uk/
  Director: Prof John France.
- E   A research centre at the University of the West of England.
- O   To promote drawing, in the widest manner

Advanced Composites and Coatings Research Centre (ACCRC)
- City Campus, Sheffield Hallam University, Sheffield, S1 1WB.
  0114-225 3500   fax 0114-225 3501
  http://www.shu.ac.uk/research/meri/centres/acc_rc.html
  Head: Prof Chris Breen.
- E   A constituent research centre within the Materials and Engineering Research Institute (qv) at Sheffield Hallam University.
- O   To conduct research in the processing, characterisation and use of advanced nanostructural materials

Advanced Composites Manufacturing Centre (ACMC) 1987
- School of Engineering, University of Plymouth, Drake Circus, Plymouth, PL4 8AA.
  01752 232651   fax 01752 232705
  http://www.tech.plymouth.ac.uk/sme/acmc/index.htm
  Project Manager: Richard Cullen.
- E   A research centre at the University of Plymouth.
- O   To conduct research and provide consultancy in all aspects of the manufacture of advanced composite materials

Advanced Computing Research Centre (ACRC)
- Faculty of Engineering, Senate House, University of Bristol, Tyndall Avenue, Bristol, BS8 1TH.
  0117-954 5163   fax 0117-954 5208
  http://www.cs.bris.ac.uk/Research/Advanced/
  Contact: Prof Nigel Smart.
- E   A department of the University of Bristol.
- O   To provide a focus for research into advanced computing systems

Advanced Concrete and Masonry Centre   (ACM)
■   Department of Civil, Structural and Environmental Engineering, University of Paisley, Paisley, PA1 2BE.
     0141-848 3279   fax 0141-848 3275
     http://www.acmcentre.com/
E   A research centre at the University of Paisley.
Note: At the time of going to press, the University of Paisley was preparing to merge with Bell College to form the University of the West of Scotland.

Advanced Design and Manufacturing Engineering Centre   (ADMEC)
■   School of Architecture, Design and the Built Environment, Nottingham Trent University, City Site, Nottingham, NG1 4BU.
     0115-848 2045
     http://www.ntu.ac.uk/research/school_research/sbe/34545gp.html
     Contact: Prof Daizhong Su.
E   A research centre at Nottingham Trent University.
O   To focus on research and consultancy activities in design and manufacturing technologies, with particular emphasis on design engineering, advanced manufacturing technology, and engineering mechanics

Advanced Institute of Management Research   (AIM)   2002
■   London Business School, 6-16 Huntsworth Mews, London, NW1 6DD.
     0870 734 3000
     http://www.aimresearch.org/
     Director: Prof Robin Wensley.
E   An ESRC funded research centre at the London Business School.
O   To significantly increase the contribution of and future capacity for world class UK research on management

Advanced Institute of Multimedia and Network Systems
     see **Brunel Advanced Institute of Multimedia and Network Systems.**

Advanced Manufacturing Research Centre   (AMRC)
■   University of Sheffield, Wallis Way, Catcliffe, Rotherham, South Yorkshire, S60 5TZ.
     0114-222 1747   fax 0114-222 7678
     http://www.amrc.co.uk/
     Commercial director: Adrian Allen.
E   A research centre at the University of Sheffield.
O   To develop innovative and advanced technology solutions for advanced materials forming

Advanced Manufacturing Technology Research Institute (CBRI)   (AMTRI)   1960
■   Hulley Road, Macclesfield, Cheshire, SK10 2NE.
     01625 425421   fax 01625 412540
     http://www.amtri.co.uk/
E   A fully commercial engineering company.
O   To supply bespoke machinery, automation systems and specialist technical services to the manufacturing sector in the UK and worldwide

Advanced Materials and Biomaterials Research Centre   (AMBRC)
■   School of Engineering, Clarke Building, Robert Gordon University, Schoolhill, Aberdeen, AB10 1FR.
     01224 262822   fax 01224 262837
     http://www.rgu.ac.uk/eng/ambrc/
     Director: Prof R H Bradley.
E   A research centre at the Robert Gordon University.

Advanced Materials Centre   (AMC)   2001
■   School of Engineering and Physical Science, University of Dundee, Dundee, DD1 4HN.
     01382 344912   fax 01382 348313
     http://www.dundee.ac.uk/elecengphysics/research/materials/advanced.html
     Contact: Prof J A Cairns.
E   A research centre at the University of Dundee.
O   To focus research on the properties of a range of materials, especially organometallic compounds which can be used in x-ray lithography and electron beam lithography, and are also suitable for decomposition by ultraviolet radiation

Advanced Materials Research Institute   (AMRI)   1998
■   School of Computing, Engineering and Information Sciences, Ellison Building, Northumbria University, Ellison Place, Newcastle upon Tyne, NE1 8ST.
     0191-227 3646   fax 0191-227 3646
     http://amri.unn.ac.uk/
     Director: Dr J S Burnell-Gray.
E   A research centre at Northumbria University.
O   To conduct research and consultancy in surface coating, surface modification, materials science and engineering, with special emphasis on high temperature corrosion

Advanced Microscopy Centre
- ■ Department of Engineering, University of Leicester, Leicester, LE1 7RH.
  0116-252 5692   fax 0116-252 2525
  http://www.le.ac.uk/eg/svh2/amc.htm
  Director: Dr Sarah Hainsworth.
- E A research centre at the University of Leicester.
- ○ To promote the advancement of research in the physical and biological sciences

Advanced Research Institute   (ARI)
- ■ Faculty of Arts, Media and Design, Mellor Building, Staffordshire University, College Road, Stoke-on-Trent, ST4 2DF.
  01782 294556
  http://www.ari.staffs.ac.uk/
  Director: Dr Dr David Durling.
- E A research institute at Staffordshire University.
- ○ To oversee art and design success

Advanced Technology Centre
> see **International Automotive Research Centre.**

Advanced Technology Institute   (ATI)
- ■ School of Electronics and Physical Sciences, University of Surrey, Guildford, Surrey, GU2 7XH.
  01483 686100   fax 01483 689404
  http://www.ati.surrey.ac.uk/
  Director: Prof Ravi Silva.
- E A department of the University of Surrey.
- ○ To conduct research in nanotechnology, photonics, ion beams and advanced theory

Advancing Skills for Professionals in the Rural Economy CETL   (Aspire)   2005
- ■ Harper Adams University College, Newport, Shropshire, TF10 8NB.
  01952 815369   fax 01952 814783
  http://www.harper-adams.ac.uk/aspire
  Director: Abigail Hind.
- E A Centre for Excellence in Teaching and Learning (CETL) at Harper Adams University College.
- Note: See **Centres for Excellence in Teaching and Learning** for more information.

Advisory Centre for Education   (ACE)   1960
- ■ 1c Aberdeen Studios, 22 Highbury Grove, London, N5 2DQ.
  020 7704 3370
  http://www.ace-ed.org.uk/
- E A registered charity and independent advice centre.
- ○ To promote fairness and opportunity in education
- ¶ Many publications available (see website).

Aerospace Centre
> see **Farnborough Aerospace Centre.**

Aerospace Manufacturing Research Centre   (AMRC)   1994
- ■ Faculty of Computing, Engineering and Mathematical Sciences, Frenchay Campus, University of the West of England, Coldharbour Lane, Bristol, BS16 1QY.
  0117-328 3500
  http://www.cems.uwe.ac.uk/amrc/AMRC.htm
  Research Director: Prof Alan Jocelyn.
- E A research centre at the University of the West of England.
- ○ To provide a national centre of expertise for aerospace manufacturing research

Aerospace Research Centre   (ARC)
- ■ Faculty of Engineering, Kingston University London, Roehampton Vale, London, SW15 3DW.
  020 8547 7704   fax 020 8547 7887
  http://engineering.kingston.ac.uk/aerospace-research-centre/index.htm
  Director: Dr Yufeng Yao.
- E A research centre at Kingston University, London.
- ○ To conduct research in avionics, astronautics and space systems

Aerospace Research Institute
> see **University of Manchester Aerospace Research Institute.**

© CBD Research Ltd · Beckenham · Kent BR3 5JS · Tel 020 8650 7745 · Fax 020 8650 0768 · E-mail cbd@cbdresearch.com · www.cbdresearch.com

Africa Centre   1961
- ■ 38 King Street, London, WC2E 8JT.
  020 7836 1973   fax 020 7836 1975
  http://www.africacentre.org.uk/
- E A company limited by guarantee and a registered charity.
- ○ To promote education in matters concerning Africa and its people; to provide cultural and social activities concerning Africa
- ● Conferences & talks - Cultural and musical events - Exhibitions of works of art & photographs - Training courses in African politics, languages, dance & literature

Africa Centre for Peace and Conflict Studies   (Africa Centre)   2002
- ■ School of Social and International Studies, University of Bradford, Pemberton Building, Bradford, West Yorkshire, BD7 1DP.
  01274 235251   fax 01274 235240
  http://www.brad.ac.uk/acad/africacentre/
  Director: Dr David Francis.
- E A centre at the University of Bradford.

Agronomy Institute   2002
- ■ Orkney College, Kirkwall, Orkney, KW15 1LX.
  01856 569000   fax 01856 569001
  http://www.agronomy.uhi.ac.uk/
- E A research centre at the University of the Highlands and Islands (UHI) Institute.
- ○ To conduct research and development in diversification in the crop sector

AHRB Centre for British Film and Television Studies   2000
- ■ Room 102, irkbeck, University of London, 43 Gordon Square, London, WC1H 0PD.
  020 7631 6137   fax 020 7631 6136
  http://www.bftv.ac.uk/
- E A research centre within the Birkbeck Institute for the Humanities (qv) at Birkbeck, University of London.
- ○ To enhance and extend research on British film and television

AHRB Centre for Byzantine Cultural History   2000
- NR School of Philosophical Studies, Queen's University Belfast, Belfast, BT7 1NN.
  028 9097 3817   fax 028 9097 5274
  http://www.byzantine-ahrb-centre.ac.uk/
  Director: Prof Margaret Mullett.
- E An interdisciplinary centre within the Institute of Byzantine Studies (qv) at Queen's University, Belfast.
- Note: A collaborative venture bringing together the literary and theological achievements of Belfast, the archaeological strengths of the University of Newcastle,and the art historical expertise of the University of Sussex.

AHRC Centre for Cultural Analysis, Theory and History
see **Centre for Cultural Analysis, Theory and History.**

AHRC Centre for Editing Lives and Letters   (CELL)   2002
- ■ Department of Humanities, Social Sciences and Law, Arts Research Centre, Queen Mary, University of London, Mile End Road, London, E1 4NS.
  020 7882 7576
  http://www.livesandletters.ac.uk/
  Director: Prof Lisa Jardine.
- E A department of Queen Mary, University of London.
- ○ To develop archive-based projects relating to the period 1500-1800, for research into collections of letters and marginalia, and the connected lives and works

AHRC Centre for Irish and Scottish Studies
- ■ Humanity Manse, 19 College Bounds, University of Aberdeen, Aberdeen, AB24 3UG.
  01224 273683   fax 01224 273677
  http://www.abdn.ac.uk/riiss/ahrccentre.shtml
  Director: Prof Cairns Craig.
- E A research centre within the Research Institute of Irish and Scottish Studies (qv) at the University of Aberdeen.
- ○ To carry out research in the history, literature and culture of Ireland and Scotland

AHRC Centre for the Study of the Domestic Interior   (CSDI)   2001
- ■ Royal College of Art, Kensington Gore, London, SW7 2EU.
  020 7590 4183   fax 020 7590 4580
  http://www.rca.ac.uk/csdi/
  Director: Jeremy Aynsley.
- E A research centre at the Royal College of Art.
- ○ To develop new histories of the home, its contents, and its representation

AHRC Research Centre for Cross-Cultural Music and Dance Performance 2002

NR   School of Arts, Digby Stuart College, Roehampton University, Roehampton Lane, London, SW15 5PH.
    020 7898 4687; 8392 3249
    http://www.roehampton.ac.uk/musicanddance/
    Director: Dr Keith Howard.
E   An interdisciplinary research centre at Roehampton University.
O   To address questions raised by the performance of sound and movement, particularly within Asian and African artistic practice, seeking a symbiosis between the performance concerns of ethnomusicology and musicology; to explore analysis methodologies utilised in theatre and dance research
Note: A collaborative venture with the School of Oriental and African Studies, University of London and with the University of Surrey.

AHRC Research Centre for Cross-Cultural Music and Dance Performance 2002

NR   Department of Music, School of Oriental and African Studies, University of London, Russell Square, London, WC1H 0XG.
    020 7898 4010   fax 020 7898 4699
    http://www.soas.ac.uk/ahrbmusicanddance/
    Director: Dr Keith Howard.
E   A research centre at the School of Oriental and African Studies, University of London.
Note: A collaborative venture with the Universities of Surrey and Roehampton (see above).

AHRC Research Centre for Cross-Cultural Music and Dance Performance

NR   Department of Dance Studies, University of Surrey, Guildford, Surrey, GU2 7XH.
    01483 689351   fax 01483 686501
    http://www.surrey.ac.uk/Dance/AHRB/index.html
    Co-ordinator: Dr Janet O'Shea.
E   A research centre at the University of Surrey.
Note: A collaborative venture with the School of Oriental and African Studies, University of London and Roehampton (see above).

AHRC Research Centre for Environmental History 2002

NR   Department of History, Room 4v3 - Cottrell Building, University of Stirling, Stirling, FK9 4LA.
    01786 466250   fax 01786 466251
    http://www.cehp.stir.ac.uk/
    Director: Fiona Watson.
E   An interdisciplinary research centre at the University of Stirling.
O   To conduct research on the history of environmental change, with particular emphasis on waste management and waste lands
Note: A joint venture with the University of St Andrews.

AHRC Research Centre for the Evolution of Cultural Diversity (CECD) 2006

■   Faculty of Social and Historical Sciences, University College London, 31-34 Gordon Square, London, WC1H 0PY.
    020 7679 4607; 4773   fax 020 7383 2572
    http://www.cecd.ucl.ac.uk/
    Director: James Steele. Administrator: Manu Davies.
E   A research centre within the UCL Institute of Archaeology (qv).
O   To advance understanding of human cultural diversity

AHRC Research Centre for the History and Analysis of Recorded Music (CHARM) 2004

NR   Department of Music, Royal Holloway, University of London, Egham, Surrey, TW20 0EX.
    01784 443361   fax 01784 439441
    http://www.charm.rhul.ac.uk/
    Co-ordinator: Carol Chan.
E   A research centre at Royal Holloway, University of London.
O   To promote the study of music as performance through a specific focus on recordings
Note: A joint research venture with King's College London and the University of Sheffield.

AHRC Research Centre for Law, Gender and Sexuality (CentreLGS) 2004

NR   University of Kent, Canterbury, Kent, CT2 7NS.
    01227 824474   fax 01227 827831
    http://www.kent.ac.uk/clgs/
    Director: Prof Davina Cooper. Co-ordinator: Anisa de Jong.
E   A research centre at the University of Kent.
O   To pioneer and facilitate work that analyses, investigates and deepens understanding of the relationship between law, gender and sexuality
Note: A joint venture with Keele University and the University of Westminster.

AHRC Research Centre for the Philosophy of Logic, Language, Mathematics and Mind (Arché) 1998

■   School of Philosophical, Anthropological and Film Studies, University of St Andrews, 17-19 College Street, St Andrews, Fife, KY16 9AL.
    01334 461796   fax 01334 462485
    http://www.st-andrews.ac.uk/~arche/
    Director: Prof Crispin Wright.
E   A research centre at the University of St Andrews.
O   To conduct teaching and research of the highest quality in analytical metaphysics and epistemology, formal and philosophical logic, philosophy of language, mathematics, and mind

© CBD Research Ltd · Beckenham · Kent BR3 5JS · Tel 020 8650 7745 · Fax 020 8650 0768 · E-mail cbd@cbdresearch.com · www.cbdresearch.com

AHRC Research Centre for Studies in Intellectual Property and Technology Law
- School of Law, Old College, University of Edinbugh, South Bridge, Edinburgh, EH8 9YL.
   0131-650 2006   fax 0131-650 6317
   http://www.law.ed.ac.uk/ahrc/
E   A research centre at the University of Edinburgh.

AHRC Research Centre for Studies of Surrealism and its Legacies
NR   Department of Art History and Theory, University of Essex, Wivenhoe Park, Colchester, Essex, CO4 3SQ.
   01206 872600   fax 01206 873003
   http://www.surrealismcentre.ac.uk/
   Director: Prof Dawn Ades.
E   A centre at the University of Essex.
O   To bring together academics and specialist curators renowned internationally for their scholarly work in dada and surrealism
Note: A joint venture with the University of Manchester.

AHRC Research Centre for Studies of Surrealism and its Legacies
NR   School of Arts, Histories and Cultures, Humanities Lime Grove Centre, University of Manchester, Oxford Road, Manchester, M13 9PL.
   0161-306 1240
   http://www.surrealismcentre.ac.uk/
E   A centre at the University of Manchester.
Note: A joint venture with the University of Essex (see above).

AHRC Research Centre for Textile Conservation and Textile Studies   2002
NR   Faculty of Law, Arts and Social Sciences, Winchester School of Art, University, Park Avenue, Winchester, Hampshire, SO23 8DL.
   023 8059 6900
   http://www.wsa.soton.ac.uk/conservation-and-museums/the-ahrc-research-centre-for-textile-conservation–textile-studies/default.asp
E   A research centre within the Textile Conservation Centre (qv) at the University of Southampton.
O   To improve the care and interpretation of historic textiles by enhancing knowledge and understanding of textiles and their conservation
Note: A collaborative venture with the Universities of Bradford and Manchester.

AIMS Centre (Applied and Integrated Medical Sciences)   (AIMS)   2005
- Department of Physiology, University of Bristol, Bristol, BS8 1TD.
   0117-928 9000
   http://www.bris.ac.uk/cetl/aims/
   Director: Judy Harris.
E   A Centre for Excellence in Teaching and Learning (CETL) at the University of Bristol.
Note: See **Centres for Excellence in Teaching and Learning** for more information.

Air Quality Management Resource Centre   (AQMRC)
- Faculty of Applied Sciences, Frenchay Campus, University of Bristol, Coldharbour Lane, Bristol, BS16 1QY.
   0117-328 3825
   http://science.uwe.ac.uk/research/
   Director: Prof James Longhurst.
E   A research centre at the University of the West of England.
O   To provide a service to all professionals working in the field of air quality management

Aircraft Design Centre
- Department of Power, Propulsion and Aerospace Engineering, Cranfield University, Cranfield, Bedfordshire, MK43 0AL.
   01234 750111   fax 01234 751550
   http://www.cranfield.ac.uk/soe/adc/
   Contact: E James.
E   A research centre at Cranfield University.
O   To focus on research, consultancy and design applied to the development and application of aircraft, (aerospace technologies and life cycle), operational and environmental issues

Alan Turing Institute
- Faculty of Engineering and Physical Sciences, PO Box 88, University of Manchester, Sackville Street, Manchester, M60 1QD.
   0161-306 9200   fax 0161-306 3755
   http://www.mace.manchester.ac.uk/
E   A research institute at the University of Manchester.
O   To conduct research in mathematics

Alcock Centre for Historical Archaeology
   see **Leslie and Elizabeth Alcock Centre for Historical Archaeology.**

Alcuin Research Resource Centre (ARRC)
- Department of Economics and Related Studies, University of York, Heslington, York, YO10 5DD.
  01904 323300
  http://www.york.ac.uk/inst/arrc/
- E   A centre at the University of York.
- O   To support those involved in health and social sciences research

Alister Hardy Religious Experience Centre
  see **Centre for Research into Religious Experience.**

Alternative Investments Research Centre (AIRC)
- Cass Business School, City University, 106 Bunhill Row, London, EC1Y 8TZ.
  020 7040 8600
  http://www.cass.city.ac.uk/airc/
  Director: Prof Harry M Kat.
- E   A centre at City University.
- O   To generate practical answers to practical questions concerning alternative investments and their role in investment portfolios

Alzheimer's Disease Research Centre (ADRC)
- Division of Pathology and Neuroscience, Ninewells Hospital and Medical School, University of Dundee, Dundee, DD1 9SY.
  01382 496589   fax 01382 633923
  http://www.dundee.ac.uk/alzheimer/
  Co-ordinator: Prof David Balfour.
- E   A centre at the University of Dundee.
- O   To increase collaboration among researchers in the field of Alzheimer's Disease

American Bureau of Shipping (ABS)   1862
- ABS House, 1 Frying Pan Alley, London, E1 7HR.
  020 7247 3255   fax 020 7377 2453
  http://www.eagle.org/
  President: Christopher J Wiernicki.
- E   An independent non-profit-distributing organisation.
- O   To promote security of life, property & the natural environment through development & verification of standards for design, construction and operational maintenance of marine-related facilities
- ¶   Annual Review. Surveyor. Rules and Guides. (see website for other publications).

American Institute
  see **Rothermere American Institute.**

American (United States) Studies Centre
- University of Essex, Wivenhoe Park, Colchester, Essex, CO4 3SQ.
  01206 873976
  http://www2.essex.ac.uk/ussc/
  Director: Dr Jeffrey Geiger.
- E   A centre at the University of Essex.
- O   To conduct research in American history, law, literature, film, politics, and sociology

Andrew Hook Centre for American Studies (CAS)   1997
- Department of History, University of Glasgow, 6 University Gardens, Glasgow, G12 8QH.
  0141-330 5697; 8281   fax 0141-330 4537
  http://www.arts.gla.ac.uk/cas/
- E   A research centre at the University of Glasgow.
- O   To encourage research on American society and culture

Anglo-Chinese Business and Management Centre (ACBMC)   2005
- Kent Business School, University of Kent, Canterbury, Kent, CT2 7PE.
  01227 827726   fax 01227 761187
  http://www.kent.ac.uk/kbs/standard.php?page_id=36
  Director: Prof Wenbin Liu.
- E   A research centre at the University of Kent.
- O   To promote world-class joint research and education on Chinese business, policy and management

Anna Freud Centre (AFC)   1952
- 21 Maresfield Gardens, London, NW3 5SD.
  020 7794 2313   fax 020 7794 6506
  http://www.annafreudcentre.org/
- E   A company limited by guarantee and a registered charity.
- O   To develop innovative psychotherapeutic treatments for adolescents and children with emotional and behavioural difficulties; to evaluate treatments and to ensure the lessons learnt are spread

© CBD Research Ltd · Beckenham · Kent BR3 5JS · Tel 020 8650 7745 · Fax 020 8650 0768 · E-mail cbd@cbdresearch.com · www.cbdresearch.com

Antibody Resource Centre   (ARC)
- Firth Court, University of Sheffield, Western Bank, Sheffield, S10 2TN.
  0114-222 7480   fax 0114-222 7483
  http://www.shef.ac.uk/arc/
- E   A research centre at the University of Sheffield.
- O   To provide both monoclonal and polyclonal antibody production

Antimicrobial Research Centre   (ARC)   1996
- Faculty of Biological Sciences, University of Leeds, Leeds, LS2 9JT.
  0113-343 5647
  http://www.leeds.ac.uk/arc/
  Director: Prof Ian Chopra.
- E   A research centre at the University of Leeds.
- Note: Also known as the Centre for Antimicrobial Research.

Ape Rescue Centre
    see **Monkey World Ape Rescue Centre.**

Applied Criminology Centre   (ACC)   1994
- School of Human and Health Sciences, CSB Level 14, University of Huddersfield, Queensgate, Huddersfield, HD1 3DH.
  01484 473676
  http://www.hud.ac.uk/hhs/
  Director: Prof Alex Hirschfield.
- E   A research centre at the University of Huddersfield.
- O   To conduct research within a broad range of areas of criminology, crime reduction and community safety

Applied Digital Signal and Image Processing Research Centre   (ADSIP)
- Technology Building, University of Central Lancashire, Preston, PR1 2HE.
  01772 893253; 893272   fax 01772 892915
  http://technology.uclan.ac.uk/adsip/index.htm
  Director: Prof Lik-Kwan Shark.
- E   A research centre at the University of Central Lancashire.
- O   To conduct research in the development and deployment of highly sophisticated and innovative signal and image processing techniques, especially in aerospace and health

Applied Educational Research Centre   (AERC)
- Department of Educational and Professional Studies, Sir Henry Wood Building, 76 Southbrae Drive, University of Strathclyde, Glasgow, G13 1PP.
  0141-950 3365   fax 0141-950 3367
  http://www.strath.ac.uk/eps/aerc/
  Contact: Katie Hunter.
- E   A research centre at the University of Strathclyde.

Applied Electromagnetics Research Centre   (AERC)
- Department of Electronic and Electrical Engineering, University of Bath, Claverton Down, Bath, BA2 7AY.
  01225 386327   fax 01225 826305
  http://www.bath.ac.uk/elec-eng/
- E   A research centre at the University of Bath.

Applied Engineering Research Centre   (AERC)
- Faculty of Engineering, Kingston University London, Friars Avenue, Roehampton Vale, London, SW15 3DW.
  020 8547 7704   fax 020 8547 7887
  http://engineering.kingston.ac.uk/applied-engineering-research-centre/
  Director: Prof Jennifer Wen.
- E   A research centre at Kingston University, London.

Applied Informatics Research Centre
- Faculty of Business, Law and the Built Environment, Maxwell Building, University of Salford, Salford, Manchester, M5 4WT.
  0161-295 5262; 5278
  http://www.iris.salford.ac.uk/degrees/subjects/appliedinformatics.php
  Director: Prof Yacine Rezgui.
- E   A research centre within the Informatics Research Institute (qv) at the University of Salford.

Applied and Integrated Medical Sciences Centre
    see **AIMS Centre (Applied and Integrated Medical Sciences).**

Applied Research Centre for Human Security   (ARCHS)   2006
- ■   Futures Institute, Coventry University, Puma Way, Coventry, CV1 2TT.
    024 7679 5757
    http://www.coventry.ac.uk/researchnet/d/176
    Director: Prof Malcolm McIntosh. Contact: Dr Alan Hunter.
- E   A centre at Coventry University.
- ○   To conduct applied research, consultancy and teaching in the general area of human security

Applied Research Centre in Sustainable Regeneration   (SURGE)   2006
- ■   Futures Institute, Coventry University Technology Park, Puma Way, Coventry, CV1 2TT.
    024 7679 5757
    http://www.coventry.ac.uk/researchnet/d/170/a/665
    Director: Nigel Berkeley
- E   A centre at Coventry University.
- ○   To support business and society in achieving sustainable regeneration through economic and social development.
- ✕   Centre for Local Economic Development; Centre for Social Justice; Rural Restructuring Research Group

Applied Vision Research Centre   (AVRC)
- ■   Department of Optometry and Visual Science, Tait Building, City University, Northampton Square, London, EC1V 0HB.
    020 7040 0193   fax 020 7040 8355
    http://www.city.ac.uk/avrc/
    Director: Prof John L Barbur.
- E   A research centre within the Institute of Health Sciences (qv) at City University.
- ○   To gain a greater understanding of the processes involved in the acquisition, analysis, storage and retrieval of visual information and the motor response

Applied Vision Research Centre
- ■   Faculty of Social Sciences and Humanities, Holywell Building, Loughborough University, Holywell Park, Loughborough, Leicestershire, LE11 3UZ.
    01509 226900   fax 01509 226960
    http://www.lboro.ac.uk/research/esri/applied-vision/
    Director: Prof Alastair G Gale.
- E   A research centre within the Ergonomics and Safety Research Institute (qv) at Loughborough University.
- ○   To conduct research in the fields of ergonomics, psychology, vision, health and human error in the development and evaluation of systems and products, in which people are an integral part

Aquaculture Technology Centre   (ATC)
- ■   University of Stirling, Stirling, FK9 4LA.
    01786 467900   fax 01786 451462
    http://www.atc.stir.ac.uk/
- E   A research centre within the Institute of Aquaculture (qv) at the University of Stirling.
- ○   To make available the expertise, experience and facilities of the Institute to companies and organisations on a commercial basis

Arabidopsis Stock Centre
    see **Nottingham Arabidopsis Stock Centre.**

Archaeological Resource Centre
Note: Has been replaced by DIG - An Archaeological Adventure, and is thus no longer within the scope of this directory.

ARP Women's Alcohol Centre   (WAC)   1984
- ■   66A Drayton Park, London, N5 1ND.
    020 7226 4581   fax 020 7354 8134
    http://www.arp-uk.org/
    Team Manager: Cordelia Mayfield.
- E   A registered charity and a company limited by guarantee.
- ○   To reduce the harm to individual women and to society, caused by alcohol-related problems
- ●   Information service - Day service (Tues-Thurs 0930-1630)
Note: ARP = Alcohol Recovery Project.

Arson Prevention Bureau   (APB)   1991
- ■   51 Gresham Street, London, EC2V 7HQ.
    020 7216 7474
    http://www.arsonpreventionbureau.org.uk/
    Chief Executive: Jane Milne.
- E   A non-profit-making subsidiary of the Association of British Insurers.
- ○   To spearhead & co-ordinate a national campaign to reduce arson & raise awareness of the problem; to bring together public & private sector organisations sharing these objectives
- ●   Conference facilities - Exhibitions

Art Design Media Subject Centre (ADM-HEA 2000
- University of Brighton, 68 Grand Parade, Brighton, East Sussex, BN2 9JY.
  - 01273 643119   fax 01273 643119
  - http://www.adm.heacademy.ac.uk/
  - Director: Prof Bruce Brown. Manager: David Clews.
- E   A Government funded national centre within the University of Brighton.
- O   To foster world-class education in art, design and the media
- ●   Education and training - Information service - Statistics
- ¶   Newsletter.

Note: One of the 24 Subject Centres of the Higher Education Academy, (qv).

Art and Design Research Centre (ADRC)
- Faculty of Arts, Media and Social Sciences, Peru Street, University of Salford, Salford, Manchester, M3 6EQ.
  - 0161-295 2801
  - http://www.adelphi.salford.ac.uk/adrc/
- E   A research centre within the Adelphi Research Institute for Creative Arts and Sciences (qv) at the University of Salford.
- O   To conduct research in the fields of art and design, with particular focus on design and innovation, heritage, creative technology, and contextualised arts practice

Art and Design Research Centre (ADRC)
- Psalter Lane Campus, Sheffield Hallam University, Sheffield, S11 8UZ.
  - 0114-225 2669   fax 0114-225 2603
  - http://www.shu.ac.uk/research/c3ri/
  - Head: Prof Chris Rust.
- E   A research centre within the Cultural, Communication and Computing Research Institute (qv) at Sheffield Hallam University.
- O   To develop research in art and design

Art and Media Arts Research Centre (AMA)
- School of Art, Cavendish North Building, Manchester Metropolitan University, Cavendish Street, Manchester, M15 6BG.
  - 0161-247 1911   fax 0161-247 6839
  - http://www.miriad.mmu.ac.uk/ama/
  - Leader: Prof Pavel Büchler.
- E   A research centre within the Manchester Institute for Research and Innovation in Art and Design (qv) at Manchester Metropolitan University.
- O   To conduct research in contemporary fine and public art, and lens-based and electronic media

Arthritis Research Centre
- Robert Jones and Agnes Hunt Orthopaedic and District General Hospital, Oswestry, Shropshire, SY10 7AG.
  - 01691 404000   fax 01691 404050
  - http://www.rjah.nhs.uk/
- E   A research centre within the Institute of Orthopaedics (qv)
- O   To specialise in a range of molecular cell biology studies

Arthur Miller Centre for American Studies
- School of American Studies, University of East Anglia, Norwich, NR4 7TJ.
  - 01603 592280   fax 01603 507728
  - http://www.uea.ac.uk/eas/
- E   A centre at the University of East Anglia.
- O   To further interest in the study of the United States; to promote major new research projects; to facilitate the movement of people between Britain and America

Arthur Rank Centre (ARC) 1972
- Stoneleigh Park, Kenilworth, Warwickshire, CV8 2LZ.
  - 024 7685 3060   fax 024 7641 4808
  - http://www.arthurrankcentre.org.uk/
- E   A registered charity.
- O   To demonstrate a practical concern for farming and countryside matters based on Christian principles and to be the national resources unit for rural churches

Article 19: International Centre against Censorship (Article 19) 1987
- 6-8 Amwell Street, London, EC1R 1UQ.
  - 020 7278 9292   fax 020 7278 7660
  - http://www.article19.org/
  - Executive Director: Dr Agnes Callamard.
- E   A registered charity and a company limited by guarantee.
- O   To promote freedom of expression internationally

Note: The Centre's name is taken from Article 19 of the United Nations Universal Declaration of Human Rights.

Artificial Intelligence Applications Institute   (AIAI)   1984
- School of Informatics, University of Edinburgh, Appleton Tower, Crichton Street, Edinburgh, EH8 9LE.
  0131-650 2732   fax 0131-650 6513
  http://www.aiai.ed.ac.uk/
- E   A research institute at the University of Edinburgh.
- ○   To promote the application of artificial intelligence research for the benefit of commercial, industrial and Government clients

Arts and Humanities Research Board
    see **AHRB**

Arts and Humanities Research Council
    see **AHRC**

Arts for Health Centre   1988
- Faculty of Art and Design, Manchester Metropolitan University, All Saints, Oxford Road, Manchester, M15 6BY.
  0161-247 1091   fax 0161-247 6390
  http://www.mmu.ac.uk/artsforhealth/
  Director: Peter Senior.
- E   A department of Manchester Metropolitan University.
- ○   To provide practical help, information and advice to all who are concerned with using art and design as a complementary part of healthcare
- Note: Also known as the International Centre for Arts in Health Care.

ArtsWork: Learning Laboratories Centre for Excellence   2005
- Bath Spa University, Newton Park, Newton St Loe, Bath, BA2 9BN.
  01225 876341   fax 01225 876340
  http://artswork.bathspa.ac.uk/
  Director: Prof Neil Sammells.
- E   A Centre for Excellence in Teaching and Learning at Bath Spa University.
- Note: See **Centres for Excellence in Teaching and Learning** for further information.

Asbestos Information Centre Ltd   (AIC)   1977
- ATSS House, Station Road East, Stowmarket, Suffolk, IP14 1RQ.
  01449 676049   fax 01449 770028
  http://www.airc.org.uk/
  Director General: Tony Hutchinson.
- E   An independent non-profit organisation and a company limited by guarantee.
- ○   To give advice on materials containing asbestos and the best practice for treatment vis-à-vis current legislation
- ●   Information service

Ashley Centre for Professional Management   (CPM)
- Staffordshire University, Leek Road, Stoke-on-Trent, ST4 2DF.
  01782 294228
  http://www.staffs.ac.uk/schools/business/cpm/
  Administrator: Sam Neal.
- E   A centre at Staffordshire University.
- ○   To provide training programmes that are customised to specific business needs
- Note: Also known as Staffordshire University Centre for Professional Management.

Ashridge Strategic Management Centre   (ASMC)   1987
- 3 Devonshire Street, London, W1W 5DT.
  020 7323 4422
  http://www.ashridge.org.uk/
  Director: Marcus Alexander.
- E   A part of the Ashridge Trust, one of Europe's leading centres for management development.
- ○   To study and provide information on management and organisational issues related to future human resource development needs, both in the UK and internationally

Asia Business Research Centre   (ABRC)   2002
- Kingston Business School, Kingston University London, Kingston Hill, Kingston-upon-Thames, Surrey, KT1 7LB.
  020 8547 2000
  http://business.kingston.ac.uk/
- E   A research centre at Kingston University, London.

Asia Research Centre
- LSE, Houghton Street, London, WC2A 2AE.
  020 7955 7388   fax 020 7107 5285
  http://www.lse.ac.uk/
  Manager: Chris Soo-Jeong Lee.
- E   A research centre at the London School of Economics and Political Science.
- ○   To encourage and co-ordinate interdisciplinary social science research in Asian studies

Asian Studies Centre   (ASC)   1982
- ■   St Antony's College, University of Oxford, Oxford, OX2 2JF.
   01865 274559   fax 01865 274559
   http://www.sant.ox.ac.uk/asian
   Director: Dr Mark Rebick.
- E   An Area Studies Centre of the University of Oxford.
- O   To bring together, in single-theme seminar series, conferences, lectures and other activities, specialists in a wide variety of different disciplines; to facilitate the exchange of ideas among scholars, to promote consideration of themes and issues that transcend national borders, and to encourage publication of its proceedings (where appropriate)
- ●   Education and training

Aspire Centre for Disability Sciences   1990
- ■   Faculty of Biomedical Sciences, Royal Free and University College Medical School, Brockley Hill, Stanmore, Middlesex, HA7 4LP.
   020 8909 5447
   http://www.ucl.ac.uk/orthopaedics/centres/aspireunits.htm
   Head: Prof Martin Ferguson-Pell.
- E   A research centre within the Institute of Orthopaedics and Musculo-Skeletal Science (qv) at University College London.
- O   To conduct research with the aim of achieving functional improvements in disability in the widest sense, including disability biomechanics, assistive technology, tissue integrity management, and structure and motion

Assessment and Learning in Practice Settings CETL   (ALPS)   2005
- ■   Fairburn House, University of Leeds, 71-75 Clarendon Road, Leeds, LS2 9PL.
   0113-343 6352   fax 0113-343 3470
   http://www.alps-cetl.ac.uk/
   Director: Prof Trudie Roberts.
- E   A Centre for Excellence in Teaching and Learning (CETL) at the University of Leeds.
- Note: See **Centres for Excellence in Teaching and Learning** for more information.

Assessment Standards Knowledge exchange CETL   (ASKe)   2005
- ■   Business School, Wheatley Campus, Oxford Brookes University, Wheatley, Oxford, OX33 1HX.
   01865 485671; 485908   fax 01865 485830
   http://www.business.brookes.ac.uk/learningandteaching/cetl.html
   Director: Margaret Price.
- E   A Centre for Excellence in Teaching and Learning (CETL) at Oxford Brookes University.
- Note: See **Centres for Excellence in Teaching and Learning** for more information.

Astbury Centre for Structural Molecular Biology   (ACSMB)   1999
- ■   Faculty of Biological Sciences, University of Leeds, Manton Building, Leeds, LS2 9JT.
   0113-343 3069
   http://www.astbury.leeds.ac.uk/
   Administrator: Donna Fletcher.
- E   A research centre at the University of Leeds.
- O   To bring together structural molecular biologists, chemists and physicists working on the structure and function of biological molecules, biomolecular assemblies and complexes

Asthma UK Centre in Allergic Mechanisms of Asthma
   see **MRC-Asthma UK Centre in Allergic Mechanisms of Asthma.**

Aston Business School Research Centre in Higher Education Learning and Management   (HELM)
- ■   Aston Business School, Aston University, Aston Triangle, Birmingham, B4 7ET.
   0121-204 3000
   http://www.abs.aston.ac.uk/newweb/research/HELM/
   Director: Dr Helen Higson.
- E   A research centre at Aston University.
- O   To advance understanding of management and pedagogy in higher education via a programme of rigorous research and application

Aston Centre for Human Resource   (ACHR)   2006
- ■   Aston Business School, Aston University, Aston Triangle, Birmingham, B4 7ET.
   0121-204 3000
   http://www.abs.aston.ac.uk/newweb/research/researchcentres.asp
   Co-Director: Pawan Budhwar. Co-Director: Judy Scully.
- E   A research centre at Aston University.

Aston Centre for Leadership Excellence   (ACLE)
- ■   Aston Business School, Aston University, Aston Triangle, Birmingham, B4 7ET.
   0121-204 3000
   http://www.abs.aston.ac.uk/newweb/research/researchcentres.asp
   Co-Director: Prof Felix Brodbeck. Co-Director: Dr Michael Grojean.
- E   A research centre at Aston University.
- O   To provide a strategic framework, to generate and transfer knowledge in leadership and leader development, by bridging academic rigour and practical relevance

Aston Centre for Research in Experimental Finance   (ACREF)   2004

■ Aston Business School, Aston University, Aston Triangle, Birmingham, B4 7ET.
  0121-204 3000
  http://www.abs.aston.ac.uk/newweb/research/ACREF/
  Contact: Jim Steeley.
E A research centre at Aston University.
○ To promote, undertake and utilize research in experimental finance and disseminate the results

Aston Centre for Voluntary Action Research   (ACVAR)   2000

■ Aston Business School, Aston University, Aston Triangle, Birmingham, B4 7ET.
  0121-204 3253   fax 0121-204 3327
  http://www.cvar.org.uk/
  Director: Ben Cairns.
E A research centre at Aston University.
○ To support the development and sustainability of voluntary and community organisations

Astronomy Centre
  see **Sussex Astronomy Centre.**

Astrophysics Research Institute   (ARI)   1992

■ Liverpool John Moores University, Twelve Quays House, Egerton Wharf, Birkenhead, CH41 1LD.
  0151-231 2919   fax 0151-231 2921
  http://www.astro.livjm.ac.uk/
  Contact: Prof Mike Bode.
E A research institute within Liverpool John Moores University.
○ To conduct research into stellar astronomy, including novae and related stars, regions of star formation, brown dwarfs, extra-solar planets and the environments of Be stars
● Information service

Athrofa Chwaraeon Cymru
  see **Welsh Institute of Sport.**

Athrofa Clyw Cymru
  see **Welsh Hearing Institute.**

Athrofa y Gymdeithas, Iechyd a Moseg Caerdydd
  see **Cardiff Institute of Society, Health and Ethics.**

Audio Visual Centre

Note: No longer in existence.

Audit Bureau of Circulations Ltd   (ABC)   1931

■ Saxon House, 211 High Street, Berkhamsted, Hertfordshire, HP4 1AD.
  01442 870800   fax 01442 200700
  http://www.abc.org.uk/
  Chief Executive: Chris Boyd.
E A membership organisation and a company limited by guarantee.
○ To certify the circulation claims of national and regional newspapers and consumer and business magazines, by professional auditors working to stringent audit rules and procedures

Australia Centre

■ King's College London, Corner of Strand and Melbourne Place, London, WC2B 4LG.
  020 7240 0220   fax 020 7240 8292
  http://www.kcl.ac.uk/
E A centre at King's College, London.
Note: Houses the Menzies Centre for Australian Studies.

Autism Research Centre   (ARC)

■ Section of Developmental Psychiatry, University of Cambridge, Douglas House, 18b Trumpington Road, Cambridge, CB2 2AH.
  01223 746057   fax 01223 746033
  http://www.autismresearchcentre.com/
  Administrator: Jenny Hannah.
E A centre at the University of Cambridge.
○ To understand the biomedical causes of autism spectrum conditions; to develop new and validated methods for assessment and intervention

Automation and Drives Centre
  see **Siemens Automation and Drives Centre.**

© CBD Research Ltd · Beckenham · Kent BR3 5JS · Tel 020 8650 7745 · Fax 020 8650 0768 · E-mail cbd@cbdresearch.com · www.cbdresearch.com

Automation Systems Centre   (ASCent)
- ■   Department of Engineering and Technology, Manchester Metropolitan University, John Dalton East, Chester Street, Manchester, M1 5GD.
     0161-247 2000   fax 0161-247 1633
     http://www.sci-eng.mmu.ac.uk/ascent/
     Manager: Andy Verwer.
- E   A research centre at Manchester Metropolitan University.
- ○   To provide training, consultancy and support for the automation community

Automotive Engineering Centre   (AEC)   1986
- ■   Faculty of Engineering and Information Sciences, University of Hertfordshire, College Lane, Hatfield, Hertfordshire, AL10 9AB.
     01707 284000   fax 01707 284115
     http://perseus.herts.ac.uk/prospectus/faculty_ei/eis_site_pages/research_commercial_pages/eis_commercial_aec.cfm#list
     Contact: Lara Dodd.
- E   A research centre within the Science and Technology Research Institute (qv) at the University of Hertfordshire.

Autonomic Neuroscience Institute   (ANI)   1995
- ■   Department of Anatomy and Developmental Biology, University College London, Gower Street, London, WC1E 6BT.
     020 7679 2000
     http://wwwcm-a.ucl.ac.uk:8090/silva/ani
     Contact: Prof G Burnstock.
- E   A research institute at University College London.
- ○   To conduct research in autonomic control

Aviation Health Institute   (AHI)   1996
- ■   17c Between Towns Road, Oxford, OX4 3LX.
     01865 715999   fax 01865 715899
     http://www.aviation-health.com/
     Director: Farrol Kahn.
- E   An independent non-profit organisation.
- ○   To provide information and comment on aviation health issues such as deep vein thrombosis (DVT), inflight disease, radiation, and cardiovascular and pulmonary risks

Babraham Institute   1948
- Babraham Research Campus, University of Cambridge, Cambridge, CB2 4AT.
  01223 496000; 496272   fax 01223 496002
  http://www.babraham.ac.uk/
  Contact: Dr Caroline Edmonds.
- E   An institute at the University of Cambridge.
- O   To conduct innovative research and training in the mechanisms of cell communication and gene regulation to understand the basis of human disease

Bach Centre
  see **Dr Edward Bach Centre.**

Bader Centre
  see **Douglas Bader Centre.**

Bagrit Centre
  see **Sir Leon Bagrit Centre.**

Bakhtin Centre   1994
- Department of Russian and Slavonic Studies, Arts Tower, University of Sheffield, Sheffield, S10 2TE.
  0114-222 7415   fax 0114-222 7416
  http://www.shef.ac.uk/bakhtin/
  Director: Prof David Shepherd.
- E   A research centre at the University of Sheffield.
- O   To promote multi- and inter-disciplinary research on the work of the Russian philosopher and theorist Mikhail Bakhtin and the Bakhtin Circle

BALTIC Centre for Contemporary Art   2005
- School of Arts and Cultures, University of Newcastle upon Tyne, Gateshead Quays, South Shore Road, Gateshead, NE8 3BA.
  0191-478 1810   fax 0191-478 1922
  http://www.balticmill.com/
  Director: Peter Doroshenko.
- E   A centre at the University of Newcastle upon Tyne.
- O   To present a dynamic, diverse and international programme of contemporary visual art

Banking Centre   (LUBC)
- Business School, Loughborough University, Loughborough, Leicestershire, LE11 3TU.
  01509 222721   fax 01509 263171
  http://www.lboro.ac.uk/departments/bs/mdc/about-bank.html
  Director: Barry Holcroft.
- E   A joint research centre within Loughborough University.
- O   To conduct research into financial institutions and their markets
Note: Also known as Loughborough University Banking Centre.

Banstead Mobility Centre
  see **Queen Elizabeth's Foundation Mobility Centre.**

Barber Institute of Fine Arts   1932
- University of Birmingham, Edgbaston, Birmingham, B15 2TS.
  0121-414 7333   fax 0121-414 3370
  http://www.barber.org.uk/
- E   A registered charity and department of the University of Birmingham.
- O   To study and encourage art and music

Basement Information Centre   (TBIC)   1992
- Riverside House, 4 Meadows Business Park, Camberley, Surrey, GU17 9AB
  01276 33155   fax 01276 606801
  http://www.basements.org.uk/
- O   To provide information about the development and use of basements in new or existing dwellings

Basil Bunting Poetry Centre   (BBPC)   1987
- Department of English Studies, University of Durham, Hallgarth House, 77 Hallgarth Street, Durham, DH1 3AY.
  0191-334 2500; 2571   fax 0191-334 2501
  http://www.dur.ac.uk/basil_bunting_poetry.centre/
- E   A research centre at the University of Durham.
- O   To foster study and research on the Northumbrian poet Basil Bunting, and on poets associated with him throughout the region, or on the modernist / post-modernist tradition

© CBD Research Ltd · Beckenham · Kent BR3 5JS · Tel 020 8650 7745 · Fax 020 8650 0768 · E-mail cbd@cbdresearch.com · www.cbdresearch.com

Bath Institute of Medical Engineering   (BIME)   1968

■   Royal United Hospital, Bath, BA1 3NG.
    01225 824103   fax 01225 824111
    http://www.bime.org.uk/
E   A registered charity.
○   To design and develop equipment for people with disabilities and for use in hospitals; to make successful designs available to
    whomever might benefit from them
●   Design and development

Bath Royal Literary and Scientific Institution   (BRLSI)   1824

■   16-18 Queen Square, Bath, BA1 2HN.
    01225 312084   fax 01225 442460
    http://www.brlsi.org/
    Chairman: David Beaugeard.
E   A research institute.
○   To conduct research and lectures in a variety of literary and scientific topics

Bayswater Institute

■   9 Orme Court, London, W2 4RL.
    020 7229 2729   fax 020 7229 2214
    http://www.bayswaterinst.org/
    Director: Prof Ken Eason.
○   To investigate human and social considerations with economic and technical ones in the design and development of organisations,
    communities and working life
●   Action research - Consultancy - Training events in group dynamics and sociotechnical systems design

BBC Television Centre

■   Wood Lane, London, W12 7RJ.
    http://www.bbc.co.uk/

BBC Weather Centre

■   Wood Lane, London, W12 7RJ.
    http://www.bbc.co.uk/weather
○   To provide UK and worldwide weather services and maps for temperature, wind, satellite, lighting, pressure, and radar

BBSRC Institute of Grassland and Environmental Research   (IGER)

■   University of Wales Aberystwyth, Plas Gogerddan, Bow Street, Aberystwyth, Ceredigion, SY23 3EB.
    01970 823000
    http://www.iger.bbsrc.ac.uk/
    Director: Prof C J Pollock.
E   A research institute within the Aberystwyth Bio Centre (qv) at the University of Wales, Aberystwyth.
○   To carry out basic, strategic and applied research into the links between ruminant animal production, agriculture and the
    environment; the Institute's principal areas of research are genetics and plant improvement, basic plant and microbial science,
    environmental and land management research, ruminant nutrition research
Note: IGER has 3 other Research stations which are based at Brecon, Okehampton and Aberystwyth.

BC   1989

■   Department of Chemistry, University of Wales Bangor, Deiniol Road, Bangor, Gwynedd, LL57 2UW.
    01248 370588   fax 01248 370594
    http://www.bc.bangor.ac.uk/
    Director: Dr Paul Fowler.
E   An interdisciplinary research centre within the Centre for Advanced and Renewable Materials at the University of Wales, Bangor.
○   To provide world leading and fundamental applied research into products and processes, based upon wood, industrial crops,
    recycled materials and industrial residues and to transfer these technologies to industry
✕   BioComposites Centre

BCCB Worldwide

Note: is now British Expertise, and thus no longer within the scope of this directory.

Beatson Institute for Cancer Research

■   University of Glasgow, Garscube Estate, Switchback Road, Glasgow, G61 1BD.
    0141-330 3953   fax 0141-942 6521
    http://www.beatson.gla.ac.uk/
    Director: Prof Karen H Vousden.
E   A company registered in Scotland and a department of the University of Glasgow.
○   To pursue research into the mechanisms that cause, or fight, cancer

Bedford Centre for the History of Women   (BCHW)   1999
- ■ Department of History and Classics, Royal Holloway University of London, Egham, Surrey, TW20 0EX.
   01784 414098   fax 01784 435841
   http://www.rhul.ac.uk/bedford-centre/
   Director: Dr Amanda Vickery. Administrator: Beverley Duguid.
- E An interdisciplinary research centre at Royal Holloway, University of London.
- ○ To bring together research in to the history of women and gender, and to promote new scholarship

Behavioural Biology Research Centre   (BBRC)
- ■ School of Biological Sciences, University of Bristol, Woodland Road, Bristol, BS8 1UG.
   0117-928 7986   fax 0117-928 7999
   http://www.bio.bris.ac.uk/research/behavior/behavior.htm
   Director: Prof J M McNamara.
- E An interdisciplinary research centre at the University of Bristol.
- ○ To foster co-operation between those who carry out observational and experimental studies of animals in the field or laboratory, and theoreticians who model behavioural, ecological and evolutionary problems
- Note: Also known as the Centre for Behavioural Biology.

Behavioural and Clinical Neurosciences Institute   (BCNI)
- ■ Department of Experimental Psychology, University of Cambridge, Downing Site, Cambridge, CB2 3EB.
   01223 333550   fax 01223 333564
   http://research.psychol.cam.ac.uk/
   Director: Prof Trevor Robbins.
- E A Medical Research Council institute at the University of Cambridge.
- ○ To link clinical research at the level of functional neural systems to basic work on the brain with a common theme of different neuroimaging modalities and neuropsychopharmacology
- Note: See **Medical Research Council Collaborative Centre** for further information.

Behavioural Neuroendocrinology Research Centre
- Note: has become the Behavioural Neuroendocrinology Research Unit and is therefore outside the scope of this directory.

Belfast e-Science Centre   (BeSC)
- ■ School of Computer Science, Queen's University Belfast, Belfast, BT7 1NN.
   028 9033 5463   fax 028 9097 5666
   http://www.qub.ac.uk/escience/dev/
   Director: Prof R H Perrott.
- E A centre at Queen's University, Belfast.
- Note: See **e-Science Centres** for further information.

Benfield Hazard Research Centre   (BHRC)   1997
- ■ Department of Earth Sciences, University College London, Gower Street, London, WC1E 6BT.
   020 7679 3449   fax 020 7679 2390
   http://www.benfieldhrc.org/
   Director: Prof Bill McGuire. Deputy Director: Dr Chris Kilburn.
- E A research centre at University College London.
- ○ To conduct strategic and applied research into natural hazards and their impact on society
- ● Conferences - Consultancy - Seminars - Workshops
- ✕ Benfield Greig Hazard Research Centre.

Bettany Centre for Entrepreneurial Performance and Economics   2006
- ■ Cranfield School of Management, Cranfield University, Cranfield, Bedfordshire, MK43 0AL.
   01234 751122   fax 01234 752136
   http://www.som.cranfield.ac.uk/som/groups/enterprise/entrep/
   Director: Prof Andrew Burke.
- E A research centre at Cranfield University.
- ○ To create a leading international business school centre which provides a stimulating entrepreneurial environment to promote high performing ventures through cutting edge entrepreneurial research, teaching and practice

BFSS National Religious Education Centre
- Note: has closed.

Bharatiya Vidya Bhavan
   see **Institute for Indian Art and Culture.**

BHF Glasgow Cardiovascular Research Centre   (BHFGCRC)   2005
- ■ University of Glasgow, 126 University Place, Glasgow, G12 8TA.
   0141-330 2045   fax 0141-330 6997
   http://www.gla.ac.uk/bhfgcrc/
   Director: Prof A Dominiczak.
- E A research centre at the University of Glasgow.
- ○ To consolidate internationally recognised cardiovascular research groups and to provide a multidisciplinary research environment

© CBD Research Ltd · Beckenham · Kent BR3 5JS · Tel 020 8650 7745 · Fax 020 8650 0768 · E-mail cbd@cbdresearch.com · www.cbdresearch.com

BHF National Centre for Physical Activity and Health   (BHFNC)
- School of Sport and Exercise Sciences, Loughborough University, Ashby Road, Loughborough, Leicestershire, LE11 3TU.
  01509 223259   fax 01509 223972
  http://www.bhfactive.org.uk/
- E   A centre at Loughborough University.
- O   To develop and promote initiatives that will help professionals stimulate more people to take more physical activity as part of everyday life

Bible and the Visual Imagination Research Centre
- Department of Theology and Religious Studies, University of Wales Lampeter, College Street, Lampeter, Ceredigion, SA48 7ED.
  01570 424708; 424866   fax 01570 424987
  http://www.imagingthebible.org/
  Director: Dr Martin O'Kane.
- E   A research centre at the University of Wales, Lampeter.
- O   To conduct research in various types of visual representation of biblical narrative - Old and New Testament

Bill Douglas Centre for the History of Cinema and Popular Culture   1994
- The Old Library, University of Exeter, Prince of Wales Road, Exeter, EX4 4SB.
  01392 264321   fax 01392 263871
  http://www.centres.ex.ac.uk/bill.douglas/
  Academic Director: Prof Steve Neale. Curator: Michelle Allen.
- E   A department of the University of Exeter.
- O   To house and care for the Bill Douglas and Peter Jewell collection of over 60,000 books, artefacts, ephemera and prints illustrating the history and prehistory of cinema
- ● Museum open Mon-Fri, 1000-1600 (free)
Note: Bill Douglas - British film maker who died in 1991.

Biocatalysis Centre
  see **Exeter Biocatalysis Centre.**

BioCentre [Aberystwyth]
  see **Aberystwyth BioCentre.**

Biocentre [Dundee]
  see **Wellcome Trust Biocentre.**

Biocentre [Manchester]
  see **Manchester Interdisciplinary Biocentre.**

BioComposites Centre
  see **BC.**

BioComputation Research Centre
  see **Liverpool BioComputation Research Centre.**

Biodeterioration Centre   1978
- Department of Biosciences, University of Hertfordshire, College Lane, Hatfield, Hertfordshire, AL10 9AB.
  01707 284545   fax 01707 285046
  http://www.herts.ac.uk/biodet/
  Contact: Richard Smith.
- E   A research centre at the University of Hertfordshire.
- O   To perform microbiological analysis and investigations for clients across the world

Biogeochemistry Research Centre
  see **Bristol Biogeochemistry Research Centre.**

Bioinformatics Research Centre   (BRC)
- Department of Computing Science, University of Glasgow, 4th Floor - Davidson Building, Glasgow, G12 8QQ.
  0141-330 2563
  http://www.brc.dcs.gla.ac.uk/
  Director: Prof David Gilbert.
- E   A research centre at the University of Glasgow.
- O   To provide an environment for collaborative interdisciplinary research in bioinformatics in the fields of systems biology, structural bioinformatics, functional genomics, databases and visualisation, e-Science and grid, and machine learning

Biological Anthropology Research Centre   (BARC)   2002
- School of Archaeological and Environmental Sciences, University of Bradford, Bradford, West Yorkshire, BD7 1DP.
  01274 233531
  http://www.barc.brad.ac.uk
- E   A centre at the University of Bradford.
- O   To specialise in the analysis of human skeletal remains, both ancient and modern

Biological Records Centre   (BRC)   1964
- ■   CEH Monks Wood, Abbots Ripton, Huntingdon, Cambridgeshire, PE28 2LS.
  01487 772407   fax 01487 773467
  http://www.brc.ac.uk/
  Head: Mark Hill.
- E   A research centre.
- O   To work with the voluntary recording community, throughout Britain and Ireland, for the recording of terrestrial and freshwater species (excluding birds)
- ●   The BRC database contains nearly 13 million records of more than 12,000 species

Biomaterials and Biomechanics Research Centre   (BBRC)   2004
- ■   Cardiff School of Dentistry, University of Wales Cardiff, Heath Park, Cardiff, CF14 4XY.
  029 2068 2161
  http://www.cardiff.ac.uk/dentistry/research/bbrc/
  Director: Prof John Middleton. Commercial Director: Prof Mark Waters.
- E   A research centre at Cardiff University.
- O   To consolidate and expand existing research initiatives in biomechanics and biomaterials

Biomedic Centre   1996
- ■   23 Manchester Street, London, W1U 4DJ.
  020 7935 6866   fax 020 7935 5114
  http://www.biomedic.co.uk/
  Director: Dr D Shakambet.
- E   A registered charity.
- O   To conduct medical research in the areas of cancer and nutrition
- ●   Conference facilities

BioMedical Centre
> see **Cranfield BioMedical Centre.**

Biomedical NMR Centre
> see **MRC Biomedical NMR Centre.**

Biomedical Research Centre   (BRC)   1992
- ■   College of Medicine, Dentistry & Nursing, Level 5 - Ninewells Hospital and Medical School, Dundee, DD1 9SY.
  01382 496669   fax 01382 669993
  http://www.dundee.ac.uk/biomedres/
  Director: Prof Roland Wolf.
- E   A centre at the University of Dundee.
- O   To provide a focus for excellence in biomedical research

Biomedical Research Centre   (BMRC)
- ■   Faculty of Health and Well Being, City Campus, Sheffield Hallam University, Howard Street, Sheffield, S1 1WB.
  0114-225 3065   fax 0114-225 3066
  http://www.shu.ac.uk/research/bmrc/
  Head: Prof Nicola Woodroofe.
- E   A research centre at Sheffield Hallam University.
- O   To conduct research in bioanalysis, biotransformation, molecular pharmacology, and neurological and chronic diseases

Biomedical Science Enterprise and Research Centre   (BSERC)
- ■   Cardiff School of Health Sciences, Llandarff Campus, University of Wales Institute Cardiff, Western Avenue, Cardiff, CF5 2YB.
  029 2041 7229
  http://www.uwic.ac.uk/sas/BSERC/bioscience_enterprise.asp
  Contact: Maninder Ahluwalia.
- E   A research centre at the University of Wales Institute, Cardiff.
- O   To conduct research in the fields of molecular and cell biology, microbiology and infection, and environmental chemistry

Biomedical Sciences Institute
> see **Essex Biomedical Sciences Institute.**

Biomedical Sciences Research Institute   2004
- ■   School of Biomedical Sciences, Coleraine Campus, University of Ulster, Cromore Road, Coleraine, County Londonderry, BT52 1SA.
  0870 040 0700
  http://www.science.ulster.ac.uk/biomed/research/institute.html
  Contact: Dr Victor A Gault.
- E   A department of the University of Ulster.
- O   To manage ten focused research groups in the fields of bioimaging, biomedical genomics, cancer and ageing, diabetes, microbial biotechnology, food and health, pharmaceutical biotechnology, stem cell and epigenetics, systems biology, and vision science

© CBD Research Ltd · Beckenham · Kent BR3 5JS · Tel 020 8650 7745 · Fax 020 8650 0768 · E-mail cbd@cbdresearch.com · www.cbdresearch.com

Biomedical Sciences Research Institute   (BRI)
- ■ Faculty of Science, Engineering and Environment, Peel Building, University of Salford, Salford, Manchester, M5 4WT.
  0161-295 3371   fax 0161-295 5015
  http://www.bri.salford.ac.uk/
  Director: Prof Geoff Hide.
- E A department of the University of Salford.
- O To co-ordinate and support the research activities in the areas of biology, biochemistry, chemistry and health-related topics

Biomedical Textiles Research Centre   (BTRC)
- ■ School of Textiles and Design, Heriot-Watt University, Netherdale, Galashiels, TD1 3HF.
  01896 892245
  http://www.hw.ac.uk/sbc/BTRC/BTRC/_private/homepage.htm
  Contact: Alex Fotheringham.
- E A research centre at Heriot-Watt University.
- O To perform research in the biomedical field, with particular emphasis on biomedical structures fabricated from textiles and their functions, conducting and medical polymers, polymer moulding and extrusion, and the medical applications of gas discharge plasma treatment

Biomolecular and Biomedical Research Centre
- ■ School of Applied Sciences, Northumbria University, Ellison Building, Ellison Place, Newcastle upon Tyne, NE1 8ST.
  0191-227 4585   fax 0191-227 3519
  http://northumbria.ac.uk/
- E A research centre at Northumbria University.
- O To conduct research within three fundamental themes - bioactive and biomimetic molecules, biochemistry and molecular biology, and microbiology and immunology

Biomolecular Sciences Research Centre   (BMSRC)   1997
- ■ School of Applied Sciences, University of Huddersfield, Queensgate, Huddersfield, HD1 3DH.
  01484 472169   fax 01484 472182
  http://www.hud.ac.uk/schools/applied_sciences/research/bmsrc/
  Director: Prof Mike Page.
- E A research centre at the University of Huddersfield.
- O To support research in biomolecular sciences, covering biochemical analysis, biological chemistry, bio-organic reaction mechanisms, biotechnology, cell and molecular physiology, food science and microbiology, molecular biology, and genetics

Biophysics Centre   2005
- ■ School of Crystallography, Birkbeck, University of London, Malet Street, Bloomsbury, London, WC1E 7HX.
  020 7631 6830   fax 020 7631 6803
  http://www.ismb.lon.ac.uk/centres.html
- E A constituent centre of the Institute of Structural Molecular Biology (qv) at Birkbeck, University of London.
- O To provide biophysics services to the wider research community

BIOS Centre
- ■ LSE, Houghton Street, London, WC2A 2AE.
  020 7955 6998   fax 020 7955 6565
  http://www.lse.ac.uk/collections/BIOS/
  Director: Prof Nikolas Rose.
- E A research centre at the London School of Economics and Political Science.
- O To conduct research into contemporary developments in the life sciences, biomedicine and biotechnology
- ✕ Centre for the Study of Bioscience, Biomedicine, Biotechnology and Society.

Biotechnology and Biological Sciences Research Council
    see **BBSRC**

Biotechnology Centre
    see **Cranfield Biotechnology Centre.**

Birkbeck Institute for the Humanities
- ■ School of English and Humanities, Birkbeck, University of London, Malet Street, Bloomsbury, London, WC1E 7HX.
  020 7631 6861
  http://www.bbk.ac.uk/bih/
  Executive Director: Donna Dickenson. International Director: Slavoj Zizek.
- E A research institute at Birkbeck, University of London.
- O To promote new ideas and forms of understanding in the humanities

Birkbeck Institute for Lifelong Learning   (BILL)
- ■ School of Continuing Education, Birkbeck, University of London, 26 Russell Square, London, WC1B 5DQ.
  020 7631 6625
  http://www.bbk.ac.uk/ce/bill/
  Director: Dr Sue Jackson.
- E An institute at Birkbeck, University of London.
- O To promote new ways of researching lifelong learning, which bridge academic, policy and community contexts, with a particular focus on pedagogics of lifelong learning

Birmingham Buddhist Centre
- 11 Park Road, Birmingham, B13 8AB.
  0121-449 5279
  http://www.birminghambuddhistcentre.org.uk/
- E   An independent non-profit-distributing organisation and a registered charity.
- O   To teach meditation and Buddhism
- ●   Education and training - The Centre provides meditation cushions and mats
- Note: For other Buddhist centres see note under **Buddhist Centres**.

Birmingham Institute of Art and Design   (BIAD)
- Birmingham City University, Gosta Green, Corporation Street, Birmingham, B4 7DX.
  0121-331 5800; 5801   fax 0121-331 7814
  http://www.biad.uce.ac.uk/
  Research Director: Nick Stanley.
- E   A faculty of Birmingham City University.
- O   To conduct research and teaching in a very broad range of subjects within art, design and media in Britain
- ×   University of Central England, Birmingham Institute of Art and Design

Blended Learning Unit CETL   (BLU)   2005
- University of Hertfordshire, College Lane, Hatfield, Hertfordshire, AL10 9AB.
  01707 284975
  http://www.herts.ac.uk/blu/
  Contact: Jon Alltree.
- E   A Centre for Excellence in Teaching and Learning (CETL) and a self contained unit within the Centre for the Enhancement of Learning and Teaching (qv) at the University of Hertfordshire.
- O   To support, promote and share new approaches to blended learning practice
- Note: See **Centres for Excellence in Teaching and Learning** for more information.

Blind Centre for Northern Ireland   (BCNI)   1978
- 70 North Road, Belfast, BT5 5NJ.
  028 9050 0999   fax 028 9065 0001
  http://www.bcni.co.uk/
- E   A registered charity and a company limited by guarantee.
- O   To enhance the quality of life for the blind and visually impaired in Northern Ireland through direct services, leisure, communication and research

Blond McIndoe Centre
    see **Queen Victoria Hospital Blond McIndoe Research Foundation.**

Bloomsbury Alexander Centre   1987
- Bristol House, 80a Southampton Row, London, WC1B 4BA.
  020 7404 5348
  http://www.alexcentre.com/
  Directors & Partner: Stephen Cooper. Director & Partner: Maya Galai.
- O   To promote the therapeutic technique devised by F Matthias Alexander (1869-1955)
- ●   Private lessons - Group introductory evening classes - One-day workshops
- Note: Affiliated to the Society of Teachers of the Alexander Technique.

Bloomsbury Centre for Bioinformatics   (BCB)
- NR   Department of Computer Science, Birkbeck, University of London, Malet Street, London, WC1E 7HX.
  020 7631 6700   fax 020 7631 6727
  http://bioinf.cs.ucl.ac.uk/bcb/
  Director: Prof David Jones. Centre Manager: Dr Jacky Pallas.
- E   A constituent centre of the Institute of Structural Molecular Biology (qv) at Birkbeck, University of London.
- O   To be at the forefront of research in protein, DNA microarray technology, genomics, and GRID-based applications for biomedical research
- Note: A joint initiative with University College London.

Bloomsbury Centre for Structural Biology   (BCSB)   1998
- School of Crystallography, Birkbeck, University of London, Malet Street, London, WC1E 7HX.
  020 7631 6830   fax 020 7631 6803
  http://www.bcsb.lon.ac.uk/
  Director: Prof Helen Saibil.
- E   A constituent centre of the Institute of Structural Molecular Biology (qv) at Birkbeck, University of London.
- O   To be a leading academic centre for translating gene sequences to protein structure and function

Bloomsbury Institute of Intensive Care Medicine
    see **Centre for Intensive Care Medicine and Bloomsbury Institute of Intensive Care Medicine.**

Bloomsbury Institute of the Natural Environment
    see **UCL Environment Institute.**

BNP Paribas Hedge Fund Centre
- ■ London Business School, Sussex Place, Regent's Park, London, NW1 4SA.
  020 7706 6804 fax 020 7724 3317
  http://www.london.edu/hedgefunds/
  Director: Narayan Naik.
- E A research centre at the London Business School.
- ○ To undertake research into all aspects of hedge fund investing, including the impact of hedge funds on the asset markets they invest in

Bobath Centre for Children with Cerebral Palsy   1951
- ■ Bradbury House, 250 East End Road, London, N2 8AU.
  020 8444 3355 fax 020 8444 3399
- E A non-profit-making company and a registered charity.
- ○ To provide treatment for children and adults with cerebral palsy; to offer training (mainly at postgraduate level) in the treatment and care of this disease - particularly for physiotherapists, speech and language therapists and occupational therapists; to undertake research into the cause, effects and treatment of cerebral palsy
- ● Assessment and consultancy service (especially for children living at a distance from London) (with the University College London and Royal Free Hospital School of Medicine) - Treatment of children per Bobath principles - Training

Bone and Mineral Centre   (BMC)
- ■ Department of Medicine, University College London, Rayne Building, 5 University Street, London, WC1E 6JF.
  020 7679 6169 fax 020 7679 6219
  http://www.ucl.ac.uk/medicine/bmc/
  Director: Prof Michael Horton.
- E A research centre at University College London.
- ○ To integrate clinical and laboratory-based research activities in the general area of skeletal biology and endocrinology of mineral metabolism, and through use of these cell and molecular methods, to study questions about diseases that affect mineralised tissues, such as osteoporosis, and hence improve diagnosis and treatment

Bookham Centre of Excellence for Optoelectronic Simulation   2005
- ■ School of Electrical and Electronic Engineering, University of Nottingham, University Park, Nottingham, NG7 2RD.
  0115-846 8296 fax 0115-951 5616
  http://www.nottingham.ac.uk/ggiemr/
- E A research centre within the George Green Institute for Electromagnetics Research (qv) at the University of Nottingham.

Borthwick Institute for Archives   1953
- ■ University of York, Heslington, York, YO10 5AR.
  01904 321160; 321166
  http://www.york.ac.uk/inst/bihr/
  Keeper of Archives: Christopher C Webb.
- E An institute at the University of York.
- ○ To keep and care for a collection of archives dating from the 12th century to the present day

Bournville Centre for Visual Arts
- ■ Birmingham Institute of Art and Design, Linden Road, Birmingham, B30 1JX.
  0121-331 5775 fax 0121-331 5779
  http://www.biad.uce.ac.uk/
- E A research centre within the Birmingham Institute of Art and Design (qv) at Birmingham City University.

BP Institute for Multiphase Flow   2000
- ■ Bullard Laboratories, University of Cambridge, Madingley Road, Cambridge, CB3 0EZ.
  01223 765700 fax 01223 765701
  http://www.bpi.cam.ac.uk/
  Contact: Catherine Pearson.
- E An institute at the University of Cambridge.
- ○ To focus research on fundamental problems involving multiphase flow

Bradford Centre for International Development   (BCID)
- ■ School of Social and International Studies, University of Bradford, Pemberton Building, Bradford, West Yorkshire, BD7 1DP.
  01274 233980 fax 01274 235280
  http://www.bradford.ac.uk/acad/bcid/
  Head of Centre: Patrick Ryan.
- E A centre at the University of Bradford.
- ○ To conduct research in development studies in economic, social and environmental policies, planning and administration, trade, business and finance, human resources and management

Bradford Disarmament Research Centre   (BDRC)
- ■ School of Social and International Studies, University of Bradford, Bradford, West Yorkshire, BD7 1DP.
  01274 234187 fax 01274 235240
  http://www.bradford.ac.uk/acad/bdrc/
  Contact: Dr Shaun Gregory.
- E A centre at the University of Bradford.
- ○ To conduct research in nuclear, chemical and biological weapons warfare disarmament

Brain and Body Centre   (B&BC)

- University of Nottingham, University Park, Nottingham, NG7 2RD.
  0115-951 5360
  http://brainbody.nottingham.ac.uk/
  Director: Prof Tomáš Paus.
- E   An interdisciplinary research centre at the University of Nottingham.
- O   To conduct studies of environmental and genetic factors that shape the structure and function of the human brain and body

Brain Imaging Centre
   see **Wolfson Brain Imaging Centre.**

Brain Repair Centre
   see **Cambridge Centre for Brain Repair.**

Brain and Repair Imaging Centre
   see **Cardiff University Brain and Repair Imaging Centre.**

Brandon Centre for Counselling and Psychotherapy for Young People   1991

- 26 Prince of Wales Road, London, NW5 3LG.
  020 7267 4792   fax 020 7267 5212
  http://www.brandon-centre.org.uk/
- E   A registered charity and a company limited by guarantee.
- O   To provide counselling, psychotherapy and advice to young people who are at risk of suicide, have severe behaviour difficulties, or abuse drugs or alcohol

Breakthrough Breast Cancer Research Centre   (BRCA)   1999

- Mary-Jean Mitchell Green Building, University of London, 237 Fulham Road, London, SW3 6JB.
  020 7153 5317   fax 020 7153 5340
  http://www.breakthroughcentre.org.uk/
  Director: Prof Alan Ashworth.
- E   A research centre within the Institute of Cancer Research (qv) at the University of London.
- O   To fight breast cancer through research and awareness

Breast Cancer Research Centre
   see **Breakthrough Breast Cancer Research Centre.**

Brickworks Conservation Centre
   see **Bursledon Brickworks Conservation Centre.**

Brighton Buddhist Centre

- 17 Tichborne Street, Brighton, East Sussex, BN1 1UR.
  01273 772090
  http://www.brightonbuddhistcentre.co.uk/
- E   An independent non-profit-distributing organisation and a registered charity.
- O   To teach meditation and Buddhism
- ● Education and training - The Centre provides meditation cushions and mats
Note: For other Buddhist centres see note under **Buddhist Centres.**

Bristol Biogeochemistry Research Centre   (BBRC)

- School of Chemistry, University of Bristol, Bristol, BS8 1TS.
  0117-928 7671   fax 0117-925 1295
  http://www.bris.ac.uk/bbrc/
  Director: Prof R P Evershed.
- E   An interdisciplinary research centre at the University of Bristol.
- O   To carry out research in the areas of atmosphere / biosphere / geosphere interactions eg ozone depletion and ecosystem response to climate change; to exploit a range of sedimentary archives, including marine and terrestrial records, to reconstruct past environments

Bristol Buddhist Centre

- 162 Gloucester Road, Bristol, BS7 8NT.
  0117-924 9991
  http://www.bristol-buddhist-centre.org/
- E   An independent non-profit-distributing organisation and a registered charity.
- O   To teach meditation and Buddhism
- ● Education and training - The Centre provides meditation cushions and mats
Note: For other Buddhist centres see note under **Buddhist Centres.**

Bristol Cancer Help Centre

Note: is now Penny Brohn Cancer Care and therefore outside the scope of this directory.

Bristol Centre for Management Accounting Research   (BRICMAR)
NR   Bristol Business School, Frenchay Campus, University of the West of England, Coldharbour Lane, Bristol, BS16 1QY.
     0117-328 2858; 3419   fax 0117-328 2289
     http://www.uwe.ac.uk/bbs/research/bricmar
     Contact: Prof Robert Luther. Contact: Prof Colwyn Jones.
E   An interdisciplinary research centre at the University of the West of England.
Note: A joint initiative with the University of Bristol.

Bristol Chemical Laboratory Sciences
     see **Bristol ChemLabS Centre for Excellence in Teaching and Learning (Bristol Chemical Laboratory Sciences).**

Bristol ChemLabS Centre for Excellence in Teaching and Learning (Bristol Chemical Laboratory Sciences)   2005
■   School of Chemistry, University of Bristol, Bristol, BS8 1TS.
     0117-928 7645   fax 0117-925 1295
     http://www.chm.bris.ac.uk/bristolchemlabs/
     Contact: Prof Guy Orpen.
E   A Centre for Excellence in Teaching and Learning (CETL) at the University of Bristol.
Note: See **Centres for Excellence in Teaching and Learning** for more information.

Bristol Genomics Research Institute   (BGRI)
■   Faculty of Applied Sciences, Frenchay Campus, University of the West of England, Coldharbour Lane, Bristol, BS16 1QY.
     0117-328 2147; 2149
     http://science.uwe.ac.uk/research/
     Co-Director: Prof Neil Avent. Co-Director: Prof Steve Neill.
E   A research institute at the University of the West of England.
O   To conduct post-genomics research, mainly on molecular plant science and molecular biomedicine

Bristol Glaciology Centre   1998
■   School of Geographical Sciences, University of Bristol, University Road, Bristol, BS8 1SS.
     0117-928 9954   fax 0117-928 7878
     http://www.bristol.ac.uk/bbrc/
     Director: Prof Martin Siebert.
E   A formal University Research Centre within the University of Bristol.
O   To carry out research into the behaviour of glaciers and ice sheets, and into the connections between the cryosphere, oceans and
     atmosphere under past, present and future climate conditions
●   Education and training
¶   See Centre's website for various publications.

Bristol Heart Institute   (BHI)   1995
■   Faculty of Medicine and Dentistry, Level 7 - Bristol Royal Infirmary, Bristol, BS2 8HW.
     0117-928 3519   fax 0117-928 3581
     http://www.bristol.ac.uk/Depts/BHI/
     Director: Dr Saadeh Suleiman.
E   A research institute at the University of Bristol.
O   To foster local, national and international cardiovascular, basic and applied research

Bristol Institute of Greece, Rome and the Classical Tradition   2000
■   Faculty of Arts, Senate House, University of Bristol, Tyndall Avenue, Bristol, BS8 1TH.
     0117-928 9000
     http://www.bristol.ac.uk/arts/birtha/centres/institute/
     Director: Prof Charles Martindale.
E   An institute within the University of Bristol.
O   To support research into any aspect of Greek and Roman civilisation, and its reception from antiquity to the present day, with
     particular emphasis on work exploring links between ancient and modern

Bristol Institute of Legal Practice   (BILP)
■   Faculty of Law, Frenchay Campus, University of the West of England, Coldharbour Lane, Bristol, BS16 1QY.
     0117-328 2604   fax 0117-328 2268
     http://www.bilp.uwe.ac.uk/
E   An institute at the University of the West of England.
O   To provide a wide variety of professional legal courses

Bristol Institute for Research in the Humanities and Arts   (BIRTHA)   2004
■   Faculty of Arts, University of Bristol, 3 Woodland Road, Bristol, BS8 1TB.
     0117-928 8892
     http://www.bristol.ac.uk/arts/birtha/
     Director: Prof Tim Unwin.
E   An institute within the University of Bristol.
O   To support, promote and disseminate the research of the Faculty of Arts

Bristol Institute for Transfusion Sciences
■ International Blood Group Reference Laboratory, Southmead Road, Bristol, BS10 5ND.
　　0117-991 2103　fax 0117-959 1660
　　http://www.blood.co.uk/ibgrl/
　　Contact: Prof David J Anstee.
E　A research institute within the National Blood Service.
Note: The Institute is a World Health Organisation **WHO Collaborating Centre** for Immunohaematology.

Britain-Russia Centre and the British East-West Centre　(BEWC)　1959
■ Willcox House, 42 Southwark Street, London, SE1 1UN.
　　020 7378 8222　fax 020 7378 8333
　　http://www.bewc.org/
E　A non-government organisation.
○　To provide information, training, consultancy and other services that support positive processes of sustainable social, political and
　　economic development in Russia

Britain Visitor Centre
■ 1 Regent Street, London, SW1Y 4NS.
　　http://www.visitbritain.org/

British Atmospheric Data Centre　(BADC)　2006
■ Space Science and Technology Department, Room 2-122 - CCLRC Rutherford Appleton Laboratory, Chilton, Didcot, Oxfordshire,
　　OX11 0QX.
　　01235 446432　fax 01235 446314
　　http://badc.nerc.ac.uk/
E　Part of the National Centre for Atmospheric Science (qv).
○　To assist UK atmospheric researchers to locate, access and interpret atmospheric data and to ensure the long-term integrity of
　　atmospheric data produced by NERC projects
Note: BDAC is one of the collaborative centres involved with the **National Centre for Atmospheric Science**.

British Broadcasting Corporation
　　see **BBC**.

British Centre for Literary Translation　(BCLT)　1989
■ School of Literature and Creative Writing, University of East Anglia, Norwich, NR4 7TJ.
　　01603 592785　fax 01603 592737
　　http://www.literarytranslation.com/
　　Director: Amanda Hopkinson. Associate Director: Maria Filippakopoulou.
E　A department of the University of East Anglia.
○　To promote and raise the profile of literature in translation and literary translators
●　Education and training - Information service - Library - Various events
¶　In Other Words (journal). New Books in German.

British East-West Centre
　　see **Britain-Russia Centre and the British East-West Centre.**

British and Foreign School Society National Religious Education Centre
Note: has closed.

British Heart Foundation...
　　see **BHF**

British Hernia Centre
■ 87 Watford Way, London, NW4 4RS.
　　020 8201 7000
　　http://www.hernia.org/
○　To treat and repair hernias

British Idealism Centre
　　see **Collingwood and British Idealism Centre.**

British Institute for Brain Injured Children　(BIBIC)　1972
■ Knowle Hall, Bridgwater, Somerset, TA7 8PJ.
　　01278 684060　fax 01278 685573
　　http://www.bibic.org.uk/
　　Chief Executive: Julie Spencer-Cingöz. Director of Fundraising: Jill Taylor.
E　A registered charity.
○　To maximise the potential of children with conditions affecting their sensory, social, communication, motor and learning abilities ·
　　caused by conditions such as autism, cerebral palsy and Down's syndrome
●　Information service

© CBD Research Ltd · Beckenham · Kent BR3 5JS · Tel 020 8650 7745 · Fax 020 8650 0768 · E-mail cbd@cbdresearch.com · www.cbdresearch.com

British Institute of Homeopathy   (BIH)   1986
- ■   Endeavour House, 80 High Street, Egham, Surrey, TW20 9HE.
     01784 473800   fax 01784 473801
     http://www.britinsthom.com/
     Director: Dr Trevor M Cook.
- E   A company limited by guarantee.
- ○   To provide education and training by distance learning programmes in homeopathy and other complementary therapies

British Institute of Human Rights   (BIHR)   1970
- ■   School of Law, King's College London, 26-29 Drury Lane, London, WC2B 5RL.
     020 7848 1818   fax 020 7848 1814
     http://www.bihr.org/
     Director: Katie Ghose.
- E   An independent charity at King's College, London.
- ○   To raise awareness and understanding about the importance of human rights

British Institute of International and Comparative Law   (BIICL)   1958
- ■   Charles Clore House, 17 Russell Square, London, WC1B 5JP.
     020 7862 5151   fax 020 7862 5152
     http://www.biicl.org/
     Director: Prof Gillian Triggs.

British Institute of Jazz Studies   (BIJS)   1964
- ■   17 The Chase, Edgcumbe Park, Crowthorne, Berkshire, RG45 6HT.
     01344 775669   fax 01344 780947
     Archivist & Secretary: Graham Langley.
- E   A registered charity.
- ○   To provide a research facility for jazz, blues and related music
- ●   Information service - Library

British Library Centre for the Book
Note: Disbanded in 2003.

British Library Document Supply Centre   (BLDSC)   1973
- ■   Boston Spa, Wetherby, West Yorkshire, LS23 7BQ.
     01937 546060   fax 01937 546333
     http://www.bl.uk/
- E   A Government-funded body.
- ○   To supply documents in various formats by loan, to customers throughout the world

British Light Aviation Centre   (BLAC)
- ■   50a Cambridge Street, London, SW1V 4QQ.
     020 7834 5631
     http://www.aopa.co.uk/
- E   The headquarters of the Aircraft Owners and Pilots Association.

British Music Information Centre   (BMIC)   1967
- ■   Lincoln House, 75 Westminster Bridge Road, London, SE1 7HS.
     020 7928 1902   fax 020 7928 2957
     http://www.bmic.co.uk/
     Director: Matthew Greenall. Production & Services Manager: Imogen Mitchell.
- E   A registered charity and a company limited by guarantee.
- ○   To encourage interest in, and performance of, British contemporary classical music from 1900 to the present day
- ●   Information service - Library - Talks and concerts
- ¶   Friends Newsletter.

British National Space Centre   (BNSC)   1985
- ■   151 Buckingham Palace Road, London, SW1W 9SS.
     020 7215 0807   fax 020 7215 0804
     http://www.bnsc.gov.uk/
     Space Minister: Lord Sainsbury of Turville.
- E   A Government organisation.
- ○   To bring together Britain's civil space interests, linking government, the public sector, the scientific community and industry; to provide a focus for expertise in earth observation and its applications, in space science and technology, in launcher systems, and satellite communications, and to provide value for money from UK Government investments in space

British Olympic Medical Centre
      see **Olympic Medical Institute.**

British Petroleum Institute for Multiphase Flow
      see **BP Institute for Multiphase Flow.**

British Philatelic Centre
Note: has closed.

British Polarographic Research Institute   (BPRI)   1955
- ■ 6 Beechvale, Hillview Road, Woking, Surrey, GU22 7NS.
  President & Research Director: Prof Wilfred Parker.
- E A private scientific-research and operational-research organisation.
- ○ To conduct fundamental research into polarisational and diffusion-based phenomena and development of theories for polarity, polarology, polarochronodynamics, polarophoton-dynamics, and polarity-operations; to conduct applied research into medical, environmental and management polarology, including cancer polarodiagnostics, cardiomotivation polarology, cardiomobility polarology, polarographic-psychotherapy
- ● Library Applied research into polarostatic fog dispersal for air ambulance landing strips, elctrochemical cold-fusion polarography, radiopolarology, radiopoloarographic deaf-mute-blind communication; and 'learning disability' communication by photon-polarography

British Regional Furniture Study Centre
- ■ Wycombe Museum, Priory Avenue, High Wycombe, Buckinghamshire, HP13 6PX.
  01494 421899

British Wildlife Rescue Centre Ltd   1991
- ■ Amerton Farm, Stowe By Chartley, Staffordshire, ST18 0LA.
  01889 271308
  http://www.thebwrc.co.uk/
  Founder & Company Director: A D Hardy.
- E An independent non-profit organisation.
- ○ To rescue, care for, rehabilitate and then release injured, sick and orphaned British wildlife
- ● Education and training - Recreational facilities
- ¶ Newsletter.

Broadcast Advertising Clearance Centre   (BACC)
- ■ 4 Roger Street (2nd floor), London, WC1N 2JX
  020 7339 4700
  http://www.bacc.org.uk/bacc
- ○ A specialist body responsible for the pre-transmission examination and clearance of television advertisements

Brook Advisory Centres   1964
- ■ 421 Highgate Studios, 53-79 Highgate Road, London, NW5 1TL.
  020 7284 6040   fax 020 7284 6050
  http://www.brook.org.uk/
- E A registered charity, registered company and a voluntary organisation.
- ○ To provide free and confidential sexual health advice and services specifically for young people under 25
Note: There are 17 Brook Advisory Centres throughout the UK.

Brooks World Poverty Institute   (BWPI)   2006
- ■ Faculty of Humanities, University of Manchester, Bridgeford Street, Oxford Road, Manchester, M13 9PL.
  0161-306 6000
  http://www.bwpi.manchester.ac.uk/
- E A research institute at the University of Manchester.
- ○ To conduct and promote world-leading research on poverty in all its manifestations

Brunel Able Children's Education Centre   (BACE)   1996
- ■ School of Sport and Education, Brunel University, Uxbridge, Middlesex, UB8 3PH.
  01895 267152   fax 01895 269805
  http://www.brunel.ac.uk/about/acad/sse/sseres/sseresearchcentres/bacehome
  Administrator: Catherina Emery.
- E A centre at Brunel University.
- ○ To offer support to professionals to make effective provision for higher ability pupils

Brunel Advanced Institute of Multimedia and Network Systems   (BRAINS)
- ■ School of Engineering and Design, Brunel University, Uxbridge, Middlesex, UB8 3PH.
  01895 265932
  http://www.brunel.ac.uk/about/acad/sed/sedres/nmc/brains
  Director: Prof Yong-Hua Song.
- E A research institute at Brunel University.
- ○ To conduct research into various fields of multimedia and network systems

© CBD Research Ltd · Beckenham · Kent BR3 5JS · Tel 020 8650 7745 · Fax 020 8650 0768 · E-mail cbd@cbdresearch.com · www.cbdresearch.com

Brunel Centre for Advanced Solidification Technology   (BCAST)
- School of Engineering and Design, Brunel University, Uxbridge, Middlesex, UB8 3PH.
  01895 274000
  http://www.brunel.ac.uk/about/acad/bcast
- E   A special research institute at Brunel University.
- O   To focus on both fundamental and applied research on advanced solidification processes for metallic materials

Brunel Centre for Contemporary Writing   (BCCW)   2002
- School of Arts, Brunel University, Uxbridge, Middlesex, UB8 3PH.
  01895 274000
  http://www.brunel.ac.uk/about/acad/sa/artresearch/bccw
- E   A centre at Brunel University.
- O   To provide a forum for cutting-edge debate, involving prominent critics, practising writers and students at all levels

Brunel Centre for Democratic Evaluation   (BCDE)
- Brunel Business School, Brunel University, Uxbridge, Middlesex, UB8 3PH.
  01895 266309
  http://www.brunel.ac.uk/about/acad/bbs/research/centres/bcde
  Director: Dr Justin Fisher.
- E   A research centre at Brunel University.
- O   To conduct research and provide consultancy in the fields of public policy, democratic procedures and public opinion

Brunel Centre for Intelligence and Security Studies   (BCISS)   2003
- Brunel Business School, Brunel University, Uxbridge, Middlesex, UB8 3PH.
  01895 265278
  http://www.brunel.ac.uk/about/acad/bbs/research/centres/bciss/
  Director: Prof Anthony Glees.
- E   A centre at Brunel University.
- O   To offer a research focus and consultancy service for work in the areas of intelligence and security worldwide

Brunel Centre for Manufacturing Metrology   (BCMM)   1985
- School of Engineering and Design, Brunel University, Uxbridge, Middlesex, UB8 3PH.
  01895 265786   fax 01895 812556
  http://www.brunel.ac.uk/about/acad/sed/sedres/dm/bcmm
  Director: Prof Barry E Jones.
- E   A centre at Brunel University.
- O   To undertake applied research, development and consultancy in all aspects of measurement science and technology, automatic inspection and quality engineering relating to manufacturing

Brunel Centre for Packaging Technology   (BCPT)   2002
- School of Engineering and Design, Brunel University, Uxbridge, Middlesex, UB8 3PH.
  01895 203253
  http://www.brunel.ac.uk/about/acad/sed/sedres/me/bcpt
  Director: Dr Lynn Gabrielson.
- E   A centre at Brunel University.
- O   To promote its packaging activities through research partnerships with industry and other organisations

Brunel Institute for Bioengineering   (BIB)   1983
- Brunel University, Uxbridge, Middlesex, UB8 3PH.
  01895 266927   fax 01895 274608
  http://www.brunel.ac.uk/about/acad/bib
  Director: Prof Ian Sutherland. Contact: Margaret Pearce.
- E   A research institute at Brunel University.
- O   To specialise in science and engineering research for space, health care and contract work for industry
- ● Laboratory facilities

Brunel Institute of Cancer Genetics and Pharmacogenomics   (BICGP)   2000
- School of Health Sciences and Social Care, Brunel University, Uxbridge, Middlesex, UB8 3PH.
  01895 274000
  http://www.brunel.ac.uk/about/acad/health/healthres/researchareas/bicgp
  Director: Prof Rob Newbold.
- E   A research institute at Brunel University.
- O   To identify and characterize new genes and molecular pathways, involved in human cancer development, that can be exploited as targets for novel therapeutic intervention

Brunel Institute of Computational Mathematics   (BICOM)
- Brunel University, Uxbridge, Middlesex, UB8 3PH.
  01895 265184
  http://www.about/acad/siscm/maths/research/bicom/
  Director: Prof J R Whiteman. Administrator: Carolyn Sellars.
- E   A research institute at Brunel University.
- O   To stimulate and execute research work within the broad areas of computational mathematics

Brunel Institute of Power Systems   (BIPS)

■ School of Engineering and Design, Brunel University, Uxbridge, Middlesex, UB8 3PH.
   01895 266809
   http://www.brunel.ac.uk/about/acad/sed/sedres/nmc/bips/
   Director: Prof Malcolm Irving.
E   A research institute at Brunel University.
O   To conduct research and devlopment of advanced computational tools (software and hardware) for the analysis, control, operation, management and design of the electricity, generation, transmission and distribution systems

Brunel Organisation and Systems Design Centre   (BOSdc)

■ Brunel Business School, Brunel University, Uxbridge, Middlesex, UB8 3PH.
   01895 265295
   http://www.brunel.ac.uk/about/acad/bbs/research/centres/osdc
   Director: Dr Nandish Patel.
E   A research centre at Brunel University.
O   To conduct basic and applied research into organisation and systems design

Brunel University Random Systems Research Centre   (BURSt)

■ Brunel University, Uxbridge, Middlesex, UB8 3PH.
   01895 265609
   http://www.brunel.ac.uk/about/acad/siscm/maths/research/burst/
   Director: Prof Geoff Rodgers.
E   A centre at Brunel University.
O   To investigate and develop the theory of random systems

BUDDHIST CENTRES

Note: There are 14 Centres in the UK and individual entries can be found under each Centre's location - see Birmingham, Brighton, Bristol, Cambridge, Croydon, Edinburgh, Glasgow, Lancashire, Leeds, London, Manchester, North London, Norwich and West London.

Building Centre

■ 26 Store Street, London, WC1E 7BT.
   020 7692 4000
   http://www.buildingcentre.co.uk/
   Chairman: Michael Rose, CBE. Chief Executive: Colin Henderson.
E   A wholly owned subsidiary of the Building Centre Trust, an independent charitable organisation.
O   To provide support for research, educational and cultural activities connected with the building environment

Built Environment Innovation Centre   (BEIC)   2003

NR   Department of Civil and Environmental Engineering, South Kensington Campus, Imperial College London, Exhibition Road, London, SW7 2AZ.
   020 7589 5111   fax 020 7823 7685
   http://www3.imperial.ac.uk/innovationstudies
   Director: Prof David Gann.
E   An EPSRC Innovative Manufacturing Research Centre within the Innovation Studies Centre (qv) at Imperial College London.
O   To bring together expertise on the study of technology innovation in the built environment industries so as to generate knowledge to help modernise the buildings and infrastructure needed for the 21st century
Note: One of the EPSRC funded centres in the UK - for further information see **EPSRC Innovative Manufacturing Research Centres.**

Burden Neurological Institute   1939

■ University of Bristol, Stoke Lane, Stapleton, Bristol, BS16 1QT.
   0117-956 7444; 970 1212
   Scientific Director: Dr Stuart Butler.
E   A registered charity and associate institute of the University of Bristol.
O   To study and investigate brain and nervous function in relation to normal and abnormal behaviour and disease; to treat, alleviate and prevent neurological, psychiatric and psychological diseases, ailments, disorders, complaints and defects

Burdett Institute of Gastrointestinal Nursing   (BIGN)   2005

■ Florence Nightingale School of Nursing and Midwifery, St Mark's Hospital, Watford Road, Harrow, Middlesex, HA1 3UJ.
   020 8869 5429   fax 020 8869 5430
   http://www.burdettinstitute.org.uk/
   Contact: Prof Christine Norton.
E   A research institute at King's College, London.
O   To improve the health and wellbeing of people with gastrointestinal disorders by promoting excellence in gastrointestinal nursing education, research and practice

© CBD Research Ltd · Beckenham · Kent BR3 5JS · Tel 020 8650 7745 · Fax 020 8650 0768 · E-mail cbd@cbdresearch.com · www.cbdresearch.com

Bureau of Analysed Samples Ltd (BAS)
- Newham Hall, Newby, Middlesbrough, TS8 9EA.
  01642 300500   fax 01642 315209
  http://www.basrid.co.uk/
  Chairman: P D Ridsdale, BSc, Ceng, MIM. Managing Director: R P Meeres, BA(Oxon).
- E A profit-making business.
- ○ To produce British Chemical Standard, Spectroscopic Standard and EURONORM certified reference materials
- ● Production of Certified Reference Materials catalogue (includes details of UK and European co-operating analysts and laboratories, British Chemical Standard certified reference materials, etc)

Bureau of Freelance Photographers (BFP) 1965
- Focus House, 497 Green Lane, London, N13 4BP.
  020 8882 3315; 3316   fax 020 8886 5174
  Director: John Tracy. Head of Members' Services: Stewart Gibson.
- E A membership organisation with c 7,000 members.
- ○ To provide information and advice about publishing markets to freelance photographers, both professional and amateur
- ● Two-year correspondence course in freelance photography and photo-journalism (BFP School of Photography)

Bureau Veritas
- Tower Bridge Court, 224-226 Tower Bridge Road, London, SE1 2TX.
  020 7550 8900   fax 020 7403 1590
  http://www.bureauveritas.com/
- E A service company with a network of 700 offices and laboratories in 140 countries worldwide.
- ○ To provide companies with quality, health, safety, environment and social accountability in the fields of certification, conformity assessment, consulting and training

Bursledon Brickworks Conservation Centre   1993
- Coal Park Lane, Southampton, SO31 7GW.
  01489 576248   fax 01489 576248
  Project Director: K Stubbs. Development Manager: C Nicholas.
- E A registered charity.
- ○ To preserve the UK's brickmaking heritage and present it to the public through the preservation and interpretation of the historic buildings and machinery; to promote enlightened conservation by encouraging the use of traditional crafts, skills and materials associated with the building industry and brickmaking; to provide an educational facility for schools, colleges, universities, professional bodies, study groups and general public at all levels, covering building conservation and environmental awareness
- ● Conference facilities - Education and training - Exhibitions - Information service - Recreational facilities

Business-to-Business Marketing Research Centre
- Kingston Business School, Kingston University London, Kingston Hill, Kingston-upon-Thames, Surrey, KT1 7LB.
  020 8547 2000
  http://business.kingston.ac.uk/
- E A research centre at Kingston University, London.
- ○ To conduct research on channel design and management, business segmentation and positioning, relationship marketing, and value creation

Business Incubation Centre
    see **Cranfield University Business Incubation Centre.**

Business, Management, Accountancy and Finance Subject Centre (BMAF) 2000
- Oxford Brookes Business School, Wheatley Campus, Oxford Brookes University, Wheatley, Oxford, OX33 1HX.
  01865 485670   fax 01865 485830
  http://www.business.heacademy.ac.uk/
- E A Government funded national centre within the Oxford Brookes University.
- ○ To foster world-class education in accountancy, business, finance and management
- ● Education and training - Information service - Statistics
- ✕ LTSN Accountancy, Business and Management Subject Centre.
Note: One of the 24 Subject Centres of the Higher Education Academy, (qv).

Business and Management Research Institute
- Faculty of Business and Management, Coleraine Campus, University of Ulster, Cromore Road, Coleraine, County Londonderry, BT52 1SA.
  028 9036 6351   fax 028 9036 6805
  http://www.business.ulster.ac.uk/researchinstitute/
  Director: Prof Paul Humphreys.
- E A research institute at the University of Ulster.
- ○ To conduct research in operations management, marketing and social economy

Business and Management Research Institute   (BMRI)
- ■   Luton Business School, Luton Campus, University of Bedfordshire, Luton, Bedfordshire, LU1 3JU.
   01582 743187
   http://www.beds.ac.uk/research/bmri/
   Director: Prof Brian Mathews.
- E   A research institute at the University of Bedfordshire.
- ○   To produce high quality research that is applied and applicable, and relevant to the needs of the business community

Business Travel Research Centre   (BTRC)
- ■   Department of Air Transport, Cranfield University, Cranfield, Bedfordshire, MK43 0AL.
   01234 754233   fax 01234 752207
   http://www.businesstravelresearch.com/
   Head: Dr Keith Mason.
- E   A research centre at Cranfield University.
- ○   To develop in-depth understanding of the complexities of the business travel sector, and its importance within the air transport industry

C4C: Collaborating for Creativity CETL   (C4C)   2005
- ■   York St John University College, Lord Mayor's Walk, York, YO31 7EX.
      01904 716774; 876306
      http://www2.yorksj.ac.uk/default.asp?Page_ID=3467
      Head: Prof Gweno Williams.
- E   A Centre for Excellence in Teaching and Learning (CETL) at the York St John University College.
- Note: See **Centres for Excellence in Teaching and Learning** for more information.

CAA Institute of Satellite Navigation   (ISN)   1993
- ■   School of Electronic and Electrical Engineering, University of Leeds, Woodhouse Lane, Leeds, LS2 9JT.
      0113-343 2090
      http://www.engineering.leeds.ac.uk/i3s/research/Sat_Nav_wire/
      Contact: Dr David Walsh.
- E   A research institute within the Institute of Integrated Information Systems (qv) at the University of Leeds.
- O   To conduct research in global navigation satellite systems

CAB International   (CABI)   1909
- ■   Nosworthy Way, Wallingford, Oxfordshire, OX10 8DE.
      01491 832111   fax 01491 833508
      http://www.cabi.org/
      Chairman: Dr John Regazzi.
- E   An international and inter-governmental organisation.
- O   To improve people's lives worldwide by providing information and applying scientific expertise to solve problems in agriculture and the environment

Caledonian Centre for Engineering Education
    see **Scottish Centre for Work Based Learning.**

Caledonian Environment Centre   (CEC)   1998
- ■   School of the Built and Natural Environment, 3rd Floor - Drummond House, Glasgow Caledonian University, 1 Hill Street, Glasgow, G3 6RN.
      0141-273 1416   fax 0141-273 1430
      http://www.caledonian.ac.uk/environment/
      Director: Prof Jim Baird.
- E   A centre at Glasgow Caledonian University.
- O   To become the leading, research and consultancy organisation in the broader environmental field
- ×   Caledonian Shanks Centre for Waste Management.

Caledonian Family Business Centre
- ■   Caledonian Business School, Hamish Wood Building, Glasgow Caledonian University, Cowcaddens Road, Glasgow, G4 0BA.
      0141-330 8280   fax 0141-330 8281
      http://www.familybusinesscentre.com/
- E   A research centre at Glasgow Caledonian University.
- O   To specialise in family business research

Caledonian Nursing and Midwifery Research Centre   2001
- ■   School of Nursing, Midwifery and Community Health, Glasgow Caledonian University, Cowcaddens Road, Glasgow, G4 0BA.
      0141-331 3463
      http://www.gcal.ac.uk/nmch/research/
      Contact: Prof Debbie Tolson.
- E   A centre at Glasgow Caledonian University.
- O   To co-ordinate the programmatic research of the School

Caledonian Shanks Centre for Waste Management
    see **Caledonian Environment Centre.**

CALL Centre
    see **Communication Aids for Language and Learning.**

Callaghan Centre for the Study of Conflict   2002
- ■   Swansea University, Singleton Park, Swansea, SA2 8PP.
      01792 205678   fax 01792 295157
      http://www.swan.ac.uk/research/centresandinstitutes/CallaghanCentrefortheStudyofConflict/
- E   An interdisciplinary research centre at Swansea University.
- O   To facilitate, co-ordinate and financially support research and informed debate on international conflict, both historical and contemporary

Cambridge Buddhist Centre
- 38 Newmarket Road, Cambridge, CB5 8DT.
  01223 577553
  http://www.cambridgebuddhistcentre.com/
- E   An independent non-profit-distributing organisation and a registered charity.
- ○   To teach meditation and Buddhism
- ●   Education and training - The Centre provides meditation cushions and mats

Note: For other Buddhist centres see note under **Buddhist Centres**.

Cambridge Centre for Brain Repair   (BRC)
- Department of Clinical Neurosciences, E D Adrian Building, University of Cambridge, Robinson Way, Cambridge, CB2 2PY.
  01223 331160   fax 01223 331174
  http://www.brc.cam.ac.uk/
- E   A centre at the University of Cambridge.
- ○   To understand, and eventually to alleviate and repair, damage to the brain and spinal cord which results from injury or
      neurodegenerative disease

Note: Also known as the Brain Repair Centre.

Cambridge Centre for Climate Change Mitigation Research   (4CMR)   2006
- Department of Land Economy, University of Cambridge, 19 Silver Street, Cambridge, CB3 9EP.
  01223 337147   fax 01223 337130
  http://www.landecon.cam.ac.uk/research/eeprg/4cmr/index.htm
- E   A research centre at the University of Cambridge.
- ○   To foresee strategies, policies and processes to mitigate human-induced climate change which are effective, efficient and equitable,
      including understanding and modelling transitions to low-carbon energy / environment / economy systems

Cambridge Centre for Economic and Public Policy   (CCEPP)
- Department of Land Economy, University of Cambridge, 19 Silver Street, Cambridge, CB3 9EP.
  01223 337147   fax 01223 337130
  http://www.landecon.cam.ac.uk/research/reuag/ccepp/ccepp.htm
  Director: Dr John McCombie.
- E   A research centre at the University of Cambridge.

Cambridge Centre for Gender Studies   (CCGS)   1997
- Room S26, University of Cambridge, 17 Mill Lane, Cambridge, CB2 1RX.
  01223 764091   fax 01223 763593
  http://www.gender.cam.ac.uk/
  Director: Prof Juliet Mitchell.
- E   A centre at the University of Cambridge.
- ○   To be a world leading institution for the study of questions relating to gender in modern society

Cambridge Centre for Housing and Planning Research   (CCHPR)   1990
- Department of Land Economy, University of Cambridge, 19 Silver Street, Cambridge, CB3 9EP.
  01223 337118   fax 01223 330863
  http://www.cchpr.landecon.cam.ac.uk/
  Director: Prof Christine Whitehead.
- E   A research centre at the University of Cambridge.

Cambridge Centre for Proteomics   (CCP)
- Cambridge System Biology Institute, Tennis Court Road, Building O, University of Cambridge, Cambridge, CB2 1QR.
  01223 765255
  http://www.bio.cam.ac.uk/proteomics/
  Facility Group Leader: Dr Kathryn Lilley.
- E   A research centre at the University of Cambridge.
- ○   To conduct research in the fields of organelle proteomics (and the study of the location within and movement between membrane
      and membrane associated proteins within cells), and power analysis of quantitative proteomics techniques

Cambridge Computational Biology Institute   (CCBI)
- Department of Applied Mathematics and Theoretical Physics, University of Cambridge, Wilberforce Road, Cambridge, CB3 0WA.
  01223 765000   fax 01223 765900
  http://www.ccbi.cam.ac.uk/
  Director: Dr Gos Micklem.
- E   A centre at the University of Cambridge.
- ○   To conduct research in a variety of fields, including basic genetics of bacteria, developmental biology, evolutionary biology,
      complex cell biology of human disease, and systems biology

© CBD Research Ltd · Beckenham · Kent BR3 5JS · Tel 020 8650 7745 · Fax 020 8650 0768 · E-mail cbd@cbdresearch.com · www.cbdresearch.com

Cambridge Crystallographic Data Centre (CCDC) 1965
■ University of Cambridge, 12 Union Road, Cambridge, CB2 1EZ.
  01223 336408   fax 01223 336033
  http://www.ccdc.cam.ac.uk/
  Executive Director: Dr Frank H Allen.
E An independent non-profit-distributing organisation, a registered charity and a company limited by guarantee, established as a teaching institution of the University of Cambridge.
O The advancement of chemistry and crystallography for the public benefit through providing high-quality information services and software
● Information service

Cambridge e-Science Centre   (CeSC)
■ Department of Applied Mathematics and Theoretical Physics, University of Cambridge, Wilberforce Road, Cambridge, CB3 0WA.
  01223 764282; 765251   fax 01223 765900
  http://www.escience.cam.ac.uk/
  Director: Prof Andy Parker.
E A research centre within the Centre for Mathematical Sciences (qv) at the University of Cambridge.
O To stimulate and sustain the development of e-Science in the UK; to contribute significantly to its international development; to ensure that its techniques are propagated rapidly to commerce and industry
Note: See **e-Science Centres** for further information.

Cambridge and East Anglia Centre for Structural Biology
■ Department of Chemistry, University of Cambridge, Lensfield Road, Cambridge, CB2 1EW.
  01223 336300   fax 01223 336362
  http://www.ch.cam.ac.uk/resources/SBI/
E A centre at the University of Cambridge.
O To study the structural biology of signalling, from receptor activation at the cell surface, and signal transduction in the cytoplasm, to the control of transcription

Cambridge Endowment for Research in Finance   (CERF)   2001
■ Judge Business School, University of Cambridge, Trumpington Street, Cambridge, CB2 1AG.
  01223 339700
  http://www.jbs.cam.ac.uk/research/cerf/
E A centre at the University of Cambridge.
O To develop an advanced understanding of how financial markets and institutions have evolved as they have, and why they behave as they do

Cambridge Engineering Design Centre   (CEDC)
NR Department of Engineering, University of Cambridge, Trumpington Street, Cambridge, CB2 1PZ.
  01223 765308   fax 01223 332662
  http://www-edc.eng.cam.ac.uk/
  Director: Prof P John Clarkson.
E An EPSRC Innovative Manufacturing Research Centre at the University of Cambridge.
O To undertake research to create knowledge, understanding, methods and tools that will contribute to improving the design process
Note: One of the EPSRC funded centres in the UK - for further information see **EPSRC Innovative Manufacturing Research Centres**.

Cambridge Entrepreneurship Centre
■ University of Cambridge, 10 Trumpington Street, Cambridge, CB2 1QA.
  01223 760339   fax 01223 764888
  http://www.enterprise.cam.ac.uk/
  Director: Teri Willey.
E A research centre at the University of Cambridge.

Cambridge Institute of Language Research   (CILR)
■ Department of Linguistics, University of Cambridge, Sidgwick Avenue, Cambridge, CB3 9DA.
  01223 331733   fax 01223 335053
  http://www.cilr.cam.ac.uk/
  Contact: Dr Gea de Jong.
E An institute at the University of Cambridge.
O To promote interdisciplinary research in languages and intellectual exchange

Cambridge Institute for Medical Research   (CIMR)
■ Wellcome Trust / MRC Building, University of Cambridge, Hill's Road, Cambridge, CB2 2XY.
  01223 762322   fax 01223 762323
  http://www.cimr.cam.ac.uk/
E An institute at the University of Cambridge.
O To conduct research into determining and understanding the molecular mechanisms of disease

Cambridge Interdisciplinary Research Centre on Ageing   (CIRCA)
- ■   Faculty of Social and Political Sciences, University of Cambridge, Free School Lane, Cambridge, CB2 3RQ.
    01223 767803
    http://www.circa.cam.ac.uk/
    Co-Director: Prof Felicia A Huppert. Co-Director: Prof Jacqueline Scott.
- E   A centre at the University of Cambridge.
- O   To advance knowledge in the field of ageing by an integrated interdisciplinary approach which crosses the traditional boundaries of the humanities, natural medical and social sciences

Cambridge-MIT Institute   (CMI)
- ■   10 Miller's Yard, Mill Lane, Cambridge, CB2 1RQ.
    01223 327207   fax 01223 765891
    http://www.cambridge-mit.org/
- E   An institute at the University of Cambridge.
- O   To enhance the competitiveness, productivity and entrepreneurship of the UK economy by improving university-industry knowledge exchange

Cambridge Research Institute [Cancer]
>   see **Cancer Research UK Cambridge Research Institute.**

Cambridge Resource Centre for Comparative Genomics
- ■   Cambridge Veterinary School, University of Cambridge, Madingley Road, Cambridge, CB3 0ES.
    01223 339553   fax 01223 337610
    http://www.vet.cam.ac.uk/genomics/
    Director: Prof Malcolm A Ferguson-Smith, FRS.
- E   A research centre within the Centre for Veterinary Science (qv) at the University of Cambridge.
- O   To help provide the comparative genomics community with high quality chromosome-specific DNA from a wide range of species for specific research projects including comparative mapping, gene localisation, and evolutionary studies

Cambridge University Health - Health Policy and Management Centre   (CUH)
- ■   Judge Business School, University of Cambridge, Trumpington Street, Cambridge, CB2 1AG.
    01223 339700   fax 01223 339701
    http://www.jbs.cam.ac.uk/research/health
- E   A centre at the University of Cambridge.
- O   To develop and harness knowledge to improve health, through promoting a shared purpose between managers, policy-makers, professionals and scholars

Cañada Blanch Centre for Contemporary Spanish Studies   1996
- ■   LSE, Cowdray House, Portugal Street, London, WC2A 2AE.
    020 7955 6119   fax 020 7955 6757
    http://www.lse.ac.uk/collections/canadaBlanch/
    Director: Prof Paul Preston.
- E   A research centre within the European Institute (qv) at the London School of Economics and Political Science.
- O   To promote the research and teaching of contemporary Spanish history, economy, sociology and culture
- ●   Archives with books, microfilm and tapes
Note: Named after D. Vicente Cañada Blanch, the founder of the Cañada Blanch Foundation in the UK.

Cancer Care Centre
>   see **Helen Rollason Cancer Care Centre.**

Cancer Care Research Centre   (CCRC)   2003
- ■   Unit 1 - Scion House, University of Stirling, Innovation Park, Stirling, FK9 4LA.
    01786 849260   fax 01786 460060
    http://www.cancercare.stir.ac.uk/
    Director: Prof Nora Kearney.
- E   A centre at the University of Stirling.
- O   To provide those people affected by cancer with the opportunity of helping shape the future of cancer services in Scotland

Cancer Research Centre [Bradford]
>   see **Tom Connors Cancer Research Centre.**

Cancer Research Centre [Manchester]
>   see **Manchester Cancer Research Centre.**

Cancer Research UK Cambridge Research Institute   (CRI)
- ■   University of Cambridge, Robinson Way, Cambridge, CB2 2RE.
    01223 404200   fax 01223 404208
    http://science.cancerresearchuk.org/cri/
- E   An institute at the University of Cambridge.
- O   To bring the scientific strengths of Cambridge to bear on practical questions of cancer diagnosis, treatment and prevention

Cancer Research UK Centre for Cancer Therapeutics

- University of London, 123 Old Brompton Road, London, SW7 3RP.
  020 7352 8133   fax 020 7370 5261
  http://www.icr.ac.uk/research/research_sections/cancer_therapeutics/
  Director: Prof Paul Workman.
- E   A research centre within the Institute of Cancer Research (qv) at the University of London.
- ○   To discover and develop novel and effective therapeutics for the treatment of cancer

Cancer Research UK Centre for Cell and Molecular Biology

- University of London, 123 Old Brompton Road, London, SW7 3RP.
  020 7352 8133   fax 020 7370 5261
  http://www.icr.ac.uk/research/research_sections/cell_and_molecular_biology/
  Director: Prof Chris Marshall.
- E   A research centre within the Institute of Cancer Research (qv) at the University of London.
- ○   To focus research on the molecular dissection of cancer genes

Cancer Research UK Institute for Cancer Studies

- Division of Cancer Studies, University of Birmingham, Vincent Drive, Edgbaston, Birmingham, B15 2TT.
  0121-414 4491   fax 0121-414 4486
  http://www.cancerstudies.bham.ac.uk/
- E   A research institute at the University of Birmingham.
- ○   To conduct cancer research, especially cancer genetics, signal transduction, viral oncology and immunology, cancer gene- and immuno-therapy and clinical trials

Cancer Research UK London Research Institute   (LRI)

- Lincoln's Inn Fields Laboratories, 44 Lincoln's Inn Fields, London, WC2A 3PX.
  020 7242 0200
  http://london-research-institute.co.uk/
- E   A registered charity and research institute.
- ○   To understand the two phenomena of cancer development and spread: 1) the nature and role of the signalling process which control the intrinsic properties of cancer cells, and their interactions with their host, and 2) how the integrity of the genome is maintained in the face of multiple environmental and endogenous insults

Note: Cancer Research also has a laboratory at South Mimms, Hertfordshire - tel 020 7269 3977.

Cancer Research UK and UCL Cancer Trials Centre   (CTC)   1997

- Department of Oncology, University College London, Stephenson House, 158-160 North Gower Street, London, NW1 2ND.
  020 7679 8040
  http://www.ucl.ac.uk/cancertrials/
  Director: Dr Jonathan Ledermann.
- E   A research centre at University College London.
- ○   To be a centre of excellence for the development, conduct and analysis of clinical trials in cancer research

Cancer Trials Centre
> see **Cancer Research UK and UCL Cancer Trials Centre.**

Canine Behaviour Centre   1998

- School of Psychology, Queen's University Belfast, Belfast, BT7 1NN.
  028 9097 4386
  http://www.psych.qub.ac.uk/Research/Clusters/BehaviourDevelopmentAndWelfare
- E   A research centre at Queen's University, Belfast.

Canine Behaviour Centre

- Farglow Farm, Greenhead, Cumbria, CA8 7JB.
  01697 747941
  http://www.caninebehaviour.co.uk/
- ○   To provide courses in dog psychology

Canolfan Astrobioleg Caerdydd
> see **Cardiff Centre for Astrobiology.**

Canolfan Astudiaeth R S Thomas
> see **R S Thomas Study Centre.**

Canolfan Astudiaethau Addysg
> see **Centre for Educational Studies [Aberystwyth].**

Canolfan Astudiaethau Awstralaidd Cymru
> see **Centre for Australian Studies in Wales.**

Canolfan Astudiaethau Canoloesol
> see **Centre for Medieval Studies (Bangor).**

Canolfan Astudiaethiau Cymru America, Prifysgol Caerdydd
see **Cardiff Centre for Welsh American Studies.**

Canolfan Astudio Crefydd mewn Cymdeithasau Celtaidd
see **Centre for the Study of Religion in Celtic Societies.**

Canolfan Bedwyr e - Gymraeg: Terminoleg a Pheirianneg Iaith
see **Centre for Standardisation of Welsh Terminology.**

Canolfan Datblygu Gwasanaethu Dementia Cymru
see **Dementia Services Development Centre [Bangor].**

Canolfan y Dechnoleg Amgen
see **Centre for Alternative Technology.**

Canolfan Dysgu Cymraeg
see **Welsh Language Teaching Centre.**

Canolfan Economeg Iechyd
see **Centre for Health Economics.**

Canolfan Efrydiau Datblygu
see **Centre for Development Studies.**

Canolfan Genedlaethol Addysg Grefyddol
see **Welsh National Centre for Religious Education.**

Canolfan Gwasanaethau'r Gymraeg
see **Centre for Welsh Language Services.**

Canolfan Gymreig Materion Rhyngwladol
see **Welsh Centre for International Affairs.**

Canolfan Hysbysrwydd Cerddoriaeth Cymru
see **Welsh Music Information Centre.**

Canolfan Hysbysrwydd Ieithyddol
see **Languages Information Centre.**

Canolfan Iechyd Cymru
see **Wales Centre for Health.**

Canolfan Materion Cyfreithiol Cymreig
see **Centre for Welsh Legal Affairs.**

Canolfan Uwch-Astudiaethau Cerddoriaeth Cymru
see **Centre for Advanced Welsh Music Studies.**

Canolfan Uwchefrydiau Crefydd yng Nghymru
see **Centre for the Advanced Study of Religion in Wales.**

Canolfan Uwchefrydiau Cymreig a Cheltaidd
see **Centre for Advanced Welsh and Celtic Studies.**

Canolfan Ymarfer Rhwng Cenedlaethau
see **Wales Centre for Intergenerational Practice.**

Canolfan Ymchwil Canser Tenovus
see **Tenovus Centre for Cancer Research.**

Canolfan Ymchwil Cymru er Gwastraff ac Adnoddau
see **Wales Waste and Resources Research Centre.**

Canolfan Ymchwil Ddaearamgylcheddol
see **Geoenvironmental Research Centre.**

© CBD Research Ltd · Beckenham · Kent BR3 5JS · Tel 020 8650 7745 · Fax 020 8650 0768 · E-mail cbd@cbdresearch.com · www.cbdresearch.com

Canolfan Ymchwil Gwyddoriaeth Iechyd
see **Centre for Health Sciences Research.**

Canolfan Ymchwil ï Lên ac Iaith Saesneg Cymru
see **Centre for Research into the English Literature and Language of Wales.**

Canolfan Ymchwili'r Amgylchedd ac Iechyd
see **Centre for Research into Environment and Health.**

Canterbury Centre for Medieval and Tudor Studies   1996
■   School of English, Rutherford College Extension, University of Kent, Canterbury, Kent, CT2 7NX.
       01227 764000; 823140   fax 01227 827060
       http://www.kent.ac.uk/mts/
       Administrator: Clare Langburn.
E   A research centre within the Kent Institute for Advanced Studies in the Humanities (qv) at the University of Kent.
O   To administer postgraduate teaching for the MA by coursework and dissertation, to promote research, and to develop links with
       Canterbury Cathedral archives and library

Capital Centre (Creativity and Performance in Teaching and Learning)   2005
■   University of Warwick, Coventry, CV4 7AL.
       024 7615 0067
       http://www2.warwick.ac.uk/fac/cross_fac/capital/
       Director: Prof Carol Chillington Rutter.

Cardiff Centre for Astrobiology   (CCAB)   2000   Canolfan Astrobioleg Caerdydd
■   Cardiff School of Mathematics, Cardiff University, Senghennydd Road, Cardiff, CF24 4AG.
       029 2087 4811   fax 029 2087 4199
       http://www.astrobiology.cf.ac.uk/
       Director: Prof N C Wickramasinghe.
E   A centre at Cardiff University.
O   To combine the expertise of astronomers, biochemists and microbiologists to generate cutting edge science that would eventually
       answer the question of where we originate from

Cardiff Centre for Ethics, Law and Society   (CCELS)   2003
■   Cardiff Law School, PO Box 427, Cardiff University, Museum Avenue, Cardiff, CF10 3XT.
       029 2087 6102   fax 029 2087 4097
       http://www.ccels.cf.ac.uk/
       Director: Prof Søren Holm.
E   A centre at Cardiff University.
O   To connect researchers and practitioners in medicine, science, the social sciences and humanities

Cardiff Centre for the History of the Crusades   2000
■   Cardiff School of History and Archaeology, Humanities Building, Cardiff University, Colum Drive, Cardiff, CF10 3EU.
       029 2087 4313   fax 029 2087 4929
       http://www.cardiff.ac.uk/hisar/history/centres.htm#crusades
       Director: Prof Peter Edbury.
E   A centre at Cardiff University.
O   To encourage and develop research collaboration, conferences and publications in the field of crusading history from the end of
       the eleventh century onwards

Cardiff Centre for Modern German History   (CCMGH)
■   Cardiff School of History and Archaeology, Humanities Building, Cardiff University, Colum Drive, Cardiff, CF10 3EU.
       029 2087 4259   fax 029 2087 4929
       http://www.history/centres.htm#German
       Director: Prof Jonathan Osmond.
E   A centre at Cardiff University.
O   To conduct research into all aspects of the history and related issues of German-speaking central Europe since 1750

Cardiff Centre for Multidisciplinary Microtechnology   (C2M2)
■   Cardiff School of Physics and Astronomy, Queen's Buildings, Cardiff University, 5 The Parade, Cardiff, CF24 3YB.
       029 2087 4992
       http://www.c2m2.cf.ac.uk/
       Contact: Dr D Westwood.
E   A centre at Cardiff University.

Cardiff Centre for Research in Genetics and Society   (CCRGS)   1991
■   Cardiff School of Social Sciences, Glamorgan Building, Cardiff University, King Edward VII Avenue, Cardiff, CF10 3WT.
       029 2087 5179   fax 029 2087 4175
       http://www.cardiff.ac.uk/socsi/research/researchcentres/researchingenetics/
E   A centre at Cardiff University.
O   To conduct critical research into the social aspects of genetic diseases and clinical genetic services

Cardiff Centre for Welsh American Studies   (CCWAS)   2001   Canolfan Astudiaethiau Cymru America, Prifysgol Caerdydd
- ■ Cardiff School of History and Archaeology, Humanities Building, Cardiff University, Colum Drive, Cardiff, CF10 3EU.
  029 2087 4843   fax 029 2087 4604
  http://www.cardiff.ac.uk/cymraeg/english/welshAmerican/welshAmerican.shtml
  Co-Director: Dr E Wyn James. Co-Director: Dr Bill Jones.
- E A research centre at Cardiff University.
- O To promote the study of the culture, language, literature and history of the Welsh in the United States, Canada and Patagonia

Cardiff Institute of Society, Health and Ethics   (CISHE)   2003   Athrofa y Gymdeithas, Iechyd a Moseg Caerdydd
- ■ Cardiff School of Social Sciences, Cardiff University, 53 Park Place, Cardiff, CF10 3AT.
  029 2087 9609   fax 029 2087 9054
  http://www.cardiff.ac.uk/socsi/cishe
  Director: Prof Laurence Moore.
- E A research institute at Cardiff University.
- O To undertake and facilitate research on tackling health inequalities

Cardiff Institute of Tissue Engineering and Repair   (CITER)
- ■ Cardiff School of Medicine, Cardiff University, 51 Park Place, Cardiff, CF10 3AT.
  029 2087 0129
  http://www.citer.org/
  Chief Executive Officer: Prof Nick Lench.
- E An institute at Cardiff University.
- O To focus on interdisciplinary research, education and clinical practice in the field of tissue engineering and repair

Cardiff Japanese Studies Centre   (CJSC)
- ■ Cardiff Business School, Aberconway Building, Cardiff University, Colum Drive, Cardiff, CF10 3EU.
  029 2087 4514; 4959
  http://www.cf.ac.uk/carbs/cjsc
  Director: Dr Christopher P Hood.
- E A centre at Cardiff University.
- O To research and develop a greater understanding of significant areas of Japanese society, politics and business

Cardiff University Brain and Repair Imaging Centre   (CUBRIC)
- ■ Cardiff School of Psychology, CUBRIC Building, Cardiff University, Park Place, Cardiff, CF10 3AT.
  029 2087 0365   fax 029 2087 0039
  http://www.cf.ac.uk/psych/cubric/
  Director: Prof Peter Halligan.
- E A centre at Cardiff University.
- O To conduct research in human-based brain imaging

Cardiff University Innovative Manufacturing Research Centre   (CUIMRC)   2004
- NR Cardiff Business School, Aberconway Building, Cardiff University, Colum Drive, Cardiff, CF10 3EU.
  029 2087 9611   fax 029 2087 9633
  http://www.cuimrc.cf.ac.uk/
  Operations Director: Dr Andrew Glanfield.
- E An EPSRC Innovative Manufacturing Research Centre at Cardiff University.
- O To assist UK manufacturing firms to develop an economically sustainable future using a combination of lean, rapid and agile management and engineering approaches together with future proof technologies
- Note: One of the EPSRC funded centres in the UK - for further information see **EPSRC Innovative Manufacturing Research Centres**.

Cardiovascular Biology Research Centre   (CBRC)
- ■ Department of Cardiological Sciences, St George's, University of London, Cranmer Terrace, London, SW17 0RE.
  020 8725 3963   fax 020 8725 3328
  http://www.sgul.ac.uk/depts/
  Director: Prof Juan Carlos Kaski.
- E A research centre at St George's, University of London.
- O To understand mechanisms of cardiovascular disease and to identify rational treatments and preventative measures

Cardiovascular Research Centre
see **BHF Glasgow Cardiovascular Research Centre**.

Cardiovascular Research Institute at Leeds   (CRISTAL)
- ■ Faculty of Medicine and Health, The Worsley Building, University of Leeds, Clarendon Way, Leeds, LS2 9JT.
  0113-343 4361
  http://www.cristal.leeds.ac.uk/
  Director: Prof Chris Peers.
- E A research institute within the Leeds Institute of Genetics, Health and Therapeutics (qv) at the University of Leeds.
- O To develop the premier cardiovascular research centre in the UK

Careers Research and Advisory Centre (CRAC) 1964

- ■   Sheraton House, Castle Park, Cambridge, CB3 0AX.
     01223 460277   fax 01223 311708
     http://www.crac.org.uk/
     Chief Executive: Jeffrey Defries. Commercial & Business Development Director: Robin Mellors-Bourne.
- E   A registered charity.
- O   To advance the education of the public, and young persons in particular, in lifelong career-related learning for all; to enable employers and the world of education to work together; to promote the highest standards of professionalism and execution amongst those offering careers advice, guidance and development
- ●   Conference facilities - Education and training

Caribbean Studies Centre (CSC) 2002

- ■   Department of Humanities, Arts and Languages, North Campus, London Metropolitan University, 166-220 Holloway Road, London, N7 8DB.
     020 7973 4898   fax 020 7753 7069
     http://www.londonmet.ac.uk/csc
     Director: Prof Jean Stubbs.
- E   A research centre affiliated to the International Institute for Culture, Tourism and Development (qv) at London Metropolitan University.
- O   To conduct research and offer undergraduate and postgraduate degrees in pan-Caribbean history and cultural studies

Carnegie National Sports Development Centre 1991

- ■   Carnegie Faculty of Sport and Education, Leeds Metropolitan University, Leeds, LS6 3QS.
     0113-283 2600
     http://www.lmu.ac.uk/ces/lss/research/consultancy.htm
     Head: Mel Welch.
- E   A department of Leeds Metropolitan University.
- O   To provide services to develop sport and recreation

Carnegie Research Institute (CRI) 1991

- ■   Carnegie Faculty of Sport and Education, Room 216 - Cavendish Hall, Leeds Metropolitan University, Headingley Campus, Leeds, LS6 3QS.
     0113-283 2600   fax 0113-283 6171
     http://www.leedsmet.ac.uk/carnegie/cri.htm
     Director: Prof Jonathan Long. Administrator: Sam Armitage.
- E   A department of Leeds Metropolitan University.
- O   To co-ordinate research and provide services to develop sport and recreation

Castings Centre 1994

- ■   University of Birmingham, Edgbaston, Birmingham, B15 2TT.
     0121-414 3446   fax 0121-414 3441
     http://www.irc.bham.ac.uk/castingcentre.htm
- E   A research centre within the Interdisciplinary Research Centre in Materials Processing (qv) at the University of Birmingham.
- O   To conduct research in combining computer-aided analysis techniques with advances in casting technology and foundry skill to achieve more efficient production

Castings Technology International (Cti) 1996

- ■   Brunel Way, Rotherham, South Yorkshire, S60 5WG.
     0114-254 1144   fax 0114-254 1155
     http://www.castingstechnology.com/
     Chief Executive: Dr Mike Ashton.
- E   A centre of excellence.
- O   To provide independent research and development, technical support and consultancy services to the castings and metal related industry
- ✕   Castings Development Centre.

Catchment Science Centre (CSC)

- ■   North Campus, University of Sheffield, Broad Lane, Sheffield, S3 7HQ.
     0114-222 5743   fax 0114-222 5701
     http://www.shef.ac.uk/csc/
     Co-Director: Prof David Lerner. Co-Director: Bob Harris.
- E   A research centre within the Kroto Research Institute (qv) at the University of Sheffield.
- O   To build a critical mass of research that focuses on the mechanistic links between the dominant pressures on water quality and quantity and freshwater ecosystem structure and functioning

Cathie Marsh Centre for Census and Survey Research (CCSR) 1995

- ■   School of Social Sciences, University of Manchester, 2nd Floor - Crawford House, Booth Street East, Manchester, M13 9PL.
     0161-275 4721   fax 0161-275 4722
     http://www.ccsr.ac.uk/
     Director: Dr Mark Elliot.
- E   An interdisciplinary research centre at the University of Manchester.
- O   To conduct applied quantitative research in the census and survey fields, with particular emphasis on aspects of confidentiality and privacy, population and places, work and employment, religion, social statistics, and elections, parties and political behaviour

Catholic Communications Centre
Note: Amalgamated in 2001 with the Catholic Media Office to become the Catholic Communications Service:

Caucasus Policy Institute   (CPI)
■ School of Social Science and Public Policy, King's College London, 138-142 Strand, London, WC2R 1HH.
 020 7848 2940   fax 020 7848 2748
 http://www.kcl.ac.uk/sspp/
 Director: Dr Dennis Corboy.
E A research institute at King's College, London.
○ To conduct and publish state-of-the-art research and policy analysis on topics relevant to the region's political, security and development challenges

CAZS Natural Resources   (CAZS-NR   1984
■ School of Agricultural and Forest Sciences, University of Wales Bangor, Deiniol Road, Bangor, Gwynedd, LL57 2UW.
 01248 382346   fax 01248 364717
 http://www.cazs.bangor.ac.uk/
 Director: Prof John Witcombe.
E A semi-autonomous self-funding centre at the University of Wales, Bangor.
○ To promote integrated agricultural and forest development in arid and semi-arid lands across Africa, Asia and Europe
✕ Centre for Arid Zone Studies.

Cecil Powell Centre for Science Education
Note: No longer in existence.

CEH Banchory
NR Hill of Brathens, Banchory, Aberdeenshire, AB31 4BW.
 01330 826300   fax 01330 823303
 http://www.ceh.ac.uk/
Note: A research site of the **Centre for Ecology and Hydrology.**

CEH Bangor
NR Orton Building, Deiniol Road, Bangor, Gwynedd, LL57 2UP.
 01248 370045   fax 01248 355365
 http://www.ceh.ac.uk/
Note: A research site of the **Centre for Ecology and Hydrology.**

CEH Dorset
NR Winfrith Newburgh, Dorchester, Dorset, DT2 8ZD.
 01305 213500   fax 01305 213600
 http://www.ceh.ac.uk/
Note: A research site of the **Centre for Ecology and Hydrology.**

CEH Edinburgh
NR Bush Estate, Penicuik, Midlothian, EH26 0QB.
 0131-445 4343   fax 0131-445 3943
 http://www.ceh.ac.uk/
Note: A research site of the **Centre for Ecology and Hydrology.**

CEH Lancaster
NR Library Avenue, Bailrigg, Lancaster, LA1 4AP.
 01524 595800   fax 01524 61536
 http://www.ceh.ac.uk/
Note: A research site of the **Centre for Ecology and Hydrology.**

CEH Monks Wood
NR Abbots Ripton, Huntingdon, Cambridgeshire, PE28 2LS.
 01487 772400   fax 01487 773467
 http://www.ceh.ac.uk/
Note: A research site of the **Centre for Ecology and Hydrology.**

CEH Oxford
NR Mansfield Road, Oxford, OX1 3SR.
 01865 281630   fax 01865 281696
 http://www.ceh.ac.uk/
Note: A research site of the **Centre for Ecology and Hydrology.**

CEH Wallingford
NR Maclean Building, Benson Lane, Wallingford, Oxfordshire, OX10 8BB.
 01491 838800   fax 01491 692424
 http://www.ceh.ac.uk/
Note: A research site of the **Centre for Ecology and Hydrology.**

CEM Centre
    see **Curriculum Evaluation and Management Centre.**

Central Cities Institute   (CCI)
- ■   School of Architecture and the Built Environment, University of Westminster, 35 Marylebone Road, London, NW1 5LS.
        020 7911 5000   fax 020 7915 5171
        http://www.centralcities.wmin.ac.uk/
        Director: Prof Marion Roberts.
- E   A research institute at the University of Westminster.
- ○   To examine the interface between the various activities and interests which make up the centres of major cities

Central European Music Research Centre   (CEMRC)
- ■   Cardiff School of Music, Cardiff University, Corbett Road, Cardiff, CF10 3EB.
        029 2087 4816   fax 029 2087 4379
        http://www.cardiff.ac.uk/music/research/cemrc/index.htm
        Director: Prof Adrian Thomas.
- E   A centre at Cardiff University.
- ○   To study the music of Central and East-Central Europe

Central London Professional Development Centre   (PDC)
- ■   London South Bank University, 103 Borough Road, London, SE1 0AA.
        020 7815 6290   fax 020 7815 6296
        http://www.lsbu.ac.uk/lluplus/pdc/
        Manager: Kay McBrien.
- E   A research centre at London South Bank University.
- ○   To act as a focal point for teachers and trainers to develop and extend their expertise in literacy, numeracy, ESOL, family learning, dyslexia support and workforce and community development

Centre for Academic Clinical Orthopaedics
- ■   Faculty of Biomedical Sciences, Royal Free and University College Medical School, Brockley Hill, Stanmore, Middlesex, HA7 4LP.
        020 8909 5825
        http://www.ucl.ac.uk/orthopaedics/centres/corthopsunits.htm#cachieve
        Head: Prof David Marsh.
- E   A research centre within the Institute of Orthopaedics and Musculo-Skeletal Science (qv) at University College London.
- ○   To conduct research in various fields of clinical orthopaedics, including arthroplasty, bone tumour surgery, metabolic bone disease, spinal surgery, peripheral nerve injury, and cartilage transplantation
- Note: Also known as Academic Centre for Clinical Orthopaedics.

Centre for Academic Practice
    see **Centre for Academic and Professional Development.**

Centre for Academic and Professional Development   (CAP)   1987
- ■   University of Warwick, Coventry, CV4 8UW.
        024 7652 4766   fax 024 7657 2736
        http://www2.warwick.ac.uk/services/cap/
        Director: Sue Bennett
- E   A research centre at the University of Warwick.
- ○   To support academic staff in the broadest sense with regard to teaching and learning, research and academic leadership / management
- ✕   Centre for Academic Practice
- Note: A Centre for Academic and Professional Development exists at most of the UK universities, each with similar aims and objectives.

Centre for Academic and Professional Literacies   (CAPLITS)
- ■   School of Culture, Language and Education, University of London, 20 Bedford Way, London, WC1H 0AL.
        020 7612 6000; 6789   fax 020 7612 6534
        http://ioewebserver.ioe.ac.uk/
        Director: Prof Ken Hyland.
- E   A research centre within the Institute of Education (qv) at the University of London.
- ○   To offer courses to help students understand and write assignments and dissertations

Centre for Academic Surgery   (CAS)   2003
- ■   Barts and the London, Queen Mary's School of Medicine and Dentistry, 4 Newark Street, London, E1 2AT.
        020 7882 2483   fax 020 7882 2200
        http://www.icms.qmul.ac.uk/centres/surgery/
- E   A research centre within the Institute of Cell and Molecular Science (qv) at Queen Mary, University of London.
- ○   To conduct research into the causes of colorectal disorders and the development of practical improvements in the selection, treatment and care of patients with these diseases

Centre for Academic Writing   (CAW)
- ■ School of Art and Design, Coventry University, Gulson Building, Priory Street, Coventry, CV1 5FB.
  024 7688 7902
  http://www.coventry.ac.uk/cu/caw
- E A department of Coventry University.
- O To offer students individualistic advice on writing essays, reports, dissertations, theses, exams and other assignments

Centre for Accelerator Science, Imaging and Medicine   (CASIM)
- NR Oliver Lodge Laboratory, University of Liverpool, Liverpool, L69 7ZE.
  0151-794 2000; 3871
  http://www.casim.ac.uk/
  Contact: Prof Peter Weightman.
- E A research centre at the University of Liverpool.
- O To advance scientific knowledge through unique accelerator and imaging technologies to benefit industry, the environment, health and the quality of life

Note: A joint venture with various other organisations, including the Universities of Lancaster, Manchester and Salford.

Centre for Accessible Environments   (CAE)   1969
- ■ 70 South Lambeth Road, London, SW8 1RL.
  020 7840 0125   fax 020 7840 5811
  http://www.cae.org.uk/
  Chief Executive Officer: Sarah Langton-Lockton. Head of Finance: Helen Carter.
- E A registered charity.
- O To advise on access to the built environment and inclusive design; to provide information, design guidance, training and access consultancy services
- ● Access consultancy - Information service
- ¶ Access by Design (journal). (see website for other publications).
- ✕ Centre on Environment for the Handicapped.

Centre for Accounting, Finance and Governance   2005
- ■ Faculty of Business, Computing and Information Management, London South Bank University, 103 Borough Road, London, SE1 0AA.
  020 7815 7891
  http://www.lsbu.ac.uk/bcim/research/afg.shtml
  Head: Dr Ken D'Silva.
- E A research centre at London South Bank University.
- O To conduct research in the areas of accounting, finance and governance

Centre for Accounting, Finance and Taxation   (CAFT)
- ■ Bournemouth Law School, Talbot Campus, Bournemouth University, Poole, Dorset, BH12 5BB.
  01202 965211   fax 01202 965261
  http://caft.bournemouth.ac.uk/
  Director: Prof Philip Hardwick.
- E A research centre within the Institute of Business and Law (qv) at Bournemouth University.
- O To conduct financial services research

Centre for Action Research in Professional Practice   (CARPP)
- ■ School of Management, University of Bath, Claverton Down, Bath, BA2 7AY.
  01225 826826   fax 01225 826473
  http://www.bath.ac.uk/carpp/
  Co-Director: Prof Peter Reason. Co-Director: Prof Judi Marshall.
- E A research centre at the University of Bath.

Centre for Active Learning in Geography, Environment and Related Disciplines   (CeAL)   2005
- ■ Department of Natural and Social Sciences, Francis Close Hall Campus, University of Gloucester, Swindon Road, Cheltenham, Gloucestershire, GL50 4AZ.
  01242 714683
  http://www.glos.ac.uk/ceal/
  Contact: Barbara Rainbow.
- E A Centre for Excellence in Teaching and Learning (CETL) at the University of Gloucestershire.
- O To promote, develop and review exemplary active learning for students in geography, environment and related disciplines, including landscape architecture, community development and heritage management

Note: See **Centres for Excellence in Teaching and Learning** for further information.

Centre for Active Lifestyles   (CAL)   2005
- ■ Carnegie Faculty of Sport and Education, Room 216 - Cavendish Hall, Headingley Campus, University of Leeds, Leeds, LS6 3QS.
  0113-283 2600   fax 0113-283 6171
  http://www.leedsmet.ac.uk/carnegie/8504.htm
  Director: Prof Jim McKenna.
- E A research centre within the Carnegie Research Institute (qv) at Leeds Metropolitan University.
- O To address two main areas of current relevance to public health - physical activity promotion and responses to physically active lifestyles
- ● Carnegie International Weight Loss Camp

Centre for Adaptive Systems   (CAS)
- School of Computing and Technology, St Peter's Campus, University of Sunderland, St Peter's Way, Sunderland, Tyne and Wear, SR6 0DD.
     0191-515 2752   fax 0191-515 2781
     http://www.cat.sunderland.ac.uk/
     Contact: John MacIntyre.
- E   A research centre at the University of Sunderland.
- O   To conduct research in the field of adaptive computing, including condition monitoring, time series analysis, non-destructive testing, medical data analysis, water treatment, process control, and intelligent tutors

Centre for Addiction Research and Education Scotland   (CARES)
- Division of Pathology and Neuroscience, Ninewells Hospital and Medical School, Dundee, DD1 9SY.
     01382 632414   fax 01382 633923
     http://www.dundee.ac.uk/psychiatry/cares/
     Director: Dr Alex Baldacchino. Administrator: Miss Jennifer Johnston.
- E   A centre at the University of Dundee.
- O   To deliver the highest quality healthcare and to improve the outcome of individuals and the Scottish community through the development of research and education in the field of drug, alchohol and tobacco dependence

Centre for Adult Oral Health   (CAOH)
- Barts and the London, Queen Mary's School of Medicine and Dentistry, Turner Street, London, E1 2AD.
     020 7377 7611   fax 020 7377 7612
     http://www.smd.qmul.ac.uk/dental/adultoralhealth
- E   A research centre within the Institute of Dentistry (qv) at Queen Mary, University of London.
- O   To conduct research and teaching in dental public health, and clinical restorative dental specialties, including prosthodontics, endodontics, operative dentistry, and periodontology

Centre for Adult and Paediatric Gastroenterology   (CAPG)   2000
- Barts and the London, Queen Mary's School of Medicine and Dentistry, 4 Newark Street, London, E1 2AT.
     020 7882 2483; 7191
     http://www.smd.qmul.ac.uk/gastro
     Head: Prof Ian Sanderson. Contact: Nici Kingston.
- E   A research centre within the Institute of Cell and Molecular Science (qv) at Queen Mary, University of London.
- O   To conduct research in various areas of gastroenterology, including development and developmental immunology, hepatobiliary, human nutrition, infection and immunity, inflammation, malignancy and transformation, and neurogastroenterology
- ×   Centre for Gastroenterology.

Centre for Advanced Development in the Creative Industries (Bangor)
     see **National Institute for Excellence in Creative Industries.**

Centre for Advanced Electronically Controlled Drives
Note: Most of the Centre's activities have now been taken over by Technelec Ltd, a company, and it is therefore no longer within the scope of this directory.

Centre for Advanced Engineering Methods   (AEM)
- Department of Power, Propulsion and Aerospace Engineering, Cranfield University, Cranfield, Bedfordshire, MK43 0AL.
     01234 754612   fax 01234 758203
     http://www.cranfield.ac.uk/soe/
     Director: Dr Marin D Guenov.
- E   A research centre at Cranfield University.
- O   To conduct internationally leading research in the areas of integrated product development, design automation, and innovative concepts for integrated engineering systems in aerospace

Centre for Advanced Historical Research
     see **Saint John's House Centre for Advanced Historical Research.**

Centre for Advanced Industry
- Royal Quays, Coble Dene, North Shields, NE29 6DE.
     0191-293 7000
- E   A purpose-built building for companies operating in high tech industries.

Centre for Advanced Instrumentation   (CfAI)
- Department of Physics, Science Laboratories, University of Durham, South Road, Durham, DH1 3LE.
     0191-334 3588
     http://www.cfai.dur.ac.uk/
- E   A research centre at the University of Durham.

Centre for Advanced Instrumentation Systems (CAIS) 1993
- University College London, 3 Taviton Street, London, WC1H 0BT.
  020 7679 4908
  http://www.ucl.ac.uk/CAIS/
  Director: Dr Steve Welch.
- E   A research centre at University College London.
- O   To promote and encourage interaction between industry and researchers working in the area of advanced instrumentation

Centre for Advanced Joining (CAJ) 1991
- Coventry University, Priory Street, Coventry, CV1 5FB.
  024 7688 8750
  http://www.lampproject.co.uk/
  Contact: Dr Colin Page.
- E   A centre at Coventry University.
- O   To focus research and development in the fields of high-energy beam processing, specifically plasma arc welding and industrial laser processing

Centre for Advanced Lipids Research
  see **Lipids Research Centre.**

Centre for Advanced Magnetic Materials and Devices
  see **Sheffield Centre for Advanced Magnetic Materials and Devices.**

Centre for Advanced Management Research (CAMR)
- Middlesex University Business School, The Burroughs, London, NW4 4BT.
  020 8411 5000
  http://mubs.mdx.ac.uk/
- E   A centre at Middlesex University.
- O   To undertake research in various fields, including enterprise and regional development, transport management, relationship marketing, and knowledge transfer

Centre for Advanced Materials and Composites
  see **Oxford Centre for Advanced Materials and Composites.**

Centre for Advanced Materials [Saint Andrews]
  see **Saint Andrews Centre for Advanced Materials.**

Centre for Advanced Microscopy [Brighton]
  see **Sussex Centre for Advanced Microscopy.**

Centre for Advanced Microscopy (CfAM)
- J J Thomson Physical Laboratory, University of Reading, Whiteknights, Reading, Berkshire, RG6 6AF.
  0118-378 6118
  http://www.rdg.ac.uk/cfam/
  Director: Geoffrey Mitchell.
- E   A research centre at the University of Reading.
- O   To provide cutting edge microscopy services and solutions for the life and physical sciences

Centre for Advanced Photography Studies
  see **Durham Centre for Advanced Photography Studies.**

Centre for Advanced Religious and Theological Studies (CARTS) 1995
- Faculty of Divinity, University of Cambridge, West Road, Cambridge, CB3 9BS.
  01223 763035   fax 01223 763003
  http://www.divinity.cam.ac.uk/advanced.html
  Director: Dr David Thompson.
- E   A centre at the University of Cambridge.
- O   To focus on current issues of social and ethical significance to the living religious traditions

Centre for Advanced and Renewable Materials (CARM)
- Department of Chemistry, University of Wales, Bangor, Deiniol Road, Bangor, Gwynedd, LL57 2UW.
  01248 364829   fax 01248 370594
  http://www.carmtechnology.com/
  Contact: Dr Robert Elias.
- E   A research centre at the University of Wales, Bangor.
- O   To help support industry through collaborative research and technology transfer projects

© CBD Research Ltd · Beckenham · Kent BR3 5JS · Tel 020 8650 7745 · Fax 020 8650 0768 · E-mail cbd@cbdresearch.com · www.cbdresearch.com

Centre for Advanced Research in English   (CARE)
- ■ Department of English, University of Birmingham, Westmere House, Edgbaston, Birmingham, B15 2TT.
   0121-414 3364   fax 0121-414 5668
   http://www.english.bham.ac.uk/visit.htm
   Director: Dr Murray Knowles.
- E A research centre at the University of Birmingham.

Centre for Advanced Research in Marketing
   see **Cranfield Centre for Advanced Research in Marketing.**

Centre for Advanced Software and Intelligent Systems   (CASIS)
- NR Department of Computer Science, University of Wales Aberstwyth, Penglais, Aberystwyth, Ceredigion, SY23 3DB.
   01970 628534
   http://www.aber.ac.uk/casis/
   Contact: Peter Simmonds.
- E A research centre at the University of Wales, Aberystwyth.
- ○ To provide industry, commerce and the public sector with innovative and cost effective solutions across a broad range of software applications
Note: A joint venture with Cardiff University.

Centre for Advanced Software Technology   (Technium CAST)
- ■ Faculty of Science and Engineering, Ffordd Penlan, University of Wales Bangor, Parc Menai, Bangor, Gwynedd, LL57 4HJ.
   01248 675005   fax 01248 675012
   http://www.technium.co.uk/index.cfm/technium/cast_technium/en6308
   Contact: Tanya Keith.
- E A centre at the University of Wales, Bangor.
- ○ To focus on exploiting the commercial potential of high performance distributed computing

Centre for Advanced Solidification Technology
   see **Brunel Centre for Advanced Solidification Technology.**

Centre for Advanced Spatial Analysis   (CASA)   1995
- ■ The Bartlett School of Architecture, University College London, 1-19 Torrington Place, London, WC1E 7HB.
   020 7679 1782   fax 020 7813 2843
   http://www.casa.ucl.ac.uk/
   Director: Prof Michael Batty.
- E An interdisciplinary research centre at University College London.
- ○ To develop emerging computer technologies in various disciplines which deal with geography, space, location, and the built environment

Centre for Advanced Studies in Architecture   (CASA)   1992
- ■ Department of Architecture and Civil Engineering, University of Bath, Claverton Down, Bath, BA2 7AY.
   01225 386526   fax 01225 383255
   http://www.bath.ac.uk/casa/
   Contact: Dr M Wilson-Jones.
- E A centre at the University of Bath.
- ○ To advance research into the built environment and its history from a scholarly perspective

Centre for Advanced Studies in Christian Ministry   (CASCM)
- ■ Department of Theology and Religious Studies, University of Glasgow, No 4 - The Square, Glasgow, G12 8QQ.
   0141-330 6526   fax 0141-330 4943
   http://www.religions.divinity.gla.ac.uk/Centre_Ministry/
   Director: Dr Heather Walton.
- E A research centre at the University of Glasgow.
- ○ To encourage research and academic debate into the changing nature of Christian ministry

Centre for Advanced Studies in Finance   (CASIF)   2005
- ■ Leeds University Business School, Maurice Keyworth Building, University of Leeds, Leeds, LS2 9JT.
   0113-343 4359   fax 0113-343 4459
   http://www.casif.leeds.ac.uk
   Administrator: Michelle Dickson.
- E A research centre at the University of Leeds.
- ○ To focus research on international finance, specifically in the fields of corporate governance, behavioural finance, mathematical finance, and financial econometrics

Centre for Advanced Studies in Nursing   (CASN)   1996
- ■ Foresterhill Health Centre, University of Aberdeen, Westburn Road, Aberdeen, AB25 2AY.
   01224 553205   fax 01224 550683
   http://www.abdn.ac.uk/nursing/
   Director: Dr Alice Kiger.
- E A centre at the University of Aberdeen.
- ○ To conduct postgraduate research and teaching, and funded research, in nursing and midwifery
- ● Education and training

Centre for Advanced Study in Film and Television
Note: No longer in existence.

Centre for the Advanced Study of Religion in Wales   1998   Canolfan Uwchefrydiau Crefydd yng Nghymru
■   Department of Theology and Religious Studies, University of Wales Bangor, Bangor, Gwynedd, LL57 2DG.
       01248 382079   fax 01248 383759
       http://www.bangor.ac.uk/trs/centres/casriw/
       Director: Dr Geraint Tudur. Secretary: Dr Robert Pope.
E   A part of the University of Wales, Bangor.
○   To promote and facilitate research into all aspects of religion in Wales
●   Conference facilities

Centre for Advanced Surface, Particle and Interface Engineering   (CASPIE)
■   School of Engineering, University of Surrey, Guildford, Surrey, GU2 7XH.
       01483 686292
       http://www.surrey.ac.uk/eng/research/caspie/
       Director: Prof John Watts.
E   A research centre at the University of Surrey.

Centre for Advanced Welsh and Celtic Studies   Canolfan Uwchefrydiau Cymreig a Cheltaidd
■   National Library of Wales, Aberystwyth, Ceredigion, SY23 3HH.
       01970 626717   fax 01970 627066
       http://www.cymru.ac.uk/newpages/external/E4000.asp
       Director: Prof Geraint H Jenkins.
○   To undertake high quality research in the language, literature and history of Wales and other Celtic countries
●   Surveying the usage of Welsh language in modern times - Research project (The Visual Culture of Wales) to be published in 3
       volumes

Centre for Advanced Welsh Music Studies   (CAWMS)   1994   Canolfan Uwch-Astudiaethau Cerddoriaeth Cymru
■   School of Music, University of Wales, Bangor, Bangor, Gwynedd, LL57 2DG.
       01248 382181
       http://www.bangor.ac.uk/music/WMI/WMI.html
       Contact: Dr Sally Harper.
E   A research centre within the Welsh Music Institute (qv) at the University of Wales, Bangor.
○   To co-ordinate and develop Welsh musical scholarship

Centre for the Advancement of Learning and Teaching   (CALT)
■   University College London, 1-19 Torrington Place, London, WC1E 6BT.
       020 7679 1604
       http://www.ucl.ac.uk/calt/
       Administrator: Carol Massey.
E   A centre at University College London.

Centre for Advancement of Women in Politics   (CAWP)   2000
■   School of Politics and International Studies, Queen's University Belfast, 19-21 University Square, Belfast, BT7 1PA.
       028 9097 3654
       http://www.qub.ac.uk/cawp/
       Director: Dr Yvonne Galligan.
E   A centre at Queen's University, Belfast.
○   To foster an appreciation of women's contribution to politics, Government and public decision making in the UK and Ireland

Centre for Advancing Innovation and Management
        see **Research Centre for Advancing Innovation and Management.**

Centre for Aegean Archaeology
        see **Sheffield Centre for Aegean Archaeology.**

Centre for Aeronautics
■   Department of Engineering, City University, Tait Building, Northampton Square, London, EC1V 0HB.
       020 7040 0113
       http://www.city.ac.uk/sems/engineering/research/aero
E   A centre at City University.
○   To support postgraduate research work in aerodynamics, aircraft structures and materials, and air transport engineering

Centre for African and Asian Studies
        see **Ferguson Centre for African and Asian Studies.**

Centre of African Studies   (ASC)   1965
■ School of the Humanities and Social Sciences, University of Cambridge, Free School Lane, Cambridge, CB2 3RQ.
   01223 334396   fax 01223 334396
   http://www.african.cam.ac.uk/
   Director: Dr Derek R Peterson.
E A centre at the University of Cambridge.
○ To support interdisciplinary research and teaching in modern African studies

Centre for African Studies   (CAS)
■ Coventry University, Priory Street, Coventry, CV1 5FB.
   024 7688 8213
   Contact: Prof Roy May.
E A centre at Coventry University.
○ To promote research and consultancy on a wide range of African issues, with particular emphasis on West, East and Central Africa

Centre of African Studies   (CAS)   1962
■ School of Social and Political Studies, University of Edinburgh, 21 George Square, Edinburgh, EH8 9LD.
   0131-650 3878   fax 0131-650 6535
   http://www.cas.ed.ac.uk/
   Director: Prof Paul Nugent.
E A department of the University of Edinburgh.
○ To conduct research and interest in teaching, publishing, networking in Africa; to promote advocacy for Africa
● Education and training - Library

Centre for African Studies [Leeds]
   see **Leeds University Centre for African Studies.**

Centre of African Studies   (CAS)   1965
■ Faculty of Arts and Humanities, University of London, Thornhaugh Street, Russell Square, London, WC1H 0XG.
   020 7898 4370   fax 020 7898 4369
   http://www.soas.ac.uk/centres/centreinfo.cfm?navid=669
E A research centre at the School of Oriental and African Studies, University of London.

Centre for Ageing and Biographical Studies   (CABS)   1995
■ Faculty of Health and Social Care, Open University, Walton Hall, Milton Keynes, MK7 6AA.
   01908 858373   fax 01908 858280
   http://www.open.ac.uk/hsc/researchCABS.htm
   Director: Rebecca Jones.
E A research centre at the Open University.
○ To conduct biographical research and studies of gerontology

Centre for Ageing and Mental Health   (CAMH)
■ Faculty of Health and Sciences, Staffordshire University, Mellor Building, Beaconside, Stafford, ST18 0AD.
   01785 353718
   http://www.staffs.ac.uk/schools/sciences/ihr/camh/
   Administrator: Mrs Elaine Stanway.
E A research centre within the Institute for Health Research (qv) at Staffordshire University.
○ To provide research, consultancy and education and to promote innovation in health and social care services for the older person

Centre for Ageing and Mental Health Sciences   (CAMHS)   2006
■ Department of Mental Health Sciences, University College London, Wolfson Building, 48 Riding House Street, London, W1Y 7EY.
   020 7679 2000
   http://www.ucl.ac.uk/mental-health-sciences/specialities/camhs.htm
   Contact: Prof Martin Orrell.
E A research centre at University College London

Centre for Ageing Population Studies
■ Department of Primary Care and Population, University College London, Royal Free and University College Medical School, Rowland Hill Street, London, NW3 2PF.
   020 7830 2239
   http://www.ucl.ac.uk/pcps/research/aps
   Director: Prof Ann Bowling.
E A research centre at University College London
○ To promote research, service development and professional education in ageing communities through population ageing research, and primary care and older people

Centre for Agri-Environmental Research (CAER) 2000
■ School of Agriculture, Policy and Development, PO Box 237, University of Reading, Earley Gate, Reading, Berkshire, RG6 6AR.
  0118-378 8938   fax 0118-378 6067
  http://www.rdg.ac.uk/caer/
  Director: Prof Ken Norris.
E A research centre at the University of Reading.
O To carry out high quality scientific research that aims to reconcile the often-conflicting demands of agricultural production and environmental protection

Centre for Agricultural and Environmental Engineering
  see **Cranfield Centre for Agricultural and Environmental Engineering.**

Centre for Agricultural Strategy (CAS) 1975
■ School of Agriculture, Policy and Development, PO Box 237, University of Reading, Earley Gate, Reading, Berkshire, RG6 6AR.
  0118-931 8150   fax 0118-935 3423
  http://www.apd.rdg.ac.uk/agristrat/
  Director: Prof Alan Swinbank.
E A research centre at the University of Reading.
O To pursue independent research of developments in the agricultural and food industries, and the rural economy and the countryside

Centre for AIDS Reagents 1989
■ National Institute for Biological Standards and Control, Blanche Lane, South Mimms, Potters Bar, Hertfordshire, EN6 3QG.
  01707 641000   fax 01707 641050
  http://www.nibsc.ac.uk/spotlight/aids.html
E A centralised facility within the National Institute for Biological Standards and Control (qv).
O To assist and support the HIV / AIDS research community through the provision of high quality, basic and specialised biological research materials
● The facility now houses over 1,900 reagents

Centre for AIDS Research 2003
■ School of Social Sciences, University of Southampton, Highfield, Southampton, SO17 1BJ.
  023 8059 4748; 8588
  http://www.aids.soton.ac.uk/
  Director: William Stones.
E A research centre at the University of Southampton.
O To conduct interdisciplinary research on the determinants and impacts of the HIV pandemic

Centre for Air Conditioning and Refrigeration
  see **Centre for Sustainable Energy Systems**

Centre for Air Transport in Remoter Regions 2000
■ Department of Air Transport, Cranfield University, Cranfield, Bedfordshire, MK43 0AL.
  01234 754239   fax 01234 752207
  http://www.cranfield.ac.uk/soe/airtransport/remoter_regions/
  Director: Dr George Williams.
E A research centre at Cranfield University.
O To conduct research into the provision of the air transport infrastructure and air services in the more remote parts of Europe

Centre in Allergic Mechanisms of Asthma
  see **MRC-Asthma UK Centre in Allergic Mechanisms of Asthma.**

Centre for Allergy Research (CAR)
■ Department of Pharmacology, Medical Sciences Building, University College London, Gower Street, London, WC1E 6BT.
  020 7679 3751
  http://www.ucl.ac.uk/allergy-research/
E A research centre at University College London.

Centre for Allied Health Professions Research (CAHPR) 2006
■ City University, Northampton Square, London, EC1V 0HB.
  020 7040 3240   fax 020 7040 8595
  http://www.city.ac.uk/ihs/cahpr
E A research centre within the Institute of Health Sciences (qv) at City University.

Centre for Alternative Technology (CAT) 1975   Canolfan y Dechnoleg Amgen
■ Machynlleth, Powys, SY20 9AZ.
  01654 705950   fax 01654 702782
  http://www.cat.org.uk/
E A registered charity.
O To inspire, inform and enable society to move towards a sustainable future
● Education and training - Information service
¶ Wide range of publications.

© CBD Research Ltd · Beckenham · Kent BR3 5JS · Tel 020 8650 7745 · Fax 020 8650 0768 · E-mail cbd@cbdresearch.com · www.cbdresearch.com

Centre for American Studies (CAS)
- Faculty of Humanities, Rutherford College, University of Kent, Canterbury, Kent, CT2 7NX.
  01227 823140   fax 01227 827060
  http://www.kent.ac.uk/amst/
  Director: Dr Karen Jones.
- E   A research centre at the University of Kent.
- O   To run study programmes on the history, literature and visual arts of the United States

Centre for American Studies [British Library]
  see **Eccles Centre for American Studies.**

Centre for American Studies [Glasgow]
  see **Andrew Hook Centre for American Studies.**

Centre for American Studies [Keele]
  see **David K E Bruce Centre for American Studies.**

Centre for American Studies [King's College, London]
  see **Research Centre for American Studies.**

Centre for American Studies [Norwich]
  see **Arthur Miller Centre for American Studies.**

Centre for American, Trans-Atlantic and Caribbean History
- Brunel University, Uxbridge, Middlesex, UB8 3PH.
  01895 274000
  http://www.brunel.ac.uk/about/acad/bbs/research/researchgroups/atlanticrg
- E   A centre at Brunel University.

Centre for Amerindian Studies (CAS)   1997
- School of Philosophical, Anthropological and Film Studies, University of St Andrews, St Andrews, Fife, KY16 9AL.
  01334 462977   fax 01334 462985
  http://www.st-andrews.ac.uk/philosophy/anthropology/centres/cas
- E   A research centre at the University of St Andrews.
- O   To promote and provide a focus for research and postgraduate teaching on the anthropology of indigenous peoples of the Americas (Andes, Amazonia and Canada), and a beginner's course on Quechua language and textuality
- ✕   Centre for Indigenous American Studies and Exchange

Centre for Amyloidosis and Acute Phase Proteins (CAAPP)
- Department of Medicine, Royal Free and University College Medical School, Rowland Hill Street, London, NW3 2PF.
  020 7433 2801   fax 020 7433 2803
  http://www.ucl.ac.uk/medicine/amyloidosis/
  Director: Prof Mark Pepys.
- E   A research centre at University College London.
- O   To conduct world leading research in all aspects of the pentraxin family of plasma proteins, and in amyloidosis, ranging from structural biology, through molecular, genetic, biochemical, physiological and pathological studies, to clinical diagnostics, patient management and new drug discovery

Centre for Anaesthesia
  see **UCL Centre for Anaesthesia.**

Centre for the Analysis of Risk and Optimisation Modelling Applications (CARISMA)
- Brunel University, Uxbridge, Middlesex, UB8 3PH.
  01895 265187   fax 01895 269732
  http://carisma.brunel.ac.uk/
  Director: Prof Gautam Mitra.
- E   A centre at Brunel University.
- O   To be a centre of excellence recognised for its research and scholarship in the analysis of risk, optimisation modelling, and the combined paradigm of risk and return quantification

Centre for Analysis of Risk and Regulation
  see **ESRC Centre for Analysis of Risk and Regulation.**

Centre for the Analysis of Social Exclusion
  see **ESRC Research Centre for the Analysis of Social Exclusion.**

Centre for the Analysis of Social Policy   (CASP)   1982
- Department of Social and Policy Sciences, University of Bath, Claverton Down, Bath, BA2 7AY.
  01225 386141   fax 01225 386381
  http://www.bath.ac.uk/casp/
  Director: Jane Millar. Secretary: Faith Howard.
- E   A research centre at the University of Bath.
- O   To conduct research into the relationship between people and the state, including issues of individual decision-making, attitudes, behaviour and needs; the delivery of welfare policies and programmes in the public, private and non-profit sectors; patterns of risk and social protection in welfare and criminal justice policy;

Centre for the Analysis of Supply Chain Innovation and Dynamics   (CASCAID)
- Faculty of Technology, Open University, Walton Hall, Milton Keynes, MK7 6AA.
  01908 653672
  http://technology.open.ac.uk/cts/
  Director: Ed Rhodes.
- E   A research centre within the Centre for Technology Strategy (qv) at the Open University.
- O   To further understanding of the dynamics of technology innovation, in product supply and distribution systems, in both manufacturing and service industries

Centre for the Analysis of Time Series   (CATS)   2000
- Department of Statistics, LSE, Columbia House, Houghton Street, London, WC2A 2AE.
  020 7955 6015   fax 020 7955 7416
  http://www.lse.ac.uk/collections/cats/
  Chairman: Prof Howell Tong. Director: Prof Leonard Smith.
- E   A research centre at the London School of Economics and Political Science.
- O   To address the question of data analysis using both physical insight and the latest statistical methods, to focus on non-linear analysis in situations of economic and physical interest - such as weather forecasting; to promote awareness of limitations of non-linear analysis and the danger of blindly transferring well-known physics to simulation modelling, and to focus on end-to-end forecasting - taking account of current uncertainty about the state of the system, model inadequacy and finite computational power

Centre for Ancient Drama and its Reception   (CADRE)   1998
- Department of Classics, University of Nottingham, University Park, Nottingham, NG7 2RD.
  0115-951 4800   fax 0115-951 4811
  http://www.nottingham.ac.uk/classics/cadre/
  Director: Prof Judith Mossman.
- E   A research centre at the University of Nottingham.
- O   To promote research on Greek and Roman drama and its impact on later traditions

Centre for Anglo-German Cultural Relations   (CAGCR)   2005
- Department of German, Arts Building, Queen Mary, University of London, Mile End Road, London, E1 4NS.
  020 7882 2683   fax 020 8980 5400
  http://www.modern-languages.qmul.ac.uk/research/anglogerman/
  Director: Prof Rüdiger Görner. Contact: Dr Angus Nicholls.
- E   A research centre at Queen Mary, University of London.
- O   To promote the study of cultural transfers and inter-relations between Britain and the German speaking world

Centre for Anglo-Saxon Studies
   see **Manchester Centre for Anglo-Saxon Studies.**

Centre for Animal Sciences   (CAS)
- Faculty of Biological Sciences, University of Leeds, Manton Building, Leeds, LS2 9JT.
  0113-343 2863   fax 0113-343 3144
  http://www.fbs.leeds.ac.uk/research/centres/cas/
  Director: Prof Peter Meyer.
- E   A research centre at the University of Leeds.

Centre for the Anthropological Study of Knowledge and Ethics   (CASKE)
- School of Philosophical, Anthropological and Film Studies, University of St Andrews, St Andrews, Fife, KY16 9AL.
  01334 462977   fax 01334 462985
  http://www.st-andrews.ac.uk/philosophy/anthropology/res.htm#caske
- E   A research centre at the University of St Andrews.
- O   To conduct research on epistemology - what and how people know things to be true, and on political morality - how different worlds of truth can be accommodated in a democratic society

Centre for Antimicrobial Research
   see **Antimicrobial Research Centre.**

© CBD Research Ltd · Beckenham · Kent BR3 5JS · Tel 020 8650 7745 · Fax 020 8650 0768 · E-mail cbd@cbdresearch.com · www.cbdresearch.com

Centre for Antiquity and the Middle Ages   (CAMA)   2003
- School of Humanities, University of Southampton, Highfield, Southampton, SO17 1BJ.
  023 8059 2206
  http://www.cama.soton.ac.uk/
  Director: Dr Brian Golding.
- E   A research centre at the University of Southampton.
- O   To create a research environment for academics and postgraduates working in the classical and medieval periods

Centre for Anxiety Disorders and Trauma
- 99 Denmark Hill, London, SE5 8AF.
  020 7919 2101; 3286   fax 020 7740 5215
  http://psychology.iop.kcl.ac.uk/cadat/
  Senior Unit Administrator: Mrs Margaret Dakin.
- E   A research centre within the Institute of Psychiatry (qv) at King's College, London.
- O   To provide specialist treatment and conduct research in a very wide range of anxiety disorders and trauma, including body dysmorphic disorder, obsessive compulsive disorder, panic disorder, post-traumatic stress disorder, social and other phobias

Centre for Appearance Research   (CAR)   1998
- School of Psychology, Frenchay Campus, University of the West of England, Coldharbour Lane, Bristol, BS16 1QY.
  0117-328 2192; 3967   fax 0117-328 3645
  http://science.uwe.ac.uk/research/
  Director: Prof Nicky Rumsey.
- E   An interdisciplinary research centre at the University of the West of England.
- O   To make a difference to the lives of the many people with appearance-related concerns through research in appearance, disfigurement and related studies

Centre for Applied Archaeological Analyses   (CAAA)   1985
- Department of Archaeology, Avenue Campus, University of Southampton, Highfield, Southampton, SO17 1BF.
  023 8059 4439   fax 023 8059 3032
  http://www.arch.soton.ac.uk/default.asp?Division=3&SubDivision=4&Page=0
  Director: Dr Elaine Morris.
- E   A research centre at the University of Southampton.
- O   To explore interdisciplinary links between archaeology and social statistics, biology, engineering, and medicine so as to investigate human ecology in its broadest sense

Centre for Applied Bioethics   (CAB)   1993
- School of Biosciences, Sutton Bonington Campus, University of Nottingham, Loughborough, Leicestershire, LE12 5RD.
  0115-951 6303   fax 0115-951 6299
  http://www.nottingham.ac.uk/bioethics/
  Director: Prof Ben Mepham.
- E   A research centre at the University of Nottingham.
- O   To conduct research in the appropriate application of biological knowledge and practice to food production, industry and medical uses of farm animals such as providing organ transplants for human patients

Centre for Applied Catalysis   (CAC)   1997
- School of Applied Sciences, University of Huddersfield, Queensgate, Huddersfield, HD1 3DH.
  01484 473138   fax 01484 472182
  http://www.hud.ac.uk/sas/research/catalysis/
  Director: Prof P A Barnes.
- E   A research centre at the University of Huddersfield.
- O   To conduct research in new techniques for catalyst preparation and characterisation, with particular emphasis on new thermal methods for materials preparation and characterisation, porous materials for catalysis and adsorption, and surface science studies

Centre for Applied Childhood Studies   (CACS)   1991
- School of Human and Health Sciences, University of Huddersfield, Queensgate, Huddersfield, HD1 3DH.
  01484 473213
  http://www.hud.ac.uk/hhs/research/acs/
  Director: Prof Nigel Parton.
- E   A research centre at the University of Huddersfield.
- O   To promote research, policy and practice which contributes to the well-being of children and young people, without discrimination on the basis of ethnicity, ability, age, gender, sexual orientation, class, or any other difference which is sensitive to them, and treats them as participants in their own right

Centre for Applied Entomology and Parasitology   (CAEP)
- School of Life Sciences, Huxley Building, Keele University, Keele, Staffordshire, ST5 5BG.
  01782 583028   fax 01782 583516
  http://www.keele.ac.uk/depts/aep/
  Director: Prof H Hurd.
- E   A research centre within the Institute for Science and Technology in Medicine (qv) at Keele University.
- O   To focus research on entomology and parasitology, particularly in the areas of chemical ecology, fish parasitology and immunology, insect ecology, malaria, molecular entomology, parasite-insect interactions, population genetics, and sandflies and leishmaniasis

Centre for Applied Ethics   (CAE)   1989
- ■   Cardiff School of English, Communication and Philosophy, Cardiff University, Colum Drive, Cardiff, CF10 3XB.
  029 2087 4025   fax 029 2087 4618
  http://www.cf.ac.uk/encap/cae
  Director: Dr Andrew Edgar.
- E   A centre at Cardiff University.
- O   To promote the study of and public interest in applied ethics

Centre for Applied Formal Methods   (CAFM)   2000
- ■   Faculty of Business, Computing and Information Management, London South Bank University, 103 Borough Road, London, SE1 0AA.
  020 7815 7413
  http://www.lsbu.ac.uk/bcimicr/research/cafm.shtml
  Head: Prof Jonathan Bowen.
- E   A research centre within the Institute for Computing Research (qv) at London South Bank University.
- O   To carry out research work with a balance of theory and practice in the general area of computer science, with particular emphasis on Z notation, functional and logic programming, high-integrity systems, real-time systems, reconfigurable computing, history of computing, online museums and web accessibility

Centre for Applied Gerontology
- ■   The Hayward Building, Selly Oak Hospital, Raddlebarn Road, Birmingham, B29 6JD.
  0121-627 8640   fax 0121-627 8304
  http://www.gerontology.bham.ac.uk/
  Director: Dr U S L Nayak, BE, ME, PhD.
- E   Part of the University of Birmingham.
- O   To work with older people, designers and manufacturers to adapt products so that older people find them easier to use

Centre for Applied Human Resource Research   (CAHRR)
- ■   Oxford Brookes Business School, Oxford Brookes University, 34 St John Street, Oxford, OX1 2LH.
  Contact: Prof William Scott-Jackson.
- E   A research centre at Oxford Brookes University.
- O   To carry out applied research that will make a real difference to organisational performance and strategy

Centre for Applied Interaction Research   (CAIR)   2006
- ■   Department of Human Communication Science, University College London, Remax House, 31-32 Alfred Place, London, WC1E 7DP.
  020 7679 4200
  http://www.ucl.ac.uk/HCS/CAIR/
- E   A research centre at University College London.
- O   To facilitate research into normal and disordered interaction, with an emphasis on analysing video- or audio-taped naturally occurring conversation in health, social and education settings, using the principles of conversation analysis

Centre for Applied Language Research   (CALR)   2004
- ■   School of Humanities, University of Southampton, Highfield, Southampton, SO17 1BJ.
  023 8059 2255
  http://www.calr.soton.ac.uk/
  Director: Prof Rosamond Mitchell.
- E   A research centre at the University of Southampton.
- O   To conduct research and advanced teaching in applied linguistics

Centre for Applied Language Studies   (CALS)   1974
- ■   Whiteknights, PO Box 241, University of Reading, Reading, Berkshire, RG6 6WB.
  0118-378 6223   fax 0118-378 5427
  http://www.cals.rdg.ac.uk/
- E   A department of the University of Reading.
- O   To offer English for Academic Purposes (EAP) courses to international students
- ●   Education and training - Information service

Centre for Applied Language Studies   (CALS)   1986
- ■   Department of Applied Linguistics, Swansea University, Singleton Park, Swansea, SA2 8PP.
  01792 602540   fax 01792 602545
  http://www.swan.ac.uk/cals/
  Leader: Dr Jim Milton.
- E   A centre at Swansea University.
- O   To run courses in English language and linguistics

Centre for Applied Laser Spectroscopy   (CALS)
- ■   Department of Environmental and Ordnance Systems, Cranfield University, Shrivenham, Swindon, Wiltshire, SN6 8LA.
  01793 785233   fax 01793 785772
  http://www.dcmt.cranfield.ac.uk/dmas/cdc/sensors/laser
  Contact: Dr S Rafi Ahmad.
- E   A research centre at Cranfield University.
- O   To conduct theoretical and experimental research into the laser ignition of energetic materials

Centre for Applied Medical Statistics (CAMS) 1996

■ School of Clinical Medicine, University of Cambridge, Robinson Way, Cambridge, CB2 2SR.
01223 330308   fax 01223 330330
http://www.phpc.cam.ac.uk/cams/
Director: Dr Chris Palmer.

E A research centre within the Institute of Public Health (qv) at the University of Cambridge.

O To provide statistical expertise for consulting and collaborating with clinical researchers on particular projects; to provide occasional short courses on introductory and specialised statistical topics

Centre for Applied Oceanography   (CAO)

■ School of Ocean Sciences, Marine Science Laboratories, University of Wales Bangor, Menai Bridge, Anglesey, Gwynedd, LL59 5EY.
01248 713808   fax 01248 716729
http://www.cao.bangor.ac.uk/
Director: Prof Alan J Elliott.

E A research centre at the University of Wales, Bangor.

O To specialise in fundamental and applied research of estuarine, nearshore and shelf sea regions

Centre for Applied Psychological Research   (CAPR)

■ Department of Behavioural Sciences, University of Huddersfield, Queensgate, Huddersfield, HD1 3DH.
01484 422288
http://www.hud.ac.uk/hhs/dbs/capr/

E A research centre at the University of Huddersfield.

Centre for Applied Psychology

■ University of Leicester, 106 New Walk, Leicester, LE1 7EA.
0116-223 1486; 252 2481
http://www.le.ac.uk/pc/

E A research centre at the University of Leicester.

Centre for Applied Psychology, Health and Culture   (CAPHC)   2006

■ Faculty of Health, Leeds Metropolitan University, Civic Quarter, Calverley Street, Leeds, LS1 3HE.
0113-283 2600   fax 0113-283 1908
http://www.leedsmet.ac.uk/health/caphcul
Co-ordinator: Mumtaz Ahmed Khan.

E A research centre at Leeds Metropolitan University.

O To focus research on psychology, health and culture

Centre for Applied Research in Economics   (CARE)

■ Middlesex University Business School, The Burroughs, London, NW4 4BT.
020 8411 5000
http://mubs.mdx.ac.uk/

E A research centre at Middlesex University.

Centre for Applied Research in Education   (CARE)   1970

■ Faculty of Social Sciences, University of East Anglia, Norwich, NR4 7TJ.
01603 592870
http://www.uea.ac.uk/care/
Director: Prof Rob Walker.

E A department of the University of East Anglia.

O To conduct field-based enquiry aimed at the improvement of educational policy and practice across the professions and the enhancement of democracy

Centre for Applied Research in Educational Technologies   (CARET)

■ University of Cambridge, 1st Floor - 16 Mill Lane, Cambridge, CB2 1SB.
01223 765040   fax 01223 765505
http://www.caret.cam.ac.uk/
Director: John Norman. Administrator: Stephanie Saunders.

E A centre at the University of Cambridge.

O To enrich the experience of education for students, teachers and researchers by providing a range of generic tools, free of charge, or producing tailor-made solutions where funding is available

Centre for Applied Research in Information Systems   (CARIS)

■ Faculty of Computing, Information Systems and Mathematics, Kingston University, London, Penrhyn Road, Kingston-upon-Thames, Surrey, KT1 2EE.
020 8547 7701   fax 020 8547 7887
http://caris.kingston.ac.uk/
Director: Chris Wills.

E A research centre at Kingston University, London.

O To provide a focus and infrastructure for applied research and consultancy projects in the area of information systems

Centre for Applied Science
- ■ School of Science and Technology, University of Teesside, Middlesbrough, TS1 3BA.
  01642 342466
  http://www.tees.ac.uk/schools/sst/
  Contact: Zulf Ali.
- E A research centre at the University of Teesside.
- O To focus research on delivering solutions to business in the fields of nanotechnology, measurement, materials, food and molecular science

Centre in Applied Sciences
  see **Research Centre in Applied Sciences.**

Centre for Applied Simulation Modelling (CASM) 1982
- ■ School of Information Systems, Computing and Mathematics, St John's Building, Brunel University, Uxbridge, Middlesex, UB8 3PH.
  01895 265975
  http://www.brunel.ac.uk/about/acad/siscm/cs/research/computing/simulation
- E A research centre at Brunel University.

Centre for Applied Social Psychology (CASP)
- ■ Department of Psychology, University of Strathclyde, 40 George Street, Glasgow, G1 1QE.
  0141-548 2582
  http://www.psych.strath.ac.uk/
- E A research centre at the University of Strathclyde.

Centre for Applied South Asian Studies (CASAS)
- ■ School of Arts, Histories and Cultures, University of Manchester, Oxford Road, Manchester, M13 9PL.
  0161-275 3605; 303 1709   fax 0161-303 1709
  http://www.art.man.ac.uk/casas/
  Contact: Dr Roger Ballard.
- E A research centre at the University of Manchester.
- O To conduct research on social, cultural and religious developments within Britain's Indian, Pakistani and Bangladeshi minorities

Centre for Applied Statistics   1979
- ■ Department of Mathematics and Statistics, Fylde College, Lancaster University, Lancaster, LA1 4YF.
  01524 593064   fax 01524 593429
  Director: Brian Francis.
- E A research centre within Lancaster University.
- O To carry out high level research in applied statistics; to provide research training through PhD programmes; to provide statistical consultancy / contract research services in social statistics and quantitative criminology to external clients to help ensure the relevance of the Centre's research programme
- ● Education and training

Centre for Applied Statistics and Systems Modelling (CASSM) 2002
- ■ School of Computing and Mathematical Sciences, Maritime Greenwich Campus, University of Greenwich, Park Row, London, SE10 9LS.
  020 8331 8717   fax 020 8331 8665
  http://www.cms1.gre.ac.uk/research/centres/appliedstatistics.asp
  Co-Director: Prof Keith Rennolls. Co-Director: Prof Vitaly Strusevitch.
- E A research centre at the University of Greenwich.
- O To co-ordinate the applied research and consultancy activities, and the provision of training courses by statisticians, management scientists and systems modellers

Centre for Applied Systems Thinking
Note: has closed.

Centre for Applied Theatre Research (CATR)
- ■ School of Arts, Histories and Cultures, University of Manchester, Lime Grove, Oxford Road, Manchester, M13 9PL.
  0161-275 3357   fax 0161-275 3049
  http://www.arts.manchester.ac.uk/subjectareas/drama/research/centreforappliedtheatreresearch/
  Contact: Prof James Thompson.
- E A research centre within the Centre for Interdisciplinary Research in the Arts (qv) at the University of Manchester.
- O To conduct research in 'applied theatre' - the practice of theatre and drama in non-traditional settings and/or with marginalised communities

Centre for Archaeological and Forensic Analysis (CAFA) 2006
- ■ Department of Materials and Medical Sciences, Cranfield University, Shrivenham, Swindon, Wiltshire, SN6 8LA.
  01793 785642   fax 01793 785772
  http://www.dcmt.cranfield.ac.uk/dmas/cmse/forensicinstitute/archaelogical/view
  Contact: Dr A J Shortland.
- E A research centre of Cranfield University.
- O To provide a wide range of scientific and analytical expertise for the archaeological and forensic communities, specialising in provenance, dating and identity especially in ceramics, glass and bone

Centre for the Archaeology of Human Origins   (CAHO)   2000
- ■   Department of Archaeology, Avenue Campus, University of Southampton, Highfield, Southampton, SO17 1BF.
  023 8059 4439   fax 023 8059 3032
  http://www.arch.soton.ac.uk/Prospectus/CAHO/
  Director: Prof Clive Gamble.
- E   A research centre at the University of Southampton.
- ○   To conduct worldwide research into the origins of humans

Centre for Architectural and Urban Studies
   see **Martin Centre for Architectural and Urban Studies.**

Centre for Archive and Information Studies   (CAIS)
- ■   School of Humanities, Tower Building, University of Dundee, Dundee, DD1 4HN.
  01382 385543   fax 01382 385523
  http://www.dundee.ac.uk/cais/
  Director: Pat Whatley.
- E   A centre at the University of Dundee.
- ○   To offer postgraduate and undergraduate distance learning programmes for information professionals and family and local
  historians

Centre for Archive Studies
   see **Liverpool University Centre for Archive Studies.**

Centre for Arid Zone Studies
   see **CAZS Natural Resources.**

Centre for Art, Design and Philosophy
- ■   Faculty of Arts, Media and Design, Staffordshire University, Mellor Building, College Road, Stoke-on-Trent, ST4 2DF.
  01782 294556
  http://www.staffs.ac.uk/research/institutes/ari.php
- E   A research centre within the Advanced Research Institute (qv) at Staffordshire University.
- ○   To promote collaborative research between art, design and philosophy as the source of unique insights into both disciplines

Centre for Art and Design and Research Experimentation   (CADRE)
- ■   School of Art and Design, University of Wolverhampton, Molineux Street, Wolverhampton, WV1 1SB.
  01902 321941
  http://www.wlv.ac.uk/Default.aspx?page=7460
  Director: Timothy Collins.
- E   A centre at the University of Wolverhampton.
- ○   To research all aspects of the arts and fine arts

Centre for the Art and Material Culture of the Middle East
   see **Khalili Research Centre for the Art and Material Culture of the Middle East.**

Centre for Arthritis
   see **Horder Centre for Arthritis.**

Centre for Artists' Books   (CAB)   1999
- ■   Duncan of Jordanstone College of Art and Design, University of Dundee, 152 Nethergate, Dundee, DD1 4DY.
  01382 388064; 388070   fax 01382 388105
  http://www.vrc.dundee.ac.uk/cab/cab.htm
  Project Co-ordinator: Vicky Hale.
- E   A research centre within the Visual Research Centre (qv) at the University of Dundee.
- Note: A combined archive and exhibition space devoted entirely to artists' books.

Centre for Arts and Humanities in Health and Medicine   (CAHHM)   2000
- ■   School of Health, Science Site, University of Durham, South Road, Durham, DH1 3LE.
  0191-334 2917   fax 0191-334 2915
  http://www.dur.ac.uk/cahhm/
  Director: Dr Jane Macnaughton.
- E   A research centre at the University of Durham.
- ○   To pursue interdisciplinary research and educational initiatives that will explore and extend the relationship between the
  humanities, the arts, and medical and healthcare practice

Centre for the Arts and Learning   (CAL)   2006
- ■   Department of Educational Studies, Goldsmiths, University of London, London, SE14 6NW.
  020 7919 7353
  http://www.goldsmiths.ac.uk/cal/
  Director: Prof D Atkinson.
- E   A research centre at Goldsmiths, University of London.
- ○   To conduct practical and theoretical exploration of learning practices across the arts within diverse social and cultural contexts

Centre for Arts Research Technology and Education (CARTE) 2000

- School of Social Sciences, Humanities and Languages, University of Westminster, 70 Great Portland Street, London, W1W 7NQ.
  020 7911 5000 ext 2675   fax 020 7915 5439
  http://www.wmin.ac.uk/sshl/page-667
  Co-Director: Jane Prophet. Co-Director: Peter Ride.
- E An interdisciplinary research centre at the University of Westminster.
- O To conduct research and teaching in visual culture from a pan-disciplinary perspective and how creative collaborations between different disciplines take place

Centre for Asia-Pacific Studies   (CAPS)

- School of Arts and Humanities, Nottingham Trent University, Clifton Lane, Nottingham, NG11 8NS.
  0115-848 6318
  http://www.ntu.ac.uk/research/school_research/hum/29517gp.html
  Contact: Dr Neil Renwick.
- E A research centre at Nottingham Trent University.
- O To promote new academic research, co-ordinate existing research, contribute to postgraduate and undergraduate study, and to provide a service to the local, regional and national communities in relation to the countries of the Asia-Pacific

Centre for Assessment Solutions   (CFAs)

- School of Education, Humanities Devas Street, University of Manchester, Oxford Road, Manchester, M13 9PL.
  0161-275 3418; 3524   fax 0161-275 8280
  http://www.education.manchester.ac.uk/research/centres/cfas/cfas/
  Director: Bill Boyle.
- E A research centre within the Centre for Formative Assessment Studies (qv) at the University of Manchester.
- O To provide large scale data management and analysis, and training programmes for formative assessment conceptualisation and strategies

Centre for Astrobiology [Cardiff]
  see **Cardiff Centre for Astrobiology.**

Centre for Astrobiology [Open University]
  see **Interdisciplinary Centre for Astrobiology.**

Centre for Astrophysics   1993

- University of Central Lancashire, Preston, PR1 2HE.
  01772 893540   fax 01772 892996
  http://www.star.uclan.ac.uk/
  Head: Prof Gordon Bromage.
- E A research centre at the University of Central Lancashire.
- O To research into the physics of stars, galaxies and the universe
- ● Seminars

Centre for Astrophysics and Planetary Science   (CAPS)

- School of Physical Sciences, Ingram Building, University of Kent, Canterbury, Kent, CT2 7NH.
  01227 823759   fax 01227 827558
  http://astro.kent.ac.uk/
  Contact: Prof Michael Smith.
- E A research centre at the University of Kent.
- O To conduct research in the solar system, star formation, astrochemistry, detector development, and the cosmic history of galaxy formation

Centre for Astrophysics Research   (CAR)

- University of Hertfordshire, College Lane, Hatfield, Hertfordshire, AL10 9AB.
  01707 284500   fax 01707 284514
  http://strc.herts.ac.uk/
  Director: Prof James Hough.
- E A research centre within the Science and Technology Research Institute (qv) at the University of Hertfordshire.
- O To carry out a wide range of research in the fields of astronomy and astrophysics

Centre for Atmospheric Science   (CAS)   1993

- Chemistry Department, University of Cambridge, Lensfield Road, Cambridge, CB2 1EW.
  01223 336473   fax 01223 763823
  http://www.atm.ch.cam.ac.uk/
  Director: Prof John Pyle.
- E A centre at the University of Cambridge.
- O To promote atmospheric research

Centre for Atomic and Molecular Quantum Dynamics   (CAMQD)   2005

- School of Mathematics and Physics, Queen's University Belfast, Belfast, BT7 1NN.
  028 9097 3546; 3941   fax 028 9097 3110
  http://www.qub.ac.uk/schools/SchoolofMathematicsandPhysics/ResearchCentres/
  InternationalResearchCentreforExperimentalPhysics/CentreforAtomicandMolecularQuantumDynamics/
- E A research centre within the International Research Centre for Experimental Physics (qv) at Queen's University, Belfast.

© CBD Research Ltd · Beckenham · Kent BR3 5JS · Tel 020 8650 7745 · Fax 020 8650 0768 · E-mail cbd@cbdresearch.com · www.cbdresearch.com

Centre for Audio Research and Engineering

■ Department of Electronic Systems Engineering, University of Essex, Wivenhoe Park, Colchester, Essex, CO4 3SQ.
01206 872414; 872905   fax 01206 872900
http://www.essex.ac.uk/ese/
Director: Prof M O J Hawksford.

E A research centre at the University of Essex.

Centre for Auditory Research   (CAR)   2005

■ Faculty of Biomedical Sciences, University College London, 332 Gray's Inn Road, London, WC1X 8EE.
020 7679 8908   fax 020 7837 9279
http://www.ucl.ac.uk/car/
Director: Prof Jonathan Ashmore.

E A research centre within the Institute of Laryngology and Otology (qv) at University College London.

○ To conduct auditory research, with particular emphasis on the molecular and cellular basis of hearing, the genetics of hearing and deafness, auditory system function, and imaging the auditory system

Centre for Australian Studies in Wales   (CASW)   1986   Canolfan Astudiaethau Awstralaidd Cymru

■ University of Wales Lampeter, College Street, Lampeter, Ceredigion, SA48 7ED.
01570 424937   fax 01570 424994
http://www.lamp.ac.uk/oz/
Director: Dr Paul Rainbird.

E A research centre at the University of Wales, Lampeter.

○ To further the study of Australia in Wales, and to strengthen links between Australia and Wales at the individual, institutional and commercial levels

Centre for Austrian Literature
see **Ingeborg Bachmann Centre for Austrian Literature.**

Centre for Austrian Studies   (CAS)

■ School of Language and Literature, King's College, University of Aberdeen, Aberdeen, AB24 3UB.
01224 272549   fax 01224 272494
http://www.abdn.ac.uk/german/
Director: Dr Janet Stewart.

E A centre at the University of Aberdeen.
○ To develop knowledge and understanding of Austrian culture

Centre for Automotive Industries Management   (CAIM)   1998

■ Nottingham Business School, Nottingham Trent University, Burton Street, Nottingham, NG1 4BU.
0115-848 8121
http://www.ntu.ac.uk/nbs/spec/caim/7398gp.html
Head: Prof Peter N C Cooke.

E A research centre at Nottingham Trent University.

○ To provide quality management training and education for the automotive industries; to undertake automotive industry funded independent pragmatic research for either internal or external application

Centre for Automotive Industry Research   (CAIR)   1991

■ Cardiff Business School, Aberconway Building, Cardiff University, Colum Drive, Cardiff, CF10 3EU.
029 2087 4281   fax 029 2087 4419
http://www.cardiff.ac.uk/carbs/research/centres_units/cair.html
Director: Prof Garel Rhys.

E A centre at Cardiff University.

○ To conduct research into the automotive industry, with particular emphasis on economic and business analysis, but supported by electrical, electronic and systems engineering

● Consultancy

Centre for Automotive Management   (CAM)   1997

■ Loughborough University Business School, Ashby Road, Loughborough, Leicestershire, LE11 3TU.
01509 228275
http://www.lboro.ac.uk/departments/bs/mdc/about-auto.html
Director: Prof Jim Saker.

E A centre at Loughborough University.

○ To provide specialist training and development for practising dealer principals, managers, supervisors and team leaders, as well as new recruits from school and aspiring managers, in automotive dealerships of all marques; to undertake research within the automotive industry

Centre for Automotive Systems, Dynamics and Control

■ Department of Engineering and Design, University of Sussex, Falmer, Brighton, East Sussex, BN1 9QT.
01273 678108
http://www.sussex.ac.uk/engineering/
Leader: Prof R K Stobart.

E A research centre at the University of Sussex.

○ To conduct research in the dynamic behaviour and control of non-linear systems with particular relevance to automotive applications

Centre for Aviation, Space and Extreme Environment Medicine   (CASE)
■   Division of Medicine, Ground Floor - Charterhouse Building, University College London, Highgate Hill, London, N19 5LW.
    020 7288 3890
    http://www.ucl.ac.uk/case/
    Research Director: Dr Hugh Montgomery.
E   A research centre within the UCL Institute for Human Health and Performance (qv).

Centre for Aviation, Transport and the Environment   (CATE)
■   Faculty of Science and Engineering, Manchester Metropolitan University, Chester Street, Manchester, M1 5GD.
    0161-247 3658   fax 0161-247 6332
    http://www.cate.mmu.ac.uk/
    Director: Prof David Raper.
E   A research centre at Manchester Metropolitan University.
O   To facilitate the integrated social, economic and environmental sustainability of the aviation industry through critical research and analysis, and through knowledge transfer between the academic, industry, regulatory and NGO sectors

Centre for Banking and Finance   (CBF)   1973
■   School of Business and Regional Development, University of Wales Bangor, Bangor, Gwynedd, LL57 2DG.
    01248 382277   fax 01248 364760
    http://sbard.bangor.ac.uk/
    Contact: Prof Ted Gardener.
E   A research centre at the University of Wales, Bangor.
O   To provide various banking and finance consultancy and research services
X   Institute for European Finance.

Centre for Battlefield Archaeology   (CBA)   2006
■   Department of Archaeology, The Gregory Building, University of Glasgow, Lilybank Gardens, Glasgow, G12 8QQ.
    0141-330 5541
    http://www.battlefieldarchaeology.arts.gla.ac.uk/
    Director: Dr Iain Banks.
E   A research centre at the University of Glasgow.
O   To provide an international centre of excellence for the burgeoning study of the archaeology of battlefields and other archaeological manifestations of human conflict

Centre for Bayesian Statistics in Health Economics   (CHEBS)   2001
■   Department of Probability and Statistics, Hicks Building, University of Sheffield, Sheffield, S3 7RH.
    0114-222 3754   fax 0114-222 3759
    http://www.shef.ac.uk/chebs/
    Director: Prof Anthony O'Hagan.
E   A research centre at the University of Sheffield.
O   To conduct research into health economic evaluation in relation to the pharmaceutical and medical technology industries, and to Governments and health care providers

Centre for Behavioural Biology
       see **Behavioural Biology Research Centre.**

Centre for Behavioural and Clinical Neuroscience
       see **Behavioural and Clinical Neurosciences Institute.**

Centre for Behavioural Medicine   2006
■   School of Pharmacy, University of London, 29-39 Brunswick Square, London, WC1N 1AX
    020 7874 1281   fax 020 7387 5693
    http://www.pharmacy.ac.uk/cbm.html
    Research Administrator: Amy Whitehead
E   A research centre at the University of London.
O   To make healthcare more efficient, by understanding and addressing the psychological and behavioural factors which explain variation in response to treatment.
Note: Has replaced the Centre for Health Care Research, University of Brighton.

Centre for Behavioural Research, Analysis, and Intervention in Developmental Disabilities   (CBRAIDD)   2000
■   School of Psychology, University of Southampton, Shackleton Building, Highfield, Southampton, SO17 1BJ.
    023 8059 3995   fax 023 8059 4597
    http://www.psychology.soton.ac.uk/research/behaviour.php
    Contact: Prof Jim Stevenson.
E   A research centre at the University of Southampton.
O   To use psychological knowledge and expertise to develop an understanding of the nature of developmental disabilities, and to enhance the treatment of individuals with such disabilities

Centre for Behavioural and Social Sciences in Medicine 2003

- Department of Medicine, University College London, 2nd Floor - Wolfson Building, 48 Riding House Street, London, W1W 7EY.
  020 7679 9476   fax 020 7679 9426
  http://www.ucl.ac.uk/medicine/behavioural-social/
  Director: Prof Stanton Newman.
- E   A department of University College London.
- O   To examine issues to do with health and illness from the perspectives of health psychology, medical sociology and medical anthropology

Centre for Biblical Studies (CBS)

- School of Arts, Histories and Cultures, University of Manchester, Oxford Road, Manchester, M13 9PL.
  0161-275 3609; 306 1255   fax 0161-275 3264
  http://www.arts.manchester.ac.uk/subjectareas/religionstheology/research/centreforbiblicalstudies/
  Contact: Prof George J Brooke. Contact: Anna Bigland.
- E   A research centre at the University of Manchester.
- O   To study the literature and cultural contexts of the Hebrew Bible (Old Testament) and of the New Testament

Centre for Bioactive Chemistry (CBC) 2005

- Department of Chemistry, University Science Laboratories, University of Durham, South Road, Durham, DH1 3LE.
  0191-334 2100
  http://www.dur.ac.uk/bioactive.chemistry/
  Co-Director: Prof R Edwards. Co-Director: Prof D Parker, FRS.
- E   An interdisciplinary research centre within the University of Durham.
- O   To facilitate research programmes in biological chemistry and bioengineering

Centre for Bioactivity Screening of Natural Products

- School of Biomedical and Health Sciences, King's College London, Strand, London, WC2B 4LG.
  020 7836 5454
  http://www.kcl.ac.uk/schools/biohealth/research/pharmsci/centres/bioactive-natt-pro-index.html
- E   A research centre at King's College, London.

Centre for BioArray Innovation

- NR   School of Biological Sciences, Laboratory for Environmental Gene Regulation, University of Liverpool, Crown Street, Liverpool, L69 7ZB.
  0151-795 4510   fax 0151-795 4431
  http://www.postgenomeconsortium.com/bioarray
  Bioarray Programme Co-ordinator: Prof Andrew Cossins.
- E   A research centre at the University of Liverpool.
- O   To conduct research in surface and nanoscale sciences, signal processing, fluorescence and amperometric detection systems to bear on problems like those posed by biologically orientated sensors and arrayed multi-sensor systems

Note: A joint venture with various other organisations, including the Universities of Cranfield, Manchester and Salford.

Centre for Biochemistry and Cell Biology (CBCB)

- School of Biomedical Sciences, Medical School, University of Nottingham, Queen's Medical Centre, Nottingham, NG7 2UH.
  0115-823 0118
  http://www.nottingham.ac.uk/biomedsci/cbcb/
  Director: Prof Peter Shaw.
- E   A research centre at the University of Nottingham.
- O   To conduct research aimed at elucidation of cellular processes at the molecular level

Centre for Bioinformatics [Cranfield]
   see **Cranfield Centre for Bioinformatics.**

Centre for Bioinformatics [Birkbeck, University of London]
   see **Bloomsbury Centre for Bioinformatics.**

Centre for Bioinformatics [Edinburgh]
   see **Edinburgh Centre for Bioinformatics.**

Centre for Bioinformatics

- Faculty of Life Sciences, South Kensington Campus, Imperial College London, Exhibition Road, London, SW7 2AZ.
  020 7594 5212; 5715   fax 020 7594 5789
  http://www.bioinformatics.ic.ac.uk/
  Director: Prof Michael J E Sternberg.
- E   A research centre at Imperial College London.
- O   To promote and co-ordinate world class research and training in bioinformatics

Centre for Bioinformatics and Medical Informatics Training

- School of Biosciences, Geoffrey Pope Building, University of Exeter, Stocker Road, Exeter, EX4 4QD.
  01392 264674   fax 01392 263700
  http://www.biosciences.ex.ac.uk/bioinformatics/
  Contact: Amanda Trick.
- E A centre at the University of Exeter.
- O To provide students with theoretical foundations and a practical understanding of computational techniques in the study of biology, especially molecular biology

Centre for Biomaterials and Tissue Engineering   (CBTE)

- North Campus, University of Sheffield, Broad Lane, Sheffield, S3 7HQ.
  0114-222 5995   fax 0114-222 5943
  http://www.cbte.group.shef.ac.uk/
  Director: Prof Sheila MacNeil.
- E A research centre within the Kroto Research Institute (qv) at the University of Sheffield.

Centre for Bio-Medical Engineering

- Faculty of Biomedical Sciences, Royal Free and University College Medical School, University College London, Brockley Hill, Stanmore, Middlesex, HA7 4LP.
  020 8954 0636
  http://www.ucl.ac.uk/orthopaedics/centres/bmeunits.htm
  Head: Prof Gordon Blunn.
- E A research centre within the Institute of Orthopaedics and Musculo-Skeletal Science (qv) at University College London.
- O To conduct research on various aspects of biomedical engineering, including development of bone tumour implants, the fixation of standard total joint arthroplasty, computer modelling, in vivo models and clinical trials, and telemetry of forces in vivo from joint replacement implants

Centre for Biomedical Engineering   (CBME)   1989

- School of Engineering, University of Durham, South Road, Durham, DH1 3LE.
  0191-334 2510
  http://www.dur.ac.uk/cbme/
  Director: Prof Anthony Unsworth.
- E A department of the University of Durham.
- O To lead multi-disciplinary research in the field of biomedical engineering
- ● Conference facilities - Education and training - Exhibitions - Information service - Library

Centre for Biomedical Engineering   (CBE)

- School of Engineering, Duke of Kent Building, University of Surrey, Guildford, Surrey, GU2 7TE.
  01483 686292
  http://portal.surrey.ac.uk/portal/page?_pageid=822,351423&_dad=portal&_schema=PORTAL
  Director: Dr David Ewins.
- E A research centre at the University of Surrey.
- O To conduct research in the design and development of equipment and measurement methods for use in healthcare, and equipment for use in hazardous situations

Centre for BioMedical Informatics   (CBI)   2006

- Faculty of Science, Technology and Medical Studies, Biosciences Laboratory, University of Kent, Canterbury, Kent, CT2 7NJ.
  01227 764000
  http://www.kent.ac.uk/bio/cbmi/
  Director: Dr Anthony Baines.
- E A research centre at the University of Kent.
- O To foster collaborative research and postgraduate teaching in the broad area of biomedical informatics

Centre for Biomedical Science
see **Royal Free Centre for Biomedical Science.**

Centre for Biomimetic and Natural Technologies   (CBNT)

- Department of Mechanical Engineering, University of Bath, Claverton Down, Bath, BA2 7AY.
  01225 826933   fax 01225 826928
  http://www.bath.ac.uk/mech-eng/biomimetics/
  Contact: Miss Sarah Fuge.
- E A centre at the University of Bath.
- O To advance research in biomimetics - the concept of taking ideas from nature and implementing them in another technology

Centre for Biomimetics   2005

- School of Construction Management and Engineering, University of Reading, Whiteknights, Reading, Berkshire, RG6 6AY.
  0118-378 8445   fax 0118-931 3327
  http://www.rdg.ac.uk/biomim/
  Director: Prof George Jeronimidis.
- E A research centre at the University of Reading.
- O To conduct research into biomimetics, ie the abstraction of good design from nature

Centre for Biomolecular Electron Microscopy (CBEM)

■ Faculty of Life Sciences, South Kensington Campus, Imperial College London, Exhibition Road, London, SW7 2AZ.
020 7594 5316   fax 020 7594 5317
http://www.cbem.ic.ac.uk/
Director: Prof Marin van Heel.
E A research centre at Imperial College London.
○ To conduct research in the area of electron microscopy and structural biology

Centre for Biomolecular Sciences   2003

■ Queen's Medical Centre, Nottingham, NG7 2UH.
0115-823 0083
http://www.nottingham.ac.uk/mol/CBS/
E A research centre at the University of Nottingham.

Centre for Biomolecular Sciences (CBMS) 1998

■ Biomolecular Sciences Building, University of St Andrews, North Haugh, St Andrews, Fife, KY16 9ST.
01334 463401   fax 01334 462595
http://biology.st-andrews.ac.uk/cbms/
Director: Prof Garry Taylor.
E A research centre at the University of St Andrews.
○ To focus research on infection and immunity, chemical biology, and DNA repair and enzymology

Centre for Biophotonics (CfB)

■ Faculty of Science, University of Strathclyde, The John Arbuthnott Building, 27 Taylor Street, Glasgow, G4 0NR.
0141-548 4694   fax 0141-548 4887
http://www.biophotonics.strath.ac.uk/
Director: Prof Paul Garside.
E A research centre within the Strathclyde Institute of Pharmacy and Biomedical Sciences (qv) at the University of Strathclyde.

Centre for Biophysics

■ Faculty of Science, Engineering and Environment, University of Salford, Peel Building, Salford, Manchester, M5 4WT.
0161-295 3371; 4912   fax 0161-295 5015
http://www.bri.salford.ac.uk/bri/m/?s=19
Contact: Prof Roger H Bisby.
E A research centre within the Biomedical Sciences Research Institute (qv) at the University of Salford.

Centre for Bioscience

■ Room 8-49n, Worsley Building, University of Leeds, Leeds, LS2 9JT.
0113-343 3001   fax 0113-343 5894
http://www.bioscience.heacademy.ac.uk/
E A Government funded national centre within the University of Leeds.
○ To foster world-class education in bioscience
● Education and training - Information service - Statistics
✕ LTSN Bioscience Subject Centre.
Note: One of the 24 Subject Centres of the Higher Education Academy, (qv).

Centre for BioScience and Society
see **UCL Centre for BioScience and Society.**

Centre for Biosciences Research (CBR)

■ Department of Life and Sports Sciences, University of Greenwich, Central Avenue, Chatham Maritime, Kent, ME4 4TB.
020 8331 8358; 9902   fax 020 8331 9805
http://www.gre.ac.uk/schools/science/research/life/biosciences
Contact: Kim Wood.
E A research centre of the University of Greenwich.
○ To conduct research in biosciences, especially biochemistry and molecular biology, biomedical research and drug discovery, and nutrition science

Centre for Biostatistics
see **Robertson Centre for Biostatistics.**

Centre for Black Professional Practice (CBPP)

■ School of Health Sciences and Social Care, Brunel University, Uxbridge, Middlesex, UB8 3PH.
01895 274000
http://www.brunel.ac.uk/about/acad/health/healthres/researchareas/cbpp
E A centre at Brunel University.
○ To establish a national network of black academics, practitioners and policymakers involved in the whole range of human service professions in the UK

Centre for Border Studies   2003
■   School of Humanities and Social Sciences, University of Glamorgan, Pontypridd, CF37 1DL.
    01443 480480
    http://www.glam.ac.uk/hassschool/research/border/
    Co-Director: Prof David Dunkerley. Co-Director: Prof Hamish Fyfe.
E   A research centre within the University of Glamorgan.
O   To achieve a better understanding of the intertwined nature of diverse national, political and cultural identities in contemporary
    Wales

Centre for Brain and Cognitive Development   (CBCD)
■   School of Psychology, Birkbeck, University of London, 32 Torrington Square, London, WC1E 7JL.
    020 7631 6372   fax 020 7631 6587
    http://www.cbcd.bbk.ac.uk/
    Director: Prof Mark Johnson.
E   A centre at Birkbeck, University of London.
O   To investigate relations between postnatal brain development and changes in perceptual, cognitive and linguistic abilities from
    birth through childhood

Centre for Brain Injury Rehabilitation and Development   (BIRD)   1982
■   131 Main Road, Broughton, Chester, CH4 0NR.
    01244 532047   fax 01244 538723
    http://www.b-i-r-d.org.uk/
    Chief Executive: John Williams.
E   A registered charity and a company limited by guarantee.
O   To radically improve the lives of brain injured patients and their carers

Centre for Brain Repair
    see **Cambridge Centre for Brain Repair.**

Centre for Brazilian and Latin American Studies   (CBLAS)
■   School of Arts, Middlesex University, Trent Park, Bramley Road, London, N14 4YZ.
    020 8411 5695
    http://www.mdx.ac.uk/schools/arts/research/brazil/
    Head of Centre: Dr Francsico Dominguez.
E   A centre at Middlesex University.
O   To promote the study and understanding of Brazilian society

Centre for Brazilian Studies   (CBS)   1997
■   92 Woodstock Road, Oxford, OX2 7ND.
    01865 284460   fax 01865 284461
    http://www.brazil.ox.ac.uk/
    Director: Prof Leslie Bethell.
E   A department of the University of Oxford.
●   Education and training

Centre for British and Comparative Cultural Studies
    see **Centre for Translation and Comparative Cultural Studies.**

Centre of British Constitutional Law and History   1988
■   School of Law, King's College London, Strand, London, WC2R 2LS.
    020 7836 2465   fax 020 7836 1799
    http://www.kcl.ac.uk/kis/schools/law/research/cbclh.html
E   A research centre at King's College, London.
O   To study British constitutional affairs
●   Conferences - Public lectures and seminars

Centre for British Film and Television Studies
    see **AHRB Centre for British Film and Television Studies.**

Centre for British Government   (CBG)   1999
■   School of Politics and International Studies, University of Leeds, Leeds, LS2 9JT.
    0113-343 4391
    http://www.leeds.ac.uk/polis/research/britGov/
    Director: Prof Kevin Theakston.
E   A research centre at the University of Leeds.
O   To provide a focus for research in British Government
●   Seminars

Centre for British Teachers
Note: is the CfBT Education Trust and therefore outside the scope of this directory.

© CBD Research Ltd · Beckenham · Kent BR3 5JS · Tel 020 8650 7745 · Fax 020 8650 0768 · E-mail cbd@cbdresearch.com · www.cbdresearch.com

Centre for Broadcasting History Research   (CBHR)   2004

■   Bournemouth Media School, Weymouth House, Talbot Campus, Bournemouth University, Poole, Dorset, BH12 5BB.
   01202 965360   fax 01202 965530
   http://media.bournemouth.ac.uk/
   Director: Prof Sean Street.
E   A centre at Bournemouth University.
○   To stimulate an interest in the study of the history of broadcasting

Centre for Broadcasting and Journalism   (CBJ)   1999

■   City Site, Nottingham Trent University, Nottingham, NG1 4BU.
   0115-848 5806   fax 0115-848 5859
   http://www.ntu.ac.uk/cbj/
E   A centre at Nottingham Trent University.
○   To provide specialist vocational training and education in the media

Centre for Buddhist Studies

■   Department of Theology and Religious Studies, Senate House, University of Bristol, Tyndall Avenue, Bristol, BS8 1TH.
   0117-331 7349   fax 0117-925 1129
   http://www.bris.ac.uk/thrs/buddhistcentre/
   Contact: Dr Rupert Gethin.
E   A research centre at the University of Bristol.
○   To conduct research into all aspects of Buddhism
●   Library - Postgraduate courses

Centre for Buddhist Studies
   see **Oxford Centre for Buddhist Studies.**

Centre of Buddhist Studies   (CBS)

■   Faculty of Arts and Humanities, University of London, Thornhaugh Street, Russell Square, London, WC1H 0XG.
   020 7898 4775   fax 020 7898 4699
   http://www.soas.ac.uk/centres/centreinfo.cfm?navid=129
   Director: Tadeusz Skorupski.
E   A research centre at the School of Oriental and African Studies, University of London.
○   To act and serve as a medium for promoting the study of, and research into, various areas of Buddhist studies

Centre for the Built Environment   (CeBE)   1992

■   School of the Built Environment, Leeds Metropolitan University, The Northern Terrace - Queen Square Court, Civic Quarter, Leeds, LS1 3HE.
   0113-283 1978; 2600   fax 0113-283 1958
   http://www.leedsmet.ac.uk/as/cebe/
   Co-Director: Prof Malcolm Bell. Co-Director: Prof Robert Ellis.
E   A research centre at Leeds Metropolitan University.
○   To carry out high quality research and consultancy activity that is of value to all concerned with the design, construction and management of the built environment

Centre for the Built Environment [London]
   see **VR Centre for the Built Environment.**

Centre for the Built Environment (Scotland)   (CBE)

NR   School of the Built and Natural Environment, Glasgow Caledonian University, 70 Cowcaddens Road, Glasgow, G4 0BA.
   0141-273 1411   fax 0141-273 1418
   http://www.gcal.ac.uk/bne/research/researchcentres-cbe.html
   Director: Dr Branka Dimitrijevic.
E   A research centre at Glasgow Caledonian University.
○   To improve the performance of the construction sector and to enhance the quality and sustainability of the built environment
Note: A joint venture with the University of Strathclyde.

Centre for Built Environment Research   (CBER)

■   School of Planning, Architecture and Civil Engineering, Queen's University Belfast, David Keir Building, Stranmillis Road, Belfast, BT7 1NN.
   028 9097 4006
   http://space.qub.ac.uk/cber/
   Director: Prof Mohammad Basheer.
E   A research centre at Queen's University, Belfast.

Centre for Bulk Solids Handling Technology
   see **Wolfson Centre for Bulk Solids Handling Technology.**

Centre for Business Excellence   (CfBE)

- Newcastle Business School, Northumbria University, Northumberland Road, Newcastle upon Tyne, NE1 8ST.
  0191-243 7507   fax 0191-227 4684
  http://northumbria.ac.uk/business/nce/expertise/bus_excel/
- E   A research centre at Northumbria University.
- O   To be an internationally valued research and development centre helping individuals and their organisations to understand, advance and sustain excellence

Centre for Business History   (CBH)   2004

- School of Business and Economics, University of Exeter, Streatham Court, Rennes Drive, Exeter, EX4 4PU.
  01392 263201   fax 01392 263210
  http://www.centres.ex.ac.uk/cbh/
  Director: A J Arnold.
- E   A centre at the University of Exeter.
- O   To promote interest in business history in general and high quality innovative research in business history in particular

Centre for Business History in Scotland   (CBH)   1987

- Department of History, University of Glasgow, Lilybank House, Bute Gardens, Glasgow, G12 8RT.
  0141-330 6890   fax 0141-330 4889
  http://www.gla.ac.uk:443/centres/businesshistory
  Director: Prof Ray Stokes.
- E   A research centre at the University of Glasgow.
- O   To encourage, facilitate and conduct research in all aspects of business history, with particular emphasis on corporate governance, innovation and organisational change

Centre for Business Information, Organisation and Process Management   (BIOPoM)   2005

- Westminster Business School, University of Westminster, 35 Marylebone Road, London, NW1 5LS.
  020 7911 5000
  http://www.wmin.ac.uk/wbs/page-742
  Director: Prof Vlatka Hlupic.
- E   An interdisciplinary research centre at the University of Westminster.
- O   To investigate how management of business information, socio-organisational aspects of business and management, and the management of business processes can contribute to the success and competitiveness of modern companies

Centre for Business Languages

- Napier University Business School, Craiglockhart Campus, Edinburgh, EH14 1DJ.
  http://www.napier.ac.uk/nubs/SchoolsandCentres/Pages/CentreforBusinessLanguages.aspx
- E   A centre at Napier University.
- ●   Education and training

Centre for Business Law and Practice

- School of Law, University of Leeds, 20 Lyddon Terrace, Leeds, LS2 9JT.
  0113-343 7573
  http://www.law.leeds.ac.uk/business/
  Director: Andrew Campbell.
- E   A research centre at the University of Leeds.
- O   To foster studies in all areas of business law and practice

Centre for Business Organisations and Society   (CBOS)

- School of Management, University of Bath, Claverton Down, Bath, BA2 7AY.
  01225 386473
  http://www.bath.ac.uk/cbos/
  Director: Dr Andrew Millington.
- E   A centre at the University of Bath.
- O   To conduct research into the relationship between corporations and the societies within which they operate, the ethical position of modern corporations in different societal contexts and the study of corporate responsibility as a strategic phenomenon

Centre for Business Performance   (CBP)

- Cranfield School of Management, Cranfield University, Cranfield, Bedfordshire, MK43 0AL.
  01234 751122   fax 01234 757409
  http://www.som.cranfield.ac.uk/som/research/centres/cbp
  Director: Mike Bourne. Contact: Angela Walters.
- E   A research centre within the Cranfield Management Research Institute (qv) at Cranfield University.
- O   To improve corporate performance by undertaking internationally recognised thought-leadership research into the measurement and management of organisational performance

Centre for Business and Professional Ethics   (CBPE)   1989

- School of Philosophy, University of Leeds, Leeds, LS2 9JT.
  0113-343 2687
  http://www.cbpe.leeds.ac.uk/
- E   A research centre at the University of Leeds.

Centre for Business Relationships, Accountability, Sustainability and Society
  see **ESRC Centre for Business Relationships, Accountability, Sustainability and Society.**

Centre for Business Research [Cambridge]
  see **ESRC Centre for Business Research.**

Centre for Business Research   (CBR)
■ Manchester Business School, University of Manchester, Booth Street West, Manchester, M15 6PB.
    0161-275 2927   fax 0161-273 5245
    http://www.mbs.ac.uk/services/consultancy-research/business-centre/
    Co-ordinator: Emma Farnworth.
E A centre at the University of Manchester.
○ To offer objective, non-partisan research and consultancy for companies, within both the private and public sector

Centre for Business in Society   2003
■ Buckingham Business School, University of Buckingham, Hunter Street, Buckingham, MK18 1EG.
    01280 814080
    http://www.buckingham.ac.uk/business/expertise/society/
    Director: Dr Ronnie Lessem.
E A centre at the University of Buckingham.
✕ Trans-Cultural Research Centre.

Centre for Business Strategy and Procurement
■ Birmingham Business School, University of Birmingham, Edgbaston, Birmingham, B15 2TT.
    0121-414 3220
    http://www.business.bham.ac.uk/cbsp
    Head: Prof Andrew Cox.
E A centre at the University of Birmingham.
○ To examine the core concerns of strategic management in the context of business-to-business interactions and the wider networks within which they take place

Centre for Business Taxation
  see **Oxford University Centre for Business Taxation.**

Centre for Business Transformation   (CBT)
■ Ashcroft International Business School, Michael A Ashcroft Building, Anglia Ruskin University, Bishop Hall Lane, Chelmsford, Essex, CM1 1SQ.
    01245 493131   fax 01245 607540
    http://www.apu.ac.uk/cbt/
    Senior Lecturer: Stephen Bloomfield.
E A research centre at Anglia Ruskin University.
○ To support companies in developing their competitive advantage through innovation and application of best practice

Centre for Byzantine Cultural History
  see **AHRB Centre for Byzantine Cultural History.**

Centre for Byzantine, Ottoman and Modern Greek Studies   (CBO&MGS)   1976
■ Arts Building, University of Birmingham, Edgbaston, Birmingham, B15 2TT.
    0121-414 5497   fax 0121-414 3595
    http://www.iaa.bham.ac.uk/bomg/
    Contact: Lena Hoff.
E A research centre within the Institute of Archaeology and Antiquity (qv) at the University of Birmingham.
○ To conduct research in the history and languages of the east Mediterranean region

Centre for Canadian Studies
■ School of Modern Languages and Cultures, Department of French, University of Leeds, Leeds, LS2 9JT.
    0113-343 3380   fax 0113-343 3477
    http://www.leeds.ac.uk/canadian_studies/
    Director: Prof Rachel Killick. Deputy Director: Prof Graham Huggan.
E A research centre at the University of Leeds.
○ To promote Canadian studies in the UK and notably in Leeds; to promote research and teaching collaborations (including student exchanges) between the University of Leeds and Canadian universities
● Education and training - Library

Centre for Canadian Studies   1982
■ Department of Geography, Birkbeck, University of London, 26 Bedford Way, London, WC1H 0AP.
    http://www.bbk.ac.uk/llc/LCCS/
    Contact: Dr Richard Dennis.
E A research centre within the Birkbeck Institute for the Humanities (qv) at Birkbeck, University of London.
○ To promote the study of Canada at all levels

Centre of Canadian Studies   (CCS)   1986

■　School of Geography, Archaeology and Palaeoecology, Queen's University, Belfast, Belfast, BT7 1NN.
　　028 9097 3927   fax 028 9097 1280
　　http://www.qub.ac.uk/schools/CentreofCanadianStudies/
　　Co-Director: Dr Susan Hodgett. Co-Director: Dr Stephen Royle.
E　A research centre at Queen's University, Belfast.

Centre of Canadian Studies   1974

■　University of Edinburgh, 21 George Square, Edinburgh, EH8 9LD.
　　0131-650 4129   fax 0131-650 4130
　　http://www.cst.ed.ac.uk/
　　Director: Dr Annis May Timpson.
E　A department of the University of Edinburgh.
O　To promote research and teaching on Canada; to encourage academic awareness about Canada in broader academic and civic communities; to encourage international connections between Canadian and UK universities through conferences and research networks
●　Education and training - Open Mon-Fri (office hours) by appointment
¶　See website for publications.

Centre for Cancer Imaging   (CCI)   2003

■　Barts and the London, Queen Mary's School of Medicine and Dentistry, Charterhouse Square, London, EC1M 6BQ.
　　020 7014 0462   fax 020 7014 0461
　　http://www.cancer.qmul.ac.uk/research/cancer_imaging/
　　Director: Prof Steve Mather.
E　A research centre within the Institute of Cancer (qv) at Queen Mary, University of London.
O　To focus research on the development of molecular targets for radionuclide-mediated diagnosis and therapy of cancer

Centre for Cancer Research and Cell Biology   (CCRCB)

■　School of Biomedical Sciences, Belfast City Hospital, Lisburn Road, Belfast, BT9 7AB.
　　028 9026 3911   fax 028 9026 3744
　　http://www.qub.ac.uk/research-centres/CentreforCancerResearchCellBiology/
　　Director: Prof Paddy Johnson.
E　A centre at Queen's University, Belfast.
O　To develop new avenues for the prevention, diagnosis and treatment of cancer; to relieve the human suffering of cancer by developing the highest quality cancer research programmes

Centre for Cancer Therapeutics
　　see **Cancer Research UK Centre for Cancer Therapeutics.**

Centre for Capital Punishment Studies   (CCPS)   1992

■　School of Law, University of Westminster, 4-12 Little Titchfield Street, London, W1W 7UW.
　　020 7911 5000 ext 2501   fax 020 7911 5821
　　http://www.wmin.ac.uk/law/page-495
　　Director: Peter Hodgkinson.
E　A research centre at the University of Westminster.
O　To conduct research in a diverse range of issues concerning the death penalty

Centre for Carbohydrate Chemistry   (CCC)

■　School of Chemical Sciences and Pharmacy, University of East Anglia, Norwich, NR4 7TJ.
　　01603 593143   fax 01603 592003
　　http://www.uea.ac.uk/cap/carbohydrate/
　　Co-Director: Prof Rob Field. Co-Director: Prof Peter Belton.
E　A centre at the University of East Anglia.
O　To act as an interface between chemistry and biology

Centre for Carbon and Silicon-Based Electronics
　　see **Wolfson Centre for Carbon and Silicon-Based Electronics.**

Centre for Cardiology and The Hatter Institute for Cardiovascular Studies

■　Department of Medicine, University College London, Grafton Way, London, WC1E 6DB.
　　020 7380 9888   fax 020 7380 5095
　　http://www.ucl.ac.uk/medicine/hatter-cardiology/
　　Director: Prof Derek M Yellon.
E　A research centre at University College London.
O　To undertake basic and clinical cardiovascular research at the very highest level, with the aim of generating new therapies for the treatment of heart disease

© CBD Research Ltd · Beckenham · Kent BR3 5JS · Tel 020 8650 7745 · Fax 020 8650 0768 · E-mail cbd@cbdresearch.com · www.cbdresearch.com

Centre for Cardiology in the Young
■ Department of Medicine, Royal Free and University College Medical School, University College London, Rowland Hill Street, London, NW3 2PF.
020 7679 2000
http://www.ucl.ac.uk/medicine/CITY
Director: Prof W McKenna.
E A research centre at University College London.

Centre for Cardiovascular Biology and Medicine   1996
■ Department of Medicine, Rayne Building, University College London, 5 University Street, London, WC1E 6JF.
020 7679 6352   fax 020 7679 6379
http://www.ucl.ac.uk/medicine/cardiovascular-biology/
Director: Prof John Martin.
E A research centre at University College London.
O To perform research into the biological mechanisms that control the integrity of the vascular wall and mediate its relationship with the blood

Centre for Cardiovascular Genetics
■ Department of Medicine, Rayne Building, University College London, 5 University Street, London, WC1E 6JF.
020 7679 6962   fax 020 7679 6212
http://www.ucl.ac.uk/medicine/cardiovascular-genetics/
Director: Prof Steve Humphries.
E A research centre at University College London.
O To conduct research so as to identify the genetic factors that contribute to an individual's risk of developing coronary heart disease

Centre for Cardiovascular Research   (CCR)
■ Department of Therapeutics and Pharmacology, Queen's University, Belfast, Whitla Medical Building, 97 Lisburn Road, Belfast, BT9 7BL.
028 9097 2193   fax 028 9043 8346
http://www.med.qub.ac.uk/research/cardio/
E A centre at Queen's University, Belfast.
O To conduct research in cardiovascular risk and disease

Centre for Career Management Skills   (CCMS)   2005
■ PO Box 217 - Blandford Lodge, University of Reading, Whiteknights, Reading, Berkshire, RG6 6AH.
0118-378 8506
http://www.rdg.ac.uk/ccms/
Contact: David Stanbury.
E A Centre for Excellence in Teaching and Learning (CETL) at the University of Reading.
Note: See **Centres for Excellence in Teaching and Learning** for more information.

Centre for Career and Skills Development
■ City University, Myddelton Building, 167-173 Goswell Road, London, EC1V 0HB.
020 7040 8093
http://www.city.ac.uk/careers/
E A centre at City University.
O To provide professional development opportunities to students at the University

Centre for Caribbean Studies
■ Department of English and Comparative Literature, Goldsmiths, University of London, London, SE14 6NW.
020 7919 7740   fax 020 7919 7743
http://www.caribbean.gold.ac.uk/
Director: Dr Joan Anim-Addo.
E A research centre at Goldsmiths, University of London.
O To promote interdisciplinary work within Caribbean studies; to develop the study of Caribbean literature

Centre for Caribbean Studies   (CCS)   1984
■ Faculty of Arts, University of Warwick, Coventry, CV4 7AL.
024 7652 3443
http://www2.warwick.ac.uk/fac/arts/ccs/
Contact: Mrs Marjorie Davies.
E A research centre at the University of Warwick.
O To stimulate teaching and research on the Caribbean

Centre for Catalan Studies   (CCS)   2006
■ Department of Hispanic Studies, Queen Mary, University of London, Mile End Road, London, E1 4NS.
020 7882 3335   fax 020 8980 5400
http://www.modern-languages.qmul.ac.uk/hispstudies/catstudies.shtml
E A research centre at Queen Mary, University of London.
O To promote Catalan language and culture internationally

Centre of the Cell   2004

■   Barts and the London, Queen Mary's School of Medicine and Dentistry, Queen Mary, University of London, 64 Turner Street, London, E1 2AB.
    020 7882 2562   fax 020 8980 9660
    http://www.smd.qmul.ac.uk/centreofthecell/
    Director: Prof Fran Balkwill. Contact: Adrian Lockwood.
E   A research centre within the Institute of Cell and Molecular Science (qv) at Queen Mary, University of London.
O   To engage young people and schools in the principles of scientific and biomedical research, in the practical work being done by researchers in the medical school and elsewhere, and in the background to many of the major scientific and ethical issues facing young people, educationally and socially

Centre for Cell Biology
    see **Wellcome Trust Centre for Cell Biology.**

Centre for Cell and Chromosome Biology   (CCCB)   2005

■   School of Health Sciences and Social Care, Brunel University, Uxbridge, Middlesex, UB8 3PH.
    01895 274000
    http://www.brunel.ac.uk/about/acad/health/healthres/researchareas/ccbg
    Director: Dr Ian Kill.
E   A research centre within the Brunel Institute of Cancer Genetics and Pharmacogenomics (qv) at Brunel University.
O   To research the fundamental aspects of cell and chromosome structure and function, particularly in the areas of genome organisation, cellular and organismal ageing, DNA damage and response mechanisms, bone metabolism, inherited disorders and chromosome aberration formation

Centre for Cell Engineering at Glasgow   (CCE)   1996

■   Department of Electronics and Electrical Engineering, University of Glasgow, Rankine Building, Oakfield Avenue, Glasgow, G12 8LT.
    0141-330 5218   fax 0141-330 4907
    http://www.gla.ac.uk/centres/cellengineering/
    Co-Director: Dr Mathis Riehle. Co-Director: Prof Chris Wilkinson.
E   A research centre at the University of Glasgow.
O   To further research into cell and tissue engineering

Centre for Cell Imaging   (CCI)

■   School of Biological Sciences, University of Liverpool, The Biosciences Building, Crown Street, Liverpool, L69 7ZB.
    0151-795 4424; 4435   fax 0151-795 4404
    http://www.liv.ac.uk/biolsci/research/groups/cci/
    Director: Prof Michael R H White.
E   A research centre at the University of Liverpool.

Centre for Cell and Integrative Biology   (CCIB)   2005

■   King's College London, DeCrespigny Park, London, SE5 8AF.
    020 7836 5454
    http://web1.iop.kcl.ac.uk/external-sites/devbio/ccib.html
E   A research centre within the Institute of Psychiatry (qv) at King's College, London.
O   To provide a focal point for research in cell and integrative biology

Centre for Cell-Matrix Research
    see **Wellcome Trust Centre for Cell-Matrix Research.**

Centre for Cell and Molecular Biology
    see **Cancer Research UK Centre for Cell and Molecular Biology.**

Centre for Cell and Molecular Dynamics   (CCMD)   2001

■   Department of Anatomy and Developmental Biology, University College London, Anatomy Building, Gower Street, London, WC1E 6BT.
    020 7679 3345   fax 020 7679 7349
    http://www.anat.ucl.ac.uk/research/dale/ccmd/
    Contact: Mrs Christine Davis.
E   A research centre at University College London.

Centre for Cell and Tissue Research

Note: The CCTR closed in August 2004.

Centre for the Cellular Basis of Behaviour   (CCBB)   2005

■   PO Box 37, King's College London, DeCrespigny Park, London, SE5 8AF.
    020 7836 5454
    http://www.iop.kcl.ac.uk/departments/?locator=622
    Business Manager: Dr Melina Carapeti-Marootian.
E   A research centre within the Centre for Cell and Integrative Biology (qv) at King's College, London.

Centre for Cement and Concrete   (CCC)
- Department of Civil and Structural Engineering, University of Sheffield, Sir Frederick Mappin Building, Mappin Street, Sheffield, S1 3JD.
  0114-222 5065   fax 0114-222 5700
  http://www.sheffield.ac.uk/ccc/
  Director: Prof Kypros Pilakoutas.
- E   A research centre at the University of Sheffield.
- O   To focus research on cement chemistry, aggregate science, binder technology, concrete technology, concrete durability, alternative concreting materials, structural performance and design, earthquake and nuclear reactor design, and finite element analysis

Centre for Census and Survey Research
  see **Cathie Marsh Centre for Census and Survey Research.**

Centre for Central and Eastern European Studies   (CCEES)   1990
- School of History, University of Liverpool, 9 Abercromby Square, Liverpool, L69 7WZ.
  0151-794 2422   fax 0151-794 2366
  http://www.liv.ac.uk/history/research/ccees.htm
  Contact: Dr Nigel Swain.
- E   An interdisciplinary research centre at the University of Liverpool.
- O   To conduct research in social, economic and politics in the Region

Centre for Central Banking Studies   (CCBS)
- 7th Floor, Bank of England, Threadneedle Street, London, EC2R 8AH.
  020 7601 4444; 4878   fax 020 7601 5460
  http://www.bankofengland.co.uk/education/ccbs/
- E   A research centre at the Bank of England.
- O   To foster monetary and financial stability worldwide; to promote the Bank of England's core activities; to provide opportunities for central banking staff to obtain broader perspectives of their own areas of expertise

Centre for Ceramics Studies, Cardiff
- Cardiff School of Art and Design, University of Wales Institute, Cardiff, Howard Gardens, Cardiff, CF24 0SP.
  029 2041 6343
  http://www.cardiffceramics.com/
  Chairman: Michael Hose. Contact: Janette Shaw.
- E   A research centre at the University of Wales Institute, Cardiff.
- O   To conduct research and teaching in a wide variety of ceramics and related disciplines

Centre for Charity Effectiveness   (CCE)   2004
- Cass Business School, City University, 106 Bunhill Row, London, EC1Y 8TZ.
  020 7040 8667   fax 020 7040 8579
  http://www.cass.city.ac.uk/charityeffectiveness/
  Director: Prof Ian Bruce.
- E   A research centre at City University.
- O   To increase the effectiveness and achievement of voluntary and community organisations

Centre Charles Péguy   (French Centre)   1954
- 16 Leicester Square, London, WC2H 7NH.
  020 7437 8339   fax 020 7494 2527
  http://www.cei-frenchcentre.com/
  General Manager: Nicolas Metalnikoff.
- E   A registered charity.
- O   To help young French people between 18-30 years old to find a place professionally (and accommodation) in Great Britain and especially in London
- ●   Information service

Centre for Chemical Physics
Note: has closed.

Centre for Chemical Sciences   (CCS)
- School of Earth, Ocean and Environmental Sciences, University of Plymouth, Drake Circus, Plymouth, PL4 8AA.
  01752 233093   fax 01752 233095
  http://www.plymouth.ac.uk/chemistry
- E   A research centre at the University of Plymouth.
- O   To offer BSc (Hons) degrees in analytical chemistry and applied chemistry

Centre for Chemometrics
- School of Chemistry, University of Bristol, Bristol, BS8 1TS.
  0117-928 7645   fax 0117-925 1295
  http://www.chm.bris.ac.uk/org/chemometrics
  Contact: Prof Richard Brereton.
- E   A research centre at the University of Bristol.

Centre for Child and Adolescent Health (CCAH)

NR   Hampton House, University of Bristol, Cotham Hill, Bristol, BS6 6JS.
        0117-331 0893   fax 0117-331 0891
        http://www.bris.ac.uk/ccah/
        Director: Prof Alan Emond.
E   A research centre at the University of Bristol.
O   To improve understanding of the complex interaction between genetic and environmental factors on child health
Note: A joint venture with the University of the West of England.

Centre for Child-focused Anthropological Research (C-FAR 1999

■   School of Social Sciences and Law, Brunel University, Uxbridge, Middlesex, UB8 3PH.
        01895 274000 ext 4840   fax 01895 203078
        http://www.brunel.ac.uk/about/acad/sssl/ssslresearch/centres/cfar/
        Director: Prof Christina Toren.
E   A centre at Brunel University.
O   To consolidate and build a comparative international approach to child-focused anthropological research

Centre for Child and Family Research (CCFR) 2001

■   Department of Social Sciences, Middlesex University, Ashby Road, Loughborough, Leicestershire, LE11 3TU.
        01509 228355   fax 01509 223943
        http://www.lboro.ac.uk/research/ccfr/
        Director: Prof Harriet Ward.
E   A research centre at Loughborough University.
O   To develop and deliver programs of research that inform, influence and support policy and practice for children, families and their communities

Centre for Child Health

■   Barts and the London, Queen Mary's School of Medicine and Dentistry, Abernethy Building, 2 Newark Street, London, E1 2AT.
        020 7882 2509   fax 020 7882 2552
        http://www.ihse.qmul.ac.uk/chs/research/childhealth
E   A research centre within the Centre for Health Sciences (qv) at Queen Mary, University of London.

Centre for Child Protection Studies

■   School of Social Work, University of Leicester, 107 Princess Road East, Leicester, LE1 7LA.
        0116-252 3760   fax 0116-252 3748
        http://www.le.ac.uk/childprotect/
        Contact: Christina Cazelet.
E   A research centre at the University of Leicester.
O   To conduct research and teaching in the field of child care

Centre for Child Research (CCR)

■   School of Applied Social Sciences, Swansea University, Vivian Building, Singleton Park, Swansea, SA2 8PP.
        01792 602491   fax 01792 602497
        http://www.swan.ac.uk/research/centresandinstitutes/CentreforChildResearch/
        Administrator: Dr Julia Davis.
E   An interdisciplinary research centre at Swansea University.
O   To conduct research in a wide variety of child-related issues

Centre for the Child and Society
        see **Glasgow Centre for the Child and Society.**

Centre for Child Studies (CCS)

■   24-32 Stephenson Way, London, NW1 2HX.
        020 7391 9150   fax 020 7391 9169
        http://www.instituteoffamilytherapy.org.uk/
        Director: Chip Chimera.
E   A research centre within the Institute of Family Therapy (qv).

Centre for Children with Cerebral Palsy
        see **Bobath Centre for Children with Cerebral Palsy.**

Centre for Children and Youth (CCY) 1997

■   University of Northampton, Boughton Green Road, Northampton, NN2 7AL.
        01604 892514
        http://www2.northampton.ac.uk/
        Director: Prof Hugh Matthews.
E   A research centre at the University of Northampton.

© CBD Research Ltd · Beckenham · Kent BR3 5JS · Tel 020 8650 7745 · Fax 020 8650 0768 · E-mail cbd@cbdresearch.com · www.cbdresearch.com

Centre for Chinese Business Development   (CCBD)   2000
- ■   University of Leeds, 14-20 Cromer Terrace, Leeds, LS2 9JT.
     0113-343 6749   fax 0113-343 6808
     http://www.smlc.leeds.ac.uk/ccbd/
- E   A research centre at the University of Leeds.
- ○   To offer the highest standards of professional expertise in Chinese language and in international business in relation to China
- ●   Information service

Centre for Chinese Business and Management Studies   1986
- ■   Manchester Business School, University of Manchester, Booth Street West, Manchester, M15 6PB.
     0161-275 6351; 7082   fax 0161-275 6335
     http://www.mbs.ac.uk/executive/centres/chinesecentre/
     Director: Prof Fang Lee Cooke
- E   A research centre at the University of Manchester.
- ○   To study the role of foreign business in China's industrial development and the promotion of mutual understanding between European and Chinese businesses; to provide advanced management development, research and consultancy
Note: Also known as the China Business Centre.

Centre for Chinese Medicine
   see **Acumedic Centre for Chinese Medicine.**

Centre for Chinese Studies   (CCS)   1997
- ■   University of Wales Lampeter, College Street, Lampeter, Ceredigion, SA48 7ED.
     01570 422351
     http://www.lamp.ac.uk/chinese/
     Director: Prof Xinzhong Yao.
- E   A research centre at the University of Wales, Lampeter.
- ○   To offer teaching and research in the area broadly defined as Chinese studies, especially in terms of Chinese culture, history, literature, media and film, philosophy and religion

Centre for Chinese Studies   (CCS)   2006
- ■   School of Languages, Linguistics and Cultures, Humanities Lime Grove, University of Manchester, Oxford Road, Manchester, M13 9PL.
     0161-275 3003   fax 0161-275 3031
     http://www.ccs.humanities.manchester.ac.uk/
- E   A research centre at the University of Manchester.

Centre of Chinese Studies   (CCS)   1992
- ■   School of Oriental & African Studies, University of London, Thornhaugh Street, Russell Square, London, WC1H 0XG.
     020 7898 4892; 4893   fax 020 7898 4489
     http://www.soas.ac.uk/centres/centreinfo.cfm?navid=4
     Manager: Jane Savory. Executive Officer: Sara Hamza.
- E   An interdisciplinary research centre at the School of Oriental and African Studies, University of London.
- ○   To facilitate and develop in the UK and Europe research, teaching and other activities relating to China
- ¶   Studies on Contemporary China (series).
Note: The Centre's publishing arm is known as the Contemporary China Institute.

Centre for Christianity and Culture   2004
- ■   Department of Theology and Religious Studies, University of Bristol, Senate House, Tyndall Avenue, Bristol, BS8 1TH.
     0117-331 7349   fax 0117-925 1129
     http://www.bristol.ac.uk/thrs/christiancentre/
     Contact: Dr Gavin D'Costa.
- E   A research centre at the University of Bristol.
- ○   To facilitate a more integrative and dynamic community of staff, students and academics who work on the history and theology of Christianity
- ●   Conferences - Seminars

Centre for Christianity and Interreligious Dialogue   (CCID)
- ■   Heythrop College, Kensington Square, London, W8 5HQ.
     020 7795 6600
     http://www.heythrop.ac.uk/ccid/
     Director: Dr Michael Barnes.
- E   A research centre at Heythrop College.
- ○   To promote an awareness and knowledge of the importance of interreligious engagement between the world's religious cultures and traditions

Centre for Chronobiology   1999

NR   School of Biomedical and Molecular Sciences, University of Surrey, Guildford, Surrey, GU2 7XH.
    01483 689341
    http://www.surrey.ac.uk/SBMS/centre_for_chronobiology/
    Co-Director: Dr Derk-Jan Dijk. Co-Director: Prof Russell Foster.
E   A research centre at the University of Surrey.
O   To foster national and international collaboration in research and research training in all aspects of chronobiology
Note: A joint venture with Imperial College London.

Centre for Church School Studies   (CCSS)

NR   Department of Theology and Religious Studies, Normal Site, University of Wales Bangor, Bangor, Gwynedd, LL57 2PZ.
    01248 382566   fax 01248 383954
    http://www.bangor.ac.uk/rs/pt/ccs/
    Director: Prof Leslie J Francis.
E   A research centre at the University of Wales, Bangor.
O   To promote and to co-ordinate conceptual and empirical research concerned with the distinctiveness and effectiveness of church
    schools, especially those of the Church of England and the Church in Wales
Note: A joint venture with the University of Durham.

Centre for Citizen Participation   (CCP)

■   School of Health Sciences and Social Care, Brunel University, Uxbridge, Middlesex, UB8 3PH.
    01895 274000
    http://www.brunel.ac.uk/about/acad/health/healthres/researchareas/ccp/
E   A centre at Brunel University.
O   To undertake research and provide education, training and consultancy in the field of user involvement and public participation

Centre for Citizenship and Community Mental Health   (CCCMH)   2004

■   School of Health Studies, University of Bradford, Bradford, West Yorkshire, BD7 1DP.
    01274 236367   fax 01274 236302
    http://www.bradford.ac.uk/acad/health/research/cccmh
E   A research centre within the Institute for Community and Primary Care Research (qv) at the University of Bradford.
O   To conduct teaching, education, research and conceptual analyses of mental health practice

Centre for Citizenship and Human Rights Education   (CCHRE)

■   School of Education, University of Leeds, Leeds, LS2 9JT.
    0113-343 4586   fax 0113-343 4541
    http://www.education.leeds.ac.uk/research/cchre/
    Director: Prof Audrey Osler.
E   A research centre at the University of Leeds.
O   To promote and develop research, consultancy and postgraduate studies in citizenship education and human rights education
●   Education and training - Consultancy

Centre for Citizenship, Identities and Governance   (CCIG)

■   Open University, Walton Hall, Milton Keynes, MK7 6AA.
    01908 654704   fax 01908 654488
    http://www.open.ac.uk/socialsciences/research/ccig
    Director: Prof Wendy Hollway. Contact: Sarah Batt.
E   An interdisciplinary research centre at the Open University.
O   To conduct and promote research, dialogue and debate that will contribute to a greater understanding of the manifold
    connections between notions of citizenship, processes of identity formation and practices of governance in the contemporary
    world

Centre of Citizenship Studies in Education   (CCSE)   1992

■   School of Education, University of Leicester, 21 University Road, Leicester, LE1 7RF.
    0116-252 3688   fax 0116-252 3653
    http://www.le.ac.uk/se/school/citizenship
E   A research centre at the University of Leicester.

Centre for City and Regional Studies   (CCRS)

■   Department of Geography, University of Hull, Cottingham Road, Hull, HU6 7RX.
    01482 465330   fax 01482 466340
    http://www.hull.ac.uk/ccrs/
    Co-Director: Prof David Gibbs. Co-Director: Prof Graham Haughton.
E   A centre at the University of Hull.
O   To focus research on national, regional and local policy for economic development and environmental protection, and in
    particular on the interface between these two areas of public policy

Centre for Civil Society   (CCS)   1987
- ■   LSE, Houghton Street, London, WC2A 2AE.
    020 7955 7205   fax 020 7955 6039
    http://www.lse.ac.uk/ccs/
    Director: Prof Jude Howell.
- E   A department of the London School of Economics and Political Science.
- O   To carry out innovative, interdisciplinary and comparative research on the study of civil society at global, national and local levels; to push theoretical frontiers and to investigate the structure and dynamics of actually existing civil societies in diverse contexts, including their benign and less benign dimensions
- ●   Conference facilities - Education and training - Grant-based research, Commissioned research and research consultancy work - The Centre is currently directing a major ESRC programme
- ¶   Annual Report. Civil Society Working Papers. (see website for full list of publications).

Centre for Clean Water Technologies   (CCWT)
- ■   School of Chemical, Environmental and Mining Engineering, University of Nottingham, University Park, Nottingham, NG7 2RD.
    0115-951 4168   fax 0115-951 4115
    http://www.cleanwatertechnologies.info/
    Director: Dr Nidal Hilal.
- E   A research centre at the University of Nottingham.
- O   To develop advanced technologies in water treatment through conducting research in the areas of drinking water treatment, waste-water treatment and re-use, and process water treatment and re-use

Centre for Climate Change
    see **Hadley Centre for Climate Change.**

Centre for Climate Change Mitigation Research
    see **Cambridge Centre for Climate Change Mitigation Research.**

Centre for Climate Change Research
    see **Tyndall Centre for Climate Change Research.**

Centre for Climate, the Environment, and Chronology
    see **Chrono Centre for Climate, the Environment, and Chronology.**

Centre for Clinical and Academic Workforce Innovation   (CCAWI)   2005
- ■   Faculty of Health, Life and Social Sciences, University of Lincoln, Mill 3 - Pleasley Vale Business Park, Outgang Lane, Mansfield, Nottinghamshire, NG19 8RL.
    01623 819140   fax 01623 811697
    http://www.lincoln.ac.uk/ccawi/
    Co-Director: Prof Tony Butterworth. Co-Director: Prof Ian Baguley.
- E   A research centre at the University of Lincoln.
- O   To be an expert resource available to Government policy strategists, and health and education economies that can create and drive clinical and academic workforce innovation
- ●   Information service

Centre for Clinical and Diagnostic Oral Sciences   (CDOS)
- ■   Barts and the London, Queen Mary's School of Medicine and Dentistry, Queen Mary's University of London, Turner Street, London, E1 2AD.
    020 7377 7611   fax 020 7377 7612
    http://www.smd.qmul.ac.uk/dental/oralscience/
    Lead: Prof F Fortune.
- E   A research centre within the Institute of Dentistry (qv) at Queen Mary, University of London.
- O   To conduct high quality research in oral and maxillofacial surgery, oral medicine, oral microbiology, and oral pathology

Centre for Clinical and Health Services Research   (CCHSR)   2005
- ■   Faculty of Health and Social Care, University of the West of England, Blackberry Hill, Stapleton, Bristol, BS16 1DD.
    0117-328 8849   fax 0117-328 8421
    http://hsc.uwe.ac.uk/net/research/
    Director: Prof Selena Gray.
- E   A research centre at the University of the West of England.
- O   To conduct clinical and health services research, including rehabilitation studies, critical and emergency care, maternal and child health, and prison health

Centre for Clinical Infection (Bloomsbury)
- ■   Department of Infection, University College London Hospital, 235 Euston Road, London, NW1 2BU.
    0845 155 5000
    http://www.ucl.ac.uk/medicalschool/infection-immunity/departments/departments.htm#CLI
    Director: Dr Vanya Gant.
- E   A research centre at University College London.
- O   To facilitate the investigation and treatment of infections in patients based at the University College London Hospital

Centre for Clinical Infection (Hampstead)

- Department of Infection, Royal Free and University College Medical School, University College London, Rowland Hill Street, London, NW3 2PF.
  020 7794 0500   fax 020 7830 2468
  http://www.ucl.ac.uk/medicalschool/infection-immunity/departments/departments.htm#CLI
  Director: Dr Michael Jacobs.
- E   A research centre at University College London.
- O   To facilitate the investigation and treatment of infections in patients based at the Royal Free Hospital

Centre for Clinical Kinaesiology
  see **Research Centre for Clinical Kinaesiology.**

Centre for Clinical Management Development   (CCMD)   2001

- Queen's Campus, University of Durham, University Boulevard, Thornaby, Stockton on Tees, TS17 6BH.
  0191-334 0386   fax 0191-334 0361
  http://www.dur.ac.uk/ccmd/
  Director: Prof Pieter Degeling.
- E   A specialist research centre within the Wolfson Research Institute (qv) at the University of Durham.
- O   To undertake research and development projects on clinician-led approaches to improving the organisation and management of clinical work

Centre for Clinical Neuroscience

- Department of Clinical Neuroscience, St George's, University of London, Cranmer Terrace, London, SW17 0RE.
  020 8725 2735   fax 020 8725 2950
  http://www.sgul.ac.uk/depts/cvs/clinical-neuroscience/clinical-neuroscience_home.cfm
  Head: Prof Hugh Markus.
- E   A research centre at St George's, University of London.

Centre for Clinical Pharmacology and Therapeutics

- Division of Medicine, University College London, Rayne Building, 5 University Street, London, WC1E 6JF.
  020 7679 6174   fax 020 7691 2838
  http://www.ucl.ac.uk/medicine/clinical-pharmaco/
  Director: Dr Raymond MacAllister.
- E   A research centre at University College London.
- O   To conduct teaching and research in the field of cardiovascular science, inflammation and the mechanisms of obesity

Centre for Clinical and Population Studies   (CCPS)

- School of Medicine and Dentistry, Queen's University, Belfast, Room 1:31 - Mulhouse, Grosvenor Road, Belfast, BT12 6BJ.
  028 9063 2627; 2746   fax 028 9063 1907
  http://www.med.qub.ac.uk/ccps/
  Director: Prof Frank Kee.
- E   A research centre at Queen's University, Belfast.

Centre for Clinical Science and Measurement   (CCSM)   1999

- School of Biomedical and Molecular Sciences, University of Surrey, Guildford, Surrey, GU2 7XH.
  01483 686400   fax 01483 686401
  http://www.surrey.ac.uk/SBMS/CCSM/
  Director: Prof Gordon Ferns.
- E   A research centre at the University of Surrey.
- O   To work with health-related organisations and industry to promote research and development in the pure and applied medical sciences

Centre for Clinical Science and Technology

- Department of Medicine, University College London, Gower Street, London, WC1E 6BT.
  020 7679 2000
  http://www.ucl.ac.uk/medicine/clinical-sci-tech
  Director: Prof J G Malone-Lee.
- E   A research centre at University College London.

Centre for Clinical Skills Education
  see **Saad Centre for Clinical Skills Education.**

Centre for Clinical Tropical Medicine
  see **Wellcome Centre for Clinical Tropical Medicine.**

© CBD Research Ltd · Beckenham · Kent BR3 5JS · Tel 020 8650 7745 · Fax 020 8650 0768 · E-mail cbd@cbdresearch.com · www.cbdresearch.com

Centre for CO₂ Technology   1997

- ■   Department of Chemical Engineering, University College London, Torrington Place, London, WC1E 7JE.
    020 7679 2315; 3805   fax 020 7383 2348
    http://www.ucl.ac.uk/chemeng/co2centre/
    Co-Director: Prof Stef Simons. Co-Director: Prof Stefano Brandani.
- E   A research centre at University College London.
- ○   To focus research on break-through technologies for the large scale reduction, removal and sequestration of carbon dioxide

Note: Formed in response to the Kyoto Protocol of 1997.

Centre for Coaching   (CFC)   2000

- ■   156 Westcombe Hill, London, SE3 7DH.
    020 8293 4334   fax 020 8293 4114
    http://www.centreforcoaching.com/
    Director: Prof Stephen Palmer. Training Director: Peter Ruddell.
- E   A profit-making business.
- ○   To promote the use of coaching and coaching psychology within personal and work domains
- ●   Education and training

Centre for Coastal and Marine Research   (CCMR)   2004

- ■   School of Environmental Sciences, Coleraine Campus, University of Ulster, Cromore Road, Coleraine, County Londonderry, BT52 1SA.
    028 7032 3083; 4429
    http://www.science.ulster.ac.uk/ccmr/
    Co-Director: Prof Andrew Cooper. Co-Director: Dr Derek Jackson.
- E   A research centre at the University of Ulster.
- ○   To examine various aspects of coastal environments, from the physical processes to the human impacts on today's coastal and marine environments

Centre for Coastal Dynamics and Engineering   (C-CoDE

- ■   Reynolds Building, University of Plymouth, Drake Circus, Plymouth, PL4 8AA.
    01752 233681   fax 01752 232638
    http://www.research.plymouth.ac.uk/c-code/
- E   A research centre at the University of Plymouth.
- ○   To conduct research on an experimental computational and theoretical basis into all aspects of coastal processes and engineering, and verifying the findings of this research with field data

Centre for Coastal Studies
    see **Scarborough Centre for Coastal Studies.**

Centre for Cognition, Computation and Culture   (CCCC)

- ■   Department of Psychology, Ben Pimlott Building, Goldsmiths, University of London, London, SE14 6NW.
    020 7078 5142
    http://www.goldsmiths.ac.uk/cccc/
    Director: Prof Jules Davidoff.
- E   A research centre at Goldsmiths, University of London.
- ○   To understand the cognitive processes, including those related to cultural differences

Centre for Cognition and Neuroimaging   (CCNI)

- ■   School of Social Sciences and Law, Brunel University, Uxbridge, Middlesex, UB8 3PH.
    01895 274000
    http://www.brunel.ac.uk/about/acad/sssl/ssslresearch/centres/ccni/
- E   A centre at Brunel University.
- ○   To conduct research into the mapping of the functions of the human brain

Centre for Cognitive Behaviour Therapy   1998

- ■   156 Westcombe Hill, London, SE3 7DH.
    020 8318 4448
    Director: Prof Stephen Palmer.
- E   A profit-making business.
- ○   To promote the use of cognitive-behaviour therapy and training in clinical work and work settings
- ●   Education and training - Courses in CBT (Introductory, Intermediate, Diploma)

Centre for Cognitive and Computational Neuroscience   (CCCN)

- ■   Department of Psychology, University of Stirling, Stirling, FK9 4LA.
    01786 467041
    http://www.cccn.stir.ac.uk/
- E   A research centre at the University of Stirling.
- ○   To conduct specialist research in computer vision, image analysis, genetic algorithms and robotics, neural computation, biophysical models, hearing, vision neuromorphic engineering, face recognition, and face composite systems

Centre for Cognitive Neuroimaging (CCNi) 2005
- ■ Department of Psychology, University of Glasgow, 58 Hillhead Street, Glasgow, G12 8QB.
  0141-330 5485   fax 0141-330 4606
  http://www.psy.gla.ac.uk/research/
- E A research centre at the University of Glasgow.
- O To provide state-of-the-art functional neuroimaging facilities for researchers in cognitive neuroscience, experimental psychology, neuropsychology, and cognitive science

Centre for Cognitive Neuroscience [Exeter]
> see **Exeter Centre for Cognitive Neuroscience.**

Centre for Cognitive Neuroscience [Oxford]
> see **Oxford McDonnell Centre for Cognitive Neuroscience.**

Centre for Cognitive Science
- ■ Department of Computer Science, University of Essex, Wivenhoe Park, Colchester, Essex, CO4 3SQ.
  01206 872686
  http://www.essex.ac.uk/academic/docs/
  Director: Dr M Poesio.
- E A research centre at the University of Essex.

Centre for Cognitive Studies
> see **Hang Seng Centre for Cognitive Studies.**

Centre for Cold Matter   (CCM)
- ■ Department of Physics, Imperial College London, Exhibition Road, London, SW7 2AZ.
  020 7594 7742; 7901
  http://www.imperial.ac.uk/research/ccm/
  Director: Prof Ed Hinds.
- E A research centre at Imperial College London.
- O To study fundamental problems in physics using the techniques of atomic and laser physics

Centre for Collaborative Intervention in the Public Sector   (CCIPS)
- ■ Lancaster University Management School, Lancaster University, Bailrigg, Lancaster, LA1 4YX.
  01524 594285
  http://www.lums.lancs.ac.uk/Departments/owt/Research/ccips/
  Director: Prof Frank Blackler. Director: Dr Suzanne Regan.
- E A research centre within Lancaster University.
- O To study and support the development of new approaches to service delivery

Centre for Colonial and Postcolonial Studies   1994
- ■ School of English, Rutherford College Extension, University of Kent, Canterbury, Kent, CT2 7NX.
  01227 764000
  http://www.kent.ac.uk/english/staff-research/centres/poco/postcolonialindex.html
- E A research centre within the Kent Institute for Advanced Studies in the Humanities (qv) at the University of Kent.
- O To conduct postgraduate research and a taught MA in postcolonial studies

Centre for Colonial and Postcolonial Studies
> see **Nottingham Trent Centre for Colonial and Postcolonial Studies.**

Centre for Colonial and Postcolonial Studies
- ■ School of Humanities, University of Sussex, Arts A 007, Falmer, Brighton, East Sussex, BN1 9SJ.
  01273 678001
  http://www.sussex.ac.uk/hums/1-3-6.html
  Contact: Prof Saul Dubow.
- E An interdisciplinary research centre at the University of Sussex.
Note: Also known as the Centre for the Study of Colonial and Postcolonial Cultures.

Centre for Combined Studies   (CCS)
- ■ Faculty of Humanities, Humanities Lime Grove Centre, University of Manchester, Oxford Road, Manchester, M13 9PL.
  0161-275 3001; 7394   fax 0161-275 3004
  http://www.humanities.manchester.ac.uk/combinedstudies/
  Director: Dr J D Hamshere.
- E An administrative unit at the University of Manchester.
- O To offer over 60 programmes of study in a wide variety of subjects
Note: Also known as the Combined Studies Centre.

Centre for Commercial Law   (CCL)

■ Faculty of Laws, University College London, Bentham House, Endsleigh Gardens, London, WC1H 0EG.
   020 7679 2000
   http://www.ucl.ac.uk/laws/commercial
   Honorary Director: The Rt.Hon. Lady Justice Arden, DBE.
E A research centre at University College London.
O To promote excellence in the research and teaching of international commercial law
Note: Also known as the Commercial Law Centre.

Centre for Commercial Law Studies   (CCLS)   1980

■ School of Law, Queen Mary, University of London, 13-14 Charterhouse Square, London, EC1M 6AX.
   020 7882 5669   fax 020 7882 6044
   http://www.ccls.edu/
   Director: Prof Janet Dine.
E A centre at Queen Mary, University of London.
O To focus on commercial law teaching and research, with particular emphasis on arbitration, intellectual property, taxation, financial law, banking law, information technology law, and European law

Centre for Commercial Law Studies   (CCLS)   1999

■ School of Law, Swansea University, Singleton Park, Swansea, SA2 8PP.
   01792 295831   fax 01792 295855
   http://www.swan.ac.uk/research/centresandinstitutes/CentreforCommercialLawStudies/
E A research centre at Swansea University.
O To conduct research in commercial law, with particular emphasis on intellectual property, asset finance, contract theory, and personal property law

Centre for Commonwealth Education   (CCE)   2005

■ Faculty of Education, University of Cambridge, 184 Hills Road, Cambridge, CB2 2PQ.
   01223 507133   fax 01223 767602
   http://www.educ.cam.ac.uk/commonwealth/
   Director: Prof Christopher Colclough.
E A centre established by the Commonwealth Institute (qv) and the University of Cambridge.
O To serve educational needs across the Commonwealth, especially in the fields of primary and secondary education. The Centre co-ordinates RECOUP - the Research Consortium on Educational Outcomes and Poverty.

Centre of Commonwealth Studies   (CCS)   1985

■ Department of English Studies, University of Stirling, Stirling, FK9 4LA.
   01786 467041
   http://www.commonwealthstudies.stir.ac.uk/
   Director: Prof Angela Smith.
E An interdisciplinary research centre at the University of Stirling.
O To specialise in pre-colonial, colonial and post-colonial studies, with an emphasis on Africa and postcolonial diasporas

Centre for Communication and Ethics in International Business   (CCEIB)

■ Ashcroft International Business School, Anglia Ruskin University, East Road, Cambridge, CB1 1PT.
   0845 271 3333
   http://www.anglia.ac.uk/ruskin/en/home/business/centre_for_communication.html
   Director: Dr Bronwen Rees.
E A research centre at Anglia Ruskin University.
O To conduct research which addresses issues in Conflict in communication, Cross-cultural communication, Ethical dilemmas, Leadership tensions, Working with diversity, and Developing and harnessing creativity

Centre for Communication Interface Research   (CCIR)

■ School of Engineering and Electronics, University of Edinburgh, The King's Buildings, Mayfield Road, Edinburgh, EH9 3JR.
   0131-650 5667   fax 0131-650 6554
   http://www.ccir.ed.ac.uk/
   Director: Prof Mervyn Jack.
E A research centre at the University of Edinburgh.
O To undertake research in usability engineering and dialogue engineering for speech recognition services (vCommerce), for Internet services (eCommerce), and for mobile services (mCommerce)

Centre for Communication Systems Research   (CCSR)   1994

■ Department of Electronic Engineering, University of Surrey, Guildford, Surrey, GU2 7XH.
   01483 686002   fax 01483 686011
   http://www.ee.surrey.ac.uk/CCSR/
   Director: Prof Barry G Evans.
E An autonomous research centre and department of the University of Surrey.
O To conduct research in mobile and satellite communication systems

Centre for Communications Research   (CCR)   1987
- ■   Faculty of Engineering, University of Bristol, Merchant Venturers Building, Woodland Road, Bristol, BS8 1UB.
      0117-954 5171   fax 0117-954 5207
      http://www.bris.ac.uk/ccr/
      Director: Prof J P McGeehan.
- E   An interdisciplinary research centre in the University of Bristol.
- O   To provide an environment in which research and teaching of the highest calibre can be undertaken in the fields of wireless communication networks and applied electromagnetics

Centre for Communications Systems   1988
- ■   School of Engineering, University of Durham, South Road, Durham, DH1 3LE.
      0191-334 2400   fax 0191-334 2407
      http://www.dur.ac.uk/comms.systems/
      Director: Prof Sana Salous.
- E   An interdisciplinary research centre at the University of Durham.
- O   To bring together the work in radio communication with the networking expertise to realise novel network architectures, with particular emphasis on mobile radio applications and the modelling of telecommunication networks with emphasis on high-speed simulation techniques
- ✕   Centre for Telecommunication Networks.

Centre for Community Arts Research and Practice
> see **Royal Bank of Scotland Centre for Community Arts Research and Practice.**

Centre for Community Justice
> see **Hallam Centre for Community Justice.**

Centre for Community and Lifelong Learning   (CCLL)
- ■   Caerleon Campus, University of Wales Newport, Newport, NP18 3YG.
      01633 432160   fax 01633 432640
      http://ccll.newport.ac.uk/
      Director: Viv Davies.
- E   A department of the University of Wales, Newport.

Centre for Community Mental Health
- ■   Faculty of Health, Birmingham City University, Perry Barr, Birmingham, B42 2SU.
      0121-331 5500
      http://www.ccmh.uce.ac.uk/
- E   A research centre at Birmingham City University.
- O   To conduct research and consultancy for the implementation of the NHS framework for people with mental health problems

Centre for Community Neurological Studies   (CNS)
- ■   Faculty of Health, Leeds Metropolitan University, Calverley Street, Leeds, LS1 3HE.
      0113-283 5918   fax 0113-283 3416
      http://www.lmu.ac.uk/health/cns/
- E   A research centre at Leeds Metropolitan University.
- O   To conduct research and teaching in epilepsy care, stroke care, Parkinson's Disease care, multiple sclerosis care, neurological care, and headache and migraine

Centre for Community Research   (CCR)
- ■   Department of Social, Community and Health Studies, University of Hertfordshire, College Lane, Hatfield, Hertfordshire, AL10 9AB.
      01707 284105
      http://perseus.herts.ac.uk/uhinfo/schools/sch/social-work/research.cfm
      Head: Dr Roger Green.
- E   A research centre within the Health and Human Sciences Research Institute (qv) at the University of Hertfordshire.
- O   To bring together a wide range of contemporary community and social themes that are grounded in the needs of professionals, community based agencies and the communities they serve

Centre for Comparative Criminology and Criminal Justice   (4CJ)   1991   Ganolfan Troseddeg Gymharol a Chyfiawnder Troseddol
- ■   School of Social Sciences, University of Wales Bangor, Bangor, Gwynedd, LL57 2DG.
      01248 382007   fax 01248 382085
      http://www.bangor.ac.uk/so/4cj/
      Acting Director: Dr Julia Wardhaugh.
- E   A research centre at the University of Wales, Bangor.
- O   To promote and conduct high quality research in a wide variety of aspects of criminology and criminal justice

Centre for Comparative Education Research
> see **UNESCO Centre for Comparative Education Research.**

Centre for Comparative European Survey Data   (CCESD)
- ■   Department of Law, Governance and International Relations, London Metropolitan University, Calcutta House, Old Castle Street, London, E1 7TP.
     020 7320 4900   fax 020 7320 4925
     http://www.londonmet.ac.uk/research/
     Director: Prof Richard Topf.
- E   A research centre at London Metropolitan University.
- ○   To provide specialist support for people wishing to work with comparative survey data sets

Centre for Comparative Genomics [Cambridge]
   see **Cambridge Resource Centre for Comparative Genomics.**

Centre for Comparative Genomics   (CCG)   2005
- ■   Department of Biology, University College London, Wolfson House, 4 Stephenson Way, London, NW1 2HE.
     020 7679 5101; 7411
     http://www.ucl.ac.uk/biology/centre-for-comparative-genomics/
     Contact: Mari Wyn-Burley. Contact: Fraser Simpson.
- E   A research centre at University College London.
- ○   To operate and run a high-throughput sequencing and genotyping facility

Centre for Comparative Housing Research   (CCHR)
- ■   Department of Public Policy, De Montfort University, Bosworth House, The Gateway, Leicester, LE1 9BH.
     0116-257 7434   fax 0116-251 7548
     http://www.cchr.net/
     Director: Dr Tim Brown.
- E   A centre at De Montfort University.
- ○   To deliver quality research and teaching in the field of housing and public policy

Centre for Comparative Infectious Diseases   (CCID)
- ■   University of Liverpool, Liverpool, L69 3BX.
     0151-794 2000   fax 0151-708 6502
     http://www.liv.ac.uk/ccid/
- E   A research centre at the University of Liverpool.
- ○   To develop and promote research in infectious diseases of animals and man

Centre for Comparative Labour Studies   (CCLS)   1993
- ■   Department of Sociology, University of Warwick, Coventry, CV4 7AL.
     024 7652 3091   fax 024 7652 3497
     http://www.warwick.ac.uk/fac/soc/complabstuds/
     Director: Dr Tony Elger.
- E   A research centre at the University of Warwick.
- ○   To provide an interdisciplinary focus for the study of questions relating to labour

Centre for Comparative Social Surveys   (CCSS)   2003
- ■   Department of Sociology, City University, Social Sciences Building, Northampton Square, London, EC1V 0HB.
     020 7040 8527
     http://www.city.ac.uk/sociology/ccss/ccss.html
     Director: Prof Roger Jowell.
- E   A centre at City University.
- ○   To improve comparative social measurement within and beyond Europe

Centre for the Comparative Study of Culture, Development and the Environment
   see **Centre for Culture, Development and the Environment.**

Centre for the Comparative Study of Modern British and European Religious History   2001
- ■   Department of Theology and Religious Studies, University of Wales Lampeter, College Street, Lampeter, Ceredigion, SA48 7ED.
     01570 424708   fax 01570 424987
     http://www.lamp.ac.uk/trs/research_centres/Mod_Brit_European.htm
     Director: Prof Nigel Yates.
- E   A research centre at the University of Wales, Lampeter.
- ○   To bring together scholars working in different European countries to undertake research into aspects of post-Reformation religious history in which useful comparisons can be made between developments in two or more different European countries

Centre for Competition Law and Policy
   see **University of Oxford Centre for Competition Law and Policy.**

Centre for Competition Policy   (CCP)
- ■   School of Management, University of East Anglia, Norwich, NR4 7TJ.
    01603 593715   fax 01603 591622
    http://www.ccp.uea.ac.uk/
    Director: Prof Catherine Waddams.
- E   A centre at the University of East Anglia.
- O   To conduct high quality independent academic research into competition and regulation

Centre for Competition and Regulation Research
    see **Cranfield Centre for Competition and Regulation Research.**

Centre for Competition and Regulatory Policy   (CCRP)   2005
- ■   Department of Economics, City University, Northampton Square, London, EC1V 0HV.
    020 7040 8533
    http://www.city.ac.uk/economics/CCRP/CCRP.html
    Director: John Cubbin.
- E   A research centre at City University.

Centre for Competitiveness   (CforC)
- ■   Northern Ireland Science Park, Queen's Road, Belfast, BT3 9DT.
    028 9073 7950   fax 028 9073 7951
    http://www.cforc.org/
- E   A private sector, not-for-profit membership organisation.
- O   To support the development of an internationally competitive economy in Northern Ireland through innovation, productivity improvement and quality excellence in the private, voluntary and public sectors

Centre for Competitiveness and Innovation   (CCI)
- ■   Judge Business School, University of Cambridge, Trumpington Street, Cambridge, CB2 1AG.
    01223 339700
    http://www.jbs.cam.ac.uk/research/cci/
- E   A centre at the University of Cambridge.
- O   To bring together organisations interested in fostering and sustaining innovation to work together to better understand how value is created, delivered and captured from product and process innovation

Centre for Complementary Care   1989
- ■   Muncaster Chase, Muncaster, Ravenglass, Cumbria, CA18 1RD.
    01229 717355   fax 01229 717355
    http://www.cccare.org/
    Director: Gretchen Stevens.
- E   A registered charity and a company limited by guarantee.
- O   To offer individual therapies of healing, counselling and acupuncture for the relief of pain, sickness and suffering, and to provide information, support and guidance to those at a point of change or loss

Centre for Complementary Healthcare and Integrated Medicine   (CCHIM)   2000
- ■   Faculty of Health and Human Sciences, Thames Valley University, Walpole House, 18-22 Bond Street, London, W5 5AA.
    020 8280 5123; 5176   fax 020 8280 5308
    http://www.cchim.com/
    Director: Prof Nicola Robinson.
- E   A research centre at Thames Valley University.
- O   To develop a range of new complementary medicine courses specifically designed to meet the professional bodies' requirements and the National Occupational Standards

Centre for Complex Cooperative Systems   (C^{3}S)   1997
- ■   Faculty of Computing, Engineering and Mathematical Sciences, Frenchay Campus, University of the West of England, Coldharbour Lane, Bristol, BS16 1QY.
    0870 901 0767   fax 0117-328 2587
    http://www.cems.uwe.ac.uk/cccs/
    Research Director: Prof Richard McClatchey.
- E   A research centre at the University of the West of England.
- O   To undertake applied, collaborative computer science research with industrial enterprises and international research institutions in the fields of large-scale distributed systems, and data and process management

Centre for Complex Fluids Processing
- ■   Swansea University, Singleton Park, Swansea, SA2 8PP.
    01792 205678
    http://www.swan.ac.uk/research/centresandinstitutes/CentreforComplexFluidsProcessing/
- E   A research centre within the Multidisciplinary Nanotechnology Centre (qv) at Swansea University.
- O   To conduct research in the fields of membrane separation processes, bioprocess technology, food technology, rheometry, colloids and interfaces, atomic force microscopy, and nanotechnology

Centre for Complex Systems Analysis
    see **York Centre for Complex Systems Analysis.**

© CBD Research Ltd · Beckenham · Kent BR3 5JS · Tel 020 8650 7745 · Fax 020 8650 0768 · E-mail cbd@cbdresearch.com · www.cbdresearch.com

Centre for Composite Materials
   see **Composites Centre.**

Centre for Composition and Performance Using Technology
- ■ UCE Birmingham Conservatoire, Birmingham City University, Paradise Place, Birmingham, B3 3HG.
   0121-331 5901; 5902
   http://www.conservatoire.uce.ac.uk/research/centre-for-composition-and-performance-using-technology
- E A research centre at Birmingham City University.
- O To draw together composers, performers, engineers and technicians in the exploration of the potential for the real-time interaction of musical performance and computer-based systems

Centre for Computational Finance and Economic Agents   (CCFEA)   2004
- ■ Department of Economics, University of Essex, Wivenhoe Park, Colchester, Essex, CO4 3SQ.
   01206 874876
   http://www.essex.ac.uk/ccfea/
   Director: Dr Sheri Markose.
- E A centre at the University of Essex.
- O To use computational and evolutionary methods to simulate markets with artificially intelligent agents and to design real time trading and risk management systems

Centre for Computational Fluid Dynamics   (CFD)   1990
- ■ University of Leeds, Houldsworth Building, Clarendon Road, Leeds, LS2 9JT.
   0113-343 2508
   http://www.leeds.ac.uk/cfd/
   Director: Dr M Pourkashanian.
- E A department of the University of Leeds.
- O To promote computational fluid dynamics in academia and industry
- ● Conference facilities - Education and training - Consultancy - Specialised courses

Centre for Computational Intelligence   (CCI)
- ■ School of Computing, De Montfort University, Gateway House, The Gateway, Leicester, LE1 9BH.
   0116-257 7539   fax 0116-207 8159
   http://www.cci.dmu.ac.uk/
   Head: Prof Robert John.
- E A centre at De Montfort University.
- O To conduct research in fuzzy logic, bio-health informatics, neural networks, mobile robotics, and creative computing

Centre for Computational Neuroscience and Robotics   (CCNR)
- ■ Department of Biochemistry, University of Sussex, John Maynard Smith Building, Falmer, Brighton, East Sussex, BN1 9QG.
   01273 872948   fax 01273 678535
   http://www.informatics.sussex.ac.uk/research/groups/ccnr/
   Joint-Co-ordinator: Prof Phil Husbands. Joint-Co-ordinator: Prof Michael O'Shea.
- E A research centre at the University of Sussex.
- O To encourage a two-way flow of ideas and methods between life sciences and computer science

Centre for Computational Science   (CCS)
- ■ Department of Chemistry, University College London, 20 Gordon Street, London, WC1H 0AJ.
   020 7679 4850
   http://ccs.chem.ucl.ac.uk/
   Director: Prof Peter V Coveney. Contact: Dr Simon Clifford.
- E A research centre at University College London.
- O To study a range of problems in theoretical and computational science, computer science, and distributed computing

Centre for Computer Graphics and Visualisation   (CCGV)   2006
- ■ Luton Campus, University of Bedfordshire, Luton, Bedfordshire, LU1 3JU.
   01582 489230   fax 01582 489212
   http://www.beds.ac.uk/research/irac/ccgv
   Director: Prof Gordon Clapworthy.
- E A research centre within the Institute for Research in Applicable Computing (qv) at the University of Bedfordshire.
- O To conduct research in computer graphics, computer animation and medical visualisation

Centre for Computer Science and Informatics Research   (CCSIR)
- ■ University of Hertfordshire, College Lane, Hatfield, Hertfordshire, AL10 9AB.
   01707 286083   fax 01707 284185
   http://perseus.herts.ac.uk/uhinfo/research/stri/stri_home.cfm
- E A research centre within the Science and Technology Research Institute (qv) at the University of Hertfordshire.

Centre for Computing in the Humanities   (CCH)

■   School of Humanities, King's College London, Kay House, 7 Arundel Street, London, WC2R 3DX.
    020 7848 2861   fax 020 7848 2980
    http://www.kcl.ac.uk/cch/
    Director & Head of Department: Harold D Short. Director of Research: Marilyn Deegan.
E   A department of King's College, London.
○   To foster awareness, understanding and skill in the scholarly applications of computing
●   Education and training - Consultancy
¶   Many publications available.
✕   Research Unit in Humanities Computing.

Centre for Computing and Social Responsibility   (CCSR)

■   School of Computing, De Montfort University, Gateway House, The Gateway, Leicester, LE1 9BH.
    0116-257 7050   fax 0116-207 8159
    http://www.ccsr.cse.dmu.ac.uk/
    Director: Prof Simon Rogerson.
E   A centre at De Montfort University.
○   To conduct research and education in the ethical and social issues related to information and communication technologies

Centre for Concurrent Systems and Very Large Scale Integration   (CCSV)   1993

■   Faculty of Business, Computing and Information Management, London South Bank University, 103 Borough Road, London,
    SE1 0AA.
    020 7815 7413
    http://www.lsbu.ac.uk/bcimicr/research/ccsv.shtml
    Head: Prof Mark Josephs.
E   A research centre within the Institute for Computing Research (qv) at London South Bank University.
○   To conduct research into asynchronous circuit design

Centre of Conflict Recovery
    see **Leonard Cheshire Centre of Conflict Recovery.**

Centre for Conflict Resolution   (CCR)   1990

■   School of Social and International Studies, University of Bradford, Bradford, West Yorkshire, BD7 1DP.
    01274 235235   fax 01274 235240
    http://www.bradford.ac.uk/acad/confres/
    Director: Prof Tom Woodhouse, BA.
E   A centre at the University of Bradford.
○   To understand and address the deep and underlying causes of conflict; to support peace constituencies seeking to end the fighting
    and to bring warring parties to the negotiating table; to enhance the roles of UN peacekeeping operations as conflict resolution
    interventions

Centre for Conservation Ecology

■   School of Conservation Sciences, Christchurch House, Talbot Campus, Bournemouth University, Poole, Dorset, BH12 5BB.
    01202 965178   fax 01202 965530
    http://www.bournemouth.ac.uk/conservation/abouttheschool/egs/egs_cecb.html
E   A centre at Bournemouth University.

Centre for Conservation and Urban Studies   (CCUS)   1996

■   School of Social Sciences, University of Dundee, 13 Perth Road, Dundee, DD1 4HN.
    01382 345236   fax 01382 204234
    http://www.trp.dundee.ac.uk/research/cpr.html
E   A research centre within the Geddes Institute (qv) at the University of Dundee.
○   To focus research and teaching activity on the practice of conservation, urban design and regeneration

Centre for Construction Innovation and Research   (CCIR)

■   School of Science and Technology, University of Teesside, Middlesbrough, TS1 3BA.
    01642 342494
    http://sst.tees.ac.uk/ccir/
    Administrator: Claire Leonard.
E   A research centre at the University of Teesside.
○   To provide high quality consultation, research and development in the built environment, to promote sustainable and cost effective
    solutions for products, processes and performance

Centre of Construction Law and Management   (CCLM)   1987

■   School of Law, King's College London, The Old Watch House, Strand, London, WC2R 2LS.
    020 7848 2685   fax 020 7872 0210
    http://www.kcl.ac.uk/schools/law/research/cclm.html
    Manager: Mrs Linda Jones.
E   A research centre at King's College, London.
○   To explore the interfaces between law, construction and management, and to bring together the various skills and strengths of the
    professions that usually make their separate contributions to the construction industry

© CBD Research Ltd · Beckenham · Kent BR3 5JS · Tel 020 8650 7745 · Fax 020 8650 0768 · E-mail cbd@cbdresearch.com · www.cbdresearch.com

Centre for Constructions and Identity   (CCI)   1998
- Department of Behavioural Sciences, University of Huddersfield, Queensgate, Huddersfield, HD1 3DH.
  01484 422288
  http://www.hud.ac.uk/hhs/dbs/cci/
  Co-Director: Dr Jim McAuley. Co-Director: Dr Trevor Butt.
- E   A research centre at the University of Huddersfield.
- O   To promote research activity and publications in the area of constructions and identity, both individually and in collaboration

Centre for Contaminated Land Remediation   (CCLR)
- Department of Earth and Environmental Sciences, University of Greenwich, Pembroke, Chatham Maritime, Kent, ME4 4TB.
  020 8331 8441; 9820   fax 020 8331 9805
  http://www.gre.ac.uk/schools/cls/
  Contact: Dr Paula Carey. Contact: Colin Hills.
- E   A centre at the University of Greenwich.

Centre for Contemporary Approaches to the Bible   2001
- Department of Theology and Religious Studies, University of Wales Lampeter, College Street, Lampeter, Ceredigion, SA48 7ED.
  01570 424708; 424866   fax 01570 424987
  http://www.lamp.ac.uk/trs/research_centres/pastoral_theology.htm
  Director: Dr Martin O'Kane.
- E   A research centre at the University of Wales, Lampeter.

Centre for Contemporary Art [Newcastle]
   see **BALTIC Centre for Contemporary Art.**

Centre for Contemporary Art
- University of Central Lancashire, 37 St Peters Street, Preston, PR1 2HE.
  01772 893993
  http://www.anotherplace.org/
  Director: Prof Lubaina Himid.
- E   A centre at the University of Central Lancashire.

Centre for Contemporary Art Research
- Faculty of Law, Arts and Social Sciences, Winchester School of Art, University of Southampton, Park Avenue, Winchester, Hampshire, SO23 8DL.
  023 8059 6900
  http://www.wsa.soton.ac.uk/
- E   A research centre at the University of Southampton.

Centre for Contemporary British History   (CCBH)   1986
- School of Advanced Study, University of London, Senate House, Malet Street, London, WC1E 7HU.
  020 7862 8810   fax 020 7862 8812
  http://www.history.ac.uk/
  Director: Prof Pat Thane.
- E   A research centre within the Institute of Historical Research (qv) at the University of London.
- O   To promote the study of recent past
- ✕   Institute of Contemporary British History.

Centre of Contemporary Central Asia and the Caucasus   (CCCAC)   2001
- Faculty of Languages and Cultures, School of Oriental & African Studies, University of London, Thornhaugh Street, Russell Square, London, WC1H 0XG.
  020 7898 4892; 4893   fax 020 7898 4489
  http://www.soas.ac.uk/centres/
  Manager: Jane Savory. Executive Officer: Sara Hamza.
- E   An interdisciplinary research centre at the School of Oriental and African Studies, University of London.
- O   To facilitate and develop in the UK and Europe research, teaching and other activities relating to Central Asia and the Caucasus

Centre for Contemporary Chinese Studies   (CCCS)   1999
- School of Government and International Affairs, University of Durham, Al-Qasimi Building, Elvet Hill Road, Durham, DH1 3TU.
  0191-334 5665   fax 0191-334 5680
  http://www.dur.ac.uk/china.studies/
  Director: Dr David Kerr.
- E   A research centre within the University of Durham.
- O   To consolidate and develop existing research on the society, culture, economy and business of China

Centre for Contemporary Civil Law Studies   (CCCLS)   1995
- Cardiff Law School, Cardiff University, PO Box 427, Cardiff, CF10 3XJ.
  029 2087 4353   fax 029 2087 4097
  http://www.law.cf.ac.uk/cccls/
- E   A centre at Cardiff University.
- O   To promote and advance knowledge of contemporary civil law systems, ie legal systems which are derived historically from Roman law

Centre for Contemporary European Studies   (CCES)
■   Paisley Business School, University of Paisley, Paisley, PA1 2BE.
   0141-848 3399   fax 0141-848 3618
   http://www.paisley.ac.uk/business/cces/
E   A research centre at the University of Paisley.
O   To conduct research on contemporary Europe, especially in the fields of politics, economics, languages, culture, and regional development
Note: At the time of going to press, the University of Paisley was preparing to merge with Bell College to form the University of the West of Scotland.

Centre for Contemporary Fiction and Narrative   (CCFN)
■   University of Northampton, Boughton Green Road, Northampton, NN2 7AL.
   01604 735500
   http://www.northampton.ac.uk/
E   A research centre at the University of Northampton.
O   To explore research in literary and cultural studies, focusing on the importance of the contemporary as a concept and periodization in fiction, in narrative more broadly understood; to address the various kinds of theory used exegetically to understand such narratives

Centre for Contemporary German Literature   (CCGL)   1993
■   Department of German, Swansea University, Singleton Park, Swansea, SA2 8PP.
   01792 205678; 295170   fax 01792 295710
   http://www.swan.ac.uk/german/
   Director: Prof Rhys W Williams.
E   A research centre at Swansea University.
O   To promote contemporary German, Swiss and Austrian authors in Wales and in Britain, and to provide stimulus for research into their works

Centre for Contemporary History and Politics
■   Faculty of Arts, Media and Social Sciences, University of Salford, Salford, Manchester, M5 4WT.
   0161-295 4948
   http://www.esri.salford.ac.uk/
   Contact: Prof Steven Fielding.
E   A research centre within the European Studies Research Institute (qv) at the University of Salford.

Centre for Contemporary Ministry   (CCM)
■   The Park, Moggerhanger, Bedfordshire, MK44 3RW.
   01767 641005   fax 01767 641515
   http://www.the-park.net/ccm/
E   A registered charity.
O   To promote the Christian faith through the provision of educational resources to envision, equip and enable leaders to be more effective in their calling to ministry

Centre for Contemporary Music   (CCM)
■   Department of Music, University of Durham, Palace Green, Durham, DH1 3RL.
   0191-334 3156   fax 0191-334 3141
   http://www.dur.ac.uk/contemporary.music/
   Director: Dr Mieko Kanno.
E   A centre at the University of Durham.
O   To address current topics in contemporary music and its culture

Centre for Contemporary Music Cultures   (CCMC)   2006
■   Music Department, Goldsmiths, University of London, London, SE14 6NW.
   020 7919 7658
   http://www.goldsmiths.ac.uk/departments/
   Director: Prof John Baily.
E   A research centre at Goldsmiths, University of London.

Centre for Contemporary Music Practice   (CCMP)   2005
■   School of Arts, Brunel University, Uxbridge, Middlesex, UB8 3PH.
   01895 274000
   http://www.brunel.ac.uk/
   Director: Prof Peter Wiegold.
E   A centre at Brunel University.
O   To conduct research on contemporary music composition

© CBD Research Ltd · Beckenham · Kent BR3 5JS · Tel 020 8650 7745 · Fax 020 8650 0768 · E-mail cbd@cbdresearch.com · www.cbdresearch.com

Centre for Contemporary and Pastoral Theology   2001
- ■   Department of Theology and Religious Studies, University of Wales Lampeter, College Street, Lampeter, Ceredigion, SA48 7ED.
  01570 424708   fax 01570 424987
  http://www.lamp.ac.uk/trs/
  Director: Dr Neil Messer.
- E   A research centre at the University of Wales, Lampeter.
- ○   To support research that constitutes a critical and constructive engagement of Christian theology with aspects of contemporary society, culture and ethics

Centre for Contemporary Spanish Studies
  see **Cañada Blanch Centre for Contemporary Spanish Studies.**

Centre for Contemporary Visual and Material Culture
- ■   Faculty of Art, Design and Architecture, Kingston University, Knights Park, Kingston-upon-Thames, Surrey, KT1 2QJ.
  020 8547 8062   fax 020 8547 8272
  http://www.kingston.ac.uk/design/research_centres.html
- E   A research centre at Kingston University, London.
- ○   To conduct research on the practice, histories and theories of contemporary visual and material culture

Centre for Contemporary Visual Arts   (CCVA)
- ■   Faculty of Arts and Architecture, University of Brighton, Mithras House, Lewes Road, Brighton, East Sussex, BN2 4AT.
  01273 600900
  http://www.brighton.ac.uk/arts/research/2_0_ccva/
- E   A centre at the University of Brighton.
- ○   To create an intellectual laboratory for the interaction of ideas and disciplines in the contemporary visual, performing arts and design

Centre for Contemporary Writing   (CCW)
- ■   School of Humanities, University of Southampton, Room 1003 - New Building, Avenue Campus, Southampton, SO17 1BJ.
  023 8059 3239   fax 023 8059 2859
  http://www.soton.ac.uk/~poetry/
  Director: Dr Nicky Marsh.
- E   A research centre at the University of Southampton.

Centre for Contemporary Writing [Uxbridge]
  see **Brunel Centre for Contemporary Writing.**

Centre for Continuing Education
  see **Møller Centre for Continuing Education.**

Centre for Corporate and Commercial Law   (3CL)   1997
- ■   Faculty of Law, University of Cambridge, 10 West Road, Cambridge, CB3 9DZ.
  01223 330042   fax 01223 330055
  http://cccl.law.cam.ac.uk/
  Administrator: Miss Felicity Eves.
- E   A centre at the University of Cambridge.
- ○   To promote further research into the areas of corporate and commercial law

Centre for Corporate Governance   (CCG)   1997
- ■   Judge Business School, University of Cambridge, Trumpington Street, Cambridge, CB2 1AG.
  01223 765330   fax 01223 756338
  http://www.jbs.cam.ac.uk/research/ccg
  Director: Prof Simon Deakin.
- E   A centre at the University of Cambridge.
- ○   To improve understanding of systems of corporate governance and their practical operation, both in the UK and internationally, through multi-disciplinary research

Centre for Corporate Governance   (CCG)
- ■   London Business School, Sussex Place, Regent's Park, London, NW1 4SA.
  020 7262 5050
  http://www.london.edu/centreforcorporategovernance.html
  Executive Director: Julia Goodbourn.
- E   A research centre at the London Business School.
- ○   To provide independent research and recommendations designed to influence the corporate governance debate, especially in relation to moving governance practices beyond mere regulatory compliance towards the creation of value for companies, policy makers, investors and other stakeholders

Centre for Corporate Governance and Regulation   (CCGR)

■   Bournemouth Law School, Talbot Campus, Bournemouth University, Poole, Dorset, BH12 5BB.
    01202 965359
    http://ccgr.bmth.ac.uk/
    Director: Robert Day.
E   A research centre within the Institute of Business and Law (qv) at Bournemouth University.
○   To conduct an economic analysis of corporate governance law and practice

Centre for Corporate Governance Research

■   Birmingham Business School, University of Birmingham, Edgbaston, Birmingham, B15 2TT.
    0121-414 2273   fax 0121-414 6678
    http://www.business.bham.ac.uk/research/accounting/ccgr/
    Director: Prof Christine Mallin.
E   A centre at the University of Birmingham.
○   To conduct and encourage high quality research in corporate governance

Centre for Corporate Law and Practice   (CCLP)   1996

■   School of Advanced Study, University of London, Charles Clore House, 17 Russell Square, London, WC1B 5DR.
    020 7862 5800   fax 020 7862 5850
    http://ials.sas.ac.uk/research/cclp/cclp.htm
E   A research centre within the Institute of Advanced Legal Studies (qv) at the University of London.

Centre for Corpus Research

■   School of Humanities, University of Birmingham, Edgbaston, Birmingham, B15 2TT.
    0121-414 5688   fax 0121-414 6053
    http://www.corpus.bham.ac.uk/
    Contact: Dr Pernilla Danielsson.
E   A centre at the University of Birmingham.
○   To facilitate corpus and text based / driven research

Centre for Corrosion Technology   (CCT)

■   City Campus, Sheffield Hallam University, Sheffield, S1 1WB.
    0114-225 4062   fax 0114-225 3501
    http://www.shu.ac.uk/research/meri/cct/
    Head: Prof Robert Akid.
E   A research centre within the Structural Materials and Integrity Research Centre (qv) at Sheffield Hallam University.
○   To provide research and business support expertise concerning the implication of materials operating within corrosive environments

Centre for Cosmic Chemistry and Physics
    see **UCL Centre for Cosmic Chemistry and Physics**.

Centre for Counselling and Psychotherapy for Young People
    see **Brandon Centre for Counselling and Psychotherapy for Young People**.

Centre for Counselling Studies   (CCS)   1992

■   Faculty of Social Sciences, University of East Anglia, Norwich, NR4 7TJ.
    01603 592807   fax 01603 451999
    http://www.uea.ac.uk/edu/
    Director: Dr Judy Moore.
E   A research centre at the University of East Anglia.

Centre for Creative Empowerment   (CCE)

■   School of Art, Design and Media, University of Portsmouth, Eldon Building, Winston Churchill Avenue, Portsmouth, PO1 2DJ.
    023 9284 3835   fax 023 9284 3808
    http://www.port.ac.uk/departments/academic/adm/
    Contact: Valerie Swales.
E   A research centre at the University of Portsmouth.
○   To study, develop and evaluate creative pedagogy and its policy implications

Centre for Creative Communities   (CCC)   1978

■   Regent House Business Centre, 24-25 Nutford Place, London, W1H 5YN.
    020 7569 3005
    http://www.creativecommunities.org.uk/
E   A registered charity and a company limited by guarantee.
○   To build sustainable and creative communities, communities in which creativity and learning have pivotal roles to play in personal, social, civic and economic development

Centre for Creative Industries [Bangor]
    see **National Institute for Excellence in Creative Industries**.

Centre for Creative Industries   (CCI)
- School of Engineering, Science and Design, Glasgow Caledonian University, Cowcaddens Road, Glasgow, G4 0BA.
  0141-331 8602   fax 0141-331 3690
  http://www.gcal.ac.uk/esd/research/centres_creative.html
- E   A research centre at Glasgow Caledonian University.
- ○   To offer a holistic approach to research, consultancy and teaching in creative industries' subject areas

Centre for Creative Industries [Plymouth]
    see **Innovate - Centre for Creative Industries.**

Centre for Creative Industry   (CCI)
- School of Management and Economics, Queen's University, Belfast, Belfast, BT7 1NN.
  028 9027 3112   fax 028 9033 5156
  http://www.creative.qub.ac.uk/creative.html
  Director: Prof Paul Jeffcutt.
- E   A centre at Queen's University, Belfast.
- ○   To concentrate on international excellence and local advantage to provide a key resource to sustain Northern Ireland at the forefront of a dynamic knowledge-based economy

Centre for Creative and Performing Arts
    see **National Institute for Excellence in Creative Industries.**

Centre for Creative Writing   (CCW)   2006
- School of English, Rutherford College Extension, University of Kent, Canterbury, Kent, CT2 7NX.
  01227 764000
  http://www.kent.ac.uk/english/creative-writing/
- E   A research centre at the University of Kent.
- ○   To support the MA in creative writing

Centre for Creative Writing and Arts   (CWA)   2006
- Department of English, University of Exeter, Queen's Building, The Queen's Drive, Exeter, EX4 4QH.
  01392 264265   fax 01392 264361
  http://www.sall.ex.ac.uk/centres/cwa/
  Head: Dr Ashley Tauchert.
- E   A centre at the University of Exeter.
- ○   To become a major centre for creative writing and arts

Centre for Creativity and Innovation   (CCI)
- Bowerham Road, Lancaster, LA1 3JD.
  01524 384672
  http://www.ucsm.ac.uk/bceu/project17.html
  Project Manager: Karl Lester.
- E   A research centre at St Martin's College.

Centre for Creativity Research
    see **National Institute for Excellence in Creative Industries.**

Centre for Creativity, Strategy and Change
Note: No longer in existence

Centre for Crime Informatics   (CCI)   2004
- Faculty of Social Sciences, Birkbeck, University of London, 23-29 Emerald Street, London, WC1N 3QS.
  020 7763 2137   fax 020 7763 2138
  http://www.lkl.ac.uk/research/crime.html
  Co-Director: Prof P J H King. Co-Director: Dr R G Johnson.
- E   A centre at Birkbeck, University of London.
- ○   To conduct research in computer support for the investigation of crime, fraud and security breaches

Centre for Crime and Justice Studies   (CCJS)   1931
- School of Law, King's College London, 26-29 Drury Lane, London, WC2B 5RL.
  020 7848 1688   fax 020 7848 1689
  http://www.kcl.ac.uk/depsta/rel/ccjs/
  Research Director: Roger Grimshaw.
- E   A research centre at King's College, London.
- ○   To initiate and promote scientific research into the causes and prevention of crime
- ¶   British Journal of Criminology (journal).

Centre for Criminal and Community Justice
    see **Newport Centre for Criminal and Community Justice.**

Centre for Criminal Justice and Criminology   (CCJC)
■ School of Applied Social Sciences, Swansea University, Vivian Building, Singleton Park, Swansea, SA2 8PP.
   01792 295318   fax 01792 595856
   http://www.swan.ac.uk/applied_social_sciences/Centres.html#Criminology_Centre
   Director: Prof Peter Raynor.
E A research centre at Swansea University.

Centre for Criminal Justice Economics and Psychology   (CCJEP)   2001
■ Department of Psychology, Wentworth College, University of York, Heslington, York, YO10 5DD.
   01904 434880   fax 01904 434881
   http://www.york.ac.uk/criminaljustice/
   Director: Prof Roger Bowles.
E A research centre at the University of York.
○ To conduct research aimed at helping to reduce the impact of crime on society and promote public safety

Centre for Criminal Justice Policy and Research   (CCJPR)   2003
■ Faculty of Law, Humanities, Development and Society, Birmingham City University, Perry Barr, Birmingham, B42 2SU.
   0121-331 6601   fax 0121-331 6938
   http://www.lhds.uce.ac.uk/criminaljustice/
   Director: Prof Douglas Sharp.
E A research centre at Birmingham City University.
○ To conduct research, consultancy and teaching in various aspects of criminal justice, including community safety, the police, prisons, penal reform, prisoner education, private security companies, vigilantism, and the experience of Muslims working within and encountering the criminal justice system

Centre for Criminal Justice Research
Note: No longer in existence.

Centre for Criminal Justice Studies   (CCJS)   1988
■ School of Law, University of Leeds, 18 Lyddon Terrace, Leeds, LS2 9JT.
   0113-343 5033   fax 0113-343 5056
   http://www.law.leeds.ac.uk/leedslaw/
   Director: Prof Adam Crawford.
E A department of the University of Leeds.
○ To develop, co-ordinate and pursue research and study into, and disseminate knowledge on, all aspects of criminal justice systems
● Conference facilities - Education and training - Information service - Library - Statistics

Centre for Criminal Law and Criminal Justice   (CCLCJ)   2006
■ Department of Law, University of Durham, 50 North Bailey, Durham, DH1 3ET.
   0191-334 2800   fax 0191-334 2801
   http://www.dur.ac.uk/cclcj/
   Director: Prof Michael Bohlander.
E A centre at the University of Durham.
○ To serve as an international forum for discussion and research in any area of criminal law and criminal law theory, criminal procedure, and criminal justice issues (including criminology)

Centre for Criminological Research
■ Chancellor's Building, Keele University, Keele, Staffordshire, ST5 5BG.
   01782 584336
   http://www.keele.ac.uk/research/lpj/research/Crim.htm
E A research centre within the Research Institute for Law, Politics and Justice (qv) at Keele University.

Centre for Criminological Research   1976
■ Department of Law, University of Sheffield, Crookesmoor Building, Conduit Road, Sheffield, S10 1FL.
   0114-222 6830
   http://www.sheffield.ac.uk/ccr/
   Director: Prof Joanna Shapland.
E A department of the University of Sheffield.
○ To pursue criminological and legal issues
● Conferences

Centre for Criminology [LSE]
   see **Mannheim Centre for the Study of Criminology and Criminal Justice.**

Centre for Criminology [Middlesex]
   see **Crime and Conflict Research Centre.**

© CBD Research Ltd · Beckenham · Kent BR3 5JS · Tel 020 8650 7745 · Fax 020 8650 0768 · E-mail cbd@cbdresearch.com · www.cbdresearch.com

Centre for Criminology   1966
■   Manor Road Building, University of Oxford, Manor Road, Oxford, OX1 3UQ.
     01865 274444   fax 01865 281924
     http://www.crim.ox.ac.uk/
     Director: Prof Ian Loader. Assistant Director: Dr Julian Roberts.
E   A department of the University of Oxford.
O   To provide undergraduate and graduate teaching to law and sociology students at the University of Oxford; to undertake research
     in criminology
●   Teaching
×   University of Oxford Centre for Criminological Research.

Centre for Criminology   2001
■   School of Humanities and Social Sciences, University of Glamorgan, 3 Forest Grove, Pontypridd, CF37 1DL.
     01443 480480   fax 01443 484507
     http://www.glam.ac.uk/hassschool/criminology/
E   A research centre within the University of Glamorgan.
O   To provide a physical base for research and teaching in criminology, including the study of crime, criminals, victims, and the
     criminal justice system including the police, the courts and prisoners
●   Education and training - Seminars

Centre for Criminology and Criminal Justice   (CCCJ)   1985
■   Department of Criminology and Sociological Studies, University of Hull, Cottingham Road, Hull, HU6 7RX.
     01482 465779; 466215
     http://www.hull.ac.uk/cass/research/centres/cccj/
     Director: Prof Peter Young.
E   A research centre at the University of Hull.

Centre for Criminology and Criminal Justice [Loughborough]
     see **Midlands Centre for Criminology and Criminal Justice.**

Centre for Criminology and Socio-Legal Studies   (CCSLS)
■   School of Law, University of Manchester, Oxford Road, Manchester, M13 9PL.
     0161-275 3874
     http://www.law.manchester.ac.uk/research/centres/ccsls/
     Director: Prof Frank Stephen. Contact: Prof Dora Kostakopoulou.
E   A research centre at the University of Manchester.
O   To study crime, the justice system and law more widely, especially in the areas of crime and criminal justice, economic analysis of
     law, regulation, global governance, legal aid, and education law

Centre for Crisis Psychology   (CCP)   1989
■   Foss House, Broughton Hall, Skipton, North Yorkshire, BD23 5SE.
     01756 796383   fax 01756 796384
     http://www.ccpdirect.co.uk/
     Business Development Manager: Anna Stewart.
E   A profit-making business.
O   To provide effective psychological management of stress, crisis or trauma within the corporate and individual domains

Centre for Critical and Cultural Theory   (CCCT)   1988
■   Cardiff School of English, Communication and Philosophy, Cardiff University, Colum Drive, Cardiff, CF10 3XB.
     029 2087 4722   fax 029 2087 4502
     http://www.cardiff.ac.uk/encap/cct/
     Chairman: Prof Chris Weedon.
E   A centre at Cardiff University.

Centre for Critical Education Policy Studies   (CeCeps)
■   School of Educational Foundations and Policy Studies, University of London, 20 Bedford Way, London, WC1H 0AL.
     020 7612 6000   fax 020 7612 6126
     http://ioewebserver.ioe.ac.uk/ioe/cms/get.asp?cid=10954
     Director: Carol Vincent.
E   A research centre within the Institute of Education (qv) at the University of London.
O   To bring together research on the processes by which education policy is shaped, implemented and experienced

Centre for Critical Social Theory
■   School of Social Sciences and Cultural Studies, Arts A, University of Sussex, Falmer, Brighton, East Sussex, BN1 9QN.
     01273 678621   fax 01273 673563
     http://www.sussex.ac.uk/spt/1-4-5.html
     Contact: Prof William Outhwaite. Contact: Dr Andrew Chitty.
E   A research centre at the University of Sussex.
O   To conduct research in the interactions between the explanatory, the normative and the ideological dimensions of social and
     political thought

Centre for Critical Theory
Note: Closed in June 2006.

Centre for Cross Border Studies   (CCBS)   1999

■   Queen's University, Belfast, 39 Abbey Street, Armagh, BT61 7EB.
028 3751 1554
http://www.crossborder.ie/
Director: Andy Pollak.
E   A centre at Queen's University, Belfast.
○   To research and develop co-operation across the Irish border in education, training, health, business, public administration, communications, agriculture and the environment

Centre for Cross-Cultural Music and Dance Performance
see **AHRC Research Centre for Cross-Cultural Music and Dance Performance.**

Centre for Cross-Cultural Research on Women
see **International Gender Studies Centre.**

Centre for Cross-Cultural Studies   (CCCS)

■   24-32 Stephenson Way, London, NW1 2HX.
020 7391 9150   fax 020 7391 9169
http://www.instituteoffamilytherapy.org.uk/
Director: Renee Singh.
E   A research centre within the Institute of Family Therapy (qv).

Centre for Cross Curricular Initiatives   (CCCI)   1991

■   Faculty of Arts and Human Sciences, London South Bank University, 103 Borough Road, London, SE1 0AA.
020 7815 5761   fax 020 7815 8160
http://www.lsbu.ac.uk/ccci/
Director: Prof Sally Inman. Administrator: Dane Austin.
E   A research centre at London South Bank University.
○   To develop educational policy and practice that promotes understanding of Global citizenship and sustainable development education, Cultural harmony and conflict resolution, Democratic schooling, and the Personal and social development of young people in schools

Centre for Crowd and Safety Management   (CCSM)

■   Buckinghamshire Chilterns University College, Queen Alexandra Road, High Wycombe, Buckinghamshire, HP11 2JZ.
01494 522141   fax 01494 524392
http://www.crowdsafetymanagement.co.uk/
Head: Mick Upton.
E   A centre at the Buckinghamshire Chilterns University College.
○   To conduct research and teaching in the field of crowd control and a safer security environment

Centre for Cultural Analysis, Theory and History   (CentreCATH at Leeds)

■   School of Fine Art, History of Art and Cultural Studies, University of Leeds, Leeds, LS2 9JT.
0113-343 5192   fax 0113-245 1977
http://www.leeds.ac.uk/cath/
Director: Prof Griselda Pollock.
E   A research centre at the University of Leeds.
✕   AHRC Centre for Cultural Analysis, Theory and History

Centre for the Cultural History of War   (CCHW)

■   School of Arts, Histories and Cultures, Humanities Lime Grove, University of Oxford, Oxford Road, Manchester, M13 9PL.
0161-306 1240
http://www.arts.manchester.ac.uk/subjectareas/history/research/cchw/
E   An interdisciplinary research centre within the Centre for Interdisciplinary Research in the Arts (qv) at the University of Manchester.
○   To conduct research and teaching dedicated to understanding the cultural attributes and representation of war in the modern world, with particular focus on population displacement, humanitarianism, and collective memory

Centre for Cultural Policy Research   (CCPR)   2001

■   Department of Theatre, Film and Television Studies, University of Glasgow, Gilmorehill Centre, 9 University Avenue, Glasgow, G12 8QQ.
0141-330 3806; 3885   fax 0141-330 4142
http://www.culturalpolicy.arts.gla.ac.uk/
Director: Christine Hamilton.
E   A research centre at the University of Glasgow.
○   To conduct research on cultural policy, with particular emphasis on cities and culture, cultural data, culture in rural areas, major events, the role of culture in social inclusion and health, cultural economics, and culture in society

Centre for Cultural Policy Studies   (CCPS)

■   Faculty of Arts, University of Warwick, Coventry, CV4 7AL.
024 7652 3020   fax 024 7652 4446
http://www2.warwick.ac.uk/fac/arts/theatre_s/cp/
E   A research centre at the University of Warwick.
○   To provide a focus for teaching and research in the fields of arts management, cultural policy and the creative industries

Centre for Cultural Resource Management   (CCRM)

■ School of Conservation Sciences, Bournemouth University, Christchurch House, Talbot Campus, Poole, Dorset, BH12 5BB.
    01202 965178   fax 01202 965530
    http://www.bournemouth.ac.uk/conservation/abouttheschool/ahe/ccrm.html
E   A centre at Bournemouth University.
O   To focus research on the identification, recording, assessment, investigation, protection, conservation, display and interpretation of all aspects of the historic environment

Centre for Cultural and Social History   2000

■ Department of History, University of Essex, Wivenhoe Park, Colchester, Essex, CO4 3SQ.
    01206 872313   fax 01206 873757
    http://www.essex.ac.uk/history/research/ccsh/
    Head: Dr Rainer Schulze.
E   A centre at the University of Essex.
O   To provide a forum for academics and graduate students working on historically based research across the University

Centre for Cultural Studies   (CCS)   1998

■ Goldsmiths, University of London, London, SE14 6NW.
    020 7919 7983   fax 020 7919 7984
    http://www.goldsmiths.ac.uk/cultural-studies/
    Director: Prof Scott Lash.
E   A research centre at Goldsmiths, University of London.
O   To provide a practical focus for the study of creative, cultural and social processes; to bring cultural studies forward into the analysis of multimedia, globalization and cultural difference under the most current socio-political conditions

Centre for Culture, Development and the Environment   (CDE)   1994

■ Department of Cultural Studies, University of Sussex, Falmer, Brighton, East Sussex, BN1 9SJ.
    01273 678722   fax 01273 623572
    http://www.sussex.ac.uk/development/
E   A department of the University of Sussex.
O   To promote research and teaching on development
✕   Centre for the Comparative Study of Culture, Development and the Environment

Centre for Cutaneous Research   (CCR)   1983

■ Barts and the London, Queen Mary's School of Medicine and Dentistry, Queen Mary, University of London, 4 Newark Street, London, E1 2AT.
    020 7882 2483   fax 020 7882 2200
    http://www.icms.qmul.ac.uk/centres/cutaneous/
    Lead: Prof Irene Leigh.
E   A research centre within the Institute of Cell and Molecular Science (qv) at Queen Mary, University of London.
O   To conduct research in the biomolecular mechanisms of keratinocyte biology, wound healing and tissue engineering, epithelial-mesenchymal interactions and skin development, the roles of viral oncogenesis and developmental genes in non-melanoma skin cancer as well as the genetics of syndromic and non-syndromic hereditary and inflammatory skin diseases

Centre for Dairy Research   (CEDAR)   1992

■ Arborfield Hall Farm, Church Lane, Reading, Berkshire, RG2 9HX.
    0118-378 8471
    http://www.apd.rdg.ac.uk/Agriculture/ASRG/dairy.htm
    Contact: Prof R H Ellis.
E   A research centre at the University of Reading.

Centre for Dance Research   (CDR)

■ School of Arts, Digby Stuart College, University of Roehampton, Roehampton Lane, London, SW15 5PH.
    020 8392 3249
    http://www.roehampton.ac.uk/researchcentres/cdr/
    Director: Prof Stephanie Jordan.
E   A research centre at Roehampton University.

Centre for Data Digitisation and Analysis   (CDDA)

■ School of Geography, Archaeology and Palaeoecology, Queen's University Belfast, Belfast, BT7 1NN.
    028 9097 3883   fax 028 9032 1280
    http://www.qub.ac.uk/cdda/
    Director: Dr Paul S Ell.
E   A centre at Queen's University, Belfast.
O   To conduct research in, and provide services in the area of, large-scale data capture from printed sources

Centre for Dead Sea Scrolls Research
    see **Manchester-Sheffield Centre for Dead Sea Scrolls Research.**

Centre for Deaf Studies, Language and Cognition
    see **Deafness Cognition and Language Research Centre.**

Centre for Deafened People
    see **Link Centre for Deafened People.**

Centre for Death and Society   (CDAS)   2005
■   Department of Social and Policy Sciences, University of Bath, Claverton Down, Bath, BA2 7AY.
       01225 386852   fax 01225 386381
       http://www.bath.ac.uk/cdas/
       Director: Dr Glennys Howarth.
E   A centre at the University of Bath.
O   To further social, policy and health research

Centre for Decision Management and Risk Management   (DARM)
■   University of Middlesex, Queensway, Enfield, Middlesex, EN3 4SA.
       020 8411 6822
       http://www.mdx.ac.uk/risk/darm/
E   A research centre at Middlesex University
O   To focus research on the development and application of decision-making and risk management strategies in public health, occupational safety, and the natural and built environment

Centre for Decision Research   (CDR)   1996
■   Leeds University Business School, University of Leeds, Maurice Keyworth Building, Leeds, LS2 9JT.
       0113-343 2622   fax 0113-343 4465
       http://www.leeds.ac.uk/decision-research/
       Director: Dr John Maule.
E   An inter-departmental centre within the University of Leeds.
O   To focus research on the way individuals and organisations make decisions

Centre for Decision Research and Experimental Economics   (CeDEx)   2000
■   School of Economics, University of Nottingham, University Park, Nottingham, NG7 2RD.
       0115-951 5620   fax 0115-951 4159
       http://www.nottingham.ac.uk/economics/cedex/
       Director: Prof Chris Starmer.
E   A research centre at the University of Nottingham.
O   To conduct research into individual and stretegic decision-making using a combination of theoretical and experimental methods

Centre for Defence Economics   (CDE)   1990
■   Department of Economics and Related Studies, Alcuin College, University of York, Heslington, York, YO10 5DD.
       01904 433788   fax 01904 433759
       http://www.york.ac.uk/depts/econ/research/associated/
E   A research centre at the University of York.
O   To undertake research into all aspects of the economics of conflict, defence, disarmament, conversion, peace and conflict

Centre for Defence and International Security Studies   (CDISS)   1990
■   The Court House, Northfield End, Henley-on-Thames, Oxfordshire, RG9 2JN.
       01491 412043   fax 01491 412082
       http://www.cdiss.org/
       Director: Maj Gen (Ret'd) Jonathan Bailey, CB, CBE, PhD.
E   An independent organisation.
O   To conduct research and analysis on international defence issues

Centre for Defence Studies   (CDS)   1990
■   School of Social Science and Public Policy, King's College, London, 138-142 Strand, London, WC2R 1HH.
       020 7848 2338   fax 020 7848 2748
       http://cds.ipi.kcl.ac.uk/
       Director: Prof Michael Clarke.
E   A research centre within King's College, London.
O   To conduct research at the highest level on British, European and international defence and security issues

Centre for Democracy and Governance   (CDG)   2006
■   Department of Behavioural Sciences, University of Huddersfield, Queensgate, Huddersfield, HD1 3DH.
       01484 422288
       http://www.hud.ac.uk/hhs/dbs/cdg/
       Director: Prof Valerie Bryson.
E   A research centre at the University of Huddersfield.
O   To promote research in governance, democracy and politics in general

Centre for Democracy Studies   (CDS)   2000
■   School of Social Sciences and Law, Gipsy Lane Campus, Oxford Brookes University, Headington, Oxford, OX3 0BP.
       01865 483924
       http://ssl.brookes.ac.uk/democracystudies/home.htm
       Director: Alan Grant.
E   A research centre at Oxford Brookes University.
O   To explore the evident significance of democracy and democratisation in the contemporary world

Centre for Democratic Evaluation
    see **Brunel Centre for Democratic Evaluation.**

Centre for Democratic Governance   (CDG)   2002
■   Department of Politics and International Studies, University of Hull, Cottingham Road, Hull, HU6 7RX.
    01482 466209   fax 01482 466208
    http://www.hull.ac.uk/pas/research/research_centre/Centre_for_Democratic_Governance/
    Co-Director: Simon Lee. Co-Director: Colin Tyler.
E   A research centre at the University of Hull.

Centre for Democratization Studies   (CDS)   1992
■   School of Education, University of Leeds, Leeds, LS2 9JT.
    0113-343 4382   fax 0113-343 4400
    Director: Dr J J Schwarzmantel.
E   A research centre at the University of Leeds.
O   To carry out research in a wide spectrum of activities within the overall fields of democracy and democratization; to organise
    lectures and seminars on current issues relating to democratic theory and practice
●   Conference facilities - Library

Centre for Dental Technology
■   Cardiff School of Health Sciences, Llandarff Campus, Cardiff University, Western Avenue, Cardiff, CF5 2YB.
    029 2041 6890   fax 029 2041 6895
    http://www.uwic.ac.uk/shss/centres/dental.asp
E   A research centre at the University of Wales Institute, Cardiff.
O   To conduct research in various dental related areas, including e-Learning with dental technology programmes, electronic storage
    of dental records, measurement of 'fit' of prostheses, orthodontic appliance / component development, professional registration,
    and non-attendance patterns of dental patients

Centre for Dental Technology Studies   (CDTS)
■   Department of Chemistry and Materials, Manchester Metropolitan University, Chester Street, Manchester, M1 5GD.
    0161-247 1437;1439   fax 0161-247 6357
    Contact: Katherine Walthall.
E   A research centre at Manchester Metropolitan University.

Centre for Design against Crime   (CDAC)   2005
■   Central Saint Martins College of Art and Design, University of the Arts, London, Southampton Row, London, WC1B 4AP.
    020 7514 7366   fax 020 7514 7050
    http://www.designagainstcrime.com/
    Co-Director: Dr Lorraine Gamman. Co-Director: Prof Paul Ekblom.
E   A research centre at the University of the Arts, London.
O   To reduce the incidence, impact and fear of crime through the design of products, services and environments that are fit for the
    purpose in all other respects

Centre for Design Innovation   (CDI)
■   Birmingham City University, Gosta Green, Corporation Street, Birmingham, B4 7DX.
    0121-331 5800; 5801   fax 0121-331 7814
    http://www.biad.uce.ac.uk/research/cssonlysite/CDI/cdi.asp
E   An interdisciplinary research centre within the Birmingham Institute of Art and Design (qv) at Birmingham City University.
O   To exhibit excellence in the creation, execution, promotion, management, development and evaluation of the design process
    across a broad range of design disciplines

Centre for Design Research   (CfDR)
■   School of Design, Northumbria University, Squires Building, Sandyford Road, Newcastle upon Tyne, NE1 8ST.
    0191-227 4124   fax 0191-227 3148
    http://www.cfdr.co.uk/
E   A research centre at Northumbria University.
O   To focus research on emerging design issues, and the application of human-centred design knowledge; to promote excellence in
    design learning

Centre for Developing Areas Research   (CEDAR)   1988
■   Department of Geography, Royal Holloway, University of London, Egham, Surrey, TW20 0EX.
    01784 443563   fax 01784 472836
    http://www.gg.rhul.ac.uk/cedar/
    Director: Prof David Simon.
E   A research centre at Royal Holloway, University of London.
O   To promote and foster geographical research, consultancy and teaching in the field of development studies

Centre for Developing and Evaluating Lifelong Learning   (CDELL)   1997

■ School of Education, Jubilee Campus, University of Nottingham, Wollaton Road, Nottingham, NG8 1BB.
   0115-951 4496   fax 0115-951 4475
   http://www.nottingham.ac.uk/education/centres/cdell/
   Director: Prof Roger Murphy.
E A research centre at the University of Nottingham.
O To provide a focus for high quality research, development and dissemination activities in relation to lifelong learning

Centre for Development and Emergency Practice   (CENDEP)   1983

■ School of the Built Environment, Gipsy Lane Campus, Oxford Brookes University, Headington, Oxford, OX3 0BP.
   01865 483413   fax 01865 483298
   http://www.brookes.ac.uk/schools/be/cendep/
E A research centre at Oxford Brookes University.
O To provide consultancy worldwide on development and emergency planning issues
● Education and training - Courses including Diploma/MSc awards in development practices

Centre for the Development of Learning and Teaching   (CDLT)   2000

■ St Martin's College, Bowerham Road, Lancaster, LA1 3JD.
   01524 384695
   http://www.cdlt.ucsm.ac.uk/
   Contact: Andy Ginty.
E A research centre at St Martin's College.

Centre for Development Policy and Research   (CDPR)

■ Faculty of Law and Social Sciences, School of Oriental and African Studies, University of London, Thornhaugh Street, Russell Square, London, WC1H 0XG.
   020 7898 4473   fax 020 7898 4559
   http://www.soas.ac.uk/centres/centreinfo.cfm?navid=12
   Director: Prof John Weeks. Administrator: Jonathan Stever.
E A research centre at the School of Oriental and African Studies, University of London.
O To develop capacity for country-driven strategies and nationally owned policies that foster the reduction of poverty

Centre for Development Studies   (CDS)   1975

■ Department of Economics and International Development, University of Bath, Claverton Down, Bath, BA2 7AY.
   01225 383642   fax 01225 383423
   http://www.bath.ac.uk/cds/
   Director: Dr Sarah White.
E A research centre at the University of Bath.
O To contribute to combating to global poverty and inequality through critical engagement with development practice and policy making, and primary research into the practical reality of global poverty

Centre for Development Studies   (CDS)   1983

■ Department of Economics, University of Glasgow, Adam Smith Building, Glasgow, G12 8RT.
   0141-330 4689   fax 0141-330 4940
   http://www.gla.ac.uk/centres/developmentstudies/
   Director: Dr Alberto Paloni.
E A research centre at the University of Glasgow.
O To conduct postgraduate studies and research in the area of development studies

Centre for Development Studies   (CDS)   1984

■ School of Politics and International Studies, University of Leeds, Leeds, LS2 9JT.
   0113-343 4393   fax 0113-343 4400
   http://www.leeds.ac.uk/devstud/
   Director: Prof Ruth Pearson.
E A department of the University of Leeds.
O To generate knowledge on the development issues in low-income countries; to pursue collaborative research with institutions in the developing world

Centre for Development Studies   (CDS)   1975   Canolfan Efrydiau Datblygu

■ Swansea University, Taliesin Building, Singleton Park, Swansea, SA2 8PP.
   01792 295332   fax 01792 295682
   http://www.swan.ac.uk/cds
   Director: Dr Neil Price. Chairman, Board of PG Studies: Dr Gerard. Clarke.
E A department of Swansea University.
O To promote the study of development processes, primarily in the Third World; to provide practical support in the appraisal, monitoring, and evaluation of development projects
● Advisory and consultancy services - Conference facilities - Education and training - Information service - Library - Courses for administrators, planners and academics working in these countries (particular emphasis is given to the social aspects of development planning) - Hours Mon-Fri 0900-1700, by appointment

© CBD Research Ltd · Beckenham · Kent BR3 5JS · Tel 020 8650 7745 · Fax 020 8650 0768 · E-mail cbd@cbdresearch.com · www.cbdresearch.com

Centre for Developmental and Biomedical Genetics   (CDBG)
- University of Sheffield, Firth Court, Western Bank, Sheffield, S10 2TN.
  0114-222 2710   fax 0114-276 5413
  http://www.cdbg.group.shef.ac.uk/
  Director: Prof Philip Ingham, FRS.
- E   A Medical Research Council centre within the Krebs Institute of Biomolecular Research (qv) at the University of Sheffield.
- O   To bring together developmental geneticists, cell biologists and human pathologists with a common interest in using model organisms to understand the genetic basis of human development and disease

Note: See **Medical Research Council Collaborative Centre** for further information.

Centre for Developmental Language Disorders and Cognitive Neuroscience   (DLDCN)   2002
- Department of Human Communication Science, University College London, 4th Floor - 123-126 Gray's Inn Road, London, WC1X 8WD.
  020 7905 1212
  http://www.ucl.ac.uk/dldcn/
  Director: Prof Heather K J van der Lely.
- E   A research centre at University College London.
- O   To investigate the development of fundamental human capacities - particularly language - to elucidate the mechanism of language acquisition and provide insight into the development of specialised cognitive systems, furthering understanding of the structure and function of the human mind and its neural instantiations

Centre for Developmental Neurobiology
> see **MRC Centre for Developmental Neurobiology.**

Centre for Diabetes and Endocrinology
- Department of Medicine, University College London, Rayne Building, 5 University Street, London, WC1E 6JF.
  020 7679 6686   fax 020 7679 6211
  http://www.ucl.ac.uk/medicine/diabetes/
  Contact: Prof Dominic J Withers.
- E   A research centre at University College London.
- O   To conduct research aimed at increasing understanding of the pathogenesis of type 2 diabetes and obesity

Centre for Diabetes, Endocrinology and Metabolism
> see **Oxford Centre for Diabetes, Endocrinology and Metabolism.**

Centre for Diabetes and Metabolic Medicine   (CDMM)
- Barts and the London, Queen Mary's School of Medicine and Dentistry, Queen Mary, University of London, 4 Newark Street, London, E1 2AT.
  020 7882 2356; 2483   fax 020 7882 2200
  http://www.icms.qmul.ac.uk/centres/diabetes/
  Lead: Prof Graham A Hitman.
- E   A research centre within the Institute of Cell and Molecular Science (qv) at Queen Mary, University of London.
- O   To conduct research on the causes and treatment of diabetes mellitus, obesity and associated disorders, and the study of inherited fever syndromes

Centre for Digital Art History
> see **Vasari Centre for Digital Art History.**

Centre for Digital Imaging   (Cdi)
- School of Media Arts and Imaging, Duncan of Jordanstone College of Art and Design, University of Dundee, Dundee, DD1 4HT.
  01382 385352
  http://imaging.dundee.ac.uk/main/facilities/
- E   A research centre at the University of Dundee.

Centre for Digital Library Research   (CDLR)   2000
- Department of Computer and Information Sciences, University of Glasgow, Livingstone Tower, 26 Richmond Street, Glasgow, G1 1XH.
  0141-548 2102
  Director: Dennis Nicholson.
- E   An interdisciplinary research centre at the University of Strathclyde.

Centre for Digital Lifestyles
> see **Digital Lifestyles Centre.**

Centre for Digital Music   (CDM)
- Department of Electronic Engineering, Queen Mary's, University of London, Mile End Road, London, E1 4NS.
  020 7882 5346   fax 020 7882 7997
  http://www.elec.qmul.ac.uk/digitalmusic
  Director: Prof Mark Sandler.
- E   A research centre at Queen Mary, University of London.
- O   To conduct research in the fields of music and audio technology, with a particular emphasis on the interface between audio and music

Centre of Digital Signal Processing   (CDSP)   2004
- ■   Cardiff School of Engineering, Cardiff University, Queen's Buildings - PO Box 925, Newport Road, Cardiff, CF24 3AA.
      029 2087 5917   fax 029 2087 4716
      http://www.cardiff.ac.uk/engin/research/informationsystems/cdsp/
      Director: Prof Jonathon Chambers.
- E   A research centre within the Institute of Information Systems and Integration Technology (qv) at Cardiff University.
- O   To undertake and publish internationally-leading research in algorithmic digital signal processing and its applications to acoustics, biomedicine, computer vision, defence systems, genomics, software, radio and wireless communications

Centre for Digital Signal Processing Research   (CDSPR)   2002
- ■   School of Physical Sciences and Engineering, King's College London, Room 34B - Main Building, Strand, London, WC2R 2LS.
      020 7848 2858
      http://www.kcl.ac.uk/schools/pse/diveng/research/cdspr/
      Director: Dr Zoran Cvetkovic.
- E   A research centre at King's College, London.
- O   To conduct research in the analysis, application and design of new algorithms for digital signal processing

Centre for Diplomatic and International Studies   (CeDIS)
- ■   Department of Politics and International Relations, University of Leicester, University Road, Leicester, LE1 7RH.
      0116-252 2702   fax 0116-252 5082
      http://www.le.ac.uk/politics/cedis/
      Director: Prof John Dumbrell.
- E   A research centre at the University of Leicester.
- O   To provide a focus for international political research in African politics, American foreign policy, diplomacy, European Union politics, and feminist international relations and politics

Centre for Director Education   (CDE)   1990
- ■   Faculty of Business and Law, Leeds Metropolitan University, Civic Quarter, Leeds, LS1 3HE.
      0113-283 7531
      http://www.leedsmet.ac.uk/lbs/cde/
      Head: Nick Beech.
- E   A centre at Leeds Metropolitan University.

Centre for Disability and the Arts
> see **Richard Attenborough Centre for Disability and the Arts.**

Centre for Disability Research
> see **Strathclyde Centre for Disability Research.**

Centre for Disability Sciences
> see **Aspire Centre for Disability Sciences.**

Centre for Disability Sport
> see **Peter Harrison Centre for Disability Sport.**

Centre for Disability Studies   (CDS)   2000
- ■   School of Sociology and Social Policy, University of Leeds, Leeds, LS2 9JT.
      0113-343 4414   fax 0113-343 4415
      http://www.leeds.ac.uk/disability-studies/
- E   A research centre at the University of Leeds.
- O   To carry out research into all aspects of disability

Centre for Discrete and Applicable Mathematics   (CDAM)   1995
- ■   Department of Mathematics, LSE, Houghton Street, London, WC2A 2AE.
      020 7955 7494   fax 020 7955 6877
      http://www.cdam.lse.ac.uk/
      Director: Prof Graham Brightwell.
- E   A research centre at the London School of Economics and Political Science.
- O   To raise the profile of mathematics in the social sciences, with particular emphasis on game theory, combinatorial optimisation, theory of economic forecasting, mathematical programming, complexity theory, discrete probabilistic analysis, mathematics in finance, social choice theory, algebraic graph theory, rendezvous search theory, and artificial neural networks and computational learning theory

Centre for Dissenting Studies
> see **Dr Williams's Centre for Dissenting Studies.**

Centre for Diversity, Equity and Inclusion   (CDEI)

■ Carnegie Faculty of Sport and Education, Leeds Metropolitan University, Room 216 - Cavendish Hall, Headingley Campus, Leeds, LS6 3QS.
 0113-283 2600   fax 0113-283 6171
 http://www.leedsmet.ac.uk/carnegie/8499.htm
E A research centre within the Carnegie Research Institute (qv) at Leeds Metropolitan University.
O To promote social change that will redress inequalities

Centre for Diversity Policy Research   (CfDPR)

■ Oxford Brookes Business School, Wheatley Campus, Oxford Brookes University, Wheatley, Oxford, OX33 1HX.
 01865 485796
 http://www.business.brookes.ac.uk/
 Director: Simonetta Manfredi.
E A research centre at Oxford Brookes University.
O To carry out research into equality and diversity issues in employment; to undertake projects that will underpin policy development and inform best practice in the workplace

Centre for Diversity and Work Psychology   (CDWP)

■ Manchester Business School, University of Manchester, Booth Street West, Manchester, M15 6PB.
 0161-306 3439   fax 0161-306 3450
 http://www.mbs.ac.uk/research/diversitypsychology/
 Co-Director: Dr Sandra Fielden. Co-Director: Prof Marilyn Davidson.
E A research centre at the University of Manchester.
O To pursue new knowledge relating to successfully managing diversity initiatives in organisations

Centre for Drawing

■ Wimbledon College of Art, Main Building, University of the Arts, London, Merton Hall Road, London, SW19 3QA.
 020 7514 9641   fax 020 7514 9642
 http://www.wimbledon.arts.ac.uk/32386.htm
E A research centre at the University of the Arts, London.

Centre for Drug Misuse Research   (CDMR)   1994

■ Faculty of Law, Business and Social Sciences, University of Glasgow, 89 Dumbarton Road, Glasgow, G11 6PW.
 0141-330 3616   fax 0141-330 2820
 http://www.gla.ac.uk/drugmisuse/
 Director: Prof Neil McKeganey.
E A research centre at the University of Glasgow.
O To conduct high quality, policy relevant research on the problem of drug misuse within Scotland

Centre for Dutch Studies   (CDS)   2005

■ University of Sheffield, University of Sheffield, Western Bank, Sheffield, S10 2TN
 0114-222 2000
 http://dutchcentre.group.shef.ac.uk/
 Director: Roel Vismans.
E A research centre at the University of Sheffield.
O To be a national and international focus for academic Dutch studies; to stimulate a wider interest in the culture of the Low Countries locally and in the region

Centre for Dynamic Macroeconomic Analysis   (CDMA)   2003

■ School of Economics and Finance, University of St Andrews, Castlecliffe, The Scores, St Andrews, Fife, KY16 9AL.
 01334 462445   fax 01334 462444
 http://www.st-andrews.ac.uk/cdma/
 Director: Prof Charles Nolan.
E A research centre at the University of St Andrews.
O To foster research in characterising the key stylised facts of the business cycle, and constructing theoretical models that can match these business cycles

Centre for e-Research

■ H H Wills Physics Laboratory, University of Bristol, Royal Fort, Tyndall Avenue, Bristol, BS8 1TL.
 0117-928 8769   fax 0117-925 5624
 http://escience.bristol.ac.uk/
E A research centre at the University of Bristol.
Note: See **e-Science Centres of Excellence** for further information.

Centre for e-Science
 see **Lancaster Centre for e-Science.**

Centre for e-Security   2003
- Faculty of Business, Computing and Information Management, London South Bank University, 103 Borough Road, London, SE1 0AA.
  020 7815 7413
  http://www.lsbu.ac.uk/bcimicr/research/esec.shtml
  Head: Prof Ali Abdallah.
- E   A research centre within the Institute for Computing Research (qv) at London South Bank University.

Centre for Early Modern Studies   (CEMS)
- School of Language and Literature, King's College, University of Aberdeen, Aberdeen, AB24 3FX.
  01224 272534   fax 01224 272624
  http://www.abdn.ac.uk/cems/
  Director: Prof Derek Hughes.
- E   A centre at the University of Aberdeen.
- O   To foster collaborative research in the fields of history, philosophy, religion, literature, and the arts

Centre for Early Modern Studies   (CEMS)
- School of Humanities, University of Sussex, Arts B 263, Falmer, Brighton, East Sussex, BN1 9SJ.
  01273 877627
  http://www.sussex.ac.uk/gchums/
  Co-Director: Andrew Hadfield. Co-Director: Brian Cummings.
- E   An interdisciplinary research centre at the University of Sussex.
- O   To pursue research in all areas of the early-modern period, broadly 1350-1800

Centre for Early Music Performance Research   (CEMPR)   1998
- Department of Music, University of Birmingham, Edgbaston, Birmingham, B15 2TT.
  0121-414 5782   fax 0121-414 5668
  http://www.music.bham.ac.uk/cempr/
  Director: Mary O'Neill.
- E   A research centre at the University of Birmingham.
- O   To bring together academic and performance research in early music at the highest professional level

Centre for Earth and Environmental Science Research   (CEESR)
- School of Earth Sciences and Geography, Kingston University, London, Penrhyn Road, Kingston-upon-Thames, Surrey, KT1 2EE.
  020 8547 2000; 7544
  http://www.kingston.ac.uk/esg/research/research.htm
  Head: Prof Gavin Gilmore.
- E   A research centre at Kingston University, London.
- O   To conduct research in the areas of geodynamics and crustal processes, environmental change, and rural geography and social change

Centre for Earth, Planetary, Space and Astronomical Research   (CEPSAR)
- Open University, Walton Hall, Milton Keynes, MK7 6AA.
  0870 333 4340
  http://cepsar.open.ac.uk/
  Director: Prof John Zarnecki. Deputy Director: Dr Ian Wright.
- E   An interdisciplinary research centre at the Open University.
- O   To study the origins, systems and processes with respect to the evolution and chemistry that form the stars and planetary bodies, the processes and natural systems that shape the environment of our habitable world now and in the past, and the essential properties of a solar system that allows life to develop on one of its planets

Centre of East Anglian Studies   (CEAS)   1967
- School of History, University of East Anglia, Norwich, NR4 7TJ.
  01603 592076; 592081   fax 01603 250434
  http://www1.uea.ac.uk/cm/home/schools/hum/his/ceas
  Director: Prof Carole Rawcliffe.
- E   A registered charity, an association with a voluntary subscribing membership and a department of the University of East Anglia.
- O   To conduct teaching and research in local and regional history
- ●   Conference facilities - Education and training - Information service - Open for public enquiries during office hours

Centre of East Asian Law   (CEAL)   1988
- Faculty of Law and Social Sciences, School of Oriental and African Studies, University of London, Thornhaugh Street, Russell Square, London, WC1H 0XG.
  020 7898 4411; 4671   fax 020 7898 4559
  http://www.oas.ac.uk/centres/centreinfo.cfm?navid=13
  Chairman: Prof Michael J E Palmer.
- E   An interdisciplinary research centre at the School of Oriental and African Studies, University of London.
- O   To focus research and practical investigation into both developing and developed legal systems in the Region

© CBD Research Ltd · Beckenham · Kent BR3 5JS · Tel 020 8650 7745 · Fax 020 8650 0768 · E-mail cbd@cbdresearch.com · www.cbdresearch.com

Centre for East Asian Studies   (CEAS)
■ University of Bristol, 8 Woodland Road, Bristol, BS8 1TN.
  0117-954 5577
  http://www.bris.ac.uk/ceas/
  Contact: Emma Holland.
E An interdisciplinary research centre in the University of Bristol.
O To bring together expertise from a wide range of disciplines to understand the societies of East Asia
● MSc in East Asian Studies

Centre of Eating, Food and Health
■ Faculty of Health, Leeds Metropolitan University, Civic Quarter, Calverley Street, Leeds, LS1 3HE.
  0113-283 2600   fax 0113-283 1908
  http://www.leedsmet.ac.uk/health/cefh/
  Director: Prof Mike Thomas.
E A research centre at Leeds Metropolitan University.
O To focus research on issues in the area of food, food composition and eating behaviours

Centre for EcoChemistry
  see **Cranfield Centre for EcoChemistry.**

Centre for Ecological Restoration
  see **Cranfield Centre for Ecological Restoration.**

Centre for Ecology and Evolution   (CEE)
■ Department of Biology, University College London, The Darwin Building, Gower Street, London, WC1E 6BT.
  020 7679 2983; 7098   fax 020 7679 7096
  http://www.ucl.ac.uk/%7Eucbtcee/cee/
  Director: Prof Linda Partridge.
E A research centre at University College London.
O To foster research and develop and extend its national and international standing as a centre of excellence in ecology and evolution

Centre for Ecology, Evolution and Conservation   (CEEC)
■ School of Environmental Sciences, University of East Anglia, Norwich, NR4 7TJ.
  01603 592537   fax 01603 507719
  http://www.uea.ac.uk/ceec/
  Director: Dr Alastair Grant.
E A research centre at the University of East Anglia.
O To conduct research in terrestrial, freshwater and marine systems, and grouped into four broad themes including, behavioural ecology and populations, contaminated environments, chemical and ecosystem ecology, conservation, and molecular ecology and evolution

Centre for Ecology and Hydrology   (CEH)   2000
NR Polaris House, North Star Avenue, Swindon, Wiltshire, SN2 1EU.
  01793 442516   fax 01793 442528
  http://www.ceh.ac.uk/
  Director: Prof Pat Nuttall, OBE. Head of Administration: Brian Butler.
E A non-profit-making research centre of the UK research councils.
O To advance through research the science and understanding of hydrology, terrestrial and freshwater, estuarine and microbial ecosystems; to monitor present, and predict future, changes in these systems and to provide data and advice to Government; to promote research findings, inventions and data; to enhance UK industrial competitiveness and our quality of life
● Education and training - Library
¶ Annual Report.
× Environmental Information Centre.
Note: The Centre has eight other sites - see **CEH**

Centre for Ecology, Law and Policy   (CELP)
■ Environment Department, University of York, Heslington, York, YO10 5DD.
  01904 432999   fax 01904 432998
  http://www.york.ac.uk/res/celp/
  Director: Dr Jon Lovett.
E An interdisciplinary research centre at the University of York.
O To integrate the disciplines of law, ecology and policy in order to reach a better understanding of how society and the environment interact

Centre for Econometric Analysis   (CEA@Cass

- Cass Business School, City University, 106 Bunhill Row, London, EC1Y 8TZ.
  020 7040 8698   fax 020 7040 8881
  http://www.cass.city.ac.uk/cea/
  Contact: Prof Giovanni Urga. Chairman: Chihwa Kao.
- E   A centre at City University.
- O   To promote and support research activities, acting as a pole of attraction for leading researchers, in the field of econometrics (methodological and applied, macro and micro), financial econometrics, and other quantitative methods used in finance, and theoretical and empirical research in financial markets and corporate finance

Centre for the Economic and Behavioural Analysis of Risk and Decision   (CEBARD)   2001

- School of Environmental Sciences, University of East Anglia, Norwich, NR4 7TJ.
  01603 593113   fax 01603 591327
  http://www.uea.ac.uk/cebard/
- E   A research centre within the Zuckerman Institute for Connective Environmental Research (qv) at the University of East Anglia.
- O   To conduct high quality research into the analysis of preferences and decision making, particularly in the context of environmental, health and safety issues

Centre for Economic Botany   (CEB)

- Royal Botanic Gardens, Kew, Richmond, Surrey, TW9 3AE.
  020 8332 5655   fax 020 8332 5768
  http://www.kew.org/scihort/ecbot/
  Director: Prof Monique Simmonds.
- E   Part of the Sustainable Uses of Plants Group at the Royal Botanic Gardens, Kew.
- O   To provide a focal point for research into plants which are useful or potentially useful; to care for the Economic Botany Collection of more than 79,000 artefacts

Centre for Economic Development and Institutions   (CEDI)   2005

- Brunel University, Uxbridge, Middlesex, UB8 3PH.
  01895 274000
  http://www.cedi.org.uk/
- E   A centre at Brunel University.
- O   To focus on how a country's economic performance is affected by its institutions - institutions that function to secure property rights, govern firms, allocate credit, redistribute wealth, select political leaders, etc

Centre for Economic Learning and Social Evolution
> see **ESRC Centre for Economic Learning and Social Evolution.**

Centre for Economic Methodology
> see **Stirling Centre for Economic Methodology.**

Centre for Economic Modelling
> see **Experian Centre for Economic Modelling.**

Centre for Economic Performance   (CEP)   1990

- LSE, Houghton Street, London, WC2A 2AE.
  020 7955 7284   fax 020 7955 6848
  http://cep.lse.ac.uk/
  Director: Prof John Van Reenen. Research Director: Prof Stephen Machin.
- E   A department of the London School of Economics and Political Science.
- O   To study the determinants of economic performance at the level of the company, the nation and the global economy by focusing on the major links between globalisation, technology and institutions, and their impact on productivity, inequality, employment, stability and wellbeing
- ¶   CentrePiece Magazine. (see website for other publications).

Centre for Economic Policy Research   (CEPR)   1983

- 90-98 Goswell Road, London, EC1V 7RR.
  020 7878 2900   fax 020 7878 2999
  http://www.cepr.org/
  Chairman: Guillermo de la Dehesa. Chief Executive Officer: Stephen Yeo.
- E   A company limited by guarantee and a non-profit-making educational charity.
- O   To promote independent, objective analysis and public discussion of open economies and relations amongst them
- ●   Colloquia and conferences - Seminars - Workshops
Note: The CEPR functions as an international organisation.

Centre for Economic and Public Policy
> see **Cambridge Centre for Economic and Public Policy.**

Centre for Economic Reform and Transformation   (CERT)   1990
- ■ School of Management and Languages, Heriot-Watt University, Riccarton, Edinburgh, EH14 4AS.
     0131-451 3485   fax 0131-451 3498
     http://www.som.hw.ac.uk/cert/
     Director: Prof Mark Schaffer.
- E A research centre at Heriot-Watt University.
- O To focus research on the transition economies of Central and Eastern Europe, the former Soviet Union, and East Asia

Centre for Economic Renewable Power Delivery   (CERPD)
- ■ Department of Electronic and Electrical Engineering, University of Strathclyde, Royal College Building, 204 George Street, Glasgow, G1 1XW.
     0141-548 2485   fax 0141-548 4872
     http://www.instee.strath.ac.uk/content/default.asp?page=s4_1_6
     Head: Prof Scott J MacGregor.
- E A research centre within the Institute for Energy and Environment (qv) at the University of Strathclyde.
- O To conduct research and education in the search for clean power
Note: A joint venture with the University of Glasgow.

Centre for Economic Renewable Power Delivery   (CERPD)   1999
- ■ Department of Electronics and Electrical Engineering, University of Glasgow, Rankine Building, Oakfield Avenue, Glasgow, G12 8LT.
     0141-330 5050; 5978   fax 0141-330 4907
     http://www.elec.gla.ac.uk/groups/cerpd/en_de2_IE.htm
     Chairman: Dr Enrique Acha.
- E A centre at the University of Glasgow.
- O To conduct research and education in the search for clean power

Centre for Economic Research and Intelligence   (CERI)
- ■ Kingston University, London, 53-57 High Street, Kingston-upon-Thames, Surrey, KT1 1LQ.
     020 8547 7221   fax 020 8547 8132
     http://www.kingston.ac.uk/business-services/ceri/ceri.htm
     Director: Peter Garside.
- E A research centre at Kingston University, London.

Centre for Economic Research on Ageing   (CERA)
- ■ Institute for Fiscal Studies, 3rd Floor - 7 Ridgmount Street, London, WC1E 7AE.
     020 7291 4800   fax 020 7323 4780
     http://www.ifs.org.uk/cera/
- E A research centre within the Institute for Fiscal Studies (qv).

Centre for Economic and Social Aspects of Genomics   (CESAGen)
- ■ Cardiff School of Social Sciences, Cardiff University, Glamorgan Building, King Edward VII Avenue, Cardiff, CF10 3WT.
     029 2087 5179   fax 029 2087 4175
     http://www.cesagen.lancs.ac.uk/
- E A centre at Cardiff University.
- O To bring together natural and social scientists to research the economic, social and ethical consequences of genomic and genetic science

Centre for Economic and Social Aspects of Genomics   (CESAGen)
- ■ Lancaster University, County South, Bailrigg, Lancaster, LA1 4YD.
     01524 510856
     http://www.cesagen.lancs.ac.uk/
     Contact: Penny Burton.
- E A research centre within the Institute for Philosophy and Public Policy (qv) at Lancaster University.
- O To bring together natural and social scientists to research the economic, social and ethical consequences of genomic and genetic science

Centre for Economics and Business Education   (CEBE)   1992
- ■ Staffordshire University, Brindley Building, Leek Road, Stoke-on-Trent, ST4 2DF.
     01782 295731
     http://www.staffs.ac.uk/schools/business/iepr/cebe.htm
- E A sub-group of the Institute for Education Policy Research (qv) at Staffordshire University.

Centre for Economics and Finance Research   (CEFR)   2005
- ■ Faculty of Business, Law and the Built Environment, University of Salford, Salford, Manchester, M5 4WT.
     0161-295 5000   fax 0161-295 2130
     http://www.mams.salford.ac.uk/mams/m/?s=7
- E An interdisciplinary research centre within the Management and Management Sciences Research Institute (qv) at the University of Salford.
- O To conduct teaching and research in overlapping fields of interest within economics, finance, accounting and banking

Centre for the Economics of Education   (CEE)   2000

NR   LSE, Houghton Street, London, WC2A 2AE.
     020 7955 7284   fax 020 7955 7595
     http://cee.lse.ac.uk/
     Director: Prof Stephen Machin.
E   A research centre within the Centre for Economic Performance (qv) at the London School of Economics and Political Science.
O   To undertake systematic and innovative research in the field of the economics of education by applying the latest techniques of empirical analysis
Note: A joint venture with the Institute of Education (qv), and the Institute for Fiscal Studies (qv).

Centre for the Economics of Health   (CEH)   Canolfan Economeg Iechyd

■   University of Wales Bangor, Dean Street Building, Bangor, Gwynedd, LL57 1UT.
     01248 388314   fax 01248 383982
     http://www.bangor.ac.uk/healtheconomics/
     Director: Dr Rhiannon Tudor Edwards.
E   A research centre within the Institute of Medical and Social Care Research (qv) at the University of Wales, Bangor.
O   To develop a programme of research and to provide policy support to the National Assembly for Wales from a standpoint of recognition of the wider economics of improving the health of the population

Centre for the Economics of Mental Health   (CEMH)

■   PO Box 24, King's College London, DeCrespigny Park, London, SE5 8AF.
     020 7848 0198   fax 020 7848 7600
     http://www.iop.kcl.ac.uk/departments/?locator=355
     Contact: Prof Martin R J Knapp.
E   A research centre within the Institute of Psychiatry (qv) at King's College, London.
O   To evaluate the economic effectiveness of the large range of treatments and services designed to help people with mental health problems

Centre for *Editing Lives and Letters*
    see **AHRC Centre for Editing Lives and Letters.**

Centre for Editorial and Intertextual Research   (CEIR)   1997

■   Cardiff School of English, Communication and Philosophy, Cardiff University, Colum Drive, Cardiff, CF10 3XB.
     029 2087 4040   fax 029 2087 4020
     http://www.cardiff.ac.uk/encap/ceir/
     Director: Prof David Skilton.
E   A centre at Cardiff University.
O   To combine traditional scholarly skills with modern technological methodologies, in order to address various aspects of textual and bibliographical research in English literary studies

Centre for *Education*
    see **Subject Centre for Education.**

Centre for Education in the Built Environment   (CEBE)   2000

■   Cardiff University, Bute Building, King Edward VII Avenue, Cardiff, CF10 3NB.
     029 2087 4600   fax 029 2087 4601
     http://www.cebe.heacademy.ac.uk/
E   A Government funded national centre within the Cardiff University.
O   To foster world-class education in the built environment, especially in the areas of architecture, landscape, planning, housing and transport
●   Education and training - Information service - Statistics
×   LTSN Built Environment Subject Centre.
Note: One of the 24 Subject Centres of the Higher Education Academy, (qv).

Centre for Education in the Built Environment   (CEBE)   2000

■   School of Construction and Property Management, University of Salford, Maxwell Building, Salford, Manchester, M5 4WT.
     0161-295 5944   fax 0161-295 5110
     http://www.cebe.heacademy.ac.uk/
E   A Government funded national centre within the University of Salford.
O   To foster world-class education in the built environment, especially in the areas of construction, surveying and real estate
●   Education and training - Information service - Statistics
×   LTSN Built Environment Subject Centre.
Note: One of the 24 Subject Centres of the Higher Education Academy, (qv).

Centre for Education and Employment Research   (CEER)

■   Department of Education, University of Buckingham, Hunter Street, Buckingham, MK18 1EG.
     01280 820219   fax 01280 822245
     http://www.buckingham.ac.uk/education/research/ceer/
     Co-Director: Prof Alan Smithers. Co-Director: Dr Pamela Robinson.
E   A centre at the University of Buckingham.
O   To describe and interpret the current state of education, for policymakers, practitioners and others who make education happen

© CBD Research Ltd · Beckenham · Kent BR3 5JS · Tel 020 8650 7745 · Fax 020 8650 0768 · E-mail cbd@cbdresearch.com · www.cbdresearch.com

Centre for Education and Finance Management   (CEFM)   1990
- ■   Red Lion House, 9-10 High Street, High Wycombe, Buckinghamshire, HP11 2AZ.
     01494 459183   fax 01494 474480
     http://www.ceduman.co.uk/
- E   An independent company.
- O   To assist schools on financial, educational, personnel and legal matters

Centre for Education and Industry   (CEI)   1987
- ■   Faculty of Social Studies, University of Warwick, Coventry, CV4 7AL.
     024 7652 3909   fax 024 7652 3617
     http://www2.warwick.ac.uk/fac/soc/cei/
     Director: Prof Prue Huddleston.
- E   A research centre within the Warwick Institute of Education (qv) at the University of Warwick.
- O   To improve knowledge and understanding of how work-related and vocational learning can enhance skills, capabilities and
     motivation to learn for all age groups; to extend and develop the range of activities through which schools and colleges can work
     with a range of partners, (including business), to provide learning experiences which enhance employability; to develop, test and
     evaluate policies, strategies, programmes and resources in education and training, particularly in work-related and vocational
     learning

Centre for Education, Leadership and Professional Development   (CELPD)
- ■   Carnegie Faculty of Sport and Education, Leeds Metropolitan University, Room 216 - Cavendish Hall, Headingley Campus, Leeds,
     LS6 3QS.
     0113-283 2600   fax 0113-283 6171
     http://www.leedsmet.ac.uk/carnegie/8507.htm
- E   A research centre within the Carnegie Research Institute (qv) at Leeds Metropolitan University.
- O   To conduct research aimed at informing the development of education practice and the enhancement of learning experiences

Centre for Education in Medicine
     see **Open University Centre for Education in Medicine.**

Centre in Education for Pluralism, Human Rights and Democracy
     see **UNESCO Centre in Education for Pluralism, Human Rights and Democracy.**

Centre for Education and Professional Practice
     see **Research Centre for Education and Professional Practice.**

Centre for Education Psychology Research   (CEPR)
- ■   Faculty of Health and Sciences, Staffordshire University, Mellor Building, College Road, Stoke-on-Trent, ST4 2DF.
     01782 294648
     http://www.staffs.ac.uk/personal/sciences/mt15/eduweb/
- E   A sub-group of the Institute for Education Policy Research (qv) at Staffordshire University.
- O   To apply psychology to educational contexts

Centre for Education Research   (CER)
- ■   Sheffield Hallam University, 33 Collegiate Crescent, Sheffield, S10 2BP.
     0114-225 5652
     http://www.shu.ac.uk/research/cer/
     Director: John Coldron. Research Administrator: Brenda Bottomley.
- E   A research centre at Sheffield Hallam University.
- O   To provide a focus for educational contract research and consultancy

Centre for Educational and Academic Practices   **(CEAP)**
- ■   City University, Drysdale Building, Northampton Square, London, EC1V 0HB.
     020 7040 0177   fax 020 7040 0178
     http://www.city.ac.uk/ceap
- E   A centre at City University.
- O   To promote a creative, innovative and scholarly approach to teaching and learning through the development of pedagogic
     research culture
              Educational Development Centre

Centre for Educational Development   (CED)
- ■   Open University, Walton Hall, Milton Keynes, MK7 6AA.
     01908 274066
     http://iet.open.ac.uk/about/maingroups/ced/
- E   A research centre within the Institute of Educational Technology (qv) at the Open University.

Centre for Educational Development, Appraisal and Research (CEDAR) 1987
- ■ Faculty of Social Studies, University of Warwick, Coventry, CV4 7AL.
  024 7652 4139   fax 024 7652 4609
  http://www2.warwick.ac.uk/fac/soc/cedar
  Director: Prof Geoff Lindsay.
- E A research centre within the Warwick Institute of Education (qv) at the University of Warwick.
- ○ To conduct research on educational appraisal, assessment and evaluation in all phases of nursery, primary, secondary, further and higher education throughout the UK
- ● Education and training - Information service

Centre for Educational Development and Materials   (CEDM)
- ■ University of Derby, Kedleston Road, Derby, DE22 1GB.
  01332 591635
  http://www.derby.ac.uk/cedm/
  Head: Chris Whitehouse.
- E A department of the University of Derby.
- ○ To support learning, teaching and the marketing of the University through the provision of diverse specialist services

Centre for Educational Innovation   (CEI)
- ■ Sussex School of Education, University of Sussex, Essex House, Falmer, Brighton, East Sussex, BN1 9QQ.
  01273 678464
  http://www.sussex.ac.uk/education/1-4-22.html
  Director: Prof Michael Fielding.
- E A research centre within the Sussex Institute (qv) at the University of Sussex.
- ○ To provide a forum for innovative work with schools and colleges in the region, primarily in the areas of leadership, pupil-centred learning and student voice

Centre for Educational Leadership   (CEL) 1997
- ■ School of Education, University of Manchester, Oxford Road, Manchester, M13 9PL.
  0161-275 3462   fax 0161-275 7970
  http://www.cel.manchester.ac.uk/
  Director: Brendan Murden.
- E A research centre at the University of Manchester.
- ○ To achieve international excellence in leadership development and organisational learning in the public sector

Centre for Educational Leadership and Management   (CELM) 1992
- ■ School of Education, University of Leicester, 162-166 Upper New Walk, Leicester, LE1 7QA.
  0116-229 7500   fax 0116-229 7501
  http://www.le.ac.uk/se/centres/celm/
  Director: Prof Clive Dimmock.
- E A research centre at the University of Leicester.
- ○ To conduct research and teaching in the field of educational ladership and management

Centre for Educational Research
Note: is now the Education Research Group and is therefore outside the scope of this directory.

Centre for Educational Sociology (CES) 1972
- ■ Department of Education and Society, University of Edinburgh, St John's Land, Holyrood Road, Edinburgh, EH8 8AQ.
  0131-651 6238   fax 0131-651 6239
  http://www.ces.ed.ac.uk/
- E A research centre at the University of Edinburgh.
- ○ To conduct multi-disciplinary research on education, training, the youth labour market and transitions to adulthood, with a complementary research interest in information systems

Centre for Educational Studies   2002   Canolfan Astudiaethau Addysg (CAA)
- ■ School of Education and Lifelong Learning, University of Wales, Aberystwyth, Yr Hen Goleg, Stryd y Brenin, Aberystwyth, Ceredigion, SY23 2AX.
  01970 622128   fax 01970 622122
  http://www.caa-aber.org.uk/
  Director: Helen Emanuel Davies.
- E An educational publishing agency and part of the University of Wales, Aberystwyth.
- ○ To publish educational titles, especially resources designed to enhance the development of Welsh as a second language and to encourage so-called 'reluctant readers'

Centre for Educational Studies   (CES)
- ■ University of Hull, Cottingham Road, Hull, HU6 7RX.
  01482 465406   fax 01482 466103
  http://www.hull.ac.uk/ces/
- E A research centre within the Institute for Learning (qv) at the University of Hull.

© CBD Research Ltd · Beckenham · Kent BR3 5JS · Tel 020 8650 7745 · Fax 020 8650 0768 · E-mail cbd@cbdresearch.com · www.cbdresearch.com

Centre for Educational Support
- ■ Department of Educational and Professional Studies, University of Strathclyde, Sir Henry Wood Building, 76 Southbrae Drive, Glasgow, G13 1PP.
   0141-950 3330   fax 0141-959 3129
   http://www.strath.ac.uk/eps/centresdivisions/ces/
   Contact: Mrs Moira McAvoy.
- E A research centre at the University of Strathclyde.

Centre for Educational Technology and Distance Learning
Note: See **Centre for Learning, Innovation and Collaboration.**

Centre for Educational Technology Interoperability Standards   (CETIS)
- ■ University of Bolton, Deane Road, Bolton, Lancashire, BL3 5AB.
   01204 903851
   http://www.cetis.ac.uk/
   Contact: Lisa Corley.
- E A research centre at the University of Bolton.

Centre for Effective Dispute Resolution   (CEDR)   1990
- ■ International Dispute Resolution Centre, 70 Fleet Street, London, EC4Y 1EU.
   020 7536 6000   fax 020 7536 6001
   http://www.cedr.co.uk/
   Chairman: Sir Peter Middleton.
- E An independent non-profit organisation.
- O To encourage and develop mediation and other cost-effective dispute resolution and prevention techniques in commercial and public-sector disputes and civil litigation

Centre for Effective Learning in Science   (CELS)   2005
- ■ School of Biomedical and Natural Sciences, Nottingham Trent University, Clifton Lane, Nottingham, NG11 8NS.
   0115-848 3915
   http://www.ntu.ac.uk/cels/
   Director: Dr Karen Moss. Administrator: Anne Rockliffe.
- E A Centre for Excellence in Teaching and Learning (CETL) at Nottingham Trent University.
- O To create a more relevant, accessible and achievable image for science, within both the higher education and school communities, through development and trials of new approaches to the teaching and presentation of science
Note: See **Centres for Excellence in Teaching and Learning** for more information.

Centre for Eighteenth Century Studies   (CECS)   2002
- ■ School of Languages, Literatures and Performing Arts, Queen's University Belfast, University Square, Belfast, BT7 1NN.
   028 9097 5363
   http://www.qub.ac.uk/schools/CentreforEighteenthCenturyStudies/
   Director: Prof Simon Davies.
- E An interdisciplinary research centre at Queen's University, Belfast.

Centre for Eighteenth Century Studies   (CECS)   1996
- ■ University of York, The King's Manor, York, YO1 7EP.
   01904 434980
   http://www.york.ac.uk/inst/cecs/
   Co-Director: Prof John Barrell. Co-Director: Prof Alan Forrest.
- E An interdisciplinary research centre at the University of York.
- O To further study and research in the 'long' eighteenth century, 1650-1850

Centre for eLearning Development   (CeLD)   2003
- ■ University of Stirling, Stirling, FK9 4LA.
   01786 467247   fax 01786 466886
   http://www.celd.stir.ac.uk/
   Manager: Simon Booth.
- E An interdisciplinary research centre at the University of Stirling.
- O To ensure that the University plays a leading part in the development of eLearning

Centre for Election Law   (CEL)
- ■ Department of Law, University of Surrey, Guildford, Surrey, GU2 7XH.
   01483 686220   fax 01483 686171
   http://www.surrey.ac.uk/law/research_centres.htm
- E A research centre at the University of Surrey.
- O To conduct research in a variety of issues connected to election law, including voting rights, campaign finance, election law and human rights, comparative election law, and election communications

Centre for Electrical Power Engineering   (CEPE)   1990

■   Department of Electronic and Electrical Engineering, University of Strathclyde, Royal College Building, 204 George Street, Glasgow, G1 1XW.
   0141-548 2485   fax 0141-548 4872
   http://www.instee.strath.ac.uk/content/default.asp?page=s1
   Head: Prof Scott J MacGregor.
E   A research centre within the Institute for Energy and Environment (qv) at the University of Strathclyde.

Centre for Electron Microscopy   (CEM)

■   University of Birmingham, Metallurgy and Materials Building, Edgbaston, Birmingham, B15 2TT.
   0121-414 5449   fax 0121-414 5449
   http://www.cem.bham.ac.uk/
   Director: Prof Ian Jones.
E   A centre at the University of Birmingham.
○   To offer facilities, services and training in electronic microscopy for both the life sciences and material sciences

Centre for Electron Microscopy and Microanalysis
   see **Sorby Centre for Electron Microscopy and Microanalysis.**

Centre for Electron Optical Studies   (CEOS)   1976

■   University of Bath, Building 3 West - Room 2-11, Claverton Down, Bath, BA2 7AY.
   01225 386681   fax 01225 386098
   http://www.bath.ac.uk/ceos/
   Experimental Officer: H R Perrott Experimental Officer: U J Potter.
E   A research centre at the University of Bath.
○   To provide facilities and expertise in carrying out electron optical investigations and x-ray analysis for researchers in both physical and life sciences
●   Contract research is undertaken

Centre for Electronic Arts
   see **Lansdown Centre for Electronic Arts.**

Centre for Electronic Commerce
   see **Centre for Internet Technologies**

Centre for Electronic Devices and Materials

■   City Campus, Sheffield Hallam University, Sheffield, S1 1WB.
   0114-225 3500   fax 0114-225 3501
   http://www.shu.ac.uk/research/meri/electronic/
   Head: Prof Jan Evans-Freeman.
E   A constituent research centre within the Materials and Engineering Research Institute (qv) at Sheffield Hallam University.
○   To conduct research in the use of functional electronic materials for novel and innovative devices

Centre for Electronic Imaging
   see **e2v Centre for Electronic Imaging.**

Centre for Electronic Media in Fine Art
   see **Slade Centre for Electronic Media in Fine Art.**

Centre for Electronic Product Engineering   (CEPE)   1994

■   School of Electronics, University of Glamorgan, Llantwit Road, Treforest, Pontypridd, CF37 1DL.
   01443 482542   fax 01443 483651
   http://www.glam.ac.uk/soeschool/CEPE/
   Manager: Clive Thomas.
E   A research centre at the University of Glamorgan.

Centre for Electronic Systems   (CES)   1995

■   School of Engineering, University of Durham, South Road, Durham, DH1 3LE.
   0191-334 2444   fax 0191-334 2390
   http://www.dur.ac.uk/ces/
   Contact: Miss Janice Smith.
E   A centre at the University of Durham.
○   To provide a focus for technology transfer activities associated with electronics and information engineering systems

Centre for Emblem Studies   (CES)

■   School of Modern Languages and Cultures, University of Glasgow, Glasgow, G12 8QQ.
    0141-330 6355   fax 0141-330 4234
    http://www.ces.arts.gla.ac.uk/
    Head: Prof Alison Adams.
E   A research centre at the University of Glasgow.
O   To conduct research in a broad range of emblems
●   Glasgow Emblem Digitisation Project - Italian Emblem Digitisation Project

Centre for Emergency Preparedness and Response
    see **Health Protection Agency Centre for Emergency Preparedness and Response.**

Centre for Empirical Finance   (CIF)

■   School of Management and Business, Cledwyn Building, University of Wales Aberystwyth, Aberystwyth, Ceredigion, SY23 2DD.
    01970 622202   fax 01970 622409
    http://www.aber.ac.uk/smba/en/research/cef/cef.shtml
    Director: Prof Owain ap Gwilym.
E   A research centre at the University of Wales, Aberystwyth.
O   To co-ordinate and conduct research in finance

Centre for Empirical Legal Research   1995

■   Faculty of Laws, University College London, Bentham House, Endsleigh Gardens, London, WC1H 0EG.
    020 7679 2000
    http://www.ucl.ac.uk/laws/socio-legal/
E   A research centre at University College London.
O   To conduct empirical research which investigates the operation and effects of law within the context of the social, economic and
        political environment
×   Centre for Socio-Legal Studies.

Centre for Employability   (CfE)

■   Fylde Building, University of Central Lancashire, Preston, PR1 2HE.
    01772 893865   fax 01772 892918
    http://www.uclan.ac.uk/facs/class/cfe/
    Contact: David Bagley.
E   A centre at the University of Central Lancashire.

Centre for Employability Through the Humanities   (CETH)   2005

■   Faculty of Design and Technology, University of Central Lancashire, Preston, PR1 2HE.
    01772 893865
    http://www.uclan.ac.uk/ceth/
    Director: David Bagley.
E   A Centre for Excellence in Teaching and Learning (CETL) at the University of Central Lancashire.
Note: See **Centres for Excellence in Teaching and Learning** for more information.

Centre for Employment Research

■   Westminster Business School, University of Westminster, 35 Marylebone Road, London, NW1 5LS.
    020 7911 5000 ext 3423   fax 020 7915 5421
    http://www.wmin.ac.uk/wbs/page-54
    Director: Peter Urwin.
E   A research centre at the University of Westminster.
O   To conduct research on employment-related issues

Centre for Enablement
    see **Oxford Centre for Enablement.**

Centre for Energy and the Environment   (CEE)   2001

■   Department of Engineering, City University, Tait Building, Northampton Square, London, EC1V 0HB.
    020 7040 0113
    http://www.city.ac.uk/sems/research/cee/
E   A centre at City University.
O   To conduct research in three main areas - flow combustion and emissions in automotive engines, industrial applications of CFD,
        and positive displacement compressors

Centre for Energy and the Environment   (CEE)   1977

■   University of Exeter, Room 303 - Physics Building, Exeter, EX4 4QL.
    01392 264141   fax 01392 264143
    http://www.centres.ex.ac.uk/cee/
    Director: Dr Trevor Preist.
E   A research centre at the University of Exeter.
O   To provide solutions to energy and environmental problems, especially in the areas of energy in buildings, transport, recycling,
        noise and vibration, water, and computer modelling

Centre for Energy, Petroleum and Mineral Law and Policy   (CEPMLP)   1977
- ■ Postgraduate School of Management and Policy, University of Dundee, Dundee, DD1 4HN.
   01382 384300   fax 01382 322578
   http://www.dundee.ac.uk/cepmlp/
- E An interdisciplinary research centre at the University of Dundee.

Centre for Energy Regulation and Obesity
   see **Aberdeen Centre for Energy Regulation and Obesity.**

Centre for Energy Research
   see **Joule Centre for Energy Research.**

Centre for Energy Studies   1983
- ■ Faculty of Engineering, Science and the Built Environment, London South Bank University, 103 Borough Road, London, SE1 0AA.
   020 7815 7656
   http://www.lsbu.ac.uk/esbe/
- E A research centre at London South Bank University.

Centre for Engineering and Applied Sciences Research   (CEASR)
- ■ University of Hertfordshire, College Lane, Hatfield, Hertfordshire, AL10 9AB.
   01707 284500   fax 01707 284514
   http://perseus.herts.ac.uk/uhinfo/research/stri/
- E A research centre within the Science and Technology Research Institute (qv) at the University of Hertfordshire.

Centre for English and Applied Linguistics
   see **Research Centre for English and Applied Linguistics.**

Centre for English Language and British Studies
Note: is now INTO University of East Anglia and is therefore no longer within the scope of this Directory.

Centre for English Language and Communication   (CELC)
- ■ School of Languages and Social Sciences, Aston University, Aston Triangle, Birmingham, B4 7ET.
   0121-204 3000
   http://www.aston.ac.uk/lss/academicgroups/english/celca/
- E An English language teaching centre at Aston University.

Centre for English Language Education   (CELE)   1987
- ■ University of Nottingham, Highfield House, University Park, Nottingham, NG7 2RD.
   0115-951 4405   fax 0115-951 4992
   http://www.cele.nottingham.ac.uk/
   Director: Rebecca Hughes.
- E A research centre at the University of Nottingham.
- ○ To provide study opportunities and support for international students, and teacher training programmes

Centre for English Language Studies   (CELS)
- ■ Department of English, University of Birmingham, Westmere House, Edgbaston, Birmingham, B15 2TT.
   0121-414 5695; 5696   fax 0121-414 3298
   http://www.cels.bham.ac.uk/
   Director: Prof C J Kennedy.
- E A centre at the University of Birmingham.
- ○ To offer postgraduate courses in various fields of English language, including special applications of linguistics, TEFL, applied linguistics, translation studies, language and lexicography, literary linguistics, etc

Centre for English Language Teacher Education   (CELTE)   1983
- ■ University of Warwick, Coventry, CV4 7AL.
   024 7652 3200; 3523   fax 024 7652 4318
   http://www2.warwick.ac.uk/fac/soc/celte/
   Director: Dr Julia P Khan.
- E A department of the University of Warwick.
- ○ To promote the development of English language teaching and aspiring professionals, particularly in relation to English as a second language and English as a foreign language
- ● Courses for English language teaching professionals wishing to develop their knowledge and skills - Courses for students whose first language is not English but who intend to take an undergraduate or postgraduate degree, or do research at a British university

Centre for English Language Teaching
   see **University of Stirling Centre for English Language Teaching.**

© CBD Research Ltd · Beckenham · Kent BR3 5JS · Tel 020 8650 7745 · Fax 020 8650 0768 · E-mail cbd@cbdresearch.com · www.cbdresearch.com

Centre for English Local History   (CELH)   1988
- ■   University of Leicester, 5 Salisbury Road, Leicester, LE1 7QR.
    0116-252 2762   fax 0116-252 5769
    http://www.le.ac.uk/elh/
    Director: Prof Christopher Dyer.
- E   A research centre within the Marc Fitch Historical Institute (qv) at the University of Leicester.

Centre for English Name-Studies
    see **Institute for Name-Studies.**

Centre for the Enhancement of Learning and Teaching   (CELT)
- ■   Robert Gordon University, Blackfriars Building, Schoolhill, Aberdeen, AB10 1FR.
    01224 262000; 262728   fax 01224 263000
    http://www.rgu.ac.uk/celt/
- E   A research centre at the Robert Gordon University.
- O   To provide intellectual stimuli, services and resources to support the developing needs of learning, teaching and assessment and pedagogic research

Centre for the Enhancement of Learning and Teaching   (CELT)
- ■   University of Hertfordshire, College Lane, Hatfield, Hertfordshire, AL10 9AB.
    01707 284000
    http://www.perseus.herts.ac.uk/uhinfo/administration/celt/celt-home-page.cfm
    Director: Prof David Bonner.
- E   A research centre at the University of Hertfordshire.

Centre for the Enhancement of Learning and Teaching   (CELT)
- ■   Lancaster University, Bowland Tower North, Lancaster, LA1 4YT.
    01524 593888   fax 01524 594748
    http://luvle.lancs.ac.uk/celt/celtweb.nsf
    Director: Paul Rodaway.
- E   A research centre at Lancaster University.
- O   To lead and support development in learning, teaching and assessment practices

Centre for Enterprise   (CFE)   2000
- ■   Manchester Metropolitan University Business School, Manchester Metropolitan University, Aytoun Building, Aytoun Street, Manchester, M1 3GH.
    0161-247 6615   fax 0161-247 6911
    http://www.business.mmu.ac.uk/centreforenterprise/
    Director: Prof Ossie Jones.
- E   A research centre within the Research Institute for Business and Management (qv) at Manchester Metropolitan University.
- O   To provide a coherent resource centre for enterprise, research and learning, through the three streams of research, business start-up and business support

Centre for Enterprise [Portsmouth]
    see **Portsmouth Centre for Enterprise.**

Centre for Enterprise and Economic Development Research   (CEEDR)
- ■   Middlesex University Business School, Middlesex University, The Burroughs, London, NW4 4BT.
    020 8411 5460   fax 020 8411 6607
    Head of Centre: David North.
- E   A research centre within the Centre for Advanced Management Research (qv) at Middlesex University.
- O   To specialise in research relating to small and medium sized enterprises, and regional economic development

Centre for Enterprise, Ethics and the Environment   (CEEE)
- ■   Huddersfield University Business School, University of Huddersfield, Queensgate, Huddersfield, HD1 3DH.
    01484 472949   fax 01484 472633
    http://www.hud.ac.uk/hubs/research/CEEE/
    Head: Dr Julia Meaton.
- E   A research centre at the University of Huddersfield.
- O   To bring together researchers from a variety of disciplines to explore the potential synergies between entrepreneurship, ethical business and environmental imperatives

Centre for Enterprise, European and Extension Services   (CEEES)
- ■   University of Wales Lampeter, College Street, Lampeter, Ceredigion, SA48 7ED.
    01570 424746   fax 01570 424991
    http://www.lamp.ac.uk/ceees/
    Director: Prof Ian Roffe. Administrator: Mrs Jenny Thomas.
- E   A centre at the University of Wales, Lampeter.

Centre for Enterprise and Innovation (CEI)

■ University of Gloucestershire, The Park, Cheltenham, Gloucestershire, GL50 2RH.
01242 714104 fax 01242 714398
http://www.glos.ac.uk/businesslinks/cei/
E A department of the University of Gloucestershire.
○ To be the gateway to the University for businesses and organisations throughout Gloucestershire and the region
● Gloucestershire Enterprise Network

Centre for Enterprise Management (CEM)

■ Postgraduate School of Management and Policy, University of Dundee, Dundee, DD1 4HN.
01382 344361; 388203
http://www.dundee.ac.uk/cem/
Chairman: Prof D Jane Bower. Administrator: Heather Henderson.
E A centre at the University of Dundee.
○ To enhance the capabilities of enterprising people and businesses in Scotland and internationally

Centre for Enterprise and the Management of Innovation   (CEMI)

■ Faculty of Engineering Sciences, University College London, Malet Place Engineering Building, Malet Place, London, WC1E 6BT.
020 7679 0446 fax 020 7679 3209
http://www.ucl.ac.uk/cemi/
Director: Prof Steven Currall.
E A department of University College London.
○ To support research and teaching that provides deep insight into management issues faced by technology-intensive organisations

Centre for Enterprise, Quality and Management (CEQM)

■ Newport Business School, University of Wales, Newport, PO Box 180, Newport, NP20 5XR.
01633 432325
http://www.ceqm.co.uk/
Director: Prof Hefin Rowlands.
E A research centre at the University of Wales, Newport.
○ To focus on research aimed at assisting organisations to achieve operational efficiency through the strategic use of technology

Centre for Enterprise and Regional Development

Note: has closed.

Centre for Enterprise Research and Innovation   (CERI)

■ Portsmouth Business School, University of Portsmouth, Richmond Building, Portland Street, Portsmouth, PO1 3DE.
023 9284 4046 fax 023 9284 4037
http://www.port.ac.uk/research/ceri/currentresearch/
E A research centre at the University of Portsmouth.

Centre for Entrepreneurial Learning (CfEL) 2003

■ Judge Business School, University of Cambridge, 2nd Floor - Keynes House, 24a Trumpington Street, Cambridge, CB2 1QA.
01223 766900 fax 01223 766922
http://www.entrepreneurs.jbs.cam.ac.uk/
E A research centre at the University of Cambridge.

Centre for Entrepreneurial Management (CEM) 2002

■ Derbyshire Business School, University of Derby, Kedleston Road, Derby, DE22 1GB.
01332 591419 fax 01332 592741
http://www.derby.ac.uk/cem/
Contact: David Rae.
E A research centre at the University of Derby.
○ To stimulate the entrepreneurial spirit, transforming individuals and organisations

Centre for Entrepreneurial Performance and Economics
see **Bettany Centre for Entrepreneurial Performance and Economics.**

Centre for Entrepreneurship [Robert Gordon]
see **Charles P Skene Centre for Entrepreneurship**

Centre for Entrepreneurship 1995

■ University of Aberdeen Business School, University of Aberdeen, Edward Wright Building, Dunbar Street, Old Aberdeen, AB24 3QY.
01224 272167
http://www.abdn.ac.uk/business/ce.shtml
E A centre at the University of Aberdeen.
○ To produce and disseminate research on entrepreneurship

Centre for Entrepreneurship
- ■ Napier University Business School, Napier University, Craiglockhart Campus, Edinburgh, EH14 1DJ.
  http://www.napier.ac.uk/nubs/CentreforEntrepreneurship.htm
- E A centre at Napier University.

Centre for Entrepreneurship
- ■ University of Greenwich Business School, University of Greenwich, Old Royal Naval College, Park Row, London, SE10 9LS.
  020 8331 9835   fax 020 8331 9684
  http://w3.gre.ac.uk/schools/business/entrepreneur/
  Director: Dr Kanes K Rajah.
- E A research centre at the University of Greenwich.
- O To conduct research into creativity and leadership in entrepreneurship

Centre for Entrepreneurship   2001
- ■ Stirling, FK9 4LA.
  01786 467041
  http://www.ent.stir.ac.uk/
- E A centre at the University of Stirling.

Centre for Entrepreneurship Research   (CER)   2002
- ■ Management School and Economics, University of Edinburgh, William Robertson Building, 50 George Square, Edinburgh, EH8 9JY.
  0131-650 3900
  http://www.man.ed.ac.uk/research/centres/cer/
- E A research centre at the University of Edinburgh.
- O To stimulate research into all aspects of entrepreneurship and small business development

Centre for Entrepreneurship Research   (CER)
- ■ School of Entrepreneurship and Business, University of Essex, Princess Caroline House, 1 High Street, Southend-on-Sea, Essex, SS1 1JE.
  01702 238653; 339888
  http://www.essex.ac.uk/entrepreneurship/research.htm
  Academic Administrator: Sheila Foster.
- E A centre at the University of Essex.
- O To provide a focus for research activity in the area of business enterprise and innovation

Centre for Entrepreneurship and Small and Medium-sized Enterprise (SME) Development
- ■ Teesside Business School, University of Teesside, Middlesbrough, TS1 3BA.
  01642 342910
  http://www.tees.ac.uk/schools/tbs/cesmed/cesmed_index.cfm
  Director: Prof Ted Fuller.
- E A research centre at the University of Teesside.
- O To help people create better futures through enterprise

Centre for the Environment [Dundee]
   see **Abertay Centre for the Environment.**

Centre for the Environment   (CfE)
- ■ University of Nottingham, University Park, Nottingham, NG7 2RD.
  0115-846 707   fax 0115-951 5249
  http://www.nottingham.ac.uk/environment/
  Director: Prof Roy Haines-Young.
- E A research centre at the University of Nottingham.

Centre for the Environment [Oxford]
   see **Oxford University Centre for the Environment.**

Centre for Environment, Fisheries and Aquaculture Science   (CEFAS)   1997
- ■ Lowestoft Laboratory, Pakefield Road, Lowestoft, Suffolk, NR33 0HT.
  01502 562244   fax 01502 513865
  http://www.cefas.co.uk/
  Chief Executive: Mark Farrar.
- E A Government Agency established by Act of Parliament.
- O To supply specialist scientific and technical support, consultancy and advice in the fields of fisheries science and management, environmental assessment, aquaculture and fish health All support is given to standards of objective enquiry agreed with its customers
- ● Conference facilities - Consultancy - Education and training - Exhibitions - Information service - Library - Statistics

Centre on Environment for the Handicapped
   see **Centre for Accessible Environments.**

Centre for Environment and Human Settlements (CEHS)

■ School of the Built Environment, Edinburgh Campus, University of Edinburgh, Riccarton, Edinburgh, EH14 4AS.
   0131-451 3866; 8062   fax 0131-451 4617
   http://www.sbe.hw.ac.uk/research/policyandplanning/cehs.htm
   Director: Prof Paul Jenkins.
E A research centre at Heriot-Watt University.
○ To provide teaching, training, research and development and other knowledge-based services and resources in the fields of environment and human settlements for the developing and urbanising world

Centre for Environment and Planning (CEP)

■ Faculty of the Built Environment, Frenchay Campus, University of the West of England, Coldharbour Lane, Bristol, BS16 1QY.
   0117-328 3102; 3378   fax 0117-328 3899
   http://www.built-environment.uwe.ac.uk/research/cep/
   Director: Prof Angela Hull.
E A research centre at the University of the West of England.
○ To conduct research in the built and natural environment

Centre for Environment and Safety Management for Business (CESMB) 1993

■ Middlesex University, Queensway, Enfield, Middlesex, EN3 4SA.
   020 8411 6067
   http://www.mdx.ac.uk/www/cesmb/
   Contact: Stewart Anthony.
E A centre at Middlesex University.
○ To help businesses and other organisations recognise how environmental management is a key factor in business competitiveness locally, nationally and internationally

Centre for Environment and Society (CES) 1997

■ Department of Biological Sciences, University of Essex, Wivenhoe Park, Colchester, Essex, CO4 3SQ.
   01206 872203   fax 01206 872592
   http://www.essex.ac.uk/ces/
   Director: Prof Ian Colbeck.
E A transdisciplinary research centre at the University of Essex.
○ To conduct a wide range of basic, applied and action-oriented environmental research

Centre for Environmental Archaeology (CEA)

■ School of Conservation Sciences, Christchurch House, Talbot Campus, Bournemouth University, Poole, Dorset, BH12 5BB.
   01202 965178   fax 01202 965530
   http://www.bournemouth.ac.uk/conservation/abouttheschool/ahe/cea.html
E A centre at Bournemouth University.
○ To focus research on the changing nature of the natural environment, the use that human communities have made of the environment, the changes that people have wrought, and the relationships between people, animals and plants

Centre for Environmental Assessment, Management and Policy (CEAMP) 2005

■ Department of Geography, King's College London, Strand, London, WC2R 2LS.
   020 7848 2610
   http://www.kcl.ac.uk/projects/ceamp/
   Director: Prof Glenn McGregor.
E An interdisciplinary research centre at King's College, London.
○ To conduct research in the solution of environmental problems and provision of postgraduate training, and to foster links between environmental assessment, management and policy systems

Centre for Environmental Biotechnology
   see **Oxford Centre for Environmental Biotechnology.**

Centre for Environmental Change and Quaternary Research (CECQR) 1995

■ Department of Natural and Social Sciences, University of Gloucestershire, Swindon Road, Cheltenham, Gloucestershire, GL50 4AZ.
   01242 714708   fax 01242 543283
   http://www.glos.ac.uk/faculties/ehs/sciences/natural/research/
   Contact: Phillip Toms.
E A research centre at the University of Gloucestershire.
○ To integrate the activities of those who work on geochronology, climate change, environmental change and human impacts, covering a wide range of different timescales - from the mid-Pleistocene to late Holocene

Centre for Environmental Control and Waste Management

Note: No longer in existence.

Centre for Environmental Data and Recording (CEDaR) 1995

■ Ulster Museum, Botanic Gardens, Belfast, BT9 5AB.
   028 9038 3153; 3154   fax 028 9038 3158
   http://www.habitas.org.uk/cedar/
E Established by the Ulster Museum, and the Environment and Heritage Service (NI).
○ To collect, store and disseminate information on the distribution of flora and fauna, and geological sites

Centre for Environmental Forensics   (CEF)
- ■   School of Conservation Sciences, University of Bournemough, Christchurch House, Talbot Campus, Poole, Dorset, BH12 5BB.
    01202 965178   fax 01202 965530
    http://www.bournemouth.ac.uk/conservation/abouttheschool/egs/egs_li.html
- E   A centre at Bournemouth University.
- O   To undertake a range of research in the field of environmental management, health and safety, and in the area of contaminated land assessment

Centre for Environmental and Geophysical Flows   (CEGF)   2002
- ■   Department of Mathematics, University of Bristol, University Walk, Bristol, BS8 1TW.
    0117-928 7978   fax 0117-928 7999
    http://www.maths.bris.ac.uk/research/labs/environmental_geophysical/
    Director: Prof R S J Sparks, FRS.
- E   An interdisciplinary research centre at the University of Bristol.
- O   To bring together expertise in modelling geological and geophysical flow processes
- ●   Seminars - Graduate course on Geological and Environmental Fluid Dynamics

Centre for Environmental Health Engineering   (CEHE)
- ■   School of Engineering, University of Surrey, Guildford, Surrey, GU2 5XH.
    01483 686292   fax 01483 686681
    http://www.surrey.ac.uk/CEHE/
    Director: Prof Barry Lloyd.
- E   A research centre at the University of Surrey.
- O   To conduct research which covers the whole water cycle, including water resources surveillance, modelling and management, water treatment, supply and regulation, wastewater treatment, disposal and safe re-use, pollution control and waste management

Centre for Environmental History
    see **AHRC Research Centre for Environmental History.**

Centre for Environmental Informatics   (CEI)
- ■   School of Health, Natural and Social Sciences, University of Sunderland, Benedict Building, St George's Way, Sunderland, Tyne and Wear, SR2 7BW.
    0191-515 3761   fax 0191-515 3762
    http://hnss-web.sunderland.ac.uk/our-research/cei/cei
    Head: Tony Alabaster.
- E   A research centre at the University of Sunderland.
- O   To conduct innovative applied research relating to private and public sector environmental, social and ethical accountability

Centre for Environmental Initiatives   (CEI)   1987
- ■   University of Surrey, The Old School House, Mill Lane, Carshalton, Surrey, SM5 2JY.
    020 8770 6611
    http://www.thecei.org.uk/
- E   A registered charity.
- O   To promote a greater awareness of environmental problems

Centre for Environmental Law   (CEL)   1990
- ■   School of Law, University of Nottingham, University Park, Nottingham, NG7 2RD.
    0115-951 5700   fax 0115-951 5696
    http://www.nottingham.ac.uk/law/research/research_Env_Centre.php
    Director: Peter Davies.
- E   A centre at the University of Nottingham.
- O   To communicate knowledge and understanding of environmental law through the promotion of courses, publications and conference facilities

Centre for Environmental Management   (CEM)
- ■   School of Geography, University of Nottingham, University Park, Nottingham, NG7 2RD.
    0115-951 5498   fax 0115-951 5249
    http://www.nottingham.ac.uk/~lgzwww/research/research%20centres/CEM/
    Director: Prof Roy Haines-Young.
- E   A research centre at the University of Nottingham.
- O   To explore ways of identifying the choices faced in developing and implementing strategies for a sustainable future

Centre for Environmental Management and Technology   (CEMT)
- ■   Bell College, Almada Street, Hamilton, ML3 0JB.
    01698 894433   fax 01698 894444
    http://www.bell.ac.uk/bdia/enviromentalcentre.htm
    Manager: Tom Fulton.
- E   A research centre at the Bell College.
- O   To provide training, management systems and technical services in the areas of environmental and health and safety practice
- ●   Education and training - Information service

Note: At the time of going to press, Bell College was preparing to merge with the University of Paisley to form the University of the West of Scotland.

Centre for Environmental Policy (CEP)

■ Faculty of Life Sciences, South Kensington Campus, Imperial College London, Exhibition Road, London, SW7 2AZ.
020 7594 9300   fax 020 7594 9334
http://www3.imperial.ac.uk/environmentalpolicy
Head: Prof John Mumford.

E A research centre at Imperial College London.

○ To focus research on environmental and development issues, including energy, pollution, conservation of natural resources, food security and poverty reduction

Centre for Environmental Policy and Governance
    see **LSE Environment: Centre for Environmental Policy and Governance.**

Centre for Environmental and Preventive Medicine (CEPM)

■ Barts and the London, Queen Mary's School of Medicine and Dentistry, Queen Mary, University of London, Charterhouse Square, London, EC1M 6BQ.
020 7882 6190   fax 020 7882 6270
http://www.wolfson.qmul.ac.uk/epm/
Director: Prof Nicholas Wald, FRS.

E A research centre within the Wolfson Institute of Preventive Medicine (qv) at Queen Mary, University of London.

○ To conduct research into the causation and prevention of disease

Centre for Environmental Research (CER)

■ School of Life Sciences, University of Sussex, John Maynard Smith Building, Falmer, Brighton, East Sussex, BN1 9QG.
01273 678085
http://www.sussex.ac.uk/cer/
Contact: Prof Michael Ramsey.

E An interdisciplinary research centre at the University of Sussex.

Centre for Environmental Research and Training (CERT)

■ University of Birmingham, Edgbaston, Birmingham, B15 2TT.
0121-414 8141   fax 0121-414 8142
http://www.cert.bham.ac.uk/
Director: Prof Geoff Petts.

E A centre at the University of Birmingham.

○ To be proactive in meeting the emerging environmental research needs of industry and commerce

Centre for Environmental Resource Management (CERM) 1996

■ University of Edinburgh, Riccarton, Edinburgh, EH14 4AS.
0131-449 5111
http://www.hw.ac.uk/cerm/
Head: Prof Mike Paul.

E A research centre at Heriot-Watt University.

○ To bring together staff and research interests in biology, ecology, conservation, marine science, engineering, and resource management

Centre for Environmental Scanning Electron Microscopy (CESEM) 1998

■ University of Edinburgh, Riccarton, Edinburgh, EH14 4AS.
0131-451 3124; 3188; 3608
http://www.pet.hw.ac.uk/cesem/
Director: Prof Adrian Todd. Facility Manager: Dr Jim Buckman.

E A research centre within the Heriot-Watt Institute of Petroleum Engineering (qv) at Heriot-Watt University.

○ To image or analyse virtually any substance, including wet, oily and outgassing samples, that cannot be analysed by more conventional scanning electroscopy methods

● Equipment used is a Philips XL30 Environmental Scanning Electron Microscope (ESEM)

Centre for Environmental Sciences (CES)

■ School of Civil Engineering and the Environment, University of Southampton, Lanchester Building, Highfield, Southampton, SO17 1BJ.
023 8059 4652   fax 023 8067 7519
http://www.civil.soton.ac.uk/es/

E A research centre at the University of Southampton.

Centre for the Environmental and Social Study of Aging (CESSA)

■ Department of Applied Social Sciences, London Metropolitan University, Ladbroke House, 62-66 Highbury Grove, London, N5 2AD.
020 7133 5082
Contact: Leonie Kellaher.

E A research centre within the Cities Institute (qv) at London Metropolitan University.

○ To conduct social and anthropological research into the material culture of ageing

© CBD Research Ltd · Beckenham · Kent BR3 5JS · Tel 020 8650 7745 · Fax 020 8650 0768 · E-mail cbd@cbdresearch.com · www.cbdresearch.com

Centre for Environmental and Spatial Analysis (CESA) 1999
- School of Applied Sciences, Northumbria University, Ellison Building, Ellison Place, Newcastle upon Tyne, NE1 8ST.
  0191-227 4585   fax 0191-227 3519
  http://northumbria.ac.uk/sd/academic/sas/sas_research/cesa/
  Director: Dr Robert MacFarlane.
- E   A research centre at Northumbria University.
- O   To focus research on geographical information systems and remote sensing

Centre for Environmental Strategy (CES)
- School of Engineering, University of Surrey, Guildford, Surrey, GU2 7XH.
  01483 686670   fax 01483 686671
  http://www.surrey.ac.uk/CES
  Director: Dr Chris France.
- E   A research centre at the University of Surrey.
- O   To conduct research in long-term environmental problems, including corporate environmental management, sustainable development, environmental strategy, and environmental life cycle management

Centre for Environmental Studies (CENS)
- Ashby Road, Loughborough, Leicestershire, LE11 3TU.
  01509 222585   fax 01509 222585
  http://www.lboro.ac.uk/research/cens/
  Director: Prof Peter Warwick.
- E   A research centre at Loughborough University.
- O   To conduct teaching and research in a wide variety of environmental topics

Centre for Environmental Studies in the Hospitality Industries (CESHI)
- Oxford Brookes Business School, Oxford Brookes University, Wheatley Campus, Wheatley, Oxford, OX33 1HX.
  01865 485908
  http://www.business.brookes.ac.uk/research/groups/ceshi.asp
- E   A research centre at Oxford Brookes University.
- O   To provide research and consultancy services to industry, Governments and academia on all aspects of sustainable development as it relates to the tourism and hospitality industries
- ● Education and training - Information service

Centre for Environmental Sustainability
> see **Aberdeen Centre for Environmental Sustainability.**

Centre for Environmental Systems Research (CESR)
- Faculty of Business, Law and the Built Environment, University of Salford, Maxwell Building, Salford, Manchester, M5 4WT.
  0161-295 4600
  http://www.buhu.salford.ac.uk/research_centres/cesr/
- E   A research centre within the Research Institute for the Built and Human Environment (qv) at the University of Salford.
- O   To conduct research in the fields of land surface processes, hydrology and hydrometeorology, ecology and sustainability

Centre for Environmental Technology
Note: No longer in existence.

Centre for Environmental and Waste Management (CEWM) 1991
- School of Engineering and Science, University of Paisley, Paisley, PA1 2BE.
  0141-848 3146
  http://www.paisley.ac.uk/es/cewm/
  Director: Dr Jennifer McQuaid-Cook.
- E   A private company wholly owned by the University of Paisley.
- O   To offer consultancy, courses and training in the specialised areas of health and safety, environmental and waste management
Note: At the time of going to press, the University of Paisley was preparing to merge with Bell College to form the University of the West of Scotland.

Centre for Epidemiology and Biostatics (CEB) 2004
- Faculty of Medicine and Health, University of Leeds, The Worsley Building, Clarendon Way, Leeds, LS2 9JT.
  0113-343 4361
  http://www.leeds.ac.uk/medhealth/light/ceb/
  Director: Prof Chris Wild.
- E   A research centre within the Leeds Institute of Genetics, Health and Therapeutics (qv) at the University of Leeds.
- O   To research disease mechanisms and aetiology

Centre for Epidemiology and Health Service Research (CEHSR)
- School of Health Sciences and Social Care, Brunel University, Uxbridge, Middlesex, UB8 3PH.
  01895 274000
  http://www.brunel.ac.uk/about/acad/health/healthres/researchareas/ehsrg
  Director: Prof Janet Peacock.
- E   A research centre at Brunel University.
- O   To undertake research and provide consultation support, in the fields of epidemiology and health service related research, with a particular emphasis on maintaining and promoting the highest methodological standards

Centre for Epilepsy
> see **Chalfont Centre for Epilepsy.**

Centre for Equality and Human Rights in Education   (CEHRE)   2007
- ■ School of Educational Foundations and Policy Studies, Institute of Education, University of London, 20 Bedford Way, London, WC1H 0AL.
  020 7612 6312   fax 020 7612 6177
  http://ioewebserver.ioe.ac.uk/ioe/cms/get.asp?cid=16215
  Head of Centre: Prof Heidi Safia Mirza.
- E A cross-departmental group within the Institute of Education (qv) at the University of London.
- ○ To undertaking research to promote the achievement of social justice and equity in education; to tackle educational inequality and undertake a range of research projects on race, class and gender in education.
- ✕ Builds on the work of the Centre for Research and Education on Gender.

Centre for Equity in Education   (CEE)
- ■ School of Education, University of Manchester, Humanities Devas Street, Oxford Road, Manchester, M13 9PL.
  0161-275 3463   fax 0161-275 3528
  http://www.education.manchester.ac.uk/research/centres/cee/
  Contact: Dr Kirstin Kerr.
- E A research centre at the University of Manchester.
- ○ To develop better understanding of the nature of the challenges facing the education service, particularly in respect to vulnerable groups

Centre for Ethics, Law and Society
> see **Cardiff Centre for Ethics, Law and Society.**

Centre for Ethics and Philosophy of Law
> see **Oxford Centre for Ethics and Philosophy of Law.**

Centre for Ethics, Philosophy and Public Affairs   (CEPPA)   1984
- ■ School of Philosophical, Anthropological and Film Studies, University of St Andrews, St Andrews, Fife, KY16 9AL.
  01334 462486   fax 01334 462485
  http://www.st-andrews.ac.uk/philosophy/ceppa/
  Director: Prof John Haldane. Secretary: Mrs Janet Kirk.
- E A department of the University of St Andrews.
- ○ To promote research in those areas of philosophy most relevant to topics of public importance, and to advance the contribution of philosophy in the discussion of these topics
- ● Conference facilities
- ¶ St Andrews Studies in Philosophy and Public Affairs (5 volumes).
- ✕ Centre for Philosophy and Public Affairs.

Centre for Ethics in Public Policy and Corporate Governance   (CEPPCG)   2005
- ■ School of Law and Social Sciences, Glasgow Caledonian University, Cowcaddens Road, Glasgow, G4 0BA.
  0141-331 3489; 8429
  http://www.gcal.ac.uk/lss/research/centres/CentreforEthics.html
  Chairman: Prof Jim Gallagher.
- E A research centre at Glasgow Caledonian University.
- ○ To promote ethics in public life

Centre for Ethnic Minority Studies   (CEMS)   1989
- ■ Equal Opportunities Consultancy Unit, Royal Holloway, University of London, Egham, Surrey, TW20 0EX.
  01784 443815   fax 01784 430680
  http://www.rhul.ac.uk/cems/
  Director: Prof Humayun Ansari. Contact: June Jackson.
- E A research unit within Royal Holloway, University of London.
- ○ To provide research and consultancy in the field of equality and diversity to organisations in the public, private and voluntary sectors
- ● Education and training
- ¶ Black and Minority Ethnic Representation in the Built Environment Professions.
- ✕ Ethnic Minority Studies Centre.

Centre for Ethnic Minority Studies   (CEMS)   1988
- ■ School of Law, School of Oriental and African Studies, University of London, Thornhaugh Street, Russell Square, London, WC1H 0XG.
  020 7637 2388   fax 020 7436 3844
  http://www.soas.ac.uk/centres/centreinfo.cfm?navid=739
  Chairman: Prof Werner Menski.
- E An interdisciplinary research centre at the School of Oriental and African Studies, University of London.
- ○ To promote teaching and research in the field of ethnic minority studies, with particular emphasis on interdisciplinary legal studies

© CBD Research Ltd · Beckenham · Kent BR3 5JS · Tel 020 8650 7745 · Fax 020 8650 0768 · E-mail cbd@cbdresearch.com · www.cbdresearch.com

Centre for Ethnicity and Gender

■ Tower Building, London Metropolitan University, 166-220 Holloway Road, London, N7 8DB.
020 7133 2927
http://www.londonmet.ac.uk/research-units/iset/research/ethnicity-gender-centre.cfm

E A research centre within the Institute for the Study of European Transformations (qv) at London Metropolitan University.

Centre for Ethnicity and Racism Studies   (CERS)

■ School of Sociology and Social Policy, University of Leeds, Leeds, LS2 9JT.
0113-343 4410   fax 0113-343 4415
http://www.leeds.ac.uk/cers/
Director: Dr Ian Law.

E An interdisciplinary research centre within the University of Leeds.

Centre for Euro-Asian Studies   1996

■ University of Reading Business School, HUMSS Building, University of Reading, PO Box 218, Reading, Berkshire, RG6 6AA.
0118-378 6637   fax 0118-378 6274
http://www.reading.ac.uk/business/default.asp?id=98
Director: Dr Yelena Kalyuzhnova.

E A research centre at the University of Reading.
O To unite researchers involved (working in both English and Russian) in politics, economics and security

Centre for Euro-Mediterranean Studies   1988

■ Graduate Institute of Political and International Studies, Whiteknights, University of Reading, PO Box 217, Reading, Berkshire, RG6 6AH.
0118-378 8378
http://www.reading.ac.uk/GIPIS/Research%207/Research%20Centres.htm

E A research centre within the Graduate Institute of Political and International Studies (qv) at the University of Reading.
O To provide a forum for research and discussion on the international relations of the Mediterranean
● Seminars

Centre for Europe   (CfE)   1989

■ 10A Tubs Hill Parade, Sevenoaks, Kent, TN13 1DH.
01732 452684   fax 01732 740446
http://www.centreforeurope.org/
Director: Roger Kercher. Director: Richard Wassell.

E An independent non-profit-distributing organisation.
● Education and training

Centre for Europe-Asia Business Research   (CEABuR)

■ Nottingham University Business School, Jubilee Campus, University of Nottingham, Wollaton Road, Nottingham, NG8 1BB.
0115-846 6602
http://www.nottingham.ac.uk/business/CEABuR.html

E A research centre at the University of Nottingham.
O To provide consultancy and research services to European business operating in Asia, and vice-versa
● Annual survey of the Malaysian economy

Centre for European and Comparative Law
see **Kent Centre for European and Comparative Law.**

Centre for European Economies in Transition
see **Strathclyde Centre for European Economies in Transition.**

Centre for European Integration   (CEI)

■ Faculty of Humanities, Law and Social Science, Manchester Metropolitan University, Geoffrey Manton Building, Rosamond Street West, Manchester, M15 6LL.
0161-247 3030
http://www.meri.mmu.ac.uk/
Convenor: Neill Nugent.

E A research centre within the Manchester European Research Institute (qv) at Manchester Metropolitan University.
O To focus research on various issues and topics related to the nature and operation of the European Union, particularly the politics and policies of the EU, small states and the EU, member states and the EU, regionalism and the EU, and problems of democracy and legitimacy in the EU

Centre for European and International Studies Research   (CEISR)

■ Faculty of Humanities and Social Sciences, University of Portsmouth, Park Building, King Henry 1 Street, Portsmouth, PO1 2DZ.
023 9284 6014   fax 023 9284 6254
http://www.port.ac.uk/research/ceisr/

E A department of the University of Portsmouth.

Centre for European Labour Market Research   (CELMR)   2000
- University of Aberdeen Business School, University of Aberdeen, Edward Wright Building, Dunbar Street, Old Aberdeen, AB24 3QY.
   01224 272167
   http://www.abdn.ac.uk/business/celmr/
- E   A centre at the University of Aberdeen.
- O   To provide a focus for the identification and implementation of high quality research projects in labour market economics

Centre for European Languages and Cultures   (CELC)
- Edgbaston, Birmingham, B15 2TT.
   0121-414 5965
   http://www.celc.bham.ac.uk/
   Director: Prof David Hill.
- E   A centre at the University of Birmingham.
- O   To undertake teaching and research in various European languages, including French, German, Italian, Portuguese, and Spanish

Centre of European Law   (CEL)   1974
- School of Law, King's College London, Strand, London, WC2R 2LS.
   020 7848 2387   fax 020 7848 2443
   http://www.kcl.ac.uk/depsta/law/research/cel/
   Director: Prof Piet Eeckhout.
- E   A research centre at King's College, London.
- O   To conduct research in various aspects of European law, including US and EC anti-trust law, sovereignty and legal systems, community trade marks, the development of private law, governance by committee, and contemporary developments in EC environmental law

Centre for European Legal Studies   (CELS)   1991
- Faculty of Law, University of Cambridge, 10 West Road, Cambridge, CB3 9DZ.
   01223 330093   fax 01223 330095
   http://cels.law.cam.ac.uk/
   Co-Director: Prof John Bell. Co-Director: Dr Claire Kilpatrick.
- E   A centre at the University of Cambridge.
- O   To provide a focus for research in European Union law and European comparative law

Centre for European Legal Studies   (CELS)   1972
- Faculty of Law, University of Exeter, Amory Building, Rennes Drive, Exeter, EX4 4RJ.
   01392 263372   fax 01392 263196
   http://www.law.ex.ac.uk/cels/
   Director: Dr C Macmaolain.
- E   A research centre within the University of Exeter.
- O   To enable an independent body of scholars to continue academic research and activities extending beyond the traditional limits of a university department; to promote research into questions of European Community law; to evaluate its effects in the UK and the other member states, and to provide a focus of information and communication in this area
- ● Specialist library (the CELS is a designated European Documentation Centre (qv)) and materials received in this capacity form part of its collection - Information service - Access to the CELEX database (which contains the entire body of EU law), and SCAD database (which contains details of all official documents and publications of the EU's institutions) - Other European databases also available, including RAPID

Centre for European Literatures and Cultures   (CELC)
- Faculty of Humanities, Law and Social Science, Manchester Metropolitan University, Geoffrey Manton Building, Rosamond Street West, Manchester, M15 6LL.
   0161-247 3030
   http://www.meri.mmu.ac.uk/
   Co-Convenor: Shelley Godsland. Co-Convenor: Carmen Herrero.
- E   A research centre within the Manchester European Research Institute (qv) at Manchester Metropolitan University.
- O   To focus research on various fields of European languages and cultures, particularly Linguistics, economies and politics of Portugal and Spain, immigration, crime and detective fiction, women's writing, Hispanic, French, Italian and German popular culture, cinema and theatre, as well as contemporary literature, autobiography and literary translation studies

Centre for European Nineteenth-Century Studies   (CENCS)
- Department of German, University of Exeter, Queen's Building, The Queen's Drive, Exeter, EX4 4QH.
   http://www.centres.ex.ac.uk/cencs/
   Contact: Dr Martina Lauster.
- E   A centre at the University of Exeter.
- O   To provide a forum for interdisciplinary research on Continental (French, German, Hispanic, Italian and Russian) culture of the nineteenth-century and its cross-cultural aspects

Centre for European Political Communications   (EurPolCom)   2000
- Faculty of Performance, Visual Arts and Communications, University of Leeds, Level 3 - Houldsworth Building, Leeds, LS2 9JT.
   0113-343 5807   fax 0113-343 1117
   http://ics.leeds.ac.uk/eurpolcom/
   Director: Prof Paul Statham.
- E   A research centre within the Institute of Communications Studies (qv) at the University of Leeds.
- O   To conduct research in the fields of political communications, the public sphere and social movements

Centre for European Politics, Economics and Society
Note: No longer in existence.

Centre for European Politics, Security and Integration   (CEPSI)
- ■   School of Slavonic and East European Studies, University College London, Gower Street, London, WC1E 6BT.
     020 7679 8764; 8772
     http://www.ssees.ac.uk/cepsi.htm
     Director: Dr Felix Ciuta. Administrator: Kelly Peaston.
- E   A research centre at University College London.

Centre for European Protected Areas Research   (CEPAR)   1998
- ■   Faculty of Continuing Education, Birkbeck, University of London, 26 Russell Square, London, WC1B 5DQ.
     020 7679 1064; 1069
     http://www.bbk.ac.uk/ce/research/cepar/
- E   A research centre at Birkbeck, University of London.
- O   To examine how sustainability can be delivered in the protected areas in the wider Europe (East and West)

Centre for European, Regional and Transport Economics   (CERTE)   1993
- ■   Department of Economics, Keynes College, University of Kent, Canterbury, Kent, CT2 7NP.
     01227 823642   fax 01227 827784
     http://www.kent.ac.uk/economics/research/certe.html
     Director: Prof Roger Vickerman.
- E   A research centre at the University of Kent.
- O   To provide a focus for research on the economics of Europe and the European Union, with particular emphasis on aspects of transport and the regional development of the EU, especially the role of transport infrastructure

Centre for European Studies   (CES)   2003
- ■   School of Social and International Studies, 12 Claremont, University of Bradford, Bradford, West Yorkshire, BD7 1DP.
     01274 233081
     http://www.bradford.ac.uk/acad/ssis/research/CES/
     Acting Director: Roberto Espíndola.
- E   A department of the University of Bradford.

Centre for European Studies
Note: Ceased operation in 2006.

Centre for European Studies   (CES)   1979
- ■   Department of Politics, Amory Building, University of Exeter, Rennes Drive, Exeter, EX4 4RJ.
     01392 263258
     http://www.centres.ex.ac.uk/ces/
     Director: Dr Susan Banducci. Contact: Dr Chris Longman.
- E   A research centre at the University of Exeter.
- O   To conduct postgraduate studies in European affairs, with an emphasis on a pan-European approach that encompasses perspectives on Western, Central and Eastern Europe and the Balkans

Centre for European Studies [London]
     see **UCL Centre for European Studies.**

Centre for European Union Studies   (CEUS)
- ■   Department of Politics and International Studies, University of Hull, Cottingham Road, Hull, HU6 7RX.
     01482 466209   fax 01482 466208
     http://www.hull.ac.uk/ceus/
     Head: Prof The Lord Norton of Louth.
- E   A research centre at the University of Hull.

Centre for Evacuee and War Child Studies
     see **Research Centre for Evacuee and War Child Studies.**

Centre for Event and Sport Research   (CESR)
- ■   School of Services Management, Bournemouth University, Dorset House, Fern Barrow, Poole, Dorset, BH12 5BB.
     01202 966966   fax 01202 515707
     http://www.bournemouth.ac.uk/services-management/research/cesr.html
     Head: Prof Adele Ladkin.
- E   A centre at Bournemouth University.
- O   To focus research on events and sport, and associated issues including hospitality, tourism and economic development

Centre for Evidence-Based Child Health   (CEBCH)   1995
- Faculty of Biomedical Sciences, University College London, 30 Guilford Street, London, WC1N 1EH.
  020 7242 9789   fax 020 7831 0488
  http://www.ich.ucl.ac.uk/ich/academicunits/Centre_for_evidence_based_child_health/Homepage
- E   A research centre within the Centre for Paediatric Epidemiology and Biostatistics (qv) at University College London.
- O   To increase the provision of effective and efficient child health care through an educational programme for health professionals

Centre for Evidence-Based Conservation   (CEBC)
- University of Birmingham, Edgbaston, Birmingham, B15 2TT.
  0121-414 7147   fax 0121-414 5925
  http://www.cebc.bham.ac.uk/
  Principal Investigator: Dr Andrew S Pullin.
- E   A research centre at the University of Birmingham.
- O   To support decision making in conservation and environmental management through the production and dissemination of systematic reviews on the effectiveness of management and policy interventions

Centre for Evidence-Based Dentistry   (CEBD)   1995
- Department of Primary Health Care, University of Oxford, Headington, Oxford, OX3 7LF.
  01865 226991   fax 01865 226845
  http://www.cebd.org/
  Director: Derek Richards.
- E   An independent research centre at the University of Oxford.
- O   To promote the teaching, learning, practice and evaluation of evidence-based dentistry

Centre for Evidence-Based Medicine   (CEBM)
- Department of Primary Health Care, Old Road Campus, University of Oxford, Headington, Oxford, OX3 7LF.
  01865 226991   fax 01865 226845
  http://www.cebm.net/
  Director: Prof Paul Glasziou. Contact: Olive Goddard.
- E   A research centre at the University of Oxford.
- Note: Also known as the Oxford Centre for Evidence-Based Medicine.

Centre for Evidence-Based Mental Health   (CEBMH)
- Department of Psychiatry, Warneford Hospital, University of Oxford, Oxford, OX3 7JX.
  01865 226476   fax 01865 793101
  http://cebmh.com/
  Director: Prof John Geddes.
- E   A research centre at the University of Oxford.
- O   To promote the teaching, practice and research in evidence-based health care throughout the UK, with special emphasis on evidence-based mental health

Centre for Evidence-Based Nursing   (CEBN)
- Department of Health Sciences, University of York, Heslington, York, YO10 5DD.
  01904 321344
  http://www.york.ac.uk/healthsciences/centres/evidence/cebn.htm
- E   A research centre at the University of York.
- O   To further evidence-based nursing through education, research and development

Centre for Evidence-Based Social Services
Note: Ceased operations in 2004.

Centre for Evidence-informed Policy and Practice in Education   (EPPI-Centre
- University of London, 18 Woburn Square, London, WC1H 0NR.
  020 7612 6131
  http://eppi.ioe.ac.uk/
- E   A research centre within the Institute of Education (qv) at the University of London.
- O   To undertake systematic revisions in research in education; to use reviews to inform policy and practice

Centre for the Evolution of Cultural Diversity
    see **AHRC Research Centre for the Evolution of Cultural Diversity.**

Centre for Evolution, Genes and Genomics   (CEGG)
- School of Biology, Sir Harold Mitchell Building, University of St Andrews, St Andrews, Fife, KY16 9TH.
  01334 463369
  http://biology.st-andrews.ac.uk/cegg
  Contact: Lianne Gibson.
- E   A research centre at the University of St Andrews.

Centre in Evolutionary Anthropology and Palaeoecology
    see **Research Centre in Evolutionary Anthropology and Palaeoecology.**

© CBD Research Ltd · Beckenham · Kent BR3 5JS · Tel 020 8650 7745 · Fax 020 8650 0768 · E-mail cbd@cbdresearch.com · www.cbdresearch.com

Centre for Excellence in Applied Research Mental Health   2001
■   Royal London House, Bournemouth University, Christchurch Road, Bournemouth, Dorset, BH1 3LT.
   01202 962114   fax 01202 962131
   http://www.bournemouth.ac.uk/ihcs/resgroupmh.html
   Contact: Prof Dawn Freshwater.
E   A research centre within the Institute of Health and Community Studies (qv) at Bournemouth University.
O   To focus on clarifying and articulating its contribution to the practice, theory and evidence base of mental health and public health disciplines

Centre for Excellence in Dynamic Career Building for Tomorrow's Musician   2005
■   Royal Northern College of Music, 124 Oxford Road, Manchester, M13 9RD.
   0161-907 5200; 5382   fax 0161-273 7611
   http://www.rncm.ac.uk/content/view/231/135/
   Director: Dr Linda Merrick. Administrator: April Robson.
E   A Centre for Excellence in Teaching and Learning (CETL) at the Royal Northern College of Music.
Note: See **Centres for Excellence in Teaching and Learning** for more information.

Centre of Excellence in Earth Observation
   see **Climate and Land-Surface Systems Interaction Centre.**

Centre for Excellence in Enquiry-Based Learning   (CEEBL)   2005
■   University of Manchester, C24 Sackville Street Building, Sackville Street, Manchester, M60 1QD.
   0161-306 6440   fax 0161-306 6455
   http://www.campus.manchester.ac.uk/ceebl/
   Director: Prof Paul O'Neill.
E   A Centre for Excellence in Teaching and Learning (CETL) at the University of Manchester.
Note: See **Centres for Excellence in Teaching and Learning** for further information.

Centre for Excellence in Healthcare Professional Education   (CETL4HealthNE)   2005
■   The Medical School, University of Newcastle upon Tyne, Framlington Place, Newcastle upon Tyne, NE2 4HH.
   0191-222 3910   fax 0191-222 5016
   http://www.cetl4healthne.ac.uk/
   Director: Geoff Hammond.
E   A Centre for Excellence in Teaching and Learning (CETL) at the University of Newcastle upon Tyne.
Note: See **Centres for Excellence in Teaching and Learning** for further information.

Centre for Excellence in Inter Professional Learning in the Public Sector   (CETL:IPPS   2005
■   Health Care Innovation Unit, University of Southampton, B62 - Level 1 - Boldrewood Campus, Bassett Crescent East, Southampton, SO16 7PX.
   023 8059 8835   fax 023 8059 8909
   http://www.ipps.soton.ac.uk/
   Director: Prof Debra Humphris.
E   A Centre for Excellence in Teaching and Learning (CETL) at the University of Southampton.
Note: See **Centres for Excellence in Teaching and Learning** for more information.

Centre of Excellence in Interdisciplinary Mental Health   (CEIMH)   2005
■   University of Birmingham, Edgbaston, Birmingham, B15 2TT.
   0121-414 5734   fax 0121-414 5726
   http://www.ceimh.bham.ac.uk/
   Director: Prof Ann Davis.
E   A Centre for Excellence in Teaching and Learning (CETL) at the University of Birmingham.
O   To enhance and expand the delivery, evaluation and dissemination of innovative, interdisciplinary mental health programmes within higher education and the mental health sector, both nationally and internationally
Note: See **Centres for Excellence in Teaching and Learning** for more information.

Centre for Excellence in Leadership and Professional Learning
■   Liverpool John Moores University, Egerton Court, 2 Rodney Street, Liverpool, L3 5UX.
   0151-231 3618
   http://www.ljmu.ac.uk/CETL
   Contact: Sue Thompson.
E   A Centre for Excellence in Teaching and Learning (CETL) at Liverpool John Moores University.
Note: See **Centres for Excellence in Teaching and Learning** for more information.

Centre for Excellence for Life Sciences   (CELS)   2003
■   University of Newcastle upon Tyne, Life Bioscience Centre, Times Square, Newcastle upon Tyne, NE1 4EP.
   0191-211 2626   fax 0191-211 2596
   http://www.celsatlife.com/
   Chief Executive: Mike Asher.
E   A research centre within the Centre for Life (qv) at the University of Newcastle upon Tyne.
O   To drive growth of the healthcare and life science economies of North East England

Centre for Excellence in Lifelong and Independent Veterinary Education
   see **LIVE Centre for Excellence in Lifelong and Independent Veterinary Education.**

Centre for Excellence in Media Practice   (CEMP)   2005

■   Bournemouth Media School, Bournemouth University, Weymouth House, Talbot Campus, Poole, Dorset, BH12 5BB.
     01202 965360   fax 01202 965530
     http://www.cemp.ac.uk/
     Director: Chris Wensley.
E   A Centre for Excellence in Teaching and Learning at Bournemouth University.
Note: See **Centres for Excellence in Teaching and Learning** for more information.

Centre of Excellence for Optoelectronic Simulation
         see **Bookham Centre of Excellence for Optoelectronic Simulation.**

Centre for Excellence in Performance Arts   (CEPA)   2005

■   Faculty of Humanities, De Montfort University, Clephan Building, The Gateway, Leicester, LE1 9BH.
     0116-207 8558
     http://www.dmu.ac.uk/cepa/
     Contact: Prof Philip Martin.
E   A Centre for Excellence in Teaching and Learning (CETL) at De Montfort University.
O   To support excellent practice and develop innovative approaches in the teaching of dance, drama and music technology
Note: See **Centres for Excellence in Teaching and Learning** for more information.

Centre for Excellence in Preparing for Academic Practice   2005

■   University of Oxford, Littlegate House, 16-17 St Ebbe's Street, Oxford, OX1 1PT.
     01865 286809
     http://www.learning.ox.ac.uk/cetl.php?page=54
     Contact: Prof Lynne McAlpine.
E   A Centre for Excellence in Teaching and Learning (CETL) within the Oxford Learning Institute (qv) at the University of Oxford.
Note: See **Centres for Excellence in Teaching and Learning** for more information.

Centre of Excellence in Product Lifecycle Management   2007

■   Swansea University, Singleton Park, Swansea, SA2 8PP.
     01792 205678
     http://www.swan.ac.uk/research/centresandinstitutes/ProductLifecycleManagement/
E   A research centre at Swansea University.
Note: Not yet open at the time of going to press.

Centre for Excellence in Professional Development Through the Use of Relevant Technologies   (ExPERT Centre)   2005

■   University of Portsmouth, St George's Building, 141 High Street, Portsmouth, PO1 2HY.
     023 9284 5222; 5321   fax 023 9284 5200
     http://www.port.ac.uk/special/ExPERTCentre/
     Director: Prof Lesley Reynolds.
E   A Centre for Excellence in Teaching and Learning (CETL) at the University of Portsmouth.
Note: See **Centres for Excellence in Teaching and Learning** for more information.

Centre for Excellence in Professional Learning from the Workplace   (CEPLW)   2005

■   University of Westminster, 309 Regent Street, London, W1B 2UW.
     020 7911 5000; 5192
     http://www.wmin.ac.uk/page-5818
     Director: Sybil Coldham.
E   A Centre for Excellence in Teaching and Learning (CETL) at the University of Westminster.
O   To prepare students for professional life using the knowledge, skills and attributes typically acquired in the workplace
Note: See **Centres for Excellence in Teaching and Learning** for more information.

Centre for Excellence in Professional Placement Learning   2005

■   University of Plymouth, Drake Circus, Plymouth, PL4 8AA.
     01752 233190
     http://www.placementlearning.org/
     Contact: Susan Lea.
E   A Centre for Excellence in Teaching and Learning (CETL) at the University of Plymouth.
Note: Also the Placement Learning in Health and Social Care CETL; see **Centres for Excellence in Teaching and Learning** for more
     information.

Centre for Excellence in Professional Training and Education
         see **Surrey Centre for Excellence in Professional Training and Education.**

Centre of Excellence for Research in Computational Intelligence and Applications   (Cercia)   2003

■   School of Computer Science, University of Birmingham, Edgbaston, Birmingham, B15 2TT.
     0121-415 8722   fax 0121-414 2799
     http://www.cercia.ac.uk/
     Director: Prof Xin Yao.
E   A centre at the University of Birmingham.

© CBD Research Ltd · Beckenham · Kent BR3 5JS · Tel 020 8650 7745 · Fax 020 8650 0768 · E-mail cbd@cbdresearch.com · www.cbdresearch.com

Centre for Excellence in Teaching and Learning in Applied Undergraduate Research Skills   (CETL-AURS   2005
- University of Reading, Whiteknights, Reading, Berkshire, RG6 6AH.
  0118-378 7948
  http://www.rdg.ac.uk/cdotl/
  Director: Dr John Creighton.
E   A Centre for Excellence in Teaching and Learning (CETL) at the University of Reading.
Note: See **Centres for Excellence in Teaching and Learning** for more information.

Centre for Excellence in Teaching and Learning in Assessment for Learning   2005
- Northumbria University, Ellison Building, Ellison Place, Newcastle upon Tyne, NE1 8ST.
  0191-215 6446
  http://northumbria.ac.uk/cetl_afl/
  Director: Liz McDowell.
E   A Centre for Excellence in Teaching and Learning (CETL) at Northumbria University.
Note: See **Centres for Excellence in Teaching and Learning** for further information.

Centre for Excellence in Teaching and Learning in Clinical and Communication Skills   (4E CETL)   2005
- Barts and the London, Queen Mary's School of Medicine and Dentistry, Queen Mary's University of London, 2 Newark Street, London, E1 2AT.
  020 7882 2509   fax 020 7882 2552
  http://www.cetl.org.uk/
E   A Centre for Excellence in Teaching and Learning (CETL) within the Institute of Health Sciences Education (qv) at Queen Mary, University of London.
Note: See **Centres for Excellence in Teaching and Learning** for more information.

Centre of Excellence in Teaching and Learning in Creativity
   see **InQbate The Centre of Excellence in Teaching and Learning in Creativity.**

Centre for Excellence in Teaching and Learning through Design   (CETLD)   2005
- Faculty of Arts and Architecture, University of Brighton, Grand Parade, Brighton, East Sussex, BN2 0JY.
  01273 600900
  http://cetld.brighton.ac.uk/
  Director: Anne Boddington.
E   A Centre for Excellence in Teaching and Learning (CETL) at the University of Brighton.
Note: See **Centres for Excellence in Teaching and Learning** for more information.

Centre for Excellence in Teaching and Learning in Developing Professionalism in Medical Students
- School of Medical Education, University of Liverpool, Cedar House, Ashton Street, Liverpool, L69 3GE.
  0151-794 8546   fax 0151-794 8763
  http://www.liv.ac.uk/cetl/
  Director: Dr Helen O'Sullivan. Secretary: Clare Hooper.
E   A Centre for Excellence in Teaching and Learning (CETL) at the University of Liverpool.
Note: See **Centres for Excellence in Teaching and Learning** for more information.

Centre for Excellence in Teaching and Learning for Education for Sustainable Development
   see **Centre for Sustainable Futures.**

Centre for Excellence in the Teaching and Learning of Enterprise
   see **White Rose Centre for Excellence in the Teaching and Learning of Enterprise.**

Centre for Excellence in Teaching and Learning in Reusable Learning Objects   2005
- Department of Computing, Communications Technology and Mathematics, London Metropolitan University, Tower Building T6-01, 166-220 Holloway Road, London, N7 8DB.
  020 7133 4340   fax 020 7133 4348
  http://www.rlo-cetl.ac.uk/
  Director: Prof Tom Boyle.
E   A Centre for Excellence in Teaching and Learning (CETL) within the Learning Technology Research Institute (qv) at London Metropolitan University.
Note: See **Centres for Excellence in Teaching and Learning** for more information.

Centre for Excellence in Teaching and Learning for Work Based Learning
Note: See **National Centre for Work Based Learning Partnerships**

Centre for Excellence in Training for Theatre   (CETT)   2004
- Embassy Theatre, Eton Avenue, London, NW3 3HY.
  020 7722 8183
  http://www.cssd.ac.uk/pages/cett.html
  Contact: Linda Cookson.
E   A Centre for Excellence in Teaching and Learning (CETL) at the Central School of Speech and Drama.
Note: See **Centres for Excellence in Teaching and Learning** for more information.

Centre for Excellence in Transport and Product Design   2005
■   School of Art and Design, Coventry University, Priory Street, Coventry, CV1 5FB.
      024 7688 8055
      http://www.coventry.ac.uk/d/893/a/2036
      Director: John Owen.
E   A Centre for Excellence in Teaching and Learning (CETL) at Coventry University.
Note: See **Centres for Excellence in Teaching and Learning** for more information.

Centre of Excellence for Work-Based Learning for Education Professionals   (WLE Centre)   2006
■   University of London, 20 Bedford Way, London, WC1H 0AL.
      020 7612 6561
      http://www.wlecentre.ac.uk/
      Director: Prof Karen Evans. Contact: Carla Cretan.
E   A Centre for Excellence in Teaching and Learning (CETL) within the Institute of Education (qv) at the University of London.
Note: See **Centres for Excellence in Teaching and Learning** for more information.

Centre for Executive Learning   (CEL)
■   Cranfield School of Management, Cranfield University, Cranfield, Bedfordshire, MK43 0AL.
      01234 751122   fax 01234 751806
      http://www.som.cranfield.ac.uk/som/research/centres/celc/
      Contact: Prof Kim Turnbull James.
E   A research centre within the Cranfield Management Research Institute (qv) at Cranfield University.
○   To understand the new challenges for executive learning and develop leading edge knowledge in the field of learning for leadership, executive development and organisational learning

Centre for Exercise and Nutrition Science   (CENS)
■   School of Applied and Health Sciences, University of Chester, Parkgate Road, Chester, CH1 4BJ.
      01244 375444
      http://www.chester.ac.uk/cens/
      Director: Prof Kevin Sykes.
E   A research centre at the University of Chester.

Centre for Experimental Economics   (EXEC)
■   Department of Economics and Related Studies, University of York, Heslington, York, YO10 5DD.
      01904 321401
      http://www.york.ac.uk/inst/exec/
E   A research centre at the University of York.

Centre for Exploitation of Science and Technology
Note: No longer in existence.

Centre for Extremophile Research   (CER)
■   Department of Biology and Biochemistry, University of Bath, Claverton Down, Bath, BA2 7AY.
      01225 386240
      http://www.bath.ac.uk/cer/
      Director: Prof Michael Danson.
E   A centre at the University of Bath.
○   To bring together interdisciplinary expertise on extremophilic micro-organisms, including microbiology, enzymology, protein crystallography, molecular biology, bioinformatics, bioprocessing, and synthetic chiral chemistry

Centre for Family, Kinship and Childhood
      see **Families, Life Course and Generations Research Centre.**

Centre for Family Research   (CFR)   1969
■   Faculty of Social and Political Sciences, University of Cambridge, Free School Lane, Cambridge, CB2 3RF.
      01223 334510   fax 01223 330574
      http://www.sps.cam.ac.uk/cfr/
      Director: Susan Golombok.
E   A department of the University of Cambridge.
○   To pursue and disseminate research related to family life

Centre for Family Studies
      see **Newcastle Centre for Family Studies.**

Centre for Fashion, the Body and Material Cultures
■   Central Saint Martins College of Art and Design, University of the Arts London, Southampton Row, London, WC1B 4AP.
      020 7514 7000
      http://www.arts.ac.uk/research/17640.htm
      Contact: Prof Helen Thomas.
E   A research centre at the University of the Arts, London.
○   To explore the nexus of fashion, material cultures and the body

    © CBD Research Ltd · Beckenham · Kent BR3 5JS · Tel 020 8650 7745 · Fax 020 8650 0768 · E-mail cbd@cbdresearch.com · www.cbdresearch.com

Centre for Fashion Studies
   see **London Centre for Fashion Studies.**

Centre for Festival and Event Management   (CFEM)
■   Napier University Business School, Napier University, Craiglockhart Campus, Edinburgh, EH14 1DJ.
   http://www.napier.ac.uk/Nubs/CentreforFestivalandEventManagement.htm
E   A centre at Napier University.

Centre for Film and Popular Culture
   see **Richard Burton Centre for Film and Popular Culture.**

Centre for Film Studies
■   Department of Film, Literature and Theatre Studies, University of Essex, Wivenhoe Park, Colchester, Essex, CO4 3SQ.
   01206 872313
   http://www.essex.ac.uk/filmstudies/
   Contact: Belinda Waterman.
E   A centre at the University of Essex.

Centre for Film Studies   (CFS)
■   School of Modern Languages, Queen Mary's University, London, Mile End Road, London, E1 4NS.
   020 7882 3335   fax 020 8980 5400
   http://www.modern-languages.qmul.ac.uk/research/filmstudies/
E   A research centre at Queen Mary, University of London.
O   To conduct research in cinema, with particular emphasis on British, European, Hollywood and Latin-American cinema

Centre for Film Studies   (CFS)   2005
■   School of Philosophical, Anthropological and Film Studies, University of St Andrews, 99 North Street, St Andrews, Fife, KY16 9AD.
   01334 476473
   http://www.st-andrews.ac.uk/filmstudies/research/institute.html
   Director: Prof Dina Iordanova.
E   An interdisciplinary research centre at the University of St Andrews.
O   To encourage research in film studies
●   Film screenings - Seminars

Centre for Finance and Financial Services   (CFFS)
■   Westminster Business School, University of Westminster, 35 Marylebone Road, London, NW1 5LS.
   020 7911 5000
   http://www.wmin.ac.uk/wbs/page-55
   Director: Dr Ben Nowman.
E   A research centre at the University of Westminster.
O   To enhance practice and student experience of financial, financial services and accounting through high-level events, research and
   publishing

Centre for Finance and Investment
   see **Xfi Centre for Finance and Investment.**

Centre for Financial Management   (CFM)
■   University of Gloucester Business School, University of Gloucester, The Park, Cheltenham, Gloucestershire, GL50 2RH.
   0870 721 0210
   http://www.glos.ac.uk/faculties/ugbs/research/financialmanagement.cfm
   Contact: Prof Bob Ryan.
E   A centre at the University of Gloucestershire.
O   To conduct research into various aspects of financial management, with particular current emphasis on the history and
   implementation of value-based accounting systems

Centre for Financial and Management Studies   (CeFiMS)
■   Department of Financial and Management Studies, School of Oriental and African Studies, University of London, Thornhaugh
   Street, Russell Square, London, WC1H 0XG.
   020 7898 4050   fax 020 7898 4089
   http://www.soas.ac.uk/departments/departmentinfo.cfm?navid=266
   Director: Prof Laurence Harris.
E   A research centre at the School of Oriental and African Studies, University of London.
O   To conduct research in various fields of finance and management, with particular emphasis on corporate governance, corporate
   finance, finance and economic growth, financial regulation, and management in China, Japan, the Middle East and North Africa

Centre for Financial Markets Research   (CFMR)
■   Management School and Economics, University of Edinburgh, 50 George Square, Edinburgh, EH8 9JY.
   0131-650 3900
   http://www.man.ed.ac.uk/research/centres/cfm/
E   A research centre at the University of Edinburgh.
O   To increase the volume and quality of financial markets research

Centre for Financial Regulation and Crime (CFRC) 2004

■ Cass Business School, City Business School, 106 Bunhill Row, London, EC1Y 8TZ.
020 7040 0166; 8600 fax 020 7040 8700
http://www.cass.city.ac.uk/cfrc/
Director: Dr Chizu Nakajima.
E A research centre at City University.
O To conduct research and teaching in all aspects of the fight against financial crime

Centre for Financial Research (CFR)

■ Judge Business School, University of Cambridge, Trumpington Street, Cambridge, CB2 1AG.
01223 339641 fax 01223 339652
http://www-cfr.jbs.cam.ac.uk/
Director: Prof Michael Dempster.
E A centre at the University of Cambridge.
O To conduct research in finance (including derivatives, risk management, foreign exchange, trading systems, real options and stock markets), logistics and telecommunications

Centre for Fine Art and Philosophy (CFAP)

■ School of Art, Design and Media, University of Portsmouth, Eldon Building, Winston Churchill Avenue, Portsmouth, PO1 2DJ.
023 9284 3835 fax 023 9284 3808
http://www.port.ac.uk/departments/
E A centre at the University of Portsmouth.
O To organise seminars, conferences and exhibitions which explore the intersection of contemporary developments in fine art practice and philosophy

Centre for Fine Art Research (CFAR)

■ Birmingham City University, Gosta Green, Corporation Street, Birmingham, B4 7DX.
0121-331 5800; 5801 fax 0121-331 7814
http://www.biad.uce.ac.uk/cssonlysite/CFAP/CFAP.asp
E A research centre within the Birmingham Institute of Art and Design (qv) at Birmingham City University.
O To engage in international art practice and exchange

Centre for Fine Print Research (CFPR)

■ Bristol School of Art, Media and Design, Bower Ashton Campus, University of the West of England, Kennel Lodge Road, Bristol, BS3 2JT.
0117-328 4716 fax 0117-328 4745
http://amd.uwe.ac.uk/cfpr/
Director: Prof Stephen Hoskins.
E A research centre at the University of the West of England.
O To conduct research in the development of quality fine print, primarily undertaken from a fine art perspective

Centre for First World War Studies 2002

■ Department of Medieval and Modern History, University of Birmingham, Arts Building, Edgbaston, Birmingham, B15 2TT.
0121-414 3983
http://www.firstworldwar.bham.ac.uk/
Director: Dr John Bourne.
E A centre at the University of Birmingham.
O To provide an intellectual and social focus for study on the First World War

Centre for Food, Physical Activity and Obesity

■ School of Health and Social Care, University of Teesside, Middlesbrough, TS1 3BA.
01642 342769; 382771
http://www.tees.ac.uk/schools/SOH/obesity.cfm
Director: Prof Carolyn Summerbell.
E A research centre within the Institute for Health Sciences and Social Care Research (qv) at the University of Teesside.
O To focus research on increasing the evidence base for prevention and treatment of obesity, and the promotion of healthy lifestyles that might contribute to reducing obesity

Centre for Foodservice Research (CFR) 1993

■ School of Services Management, Bournemouth University, Dorset House, Fern Barrow, Poole, Dorset, BH12 5BB.
01202 965127
http://www.bournemouth.ac.uk/services-management/research/cfr.html
Head: Prof John Edwards.
E A centre at Bournemouth University.
O To undertake projects, primarily in the public sector, involving the quality of food provision

Centre for Forecasting
        see **Lancaster Centre for Forecasting.**

© CBD Research Ltd · Beckenham · Kent BR3 5JS · Tel 020 8650 7745 · Fax 020 8650 0768 · E-mail cbd@cbdresearch.com · www.cbdresearch.com

Centre for Forensic Computing   (CFFC)
- Department of Information Systems, Cranfield University, Shrivenham, Swindon, Wiltshire, SN6 8LA.
  01793 785270
  http://www.dcmt.cranfield.ac.uk/dois/cffc
  Contact: Miss L C Sheppard.
- E   A research centre at Cranfield University.
- O   To conduct research, education and training programmes in various areas of forensic computing

Centre for Forensic and Family Psychology   (CFFP)   1991
- School of Psychology, University of Birmingham, Edgbaston, Birmingham, B15 2TT.
  0121-414 3319; 3402   fax 0121-414 8248
  http://psg275.bham.ac.uk/forensic_centre/index.htm
  Director: Prof Kevin Browne.
- E   A centre at the University of Birmingham.
- O   To conduct research into the causes and consequences of family violence, child maltreatment and serious crime, and the study of prevention through prediction, assessment and treatment of victims and offenders
Note: The CFFP is a World Health Organisation **WHO Collaborating Centre** for Child Care and Protection.

Centre for Forensic Investigation   (CFI)   2005
- School of Engineering, Science and Design, Glasgow Caledonian University, Cowcaddens Road, Glasgow, G4 0BA.
  0141-331 3679
  http://www.gcal.ac.uk/esd/research/centres_forensic.html
  Contact: Dr Ray Ansell.
- E   A research centre at Glasgow Caledonian University.
- O   To advance forensic investigation in the widest sense through postgraduate teaching, research, professional practice and consultancy

Centre for Forensic Investigation   (CFI)
- School of Science and Technology, University of Teesside, Middlesbrough, TS1 3BA.
  01642 342427   fax 01642 342401
  http://www.tees.ac.uk/researchcentres/cfi/
  Dean: Brian Hobbs.
- E   A research centre at the University of Teesside.
- O   To enhance and expand the existing range of activities in crime scene science, forensic science, forensic investigation, disaster management and related areas

Centre for Forensic and Legal Medicine   (CFLM)
- School of Medicine, University of Dundee, Fleming Gymnasium Building, Dundee, DD1 4HN.
  01382 388020   fax 01382 388021
  http://www.dundee.ac.uk/forensicmedicine/
  Director: Prof Derrick J Pounder.
- E   A research centre at the University of Dundee.

Centre for Forensic Science   (CFS)
- Department of Pure and Applied Chemistry, University of Strathclyde, Thomas Graham Building, 295 Cathedral Street, Glasgow, G1 1XL.
  0141-548 2019; 2282   fax 0141-548 4822
  http://www.chem.strath.ac.uk/research.php?id=1
  Director: Prof Jim Fraser.
- E   A research centre at the University of Strathclyde.

Centre for Forensic Statistics and Legal Reasoning
   see **Joseph Bell Centre for Forensic Statistics and Legal Reasoning.**

Centre for Formative Assessment Studies   (CFAS)   1988
- School of Education, University of Manchester, Humanities Devas Street, Oxford Road, Manchester, M13 9PL.
  0161-275 3418; 3524   fax 0161-275 8280
  http://www.education.manchester.ac.uk/research/centres/cfas/
  Director: Bill Boyle. Manager: Andrew Fryers.
- E   A research centre at the University of Manchester.
- O   To conduct a range of national and international research encompassing developments in teaching, learning and assessment, the monitroring of curriculum implementation and evaluations of organisations and programmes

Centre for Fraud Risk Management
   see **International Fraud Prevention Research Centre.**

Centre for French History and Culture   (CFHC)   2005
- School of History, University of St Andrews, St Andrews, Fife, KY16 9AL.
  01334 462886; 462902   fax 01334 462927
  http://www.st-andrews.ac.uk/history/frenchcentre/
  Director: Dr Guy Rowlands.
- E   A research centre at the University of St Andrews.
- O   To conduct research in any field and on any period related to the history of France and its possessions

Centre for Fun and Families   1990

■   177-179 Narborough Road, Leicester, LE3 0PE.
    0116-223 4254   fax 0116-275 8558
    http://www.funandfamilies.co.uk
    Co-Manager: Jayne Ballard. Co-Manager: Rita Nag.
E   A registered charity.
O   To assist families where parents are experiencing behaviour and communication difficulties with their children; to offer practical help to parents with children of all ages; to equip workers with the necessary skills and resources to run Fun and Family groups
●   Training packages - Workshops

Centre for Functional Genomics   2003

■   School of Biomedical Sciences, Coleraine Campus, University of Ulster, Cromore Road, Coleraine, County Londonderry, BT52 1SA.
    028 7032 4159   fax 028 7032 4956
    http://www.science.ulster.ac.uk/biomed/research/cfg.html
    Contact: Dr Victor A Gault, BSc.
E   A research centre within the Biomedical Sciences Research Institute (qv) at the University of Ulster.
O   To research into genetics, in particular how specific genes can be used to target life-threatening medical conditions such as cancer and diabetes

Centre for Functional Magnetic Resonance Imaging of the Brain
    see **Oxford Centre for Functional Magnetic Resonance Imaging of the Brain.**

Centre for Fundamental Physics
    see **Ogden Centre for Fundamental Physics.**

Centre for Fusion Studies and Plasma Engineering

■   Blackett Laboratory, Imperial College London, Prince Consort Road, London, SW7 2UW.
    020 7594 7656
    http://www3.imperial.ac.uk/courses/azofdepartmentsandcentres/fusionstudiesandplasmaengineering
    Director: Prof Malcolm Haines.
E   A research centre at Imperial College London.

Centre for Fusion, Space and Astrophysics   (CFSA)   1995

■   Department of Physics, University of Warwick, Coventry, CV4 7AL.
    024 7652 3965   fax 024 7669 2016
    http://www2.warwick.ac.uk/fac/sci/physics/research/cfsa/
    Co-Director: Prof S C Chapman. Co-Director: Prof R O Dendy.
E   A centre attached to the University of Warwick.
O   To focus research on plasma physics applied to the grand challenges of fusion power, space physics, solar physics and astrophysics

Centre for Future Communications
    see **Research Centre for Future Communications.**

Centre for Future and Emerging Technologies - Research and Applications   (CFERA)

■   Informatics Research Institute, University of Salford, Salford, Manchester, M5 4WT.
    0161 295 5292
    http://www.iris.salford.ac.uk/iris/p/?s=3&pid=2
    Director: Prof Alison Adam.
E   A centre within the Informatics Research Institute (qv) of the University of Salford.

Centre for Future Studies

■   Stelling Minnis, Canterbury, Kent, CT4 6AQ.
    01227 709575
    http://www.futurestudies.co.uk/
E   An independent think tank.

Centre for Gastroenterology
    see **Centre for Adult and Paediatric Gastroenterology.**

Centre for Gastroenterology and Nutrition

■   Department of Medicine, University College London Hospital, 235 Euston Road, London, NW1 2BU.
    0845 155 5000   fax 020 8342 8308
    http://www.ucl.ac.uk/medicine/gastroenterology/
    Director: Prof Alastair Forbes.
E   A research centre at University College London.
O   To conduct research in a very wide variety of fields within gastroenterology and nutrition, including tissue engineering, neurogastroenterology, inflammatory bowel disease, neuroendocrine tumours, specialist and invasive endoscopy techniques, gastrointestinal cancer, radiation enteritis, pancreatic disease, hepatitis, cell signalling, paediatric gastroenterology, and nutritional science

 © CBD Research Ltd · Beckenham · Kent BR3 5JS · Tel 020 8650 7745 · Fax 020 8650 0768 · E-mail cbd@cbdresearch.com · www.cbdresearch.com

Centre for Gender and Religions Research   (GRR)   2001

■   Faculty of Arts and Humanities, School of Oriental and African Studies, University of London, Thornhaugh Street, Russell Square, London, WC1H 0XG.
   020 7898 4774   fax 020 7436 3844
   http://www.soas.ac.uk/Religions/grr/
   Chairman: Prof Brian Bocking.
E   A research centre at the School of Oriental and African Studies, University of London.
O   To promote the cross-cultural study of gender and religion
●   Conferences - Seminars
Note: Also known as the Gender and Religion Research Centre.

Centre for Gender Research   (CGR)

■   Department of Sociology, Social Sciences Building, Northampton Square, London, EC1V 0HB.
   020 7040 5060   fax 020 7040 5070
   http://www.city.ac.uk/sociology/GenderResearch/GenderCentre.html
E   A centre at City University.
O   To provide national and international research, consultancy and policy advice on questions of gender and contemporary social change

Centre for Gender, Sexuality and Writing

■   School of English, Rutherford College Extension, City University, Canterbury, Kent, CT2 7NX.
   01227 764000
   http://www.kent.ac.uk/english/staff-research/centres/gswcentre.html
E   A research centre at the University of Kent.

Centre for Gender Studies   (CGS)

■   School of Social Science, University of Aberdeen, Edward Wright Building, Dunbar Street, Old Aberdeen, AB24 3QY.
   01224 272768   fax 01224 272552
   http://www.abdn.ac.uk/genderstudies/
   Director: Dr Marysia Zalewski.
E   An interdisciplinary research centre at the University of Aberdeen.
O   To conduct research and teaching in the role of men and women in society

Centre for Gender Studies   (CGS)

■   School of Social Sciences and Cultural Studies, University of Sussex, Arts D 335, Falmer, Brighton, East Sussex, BN1 9RQ.
   01273 678442   fax 01273 678835
   http://www.sussex.ac.uk/gender/
   Director: Dr Jacqueline O'Reilly.
E   A department of the University of Sussex.
O   To study ideas about masculinity and femininity

Centre for Gender Studies [Cambridge]
   see **Cambridge Centre for Gender Studies.**

Centre in Gender Studies [Strathclyde]
   see **Strathclyde Centre in Gender Studies.**

Centre for Gender Studies   (CGS)

■   Faculty of Languages and Cultures, School of Oriental and African Studies, University of London, Thornhaugh Street, Russell Square, London, WC1H 0XG.
   020 7898 4247   fax 020 7898 4399
   http://www.soas.ac.uk/centres/centreinfo.cfm?navid=1052
   Director: Dr Rachel Harrison.
E   An interdisciplinary research centre at the School of Oriental and African Studies, University of London.
O   To promote research and teaching in the field of gender studies, with particular reference to Africa and Asia

Centre for Gender Studies   (CGS)

■   Department of French, University of Sheffield, Arts Tower, Sheffield, S10 2TN.
   0114-222 4386   fax 0114-275 1198
   http://www.genderstudies.group.shef.ac.uk/
   Director: Prof Máire Cross.
E   A research centre at the University of Sheffield.
O   To bring together researchers working in the field of gender studies

Centre for Gender and Women's Studies   (CGWS)   1996

■   School of Geography, Politics and Sociology, University of Newcastle upon Tyne, Newcastle upon Tyne, NE1 7RU.
   0191-222 7643
   http://www.ncl.ac.uk/cgws/
   Director: Prof Diane Richardson.
E   A research centre at the University of Newcastle upon Tyne.
O   To promote teaching and research on gender and women's studies

Centre for General Practice (CGP)

■ Bournemouth University, Royal London House, Christchurch Road, Bournemouth, Dorset, BH1 3LT.
01202 962114   fax 01202 962131
http://www.bournemouth.ac.uk/ihcs/gpcentre.html
E   A research centre within the Institute of Health and Community Studies (qv) at Bournemouth University.

Centre for General Practice and Primary Care

■ Barts and the London, Queen Mary's School of Medicine and Dentistry, Queen Mary's, University of London, Abernethy Building, 2 Newark Street, London, E1 2AT.
020 7882 2509
http://www.ihse.qmul.ac.uk/chs/research/gppc/
E   A research centre within the Centre for Health Sciences (qv) at Queen Mary, University of London.

Centre for Genetic Anthropology (TCGA) 1996

■ Department of Biology, University College London, The Darwin Building, Gower Street, London, WC1E 6BT.
020 7679 2654   fax 020 7679 7096
http://www.ucl.ac.uk/tcga/
Chairman: Dr Neil Bradman.
E   A research centre at University College London.
O   To pursue research on the evolutions and migrations of human populations in North Africa, East Africa, the Near East, Asia and Europe

Centre for Genomics in Society
see **ESRC Centre for Genomics in Society.**

Centre for Geo-Information Studies (GIS)

■ School of Computing and Technology, Docklands Campus, University of East London, 4-6 University Way, London, E16 2RD.
020 8223 2352   fax 020 8223 2918
http://www.uel.ac.uk/geo-information/
Director: Prof Allan J Brimicombe.
E   A research centre at the University of East London.
O   To specialise in all aspects of geo-information science, systems and engineering applied broadly to areas of the physical, social and cultural environment

Centre for Geographical Information Management
see **Cranfield Centre for Geographical Information Management.**

Centre for Geomechanics
see **Nottingham Centre for Geomechanics.**

Centre for Geomorphology

■ School of Conservation Sciences, Bournemouth University, Christchurch House, Talbot Campus, Poole, Dorset, BH12 5BB.
01202 965178   fax 01202 965530
http://www.bournemouth.ac.uk/conservation/abouttheschool/egs/centre_geomorphology.html
Director: Prof Matthew Bennett.
E   A centre at Bournemouth University.
O   To focus research on a range of natural landscapes

Centre for Geophysical and Astrophysical Fluid Dynamics

■ School of Engineering, Computer Science and Mathematics, University of Exeter, Harrison Building, North Park Road, Exeter, EX4 4QE.
01392 263650   fax 01392 264067
http://www.secam.ex.ac.uk/index.php?nav=89
Director: Prof Keke Zhang.
E   A research centre at the University of Exeter.
O   To provide a focus for a wide range of research activity in applied mathematics, theoretical physics and numerical modelling relevant to weather, climate and magnetic field generation, all of which are determined by fluid flow on planetary scales

Centre for Geospatial Science (CGS) 2005

■ School of Geography, University of Nottingham, University Park, Nottingham, NG7 2RD.
0115-846 8130   fax 0115-951 5249
http://www.nottingham.ac.uk/cgs/
Director: Prof Mike Jackson.
E   A research centre at the University of Nottingham.
O   To undertake research in the fields of Geospatial intelligence, Geospatial interoperability, Mobile location based services, and Positioning, routing and tracking

Centre for German and Austrian Exile Studies
see **Research Centre for German and Austrian Exile Studies.**

Centre for German-Jewish Studies   (CGJS)   1994
- School of Humanities, University of Sussex, Falmer, Brighton, East Sussex, BN1 9SJ.
  01273 678771
  http://www.sussex.ac.uk/cgjs/
  Contact: Prof Edward Timms. Contact: Diana Franklin.
- E   An interdisciplinary research centre at the University of Sussex.
- O   To conduct teaching and research in the history, culture and thought of Jews in central Europe

Centre for Gerontological Practice   (CGP)   2003
- School of Nursing, Midwifery and Community Health, Glasgow Caledonian University, Cowcaddens Road, Glasgow, G4 0BA.
  0141-331 8311; 8492   fax 0141-331 8312
  http://www.gcal.ac.uk/nmch/research/cogp.html
  Administrator: Margaret McLay.
- E   A research centre at Glasgow Caledonian University.
- O   To enable expansion of interdisciplinary work related to the care of older people

Centre for Glaciology   1996
- Llandinam Building, University of Wales Aberystwyth, Aberystwyth, Ceredigion, SY23 2DB.
  01970 621860; 622606
  http://www.aber.ac.uk/glaciology/
  Director: Prof Mike Hambrey.
- E   A research centre within the Institute of Geography and Earth Sciences (qv) at the University of Wales, Aberystwyth.
- O   To conduct research in glaciology, snow processes and glacial geology

Centre for Glass Research   (CGR)
- Department of Engineering Materials, University of Sheffield, Sir Robert Hadfield Building, Mappin Street, Sheffield, S1 3JD.
  0114-222 5467; 5941   fax 0114-222 5943
  http://www.sheffield.ac.uk/materials/research/centres/glass/
  Co-Director: Dr J M Parker. Co-Director: Dr R J Hand.
- E   A research centre at the University of Sheffield.
- O   To focus research on various applications with glass, including glass melting, crystallisation, glass ceramics, strength and durability

Centre for Global Atmospheric Modelling
Note: has become the NCAS Climate @ Reading Programme and is therefore outside the scope of this directory.

Centre for Global Education
    see **MUNDI Centre for Global Education.**

Centre for Global Energy Studies   (CGES)   1989
- 17 Knightsbridge, London, SW1X 7LY.
  020 7235 4334   fax 020 7235 4338
  http://www.cges.co.uk/
  Marketing and Business Development Manager: Jenni Wilson.
- E   An independent non-profit-distributing organisation.
- O   To carry out research on global energy issues, and to act as a forum for world energy debate

Centre for Global Political Economy   (CGPE)
- Department of International Relations, University of Sussex, Arts 327, Falmer, Brighton, East Sussex, BN1 9SJ.
  01273 678064   fax 01273 673563
  http://www.sussex.ac.uk/ir/1-4-7.html
  Director: Prof Kees van der Pijl.
- E   A research centre at the University of Sussex.

Centre for Globalisation, Education and Societies
    see **CLIO Centre for Globalisation, Education and Societies.**

Centre for Globalisation Research   (CGR)   2005
- School of Business and Management, Queen Mary, University of London, Mile End Road, London, E1 4NS.
  020 7882 3167   fax 020 7882 3615
  http://www.busman.qmul.ac.uk/cgr/
  Co-Director: Prof Brigitte Granville. Co-Director: Teresa da Silva Lopes.
- E   A research centre at Queen Mary, University of London.
- O   To conduct research on globalisation and the institutions and policies needed to enhance it

Centre for Government and Charity Management   (CGCM)   2002
- Faculty of Business, Computing and Information Management, London South Bank University, London Road Building, 103 Borough Road, London, SE1 0AA.
  020 7815 7886
  http://www.lsbu.ac.uk/bcim/cgcm/
  Director: Prof Alex Murdock.
- E   A research centre at London South Bank University.
- O   To encourage and facilitate study into the distinctive characteristics of voluntary organisations and the not-for-profit sector

Centre for Graduate Medical Education and Research
   see **Trafford Centre for Graduate Medical Education and Research.**

Centre for Grain Process Engineering
   see **Satake Centre for Grain Process Engineering.**

Centre for Grid Computing
■   Department of Process and Systems Engineering, Cranfield University, Building 63, Cranfield, Bedfordshire, MK43 0AL.
   01234 754213
   http://www.cranfield.ac.uk/soe/amac/computing/
   Director: Prof Frank Zhigang Wang.
E   A research centre at Cranfield University.
○   To conduct research on data storage, data mining, data warehousing and data-intensive computing on grid platforms, within the
   context of the Cambridge-Cranfield High Performance Computing Facility

Centre for Growing Businesses
■   Nottingham Business School, Nottingham Trent University, Burton Street, Nottingham, NG1 4BU.
   0115-848 6128
   http://www.nbs.ntu.ac.uk/cgb/
E   A centre at Nottingham Trent University.

Centre for Growth and Business Cycle Research   (CGBCR)
■   School of Social Sciences, University of Manchester, Dover Street, Manchester, M13 9PL.
   0161-275 3908
   http://www.ses.man.ac.uk/cgbcr/
   Co-Director: Prof Keith Blackburn. Co-Director: Prof Pierre-Richard Agénor.
E   A research centre at the University of Manchester.
○   To provide a focus for the thriving wide-ranging research on growth and business cycles

Centre for Guidance Studies   (CeGS)
■   School of Education, University of Derby, Kedleston Road, Derby, DE22 1GB.
   01332 591266
   http://www.derby.ac.uk/cegs/
   Contact: Deirdre Hughes.
E   A research centre at the University of Derby.
○   To bridge the gap between guidance theory and practice in support of lifelong learning

Centre for Haematology
■   Barts and the London, Queen Mary's School of Medicine and Dentistry, Queen Mary, University of London, 4 Newark Street,
   London, E1 2AT.
   020 7377 7180; 7882 2483   fax 020 7882 2200
   http://www.icms.qmul.ac.uk/centres/haematology/
   Lead: Prof Adrian C Newland.
E   A research centre within the Institute of Cell and Molecular Science (qv) at Queen Mary, University of London.
○   To conduct research in various areas of haematology, with particular focus on autoimmune thrombocytopenia, dendritic cell
   biology, lymphoproliferation, Down's Leukaemia and myeloproliferation, and forensic genetics

Centre for Hazard and Risk Management   (CHaRM)
■   Loughborough University Business School, Loughborough University, Loughborough, Leicestershire, LE11 3TU.
   01509 222175; 263171   fax 01509 223991
   http://www.lboro.ac.uk/departments/charm/
E   A research centre at Loughborough University.
○   To provide postgraduate training in the management of back care, healthcare risk, occupational health and safety, and security
●   Education and training

Centre for Health Care Research
   see **Centre for Behavioural Medicine.**

Centre for Health Economics   (CHE)   1983
■   Department of Economics and Related Studies, University of York, Alcuin College, Heslington, York, YO10 5DD.
   01904 321401   fax 01904 321402
   http://www.york.ac.uk/inst/che/
   Director: Prof Peter C Smith.
E   A research centre at the University of York.
○   To undertake high quality research that is capable of influencing health policy decisions

Centre for Health Ergonomics
   see **Robens Centre for Health Ergonomics.**

Centre for Health, Exercise and Rehabilitation   (CHER)
- School of Sport, Health and Exercise Sciences, University of Wales Bangor, George Building, Normal Site, Bangor, Gwynedd, LL57 2PZ.
  01248 382756   fax 01248 371053
  http://www.shes.bangor.ac.uk/
- E   A research centre within the Institute for Rehabilitation (qv) at the University of Wales, Bangor.

Centre for Health Improvement and Leadership in Lincoln   (CHILL)   2005
- Brayford Pool, Lincoln, LN6 7TS.
  01522 837060
  http://www.lincoln.ac.uk/home/chill/
  Director: Gerry McSorley.
- E   A research centre at the University of Lincoln.
- O   To support health and social care organisations in transforming their services so as to achieve excellence in care delivery

Centre for Health Informatics [City]   (CHI)   1983
- School of Informatics, City University, Northampton Square, London, EC1V 0HB.
  020 7040 8369   fax 020 7040 8364
  http://www.soi.city.ac.uk/organisation/chi/
  Executive Officer: Mrs Gill Smith.
- E   An independent research centre and department of City University.
- O   To develop advanced concepts, methods and techniques of medical and health informatics for application in the solution of clinical and healthcare problems
Note: Formally launched in 2005 as the Centre for Health Informatics.

Centre for Health Informatics [Leeds]
>   see **Yorkshire Centre for Health Informatics.**

Centre for Health Informatics [Newcastle]
>   see **Sowerby Centre for Health Informatics.**

Centre for Health Informatics and Multiprofessional Education   (CHIME)   1995
- Archway Campus, University College London, Highgate Hill, London, N19 5LW.
  020 7288 5966
  http://www.chime.ucl.ac.uk/
- E   An interdisciplinary research centre at University College London.
- O   To undertake research and provide undergraduate and postgraduate education in information and quality management, to support clinical practice and to benefit local communities - both patients and health care professionals
Note: CHIME is a World Health Organisation **WHO Collaborating Centre** for Community Control of Hereditary Disorders.

Centre for Health Information, Research and Evaluation   (CHIRAL)
- School of Medicine, Swansea University, Singleton Park, Swansea, SA2 8PP.
  01792 513400   fax 01792 513430
  http://www.chiral.swansea.ac.uk/
  Executive Director: David Ford.
- E   An interdisciplinary research centre within the Institute of Life Science (qv) at Swansea University.
- O   To undertake research at the individual, organisational and population levels to improve the quality of patient care, maximise the cost-effectiveness of service delivery, develop primary prevention strategies directed at important public health problems, and evaluate the effectiveness of new initiatives in health and social care

Centre for Health and International Relations   (CHAIR)   2003
- Department of International Politics, University of Wales, Aberystwyth, Penglais, Aberystwyth, Ceredigion, SY23 3FE.
  01970 621799
  http://www.aber.ac.uk/interpol/research_index.html
  Director: Prof Colin McInnes.
- E   A research centre at the University of Wales, Aberystwyth.
- O   To conduct research on the relationships between health and international politics

Centre for Health Management   (CHM)
- Tanaka Business School, South Kensington Campus, Imperial College London, Exhibition Road, London, SW7 2AZ.
  020 7594 9217
  http://www3.imperial.ac.uk/healthmanagement
  Director: Prof Rifat A Atun.
- E   A research centre at Imperial College London.
- O   To conduct health section research, education and development that is international in orientation, and with a particular emphasis on Europe, Central Asia and Latin America

Centre for Health, Medicine and Society

■ School of Arts and Humanities, Oxford Brookes University, Oxford, OX3 0BP.
  01865 483665
  http://www.ah.brookes.ac.uk/index.php/historyofmedicine/
  Director: Prof Steven King.
E A research centre at Oxford Brookes University.
O To promote the study of the social and cultural history of medicine

Centre for Health Planning and Management (CHPM) 1986

■ School of Economics and Management Studies, Keele University, Darwin Building, Keele, Staffordshire, ST5 5BG.
  01782 583191   fax 01782 711737
  http://www.keele.ac.uk/depts/hm/
E A research centre within the Research Institute for Public Policy and Management (qv) at Keele University.
O To improve health through better planning and management

Centre for Health Promotion Research (CHPR) 1997

■ Faculty of Health, Leeds Metropolitan University, Civic Quarter, Calverley Street, Leeds, LS1 3HE.
  0113-283 2600   fax 0113-283 1908
  http://www.leedsmet.ac.uk/health/healthpromotion/chpr/chpr.htm
  Administrator: Marianne Kennedy.
E A research centre at Leeds Metropolitan University.
O To conduct research on the develoment and evaluation of health education materials

Centre for Health Psychology (CHP)

■ Corstophine Campus, Queen Margaret University, Clerwood Terrace, Edinburgh, EH12 8TS.
  0131-317 3000
  http://www.qmuc.ac.uk/psych/chp.htm
E A research centre at Queen Margaret University.

Centre for Health Psychology (CHP)

■ Faculty of Health and Sciences, Staffordshire University, Mellor Building, College Road, Stoke-on-Trent, ST4 2DF.
  01782 294648   fax 01782 294986
  http://www.staffs.ac.uk/schools/sciences/ihr/chp/
  Director: Prof David White.
E A research centre within the Institute for Health Research (qv) at Staffordshire University.
O To provide training for health psychologists; to promote psychological research into illness and health and into health care delivery

Centre for Health and Public Services Management (CHPSM)

■ Department of Management Studies, University of York, Heslington, York, YO10 5DD.
  01904 432222   fax 01904 434163
  http://www.york.ac.uk/management/chpsm/
  Director: Dr Russell Mannion.
E A research centre at the University of York.
O To conduct research and teaching in health and public services management

Centre for Health Research and Evaluation (CHRE)

■ School of Health and Social Care, University of Greenwich, Park Row, London, SE10 9LS.
  http://www.gre.ac.uk/schools/health/research
E A research centre at the University of Greenwich.
O To conduct research in the fields of primary care, public health, health promotion and clinical effectiveness

Centre for Health Research and Practice Development (CHRPD)

■ St Martin's College, Fusehill Street, Carlisle, Cumbria, CA1 2HH.
  01228 616364
  http://www.ucsm.ac.uk/faculties/health-research.php
  Director: Dr Ruth Balogh.
E A research centre at St Martin's College.

Centre for Health, Safety and Environment (CHSE)

■ Cardiff School of Health Sciences, Llandarff Campus, Cardiff University, Western Avenue, Cardiff, CF5 2YB.
  029 2041 6070; 6802; 6856
  http://www.chse.uwic.ac.uk/
  Director: John Wildsmith.
E A research centre at the University of Wales Institute, Cardiff.
O To act as a focal point to those organisations wishing to ensure legal compliance and enhance their health, safety and environmental performance

© CBD Research Ltd · Beckenham · Kent BR3 5JS · Tel 020 8650 7745 · Fax 020 8650 0768 · E-mail cbd@cbdresearch.com · www.cbdresearch.com

Centre for Health Sciences   (CHS)   2005

■   Barts and the London, Queen Mary's School of Medicine and Dentistry, Queen Mary's, University of London, Abernethy Building, 2 Newark Street, London, E1 2AT.
    020 7882 2509   fax 020 7882 2552
    http://www.ihse.qmul.ac.uk/chs/
    Director: Prof Sheila Hillier.
E   A research centre within the Institute of Health Sciences Education (qv) at Queen Mary, University of London.
○   To conduct research in the general area of health sciences

Centre for Health Sciences Research   (CHSR)   Canolfan Ymchwil Gwyddoriaeth Iechyd

■   Cardiff University, Upper Ground Floor, Heath Park, Cardiff, CF14 4XN.
    029 2074 2478   fax 029 2074 2898
    http://medweb.cf.ac.uk/chsr/
E   A centre at Cardiff University.
○   To better understand the determinants of ill health

Centre for Health Services Research
    see **Institute for Health and Society.**

Centre for Health Services Studies   (CHSS)   1989

■   School of Social Policy, Sociology and Social Research, University of Kent, Cornwallis George Allen Wing, Canterbury, Kent, CT2 7NF.
    01227 824057   fax 01227 827868
    http://www.kent.ac.uk/chss/
    Director: Prof Andy Alaszewski. Executive Officer: Peta Hampshire.
E   An interdisciplinary research centre at the University of Kent.
○   To support research in the NHS in Kent, Surrey and Sussex; to conduct a programme of national and international health services research

Centre for Health and Social Care

■   Faculty of Medicine and Health, University of Leeds, 15 Hyde Terrace, Leeds, LS2 9JT.
    0113-343 6357; 6905
    http://www.leeds.ac.uk/hsphr/hsc/
    Senior Secretary: Julie Prudhoe.
E   A research centre within the Leeds Institute of Health Sciences (qv) at the University of Leeds.
○   To conduct research that focuses on the organisation and delivery of health and social care, processes of inclusion and exclusion, and methodological development

Centre for Health and Social Care Improvement   (CHSCI)

■   School of Health, Mary Seacole Building, City Campus - North, University of Wolverhampton, Wolverhampton, WV1 1SB.
    01902 518614   fax 01902 518660
    http://www.wlv.ac.uk/chsci/
    Director: Prof Mel Chevannes.
E   A centre at the University of Wolverhampton.
○   To improve continuously upon the science and art of preventing disease and promoting health in partnership with health service organisations; to contribute to the development of appropriate policies and interventions locally, regionally and nationally

Centre for Health and Social Care Informatics   (CHaSCI)

■   Faculty of Health and Applied Social Sciences, Liverpool John Moores University, North Street, Liverpool, L3 2AY.
    http://www.ljmu.ac.uk/chasci/
    Head: Dr Farath Arshad.
E   A research centre within Liverpool John Moores University.
○   To bring together multidisciplinary skills from the areas of health sciences, computing and mathematical sciences, and engineering and sport science

Centre for Health and Social Care Research   (CHSCR)   2003

■   School of Human and Health Sciences, University of Huddersfield, Queensgate, Huddersfield, HD1 3DH.
    01484 473974
    http://www.hud.ac.uk/hhs/research/chscr
    Director: Prof Annie Topping.
E   A research centre at the University of Huddersfield.
○   To undertake research and consultancy in health and social care at local, national and international levels, and with particular emphasis on Ageing and mental health, Assisted conception and infertility, Mental health, Nursing and midwifery, and Primary care

Centre for Health and Social Care Research   (HSC)

■   Faculty of Health and Well Being, Collegiate Campus, Sheffield Hallam University, Sheffield, S10 2BP.
    0114-225 5854   fax 0114-225 4341
    http://www.shu.ac.uk/research/hsc/
    Director: Dr Gail Mountain.
E   A research centre at Sheffield Hallam University.
○   To focus research within various themes, including education, rehabilitation, older people, workforce and organisational development, the impact of pain, and children, young people and families

Centre for Health and Social Evaluation   (CHASE)
- School of Health and Social Care, University of Teesside, Centuria Building, Middlesbrough, TS1 3BA.
  01642 342969; 384110   fax 01642 384105
  http://www.tees.ac.uk/researchcentres/CHASE/
  Co-Director: Prof Robin Bunton. Co-Director: Prof Janet Shucksmith.
- E   A research centre within the Institute for Health Sciences and Social Care Research (qv) at the University of Teesside.
- O   To provide evaluation and research expertise for agencies in health and social care fields

Centre for Health and Social Research   (CHSR)
- Glenrothes House, North Street, Glenrothes, Fife, KY7 5PB.
  01592 754355

Centre for Healthcare Architecture & Design   (CHAD)   2001
- NHS Estates, 1 Trevelyan Square, Boar Lane, Leeds, LS1 6AE.
  http://chad.nhsestates.gov.uk
  Head: Chris Farrah
- E   A centre established by NHS Estates.
- O   To improve the design of the built environment of the NHS.

Centre for Healthcare Associated Infections   (CHAI)   2007
- University of Nottingham, CBS Building, University Park, Nottingham, NG7 2RD.
  http://hcai.nottingham.ac.uk/HCAI_home.htm
  Director: Professor Richard James
- E   A research centre at the University of Nottingham,
- O   To study a range of bacterial infections for basic and translational research purposes. The centre concentrates on the transmission of Clostridia, E.Coli, MRSA and other staphylococci and works on remedies and solutions such as the discovery of novel antibacterial agents, novel therapies and microbiological screening and diagnostics.

Centre for Healthcare Ethics
  see **Linacre Centre for Healthcare Ethics.**

Centre for Healthy Cities and Urban Policy
  see **WHO Collaborating Centre for Healthy Cities and Urban Policy.**

Centre for Hebrew and Jewish Studies
  see **Oxford Centre for Hebrew and Jewish Studies.**

Centre for Hellenic Studies   (CHS)   1989
- Department of Byzantine and Modern Greek Studies, King's College London, Strand, London, WC2R 2LS.
  020 7848 2212; 2343   fax 020 7848 2830
  http://www.kcl.ac.uk/schools/humanities/hrc/chs/
  Director: Dr Karim Arafat.
- E   A research centre within King's College, London.
- O   To promote Hellenic studies through a continuous programme of lectures, colloquia, conferences and publications, including 7 major volumes and an annual newsletter; to collaborate with many international cultural organisations and maintain close relations with the Greek government and Greek cultural organisations, especially the Greek community in the UK
- ●   Library (including modern Greek holdings of major importance) - Postgraduate scholarship
- ¶   Newsletter. Volumes. (many other publications).

Centre for Hellenic Studies   (CHS)
- Whiteknights, PO Box 216, University of Reading, Reading, Berkshire, RG6 6AA.
  0118-378 8420   fax 0118-378 6661
  http://www.rdg.ac.uk/chs/
  Director: Dr Timothy E Duff.
- E   A research centre at the University of Reading.

Centre for Hellenistic and Greco-Roman Culture
  see **Exeter Centre for Hellenistic and Greco-Roman Culture.**

Centre for Hepatology
  see **UCL Institute of Hepatology.**

Centre for Heritage Research
- School of Philosophy, University of Leeds, Leeds, LS2 9JT.
  0113-343 3274
  http://www.leeds.ac.uk/heritage/
  Contact: Graeme Gooday.
- E   A research centre at the University of Leeds.

Centre for Heuristic Optimisation   (CHO)
- Kent Business School, University of Kent, Canterbury, Kent, CT2 7PE.
   01227 827726   fax 01227 761187
   http://www.kent.ac.uk/kbs/standard.php?page_id=34
   Director: Prof Said Salhi.
- E   A research centre at the University of Kent.
- O   To concentrate on new applied research developments, in heuristic search and practical optimisation; to tackle real life problems arising in both in the public and the private sectors, including scheduling and routing, logistics, facility location, security enhancement, data mining and aspects of health management and medicine, finance and the environment

Centre for High Frequency Engineering   (CHFE)   1999
- Cardiff School of Engineering, Queen's Buildings, Cardiff University, Newport Road, Cardiff, CF24 3AA.
   029 2087 4423
   http://www.engin.cf.ac.uk/research/group.asp?GroupNo=46
   Group Leader: Prof Paul J Tasker.
- E   A research centre within the Institute of Information Systems and Integration Technology (qv) at Cardiff University.
- O   To undertake research projects aimed at solving, for business, the RF/microwave dynamic voltage and current waveform measurements and active source- and load pull concepts

Centre for Higher Education Development
   see **Centre for the Study of Higher Education.**

Centre in Higher Education Learning and Management
   see **Aston Business School Research Centre in Higher Education Learning and Management.**

Centre for Higher Education Policy Studies
   see **Oxford Centre for Higher Education Policy Studies.**

Centre for Higher Education Research and Information   (CHERI)   1992
- Open University, 44 Bedford Row, London, WC1R 4LL.
   020 7447 2561   fax 020 7447 2556
   http://www.open.ac.uk/cheri/
   Director: John Brennan.
- E   A research centre at the Open University.
- O   To conduct research on the relationship between higher education and society, with particular emphasis on higher education and work, access and widening participation, and quality assurance and evaluation

Centre for Higher Education Studies   (CHES)   1985
- University of London, 20 Bedford Way, London, WC1H 0AL.
   020 7612 6000   fax 020 7612 6126
   http://ioewebserver.ioe.ac.uk/ioe/cms/get.asp?cid=14045
   Co-Director: Prof Sir David Watson. Co-Director: Prof Ronald Barnett.
- E   A research centre within the Institute of Education (qv) at the University of London.

Centre for Hindu Studies
   see **Oxford Centre for Hindu Studies.**

Centre for Historical Archaeology
   see **Leslie and Elizabeth Alcock Centre for Historical Archaeology.**

Centre for Historical Economics and Related Research at York   (CHERRY)
- Department of Economics and Related Studies, University of York, Heslington, York, YO10 5DD.
   01904 432981
   http://www.york.ac.uk/res/cherry/
- E   An interdisciplinary research centre at the University of York.
- O   To promote and further shared expertise and interests in the understanding of the historical past

Centre for History
   see **UHI Centre for History.**

Centre for the History of Cinema and Popular Culture
   see **Bill Douglas Centre for the History of Cinema and Popular Culture.**

Centre for History, Classics and Archaeology
   see **Subject Centre for History, Classics and Archaeology**.

Centre for the History of the Crusades
   see **Cardiff Centre for the History of the Crusades.**

Centre for History and Cultural Studies of Science
  see **Centre for the History of Science, Technology and Medicine [Kent]**

Centre for the History of Culture and Medicine
- ■ Faculty of Arts and Humanities, School of Oriental and African Studies, University of London, Thornhaugh Street, Russell Square, London, WC1H 0XG.
  020 7898 4020   fax 020 7898 4699
  http://www.soas.ac.uk/centres/centreinfo.cfm?navid=15
  Chairman: Prof David Arnold.
- E   A research centre at the School of Oriental and African Studies, University of London.
- O   To promote the study of disease, medicine and related fields of science and technology, in the context of Africa, Asia and other parts of the extra-European world

Centre for the History of the Mathematical Sciences   (CHMS)   2001
- ■ Open University, Walton Hall, Milton Keynes, MK7 6AA.
  0870 333 4340
  http://puremaths.open.ac.uk/pmd_research/CHMS/res.html
  Director: Prof Jeremy Gray.
- E   A research centre at the Open University.
- O   To conduct research in the history of the mathematical sciences, covering pure and applied mathematics, statistics, mathematics education and computing

Centre for the History of Medicine   (CHM)   2000
- ■ Ground Floor - The Medical School, University of Birmingham, Edgbaston, Birmingham, B15 2TT.
  0121-415 8174   fax 0121-414 6036
  http://www.medicine.bham.ac.uk/histmed/
  Director: Dr Robert Arnott. Contact: Miss Michelle Lee.
- E   A centre at the University of Birmingham.
- O   To provide a stimulating and supportive environment for those involved in the history of medicine

Centre for the History of Medicine   (CHM)   1999
- ■ Faculty of Arts, University of Warwick, Gibbet Hill Road, Coventry, CV4 7AL.
  024 7657 2601   fax 024 7652 3437
  http://www2.warwick.ac.uk/fac/arts/history/chm/
  Director: Prof Hilary Marland.
- E   A research centre at the University of Warwick.

Centre for the History of Medicine   (CHM)   1985
- ■ Department of Economic and Social History, University of Glasgow, Lilybank House, Bute Gardens, Glasgow, G12 8RT.
  0141-330 6071   fax 0141-330 3511
  http://www.arts.gla.ac.uk/History/Medicine/
  Director: Dr M Nicolson.
- E   A centre at the University of Glasgow.
- O   To conduct research on the history of medicine in Scotland and Britain more generally, from the early modern period to the 20th century, especially on medicine and the Enlightenment, women and medicine, the social history of medicine, including hospitals and the development of the medical profession, and the history of diagnostics and of 20th century biomedical science

Centre for the History of Medicine   (CHM)
- ■ Faculty of Humanities and Social Sciences, University of Newcastle upon Tyne, 7th Floor - Daysh Building, Newcastle upon Tyne, NE1 7RU.
  0191-222 8679
  http://www.ncl.ac.uk/niassh/hom/
- E   A research centre within the Newcastle Institute for the Arts, Social Sciences and Humanities (qv) at the University of Newcastle upon Tyne.
- O   To conduct research and teaching in the history of medicine and science, with particular emphasis on the whole Western medical tradition from antiquity until the twentieth century

Centre for the History of Medicine and Disease   (CHMD)   2001
- ■ Queen's Campus, University of Durham, University Boulevard, Thornaby, Stockton on Tees, TS17 6BH.
  0191-334 0701   fax 0191-334 0374
  http://www.dur.ac.uk/chmd/
  Director: Prof Andreas-Holger Maehle.
- E   A research centre and part of the Northern Centre for the History of Medicine (qv) within the Wolfson Research Institute (qv) at the University of Durham.
- O   To provide a focus for research and postgraduate education in the history of medicine, health, disease and medical ethics

Centre for the History of Philosophical Theology   (CHPT)   2003
- ■ School of Humanities, King's College London, Strand, London, WC2R 2LS.
  020 7836 5454
  http://www.kcl.ac.uk/schools/humanities/hrc/chpt/
  Director: Dr Maria Rosa Antognazza.
- E   A research centre at King's College, London.
- O   To provide a focus for research into and commentary upon, philosophical accounts of the divine in the history of Western thought

Centre for the History of Political Thought   (CHPT)

- School of Government and International Affairs, University of Durham, The Al-Qasimi Building, Elvet Hill Road, Durham, DH1 3TU.
   0191-334 7182; 7183
   http://www.dur.ac.uk/chpt/
   Director: Dr P M R Stirk.
- E   A centre at the University of Durham.
- O   To promote the historical study of political thought over the broadest possible front; to encourage scholarly research and publication

Centre for the History of Science, Technology and Medicine   (CHoSTM)   1992

- Faculty of Physical Sciences, South Kensington Campus, Imperial College London, Exhibition Road, London, SW7 2AZ.
   020 7594 9360   fax 020 7594 9353
   http://www3.imperial.ac.uk/historyofscience
   Director: Prof Andrew Warwick. Administrator: Robert Powell.
- E   A research centre within the London Centre for the History of Science, Medicine and Technology (qv) at Imperial College London.
- O   To conduct research and teaching programmes in the history of science, technology and medicine

Centre for History of Science, Technology and Medicine   (CHSTM)   1994

- School of History, Rutherford College, University of Kent, Canterbury, Kent, CT2 7NX.
   01227 823837; 827665   fax 01227 827258
   http://www.kent.ac.uk/history/
   Director: Prof Crosbie Smith.
- E   A research centre at the University of Kent.
- O   To promote research in the field of cultural history of science, including technology and medicine

Note: Centre for History and Cultural Studies of Science

Centre for the History of Technology, Science and Society

Note: is no longer active.

Centre for the History of Wales and its Borderlands   (CHWB)

- Department of History, Swansea University, James Callaghan Building, Singleton Park, Swansea, SA2 8PP.
   01792 295227   fax 01792 295746
   http://www.swan.ac.uk/history/research/chwb
   Director: Prof Chris Williams.
- E   A research centre at Swansea University.
- O   To conduct research into the history of Wales as viewed against other Celtic regions, other coalfield societies in America, Asia and Europe, and the UK as a whole

Centre for the History of Women
   see **Bedford Centre for the History of Women.**

Centre for the Holocaust and 20th-Century History
   see **Research Centre for the Holocaust and 20th-Century History.**

Centre for Holocaust Studies
   see **Stanley Burton Centre for Holocaust Studies.**

Centre for Hospitality Management and Retailing   (CHMR)

- Leslie Silver International Facility, Leeds Metropolitan University, Civic Quarter, Calverley Street, Leeds, LS1 3HE.
   0113-283 5937
   http://www.leedsmet.ac.uk/international/the/hospitality_retail.htm
   Head: Isabell Hodgson.
- E   A research centre at Leeds Metropolitan University.
- O   To be a leading provider of hospitality education at both under and post-graduate level

Centre for Housing and Community Research   (CHCR)   1989

- London Metropolitan University, Ladbroke House, 62-66 Highbury Grove, London, N5 2AD.
   020 7133 5105   fax 020 7133 5123
   http://www.citiesinstitute.org/chcr.html
   Director: Dr Joan Smith.
- E   An interdisciplinary research centre within the Cities Institute (qv) at London Metropolitan University.
- O   To conduct research into the concepts, policies and practices that help explain and influence the success of particular cities and urban quality of life

Centre for Housing and Planning Research
   see **Cambridge Centre for Housing and Planning Research.**

Centre for Housing Policy (CHP) 1990
- Department of Social Policy and Social Work, University of York, Heslington, York, YO10 5DD.
  01904 433691   fax 01904 432318
  http://www.york.ac.uk/inst/chp/
  Director: Prof Suzanne Fitzpatrick.
- E A research unit at the University of York.
- O To conduct research into the interface between housing and other aspects of social policy, which is becoming increasingly important in practice, particularly with respect to homelessness, community care and the management of social housing and the sustainability of owner occupation
- ● Quantitive and qualitative research

Centre for Human Communication
  see UCL Centre for Human Communication.

Centre for Human Computer Interaction Design   1991
- School of Informatics, City University, Northampton Square, London, EC1V 0HB.
  020 7040 8427   fax 020 7040 8859
  http://hcid.soi.city.ac.uk/
  Head: Prof Neil Maiden.
- E An independent research centre and department of City University.
- O To research the relationship between people and technology with the aim of creating more useful and easier to use systems
Note: Also known as Centre for HCI Design.

Centre for Human Ecology (CHE)   1972
- 54 Manor Place, Edinburgh, EH3 7EH.
  0845 119 2001   fax 0845 119 2002
  http://www.che.ac.uk/
- E An independent think tank.
- O To effect practical change and develop new thinking that influences local, national and international policy and practice for ecological sustainability and social justice

Centre for Human Evolutionary Studies
  see Leverhulme Centre for Human Evolutionary Studies.

Centre for Human Genetics   (CHG)
- Department of Biology, University College London, The Darwin Building, Gower Street, London, WC1E 6BT.
  020 7679 7098
  http://www.gene.ucl.ac.uk/chg/
  Co-ordinator: Prof Sue Povey. Administrator: Michelle Bush.
- E A research centre at University College London.

Centre for Human Genetics [Oxford]
  see Wellcome Trust Centre for Human Genetics.

Centre for Human Molecular Genetics
- Department of Paediatrics and Child Health, University College London, Rayne Building, 5 University Street, London, WC1E 6JJ.
  020 7679 6101
  http://www.ucl.ac.uk/paediatrics/paediatrics/research.htm
- E A research centre at University College London.

Centre for Human Nutrition Research
  see MRC Resource Centre for Human Nutrition Research.

Centre for Human Palaeoecology   (CHP)
- University of York, Heslington, York, YO10 5DD.
  01904 433934; 433946   fax 01904 433902
  http://www.york.ac.uk/inst/chumpal/welcome.htm
  Contact: Prof Don Brothwell.
- E A research centre at the University of York.
- O To foster links between archaeology, biology and environmental science, to enable the fully integrated study of the individual, population, and community ecology of past peoples

Centre for Human Performance
- Royal Veterinary College, University of London, Hawkshead Lane, North Mymms, Hatfield, Hertfordshire, AL9 7DY.
  01707 666259; 666327   fax 01707 666371
  http://www.rvc.ac.uk/SML/IHP_Directions.cfm
  Contact: Alan Wilson.
- E A research centre at the Royal Veterinary College, University of London.
- O To undertake fundamental and applied research into musculo-skeletal function

Centre for Human Resource
> see **Aston Centre for Human Resource.**

Centre on Human Rights in Conflict   (CHRC)
- ◼ School of Law, University of East London, Duncan House, Stratford High Street, London, E15 2JB.
  020 8223 3361   fax 020 8223 2927
  http://www.uel.ac.uk/chrc/
  Director: Prof Chandra Lekha Sriram.
- E An interdisciplinary research centre at the University of East London.
- ○ To promote policy-relevant research and events aimed at developing greater knowledge of human rights and armed conflict, Islamic human rights, and human rights and civil liberties in the war on terror

Centre for Human Science and Medical Ethics
Note: has become an academic unit within the **Centre for Health Sciences.**

Centre for Human Sciences
- ◼ Cody Technology Park, Iveley Road, Farnborough, Hampshire, GU14 0LX.
  0870 010 0942
  http://www.qinetiq.com/home/technologies/technologies/Sub_Landing1.html
- E A research centre within QinetiQ, one of the world's leading defence technology and security companies.

Centre for Human Service Technology   (CHST)
- ◼ School of Social Sciences, University of Southampton, Highfield, Southampton, SO17 1BJ.
  023 8059 2925   fax 023 8059 2779
  http://www.chst.soton.ac.uk/
  Director: Jackie Rafferty.
- E A research centre at the University of Southampton.
- ○ A research, development and service centre for social work

Centre for Humanities Research
> see **Humanities Research Centre [Sheffield Hallam].**

Centre for Illuminated Manuscripts
> see **Research Centre for Illuminated Manuscripts.**

Centre for Images in Practice   (CIP)
- ◼ School of Art, Design and Media, University of Portsmouth, Eldon Building, Winston Churchill Avenue, Portsmouth, PO1 2DJ.
  023 9284 3835   fax 023 9284 3808
  http://www.envf.port.ac.uk/illustration/images/
  Contact: Dr Jackie Batey.
- E A research centre at the University of Portsmouth.
- ○ To bring together research on visual response to image qualities, interactive systems and collaborative elaboration of complex net-based cultural artefacts and other experimental contexts for image-based communication

Centre for Immune Regulation
> see **MRC Centre for Immune Regulation.**

Centre for Immunodeficiency
- ◼ Department of Immunology and Molecular Pathology, Royal Free and University College Medical School, University College London, Rowland Hill Street, London, NW3 2PF.
  020 7829 8490
  http://www.ucl.ac.uk/medicalschool/infection-immunity/departments/departments.htm
  Director: Prof Adrian Thrasher.
- E A research centre at University College London.
- ○ To link work on paediatric inherited immuno-deficiency at the Institute of Child Health (qv) with research on inherited and acquired immuno-deficiencies at the Royal Free Hospital

Centre for Imperial and Maritime Studies   (CIMS)   2005
- ◼ National Maritime Museum, London, SE10 9NF.
  020 8312 6716   fax 020 8312 6592
  http://www.nmm.ac.uk/server/show/nav.005002007008
  Head: Dr Nigel Rigby.
- E An interdisciplinary research centre at the National Maritime Museum.
- ○ To support and advance research on the Museum's imperial and maritime collections
- ● Library (over 100,000 specialist volumes)
- ¶ Journal for Maritime Research.

Centre for Imperial and Post-Colonial Studies   (CIPCS)   2006
- School of Humanities, University of Southampton, Highfield, Southampton, SO17 1BJ.
  023 8059 7245
  http://www.history.soton.ac.uk/cipcs/
  Contact: Dr Adrian Smith.
- E   A research centre at the University of Southampton.

Note: The Centre is developing the work of the previous Centre for the Study of Britain and its Empire.

Centre for Inclusion and Diversity
- School of Health Studies, University of Bradford, 25 Trinity Road, Bradford, West Yorkshire, BD5 0BB.
  01274 236347   fax 01274 236443
  http://www.bradford.ac.uk/acad/health/research/cid/
  Director: Prof Uduak Archibong.
- E   A centre at the University of Bradford.
- O   To develop a world class centre of expertise in applied research, knowledge transfer, policy and programme development, and consultancy on inclusion and diversity

Centre for Indigenous American Studies and Exchange
  see **Centre for Amerindian Studies.**

Centre for Individual and Organisational Development   (CIOD)
- City Campus, Sheffield Hallam University, Sheffield, S1 1WB.
  0114-225 5555
  http://www.shu.ac.uk/research/ciod/
  Director: Dr Gareth G Morgan.
- E   A research centre at Sheffield Hallam University.
- O   To support delivery of change initiatives at both personal and organisational levels, especially organisational development, team working and inter-organisational relationships

Centre for Industrial and Applied Mathematics
  see **Oxford Centre for Industrial and Applied Mathematics.**

Centre for Industrial Automation and Manufacture   (CIAM)   1991
- School of Engineering, University of Durham, Science Site, Durham, DH1 3LE.
  0191-334 2432   fax 0191-334 2377
  http://www.dur.ac.uk/ciam/
- E   A centre at the University of Durham.
- O   To conduct research of direct relevance to the development of techniques for the advancement of industrial automation and excellence in manufacture

Centre for Industrial Bulk Solids Handling   (CIBSH)
- School of Engineering, Science and Design, Glasgow Caledonian University, Cowcaddens Road, Glasgow, G4 0BA.
  0141-331 3711   fax 0141-331 3394
  http://cibsh.gcal.ac.uk/
  Contact: Andrew Cowell.
- E   A research centre at Glasgow Caledonian University.
- O   To focus on fundamental and applied research in the areas of pneumatic conveying, bulk solids characterisation and bulk solids handling technology

Centre for Industrial and Commercial Optoelectronics   (ICON)
- Schools of Electronic Engineering and Computer Science, University of Wales Bangor, Dean Street, Bangor, Gwynedd, LL57 1UT.
  01248 382686   fax 01248 361429
  http://www.iconphotonics.co.uk/
- E   A research centre at the University of Wales, Bangor.
- O   To conduct research, testing and innovation in a range of optoelectronic and electronic devices

Centre for Industrial Mathematical Modelling   (CIMM)
- School of Mathematical Sciences, University of Nottingham, University Park, Nottingham, NG7 2RD.
  0115-951 3838   fax 0115-951 3837
  http://www.maths.nottingham.ac.uk/research/cimm/
  Director: Prof J Billingham.
- E   A research centre at the University of Nottingham.
- O   To enhance the understanding of industrial processes; to perform troubleshooting studies of industrial problems through the use of state-of-the-art mathematical tools

Centre for Infections
  see **Health Protection Agency Centre for Infections.**

© CBD Research Ltd · Beckenham · Kent BR3 5JS · Tel 020 8650 7745 · Fax 020 8650 0768 · E-mail cbd@cbdresearch.com · www.cbdresearch.com

Centre for Infectious Disease (CID) 2003

- Barts and the London, Queen Mary's School of Medicine and Dentistry, Queen Mary's, University of London, 4 Newark Street, London, E1 2AT.
  020 7882 2308   fax 020 7882 2181
  http://www.smd.qmul.ac.uk/cid/
  Lead: Prof Judy Breuer.
- E A research centre within the Institute of Cell and Molecular Science (qv) at Queen Mary, University of London.
- O To focus research on the study of host and pathogen determinants of infection, with the aim of identifying targets for drug and vaccine development

Centre for Infectious Disease (CID) 2001

- Queen's Campus, University of Durham, University Boulevard, Thornaby, Stockton on Tees, TS17 6BH.
  0191-334 0465   fax 0191-334 0468
  http://www.dur.ac.uk/cid/
  Chairman: Prof Adrian R Walmsley.
- E A research centre within the Wolfson Research Institute (qv) at the University of Durham.
- O To develop research interests that address some of the challenges for treating infectious diseases in the future

Centre for Infectious Disease Epidemiology (CIDE)

- Department of Primary Care and Population, University College London, Royal Free and University College Medical School, Rowland Hill Street, London, NW3 2PF.
  020 7830 2239
  http://www.ucl.ac.uk/pcps/research/cide/
  Head: Prof Anne Johnson.
- E A research centre at University College London
- O To undertake research, particularly among vulnerable populations in primary care, on the epidemiology, prevention and treatment of infections including sexually transmitted diseases, influenza, tuberculosis, antimicrobial resistance, hospital infection control, and other common problems

Centre for Infectious Diseases and International Health

- Department of Infection, University College London, Windeyer Building, 46 Cleveland Street, London, W1T 4JF.
  020 7679 9153
  http://windeyer.ucl.ac.uk/infectious-diseases/
  Director: Prof Ali Zumla.
- E A research centre at University College London.
- O To conduct research in mycobacteria and the pathogenesis of diseases such as tuberculosis, with particular reference to the introduction of novel modalities of vaccination and immunotherapy

Centre for Inflammation Research
> see **MRC-University of Edinburgh Centre for Inflammation Research.**

Centre for Informatics Education Research (CIER)

- Faculty of Mathematics and Computing, Open University, Walton Hall, Milton Keynes, MK7 6AA.
  01908 653037
  http://www.computing.open.ac.uk/Themes/IE
  Co-ordinator: Dr Pete Thomas.
- E A research centre at the Open University.

Centre for Information Behaviour and the Evaluation of Research (CIBER)

- School of Library, Archive and Information Studies, University College London, Henry Morley Building, Gower Street, London, WC1E 6BT.
  020 7679 2000; 2477   fax 020 7383 0557
  http://www.ucl.ac.uk/slais/research/ciber/
  Contact: Prof David Nicholas.
- E A research centre within the UCL Centre for Publishing (qv) at University College London.
- O To map, monitor and evaluate digital information systems, platforms, services and environments, using research methods that provide strategic data for policy makers

Centre for Information and Computer Sciences [Loughborough]
> see **Subject Centre for Information and Computer Sciences [Loughborough].**

Centre for Information and Computer Sciences [Newtownabbey]
> see **Subject Centre for Information and Computer Sciences [Newtownabbey].**

Centre for Information on Language Teaching and Research
> see **CILT, The National Centre for Languages.**

Centre for Information Management   (CIM)   2000

- School of Management, University of Bath, Claverton Down, Bath, BA2 7AY.
  01225 386473
  http://www.bath.ac.uk/cim/
- E A research centre at the University of Bath.
- O To conduct high quality research in key areas of information systems

Centre for Information Management and E-Business

- Faculty of Business, Computing and Information Management, London South Bank University, 103 Borough Road, London, SE1 0AA.
  020 7815 7429
  http://www.lsbu.ac.uk/bcimicr/research/imeb.shtml
  Contact: Prof Dilip Patel.
- E A research centre at London South Bank University.

Centre for Information Management and Technology   (Cimtech)   1967

- University of Hertfordshire, Innovation Centre, College Lane, Hatfield, Hertfordshire, AL10 9AB.
  01707 281060   fax 01707 281061
  http://www.cimtech.co.uk/
- E A research centre and membership organisation at the University of Hertfordshire.
- O To be a centre for expertise on all aspects of information management and technology

Note: Often referred to as **Cimtech Ltd**.

Centre for Information Policy Studies   (CIPS)

- Department of Information Science, City University, Northampton Square, London, EC1V 0HB.
  020 7040 8389   fax 020 7040 8584
  http://www.soi.city.ac.uk/organisation/is/research/cips/
- E A centre at City University.
- O To study strategic thinking on information policy with its foundation in information domains and information behaviour; to develop new understanding and fresh insights into the social, economic and cultural opportunities and challenges brought about by unprecedented access to information systems and resources

Centre for Information Quality Management   (CIQM)   1993

- Penbryn, Bronant, Aberystwyth, Ceredigion, SY23 4TJ.
  01974 251441   fax 01974 251441
  Director: C J Armstrong.
- E A profit-making business and a company limited by guarantee.
- O To improve the quality of e-resources and in so doing, work towards developing a set of metrics by which e-resource quality can be measured, and a methodology to guarantee it to users

Centre for Information Technology in Construction
  see **Centre for IT in Construction.**

Centre for Information Technology in Language Learning   (CITLL)

- University of Coventry, Priory Street, Coventry, CV1 5FB.
  024 7679 8256
  http://www.stile.coventry.ac.uk/public/rcon/citl.htm
  Contact: Marina Orsini-Jones.
- E A centre at Coventry University.
- O To undertake research and development in computer-assisted language learning (CALL), and creation of collaborative learning environments to teach languages and to enhance translation studies via network based language teaching and learning

Centre for Infrastructure Management   (CIM)

- City Campus, Sheffield Hallam University, Howard Street, Sheffield, S1 1WB.
  0114-225 3339   fax 0114-225 4546
  http://www.shu.ac.uk/research/cim/
  Director: Prof Pal Mangat.
- E A research centre within the Structural Materials and Integrity Research Centre (qv) at Sheffield Hallam University.
- O To provide a professional service to the construction and infrastructure sector in the fields of infrastructure management, environmental protection and recycling solutions

Centre for Innovation in Healthcare Technology   (CIHT)

- Glasgow Caledonian University, 6th Floor - Govan Mbeki Health Building, Cowcaddens Road, Glasgow, G4 0BA.
  0141-331 8877; 8880   fax 0141-331 8887
  http://www.ciht.gcal.ac.uk/
  Director: John Marshall.
- E A research centre at Glasgow Caledonian University.
- O To assist the commercialisation of the outputs of the University's research in the areas of medical device development, biomedicine and the wider aspects of healthcare

© CBD Research Ltd · Beckenham · Kent BR3 5JS · Tel 020 8650 7745 · Fax 020 8650 0768 · E-mail cbd@cbdresearch.com · www.cbdresearch.com

Centre for Innovation, Knowledge and Development   (IKD)
■   Faculty of Technology, Open University, Walton Hall, Milton Keynes, MK7 6AA.
     01908 652764   fax 01908 654355
     http://www.open.ac.uk/ikd/
     Director: Prof Joanna Chataway. Secretary: Gill Buckland.
E   An interdisciplinary research centre at the Open University.

Centre for Innovation in Mathematics Teaching   (CIMT)   1986
■   Exmouth Campus, University of Plymouth, Douglas Avenue, Exmouth, Devon, EX8 2AT.
     01395 255521   fax 01395 255422
     http://www.cimt.plymouth.ac.uk/
     Director: Prof David Burghes.
E   A research centre at the University of Plymouth.

Centre for Innovation in Raising Educational Achievement   (CIREA)
■   School of Education, University of Leicester, 21 University Road, Leicester, LE1 7RF.
     0116-252 3688   fax 0116-252 3653
     http://www.le.ac.uk/se/schoolcentres/cirea/
E   A research centre at the University of Leicester.

Centre for Innovation and Research in Science Education   (CIRSE)   2005
■   Department of Educational Studies, Alcuin College, University of York, Heslington, York, YO10 5DD.
     01904 432601   fax 01904 432605
     http://www.york.ac.uk/depts/educ/projs/CIRSE%20homepage.htm
     Contact: Mrs S L Wilmott.
E   A research centre at the University of York.

Centre for Innovative and Collaborative Engineering   (CICE)   1999
■   Loughborough University, Ashby Road, Loughborough, Leicestershire, LE11 3TU.
     01509 228549   fax 01509 223982
     http://www.lboro.ac.uk/cice/
     Director: Prof Chimay Anumba.
E   A research centre at Loughborough University.
O   To advance training and research in engineering and management

Centre for Innovative Manufacture and Machine Vision Systems   (CIMMS)
■   Faculty of Computing, Engineering and Mathematical Sciences, Frenchay Campus, University of the West of England, Coldharbour
     Lane, Bristol, BS16 1QY.
     0117-344 2629   fax 0117-344 3800
     http://www.uwe.ac.uk/cems/research/centres/cimms.html
     Director: Dr Sagar Midha.
E   A research centre at the University of the West of England.
O   To conduct fundamental and applied research, aimed at developing state-of-the-art technologies and systems, that could be
     beneficially applied to various stages of the product life cycle

Centre for Innovative Products and Services
■   Cranfield School of Management, Cranfield University, Cranfield, Bedfordshire, MK43 0AL.
     01234 751122
     http://www.som.cranfield.ac.uk/som/research/centres/cips/
     Contact: Prof Keith Goffin.
E   A research centre within the Cranfield Management Research Institute (qv) at Cranfield University.
Note: In process of re-organisation.

Centre for Inquiry-based Learning in the Arts and Social Sciences   (CILASS)   2005
■   University of Sheffield, 65 Wilkinson Street, Sheffield, S10 2GJ.
     0114-222 2638; 5270   fax 0114-222 5279
     http://www.sheffield.ac.uk/cilass/
     Director: Dr Phil Levy.
E   A Centre for Excellence in Teaching and Learning (CETL) at the University of Sheffield.
Note: See **Centres for Excellence in Teaching and Learning** for more information.

Centre for Insolvency Law and Policy   (CILP)
■   School of Law, Kingston University, London, Kingston Hill, Kingston-upon-Thames, Surrey, KT1 7LB.
     020 8547 2000   fax 020 8547 7038
     http://www.kingston.ac.uk/cilp/
     Contact: J Tribe.
E   A research centre at Kingston University, London.
O   To promote a knowledge and understanding of insolvency law

Centre for Institutional Performance   (CIP)

■   University of Reading Business School, University of Reading, HUMSS Building, PO Box 218, Reading, Berkshire, RG6 6AA.
   0118-378 8226
   http://www.reading.ac.uk/business/default.asp?id=82
   Director: Prof Mark Casson.
E   A research centre at the University of Reading.
○   To study and assess institutional arrangements between markets (firms, industries and regulation), governments and non-governmental organisations (non-profit institutions such as charities) with the aim to support policy makers in understanding how policies translate into institutional arrangements

Centre for Institutional Research   (CIR)

■   Open University, Walton Hall, Milton Keynes, MK7 6AA.
   01908 274066
   http://iet.open.ac.uk/about/maingroups/cir/
E   A research centre within the Institute of Educational Technology (qv) at the Open University.

Centre for Institutional Studies   (CIS)   1970

■   School of Social Sciences, Media and Cultural Studies, Docklands Campus, University of East London, 4-6 University Way, London, E16 2RD.
   020 8223 4230   fax 020 8223 4278
   http://www.uel.ac.uk/ssmcs/research/cis/
   Director: Michael Locke. Administrator: Irene Smith.
E   A department of the University of East London.
○   To undertake research which contributes to the improvement of public policies
●   Education and training - Research projects on Evaluations of urban regeneration and community-based services, Faith-based community action, Volunteering, Development and governance of voluntary organisations
¶   Commentary Series.

Centre for Integral Excellence   (CIE)

■   City Campus, Sheffield Hallam University, Sheffield, S1 1WB.
   0114-225 2044   fax 0114-225 4207
   http://www.shu.ac.uk/research/integralexcellence/
   Development Manager: Paul Beresford.
E   A research centre at Sheffield Hallam University.
○   To help support organisations develop an integrated approach to managing and enhancing organisational excellence

Centre for Integrated Diagnostic Systems   (CIDS)

■   Thomson Building, University of Glasgow, Glasgow, G12 8QQ.
   0141-330 2021   fax 0141-330 2483
   http://www.gla.ac.uk/centres/cids/
   Manager: Sylvia Morrison.
E   An interdisciplinary research centre at the University of Glasgow.
○   To bring together researchers in the fields of immunology, biochemistry, medicine, veterinary medicine, haematology, molecular biology, genomics, electronics, bioengineering and informatics to conduct research in diagnostics and screening applications in cancers, infectious, cardiovascular, parasitic and infectious diseases

Centre for Integrated Genomic Medical Research   (CIGMR)   2001

■   School of Medicine, University of Manchester, Stopford Building, Oxford Road, Manchester, M13 9PT.
   0161-275 5698
   http://www.medicine.manchester.ac.uk/cigmr/
   Manager: Mrs Sue Hookway.
E   A research centre at the University of Manchester.
○   To provide a scientific and technical foundation on which post-genome knowledge is being translated into applied clinical research and healthcare

Centre for Integrated Health Care Research   (CIHCR)

■   Queen's Campus, University of Durham, University Boulevard, Thornaby, Stockton on Tees, TS17 6BH.
   0191-334 0373   fax 0191-334 0374
   http://www.dur.ac.uk/cihcr/
   Director: Prof A P S Hungin, OBE.
E   A research centre within the Wolfson Research Institute (qv) at the University of Durham.
○   To conduct clinical research, particularly around the management of patients across the primary / secondary care interface

Centre for Integrated Healthcare Research   (CIHR)   2004

■   Corstorphine Campus, Queen Margaret University, 36 Clerwood Terrace, Edinburgh, EH12 8TS.
   0131-317 3475   fax 0131-317 3162
   http://www.cihr.org.uk/
   Director: Prof James Law.
E   A research centre at Queen Margaret University.
○   To develop research capacity in nursing, midwifery and the allied health professions

© CBD Research Ltd · Beckenham · Kent BR3 5JS · Tel 020 8650 7745 · Fax 020 8650 0768 · E-mail cbd@cbdresearch.com · www.cbdresearch.com

Centre for Integrated Optoelectronic Systems   (CIOS)   1990
■   Department of Physics, University of Edinburgh, Riccarton, Edinburgh, EH14 4AS.
       0131-449 5111; 451 3036   fax 0131-449 5542
       http://www.phy.hw.ac.uk/resrev/233.htm
       Director: Prof Andy C Walker.
E   A research centre at Heriot-Watt University.
O   To promote the multi-disciplinary research into the applications of optoelectronics to information technology

Centre for Integrated Systems Biology and Medicines   (CISBM)
■   School of Biomedical Sciences, Queen's Medical Centre, University of Nottingham, Nottingham, NG7 2UH.
       0115-823 0141   fax 0115-823 0142
       http://www.nottingham.ac.uk/cisbm/
E   A research centre within the Institute of Clinical Research (qv) at the University of Nottingham.
O   To use integrated systems approaches to answer questions of clinical relevance

Centre for Integrative Learning   2005
■   Hallward Library, University of Nottingham, University Park, Nottingham, NG7 2RD.
       0115-846 7787; 951 5274   fax 0115-846 6777
       http://www.nottingham.ac.uk/integrativelearning/
       Director: Prof Martin Binks.
E   A Centre for Excellence in Teaching and Learning (CETL) within the University of Nottingham Institute for Enterprise and Innovation
       (qv) at the University of Nottingham.
O   To support high quality student learning
Note: See **Centres for Excellence in Teaching and Learning** for further information.

Centre for Integrative Systems Biology [Manchester]
       see **Manchester Centre for Integrative Systems Biology.**

Centre for Integrative Systems Biology at Imperial College   (CISBIC)
■   Faculty of Life Sciences, Imperial College London, Flowers Building, Armstrong Road, London, SW7 2AZ.
       020 7594 3094; 3962   fax 020 7594 3076
       http://www3.imperial.ac.uk/cisbic
       Director: Prof Douglas Young. Administrator: Miss Sophie Kemp.
E   A research centre at Imperial College London.
O   To bring scientists together within an iterative cycle, with data from cutting edge bioscience feeding into the development of
       innovative modelling methods that in turn inspire new directions for experimental approaches and biological insights

Centre for Intellectual History
       see **Sussex Centre for Intellectual History.**

Centre for Intellectual Property in the Creative Industries
       see **National Institute for Excellence in Creative Industries.**

Centre for Intellectual Property and Information Law   (CIPIL)   2004
■   Faculty of Law, University of Cambridge, 10 West Road, Cambridge, CB3 9DZ.
       01223 330081   fax 01223 330086
       http://cipil.law.cam.ac.uk/
       Director: Prof Lionel Bently.
E   A centre at the University of Cambridge.
O   To foster the study of all aspects of intellectual property law, information law and associated subjects

Centre for Intellectual Property Policy and Management   (CIPPM)   2000
■   Bournemouth Law School, Bournemouth University, Talbot Campus, Poole, Dorset, BH12 5BB.
       01202 965211   fax 01202 965261
       http://www.cippm.org.uk/
       Co-Director: Martin Kretschmer. Co-Director: Ruth Soetendorp.
E   A research centre within the Institute of Business and Law (qv) at Bournemouth University.
O   To conduct interdisciplinary research in the governance and application of innovation and creativity

Centre for Intelligence and International Security Studies   (CIISS)   2004
■   Department of International Politics, University of Wales Aberystwyth, Penglais, Aberystwyth, Ceredigion, SY23 3FE.
       01970 628563
       http://www.aber.ac.uk/interpol/research/CIISS.htm
       Director: Prof Len Scott.
E   A research centre at the University of Wales, Aberystwyth.
O   To facilitate and promote the study of intelligence and international security

Centre for Intelligence and Security Studies
       see **Brunel Centre for Intelligence and Security Studies.**

Centre for Intelligent Environmental Systems   (CIES)
- ■   Staffordshire University, Mellor Building, College Road, Stoke-on-Trent, ST4 2DF.
     http://www.cies.staffs.ac.uk/
     Centre Manager: Martin Paisley.
- E   A centre at Staffordshire University.
- ○   To specialise in the application of artifical intelligence to problems affecting the natural environment

Centre for Intelligent Monitoring Systems   (CIMS)
- ■   Department of Electrical Engineering and Electronics, University of Liverpool, Brownlow Hill, Liverpool, L69 3GJ.
     0151-794 4518; 4615   fax 0151-794 4568
     http://www.cims.org.uk/
- E   A research centre at the University of Liverpool.

Centre for Intelligent Systems and their Applications   (CISA)
- ■   School of Informatics, University of Edinburgh, Appleton Tower, Crichton Street, Edinburgh, EH8 9LE.
     0131-650 2732   fax 0131-650 6513
     http://www.inf.ed.ac.uk/research/cisa/
     Director: Dr Dave Robertson.
- E   A research centre at the University of Edinburgh.
- ○   To conduct basic and applied research and development in knowledge representation and reasoning

Centre for Intensive Care Medicine and Bloomsbury Institute of Intensive Care Medicine
- ■   Department of Medicine, The Middlesex Hospital, Mortimer Street, London, W1T 3AA.
     020 7679 9666   fax 020 7679 9660
     http://www.ucl.ac.uk/medicine/intensive-care/
     Director: Prof Mervyn Singer.
- E   A research centre at University College London.
- ○   To promote and maintain good clinical practice in intensive care medicine, with research emphasis on the study and management of critical illness, tissue oxygenation, vascular hyporeactivity and mitochondrial dysfunction in sepsis, utilising both clinical and laboratory investigations
- ●   Educational programme

Centre for Interactive Assessment Development   (CIAD)
- ■   University of Derby, Kedleston Road, Derby, DE22 1GB.
     01332 591720
     http://www.derby.ac.uk/ciad/
     Contact: Don Mackenzie.
- E   A centre at the University of Derby.
- ○   To provide design consultancy, production, delivery and a results reporting service for computer based assessments across the University

Centre for Interactive Intelligent Systems   (CIIS)
- ■   School of Computing, Communications and Electronics, University of Plymouth, Drake Circus, Plymouth, PL4 8AA.
     01752 600600
     http://www.tech.plym.ac.uk/Research/computer_science_and_informatics/
     Contact: Prof Eduardo Reck Miranda.
- E   A research centre at the University of Plymouth.

Centre for Interactive Media   (CIM)
- ■   School of Computing, De Montfort University, Gateway House, The Gateway, Leicester, LE1 9BH.
     0116-257 7456
     http://www.dmu.ac.uk/faculties/cse/research_consultancy/computing/research_groups.jsp#csr
     Director: Dr Ian Sexton.
- E   A centre at De Montfort University.

Centre for Interactive Network Arts   (CINA)
- ■   Wimbledon College of Art, University of the Arts, London, Main Building, Merton Hall Road, London, SW19 3QA.
     020 7514 9641   fax 020 7514 9642
     http://www.wimbledon.arts.ac.uk/research-wimbledon.htm
- E   A research centre at the University of the Arts, London.

Centre for Interactive Systems Engineering   (CISE)
- ■   Faculty of Business, Computing and Information Management, London South Bank University, 103 Borough Road, London, SE1 0AA.
     020 7815 7434
     http://www.lsbu.ac.uk/bcimicr/research/cise.shtml
     Director: Prof Fintan Culwin.
- E   A research centre at London South Bank University.
- ○   To conduct research in novel approaches to usability evaluation, computer-mediated communication (CMC), web design, computer-mediated distance education, the influence of gender in CMC, and pro-active anti-plagiarism

Centre for Interactive Systems Research   (CISR)   1987
■   Department of Information Science, City University, Northampton Square, London, EC1V 0HB.
      020 7040 8386   fax 020 7040 8389
      http://www.soi.city.ac.uk/organisation/is/research/cisr/
E   A department of City University.
O   To bring together research interests in the areas of information retrieval system design and evaluation and the associated study of
      users and information-seeking behaviour

Centre for Intercultural Development   (CI-CD)   1993
■   27 Langland Gardens, London, NW3 6QE.
      020 7431 1712
      http://www.diversityworks.co.uk/CICDhomepage.htm
      Director: John Twitchin. Co-Director: Tamara Lewis.
E   A company limited by guarantee.
O   To research, design and deliver training courses in intercultural communication skills
●   Education and training - Information service - Library
¶   Employment Law. The Law and You. Trading in. . .[series of 5 publications - one each for China, France, Germany, Poland, and
      the UK].

Centre for Intercultural Music
■   Department of Music, City University, Northampton Square, London, EC1V 0HB.
      020 7040 8284
      http://www.city.ac.uk/music/staff/intercultural.html
E   A research centre at City University.

Centre for Intercultural Studies   (CIS)   1992
■   School of Modern Languages and Cultures, University of Glasgow, 16 University Gardens, Glasgow, G12 8QL.
      0141-330 5377   fax 0141-330 3512
      http://www.cis.arts.gla.ac.uk/
      Director: Prof R H Stephenson. Contact: Mrs Meta Jamison.
E   A research centre at the University of Glasgow.
✕   Centre for Intercultural Germanistics.

Centre for Intercultural Studies   (CIS)
■   Department of Dutch, University College London, Gower Street, London, WC1E 6BT.
      020 7679 3117
      http://www.ucl.ac.uk/ics/
      Director: Prof Theo Hermans.
E   A research centre at University College London.

Centre for Interdisciplinary Gender Research
      see **Mary Ann Baxter Centre for Interdisciplinary Gender Research.**

Centre for Interdisciplinary Gender Studies   (CIGS)
■   Faculty of Education, Social Sciences and Law, University of Leeds, Social Studies Building, Leeds, LS2 9JT.
      0113-343 3770   fax 0113-343 4415
      http://www.leeds.ac.uk/gender-studies/
      Director: Dr Ruth Holliday.
E   An interdisciplinary research centre at the University of Leeds.
O   To offer programmes of study leading to various degrees in gender studies
●   Education and training

Centre for Interdisciplinary Mathematical Research   (CIMR)   2000
■   School of Mathematics, University of East Anglia, Norwich, NR4 7TJ.
      01603 592844   fax 01603 593868
      http://www.cimr.uea.ac.uk/
      Director: Prof Jean-Marc Vanden-Broeck.
E   An interdisciplinary research centre at the University of East Anglia.
O   To use mathematics to solve problems arising in other disciplines, and to develop new mathematical ideas motivated by the
      challenges of interdisciplinary research

Centre for Interdisciplinary Practice
      see **Interface - The Centre for Interdisciplinary Practice.**

Centre for Interdisciplinary Research in the Arts   (CIDRA)   2005
■   School of Arts, Histories and Cultures, University of Manchester, Humanities Lime Grove Centre, Oxford Road, Manchester,
      M13 9PL.
      0161-275 8965
      http://www.arts.manchester.ac.uk/cidra/
      Director: Prof Frank Mort.
E   An interdisciplinary research centre at the University of Manchester.
O   To foster, develop and promote high-quality research and teaching in arts subjects

Centre for Interdisciplinary Research in Computational Algebra   (CIRCA)   2000
- School of Computer Science, University of St Andrews, North Haugh, St Andrews, Fife, KY16 9SS.
   01334 463269   fax 01334 463278
   http://www-circa.mcs.st-and.ac.uk/
   Director: Prof S A Linton.
- E   An interdisciplinary research centre at the University of St Andrews.
- O   To undertake mathematical research, with computer assistance, into developing new techniques for computation in abstract algebra, and to develop and distribute software implementing these techniques

Centre for Interdisciplinary Studies of Higher Education   (CISHE)   2003
- University College London, Gower Street, London, WC1E 6BT.
   020 7679 2000
   http://www.ucl.ac.uk/cishe/
- E   A research centre at University College London.

Centre for Inter-Faith Studies   2001
- Department of Theology and Religious Studies, University of Glasgow, 4 The Square, Glasgow, G12 8QQ.
   0141-330 6526
   http://www.religions.divinity.gla.ac.uk/Centre-Interfaith/
   Co-Director: Prof Dr Perry Schmidt-Leukel. Co-Director: Dr Kyoshi Tsuchiya.
- E   A centre at the University of Glasgow.
- O   To encourage research in inter-faith studies

Centre for Interfaces and Materials   (CIM)
- Department of Chemistry, University of Warwick, Coventry, CV4 7AL.
   024 7657 4009
   http://www2.warwick.ac.uk/fac/sci/chemistry/cim/
   Contact: Dr Stefan Bon.
- E   A research centre within the University of Warwick.
- ●   Conferences

Centre for Interfacial Science and Technology
   see **Imperial College Centre for Interfacial Science and Technology.**

Centre for Interfirm Comparison   (CIFC)   1959
- 32 St Thomas Street, Winchester, Hampshire, SO23 9HJ.
   01962 844144   fax 01962 843180
   Director: H W Palmer.
- E   Established by the British Institute of Management in association with the British Productivity Council.
- O   To help businesses of every kind to assess their performance and then take steps to improve it through benchmarking and interfirm comparison
- ●   Education and training - Information service - Management consultancy - Statistics

Centre for Intergenerational Practice   (CIP)   2002
- Beth Johnson Foundation, Parkfield House, 64 Princes House, Stoke-on-Trent, ST4 7JL.
   01782 844036   fax 01782 746940
   http://www.centreforip.org.uk/
   Co-ordinator: Louise Middleton.
- E   A centre at the Beth Johnson Foundation.

Centre for Intermedia
- Department of Drama, University of Exeter, Thornlea, New North Road, Exeter, EX4 4LA.
   01392 262332   fax 01392 264594
   http://www.spa.ex.ac.uk/drama/research/intermedia/welcome.shtml
   Contact: Prof Nick Kaye. Contact: Linda Dowsett.
- E   A centre at the University of Exeter.
- O   To promote transdisciplinary research in performance and the arts through collaborations between artists, academics and scientists from a range of disciplines

Centre for International Borders Research   (CIBR)
- School of Sociology, Social Policy and Social Work, Queen's University, Belfast, 1-3 College Park East, Belfast, BT7 1NN.
   028 9097 5117   fax 028 9097 3943
   http://www.qub.ac.uk/cibr/
   Director: Prof Liam O'Dowd.
- E   A centre at Queen's University, Belfast.
- O   To be an interdisciplinary centre for empirical, comparative, historical, and theoretical study of international borders and border regions

Centre for International Briefing   (CIB)   1953

■   Farnham Castle, Castle Street, Farnham, Surrey, GU9 0AG.
    01252 721194
    http://www.farnhamcastle.com/
E   A registered charity and a company limited by guarantee.
O   To provide comprehensive country and business briefings, language tuition and cross-cultural skills training for those taking up long and short term contracts anywhere in the world

Centre for International Business History   (CIBH)   1997

■   University of Reading Business School, University of Reading, HUMSS Building, PO Box 218, Reading, Berkshire, RG6 6AA.
    0118-378 5435   fax 0118-378 6229
    http://www.reading.ac.uk/business/Research/Centres/bus-CIBH.asp
    Director: Dr Peter Scott.
E   A research centre at the University of Reading.
O   To promote the study of the past development and future evolution of business in an international and comparative context

Centre for International Business and Innovation   (CIBI)   2005

■   Manchester Metropolitan University Business School, Manchester Metropolitan University, Aytoun Building, Aytoun Street, Manchester, M1 3GH.
    0161-247 3742; 3808
    http://www.business.mmu.ac.uk/cibi
    Director: Prof Heinz Tuselmann.
E   A research centre within the Research Institute for Business and Management (qv) at Manchester Metropolitan University.
O   To bring together the expertise and international level research of scholars in the research fields of international business and innovation studies into a dedicated centre

Centre for International Business and Management   (CIBAM)

■   Judge Business School, University of Cambridge, Trumpington Street, Cambridge, CB2 1AG.
    01223 339618   fax 01223 766815
    http://www.jbs.cam.ac.uk/research/cibam/
    Director: Dr Christos Pitelis.
E   A centre at the University of Cambridge.
O   To deepen the understanding internationalisation and managing in the global economy

Centre for International Business Policy   (CIBP)

■   Kingston Business School, University of Kingston, London, Kingston Hill, Kingston-upon-Thames, Surrey, KT1 7LB.
    020 8547 2000
    http://business.kingston.ac.uk/CIBP.php
    Contact: Issam Tlemsani.
E   A research centre at Kingston University, London.
O   To conduct research and consultancy in global business in the range of transition problems (especially in Russia and the Maghreb), global business strategy, modelling complexity in organisational behaviour, and inter-cultural issues

Centre for International Business, Research and Development   (CIB)

■   Ashcroft International Business School, University of Cambridge, East Road, Cambridge, CB1 1PT.
    0845 196 2479
    http://www.anglia.ac.uk/ruskin/en/home/business/cib.html
    Director: Prof Lester Lloyd-Reason.
E   A research centre at Anglia Ruskin University.
O   To conduct research in the area of skills and knowledge development of international small- and medium-sized enterprises

Centre for International Business and Strategy   (CIBS)

■   University of Reading Business School, University of Reading, HUMSS Building, PO Box 218, Reading, Berkshire, RG6 6AA.
    0118-378 5247   fax 0118-975 0236
    http://www.reading.ac.uk/business/Research/Centres/bus-CIBS.asp
    Director: Prof Rajneesh Narula.
E   A research centre at the University of Reading.
O   To research the impact of international business on economic issues

Centre for International Business Studies   (CIBS)   1992

■   Faculty of Business, Computing and Information Management, London South Bank University, 103 Borough Road, London, SE1 0AA.
    020 7815 8281   fax 020 7815 8250
    http://www.lsbu.ac.uk/cibs/
    Director: Prof Grazia Ietto-Gillies.
E   A centre at London South Bank University.
O   To foster excellence in research, teaching and consultancy in the field of international business

Centre for International Business, University of Leeds   (CIBUL)   1995
- ■ Leeds University Business School, University of Leeds, Maurice Keyworth Building, Leeds, LS2 9JT.
  0113-343 4592
  http://lubswww.leeds.ac.uk/cibul/
  Director: Prof Peter J Buckley.
- E   A research centre at the University of Leeds.
- O   To focus research on all aspects of international business

Centre for International Capital Markets   (CICM)
- ■ Department of Economics, Finance and International Business, London Metropolitan University, 84 Moorgate, London, EC2M 6SQ.
  020 7320 1000; 1464   fax 020 7320 1414
  http://www.londonmet.ac.uk/depts/efib/research/cicm.cfm
  Director: Prof Nicholas Sarantis.
- E   A research centre at London Metropolitan University.
- O   To conduct research, teaching, supervision of PhD students and consultancy in the broad areas of modelling and forecasting of financial markets, international finance, financial derivatives and risk management, portfolio investment, and banking

Centre for International Communications and Society
- ■ Department of Sociology, City University, Social Sciences Building, Northampton Square, London, EC1V 0HB.
  020 7040 5060   fax 020 7040 5070
  http://www.city.ac.uk/sociology/journ/
  Contact: Prof Frank Webster.
- E   A centre at City University.
- O   To conduct research in various fields of international communications, including media policy / regulation, media and contemporary social change, ethnicity and media relations, comparative media studies, promotional culture, political communications, media professionals, media organisation, transnational and international media, journalism, consumption, news media / communications, and information society studies

Centre for International Communications Research   (CICR)
- ■ Faculty of Performance, Visual Arts and Communications, University of Leeds, Level 3, Houldsworth Building, Leeds, LS2 9JT.
  0113-343 7608   fax 0113-343 1117
  http://ics.leeds.ac.uk/papers/index.cfm?outfit=cicr
  Director: Dr Katharine Sarikakis.
- E   A research centre within the Institute of Communications Studies (qv) at the University of Leeds.

Centre for International and Comparative Studies
> see **CLIO Centre for International and Comparative Studies.**

Centre for International Co-operation and Security   (CICS)   2002
- ■ School of Social and International Studies, University of Bradford, Bradford, West Yorkshire, BD7 1DP.
  01274 235172
  http://www.bradford.ac.uk/acad/cics/
  Director: Dr Owen Greene.
- E   A centre at the University of Bradford.
- O   To conduct research and training in international affairs and transnational issues, particularly in the areas of conflict, security, development and environment

Centre for International Courts and Tribunals   (CICT)   2002
- ■ Faculty of Laws, University College London, Bentham House, Endsleigh Gardens, London, WC1H 0EG.
  020 7679 1455   fax 020 7679 1440
  http://www.ucl.ac.uk/laws/cict/
  Director: Prof Philippe Sands. Administrator: Kate Barber.
- E   A research centre at University College London.
- O   To facilitate access to and transparency in the work of international courts and tribunals; to enhance the effectiveness and promote greater knowledge about courts and tribunals
Note: The Centre serves as the London home of the Project on International Courts and Tribunals (PICT), which was established in 1997.

Centre for International Development
> see **Bradford Centre for International Development.**

Centre for International Drylands Research
> see **Sheffield Centre for International Drylands Research.**

Centre for International Economic Studies
> see **Surrey Centre for International Economic Studies.**

© CBD Research Ltd · Beckenham · Kent BR3 5JS · Tel 020 8650 7745 · Fax 020 8650 0768 · E-mail cbd@cbdresearch.com · www.cbdresearch.com

Centre for International Education   (CIE)

■ Sussex School of Education, University of Sussex, Essex House, Falmer, Brighton, East Sussex, BN1 9QQ.
   01273 877888   fax 01273 877534
   http://www.sussex.ac.uk/education/1-4-21.html
   Director: Prof Keith Lewin.
E   A research centre within the Sussex Institute (qv) at the University of Sussex.
O   To provide a focal point for work on education and development in low-income countries

Centre for International Education and Research   (CIER)

■ School of Education, University of Birmingham, Edgbaston, Birmingham, B15 2TT.
   0121-414 4866   fax 0121-414 4865
   http://www.education.bham.ac.uk/research/cier/
E   A research centre at the University of Birmingham.

Centre for International and European Studies   (CIES)

■ Coventry University, Priory Street, Coventry, CV1 5FB.
   024 7688 8177
   http://www.stile.coventry.ac.uk/public/rcon/cies_f.htm
   Contact: Prof Brian Hocking.
E   A centre at Coventry University.
O   To provide a focus for research on a range of international and European issues

Centre for International Exchange and Languages   (CIEL)

■ School of Humanities, Keele University, Walter Moberly Building, Keele, Staffordshire, ST5 5BG.
   01782 621111   fax 01782 584238
   http://www.keele.ac.uk/depts/solcca/ciel/
   Head: Annette Kratz.
E   A research centre at Keele University.

Centre for International Family Law Studies   (CIFLS)

■ Cardiff Law School, Cardiff University, PO Box 427, Cardiff, CF10 3XJ.
   029 2087 6705   fax 029 2087 4097
   http://www.law.cf.ac.uk/family/
   Director: Prof Nigel Lowe.
E   A centre at Cardiff University.
O   To gather together existing knowledge on the international aspects of family law; to promote further understanding of the field by research and analysis

Centre for International Governance   (CfIG)   2006

■ School of Law, University of Leeds, 20 Lyddon Terrace, Leeds, LS2 9JT.
   0113-343 5033   fax 0113-343 5056
   http://www.law.leeds.ac.uk/leedslaw/
   Contact: Steve Wheatley.
E   A research centre at the University of Leeds.
O   To pursue research activities concerned with aspects of international governance

Centre for International Health and Development
   see **Nuffield Centre for International Health and Development.**

Centre for International Health and Development
   see **UCL Centre for International Health and Development.**

Centre for International Health Studies
   see **Institute for International Health and Development.**

Centre for International Hospitality Management Research   (CIHMR)   1972

■ Faculty of Organisation and Management, Sheffield Hallam University, Howard Street, Sheffield, S1 1WB.
   0114-225 2948; 3320   fax 0114-225 3343
   http://www.shu.ac.uk/research/cihmr/
   Director: Prof Stephen Ball.
E   A research centre at Sheffield Hallam University.
O   To carry out research in hospitality management and the hospitality industry

Centre for International Labour Market Studies   (CILMS)   2000

■ Aberdeen Business School, Robert Gordon University, Management Building, Garthdee Road, Aberdeen, AB10 7QE.
   01224 263400   fax 01224 263434
   http://www.rgu.ac.uk/abs/centres/page.cfm?pge=5631
   Director: David Gibbons-Wood.
E   A research centre at the Robert Gordon University.
O   To undertake research and consultancy in the areas of education, training, skills, employment and local, national and international labour market policy

Centre for International Law [Cambridge]
   see **Lauterpacht Centre for International Law.**

Centre for International Law [Hull]
   see **McCoubrey Centre for International Law.**

Centre for International Law and Colonialism   (CILC)   2006
■   Faculty of Law and Social Sciences, School of Oriental and African Studies, University of London, Thornhaugh Street, Russell Square, London, WC1H 0XG.
   020 7898 4411   fax 020 7898 4559
   http://www.soas.ac.uk/centres/centreinfo.cfm?navid=1046
E   A research centre at the School of Oriental and African Studies, University of London.
O   To examine the historical and contemporary relationship of colonialism and international law

Centre for International Media Analysis   (CIMA)
■   Luton Campus, University of Bedfordshire, Luton, Bedfordshire, LU1 3JU.
   01234 400400
   http://www.beds.ac.uk/research/rimad/cima
   Director: Prof Garry Whannel.
E   A research centre within the Research Institute for Media, Art and Design (qv) at the University of Bedfordshire.
O   To focus research on world cinema, media economics, and image and representation

Centre for International Politics   (CIP)
■   City University, Northampton Square, London, EC1V 0HB.
   http://www.city.ac.uk/intpol/
   Contact: Dr Jamie Munn.
E   A research centre at City University.

Centre for International Poverty Research
   see **Townsend Centre for International Poverty Research.**

Centre for International and Public Law   (CIPL)   2004
■   School of Social Sciences and Law, Brunel University, Uxbridge, Middlesex, UB8 3PH.
   01895 266230   fax 01895 266239
   http://www.brunel.ac.uk/about/acad/law/research/cipl
   Co-Director: Prof Ben Chigara. Co-Director: Dr George Letsas.
E   A centre at Brunel University.
O   To promote excellence in the research and teaching of public law and international law

Centre for International Research in Arts and Society
   see **Glenamara Centre for International Research in Arts and Society.**

Centre for International Research on Creativity and Learning in Education   (CIRCLE)   2005
■   School of Education, Roehampton University, Erasmus House, Roehampton Lane, London, SW15 5PU.
   020 8392 3000
   http://www.roehampton.ac.uk/researchcentres/circle
   Director: Prof David Hargreaves. Administrator: Caroline Freeland.
E   A research centre at Roehampton University.
O   To conduct research in creativity and learning in education in the fields of art, design and technology, English and music

Centre for International Security Studies and Non-proliferation
■   Graduate Institute of Political and International Studies, University of Reading, Whiteknights, PO Box 217, Reading, Berkshire, RG6 6AH.
   0118-378 8378
   http://www.rdg.ac.uk/GIPIS/Research%207/Research%20Centres.htm
E   A research centre within the Graduate Institute of Political and International Studies (qv) at the University of Reading.
O   To conduct research on issues of international and global security

Centre of International Studies   (CIS)   1977
■   University of Cambridge, 1st floor - 17 Mill Lane, Cambridge, CB2 1RX.
   01223 767235   fax 01223 767237
   http://www.intstudies.cam.ac.uk/
   Director: Prof Christopher Hill.
E   A centre at the University of Cambridge.
O   To be one of the world's leading institutions in research and the teaching of international relations

Centre for International Studies   (CIS)
- School of Politics and International Studies, University of Leeds, Leeds, LS2 9JT.
  0113-343 4382
  http://www.leeds.ac.uk/polis/research/intStd/
  Director: Prof Christoph Bluth.
- E   A research centre at the University of Leeds.

Centre for International Studies   (CIS)   1967
- LSE, Room Q501, Sheffield Street, London, WC2A 2AE.
  020 7405 7686
  http://lse.ac.uk/collections/CIS/
  Chairman: Dr John Kent.
- E   A department of the London School of Economics and Political Science.
- O   To encourage individual research in international studies, especially Russia, China, the Middle East, Asia and Europe

Centre for International Studies   (CIS)   1992
- Department of Politics and International Relations, University of Oxford, Queen Elizabeth House, Mansfield Road, Oxford, OX1 3TB.
  01865 288569   fax 01865 278725
  http://cis.politics.ox.ac.uk/
  Director: Dr Andrew Hurrell.
- E   A centre at the University of Oxford.
- O   To promote and advance current issues in international studies

Centre for International Studies [Southampton]
  see **Mountbatten Centre for International Studies.**

Centre for International Studies and Diplomacy   (CISD)   2000
- Faculty of Languages and Cultures, School of Oriental and African Studies, University of London, Thornhaugh Street, Russell Square, London, WC1H 0XG.
  020 7898 4830; 4840   fax 020 7898 4839
  http://www.cisd.soas.ac.uk/
  Academic Director: Dr Peter Slinn.
- E   An interdisciplinary research centre at the School of Oriental and African Studies, University of London.
- O   To promote research and teaching in area studies and diplomacy

Centre for International Studies in Education, Management and Training   (CISEMT)   1991
- University of Reading, Bulmershe Court, Earley, Reading, Berkshire, RG6 1HY.
  0118-378 8811
  http://www.education.rdg.ac.uk/cisemt/
- E   A research centre within the Institute of Education (qv) at the University of Reading.
- O   To study the different facets of educational development within an international context

Centre for International Transport Management   (CITM)   1992
- Department of Business and Service Sector Management, London Metropolitan University, 84 Moorgate, London, EC2M 6SQ.
  020 7320 1357
  http://www.londonmet.ac.uk/depts/bssm/research/citm/home.cfm
  Director: Dr Heather Leggate. Director: Prof James McConville.
- E   A department of London Metropolitan University.
- O   To promote training in international transport, especially shipping and civil aviation (which is a separate department)
- ●   Education and training - Library
- ¶   UK Seafarers (annual).

Centre for Internationalisation and Usability
- Thames Valley University, Wellington Street, Slough, Berkshire, SL1 1YG.
  01753 697732   fax 01753 697750
  http://iit.tvu.ac.uk/research.html
  Administrator: Alex Bussey.
- E   A research centre within the Institute of Information Technology (qv) at Thames Valley University.
- O   To support software developers in building systems that meet all the needs of end users within the discipline of human-computer interaction

Centre for Internet Computing
Note: Since 1 August 2006 is the School of Arts and New Media, Scarborough.

Centre for Internet Technologies   (CIT)   2005
- School of Computing and Technology, University of Sunderland, St Peter's Campus, St Peter's Way, Sunderland, Tyne and Wear, SR6 0DD.
  0191-515 2752   fax 0191-515 2781
  http://www.cit.sunderland.ac.uk/
  Contact: John Tait.
- E   A research centre at the University of Sunderland.
- O   To conduct research in a wide range of internet technologies

Centre for Interprofessional e-Learning in Health and Social Care   (CIPeL)   2005
- Faculty of Health and Life Sciences, University of Coventry, Richard Crossman Building, Priory Street, Coventry, CV1 5FB.
  024 7679 5959   fax 024 7679 5950
  http://www.cipel.ac.uk
  Director: Dr Lynn Clouder.
- E   A Centre for Excellence in Teaching and Learning (CETL) at Coventry University.
- Note: See **Centres for Excellence in Teaching and Learning** for more information.

Centre for Interprofessional Practice   (CIPP)
- University of East Anglia, Norwich, NR4 7TJ.
  01603 593681
  http://www1.uea.ac.uk/cm/home/schools/foh/cipp
- E   A research centre at the University of East Anglia.
- O   To work across the schools within the IOH to deliver inter-professional learning opportunities to all students in the Institute

Centre for Ion Conducting Membranes   (CICM)
- T H Huxley School of Environment, Earth Sciences and Engineering, Imperial College London, Flowers Building, Armstrong Road, London, SW7 2AZ.
  020 7594 7594   fax 020 7594 7444
  http://www3.imperial.ac.uk/courses/azofdepartmentsandcentres/ionconductingmembranes
  Director: Dr Nigel Brandon.
- E   A research centre at Imperial College London.

Centre for Iranian Studies   (CIS)   1999
- School of Government and International Affairs, University of Durham, The Al-Qasimi Building, Elvet Hill Road, Durham, DH1 3TU.
  0191-334 5664   fax 0191-334 5661
  http://www.dur.ac.uk/iranian.studies/
  Director: Dr Mahjoob Zweiri.
- E   A subsidiary research centre of the Institute for Middle Eastern and Islamic Studies (qv) at the University of Durham.
- O   To facilitate and encourage debate, research and the growth of Iranian studies in the UK

Centre for Iris Murdoch Studies   2006
- Faculty of Arts and Social Sciences, Kingston University, London, Penrhyn Road, Kingston-upon-Thames, Surrey, KT1 2EE.
  020 8547 2000
  http://fass.kingston.ac.uk/research/centres/Iris_Murdoch/
  Contact: Dr Anne Rowe.
- E   A research centre at Kingston University, London.
- O   To conduct research on the life and work of author Iris Murdoch

Centre for Irish Politics   (CIP)   1994
- School of Politics and International Studies, Queen's University, Belfast, 19-21 University Square, Belfast, BT7 1PA.
  028 9027 3657
  http://www.qub.ac.uk/cip/
  Contact: Dr Margaret O'Callaghan.
- E   A centre at Queen's University, Belfast.
- O   To promote research on Irish politics

Centre for Irish and Scottish Studies
   see **AHRC Centre for Irish and Scottish Studies.**

Centre of Islamic and Middle East Law   (CIMEL)   1990
- Faculty of Law and Social Sciences, School of Oriental and African Studies, University of London, Thornhaugh Street, Russell Square, London, WC1H 0XG.
  020 7898 4672   fax 020 7898 4559
  http://www.soas.ac.uk/centres/centreinfo.cfm?navid=17
  Director: Dr Lynn Welchman.
- E   A research centre at the School of Oriental and African Studies, University of London.
- O   To act as a scholarly legal bridge for research and practice at the crossroad of Islam, the Middle East and the West

Centre of Islamic Studies   (CIS)   1995
- Faculty of Arts and Humanities, School of Oriental and African Studies, University of London, Thornhaugh Street, Russell Square, London, WC1H 0XG.
  020 7898 4325   fax 020 7898 4379
  http://www.soas.ac.uk/centres/centreinfo.cfm?navid=18
  Director: Prof MAS Abdel Haleem.
- E   A research centre at the School of Oriental and African Studies, University of London.
- O   To promote scholarship and research in all areas of Islamic studies, past and present - and with particular emphasis on the study of the Qur'an and Hadith from the Arabic texts, and the analysis and translation of Islamic texts from Arabic into English; to promote the study of Islamic culture and relations between Muslims and the wider world

Centre for Islamic Studies [Oxford]
   see **Oxford Centre for Islamic Studies.**

© CBD Research Ltd · Beckenham · Kent BR3 5JS · Tel 020 8650 7745 · Fax 020 8650 0768 · E-mail cbd@cbdresearch.com · www.cbdresearch.com

Centre for Israeli Studies

■   Department of Hebrew and Jewish Studies, University College London, Foster Court, Gower Street, London, WC1E 6BT.
     020 7679 7171   fax 020 7209 1026
     http://www.ucl.ac.uk/hebrew-jewish/graduate/dept_resources.php#cis
E   A research centre at University College London.

Centre for IT in Construction

■   Faculty of Business, Law and the Built Environment, University of Salford, Maxwell Building, Salford, Manchester, M5 4WT.
     0161-295 5128   fax 0161-295 5011
     http://www.buhu.salford.ac.uk/research_centres/constructit/
     Director: Prof Mustafa Alshawi.
E   A research centre within the Research Institute for the Built and Human Environment (qv) at the University of Salford.
O   To improve constructive industry performance through the innovative application of IT

Centre for Italian Studies   (CIS)

■   Department of Italian, University College London, Gower Street, London, WC1E 6BT.
     020 7380 7365; 7679 7024   fax 020 7380 7380
     http://www.ucl.ac.uk/italian/pages/centre.html
     Director: Enrico Palandri.
E   An interdisciplinary research centre at University College London.
O   To provide a forum for research relating to all aspects of Italian culture

Centre of Jaina Studies   (COJS)   2005

■   Faculty of Arts and Humanities, School of Oriental and African Studies, University of London, Thornhaugh Street, Russell Square, London, WC1H 0XG.
     020 7898 4020; 4776   fax 020 7898 4699
     http://www.soas.ac.uk/centres/centreinfo.cfm?navid=863
     Chairman: Dr Peter Flûgel.
E   A research centre at the School of Oriental and African Studies, University of London.
O   To promote teaching, research and study in the field of Jaina studies

Centre for Jewish Education
     see **Leo Baeck College - Centre for Jewish Education.**

Centre for Jewish Studies   (CJS)

■   School of Fine Art, History of Art and Cultural Studies, University of Leeds, Old Mining Building, Leeds, LS2 9JT.
     0113-343 5192   fax 0113-245 1977
     http://www.leeds.ac.uk/fine_art/cejs/
     Director: Dr Eva Frojmovic.
E   A research centre at the University of Leeds.

Centre for Jewish Studies   (CJS)

■   Faculty of Languages and Cultures, School of Oriental and African Studies, University of London, Thornhaugh Street, Russell Square, London, WC1H 0XG.
     020 7898 4101   fax 020 7898 4399
     http://www.soas.ac.uk/centres/centreinfo.cfm?navid=20
     Chairman: Dr Colin Shindler.
E   A centre at the School of Oriental and African Studies, University of London.
O   To discuss various topics with relation to Jewish history
●   Seminars

Centre for Jewish Studies   (MUCJS)   1997

■   School of Arts, Histories and Cultures, University of Manchester, Oxford Road, Manchester, M13 9PL.
     0161-275 3614   fax 0161-275 3613
     http://www.mucjs.org/
     Co-Director: Prof Philip Alexander. Co-Director: Prof Bernard Jackson.
E   An interdisciplinary research centre at the University of Manchester.
O   To maximise the teaching of Jewish studies, at undergraduate and postgraduate level

Centre for Journalism Studies   (CJS)   1970

■   Cardiff School of Journalism, Media and Cultural Studies, Cardiff University, The Bute Building, King Edward VII Avenue, Cardiff, CF10 3NB.
     029 2087 4000   fax 029 2023 8832
     http://www.cardiff.ac.uk/jomec/en/groups/298.html
     Director: Prof Richard Tait.
E   A research centre at Cardiff University.
O   To provide professional training to new graduates; to provide mid-career journalists with the oportunity to study for higher degrees and to conduct research

Centre for Judaism
     see **Sternberg Centre for Judaism.**

Centre for Knowledge Management (CKM) 2000
- ■ Aberdeen Business School, Robert Gordon University, Management Building, Garthdee Road, Aberdeen, AB10 7QE.
  01224 263884
  http://www.rgu.ac.uk/abs/centres/page.cfm?pge=5649
  Director: Simon Burnett.
- E A research centre at the Robert Gordon University.
- O To enable organisations to build sustainable competitive advantage through management of knowledge

Centre for Knowledge Transfer   2002
- ■ London South Bank University, Technopark, 90 London Road, London, SE1 6LN.
  020 7815 6922   fax 020 7815 6915
  http://www.ktplondon.co.uk/
- E A centre at London South Bank University.
- O To implement the Knowledge Transfer Partnership (KTP) programme, a programme aiming to bring top employees and university resources to business

Centre of Korean Studies (CKS) 1987
- ■ School of Oriental and African Studies, University of London, Thornhaugh Street, Russell Square, London, WC1H 0XG.
  020 7898 4892; 4893   fax 020 7898 4489
  http://www.soas.ac.uk/centres/centreinfo.cfm?navid=6
  Manager: Jane Savory. Executive Officer: Sara Hamza.
- E An interdisciplinary research centre at the School of Oriental and African Studies, University of London.
- O To facilitate and develop, in the UK and Europe, research, teaching and other activities relating to Korea

Centre for Labour Market Studies   (CLMS)
- ■ University of Leicester, 7-9 Salisbury Road, Leicester, LE1 7QR.
  0116-252 5949   fax 0116-252 5953
  http://www.clms.le.ac.uk/
  Head: John Goodwin, BSc.
- E A research centre at the University of Leicester.
- O To offer a range of courses on various aspects of labour market studies

Centre for Land-Based Studies (CLBS) 1993
- ■ School of Services Management, Bournemouth University, Dorset House, Fern Barrow, Poole, Dorset, BH12 5BB.
  01202 965184
  http://www.bournemouth.ac.uk/services-management/research/clbs.html
  Head: Dr Jonathan Edwards.
- E A centre at Bournemouth University.
- O To conduct research into activities that are dependent, either directly or indirectly, upon land and landscapes

Centre for Land Use and Water Resources Research   (CLUWRR)
- ■ University of Newcastle, 3rd Floor - Devonshire Building, Claremont Road, Newcastle upon Tyne, NE1 7RU.
  0191-246 4882   fax 0191-246 4961
  http://www.cluwrr.ncl.ac.uk/
  Director: Prof Ian Calder.
- E A research centre at the University of Newcastle upon Tyne.
- O To develop integrating methodologies for linking ecology, hydrology, and economics, taking account of issues of sustainability, equity, socio-economics and stakeholder participation

Centre for Landscape and Townscape Archaeology (CLTA)
- ■ School of Conservation Sciences, Bournemouth University, Christchurch House, Talbot Campus, Poole, Dorset, BH12 5BB.
  01202 965178   fax 01202 965530
  http://www.bournemouth.ac.uk/conservation/abouttheschool/ahe/clta.html
- E A centre at Bournemouth University.
- O To conduct research in understanding and explaining patterning in the way that human communities have engaged with, modified, and constructed their surroundings

Centre for Language Assessment Research (CLARe) 2000
- ■ School of Arts, Roehampton University, Digby Stuart College, Roehampton Lane, London, SW15 5PH.
  020 8392 3249
  http://www.roehampton.ac.uk/researchcentres/clare/
- E A research centre at Roehampton University.
- O To offer scholars, examining boards and government organisations, both domestic and foreign, a centre in London that can provide and assist in quality research and development in the areas of language test development, evaluation and validation

Centre for Language and Communication Research   (CLCR)

■   Cardiff School of English, Communication and Philosophy, Cardiff University, Humanities Building, Colum Drive, Cardiff, CF10 3EU.
   029 2087 6049
   http://www.cardiff.ac.uk/encap/clcr/resact.html
   Director: Prof Nik Coupland.
E   A centre at Cardiff University.
○   To provide a focus for research and research training in social, applied and interactional areas of language, linguistics and human communication

Centre for Language and Culture

■   School of Languages, University of Salford, Salford, Manchester, M5 4WT.
   0161-295 4948   fax 0161-295 5335
   http://www.esri.salford.ac.uk/esri/m/?s=7
   Contact: Prof Diane Blakemore.
E   A research centre within the European Studies Research Institute (qv) at the University of Salford.
○   To provide a stimulating environment for research in linguistics, translation studies, literature and cultural studies; to research a variety of languages - Arabic, French, German, Italian, Portuguese and Spanish
●   Education and training

Centre for Language, Discourse and Communication   (LDC)   2006

■   King's College London, Franklin-Wilkins Building, Waterloo Road, London, SE1 9NH.
   020 7848 3189   fax 020 7848 3182
   http://www.kcl.ac.uk/projects/ldc/
   Administrator: Melissa de Graaff.
E   A research centre at King's College, London.
○   To conduct basic and applied research on language, communication, society and education, with a particular focus on the dynamics of language and literacy within globalisation and intercultural contact

Centre for Language Learning Research

■   Department of Educational Studies, University of York, Heslington, York, YO10 5DD.
   01904 430000
   http://www.york.ac.uk/depts/educ/LanguageResGrp.htm
   Contact: Nick Page.
E   A research centre at the University of York.

Centre for Language in Social Life

■   Department of Linguistics, Lancaster University, Lancaster, LA1 4YT.
   01524 592175   fax 01524 843085
   http://www.ling.lancs.ac.uk/groups/clsl/index.htm/
   Director: Dr Mark Sebba.
E   A department of Lancaster University.
○   To study and research language and communication from a social perspective and in a wide variety of social settings

Centre for Language Studies   (CLS)   1975

■   School of Arts, Communication and Humanities, University of Surrey, Guildford, Surrey, GU2 7XH.
   01483 689178   fax 01483 689505
   http://www.surrey.ac.uk/tlc/
   Director: Andrea Dlaska. Deputy Director: Ewan Dow.
E   A department of the University of Surrey.
○   To offer a variety of modern language programmes for students and adult learners through various modes of study; to provide a variety of language solutions for business customers as well as translation services
●   Education and training (programmes include academic, general and business English, preparation and tests
×   English Language Institute.

Centre for Language Studies   (CLS)

■   School of Arts, City University, Northampton Square, London, EC1V 0HB.
   020 7040 8865   fax 020 7040 8575
   http://www.city.ac.uk/languages/
   Director: Prof Tim Connell.
E   A department of City University.
○   To create links between linguists and the professions, as well as developing language skills for students across the University

Centre for Language Study   (CLS)

■   School of Humanities, University of Southampton, Highfield, Southampton, SO17 1BJ.
   023 8059 2256   fax 023 8059 3288
   http://www.lang.soton.ac.uk/cls/courses.html
   Director: Vicky Wright.
E   A research centre at the University of Southampton.
○   To provide courses in approximately 20 foreign languages

Centre for Languages, English and Media in Education   (CLEME)
- University of Reading, Bulmershe Court, Earley, Reading, Berkshire, RG6 1HY.
  0118-378 8811
  http://www.education.rdg.ac.uk/cleme/
- E   A research centre within the Institute of Education (qv) at the University of Reading.
- O   To facilitate and promote a broad range of educational activities in modern languages, English and media studies
- ●   Education and training

Centre for Languages, Linguistics and Area Studies
   see **Subject Centre for Languages, Linguistics and Area Studies**.

Centre for Late Antique and Byzantine Studies
   see **Research Centre for Late Antique and Byzantine Studies.**

Centre for Late Antique and Medieval Studies   (CLAMS)   1988
- Department of History, King's College London, Strand, London, WC2R 2LS.
  020 7848 1088
  http://www.kcl.ac.uk/schools/humanities/hrc/clams.html
  Director: Prof David Carpenter.
- E   A research centre at King's College, London.

Centre for Late Antique Religion and Culture   (CLARC)
- Cardiff School of Religious and Theological Studies, Cardiff University, Humanities Building, Colum Drive, Cardiff, CF10 3EU.
  029 2087 5499   fax 029 2087 4500
  http://www.cardiff.ac.uk/schoolsanddivisions/academicschools/relig/research/centres/lateantiquity/
  Contact: Dr Josef Lössl.
- E   A centre at Cardiff University.
- O   To promote and support the study of late antique religion and culture from the late Hellenistic period to the early Middle Ages, also in relation to earlier and later periods, in particular classical antiquity and the modern world

Centre for Late Antiquity   (CLA)   1996
- School of Arts, Histories and Cultures, University of Manchester, Humanities Lime Grove, Oxford Road, Manchester, M13 9PL.
  0161-275 3598
  http://www.arts.manchester.ac.uk/cla/
  Director: Dr Kate Cooper.
- E   An interdisciplinary research centre within the Centre for Interdisciplinary Research in the Arts (qv) at the University of Manchester.
- O   To foster teaching and research into the history and cultures of the late ancient and early medieval Mediterranean

Centre for Latin American Cultural Studies   (CLACS)
- Department of Spanish and Spanish American Studies, King's College London, 3rd Floor - Strand Building, Strand, London, WC2R 2LS.
  020 7873 2205
  http://www.kcl.ac.uk/
- E   An interdisciplinary research centre at King's College, London.
- O   To conduct research in Latin American culture

Centre for Latin American Cultural Studies   (CLACS)
- School of Languages, Linguistics and Cultures, University of Manchester, Humanities Lime Grove Centre, Oxford Road, Manchester, M13 9PL.
  0161-275 3998
  http://www.llc.manchester.ac.uk/Research/Centres/CentreforLatinAmericanCulturalStudies/
  Co-Director: Prof John Gledhill. Co-Director: Prof Lúcia Sá.
- E   A research centre at the University of Manchester.
- O   To be a focal point for the diverse and geographically dispersed research activities associated with Latin American cultural studies

Centre for Latin American Research   (CLAR)
- University of Glasgow, East Quadrangle, Glasgow, G12 8QQ.
  0141-330 4789   fax 0141-330 4894
  http://www.gla.ac.uk/centres/clar/
- E   A research centre at the University of Glasgow.
- O   To raise the profile of Latin American research

Centre of Latin American Studies   (CLAS)   1966
- University of Cambridge, 17 Mill Lane, Cambridge, CB2 1RX.
  01223 335390   fax 01223 335397
  http://www.latin-american.cam.ac.uk/
- E   A centre at the University of Cambridge.
- O   To promote research and teaching on Latin America
- ●   Library of 11,000 volumes

Centre for Latin American Studies (CLAS) 1964

■ University of Essex, Wivenhoe Park, Colchester, Essex, CO4 3SQ.
   01206 873565   fax 01206 874043
   http://www.essex.ac.uk/centres/lastud/
   Director: Dr Andrew Canessa.
E A centre at the University of Essex.
O To conduct research in the politics, sociology, history, art, literature and architecture of Latin America

Centre for Latin American Studies (CLAS)

■ School of Arts, Languages and Literatures, University of Exeter, Queen's Building, The Queen's Drive, Exeter, EX4 4QH.
   01392 661000
   http://www.centres.ex.ac.uk/clas/
   Director: Dr Claudio Canaparo.
E A centre at the University of Exeter.
O To carry out research, supervision and teaching within the area of Latin American studies, and in many different fields of the sciences, social sciences and humanities

Centre for Law and Conflict (CLC) 2002

■ Faculty of Law and Social Sciences, School of Oriental and African Studies, University of London, Thornhaugh Street, Russell Square, London, WC1H 0XG.
   020 7898 4411   fax 020 7898 4559
   http://www.soas.ac.uk/centres/centreinfo.cfm?navid=593
   Director: Catherine Jenkins.
E A research centre at the School of Oriental and African Studies, University of London.
O To highlight and promote the use of international law and human rights

Centre for Law and the Environment (CLE) 2001

■ Faculty of Laws, University College London, Bentham House, Endsleigh Gardens, London, WC1H 0EG.
   020 7679 1440
   http://www.ucl.ac.uk/laws/environment
   Director: Prof Richard Macrory.
E A research centre at University College London.
O To advance research and teaching, and to explore the role of law in meeting contemporary environmental challenges

Centre for Law, Ethics and Society

■ Keele University, Chancellor's Building, Keele, Staffordshire, ST5 5BG.
   01782 584336
   http://www.keele.ac.uk/research/lpj/research/LES.htm
   Director: Dr Barry Godfrey.
E A research centre within the Research Institute for Law, Politics and Justice (qv) at Keele University.

Centre for the Law of the European Union

■ Faculty of Laws, University College London, Bentham House, Endsleigh Gardens, London, WC1H 0EG.
   020 7679 2000
   http://www.ucl.ac.uk/laws/
E A research centre at University College London.
O To conduct research and teaching in all major areas of European Community and Union law

Centre for Law and Governance in Europe (CLGE)

■ Faculty of Laws, University College London, Bentham House, Endsleigh Gardens, London, WC1H 0EG.
   020 7679 1407   fax 020 7679 1520
   http://www.ucl.ac.uk/laws/clge
   Director: Prof Joanne Scott. Administrator: Manuella Romeres.
E A research centre at University College London.
O To conduct research and teaching in all areas of EU law and governance

Centre for Law and Religion (CLR)

■ Cardiff Law School, Cardiff University, PO Box 427, Cardiff, CF10 3XJ.
   029 2087 4348   fax 029 2087 4097
   http://www.law.cf.ac.uk/clr/
   Director: Prof Norman Doe.
E A centre at Cardiff University.
O To develop professional academic study of the relationship between two major spheres of human activity

Centre for Law and Society 1983

■ School of Law, University of Edinburgh, Old College, South Bridge, Edinburgh, EH8 9YL.
   0131-650 2006   fax 0131-650 6317
   http://www.law.ed.ac.uk/cls/
E A research centre at the University of Edinburgh.

Centre for Leadership in Creativity   1990
- ■   138 Iffley Road, London, W6 0PE.
      020 8748 2553
      Chairman & Chief Executive Officer: John Whatmore.
- E   A profit-making business.
- ○   To understand and develop the skills of managing creativity and innovation
- ●   Consultancy - Education and training - Information service
- ¶   Wide range of publications.

Centre for Leadership Excellence
      see **Aston Centre for Leadership Excellence.**

Centre for Leadership, Learning and Change   (CLLC)   2006
- ■   Cass Business School, City University, 106 Bunhill Row, London, EC1Y 8TZ.
      020 7040 8658   fax 020 7040 8898
      http://www.cass.city.ac.uk/cllc/
      Contact: Christopher Seymour.
- E   A research centre at City University.

Centre for Leadership and Organisational Change   (CLOC)
- ■   Teesside Business School, University of Teesside, Middlesbrough, TS1 3BA.
      01642 342800; 342910
      http://www.tees.ac.uk/schools/tbs/cloc/cloc_index.cfm
      Director: Prof Paul Iles.
- E   A research centre at the University of Teesside.
- ○   To provide a platform for the growth of human resource management, leadership and change management

Centre for Leadership and Practice Innovation   (CLPI)   2004
- ■   Faculty of Health and Social Care, London South Bank University, 103 Borough Road, London, SE1 0AA.
      020 7815 8463
      http://www.lsbu.ac.uk/health/clpi/
      Director: Prod Susan McLaren.
- E   A research centre at London South Bank University.
- ○   To achieve excellence in research, leadership, practice innovation and postgraduate education in partnership with health providers, commissioners and other centres of excellence

Centre for Leadership Studies   (CLS)   1997
- ■   School of Business and Economics, University of Exeter, Xfi Building, Rennes Drive, Exeter, EX4 4ST.
      01392 262555   fax 01392 262559
      http://www.leadership-studies.com/
      Director: Prof Jonathan Gosling.
- E   A centre at the University of Exeter.
- ○   To be the first port of call for those interested in leading, in leadership development, or in the study and critique of leadership and its social significance

Centre for Learning Development   (CLD)
- ■   University of Hull, Cottingham Road, Hull, HU6 7RX.
      01482 466227   fax 01482 341334
      http://www.hull.ac.uk/cld/
      Head of Centre: Simon Atkinson.
- E   A research centre within the Institute for Learning (qv) at the University of Hull.
- ○   To promote and facilitate innovation and quality in learning, teaching, assessment and learning support, in order to enhance the student learning experience

Centre for Learning and Enterprise in Organisations   (CLEO)
- ■   University of Northampton, Boughton Green Road, Northampton, NN2 7AL.
      01604 892976
      http://www.cleobusiness.co.uk/
- E   A research centre at the University of Northampton.
- ○   To provide an opportunity for young business people to kick start their own business ventures and gain experience in the world of business

Centre for Learning, Innovation and Collaboration   (CLIC)
- ■   Department of Electronic, Electrical and Computer Engineering, University of Birmingham, Gisbert Kapp Buildng, Edgbaston, Birmingham, B15 2TT.
      0121-414 2747   fax 0121-414 4291
      http://www.clic.bham.ac.uk/
      Director: Dr Theodoros N Arvanitis.
- E   A centre at the University of Birmingham.
- ○   To be a world-leading facility for research and development in e-learning
- ✕   Centre for Educational Technology and Distance Learning

© CBD Research Ltd · Beckenham · Kent BR3 5JS · Tel 020 8650 7745 · Fax 020 8650 0768 · E-mail cbd@cbdresearch.com · www.cbdresearch.com

Centre for Learning, Knowing and Interactive Technologies
> see **CLIO Centre for Learning, Knowing and Interactive Technologies.**

Centre for the Learning Society
> see **Research Centre for the Learning Society.**

Centre for Learning and Teaching   (CLT)
■   Faculty of Education and Sport, University of Brighton, Mayfield House, Falmer, Brighton, East Sussex, BN1 9PH.
> 01273 643446
> http://staffcentral.brighton.ac.uk/clt/
> Co-ordinator: Dr Barry Stierer.
E   A centre at the University of Brighton.
O   To co-ordinate and develop new approaches to learning, teaching and assessment
Note: Many such centres exist at major UK educational institutions, all with similar objectives.

Centre for Learning and Teaching Research   (CLTR)
■   Edge Hill College of Higher Education, LINC Building, Edge Hill, Ormskirk, Lancashire, L39 4QP.
> 01695 584153
> http://www.edgehill.ac.uk/Sites/CLTR/
> Contact: Jennie Barnsley.
E   A research centre at Edge Hill College of Higher Education.
O   To conduct research, learning and teaching in the post-compulsory education sector

Centre for Learning, Teaching and Research in Higher Education   (CLTRHE)   1999
■   School of Education, University of Durham, Leazes Road, Durham, DH1 1TA.
> 0191-334 8310   fax 0191-334 8311
> http://www.dur.ac.uk/education/ctlrhe/
> Director: Prof Erik Meyer.
E   A centre at the University of Durham.
O   To further the University's strategies for teaching and learning, and for academic staff development

Centre for Learning and Teaching Sociology, Anthropology and Politics
> see **Subject Network for Sociology, Anthropology, Politics.**

Centre for Learning and Workforce Research   (CLWR)
■   Faculty of Health and Social Care, University of the West of England, Blackberry Hill, Stapleton, Bristol, BS16 1DD.
> 0117-328 8777
> http://hsc.uwe.ac.uk/net/research/Default.aspx?pageid=15
> Director: Prof Margaret Miers.
E   A research centre at the University of the West of England.
O   To be a focus for research, consultancy and scholarship in interprofessional learning, e-learning and health informatics, values and ethics in professional practice, action learning, professional and workforce development, and historical perspectives on health and welfare

Centre for Lebanese Studies   (CLS)   1984
■   14a Airlie Gardens, London, W8 7AL.
> 020 7221 3809
> http://www.lebanesestudies.com/
E   An independent research organisation.

Centre for Legal Practice   (CLP)   1992
■   School of Law and Social Science, University of Plymouth, 20 Portland Villas, Drake Circus, Plymouth, PL4 8AA.
> 01752 233200; 232864   fax 01752 233201
> http://www.plymouth.ac.uk/pages/view.asp?page=15237
E   A centre at the University of Plymouth.

Centre for Legal Research   (CLR)   2002
■   Faculty of Law, Frenchay Campus, University of the West of England, Coldharbour Lane, Bristol, BS16 1QY.
> 0117-328 2604   fax 0117-328 2268
> http://law.uwe.ac.uk/faculty/research/
> Director: Prof Ed Cape.
E   A research centre at the University of the West of England.
O   To co-ordinate and promote research activity, with particular emphasis on criminal justice, commercial law, Burgess Salmon environmental law, and international law and human rights

Centre for Legal Research   (CLR)
■   Middlesex University Business School, Middlesex University, The Burroughs, London, NW4 4BT.
> 020 8411 5000
> http://mubs.mdx.ac.uk/Research/Research_Centres/CLR/
> Director: Prof Indira Carr.
E   A centre at Middlesex University.
O   To specialise in research in international and EU law, and the law relating to employment and disability

Centre for Legal Research (CLR) 1996

- ■ Nottingham Law School, Nottingham Trent University, Chaucer Street, Nottingham, NG1 5LP.
  0115-848 4174   fax 0115-848 6489
  http://ntu.ac.uk/nls/centreforlegalresearch
  Head: Prof Mary Seneviratne. Administrator: Carole Vaughan.
- E   A research centre at Nottingham Trent University.
- O   To carry out research projects designed to inform and influence all branches of the legal profession and their regulatory bodies, on policy matters; to carry our applied research programmes for commercial, governmental and quasi-governmental clients from the UK and other jurisdictions
- ●   Electronic Online Library

Centre for Legal Research and Policy Studies (CLRPS) 1998

- ■ School of Social Sciences and Law, Gipsy Lane Campus, Oxford Brookes University, Headington, Oxford, OX3 0BP.
  01865 484901
  http://ssl.brookes.ac.uk/legalResearchCentre/home.htm
- E   A research centre at Oxford Brookes University.
- O   To focus research on the part played by courts in the implementation of policy by Government and its agencies and the inter-relationship between politicians, judges and citizens in policy formulation

Centre for Legislative Studies (CLS) 1992

- ■ Department of Politics and International Studies, University of Hull, Cottingham Road, Hull, HU6 7RX.
  01482 466209   fax 01482 466208
  http://www.hull.ac.uk/cls/
- E   A research centre at the University of Hull.

Centre for Legislative Studies [London]
  see **Sir William Dale Centre for Legislative Studies.**

Centre for Leisure Retailing (CLR) 2003

- ■ Nottingham Business School, Nottingham Trent University, Burton Street, Nottingham, NG1 4BU.
  0115-848 4488
  https://www.ntu.ac.uk/nbs/spec/clr/
  Head: Prof Conrad Lashley.
- E   A research centre at Nottingham Trent University.
- O   To focus on management development and research and consultancy services for firms operating in the leisure retail sector

Centre for Leisure, Tourism and Society (CELTS)

- ■ Faculty of the Built Environment, Frenchay Campus, University of the West of England, Coldharbour Lane, Bristol, BS16 1QY.
  0117-328 3000
  http://www.built-environment.uwe.ac.uk/research/tourism/
  Director: Prof Cara Aitchison.
- E   An interdisciplinary research centre at the University of the West of England.
- O   To investigate and explain the place of tourism and leisure in shaping wider social, economic and environmental relations within society

Centre for Leisure and Tourism Studies (CELTS) 1986

- ■ London Metropolitan University, Stapleton House, 277-281 Holloway Road, London, N7 8HN.
  020 7133 3035   fax 020 7133 3082
  http://www.londonmet.ac.uk/research-units/iictd/about/
- E   A research centre within the International Institute for Culture, Tourism and Development (qv) at London Metropolitan University.

Centre for Life 2001

- ■ University of Newcastle upon Tyne, Times Square, Newcastle upon Tyne, NE1 4EP.
  0191-243 8210   fax 0191-243 8201
  http://www.life.org.uk/
- E   A registered charity under the title International Centre for Life Trust at the University of Newcastle upon Tyne.
- O   To foster an informed climate within which science can flourish, and to encourage young people to develop a curiosity about science and scientific endeavour
- ●   Exhibition - Schools programme - Annual lecture - Science fesival - Laboratory

Centre for Life History Research (CLHR) 1999

- ■ University of Sussex, Sussex House, Falmer, Brighton, East Sussex, BN1 9RH.
  01273 606755   fax 01273 678335
  http://www.sussex.ac.uk/clhr/
- E   An interdisciplinary research centre at the University of Sussex.

Centre for Life Sciences (CLS) 2003

- ■ School of Biological and Chemical Sciences, Queen Mary, University of London, Mile End Road, London, E1 4NS.
  020 7882 3200   fax 020 8983 0973
  http://www.biology.qmul.ac.uk/srif
- E   A research centre at Queen Mary, University of London.
- O   To conduct research so as to improve knowledge of biological processes at the level of the molecule, the cell and the whole organism

© CBD Research Ltd · Beckenham · Kent BR3 5JS · Tel 020 8650 7745 · Fax 020 8650 0768 · E-mail cbd@cbdresearch.com · www.cbdresearch.com

Centre for Lifelong Learning
 see **Centres for Lifelong Learning.**

Centre for Linguistic Research   (CLR)   2002

- School of Language and Literature, King's College, University of Aberdeen, Aberdeen, AB24 3UB.
  01224 272625   fax 01224 272624
  http://www.abdn.ac.uk/langling/clr.htm
- E   A research centre at the University of Aberdeen.
- O   To conduct research into linguistics, and especially sociolinguistics, with a special emphasis on variation and change in varieties of English, immigrant varieties, forensic linguistics and phonetics

Centre for Linguistics and Philology

- University of Oxford, Walton Street, Oxford, OX1 2HG.
  01865 280400   fax 01865 280412
  http://www.ling-phil.ox.ac.uk/pages/facilities.html
  Secretary: Kate Dobson.
- E   A research centre at the University of Oxford.
- O   To teach and research in linguistic subjects

Centre for Literacy in Primary Education   (CLPE)   1971

- Webber Street, London, SE1 8QW.
  020 7401 3382; 7633 0840   fax 020 7928 4624
  http://www.clpe.co.uk/
  Co-Director: Sue Ellis. Co-Director: Julia Eccleshare.
- E   An independent charitable trust.
- O   To provide training courses and consultancy for schools and teachers, teaching assistants, other educators, parents and families in London and nationally

Centre for Literacy Research   (CLR)   1996

- School of Education, Jubilee Campus, University of Nottingham, Wollaton Road, Nottingham, NG8 1BB.
  0115-951 4441   fax 0115-951 4322
  http://www.nottingham.ac.uk/education/centres/clr/
  Director: Prof Colin Harrison.
- E   A research centre at the University of Nottingham.
- O   To promote high quality research, and its effective communication, in areas related to children's literacy, and to maintaining strong partnerships with schools and the wider educational community through work in continuing professional development, taught courses and research supervision

Centre for Literature and Cultural History
 see **Research Centre for Literature and Cultural History.**

Centre for Local Democracy   (CLD)

- Faculty of Health and Social Care, University of the West of England, Blackberry Hill, Bristol, BS16 1DD.
  0117-328 8788   fax 0117-328 8421
  http://hsc.uwe.ac.uk/net/research/Default.aspx?pageid=57
  Research Administrator: Jan Green.
- E   A research centre at the University of the West of England.
- O   To conduct research in the ways in which citizens and communities experience, understand, and engage with issues of power and the processes of decision-making, which shape their lives and localities

Centre for Local Economic Development
 see **Applied Research Centre in Sustainable Regeneration.**

Centre for Local Economic Strategies   (CLES)

- 1 George Leigh Street, Manchester, M4 5DL.
  0161-236 7036   fax 0161-236 1891
  http://www.cles.org.uk/
- E   An independent organisation and a registered charity.
- O   To bring together a network of subscribing organisations, including regeneration partnerships, local authorities, regional bodies, community groups and voluntary organisations, to explain national and European policy at the local level

Centre for Local Enterprise and Skills   (CLES)

- Staffordshire University, Mellor Building, College Road, Stoke-on-Trent, ST4 2DF.
  01782 294110
  http://www.staffs.ac.uk/schools/sciences/geography/links/IESR//CLES.html
- E   A research centre within the Institute for Environment and Sustainability Research (qv) at Staffordshire University.
- O   To apply different business disciplines to project work for local organisations in both the public and private sectors

Centre for Local Governance   (CfLG)   2006
- ■   School of Education, University of Manchester, Oxford Road, Manchester, M13 9PL.
       0161-275 3462   fax 0161-275 7970
       http://www.cflg.manchester.ac.uk/
- E   A research centre within the Centre for Educational Leadership (qv) at the University of Manchester.

Centre for Local History   (CLH)
- ■   Department of History, University of Essex, Wivenhoe Park, Colchester, Essex, CO4 3SQ.
       01206 872302
       http://www.essex.ac.uk/history/research/local-history/
       Contact: Dr Chris Thornton.
- E   A centre at the University of Essex.
- ○   To provide a forum for research and teaching in local and regional history in Essex and Suffolk

Centre for Local History   (CLH)
- ■   School of Education, Jubilee Campus, University of Nottingham, Wollaton Road, Nottingham, NG8 1BB.
       0115-846 6466   fax 0115-951 6556
       http://www.nottingham.ac.uk/education/centres/clh/
- E   A centre at the University of Nottingham.
- ○   To provide a forum for research and teaching in local and regional history in Nottinghamshire and the East Midlands

Centre for Local History Studies   (CLHS)
- ■   Faculty of Arts and Social Sciences, Kingston University, London, Penrhyn Road, Kingston-upon-Thames, Surrey, KT1 2EE.
       020 8547 7359
       http://localhistory.kingston.ac.uk/
       Director: Dr Chris French.
- E   A research centre at Kingston University, London.
- ○   To encourage research on the local region by undertaking research projects centred on Kingston and its locality

Centre for Local and Regional Economic Analysis   (CLREA)
- ■   Department of Economics, University of Portsmouth, Richmond Building, Portland Street, Portsmouth, PO1 3DE.
       023 9284 4600
       http://www.port.ac.uk/departments/academic/economics/research/clrea/
       Director: Jeff Grainger.
- E   A research centre at the University of Portsmouth.
- ○   To conduct research in local and economic analysis

Centre for Local and Regional Government Research   (CLRGR)
- ■   Cardiff Business School, Cardiff University, Aberconway Building, Colum Drive, Cardiff, CF10 3EU.
       029 2087 4000   fax 029 2087 4419
       http://www.clrgr.cf.ac.uk/
       Director: Prof Stephen Martin.
- E   A centre at Cardiff University.
- ○   To be a leading centre for academic research on UK local Government

Centre for Local and Regional History
- ■   Department of History, University of Essex, Wivenhoe Park, Colchester, Essex, CO4 3SQ.
       01206 872302
       http://www.essex.ac.uk/history/research/local-history/
       Director: Dr Chris Thornton.
- E   A research centre at the University of Essex.

Centre for Longitudinal Studies   (CLS)
- ■   Bedford Group for Lifecourse and Statistical Studies, University of London, 20 Bedford Way, London, WC1H 0AL.
       020 7612 6875   fax 020 7612 6880
       http://www.cls.ioe.ac.uk/
       Director: Prof Heather Joshi.
- E   A research centre within the Institute of Education (London) (qv) at the University of London.
- ○   To collect, manage and analyse large-scale longitudinal data, with particular emphasis on family life and parenting, family economics, youth, life course transitions, gender, spatial issues, and longitudinal methodology
- ●   The Centre houses three birth cohort studies - National Child Development Study (1958), British Cohort Study (1970), and Millennium Cohort Study

Centre for the Magic Arts
- ■   12 Stephenson Way, London, NW1 2HD.
       020 7387 2222
       http://www.themagiccircle.co.uk/
- E   The headquarters of the Magic Circle.

Centre for Magnetic Resonance
       see **Manchester Centre for Magnetic Resonance.**

Centre for Magnetic Resonance Investigations (CMRI) 1992

■ Hull Royal Infirmary, Anlaby Road, Hull, HU3 2JZ.
01482 674082 fax 01482 320137
http://www.hull.ac.uk/mri/
Scientific Director: Prof L W Turnbull.
E A department of the University of Hull.
O To undertake clinical cancer-related research of the breast, prostate, brain and uterus using 3T magnetic resonance imaging and spectroscopy as the main investigative tools
● Education and training - Equipment includes MR Imager (IGE Signa Echo-speed), 3T GE LX whole body scanner - Clinical scanning by appointment

Centre for Magnetics Technology
see **Wolfson Centre for Magnetics Technology.**

Centre for Management Accounting Research
see **Bristol Centre for Management Accounting Research.**

Centre for Management and Business Research (CMBR)

■ Lincoln Business School, University of Lincoln, Brayford Pool, Lincoln, LN6 7TS.
01522 882000
http://www.lincoln.ac.uk/lbs/research/cmbr/
Contact: Prof Andrew Atherton.
E A research centre at the University of Lincoln.
O To encourage and stimulate business research
● Information service

Centre for Management Buy-Out Research (CMBOR) 1986

■ Nottingham University Business School, Jubilee Campus, University of Nottingham, Wollaton Road, Nottingham, NG8 1BB.
0115-846 6602; 951 5505 fax 0115-846 6667
http://www.nottingham.ac.uk/business/CMBOR.html
Director: Prof Alistair Bruce.
E A research centre at the University of Nottingham.
O To monitor and analyse management buy-outs
● Database of 20,000 companies

Centre for Management in China
see **Lancaster Centre for Management in China.**

Centre for Management Creativity (CMC) 1988

■ High Trenhouse, Malham Moor, Settle, North Yorkshire, BD24 9PR.
01729 830322 fax 01729 830519
http://www.changeandinnovation.com/
Chief Executive Officer: John Varney. Managing Director: Bernadette Schutte.
E A profit-making business.
O To promote authentic leadership, whole system understanding, creativity and innovation, in organisations and education
● Conference facilities - ET - Logo visual thinking methodology, tools and software - Recreational facilities - Strategy innovation
¶ Newsletter. Making Meaning. Logo Visual Thinking: A guide to making sense.

Centre for Management Development
see **Hull Centre for Management Development.**

Centre for Management Learning and Development (CMLD)

■ School of Management, University of Surrey, Guildford, Surrey, GU2 7XH.
01483 686300
http://www.som.surrey.ac.uk/business/cmld/
Director: Prof Eugene Sadler-Smith.
E A research centre at the University of Surrey.
O To conduct research into understanding the processes which facilitate the learning, development, growth and transformation of individuals and the organisations of which they are a part

Centre for the Management of Professional Service Firms
see **Clifford Chance Centre for the Management of Professional Service Firms.**

Centre for Management under Regulation (CMuR)

■ Warwick Business School, University of Warwick, Coventry, CV4 7AL.
024 7652 4153 fax 024 7652 4965
http://users.wbs.ac.uk/group/cmur/
Director: Prof Martin Cave.
E A research centre at the University of Warwick.
O To undertake independent research on the effect of regulation on the management and operations of regulated organisations

Centre for Management Research
　　see **Huck Centre for Management Research.**

Centre for Managing Security in Transitional Societies   2002
- ■　Department of Defence Management and Security, Cranfield University, Shrivenham, Swindon, Wiltshire, SN6 8LA.
　　01793 785290
　　http://www.dcmt.cranfield.ac.uk/ddmsa/msts
　　Contact: Mrs S Stonham.
- E　A research centre at Cranfield University.
- O　To conduct a broad range of research into wider security issues and the implications for policy development and capacity building

Centre for Manufacturing
- ■　School of Engineering and Technology, De Montfort University, The Gateway, Leicester, LE1 9BH.
　　0116-257 7456
　　http://www.dmu.ac.uk/faculties/cse/research_consultancy/eng_and_tech/
- E　A centre at De Montfort University.

Centre for Manufacturing Metrology
　　see **Brunel Centre for Manufacturing Metrology.**

Centre for Manuscript and Print Studies   (CMPS) 2001
- ■　School of Advanced Study, University of London, Room 305 - Senate House, Malet Street, London, WC1E 7HU.
　　020 7862 8675; 8680　fax 020 7862 8720
　　http://ies.sas.ac.uk/cmps
　　Director: Prof Warwick Gould.
- E　A research centre within the Institute of English Studies (qv) at the University of London.
- O　To develop individual and collective research projects on national and international subjects within manuscript and print studies, and including palaeography, codicology, diplomatic and calligraphy, history of printing, manuscript and print relations, history of publishing and the book trade, ephemera studies, history of reading, history of libraries, collecting and scholarships, analytical, descriptive and historical bibliography, textual criticism and textual theory, and the electronic book

Centre for Manx Studies   (CMS) 2001   Laare-Studeyrys Manninagh
- ■　6 Kingswood Grove, Douglas, Isle of Man, IM1 3LX.
　　01624 673074　fax 01624 678752
　　http://dbweb.liv.ac.uk/manninagh/
　　Director: Dr Peter Davey.
- E　A research centre at the University of Liverpool.
- O　To teach students and conduct research in Manx archaeological, cultural, environmental and historical studies

Centre for Marine Biodiversity and Biotechnology   (CMBB) 1999
- ■　School of Life Sciences, Heriot-Watt University, Riccarton, Edinburgh, EH14 4AS.
　　0131-451 3455　fax 0131-451 3009
　　http://www.bio.hw.ac.uk/
　　Co-ordinator: Dr Paul Kingston.
- E　A research centre at Heriot-Watt University.
- O　To establish a unit for molecular genetic analysis of marine organisms that could be applied to taxonomic problems, monitoring marine pollution and the biotechnical exploitation of naturally occurring substances

Centre for Marine and Coastal Archaeology   (CMCA)
- ■　School of Conservation Sciences, Bournemouth University, Christchurch House, Talbot Campus, Poole, Dorset, BH12 5BB.
　　01202 965178　fax 01202 965530
　　http://www.bournemouth.ac.uk/conservation/abouttheschool/ahe/cmca.html
　　Senior Lecturer: Dave Parham.
- E　A centre at Bournemouth University.
- O　To conduct research in marine spatial planning and GIS, the archaeology of seafaring and the development of ships, site formation and in-situ preservation, marine environmental processing, diving project management, and coastal studies
- ●　BSc in Marine Archaeology

Centre of Marine Hydrodynamics   (CMH)
- ■　Department of Naval Architecture and Marine Engineering, University of Strathclyde, 100 Montrose Street, Glasgow, G4 0LZ.
　　0141-548 4094　fax 0141-552 2879
　　http://www.na-me.ac.uk/index_2.htm
- E　A research centre at the University of Strathclyde.

Centre for Marine Law and Policy
Note: No longer in existence.

© CBD Research Ltd · Beckenham · Kent BR3 5JS · Tel 020 8650 7745 · Fax 020 8650 0768 · E-mail cbd@cbdresearch.com · www.cbdresearch.com

Centre for Marine Resources and Mariculture   (C-Mar
- ■ School of Biology and Biochemistry, Queen's University, Belfast, 12 The Strand, Portaferry, County Down, BT22 1PF.
    028 4272 9648   fax 028 4272 9672
    http://www.qub.ac.uk/bb/cmar/
    Director: Dr Dai Roberts.
- E A centre at Queen's University, Belfast.
- ○ To facilitate and stimulate environmentally acceptable development of existing and new mariculture enterprises in an all-Ireland context

Centre for Maritime Archaeology [Oxford]
    see **Oxford Centre for Maritime Archaeology.**

Centre for Maritime Archaeology   (CMA)
- ■ Department of Archaeology, Avenue Campus, University of Southampton, Highfield, Southampton, SO17 1BF.
    023 8059 4439   fax 023 8059 3032
    http://www.cma.soton.ac.uk/
    Contact: Dr Jonathan Abrams.
- E A research centre at the University of Southampton.
- ○ To provide a focus for maritime archaeological research

Centre for Maritime Historical Studies   (CMHS)   1990
- ■ Department of History, University of Exeter, Amory Building, Rennes Drive, Exeter, EX4 4RJ.
    01392 264297   fax 01392 263305
    http://www.centres.ex.ac.uk/cmhs/
    Director: Dr Michael Duffy.
- E A centre at the University of Exeter.
- ○ To promote research into economic, social, political, naval and environmental aspects of the British maritime past, from the earliest times to the present day, drawing also on European and international experience

Centre for Market and Public Organisation   (CMPO)   1998
- ■ Department of Economics, University of Bristol, 8 Woodland Road, Bristol, BS8 1TN.
    0117-928 8436   fax 0117-954 6997
    http://www.bris.ac.uk/cmpo/
    Director: Prof Simon Burgess.
- E A research centre at the University of Bristol.
- ○ To study the intersection between the public and private sectors of the economy, and in particular to understand the right way to organise and deliver public services

Centre for Marketing   (CM)
- ■ London Business School, Sussex Place, Regent's Park, London, NW1 4SA.
    020 7262 5050   fax 020 7724 1145
    http://www.london.edu/marketing/
    Director: Nirmalya Kumar. Manager: Sophie Linguri.
- E An outreach activity of the Marketing Department of London Business School.
- ○ To provide a forum for showcasing research and a platform for discussion on marketing, and a resource for its corporate supporters
- ● Consultancy - Education and training - Seminars - Workshops
- ¶ Marketing Insight. Many other reports and working papers available.

Centre for Mass Communication Research   (CMCR)   1966
- ■ University of Leicester, Attenborough Tower, University Road, Leicester, LE1 7RH.
    0116-252 3863   fax 0116-252 5276
    http://www.le.ac.uk/cmcr/research/cmcr.html
    Director: Prof Barrie Gunter.
- E A postgraduate research and teaching unit of the University of Leicester.
- ○ To contribute to public debate and inform policy on the major media and communication issues of our time; to engage in a multidisciplinary approach to systematic study of all aspects of media institutions and the communication process generally
- ● National and international research co-operation - Media archive - Education and training - Consultancy to media, government, research and international agencies Equipment includes TV recording suite and on-line facilities

Centre for Mass Spectrometry
    see **Michael Barber Centre for Mass Spectrometry.**

Centre for Materials
    see **Wolfson Centre for Materials Processing.**

Centre in Materials Processing [Birmingham]
    see **Interdisciplinary Research Centre in Materials Processing.**

Centre for Materials Processing [Brunel]
    see **Wolfson Centre for Materials Processing.**

Centre for Materials Research   (CMR)

■   Department of Materials, Queen Mary, University of London, Mile End Road, London, E1 4NS.
      020 7882 5150   fax 020 8981 9804
      http://www.cmr.qmul.ac.uk/
      Contact: Prof Paul Hogg.
E   A research centre at Queen Mary, University of London.
O   To foster a stronger community for materials research

Centre for Materials Research   (CMR)

■   Department of Physics and Astronomy, University College London, Gower Street, London, WC1E 6BT.
      020 7391 1377   fax 020 7391 1360
      http://www.cmr.ucl.ac.uk/
E   An interdisciplinary research centre at University College London.

Centre for Materials Science   (CMS)   1998

■   Preston, PR1 2HE.
      01772 893540   fax 01772 892996
      http://www.uclan.ac.uk/pasm/research/materialsscience/
      Director: Dr Colin Boxall.
E   A centre at the University of Central Lancashire.
O   To conduct research on various fields of materials science, including biodegration of materials, batalytic materials, lquid crystals, magnetic materials, microwave processing of materials, particle reinforced resins, photocatalytic materials, sensors, tribology, and ultra fast laser methods
●   Consultancy - Education and training - Measurement service

Centre for Materials Science and Engineering   (CMSE)

■   College of Science and Engineering, University of Edinburgh, The King's Buildings, Mayfield Road, Edinburgh, EH9 3JL.
      0131-650 5566   fax 0131-667 3677
      http://www.cmse.ed.ac.uk/
      Director: Prof Christopher Hall.
E   A centre at the University of Edinburgh.
O   To promote high quality work in materials (broadly defined)

Centre for Materials Science and Engineering   (CMSE)

■   Department of Materials and Medical Sciences, Cranfield University, Shrivenham, Swindon, Wiltshire, SN6 8LA.
      01793 785399   fax 01793 785772
      http://www.dcmt.cranfield.ac.uk/dmas/cmse/
      Director: Prof Keith Rogers.
E   A research centre at Cranfield University.
O   To provide a focus for materials development and fabrication, physical testing and failure analysis, materials composition and structure characterisation, the effects of radiation on materials and the application of materials in a wide range of industrial sectors

Centre for Materials Science Research   (CMSR)

■   Department of Chemistry and Materials, Manchester Metropolitan University, Chester Street, Manchester, M1 5GD.
      0161-247 1437
      http://www.chem-mats.mmu.ac.uk/Research/research_home.html
      Director: Prof Norman Allen.
E   A research centre at Manchester Metropolitan University.
O   To conduct research in the production of novel materials and the modification of surfaces for a wide range of applications, with particular focus on organic polymers and their properties, surface coatings and characterisation, synthesis, properties and applications of advanced materials, and materials in biological and food science

Centre for Materials, Surfaces and Structural Systems   (MaSSS)

■   School of Engineering, University of Surrey, Guildford, Surrey, GU2 7XH.
      01483 686600
      http://portal.surrey.ac.uk/eng/research/masss
      Head: Prof John F Watts.
E   A research centre at the University of Surrey.
O   To conduct research across the complete range of length scales from nanomaterials and nanocharacterisation, through solid mechanics and materials engineering, to large scale structures and reliability engineering of large infrastructural systems

Centre for Mathematical Biology   (CMB)   1994

■   Department of Mathematical Sciences, University of Bath, Claverton Down, Bath, BA2 7AY.
      01225 386005   fax 01225 386492
      http://www.bath.ac.uk/cmb/
      Director: Dr N F Britton.
E   A research centre at the University of Bath.
O   To encourage collaboration between mathematicians and biologists interested in interdisciplinary research

   © CBD Research Ltd · Beckenham · Kent BR3 5JS · Tel 020 8650 7745 · Fax 020 8650 0768 · E-mail cbd@cbdresearch.com · www.cbdresearch.com

Centre for Mathematical Biology (CMB) 1983

- University of Oxford, 24-29 St Giles', Oxford, OX1 3LB.
  01865 283889   fax 01865 270515
  http://www.maths.ox.ac.uk/cmb/
  Head: Prof Philip K Maini.
- E   A research centre within the Mathematical Institute (qv) at the University of Oxford.
- O   To co-ordinate mathematicians, physicists, and biologists from various fields to carry out research in mathematical biology

Centre for Mathematical Medicine (CMM)

- School of Mathematical Sciences, University of Nottingham, University Park, Nottingham, NG7 2RD.
  0115-951 3838   fax 0115-951 3837
  http://www.maths.nottingham.ac.uk/research/cmmb/
  Director: Prof Helen Byrne.
- E   A research centre at the University of Nottingham.
- O   To promote the application of mathematical modelling to medicine and the biomedical sciences; to stimulate research

Centre for Mathematical Modelling and Flow Analysis (CMMFA) 1993

- Department of Computing and Mathematics, Manchester Metropolitan University, John Dalton Building, Chester Street, Manchester, M1 5GD.
  0161-247 1500; 3581   fax 0161-247 6337
  http://www.doc.mmu.ac.uk/cmmfa/
  Co-Director: Prof Derek M Causon. Co-Director: Clive G Mingham.
- E   A research centre at Manchester Metropolitan University.
- O   To be a centre of excellence in computational fluid dynamics (CFD), and to specialise in the development and application of hydroinformatics and industrial blastwave hazard analysis

Centre for Mathematical Science (CMS)

- School of Engineering and Mathematical Sciences, City University, Tait Building, Northampton Square, London, EC1V 0HB.
  020 7040 5060; 8465
  http://www.city.ac.uk/sems/mathematics/
  Director: Dr Oliver Kerr.
- E   A centre at City University.
- O   To conduct research in various fields of mathematics, including algebraic representation theory, fluid dynamics, high intensity laser physics, integral quantum field theory, low-dimensional magnetic structures, and statistical mechanics

Centre for Mathematical Sciences (CMS)

- Department of Applied Mathematics and Theoretical Physics, University of Cambridge, Wilberforce Road, Cambridge, CB3 0WA.
  01223 765000   fax 01223 765900
  http://www.cms.cam.ac.uk/site/
- E   A centre at the University of Cambridge.
- O   To conduct research in mathematical sciences

Centre for Mathematics Applied to the Life Sciences (CMALS)

- Department of Mathematics, University of Glasgow, University Gardens, Glasgow, G12 8QW.
  0141-330 2058   fax 0141-330 4111
  http://www.maths.gla.ac.uk/cmals/
  Contact: Dr Martin A Bees.
- E   A research centre within the Institute of Biomedical and Life Sciences (qv) at the University of Glasgow.
- O   To promote interdisciplinary research and scholarship in mathematical biology - mathematical modelling applied to all aspects of medicine and biology and related activities

Centre for Mathematics Education

Note: Now the Department of Mathematics at the Open University.

Centre for Mathematics and Physics in the Life Sciences and Experimental Biology (CoMPLEX) 1998

- University College London, Wolfson House, 4 Stephenson Way, London, NW1 2HE.
  020 7679 5033; 5063   fax 020 7679 5007
  http://www.ucl.ac.uk/complex/
  Contact: Prof Anne Warner. Contact: Rachel Woolfson.
- E   An interdisciplinary research centre at University College London.
- O   To provide a forum for teaching and research in the problems and challenges arising from complexity in biology and medicine

Centre for Mathematics and Statistics

- Napier University Business School, Napier University, Craiglockhart Campus, Edinburgh, EH14 1DJ.
  http://www.napier.ac.uk/Nubs/CentreforMathematicsandStatistics.htm
- E   A centre at Napier University.

Centre for Measurement and Information in Medicine

Note: has closed.

Centre for Mechatronics and Manufacturing Systems   (CMMS)   1992
- ■   School of Physical Sciences and Engineering, King's College London, Office 120 - Strand Building, Strand, London, WC2R 2LS.
  020 7848 2236
  http://kcl.ac.uk/schools/pse/diveng/research/cmms/
  Director: Prof Lakmal Seneviratne.
- E   A research centre at King's College, London.
- O   To conduct research in the main core disciplines in mechatronics and manufacturing systems, including control and automation, robotics, CAD/CAM, material and manufacturing processes, and monitoring and inspection systems

Centre for Media, Arts and Performance   (CeMAP)
- ■   Department of Media and Communication, Coventry University, Priory Street, Coventry, CV1 5FB.
  024 7679 2481
  http://www.coventry.ac.uk/researchnet/d/194
  Director: Prof Karen Ross.
- E   A centre at Coventry University.
- O   To provide a context, focus and structure for the development of research, scholarship and practice in the creative and performing arts, media, art practice and communication

Centre for Media and Film Studies   (CMFS)   1997
- ■   Faculty of Arts and Humanities, School of Oriental and African Studies, University of London, Thornhaugh Street, Russell Square, London, WC1H 0XG.
  020 7898 4422
  http://www.soas.ac.uk/mediaandfilm/
  Director: Prof Annabelle Sreberny, FRSA.
- E   A department of the School of Oriental and African Studies, University of London.
- O   To conduct teaching and research in the study of non-Western media and film

Centre for Media: Globalisation: Risk   (CGMR)
- ■   School of Social Sciences and Law, Brunel University, Uxbridge, Middlesex, UB8 3PH.
  01895 265460
  http://www.brunel.ac.uk/about/acad/sssl/ssslresearch/centres/cgmr
  Director: Prof John Tulloch.
- E   A centre at Brunel University.
- O   To conduct research into the relationships between media, insecurity and risk, and globalisation, communication and culture

Centre for Media Research [Cardiff]
  see **Tom Hopkinson Centre for Media Research.**

Centre for Media Research   (CMR)   2004
- ■   School of Creative and Performing Arts, Coleraine Campus, University of Ulster, Cromore Road, Coleraine, County Londonderry, BT52 1SA.
  028 7032 3361
  http://www.ulster.ac.uk/
  Manager: Mrs Barbara Butcher.
- E   A research centre at the University of Ulster.
- O   To carry out research into the visual history of Ireland, digital cultures, comparative film and media studies, and media policy

Centre for Media Sound
- ■   University of Wales Bangor, Bangor, Gwynedd, LL57 2DG.
  01248 383215
  http://www.bangor.ac.uk/creative_industries/index.php.en
- E   A research centre within the National Institute for Excellence in Creative Industries (qv) at the University of Wales, Bangor.

Centre for Medical Education   (CME)   1972
- ■   School of Medicine, University of Dundee, Tay Park House, 484 Perth Road, Dundee, DD2 1LR.
  01382 381952   fax 01382 645748
  http://www.dundee.ac.uk/meded/
  Head: Prof Margery H Davis.
- E   A centre at the University of Dundee.

Centre for Medical Education   (CME)   2006
- ■   Lancaster University, Faraday Building, Lancaster, LA1 4YA.
  01524 592073
  http://www.cme.lancs.ac.uk/
  Director: Prof Anne Garden.
- E   A research centre at Lancaster University.
- O   To establish undergraduate medical education in North Lancashire and Cumbria

© CBD Research Ltd · Beckenham · Kent BR3 5JS · Tel 020 8650 7745 · Fax 020 8650 0768 · E-mail cbd@cbdresearch.com · www.cbdresearch.com

Centre for Medical Education   (CME)
■　Barts and the London, Queen Mary's School of Medicine and Dentistry, Queen Mary, University of London, St Bartholomew's Hospital, West Smithfield, London, EC1A 7BE.
　　020 7601 7600
　　http://www.ihse.qmul.ac.uk/cme/
　　Lead: Dr Jon Fuller.
E　A research centre within the Institute of Health Sciences Education (qv) at Queen Mary, University of London.
○　To conduct high quality teaching and research in medical education

Centre for Medical Engineering and Technology   (CMET)
■　University of Hull, Wolfson Building, Cottingham Road, Hull, HU6 7RX.
　　01482 465777　fax 01482 466664
　　http://www.hull.ac.uk/cmet/
　　Director: Dr M J Fagan.
E　A research centre within the Clinical Biosciences Institute (qv) at the University of Hull.

Centre for Medical Genetics and Policy
Note: reported to us as no longer in existence.

Centre for Medical and Healthcare Education   (CMHE)   2005
■　St George's, University of London, Cranmer Terrace, London, SW17 0RE.
　　020 8725 2735　fax 020 8725 2950
　　http://www.sgul.ac.uk/cmhe/
　　Director: Prof Peter McCrorie.
E　A division of St George's, University of London.

Centre for Medical History   (CMH)   1997
■　School of Humanities and Social Sciences, University of Exeter, Amory Building, Rennes Drive, Exeter, EX4 4RJ.
　　01392 263289　fax 01392 263305
　　http://www.centres.ex.ac.uk/medhist/
　　Director: Prof Mark Jackson.
E　A centre at the University of Exeter.
○　To advance methods and areas of research within the history of medicine, and for the social study of contemporary medical and health-related activities

Centre for Medical Image Computing   (MedIC)   2005
■　Department of Computer Science, University College London, Malet Place Engineering Building, Malet Place, London, WC1E 6BT.
　　020 7679 0250
　　http://cmic.cs.ucl.ac.uk/
　　Administrator: Karen Cardy.
E　A research centre at University College London.
○　To focus research on detailed structural and functional analysis in neurosciences, imaging to guide interventions, image analysis in drug discovery, imaging in cardiology, and imaging in oncology, with a particular emphasis on e-science technologies

Centre of Medical Law and Ethics   (CMLE)   1978
■　School of Law, Birkbeck, University of London, Strand, London, WC2R 2LS.
　　020 7873 2382　fax 020 7873 2575
　　http://www.kcl.ac.uk/schools/law/research/cmle/
　　Director: Prof Jonathan Glover. Administrator: Peter Niven.
E　A research centre at King's College, London.
○　To encourage and facilitate teaching and research in medical ethics and law; to contribute to informed scholarly and public debate on medical ethics and law by serving as a centre of information and expertise; to maintain a specialist library
●　Library - Public lectures - Research degrees (MA in Medical Ethics and Law, PGDip/MA in Human Values and Contemporary Global Ethics)

Centre for Medical Microbiology   (CMM)
■　Department of Infection, Royal Free and University College Medical School, University College London, Rowland Hill Street, London, NW3 2PF.
　　020 7794 0500 ext 3539
　　http://www.ucl.ac.uk/medicalschool/infection-immunity/departments/departments.htm
　　Director: Prof Stephen Gillespie.
E　A research centre at University College London.
○　To conduct research in medical microbiology, with a particular emphasis on the pathogenesis of respiratory tract infections

Centre for Medical Molecular Virology
　　see **MRC UCL Centre for Medical Molecular Virology.**

Centre for Medical Oncology   (CMO)

■   Barts and the London, Queen Mary's School of Medicine and Dentistry, Queen Mary, University of London, Charterhouse Square, London, EC1M 6BQ.
     020 7014 0462   fax 020 7014 0461
     http://www.cancer.qmul.ac.uk/research/medical_oncology
     Director: Prof Andrew Lister.
E   A research centre within the Institute of Cancer (qv) at Queen Mary, University of London.
O   To conduct research in haemato-oncology, urological and paediatric malignancies

Centre for Medicine, Dentistry and Veterinary Medicine
     see **Subject Centre for Medicine, Dentistry and Veterinary Medicine**.

Centre for Medicines Research
     see **CMR International.**

Centre for Medico-Legal Studies   (CMLS)   1993

■   Cardiff Law School, PO Box 427, Cardiff University, Museum Avenue, Cardiff, CF10 3XJ.
     029 2087 4345   fax 029 2087 4097
     http://www.law.cf.ac.uk/medico/
     Director: Prof Viv Harpwood.
E   A centre at Cardiff University.
O   To raise the profile of the Law School's activities in the field of health care law

Centre for Medieval and Renaissance Studies   (CMRS)

■   Durham, DH1 3HP.
     0191-334 2000
     http://www.dur.ac.uk/cmrs/
E   An interdisciplinary research centre at the University of Durham.

Centre for Medieval and Renaissance Studies [Glasgow]
     see **Glasgow Centre for Medieval and Renaissance Studies.**

Centre for Medieval Studies   (CMS)   2005   Canolfan Astudiaethau Canoloesol

■   Department of English, University of Wales Bangor, Bangor, Gwynedd, LL57 2DG.
     01248 382110
     http://www.bangor.ac.uk/english/medieval/
     Director: Dr Raluca Radulescu.
E   A research centre at the University of Wales, Bangor.

Centre for Medieval Studies   (CMS)   1994

■   Department of Historical Studies, University of Bristol, 13 Woodland Road, Bristol, BS8 1TB.
     0117-928 8892
     http://www.bris.ac.uk/medievalcentre/
     Director: Prof Pamela King.
E   A research centre at the University of Bristol.
O   To conduct research into all aspects of the history, culture, art and representation of Medieval Europe
●   Conferences - Seminars

Centre for Medieval Studies   (CMS)

■   University of Exeter, The Queen's Drive, Exeter, EX4 4QJ.
     01392 264364
     http://www.centres.ex.ac.uk/medievalstudies/
     Director: Dr Yolanda Plumley.
E   A centre at the University of Exeter.
O   To provide the focal point for interdisciplinary scholarship and learning in a wide variety of subjects relating to the Middle Ages

Centre for Medieval Studies [Liverpool]
     see **Liverpool Centre for Medieval Studies.**

Centre for Medieval Studies [Reading]
     see **Graduate Centre for Medieval Studies.**

Centre for Medieval Studies   (CMS)   1968

■   Department of Archaeology, University of York, The King's Manor, York, YO1 7EP.
     01904 433910   fax 01904 433918
     http://www.york.ac.uk/inst/cms/
     Director: Prof J D Richards. Director: Dr S Rees Jones.
E   A department of the University of York.
O   To further the study and interdisciplinary research into the Middle Ages (400-1550 AD)
●   Education and training

© CBD Research Ltd · Beckenham · Kent BR3 5JS · Tel 020 8650 7745 · Fax 020 8650 0768 · E-mail cbd@cbdresearch.com · www.cbdresearch.com

Centre for Medieval and Tudor Studies
   see **Canterbury Centre for Medieval and Tudor Studies.**

Centre for Mediterranean Studies   (CMS)   1992
■   School of Humanities and Social Sciences, University of Exeter, Stocker Road, Exeter, EX4 4ND.
     01392 264036   fax 01392 264035
     http://www.huss.ex.ac.uk/iais/research/med.htm
E   A research centre within the Institute of Arab and Islamic Studies (qv) at the University of Exeter.
○   To promote interdisciplinary research and teaching on the Mediterranean region

Centre for Mediterranean Studies   (CMS)
■   Faculty of Arts, University of Leeds, Room LG18 - Michael Sadler Building, Leeds, LS2 9JT.
     0113-343 3569   fax 0113-343 3568
     http://www.leeds.ac.uk/cmdtr/
     Director: Prof Dionisius A Agius.
E   An interdisciplinary research centre at the University of Leeds.

Centre for Men's Health   (CMH)
■   Faculty of Health, Leeds Metropolitan University, Civic Quarter, Calverley Street, Leeds, LS1 3HE.
     0113-283 2600   fax 0113-283 1908
     http://www.leedsmet.ac.uk/health/menshealth/
     Leader: Prof Alan White.
E   A research centre at Leeds Metropolitan University.
○   To conduct research in men's health

Centre for Mental Health
   see **Sainsbury Centre for Mental Health.**

Centre for Mesoscience and Nanotechnology
   see **Manchester Centre for Mesoscience and Nanotechnology.**

Centre for Metalloprotein Spectroscopy and Biology   (CMSB)   1991
■   School of Biological Sciences, University of East Anglia, Norwich, NR4 7TJ.
     01603 592269   fax 01603 592250
     http://www1.uea.ac.uk/cm/home/schools/sci/bio/res/cmsb
     Co-Director: Prof Andrew Thomson. Co-Director: Prof David Richardson.
E   A centre at the University of East Anglia.
○   To research and to understand the activation and redox cycling of inorganic substrates involved in the bacterial nitrogen, oxygen and sulphur cycles, metal ion metabolism and metal-microbe interactions, and protein interactions in bacterial and plant metabolism

Centre for Metropolitan History   (CMH)   1988
■   School of Advanced Study, University of London, Malet Street, London, WC1E 7HU.
     020 7862 8790   fax 020 7862 8793
     http://www.history.ac.uk/cmh/cmh.main.html
     Director: Matthew Davies.
E   A research centre within the Institute of Historical Research (qv) at the University of London.
○   To promote the study and wide appreciation of London's character and development from its beginnings to the present day, and to set the history of London in the wider context provided by knowledge of other metropolises

Centre for Micro-Assisted Communication   (CENMAC)   1968
■   Charlton Park, Charlton Park Road, London, SE7 8JB.
     020 8854 1019   fax 020 8854 1143
     http://www.cenmac.com
     Team Leader: Trish Davidson.
E   A statutory organisation.
○   To support pupils and students, with physical disabilities, who are receiving their education in special and mainstream schools throughout Inner London

Centre on Micro-Social Change
   see **ESRC Research Centre on Micro-Social Change.**

Centre for MicroEnterprise   (CME)   2003
■   Department of Management and Professional Development, London Metropolitan University, 84 Moorgate, London, EC2M 6SQ.
     020 7320 1573
     http://www.londonmet.ac.uk/depts/mpd/research/micro_ent/home.cfm
     Contact: Valerie Mills. Contact: Hilary Farnworth.
E   A research centre at London Metropolitan University.
○   To conduct research and training for women entrepreneurs, and owners of micro-enterprises and small businesses

Centre for Micromorphology 2003

NR Department of Geography, Queen Mary, University of London, Mile End Road, London, E1 4NS.
     020 7882 5400   fax 020 8981 6276
     http://www.geog.qmul.ac.uk/micromorphology/
E   A research centre at Queen Mary, University of London.
O   To conduct microscopic studies of soils and sediments
Note: A joint venture with Royal Holloway, University of London.

Centre of Middle Eastern and Islamic Studies   (CMEIS) 1960

■   Faculty of Oriental Studies, University of Cambridge, Sidgwick Avenue, Cambridge, CB3 9DA.
     01223 335103   fax 01223 335110
     http://www.cmeis.cam.ac.uk/
     Director: Dr Amira K Bennison. Senior Secretary: Phoebe Luckyn-Malone.
E   A department of the University of Cambridge.
O   To promote Middle Eastern and Islamic studies amongst academics and the public
●   Conferences - Education and training - Exhibitions - Library - Concerts - Annual lecture series during full term (Thursday at 1700 in the Faculty of Orental Studies)
¶   Newsletter.

Centre for Middle Eastern and Islamic Studies [Durham]
     see **Institute for Middle Eastern and Islamic Studies.**

Centre on Migration, Policy and Society   (COMPAS)

■   University of Oxford, 58 Banbury Road, Oxford, OX2 6QS.
     01865 274711   fax 01865 274718
     http://www.compas.ox.ac.uk/
     Director: Steven Vertovec.
E   A centre at the University of Oxford.
O   To conduct high quality research on migration, in order to develop theory and knowledge; to inform public opinion and contribute to policy debates

Centre for Migration Research
     see **Sussex Centre for Migration Research.**

Centre for Migration Studies at the Ulster-American Folk Park   (CMS) 1998

■   2 Mellon Road, Castletown, Omagh, County Tyrone, BT78 5QY.
     028 8225 6315   fax 028 8224 2241
     http://www.folkpark.com/centre_for_migration_studies/
     Chairman: Sir Peter Froggatt.
E   A research centre at the Ulster-American Folk Park.
O   To serve the community as a leading international institution for the study of human migration, focusing on the peoples of Ireland worldwide

Centre for Military Archives
     see **Liddell Hart Centre for Military Archives.**

Centre for Military Health Research
     see **King's Centre for Military Health Research.**

Centre for Mindfulness Research and Practice   (CMRP) 2001

■   University of Wales Bangor, Dean Street Building, Bangor, Gwynedd, LL57 1UT.
     01248 382939   fax 01248 383982
     http://www.bangor.ac.uk/mindfulness/
     Co-ordinator and Administrator: Caroline Creasey.
E   A research centre within the Institute of Medical and Social Care Research (qv) at the University of Wales, Bangor.
O   To promote and expand the development and availability of mindfulness-based approaches in health care and other settings

Centre for Ministry Studies   (CMS) 2001

■   Department of Theology and Religious Studies, University of Wales Bangor, Normal Site, Bangor, Gwynedd, LL57 2PZ.
     01248 382566   fax 01248 383954
     http://www.bangor.ac.uk/rs/pt/
     Director: Revd Dr Andrew Village.
E   A research centre at the University of Wales, Bangor.
O   To conduct research and teaching in practical theology and ministry studies

Centre for Mission Studies
     see **Oxford Centre for Mission Studies.**

© CBD Research Ltd · Beckenham · Kent BR3 5JS · Tel 020 8650 7745 · Fax 020 8650 0768 · E-mail cbd@cbdresearch.com · www.cbdresearch.com

Centre for Mobile Communications Research   (CMCR)   1998
- Department of Electronic and Electrical Engineering, Loughborough University, Ashby Road, Loughborough, Leicestershire, LE11 3TU.
  01509 227089   fax 01509 227006
  http://www.lboro.ac.uk/departments/el/research/comms-cmcr.html
  Director: Prof Yiannis Vardaxoglou.
- E   A research centre at Loughborough University.
- O   To conduct specialist research into antennas and associated devices for mobile telephony

Centre for Mobilities Research   (CeMoRe)
- Department of Sociology, Lancaster University, County South, Bailrigg, Lancaster, LA1 4YD.
  01524 593148   fax 01524 594256
  http://www.lancs.ac.uk/fss/sociology/cemore/
  Director: John Urry.
- E   A research centre within Lancaster University.
- O   To study and research all aspects of mobilities (the large-scale movements of people, objects, capital and information across the world), as well as the more local processes of daily transportation, movement through public space, and the travel of material things within everyday life

Centre in Modern and Contemporary Poetry
　　see **Research Centre in Modern and Contemporary Poetry.**

Centre Modern and Contemporary Wales   (CMCW)
- School of Humanities and Social Sciences, University of Glamorgan, Pontypridd, CF37 1DL.
  01443 654269
  http://hass.glam.ac.uk/research/modernwales/
- E   A research centre within the University of Glamorgan.
- O   To encourage interdisciplinary research on contemporary Wales

Centre for Modern German History
　　see **Cardiff Centre for Modern German History.**

Centre for Modern Language Teaching
　　see **Northern Ireland Centre for Information on Language Teaching and Research.**

Centre for Modern Languages
- University of Birmingham, Edgbaston, Birmingham, B15 2TT.
  0121-414 3324; 5589   fax 0121-414 5919
  http://www.cml.bham.ac.uk/
  Director: Prof John Klapper, BA, MLitt, PGCE, PhD, ILTM.
- E   A department of the University of Birmingham.
- O   To deliver tailor-made language courses
Note: Many such centres exist within major UK educational institutions.

Centre for Modern Poetry
- School of English, Rutherford College Extension, University of Kent, Canterbury, Kent, CT2 7NX.
  01227 764000
  http://www.kent.ac.uk/english/staff-research/centres/mopoindex.html
- E   A research centre at the University of Kent.
- O   To promote the reading of poetry and research into modern poetry at graduate level and beyond

Centre for Modernist Studies   (CMS)
- School of Humanities, University of Sussex, Arts A, Falmer, Brighton, East Sussex, BN1 9SJ.
  01273 873216
  http://www.sussex.ac.uk/modernist/
  Co-Director: Dr Laura Marcus. Co-Director: Prof Peter Nicholls.
- E   An interdisciplinary research centre at the University of Sussex.
- O   To conduct research in Anglo-American and European traditions in literary and cultural modernism

Centre for Molecular Biosciences   (CMB)   2001
- School of Biomedical Sciences, University of Ulster, Coleraine Campus, Cromore Road, Coleraine, County Londonderry, BT52 1SA.
  028 7032 4121   fax 028 7032 4375
  http://www.science.ulster.ac.uk/cmb/
  Director: Prof Stephen Downes.
- E   A research centre within the Biomedical Sciences Research Institute (qv) at the University of Ulster.
- O   To establish Northern Ireland as a centre of excellence in molecular biosciences

Centre for Molecular Cell Biology

■ Department of Medicine, Royal Free and University College Medical School, University College London, Rowland Hill Street, London, NW3 2PF.
   020 7433 2822   fax 020 7433 2817
   http://www.ucl.ac.uk/medicine/mcb/
   Director: Dr Justin Hsuan.
E   A research centre at University College London.
O   To conduct a wide range of advanced molecular approaches, in order to understand how biochemical signals, which regulate many vital cell functions, are organised in different parts of a cell

Centre for Molecular Design   (CMD)   1993

■ School of Pharmacy and Biomedical Sciences, University of Portsmouth, King Henry 1 Street, Portsmouth, PO1 2DY.
   023 9284 3020; 3612   fax 023 9284 3722
   http://www.port.ac.uk/research/cmd/
   Director: Prof Martyn Ford.
E   An interdisciplinary research centre at the University of Portsmouth.
O   To provide a central facility for research into molecular design

Centre for Molecular Drug Design   (CMDD)

■ Faculty of Science, Engineering and Environment, Cockcroft Building, University of Salford, Salford, Manchester, M5 4WT.
   0161-295 4851
   http://www.bri.salford.ac.uk/bri/m/?s=3
   Contact: Prof Alan T McGown.
E   A research centre within the Biomedical Sciences Research Institute (qv) at the University of Salford.
O   To conduct research aimed at improving the knowledge of how existing anti-cancer drugs work against cancer cells, and the effect these drugs may have on adults and children

Centre for Molecular Environmental Science
   see **Williamson Research Centre for Molecular Environmental Science.**

Centre for Molecular Medicine

■ Department of Medicine, University College London, Rayne Building, 5 University Street, London, WC1E 6JF.
   020 7679 6175   fax 020 7679 6175
   http://www.ucl.ac.uk/medicine/molecular-medicine
   Director: Prof A W Segal.
E   A research centre at University College London.

Centre for Molecular Microbiology and Infection   (CMMI)

■ Faculty of Life Sciences, Imperial College London, Flowers Building, Armstrong Road, London, SW7 2AZ.
   020 7594 3201; 3962   fax 020 7594 3076
   http://www.imperial.ac.uk/cmmi/
   Director: Prof Douglas Young.
E   A research centre at Imperial College London.
O   To undertake research in infectious diseases

Centre for Molecular and Nanoscale Electronics   1987

■ Science Laboratories, University of Durham, South Road, Durham, DH1 3LE.
   0191-334 2419   fax 0191-334 2407
   http://www.dur.ac.uk/molecular.electronics/
   Director: Prof M C Petty. Director: Prof M R Bryce.
E   A research centre within the University of Durham.
O   To consolidate and promote activities in the strategic and highly interdisciplinary subject of molecular electronics; to conduct research on biological membranes, chemical and biological sensors, liquid crystal devices, neural networks, nonlinear optics, organic conductors, pyroelectric detectors, and organic magnets
●   Short courses covering molecular electronics, conducting polymers, and Langmuir-Blodgett films - Analytical techniques available include electron diffraction, x-ray diffraction, infra-red spectroscopy, together with a number of instrumental services
✕   Centre for Molecular Electronics.

Centre for Molecular Oncology   (CMO)

■ Barts and the London, Queen Mary's School of Medicine and Dentistry, Queen Mary, University of London, Charterhouse Square, London, EC1M 6BQ.
   020 7014 0462   fax 020 7014 0461
   http://www.cancer.qmul.ac.uk/research/molecular_oncology/
   Director: Prof Nicholas Lemoine.
E   A research centre within the Institute of Cancer (qv) at Queen Mary, University of London.
O   To focus research on the development of innovative therapeutic and diagnostic approaches to cancer, including gene therapy

Centre for Molecular Parasitology
   see **Wellcome Centre for Molecular Parasitology.**

Centre for Molecular Science Informatics
   see **Unilever Centre for Molecular Science Informatics.**

 © CBD Research Ltd · Beckenham · Kent BR3 5JS · Tel 020 8650 7745 · Fax 020 8650 0768 · E-mail cbd@cbdresearch.com · www.cbdresearch.com

Centre for Molecular Sciences
  see **Oxford Centre for Molecular Sciences.**

Centre for Mountain Studies   (CMS)   2000

■   Perth College, University of the Highlands and Islands (UHI) Institute, Webster Building, Crieff Road, Perth, PH1 2NX.
  01738 877761   fax 01738 877018
  http://www.cms.uhi.ac.uk/
  Director: Prof Martin Price.
E   A research centre at the University of the Highlands and Islands (UHI) Institute.
O   To conduct research and teaching on issues relating to sustainable development in mountain regions

Centre for Multi-Cultural Studies in Law and the Family   2001

■   Law School, University of Buckingham, Hunter Street, Buckingham, MK18 1EG.
  01280 828274
  http://www.buckingham.ac.uk/law/aboutdept/multi.html
  Co-Director: Dr Mary Welstead. Co-Director: Prof Susan Edwards.
E   A centre at the University of Buckingham.
O   To study law based on a multi-cultural approach which reflects the religious, ethnic and cultural diversity of society

Centre for Multidisciplinary Microtechnology
  see **Cardiff Centre for Multidisciplinary Microtechnology.**

Centre of Multimedia Performance History   (COMPH)

■   Department of Drama and Theatre, Royal Holloway, University of London, Egham, Surrey, TW20 0EX.
  01784 443922   fax 01784 431018
  http://www.rhul.ac.uk/drama/comph/
  Contact: Jacky Bratton.
E   A research centre at Royal Holloway, University of London.
O   To investigate new ways of interacting with live theatre through imaginative use of digital technology, and creating new interfaces for traditional research materials and experimenting with the use of digital technologies in live performance; to facilitate in-depth research of theatrical working processes through the study of individual productions and the work of individual practitioners
●   To promote and facilitate further production research by bringing together primary materials including production images, set designs, costume designs and interviews with creative practitioners

Centre for Museology   2002

■   School of Arts, Histories and Cultures, University of Manchester, Humanities Bridgeford Street, Oxford Road, Manchester, M13 9PL.
  0161-275 3311   fax 0161-275 3331
  http://www.arts.manchester.ac.uk/museology/
  Director: Dr Helen Rees Leahy.
E   A research centre at the University of Manchester.
O   To develop and promote research and teaching in museum theory and practice

Centre for Music in Culture
  see **Manchester Centre for Music in Culture.**

Centre for Music Technology   (CMT)

■   Faculty of Science, Technology and Medical Studies, University of Kent, Medway Building, Chatham Maritime, Chatham, Kent, ME4 4AG.
  01227 827833   fax 01227 827154
  http://www.kent.ac.uk/musictechnology/
  Contact: Clive Arundell.
E   A research centre at the University of Kent.
O   To explore the area of electronic and computer technology within the specific field of music

Centre for Music Technology   (CMT)

■   Department of Music and Department of Electronics and Electrical Engineering, University of Glasgow, 14 University Gardens, Glasgow, G12 8QH.
  0141-330 4903   fax 0141-330 6065
  http://markov.music.gla.ac.uk/
  Co-Director: Dr Nick Bailey. Co-Director: Carola Böhm.
E   A centre at the University of Glasgow.
O   To provide a framework in support of an interaction between artists, engineers and scientists, university external and internal organisations and individuals, in order to collaborate on activities within music technology

Centre for Music Theatre   (CMT)

■   School of Creative Arts, Film and Media, University of Portsmouth, University House, Winston Churchill Avenue, Portsmouth, PO1 2UP.
  023 9284 6104; 6132
  http://www.port.ac.uk/departments/academic/scafm/researchcentres/musictheatre/
  Co-Director: Dominic Symonds. Co-Director: George Burrows.
E   An interdisciplinary research centre at the University of Portsmouth.
O   To conduct research in a wide variety of music, theatre, musical theatre and opera

Centre for Nanoporous Materials   (CNM)   1995
■   School of Chemistry and School of Chemical Engineering and Analytical Science, PO Box 88, University of Manchester, Sackville Street, Manchester, M60 1QD.
  0161-306 4527   fax 0161-306 4559
  http://www.chemistry.manchester.ac.uk/
  Director: Prof Mike Anderson.
E   A research centre at the University of Manchester.
O   To provide a focus for projects on nanoporous materials in collaboration with industry and many academic institutions

Centre for Nanoscale Science   (CNS)
■   Department of Chemistry, University of Liverpool, Oxford Street, Liverpool, L69 7ZD.
  0151-794 3493   fax 0151-794 3588
  http://www.liv.ac.uk/nano/
E   A research centre at the University of Liverpool.

Centre for Nanostructured Media   (CNM)   2005
■   School of Mathematics and Physics, Queen's University, Belfast, Belfast, BT7 1NN.
  028 9097 3546; 3941   fax 028 9097 3110
  http://www.qub.ac.uk/schools/SchoolofMathematicsandPhysics/con/
E   A research centre within the International Research Centre for Experimental Physics (qv) at Queen's University, Belfast.

Centre for Nanotechnology and Microfabrication
  see **Teesside Centre for Nanotechnology and Microfabrication.**

Centre for Narrative Research   (CNR)
■   School of Social Sciences, Media and Cultural Studies, Docklands Campus, University of East London, 4-6 University Way, London, E16 2RD.
  020 8223 7690
  http://www.uel.ac.uk/cnr/
E   A research centre at the University of East London.

Centre for Narratives and Transformative Learning
  see **CLIO Centre for Narratives and Transformative Learning.**

Centre of Near and Middle Eastern Studies
Note: Now incorporated into the London Middle East Institute (qv).

Centre for Nephrology
■   Department of Medicine, Royal Free and University College Medical School, University College London, Rowland Hill Street, London, NW3 2PF.
  020 7830 2930   fax 020 7317 8591
  http://www.ucl.ac.uk/medicine/nephrology-rf
  Director: Prof S Powis.
E   A research centre at University College London.
O   To conduct research so as to improve outcomes for patients with chronic kidney disease by slowing the progression of kidney damage, optimising treatment of complications and developing better therapies for individuals who reach end-stage kidney failure

Centre for Network Research
■   Department of Electronic Systems Engineering, University of Essex, Wivenhoe Park, Colchester, Essex, CO4 3SQ.
  01206 872277   fax 01206 873012
  http://www.essex.ac.uk/
  Director: Dr A Vickers.
E   A research centre within the University of Essex.

Centre for Networking and Telecommunications Research   (CNTR)
■   Faculty of Business, Law and the Built Environment, Maxwell Building, University of Salford, Salford, Manchester, M5 4WT.
  0161-295 3223   fax 0161-295 5575
  http://www.cntr.salford.ac.uk/
  Director: Prof Nigel Linge.
E   A research centre within the Informatics Research Institute (qv) at the University of Salford.
O   To undertake both pure and applied research into the development of computer networking technologies and multimedia application systems, which is fundamental to the future of the information age

Centre for Neurodegenerative Research
  see **MRC Centre for Neurodegenerative Research.**

© CBD Research Ltd · Beckenham · Kent BR3 5JS · Tel 020 8650 7745 · Fax 020 8650 0768 · E-mail cbd@cbdresearch.com · www.cbdresearch.com

Centre for Neuroendocrinology
- ■ Department of Medicine, University College London, Rayne Building, 5 University Street, London, WC1E 6JJ.
  020 7679 2000
  http://www.ucl.ac.uk/medicine/neuroendocrinology/
  Director: Dr P Bouloux.
- E A research centre at University College London.

Centre for Neuroimaging Techniques
  see **UCL Centre for Neuroimaging Techniques.**

Centre for Neurology and Neurosurgery
  see **Walton Centre for Neurology and Neurosurgery.**

Centre for Neuroscience
  see **Sussex Centre for Neuroscience.**

Centre for Neuroscience in Education   (CNE)
- ■ Faculty of Education, University of Cambridge, 184 Hills Road, Cambridge, CB2 2PQ.
  01223 767600   fax 01223 767602
  http://www.educ.cam.ac.uk/neuroscience/
  Co-Director: Prof Usha Goswami. Co-Director: Dr Denes Szucs.
- E A centre at the University of Cambridge.
- O To establish the basic parameters of brain development in the cognitive skills critical for reading and mathematics

Centre for Neuroscience Research   (CNR)
- ■ University of Edinburgh, Summerhall, Edinburgh, EH9 1QH.
  0131-650 3520
  http://www.cnr.ed.ac.uk/
- E A research centre at the University of Edinburgh.
- O To conduct research and teaching in all aspects of basic and clinical neuroscience

Centre for New and Emerging Markets   (CNEM)
- ■ London Business School, Sussex Place, Regent's Park, London, NW1 4SA.
  020 7000 7000   fax 020 7000 7001
  http://www.london.edu/cnem.html
- E A centre at the London Business School.
- O To promote a better understanding of the ways in which the private sector can contribute positively to development of markets

Centre for New Media Research   (CNMR)
- ■ School of Art, Design and Media, University of Portsmouth, Eldon Building, Winston Churchill Avenue, Portsmouth, PO1 2DJ.
  023 9284 3835   fax 023 9284 3808
  http://www.envf.port.ac.uk/newmedia/first.html
  Contact: Dr Paul Newland.
- E A research centre at the University of Portsmouth.
- O To investigate cumulative processes in digital cultures, integrating experimental work in origination and authoring with strategies of data management and cultural research on patterns of inter-activity

Centre for New Religions
Note: No longer in existence.

Centre for New Technologies Research in Education   (CeNTRE)   1998
- ■ University of Warwick, Coventry, CV4 7AL.
  024 7657 2911   fax 024 7652 4609
  http://www2.warwick.ac.uk/fac/soc/wie/research/centre/
  Manager: Yvette Kingston.
- E A research centre within the Warwick Institute of Edication (qv) at the University of Warwick.
- O To be a leading centre for teaching, development and research in information and communications technology (ICT)
- ● Education and training

Centre for New Technologies, Innovation and Entrepreneurship   (CENTIVE)   2006
- ■ Cass Business School, City University, 106 Bunhill Row, London, EC1Y 8TZ.
  020 7040 8666
  http://www.cass.city.ac.uk/centive/
  Director: Prof Chris Hendry.
- E A research centre at City University.

Centre for Nineteenth-Century Studies   1996
- ■ School of English and Humanities, Birkbeck, University of London, Malet Street, Bloomsbury, London, WC1E 7HX.
  020 7631 6861
  http://www.bbk.ac.uk/eh/research/centreforc19thstudies
  Contact: Prof Hilary Fraser.
- E   A research centre within the Birkbeck Institute for the Humanities (qv) at Birkbeck, University of London.
- O   To conduct research from the French Revolutionary period to World War One (1790-1914)

Centre for Nineteenth-Century Studies
- ■ Department of English Literature, University of Sheffield, Sheffield, S10 2TN.
  0114-282 8450; 8499   fax 0114-282 8481
  http://c19.group.shef.ac.uk/
  Contact: Claire Penny.
- E   A research centre at the University of Sheffield.
- O   To promote research in the 'long' nineteenth century (1789-1914), covering British, American and European history, culture and literature

Centre in Non-destructive Evaluation
  see **Research Centre in Non-destructive Evaluation**

Centre for Nonlinear Dynamics
  see **Manchester Centre for Nonlinear Dynamics.**

Centre for Nonlinear Dynamics and its Applications   (CNDA)   1991
- ■ Department of Civil and Environmental Engineering, University College London, Gower Street, London, WC1E 6BT.
  020 7679 7729
  http://www.ucl.ac.uk/cnda/
  Director: Prof J M T Thompson. Contact: Prof Steve Bishop.
- E   An interdisciplinary research centre at University College London.
- O   To conduct research into the theory of nonlinear dynamics and its applications to science and engineering

Centre for Nonlinear Mathematics and Applications
- ■ Department of Mathematical Sciences, Loughborough University, Ashby Road, Loughborough, Leicestershire, LE11 3TU.
  01509 222861   fax 01509 223969
  http://www.lboro.ac.uk/departments/ma/research/cnlma/
  Director: Prof Roger Grimshaw.
- E   A research centre at Loughborough University.
- O   To focus, support and enhance research activities in nonlinear mathematics and its applications, with a particular emphasis on integrable systems, Hamiltonian dynamics, applied dynamical systems, nonlinear waves, nonlinear partial differential equations, reaction-diffusion equations, biological systems, waves and vortices in geophysical fluid dynamics

Centre for Nonlinear Mechanics   (CNM)
- ■ University of Bath, Claverton Down, Bath, BA2 7AY.
  01225 826241; 826796
  http://www.bath.ac.uk/cnm/
  Co-Director: Prof Chris Budd. Co-Director: Prof Giles Hunt.
- E   A research centre at the University of Bath.
- O   To encourage interdisciplinary research between engineers, scientists, mathematicians and industry, through the modelling and application of nonlinear systems

Centre for Nonprofit and Voluntary Section Management   (CNPVSM)   2001
- ■ School of Business and Social Sciences, Southlands College, University of Roehampton, 80 Roehampton Lane, London, SW15 5SL.
  020 8392 3862   fax 020 8392 3518
  http://www.roehampton.ac.uk/cnpvsm/
  Director: Colin Rochester.
- E   A research centre at Roehampton University.
- O   To conduct research, postgraduate teaching, consultancy and training for voluntary sector organisations

Centre for Nordic Studies   (CNS)   2006
- ■ Orkney College, University of the Highlands and Islands (UHI) Institute, Kirkwall, Orkney, KW15 1LX.
  01856 569000   fax 01856 569001
  http://www.uhi.ac.uk/research/research-centres/centre-for-nordic-studies
- E   A research centre at the University of the Highlands and Islands (UHI) Institute.
Note: The Centre is in the process of formation and will also have a base in the Shetland Islands

© CBD Research Ltd · Beckenham · Kent BR3 5JS · Tel 020 8650 7745 · Fax 020 8650 0768 · E-mail cbd@cbdresearch.com · www.cbdresearch.com

Centre for North-West Regional Studies (CNWRS) 1974

■ Fylde College, Lancaster University, Lancaster, LA1 4YF.
　01524 593770　fax 01524 594725
　http://www.lancs.ac.uk/users/cnwrs/
　Director: Jacqueline Whiteside. Co-ordinator: Dr Jean Turnbull.
E An association with a voluntary subscribing membership and a department of Lancaster University.
○ To encourage, develop and co-ordinate research into North-West England; to store and disseminate information relevant to research; to develop contacts with learned bodies and members of the professions and the public
● Conference facilities - Education and training - Postgraduate courses - Oral history archives open by appointment
¶ Centre Words (annual).

Centre for The Novel

■ English Department, King's College, University of Aberdeen, Aberdeen, AB24 3UB.
　01224 272625
　http://www.abdn.ac.uk/english/novel/
　Director: Janet Todd.
E A research centre at the University of Aberdeen.
○ To explore the regional, national and international significance of the novel as an art form; to address such general topics as subjectivity and identity, medical theory and fiction, aesthetics, print culture, the sociology of reading, mass and elite fiction, and issues of race, class, nation and gender

Centre for Novel Agricultural Products (CNAP) 1999

■ Department of Biology, University of York, Heslington, York, YO10 5DD.
　01904 328763　fax 01904 328801
　http://www.york.ac.uk/org/cnap/
　Director: Prof Dianna Bowles.
E A research centre at the University of York.
○ To conduct specialist research in gene discovery with plant- and microbial-based applications, using biology to benefit society and to provide a sustainable future

Centre for Novel Computing (CNC) 1990

■ School of Computer Science, University of Manchester, Kilburn Building, Oxford Road, Manchester, M13 9PL.
　0161-275 6134　fax 0161-275 6204
　http://www.cs.manchester.ac.uk/cnc/
　Contact: Dr Len Freeman.
E An interdisciplinary research group at the University of Manchester.
○ To investigate techniques, and develop associated tools, for support of high performance computing with a focus on shared parallel resources

Centre for Nuclear and Radiation Physics   (CNRP)

■ Department of Physics, University of Surrey, Guildford, Surrey, GU2 7XH.
　01483 686800　fax 01483 686781
　http://www.ph.surrey.ac.uk/cnrp
　Chairman: Prof Ian Thompson.
E A research centre at the University of Surrey.
○ To bring together expertise in both pure and applied nuclear physics, radiation physics, and medical physics applications

Centre for Numerical Modelling and Process Analysis (CNMPA) 1983

■ School of Computing and Mathematical Sciences, University of Greenwich, Queen Anne Building, 30 Park Row, London, SE10 9LS.
　020 8331 8702
　http://www.cms1.gre.ac.uk/research/cnmpa/
　Contact: Prof Mark Cross.
E A research centre at the University of Greenwich.
○ To provide a centre of excellence for applied research in numerical modelling and analysis of physical systems

Centre for Nursing and Allied Health Professionals Research   (CNAHPR)

■ University College London, Level 7 - Old Building, Great Ormond Street, London, WC1N 3JH.
　020 7405 9200 ext 5833　fax 020 7829 8602
　http://www.ich.ucl.ac.uk/ich/academicunits/Centre_for_nursing_and_allied_health_professions_research/
　Head: Prof Linda S Franck. Contact: Razia Nuur.
E A research centre within the UCL Institute of Child Health (qv) at University College London.
○ To conduct child and family focused research

Centre for Nursing, Midwifery and Collaborative Research
　see **Salford Centre for Nursing, Midwifery and Collaborative Research.**

Centre for Nursing and Midwifery Research (CNMR)

■ Faculty of Health, University of Brighton, Westlain House, Village Way, Brighton, East Sussex, BN1 9PH.
　01273 644013　fax 01273 644010
　http://www.brighton.ac.uk/inam/research
E A research centre at the Institute of Nursing and Midwifery (qv) within the University of Brighton.
○ To offer full and part-time research study opportunities to people working on clinical practice or education

Centre for Nursing Practice
see **Mary Seacole Centre for Nursing Practice.**

Centre for Nutritional Epidemiology in Cancer Prevention and Survival
see **MRC Centre for Nutritional Epidemiology in Cancer Prevention and Survival.**

Centre for Observation of Air-Sea Interactions and Fluxes   (CASIX)

■   Plymouth Marine Laboratory, University of Plymouth, Prospect Place, Plymouth, PL1 3DH.
     01752 633429
     http://www.pml.ac.uk/casix/
     Contact: Prof Jim Aiken.
E   A Natural Environment Research Council collaborative research centre at the University of Plymouth.
O   To study chemical movements between the oceans and the atmosphere, with the goal of quantifying accurately the global air-sea
     movements of carbon dioxide

Centre for the Observation and Modelling of Earthquakes and Tectonics   (COMET)

NR   Department of Earth Sciences, University of Oxford, Parks Road, Oxford, OX1 3PR.
      01865 272030   fax 01865 272072
      http://comet.nerc.ac.uk/
      Contact: Prof Barry Parsons.
E   A Natural Environment Research Council collaborative research centre at the University of Oxford.
O   To use satellite observations to model the deformation of the Earth's crust over periods ranging from days to millions of years, and
     over areas ranging from tens to thousands of kilometres
Note: A collaborative venture with the University of Cambridge and University College London.

Centre for Occupational Health and Safety   (COHS)   2000

■   School of Engineering and Physical Sciences, Heriot-Watt University, Riccarton, Edinburgh, EH14 4AS.
     0131-451 8245   fax 0131-451 3129
     http://www.hw.ac.uk/cohs/
     Co-Director: Prof Bob Reuben. Co-Director: Dr Julian Goodwin.
E   A research centre and department of Heriot-Watt University.
O   To help focus the University's established expertise in the health and safety arena

Centre for Occupational Health and Safety [Surrey]
see **Robens Centre for Occupational Health and Safety.**

Centre for the Older Person's Agenda
see **Royal Bank of Scotland Centre for the Older Person's Agenda.**

Centre for Olympic Studies and Research   (COS&R)   2004

■   School of Sport and Exercise Sciences, Loughborough University, Ashby Road, Loughborough, Leicestershire, LE11 3TU.
     01509 226302
     http://www.lboro.ac.uk/departments/sses/institutes/cos
     Director: Prof Ian Henry.
E   A research centre at Loughborough University.
O   To promote, facilitate and conduct research into Olympism, the Olympic Games, the Olympic Movement, and Olympic sport

Centre for Ombudsman and Governance Studies   (COGS)   1989

■   Graduate Institute of Political and International Studies, University of Reading, Whiteknights, PO Box 217, Reading, Berkshire,
     RG6 6AH.
      0118-378 8378
      http://www.reading.ac.uk/GIPIS/The%20Institute%203/Research.htm
E   A research centre within the Graduate Institute of Political and International Studies (qv) at the University of Reading.
O   To conduct research and study of Ombudsman and Ombudsman-related schemes in the public sectors world-wide

Centre for Oncology
see **Clatterbridge Centre for Oncology.**

Centre for Oncology and Applied Pharmacology

■   University of Glasgow, Garscube Estate, Switchback Road, Glasgow, G61 1BD.
     0141-330 4161   fax 0141-330 4127
     http://www.gla.ac.uk/cancerpathology/
     Contact: Prof Jim Cassidy.
E   A research centre within the Beatson Institute for Cancer Research (qv) at the University of Glasgow.

Centre for Open Learning in Mathematics, Science, Computing and Technology   (COLMSCT)   2005
- ■   Open University, Walton Hall, Milton Keynes, MK7 6AA.
   01908 655792
   http://www.open.ac.uk/colmsct/
   Director: Prof Stephen Swithenby. Contact: Diane Ford.
- E   A Centre for Excellence in Teaching and Learning (CETL) at the Open University.
- Note: See **Centres for Excellence in Teaching and Learning** for more information.

Centre for Operational Research and Applied Statistics   (CORAS)   1988
- ■   Faculty of Business, Law and the Built Environment, University of Salford, Salford, Manchester, M5 4WT.
   0161-295 4022   fax 0161-295 4947
   http://www.mams.salford.ac.uk/mams/m/?s=6
   Contact: A H Christer.
- E   An interdisciplinary research centre within the Management and Management Sciences Research Institute (qv) at the University of Salford.
- O   To focus on areas of operational research and applied statistics, and specifically methodology, health, strategy modelling, maintenance, warranty risk, condition monitoring, sport, and intelligent decision support in operations

Centre for Operational Research, Management Science and Information Systems   (CORMSIS)
- ■   School of Management, University of Southampton, Highfield, Southampton, SO17 1BJ.
   023 8059 3567   fax 023 8059 3844
   http://www.cormsis.soton.ac.uk/
   Director: Dr Sally Brailsford.
- E   A research centre at the University of Southampton.

Centre for Oral Growth and Development   (COGD)
- ■   Barts and the London, Queen Mary's School of Medicine and Dentistry, Queen Mary's, University of London, Queen Mary, University of London, Turner Street, London, E1 2AD.
   020 7377 7611   fax 020 7377 7612
   http://www.smd.qmul.ac.uk/dental/oralgrowdev/
- E   A research centre within the Institute of Dentistry (qv) at Queen Mary, University of London.
- O   To conduct research in oral growth and development, with particular emphasis on the fields of dental biomaterials, dental biophysics, paediatric dentistry, and orthodontics

Centre for Ordnance Science and Technology   (COST)
- ■   Department of Materials and Applied Science, Defence College of Management and Technology, Cranfield University, Shrivenham, Swindon, Wiltshire, SN6 8LA.
   01793 782551
   http://www.dcmt.cranfield.ac.uk/dmas/cost/
   Contact: Dr S G Murray.
- E   A research centre at Cranfield University.

Centre for Organic and Biological Chemistry   (COBC)
- ■   Department of Chemistry, University of Hull, Cottingham Road, Hull, HU6 7RX.
   01482 465221
   http://www.hull.ac.uk/chemistry/
- E   A centre at the University of Hull.

Centre for Organisation and Innovation
> see **ESRC Centre for Organisation and Innovation.**

Centre for Organisational Effectiveness   (COE)   1998
- ■   Bournemouth Law School, Talbot Campus, Bournemouth University, Poole, Dorset, BH12 5BB.
   01202 967231; 967422
   http://coe.bournemouth.ac.uk/
   Co-Director: Prof Colin Armistead. Co-Director: Dr Julia Kiely.
- E   A research centre within the Institute of Business and Law (qv) at Bournemouth University.
- O   To improve the effectiveness of private and public organisations through its research, consultancy and specialist management development programmes

Centre for Organisational Excellence
> see **Research Centre for Organisational Excellence.**

Centre for Organisational Transformation   (COT)
- ■   Cranfield School of Management, Cranfield University, Cranfield, Bedfordshire, MK43 0AL.
   01234 751122   fax 01234 751806
   http://www.som.cranfield.ac.uk/som/research/centres/cot/
- E   A research centre at Cranfield University.
- O   To study incremental, radical, large scale and strategic change in organisations

Centre for Ornithology
- School of Biosciences, University of Birmingham, Edgbaston, Birmingham, B15 2TT.
  0121-414 5400   fax 0121-414 5925
  http://www.ornithology.bham.ac.uk/
  Chairman: Prof Graham Martin.
- E   A centre at the University of Birmingham.
- O   To research in various aspects of birds and bird behaviour, including macroecology and clock genes through phsyiology, energetics, sensory systems, behaviour, cognition, and reproductive biology

Centre for Orthopaedic Biomechanics   (COB)
- Department of Mechanical Engineering, University of Bath, Claverton Down, Bath, BA2 7AY.
  01225 386371   fax 01225 826928
  http://www.bath.ac.uk/ortho-biomechanics/
  Director: Prof Tony Miles.
- E   A centre at the University of Bath.
- O   To provide a resource for multidisciplinary research linking engineering and clinical orthopaedics

Centre for Osmosis Research and Applications   (CORA)   2003
- School of Engineering, University of Surrey, Guildford, Surrey, GU2 7XH.
  01483 686292
  http://www.surrey.ac.uk/eng/research/fluids/cora
  Director: Dr Adel Sharif.
- E   A research centre at the University of Surrey.
- O   To conduct research in low cost desalination technologies

Centre for Outcomes Research and Effectiveness   (CORE)   1995
- Department of Psychology, University College London, 1-19 Torrington Place, London, WC1E 7HB.
  020 7679 1785   fax 020 7916 8511
  http://www.psychol.ucl.ac.uk/CORE/
  Director: Stephen Pilling.
- E   A British Psychological Society research centre at University College London.
- O   To apply psychological expertise to the promotion of clinical effectiveness, and to evaluate health services and health interventions

Centre for Packaging Technology
  see **Brunel Centre for Packaging Technology.**

Centre for Paediatric and Adolescent Rheumatology
- Department of Medicine, University College London, Windeyer Building, 46 Cleveland Street, London, W1T 4JF.
  020 7679 9148
  http://www.ucl.ac.uk/medicine/paediatric-rheumatology/
  Director: Prof Pat Woo.
- E   A research centre at University College London.
- O   To offer a national tertiary referral centre for all rheumatological disorders affecting children and adolescents; to conduct research which deals with technologies which improve diagnosis as well as therapeutic trials

Centre for Paediatric Epidemiology and Biostatistics
- Faculty of Biomedical Sciences, University College London, 30 Guilford Street, London, WC1N 1EH.
  020 7242 9789   fax 020 7831 0488
  http://www.ich.ucl.ac.uk/website/ich/academicunits/Paediatric_Epidemiology_and_Biostatistics/
- E   A research centre within the UCL Institute of Child Health (qv) at University College London.

Centre for Paediatric Infectious Diseases and Microbiology
  X   is now the Infectious Diseases and Microbiology Unit of the **Hugh and Catherine Stevenson Centre for Childhood Infectious Diseases and Immunology** and is therefore no longer within the scope of this Directory.

Centre for Pain Research   (CPR)
- Faculty of Health, Leeds Metropolitan University, Civic Quarter, Calverley Street, Leeds, LS1 3HE.
  0113-283 2600   fax 0113-283 1908
  http://www.leedsmet.ac.uk/health/painresearch
  Leader: Prof Mark I Johnson.
- E   A research centre at Leeds Metropolitan University.
- O   To conduct research in the use of non-invasive approaches to manage pain

Centre for Palliative and End of Life Studies
  see **Sue Ryder Care Centre for Palliative and End of Life Studies.**

Centre for Parallel Computing   (CPC)

■   Cavendish School of Computer Science, University of Westminster, 115 New Cavendish Street, London, W1B 2UW.
      020 7911 5000 ext 3625   fax 020 7911 5089
      http://www.wmin.ac.uk/cscs/page-26
      Director: Prof Stephen Winter.
E   A research centre at the University of Westminster.
○   To conduct research in the technology and applications of parallel and distributed computations

Centre for Parent and Child Support   (CPCS)

■   Guy's Hospital, 66 Snowfields, London, SE1 3SS.
      020 7378 3235   fax 020 7378 3243
      http://www.cpcs.org.uk/
E   A research centre within the Institute of Psychiatry (qv) at King's College, London.

Centre for Particle Characterisation and Analysis

■   School of Engineering and Science, University of Paisley, Paisley, PA1 2BE.
      0141-848 3101   fax 0141-848 3663
      http://www.paisley.ac.uk/es/consultancy.asp#cpca
      Contact: Dr Ciaran Ewins.
E   A research centre at the University of Paisley.
Note: At the time of going to press, the University of Paisley was preparing to merge with Bell College to form the University of the West
      of Scotland.

Centre for Particle Physics   (CPP)

■   Department of Physics, Royal Holloway, University of London, Egham, Surrey, TW20 0EX.
      01784 443448   fax 01784 472794
      http://www.pp.rhul.ac.uk/
E   A centre at Royal Holloway, University of London.

Centre for Particle Theory   (CPT)   1988

■   University of Durham, South Road, Durham, DH1 3LE.
      0191-334 3635   fax 0191-334 3645
      http://www.dur.ac.uk/cpt/
E   A research centre within the University of Durham.
○   To conduct research and development in particle physics and related areas

Centre for Parties and Democracy in Europe   (CPDE)

■   Department of Politics and Contemporary European Studies, University of Sussex, EDB 226, Falmer, Brighton, East Sussex,
      BN1 9SJ.
      01273 678578
      http://www.sussex.ac.uk/sei/1-4-4.html
      Contact: Amanda Sims.
E   A research centre within the Sussex European Institute (qv) at the University of Sussex.
○   To conduct research on contemporary party politics

Centre for Peace and Conflict Studies   (CPCS)   2005

■   School of International Relations, University of St Andrews, Arts Building, St Andrews, Fife, KY16 9AJ.
      01334 462943   fax 01334 462937
      http://www.st-andrews.ac.uk/intrel/cpcs/CPCS.html
      Director: Prof Oliver Richmond.
E   A research centre at the University of St Andrews.

Centre for Peace and Reconciliation Studies   (CPRS)

■   School of International Studies and Social Sciences, University of Coventry, Priory Street, Coventry, CV1 5FB.
      024 7688 7862   fax 024 7688 8679
      http://www.coventry.ac.uk/researchnet/d/224
      Director: Prof Andrew Rigby
E   A centre at Coventry University.
○   To be a centre of research, teaching and related activities which will contribute to the deeper understanding and promotion of
      processes of peace and reconciliation throughout the world

Centre for Penal Theory and Penal Ethics   2000

■   University of Cambridge, Sidgwick Avenue, Cambridge, CB3 9DT.
      01223 335364   fax 01223 335356
      http://www.crim.cam.ac.uk/research/cpt/
      Director: Prof Andrew von Hirsch. Administrator: Ann Phillips.
E   A research centre within the Institute of Criminology (qv) at the University of Cambridge.
○   To explore conceptual and ethical issues in criminal law and policy

Centre for Pentecostal and Charismatic Studies   (CPCS)   2001

- Department of Theology and Religious Studies, University of Wales, Bangor, Normal Site, Bangor, Gwynedd, LL57 2PZ.
  01248 382566   fax 01248 383954
  http://www.bangor.ac.uk/rs/pt/pcs/
  Director: Revd Dr William K Kay.
- E   A research centre at the University of Wales, Bangor.
- ● Database of Pentecostal and Charismatic Churches in the UK

Centre for Performance Analysis   (CPA)   1992

- Cardiff School of Sport, University of Wales Institute, Cardiff, Cyncoed Road, Cardiff, CF23 6XD.
  029 2041 6591   fax 029 2041 6589
  http://cpa.uwic.ac.uk/
  Director: Mike Hughes.
- E   A research centre at the University of Wales Institute, Cardiff.

Centre for Performance Enhancement   (CPE)

- Department of Sport and Exercise Science, University of Portsmouth, St Michael's Building, White Swan Road, Portsmouth, PO1 2DT.
  023 9284 3005
  http://www.port.ac.uk/departments/academic/sportscience/centreforperformanceenhancement/
- E   A centre at the University of Portsmouth.
- ○ To offer support services to all standards of sports performers and to those who have an interest in general exercise

Centre for Performance Evaluation and Resource Management   (CPERM)

- Department of Economics and Related Studies, University of York, Heslington, York, YO10 5DD.
  01904 433761; 488674   fax 01904 488674
  http://www.york.ac.uk/depts/econ/research/associated/cperm.htm
  Director: Prof David Mayston.
- E   A research centre at the University of York.

Centre for Performance History, incorporating the Museum of Instruments   (CPH)

- Royal College of Music, Prince Consort Road, South Kensington, London, SW7 2BS.
  020 7589 3643; 7591 4340   fax 020 7589 7740
  http://www.cph.rcm.ac.uk/
  Head: Dr Paul Banks.
- E   A centre at the Royal College of Music.
- ○ To house and care for a diverse collection relating to the history of perfomance, comprising 340 portraits and 10,000 prints and photographs of musicians in the UK, 600,000 concert programmes from 1720 to today, and extensive holdings of opera, instrument, title-page and concert-hall design
- ● Library - Museum of Instruments from 15th century to present day open Tues-Fri (1400-1630)

Centre for Performance Measurement and Management   (CEPMMA)

- Aston Business School, Aston University, Aston Triangle, Birmingham, B4 7ET.
  0121-204 3000
  http://www.abs.aston.ac.uk/newweb/research/CEPMMA/
  Director: Emmanuel Thanassoulis.
- E   A research centre at Aston University.
- ● Education and training - Degrees

Centre for Performance Research   (CPR)

- University of Wales, Aberystwyth, 6 Science Park, Aberystwyth, Ceredigion, SY23 3AH.
  01970 622133   fax 01970 622132
  http://www.thecpr.org.uk/
- E   A centre at the University of Wales, Aberystwyth.
- ○ To develop and improve the knowledge, understanding and practice of theatre in its broadest sense
- ● Conferences - Lectures - Masterclasses - Workshops

Centre for Performance Science   (CPS)   2007

- Royal College of Music, Prince Consort Road, South Kensington, London, SW7 2BS.
  020 7589 3643   fax 020 7589 7740
  http://www.cps.rcm.ac.uk/
  Head: Aaron Williamon.
- E   An interdisciplinary research centre at the Royal College of Music.
- ○ To lead and facilitate research in performance studies, including the investigation of music perception and cognition, group dynamics and social interaction to the study of peak performance
- Note: has replaced the Centre for the Study of Music Performance.

© CBD Research Ltd · Beckenham · Kent BR3 5JS · Tel 020 8650 7745 · Fax 020 8650 0768 · E-mail cbd@cbdresearch.com · www.cbdresearch.com

Centre for Performance Sport   (CPS)

■ Carnegie Faculty of Sport and Education, Leeds Metropolitan University, Room 216 - Cavendish Hall, Headingley Campus, Leeds, LS6 3QS.
  0113-283 2600   fax 0113-283 6171
  http://www.leedsmet.ac.uk/carnegie/8510.htm
  Director: Prof Carlton Cooke.
E A research centre within the Carnegie Research Institute (qv) at Leeds Metropolitan University.
○ To conduct research on sport and physical education performance through focusing on dietary supplementation, sports drinks, effect, coping in sport, body composition and talent development

Centre for Performance Translation and Dramaturgy
  see **Performance Translation Centre.**

Centre for Perinatal Brain Research

■ Department of Paediatrics and Child Health, University College London, Rayne Building, 5 University Street, London, WC1E 6JJ.
  020 7679 6101
  http://www.ucl.ac.uk/paediatrics/paediatrics/research.htm
E A research centre at University College London.

Centre for Pest Management
  see **Silwood Centre for Pest Management.**

Centre for Philosophical and Religious Studies
  see **Subject Centre for Philosophical and Religious Studies**.

Centre for Philosophical Studies   (CPS)   1989

■ Department of Philosophy, King's College London, Strand, London, WC2R 2LS.
  020 7848 2118; 2230
  http://www.kcl.ac.uk/schools/humanities/hrc/cps/
  Co-Director: Dr Thomas Pink. Co-Director: Dr Peter Adamson.
E A research centre at King's College, London.

Centre for the Philosophy of Logic, Language, Mathematics and Mind
  see **AHRC Research Centre for the Philosophy of Logic, Language, Mathematics and Mind.**

Centre for Philosophy of Natural and Social Science   (CPNSS)   1990

■ LSE, Lakatos Building, Houghton Street, London, WC2A 2AE.
  020 7955 7573   fax 020 7955 6869
  http://www.lse.ac.uk/collections/CPNSS/
  Director: Dr Stephan Hartman. Deputy Director: Dr Eleonora Montuschi.
E A research centre within the London School of Economics and Political Science.
○ To promote interdisciplinary research in fundamental questions of the natural and social sciences, partly on the important and methodological and philosophical issues that arise, specifically, in biology, medicine, physics, economics and the social sciences The Centre also has a special interest in those methodological issues that arise when insights from both natural and social scientists are clearly needed to solve problems of practical concern
● Conference facilities Some of its projects investigate, for example, the impact on policy making of knowledge acquired from the natural sciences, and the roles that different kinds of information play in economic models

Centre for Philosophy and Public Affairs
  see **Centre for Ethics, Philosophy and Public Affairs.**

Centre for Philosophy and Religion

■ Department of Theology and Religious Studies, University of Glasgow, 4 The Square, Glasgow, G12 8QQ.
  0141-330 6526
  http://www.religions.divinity.gla.ac.uk/Centre_Philosophy
  Director: Prof Joseph Houston.
E A centre at the University of Glasgow.
○ To encourage mutual co-operation between researchers of philosophy and religion

Centre for Philosophy of the Social Sciences

Note: is the Philosophy of Social Science Group of the University of Exeter and therefore outside the scope of this directory.

Centre for Philosophy and Value   1997

■ Department of Philosophy, University of Southampton, Southampton, SO17 1BJ.
  023 8059 5753   fax 023 8059 3032
  http://www.philosophy.soton.ac.uk/postgraduate_pages/centre.htm
  Contact: Prof Aaron Ridley.
E A research centre at the University of Southampton.

Centre for Phosphors and Display Materials   (CPDM)   1968
- Brunel University, Uxbridge, Middlesex, UB8 3PH.
   01895 265628   fax 01895 269737
   http://www.brunel.ac.uk/about/acad/wolfson/cpdm
   Director: Prof Jack Silver.
- E   A research centre within the Wolfson Centre for Materials Processing (qv) at Brunel University.
- O   To conduct research into luminescent materials, with a particular interest in displays and lighting in industrial sectors

Centre for Photographic Research   2000
- Newport School of Art, Media and Design, Caerleon Campus, PO Box 101, University of Wales, Newport, Newport, NP18 3YG.
   01633 432210; 432432   fax 01633 432046
   http://artschool.newport.ac.uk/photographicresearch.html
   Director: Prof Paul Seawright.
- E   A research centre at the University of Wales, Newport.
- O   To conduct postgraduate teaching and research in photography

Centre for Photonics and Photonic Materials   (CPPM)
- Department of Physics, University of Bath, Claverton Down, Bath, BA2 7AY.
   01225 383042   fax 01225 386110
   http://www.bath.ac.uk/physics/groups/cppm/
   Director: Prof Jonathan Knight.
- E   A centre at the University of Bath.
- O   To perform cutting edge research in photonics

Centre for Photosynthesis Research
   see **Robert Hill Institute.**

Centre for Physical Education and Sport Pedagogy   (CPESP)
- Carnegie Faculty of Sport and Education, Room 216 - Cavendish Hall, Headingley Campus, Leeds Metropolitan University, Leeds, LS6 3QS.
   0113-283 2600   fax 0113-283 6171
   http://www.leedsmet.ac.uk/carnegie/9193.htm
   Director: Prof David Kirk.
- E   A research centre within the Carnegie Research Institute (qv) at Leeds Metropolitan University.
- O   To draw together physical education and sport in school and community contexts by focusing around the theme of pedagogy

Centre for Physical Electronics and Materials   (PEM)   1994
- Faculty of Engineering, Science and the Built Environment, London South Bank University, 103 Borough Road, London, SE1 0AA.
   020 7815 7559
   http://ecce1.lsbu.ac.uk/research/pem/
   Leader: Prof Neil Alford.
- E   A research centre at London South Bank University.
- O   To investigate the electrical and physical properties of materials with applications to electrical engineering

Centre for Physical Electronics and Quantum Technology   (PEQT)
- Department of Engineering and Design, University of Sussex, Falmer, Brighton, East Sussex, BN1 9QT.
   01273 678087; 872577   fax 01273 686670
   http://www.sussex.ac.uk/pei/
   Contact: Dr Robert J Prance. Contact: Dr Helen Prance.
- E   A research centre at the University of Sussex.
- O   To conduct research in the experimental and theoretical working of superconducting devices, and the development of ultra-sensitive, room temperature electric and magnetic field sensors

Centre for Pipeline Engineering   (CPE)   2005
- School of Marine Science and Technology, University of Newcastle upon Tyne, Armstrong Building, Newcastle upon Tyne, NE1 7RU.
   0191-222 6718   fax 0191-222 5491
   http://www.ncl.ac.uk/marine/pipelineeng/
   Director: Prof Phil Hopkins.
- E   A research centre at the University of Newcastle upon Tyne.
- O   To conduct research and learning in pipeline engineering

Centre for Planetary Science and Astrobiology   (CPSA)
- University of East London, Malet Street, Bloomsbury, London, WC1E 7HX.
   020 7631 6000
   http://zuserver2.star.ucl.ac.uk/astrobiology/
   Director: Dr Ian Crawford.
- E   A centre at Birkbeck, University of London.
- O   To facilitate and enhance research in planetary science

Centre for Planning and Resource Control
Note: The Centre closed in 2005.

© CBD Research Ltd · Beckenham · Kent BR3 5JS · Tel 020 8650 7745 · Fax 020 8650 0768 · E-mail cbd@cbdresearch.com · www.cbdresearch.com

Centre of Planning Studies   (CoPS)
- ■   University of Reading Business School, University of Reading, Reading, Berkshire, RG6 6AW.
    0118-378 8170
    http://www.reading.ac.uk/cops/
- E   An interdepartmental centre of the University of Reading.
- ○   To undertake research and teaching in the field of town and country planning to the highest standard
- ●   Education and training

Centre for Plant Sciences   (CPS)
- ■   Faculty of Biological Sciences, University of Leeds, Miall Building, Leeds, LS2 9JT.
    0113-343 2863   fax 0113-343 3144
    http://www.plants.leeds.ac.uk/
    Director: Dr Brendan Davies.
- E   A research centre within the Institute of Integrative and Comparative Biology (qv) at the University of Leeds.
- ○   To provide a stimulating research environment for studies in both fundamental and applied aspects of plant molecular sciences

Centre for Plasma Physics   (CPP)   2005
- ■   School of Mathematics and Physics, Queen's University, Belfast, Belfast, BT7 1NN.
    028 9097 3546; 3941   fax 028 9097 3110
    http://www.qub.ac.uk/schools/SchoolofMathematicsandPhysics/plip/
- E   A research centre within the International Research Centre for Experimental Physics (qv) at Queen's University, Belfast.

Centre for Podcasting Research
- ■   University of Wales, Bangor, Bangor, Gwynedd, LL57 2DG.
    01248 383215
    http://www.bangor.ac.uk/creative_industries/research.php.en?subid=0
- E   A research centre within the National Institute for Excellence in Creative Industries (qv) at the University of Wales, Bangor.

Centre for Polar Observation and Modelling   (CPOM)
- NR   Department of Earth Sciences, University College London, Pearson Building, Gower Street, London, WC1E 6BT.
    020 7679 3031   fax 020 7679 7883
    http://www.cpom.org/
    Contact: Prof Duncan Wingham.
- E   A Natural Environment Research Council collaborative research centre at University College London.
- ○   To study processes in the Earth's polar latitudes that may affect the Earth's albedo, polar atmosphere and ocean circulation, and global sea level
- Note: CPOM also has sites at the Universities of Bristol and Edinburgh.

Centre for Policing and Community Safety
    see **John Grieve Centre for Policing and Community Safety.**

Centre for Policy on Ageing   (CPA)   1947
- ■   25-31 Ironmonger Row, London, EC1V 3QP.
    020 7553 6500   fax 020 7553 6501
    http://www.cpa.org.uk/
    Director: Gillian Crosby.
- E   A company limited by guarantee and a registered charity.
- ○   To formulate and encourage social policies which will enable everyone to live life as fully as possible in older age; to promote informed debate about issues affecting older age groups; to stimulate awareness of the needs of older people and encourage the spread of good practice

Centre for Policy Evaluation   (CPE)   2005
- ■   School of Economics, University of Nottingham, University Park, Nottingham, NG7 2RD.
    0115-951 5469   fax 0115-951 5552
    http://www.nottingham.ac.uk/economics/cpe/
    Co-Director: Prof Richard Disney. Co-Director: Prof Alan Duncan.
- E   A research centre at the University of Nottingham.
- ○   To provide a forum for the development of new research initiatives that contribute to our understanding of the economic effects of public policy

Centre for Policy Modelling   (CFPM)
- ■   Manchester Metropolitan University Business School, Manchester Metropolitan University, Aytoun Building, Aytoun Street, Manchester, M1 3GH.
    0161-247 6482   fax 0161-247 6802
    http://www.cfpm.org/
- E   A research centre within the Research Institute for Business and Management (qv) at Manchester Metropolitan University.

Centre for Policy Studies   (CPS)   1974
■   57 Tufton Street, London, SW1P 3QL.
    020 7222 4488   fax 020 7222 4388
    http://www.cps.org.uk/
    Chairman: Lord Blackwell. Deputy Chairman: Tessa Keswick.
E   A company limited by guarantee and an independent non-profit-distributing organisation.
●   Conferences - Publishing - Seminars

Centre for Policy Studies in Education   (CPSE)   1993
■   School of Education, University of Leeds, Leeds, LS2 9JT.
    0113-233 4656   fax 0113-233 4541
    http://www.cpse.leeds.ac.uk/
    Director: Prof David Sugden. Administrator: Dr Janet Coles.
E   A research centre at the University of Leeds.
○   To bring together researchers in all the aspects of educational policy, other social scientists with an interest in how policies are
    made, and practitioners engaged in making, implementing and influencing policies in schools, colleges and universities
●   Guest seminars and lectures - Research workshops - Visiting fellows - Collaborative research - Conferences

Centre for Political and Diplomatic Studies   (CPDS)   1993
■   Hill House, Shotover Park, Oxford, OX33 1QN.
    01865 873001   fax 01865 873002
    http://www.cpds.co.uk/
    Contact: Dr John Hemery.
E   An independent organisation.
○   To design and conduct programmes of professional, political and international studies for officials and elected politicians, from
    states developing the institutions of democracy and good governance

Centre for Political Song
■   Glasgow Caledonian University, Saltire House, Cowcaddens Road, Glasgow, G4 0BA.
    0141-273 1189
    http://www.caledonian.ac.uk/politicalsong/
    Manager: John Powles.
E   A research centre at Glasgow Caledonian University.
○   To promote and foster an awareness of all forms of political song
●   Maintenance of a Political Song Catalogue

Centre for Political Theory and Ideologies   (CPTI)
■   Department of Politics, University of Sheffield, Elmfield, Northumberland Road, Sheffield, S10 2TU.
    0114-222 1700   fax 0114-222 1717
    http://www.shef.ac.uk/politics/research/centres/cpti.html
E   A research centre at the University of Sheffield.
○   To promote and develop the study of political ideologies as a major focus in political studies

Centre for Politics and International Studies
■   Keele University, Chancellor's Building, Keele, Staffordshire, ST5 5BG.
    01782 584336
    http://www.keele.ac.uk/research/lpj/research/Pol&Int.htm
E   A research centre within the Research Institute for Law, Politics and Justice (qv) at Keele University.

Centre in Polymer Science and Technology
    see **Interdisclipinary Research Centre in Polymer Science and Technology.**

Centre for Polymer Therapeutics   (CPT)   2000
■   Welsh School of Pharmacy, Cardiff University, Redwood Building, King Edward VII Avenue, Cardiff, CF10 3XF.
    029 2087 4180   fax 029 2087 4536
    http://www.cardiff.ac.uk/phrmy/CPolyT/
    Director: Prof Ruth Duncan.
E   A centre at Cardiff University.
○   To focus research on compounds and drug delivery technologies which use water soluble polymers as polymeric drugs or
    components of polymer-drug conjugates

Centre for Population Biology
    see **NERC Centre for Population Biology.**

Centre for Population Research
    see **Oxford Centre for Population Research.**

© CBD Research Ltd · Beckenham · Kent BR3 5JS · Tel 020 8650 7745 · Fax 020 8650 0768 · E-mail cbd@cbdresearch.com · www.cbdresearch.com

Centre for Population Sciences   (CPS)
- ■   School of Community Health Sciences, University of Nottingham, The Tower, University Park, Nottingham, NG7 2RD.
    0115-846 6901
    http://www.nottingham.ac.uk/cps/
    Director: Prof Mike Pringle.
- E   A research centre within the Institute of Clinical Research (qv) at the University of Nottingham.
- O   To become internationally renowned for thematic research using community populations or in community settings

Centre for Port and Maritime History   (CPMH)   1996
- ■   School of History, University of Liverpool, Liverpool, L69 3BX.
    0151-794 2413   fax 0141-794 2366
    http://www.liv.ac.uk/history/research/cpmh.htm
    Co-Director: Prof W R Lee. Co-Director: Adrian Jarvis.
- E   A research centre at the University of Liverpool.
- O   To conduct research and teaching in maritime history
Note: A joint venture with the National Museums Liverpool.

Centre for Post Qualifying Social Work   (PQSW)   2000
- ■   Bournemouth University, 4th Floor - Royal London House, Christchurch Road, Bournemouth, Dorset, BH1 3LT.
    01202 964765   fax 01202 964025
    http://www.bournemouth.ac.uk/ihcs/pqsw.html
    Head: Keith Brown.
- E   A research centre within the Institute of Health and Community Studies (qv) at Bournemouth University.

Centre for Postgraduate Studies and Research Ltd   2000
- ■   PO Box 443, Harpenden, Hertfordshire, AL5 4WW.
    01582 712161   fax 01582 712161
    http://www.studiesandresearch.com/
    Co-Director: Kate Thomas. Co-Director: Prof Stephen Palmer.
- E   A profit-making business.
- O   To promote effective forms of coaching, training and psychotherapy
- ●   Education and training

Centre for Power Transmission and Motion Control   (PTMC)   1968
- ■   Department of Mechanical Engineering, University of Bath, Claverton Down, Bath, BA2 7AY.
    01225 826371   fax 01225 826928
    http://www.bath.ac.uk/ptmc
- E   A department of the University of Bath.
- O   To conduct research, consultancy and teaching in all aspects of fluid power systems
- ●   Consultancy - Education and training

Centre for Practical Ethics
>   see **Oxford Uehiro Centre for Practical Ethics.**

Centre for Practice Development   (CPD)
- ■   Bournemouth University, Royal London House, Christchurch Road, Bournemouth, Dorset, BH1 3LT.
    01202 962210
    http://www.bournemouth.ac.uk/ihcs/
    Head: Clive Andrewes.
- E   A research centre within the Institute of Health and Community Studies (qv) at Bournemouth University.
- O   To conduct research into ways of enabling individuals and teams to develop better ways of working, by developing new
    approaches, bringing about a positive change, and improving the quality of life for residents, patients and carers

Centre for Practice as Research in the Arts   (CPaRA)
- ■   School of Arts and Media, University of Chester, Parkgate Road, Chester, CH1 4BJ.
    01244 511000   fax 01244 511300
    http://www.chester.ac.uk/cpra/
- E   A research centre at the University of Chester.

Centre for Practice-led Research in the Arts
- ■   University of Northampton, Boughton Green Road, Northampton, NN2 7AL.
    01604 735500
    http://www2.northampton.ac.uk/portal/page/portal/Arts/home/research/cplrinthearts
- E   A research centre at the University of Northampton.
- O   To develop new knowledge, understanding and insight in the arts

Centre for Precision Farming
>   see **Cranfield Centre for Precision Farming.**

Centre for Precision Technologies   (CPT)   1993
■   School of Computing and Engineering, University of Huddersfield, Queensgate, Huddersfield, HD1 3DH.
01484 472037
http://cpt.hud.ac.uk/
Director: Prof Liam Blunt.
E   A research centre at the University of Huddersfield.

Centre for Pregnancy Nutrition   1989
■   Department of Obstetrics and Gynaecology, University of Sheffield, The Jessop Wing, Tree Root Lane, Sheffield, S10 2SF.
0114-226 8544   fax 0114-226 8538
http://www.shef.ac.uk/pregnancy_nutrition/
Contact: Fiona Ford.
E   A department of the University of Sheffield.
O   To provide focus for continuing research programmes into nutritional physiology of human pregnancy; to maintain a database of nutritional interventions in pregnancy and lactation for information and advice purposes
●   Information service The Centre runs the 'Eating for Pregnancy' helpline - 0845 130 3646 / Mon-Fri 1000-1600, to answer enquiries from members of the public, the media, fellow scientists and health professionals

Centre for Primary Care   (CPC)
■   Faculty of Health and Sciences, Staffordshire University, Mellor Building, College Road, Stoke-on-Trent, ST4 2DF.
01782 294648   fax 01782 294986
http://www.staffs.ac.uk/schools/sciences/ihr/cpc/
E   A research centre within the Institute for Health Research (qv) at Staffordshire University.
O   To provide a vision and focus on integrated learning between various health settings within the NHS

Centre for Primary Health and Social Care
■   Department of Applied Social Sciences, London Metropolitan University, Ladbroke House, 62-66 Highbury Grove, London, N5 2AD.
020 7133 5098
http://www.londonmet.ac.uk/depts/dass/research/cphsc/
Head: Prof John Gabriel.
E   An interdisciplinary research centre at London Metropolitan University.
O   To provide a range of activities which support the development of best practice and outcomes in health and social care, in partnership with social services departments, NHS workforce development confederations, trusts and authorities

Centre for Primary Health Care Studies   (CPHCS)   1998
■   Warwick Medical School, University of Warwick, Coventry, CV4 7AL.
024 7657 2950   fax 024 7652 8375
http://www2.warwick.ac.uk/fac/med/research/hsri/primary_care/
Director: Prof Jeremy Dale.
E   A research centre within the Health Sciences Research Institute (qv) at the University of Warwick.
O   To focus research on self-management and patient-centred care, decision making, service modernisation and policy, and emergency care and rehabilitation

Centre for Printing and Coating
   see **Welsh Centre for Printing and Coating.**

Centre for Problem-Focused Training and Therapy
■   156 Westcombe Hill, London, SE3 7DH.
020 8293 4114   fax 020 8293 1441
O   To offer training and consultancy in problem-focused therapy techniques

Centre for Process Analytics and Control Technology   (CPACT)
NR   Faculty of Engineering, University of Strathclyde, Room 6-16 - Colville Building, 48 North Portland Street, Glasgow, G1 1XN.
0141-548 4836   fax 0141-548 4713
http://www.cpact.com/
Chairman: Dr Frank Cottee. Co-ordinator: Natalie Driscoll.
E   A research centre at the University of Strathclyde.
O   To provide research and advice to companies seeking information on process control, including analytical chemistry, process optimisation, chemometrics and actuation
Note: A collaborative venture with the Universities of Hull and Newcastle upon Tyne.

Centre for Process and Information Systems Engineering   (PRISE)
■   School of Engineering, University of Surrey, Guildford, Surrey, GU2 7XH.
01483 686573   fax 01483 686581
http://www.surrey.ac.uk/eng/research/prise/
Director: Prof Antonis C Kokossis.
E   A research centre at the University of Surrey.
O   To conduct research in the use of advanced computing and systems engineering technology for the systematic development of industrial processes

Centre for Process Integration   (CPI)   1984

- ■ School of Chemical Engineering and Analytical Sciences, PO Box 88, University of Manchester, Sackville Street, Manchester, M60 1QD.
     0161-200 4393   fax 0161-236 7439
     http://www.ceas.manchester.ac.uk/research/centres/centreforprocessintegration/
     Director: Prof Robin Smith.
- E A department of the University of Manchester.
- ○ To conduct environmental research and teaching at MSc and PhD levels
- ● Conference facilities - Exhibitions - Library - Teaching

Centre for Process Integration and Membrane Technology   (CPIMT)

- ■ School of Engineering, Robert Gordon University, Clarke Building, Schoolhill, Aberdeen, AB10 1FR.
     01224 262348   fax 01224 262444
     http://www.rgu.ac.uk/eng/cpi/
     Director: Edward Gobina.
- E A research centre at the Robert Gordon University.
- ○ To conduct research and teaching in various fields of engineering, including oil and gas engineering, electronic and electrical engineering, computer network management and design, mechanical engineering, engineering design, engineering for sustainability and the environment, electronic and communication engineering, mechanical and offshore engineering, artificial intelligence and robotics, and electronic and computer engineering

Centre for Process Systems Engineering   (CPSE)   1989

- NR Department of Chemical Engineering, South Kensington Campus, Imperial College London, Exhibition Road, London, SW7 2AZ.
     020 7594 5592
     http://www.ps.ic.ac.uk/
     Director: Prof Stratos Pistikopoulos.
- E An interdisciplinary research centre at Imperial College London.
- ○ To investigate and perform advanced research aimed at developing new approaches, methodologies and tools
- Note: A joint venture with University College London.

Centre for Professional Accounting and Financial Services   (CPA)

- ■ Manchester Metropolitan University Business School, Aytoun Building, Aytoun Street, Manchester, M1 3GH.
     0161-247 3789
     http://www.business.mmu.ac.uk/about/division.php?code=cpa
     Director: Prof Robert Sweeting.
- E A research centre within the Research Institute for Business and Management (qv) at Manchester Metropolitan University.
- ○ To work at the leading edge of research, opinion forming and teaching, of all aspects of applied professional accounting

Centre for Professional Development   (CPD)

- ■ Imperial College London, Room 212 - Mechanical Engineering Building, South Kensington Campus, London, SW7 2AZ.
     020 7594 6882; 6886   fax 020 7594 6883
     http://www.imperial.ac.uk/cpd/
     Director: Dr Mervyn Jones.
- E A centre at Imperial College London.
- ○ To present a diverse range of intensive short courses for professionals working in science, technology, medicine and management

Centre for Professional Development in Art and Design   (CPD)

- ■ Duncan of Jordanstone College of Art and Design, University of Dundee, Perth Road, Dundee, DD1 4HT.
     01382 385290
     http://www.dundee.ac.uk/djcad/cpd
- E A centre at the University of Dundee.
- ○ To conduct a comprehensive range of art and design courses

Centre for Professional Ethics   (PEAK)   2002

- ■ School of English, Keele University, Keele Hall, Keele, Staffordshire, ST5 5BG.
     01782 584297   fax 01782 584239
     http://www.keele.ac.uk/depts/pk/
     Director: Dr Jonathan Hughes.
- E A research centre at Keele University.
- ○ To be a leading centre for research, teaching and consultancy in the fields of applied and professional ethics

Centre for Professional Ethics   (CPE)   1993

- ■ University of Central Lancashire, Vernon Building, Preston, PR1 2HE.
     01772 892541   fax 01772 892942
     http://www.uclan.ac.uk/facs/health/ethics/
     Contact: Dr Doris Schroeder.
- E A centre at the University of Central Lancashire.
- ○ To study issues, relating to particular professions and themes common to all professions, in light of changing economic conditions
- ● Education and training - Various programmes in bioethics and philosophy

Centre for Professional Legal Studies (CPLS) 1986
- ■ The Law School, University of Strathclyde, Stenhouse Building, 173 Cathedral Street, Glasgow, G4 0RQ.
  http://www.law.strath.ac.uk/cpls/
- E A research centre at the University of Strathclyde.

Centre for Professional Management
   see **Ashley Centre for Professional Management.**

Centre for Professional and Organisation Development   (CPOD)
- ■ Faculty of Health and Well Being, Sheffield Hallam University, Collegiate Campus, Sheffield, S10 2BP.
  0114-225 5619   fax 0114-225 2430
  http://www.shu.ac.uk/research/cpod/
  Head: Iain Snelling.
- E A research centre at Sheffield Hallam University.
- ○ To play a full and active part in the modernisation of health and social care, supporting the development of managers of health and social services at all levels

Centre for Professionals Complementary to Dentistry
- ■ Barts and the London, Queen Mary's School of Medicine and Dentistry, Queen Mary, University of London, Turner Street, London, E1 2AD.
  020 7377 7611   fax 020 7377 7612
  http://www.smd.qmul.ac.uk/dental/cpcd/
  Lead: Prof Kevin Seymour.
- E A research centre within the Institute of Dentistry (qv) at Queen Mary, University of London.
- ○ To teach those people wishing to enter the dental healthcare profession to work alongside the dental surgeon, including dental nurses, dental hygienists and therapists, and dental technicians

Centre for Professions and Professional Work
Note: No longer in existence.

Centre for Project Management   (C4PM)
- ■ School of the Built Environment, Leeds Metropolitan University, The Northern Terrace - Queen Square Court, Civic Quarter, Leeds, LS1 3HE.
  0113-283 1999   fax 0113-283 1958
  http://www.leedsmet.ac.uk/c4pm/
  Head: Mike Bates.
- E A research centre at Leeds Metropolitan University.
- ○ To promote the profession of project management; to provide education, training, research and consultancy in all facets of generic project management

Centre for Promoting Learner Autonomy (CPLA) 2005
- ■ City Campus, Sheffield Hallam University, Sheffield, S1 1WB.
  0114-225 2979; 4735   fax 0114-225 4755
  http://www.shu.ac.uk/cetl/autonomy/
  Contact: Prof Anthony Rosie.
- E A Centre for Excellence in Teaching and Learning (CETL) at Sheffield Hallam University.
Note: See **Centres for Excellence in Teaching and Learning** for more information.

Centre for Property Law   2001
- ■ Aberdeen University School of Law, University of Aberdeen, Taylor Building, Aberdeen, AB24 3UB.
  01224 272442
  http://www.abdn.ac.uk/law/propcent.shtml
  Contact: David L Carey Miller.
- E A research centre at the University of Aberdeen.

Centre for Property Research   (CPR)
- ■ University of Aberdeen Business School, University of Aberdeen, Edward Wright Building, Dunbar Street, Aberdeen, AB24 3QY.
  01224 272167
  http://www.abdn.ac.uk/business/property.shtml
  Director: Prof Norman Hutchison.
- E A research centre at the University of Aberdeen.

Centre for Protein Engineering
   see **MRC Centre for Protein Engineering.**

Centre for Protein and Membrane Structure and Dynamics (CPMSD) 2000
- ■ School of Crystallography, Birkbeck, University of London, Malet Street, Bloomsbury, London, WC1E 7HX.
  020 7631 6800   fax 020 7631 6803
  http://www.srs.dl.ac.uk/VUV/CD/cpmsd.html
  Director: Prof Bonnie Wallace.
- E A centre at Birkbeck, University of London.

© CBD Research Ltd · Beckenham · Kent BR3 5JS · Tel 020 8650 7745 · Fax 020 8650 0768 · E-mail cbd@cbdresearch.com · www.cbdresearch.com

Centre for Proteins and Peptides

■ School of Biological and Molecular Sciences, Gipsy Lane Campus, Oxford Brookes University, Headington, Oxford, OX3 0BP.
01865 483255; 483294   fax 01865 483928
http://www.brookes.ac.uk/lifesci/protein_peptides.html!
Director: Prof Nigel Groome.
E A research centre at Oxford Brookes University.
O To conduct research into the development of assays for the quantitative analysis of inhibin and activin levels in human and animal research

Centre for Proteomics
see **Cambridge Centre for Proteomics.**

Centre for Psychiatry   (CfP)

■ Barts and the London, Queen Mary's School of Medicine and Dentistry, Queen Mary, University of London, Charterhouse Square, London, EC1M 6BQ.
020 7882 2021   fax 020 7882 5728
http://www.wolfson.qmul.ac.uk/psychiatry/
Director: Prof Stephen Stansfeld.
E A research centre within the Wolfson Institute of Preventive Medicine (qv) at Queen Mary, University of London.
O To provide undergraduate and postgraduate education and conduct research on epidemiological, social and environmental influences on mental health and wellbeing

Centre for Psychoanalysis   1993

■ School of Health and Social Sciences, Middlesex University, Queensway, Enfield, Middlesex, EN3 4SA.
http://www.mdx.ac.uk/www/issr/research/cen4psy/
Director: Prof Bernard Burgoyne.
E A centre at Middlesex University.
O To facilitate individual and collaborative research in psychoanalysis

Centre for Psychoanalytic Studies

■ University of Essex, Wivenhoe Park, Colchester, Essex, CO4 3SQ.
01206 873745   fax 01206 872746
http://www.essex.ac.uk/centres/psycho/
Director: Prof Karl Figlio.
E A department of the University of Essex.
O To promote the grounds of psychoanalytic knowledge including experiential components and clinically oriented teaching
● MA degrees
Note: The staff are practitioners as well as scholars, who share an interest in psychoanalytic thinking and methods, as well as in fields that can be enriched by psychoanalytic understanding and that, in turn, can enrich psychoananalysis itself.

Centre for Psychological Astrology   (CPA)   1983

■ BCM Box 1815, London, WC1N 3XX.
020 8749 2330   fax 020 8749 2330
http://www.cpalondon.com/
Administrator: Juliet Sharman-Burke.
E An independent organisation.
O To provide a workshop and professional training programme, designed to foster the cross-fertilisation of the fields of astrology and of depth, humanistic, and transpersonal psychology

Centre for Psychological Research in Human Behaviour

■ University of Derby, Kedleston Road, Derby, DE22 1GB.
01332 592223
http://ibs.derby.ac.uk/centre/
Contact: Dr Rebecca Knibb.
E A research centre at the University of Derby.
O To investigate the many theoretical and applied issues related to human behaviour and why people act the way they do

Centre for Psychology and Learning in Context   (CAP)

■ Graduate School of Education, University of Bristol, 35 Berkeley Square, Bristol, BS8 1JA.
0117-928 7073   fax 0117-925 5412
http://www.bristol.ac.uk/education/research/centres/cplic
Co-Ordinator: Sue Pickering

Centre for Psycho-Social Studies

■ Faculty of Humanities, Languages and Social Sciences, Frenchay Campus, University of the West of England, Coldharbour Lane, Bristol, BS16 1QY.
0117-328 2244; 2366   fax 0117-344 2295
http://www.uwe.ac.uk/hlss/research/cpss
Co-Director: Prof Paul Hoggett. Co-Director: Prof Simon Clarke.
E A research centre at the University of the West of England.
O To encompass a wide range of research interests and theoretical positions which have a common commitment to psychoanalytic and other non-rationalist understandings of the human subject

Centre for Psychosocial and Disability Research
>   see **UnumProvident Centre for Psychosocial and Disability Research.**

Centre for Psychosocial Studies   (CPS)   2000
■   School of Psychology, Birkbeck, University of London, Malet Street, Bloomsbury, London, WC1E 7HX.
>   020 7631 6535   fax 020 7631 6312
>   http://www.psyc.bbk.ac.uk/cps/
E   A centre at Birkbeck, University of London.
○   To conduct innovative, interdisciplinary research and teaching focused on the interweaving of psychological and social concerns

Centre for Public Communication Research   (CPCR)   2003
■   Bournemouth Media School, Bournemouth University, Weymouth House, Talbot Campus, Poole, Dorset, BH12 5BB.
>   01202 524111; 965360   fax 01202 965530
>   http://www.cpcr.org.uk/
>   Contact: Prof Barry Richards.
E   A centre at Bournemouth University.
○   To produce creative and rigorous research into public communication and the public sphere in the UK and abroad

Centre for Public Economics
Note: has closed

Centre for Public Engagement in Mental Health Sciences
>   see **Mental Health Knowledge Centre.**

Centre for Public and Environmental Health
>   see **Robens Centre for Public and Environmental Health.**

Centre for Public Health   (CPH)
■   Faculty of Health and Applied Social Sciences, Liverpool John Moores University, North Street, Liverpool, L3 2AY.
>   0151-231 4511   fax 0151-231 4515
>   http://www.cph.org.uk/
>   Director: Mark Bellis.
E   A research centre within Liverpool John Moores University.
○   To work in partnership with health services, local authorities, judicial bodies, environmental services and community groups to deliver health at local, regional, national and international level

Centre for Public Health Research   (CPHR)
■   Faculty of Health and Social Care, University of the West of England, Blackberry Hill, Stapleton, Bristol, BS16 1DD.
>   0117-328 8836
>   http://hsc.uwe.ac.uk/net/research/Default.aspx?pageid=24
>   Director: Judy Orme.
E   A research centre at the University of the West of England.
○   To encourage national improvements in public through alcohol and drugs research, arts and health research, children, young people and communities research, involving service users and communities research, and Primary care practice research

Centre for Public Health Research   (CPHR)
■   School of Applied and Health Sciences, University of Chester, Parkgate Road, Chester, CH1 4BJ.
>   01244 512029
>   http://www.chester.ac.uk/cphr/
>   Director: Prof Miranda N Thurston.
E   A research centre at the University of Chester.

Centre for Public Health Research   (CPHR)
■   Faculty of Health and Social Care, University of Salford, Allerton Building, Salford, Manchester, M6 6PU.
>   0161-295 2814
>   http://www.ihscr.salford.ac.uk/CPHR/
>   Director: Prof Deborah Baker.
E   A research centre within the Institute for Health and Social Care Research (qv) at the University of Salford.
○   To study the social and environmental determinants of health, with particular emphasis on the health of women, children and families
×   Institute of Public Health Research and Policy.

Centre for Public Health Research   (CPHR)   2005
■   Brunel University, 3rd floor, Mary Seacole Building, Kingston Lane, Uxbridge, Middlesex, UB8 3PH.
>   01895 274000
>   http://www.brunel.ac.uk/research/centres/cphr
E   A centre at Brunel University.
○   To identify and address local, national and global public health challenges

Centre for Public Law   (CPL)   1998

■   Faculty of Law, University of Cambridge, 10 West Road, Cambridge, CB3 9DZ.
   01223 330042   fax 01223 330055
   http://www.law.cam.ac.uk/centres/index.php#cpl
E   A research centre at the University of Cambridge.
O   To promote and conduct research into public law, with particular interest in the legal relationship between the UK and Europe

Centre for the Public Library and Information in Society   (CPLIS)

■   Department of Information Studies, University of Sheffield, Regent Court, 211 Portobello Street, Sheffield, S1 4DP.
   0114-222 2653
   http://cplis.shef.ac.uk/
   Director: Briony Train.
E   A research centre at the University of Sheffield.
O   To carry out research and consultancy for public library services, and for other information and advice agencies in the public and voluntary sectors
●   Consultancy

Centre for Public Policy   (CPP)   2002

■   School of Arts and Social Sciences, Northumbria University, Lipman Building, Newcastle upon Tyne, NE1 8ST.
   0191-243 7426   fax 0191-243 7434
   http://northumbria.ac.uk/sd/academic/sass/res_con/cpp_main/
   Director: Prof Lynn Dobbs. Research Manager: Jane Ashby.
E   A research centre at Northumbria University.
O   To focus research on public policy and governance issues

Centre for Public Policy and Health

■   School for Health, Queen's Campus, University of Durham, University Boulevard, Stockton on Tees, TS17 6BH.
   0191-334 0360   fax 0191-334 0361
   http://www.dur.ac.uk/public.health/
   Director: Prof D J Hunter.
E   A research centre within the Wolfson Research Institute (qv) at the University of Durham.

Centre for Public Policy and Management   (CPPM)

■   Aberdeen Business School, Robert Gordon University, Management Building, Garthdee Road, Aberdeen, AB10 7QE.
   01224 263111   fax 01224 263434
   http://www2.rgu.ac.uk/publicpolicy/cppm/
   Director: Prof Paul Spicker.
E   A research centre at the Robert Gordon University.
O   To undertake research and consultancy in Scottish and European public policy in the public, voluntary, non-profit and commercial fields

Centre for Public Policy and Management   (CPPM)

■   Caledonian Business School, Glasgow Caledonian University, Cowcaddens Road, Glasgow, G4 0BA.
   0141-331 3150
   http://www.gcal.ac.uk/cppm/
   Director: Prof Robert Pyper.
E   A research centre at Glasgow Caledonian University.
O   To advance research across the wide range of contemporary public policy and management issues

Centre for Public Policy and Management   (CPPM)   2004

■   Manchester Business School, University of Manchester, Booth Street West, Manchester, M15 6PB.
   0161-275 2908   fax 0161-273 5245
   http://www.mbs.ac.uk/research/publicpolicy/
E   A research centre at the University of Manchester.
O   To contribute to the advancement of public policy and to the management and leadership of public services and public organisations, through the generation and application of knowledge, skills and learning in research, education and development

Centre for Public Policy and Management   (CPPM)

■   School of Management, University of St Andrews, The Gateway, North Haugh, St Andrews, Fife, KY16 9SS.
   01334 462878   fax 01334 462812
   http://www.st-andrews.ac.uk/~cppm/
   Co-Director: Prof Huw Davies. Co-Director: Prof Sandra Nutley.
E   A research centre at the University of St Andrews.
O   To contribute to the intellectual and practical debates on public policy and management, through high quality research and scholarship

Centre for Public Policy for Regions   (CPPR)

NR   Department of Economics, Ivy Lodge, 63 Gibson Street, Glasgow, G12 8LR.
     0141-330 8563   fax 0141-330 1880
     http://www.cppr.ac.uk/
     Director: Prof Richard Harris.
E   A research centre at the University of Glasgow, run jointly with the University of Strathclyde (Sir William Duncan Building,
     130 Rottenrow, Glasgow, G4 0GE)
O   To look at the role of public policy in promoting economic and social development in Scotland and beyond
Note: A joint venture with the University of Strathclyde.

Centre for Public Policy Research   (CPPR)

■   School of Social Science and Public Policy, King's College London, 138-142 Strand, London, WC2R 1HH.
     020 7848 3138; 3151
     http://www.kcl.ac.uk/schools/sspp/education/research/groups/cppr/
     Contact: Alan Cribb. Contact: Sharon Gewirtz.
E   A research centre at King's College, London.
O   To use research to inform public policy debate, with particular research foci on public sector restructuring, professional change and
     professional development, professional values and ethics, and equality and social justice

Centre for Public Scrutiny   (CfPS)   2003

■   Laydon House, 76-86 Turnmill Street, London, EC1M 5LG.
     020 7296 6451
     http://www.cfps.org.uk/
     Executive Director: Jessica Crowe.
E   An independent centre.
O   To promote the value of scrutiny in modern and effective Government

Centre for Public Services

Note: The work of this Centre is being continued by the European Services Strategy Unit of Northumbria University, which is outside the
     scope of this directory.

Centre for Public Services Management   (CPSM)   2003

■   Teesside Business School, University of Teesside, Middlesbrough, TS1 3BA.
     01642 342871; 342910
     http://www.tees.ac.uk/schools/tbs/copum/COPUM_index.cfm
     Director: Dr Michael Macaulay.
E   A research centre at the University of Teesside.
O   To conduct research and teaching in public services management

Centre for Public Services Management (Nottingham)   (PSM)

■   Nottingham Business School, Nottingham Trent University, Burton Street, Nottingham, NG1 4BU.
     0115-848 2432
     http://www.ntu.ac.uk/nbs/spec/psu/7371gp.html
E   A centre at Nottingham Trent University.
O   To provide courses in public services management

Centre for Public Services Organisations   (CPSO)   2003

■   School of Management, Royal Holloway, University of London, Egham, Surrey, TW20 0EX.
     01784 443780   fax 01784 276100
     http://www.rhul.ac.uk/management/Research/public.html
     Director: Prof Ewan Ferlie.
E   A research centre at Royal Holloway, University of London.
O   To further rigorous and relevant research into organisational and managerial issues in contemporary public services organisations,
     in particular focusing on the core themes of organisational change, organisational learning, and decision-making

Centre for Public Theology
     see **Manchester Centre for Public Theology.**

Centre for Publishing
     see **UCL Centre for Publishing.**

Centre for Publishing Studies   (PS)   1982

■   Department of English Studies, University of Stirling, Stirling, FK9 4LA.
     01786 467510   fax 01786 466210
     http://www.pubstd.stir.ac.uk/
     Director: Andrew Wheatcroft.
E   A research centre at the University of Stirling.
O   To conduct research in contemporary publishing worldwide, with particular emphasis on Modernist and contemporary, Scottish
     literature and identity, Commonwealth and post-colonial, Early modern studies, Critical theory, and Romantic, Victorian and
     Gothic literature

Centre for Qualitative Research (CQR)

■ Bournemouth University, Royal London House, Christchurch Road, Bournemouth, Dorset, BH1 3LT.
  01202 962763   fax 01202 962194
  http://www.bournemouth.ac.uk/ihcs/rescqr.html
  Co-Director: Prof Immy Holloway. Co-Director: Prof Les Todres.
E A research centre within the Institute of Health and Community Studies (qv) at Bournemouth University.
○ To conduct research into ways of improving the everyday lives of health and social care users

Centre for Quality in the Global Supply Chain (CQGSC)

■ Nottingham University Business School, Jubilee Campus, University of Nottingham, Wollaton Road, Nottingham, NG8 1BB.
  0115-951 4023   fax 0115-951 3800
  http://www.nottingham.ac.uk/cqgsc/
  Contact: Dr James Tannock.
E A research centre at the University of Nottingham.
○ To conduct research on the issues associated with quality and its management

Centre for Quality, Innovation and Support (CQIS) 2006

■ Manchester Metropolitan University, 799 Wilmslow Road, Didsbury, Manchester, M20 2RR.
  0161-247 5081
  http://www.ioe.mmu.ac.uk/cqis/
  Director: Ray Moorcroft.
E A research centre within the Institute of Education (qv) at Manchester Metropolitan University.
○ To provide administrative support for the Institute of Education

Centre for Quantitative Finance (CQF)

■ Tanaka Business School, Imperial College London, London, SW7 2AZ.
  020 7594 9166   fax 020 7581 8809
  http://www3.imperial.ac.uk/tanaka/research/quantitativefinance
  Director: Prof Nicos Christofides.
E A research centre at Imperial College London.
○ To conduct research and teaching on different aspects of pricing contingent claims, risk management and other financial modelling problems

Centre for Quantitative Finance [Oxford]
  see **Nomura Centre for Quantitative Finance.**

Centre for Quantum Computation (CQC)

■ Department of Applied Mathematics and Theoretical Physics, University of Cambridge, Wilberforce Road, Cambridge, CB3 0WA.
  01223 760394   fax 01223 765900
  http://cam.qubit.org/
  Contact: Mrs Kaija Hampson.
E A research centre at the University of Cambridge.
○ To conduct theoretical and experimental research into all aspects of quantum information processing, and into the implications of the quantum theory of computation for physics itself

Centre for Quantum Computation (CQC)

■ Department of Physics, Clarendon Laboratory, University of Oxford, Parks Road, Oxford, OX1 3PU.
  http://www.qubit.org/
E A centre at the University of Oxford.
○ To conduct theoretical and experimental research into all aspects of quantum information processing, and into the implications of the quantum theory of computation for physics itself

Centre for Quaternary Research (CQR) 1990

■ Department of Geography, Royal Holloway University, Egham, Surrey, TW20 0EX.
  01784 443563   fax 01784 472836
  http://www.gg.rhul.ac.uk/cqr/
  Director: Prof Jim Rose.
E A research centre at Royal Holloway, University of London.
○ To investigate a wide range of problems relevant to the understanding of late Pleistocene dynamics in the North Atlantic region and its hinterland, the Mediterranean, central Asia and the Canadian Arctic

Centre for Quebec Studies   Centre d'études québécoises

■ University of Leicester, Attenborough Tower, University Road, Leicester, LE1 7QH.
  0116-252 2694   fax 0116-252 3633
  http://www.le.ac.uk/ml/quebec/coord.html
E A research centre at the University of Leicester.

Centre for Radiation, Chemical and Environmental Hazards
  see **Health Protection Agency Centre for Radiation, Chemical and Environmental Hazards.**

Centre for Radiochemistry Research   (CRR)   1999
- School of Chemistry, University of Manchester, Oxford Road, Manchester, M13 9PL.
  0161-306 9260   fax 0161-275 4598
  http://www.dalton.manchester.ac.uk/research/areas/radiochemistry/
  Director: Prof Francis Livens.
- E   A research centre at the University of Manchester.
- O   To conduct research in all aspects of the nuclear fuel cycle, including fundamental research relevant to process chemistry, waste management and reducing environmental impact

Centre for Rail Human Factors   (CRHF)
- School of Mechanical Materials and Manufacturing Engineering, University of Nottingham, University Park, Nottingham, NG7 2RD.
  0115-951 4040   fax 0115-846 6771
  http://www.virart.nottingham.ac.uk/railhf.htm
- E   A research centre within the Institute for Occupational Ergonomics (qv) at the University of Nottingham.
- O   To be a focus for research and consultancy into ergonomics and human factors of all aspects of rail transport

Centre for Railway Research
> see **Newcastle Centre for Railway Research.**

Centre for Rational Design of Molecular Diagnostics
> see **Wolfson Centre for Rational Design of Molecular Diagnostics.**

Centre for Rational-Emotive Behaviour Therapy   1990
- 156 Westcombe Hill, London, SE3 7DH.
  020 8293 4114   fax 020 8293 1441
  Director: Dr Stephen Palmer. Associate Director: Michael Neenan.
- E   A profit-making business.
- O   To promote rational-emotive behaviour therapy (REBT) and counselling; to promote the use of REBT in industry to reduce stress and increase performance
- ●   Courses in REBT and counselling - Education and training - Information service

Centre for Reading and Language   (CRL)
- Department of Psychology, University of Reading, Heslington, York, YO10 5DD.
  01904 434366   fax 01904 433181
  http://www.york.ac.uk/res/crl/
  Secretary: Sally Stephenson.
- E   A research centre at the University of York.
- O   To conduct high-quality research into the nature and causes of reading and language difficulties

Centre for Real Estate Research   (CRER)   2002
- University of Reading Business School, HUMSS Building, PO Box 218, University of Reading, Reading, Berkshire, RG6 6AA.
  0118-378 8226
  http://www.reading.ac.uk/crer/
  Director: Prof Peter Byrne.
- E   A research centre at the University of Reading.
- O   To conduct pure and applied research in real estate investment, finance, appraisal and management

Centre for Recovery Research
> see **Raymond Williams Centre for Recovery Research.**

Centre for Recovery in Severe Psychosis   (CRiSP)
- King's College London, Henry Wellcome Building, DeCrespigny Park, London, SE5 8AF.
  020 7848 0430   fax 020 7848 5006
  http://www.iop.kcl.ac.uk/departments/?locator=433
  Business Co-ordinator: Elizabeth R Hutt.
- E   A research centre within the Institute of Psychiatry (qv) at King's College, London.
- O   To conduct research in cognitive remediation therapy (CRT) to help people improve their thinking skills

Centre for Reformation and Early Modern Studies   (CREMS)   2004
- School of Historical Studies, University of Birmingham, Arts Building, Edgbaston, Birmingham, B15 2TT.
  http://www.crems.bham.ac.uk/
  Contact: Dr Alec Ryrie.
- E   A centre at the University of Birmingham.
- O   To support research into the history of the Reformation and early modern Britain and Europe from c1450-1750

Centre for Regenerative Medicine   (CRM)
- Department of Biology and Biochemistry, University of Bath, Claverton Down, Bath, BA2 7AY.
  01225 386597   fax 01225 386779
  http://www.bath.ac.uk/crm/
  Director: Prof J Slack.
- E   A research centre at the University of Bath.
- O   To bring together groups working on developmental biology, stem cell biology and tissue engineering

Centre for Regional Business Productivity   (CRBP)
- Kent Business School, University of Kent, Canterbury, Kent, CT2 7PE.
  01227 827726   fax 01227 761187
  http://www.kent.ac.uk/kbs/crbp/
  Contact: M W Gilman.
- E   A research centre at the University of Kent.
- O   To develop world-class research delivering understanding of efficiency and productivity improvement to academia, business and social partners

Centre for Regional Economic Development   (CRED)   1996
- Cumbria Business School, University of Central Lancashire, Paternoster Row, Carlisle, Cumbria, CA3 8TB.
  01772 895240   fax 01772 895295
  http://www.uclan.ac.uk/carlisle/cred/
  Director: Prof Frank Peck.
- E   A centre at the University of Central Lancashire.
- O   To conduct academic and commercial research around the broad theme of economic development

Centre for Regional Economic and Social Research   (CRESR)   1990
- City Campus, Sheffield Hallam University, Howard Street, Sheffield, S1 1WB.
  0114-225 3073   fax 0114-225 2197
  http://www.shu.ac.uk/research/cresr/
  Director: Prof Ian Cole.
- E   A research centre at Sheffield Hallam University.
- O   To deliver high quality and cost-effective research, advisory and consultancy services in the fields of social, urban and housing policy

Centre for Regional History
   see **Manchester Centre for Regional History.**

Centre for Regional and Local Historical Research   (CRLHR)   1995
- School of Arts and Media, University of Teesside, Middlesbrough, TS1 3BA.
  01642 384019
  http://www.tees.ac.uk/schools/sam/research.cfm
  Contact: Dr Diane Newton.
- E   A research centre at the University of Teesside.
- O   To conduct research on the history of England's North Eastern counties, and on the history of regions and localities

Centre for Regional Public Finance   (CRPF)   2000
- Department of Accountancy and Finance, University of Aberdeen, Edward Wright Building, Dunbar Street, Aberdeen, AB24 3QY.
  01224 272213
  http://www.abdn.ac.uk/crpf/
  Director: Prof David Heald.
- E   A centre at the University of Aberdeen.
- O   To promote research on the public finances of the newly devolved Scotland

Centre for Regulation and Competition   (CRC)   2000
- School of Environment and Development, University of Manchester, Harold Hankins Building, Booth Street West, Manchester, M13 9QH.
  0161-275 0410; 2798   fax 0161-275 0808
  http://www.competition-regulation.org.uk/
  Director: Prof Paul Cook.
- E   A research centre within the Institute for Development Policy and Management (qv) at the University of Manchester.
- O   To conduct research into rules-based systems and processes, of regulation and competition, in developing countries and their contribution to poverty reduction

Centre for Regulatory Governance   (CeReGo)   2005
- Department of Politics, University of Exeter, Amory Building, Rennes Drive, Exeter, EX4 4RJ.
  01392 263164   fax 01392 263164
  http://www.huss.ex.ac.uk/politics/research/crg/
  Head: Dr Tim Dunne.
- E   A research centre at the University of Exeter.
- O   To specialise in the analysis of regulatory policy - the rules and institutions that govern markets and the public sector

Centre for Rehabilitation Engineering   (CRE)
- Department of Mechanical Engineering, University of Glasgow, James Watt (South) Building, Glasgow, G12 8QQ.
  0141-330 2528; 4340
  http://fesnet.eng.gla.ac.uk/CRE/
  Director: Prof Ken Hunt.
- E   A research centre at the University of Glasgow.
- O   To carry out basic and applied research into spinal cord injury rehabilitation, and on the control of functional electrical stimulation (FES) and its application to function restoration and exercise therapy

Centre for Rehabilitation and Human Performance Research (CRHPR)

- ■ Faculty of Health and Social Care, University of Salford, Brian Blatchford Building, Salford, Manchester, M6 6PU.
  0161-295 2275   fax 0161-295 2268
  http://www.hscr.salford.ac.uk/CRHPR/
  Director: Prof David Howard.
- E A research centre within the Institute for Health and Social Care Research (qv) at the University of Salford.
- O To undertake leading edge and basic clinical research into human movement, its disorders and rehabilitation

Centre for Rehabilitation Research

- ■ Jordanstown campus, University of Ulster, Shore Road, Newtownabbey, Co. Antrim, BT37 0QB.
  http://www.science.ulster.ac.uk/hrsri/facilities.html
- E A centre within the Health and Rehabilitation Sciences Research Institute (qv) at the University of Ulster.

Centre for Rehabilitation Robotics

- ■ Faculty of Arts, Media and Design, University of Staffordshire, Mellor Building, College Road, Stoke-on-Trent, ST4 2DF.
  01782 294556
  http://www.staffs.ac.uk/research/institutes/ari.php
- E A research centre within the Advanced Research Institute (qv) at Staffordshire University.
- O To produce innovative design and development of robotic devices for severely disabled persons

Centre for Rehabilitation Sciences (TCRS)

- ■ School of Health and Social Care, University of Teesside, Centuria Building, Middlesbrough, TS1 3BA.
  01642 854324
  http://www.tees.ac.uk/schools/SOH/rehab.cfm
  Director: Prof Keith Rome.
- E A research centre within the Institute for Health Sciences and Social Care Research (qv) at the University of Teesside.
- O To focus research on increasing the evidence base for rehabilitation

Centre for Religion and the Biosciences (CRB)

- ■ School of Humanities, University of Chester, Parkgate Road, Chester, CH1 4BJ.
  01244 511036
  http://www.chester.ac.uk/crb/
  Director: Celia Deane-Drummond.
- E A research centre at the University of Chester.

Centre for Religion and Political Culture (CRPC)

- ■ School of Arts, Histories and Cultures, University of Manchester, Oxford Road, Manchester, M13 9PL.
  0161-306 1240
  http://www.arts.manchester.ac.uk/crpc/
  Director: Prof Graham Ward.
- E A research centre at the University of Manchester.
- O To assess and examine the relationship between religion and political life in the contemporary world

Centre for Religious Education
  see **Welsh National Centre for Religious Education.**

Centre for Remote Sensing and Environmental Monitoring (CRSEM)

- ■ School of Engineering and Physical Science, University of Dundee, Dundee, DD1 4HN.
  01382 345446
  http://www.dundee.ac.uk/crsem/
  Director: Dr Robin Vaughan.
- E A centre at the University of Dundee.
- O To understand and model the physical processes involved in the acquisition of remote sensing data

Centre for Renaissance and Early Modern Studies (CREMS) 2005

- ■ Department of Humanities, Social Sciences and Law, Queen Mary, University of London, Mile End Road, London, E1 4NS.
  020 7882 5555   fax 020 7882 5556
  http://www.qmul.ac.uk/renaissance/
  Director: Prof Kevin Sharpe.
- E A department of Queen Mary, University of London.
- O To consider how new scholarship and new interdisciplinary methods and approaches have refigured understanding of developments traditionally associated with the term and period of the Renaissance

Centre for Renaissance and Early Modern Studies (CREMS)

- ■ University of York, Heslington, York, YO10 5DD.
  01904 433592
  http://www.york.ac.uk/crems/
  Co-Director: Prof William Sherman. Co-Director: Prof David Wootton.
- E An interdisciplinary research centre at the University of York.
- O To further study and research in the period 1500-1700

Centre for Renaissance Studies   (CRS)
- Department of History, University of Hull, Cottingham Road, Hull, HU6 7RX.
  01482 346311
  http://www.hull.ac.uk/history/research/researchunits.htm
E   A research centre at the University of Hull.

Centre for Renewable Energy
  see **Durham Centre for Renewable Energy.**

Centre for Renewable Energy Systems Technology   (CREST)   1993
- Department of Electronic and Electrical Engineering, Loughborough University, Ashby Road, Loughborough, Leicestershire, LE11 3TU.
  01509 227087   fax 01509 227118
  http://www.lboro.ac.uk/departments/el/research/power-crest.html
  Director: Prof David Infield. Contact: Julie Allen.
E   A research centre at Loughborough University.
O   To advance renewable energy technology so as to provide substantial and benign energy options for present and future generations

Centre for Reproduction and Early Life   (CREL)
- Medical School, University of Nottingham, Queen's Medical Centre, Nottingham, NG7 2UH.
  0115-951 5151 ext 30611
  http://www.nottingham.ac.uk/crel/
  Director: Prof Michael Symonds.
E   A research centre within the Institute of Clinical Research (qv) at the University of Nottingham.

Centre for Reputation Management through People   (CRMP)
- School of Business and Management, West Quadrangle, University of Glasgow, Glasgow, G12 8QQ.
  0141-330 5993   fax 0141-330 5669
  http://www.gla.ac.uk/centres/crmp/
  Director: Prof Graeme Martin.
E   A centre at the University of Glasgow.
O   To help Scottish-based organisations create a virtuous circle linking highly engaged and talented people with enhanced external and internal reputations and superior organisational performance

Centre for Research in Accounting, Accountability and Governance   (CRAAG)
- School of Management, University of Southampton, Highfield, Southampton, SO17 1BJ.
  023 8059 3067
  http://www.management.soton.ac.uk/research/centre-for-accounting-accountability-and-governance.php
  Director: Prof Andrew Goddard.
E   A research centre at the University of Southampton.
O   To conduct and encourage high quality research into the relationship between accounting, accountability and governance

Centre for Research on Ageing
  see **UCL Centre for Research on Ageing.**

Centre for Research on Ageing and Gender   (CRAG)   2000
- Department of Sociology, University of Surrey, Guildford, Surrey, GU2 7XH.
  01483 683964   fax 01483 689551
  http://www.crag.surrey.ac.uk/
  Co-Director: Kate Davidson. Co-Director: Sara Arber.
E   A research centre at the University of Surrey.
O   To focus research on the interconnections between gender and ageing

Centre for Research into Alcohol, Alcoholism and Drug Addiction
  see **Sussex Centre for Research into Alcohol, Alcoholism and Drug Addiction.**

Centre for Research in Allied Health Professions   (CeRAHP)   1998
- Faculty of Health and Social Care, London South Bank University, 103 Borough Road, London, SE1 0AA.
  020 7815 8463   fax 020 7815 8490
  http://www.lsbu.ac.uk/health/cerahp1.shtml
  Director: Mary Lovegrove. Administrator: Cheryl Pinder.
E   A research centre at London South Bank University.
O   To conduct research into the organisation and delivery of health services involving allied health professionals

Centre for Research and Analysis of Migration   (CReAM)
- Department of Economics, University College London, Drayton House, 30 Gordon Street, London, WC1H 0AX.
  020 7679 5888   fax 020 7916 2775
  http://www.econ.ucl.ac.uk/cream/
  Contact: Anne Usher.
E   A research centre at University College London.

Centre for Research in Analytical, Materials and Sensor Science   (CRAMSS)

■   Faculty of Applied Sciences, Frenchay Campus, University of the West of England, Coldharbour Lane, Bristol, BS16 1QY.
      0117-328 3815   fax 0117-328 2904
      http://science.uwe.ac.uk/research/homePage.aspx?pageId=cramssHome
      Director: Prof John Duffield.
E   A research centre at the University of the West of England.
O   To conduct research in the applications of sensors for the agri-food, environmental and biomedical sectors

Centre for Research in Applied Linguistics   (CRAL)

■   School of English Studies, University of Nottingham, University Park, Nottingham, NG7 2RD.
      0115-951 5899   fax 0115-951 5924
      http://www.nottingham.ac.uk/english/research/cral/doku.php
      Contact: Norbert Schmitt.
E   An interdisciplinary research centre at the University of Nottingham.
O   To conduct research in the understanding of language as it is acquired and used in the real world, both in monolingual and bilingual contexts

Centre for Research Architecture   (CRA)

■   Visual Cultures Department, Goldsmiths, University of London, New Cross, London, SE14 6NW.
      020 7919 7498   fax 020 7919 7398
      http://www.goldsmiths.ac.uk/architecture/
      Director: Eyal Weizman.
E   A research centre at Goldsmiths, University of London.

Centre for Research in the Arts, Social Sciences, and the Humanities   (CRASSH)   2001

■   17 Mill Lane, Cambridge, CB2 1RX.
      01223 766886   fax 01223 765276
      http://www.crassh.cam.ac.uk/
      Director: Prof Mary Jacobus.
E   A centre at the University of Cambridge.

Centre for Research in Beliefs, Rights and Values in Education   (BRaVE)

■   School of Education, University of Roehampton, Erasmus House, Roehampton Lane, London, SW15 5PU.
      020 8392 3000; 3374
      http://www.roehampton.ac.uk/researchcentres/brave/
      Director: Prof Ron Best. Administrator: Caroline Freeland.
E   A research centre at Roehampton University.
O   To conduct research in beliefs, rights and values in education, with particular emphasis on religious education, pastoral care and citizenship education

Centre for Research in Biomedicine   (CRiB)

■   School of Biomedical Sciences, Frenchay Campus, University of the West of England, Coldharbour Lane, Bristol, BS16 1QY.
      0117-328 2147   fax 0117-328 2904
      http://science.uwe.ac.uk/research/homePage.aspx?pageId=cribHome
      Director: Prof Neil Avent.
E   A research centre at the University of the West of England.
O   To conduct research in biomedical sciences, in particular the cellular processes in disease

Centre for Research in Brand Marketing

■   Birmingham Business School, University of Birmingham, Edgbaston, Birmingham, B15 2TT.
      0121-414 2299   fax 0121-414 7791
      http://www.crbm.bham.ac.uk
      Director: Prof Leslie de Chernatony.
E   A centre at the University of Birmingham.
O   To bring together people who share an interest in understanding how to grow brands

Centre for Research in Business, Economics and Management   (CeRAeBEM)   2001

■   Business School, Staffordshire University, College Road, Stoke-on-Trent, ST4 2DE.
      01782 294000; 294083
      http://www.staffs.ac.uk/schools/business/webpages/research/mainresearch.html
      Contact: Dr Peter Reynolds.
E   A research centre at Staffordshire University.

© CBD Research Ltd · Beckenham · Kent BR3 5JS · Tel 020 8650 7745 · Fax 020 8650 0768 · E-mail cbd@cbdresearch.com · www.cbdresearch.com

Centre for Research on the Child and Family   (CRCF)   1996

■   School of Social Work and Psychosocial Sciences, University of East Anglia, Elizabeth Fry Building, Norwich, NR4 7TJ.
01603 592068   fax 01603 593552
http://www.uea.ac.uk/swk/research/centre/welcome.htm
Co-Director: Prof Margaret O'Brien. Co-Director: Dr Gillian Schofield.
E   A department of the University of East Anglia.
O   To work in collaboration with or on behalf of welfare agencies in the statutory, voluntary and private sectors in the UK and overseas; to contribute to and disseminate knowledge which will enhance the well-being of children in adversity and their families; to seek funding to allow members to undertake research which will contribute to the development of knowledge of children and families in adversity, and of services which may enhance their well-being
●   Education and training - Commissioned research, developing new research methodologies, provision of training and advice on research matters and dissemination of research findings to academic colleagues, parents, children and their carers

Centre for Research into Childhood   (CRinCH)   2006

■   Carnegie Faculty of Sport and Education, Leeds Metropolitan University, Room 216 - Cavendish Hall, Headingley Campus, Leeds, LS6 3QS.
0113-283 2600   fax 0113-283 6171
http://www.leedsmet.ac.uk/carnegie/9583.htm
Director: Prof Pat Broadhead.
E   A research centre within the Carnegie Research Institute (qv) at Leeds Metropolitan University.
O   To undertake and disseminate research that demonstrates a commitment to children's rights, child-centred approaches and social justice for children

Centre for Research in Cognition, Emotion and Interaction   (CRICEI)   2001

■   School of Human and Life Sciences, Whitelands College, University of Roehampton, Holybourne Avenue, London, SW15 4JD.
020 8392 3500   fax 020 8392 3531
http://www.roehampton.ac.uk/researchcentres/cricei/
Director: Dr Joe Levy.
E   An interdisciplinary research centre at Roehampton University.
O   To foster collaboration in the intersections between cognition, emotion and social interaction

Centre for Research in Cognitive Science   (COGS)   2003

■   School of Science and Technology, University of Sussex, Falmer, Brighton, East Sussex, BN1 9RE.
01273 678581
http://www.sussex.ac.uk/cogs/
Director: Dr Ron Chrisley.
E   A research centre at the University of Sussex.
O   To foster collaboration among those working in cognitive science, including researchers in artificial intelligence, psychology, linguistics, neuroscience, and philosophy

Centre for Research on Communication and Language   (CRCL)

■   Department of English Studies, University of Stirling, Stirling, FK9 4LA.
01786 467041
http://www.crcl.stir.ac.uk/
E   A research centre at the University of Stirling.
O   To specialise in English language teaching and the intercultural curriculum, and communication in health care relationships

Centre for Research into Communications and Subjectivity

Note: is the Communications and Subjectivity Research Group of London Metropolitan University, and therefore not eligible for this directory.

Centre for Research in Computer Science

■   School of Computing and Mathematical Sciences, Maritime Greenwich Campus, University of Greenwich, Park Row, London, SE10 9LS.
020 8331 8503   fax 020 8331 8665
http://www.cms.gre.ac.uk/research/centres/computerscience.asp
E   A research centre at the University of Greenwich.
O   To specialise in the application of software engineering and artificial intelligence techniques to real life industrial and commercial problems

Centre for Research in Computing   (CRC)

■   Open University, Walton Hall, Milton Keynes, MK7 6AA.
0870 333 4340
http://crc.open.ac.uk/
E   An interdisciplinary research centre at the Open University.
O   To undertake distinctive, leading edge research in software and processes that underpin knowledge management, communication, learning and interactions among humans and machines

Centre for Research in Corporate Governance   (CRCG)

■   Cass Business School, City Business School, 106 Bunhill Row, London, EC1Y 8TZ.
020 7040 8738
http://www.cass.city.ac.uk/crcg/
E   A research centre at City University.

Centre for Research into Creation in the Performing Arts   (ResCen)   1999
- School of Arts, Middlesex University, Trent Park, Bramley Road, London, N14 4YZ.
  020 8411 6288
  http://www.mdx.ac.uk/rescen/
  Director: Prof Christopher Bannerman.
- E   A centre at Middlesex University.
- O   To provide a supportive resource for artists and their work
- ● Seminars

Centre for Research into the Delivery of Legal Services
- School of Law, University of Westminster, 4-12 Little Titchfield Street, London, W1W 7UW.
  020 7911 5000   fax 020 7911 5821
  http://www.wmin.ac.uk/law/page-496
- E   A research centre at the University of Westminster.

Centre for Research and Development   (CRD)
- Faculty of Arts and Architecture, University of Brighton, Mithras House, Lewes Road, Brighton, East Sussex, BN2 4AT.
  01273 600900
  http://www.brighton.ac.uk/arts/research/
- E   A centre at the University of Brighton.

Centre for Research and Development in Adult and Lifelong Learning   (CRADALL)   2006
- Department of Adult and Continuing Education, University of Glasgow, St Andrew's Building, 11 Eldon Street, Glasgow, G3 6NH.
  0141-330 1833   fax 0141-330 1821
  http://www.gla.ac.uk/centres/cradall/
  Director: Prof Julia Preece.
- E   A centre at the University of Glasgow.
- O   To be an international research facility for the study of adult education and lifelong learning for social justice, social inclusion and reduction of poverty

Centre for Research and Development in Catholic Education   (CRDCE)
- School of Curriculum, Pedagogy and Assessment, University of London, 20 Bedford Way, London, WC1H 0AL.
  020 7612 6000; 6889
  http://ioewebserver.ioe.ac.uk/ioe/cms/get.asp?cid=5604&5604_0=5606
  Director: Prof Gerald Grace.
- E   A research centre within the Institute of Education (qv) at the University of London.
- O   To engage in research and publication related to the distinctive history, ethos, curricula, school leadership and school effectiveness of Catholic education, nationally and internationally

Centre for Research in Development, Instruction and Training
see **ESRC Centre for Research in Economic Development and International Trade.**

Centre for Research and Development in Religious Education
see **Keswick Hall Centre for Research and Development in Religious Education.**

Centre for Research in Distributed Technologies   (CREDIT)
- Luton Campus, University of Bedfordshire, Luton, Bedfordshire, LU1 3JU.
  01582 489230   fax 01582 489212
  http://www.beds.ac.uk/research/irac/credit
  Director: Prof Gordon Clapworthy.
- E   A research centre within the Institute for Research in Applicable Computing (qv) at the University of Bedfordshire.
- O   To focus research on secure services, communications and networks, and distributed processing

Centre for Research on Drugs and Health Behaviour   (CRDHB)   1990
- London School of Hygiene and Tropical Medicine, University of London, Keppel Street, London, WC1E 7HT.
  020 7636 8636
  http://www.lshtm.ac.uk/crdhb/
- E   A research centre at the London School of Hygiene and Tropical Medicine, University of London.

Centre for Research in East Roman Studies   (CRERS)
- Faculty of Arts, University of Warwick, Coventry, CV4 7AL.
  024 7652 3023   fax 024 7652 4973
  http://www2.warwick.ac.uk/study/postgraduate/courses/researchcentres/crers/
  Director: Prof S Swain, MA, DPhil Oxf.
- E   A research centre at the University of Warwick.
- O   To encourage and co-ordinate research in the history, archaeology, literature, religion, economy and palaeo-ecology of the eastern Roman Empire

Centre for Research into Ecological and Environmental Modelling   (CREEM)   1993
- ■   University of St Andrews, The Observatory, Buchanan Gardens, St Andrews, Fife, KY16 9LZ.
     01334 461842   fax 01334 461800
     http://www.creem.st-and.ac.uk/
     Director: Prof John Harwood.
- E   An interdisciplinary research centre at the University of St Andrews.
- O   To develop and apply advanced mathematical and statistical methods to practical problems in biology, ecology and geography

Centre for Research in Ecology and the Environment   (CREE)
- ■   School of Human and Life Sciences, Whitelands College, University of Roehampton, Holybourne Avenue, London, SW15 4JD.
     020 8392 3500   fax 020 8392 3531
     http://www.roehampton.ac.uk/researchcentres/cree/
     Director: Dr Peter Shaw.
- E   A research centre at Roehampton University.
- O   To act as a supplier of ecological and environmental expertise in the fields of academic research and applied consultancy work

Centre for Research into Economics and Finance in Southern Africa   (CREFSA)   1990
- ■   LSE, St Philips Building, Houghton Street, London, WC2A 2AE.
     020 7955 7280   fax 020 7955 6954
     http://www.lse.ac.uk/Depts/CREFSA/
     Director: Dr Jonathan Leape.
- E   A research centre at the London School of Economics and Political Science.
- O   To conduct independent research into the determinants of cross-border capital flows and their implications for macroeconomic policy in Southern Africa, the structure and development of the financial system and the framework for financial regulation in the region, and prospects for regional integration in Eastern and Southern Africa

Centre for Research in Education   (CRE)
- ■   Department of Education and Lifelong Learning, City University, Northampton Square, London, EC1V 0HB.
     020 7040 8315   fax 020 7040 8256
     http://www.city.ac.uk/cre/
     Contact: Prof Yvonne Hillier.
- E   A centre at City University.
- O   To promote research in post-compulsory education, particularly focusing on education policy, teaching and learning in higher education and professional education

Centre for Research and Education in Art and Media   (CREAM)
- ■   School of Media, Arts and Design, University of Westminster, Watford Road, Northwick Park, Harrow, Middlesex, HA1 3TP.
     020 7911 5903; 5944   fax 020 7911 5943
     http://www.wmin.ac.uk/mad/page-569
     Director: Rosie Thomas.
- E   A research centre at the University of Westminster.
- O   To conduct research in the media, arts and cultures across the subject areas of film, photography, digital arts, visual arts and ceramics

Centre for Research in Education and Democracy   (CRED)   2004
- ■   Faculty of Education, Frenchay Campus, University of the West of England, Coldharbour Lane, Bristol, BS16 1QY.
     0117-328 4226
     http://edu.uwe.ac.uk/cred/
     Director: Prof Saville Kushner.
- E   A research centre at the University of the West of England.
- O   To explore the inter-relationship of education and democracy

Centre for Research in Education and Educational Technology   (CREET)   2003
- ■   Faculty of Education and Language Studies, Open University, Walton Hall, Milton Keynes, MK7 6AA.
     0870 333 4340
     http://creet.open.ac.uk/
- E   An interdisciplinary research centre at the Open University.
- O   To pursue educational research of the highest quality, with the aims of informing educational practice, improving modern learning technology, and influencing international conceptualisations of educational processes, policies and practices

Centre for Research in Education and the Environment   (CREE)
- ■   Department of Education, University of Bath, Claverton Down, Bath, BA2 7AY.
     01225 386648   fax 01225 386113
     http://www.bath.ac.uk/cree/
- E   A centre at the University of Bath.
- O   To focus on educational issues relating to the environment and sustainability

Centre for Research and Education on Gender
>   see **Centre for Equality and Human Rights in Education.**

Centre for Research in Education Inclusion and Diversity   (CREID)

- Moray House School of Education, University of Edinburgh, Holyrood Road, Edinburgh, EH8 8AQ.
  0131-651 6459
  http://www.creid.ed.ac.uk/

E   A research centre at the University of Edinburgh.

Centre for Research in Education Policy and Professionalism   (CeREPP)   2005

- School of Education, University of Roehampton, Erasmus House, Roehampton Lane, London, SW15 5PU.
  020 8392 3000
  http://www.roehampton.ac.uk/researchcentres/cerepp/
  Director: Prof Christine Skelton.

E   A research centre at Roehampton University.
O   To advance, encourage and conduct research in a wide range of topics which fall within education policy and professionalism

Centre for Research, Education and Training in Energy   (CREATE)   1988

- PO Box 561, Standish, Wigan, WN1 9DU.
  01257 422800
  http://www.create.org.uk/

E   A not-for-profit organisation.
O   To work with communities and organisations to reduce the effect of climate change and build a sustainable future

Centre for Research in Electronic Art and Communication   (CREAC)

- School of Art and Design, University of Hertfordshire, College Lane, Hatfield, Hertfordshire, AL10 9AB.
  01707 284000   fax 01707 284115
  http://www.herts.ac.uk/artdes1/research/creac/
  Co-ordinator: Malcolm Ferris.

E   A research centre within the Social Sciences, Arts and Humanities Research Institute (qv) at the University of Hertfordshire.
O   To foster connections across the cognate fields of fine art, design, theory and technology

Centre for Research on Emerging Economies   (CREE)   2005

- Staffordshire University, Mellor Building, College Road, Stoke-on-Trent, ST4 2DF.
  01782 294110
  http://www.staffs.ac.uk/schools/sciences/geography/links/IESR/CREE.html

E   A research centre within the Institute for Environment and Sustainability Research (qv) at Staffordshire University.
O   To focus research and consultancy activities in emerging market economies, particularly in Central and South-Eastern Europe

Centre for Research in Emotion Work   (CREW)

- Brunel Business School, Brunel University, Uxbridge, Middlesex, UB8 3PH.
  01895 265298   fax 01895 203191
  http://www.brunel.ac.uk/about/acad/bbs/research/centres/crew/
  Director: Dr Nelarine Cornelius.

E   A centre at Brunel University.
O   To study, manage and practice emotion work, ie work that transforms the emotional state of others

Centre for Research in Employment Studies   (CRES)   1995

- Business School, De Havilland Campus, University of Herfordshire, College Lane, Hatfield, Hertfordshire, AL10 9AB.
  01707 284800   fax 01707 284870
  http://perseus.herts.ac.uk/prospectus/faculty_bs/uhbs/research/cres/cres_home.cfm
  Director: Prof Gregor Gall.

E   A research centre within the Social Sciences, Arts and Humanities Research Institute (qv) at the University of Hertfordshire.
O   To provide a focus for the study of employment issues from a critical, analytical and multidisciplinary standpoint

Centre for Research in Energy and the Environment   (CRE+E

- School of Engineering, Robert Gordon University, Clarke Building, Schoolhill, Aberdeen, AB10 1FR.
  01224 262380   fax 01224 262222
  http://www.rgu.ac.uk/cree/
  Director: Prof Peter Robertson.

E   A research centre at the Robert Gordon University.
O   To deliver research expertise in renewable energy, advanced water and air treatment technology, environmental sensing and environmental catalysis

Centre for Research in Energy, Waste and the Environment

- Cardiff School of Engineering, PO Box 925, Cardiff University, Newport Road, Cardiff, CF24 0YF.
  029 2087 4280
  http://www.engin.cf.ac.uk/research/group.asp?GroupNo=39
  Leader: Prof N Syred.

E   An integrated research centre within the Institute of Sustainability, Energy and Environmental Management (qv) at Cardiff University.
O   To carry out research on a wide range of problems relating to energy, electricity generation, solid, liquid and gaseous pollutants

Centre for Research in English Language Learning and Assessment   (CRELLA)   2005
- ■   Luton Business School, University of Bedfordshire, Putteridge Bury, Hitchin Road, Luton, Bedfordshire, LU2 8LE.
     01582 489303
     http://www.beds.ac.uk/research/bmri/crella
     Director: Prof Cyril Weir.
- E   A research centre within the Business and Management Research Institute (qv) at the University of Bedfordshire.
- O   To focus research on various aspects of language test validity
- ●   Education and training - Various courses

Centre for Research into the English Literature and Language of Wales   (CREW)   Canolfan Ymchwil ï Lên ac Iaith Saesneg Cymru
- ■   Department of English, Swansea University, Singleton Park, Swansea, SA2 8PP.
     01792 295926   fax 01792 295761
     http://www.swan.ac.uk/english/crew/
     Director: Prof M Wynn Thomas.
- E   A research centre within the Centre for Translation Research and Multilingualism (qv) at Swansea University.
- ●   David Parry Archive - Specialist Library

Centre for Research in English and Local History   (CRELH)
- ■   School of Arts, Digby Stuart College, University of Roehampton, Roehampton Lane, London, SW15 5PH.
     020 8392 3249
     http://www.roehampton.ac.uk/researchcentres/crelh/
     Director: Prof Margaret Spufford.
- E   A research centre at Roehampton University.
- ●   Hearth Tax Project

Centre for Research into Environment and Health   (CREH)
- NR   University of Wales, Aberystwyth, Llandinam Building, Aberystwyth, Ceredigion, SY23 2DB.
     01970 622634   fax 01970 622634
     http://www.grenville10.freeserve.co.uk/
     Director: Prof David Kay.
- E   A research centre within the Institute of Geography and Earth Sciences (qv) at the University of Wales, Aberystwyth.
- O   To further the improvement of the environment and health by research and education
- Note: One of the 5 CREH offices - see other CREH entries below.

Centre for Research into Environment and Health   (CREH)
- NR   Cardiff University, 10 Grenville Road, Pen-Y-Lan, Cardiff, CF23 5BP.
     029 2048 9067   fax 029 2048 9067
     http://www.grenville10.freeserve.co.uk/
     Contact: Tony Smith.
- E   A research centre at the Cardiff University.
- Note: One of the 5 CREH offices - see CREH Aberystwyth for full details.

Centre for Research into Environment and Health
- NR   5 Quakers Coppice, Crewe Gates Farm, Crewe, Cheshire, CW1 6FA.
     01270 250583   fax 01270 589761
     http://www.grenville10.freeserve.co.uk/
     Contact: Dr Lorna Fewtrell.
- Note: One of the 5 CREH offices - see CREH Aberystwyth for full details.

Centre for Research into Environment and Health   (CREH)   Canolfan Ymchwili'r Amgylchedd ac Iechyd
- NR   University of Wales, Lampeter, College Street, Lampeter, Ceredigion, SA48 7ED.
     01570 423565   fax 01570 423565
     http://www.grenville10.freeserve.co.uk/
     Contact: Dr Mark Wyer.
- E   A research centre at the University of Wales, Lampeter.
- Note: One of the 5 CREH offices - see CREH Aberystwyth for full details.

Centre for Research into Environment and Health
- NR   Hoyland House, 50 Back Lane, Leeds, LS18 4RS.
     0113-281 9849   fax 0113-281 9850
     http://www.grenville10.freeserve.co.uk/
     Technical Director: John Watkins. Contact: Miss Carol Francis.
- E   An analytical research centre.
- Note: One of the 5 CREH offices - see CREH Aberystwyth for full details.

Centre for Research in Environmental Appraisal and Management   (CREAM)
- ■   School of Architecture, Planning and Landscape, University of Newcastle upon Tyne, Newcastle upon Tyne, NE1 7RU.
     0191-222 7807   fax 0191-222 8811
     http://www.ncl.ac.uk/cream/
     Director: Ken Willis.
- E   A research centre at the University of Newcastle upon Tyne.
- O   To provide a sound scientific framework in research on the economic analysis of environmental issues, regulations and policies

Centre for Research in Environmental History
    see **AHRC Research Centre for Environmental History.**

Centre for Research in Environmental Sciences   (CRES)
■   Department of Environmental Sciences, Frenchay Campus, University of the West of England, Coldharbour Lane, Bristol,
    BS16 1QY.
        0117-328 3692   fax 0117-328 2132
        http://science.uwe.ac.uk/research/homePage.aspx?pageId=cresHome
        Contact: Prof James Longhurst.
E   A research centre at the University of the West of England.
O   To promote research into the environment, the damaging effects of pollution and how to remedy this damage

Centre for Research in Equality and Diversity   (CRED)   2002
■   School of Business and Management, Queen Mary, University of London, Mile End Road, London, E1 4NS.
        020 7882 3167   fax 020 7882 3615
        http://www.busman.qmul.ac.uk/research/research-equality-diversity.htm
        Director: Prof Geraldine M Healy.
E   A research centre at Queen Mary, University of London.
O   To conduct research on equality and diversity, both nationally and internationally

Centre for Research into Equity and Diversity in Education   (CREDE)
■   School of Education, Jubilee Campus, University of Nottingham, Wollaton Road, Nottingham, NG8 1BB.
        0115-846 7248   fax 0115-846 6188
        http://www.nottingham.ac.uk/education/centres/crede/index.phtml?enu=crede&sub=crede
        Director: Prof Patricia Thomson.
E   A research centre at the University of Nottingham.
O   To focus research on the everyday lives of those children, young people and adults who are marginalised by educational, social
        and political institutions

Centre for Research on Equity and Impact in Education
■   Department of Educational Studies, Alcuin College, University of York, Heslington, York, YO10 5DD.
        01904 433455
        http://www.york.ac.uk/depts/educ/equity/
        Contact: Prof Stephen Gorard.
E   A research centre at the University of York.
O   To conduct research that assesses, understands and improves both equity and impact in education throughout the lifecourse

Centre for Research in Ethnic Minority Entrepreneurship   (CREME)
■   Leicester Business School, De Montfort University, Innovation Centre, 49 Oxford Street, Leicester, LE1 5XY.
        0116-207 8923; 8926   fax 0116-207 8924
        http://www.creme-dmu.org.uk/
        Director: Prof Monder Ram.
E   A centre at De Montfort University.
O   To provide an international centre of excellence for research and practice on issues related to ethnic minority entrepreneurship

Centre for Research in Ethnic Relations   (CRER)   1970
■   Faculty of Social Studies, University of Warwick, Coventry, CV4 7AL.
        024 7652 4869   fax 024 7652 4324
        http://www2.warwick.ac.uk/study/postgraduate/courses/researchcentres/crer/
        Director: Prof Daniéle Jolly.
E   A department of the University of Warwick.
O   To increase knowledge, promote better understanding and influence other agencies and bodies concerned with racism, migration
        and ethnic relations
●   Conference facilities - Education and training - Exhibitions - Information service - Library - Statistics

Centre for Research on European Financial Markets and Institutions   (CREFMI)
■   Cass Business School, City University, 106 Bunhill Row, London, EC1Y 8TZ.
        020 7040 8738   fax 020 7040 8881
        http://www.cass.city.ac.uk/crefmi/
        Director: Dr Alistair Milne.
E   A research centre at City University.
O   To analyse the efficiency, safety and global competitiveness of Europe's financial services industry, and the sustainability of the
        UK's leading position in many aspects of financial services

Centre for Research in European Studies   (CREST)   1997
■   School of Political, Social and International Studies, University of East Anglia, Norwich, NR4 7TJ.
        01603 456161   fax 01603 458553
        http://www.uea.ac.uk/psi/Crest/
        Director: Dr Vassiliki Koutrakou.
E   A centre at the University of East Anglia.
O   To promote research in contemporary European affairs

Centre for Research and Evaluation   (CRE)
- ■   City Campus, Sheffield Hallam University, Howard Street, Sheffield, S1 1WB.
   0114-225 4973   fax 0114-225 5186
   http://www.shu.ac.uk/research/cre/
   Director: Prof Lee Harvey.
- E   A research centre at Sheffield Hallam University.
- O   To undertake a wide variety of educational and public sector research and evaluation in any area of the public sector, including gerontology and health, education, employability, satisfaction, and community and citizenship

Centre for Research in Evolutionary Anthropology   (CREA)   2002
- ■   School of Human and Life Sciences, Whitelands College, University of Roehampton, Holybourne Avenue, London, SW15 4JD.
   020 8392 3500   fax 020 8392 3531
   http://www.roehampton.ac.uk/researchcentres/crea
   Director: Prof Ann MacLarnon.
- E   A research centre at Roehampton University.
- O   To conduct research in evolutionary aspects of biological anthropology in the fields of primatology, socioecology, life history strategies, communication, cognition, welfare, reproductive endocrinology, comparative morphology, and crop raiding behaviour

Centre for Research Excellence in Religion and Theology   (CRERT)   2004
- ■   St Martin's College, Bowerham Road, Lancaster, LA1 3JD.
   01524 384384   fax 01524 384385
   http://www.ucsm.ac.uk/research/religion/
- E   A research centre at St Martin's College.

Centre for Research in Experimental Finance
   see **Aston Centre for Research in Experimental Finance.**

Centre for Research on Families and Relationships   (CRFR)
- ■   University of Edinburgh, 23 Buccleuch Place, Edinburgh, EH8 9LN.
   0131-651 1832
   http://www.crfr.ac.uk/
   Centre Manager: Vivien Smith.
- E   A research centre at the University of Edinburgh.
- O   To generate high quality research on families and relationships

Centre for Research in Film and Audiovisual Cultures   (CRFAC)
- ■   School of Humanities and Cultural Studies, University of Roehampton, Roehampton Lane, London, SW15 5PU.
   020 8392 3249; 3513   fax 020 8392 3687
   http://www.crfac.org/
   Director: Dr Paul McDonald.
- E   A research centre at Roehampton University.
- O   To advance critical, historical and analytic research relating to film and other audiovisual media

Centre for Research into Film Studies
- ■   Department of Film Studies, University of Exeter, Queen's Building, The Queen's Drive, Exeter, EX4 4QH.
   01392 264306; 264342
   http://www.sml.ex.ac.uk/languages/content/view/743/403/
   Director: Prof Susan Hayward.
- E   A centre at the University of Exeter.

Centre for Research in Finance and Accounting   (CRiFA)   2005
- ■   Business School, De Havilland Campus, University of Hertfordshire, College Lane, Hatfield, Hertfordshire, AL10 9AB.
   01707 284800   fax 01707 284870
   http://perseus.herts.ac.uk/uhinfo/prospectus/faculty_bs/uhbs/research/centre-for-research-in-finance-and-accounting/
   Director: Prof Colin Haslam.
- E   A research centre within the Social Sciences, Arts and Humanities Research Institute (qv) at the University of Hertfordshire.
- O   To consolidate a critical research agenda in areas covering financial markets and intermediation, financial reporting and governance, management control in the private and public sector, business analysis, and corporate performance

Centre for Research in Fire and Explosion Studies   (CRFES)   1994
- ■   Department of Built Environment, University of Central Lancashire, Preston, PR1 2HE.
   01772 893222   fax 01772 892216
   http://www.uclan.ac.uk/facs/destech/builtenv/firecentre
   Director: Prof Georgy Makhviladze.
- E   A research centre at the University of Central Lancashire.
- O   To conduct state-of-the-art research in combustion, explosion and fluid dynamics of reacting media, linking together with applications to safety engineering, technological and environmental problems

Centre for Research into Freemasonry   2001

- ■ University of Sheffield, 34 Gell Street, Sheffield, S3 7QW.
  0114-222 9890   fax 0114-222 9894
  http://www.freemasonry.dept.shef.ac.uk/
  Director: Prof D G Shepherd.
- E A research centre within the Humanities Research Institute (qv) at the University of Sheffield.
- O To undertake and promote objective scholarly research into the historical, social and cultural impact of freemasonry, particularly in Britain

Centre for Research into Gender in Culture and Society   (GENCAS)   2003

- ■ Department of English, Swansea University, Singleton Park, Swansea, SA2 8PP.
  01792 295926
  http://www.swan.ac.uk/english/gender
  Director: Dr Sarah Gamble.
- E An interdisciplinary research centre at Swansea University.
- O To conduct research in various fields, including classic and medieval culture, women's writing, masculinities, gender and sexuality, and representations of gender in art, the media and film

Centre for Research in Genetics and Society
   see **Cardiff Centre for Research in Genetics and Society.**

Centre for Research on Globalization and Economic Policy
   see **Leverhulme Centre for Research on Globalization and Economic Policy.**

Centre for Research in Health Behaviour   1991

- ■ Department of Psychology, Keynes College, University of Kent, Canterbury, Kent, CT2 7NP.
  01227 823082   fax 01227 827032
  http://www.kent.ac.uk/psychology/department/research-groups/crhb
  Director: Prof Derek Rutter.
- E A research centre at the University of Kent.
- O To conduct basic theoretical research into the effects of psychological processes on health, with particular emphasis on the psychobiological mechanisms involved in physical illness

Centre for Research in Health and Medicine   (CRHaM)

- ■ School of Social Sciences and Cultural Studies, University of Sussex, Arts C, Falmer, Brighton, East Sussex, BN1 9SJ.
  01273 678612
  http://www.sussex.ac.uk/soccul/1-3-1.html
  Co-Director: Prof Charles Abraham. Co-Director: Prof John Abraham.
- E An interdisciplinary research centre at the University of Sussex.
- O To investigate health-related behaviour, patient-professional interactions in health care, medicines policy, the social determinants of health, and general health issues

Centre for Research in Health and Social Care   (CRHSC)   2001

- ■ Department of Advanced Practice and Research, Anglia Ruskin University, East Road, Cambridge, CB1 1PT.
  0845 271 3333
  http://www.anglia.ac.uk/ruskin/en/home/faculties/ihsc/departments/practice_research/crhsc.html
  Director: Prof Diane DeBell.
- E A research centre at Anglia Ruskin University.

Centre for Research in Health and Social Issues
   see **Crichton Centre for Research in Health and Social Issues.**

Centre for Research into Higher Education   (CRHE)

- ■ University of Glasgow, Glasgow, G12 8QQ.
  0141-330 4997
  http://www.gla.ac.uk/crhe/
  Co-ordinator: Erica McAteer.
- E A centre at the University of Glasgow.

Centre for Research in the History of Art
   see **Sussex Centre for Research in the History of Art.**

Centre for Research in Human Rights   (CRHR)

- ■ School of Business and Social Sciences, Southlands College, University of Roehampton, 80 Roehampton Lane, London, SW15 5SL.
  020 8392 3227
- E A research centre at Roehampton University.

© CBD Research Ltd · Beckenham · Kent BR3 5JS · Tel 020 8650 7745 · Fax 020 8650 0768 · E-mail cbd@cbdresearch.com · www.cbdresearch.com

Centre for Research and Implementation of Clinical Practice   (CRICP)

■ Faculty of Health and Human Sciences, Thames Valley University, Westel House, 32-38 Uxbridge Road, London, W5 2BS.
http://cricp.org/
E A research centre at Thames Valley University.
○ To implement research evidence into clinical practice

Centre for Research on Indoor Climate and Health   (RICH)   2003

■ School of Engineering, Science and Design, Glasgow Caledonian University, Cowcaddens Road, Glasgow, G4 0BA.
0141-331 8849
http://www.gcal.ac.uk/rich/
Director: Chris Sanders. Contact: Denise Smith.
E A research centre at Glasgow Caledonian University.
○ To focus research on the factors that determine the indoor environment (primarily in buildings but also including transportation) and the consequent effect on the health of the occupants

Centre for Research into Industry, Enterprise, Finance and the Firm   (CRIEFF)   1991

■ School of Economics and Finance, St Salvator's College, University of St Andrews, St Andrews, Fife, KY16 9AL.
01334 462438   fax 01334 462444
http://www.st-andrews.ac.uk/crieff/CRIEFF.html
Director: Prof Gavin C Reid.
E A research centre at the University of St Andrews.
○ To foster rigorous research in industrial economics, with a commitment to applying advanced theoretical, quantitative and qualitative methods to contemporary problems of industrial organisation; and taking explicit account of the relevant institutional framework

Centre for Research on Inequality, Human Security and Ethnicity   (CRISE)

■ Department of International Development, University of Oxford, Queen Elizabeth House, Mansfield Road, Oxford, OX1 3TB.
01865 281810   fax 01865 281801
http://www.crise.ox.ac.uk/
Director: Frances Stewart.
E A centre at the University of Oxford.
○ To investigate relationships between ethnicity, inequality and conflict, with the aim of identifying economic, political, social and cultural policies which promote stable and inclusive multi-ethnic societies

Centre for Research in Infant Behaviour   (CRIB)

■ School of Social Sciences and Law, Brunel University, Uxbridge, Middlesex, UB8 3PH.
01895 274000
http://www.brunel.ac.uk/about/acad/sssl/ssslresearch/centres/research
E A research centre at Brunel University.

Centre for Research in Information Management

Note: No longer in existence.

Centre for Research and Innovation
see **Salford Centre for Research and Innovation.**

Centre for Research on Innovation and Competition
see **ESRC Centre for Research on Innovation and Competition.**

Centre for Research, Innovation and Graduate Studies

Note: is now the Research, Business and Innovation department of the University of the West of England and is therefore outside the scope of this directory.

Centre for Research in Innovation Management   (CENTRIM)   1987

■ Faculty of Management and Information Sciences, University of Brighton, The Freeman Centre, Falmer, Brighton, East Sussex, BN1 9PH.
01273 877980
http://www.centrim.bus.brighton.ac.uk/
Director: Prof Howard Bush.
E A centre at the University of Brighton.
○ To help improve the understanding and management of innovation for firms trying to develop and introduce new products, organisations implementing changes, and governments and other bodies trying to create a supportive and enabling environment in which innovation can flourish

Centre for Research in Institutional Economics   (CRIE)   1999

■ Business School, De Havilland Campus, University of Hertfordshire, College Lane, Hatfield, Hertfordshire, AL10 9AB.
01707 284800   fax 01707 284870
http://perseus.herts.ac.uk/prospectus/faculty_bs/uhbs/research/crie/crie_home.cfm
Research Leader: Prof Geoff Hodgson.
E A research centre within the Social Sciences, Arts and Humanities Research Institute (qv) at the University of Hertfordshire.
○ To develop cutting-edge research on the theoretical frontiers of institutional economics

Centre for Research into Interactive Learning   (CRIL)   1992
- Department of Psychology, University of Strathclyde, 40 George Street, Glasgow, G1 1QE.
  0141-548 2582   fax 0141-552 6948
  http://www.psych.strath.ac.uk/research/centre-for-research-into-interactive-learning/
  Director: Dr Andrew Tolmie.
- E   A research centre at the University of Strathclyde.

Centre for Research in Ion Beam Applications
   see **Surrey Ion Beam Centre.**

Centre for Research in Knowledge Science and Society   (KNOSSOS)
- Herschel Building, University of Newcastle, Newcastle upon Tyne, NE1 7RU.
  0191-222 7302; 7379   fax 0191-222 7361
  http://www.phil.ncl.ac.uk/
  Director: Prof Milan Jaros. Secretary: Julie Coomber.
- E   A research centre at the University of Newcastle upon Tyne.

Centre for Research and Knowledge Transfer   (CRKT)
- Melbury House (4th floor), 1-3 Oxford Road, Bournemouth University, Bournemouth, Dorset, BH8 8ES.
  01202 961200
  http://www.bournemouth.ac.uk/CRKT.html
- E   A centre at Bournemouth University.
- O   To serve as a focal point for mutually beneficial partnerships in setting the agenda for economic development throughout South West England

Centre for Research on Language and Education
   see **CLIO Centre for Research on Language and Education.**

Centre for Research in Language Education   (CRILE)   1989
- Department of Linguistics and Modern English Language, Lancaster University, Lancaster, LA1 4YT.
  01524 594641   fax 01524 843085
  http://www.ling.lancs.ac.uk/groups/crile/
- E   A research centre at Lancaster University.

Centre for Research on Leather and Materials Science   (CROLMS)   2004
- School of Applied Sciences, Park Campus, University of Northampton, Boughton Green Road, Northampton, NN2 7AL.
  01604 735500
  http://www.northampton.ac.uk/research/centres/
  Contact: Prof Geoff Attenburrow.
- E   A research centre at the University of Northampton.
- O   To maintain and build an applied science research group devoted to the area of leather and materials science
- ● Information service

Centre for Research in Library and Information Management   (CERLIM)   1993
- Department of Information and Communications, Manchester Metropolitan University, Geoffrey Manton Building, Rosamond Street West, Manchester, M15 6LL.
  0161-247 6142   fax 0161-247 6979
  http://www.cerlim.ac.uk/
  Director: Prof Peter Brophy.
- E   A research centre at Manchester Metropolitan University.
- O   To conduct a wide range of research in the field of library and information management, with particular emphasis on technological and social issues such as community cultural development, distributed delivery of library and information services, accessibility and usability of information, and quality management techniques and performance measurement

Centre for Research in Lifelong Learning   (CRLL)   1999
- NR   Glasgow Caledonian University, Floor 2 - 6 Rose Street, Glasgow, G3 6RN.
  0141-273 1347   fax 0141-273 1318
  http://crll.gcal.ac.uk/
  Co-Director: Prof Jim Gallacher. Co-Director: Prof Mike Osborne.
- E   A research centre at Glasgow Caledonian University.
- O   To engage in a range of research and related activities to inform policy and provision in the field of lifelong learning in the post-compulsory sector in Scotland and beyond

Note: A joint venture with the University of Stirling.

Centre for Research into the Management of Expatriation   (CReME)   1999
- Cranfield School of Management, Cranfield University, Cranfield, Bedfordshire, MK43 0AL.
  01234 751122   fax 01234 751806
  http://www.som.cranfield.ac.uk/som/research/centres/creme/
  Contact: Dr Michael Dickmann.
- E   A research centre within the Cranfield Management Research Institute (qv) at Cranfield University.
- O   To conduct innovative, rigorous and relevant research into international Human Resources Management, management of global assignments and intercultural management

Centre for Research in Marketing   (CRM)
■   School of Management and Business, University of Wales Aberystwyth, Cledwyn Building, Aberystwyth, Ceredigion, SY23 2DD.
      01970 622202   fax 01970 622409
      http://www.aber.ac.uk/smba/en/research/crm/crm.shtml
      Director: Prof Nicholas Alexander.
E   A research centre at the University of Wales, Aberystwyth.
○   To co-ordinate and conduct research in marketing

Centre for Research in Marketing   (CREAM)   2005
■   Brunel Business School, Brunel University, Elliot Jaques Building, Uxbridge, Middlesex, UB8 3PH.
      01895 265859   fax 01895 269775
      http://www.brunel.ac.uk/about/acad/bbs/research/centres/crim
      Director: Professor TC Melewar.
E   A research centre at Brunel University.
○   To develop, promote and facilitate research on various aspects of marketing.

Centre for Research in Marketing   (CERMARK)
■   Department of Business and Service Sector Management, London Metropolitan University, 84 Moorgate, London, EC2M 6SQ.
      020 7320 1577   fax 020 7320 1465
      http://www.londonmet.ac.uk/depts/bssm/research/cermark/
      Director: Prof Roger Bennett.
E   A research centre at London Metropolitan University.
○   To conduct research in the marketing communications of charitable organisations, museums, art galleries and theatres, and Western firms operating in Eastern Europe

Centre for Research in Marketing   (CRM)
■   Westminster Business School, University of Westminster, 35 Marylebone Road, London, NW1 5LS.
      020 7911 5000
      http://www.wmin.ac.uk/wbs/page-56
E   A research centre at the University of Westminster.

Centre for Research in Marketing   (CRM)   1990
■   Faculty of Business, Law and the Built Environment, University of Salford, Salford, Manchester, M5 4WT.
      0161-295 2247   fax 0161-295 5022
      http://www.mams.salford.ac.uk/CRM
      Director: Dr Tony Conway.
E   A research centre within the Management and Management Sciences Research Institute (qv) at the University of Salford.
○   To provide a forum for researchers; to provide a mechanism for the dissemination of research findings through seminars and workshops; to promote greater integration in the marketing field between academics and industry
✕   North West Centre for European Marketing.

Centre for Research in Marketing [South Bank]
      see **Ehrenberg Centre for Research in Marketing.**

Centre for Research in Media and Cultural Studies
■   School of Arts, Design, Media and Culture, University of Sunderland, The Media Centre, St Peter's Way, Sunderland, Tyne and Wear, SR6 0DD.
      0191-515 3231   fax 0191-515 3807
      http://www.solutions.sunderland.ac.uk/page.asp?id=99
E   A research centre at the University of Sunderland.
○   To promote excellence in research across the whole range of academic activities which characterise media and cultural studies

Centre for Research in Medical and Dental Education   (CRMDE)
■   School of Education, University of Birmingham, Edgbaston, Birmingham, B15 2TT.
      0121-414 3422   fax 0121-414 4865
      http://www.education.bham.ac.uk/research/crmde/
      Contact: Liz Potts.
E   A research centre at the University of Birmingham.

Centre for Research in Medical Sociology and Health Policy   (CRMSHP)   1997
■   School of Sociology and Social Policy, University of Nottingham, University Park, Nottingham, NG7 2RD.
      0115-951 5239   fax 0115-951 5232
      http://www.nottingham.ac.uk/sociology/
      Director: Dr Ian Shaw.
E   A research centre at the University of Nottingham.
○   To focus research on the lay concepts of health and illness, mental health and primary care

Centre for Research in Midwifery and Childbirth   (CeMaC)   2003
- Faculty of Health and Human Sciences, Royal Berkshire Hospital, London Road, Reading, Berkshire, RG1 5AN.
  0118-987 7647
    http://www.health.tvu.ac.uk/mid/research/index.asp
- E A research centre at Thames Valley University.
- O To develop, synthesise and facilitate translation of evidence, from all relevant sources, to inform midwifery practice and education in order to enhance care for women, their babies and families before, during and after birth

Centre for Research in Modern European Philosophy   (CRMEP)   1994
- School of Arts, Middlesex University, Trent Park, Bramley Road, London, N14 4YZ.
  http://www.mdx.ac.uk/www/crmep/
- E A centre at Middlesex University.
- O To focus on research and teaching in the field of post-Kantian European philosophy

Centre for Research on Nationalism, Ethnicity and Multiculturalism   (CRONEM)
- NR School of Arts, Communication and Humanities, University of Surrey, Austin Pearce Building, Guildford, Surrey, GU2 7XH.
  01483 686200   fax 01483 686201
    http://www.surrey.ac.uk/Arts/CRONEM/
  Executive Director: Prof John Eade. Administrator: Mirela Dumic.
- E A research centre at the University of Surrey.
- O To focus on crucial developments within contemporary society in the fields of nationalism, ethnicity and multiculturalism
Note: A joint venture with Roehampton University.

Centre for Research in Nursing and Midwifery Education   (CRNME)   1998
- University of Surrey, Duke of Kent Building, Guildford, Surrey, GU2 7XH.
  01483 683120   fax 01483 686711
    http://www.portal.surrey.ac.uk/eihms/research/specgroup/crnme/
  Director: Prof Pam Smith.
- E An interdisciplinary research centre within the European Institute of Health and Medical Sciences (qv) at the University of Surrey.
- O To conduct research into nursing and midwifery education

Centre for Research in Opera and Music Theatre   (CROMT)   2004
- Department of Music, University of Sussex, Arts B 159, Falmer, Brighton, East Sussex, BN1 9SJ.
  01273 678693
    http://www.sussex.ac.uk/cromt/
  Director: Dr Nicholas Till.
- E A research centre at the University of Sussex.
- O To conduct research and development in the practice and theory of contemporary opera, music-based theatre and other forms of musical multi-media performance

Centre for Research in Pain Management
   see **Pain Management Research Centre.**

Centre for Research in Performance
   see **Pinter Centre for Research in Performance.**

Centre for Research in Philosophy and Literature   (CRPL)
- Faculty of Social Studies, University of Warwick, Coventry, CV4 7AL.
  024 7652 2582   fax 024 7652 3019
    http://www2.warwick.ac.uk/fac/soc/philosophy/research/phillit/
  Director: Prof Michael Bell. Programme Director: Dr Darren Ambrose.
- E A centre attached to the University of Warwick.
- O To stimulate and focus work exploring the relations between philosophy and literature; to develop links between scholars in different universities and institutions in the UK and abroad; to offer a visiting fellows programme
- ● Conferences - Lectures - Symposia To contribute to the Philosophy and Literature MA programme

Centre for Research in Plant Science   (CRIPS)
- Faculty of Applied Sciences, Frenchay Campus, University of the West of England, Coldharbour Lane, Bristol, BS16 1QY.
  0117-328 3815
    http://science.uwe.ac.uk/research/homePage.aspx?pageId=cripsHome
  Director: Prof Steve Neill.
- E A research centre at the University of the West of England.
- O To conduct research in plant sciences

Centre for Research in Polish History   (CRPH)
- Department of History, University of Stirling, Stirling, FK9 4LA.
  01786 467041
    http://www.history.stir.ac.uk/research/CentreforResearchinPolishHistory.php
- E A research centre at the University of Stirling.
- O To conduct research on the history of Poland

Centre for Research into Post-Communist Economies   (CRCE)   1983

- 57 Tufton Street, London, SW1P 3QL.
  020 7233 1050   fax 020 7222 4299
  http://www.crce.org.uk/
  Director: Dr Ljubo Sirc, CBE. Administrative Director: Miss Lisl Biggs-Davison.
- E   A registered charity.
- O   To carry out research into the problems of communist economies and in economies making the transition from communism to democracy and market economies
- ¶   Wide range of publications.

Centre for Research in Postcolonial and Transcultural Studies

- School of Arts, Digby Stuart College, University of Roehampton, Roehampton Lane, London, SW15 5PH.
  020 8392 3249
  http://www.roehampton.ac.uk/researchcentres/postcolonial/
  Contact: Dr Patrick Corcoran. Contact: Dr Dorothy Rowe.
- E   An interdisciplinary research centre at Roehampton University.

Centre for Research in Primary Care

Note: is the Academic Unit of Primary Care at the University of Leeds and is therefore outside the scope of this directory.

Centre for Research in Primary and Community Care   (CRIPACC)   1996

- University of Hertfordshire, College Lane, Hatfield, Hertfordshire, AL10 9AB.
  01707 285990   fax 01707 285995
  http://perseus.herts.ac.uk/uhinfo/research/hhsri-new/cripacc/cripacc_home.cfm
  Director: Prof Sally Kendall.
- E   A research centre within the Health and Human Sciences Research Institute (qv) at the University of Hertfordshire.
- O   To conduct research and training in evidence based health care within the area of primary care

Centre for Research in Primary Science and Technology   (CRIPSAT)

- University of Liverpool, 126 Mount Pleasant, Liverpool, L69 3BX.
  0151-794 3270   fax 0151-794 3271
  http://www.cripsat.org.uk/
  Director: Prof Terry Russell. Deputy Director: Dr Linda McGuigan.
- E   A department of the University of Liverpool.
- O   To provide a consultation service to individuals, schools and other institutions, locally, nationally and internationally; to explore educationally-orientated links with industry and non-formal educational settings and organisations; to act as a base for the overview and consolidation of on-going work in primary science and provide a focus for further research; to develop relations (from the many already existing) with educators and researchers in other countries, leading to comparative work and attracting visiting scholars to the Centre
- ●   Education and training - Consultancy - Curriculum development - Enquiries welcomed during office hours - The Centre also has DTP and database facilities

Centre for Research into Quality   (CRQ)

- Birmingham City University, 90 Aldridge Road, Perry Barr, Birmingham, B42 2TP.
  0121-331 5715   fax 0121-331 6379
  http://www.uce.ac.uk/crq/
  Director: Morag MacDonald.
- E   A research centre at Birmingham City University.
- O   To deliver high quality policy research into higher education at institutional, national and international levels, informed by researching perceptions of the various stakeholders in higher education - staff, students, employers and professional bodies

Centre for Research on Racism, Ethnicity and Nationalism   (CRREN)   2005

- Department of Sociology, Anthropology and Applied Social Sciences, University of Glasgow, Adam Smith Building, 40 Bute Gardens, Glasgow, G12 8RT.
  0141-330 5355
  http://www.gla.ac.uk/departments/sociology/crren.html
  Director: Prof Satnam Virdee.
- E   A research centre at the University of Glasgow.
- O   To promote the comparative study of the historically specific ways in which racism, ethnicity and nationalism have shaped the development of modern society

Centre for Research in Rehabilitation   (CRR)

- School of Health Sciences and Social Care, Brunel University, Uxbridge, Middlesex, UB8 3PH.
  01895 274000
  http://www.brunel.ac.uk/about/acad/health/healthres/researchareas/crr
  Director: Prof Lorraine DeSouza.
- E   A research centre at Brunel University.
- O   To carry out high quality research of practical importance, which enables people with disabilities to fulfil their potential for health and personal development

Centre for Research into Religious Experience   (CRRE)   1969

■   Department of Theology and Religious Studies, University of Wales Lampeter, College Street, Lampeter, Ceredigion, SA48 7ED.
      01570 424708   fax 01570 424987
      http://www.lamp.ac.uk/trs/research_centres/religions_experience.htm
      Contact: Dr Wendy Dossett.
E   A research centre at the University of Wales, Lampeter.
O   To conduct research into various accounts of religious experience
●   Care and maintenance of archives of accounts of religious experience (started by Prof Sir Alister Hardy (marine biologist), in 1969)
✕   Alister Hardy Religious Experience Centre.

Centre for Research in Renaissance Studies   (CRRS)

■   School of Arts, Digby Stuart College, University of Roehampton, Roehampton Lane, London, SW15 5PH.
      020 8392 3249
      http://www.roehampton.ac.uk/renaissance/
      Director: Prof Robin Headlam Wells.
E   An interdisciplinary research centre at Roehampton University.
O   To conduct research and teaching in Renaissance studies, and covering the fields of Italian history, English literature, history and politics, theatre and performance history, and the Jacobean masque

Centre for Research in Romanticism   (CRR)

■   School of Arts, Digby Stuart College, University of Roehampton, Roehampton Lane, London, SW15 5PH.
      020 8392 3249
      http://www.roehampton.ac.uk/romanticism/
      Director: Dr Ian Haywood.
E   A research centre at Roehampton University.
O   To provide a focus for research in the area of Romantic and eighteenth century literature and culture

Centre for Research and Scholarship in History, Education and Cultural Heritage   (HECH)   2004

■   St Martin's College, Bowerham Road, Lancaster, LA1 3JD.
      01524 384384   fax 01524 384385
      http://www.ucsm.ac.uk/research/HECH/
E   A research centre at St Martin's College.

Centre for Research into Second and Foreign Language Pedagogy

Note: is the Second and Foreign Language Pedagogy Group of the University of Nottingham and is therefore outside the scope of this directory.

Centre for Research on Self and Identity   (CRSI)

■   School of Psychology, University of Southampton, Shackleton Building, Highfield, Southampton, SO17 1BJ.
      023 8059 3995   fax 023 8059 4597
      http://www.psychology.soton.ac.uk/research/crsi.php
      Contact: Prof Constantine Sedikides.
E   A research centre at the University of Southampton.
O   To carry out programmatic research on themes surrounding the topics of self and identity

Centre for Research in Service   (CeReS)

■   University of Gloucester Business School, The Park, Cheltenham, Gloucestershire, GL50 2RH.
      01242 544059
      http://www.glos.ac.uk/faculties/ugbs/
      Head: Dr Stuart Hanmer-Lloyd.
E   A research centre at the University of Gloucestershire.
O   To provide a focus for the development of research and consultancy in all aspects of service and service provision, within all areas of the economy

Centre for Research in Six Sigma and Process Improvement   (CRISSPI)   2004

■   Caledonian Business School, Glasgow Caledonian University, Cowcaddens Road, Glasgow, G4 0BA.
      0141-331 8475   fax 0141-331 8496
      http://www.gcal.ac.uk/crisspi/
      Director: Prof Jiju Antony.
E   A research centre at Glasgow Caledonian University.
O   To offer comprehensive knowledge and training to senior managers, executives, directors and technical personnel, who are seeking methods for improving the quality of their products and services

Centre for Research in Social Inclusion and Social Justice   2000

■   Department of Criminology and Sociological Studies, University of Hull, Cottingham Road, Hull, HU6 7RX.
      01482 465780
      http://www.hull.ac.uk/cass/research/centres/sjsi/
      Director: Prof Gary Craig.
E   A research centre at the University of Hull.

© CBD Research Ltd · Beckenham · Kent BR3 5JS · Tel 020 8650 7745 · Fax 020 8650 0768 · E-mail cbd@cbdresearch.com · www.cbdresearch.com

Centre for Research in Social Policy   (CRSP)   1983
- Department of Social Sciences, Loughborough University, Loughborough, Leicestershire, LE11 3TU.
    01509 223372   fax 01509 213409
    http://www.crsp.ac.uk/
    Director: Dr Bruce Stafford. Director: Mrs Sue Middleton.
- E   A research centre at Loughborough University.
- O   To conduct research in the field of social policy; to improve the quality and flow of information on which policy decisions are made; to promote contacts between policy makers, practitioners and the research community
- The Centre has PC based computing resources, with access to the University's Hewlett-Packard mainframe, giving access to the Joint Academic Network (JANET)

Centre for Research in Social and Political Sciences   (CRSPS)
- School of Languages and Social Sciences, Aston University, Aston Triangle, Birmingham, B4 7ET.
    0121-204 3752   fax 0121-204 3766
    http://www.aston.ac.uk/lss/research/centres/crsp.jsp
    Contact: Mary Bodfish.
- E   A research centre at Aston University.

Centre for Research in Social Simulation   (CRESS)
- Department of Sociology, University of Surrey, Guildford, Surrey, GU2 7XH.
    01483 689173
    http://cress.soc.surrey.ac.uk/
    Director: Prof Nigel Gilbert.
- E   A research centre at the University of Surrey.
- O   To bring together the social sciences, software engineering and agent-based computing to promote and support the use of social simulation in research in the human sciences

Centre for Research into Socially Inclusive Services   (CRSIS)
- School of the Built Environment, Edinburgh Campus, Heriot-Watt University, Riccarton, Edinburgh, EH14 4AS.
    0131-451 8181   fax 0131-451 4617
    http://www.sbe.hw.ac.uk/crsis
    Director: Prof Glen Bramley.
- E   A research centre at Heriot-Watt University.
- O   To undertake and disseminate research into the provision and use of local private and public services in deprived areas

Centre for Research on Socio-Cultural Change
   see **ESRC Centre for Research on Socio-Cultural Change.**

Centre for Research into Sport and Society [Leicester]
   see **Centre for the Sociology of Sport.**

Centre for Research into Sport in Society [Chester]
   see **Chester Centre for Research into Sport in Society.**

Centre for Research in Statistical Methodology   (CRiSM)
- Department of Statistics, University of Warwick, Coventry, CV4 7AL.
    024 7652 4553   fax 024 7652 4532
    http://www2.warwick.ac.uk/study/postgraduate/courses/researchcentres/crism/
    Contact: Mrs Susan Castle.
- E   A research centre at the University of Warwick.
- O   To help safeguard the UK's knowledge base in statistics by encouraging top-quality research

Centre for Research in Strategic Processes and Operations
   see **eXeter Centre for Research in Strategic Processes and Operations.**

Centre for Research into Strategic Purchasing and Supply   (CRiSPS)   1994
- School of Management, University of Bath, Claverton Down, Bath, BA2 7AY.
    01225 383492
    http://www.bath.ac.uk/crisps/
    Director: Prof Christine Harland, BA, PhD, FCIPS.
- E   A centre at the University of Bath.
- O   To identify and research contemporary and future aspects of supply management

Centre for Research into Sustainability   (CRIS)   2004
- School of Management, Royal Holloway, University of London, Egham, Surrey, TW20 0EX.
    01784 439854; 443780   fax 01483 472836
    http://www.rhul.ac.uk/Management/cris/
    Director: Prof Dirk Matten.
- E   An interdisciplinary research centre at Royal Holloway, University of London.
- O   To conduct teaching, research and consultancy in sustainability, with particular emphasis on protection of the global environment, corporate social responsibility, and social progress recognising the needs of all groups of society

Centre for Research on Teacher and School Development
  see **Teacher and Leadership Research Centre.**

Centre for Research in Tertiary Education   (CreaTE)
■   The Graduate School, Ealing Campus, Thames Valley University, St Mary's Road, London, W5 5RF.
    http://www.tvu.ac.uk/research/1centres/create.jsp
    Director: Prof Bruce Macfarlane.
E   A research centre at Thames Valley University.
O   To investigate the management of change in dual-sector educational (FE-HE) institutions

Centre for Research in Translation
■   School of Arts, Trent Park, Middlesex University, Bramley Road, London, N14 4YZ.
    http://www.mdx.ac.uk/research/centres/
E   A research centre within the Middlesex University Translation Institute (qv) at Middlesex University.
O   To encourage research in the theory and practice of translation and the development of translation studies as an academic
      discipline

Centre for Research on the Wider Benefits of Learning   (WBL)
■   Bedford Group for Lifecourse and Statistical Studies, 20 Bedford Way, London, WC1H 0AL.
    020 7612 6291   fax 020 7612 6880
    http://www.learningbenefits.net/
    Director: Leon Feinstein.
E   A research centre within the Institute of Education (qv) at the University of London.
O   To clarify, model and quantify the outcomes of all forms of intentional learning so as to inform the funding, implementation and
      practice of educational provision through the life course

Centre for Research on Women's Health
  see **Dugald Baird Centre for Research on Women's Health.**

Centre for Resource Management and Efficiency   (CRM&E)
■   Sustainable Systems Department, Building 61, Cranfield University, Cranfield, Bedfordshire, MK43 0AL.
    01234 754101
    http://www.cranfield.ac.uk/sas/resource/
    Director: Dr Phil Longhurst.
E   A research centre at Cranfield University.
O   To conduct research, training, education and consultancy in waste management
Note: Integrated Waste Management Centre.

Centre for Respiratory Research
■   Department of Medicine, University College London, Rayne Building, 5 University Street, London, WC1E 6JF.
    020 7679 6974   fax 020 7679 6973
    http://www.ucl.ac.uk/medicine/respiratory-research/
    Director: Prof Geoffrey Laurent.
E   A research centre at University College London.
O   To conduct research aimed at improving understanding of the pathogenesis of debilitating respiratory diseases, including asthma,
      lung cancer, acute lung injury, pulmonary infections, chronic obstructive pulmonary diseases and fibrotic lung disorders

Centre for Respiratory Research   (CRR)
■   Clinical Sciences Building, City Hospital, Nottingham, NG5 1PB.
    0115-823 1713
    http://www.nottingham.ac.uk/ctrr/
    Director: Prof Alan Knox.
E   A research centre within the Institute of Clinical Research (qv) at the University of Nottingham.
O   To provide a centre of excellence in respiratory research and to facilitate the integration and training of new researchers who want
      to carry out high quality research in respiratory diseases

Centre for Retail Research   (CRR)   1994
■   Lenton Business Centre, Lenton Boulevard, Nottingham, NG7 2BY.
    0115-970 0555   fax 0845 130 5618
    http://www.retailresearch.org/
E   A profit-making business.
O   To study and report on the impact of technology upon retail futures with special emphasis on consumers and retail crime
●   Statistics
¶   European Retail Theft Barometer. (many other publications - see website).

Centre for Retailing
  see **Glasgow Centre for Retailing.**

Centre for Reviews and Dissemination (CRD) 1994

- ■ Department of Economics and Related Studies, University of York, Alcuin B Block, Heslington, York, YO10 5DD.
  01904 321040   fax 01904 321041
  http://www.york.ac.uk/inst/crd/
  Director: Prof Jos Kleijnen. Administrator: Caroline Horwood.
- E A department of the University of York.
- ○ To undertake reviews of research about the effects of interventions used in health and social care
- ● Education and training - Information service - Library
- ¶ CRD Reports.

Centre for Rhetoric and Cultural Poetics

- ■ School of Humanities, University of Southampton, Highfield, Southampton, SO17 1BF.
  023 8059 3409
  http://www.english.soton.ac.uk/centres.htm
  Contact: Prof Peter Middleton.
- E A research centre at the University of Southampton.

Centre for Rheumatology (CR)

- ■ Department of Immunology and Molecular Pathology, University College London, Windeyer Building, 46 Cleveland Street, London, W1T 4JF.
  020 7679 9431
  http://www.ucl.ac.uk/medicine/bloomsbury-rheumatology/
  Director: Prof David Isenberg.
- E A research centre at University College London.
- ○ To conduct research in the structure, function and origin of auto-antibodies in the context of the auto-immune rheumatic diseases, utilising both molecular biological and immunological approaches

Centre for Rheumatology and Connective Tissue Disease

- ■ Department of Medicine, Royal Free and University College Medical School, University College London, Rowland Hill Street, London, NW3 2PF.
  020 7794 0500 ext 4049   fax 020 7435 0432
  http://www.ucl.ac.uk/medicine/rheumatology-RF/
  Director: Prof Carol Black.
- E A research centre at University College London.
- ○ To conduct clinical and serological research in connective tissue disease, chiefly scleroderma

Centre for Rights, Understanding and Citizenship Based on Learning through Experience
see **CRUCiBLE: Centre for Rights, Understanding and Citizenship Based on Learning through Experience.**

Centre for Risk and Governance
see **Cullen Centre for Risk and Governance.**

Centre for Risk and Insurance Studies (CRIS) 1991

- ■ Nottingham University Business School, Jubilee Campus, University of Nottingham, Wollaton Road, Nottingham, NG8 1BB.
  0115-846 6607   fax 0115-846 6684
  http://www.nottingham.ac.uk/business/CRIS.html
  Centre Director: Chris O'Brien.
- E A department of the University of Nottingham.
- ○ To enhance understanding of risk and insurance by research and its dissemination, education at undergraduate and postgraduate (including MBA) level, and providing data about the insurance industry
- ● Conferences - Education and training - Information service - Statistics
- ¶ Insurance Company Performance (2 parts).

Centre for Risk Management
see **King's Centre for Risk Management.**

Centre for Risk Management, Reliability and Maintenance

- ■ Department of Engineering, City University, Tait Building, Northampton Square, London, EC1V 0HB.
  020 7040 0113
  http://www.city.ac.uk/sems/research/risk/
- E A centre at City University.
- ○ To carry out research, consultancy, education and training in the scientific management of risk, reliability and maintenance

Centre for Risk Research (CRR) 1990

- ■ School of Management, University of Southampton, Highfield, Southampton, SO17 1BJ.
  023 8059 2546
  http://www.risk.soton.ac.uk/
  Contact: Prof Johnnie Johnson.
- E A research centre at the University of Southampton.
- ○ To encourage a deeper appreciation of the nature of risk, to develop approaches to its analysis, and to assist organisations to effectively manage risk and uncertainty

---

© CBD Research Ltd · Beckenham · Kent BR3 5JS · Tel 020 8650 7745 · Fax 020 8650 0768 · E-mail cbd@cbdresearch.com · www.cbdresearch.com   227

Centre for Robotics and Automation   (CRA)   1987
- ■   Faculty of Business, Law and the Built Environment, University of Salford, Maxwell Building, Salford, Manchester, M5 4WT.
  0161-295 5262; 5278
  http://www.iris.salford.ac.uk/
  Director: Prof J O Gray.
- E   A research centre within the Informatics Research Institute (qv) at the University of Salford.
- O   To be at the forefront of research in robotics and automation, including legged robots and walking systems, bipedal and quadrapedal automata, robot and machine design, actuation systems, sensors and signal processing, etc

Centre for Roman Cultural Studies
  see **Durham Centre for Roman Cultural Studies.**

Centre for Romantic Studies   (CRS)
- ■   Department of English, University of Bristol, Woodland Road, Bristol, BS8 1TB.
  0117-928 7786   fax 0117-928 8860
  http://www.bristol.ac.uk/romanticstudies/
  Director: Dr Nick Groom.
- E   A research centre at the University of Bristol.
- O   To broaden fundamentally the scope of romantic studies so that it includes all aspects of history, culture and society for the period 1700-1850

Centre for Rural Economy   (CRE)
- ■   School of Agriculture, Food and Rural Development, University of Newcastle upon Tyne, Newcastle upon Tyne, NE1 7RU.
  0191-222 6623
  http://www.ncl.ac.uk/cre/
  Director: Prof Neil Ward.
- E   A research centre at the University of Newcastle upon Tyne.
- O   To specialise in interdisciplinary social science and applied policy research oriented towards the achievement of a rural economy

Centre for Rural Enterprise
  see **Crichton Centre for Rural Enterprise.**

Centre for Rural Health Research and Policy   (CRH)   2004
- ■   University of Aberdeen, The Greenhouse, Beechwood Business Park, Inverness, IV2 3BL.
  01463 667322   fax 01463 667310
  http://www.abdn.ac.uk/crh/
  Director: Prof David J Godden MD, FRCP(Edin), FRCP(Glas).
- E   A research centre at the University of Aberdeen.
- O   To advance knowledge of health and health services in rural and remote communities
- ✕   Highlands and Islands Health Research Institute.

Centre for Rural Innovation   (CfRI)   2003
- ■   Harper Adams University College, Newport, Shropshire, TF10 8NB.
  01952 820280
  http://www.cfri.co.uk/
- E   A research centre at Harper Adams University College.
- O   To conduct research and provide consultancy on rural entrepreneurship and social enterprise, innovation for sustainable farming, food chain safety, linking urban and rural economies and communities, sustainable technology and the rural economy, rural advisers and agencies, and rural professional practice

Centre for Rural Research   (CRR)
- ■   School of Geography, Archaeology and Earth Resources, University of Exeter, Lafrowda House, St German's Road, Exeter, EX4 6TL.
  01392 263836   fax 01392 263852
  http://www.centres.ex.ac.uk/crr/
  Director: Prof Michael Winter. Administrator: Liz Saunders.
- E   A centre at the University of Exeter.
- O   To advance the study of food, environment and rural issues regionally, nationally and internationally, with particular emphasis on farm economics studies, rural development and policy appraisal, animal health and welfare economics, transition in Central and Eastern Europe, and ad hoc regional and local studies

Centre for Russian, Central and East European Studies   (CRCEES)   1990
- NR   Department of Central and East European Studies, University of Glasgow, Hetherington Building, Bute Gardens, Glasgow, G12 8RS.
  0141-330 5259
  http://www.gla.ac.uk/crcees/
  Head: Richard Berry. Contact: Mrs Maggie Baister.
- E   A research centre at the University of Glasgow.
- O   To create a world-class cadre of researchers who will enhance the UK's understanding of central and eastern Europe and the former Soviet Union, and covering various research themes including, aspects of identity and culture and their social, political and economic implications, economic and social transformation, political transformation and international relations, literary, cinematic and cultural developments in the area, and the politics of language

Note: A consortium of the Universities of Aberdeen, Edinburgh, Glasgow, Newcastle, Nottingham, Paisley, St Andrews, and Strathclyde.

Centre for Russian and East European Cultural Studies   (CREECS)   2000
- ■   Faculty of Arts, University of Bristol, Senate House, Tyndall Avenue, Bristol, BS8 1TH.
     0117-331 7349   fax 0117-925 1129
     http://www.bris.ac.uk/creecs/
     Contact: Birgit Beumers.
- E   A research centre at the University of Bristol.
- ○   To conduct research into all aspects of Russian and East European culture
- ●   Seminars

Centre for Russian and East European Studies   (CREES)   1963
- ■   University of Birmingham, Edgbaston, Birmingham, B15 2TT.
     0121-414 6346   fax 0121-414 3423
     http://www.bham.ac.uk/crees/
     Director: Dr Kataryna Wolczuk. Secretary: Tricia Carr.
- E   A research centre within the European Research Institute (qv) at the University of Birmingham.
- ○   To conducting teaching and research on the former USSR, in particular Russia and Ukraine, and Eastern Europe, with particular emphasis on the economy, politics, society and history
- ●   Conferences - Education and training - Information service - Lectures to outside bodies - Seminars - Teaching at undergraduate and postgraduate level

Centre for Russian and Eurasian Studies   (CRES)   2004
- ■   School of Languages, Linguistics and Cultures, University of Manchester, Humanities Lime Grove Centre, Oxford Road, Manchester, M13 9PL.
     0161-275 3140
     http://www.llc.manchester.ac.uk/SubjectAreas/RussianStudies/CentreforRussianandEurasianStudies/
     Contact: Prof Vera Tolz.
- E   A research centre at the University of Manchester.
- ○   To conduct research, teaching and postgraduate supervision between academic staff with expertise in Russia, other countries of the former Soviet Union and Eastern and East Central Europe

Centre for Russian Music   (CRM)   1997
- ■   Music Department, Goldsmiths, University of London, London, SE14 6NW.
     020 7919 7640   fax 020 7919 7644
     http://www.goldsmiths.ac.uk/departments/music/crm/
     Director: Prof Alexander Ivashkin.
- E   A research centre at Goldsmiths, University of London.
- ○   To promote research, publication and performance of Russian music

Centre for Russian, Soviet and Central and Eastern European Studies   (CRSCEES)   1990
- ■   School of International Relations, University of St Andrews, St Andrews, Fife, KY16 9AL.
     01334 462907   fax 01334 462927
     http://www.st-andrews.ac.uk/crscees/
     Director: Dr Roger Keys.
- E   A research centre at the University of St Andrews.
- ○   To conduct research in a wide area of Russian, Central and Eastern European politics, culture and 19th and 20th century history
Note: See above University of Aberdeen entry for full details.

Centre for Russian Studies   (CRS)
- ■   School of Slavonic and East European Studies, University College London, Gower Street, London, WC1E 6BT.
     020 7679 8823
     http://www.ssees.ac.uk/russstud.htm
     Director: Prof Lindsey Hughes.
- E   A research centre at University College London.

Centre for Science Communication   (SciCOMM)
- ■   School of Applied and Health Sciences, University of Chester, Parkgate Road, Chester, CH1 4BJ.
     01244 221204   fax 01244 511341
     http://www.chester.ac.uk/scicomm/
     Director: Prof Graham Bonwick.
- E   A research centre at the University of Chester.

Centre for Science Education   (CSE)   1975
- ■   Department of Educational Studies, University of Glasgow, St Andrew's Building, 11 Eldon Street, Glasgow, G3 6NH.
     0141-330 5172; 6565   fax 0141-330 3755
     http://www.gla.ac.uk/centres/scienceeducation/
     Director: Dr Norman Reid.
- E   A centre at the University of Glasgow.

Centre for Science Education   (CSE)
- ■   City Campus, Sheffield Hallam University, Sheffield, S1 1WB.
   0114-225 4870   fax 0114-225 4872
   http://extra.shu.ac.uk/cse/
   Administrator: Leon Snell.
- E   A research centre at Sheffield Hallam University.
- O   To inspire and capture the imagination of young people in science through the development of 'creativity rich' resources and activities

Centre for Science at Extreme Conditions   (CSEC)
- ■   University of Edinburgh, Erskine Williamson Building, The King's Buildings, Edinburgh, EH9 3JZ.
   0131-651 7228   fax 0131-651 7049
   http://www.csec.ed.ac.uk/
   Secretary: Mrs Anne Roberts.
- E   A research centre at the University of Edinburgh.
- O   To promote the study of materials at extremes of temperature and pressure, and in electromagnetic fields, using both in-house and synchrotron and neutron techniques

Centre for Science of the Mind
   see **Oxford Centre for Science of the Mind.**

Centre for Science Studies   (CSS)   1985
- ■   Faculty of Social Sciences, Lancaster University, County South, Bailrigg, Lancaster, LA1 4YD.
   01524 594178   fax 01524 594256
   http://www.lancs.ac.uk/fass/centres/css/
   Director: John Law, MA.
- E   A department of Lancaster University.
- O   To provide a point of focus and stimulus for research in the fields of science policy, the history of science, the philosophy of science, and related areas

Centre for Scientific Computing   (CSC)   2001
- ■   Faculty of Science, University of Warwick, Gibbet Hill Road, Coventry, CV4 7AL.
   024 7657 4111   fax 024 7657 3133
   http://www2.warwick.ac.uk/fac/sci/csc/
   Director: Prof Andrew Stuart.
- E   A research centre at the University of Warwick.
- O   To conduct research in molecular dynamics and modelling, Monte Carlo methods, computational partial differential equations (PDEs), quantum simulations, computational fluid dynamics, and computational systems biology

Centre for Scientific and Cultural Research in Sport   (CSCRS)
- ■   School of Human and Life Sciences, Whitelands College, University of Roehampton, Holybourne Avenue, London, SW15 4JD.
   020 8392 3500   fax 020 8392 3531
   http://www.roehampton.ac.uk/researchcentres/cscrs/
- E   A research centre at Roehampton University.
- O   To promote research on sport, leisure and physical activities across disciplinary boundaries including biomechanics, sociology, psychology, nutrition and physiology

Centre for Scientific Enterprise   (CSEL)   2000
- NR   London Business School, 17 Linhope Street, London, NW1 6HT.
   0870 765 7604   fax 0870 765 7606
   http://www.cselondon.com/
   Chief Executive Officer: Peter Reid.
- E   A centre at the London Business School.
- O   To promote entrepreneurship within the fields of science and technology
Note: A joint venture with University College London.

Centre for Scottish and Gaelic Studies   (CSGS)   2005
- ■   Department of Celtic, University of Glasgow, Modern Languages Building, 16 University Gardens, Glasgow, G12 8QQ.
   0141-330 4222   fax 0141-330 4222
   http://www.arts.gla.ac.uk/scottishstudies/
   Director: Prof Thomas Owen Clancy.
- E   A research centre at the University of Glasgow.
- O   To conduct research on various aspects of Scottish and Gaelic history, focusing particularly on two projects - the Scottish Chronicle Project and the Scottish Charters Project

Centre for Scottish Studies   (CSS)   1971
- ■   University of Aberdeen, Room G09 - Crombie Annex, King's College, Aberdeen, AB24 3FX.
   01224 272195
   http://www.abdn.ac.uk/css/
   Director: Prof David Dumville.
- E   A centre at the University of Aberdeen.

Centre for Scottish Studies [Stirling]
  see **Stirling Centre for Scottish Studies.**

Centre for Screen Studies   (CSS)
■   Department of Theatre, Film and Television Studies, University of Glasgow, Gilmorehill Centre, 9 University Avenue, Glasgow, G12 8QQ.
    0141-330 3809   fax 0141-330 4142
    http://www.tfts.arts.gla.ac.uk/centrescreenstuds.htm
    Head: Prof Christine Geraghty.
E   A research centre within the University of Glasgow.
O   To bring together academics and students who are interested in the study of film and television

Centre for Screen Studies   (CSS)   1998
■   School of Arts, Histories and Cultures, University of Manchester, Humanities Lime Grove, Oxford Road, Manchester, M13 9PL.
    0161-275 3352   fax 0161-275 3349
    http://www.arts.manchester.ac.uk/subjectareas/drama/research/centreforscreenstudies/
    Director: Dr Alan Marcus.
E   A research centre within the Centre for Interdisciplinary Research in the Arts (qv) at the University of Manchester.
O   To foster and facilitate research in film and television studies

Centre for Security and Crime Science
  see **UCL Centre for Security and Crime Science.**

Centre for Security Studies   (CSS)
■   Department of Politics and International Studies, University of Hull, Cottingham Road, Hull, HU6 7RX.
    01482 466209   fax 01482 466208
    http://www.hull.ac.uk/securitystudies/
E   A research centre at the University of Hull.

Centre for Self-Organising Molecular Systems   (SOMS)
■   Faculty of Mathematics and Physical Sciences, University of Leeds, Leeds, LS2 9JT.
    http://www.soms.leeds.ac.uk/
    Acting Director: Dr R W Kelsall.
E   A research centre within the University of Leeds.
O   To understand the science of molecular self-assembly and self-organisation; to engineer new functional exploitable materials and devices

Centre for Sensory Impaired People   (CSIP)   1997
■   17 Gullane Street, Glasgow, G11 6AH.
    0141-334 5530   fax 0141-334 5530
    Manager: Jim Agnew.
E   A local authority body.

Centre for Sentencing Research   (CSR)
■   The Law School, University of Strathclyde, Stenhouse Building, 173 Cathedral Street, Glasgow, G4 0RQ.
    0141-548 3274; 3338   fax 0141-553 1546
    http://www.law.strath.ac.uk/csr/
E   A research centre at the University of Strathclyde.
O   To develop, disseminate and promote the study of sentencing, punishment and society

Centre for Service Management   (CREAM)
■   Buckingham Business School, University of Buckingham, Hunter Street, Buckingham, MK18 1EG.
    01280 820144   fax 01280 820151
    http://www.buckingham.ac.uk/business/expertise/service/
E   A centre at the University of Buckingham.
O   To help organisations improve their service, from turnkey projects, on issues critical to them, to full-blown organisation transformation projects

Centre for Service Research   (CServ)
■   School of Business and Economics, University of Exeter, Streatham Court, Rennes Drive, Exeter, EX4 4PU.
    01392 263458   fax 01392 263242
    http://www.centres.ex.ac.uk/cserv/
    Co-Director: Dr Irene C L Ng. Co-Director: Prof Roger Maull.
E   A centre at the University of Exeter.
O   To advance knowledge and understanding of activities in services; to gain a better understanding of activities involving service components in goods as well as goods components in services

Centre for Sexual Health and HIV Research   1979
- ■ Department of Primary Care and Population, University College London, Mortimer Market Centre, off Capper Street, London, WC1E 6JB.
  020 7380 9660   fax 020 7388 4179
  http://www.ucl.ac.uk/sexual-health/
  Director: Prof Graham Hart.
- E A research centre within the Mortimer Market Centre (qv) at University College London

Centre for Sexual Health Research   (CSHR)   1994
- ■ School of Psychology, University of Southampton, Shackleton Building, Highfield, Southampton, SO17 1BJ.
  023 8059 7770   fax 023 8059 3846
  http://www.socstats.soton.ac.uk/cshr/
  Contact: Dr Roger Ingham.
- E A research centre at the University of Southampton.
- O To provide a focus for research on sexual health issues

Centre for Sheltered Housing Studies   (CSHS)   1990
- ■ First Floor - Elgar House, Shrub Hill Road, Worcester, WR4 9EE.
  01906 21155
  http://www.cshs.co.uk/
- E A charitable organisation.
- O To provide professional validated training and education programmes for all who work in the sheltered housing service and related care sector

Centre for Signal Processing in Neuroimaging and Systems Neuroscience   (SpiNSN)   2004
- ■ Department of Psychology, University of Sheffield, Sheffield, S10 2TP.
  0114-222 6511   fax 0114-276 6515
  http://www.spinsn.group.shef.ac.uk/
  Contact: Dr Ying Zheng.
- E A research centre at the University of Sheffield.
- O To provide the signal processing and data analysis expertise to support the emerging neuro-imaging and computational neuroscience programme at the University

Centre on Skills, Knowledge and Organisational Performance and Organisational Performance
  see **ESRC Centre on Skills, Knowledge and Organisational Performance.**

Centre for Small and Medium Sized Enterprises   (CSME)   1984
- ■ Warwick Business School, University of Warwick, Coventry, CV4 7AL.
  024 7652 3741   fax 024 7652 3747
  http://www.wbs.ac.uk/faculty/research/csme.cfm
  Director: Prof David Storey.
- E A research centre at the University of Warwick.
- O To conduct research into small and medium-sized enterprises

Centre for Social Action   1989
- ■ School of Applied Social Sciences, De Montfort University, Hawthorn Building, The Gateway, Leicester, LE1 9BH.
  0116-257 7777   fax 0116-257 7778
  http://www.dmu.ac.uk/dmucsa/
  Director: Jennie Fleming.
- E A centre at De Montfort University.
- O To achieve positive social change through community, project and professional development

Centre for Social Anthropology and Computing   (CSAC)   1986
- ■ Department of Anthropology, University of Kent, Marlowe Building, Canterbury, Kent, CT2 7NZ.
  01227 764000
  http://lucy.ukc.ac.uk/
  Director: M D Fischer.
- E A department of the University of Kent.
- O To conduct research and teaching in biological and social anthropology

Centre for Social and Business Informatics
  see **Newcastle Centre for Social and Business Informatics.**

Centre for Social Care Studies
- ■ School of Applied Social Sciences, De Montfort University, The Gateway, Leicester, LE1 9BH.
  0116-257 7700
  http://www.dmu.ac.uk/faculties/hls/research/centreforsocialcare/cscindex.jsp
  Administrator: Joanne Drury.
- E A centre at De Montfort University.
- O To offer information, research, consultancy, education and training for people living and working in or with group care settings and the provider side of community care such as children's homes, hostels, home care services, inspection and registration teams, supported and special needs housing, and older people's homes

Centre for Social and Economic Research on the Global Environment   (CSERGE)   1991

■   School of Environmental Sciences, University of East Anglia, Norwich, NR4 7TJ.
   01603 593738   fax 01603 593739
   http://www.uea.ac.uk/env/cserge/
   Director: Prof Kerry Turner, CBE. Contact: Dawn Turnbull.
E   An interdisciplinary research centre within the Zuckerman Institute for Connective Environmental Research (qv) at the University of East Anglia.
O   To focus on the study of environmental change with particular emphasis on sustainable development, environmental valuation, natural resources, and waste and energy

Centre for Social and Economic Research on Innovation in Genomics
   see **Innogen - ESRC Centre for Social and Economic Research on Innovation in Genomics.**

Centre for Social Entrepreneurship
   see **Skoll Centre for Social Entrepreneurship**.

Centre for Social and Environmental Accounting Research   (CSEAR)   1991

■   School of Management, University of St Andrews, The Gateway, North Haugh, St Andrews, Fife, KY16 9SS.
   01334 462805   fax 01334 462812
   http://www.st-andrews.ac.uk/management/csear/
   Director: Prof Rob Gray.
E   A research centre at the University of St Andrews.
O   To provide a mechanism for all those with an interest in the practice and theory of social and environmental accounting and reporting; to make contact and support each other

Centre for Social Ethics and Policy   (CSEP)

■   School of Law, University of Manchester, Oxford Road, Manchester, M13 9PL.
   0161-275 3473
   http://www.law.manchester.ac.uk/research/centres/csep/
   Director: Prof John Harris.
E   A research centre at the University of Manchester.
O   To conduct research in bioethics and biolaw

Centre for Social Evaluation Research   (CSER)

■   Department of Applied Social Sciences, London Metropolitan University, Calcutta House, Old Castle Street, London, E1 7NT.
   020 7320 1276
   http://www.londonmet.ac.uk/depts/dass/
   Director: Simon Hallsworth. Administrator: Karen Hobbs.
E   A research centre at London Metropolitan University.
O   To undertake a broad range of social research for statutory and non-statutory organisations

Centre for Social Gerontology   (CSG)   1987

■   Keele University, Keele, Staffordshire, ST5 5BG.
   01782 584066
   http://www.keele.ac.uk/depts/so/csg/
   Director: Prof Thomas Scharf.
E   A research centre within the Research Institute for Life Course Studies (qv) at Keele University.

Centre for Social History

Note: Now known as the Social History Society - www.socialhistory.org.uk.

Centre for the Social History of Health and Healthcare   (CSHHH)

NR   Department of History, University of Strathclyde, McCance Building, 16 Richmond Street, Glasgow, G1 1XQ.
   0141-548 2208
   http://www.strath.ac.uk/Departments/History/
   Director: Dr Jim Mills.
E   A research centre at the University of Strathclyde.
Note: A joint venture with Glasgow Caledonian University (see above).

Centre for the Social History of Health and Healthcare   (CSHHH)

NR   School of Law and Social Sciences, Glasgow Caledonian University, Cowcaddens Road, Glasgow, G4 0BA.
   0141-330 3494
   http://www.gcal.ac.uk/historyofhealth/
   Deputy Director: Dr Jim Mills.
E   A research centre at Glasgow Caledonian University.
O   To produce high quality research on the social history of health and healthcare, with special emphasis on occupational health and healthcare, medicalisation of life and death in Scotland, and colonialism and medical markets
Note: A joint venture with the University of Strathclyde.

Centre for Social Inclusion   (CSI)
- City Campus, Sheffield Hallam University, 33 Collegiate Crescent, Sheffield, S10 2BP.
  0114-225 5786   fax 0114-225 5706
  http://www.shu.ac.uk/research/csi/
  Director: John Coldron.
- E   A research centre at Sheffield Hallam University.
- O   To take forward an active programme of research and evaluation relating to social inclusion / exclusion in the fields of gender and equalities, care, caring, carers and care workers, housing law socio-legal issues, and sexualities and health

Centre for Social Justice
Note: see **Applied Research Centre in Sustainable Regeneration.**

Centre for Social Justice   (CSJ)
- 9 Westminster Palace Gardens, Artillery Row, London, SW1P 1RL.
  020 7340 9650
  http://www.centreforsocialjustice.org.uk/
  Executive Director: Philippa Stroud.
- O   To work to narrow the gap between the rich and the poor and to reduce corporate domination

Centre for Social Learning and Cognitive Evolution
- School of Psychology, St Mary's College, University of St Andrews, South Street, St Andrews, Fife, KY16 9JP.
  01334 462157   fax 01334 463042
  http://culture.st-and.ac.uk:16080/
  Co-ordinator: Prof Andrew Whiten.
- E   An interdisciplinary research centre at the University of St Andrews.
- O   To conduct research in social learning, culture and cognitive evolution of wild and captive animals, as well as humans
- Note: Often referred to by its shortened title Centre for SoLaCE.

Centre for Social Marketing
Note: No longer in existence.

Centre for Social and Organisational Learning as Action Research   (SOLAR)
- Faculty of Health and Social Care, University of the West of England, Blackberry Hill, Stapleton, Bristol, BS16 1DD.
  0117-328 1115
  http://hsc.uwe.ac.uk/net/research/Default.aspx?pageid=56
  Co-Director: Prof Susan Weil. Co-Director: Prof Danny Burns.
- E   An interdisciplinary research centre at the University of the West of England.
- O   To specialise in new forms of action research and co-inquiry to support learning and change in complex social and organisational systems

Centre for Social and Policy Research   (CSPR)
- School of Social Sciences and Law, Teesside University, Middlesbrough, TS1 3BA.
  01642 342346
  http://www.tees.ac.uk/depts/socialfutures/CSPRprofile.cfm
  Director: Prof Eileen Green.
- E   A research centre within the Social Futures Institute (qv) at the University of Teesside.
- O   To deliver external research projects in social exclusion, difference and diversity

Centre for Social Policy Research and Development   (CSPRD)   1986
- Neuadd Ardudwy, Normal Site, University of Wales, Bangor, Bangor, Gwynedd, LL57 2PX.
  01248 382225   fax 01248 382229
  http://www.bangor.ac.uk/csprd/
  Director: Dr Vanessa Burholt. Administrator: Sue Howard.
- E   A research centre within the Institute of Medical and Social Care Research (qv) at the University of Wales, Bangor.
- O   To conduct well founded scientific research in social gerontology; to focus on multidisciplinary collaborative research at the local, national and international level with the aims - to empower older people and to promote social inclusion - to be receptive to input from older people, service providers and politicians which highlight important areas of enquiry; to influence the integration of services between sectors to match older people's needs

Centre for Social Policy and Social Work
   see **Subject Centre for Social Policy and Social Work.**

Centre for Social Research   (CSR)   1990
- School of Sociology and Social Policy, Queen's University, Belfast, Belfast, BT7 1NN.
  028 9033 5970
  http://www.qub.ac.uk/ss/csr/
- E   A centre at Queen's University, Belfast.
- O   To run a research affiliate programme at the University

Centre for Social Research in Health and Health Care   (CSRHHC)   2003
- ■ School of Education, Jubilee Campus, University of Nottingham, Wollaton Road, Nottingham, NG8 1BB.
     0115-951 5403
     http://www.nottingham.ac.uk/csrhhc/
     Contact: Prof Elizabeth Murphy.
- E   An interdisciplinary research centre at the University of Nottingham.
- O   To conduct investigation of the delivery and experience of health and health care, in the context of current developments in UK health policy, and the associated restructuring of the education of health professionals

Centre for Social Responsibility in Accounting and Management
- ■ Department of Accounting, Finance and Management, University of Essex, Wivenhoe Park, Colchester, Essex, CO4 3SQ.
     01206 872364
     Director: Dr Harro Höpfl.
- E   A research centre at the University of Essex.

Centre for Social Sciences
     see **Research Centre for Social Sciences.**

Centre for Social Work
- ■ School of Sociology and Social Policy, University of Nottingham, University Park, Nottingham, NG7 2RD.
     0115-951 5231   fax 0115-951 5232
     http://www.nottingham.ac.uk/sociology/centre-socialwork.php
- E   A research centre at the University of Nottingham.
- O   To offer a range of social work degree programmes, and conduct research in various areas of social work, including critical evaluation of the 'modernisation' of social work, protection of vulnerable children and adults, race, ethnicity and social work, and the interface between social work and health

Centre for Social Work Research [London]   (CSWR)   2006
- ■ School of Social Sciences, Media and Cultural Studies, Docklands Campus, University of East London, 4-6 University Way, London, E16 2RD.
     020 8223 2768
     http://www.uel.ac.uk/ssmcs/research/cswr/
     Director: Dr Stephen Briggs. Administrator: Sylvie Hudson.
- E   A research centre at the University of East London.
- O   To make a significant contribution to the generation of knowledge in social work, and to enhance research in the profession

Centre for Social Work Research [Manchester]
     see **Salford Centre for Social Work Research.**

Centre for Socio-Legal Studies [UCL]
     see **Centre for Empirical Legal Research.**

Centre for Socio-Legal Studies   1972
- ■ University of Oxford, Manor Road, Oxford, OX1 3UQ.
     01865 284220   fax 01865 284221
     http://www.csls.ox.ac.uk/
     Director: Prof Dennis J Galligan.
- E   A centre at the University of Oxford.
- O   To conduct innovative, interdisciplinary research into the interaction of law and society

Centre for Sociocultural and Activity Theory Research   (CSAT)   2005
- ■ Department of Education, University of Bath, Claverton Down, Bath, BA2 7AY.
     01225 385256
     http://www.bath.ac.uk/csat/
     Contact: Prof H Daniels.
- E   A research centre at the University of Bath.

Centre for Socioeconomic Research
     see **Welsh School of Pharmacy Centre for Socioeconomic Research.**

Centre for the Sociology of Sport
- ■ Department of Sociology, University of Leicester, University Road, Leicester, LE1 7RH.
     0116-252 2745
     http://www.le.ac.uk/so/css/
     Head: John Williams.
- E   A research centre at the University of Leicester.
- O   To conduct research on various aspects of playing and spectating in professional sports
- X   Centre for Research into Sport and Society, and the Sir Norman Chester Centre for Football Research.

Centre for Software Maintenance
     see **Research Institute in Software Evolution.**

Centre for Software Process Technologies   (CSPT)
- Faculty of Informatics, University of Ulster, Shore Road, Newtownabbey, County Antrim, BT37 0QB.
  028 9036 8887
  http://www.infc.ulst.ac.uk/informatics/cspt/
  Director: Dr George Wilkie.
- E   A research centre at the University of Ulster.
- O   To conduct research into the quality and effectiveness of both software development processes and products, from process measurement, through business process co-evolution, to object oriented software complexity metrics

Centre for Software Reliability   (CSR)   1983
- School of Informatics, City University, Northampton Square, London, EC1V 0HB.
  020 7040 8423   fax 020 7040 8585
  http://www.csr.city.ac.uk/
  Director: Prof Robin Bloomfield.
- E   An independent research centre and department of City University.
- O   To conduct research in methods for computer software reliability, measurement, modelling and safety

Centre for Software Reliability   (CSR)   1984
- School of Computing Science, University of Newcastle upon Tyne, 11th Floor - Claremont Tower, Newcastle upon Tyne, NE1 7RU.
  0191-222 7997   fax 0191-222 8788
  http://www.csr.ncl.ac.uk/
- E   A research centre at the University of Newcastle upon Tyne.
- O   To conduct research on how to make computing systems more reliable

Centre for SoLaCE
> see **Centre for Social Learning and Cognitive Evolution.**

Centre for Sonochemistry
- Coventry University, Priory Street, Coventry, CV1 5FB.
  024 7688 8173
  http://www.www.coventry.ac.uk/sonochemistry
  Contact: Prof Tim Mason. Contact: Prof Phil Lorimer.
- E   A centre at Coventry University.
- O   To study the effects of acoustic cavitation in a liquid medium produced by power ultrasound

Centre for Sound and Experimental Environments   (CSEE)
- School of Art, Design and Media, University of Portsmouth, Eldon Building, Winston Churchill Avenue, Portsmouth, PO1 2DJ.
  023 9284 3835   fax 023 9284 3808
  http://www.port.ac.uk/departments/academic/adm/research/
  Contact: Dr Chris Creed.
- E   An interdisciplinary research centre at the University of Portsmouth.
- O   To conduct research on embodied multi-sensory experience of space

Centre for South Asian Studies
- Department of Cultural Studies, University of Sussex, Falmer, Brighton, East Sussex, BN1 9SJ.
  01273 678722
  http://www.sussex.ac.uk/development/1-4-6.html
  Contact: Dr Vinita Damodaran.
- E   A research centre within the Centre for the Comparative Study of Culture, Development and the Environment (qv) at the University of Sussex.

Centre of South Asian Studies   1964
- University of Cambridge, Laundress Lane, Cambridge, CB2 1SD.
  01223 338094   fax 01223 767094
  http://www.s-asian.cam.ac.uk/
  Director: Dr R S Chandavarkar.
- E   A department of the University of Cambridge.
- O   To promote the study of South Asia within the University; to maintain an archive of unique materials comprising approximately 600 written collections, 80 hours of cine film in 200 reels, 400 tape recordings, 300 maps and 125,000 photographs
- ● Conferences - Seminars - Workshops - The Centre's library contains some 32,000 monographs, 5,500 volumes of serials and 10,000 microfilms and microforms; countries covered are: Afghanistan, Bangladesh, Cambodia, the Himalayan Kingdoms, Hong Kong, India, Indonesia, Laos, Malaysia, Myanmar (Burma), Pakistan, Philippines, Singapore, Sri Lanka, Thailand, and Vietnam

Centre for South Asian Studies   (CSAS)   1998
- Coventry University, Priory Street, Coventry, CV1 5FB.
  024 7688 8198
  http://www.stile.coventry.ac.uk/public/rcon/csea/
  Contact: Prof Ian Talbot.
- E   A centre at Coventry University.
- O   To co-ordinate research activities and interests across the disciplines of history, politics, geography, economics and religious studies, with particular emphasis on the historical development of the Indian subcontinent and on the peoples of the region who have migrated to Europe and North America

Centre for South Asian Studies   (CSAS)   1988
- School of Social and Political Studies, University of Edinburgh, Adam Ferguson Building, George Square, Edinburgh, EH9 1TZ.
  0131-650 3878   fax 0131-650 6535
  http://www.csas.ed.ac.uk/
  Convener: Roger Jeffery.
- E   A department of the University of Edinburgh.
- O   To advance the study of South Asia
- ● Conference facilities - Education and training - Library

Centre of South Asian Studies   (CSAS)   1966
- School of Oriental and African Studies, University of London, Thornhaugh Street, Russell Square, London, WC1H 0XG.
  020 7898 4892; 4893   fax 020 7898 4489
  http://www.soas.ac.uk/centres/centreinfo.cfm?navid=8
  Manager: Jane Savory. Executive Officer: Sara Hamza.
- E   An interdisciplinary research centre at the School of Oriental and African Studies, University of London.
- O   To facilitate and develop in the UK and Europe research, teaching and other activities relating to South Asia

Centre of South East Asian Studies   (CSEAS)
- School of Oriental and African Studies, University of London, Thornhaugh Street, Russell Square, London, WC1H 0XG.
  020 7898 4892; 4893   fax 020 7898 4489
  http://www.soas.ac.uk/centres/centreinfo.cfm?navid=9
  Manager: Jane Savory. Executive Officer: Sara Hamza.
- E   An interdisciplinary research centre at the School of Oriental and African Studies, University of London.
- O   To facilitate and develop in the UK and Europe research, teaching and other activities relating to South East Asia

Centre for South-East European Studies   (CSEES)
- School of Slavonic and East European Studies, University College London, Gower Street, London, WC1E 6BT.
  020 7679 8773; 8821   fax 020 7679 8755
  http://www.ssees.ac.uk/seecent.htm
  Co-Director: Dr Peter Siani-Davies. Co-Director: Dr Vesna Popovski.
- E   A research centre at University College London.

Centre for Space, Atmospheric and Oceanic Science   (CSAOS)   2005
- Department of Electronic and Electrical Engineering, University of Bath, Claverton Down, Bath, BA2 7AY.
  01225 386327   fax 01225 826305
  http://www.bath.ac.uk/csaos/
  Director: Prof N J Mitchell.
- E   A research centre at the University of Bath.
- O   To conduct research into remote-sensing techniques in relation to the natural environment of the Earth, its atmosphere, ionosphere and oceans

Centre for Spatial Analysis in Public Health   (C-SAPH   2006
- PEHRU, London School of Hygiene and Tropical Medicine, University of London, Keppel Street, London, WC1E 7HT.
  020 7927 2441
  http://www.lshtm.ac.uk/csaph/
  Contact: Chris Grundy.
- E   A research centre at the London School of Hygiene and Tropical Medicine, University of London.

Centre for Spatial and Real Estate Economics   (CSpREE)   1995
- University of Reading Business School, University of Reading, HUMSS Building, PO Box 218, Reading, Berkshire, RG6 6AA.
  0118-378 8826
  http://www.reading.ac.uk/business/default.asp?id=107
  Director: Prof Alan Evans.
- E   A research centre at the University of Reading.

Centre for Special Needs Education and Research   (CeSNER)   2000
- University of Northampton, Boughton Green Road, Northampton, NN2 7AL.
  01604 735500
  http://www2.northampton.ac.uk/education/home1/cesner
  Contact: Liz Bonnett.
- E   A research centre at the University of Northampton.
- O   To support practitioner research in the promotion of an inclusive education system

Centre for Speech, Language and the Brain
- Department of Experimental Psychology, University of Cambridge, Downing Street, Cambridge, CB2 3EB.
  01223 766458   fax 01223 766452
  http://csl.psychol.cam.ac.uk/
  Director: Prof Lorraine K Tyler.
- E   A centre at the University of Cambridge.
- O   To investigate the neural basis of conceptual knowledge and language

Centre for Speech Technology Research (CSTR) 1984

- University of Edinburgh, 2 Buccleuch Place, Edinburgh, EH8 9LW.
  0131-650 4434   fax 0131-650 6626
  http://www.cstr.ed.ac.uk/
  Director: Prof Steve Renals.
- E A centre at the University of Edinburgh.
- O To conduct interdisciplinary research in all areas of speech technology including speech recognition, speech synthesis, speech signal processing, information access, multimodal interfaces and dialogue systems

Centre for Spinal Disorders

- Robert Jones and Agnes Hunt Orthopaedic and District General Hospital,Oswestry, Shropshire, SY10 7AG.
  01691 404000   fax 01691 404050
  http://www.keele.ac.uk/depts/rjah/
- E A research centre within the Institute of Orthopaedics (qv)
- O To conduct clinical and basic sciences research into back pain and spinal deformities such as scoliosis

Centre for Spinal Studies 1987

- Robert Jones and Agnes Hunt Orthopaedic and District General Hospital, Oswestry, Shropshire, SY10 7AG.
  01691 655311
  http://www.rjah.nhs.uk/Default.aspx?tabid=875
- E A registered charity.
- O To undertake research in all aspects of spinal disorders

Centre for Spirituality, Health and Disability

- School of Divinity, History and Philosophy, King's College, University of Aberdeen, Aberdeen, AB24 3UB.
  01224 273224   fax 01224 273750
  http://www.abdn.ac.uk/cssh/
  Director: Prof John Swinton.
- E A research centre at the University of Aberdeen.

Centre in Sport, Exercise and Performance
    see **Research Centre in Sport, Exercise and Performance**

Centre for Sport and Exercise Research (CSER) 2002

- Faculty of Health and Sciences, Staffordshire University, Brindley Building, Leek Road, Stoke-on-Trent, ST4 2DF.
  01782 295855
  http://www.staffs.ac.uk/schools/sciences/ihr/cser/
  Director: Prof Tom Cochrane.
- E A research centre within the Institute for Health Research (qv) at Staffordshire University.
- O To support and promote international excellence in applied research with communities, professionals and practitioners

Centre for Sport and Exercise Science (CSES) 1999

- Faculty of Health and Well Being, City Campus, Sheffield Hallam University, 33 Collegiate Crescent, Sheffield, S10 2BP.
  0114-225 2544   fax 0114-225 4341
  http://www.shu.ac.uk/cses/
  Director: Prof Ian Maynard.
- E A research centre at Sheffield Hallam University.
- O To conduct research and provide consultancy in education and training for physical activity and well-being, performance enhancement, and sports engineering

Centre for Sports and Exercise Medicine (CSEM)

- Barts and the London, Queen Mary's School of Medicine and Dentistry, Queen Mary, University of London, Turner Street, London, E1 2AD.
  020 7882 5555
  http://www.smd.qmul.ac.uk/sportsmed/
- E A research centre within the Institute of Health Sciences Education (qv) at Queen Mary, University of London.

Centre for Sports and Exercise Science (CSES)

- Department of Biological Sciences, University of Essex, Wivenhoe Park, Colchester, Essex, CO4 3SQ.
  01206 873326
  http://www.essex.ac.uk/bs/cses/
  Director: Dr Martin Sellens, BSc.
- E A centre at the University of Essex.

Centre for Sports Science and History

Note: has amalgamated with the Medical School Library of the University of Birmingham and is therefore no longer within the scope of this Directory.

© CBD Research Ltd · Beckenham · Kent BR3 5JS · Tel 020 8650 7745 · Fax 020 8650 0768 · E-mail cbd@cbdresearch.com · www.cbdresearch.com

Centre for Sports Studies   (CSS)
- ■   Faculty of Social Sciences, University of Kent, Medway Building, Chatham Maritime, Chatham, Kent, ME4 4AG.
    01634 888807   fax 01634 888890
    http://www.kent.ac.uk/sports-studies/
    Director: Steve Uglow.
- E   A research centre at the University of Kent.
- O   To offer a programme of undergraduate degree courses in sports and exercise

Centre for Sports Surfaces
    see **Cranfield Centre for Sports Surfaces.**

Centre for Staff and Learning Development
    see **Oxford Centre for Staff and Learning Development.**

Centre for Stakeholder Learning Partnerships   (CSLP)   2005
- ■   Faculty of Health, Birmingham City University, Ravensbury House, Westbourne Road, Birmingham, B15 3TN.
    0121-331 6082
    http://www.hcc.uce.ac.uk/cetl/
    Director: Dr Stuart Brand.
- E   A Centre for Excellence in Teaching and Learning (CETL) at Birmingham City University.
- Note: See **Centres for Excellence in Teaching and Learning** for more information.

Centre for Stakeholding and Sustainable Enterprise   (CSSE)   1997
- ■   Kingston Business School, Kingston University, Kingston Hill, Kingston-upon-Thames, Surrey, KT1 7LB.
    020 8547 7454
    http://business.kingston.ac.uk/CSSE.php
    Contact: Charles Jackson.
- E   A research centre at Kingston University, London.
- O   To promote sustainable development in business through the successful engagement of stakeholders

Centre for Stammering Children
    see **Michael Palin Centre for Stammering Children.**

Centre for Standardisation of Welsh Terminology   Canolfan Bedwyr e - Gymraeg: Terminoleg a Pheirianneg Iaith
- ■   Department of Welsh Language and Literature, University of Wales Bangor, Bangor, Gwynedd, LL57 2DG.
    01248 383293   fax 01248 383293
    http://www.e-gymraeg.org/
- E   A centre at the University of Wales, Bangor.

Centre for Statistical Education
    see **Royal Statistical Society Centre for Statistical Education.**

Centre for Statistics
- ■   Department of Mathematical Sciences, Queen Mary, University of London, Mile End Road, London, E1 4NS.
    020 7882 5555   fax 020 7882 5556
    http://www.stats.qmul.ac.uk/
    Director: Prof Steven Gilmour.
- E   An interdisciplinary research centre at Queen Mary, University of London.

Centre for Stem Cell Biology   (CSCB)
- ■   Department of Biomedical Science, University of Sheffield, Addison Building, Western Bank, Sheffield, S10 2TN.
    0114-222 1082   fax 0114-276 5413
    http://cscb.shef.ac.uk/
- E   A research centre within the Krebs Institute of Biomolecular Research (qv) at the University of Sheffield.
- O   To undertake research and provide training in stem cell biology
- ●   Education and training - Seminars

Centre for Stem Cell Biology and Medicine
    see **MRC Centre for Stem Cell Biology and Medicine.**

Centre for Stem Cell Biology and Regenerative Medicine
- ■   School of Biological and Biomedical Sciences, University of Durham, South Road, Durham, DH1 3LE.
    0191-334 1200
    http://www.dur.ac.uk/stem.cells/
- E   An interdisciplinary research centre at the University of Durham.
- O   To characterise stem cells, to identify how to manipulate their fate, and to develop new therapies for degenerative human disease

Centre for Stem Cell Research
    see **Institute for Stem Cell Research.**

Centre for Stem Cell Research and Institute for Stem Cell Biology
　　see **Wellcome Trust Centre for Stem Cell Research and Institute for Stem Cell Biology.**

Centre for Storytelling
　　see **George Ewart Evans Centre for Storytelling.**

Centre for Strategic Leadership
- National School of Government, Larch Avenue, Ascot, Berkshire, SL5 0QE.
  　01344 634000　fax 01344 634233
  　http://www.nationalschool.gov.uk/leadership/
  　Head: Robin Hyde.
- E　A centre at the National School of Government.
- O　To support and lead strategic change across Government

Centre for Strategic Studies [Anglia Ruskin]　(CSS)
- Ashcroft International Business School, Anglia Ruskin University, East Road, Cambridge, CB1 1PT.
  　0845 271 3333
  　http://www.anglia.ac.uk/ruskin/en/home/business/css.html
- E　A research centre at Anglia Ruskin University.
- O　To provide an environment in which corporate and academic partners work together to drive forward thinking on strategic management approaches through the exchange of ideas of leading theory and practice

Centre for Strategic Studies [London]
　　see **Gulf Centre for Strategic Studies.**

Centre for Strategic Studies [Reading]　2000
- Graduate Institute of Political and International Studies, Whiteknights, PO Box 217, University of Reading, Reading, Berkshire, RG6 6AH.
  　0118-378 8378
  　http://www.rdg.ac.uk/GIPIS/Research%207/Research%20Centres.htm
- E　A research centre within the Graduate Institute of Political and International Studies (qv) at the University of Reading.
- O　To conduct research and dialogue on all matters relating directly to the threat and use of organised force for political purposes

Centre for Stress Management　1987
- 156 Westcombe Hill, London, SE3 7DH.
  　020 8293 4334　fax 020 8293 4114
  　Director: Prof Stephen Palmer. Administrator: Dawn Cope.
- E　A profit-making business.
- O　To promote the use of stress management; to provide certificate and diploma courses on stress management, cognitive therapy, multimodal therapy and coaching
- ● Coaching - Consultancy and stress audits - Counselling - Training - Short courses and workshops for health professionals

Centre for Stress Research [Chester]
　　see **Chester Centre for Stress Research.**

Centre for Stress Research　1991
- Room 6 - Building 44, London Road, University of Reading, Reading, Berkshire, RG1 5AQ.
  　0118-975 6059
  　Director: Dean Juniper.
- E　A private venture within the University of Reading.
- O　To further research into the causes and amelioration of stress
- ● Conference facilities - Education and training

Centre for Structural and Architectural Engineering　(CSAE)
- Department of Architecture and Civil Engineering, University of Bath, Claverton Down, Bath, BA2 7AY.
  　01225 386526　fax 01225 383255
  　http://www.bath.ac.uk/csae/
  　Contact: Dr T Ibell.
- E　A centre at the University of Bath.
- O　To conduct research into the application of engineering to the structural and material aspects of building structures

Centre for Structural Biology [Cambridge]
　　see **Cambridge and East Anglia Centre for Structural Biology.**

Centre for Structural Biology　(CSB)
- Faculty of Life Sciences, Imperial College London, Wolfson Building, Exhibition Road, London, SW7 2AZ.
  　020 7594 3064　fax 020 7594 3022
  　http://www.imperial.ac.uk/structuralbiology/
  　Director: Prof So Iwata.
- E　A research centre at Imperial College London.
- O　To promote internationally competitive structural biology research and training

Centre for Structural Biology [London, WC1E]
see **Bloomsbury Centre for Structural Biology.**

Centre for Structural Molecular Biology
see **Astbury Centre for Structural Molecular Biology.**

Centre for Studies in Advanced Learning Technology   (CSALT)   1992
- ■   Department of Educational Research, Lancaster University, County College South, Lancaster, LA1 4YL.
  01524 592685
  http://csalt.lancs.ac.uk/
  Director: Prof David McConnell.
- E   A research centre at Lancaster University.

Centre for Studies in Democratization   (CSD)   1992
- ■   Department of Politics and International Studies, University of Warwick, Coventry, CV4 7AL.
  024 7652 3302   fax 024 7652 4221
  http://www2.warwick.ac.uk/fac/soc/pais/research/csd/
  Contact: Peter Ferdinand.
- E   An interdisciplinary research centre at the University of Warwick.
- O   To provide a focal point for studies in democratization

Centre for Studies in Implicit Religion   (CSIR)   2001
- ■   Department of Theology and Religious Studies, Normal Site, University of Wales Bangor, Bangor, Gwynedd, LL57 2PZ.
  01248 382566   fax 01248 383954
  http://www.bangor.ac.uk/rs/pt/ir/
  Director: Revd Canon Prof Edward Bailey.
- E   A research centre at the University of Wales, Bangor.
- O   To conduct research into the many ways in which religion and spirituality are given expression in today's society, outside the framework of the Christian churches and outside the framework of other world faiths

Centre for Studies on Inclusive Education   (CSIE)   1982
- ■   University of the West of England, New Redland, Coldharbour Lane, Bristol, BS16 1QU.
  0117-328 4007   fax 0117-328 4005
  http://inclusion.uwe.ac.uk/csie/
- E   A registered charity, a company limited by guarantee and part of the University of the West of England.
- O   To work in the UK and overseas to end the practice of segregated education for disabled children

Centre for Studies in Intellectual Property and Technology Law
see **AHRC Research Centre for Studies in Intellectual Property and Technology Law.**

Centre for Studies in Rural Ministry   (CSRM)   2001
- ■   Department of Theology and Religious Studies, Normal Site, University of Wales Bangor, Bangor, Gwynedd, LL57 2PZ.
  01248 382566   fax 01248 383954
  http://www.bangor.ac.uk/rs/pt/rm/
  Co-Director: Prof Leslie J Francis, PhD, ScD, DD. Co-Director: Revd Canon Jeremy Martineau.
- E   A research centre at the University of Wales, Bangor.
- O   To be a research and education resource for the rural churches

Centre for Studies in Science and Mathematics Education   (CSSME)   1971
- ■   School of Education, University of Leeds, Leeds, LS2 9JT.
  0113-343 4675   fax 0113-343 4683
  http://www.education.leeds.ac.uk/research/cssme/
  Director: Prof Phil Scott.
- E   An interdisciplinary research centre at the University of Leeds.
- O   To provide and monitor courses for the initial training of graduates for the teaching profession at primary and secondary level; to provide courses for students reading for higher degrees and to develop them in the light of changing conditions
- ●   Conference facilities - Education and training

Centre for Studies in Security and Diplomacy   (CSSD)   1998
- ■   University of Birmingham, Edgbaston, Birmingham, B15 2TT.
  0121-414 6950   fax 0121-414 2596
  http://www.cssd.bham.ac.uk/
  Centre Manager: Amanda Griffiths.
- E   A research centre within the European Research Institute (qv) at the University of Birmingham.
- O   To promote common sustainable agendas between policy makers and academics in security and diplomacy

Centre for Studies of Surrealism and its Legacies [Essex]
see **AHRC Research Centre for Studies of Surrealism and its Legacies [Essex].**

Centre for Studies of Surrealism and its Legacies [Manchester]
see **AHRC Research Centre for Studies of Surrealism and its Legacies [Manchester].**

Centre for Studies in the Visual Culture of Religion   (CSVCR)   1999
- School of Art, Buarth Mawr, Aberystwyth, Ceredigion, SY23 1NG.
   01970 622460   fax 01970 622461
   http://www.visual-religion.co.uk/
   Director: John Harvey.
- E A research centre at the University of Wales, Aberystwyth.
- O To examine the visual culture of churches, sects, and systems of belief outside the established church traditions

Centre for the Study of African Economies   (CSAE)
- Department of Economics, University of Oxford, Manor Road, Oxford, OX1 3UQ.
   01865 271084   fax 01865 281447
   http://www.csae.ox.ac.uk/
   Director: Prof P Collier.
- E A centre at the University of Oxford.
- O To conduct research into both macro- and micro-economic problems facing individuals, organisations and countries

Centre for the Study of Ancient Documents   (CSAD)   1995
- University of Oxford, The Old Boys' School, George Street, Oxford, OX1 2RL.
   01865 288180   fax 01865 288262
   http://www.csad.ox.ac.uk/
   Director: Alan K Bowman, MA, PhD, FBA.
- E A centre at the University of Oxford.
- O To provide a focus within Oxford for the study of ancient documents

Centre for the Study of Ancient Systems of Knowledge
   see **Logos: Centre for the Study of Ancient Systems of Knowledge.**

Centre for the Study of Anomalous Psychological Processes   (CSAPP)
- School of Social Sciences, University of Northampton, Boughton Green Road, Northampton, NN2 7AL.
   01604 735500
   http://www.northampton.ac.uk/research/centres/
   Director: Prof Deborah Delanoy.
- E A research centre at the University of Northampton.
- O To become a recognised national and international centre in the areas of parapsychological and transpersonal psychological research

Centre for the Study of the Bible in the Modern World
- Department of Biblical Studies, Arts Tower, University of Sheffield, Western Bank, Sheffield, S10 2TN.
   0114-222 0507; 0508
   http://www.shef.ac.uk/bibs/modernworld
   Director: Prof J Cheryl Exum.
- E A research centre at the University of Sheffield.
- O To develop a centre of international excellence, identifying the Bible in the modern world as an essential theme for biblical research, as a significant element in contemporary culture, and as a strategic interface between the scholarly world and centres of cultural understanding and influence, such as the media

Centre for the Study of Bioscience, Biomedicine, Biotechnology and Society
   see **BIOS Centre.**

Centre for the Study of Britain and its Empire
   see **Centre for Imperial and Post-Colonial Studies.**

Centre for the Study of Byron and Romanticism   (CSBR)
- School of English Studies, University of Nottingham, University Park, Nottingham, NG7 2RD.
   0115-951 4610   fax 0115-951 5924
   http://byron.nottingham.ac.uk/
   Director: Dr Matt Green.
- E A research centre at the University of Nottingham.
- O To broaden understanding of cultural interaction in the Romantic period, particularly between figures like Byron and other writers from the late eighteenth and early nineteenth centuries, including lesser known writers in Britain and beyond

Centre for the Study of Cartoons and Caricature
Note: has become the British Cartoon Archive and is therefore outside the scope of this directory

Centre for the Study of Central Europe   (CSCE)
- School of Slavonic and East European Studies, University College London, Gower Street, London, WC1E 6BT.
   020 7679 8774
   http://www.ssees.ac.uk/csce.htm
   Director: Dr Rebecca Haynes. Administrator: Susie Rizvi.
- E A research centre at University College London.

Centre for the Study of Child, the Family and the Law   (CSCFL)

■   Liverpool School of Law, University of Liverpool, Liverpool, L69 7ZS.
      0151-794 3819   fax 0151-794 2884
      http://www.liv.ac.uk/law/cscfl/
      Co-Director: Prof Christina Lyon. Co-Director: Stephanie Petrie.
E   A research centre at the University of Liverpool.

Centre for the Study of Childhood and Youth   (CSCY)   2002

■   University of Sheffield, Western Bank, Sheffield, S10 2TN.
      0114-222 2000
      http://www.cscy.group.shef.ac.uk/
      Director: Dr Alan France.
E   A research centre at the University of Sheffield.
○   To contribute to the improvement of children and young people's lives

Centre for the Study of Children, Youth and Media   (CSCYM)

■   School of Culture, Language and Education, London Knowledge Lab, University of London, 23-29 Emerald Street, London, WC1N 3QS.
      020 7763 2180   fax 020 7763 2144
      http://www.childrenyouthandmediacentre.co.uk/
      Contact: Prof David Buckingham.
E   A research centre within the Institute of Education (qv) at the University of London.
○   To focus on a wide range of aspects relating to young people both as consumers and producers of media, including media texts, media industries and media audiences

Centre for the Study of the Christian Church   (CSCC)

■   Department of Theology, University of Exeter, Queen's Building, The Queen's Drive, Exeter, EX4 4QH.
      01392 264242
      http://www.centres.ex.ac.uk/CSCC
      Contact: Dr Paul Avis.
E   A centre at the University of Exeter.
○   To promote the scholarly study of the Christian Church, in particular its nature, unity, ministry and mission

Centre for the Study of Cities and Regions   (CSCR)

■   Queen's Campus, University of Durham, University Boulevard, Thornaby, Stockton-on-Tees, TS17 6BH.
      0191-334 0455
      http://www.dur.ac.uk/cscr/
      Director: Prof Joe Painter.
E   A specialist research centre within the Wolfson Research Institute (qv) at the University of Durham.
○   To undertake research on urban and regional change, and on policies for urban and regional development

Centre for the Study of the Civil Law Tradition   1994

■   Aberdeen University School of Law, University of Aberdeen, Taylor Building, Aberdeen, AB24 3UB.
      01224 272441   fax 01224 272442
      http://www.abdn.ac.uk/law/civillawcentre/
E   A research centre at the University of Aberdeen.
○   To research the classical Roman law, its second life in Europe, and the means by which it was transmitted into modern legal systems
Note: Also known as the Civil Law Centre.

Centre for the Study of Colonial and Postcolonial Cultures
      see **Centre for Colonial and Postcolonial Studies (Sussex).**

Centre for the Study of Colonial and Postcolonial Societies

■   Faculty of Arts, University of Bristol, Senate House, Tyndall Avenue, Bristol, BS8 1TH.
      0117-928 7930   fax 0117-928 8276
      http://www.bris.ac.uk/colonialstudies/
      Director: Prof Robert Bickers.
E   An interdisciplinary research centre at the University of Bristol.
○   To explore all facets of the history, culture, representation and legacy of colonialism in comparative perspective - across time and across empires - and amongst the colonised and the coloniser

Centre for Study of Comparative Change and Development   (CCCD)

■   Department of Criminology and Sociological Studies, University of Hull, Cottingham Road, Hull, HU6 7RX.
      01482 346311
      http://www.hull.ac.uk/cccd/
E   A research centre at the University of Hull.

Centre for the Study of Comprehensive Schools (CSCS) 1981

NR   The Knowledge Exchange, University of Northampton, Boughton Green Road, Northampton, NN2 7AL.
01604 892711   fax 01604 791114
http://www.cscs.org.uk/
Director: Tim Bartlett. Administrator: Alison Paget.

E   A charitable trust, affiliated to the University of Leicester and based at the University of Northampton.

○   To support and promote education of quality in schools through studies of good practice, and by provision of opportunities; to share knowledge and experiences of comprehensive education through a network of schools, local education authorities, industry and higher and further education institutions

Centre for the Study of Composition for Screen (CSCS) 1998

■   Royal College of Music, Prince Consort Road, South Kensington, London, SW7 2BS.
020 7589 3643   fax 020 7589 7740
http://www.rcm.ac.uk/jkcm/default.aspx?pg=2037
Head of Music Technology: David Burnand.

E   A research centre at the Royal College of Music.

○   To promote education and research in music for film and television, with a particular emphasis on practice-based research

Centre for the Study of Conflict
    see **Callaghan Centre for the Study of Conflict.**

Centre for the Study of Constitutionalism and National Identity
    see **Cunliffe Centre for the Study of Constitutionalism and National Identity.**

Centre for the Study of the Country House 2006

■   Department of History of Art and Film, University of Leicester, Leicester, LE1 7RH.
0116-252 2866
http://www.le.ac.uk/ha/countryhouse/
Director: Dr Phillip Lindley.

E   A research centre at the University of Leicester.

○   To promote all aspects of the study of great historic houses and their surroundings, their design, construction and conservation

Centre for the Study of Crime
    see **Vauxhall Centre for the Study of Crime.**

Centre for the Study of Criminology and Criminal Justice
    see **Mannheim Centre for the Study of Criminology and Criminal Justice.**

Centre for the Study of Democracy (CSD) 1989

■   School of Social Sciences, Humanities and Languages, University of Westminster, 32-38 Wells Street, London, W1T 3UW.
020 7911 5138   fax 020 7911 5164
http://www.wmin.ac.uk/sshl/page-1
Director: Dr Simon Joss.

E   A research centre at the University of Westminster.

○   To conduct research and teaching in international relations, political theory and cultural studies

Centre for the Study of the Design of the Modern Interior
    see **Modern Interiors Research Centre.**

Centre for the Study of the Domestic Interior
    see **AHRC Centre for the Study of the Domestic Interior**

Centre for the Study of Economic and Social Change in Europe (CSESCE)

■   School of Slavonic and East European Studies, University College London, Gower Street, London, WC1E 6BT.
020 7679 8757; 8810
http://www.ssees.ac.uk/csesce.htm
Director: Dr Tomasz Mickiewicz. Administrator: Hannah Spikesley.

E   A research centre at University College London.

Centre for the Study of Education in an International Context (CEIC)

■   Department of Education, University of Bath, Claverton Down, Bath, BA2 7AY.
01225 386120
http://www.bath.ac.uk/ceic/
Director: Dr Mary Hayden.

E   A research centre at the University of Bath.

© CBD Research Ltd · Beckenham · Kent BR3 5JS · Tel 020 8650 7745 · Fax 020 8650 0768 · E-mail cbd@cbdresearch.com · www.cbdresearch.com

Centre for the Study of Education and Training   (CSET)
■   Faculty of Social Sciences, Lancaster University, County South, Bailrigg, Lancaster, LA1 4YD.
    01524 592679   fax 01524 592914
    http://www.lancs.ac.uk/fss/centres/cset/cset.htm
    Director: Prof M Saunders.
E   A department of Lancaster University.
○   To conduct research in the fields of adult learning, basic skills and literacy, competence based qualifications and core skills,
    education and work, evaluation and quality, guidance, careers, individual action plans and records of achievement, higher and
    further education, teacher support and professional development, teaching and learning strategies, training strategies and
    management development
●   Consultancy - The Centre carries out work with all sectors of the education and training community

Centre for the Study of Educational Technologies   (CSET)
■   Walton Hall, Milton Keynes, MK7 6AA.
    01908 274066
    http://iet.open.ac.uk/about/maingroups/cset/
E   A research centre within the Institute of Educational Technology (qv) at the Open University.

Centre for the Study of Emotion and Motivation   (CSEM)
■   School of Psychology, University of Southampton, Shackleton Building, Highfield, Southampton, SO17 1BJ.
    023 8059 3995   fax 023 8059 4597
    http://www.psychology.soton.ac.uk/research/emotion.php
    Co-Director: Prof Brendan Bradley. Co-Director: Prof Karin Mogg.
E   A research centre at the University of Southampton.
○   To act as a focus for research into normal and abnormal aspects of emotional and motivational processes

Centre for the Study of Environmental Change   (CSEC)   1991
■   Department of Sociology, Lancaster University, Furness College, Lancaster, LA1 4YG.
    01524 594178   fax 01524 594256
    http://csec.lancs.ac.uk/
    Director: Bronislaw Szerszynski.
E   A research centre within Lancaster University.
○   To research into issues now regarded as environmental and central to the agendas of political institutions, industries, social
    organisations and individuals worldwide; to look into new (and proliferating) forms of regulation, economic incentive and
    partnership aimed at addressing such problems both nationally and internationally

Centre for the Study of Environmental Change and Sustainability   (CECS)
■   University of Edinburgh, The King's Buildings, Mayfield Road, Edinburgh, EH9 3JK.
    0131-650 4866   fax 0131-650 7214
    http://www.geos.ed.ac.uk/research/cecs/
    Director: Dr Andy McLeod.
E   A research centre at the University of Edinburgh.
○   To pursue active research into the causes and impacts of global environmental change and the technologies and policies needed
    to achieve sustainable development

Centre for the Study of Esotericism
        see **Exeter Centre for the Study of Esotericism.**

Centre for the Study of Ethnic Conflict   (CSEC)   1998
■   School of Politics and International Studies, Queen's University of Belfast, 19-21 University Square, Belfast, BT7 1PA.
    028 9097 5028   fax 028 9023 5373
    http://www.qub.ac.uk/csec/
    Director: Prof Adrian Guelke.
E   A centre at Queen's University, Belfast.
○   To promote research into societies that are or have been deeply divided in terms of their ethnic and national identities

Centre for the Study of Ethnicity and Citizenship   1999
■   Department of Sociology, University of Bristol, 12 Woodland Road, Bristol, BS8 1UQ.
    0117-928 8218   fax 0117-954 6609
    http://www.bristol.ac.uk/sociology/ethnicitycitizenship/
    Director: Prof Tariq Modood. Assistant Director: Prof Steve Fenton.
E   A part of the University of Bristol.
○   To stimulate debate and discussion on social change that affects ethnic minority communities in Europe

Centre for the Study of European Governance   (CSEG)
■   School of Politics and International Relations, University of Nottingham, University Park, Nottingham, NG7 2RD.
    0115-951 4862
    http://www.nottingham.ac.uk/politics/research/research_cseg.php
    Director: Dr Catherine Fieschi.
E   A research centre at the University of Nottingham.
○   To encourage research that explores issues of governance and European politics through a variety of theoretical means and
    methodological approaches

Centre for the Study of Evolution   (CSE)
- ■ Department of Biochemistry, University of Sussex, John Maynard Smith Building, Falmer, Brighton, East Sussex, BN1 9QG.
  01273 678480   fax 01273 877586
  http://www.lifesci.sussex.ac.uk/CSE
  Contact: Adam Eyre-Walker.
- E   A cross-disciplinary research centre at the University of Sussex.
- O   To develop and utilize evolutionary ideas

Centre for the Study of Expertise   (CSE)
- ■ School of Social Sciences and Law, Brunel University, Uxbridge, Middlesex, UB8 3PH.
  01895 265484
  http://www.brunel.ac.uk/about/acad/sssl/ssslresearch/centres/researchs
  Director: Prof Fernand Gobet.
- E   A research centre at Brunel University.
- O   To understand the perceptual and cognitive mechanisms underpinning expert behaviour, and how knowledge and skill are acquired over time

Centre for the Study of Financial Innovation   (CSFI)   1993
- ■ 5 Derby Street, London, W1J 7AB.
  020 7493 0173   fax 020 7493 0190
  http://www.csfi.org.uk/
- E   A registered charity and membership organisation.
- O   To provide a forum for research and debate into new developments in the financial services industry

Centre for the Study of Gambling   (CSG)   1994
- ■ Salford Business School, University of Salford, Maxwell Building, Salford, Manchester, M5 4WT.
  0161-295 6200
  http://www.gamblingstudies.salford.ac.uk/
  Director: Prof Peter Collins. Executive Officer: Kath Milhench.
- E   A research centre at the University of Salford.
- O   To conduct research relating to the gambling industry; to conduct teaching for people interested in developing a career within the industry; to increase understanding of the industry by the wider public

Centre for the Study of Global Change and Governance
- ■ Graduate Institute of Political and International Studies, University of Reading, Whiteknights, PO Box 217, Reading, Berkshire, RG6 6AH.
  0118-378 8378
  http://www.reading.ac.uk/GIPIS/Research%207/Research%20Centres.htm
- E   A research centre within the Graduate Institute of Political and International Studies (qv) at the University of Reading.
- O   To conduct research into the implications for human governance, at all levels, of a wide range of environmental, economic, political and social changes within the global system

Centre for the Study of Global Ethics   (CSGE)
- ■ School of Social Sciences, University of Birmingham, Edgbaston, Birmingham, B15 2TT.
  0121-414 8442   fax 0121-414 8453
  http://www.globalethics.bham.ac.uk/
  Director: Prof Tim Sorrell.
- E   A centre at the University of Birmingham.
- O   To undertake a collaborative and multidisciplinary approach to research into the ethical issues of our time

Centre for the Study of Global Governance   (CSGG)   1992
- ■ LSE, Houghton Street, London, WC2A 2AE.
  020 7955 7583
  http://www.lse.ac.uk/Depts/global/
  Co-Director: Prof David Held. Co-Director: Prof Mary Kaldor.
- E   A research centre at the London School of Economics and Political Science.
- O   To increase understanding and knowledge of global issues in relation to global governance

Centre for the Study of Globalisation and Regionalisation   (CSGR)   1997
- ■ Faculty of Social Studies, Coventry University, Coventry, CV4 7AL.
  024 7657 2533   fax 024 7657 2548
  http://www2.warwick.ac.uk/fac/soc/csgr/
  Director: Prof Richard Higgott.
- E   A designated research centre of the Economic and Social Research Council at the University of Warwick.
- O   To develop research that can better define, measure, explain and evaluate a world with more pronounced global and regional qualities

© CBD Research Ltd · Beckenham · Kent BR3 5JS · Tel 020 8650 7745 · Fax 020 8650 0768 · E-mail cbd@cbdresearch.com · www.cbdresearch.com

Centre for the Study of Governance in the European Union   (CSGEU)
- ■ School of Politics and International Studies, University of Leeds, Leeds, LS2 9JT.
   0113-343 4382
   http://www.leeds.ac.uk/polis/research/csgeu/
   Director: Dr Neil Winn.
- E A research centre within the University of Leeds.
- O To produce cutting-edge research into the changing governance of the European Union

Centre for the Study of Group Processes   (CSGP)   1990
- ■ Department of Psychology, Keynes College, University of Kent, Canterbury, Kent, CT2 7NP.
   01227 823961   fax 01227 827030
   http://www.kent.ac.uk/psychology/
   Director: Prof Dominic Abrams.
- E A research centre at the University of Kent.
- O To conduct social psychological research into group processes and intergroup relations

Centre for the Study of Health and Illness   (CSHI)   1989
- ■ School of Social Sciences and Law, Brunel University, Uxbridge, Middlesex, UB8 3PH.
   01895 274000
   http://www.brunel.ac.uk/
   Director: Prof Clive Seale.
- E A centre at Brunel University.
- O To carry out research into the individual, social and cultural processes through which disease, illness, sickness, health and disablement are defined, explained and managed

Centre for the Study of Higher Education   (CSHE)   2006
- ■ School of Art and Design, Coventry University, Priory Street, Coventry, CV1 5FB.
   024 7688 7588
   http://www.corporate.coventry.ac.uk/cms/
   Director: Prof Paul Blackmore. Administration Manager: Maggie Eggar.
- E A department of Coventry University.
- O To undertake research, development and consultancy in academic practice in relation to academic leadership and management, and teaching and learning (including online learning and WebCT support
- × Centre for Higher Education Development.

Centre for the Study of the History of Social Investigation
   see **Charles Booth Centre for the Study of the History of Social Investigation.**

Centre for the Study of Human Development and Well-Being   (CHDW)   2003
- ■ Department of Psychology, City University, Northampton Square, London, EC1V 0HB.
   020 7040 8531
   http://www.city.ac.uk/psychology/research/chdw/
- E A centre at City University.
- O To be a focal point for research on questions of human development across the life course, psychosocial well-being and health

Centre for the Study of Human Relations   (CSHR)   1990
- ■ School of Education, Jubilee Campus, University of Nottingham, Wollaton Road, Nottingham, NG8 1BB.
   0115-951 4457   fax 0115-846 6600
   http://www.nottingham.ac.uk/education/centres/cshr/
   Contact: Dr Max Biddulph.
- E A research centre at the University of Nottingham.

Centre for the Study of Human Rights   (CSHR)   2000
- ■ LSE, Houghton Street, London, WC2A 2AE.
   020 7955 6554   fax 020 7955 6934
   http://www.lse.ac.uk/Depts/human-rights/
   Director: Prof Conor Gearty.
- E A research centre at the London School of Economics and Political Science.
- O To promote the study of human rights in a dynamic and critically-aware fashion, thereby engaging the interest and excitement of the scholarly community, human rights practitioners and the wider public

Centre for the Study of Human Rights Law   (CSHRL)   1999
- NR School of Law, University of Glasgow, Stair Building, 5-8 The Square, Glasgow, G12 8QQ.
   0141-330 3583   fax 0141-330 4900
   http://www.law.strath.ac.uk/chrl/
   Co-Director: Prof Jim Murdoch.
- E A research centre at the University of Glasgow.
- O To study all aspects of human rights law
- Note: A joint operation with Strathclyde University.

Centre for the Study of Human Rights Law   (CSHRL)   1999

NR   The Law School, University of Strathclyde, Stenhouse Building, 173 Cathedral Street, Glasgow, G4 0RQ.
     0141-548 4264; 4428 fax 0141-548 3119
     http://www.law.strath.ac.uk/chrl/
     Co-Director: Prof Noel Whitty.
E   A research centre at the University of Strathclyde.
Note: A joint venture with the University of Glasgow (see above).

Centre for the Study of Information and Technology in Peace, Conflict Resolution and Human Rights
    see **Praxis Centre - Centre for the Study of Information and Technology in Peace, Conflict Resolution and Human Rights.**

Centre for the Study of International Governance   (CSIG)   2006

■   Department of Politics, International Relations and European Studies, Loughborough University, Loughborough, Leicestershire, LE11 3TU.
     01509 222991 fax 01509 223917
     http://www.lboro.ac.uk/departments/eu/CSIG/
     Co-Director: Prof Brian Hocking. Co-Director: Prof Michael Smith.
E   A research centre at Loughborough University
○   To provide a focus for research on the changing nature of world politics and the challenges posed by managing relationships between an increasingly diverse range of actors at the global, regional, national and subnational levels.

Centre for the Study of Invention and Social Process   (CSISP)

■   Department of Sociology, Goldsmiths, University of London, London, SE14 6NW.
     020 7919 7731 fax 020 7919 7713
     http://www.goldsmiths.ac.uk/csisp/
     Director: Dr Mariam Fraser.
E   A research centre at Goldsmiths, University of London.

Centre for the Study of Islam   (CSI)   1998

■   Department of Theology and Religious Studies, University of Glasgow, 4 The Square, Glasgow, G12 8QQ.
     0141-330 6526 fax 0141-330 4943
     http://www.religions.divinity.gla.ac.uk/
     Head: Dr Mona Siddiqui.
E   A research centre at the University of Glasgow.
○   To develop the field of Islamic studies and to promote a better understanding of Islam and Muslims

Centre for the Study of Islam in the UK   (CSI-UK   2005

■   Cardiff School of Religious and Theological Studies, Cardiff University, Humanities Building, Colum Drive, Cardiff, CF10 3EU.
     029 2087 6125 fax 029 2087 4500
     http://www.cardiff.ac.uk/schoolsanddivisions/academicschools/relig/research/centres/islam-uk/
     Director: Dr Sophie Gilliat-Ray.
E   A centre at Cardiff University.
○   To promote scholarly understanding of Islam and the life of Muslim communities in the UK

Centre for the Study of Japanese Religions   (CSJR)   1999

■   Faculty of Languages and Cultures, School of Oriental and African Studies, University of London, Thornhaugh Street, Russell Square, London, WC1H 0XG.
     020 7898 4101 fax 020 7898 4399
     http://www.soas.ac.uk/centres/centreinfo.cfm?navid=19
     Director: Dr Lucia Dolce.
E   A research centre at the School of Oriental and African Studies, University of London.
○   To promote the academic study of Japanese religions past and present

Centre for the Study of Jewish-Christian Relations   (CJCR)

■   University of Cambridge, Wesley House, Jesus Lane, Cambridge, CB5 8BJ.
     01223 741048
     http://www.cjcr.cam.ac.uk/
     Director: Dr Edward Kessler.
E   A centre at the University of Cambridge.
○   To dedicate itself to the study and teaching of all aspects of the encounter between Christians and Jews throughout the ages

Centre for the Study of Knowledge, Expertise and Science   (KES)

■   Cardiff School of Social Sciences, Cardiff University, Glamorgan Building, King Edward VII Avenue, Cardiff, CF10 3WT.
     029 2087 5179
     http://www.cardiff.ac.uk/socsi/research/researchcentres/kes/
E   A centre at Cardiff University.
○   To conduct specialist research in sociology and history of science, sociology of scientific and medical knowledge, and studies of the nature of expertise as a form of knowledge

Centre for the Study of Law and Policy in Europe   (CSLPE)   1993
- School of Law, University of Leeds, 31 Lyddon Terrace, Leeds, LS2 9JT.
   0113-343 7040
   http://www.law.leeds.ac.uk/leedslaw/
   Director: Prof Louise Ackers.
- E   A research centre at the University of Leeds.
- O   To promote research activities in European legal studies
- ● Education and training

Centre for the Study of Law, Society and Popular Culture
- School of Law, University of Westminster, 4-12 Little Titchfield Street, London, W1W 7UW.
   020 7911 5000   fax 020 7911 5821
   http://www.wmin.ac.uk/law/page-497
   Co-Director: Steve Greenfield. Co-Director: Guy Osborn.
- E   A research centre at the University of Westminster.

Centre for the Study of Liberty
   see **Max Beloff Centre for the Study of Liberty.**

Centre for the Study of Literature, Theology and the Arts   1982
- Department of Theology and Religious Studies, University of Glasgow, 4 The Square, Glasgow, G12 8QQ.
   0141-330 6526   fax 0141-330 4943
   http://www.religions.divinity.gla.ac.uk/Centre_Literature/
   Co-Director: Yvonne Sherwood. Co-Director: Heather Walton.
- E   A research centre at the University of Glasgow.
- O   To conduct research into theology in its widest sense and including Christianity, Judaism, Islam, Buddhism, Hinduism, Chinese Religions, and in most kinds of visual arts

Centre for the Study of Liturgy and Architecture   2001
- Department of Theology and Religious Studies, University of Wales Lampeter, College Street, Lampeter, Ceredigion, SA48 7ED.
   01570 424708   fax 01570 424987
   http://www.lamp.ac.uk/trs/Main_pages/dept_research_centres.htm
   Director: Dr Juliette Day.
- E   A research centre at the University of Wales, Lampeter.

Centre for the Study of Long Wave Events
   see **LSE Mackinder Centre for the Study of Long Wave Events.**

Centre for the Study of Mathematics Education   (CSME)
- School of Education, Jubilee Campus, University of Nottingham, Wollaton Road, Nottingham, NG8 1BB.
   0115-951 4432   fax 0115-951 4599
   http://www.nottingham.ac.uk/education/centres/csme/
   Contact: Dr Peter Gates.
- E   A research centre at the University of Nottingham.

Centre for the Study of Medieval Society and Culture   (CSMSC)
- Cardiff School of History and Archaeology, Cardiff University, PO Box 909, Cardiff, CF10 3XU.
   029 2087 4625   fax 029 2087 4502
   http://www.cf.ac.uk/hisar/research/centres/csmsc/
   Co-Director: Prof Peter Coss. Co-Director: Prof John Hines.
- E   A centre at Cardiff University.
- O   To bring together medievalists from a variety of subject areas who wish to co-operate in research and in teaching at graduate level

Centre for the Study of Migration   (CSM)
- Department of Humanities, Social Sciences and Law, Queen Mary, University of London, Mile End Road, London, E1 4NS.
   020 7882 5003; 5009
   http://www.politics.qmul.ac.uk/research/migration/
   Director: Dr Anne J Kershen.
- E   A department of Queen Mary, University of London.
- O   To conduct research and study of the movements of people locally, nationally and internationally

Centre for the Study of Mission and World Christianity
   see **Henry Martyn Centre for the Study of Mission and World Christianity.**

Centre for the Study of Music Performance
   see **Centre for Performance Science.**

Centre for the Study of No Drama
Note: No longer in existence.

Centre for the Study of Perceptual Experience   (CSPE)
- Department of Philosophy, University of Glasgow, 67-69 Oakfield Avenue, Glasgow, G12 8QQ.
  0141-330 5692   fax 0141-330 4112
  http://www.gla.ac.uk/Acad/Philosophy/CSPE/
  Contact: Prof Dudley Knowles.
- E   A research centre at the University of Glasgow.

Centre for the Study of Policy and Practice in Health and Social Care   (CSPP)   2003
- Faculty of Health and Human Sciences, Thames Valley University, Westel House, 32-38 Uxbridge Road, London, W5 2BS.
  020 8280 5297; 5319
  http://www.cspp.health.tvu.ac.uk/
  Director: Prof Charles Easmon, CBE.
- E   A research centre at Thames Valley University.

Centre for the Study of Post-Conflict Cultures   2004
- School of Modern Languages and Cultures, University of Nottingham, University Park, Nottingham, NG7 2RD.
  0115-951 5799   fax 0115-846 7309
  http://www.nottingham.ac.uk/critical-theory/post-conflict-cultures/
- E   A research centre at the University of Nottingham.
- O   To facilitate cutting-edge research into the inter-relations between war, conflict, history, culture, gender and national identity

Centre for the Study of Poverty of Social Justice   (CSPSJ)   1998
- School for Policy Studies, University of Bristol, 8 Priory Road, Bristol, BS8 1TZ.
  0117-954 6755   fax 0117-954 6756
  http://www.bristol.ac.uk/sps/research/cpsj/default.shtml
  Contact: Dr Dave Gordon.
- E   A research centre at the University of Bristol.
- O   To conduct research into the nature and extent of social exclusion and injustice

Centre for the Study of Propaganda   (CSPW)   1993
- School of History, Rutherford College, University of Kent, Canterbury, Kent, CT2 7NX.
  01227 823837; 827665   fax 01227 827258
  http://www.kent.ac.uk/history/centres/prop.html
  Director: Prof David Welch.
- E   An interdisciplinary research centre at the University of Kent.
- O   To conduct a systematic study of propaganda in its widest possible historical context; to promote a greater understanding of propaganda theory and its practice

Centre for the Study of Public Policy   (CSPP)   1976
- School of Social Science, University of Aberdeen, Aberdeen, AB24 3QY.
  01224 272726
  http://www.abdn.ac.uk/cspp/
  Director: Prof Richard Rose, FBA.
- E   A centre at the University of Aberdeen.
- O   To join the world of ideas and the world of practice, with special reference to the problems of post-communist societies in transition

Centre for the Study of Race and Ethnicity   (CSRE)   2003
- Department of Sociology, City University, Social Sciences Building, Northampton Square, London, EC1V 0HB.
  020 7040 5060   fax 020 7040 5070
  http://www.city.ac.uk/sociology/csre/Centre.html
- E   A centre at City University.
- O   To provide a research focus for both empirical and theoretical work in the core areas of race and ethnic studies, racism, refugee studies, and globalisation and migration

Centre for the Study of Radicalisation and Contemporary Political Violence   (CSRV)
- Department of International Politics, University of Wales Aberystwyth, Penglais, Aberystwyth, Ceredigion, SY23 3FE.
  01970 622741
  http://www.aber.ac.uk/interpol/research/CSRV/CSRV.html
  Director: Dr Marie Breen Smyth.
- E   A research centre at the University of Wales, Aberystwyth.
- O   To deepen the understanding of processes of (de)-radicalisation and the relationship between radicalisation, political terror and counter terrorism

Centre for the Study and Reduction of Hate Crimes, Bias and Prejudice
see **Nottingham Centre for the Study and Reduction of Hate Crimes.**

© CBD Research Ltd · Beckenham · Kent BR3 5JS · Tel 020 8650 7745 · Fax 020 8650 0768 · E-mail cbd@cbdresearch.com · www.cbdresearch.com

Centre for the Study of Regulated Industries   (CRI)   1991
- ■ School of Management, University of Bath, Claverton Down, Bath, BA2 7AY.
    01225 386473
    http://www.bath.ac.uk/cri/
    Director: Peter Vass.
- E   A research centre at the University of Bath.
- ○   To investigate how competition and regulation are working in practice, both in the UK and globally
- ●   Conference facilities - Information service - Library - Statistics

Centre for the Study of Relationships and Personal Life
   see **Morgan Centre for the Study of Relationships and Personal Life.**

Centre for the Study of Religion in Celtic Societies   1999   Canolfan Astudio Crefydd mewn Cymdeithasau Celtaidd
- ■ Department of Theology and Religious Studies, University of Wales Lampeter, College Street, Lampeter, Ceredigion, SA48 7ED.
    01570 424708   fax 01570 424987
    http://www.lamp.ac.uk/celtic/
    Director: Dr Jonathan Wooding.
- E   A research centre at the University of Wales, Lampeter.
- ○   To promote the study of the religious dimension in the Celtic-speaking cultures of the early, medieval and modern periods

Centre for the Study of Religion, Ideas and Society   (CRIS)
Note: The Centre has temporarily suspended its activities while new staff are being appointed.

Centre for the Study of Religion and Politics   (CSRP)   2004
- ■ School of Divinity, University of St Andrews, South Street, St Andrews, Fife, KY16 9JU.
    01334 462850   fax 01334 462852
    http://www.st-andrews.ac.uk/divinity/csrp.html
    Director: Prof Mario I Aquilar.
- E   A research centre at the University of St Andrews.
- ○   To conduct collaborative research on the relation of the practice of religion and its political context

Centre for the Study of Religion and Popular Culture
- ■ School of Humanities, University of Chester, Parkgate Road, Chester, CH1 4BJ.
    01244 511031
    http://www.chester.ac.uk/trs/research_culture.html
    Contact: Prof Christopher Partridge.
- E   A research centre at the University of Chester.

Centre for the Study of the Renaissance   (CRS)
- ■ Faculty of Arts, University of Warwick, Coventry, CV4 7AL.
    024 7652 3523   fax 024 7646 1606
    http://www2.warwick.ac.uk/fac/arts/ren/
- E   A research centre at the University of Warwick.
- ●   Education and training - MA in the Culture of the European Renaissance

Centre for the Study of Retailing in Scotland   (CSRS)   2002
- NR   Department of Marketing, University of Stirling, Stirling, FK9 4LA.
    01786 467384
    http://www.csrs.ac.uk/
    Director: Prof Leigh Sparks.
- E   An independent research centre at the University of Stirling.
- ○   To provide a resource to support and develop research on retailing in Scotland; to create and maintain a retail information
    database for Scotland, and train future researchers in retailing
Note: A joint venture with the Universities of Edinburgh and Strathclyde.

Centre for the Study of Rights and Conflict
   see **Helen Bamber Centre for the Study of Rights and Conflict.**

Centre for the Study of Safety and Well-Being   (SWELL)
- ■ School of Health and Social Studies, University of Warwick, Coventry, CV4 7AL.
    024 7652 3543   fax 024 7652 4415
    http://www2.warwick.ac.uk/fac/soc/shss/swell/
    Director: Dr Cathy Humphreys.
- E   A research centre at the University of Warwick.
- ○   To focus on the safety and well-being of vulnerable groups, particularly children, young people and women, who have experienced
    abuse and violence

Centre for the Study of Sexual Dissidence   (CSSD)

■   School of Humanities, University of Sussex, Arts E 432, Falmer, Brighton, East Sussex, BN1 9SN.
     01273 678412
     http://www.sussex.ac.uk/cssd/
     Convener: Dr Vincent Quinn.
E   A research centre at the University of Sussex.
○   To draw together existing work, and promote new work, on texts and issues in lesbian, gay, bisexual, queer, transsexual and transgender studies, and on their intersections with imperatives of race, gender and class

Centre for the Study of Sexuality and Culture   (CSSC)   2003

■   School of Arts, Histories and Cultures, University of Manchester, Humanities Lime Grove, Oxford Road, Manchester, M13 9PL.
     0161-306 1240
     http://www.arts.manchester.ac.uk/subjectareas/englishamericanstudies/research/cssc/
     Co-Director: Dr David Alderson. Co-Director: Prof Laura Doan.
E   An interdisciplinary research centre within the Centre for Interdisciplinary Research in the Arts (qv) at the University of Manchester.
○   To focus research on the inter-relationships of sexuality, gender, culture and history

Centre for the Study of Social and Global Justice   (CSSGJ)   2005

■   School of Politics and International Relations, University of Nottingham, University Park, Nottingham, NG7 2RD.
     0115-846 8135   fax 0115-951 4859
     http://www.nottingham.ac.uk/politics/research/research_CSSGJ.php
     Director: Prof Simon Tormey.
E   A research centre at the University of Nottingham.
○   To focus research on the various aspects of how justice has been thought about, sought after and implemented within and beyond the state

Centre for the Study of Social and Political Movements   (CSSPM)   1992

■   School of Social Policy, Sociology and Social Research, University of Kent, Cornwallis North East, Canterbury, Kent, CT2 7NF.
     01227 827150; 827251   fax 01227 827005
     http://www.kent.ac.uk/sspssr/polsoc/
     Director: Christopher A Rootes.
E   A research centre at the University of Kent.
○   To promote and undertake the study of social and political movements, protest and political contention

Centre for the Study of Socialist Theory and Movement   (CSSTM)

■   University of Glasgow, Glasgow, G12 8QQ.
     0141-339 8855
     http://www.gla.ac.uk/centres/csstm/
     Contact: Bridget Fowler.
E   A centre at the University of Glasgow.

Centre for the Study of Sport in Society
     see **Warwick Centre for the Study of Sport in Society.**

Centre for the Study of Technology and Organisations   (CSTO)

■   Lancaster University Management School, Lancaster University, Bailrigg, Lancaster, LA1 4YX.
     01524 594285
     http://www.lums.lancs.ac.uk/Research/Centres/CSTO/
     Director: Prof Brian Bloomfield.
E   A research centre at Lancaster University.

Centre for the Study of Terrorism and Political Violence   (CSTPV)   1994

■   School of International Relations, University of St Andrews, Arts Building, St Andrews, Fife, KY16 9AJ.
     01334 462935   fax 01334 461922
     http://www.st-andrews.ac.uk/intrel/research/cstpv/
     Director: Prof Alex P Schmid.
E   A research centre at the University of St Andrews.
○   To study the determinants, manifestations and consequences of terrorism and other forms of political violence; to investigate the responses of states, civil society and international organisations to violent modes of waging conflict

Centre for the Study of Urban and Regional Governance   (CURG)

■   School of Social Sciences, Humanities and Languages, University of Westminster, 309 Regent Street, London, W1B 2UW.
     020 7911 5000   fax 020 7911 5106
     http://www.wmin.ac.uk/sshl/page-950
     Co-Director: Dr Tassilo Herrschel. Co-Director: Dr Peter Newman.
E   An interdisciplinary research centre at the University of Westminster.
○   To develop research into all aspects of the dynamics of governing cities, regions and city-regions

© CBD Research Ltd · Beckenham · Kent BR3 5JS · Tel 020 8650 7745 · Fax 020 8650 0768 · E-mail cbd@cbdresearch.com · www.cbdresearch.com

Centre for the Study of the Viking Age
- School of English Studies, University of Nottingham, University Park, Nottingham, NG7 2RD.
  0115-951 5900; 5925   fax 0115-951 5924
  http://www.nottingham.ac.uk/english/csva/
  Contact: Prof Judith Jesch.
- E   A research centre at the University of Nottingham.
- O   To foster, develop and co-ordinate research into all aspects of the Viking age, with special emphasis on Scandinavian contacts with the British Isles, and on literary and linguistic sources for the period

Centre for the Study of Violence
   see **Glasgow Centre for the Study of Violence.**

Centre for the Study of War, State and Society   2005
- Department of History, University of Exeter, Amory Building, Rennes Drive, Exeter, EX4 4RJ.
  01392 264297   fax 01392 263305
  http://www.huss.ex.ac.uk/history/research/wss/
  Director: Dr Martin Thomas.
- E   A research centre at the University of Exeter.
- O   To support research and postgraduate teaching on the effects of armed conflict on states, societies and cultures throughout history

Centre for the Study of Women and Gender   1993
- Department of Sociology, University of Warwick, Coventry, CV4 7AL.
  024 7657 5122   fax 024 7652 3497
  http://www2.warwick.ac.uk/fac/soc/sociology/gender/
  Director: Prof Nickie Charles.
- E   An interdisciplinary research centre at the University of Warwick.

Centre for Suburban Studies   (CSS)
- Faculty of Arts and Social Sciences, Kingston University, Penrhyn Road, Kingston-upon-Thames, Surrey, KT1 2EE.
  020 8547 2000
  http://www.kingston.ac.uk/research/centres/suburban_studies/
- E   A research centre at Kingston University, London.
- O   To pioneer interdisciplinary approaches to the study of suburbia

Centre for Successful Schools   1989
- Keele University, Keele, Staffordshire, ST5 5BG.
  01782 583579   fax 01782 583555
  http://www.keele.ac.uk/cfss/
  Contact: Melanie Broad.
- E   A research centre at Keele University.
- O   To pursue research into 'success' in schooling and disseminate the findings

Centre for Suicide Research
   see **University of Oxford Centre for Suicide Research.**

Centre in Superconductivity
   see **Interdisciplinary Research Centre in Superconductivity.**

Centre for Supply Chain Management   (CSCM)
- 1 Todd Campus - West of Scotland Science Park, University of Glasgow, Maryhill Road, Glasgow, G20 0XA.
  0141-945 6461   fax 0141-945 0427
  http://www.cscm.org.uk/
- E   A centre at the University of Glasgow.
- O   To support the development and dissemination of knowledge in the field of supply chain management

Centre for Supply Chain Research   (CSCR)
- Kent Business School, University of Kent, Canterbury, Kent, CT2 7PE.
  01227 827726   fax 01227 761187
  http://www.kent.ac.uk/kbs/cscr/
  Director: Dr Andrew Fearne.
- E   A research centre at the University of Kent.
- O   To identify best-practice in supply chain management and promote its adoption in the food and construction sectors

Centre for Supramolecular Technology
   see **Cranfield Centre for Supramolecular Technology.**

Centre for Surgical Science   (CSS)

■   Barts and the London, Queen Mary's School of Medicine and Dentistry, Queen Mary, University of London, Charterhouse Square, London, EC1M 6BQ.
         020 7014 0462   fax 020 7014 0461
         http://www.cancer.qmul.ac.uk/research/surgical_science/
         Director: Prof Ajay Kakkar.
E   A research centre within the Institute of Cancer (qv) at Queen Mary, University of London.
O   To conduct research in defining the role of thrombosis in the genesis and progression of cancer, and to develop novel approaches to antithrombotic therapy

Centre for Sustainable Aquaculture Research   (CSAR)

■   School of the Environment and Society, Swansea University, Singleton Park, Swansea, SA2 8PP.
         01792 295361
         http://www.swan.ac.uk/research/centresandinstitutes/CentreforSustainableAquacultureResearch/
E   A research centre within the Institute of Environmental Sustainability (qv) at Swansea University.
O   To research methods of cultivating fish and shellfish under environmentally friendly conditions

Centre for Sustainable Consumption   (CSC)   1996

■   City Campus, Sheffield Hallam University, Sheffield, S1 1WB.
         0114-225 4838   fax 0114-225 2881
         http://www.shu.ac.uk/research/csc/
         Head: Dr Tim Cooper.
E   A research centre at Sheffield Hallam University.
O   To focus research on consumer behaviour and the environmental impact of household goods

Centre for Sustainable Design   (CfSD)

■   University College for the Creative Arts at Farnham, Falkner Road, Farnham, Surrey, GU9 7DS.
         01252 892772   fax 01252 892747
         http://www.cfsd.org.uk/
         Director: Prof Martin Charter.
E   A research centre at the University College for the Creative Arts.
O   To enable research and discussion on the subjects of eco-design and environmental, economic, ethical and social (e3s) considerations in product and service development and design
●   Conferences - Consultancy - Education and training - Seminars - Workshops

Centre for Sustainable Development   (CfSD)   1998

■   School of Architecture and the Built Environment, University of Westminster, 35 Marylebone Road, London, NW1 5LS.
         020 7911 5000 ext 3090   fax 020 7915 5057
         http://www.wmin.ac.uk/cfsd/
         Contact: Dr Karen Lucas.
E   An interdisciplinary research centre at the University of Westminster.
O   To provide a forum for collaborative research initiatives in the field of sustainable development

Centre for Sustainable Energy Systems

■   Faculty of Engineering, Science and the Built Environment, London South Bank University, 103 Borough Road, London, SE1 0AA.
         020 7815 7676
         http://www.lsbu.ac.uk/esbe/engineering/cses.shtml
         Head: Dr John Missenden.
E   A research centre at London South Bank University.
✕   Centre for Air Conditioning & Refrigeration

Centre for Sustainable Futures   (CSF)   2005

■   University of Plymouth, Drake Circus, Plymouth, PL4 8AA.
         01395 255493
         http://csf.plymouth.ac.uk/
         Director: Prof David Selby.
E   A Centre for Excellence in Teaching and Learning (CETL) at the University of Plymouth.
Note: funded by the Higher Education Funding Council of England (HEFCE) as the Centre for Excellence in Teaching and Learning (CETL) in Education for Sustainable Development (ESD) See **Centres for Excellence in Teaching and Learning** for more information.

Centre for Sustainable Heritage
         see **UCL Centre for Sustainable Heritage.**

Centre for Sustainable Power Distribution   (CSPD)

■   Department of Electronic and Electrical Engineering, University of Bath, Claverton Down, Bath, BA2 7AY.
         01225 386327   fax 01225 826305
         http://www.bath.ac.uk/elec-eng/cspd/
         Director: Prof Raj Aggarwal.
E   A research centre at the University of Bath.
O   To conduct research in electrical power and electrical systems

    © CBD Research Ltd · Beckenham · Kent BR3 5JS · Tel 020 8650 7745 · Fax 020 8650 0768 · E-mail cbd@cbdresearch.com · www.cbdresearch.com

Centre for Sustainable Technologies   (CST)
- Faculty of Engineering, University of Uister, Jordanstown, Newtownabbey, County Antrim, BT37 0QB.
  028 9036 6329   fax 028 9036 6863
  http://www.engj.ulst.ac.uk/CST
E   A research centre at the University of Ulster.

Centre for Sustainable Urban and Regional Futures   (SURF)   1999
- Faculty of Business, Law and the Built Environment, University of Bath, 113-115 Portland Street, Salford, Manchester, M1 6DW.
  0161-295 4018   fax 0161-295 5880
  http://www.surf.salford.ac.uk/
  Contact: Pam Allen.
E   An interdisciplinary research centre within the Research Institute for the Built and Human Environment (qv) at the University of Salford.
O   To advance understanding of how economic, social, environmental and technological changes interact to affect urban and regional futures

Centre for Sustainable Wastes Management
   see **SITA Centre for Sustainable Wastes Management.**

Centre for Synaptic Plasticity
   see **MRC Centre for Synaptic Plasticity.**

Centre for Syrian Studies   (CSS)   2006
- School of International Relations, United College, University of St Andrews, St Andrews, Fife, KY16 9AL.
  01334 462861   fax 01334 462937
  http://www.st-andrews.ac.uk/intrel/syrian/
  Director: Prof Raymond Hinnebusch.
E   A research centre within the Institute of Middle East, Central Asia and the Caucasus Studies (qv) at the University of St Andrews.

Centre for System Analysis   (CSA)
- School of Informatics, University of Westminster, 115 New Cavendish Street, London, W1W 6UW.
  020 7911 5831
  http://www.wmin.ac.uk/cscs/page-1134
  Leader: Dr Andrzej Tarczynski.
E   A research centre at the University of Westminster.
O   To conduct research in signal processing, control engineering, system modelling and system theory

Centre for Systems Biology   (CSB)
- Department of Biological Sciences, University of Essex, Wivenhoe Park, Colchester, Essex, CO4 3SQ.
  01206 872118   fax 01206 872592
  http://csb.essex.ac.uk/
  Director: Prof Phil Mullineaux.
E   A centre at the University of Essex.
O   To harness powerful tools from mathematics, computing, and physical and engineering sciences to address biological questions

Centre for Systems Biology at Edinburgh   (CSBE)
- University of Edinburgh, C H Waddington Building, King's Buildings Science Campus, Edinburgh, EH9 3JF.
  0131-651 3325; 3837
  http://csbe.bio.ed.ac.uk/
  Co-Director: Prof Andrew Millar. Co-Director: Prof Igor Goryanin.
E   A research centre at the University of Edinburgh.
O   To develop broadly applicable methods and large-scale infrastructure for modelling the temporal aspects of biological phenomena

Centre for Systems and Control   (CSC)
- Department of Electronics and Electrical Engineering, University of Glasgow, Glasgow, G12 8QQ.
  0141-330 2411; 4302; 4984   fax 0141-330 6004
  http://www.mech.gla.ac.uk/Research/Control/
  Convener: Prof David Murray-Smith.
E   An interdisciplinary research centre at the University of Glasgow.
O   To conduct research in the field of systems and control, including fault detection and model validation, multi-variable control, nonlinear control, robust control, predictive control, neural networks, and genetic algorithms

Centre for Systems Engineering [University College London]
   see **UCL Centre for Systems Engineering.**

Centre for Systems Engineering   (CSE)   1998

■   Engineering Systems Department, Cranfield University, Shrivenham, Swindon, Wiltshire, SN6 8LA.
     01793 785289
     http://www.dcmt.cranfield.ac.uk/esd/syseng/
     Contact: Mrs B Holden.
E   A research centre at Cranfield University.
O   To deliver systems engineering expertise, to the defence and non-defence communities, in order to equip them to tackle today's complex systems problems

Centre for Systems and Modelling   (CSM)

■   Department of Engineering, City University, Tait Building, Northampton Square, London, EC1V 0HB.
     020 7040 0113
     http://www.city.ac.uk/sems/research/csm/
E   A centre at City University.
O   To undertake fundamental and applied research for developing holistic, engineering type approaches and methodologies to challenging new problems

Centre for Systems and Software Engineering   (CSSE)   1986

■   Faculty of Business, Computing and Information Management, London South Bank University, 103 Borough Road, London, SE1 0AA.
     020 7815 7471
     http://myweb.lsbu.ac.uk/~blackse/CSSE.html
     Head: Dr Sue Black.
E   A research centre within the Institute for Computing Research (qv) at London South Bank University.
O   To carry out research in software engineering

Centre of Taiwan Studies   (CTS)   1999

■   Faculty of Languages and Cultures, School of Oriental and African Studies, University of London, Thornhaugh Street, Russell Square, London, WC1H 0XG.
     020 7898 4206
     http://www.soas.ac.uk/centres/centreinfo.cfm?navid=1062
     Director: Dr Dafydd Fell.
E   A research centre at the School of Oriental and African Studies, University of London.
O   To conduct research and teaching on Taiwan's society, culture, politics, language and economics

Centre for Tax Law   (CTL)   2000

■   Faculty of Law, University of Cambridge, 10 West Road, Cambridge, CB3 9DZ.
     01223 330033   fax 01223 330055
     http://ctl.law.cam.ac.uk/
     Director: Prof John Tiley.
E   A centre at the University of Cambridge.
O   To promote encouragement of tax law scholarship; to encourage work on the subject of tax history
●   Education and training - Workshops

Centre for Teaching Chinese as a Foreign Language   (CTCFL)   1999

■   Faculty of Oriental Studies, University of Oxford, Clarendon Institute Building, Walton Street, Oxford, OX1 2HG.
     01865 280393   fax 01865 280431
     http://www.ctcfl.ox.ac.uk/
     Contact: Mr Shio-yun Kan.
E   A research centre within the Institute for Chinese Studies (qv) at the University of Oxford.

Centre for Teaching, Learning and Assessment   (TLA)

■   University of Edinburgh, Holyrood Road, Edinburgh, EH8 8AQ.
     0131-651 6661   fax 0131-651 6664
     http://www.tla.ed.ac.uk/
     Director: Prof Carolin Kreber.
E   A centre at the University of Edinburgh.

Centre for Technological Education
     see **Robert Clark Centre for Technological Education.**

Centre for Technology and the Arts
     see **Centre for Textual Scholarship.**

Centre for Technology Management   (CTM)

■   Department of Engineering, University of Cambridge, Mill Lane, Cambridge, CB2 1RX.
     01223 766401   fax 01223 766400
     http://www.ifm.eng.cam.ac.uk/ctm/
E   A research centre within the Institute for Manufacturing (qv) at the University of Cambridge.
O   To bridge the gap between industry and university research for all topics concerned with the effective integration of technological considerations into business decision making

Centre for Technology, Production and Ancient Materials   (CTPAM)

■   School of Conservation Sciences, Bournemouth University, Christchurch House, Talbot Campus, Poole, Dorset, BH12 5BB.
01202 965178   fax 01202 965530
http://www.bournemouth.ac.uk/conservation/abouttheschool/ahe/ctpa.html
E   A centre at Bournemouth University.
O   To focus research on ancient technology, including the use, trade and exchange of ancient artefacts and materials, the physical and socially constructed properties of artefacts made of ceramic, metal, glass and other inorganic substances, and the sourcing of materials and objects

Centre for Technology Strategy   (CTS)   1988

■   Faculty of Technology, Open University, Walton Hall, Milton Keynes, MK7 6AA.
01908 653672
http://technology.open.ac.uk/cts/
Director: Prof Stephen Potter.
E   A centre and federation of research groups at the Open University.
O   To conduct research in various technological areas, the key foci being innovation, environment and development

Centre for Telecommunication Networks
see **Centre for Communications Systems.**

Centre for Telecommunications Research   (CTR)   1994

■   School of Physical Sciences and Engineering, King's College London, 26-29 Drury Lane, London, WC2B 5RL.
020 7848 2898
http://www.kcl.ac.uk/schools/pse/diveng/research/ctr/
Director: Prof Hamid Aghvami.
E   A department of King's College, London.
O   To conduct research on various areas of telecommunications, particularly radio access, networking, reconfigurability and radio

Centre for Terrestrial Carbon Dynamics   (CTCD)

■   University of Sheffield, Hicks Building, Hounsfield Road, Sheffield, S3 7RH.
0114-222 3803   fax 0114-222 3809
http://ctcd.group.shef.ac.uk/
Director: Prof Shaun Quegan.
E   A Natural Environment Research Council collaborative research centre at the University of Sheffield.
O   To solve the equations for the terrestrial carbon balance, at a variety of scales, by a combination of modelling and data

Centre for Textile Conservation and Textile Studies
see **AHRB Research Centre for Textile Conservation and Textile Studies.**

Centre for Textual Scholarship   (CTS)   2006

■   Faculty of Humanities, De Montfort University, The Gateway, Leicester, LE1 9BH.
0116-207 8410
http://www.cts.dmu.ac.uk/
Director: Prof Peter Shillingsburg.
E   A centre at De Montfort University.
O   To conduct scholarly research in the fields of textual studies and the history of the book, and in the emerging technologies that support them
X   Centre for Technology and the Arts.

Centre for Theatre and the Community   (CTC)

■   School of Creative Arts, Film and Media, University of Portsmouth, University House, Winston Churchill Avenue, Portsmouth, PO1 2UP.
023 9284 6104; 6132
http://www.port.ac.uk/departments/academic/scafm/researchcentres/theatreandthecommunity/
Director: Stuart Olesker.
E   A centre at the University of Portsmouth.
O   To assist people, with a diversity of abilities, disabilities and backgrounds, to devise theatre of various kinds

Centre for Theatre Research in Europe   (CTRE)

■   School of Arts, Digby Stuart College, University of Roehampton, Roehampton Lane, London, SW15 5PH.
020 8392 3249
http://www.roehampton.ac.uk/researchcentres/theatreresearch/
Contact: Dr Joe Kelleher.
E   A research centre at Roehampton University.
O   To examine relationships between hegemonic national theatre forms in Europe and resistant, alternative forms of performance outside the mainstream

Centre for Theatre Studies   (CTS)
■   Department of Film, Literature and Theatre Studies, University of Essex, Wivenhoe Park, Colchester, Essex, CO4 3SQ.
01206 872806   fax 01206 872940
http://www.essex.ac.uk/theatre/
Administrator: Penny Woollard.
E   A centre at the University of Essex.
O   To give students experience in theatre-making

Centre for Theology, Religion and Culture   (CTRC)
■   Department of Education and Professional Studies, King's College London, Franklin Wilkins Building, Waterloo Road, London, SE1 9JN.
020 7848 3148; 3243   fax 020 7872 3182
http://www.kcl.ac.uk/schools/schools/sspp/education/research/groups/ctrc/
Academic Leader: Prof Andrew Walker.
E   A research centre at King's College, London.

Centre for Theoretical and Computational Neuroscience
■   University of Plymouth, Room A223 - Portland Square Building, Plymouth, PL4 8AA.
01752 233359   fax 01752 233349
http://www.plymneuro.org.uk/
Director: Prof Mike Denham.
E   A research centre at the University of Plymouth.

Centre for Theoretical Modelling in Medicine   (CTMM)   1999
■   Department of Mathematics, Heriot-Watt University, Riccarton, Edinburgh, EH14 4AS.
0131-451 8003   fax 0131-451 3249
http://www.ma.hw.ac.uk/maths/medicine
E   A research centre at Heriot-Watt University.
O   To conduct research on the application of mathematics to a wide range of problems in laboratory and clinical medicine

Centre for Theoretical Studies in the Humanities and the Social Sciences
■   University of Essex, Wivenhoe Park, Colchester, Essex, CO4 3SQ.
01206 872178   fax 01206 872178
http://www.essex.ac.uk/centres/theostud/
Secretary: Noreen Harburt.
E   A research centre within the University of Essex.
O   To encourage co-operation between academics using different theoretical approaches and disciplines
●   Mini courses and seminars - Lectures - Workshops

Centre for the Theory and Application of Catalysis   (CenTACat)
■   School of Chemistry and Chemical Engineering, Queen's University, Belfast, David Keir Building, Stranmillis Road, Belfast, BT9 5AG.
028 9097 5418
http://www.ch.qub.ac.uk/
Director: Prof Chris Hardacre.
E   A research centre at Queen's University, Belfast.
O   To conduct research in fundamental computational chemistry and the engineering of catalysis

Centre for Therapeutic Education
      see **Research Centre for Therapeutic Education.**

Centre for Thermal Studies   (CTS)
■   School of Applied Sciences, University of Huddersfield, Queensgate, Huddersfield, HD1 3DH.
01484 422288   fax 01484 472182
http://www.hud.ac.uk/schools/applied_sciences/research/cts/
Director: Prof E Charsley.
E   A research centre at the University of Huddersfield.
O   To conduct contract research in thermal analysis and calorimetry

Centre for Thinking and Language   1998
■   School of Psychology, University of Plymouth, Portland Square, Drake Circus, Plymouth, PL4 8AA.
01752 233157
http://www.psy.plymouth.ac.uk/research/cftal/
Head: Prof Tim Perfect.
E   A research centre at the University of Plymouth.
O   To conduct research projects in the fields of human reasoning in adults and children, decision making, hypothesis testing, probability judgement, child language, second language learning and auditory warnings

Centre for Timber Engineering   (CTE)   2002
■   School of the Built Environment, Merchiston Campus, University of Edinburgh, 10 Colinton Road, Edinburgh, EH10 5DT.
      0131-455 2819   fax 0131-455 2239
      http://cte.napier.ac.uk/
      Director: Prof Philip Turner.
E   A centre at Napier University.
O   To be a focus for excellence in providing education, research and consultancy in the various constructional uses of timber
●   Consultancy - Education and training - Information service

Centre for Tissue Regeneration Science
■   Faculty of Biomedical Sciences, Royal Free and University College Medical School, University College London, Brockley Hill, Stanmore, Middlesex, HA7 4LP.
      020 8909 5845
      http://www.ucl.ac.uk/orthopaedics/
      Head: Prof Robert Brown.
E   A research centre within the Institute of Orthopaedics and Musculo-Skeletal Science (qv) at University College London.
O   To conduct research into the responses of skeletal tissues to biological and biomechanical environments in terms of modelling, repair, neoplasia, replacement and regeneration in the areas of bone cell biology, cartilage tissue engineering, bone repair, intervertebral disc replacement, and skeletal neoplasia

Centre for Tobacco Control Research   (CTCR)   1999
■   University of Stirling, Stirling, FK9 4LA.
      01786 467390   fax 01786 464745
      http://www.ctcr.stir.ac.uk/
      Director: Prof Gerard Hastings.
E   A research centre within the Institute for Social Marketing (qv) at the University of Stirling.
Note: A joint venture with the Open University.

Centre for Tomorrow's Company   1996
■   NIOC House, 4 Victoria Street, London, SW1H 0NE.
      020 7222 7443   fax 020 7222 7585
      http://www.tomorrowscompany.com/
      Director: Mark Goyder.
E   A research and education charity.
O   To create a future for business which makes equal sense to staff, shareholders and society

Centre for Tourism
■   School of Architecture and the Built Environment, University of Westminster, 35 Marylebone Road, London, NW1 5LS.
      020 7911 5000
      http://www.wmin.ac.uk/sabe/page-629
E   A centre at the University of Westminster.
O   To offer undergraduate degree programmes in tourism management, business and planning

Centre for Tourism and Cultural Change   (CTCE)
■   Old School Board, Calverley Street, Leeds, LS1 3ED.
      0113-283 8540   fax 0113-283 8544
      http://www.tourism-culture.com/
      Contact: Prof Mike Robinson.
E   A research centre at Leeds Metropolitan University.

Centre for Tourism in Islands and Coastal Areas   (CENTICA)
■   Kent Business School, University of Kent, Level 3 - The Medway Building, Chatham Maritime, Chatham, Kent, ME4 4AG.
      01634 888801; 888863   fax 01634 888890
      http://www.kent.ac.uk/kbs/standard.php?page_id=33
      Director: Dr Mark Hampton.
E   A research centre at the University of Kent.
O   To conduct high quality applied research on the development and management challenges facing tourism in islands and coastal areas

Centre for Toxicology   (CfT)   2001
■   School of Biomedical and Molecular Sciences, Guildford, Surrey, GU2 7XH.
      01483 689204   fax 01483 300374
      http://www.centrefortoxicology.com/
E   A research centre at the University of Surrey.
O   To offer a mechanism for addressing novel questions and solving novel problems of a toxicological nature

Centre for Trade Union Studies   (CTUS)   1984
■   31 Jewry Street, London, EC3N 2EY.
      020 7320 3042
E   An autonomous centre within the Working Lives Research Institute (qv) at London Metropolitan University.
O   To provide research and consultancy for trade unions and the labour movement; to provide bespoke short courses for trade unions

Centre for Transcultural Research   (CTR)

■ Department of Humanities, Arts and Languages, City Campus, London Metropolitan University, 100 Minories, London, EC3N 1JY.
   020 7320 1666
   http://www.londonmet.ac.uk/depts/hal/
   Contact: Dr Karen Seago.
E An interdisciplinary research centre at London Metropolitan University.
○ To conduct research in cultural transmissions, both within and between dominant and marginal communities, and the shaping of (trans)national identities through language

Centre for Transcultural Studies in Health
   see **Research Centre for Transcultural Studies in Health.**

Centre for Translating and Interpreting Studies in Scotland   (CTISS)

■ Department of Languages and Intercultural Studies, University of Edinburgh, Henry Prais Building, Riccarton, Edinburgh, EH14 4AS.
   0131-451 4201   fax 0131-451 3079
   http://www.sml.hw.ac.uk/ctiss/
   Director: Prof Graham Turner.
E A research centre at Heriot-Watt University.
○ To investigate the nature of the process of translating, to disseminate research; to promote awareness of issues relating to the profession and, especially, to the training of interpreters and translators

Centre for Translation and Comparative Cultural Studies   (CTCCS)   1965

■ Faculty of Arts, University of Warwick, Coventry, CV4 7AL.
   024 7652 3655   fax 024 7652 4468
   http://www2.warwick.ac.uk/fac/arts/ctccs/
   Director: Dr Piotr Kuhiwczak.
E A department of the University of Warwick.
○ To provide postgraduate education in translation studies, comparative literary theory, Colonial and post-Colonial literature in English, British cultural studies and modern British studies
● Education and training (including MA and PhD programmes)
✕ Centre for British and Comparative Cultural Studies.

Centre for Translation and Intercultural Studies   (CTIS)

■ School of Languages, Linguistics and Cultures, University of Manchester, Humanities Lime Grove Centre, Oxford Road, Manchester, M13 9PL.
   0161-275 3003   fax 0161-275 3031
   http://www.llc.manchester.ac.uk/Research/Centres/CentreforTranslationandInterculturalStudies/
E A research centre at the University of Manchester.
● Translational English Corpus (world's largest computerised collection of translated English text)

Centre for Translation Research and Multilingualism   (TRAM)   2003

■ Department of French, Swansea University, Singleton Park, Swansea, SA2 8PP.
   01792 295968   fax 01792 295978
   http://www.swan.ac.uk/tram/
   Contact: Prof Andrew Rothwell.
E An interdisciplinary research centre at Swansea University.
○ To act as a focus for research activity in the areas of literary translation, language technology, community interpreting, and second language acquisition and multilingualism

Centre for Translation Studies   (CTS)   1982

■ Department of Culture, Media and Communication, University of Surrey, Guildford, Surrey, GU2 7XH.
   01483 689969   fax 01483 689528
   http://www.surrey.ac.uk/translation
   Director: Dr Margaret Rogers.
E A research centre at the University of Surrey.
○ To conduct teaching, scholarship and research in translation and translation studies

Centre for Translation Studies

■ School of Modern Languages and Cultures, University of Leeds, Leeds, LS2 9JT.
   0113-343 3234   fax 0113-343 6631
   http://www.smlc.leeds.ac.uk/cts/
   Director: Prof Tony Hartley.
E A research centre at the University of Leeds.
○ To model translation in all its forms
● Consultancy - Information service

© CBD Research Ltd · Beckenham · Kent BR3 5JS · Tel 020 8650 7745 · Fax 020 8650 0768 · E-mail cbd@cbdresearch.com · www.cbdresearch.com

Centre for Translational Oncology   (CTO)

■   Barts and the London, Queen Mary's School of Medicine and Dentistry, Queen Mary, University of London, Charterhouse Square, London, EC1M 6BQ.
020 7014 0462   fax 020 7014 0461
http://www.cancer.qmul.ac.uk/research/translational_oncology/
Director: Prof Fran Balkwill.
E   A research centre within the Institute of Cancer (qv) at Queen Mary, University of London.
O   To conduct research on the interactions between cancer and the process of inflammation, using ovarian and skin cancer as the disease model, and with particular focus on the role of cytokines, chemokines and inflammatory stroma in the development and spread of epithelial tumours

Centre for Translational Research
see **Wolfson Centre for Translational Research.**

Centre for Transnational Studies   (TNS)   2003

■   School of Humanities, University of Southampton, Highfield, Southampton, SO17 1BJ.
023 8059 2255   fax 023 8059 3288
http://www.transnational.soton.ac.uk/
Director: Prof Ulrike H Meinhof.
E   A research centre at the University of Southampton.

Centre for Transpersonal Psychology   (CTP)   1973

■   Breasy Place, 9 Burroughs Gardens, London, NW4 4AU.
0845 004 5359
http://www.transpersonalcentre.co.uk/
Co-Chairman: Jan Mojsa. Co-Chairman: Rupert Tower.
E   A registered charity.
O   To foster the development of an eclectic spiritual psychology, based on modern research and ancient wisdom, height and depth approaches, and oriental and occidental sources; to train counsellors and therapists in transpersonal perspectives and skills, and to develop a therapeutic referral network

Centre for Transport Policy   (CfTP)

■   Aberdeen Business School, Robert Gordon University, Management Building, Schoolhill, Aberdeen, AB10 1FR.
01224 263134   fax 01224 263129
http://www.rgu.ac.uk/abs/centres/page.cfm?pge=5911
Director: Prof David Gray.
E   A research centre at the Robert Gordon University.
O   To analyse transport problems, recommend solutions and improve understanding of transport related issues among decision-makers in the public and private sector, the media and the public at large

Centre for Transport and Society   (CTS)   2004

■   Faculty of the Built Environment, Frenchay Campus, University of the West of England, Coldharbour Lane, Bristol, BS16 1QY.
0117-328 3000; 3219   fax 0117-328 3899
http://www.transport.uwe.ac.uk/
Director: Prof Glenn Lyons.
E   A research centre at the University of the West of England.
O   To improve and promote understanding of the inherent links between lifestyles and personal travel in the context of continuing social and technological change

Centre for Transport Studies [Clitheroe]
see **Whalley Centre for Transport Studies.**

Centre for Transport Studies   (CTS)

■   Department of Civil and Environmental Engineering, Imperial College London, Exhibition Road, London, SW7 2AZ.
020 7594 6100   fax 020 7594 6102
http://www.cts.cv.ic.ac.uk/
Head: Prof John Polak.
E   A research centre at Imperial College London.
O   To conduct research and teaching in a wide variety of transport subjects, including transport engineering, planning, operations and management, geomatic engineering and surveying
Note: A centre run jointly with University College London.

Centre for Transport Studies   (CTS)

■   Department of Civil and Environmental Engineering, Chadwick Building, University College London, Gower Street, London, WC1E 6BT.
020 7679 7009
http://www.cts.ucl.ac.uk/
Head: Prof B Heydecker.
E   A research centre at University College London.
O   To conduct research in the fields of safety, transport modelling and analysis, institutional and behavioural aspects of transport policy, public transport, the theory and practice of traffic control, transport in developing countries
Note: A centre run jointly with Imperial College London.

Centre for Trauma Research
    see **Aberdeen Centre for Trauma Research.**

Centre for Trauma, Resilience and Growth   1998
■   University of Nottingham, Burton Street, Nottingham, NG1 4BU.
        0115-941 8418
        http://www.nottinghamshirehealthcare.nhs.uk/trauma
E   A research centre at Nottingham Trent University.

Centre for Travel and Tourism Business Development
    see **Moffat Centre for Travel and Tourism Business Development.**

Centre for Travel Writing Studies
    see **Nottingham Trent Centre for Travel Writing Studies.**

Centre for Tumour Biology   (CTB)
■   Barts and the London, Queen Mary's School of Medicine and Dentistry, Queen Mary, University of London, Charterhouse Square,
        London, EC1M 6BQ.
        020 7014 0462   fax 020 7014 0461
        http://www.cancer.qmul.ac.uk/research/tumour_biology/
        Director: Prof Ian Hart.
E   A research centre within the Institute of Cancer (qv) at Queen Mary, University of London.
○   To focus research on understanding the role that cytoadhesion plays in modulating cancer spread, with particular emphasis on the
        involvement of members of the integrin family of adhesion receptors

Centre for Ultrasonic Engineering   (CUE)   1981
NR   Department of Electronic and Electrical Engineering, University of Strathclyde, Royal College Building, 204 George Street,
        Glasgow, G1 1XW.
        0141-548 2485
        http://www.cue.ac.uk/
E   A research centre at the University of Strathclyde.
Note: A joint venture with the University of Edinburgh and Glasgow Caledonian University.

Centre for Undergraduate Research
    see **Reinvention Centre for Undergraduate Research.**

Centre for the Urban Built Environment   (CUBE)
■   CUBE Building, 113-115 Portland Street, Manchester, M1 6DW.
        http://www.cube.org.uk/
        Contact: Janice Parkinson.

Centre for Urban and Community Research   (CUCR)   1994
■   Goldsmiths, University of London, London, SE14 6NW.
        020 7919 7390   fax 020 7919 7383
        http://www.goldsmiths.ac.uk/cucr/
        Director: Prof Michael Keith.
E   A research centre at Goldsmiths, University of London.
○   To develop work that is both rooted in contemporary debates in urban social theory and committed to an ethical engagement with
        contemporary city life

Centre for Urban Culture   (CUC)
■   School of History, University of Nottingham, University Park, Nottingham, NG7 2RD.
        0115-951 5947   fax 0115-951 5948
        http://www.nottingham.ac.uk/history/cuc/
        Director: Prof Helen Meller.
E   An interdisciplinary research centre at the University of Nottingham.
○   To conduct research on urban culture in cities worldwide

Centre for Urban Development and Environmental Management   (CUDEM)   1989
■   School of the Built Environment, Leeds Metropolitan University, The Northern Terrace - Queen Square Court, Calverley Street,
        Leeds, LS1 3HE.
        0113-283 2600   fax 0113-283 1958
        http://www.leedsmet.ac.uk/as/cudem/
        Director: Prof Simin Davoudi.
E   A research centre at Leeds Metropolitan University.
○   To conduct an integrated set of courses and research programmes around spatial planning, governance, sustainability and urban
        and regional regeneration themes

Centre for Urban Education   (CUE)   2006
- Manchester Metropolitan University, 799 Wilmslow Road, Didsbury, Manchester, M20 2RR.
  0161-247 2606
  http://www.ioe.mmu.ac.uk/cue/
  Leader: Marilyn Eccles.
- E   A research centre within the Institute of Education (qv) at Manchester Metropolitan University.
- O   To work with pupils, school staff, academics, researchers, cultural organisations and higher education institutions to meet the challenges and harness the opportunities of urban education

Centre for Urban History   (CUH)   1985
- University of Leicester, 3-5 Salisbury Road, Leicester, LE1 7QR.
  0116-252 2378   fax 0116-252 5769
  http://www.le.ac.uk/ur/
- E   A research centre within the Marc Fitch Historical Institute (qv) at the University of Leicester.
- O   To promote interdisciplinary research and teaching in the field of urban history from classical times to the present, through national and international collaboration

Centre for Urban and Metropolitan Research
  see **LSE London Centre for Urban and Metropolitan Research.**

Centre for Urban Policy Studies   (CUPS)
- School of Environment and Development, University of Manchester, Oxford Road, Manchester, M13 9PL.
  0161-275 3639   fax 0161-275 7878
  http://www.sed.manchester.ac.uk/geography/research/cups/
  Director: Prof Brian Robson.

Centre for Urban Quality
- Faculty of Business, Law and the Built Environment, Maxwell Building, University of Salford, Salford, Manchester, M5 4WT.
  0161-295 4600   fax 0161 295 5011
  http://www.buhu.salford.ac.uk/research_centres/csc/
- E   A centre within the Research Institute for the Built and Human Environment (qv) at the University of Salford.

Centre for Urban and Regional Development Studies   (CURDS)   1977
- School of Geography, Politics and Sociology, University of Newcastle upon Tyne, Newcastle upon Tyne, NE1 7RU.
  0191-222 7741; 8604
  http://www.ncl.ac.uk/curds/
  Director: Prof John Tomaney.
- E   A research centre within the Institute for Policy and Practice (qv) at the University of Newcastle upon Tyne.
- O   To undertake basic research aimed at improving the understanding of the process of area development in advanced economies

Centre for Urban and Regional Ecology   (CURE)   1999
- School of Environment and Development, University of Manchester, Oxford Road, Manchester, M13 9PL.
  0161-275 6920; 6938   fax 0161-275 6917
  http://www.sed.manchester.ac.uk/research/cure/
  Director: Prof John Handley.
- E   A research centre at the University of Manchester.
- O   To promote and provide high quality research in relation to the new academic agendas of regionalism, sustainability and the re-building of environmental capital

Centre for Urban and Regional Studies   (CURS)   1966
- School of Public Policy, University of Birmingham, J G Smith Building, Edgbaston, Birmingham, B15 2TT.
  0121-414 5028   fax 0121-414 3279
  http://www.curs.bham.ac.uk/
  Director: Richard Groves.
- E   A centre at the University of Birmingham.
- O   To be a leading international centre for research and teaching in housing, regional and local economic development, urban policy, and regional and urban regeneration

Centre for Urban Research
  see **LSE Centre for Urban Research.**

Centre for Urban Theory
- Swansea University, Singleton Park, Swansea, SA2 8PP.
  01792 205678
  http://www.swan.ac.uk/research/centresandinstitutes/CentreforUrbanTheory/
- E   An interdisciplinary research centre at Swansea University.
- O   To advance cutting-edge, internationally renowned understandings of the changing nature of urban society and space

Centre for Usable Home Technology   (CUHTec)

■   Department of Psychology, University of York, Heslington, York, YO10 5DD.
       01904 433148; 433178   fax 01904 433181
       http://www.cuhtec.org.uk/
       Director: Prof Andrew Monk. Administrator: Rachel Dare.
E   An interdisciplinary research centre at the University of York.

Centre for Vascular Inflammation
       see **Eric Bywaters Centre for Vascular Inflammation.**

Centre for Very Large-Scale Integration and Computer Graphics
       see **Centre for VLSI and Computer Graphics.**

Centre for Veterinary Science   (CVS)

■   Cambridge Veterinary School, University of Cambridge, Madingley Road, Cambridge, CB3 0ES.
       01223 339553
       http://www.vet.cam.ac.uk/research
E   A centre at the University of Cambridge.

Centre for Victorian Art and Architecture
       see **Centre for Victorian Studies (Royal Holloway)**

Centre for Victorian Studies   (CVS)   1992

■   School of Humanities, University of Chester, Parkgate Road, Chester, CH1 4BJ.
       01244 375444
       http://www.chester.ac.uk/history/victorian.html
       Head: Dr Ronald J Barr.
E   A research centre at the University of Chester.

Centre for Victorian Studies   (CVS)

■   School of English, University of Exeter, Queen's Building, The Queen's Drive, Exeter, EX4 4QH.
       01392 264265   fax 01392 264361
       http://www.centres.ex.ac.uk/cvs/
       Contact: Dr John Plunkett.
E   A centre at the University of Exeter.
○   To promote interdisciplinary research and teaching in all aspects of nineteenth-century literature, culture and media

Centre for Victorian Studies

■   Royal Holloway, University of London, Egham, Surrey, TW20 0EX.
       01784 434455
       http://www.rhul.ac.uk/Victorian-Centre/
E   An interdisciplinary research centre at Royal Holloway, University of London.
              Centre for Victorian Art and Architecture

Centre for Video Communications   (CVC)

■   School of Engineering, Robert Gordon University, Schoolhill, Aberdeen, AB10 1FR.
       01224 262320   fax 01224 262444
       http://www.rgu.ac.uk/eng/cvc/
       Director: Dr Iain E G Richardson.
E   A research centre at the Robert Gordon University.
○   To conduct research and development in imaging and communication, including image and video compression, compression
       standards, low complexity video coding, visual perception and video coding, applied visual communications, medical imaging,
       and the transport of compressed multimedia data across networks

Centre for Virology

■   Department of Infection, Windeyer Building, University College London, 46 Cleveland Street, London, W1T 4JF.
       020 7679 9482
       http://www.vgb.ucl.ac.uk/
       Director: Dr Deenan Pillay.
E   A research centre at University College London.
○   To concentrate research on viruses of clinical importance in human health, including all aspects of human hepatitis and retrovirus
       infections

Centre for Virtual Environments   (CVE)   1994

■   Faculty of Business, Law and the Built Environment, Business House, University of Salford, Salford, Manchester, M5 4WT.
       0161-295 2917   fax 0161-295 2925
       http://www.nicve.salford.ac.uk/
       Leader: Rob Aspin.
E   A research centre within the Informatics Research Institute (qv) at the University of Salford.
○   To undertake scientific investigation into the application of virtual environments to engineering, construction and medicine

Centre for Virtual Organisation Technology Enabling Research
   see **SRIF Centre for Virtual Organisation Technology Enabling Research.**

Centre for Vision Sciences and Vascular Biology   (CVS)
- ■   School of Biomedical Sciences, Royal Victoria Hospital, Grosvenor Road, Belfast, BT12 6BA.
    028 9063 2729   fax 028 9063 2699
    http://www.qub.ac.uk/research-centres/CentreforVisionSciences/
    Director: Prof Alan Stitt.
- E   A centre at Queen's University, Belfast.
- O   To build on proven strengths that are focused on fundamental and clinical investigative aspects of retinal microvascular and degenerative diseases

Centre for Vision, Speech and Signal Processing   (CVSSP)
- ■   Department of Electronic Engineering, University of Surrey, Guildford, Surrey, GU2 7XH.
    01483 686030   fax 01483 686031
    http://www.ee.surrey.ac.uk/CVSSP/
    Director: Prof Josef Kittler.
- E   An autonomous research centre and department of the University of Surrey.
- O   To advance the state of the art in multimedia signal processing and computer vision, with an emphasis on image, video and audio applications

Centre for Vision and Visual Cognition   (CVVC)
- ■   Department of Psychology, University of Durham, Science Laboratories, South Road, Durham, DH1 3LE.
    0191-334 3240   fax 0191-334 3241
    http://www.dur.ac.uk/cvvc.durham/
    Director: Prof John M Findlay.
- E   A research centre at the University of Durham.

Centre for Visual Anthropology   (CVA)
- ■   Anthropology Department, Goldsmiths, University of London, London, SE14 6NW.
    020 7919 7805
    http://www.goldsmiths.ac.uk/visual-anthropology/
    Director: Prof Stephen Nugent.
- E   A research centre at Goldsmiths, University of London.

Centre for Visual Anthropology [Manchester]
   see **Granada Centre for Visual Anthropology.**

Centre for Visual Arts [Norwich]
   see **Sainsbury Centre for Visual Arts.**

Centre for Visual Arts [Birmingham City University]
   see **Bournville Centre for Visual Arts.**

Centre for Visual Studies   (CVS)   2004
- ■   School of Humanities, University of Sussex, Falmer, Brighton, East Sussex, BN1 9SN.
    01273 877627
    http://www.sussex.ac.uk/gchums/1-4-3.html
- E   An interdisciplinary research centre at the University of Sussex.
- O   To bring together research in a wide range of interests on visual studies across media, disciplines and cultures

Centre for Visual Studies   (CVS)   1999
- ■   Department of History of Art, University of Oxford, Littlegate House, 16-17 St Ebbe's Street, Oxford, OX1 1PT.
    01865 286830   fax 01865 286831
    http://www.history.ox.ac.uk/hoa/resources/centre.htm
    Director: Prof Martin Kemp.
- E   A centre at the University of Oxford.
- O   To provide teaching for, and research in, art history and visual media, to show how visual styles at different times and in different places can be understood in relation to the aesthetic, intellectual and social facets of different cultures

Centre for VLSI and Computer Graphics
- ■   Department of Informatics, University of Sussex, Falmer, Brighton, East Sussex, BN1 9QT.
    01273 678050   fax 01273 690816
    http://139.184.100.112/vlsi/index.jsp
    Director: Prof Paul Lister.
- E   A research centre at the University of Sussex.
- O   To conduct research in the design and development of advanced hardware and software systems for computer graphics, virtual reality, augmented reality and virtual prototyping
Note: VLSI = Very Large-Scale Integration.

Centre for the Vocational Training of Musicians
    see **Research Centre for the Vocational Training of Musicians**.

Centre for Voluntary Action Research
    see **Aston Centre for Voluntary Action Research**.

Centre for Voluntary Action Studies (CVAS) 1995
- ■ School of Policy Studies, Coleraine Campus, University of Ulster, Cromore Road, Coleraine, County Londonderry, BT52 1SA.
    028 7032 4865 fax 028 7032 4881
    http://www.ulster.ac.uk/cvas/
- E   A research centre at the University of Ulster.
- ○   To promote, develop, conduct and disseminate research on voluntary action, for the voluntary sector in Ireland and internationally, as a contribution to scholarship and as a resource for social and public policy

Centre for Waste Management (CWM)
- ■ School of Natural Resources, University of Central Lancashire, Leighton Building, Preston, PR1 2HE.
    01772 201201
    http://www.uclan.ac.uk/facs/science/cwm/
    Director: Prof Glynn Morton.
- E   A research centre at the University of Central Lancashire.
- ○   To provide a focus for existing waste / environmental research and course provision

Centre for Water Law, Policy and Science
    see **UNESCO Centre for Water Law, Policy and Science**.

Centre for Water Policy and Development (CWPD)
- ■ Faculty of Environment, University of Leeds, Woodhouse Lane, Leeds, LS2 9JT.
    0113-343 5241
    http://www.leeds.ac.uk/cwpd/
- E   A research centre at the University of Leeds.

Centre for Water Research [Oxford]
    see **Oxford Centre for Water Research**.

Centre for Water Science (CWS) 2006
- ■ Sustainable Systems Department, Cranfield University, Building 61, Cranfield, Bedfordshire, MK43 0AL.
    01234 754173
    http://www.cranfield.ac.uk/sas/water/
    Director: Prof Simon Judd.
- E   A research centre at Cranfield University.
- ○   To offer research, consultancy and training specialising in the science, engineering and management of water

Centre for Water Systems (CWS)
- ■ Department of Engineering, University of Exeter, Tait Building, North Park Road, Exeter, EX4 4QF.
    01392 263637 fax 01392 217965
    http://www.projects.ex.ac.uk/cws/
    Contact: Prof Dragan Savic.
- E   A centre at the University of Exeter.
- ○   To conduct research into water systems engineering

Centre for Wave Dynamics
    see **Keele Centre for Wave Dynamics**.

Centre for Well-being in Public Policy (CWiPP) 2004
- ■ University of Sheffield, Regent Court, 30 Regent Street, Sheffield, S1 4DA.
    0114-222 5454 fax 0114-272 4095
    http://www.shef.ac.uk/cwipp/
    Director: Prof Paul Dolan.
- E   A research centre at the University of Sheffield.
- ○   To consider how people's health and well-being can be defined and measured in ways that help policy-makers determine the best use of scarce resources

Centre for Welsh American Studies
    see **Cardiff Centre for Welsh American Studies**.

Centre for Welsh Language Services   (CWLS)   Canolfan Gwasanaethau'r Gymraeg
- ■   Old College, University of Wales Aberystwyth, King Street, Aberystwyth, Ceredigion, SY23 2AX.
     01970 622040; 622049   fax 01970 611446
     http://www.aber.ac.uk/canolfangymraeg/welcome/
     Manager: Mari Elin Jones.
- E   A centre at the University of Wales, Aberystwyth.
- ○   To facilitate the use of Welsh

Centre for Welsh Legal Affairs   (CWLA)   1999   Canolfan Materion Cyfreithiol Cymreig (CMCC)
- ■   Department of Law, University of Wales Aberystwyth, Penglais, Aberystwyth, Ceredigion, SY23 3DY.
     01970 622712   fax 01970 622729
     http://www.aber.ac.uk/cwla/
     Director: Ann Sherlock.
- E   A research centre at the University of Wales, Aberystwyth.
- ○   To facilitate research into Welsh legal affairs, emphasising not only the the operation of the law within Wales but also in the UK, European and international contexts

Centre of West African Studies   (CWAS)   1963
- ■   School of Historical Studies, University of Birmingham, Edgbaston, Birmingham, B15 2TT.
     0121-414 5128   fax 0121-414 3228
     http://www.cwas.bham.ac.uk/
     Director: Dr Stewart Brown.
- E   A department of the University of Birmingham.
- ○   To undertake teaching and research in African studies, focusing particularly on West Africa

Centre for Whistler Studies   (CWS)
- ■   Department of History of Art, Reading Room, University of Glasgow, University Avenue, Glasgow, G12 8QQ.
     0141-330 5631   fax 0141-330 8602
     http://www.whistler.arts.gla.ac.uk/
     Director: Prof Nigel Thorp.
- E   A centre and constituent member of the Institute for Art History (qv) at the University of Glasgow.
- ○   To be the primary focus for scholarship on the artist James McNeill Whistler (1834-1903), and his circle

Centre for Widening Participation Policy Studies
     see **Continuum - Centre for Widening Participation Policy Studies.**

Centre for Widening Participation and Social Inclusion   1998
- ■   Old College, University of Wales Aberystwyth, King Street, Aberystwyth, Ceredigion, SY23 2AX.
     01970 621890   fax 01970 627410
     http://www.aber.ac.uk/wpsi/
     Secretary: Gary Griffiths.
- E   A centre at the University of Wales, Aberystwyth.
- ○   To work with a range of partners to widen access for people who traditionally have been under-represented in higher education

Centre for Window and Cladding Technology   (CWCT)   1989
- ■   Faculty of Engineering & Design, University of Bath, Claverton Down, Bath, BA2 7AY.
     01225 386541   fax 01225 386556
     http://www.cwct.co.uk/
     Director: Stephen Ledbetter. Administration Manager & PRO: Brenda Apted.
- E   A company limited by guarantee within the University of Bath.
- ○   To establish and promote the highest standards for UK windows, cladding and curtain walling through targeted research and education
- ●   Consultancy - Education and training - Facilities include laboratory testing and computer analysis equipment
- ¶   List of publications available.

Centre for Wireless Network Design   (CWIND)   2006
- ■   Luton Campus, University of Bedfordshire, Luton, Bedfordshire, LU1 3JU.
     01582 489230   fax 01582 489212
     http://www.beds.ac.uk/research/irac/cwind
     Director: Dr Jie Zhang.
- E   A research centre within the Institute for Research in Applicable Computing (qv) at the University of Bedfordshire.
- ○   To develop novel approaches that will solve telecommunications network planning and optimisation problems of real industrial interests

Centre for Women in Business
     see **Lehman Brothers Centre for Women in Business.**

Centre for Women Business Leaders
- Cranfield School of Management, Cranfield University, Cranfield, Bedfordshire, MK43 0AL.
  01234 751122 fax 01234 751806
  http://www.som.cranfield.ac.uk/som/research/centres/cdwbl/
  Director: Prof Susan Vinnicombe, OBE. Administrator: Alison Southgate.
- E A research centre within the Cranfield Management Research Institute (qv) at Cranfield University.
- O To understand the issues facing senior women managers, and the impact of organisational and personal factors on women's managerial careers

Centre for Women's Studies (WSC) 1994
- Department of European Studies and Modern Languages, University of Bath, Claverton Down, Bath, BA2 7AY.
  01225 386171 fax 01225 386099
  http://www.bath.ac.uk/esml/wsc/
  Contact: Dr A Giorgio.
- E A research centre at the University of Bath.
- O To provide a distinctive focus for the research and teaching in women's studies
- Note: Also known as the Women's Studies Centre.

Centre for Women's Studies (CWS) 1984
- Department of Sociology, University of York, Heslington, York, YO10 5DD.
  01904 433671 fax 01904 433670
  http://www.york.ac.uk/inst/cws/
  Director: Prof Stevi Jackson.
- E An interdisciplinary research centre at the University of York.
- O To conduct women-centred research in the changing nature of both women's experiences and gender relations

Centre for Work and Learning   (CWAL)
- Partnership Development Office, University of Kent, Gillingham Building, Chatham Maritime, Chatham, Kent, ME4 4AG.
  01634 888953 fax 01634 888890
  http://www.kent.ac.uk/departments/results.html?action=deptcard&deptid=273
- E A centre at the University of Kent.

Centre for Working Life Research (CWLR) 2000
- Kingston Business School, University of Kingston, Kingston Hill, Kingston-upon-Thames, Surrey, KT1 7LB.
  020 8547 7404
  http://business.kingston.ac.uk/cwlr.php
  Contact: Sue Preston.
- E A research centre at Kingston University, London.
- O To bring together individuals and organisations studying and contributing to the process of change

Centre for Working Memory and Learning   (WML)
- NR Department of Psychology, University of York, Heslington, York, YO10 5DD.
  01904 433190 fax 01904 433181
  http://www.york.ac.uk/res/wml/
  Administrator: Lindsay Bowes.
- E A research centre at the University of York.
- O To focus research on the cognitive mechanisms involved in working memory and the associated processes involved in long-term memory and learning
- Note: A joint venture with the University of Durham.

Centre for Workplace Health (CWH) 2005
- Harpur Hill, Buxton, Derbyshire, SK17 9JN.
  01298 218447
  http://www.hsl.gov.uk/cwh/
- E A Health and Safety Laboratory centre with close links to the University of Sheffield.
- O To use high quality research and development to develop simple practical solutions to workplace problems

Centre for World Cinemas
- School of Modern Languages and Cultures, University of Leeds, Leeds, LS2 9JT.
  0113-343 7069 fax 0113-343 3505
  http://www.leeds.ac.uk/worldcinemas/
  Director: Prof Lúcia Nagib.
- E A research centre within the University of Leeds.
- O To establish an international centre for research and teaching on world cinemas
- ● Education and training - Information service

Centre for World Environmental History (CWEH) 2002
- Department of Cultural Studies, University of Sussex, Arts C 146, Falmer, Brighton, East Sussex, BN1 9SJ.
  01273 606755 ext 2222
  http://www.sussex.ac.uk/development/1-4-5.html
  Director: Dr Vinita Damodaran. Research Director: Dr Richard Grove.
- E A research centre at the University of Sussex.
- O To focus research on environment and development issues in the tropics

© CBD Research Ltd · Beckenham · Kent BR3 5JS · Tel 020 8650 7745 · Fax 020 8650 0768 · E-mail cbd@cbdresearch.com · www.cbdresearch.com

Centre for Writing
- School of Media, Critical and Creative Arts, Liverpool John Moores University, Dean Walters Building, St James Road, Liverpool, L1 7BR.
    0151-231 5196   fax 0151-231 5049
    http://www.ljmu.ac.uk/mcc/englishresearch/
    Contact: Amanda Greening.
- E   A research centre within the Research Centre for Literature and Cultural History (qv) at Liverpool John Moores University.
- O   To offer a single and joint honours BA in imaginative writing, MAs in writing and screenwriting, and other programmes

Centre for Young Musicians   (CYM)   1970
- Morley College, London, 61 Westminster Bridge Road, London, SE1 7HT.
    020 7928 3844   fax 020 7928 3454
    http://www.cym.org.uk/
    Director: Stephen Dagg.
- E   A non-profit-distributing organisation based at Morley College, London.
- O   To provide a high quality instrumental and vocal service for pupils in London schools, with a special focus on helping those who may be in financial difficulty

Centre for Young Musicians [Manchester]
    see **RNCM Centre for Young Musicians.**

Centre for Youth Work Studies
- Department of Educational and Professional Studies, University of Strathclyde, Sir Henry Wood Building, 76 Southbrae Drive, Glasgow, G13 1PP.
    0141-950 3378   fax 0141-950 3374
    http://www.strath.ac.uk/Departments/CommunEdu/research/youthstudies.html
    Co-Director: Annette Coburn. Co-Director: Brian McGinley.
- E   A research centre at the University of Strathclyde.
- O   To undertake research in youth work and promote practice development

Centre for Youth Work Studies   (CYWS)   1991
- School of Sport and Education, Brunel University, Uxbridge, Middlesex, UB8 3PH.
    01895 274000
    http://www.brunel.ac.uk/
- E   A centre at Brunel University.
- O   To focus research on professional work, with young people and communities, in the broad field of informal education

CENTRES for CONTINUING EDUCATION
Note: There are many Centres for Continuing Education and most are departments of universities. Each centre supports adults who are re-entering the education arena for part- or full-time courses.

Centres of Cricketing Excellence
    see **University Centres of Cricketing Excellence Scheme.**

Centres for European Studies
    see **Jean Monnet Centres.**

CENTRES for EXCELLENCE in TEACHING and LEARNING   (CETLs)
Note: An initiative of the Higher Education Funding Council for England which provides funding for each centre. Currently there are over 70 CETLs in the United Kingdom.

CENTRES for LIFELONG LEARNING
Note: Lifelong Learning Centres exist at many UK universities; their broad remit is to promote wider access to higher education.

Chalfont Centre for Epilepsy
- Chesham Lane, Chalfont St Peter, Buckinghamshire, SL9 0RJ.
    01494 601300; 601400 (helpline)   fax 01494 871927
- E   The headquarters of the National Society for Epilepsy.

Charities Information Bureau   (CIB)   1981
- 93 Lawefield Lane, Wakefield, West Yorkshire, WF2 8SU.
    01924 239063   fax 01924 239431
    http://www.fit4funding.org.uk/
    Director: Chris Hollins.
- E   A registered charity and a company limited by guarantee.
- O   To provide funding and management information, training and advice for voluntary and community organisations

Charles Booth Centre for the Study of the History of Social Investigation   1985
- ■ Department of History, Open University, Walton Hall, Milton Keynes, MK7 6AA.
  01908 652477   fax 01908 653750
  http://www.open.ac.uk/Arts/history/booth-centre/
  Director: Prof Rosemary O'Day. Contact: Dr Donna Loftus.
- E A research centre at the Open University.

Charles P Skene Centre for Entrepreneurship   (CfE)   1995
- ■ Aberdeen Business School, Robert Gordon University, Kaim House, Garthdee Road, Aberdeen, AB10 7QE.
  01224 263895
  http://www.rgu.ac.uk/abs/centres/page.cfm?pge=5256
  Director: Prof Alistair Anderson. Contact: Susan Moult.
- E A research centre at the Robert Gordon University.
- O To achieve academic excellence in both teaching and research in entrepreneurship

Charles Salt Research Centre   1965
- ■ Robert Jones & Agnes Hunt Orthopaedic & District Hospital NHS Trust, Oswestry, Shropshire, SY10 7AG.
  01691 404000; 404476   fax 01691 404050
  http://www.rjah.nhs.uk/Default.aspx?tabid=874
  Director of Research: Dr Michael Davie.
- E A research centre within the Institute of Orthopaedics (qv).
- O To specialise in research into osteoporosis, fracture prevalence and bone densitometry; to provide a more patient-friendly
  screening and monitoring service for osteoporosis
- ● Education and training - Information service - Bone densitometry 0900-1700 (by appointment)

Chelsea School Research Centre   (CSCR)   1986
- ■ Faculty of Education and Sport, University of Brighton, Hillbrow, Denton Road, Eastbourne, East Sussex, BN20 7SR.
  01273 643707   fax 01273 643704
  http://www.brighton.ac.uk/chelsea/research/
  Head of School: Prof Jonathan Doust.
- E A centre at the University of Brighton.
- O To provide innovative courses in sport and exercise science, PE and dance, sport journalism, and sport and leisure cultures

Cheltenham International Language Centre   (CILC)   1987
- ■ Cornerways, The Park, Cheltenham, Gloucestershire, GL50 2RH.
  0870 721 0210
  http://www.glos.ac.uk/int/prospective/cilc/
  Director: Piers Wall.
- E A department of the University of Gloucestershire.
- O To conduct teaching of the English language
- ● Education and training

Chemical Biology Centre   (CBC)
- ■ University of Gloucester, Room 265 - Chemistry Building, Imperial College London, Exhibition Road, London, SW7 2AZ.
  020 7594 5880
  http://www.chemicalbiology.ac.uk/
- E A research centre at Imperial College London.
- O To bring together life scientists and physical scientists from the Institute of Cancer Research (qv), the Cancer Research UK London
  Research Institute (qv) and Imperial College, to conduct research in understanding the molecular details of biological activity at
  the membrane

Chemical Biology Centre   (CBC)   2006
- ■ School of Crystallography, Birkbeck, University of London, Malet Street, Bloomsbury, London, WC1E 7HX.
  020 7631 6830   fax 020 7631 6803
  http://www.ismb.lon.ac.uk/centres.html
  Contact: Prof Steve Caddick.
- E A constituent centre of the Institute of Structural Molecular Biology (qv) at Birkbeck, University of London.

Chemical Dependency Centre   (CDC)   1985
- ■ 11 Redcliffe Gardens, London, SW10 9BG.
  020 7351 0217
  http://www.thecdc.org.uk/
- E A registered charity.
- O To offer a variety of client oriented services to reduce the harm to anyone whose life has been adversely affected by substance
  misuse; to provide out-patient and residential services with which it supports and encourages those involved to improve the
  quality of their lives, and to fulfil their potential without recourse to the use of alcohol and/or drugs
- ● The Centre runs four treatment centres - three in London and one in Liverpool

© CBD Research Ltd · Beckenham · Kent BR3 5JS · Tel 020 8650 7745 · Fax 020 8650 0768 · E-mail cbd@cbdresearch.com · www.cbdresearch.com

Chemical Industry Education Centre (CIEC) 1998
- ■ Department of Chemistry, University of York, Heslington, York, YO10 5DD.
  01904 432523   fax 01904 434460
  http://www.ciec.org.uk/
- E   A centre at the University of York.
- O   To enhance the effective teaching of science and technology

ChemLabS
  see **Bristol ChemLabS Centre for Excellence in Teaching and Learning (Bristol Chemical Laboratory Sciences).**

Chester Centre for Research into Sport in Society (CCRSS)
- ■ School of Applied and Health Sciences, University of Chester, Parkgate Road, Chester, CH1 4BJ.
  01244 513440
  http://www.chester.ac.uk/ccrss/
  Co-Director: Dr Daniel Bloyce. Co-Director: Dr Katie Liston.
- E   A research centre at the University of Chester.

Chester Centre for Stress Research (CCSR)
- ■ School of Applied and Health Sciences, University of Chester, Parkgate Road, Chester, CH1 4BJ.
  01244 375444
  http://www.chester.ac.uk/ccsr/
  Director: Prof John Williams.
- E   A research centre at the University of Chester.

Child Development and Well-Being Interdisciplinary Research Centre (CDW)
- ■ Department of Social Policy and Social Work, University of York, Alcuin 'B' Block, Heslington, York, YO10 5DD.
  01904 321981   fax 01904 321953
  http://www.york.ac.uk/inst/cdw/
  Co-Director: Kathleen Kiernan. Co-Director: Charles Hulme.
- E   An interdisciplinary research centre at the University of York.
- O   To focus research on the relationship between children's cognitive, social and emotional 'competence', and their current and future social lives

Child Exploitation and Online Protection Centre (CEOP)
- ■ 33 Vauxhall Bridge Road, London, SW1V 2WG.
  0870 000 3344
  http://www.ceop.gov.uk/
  Chief Executive: Jim Gamble.

Childhood and Families Research and Development Centre (CAF)
- ■ Faculty of Education, University of Strathclyde, Sir Henry Wood Building, 76 Southbrae Drive, Glasgow, G13 1PP.
  0141-950 3590
  http://www.strath.ac.uk/centres/caf/
  Director: Peter Lee.
- E   A research centre at the University of Strathclyde.
- O   To enhance the quality of childhood and family experience by working in partnership with parents, professionals and policy makers

Children's Health and Exercise Research Centre (CHERC) 1987
- ■ University of Exeter, Heavitree Road, Exeter, EX1 2LU.
  01392 264812   fax 01392 264706
  http://www.exeter.ac.uk/cherc/
  Director: Prof Neil Armstrong. Deputy Director: Dr Jo Welsman.
- E   A department of the University of Exeter.
- O   To initiate research in pediatric physiology and disseminate the findings; to promote young people's health and well-being
- ● Equipment includes magnetic resonance imaging, DEXA, ass spectroscopy Doppler laser, NIRS, respiratory, cardiac and blood analysis
- ¶ Young People and Physical Activity. Paediatric Exercise Science and Medicine. Various academic papers in medical and science journals published each year.

Children's Legal Centre 1981
- ■ University of Essex, Wivenhoe Park, Colchester, Essex, CO4 3SQ.
  01206 872466   fax 01206 874026
  http://www.childrenslegalcentre.com/
  Managing Director: Carolyn Hamilton. International Programme Director: George Lane.
- E   A registered charity and part of the University of Essex.
- O   To give free and confidential advice and information on all aspects of law and policy affecting children and young people
- ● Education - Legal Advocacy Unit providing free legal representation to children and parents in SE England and telephone advice elsewhere - Consultancy and research services
- ¶ Many publications available.

Children's Research Centre   (CRC)

- Open University, Briggs Building, Walton Hall, Milton Keynes, MK7 6AA.
  01908 653295
  http://childrens-research-centre.open.ac.uk/
  Director: Mary Kellett.
- E A research centre at the Open University.

China Business Centre
  see **Centre for Chinese Business and Management Studies.**

China Centre
  see **China and Transitional Economics Research Centre.**

China Media Centre   2004

- School of Media, Arts and Design, University of Westminster, Watford Road, Northwick Park, Harrow, Middlesex, HA1 3TP.
  020 7911 5903; 5944   fax 020 7911 5943
  http://www.wmin.ac.uk/mad/page-933
- E A centre at the University of Westminster.

China Policy Institute   (CPI)

- China House, University Park, Nottingham, NG7 2RD.
  0115-846 7769   fax 0115-846 7900
  http://www.nottingham.ac.uk/china-policy-institute/
  Chairman: Elizabeth Wright. Director: Richard Pascoe.
- E An institute within the Centre for the Environment (qv) at the University of Nottingham.
- O To analyse critical policy challenges faced by China in its rapid development, and to expand the knowledge and understanding of contemporary China in Britain, Europe and worldwide

China and Transitional Economics Research Centre   (CTERC)   1999

- Northampton Business School, University of Nottingham, Park Campus, Boughton Green Road, Northampton, NN2 7AL.
  01604 892163   fax 01604 721214
  http://thechinacentre.org.uk/
  Director: Dr Richard Sanders.
- E A research centre at the University of Northampton.
- O To encourage research activity and scholarly exchanges between Britain and China
- ● Education and training - Information service
- Note: Also known as the China Centre.

Chinese Boxing Centre
  see **Wu Shu Kwan Chinese Boxing Centre.**

Chiron Centre Ltd   (CCBP)   1984

- 26 Eaton Rise, London, W5 2ER.
  020 8997 5219   fax 020 8997 5219
  http://www.chiron.org/
  Managing Director: Bernd Eiden.
- E A company limited by guarantee.
- O To offer individual body psychotherapy, biodynamic massage, group psychotherapy and advanced training / continuing professional development (CPD) in body psychotherapy
- ● Education and training

Christel DeHaan Tourism and Travel Research Institute   (TTRI)

- Nottingham University Business School, University of Nottingham, Jubilee Campus, Wollaton Road, Nottingham, NG8 1BB.
  0115-846 6602; 951 5505   fax 0115-846 6667
  http://www.nottingham.ac.uk/ttri/
- E A research institute at the University of Nottingham.
- O To carry out high quality research to contribute to policy formation by business, governments and international organisations, with particular expertise in economic impact modelling, tourism taxation, economic development and sustainability, tourism marketing and rural tourism

Chronic Poverty Research Centre   (CPRC)   2000

- School of Environment and Development, University of Manchester, Harold Hankins Building, Booth Street West, Manchester, M13 9QH.
  0161-275 2810   fax 0161-273 8829
  http://www.chronicpoverty.org/
  Director: Dr Andrew Shepherd.
- E A research centre within the Institute for Development Policy and Management (qv) at the University of Manchester.
- O To focus attention on chronic poverty, to deepen understanding of its causes; to provide research, analysis and policy guidance that will contribute to the reduction of poverty
- Note: A collaborative venture with a number of different Universities.

Chrono Centre for Climate, the Environment, and Chronology   (CHRONO)
■　School of Archaeology and Palaeoecology, Queen's University, Belfast, 42 Fitzwilliam Street, Belfast, BT7 1NN.
　　http://www.chrono.qub.ac.uk/
　　Director: Dr Paula J Reimer.
E　A centre at Queen's University, Belfast.

Churchill Archives Centre   1960
■　Churchill College, University of Cambridge, Cambridge, CB3 ODS.
　　01223 336087　fax 01223 336135
　　http://www.chu.cam.ac.uk/archives/
　　Director: Allen Packwood. Archivist & Information Services Manager: Natalie Adams.
E　A registered charity and part of the University of Cambridge.
O　To collect, care for and make available to scholars the archives of the 'Churchill era', including political, scientific, military and
　　diplomatic material
●　Conference facilities - Education and training - Exhibitions - Information service

CILT, The National Centre for Languages   1966
■　20 Bedfordbury, London, WC2N 4LB.
　　020 7379 5101　fax 020 7379 5082
　　http://www.cilt.org.uk/
　　Director: Isabella Moore.
E　A registered charity and a company limited by guarantee.
O　To promote a greater national capability in languages, and in particular to provide professional support for teachers of languages
●　Continuing professional development - Information service - Language teaching library
¶　Wide range of publications (catalogue available).
×　Centre for Information on Language Teaching and Research.

Cimtech Ltd
　　see **Centre for Information Management and Technology.**

Cities Institute   (CI)
■　Department of Applied Social Sciences, London Metropolitan University, Ladbroke House, 62-66 Highbury Grove, London,
　　N5 2AD.
　　020 7133 5105　fax 020 7133 5123
　　http://www.citiesinstitute.org/
E　A research institute at London Metropolitan University.
O　To undertake research into urban society in its human, physical and economic dimensions

Cities Research Centre   (CRC)
■　Faculty of the Built Environment, Frenchay Campus, University of the West of England, Coldharbour Lane, Bristol, BS16 1QY.
　　0117-328 3000
　　http://www.built-environment.uwe.ac.uk/research/cities/
E　An interdisciplinary research centre at the University of the West of England.
O　To explore the challenges of urban change through original research, evaluation, action research and policy analysis

Citizens Advice Bureaux   (CAB)
■　Myddelton House, 115-123 Pentonville Road, London, N1 9LZ.
　　020 7833 2181　fax 020 7833 4371
　　http://www.citizensadvice.org.uk/
　　Chief Executive: David Harker.
Note: There are over 700 Citizens Advice Bureaux in England and Wales. Each Bureau is a registered charity reliant on trained
　　volunteers and funds to help people resolve their legal, monetary and other problems by providing free, independent and
　　confidential Each local advice bureau is supported by one of a network of six regional offices in England and three in Wales; all
　　are overseen by its headquarters shown above.

Citizens Income Study Centre
Note: Now the Citizen's Income Trust, which can be contacted on 020 8305 1222.

City and Guilds of London Institute   1878
■　1 Giltspur Street, London, EC1A 9DD.
　　020 7294 2800　fax 020 7294 2405
　　http://www.city-and-guilds.co.uk/
E　The UK's leading vocational awarding body.
O　To offer more than 500 qualifications over 28 industry sectors, through 8,500 approved centres in around 100 countries
　　worldwide

City Health Economics Centre   (CHEC)
■　Department of Economics, City University, Northampton Square, London, EC1V 0HB.
　　020 7040 0168; 0171
　　http://www.city.ac.uk/economics/research/chec/
E　A centre at City University.
O　To conduct research into theoretical and empirical developments in economics generally, as applied to health and health care

City Literary Institute   (City Lit)   1919
■   Keeley Street, London, WC2B 4BA.
    020 7831 2600   fax 020 7492 2735
    http://www.citylit.ac.uk/
E   An independent non-profit-distributing organisation, a registered charity and a company limited by guarantee.
O   To provide adult learning opportunities, in a very wide range of subjects, for over 24,000 students every year

Civil and Computational Engineering Centre   (CCEC)
■   School of Engineering, Swansea University, Singleton Park, Swansea, SA2 8PP.
    01792 205678
    http://www.swan.ac.uk/engineering/Research/CivilandComputationalEngineeringCentre/
    Head: Prof K Morgan.
E   A research centre at Swansea University.
O   To conduct research in a number of topics in the area of computational and applied mechanics

Civil Law Centre
   see **Centre for the Study of the Civil Law Tradition.**

Clatterbridge Centre for Oncology   (CCO)   1958
■   Clatterbridge Road, Wirral, CH63 4JY.
    0151-334 1155   fax 0151-482 7817
    http://www.ccotrust.nhs.uk/
O   A specialist cancer treatment centre

Clean Environment Management Centre   (CLEMANCE)
■   School of Science and Technology, University of Teesside, Borough Road, Middlesbrough, TS1 3BA.
    01642 384418   fax 01642 384418
    http://www.tees.ac.uk/depts/clemance/
    Director: Prof Graham Street.
E   A research centre at the University of Teesside.
O   To provide clean technology solutions to the environmental problems of industry in the North East

Clifford Chance Centre for the Management of Professional Service Firms
■   Saïd Business School, University of Oxford, Park End Street, Oxford, OX1 1HP.
    01865 288949   fax 01865 288553
    http://www.sbs.ox.ac.uk/ccc
E   A research centre at the University of Oxford.

Climate and Land-Surface Systems Interaction Centre   (CLASSIC)
■   School of the Environment and Society, Swansea University, Singleton Park, Swansea, SA2 8PP.
    01792 295361
    http://www.swan.ac.uk/research/centresandinstitutes/CLASSIC/
E   A Natural Environment Research Council collaborative research centre within the Institute of Environmental Sustainability (qv) at
    Swansea University.
Note: Also known as the Centre of Excellence in Earth Observation.

Clinical Biosciences Institute   (ClinBio)
■   University of Hull, Wolfson Building, Cottingham Road, Hull, HU6 7RX.
    01482 465777   fax 01482 466664
    http://www.hull.ac.uk/clinbio/
    Director: Dr John Greenman.
E   A research Institute at the University of Hull.
O   To provide advances in disease diagnosis and treatment through excellence in basic and translational research, especially for
    cancer, cardiovascular disease, and musculoskeletal disorders

Clinical and Health Psychology Research Centre   (CHP)
■   School of Human and Life Sciences, Whitelands College, University of Roehampton, Holybourne Avenue, London, SW15 4JD.
    020 8392 3500   fax 020 8392 3531
    http://www.roehampton.ac.uk/researchcentres/chp
E   A research centre at Roehampton University.
O   To focus on the interaction of biological, behavioural, socio-cultural and environmental factors in aetiology, maintenance and
    prevention of health problems and the promotion of healthy human development

Clinical Neuroscience Centre   2005
■   Department of Psychology, University of Hull, 2nd Floor - Cohen Building, Cottingham Road, Hull, HU6 7RX.
    01482 466793   fax 01482 466664
    http://www.hull.ac.uk/psychology/neuroscience.htm
    Director: Dr M F Shanks.
E   A research centre at the University of Hull.

Clinical Research Centre

- School of Health and Social Care, Glasgow Caledonian University, Cowcaddens Road, Glasgow, G4 0BA.
  0141-330 8300
  http://www.gcal.ac.uk/shsc/research/centres_crc.html
- E   A research centre at Glasgow Caledonian University.
- O   To encourage a holistic approach to patient investigations, including functional assessment, biomechanical analysis, physiological measures, and social parameters where appropriate

Clinical Research Centre for Health Professions   (CRC)   1993

- Faculty of Health, University of Brighton, 49 Darley Road, Eastbourne, East Sussex, BN20 7UR.
  http://www.brighton.ac.uk/health/crc/
  Director: Prof Ann Moore.
- E   A centre at the University of Brighton.
- O   To embrace research in occupational therapy, physiotherapy and podiatry

Clinical Sciences Centre
> see **MRC Clinical Sciences Centre.**

Clinical Sciences Research Institute   (CSRI)   2003

- Warwick Medical School, University of Warwick, Gibbet Hill Road, Coventry, CV4 7AL.
  024 7657 4880   fax 024 7657 3079
  http://www2.warwick.ac.uk/fac/med/research/csri/
  Director: Prof Victor Zammit.
- E   A research institute at the University of Warwick.
- O   To focus research on cardiovascular disease and diabetes, cardiovascular medicine and epidemiology, clinical pharmacology, endocrinology and metabolism, ethnicity and health, metabolic health, orthopaedics, reproductive health, and sleep research

Clinical Skills Centre   (CSC)

- School of Nursing and Midwifery, Robert Gordon University, Garthdee Road, Aberdeen, AB10 7QG.
  01224 262976
  http://www.rgu.ac.uk/nursing/
  Senior Lecturer: Caroline MacDonald.
- E   A centre at the Robert Gordon University.
- O   To promote the development of clinical skills through fostering learning, educational innovation, collaboration and research, to achieve the highest possible standard of care for patients and clients

Clinical Skills Centre   1997

- University of Aberdeen, Westburn Centre, Westburn Road, Aberdeen, AB25 2XG.
  01224 551162
  http://www.abdn.ac.uk/clinicalskills/
  Director: Dr Rona Patey.
- E   A centre at the University of Aberdeen.
- O   To provide users with transferable clinical skills, encourage independent learning, and promote shared / multi professional learning

Clinical Skills Centre   (CSC)   1997

- College of Medicine, Dentistry and Nursing, Ninewells Hospital and Medical School, University of Dundee, Dundee, DD1 9SY.
  01382 633937   fax 01382 633950
  http://www.dundee.ac.uk/clinskills/
  Director: Dr Jean Ker.
- E   A centre at the University of Dundee.
- O   To allow postgraduate and undergraduate students the opportunity to acquire, or refine, various clinical skills by bridging the gap between theory and practice using simulation

CLIO Centre for Globalisation, Education and Societies   (GES)

- Graduate School of Education, University of Bristol, 35 Berkeley Square, Bristol, BS8 1JA.
  0117-928 7073   fax 0117-925 5412
  http://www.bristol.ac.uk/education/research/centres/ges
  Co-ordinator: Prof Susan Robertson.
- E   A research centre at the University of Bristol.

CLIO Centre for International and Comparative Studies   (ICS)

- Graduate School of Education, University of Bristol, 35 Berkeley Square, Bristol, BS8 1JA.
  0117-928 7073   fax 0117-925 5412
  http://www.bristol.ac.uk/education/research/centres/ics
  Co-ordinator: Prof Michael Crossley.
- E   A research centre at the University of Bristol.

CLIO Centre for Learning, Knowing and Interactive Technologies   (L-KIT

- Graduate School of Education, University of Bristol, 35 Berkeley Square, Bristol, BS8 1JA.
  0117-928 7073   fax 0117-925 5412
  http://www.bristol.ac.uk/education/research/centres/l-kit
  Co-ordinator: Prof Sally Barnes.
- E   A research centre at the University of Bristol.

CLIO Centre for Narratives and Transformative Learning   (CeNTRAL)

- Graduate School of Education, University of Bristol, 35 Berkeley Square, Bristol, BS8 1JA.
  0117-928 7073   fax 0117-925 5412
  http://www.bristol.ac.uk/education/research/centres/central
  Co-ordinator: Jane Speedy.
- E   A research centre at the University of Bristol.

CLIO Centre for Research on Language and Education   (CREOLE)

- Graduate School of Education, University of Bristol, 35 Berkeley Square, Bristol, BS8 1JA.
  0117-928 7073   fax 0117-925 5412
  http://www.bristol.ac.uk/education/research/centres/creole
  Co-ordinator: Pauline Rae-Dickins.
- E   A research centre at the University of Bristol.

CLRC e-Science Centre   (CLRCeSC)

- Rutherford Appleton Laboratory, Chilton, Didcot, Oxfordshire, OX11 0QX.
  01235 446084   fax 01235 445945
  http://www.e-science.clrc.ac.uk/
  Director: Dr Neil Geddes.

CMR International   (CMR)   1981

- Novellus Court, 61 South Street, Epsom, Surrey, KT18 7PX.
  01372 846100   fax 01372 846101
  http://www.cmr.org/
- E   Established by the Association of the British Pharmaceutical Industry as an independent scientific research unit.
- O   To conduct research on the scientific, economic and sociological aspects of the research and development of new medicines

Note: CMR = Centre for Medicines Research.

Cochlear Implant Centre
   see **South of England Cochlear Implant Centre.**

Cockcroft Institute: An International Centre for Research in Accelerator Science and Technology   2004

- NR   Daresbury Laboratory, Daresbury, Warrington, Cheshire, WA4 4AD.
  01925 603820
  http://www.cockcroft.ac.uk/
- E   A research institute.

Note: A collaborative venture involving various research councils and the Universities of Liverpool, Manchester and Lancaster. Named after Sir John Cockcroft, FRS - Nobel prizewinner and pioneer of modern accelerator research.

Coffee Science Information Centre   (CoSIC)   1990

- 12 Market Street, Chipping Norton, Oxfordshire, OX7 5NQ.
  01608 645566   fax 01608 645300
  http://www.cosic.org/
  Director: Roger Cook.
- E   Established by the former Institute for Scientific Information on Coffee.
- O   To assess all the on-going and past medical research on coffee and caffeine being undertaken around the world, and to provide accurate, balanced and consistent information to all audiences across Europe who have an interest in coffee, caffeine and health

COGNIT Research Centre

- School of Biological Sciences, University of Bristol, Woodland Road, Bristol, BS8 1UG.
  0117-928 8565
  http://cognit.psy.bris.ac.uk/
  Contact: Prof Tom Troscianko.
- E   An interdisciplinary research centre at the University of Bristol.
- O   To understand the manner in which information is handled in biological systems

Cold War Studies Centre   (CWSC)

- LSE, Houghton Street, London, WC2A 2AE.
  020 7852 3626   fax 020 7955 6514
  http://www.lse.ac.uk/collections/CWSC/
  Co-Director: Prof Michael Cox. Co-Director: Prof Odd Arne Westad.
- E   A research centre at the London School of Economics and Political Science.
- O   To conduct advanced study and research into the key political, social, intellectual, economic and military aspects of the Cold War, their historical origins, and their contemporary repercussions

Collaborating for Creativity CETL
  see **C4C: Collaborating for Creativity CETL.**

Collaboratory for Quantitative e-Social Science [Research Centre]   (CQeSS)   2004
NR   Lancaster University, C Floor - Bowland Annexe, Lancaster, LA1 4YT.
       01524 592175   fax 01524 594459
       http://www.ncess.ac.uk/research/nodes/CQeSS/
E   A research centre within the Lancaster Centre for e-Science (qv) at Lancaster University.
O   To ensure the effective development and use of grid-enabled quantitative methods
Note: A research node of the **National Centre for e-Social Science**.

Collingwood and British Idealism Centre   1994
■   Cardiff School of European Studies, Cardiff University, 65-68 Park Place, Cardiff, CF10 3AS.
       029 2087 4885   fax 029 2087 4885
       http://www.cf.ac.uk/euros/collingwood/
       Contact: Lisa Chivers.
E   A centre at Cardiff University.
O   To promote and encourage research into the life and philosophy of R G Collingwood (1889-1943)

Colour Design Research Centre   (CDRC)
■   Faculty of Art, Design and Architecture, Kingston University, Knights Park, Kingston-upon-Thames, Surrey, KT1 2QJ.
       020 8547 8062   fax 020 8547 8272
       http://www.kingston.ac.uk/design/research_centres.html
       Leader: Hilary Dalke.
E   A research centre at Kingston University, London.
O   To conduct research on the effect of colour and design on people suffering from long-term illnesses

Combined Studies Centre
  see **Centre for Combined Studies.**

Commercial Law Centre
  see **Centre for Commercial Law (UCL)..**

Common Cold and Nasal Research Centre   (CCC)   1988
■   Cardiff School of Biosciences, Cardiff University, Museum Avenue - PO Box 911, Cardiff, CF10 3US.
       029 2087 4099   fax 029 2087 4093
       http://www.cf.ac.uk/uwc/biosi/associates/cold/
       Director: Prof Ronald Eccles, BSc, PhD, DSc. Medical Officer: Dr Martez Jawad.
E   A department of Cardiff University.
O   To test new medications for the treatment of the common cold and hay fever; to undertake basic research on the nature of the
       related symptoms
●   Clinical trials - Information service - Hours Mon-Fri (0930-1630)

Commonwealth Institute   1962
■   New Zealand House, 80 Haymarket, London, SW1Y 4TQ.
       020 7024 9822   fax 020 7024 9833
       http://www.commonwealth.org.uk/
E   A registered charity and a company limited by guarantee.
O   To advance education in the Commonwealth; to promote industry and commerce in the Commonwealth for the public benefit by
       all means

Commonwealth Resource Centre   1962
■   New Zealand House, 80 Haymarket, London, SW1Y 4TQ.
       020 7024 9822   fax 020 7024 9833
       http://www.commonwealth.org.uk/
E   A research centre within the Commonwealth Institute (qv).

Communicable Disease Surveillance Centre
  see **Health Protection Agency Centre for Infections.**

Communication Aid Centre   (CAC)   1983
■   Speech and Language Therapy Department, Frenchay Hospital, Bristol, BS34 6RN.
       0117-975 3946   fax 0117-918 6558
       http://www.cacfrenchay.nhs.uk/
       Manager & Consultant: Judith de Ste Croix.
E   A statutory organisation.
O   To provide an established service to people (aged 11 years and over) with severe speech impairment; to act as a resource centre to
       provide up to date information regarding AAC related issues; to evaluate prototype and commercially available communication
       aids, and to provide a bank of equipment for loan to patients who have been assessed within the Centre
●   Education and training - Exhibitions - Information service - Statistics
¶   Wide range of publications.

Communication Aids for Language and Learning (CALL Centre) 1982
- ■ Paterson's Land, Holyrood Road, Edinburgh, EH8 8AQ.
   0131-651 6235   fax 0131-651 6234
   http://www.callcentre.education.ed.ac.uk/
   Joint Co-ordinator: Paul Nisbet. Joint Co-ordinator: Sally Millar.
- E A department of the University of Edinburgh.
- ○ To provide services and carry out research and development projects, working with all those involved in meeting the needs of people who require augmentative communication and/or specialised technology particularly in education
- ● Education and training - Exhibitions - Information service - Library - Assessment and support Mon-Fri (0900-1700)
- ¶ Wide range of publications.
- × CALL Centre.

Communication and Computing Research Centre (CCRC)
- ■ Sheffield Hallam University, Mundella House, Collegiate Crescent Campus, Sheffield, S10 2BP.
   0114-225 2259   fax 0114-225 4363
   http://www.shu.ac.uk/research/c3ri/ccrc.html
   Head: Dr Simeon Yates.
- E A research centre within the Cultural, Communication and Computing Research Institute (qv) at Sheffield Hallam University.
- ○ To consider the analysis, design, use and evaluation of all forms of communication, be it human-human, human-system or system-system

Communication, Cultural and Media Studies Research Centre (CCM)
- ■ Faculty of Arts, Media and Social Sciences, University of Salford, Adelphi House, Salford, Manchester, M3 6EN.
   0161-295 2694
   http://www.ccm.salford.ac.uk/
   Director: Prof George McKay.
- E A research centre within the Institute for Social, Cultural and Policy Research (qv) at the University of Salford.
- ○ To bring together researchers across the University whose work informs communication, cultural and media studies

Communication and Media Research Institute (CAMRI)
- ■ School of Media, Arts and Design, University of Westminster, Watford Road, Northwick Park, Harrow, Middlesex, HA1 3TP.
   020 7911 5903; 5944   fax 020 7911 5943
   http://www.wmin.ac.uk/mad/page-561
   Director: Prof Colin Sparks.
- E A research institute at the University of Westminster.
- ○ To conduct research into the full range of the media, from telecommunications through broadcasting to the printed media

Communications Research Centre (CRC)
- ■ Cardiff School of Engineering, Cardiff University, Queen's Buildings, Newport Road, Cardiff, CF24 3AA.
   029 2087 4071
   http://www.engin.cf.ac.uk/research/group.asp?GroupNo=45
   Group Leader: Prof Kenneth V Lever.
- E A research centre within the Institute of Information Systems and Integration Technology (qv) at Cardiff University.
- ○ To research communication in a very wide sense, ranging from novel device and subsystem technologies to new signal processing, data fusion and information fusion techniques, including human factors engineering

Communications Research Centre (CRC) 1991
- ■ Department of Social Sciences, Loughborough University, Loughborough, Leicestershire, LE11 3TU.
   01509 223370
   http://www.lboro.ac.uk/departments/ss/centres/crc.html
   Co-Director: Prof Michael Billig. Co-Director: Prof P Golding.
- E A research centre at Loughborough University.
- ○ To conduct communication and media research

Communications and Software Systems Engineering Research Centre (CSSERC) 2001
- ■ Department of Computing, Communications Technology and Mathematics, North Campus, London Metropolitan University, 166-220 Holloway Road, London, N7 8DB.
   020 7353 5070
   http://cctmdev2.londonmet.ac.uk/AlgirdasP//CET/Research/CSSERC/
   Director: Prof Algirdas Pakstas.
- E A research centre at London Metropolitan University.
- ○ To conduct theoretical and applied research into the use of methods and tools for design and development of communications, software and other systems

Community Audit and Evaluation Centre (CAEC)
- ■ Faculty of Health, Social Care and Education, Manchester Metropolitan University, 799 Wilmslow Road, Didsbury, Manchester, M20 2RR.
   0161-247 2114; 2134
   http://www.did.stu.mmu.ac.uk/caec/
   Director: Carol Packham.
- E A research centre at Manchester Metropolitan University.
- ○ To undertake participatory research and evaluations of services and organisations such as local authorities, health care trusts, and the private and voluntary sector

© CBD Research Ltd · Beckenham · Kent BR3 5JS · Tel 020 8650 7745 · Fax 020 8650 0768 · E-mail cbd@cbdresearch.com · www.cbdresearch.com

Community Care Works   (CCW)
- Division of Community Based Sciences, University of Glasgow, 1 Lilybank Gardens, Glasgow, G12 8RZ.
  0141-330 4039   fax 0141-330 5018
  http://www.gla.ac.uk/centres/nuffield/
  Contact: Kathryn Berzins.
- E   A centre at the University of Glasgow.
- O   To focus on the evaluation, promotion and dissemination of community care policy and practice
- ✕   Nuffield Centre for Community Care Studies.

Community Information Systems Centre   (CISC)
- Faculty of Computing, Engineering and Mathematical Sciences, Frenchay Campus, University of the West of England, Coldharbour Lane, Bristol, BS16 1QY.
  0117-328 3136
  http://cisc.uwe.ac.uk/
  Director: Dr Rob Stephens.
- E   A research centre at the University of the West of England.
- O   To work in partnership with people in their own community settings to use, understand, develop or optimise information systems in line with their particular needs and practices

Community Regeneration Research Centre
- University of Derby, Kedleston Road, Derby, DE22 1GB.
  01332 591849
  Co-ordinator: Gordon Riches.
- E   A research centre at the University of Derby.
- O   To support individuals, groups and organisations working to enhance the quality of social life in urban, suburban and rural settings

Comparative Organisation and Equality Research Centre   (COERC)
- Department of Management and Professional Development, London Metropolitan University, Stapleton House, 277-281 Holloway Road, London, N7 8HN.
  020 7753 5063   fax 020 7753 5051
  http://www.workinglives.org/
  Contact: Fiona Colgan. Contact: Dr Stephen Perkins.
- E   An affiliate centre of the Working Lives Research Institute (qv) at London Metropolitan University.
- O   To provide a platform for interdisciplinary research into employment, work organisation and equality and diversity in a comparative and international perspective

Compass Centre   2000
- Department of Language and Computer Science, City University, Northampton Square, London, EC1V 0HB.
  020 7040 8288
  http://www.city.ac.uk/lcs/compass/compasshome.html
  Contact: J Topping.
- E   A centre at City University.
- O   To offer a range of cutting-edge intervention services for clients; to provide an excellent quality of supervision for speech and language therapy students; to promote the development of well-designed research

Complex Product Systems Innovation Centre   (CoPS)
- SPRU - Science and Technology Policy Research, The Freeman Centre, University of Sussex, Falmer, Brighton, East Sussex, BN1 9QE.
  01273 678177   fax 01273 877977
  http://www.cops.ac.uk/
  Contact: Prof Mike Hobday.
- E   A research centre at the University of Sussex.
- O   To make a fundamental contribution to the understanding and management of innovation in complex high value, capital goods, industrial products, systems, constructs and networks

Complex Systems Management Centre
- Cranfield School of Management, Cranfield University, Cranfield, Bedfordshire, MK43 0AL.
  01234 758080
  http://www.som.cranfield.ac.uk/som/research/centres/csmc.asp
  Contact: Prof Peter Allen.
- E   A research centre within the Cranfield Management Research Institute (qv) at Cranfield University.
- O   To apply complex systems thinking to a wide variety of issues, including new product / service definition and development, organising for innovation, and the evolution of market systems and business sectors

Complexity and Management Centre   1995
- Business School, De Havilland Campus, University of Hertfordshire, College Lane, Hatfield, Hertfordshire, AL10 9AB.
  01707 284800   fax 01707 284870
  http://perseus.herts.ac.uk/prospectus/faculty_bs/uhbs/research/complexity-and-management-centre/complexity-and-management-centre_home.cfm
  Research Leader: Prof Ralph Stacey.
- E   A research centre within the Social Sciences, Arts and Humanities Research Institute (qv) at the University of Hertfordshire.
- O   To create links between academic work and organisational practice using a complexity perspective, in which the inevitable paradoxes and ambiguities of organisational life are not finally resolved but held in creative tension

Complexity Science Research Centre   (CSRC)   2001
- Faculty of Technology, Open University, Walton Hall, Milton Keynes, MK7 6AA.
  01908 652103
  http://technology.open.ac.uk/cts/
  Contact: Olivia Acquah.
- E   A research centre within the Centre for Technology Strategy (qv) at the Open University.
- O   To establish itself as a leading centre of excellence and expertise in complexity science research via exploration, design, innovation and implementation

Composites Centre
- Materials Department, Cranfield University, Building 61, Cranfield, Bedfordshire, MK43 0AL.
  01234 754062
  http://www.cranfield.ac.uk/sas/materials/polymers/
  Contact: Dr Sue Impey.
- E   A research centre at Cranfield University.
- O   To conduct research on the behaviour of continuous fibre reinforced composites, mainly those based on thermosetting resins

Composites Centre   1983
- Department of Aeronautics, South Kensington Campus, Imperial College London, Exhibition Road, London, SW7 2AZ.
  020 7594 5084   fax 020 7594 5083
  http://www.imperial.ac.uk/aeronautics/composites/
  Director: Dr Paul Robinson.
- E   An interdisciplinary research centre at Imperial College London.
- O   To co-ordinate and expand research activities in composites, and educate and train young engineers and scientists
- ×   Centre for Composite Materials.

Computational Biology Institute
  see **Cambridge Computational Biology Institute.**

Computational Engineering and Design Centre   (CEDC)
- Department of Mechanical Engineering, University of Southampton, Highfield, Southampton, SO17 1BJ.
  023 8059 2944   fax 023 8059 3220
  http://www.soton.ac.uk/ses/research/ced/
- E   A research centre at the University of Southampton.
- O   To develop and exploit models of engineering systems using powerful computational facilities

Computer Centre for People with Disabilities
  see **National Network of Assessment Centres.**

Computer Learning Research Centre   (CLRC)
- Department of Computer Science, Royal Holloway University of London, Egham, Surrey, TW20 0EX.
  01784 414024   fax 01784 436332
  http://www.clrc.rhul.ac.uk/
  Director: Prof Alex Gammerman.
- E   A research centre at Royal Holloway, University of London.
- O   To develop machine learning theory, and design and implement software based on the algorithms and theory developed by the Centre

Computer Science Research Institute
- Faculty of Engineering, University of Ulster, Cromore Road, Coleraine, County Londonderry, BT52 1SA.
  028 9036 6553   fax 028 9036 6803
  http://www.informatics.ulster.ac.uk/research/
- E   A research institute at the University of Ulster.

Computer Security and Audit Centre   (CSAC)   1997
- School of Computing and Mathematical Sciences, Maritime Greenwich Campus, University of Greenwich, Park Row, London, SE10 9LS.
  020 8331 8509; 9709
  http://www.cms.gre.ac.uk/research/centres/securityaudit.asp
  Co-ordinator: David Chadwick. Co-ordinator: Diane Gan.
- E   A research centre at the University of Greenwich.
- O   To focus on research and teaching in the areas of network security, application security (databases, spreadsheets and websites), security management, operating systems security, software quality, and auditing and information ethics
- ×   Information Integrity Research Centre.

Computer Security Research Centre
Note: is now the Information Systems Integrity Group of the London School of Economics and is therefore outside the scope of this directory.

Concrete Centre   2001
- Riverside House, 4 Meadows Business Park, Camberley, Surrey, GU17 9AB.
  0700 822 822   fax 01276 606801
  http://www.concretecentre.com/
  Marketing Intelligence Officer: Reuben Speed.
- ○ To provide a new focus for excellence in concrete design and construction that will enable all those who design and construct in concrete; to realise the full potential of concrete and to become knowledgeable about the products and design options available
- ● Conferences - Education and training - Meetings - Picture library - Visits
- ¶ Concrete Centre News. Concrete Quarterly.

Confucius Institute   2006
- School of Languages, Linguistics and Cultures, University of Manchester, Humanities Lime Grove Centre, Oxford Road, Manchester, M13 9PL.
  0161-275 3003   fax 0161-275 3031
  http://www.confuciusinstitute.manchester.ac.uk/
- E   An institute at the University of Manchester.

Note: A partnership between the University, the Office of Chinese Language Council International, and Beijing Normal University.

Constance Howard Resource and Research Centre in Textiles
- Goldsmiths, University of London, Deptford Town Hall, New Cross Road, London, SE14 6AF.
  020 7717 2210
  http://www.goldsmiths.ac.uk/constance-howard/
- E   A independent research centre at Goldsmiths, University of London.

Construction and Property Research Centre   (CPRC)   1998
- Faculty of the Built Environment, Frenchay Campus, University of the West of England, Coldharbour Lane, Bristol, BS16 1QY.
  0117-328 3000
  http://www.built-environment.uwe.ac.uk/research/cprc/
- E   A research centre at the University of the West of England.
- ○ To conduct research in the development and application of integrated innovative solutions to technical, social and economic problems related to the management of construction and property

Constructive Teaching Centre   (CTC)   1960
- 18 Lansdowne Road, London, W11 3LL.
  020 7727 7222
  Joint Director: W H M Carrington. Joint Director: Mrs D M G Carrington.
- E   A company limited by guarantee.
- ○ To train people to teach the technique developed by F M Alexander to improve posture
- ● Education and training - Information service

Contaminated Land Assessment and Remediation Research Centre   (CLARRC)
- University of Edinburgh, The King's Buildings, Mayfield Road, Edinburgh, EH9 3JR.
  0131-650 7328   fax 0131-650 6554
  http://www.clarrc.ed.ac.uk/
  Director: Colin Cunningham.
- E   A research centre at the University of Edinburgh.
- ○ To develop technologies for sustainable, cost-effective assessment and remediation of contaminated environments, and promoting their transfer to industry

Contemporary China Institute
Note: The Institute is the publishing arm of the Centre of Chinese Studies(qv).

Contemporary Poetics Research Centre   (CPRC)
- School of English and Humanities, Birkbeck, University of London, Malet Street, Bloomsbury, London, WC1E 7HX.
  020 7631 6861
  http://www.bbk.ac.uk/eh/research/contemppoeticscentre
- E   A research centre within the Birkbeck Institute for the Humanities (qv) at Birkbeck, University of London.
- ○ To be involved in the living arts as matters of intellectual concern and in policy debate about the arts in society

Contextual, Public and Commemorative Art Research Centre   (CPCA)
- Bristol School of Art, Media and Design, Bower Ashton Campus, University of the West of England, Kennel Lodge Road, Bristol, BS3 2JT.
  0117-328 4716
  http://www.uwe.ac.uk/amd/cpca/
  Director: Prof Paul Gough.
- E   A research centre at the University of the West of England.

Continuous Mortality Investigation Bureau
- Staple Inn Hall, High Holborn, London, WC1V 7QJ.
  020 7632 2100   fax 020 7632 2111
  http://www.cmib.org.uk/
- E   A research organisation within the Institute of Actuaries.
- ○ To conduct research into the disease and death rates of people with long term risk contracts issued by life assurance offices

Continuum - Centre for Widening Participation Policy Studies

■ Docklands Campus, University of East London, 4-6 University Way, London, E16 2RD.
020 8223 2162   fax 020 8223 3394
http://www.uel.ac.uk/continuum/
Director: Prof John Storan.

E A research centre at the University of East London.

O To provide a focus for critical understanding of widening participation policy and practice

Control Engineering Research Centre   (CERC)   1983

■ Department of Engineering, City University, Tait Building, Northampton Square, London, EC1V 0HB.
020 7040 0113
http://www.city.ac.uk/sems/research/cerc/

E A centre at City University.

O To undertake education and research in the field of control engineering

Control Systems Centre

■ School of Computing and Technology, University of Sunderland, St Peter's Campus, St Peter's Way, Sunderland, Tyne and Wear, SR6 0DD.
0191-515 2752   fax 0191-515 2781
http://www.sunderland.ac.uk/~ts0aad/csc/
Director: Prof Chris Cox.

E A research centre at the University of Sunderland.

O To conduct research in a wide spectrum of interests relating to the modelling, simulation, analysis and design of process control systems

Control Theory and Applications Centre   (CTAC)   1992

■ School of Mathematical and Information Sciences, University of Coventry, Priory Street, Coventry, CV1 5FB.
024 7688 8052; 8189
http://www.ctac.mis.coventry.ac.uk/
Director: Prof Keith J Burnham.

E An interdisciplinary research centre at Coventry University.

O To conduct research in control theory and applications, including adaptive control and fault detection, biomedical engineering systems, computational intelligence and optimisation, industrial computing, industrial control applications, and robust control system theory and design

Co-operative Bank plc National Centre of Business and Ecology
see **Sustainability Northwest and National Centre for Business and Sustainability.**

Corrosion and Protection Centre   1972

■ School of Materials, PO Box 88, University of Manchester, Sackville Street, Manchester, M60 1QD.
0161-306 6000
http://www.materials.manchester.ac.uk/research/groups/corrosionandprotection/
Contact: Prof George Thompson.

E A research centre at the University of Manchester.

O To conduct research in corrosion and its control

Costume and Fashion Research Centre
see **Museum of Costume and Fashion Research Centre.**

Counterfeiting Intelligence Bureau
see **ICC Counterfeiting Intelligence Bureau.**

Courtauld Institute of Art   1932

■ Somerset House, Strand, London, WC2R 0RN.
020 7848 2777   fax 020 7848 2410
http://www.courtauld.ac.uk/
Secretary & Registrar: Michael Arthur.

E A college of the University of London.

O To be a world leading institute for teaching and research in the history of art and conservation

Note: The Institute is named after Samuel Courtauld, textile magnate and art lover, who, in 1932, made over his house in Portman Square for the

Coventry University Design Institute

■ School of Art and Design, University of Coventry, Priory Street, Coventry, CV1 5FB.
024 7688 7688
http://www.corporate.coventry.ac.uk/cms/jsp/polopoly.jsp?d=844

E A research institute at Coventry University.

O To achieve excellence in research and design science relevant to a wide range of design domains; to contribute to industrial and postgraduate courses in design; to provide consultancy in design and related topics to industry

Craft and Design Research Centre

■ School of Art, Manchester Metropolitan University, Cavendish North Building, Cavendish Street, Manchester, M15 6BG.
 0161-247 5389
 http://www.miriad.mmu.ac.uk/craftdesign/
 Leader: Stephen Dixon.
E A research centre within the Manchester Institute for Research and Innovation in Art and Design (qv) at Manchester Metropolitan University.
○ To promote the development of research activity in the theory and practice of craft and design

Crafts Study Centre   (CSC)   1970

■ Farnham Campus, University College for the Creative Arts, Falkner Road, Farnham, Surrey, GU9 7DS.
 01252 722441   fax 01252 892616
 http://www.csc.ucreative.ac.uk/
 Chairman: Prof Edmund de Waal.
E A registered charity and centre at University College for the Creative Arts.
○ To capture, safeguard and offer wide access to a unique craft collection; to facilitate a deeper understanding and enjoyment of the crafts by fostering and articulating the underpinning values that exist between makers, craft practice and the collection; to safeguard and develop the Centre's collections and make them accessible to the widest possible audiences

Craighalbert Centre
 see **Scottish Centre for Children with Motor Impairments.**

Cranfield BioMedical Centre

■ Cranfield Health, Cranfield University, Silsoe, Bedfordshire, MK45 4DT.
 01525 863517   fax 01525 863533
 http://www.cranfield.ac.uk/ibst/cbmc/
 Head: Dr Anthony Woodman.
E A research centre at Cranfield University.
○ To provide solutions in research and training for in vivo and in vitro diagnostic medicine

Cranfield Biotechnology Centre   (CBC)   1981

■ Cranfield Health, Cranfield University, Silsoe, Bedfordshire, MK45 4DT.
 01525 863168   fax 01525 863080
 http://www.cranfield.ac.uk/biotech/
 General Manager: Ned Ashby.
E A research centre at Cranfield University.
○ To conduct research in various areas of biotechnology including, applied mycology, astrobiology and astrobiotechnology, plant science, surface science, and sensors, arrays and diagnostics

Cranfield Centre for Advanced Research in Marketing   (CCARM)

■ Cranfield School of Management, Cranfield University, Cranfield, Bedfordshire, MK43 0AL.
 01234 754408
 http://www.som.cranfield.ac.uk/som/research/centres/ccarm/
 Director: Prof Adrian Payne.
E A research centre within the Cranfield Management Research Institute (qv) at Cranfield University.
○ To work with the operating boards of various multinational companies in the areas of customer relationship management, key account management, multi-channel marketing, new marketing, and brand management

Cranfield Centre for Agricultural and Environmental Engineering   (CAEE)

■ Natural Resources' Department, Cranfield University, Silsoe, Bedfordshire, MK45 4DT.
 01525 863050; 863056
 http://www.silsoe.cranfield.ac.uk/caee/
 Contact: Prof R J Godwin.
E A research centre within the National Soil Resources Institute (qv) at Cranfield University.
○ To deliver education, research and professional training in the areas of machinery and land systems engineering

Cranfield Centre for Bioinformatics

■ Cranfield Health, Cranfield University, Silsoe, Bedfordshire, MK45 4DT.
 01525 863279
 http://www.cranfield.ac.uk/dasi/research/bioinfo.htm
E A research centre at Cranfield University.
○ To provide research and postgraduate training, with specific expertise in proteomic bioinformatics, microarray informatics and systems biology, high performance computing and the grid, and knowledge technologies

Cranfield Centre for Competition and Regulation Research   (CCORR)

■ Cranfield School of Management, Cranfield University, Cranfield, Bedfordshire, MK43 0AL.
 01234 754378
 http://www.som.cranfield.ac.uk/som/research/centres/ccorr.asp
 Director: Prof David Parker.
E A research centre within the Cranfield Management Research Institute (qv) at Cranfield University.
○ To advance research on competition and regulation

Cranfield Centre for EcoChemistry

- Cranfield University, Silsoe, Bedfordshire, MK45 4DT.
  01525 863000   fax 01525 863533
  http://www.silsoe.cranfield.ac.uk/ecochemistry/
  Contact: Helen Noble.
- E   A research centre within the Institute of Water and Environment (qv) at Cranfield University.
- O   To promote understanding and study of the fate, effects and risk assessment of chemicals released into the environment

Cranfield Centre for Ecological Restoration   (CCER)

- Cranfield University, Silsoe, Bedfordshire, MK45 4DT.
  01525 863141   fax 01525 863344
  http://www.silsoe.cranfield.ac.uk/ccer/
  Director: Prof Jim Harris.
- E   A research centre within the Institute of Water and Environment (qv) at Cranfield University.
- O   To conduct research and teaching in the area of land reclamation and restoration, to promote effective and sustainable restoration programmes

Cranfield Centre for Geographical Information Management   (CCGIM)

- Natural Resources' Department, Cranfield University, Silsoe, Bedfordshire, MK45 4DT.
  01525 863062
  http://www.silsoe.cranfield.ac.uk/ccgim/
  Contact: Tim Brewer.
- E   A research centre within the National Soil Resources Institute (qv) at Cranfield University.
- O   To create and promote innovative solutions for the rational management of resources based on the integration of the component technologies of remote sensing, geographical information systems (GIS) and global positioning systems (GPS)

Cranfield Centre for Precision Farming   (CCPF)   1996

- Natural Resources' Department, Cranfield University, Silsoe, Bedfordshire, MK45 4DT.
  01525 863052   fax 01525 863099
  http://www.silsoe.cranfield.ac.uk/cpf
  Contact: Prof Dick Godwin.
- E   A research centre within the National Soils Resources Institute (qv) at Cranfield University.
- O   To provide a forum for farmers, the supply industry and other research organisations, for the management of within-field variation, helping farmers to grow crops more efficiently, and at competitive prices, whilst reducing waste to the environment

Cranfield Centre for Sports Surfaces   (CCSS)

- Natural Resources' Department, Cranfield University, Silsoe, Bedfordshire, MK45 4DT.
  01525 863000   fax 01525 863001
  http://www.silsoe.cranfield.ac.uk/ccss
- E   A research centre within the National Soil Resources Institute (qv) at Cranfield University.
- O   To deliver education, research and professional training to the sports turf industry

Cranfield Centre for Supramolecular Technology   (CCST)

- Cranfield Health, Cranfield University, Silsoe, Bedfordshire, MK45 4DT.
  01525 863584   fax 01525 863533
  http://www.cranfield.ac.uk/ibst/ccst/
  Head: Prof Sergey Piletsky.
- E   A research centre at Cranfield University.
- O   To develop world class polymer science for solving problems in separation and sensing

Cranfield Impact Centre   (CIC)

- Cranfield University, Building 56, Cranfield, Bedfordshire, MK43 0AL.
  01234 751361   fax 01234 754280
  http://www.cicl.co.uk/
  Contact: K A H Montgomery.
- E   A research centre at Cranfield University.
- O   To be a leader in the field of safety and safety structures, with special emphasis on vehicle and vehicle occupant simulation, pedestrian impact modelling, design for crashworthiness and crash protection, and analysis, design, development and testing of safety structures

Cranfield Innovative Manufacturing Research Centre   (IMRC)   2002

- NR   School of Applied Sciences, Cranfield University, Cranfield, Bedfordshire, MK43 0AL.
  01234 758090   fax 01234 750111
  http://www.cranfield.ac.uk/imrc/
  Director: Prof David Stephenson. Research Manager: Dr Ian Walton.
- E   An EPSRC Innovative Manufacturing Research Centre at Cranfield University.
- O   To grow the existing world-class research activity, through the development and interaction between manufacturing technologies and product / service systems that move UK manufacturing up the value chain, to provide high added value manufacturing business opportunities

Note: One of the EPSRC funded centres in the UK - for further information see EPSRC Innovative Manufacturing Research Centres.

© CBD Research Ltd · Beckenham · Kent BR3 5JS · Tel 020 8650 7745 · Fax 020 8650 0768 · E-mail cbd@cbdresearch.com · www.cbdresearch.com

Cranfield Institute for Safety, Risk and Reliability   (CISRR)

■ School of Applied Sciences, Cranfield University, Building 83, Cranfield, Bedfordshire, MK43 0AL.
   01234 750111   fax 01234 750728
   http://www.cranfield.ac.uk/safety/
   Director: Prof Helen Muir.
E A research institute at Cranfield University.
O To conduct trans-disciplinary and multi-sector approaches to safety research, consultancy and teaching in all the major safety-critical sectors including, agriculture, aviation, automotive and road, defence, education, food, rail, medicine and health, offshore engineering, and water

Cranfield Management Research Institute   (CMRI)

■ Cranfield School of Management, Cranfield University, Cranfield, Bedfordshire, MK43 0AL.
   01234 751122   fax 01234 752136
   http://www.som.cranfield.ac.uk/som/research/
   Contact: Andrew Kirchner.
E An institute at Cranfield University.
O To bring together various management research centres at the University

Cranfield Mine Action and Disaster Management Centre   (CMA&DMC)   2003

■ Department of Defence Management and Security Analysis, Cranfield University, Shrivenham, Swindon, Wiltshire, SN6 8LA.
   01793 785950
   http://www.dcmt.cranfield.ac.uk/
   Contact: Miss Hilary Tonks.
E A research centre at Cranfield University.
O To assist countries and organisations enhance their leadership and management capabilities, and thus enable them to prepare for and respond better to disasters, complex emergencies and post-conflict challenges

Cranfield Ordnance Test and Evaluation Centre   (COTEC)

■ Department of Materials and Applied Science, Cranfield University, Shrivenham, Swindon, Wiltshire, SN6 8LA.
   01380 813251   fax 01380 813251
   http://www.dcmt.cranfield.ac.uk/dmas/cost/cotec/
   Contact: Andrew Norton.
E A research centre within the Centre for Ordnance Science and Technology (qv) at Cranfield University.
O To undertake demilitarisation and test and evaluation of munitions, weapon systems, pyrotechnic and explosive stores

Cranfield Resilience Centre   (CRC)   1984

■ Department of Defence Management and Security Analysis, Cranfield University, Shrivenham, Swindon, Wiltshire, SN6 8LA.
   01793 782551   fax 01793 783878
   http://www.dcmt.cranfield.ac.uk/ddmsa/resilience
   Director: Ivar Hellberg, OBE.
E A research centre at Cranfield University.
O To improve the capacity of organisations to respond to emergency and disruptive challenges - whether natural, accidental or deliberate - through the provision of relevant education, training, research and operational support

Cranfield Safety and Accident Investigation Centre   (CSAIC)   1977

■ Department of Air Transport, Cranfield University, Cranfield, Bedfordshire, MK43 0AL.
   01234 754252   fax 01234 752207
   http://www.cranfield.ac.uk/soe/airtransport/csaic.htm
   Director: Dr Graham Braithwaite.
E A research centre within the Cranfield Institute for Safety, Risk and Reliability (qv) at Cranfield University.
O To conduct training courses and research in accident investigation and safety matters involving various modes of transport

Cranfield Space Research Centre

■ Department of Power, Propulsion and Aerospace Engineering, Cranfield University, Cranfield, Bedfordshire, MK43 0AL.
   01234 750111   fax 01234 758203
   http://www.cranfield.ac.uk/soe/space/
   Senior Lecturer: Dr Stephen Hobbs.
E A research centre at Cranfield University.
O To teach and research in a wide range of space engineering, space systems and space applications

Cranfield University Business Incubation Centre   (CUBIC)

■ Cranfield School of Management, Cranfield University, Building 45, Cranfield, Bedfordshire, MK43 0AL.
   01234 754017
   http://www.businessgateway.cranfield.ac.uk/
   Contact: Paul Kitson.
E A centre at Cranfield University.
O To support and encourage hi-tech and knowledge-based pre-start and early start companies during the formative stages of their development

Creative Learning in Practice Centre for Excellence in Teaching and Learning   (CLIP)   2005

- ■ London College of Fashion, University of the Arts, London, Room 148, 20 John Princes Street, London, W1G 0BJ.
  020 7514 8723
  http://www.arts.ac.uk/cetl.htm
- E A Centre for Excellence in Teaching and Learning (CETL) at the University of the Arts, London.
- O To identify, evaluate and disseminate effective practice-based teaching and learning in the creative industries
- Note: See **Centres for Excellence in Teaching and Learning** for further information.

Credit Management Research Centre   (CMRC)   1996

- ■ Leeds University Business School, University of Leeds, Maurice Keyworth Building, Leeds, LS2 9JT.
  0113-343 5750   fax 0113-343 5753
  http://www.cmrc.co.uk/
  Director: Prof Nick Wilson.
- E A research centre at the University of Leeds.
- O To carry out academic research and develop educational programmes in the credit and financial services sectors

Crichton Centre for Research in Health and Social Issues   2003

- ■ Crichton University Campus, University of Glasgow, Rutherford-McCowan Building, Dumfries, DG1 4ZL.
  01387 702001
  http://www.cc.gla.ac.uk:443/layer1/hs_research.htm
  Director: Dr Carol Hill.
- E A research centre at the University of Glasgow.
- O To develop research and scholarship in the broad field of health and social issues

Crichton Centre for Rural Enterprise   (CCRE)   2002

- ■ Paisley Business School, University of Paisley, Paisley, PA1 2BE.
  http://www.paisley.ac.uk/business/perc/
  Contact: Carole Naylor.
- E Part of the Paisley Enterprise Research Centre (qv) at the University of Paisley.
- O To conduct research on rural enterprise issues
- Note: At the time of going to press, the University of Paisley was preparing to merge with Bell College to form the University of the West of Scotland.

Crichton Tourism Research Centre   (CTRC)

- ■ Crichton University Campus, University of Glasgow, Rutherford-McCowan Building, Dumfries, DG1 4ZL.
  01387 702021
  http://www.cc.gla.ac.uk:443/crc/
  Director: Dr Valentina Bold.
- E A research centre at the University of Glasgow.
- O To explore issues relating to tourism, cultural and natural heritage, heritage management and related areas, such as development

Crime and Conflict Research Centre   (CCRC)   1986

- ■ School of Health and Social Sciences, Middlesex University, Queensway, Enfield, Middlesex, EN3 4SA.
  020 8411 5657   fax 020 8411 6404
  http://www.mdx.ac.uk/hssc/research/centres/csccc/
  Administrator: Sandra Dias.
- E A centre at Middlesex University.
- O To focus research on the areas of crime, policing, community safety, justice and victimisation, social movements, international conflicts, political violence, and terrorism
- × Centre for Criminology.

Crime Fictions Research Centre   (CFRC)

- ■ Faculty of Humanities, Law and Social Science, Manchester Metropolitan University, Geoffrey Manton Building, Rosamond Street West, Manchester, M15 6LL.
  0161-247 3030
  http://www.hlss.mmu.ac.uk/languages/research/cfrc/
  Co-Convenor: Shelley Godsland. Co-Convenor: Carmen Herrero.
- E A research centre within the Centre for European Literatures and Cultures (qv) at Manchester Metropolitan University.

Criminal Justice Centre [Kent]
  see **Kent Criminal Justice Centre.**

Criminal Justice Centre   1993

- ■ Ealing Law School, Thames Valley University, Walpole House, 18-20 Bond Street, London, W5 5AA.
  020 8579 5000
  http://www.tvu.ac.uk/research/1centres/cjc.jsp
  Director: Prof Malcolm Davies.
- E A research centre at Thames Valley University.
- O To encourage research in the field of criminal justice

© CBD Research Ltd · Beckenham · Kent BR3 5JS · Tel 020 8650 7745 · Fax 020 8650 0768 · E-mail cbd@cbdresearch.com · www.cbdresearch.com

Criminal Justice Research Centre   (CJRC)

- University of Coventry, Priory Street, Coventry, CV1 5FB.
  024 7688 8761
  http://www.stile.coventry.ac.uk/public/rcon/ccj_f.htm
  Director: Prof Barry Mitchell.
- E   A centre at Coventry University.
- O   To pursue quality research in criminal justice

Criminal Justice Social Work Development Centre for Scotland   (CJSW)

- Old College, University of Edinburgh, South Bridge, Edinburgh, EH8 9YL.
  0131-651 1464
  http://www.cjsw.ac.uk/
- E   A research centre at the University of Edinburgh.
- O   To provide a range of services to those working in, or concerned about, criminal and youth justice social work services

Criminal Records Bureau   (CRB)   2005

- PO Box 110, Liverpool, L69 3EF.
  0870 909 0811
  http://www.crb.gov.uk/
- E   An executive agency of the Home Office.
- O   To help organisations, in the public, private and voluntary sectors, by identifying candidates who may be unsuitable to work with children or other vulnerable members of society

Crisis States Research Centre   (CSRC)

- LSE, Connaught House, Houghton Street, London, WC2A 2AE.
  020 7849 4631   fax 020 7955 6421
  http://www.crisisstates.com/
  Director: Dr James Putzel.
- E   A research centre within the Development Studies Institute (qv) at the London School of Economics and Political Science.
- O   To provide new understanding of the causes of crisis and breakdown in the developing world and the processes of avoiding or overcoming them

Cromarty Training Centre   2004

- Old Brewery, Burnside Place, Cromarty, Ross-shire, IV11 8XQ.
  01381 600277
  http://www.cromarty-training.com/
  Manager: Mairi Macneil.
- E   A company limited by guarantee.
- O   A training and conference centre

Crown Agents Stamp Bureau   (CASB)

- 3rd Floor - St Nicholas House, St Nicholas Road, Sutton, Surrey, SM1 1EL.
  020 8770 0707   fax 020 8642 0769
  http://www.casb.co.uk/
- O   To deliver the advice and support required to meet the ever-changing requirements of the philatelic business

Croydon Buddhist Centre

- 98 High Street, Croydon, Surrey, CR0 1ND.
  020 8688 8624   fax 020 8649 9375
  http://www.buddhistcentrecroydon.org/
- E   An independent non-profit-distributing organisation and a registered charity.
- O   To teach meditation and Buddhism
- ●   Education and training - The Centre provides meditation cushions and mats

Note: For other Buddhist centres see note under **Buddhist Centres**.

CRUCiBLE: Centre for Rights, Understanding and Citizenship Based on Learning through Experience   (CRUCiBLE)   2005

- School of Business and Social Sciences, Southlands College, University of Roehampton, 80 Roehampton Lane, London, SW15 5SL.
  020 8392 3091; 3336
  http://www.roehampton.ac.uk/crucible/
  Head: David Woodman.
- E   A Centre for Excellence in Teaching and Learning (CETL) at Roehampton University.

Note: See **Centres for Excellence in Teaching and Learning** for more information.

Crystallographic Data Centre
> see **Cambridge Crystallographic Data Centre.**

Cullen Centre for Risk and Governance   (CRaG)

■   Caledonian Business School, Glasgow Caledonian University, Cowcaddens Road, Glasgow, G4 0BA.
  0141-331 3159   fax 0141-331 3229
  http://www.caledoniancrag.com/
  Executive Director: Dr Bill Stein.
E   A research centre at Glasgow Caledonian University.
○   To identify, with a range of relevant stakeholders, the principal governance and risk management needs and/or deficits of agents in the public, voluntary and private sectors

Cult Information Centre   1987

■   BCM Cults, London, WC1N 3XX.
  0870 777 3800
  http://www.cultinformation.org.uk/
  General Secretary: Ian Haworth.
E   A registered charity.
○   To provide information on cults and their damaging methods; to offer advice and an international network of contacts for counselling and further information to people with cult-related problems
●   Education and training - Helpline - Information service - Lectures - Statistics

Cultural, Communication and Computing Research Institute   (C3RI)

■   Psalter Lane Campus, Sheffield Hallam University, Sheffield, S11 8UZ.
  0114-225 2669   fax 0114-225 2603
  http://www.shu.ac.uk/research/c3ri/
  Director: Prof Jim Roddis. Research Support Officer: Sarah Owen.
E   A department of Sheffield Hallam University.
○   To develop research in the arts and humanities
●   Education and training - Statistics
Note: C3RI has two centres: the Art and Design Research Centre and the Communicationand Computing Research Centre
✕   Cultural Research Institute.

Cultural Informatics Research Centre in the Arts and Humanities   (CIRCAh)   2005

■   School of Library, Archive and Information Studies, University College London, Henry Morley Building, Gower Street, London, WC1E 6BT.
  020 7679 2000
  http://www.ucl.ac.uk/slais/research/circah/
  Contact: Dr Claire Warwick.
E   A research centre at University College London.
○   To study the application of computing to the arts and humanities

Cultural Research Institute
  see **Cultural, Communication and Computing Research Institute.**

Cultural Theory Institute   (CTI)   2004

■   School of Arts, Histories and Cultures, University of Manchester, 178 Waterloo Place, Oxford Road, Manchester, M13 9PG.
  0161-275 8997
  http://www.cti.man.ac.uk/
  Director: Lisa Adkins.
E   An interdisciplinary research institute at the University of Manchester.
○   To rethink the contested ground of culture

Culture, Development and the Environment Centre   (CDE)

■   School of Social Sciences and Cultural Studies, Arts C, University of Sussex, Falmer, Brighton, East Sussex, BN1 9SJ.
  01273 678261; 678722   fax 01273 623572
  http://www.sussex.ac.uk/development/
  Contact: Clare Rogers.
E   A research centre at the University of Sussex.

Cunliffe Centre for the Study of Constitutionalism and National Identity   1991

■   School of Humanities, University of Sussex, Falmer, Brighton, East Sussex, BN1 9QN.
  01273 606755; 678098   fax 01273 625972
  http://www.sussex.ac.uk/Units/cunliffe/
  Director: Prof Vivien Hart.
E   An interdisciplinary research centre at the University of Sussex.
○   To bring together international scholars to study constitutionalism, national identity and related issues
Note: The Centre is named in honour of Marcus Cunliffe (1922-1990), Professor of American Studies at the University from 1965-1980.

Curriculum Evaluation and Management Centre   (CEM)   1983
- ■   Mountjoy Research Centre, University of Durham, Block 4, Stockton Road, Durham, DH1 3UZ.
         0191-334 4189   fax 0191-334 4180
         http://www.cemcentre.org/
         Director: Prof P B Tymms.
- E   A department of the University of Durham.
- ○   To conduct research and development in education and related areas

Note: Usually known as the CEM Centre.

Cymru Centre for Intergenerational Practice
         see **Wales Centre for Intergenerational Practice.**

D H Lawrence Research Centre   1990

■   School of English Studies, University of Nottingham, University Park, Nottingham, NG7 2RD.
0115-951 5900   fax 0115-951 5924
http://www.dh-lawrence.org/
E   A research centre at the University of Nottingham.
O   To bring together those interested in research in Lawrence and his contemporaries, and to help focus and develop that research

Dalton Nuclear Institute

■   Faculty of Engineering and Physical Sciences, University of Manchester, Simon Building, Oxford Road, Manchester, M13 9PL.
0161-275 4431
http://www.eps.manchester.ac.uk/dalton/
Director: Prof Richard Clegg.
E   A department of the University of Manchester.
O   To be the focal point for the University's nuclear research activities

Dalton Research Institute

■   Faculty of Science and Engineering, Manchester Metropolitan University, John Dalton Building, Chester Street, Manchester, M1 5GD.
0161-247 1629   fax 0161-247 6315
http://www.dri.mmu.ac.uk/
E   A department of Manchester Metropolitan University.
O   To manage and promote research in the areas of environmental science, material science, computer science and general engineering

Danish Cultural Institute

■   3 Doune Terrace, Edinburgh, EH3 6DY.
0131-225 7189   fax 0131-220 6162
Director: Kim Caspersen.

Data Assimilation Research Centre   (DARC)   2001

■   Department of Meteorology, PO Box 243, University of Reading, Earley Gate, Reading, Berkshire, RG2 2BB.
0118-378 6728
http://darc.nerc.ac.uk/
Contact: Prof Alan O'Neill.
E   A Natural Environment Research Council collaborative research centre at the University of Reading.
O   To take satellite data and information from other sources in order to create a complete picture of how the oceans, land and atmosphere interact

David Davies Memorial Institute   (DDMI)

■   Department of International Politics, University of Wales Aberystwyth, Penglais, Aberystwyth, Ceredigion, SY23 3FE.
01970 628563
http://www.aber.ac.uk/interpol/research/DDMI/DavidDavies.htm
E   A research institute at the University of Wales, Aberystwyth.

David Hope RE Centre in York   1976

■   Fountains Learning Centre, University of York, Lord Mayor's Walk, York, YO31 7EX.
01904 716605
http://www2.yorksj.ac.uk/default.asp?Page_ID=345&Parent_ID=341
Development Officer: Imelda O'Grady. Professional Adviser & Project Director: Eileen Bellett.
E   A department of the York St John University College.
O   To provide resources and a consultancy service for teachers in both the primary and secondary sectors; to give service to church ministers, youth workers and others involved in religious education both within their own faith community and in the wider community
●   Education and training - Information service - Library
✕   York Religious Education Centre.

David K E Bruce Centre for American Studies   (DBC)   1969

■   Research Institute for the Humanities, Keele University, Chancellor's Building, Keele, Staffordshire, ST5 5BG.
01782 583010   fax 01782 583460
http://www.keele.ac.uk/depts/as/Dbruce/bruce.htm
Director: Dr Axel R Schäfer. Honorary President: Prof David K Adams.
E   A department of Keele University.
O   To further and encourage research in matters relating to the United States
●   Conference facilities - Library - Academic seminars and colloquia - Sponsorship of visiting faculty - Student burseries and research grants

David Lewis National Epilepsy Centre   1904

■   Mill Lane, Warford, Alderley Edge, Cheshire, SK9 7UD.
01565 640000   fax 01565 640100
http://www.davidlewis.org.uk/
E   A registered charity and a company limited by guarantee.
O   To offer residential assessment, treatment and rehabilitation of people, including schoolchildren, suffering from epilepsy; to promote the welfare for all people with epilepsy; to conduct research into epilepsy and related disorders

© CBD Research Ltd · Beckenham · Kent BR3 5JS · Tel 020 8650 7745 · Fax 020 8650 0768 · E-mail cbd@cbdresearch.com · www.cbdresearch.com

David Livingstone Institute of International Development Studies   (DLIIDS)   1973
■   Department of Civil Engineering, University of Strathclyde, John Anderson Building, 107 Rottenrow, Glasgow, G4 0NG.
     0141-548 3277   fax 0141-553 2066
     http://www.strath.ac.uk/Departments/Civeng/dliids
     Director: Prof George Fleming.

Deafness, Cognition and Language Research Centre   (DCAL)
■   Department of Human Communication Science, University College London, 49 Gordon Square, London, WC1H 0PD.
     020 7679 8679   fax 020 7679 8691
     http://www.dcal.ucl.ac.uk/
     Director: Prof Bencie Woll.
E   A research centre at University College London.
O   To conduct research in a wide variety of language and cognition fields, including language development, face-to-face communication, atypical language, language processing, the Deaf individual and the community, and normative data and assessment tools for British sign language

Decision Engineering Centre   (DEC)
■   Manufacturing Department, Cranfield University, Building 50, Cranfield, Bedfordshire, MK43 0AL.
     01234 750111   fax 01234 751806
     http://www.cranfield.ac.uk/sas/mem/decisionengineering/
     Head: Prof Rajkumar Roy.
E   A research centre at Cranfield University.
O   To conduct research in cost engineering, applied soft computing and product engineering which provides facts, techniques and infrastructure required for competitive design

Decommissioning and Environmental Remediation Centre
     see **UHI Decommissioning and Environmental Remediation Centre.**

Deer Study and Resource Centre
■   Trentham Gardens, Trentham, Stoke-on-Trent, ST4 8AX.
     01782 657717   fax 01782 657717
     http://www.deerstudy.com/
E   Established by the Deer in the Environment Educational Resource Fund, a registered charity.
O   To offer advice to anyone involved with deer

Defence Animal Centre   (DAC)   1993
■   Asfordby Road, Melton Mowbray, Leicestershire, LE13 0SL.
     01664 418600   fax 01664 418684
     http://www.defenceanimalcentre.co.uk/
E   A training centre.
O   To provide year round training for individuals who will maintain and handle working animals

Dementia Services Development Centre   (DSDC)   1989
■   Department of Applied Social Science, University of Stirling, Iris Murdoch Building, Stirling, FK9 4LA.
     01786 467440   fax 01786 466846
     http://www.dementia.stir.ac.uk/
     Director: June Andrews. Planning Consultant: Sylvia Cox.
E   A registered charity and a department of the University of Stirling.
O   To provide and encourage the development and initiation of services for people with dementia and their carers both on a national and international level
●   Conferences - Advice and information services - Training - Seminars and workshops - Hours Mon-Fri 0900-1700 (no appointment necessary for information, but advisable for visits)
¶   Annual Report. Very wide range of other publications - list available.

Dementia Services Development Centre Wales   (DSDC)   Canolfan Datblygu Gwasanaethu Dementia Cymru
■   Neuadd Ardudwy, Normal Site, University of Wales Bangor, Bangor, Gwynedd, LL57 2PX.
     01248 383719   fax 01248 382229
     http://www.bangor.ac.uk/dsdc/
     Co-Director: Prof Bob Woods. Research Director: Dr Linda Clare.
E   A research centre within the Institute of Medical and Social Care Research (qv) at the University of Wales, Bangor.

Dental Institute [Edinburgh]
     see **Edinburgh Dental Institute.**

Dental Institute [Leeds]
     see **Leeds Dental Institute.**

Dental Institute [London]
     see **UCL Eastman Dental Institute.**

Derbyshire Further Mathematics Centre   2006
- University of Derby, Kedleston Road, Derby, DE22 1GB.
  01332 591891
  http://www.fmnetwork.org.uk/centre/index.php?centre=der
  Contact: Simon Butt.
- E   A centre at the University of Derby.
- ○   To promote A and AS level mathematics in schools and colleges across the county

Design Enterprise Centre   (DEC)
- University of Hull, Newlands Science Park, Inglemire Lane, Hull, HU6 7RX.
  01482 466470
  http://www.hull.ac.uk/dec/
  Manager: Dr Stuart Brown.
- E   A centre at the University of Hull.
- ○   To provide industry with practical support and access to expertise and technology to further the design and development of products and processes

Design Institute
  see **Coventry University Design Institute.**

Design Research Centre   (DRC)
- Department of Mechanical Engineering, University College London, Torrington Place, London, WC1E 7JE.
  020 7679 3874; 7178
  http://www.mecheng.ucl.ac.uk/research/marine-systems/design-research/
  Contact: Prof David A Andrews.
- E   A research centre at University College London.
- ○   To conduct research into the use of computer aided design (CAD) for the architectural design of marine vehicles

Development Research Centre on Migration, Globalisation and Poverty   (DRC)   2003
- Department of Cultural Studies, University of Sussex, Arts C, Falmer, Brighton, East Sussex, BN1 9SJ.
  01273 877568   fax 01273 873158
  http://www.migrationdrc.org/
  Director: Prof Richard Black.
- E   A research centre within the Centre for Culture, Development and the Environment (qv) at the University of Sussex.
- ○   To promote new policy approaches that will help to maximise the potential benefits of migration for poor people, whilst minimising its risks and costs

Development Studies Institute   (DESTIN)   1990
- LSE, Houghton Street, London, WC2A 2AE.
  020 7955 7425   fax 020 7955 6844
  http://www.lse.ac.uk/collections/DESTIN/
  Head: Prof Jo Beall.
- E   An interdisciplinary institute at the London School of Economics and Political Science.
- ○   To promote teaching and research on processes of social, political and economic development and change

Diamond-like Carbon Coating Centre
- School of Engineering and Design, Brunel University, Uxbridge, Middlesex, UB8 3PH.
  01895 265863   fax 01895 812556
  http://www.brunel.ac.uk/about/acad/sed/sedres/me/dlc
  Director: Prof Joe Franks.
- E   A centre at Brunel University.
- ○   To provide an industrial service for coating components with diamond-like carbon and to manufacture custom built diamond-like carbon coating

Dictionary Research Centre   (DRC)   2001
- Department of English, University of Birmingham, Westmere House, Edgbaston, Birmingham, B15 2TT.
  0121-414 3076; 3364   fax 0121-414 5668
  http://www.english.bham.ac.uk/drc/
  Contact: Dr Rosamund Moon.
- E   A research centre at the University of Birmingham.
- ○   To conduct teaching and research in lexicography and dictionaries

Didcot Railway Centre   1961
- Didcot, Oxfordshire, OX11 7NJ.
  01235 817200   fax 01235 510621
  http://www.didcotrailwaycentre.org.uk/
- E   A registered charity and a company limited by guarantee.
- ○   To preserve the Great Western Railway (GWR) in all its aspects

Digestive Disease Research Centre   (DDRC)

■   Barts and the London, Queen Mary's School of Medicine and Dentistry, Queen Mary, University of London, 4 Newark Street, London, E1 2AT.
    020 7882 7196
    http://www.smd.qmul.ac.uk/gastro
    Head: Prof Parveen Kumar.
E   A research group within the Centre for Adult and Paediatric Gastroenterology (qv) at Queen Mary, University of London.

Digestive Diseases Centre
    see **Wolfson Digestive Diseases Centre.**

Digital Curation Centre   (DCC)

■   University of Edinburgh, Appleton Tower, Crichton Street, Edinburgh, EH8 9LE.
    0131-651 1239
    http://www.dcc.ac.uk/
E   A research centre at the University of Edinburgh.
O   To support UK institutions who store, manage and preserve data to help ensure their enhancement and their continuing long-term use
Note: See **e-Science Centres** for further information.

Digital Imaging Research Centre   (DIRC)   2000

■   Faculty of Computing, Information Systems and Mathematics, Kingston University, Penrhyn Road, Kingston-upon-Thames, Surrey, KT1 2EE.
    020 8547 7769   fax 020 8547 7824
    http://dircweb.kingston.ac.uk/
    Director: Prof Graeme A Jones.
E   A research centre at Kingston University, London.
O   To conduct research in the increasingly convergent fields of digital image capture, digital processing of images, computer graphical modelling, and digital rendering of virtual environments

Digital Lifestyles Centre

■   Ross Building - PP1, Adastral Park, Ipswich, Suffolk, IP5 3RE.
    01473 631182
    http://digital-lifestyles.essex.ac.uk/
    Contact: Mark Brady.
E   An interdisciplinary research centre at the University of Essex.
Note: Also known as the Centre for Digital Lifestyles.

Digital Media Research Centre   (DMRC)

■   Bristol School of Art, Media and Design, Bower Ashton Campus, University of the West of England, Kennel Lodge Road, Bristol, BS3 2JT.
    0117-966 0222 ext 4755 and 4794   fax 0117-976 3946
    http://www.media.uwe.ac.uk/
    Contact: Judith Aston.
E   A research centre at the University of the West of England.
O   To support projects concerned with content creation through digital media

Digital and Photographic Imaging Centre   (DPIC)

■   School of Biological and Chemical Sciences, Queen Mary, University of London, Mile End Road, London, E1 4NS.
    020 7882 3352
    http://www.dpic.qmul.ac.uk/
    Contact: Ray Crundwell.
E   A centre at Queen Mary, University of London.
O   To offer a wide range of photographic services, including photography, poster printing, digital photo-quality printing, 35mm slides, slide to CD transfer, scanning, etc

Digital World Research Centre   (DWRC)   1998

■   Department of Psychology, University of Surrey, Guildford, Surrey, GU2 7XH.
    01483 683973   fax 01483 689550
    http://www.dwrc.surrey.ac.uk/
    Research Director: Prof David Frohlich.
E   A research centre at the University of Surrey.
O   To develop and apply innovation in digital technology for the consumer market, based on the interplay of user, design, business and technology research

Disarmament Research Centre
    see **Bradford Disarmament Research Centre.**

Disaster and Development Centre (DDC)

■ School of Applied Sciences, Northumbria University, Ellison Building, Ellison Place, Newcastle upon Tyne, NE1 8ST.
   0191-227 3754   fax 0191-227 4715
   http://northumbria.ac.uk/sd/academic/sas/sas_research/ddc/
   Director: Andrew Collins.
E   A research centre at Northumbria University.
○   To develop, through research, teaching and learning, the knowledge and skills to address hazards, disasters and complex emergencies from the perspective of different development debates and experience
●   Education and training

Disaster Management Centre (DMC) 1985

■ Department of Defence Management and Security, Cranfield University, Shrivenham, Swindon, Wiltshire, SN6 8LA.
   01793 785126   fax 01793 780341
   http://www.dcmt.cranfield.ac.uk/ddmsa/dmc/
   Contact: Mrs Michelle Addison.
E   A research centre at Cranfield University.
○   To save lives and livelihoods at risk from disaster impact through the promotion of risk and vulnerability reduction, preparedness and effective disaster response

Diving Diseases Research Centre Ltd (DDRC) 1980

■ The Hyperbaric Medical Centre, Tamar Science Park, Research Way, Plymouth, PL6 8BU.
   01752 209999   fax 01752 209115
   http://www.ddrc.org/
   Chief Executive: Mrs Karena Pring. Medical Director: Dr Phillip Bryson.
E   A registered charity.
○   To develop as a centre of excellence in Europe for baromedical research, education and treatment; to promote, provide and increase the availability of high quality cost-effective hyperbaric oxygen therapies
●   Education and training - Medical services - 24-hour emergency call-out
¶   Various Scientific Research publications.

Doctoral Training Centre in Medical Devices (DTC) 2006

■ Department of Bioengineering, University of Strathclyde, Glasgow, G4 0NW.
   0141-548 3781   fax 0141-552 6098
   http://www.strath.ac.uk/dtc
   Administrator: Ruth Kirk.
E   A training centre at the University of Strathclyde.
○   To provide engineers and physical scientists with full research training at the life sciences interface that is relevant to medical devices and related materials / technologies

Dorothy L Sayers Centre 1992

■ Witham Library, 18 Newland Street, Witham, Essex, CM8 2AQ.
   01376 519625   fax 01376 501913
E   An independent non-profit-distributing organisation.
○   To maintain a reference collection of works by, and about, Dorothy L Sayers; to provide access to the collection for study
●   Information service - Library

Doughty Centre for Corporate Responsibility 2006

■ Cranfield School of Management, Building 45, Cranfield University, Cranfield, Bedfordshire, MK43 0AL.
   01234 754017
   http://www.som.cranfield.ac.uk/som/research/centres/ccr/
E   A research centre at Cranfield University.

Douglas Bader Centre

■ University of Roehampton, Roehampton Lane, London, SW15 5DZ.
   020 8487 6040; 8788 1551
   http://www.douglasbaderfoundation.co.uk/content/DBF/DBF_Information/AboutTheDBF.html
E   A registered charity.
○   To provide sporting, recreational and leisure facilities and opportunities to those with disabilities, and to assist rehabilitation

Dr Edward Bach Centre 1936

■ Mount Vernon, Bakers Lane, Brightwell-cum-Sotwell, Oxfordshire, OX10 0PZ.
   01491 834678   fax 01491 825022
   http://www.bachcentre.com/
E   A registered charity and a company limited by guarantee.
○   To continue and uphold the work of Dr Edward Bach; to promote the use of the Bach Flower Remedies

Dr Williams's Centre for Dissenting Studies   2004
- School of English and Drama, Queen Mary, University of London, Mile End Road, London, E1 4NS.
  020 7882 3172   fax 020 7882 3357
  http://www.english.qmul.ac.uk/drwilliams/
  Co-Director: Prof Isabel Rivers. Co-Director: Dr David Wykes.
- E   A research centre at Queen Mary, University of London.
- O   To promote the use of the Library's unique holdings of puritan, Protestant nonconformist and dissenting books and manuscripts

Note: The Library is based at 14 Gordon Square, London, WC1H 0AR, and was established in the early 18th century under the will of Dr Daniel Williams.

Drama, Dance and Performing Arts Research Centre   (DDP)
- Department of Contemporary Arts, Alsager Campus, Manchester Metropolitan University, Hassal Road, Alsager, Cheshire, ST7 2HL.
  0161-247 5305; 5443   fax 0161-247 6377
  http://www.miriad.mmu.ac.uk/ddp/
  Contact: Dr Jonathan Pitches.
- E   A research centre within the Manchester Institute for Research and Innovation in Art and Design (qv) at Manchester Metropolitan University.
- O   To conduct research into various areas of contemporary arts

Drug Control Centre   (DCC)   1978
- School of Biomedical and Health Sciences, King's College London, Strand, London, WC2R 2LS.
  020 7836 5454
  http://www.kcl.ac.uk/schools/biohealth/research/drugcontrol/
  Director: Prof David Cowan.
- E   A research centre at King's College, London.
- O   To conduct scientific detection and control of drug abuse in sport

DrugScope   2000
- 32-36 Loman Street, London, SE1 0EE.
  020 7928 1211   fax 020 7928 1771
  http://www.drugscope.org.uk/
  Chief Executive: Martin Barnes. Chairman: Sylvie Pierce.
- E   A registered charity.
- O   To inform policy development and reduce drug-related risk; to provide quality drug information, promote effective responses to drug taking, undertake research at local, national and international levels; to advise on policy-making, encourage informed debate and speak for member organisations working on the ground
- ●   Information service - Library
- ¶   Druglink (journal). See website for other publications.
- ×   Institute for the Study of Drug Dependence.

Dugald Baird Centre for Research on Women's Health   (DBC)   1995
- Department of Obstetrics and Gynaecology, Aberdeen Maternity Hospital, Cornhill Road, Aberdeen, AB25 2ZL.
  01224 553621   fax 01224 553708
  http://www.abdn.ac.uk/dugaldbairdcentre/
  Director: Prof Siladitya Bhattacharya.
- E   A centre at the University of Aberdeen.
- O   To improve the reproductive health of women and the health of their families

Dundee Limb Fitting Centre   1965
- Section of Orthopaedic and Trauma Surgery, TORT Centre, Ninewells Hospital and Medical School, Dundee, DD1 9SY.
  01382 425746   fax 01382 496200
  http://www.dundee.ac.uk/orthopaedics/
- E   A specialist centre within the Tayside Orthopaedic and Rehabilitation Technology Centre (qv) at the University of Dundee.
- O   To help people facing the physical and psychological challenges of life without one or more limbs, often in association with debilitating diseases such as generalised vascular disease and diabetes

Durham Centre for Advanced Photography Studies   (DCAPS)   2005
- School of Modern Languages and Cultures, University of Durham, Elvet Riverside, New Elvet, Durham, DH1 3JT.
  0191-334 3450   fax 0191-334 3421
  http://www.dur.ac.uk/dcaps/
- E   A centre at the University of Durham.
- O   To bring together activities related to research on the photographic image

Durham Centre for Renewable Energy   (DCRE)   2005
- Department of Physics, University of Durham, Science Laboratories, South Road, Durham, DH1 3LE.
  0191-334 3595
  http://www.dur.ac.uk/renewable.energy/
  Director: Ken Durose.
- E   A research centre at the University of Durham.

Durham Centre for Roman Cultural Studies   1996
■   Department of Archaeology, University of Durham, Durham, DH1 3HP.
   0191-334 1100; 1164
   http://www.dur.ac.uk/roman.centre/
E   A centre at the University of Durham.
○   To foster and develop research into all aspects of the Roman world

Durham European Law Institute   (DELI)
■   Department of Law, University of Durham, 50 North Bailey, Durham, DH1 3ET.
   0191-334 2830   fax 0191-334 2819
   http://www.dur.ac.uk/deli/
   Director: Dr Eleanor Spaventa.
E   An institute within the University of Durham.
○   To conduct research and teaching in various aspects of European law, notably European social law, European institutional law, European competition law, EC external trade law, and intellectual property law

Durrell Institute of Conservation and Ecology   (DICE)   1989
■   Department of Anthropology, University of Kent, Marlowe Building, Canterbury, Kent, CT2 7NR.
   01227 764000   fax 01227 827289
   http://www.kent.ac.uk/anthropology/department/dice.html
E   A research institute at the University of Kent.
○   To undertake research necessary to conserve biodiversity and the functioning ecosystems upon which people depend

Dyslexia Centre
   see **Helen Arkell Dyslexia Centre.**

Dyslexia Teaching Centre   (DTC)   1978
■   23 Kensington Square, London, W8 5HN.
   020 7361 4790   fax 020 7938 4816
   http://www.dyslexia-teaching-centre.org.uk/
E   A registered charity and an independent non-profit-distributing organisation.
○   To teach learning and organisational skills to dyslexic children and adults to enable them to achieve their full potential in education and / or careers

© CBD Research Ltd · Beckenham · Kent BR3 5JS · Tel 020 8650 7745 · Fax 020 8650 0768 · E-mail cbd@cbdresearch.com · www.cbdresearch.com

e-Business Research Centre

NR   University of Liverpool Management School, University of Liverpool, Chatham Street, Liverpool, L69 7ZH.
      0151-794 4691
      http://www.ebrc.liv.ac.uk/
      Director: Prof Dennis Kehoe.
E   An EPSRC Innovative Manufacturing Research Centre at the University of Liverpool.
O   To focus on developing new business models, prototyping these using rapid application technologies and finally evaluating them using modelling and simulation tools
Note: One of the EPSRC funded centres in the UK - for further information see EPSRC Innovative Manufacturing Research Centres.

e-Horizons Institute

■   University of Oxford, 1 St Giles, Oxford, OX1 3PJ.
      01865 273229
      http://www.e-horizons.ox.ac.uk/
      Co-Director: Prof Paul Jeffreys. Co-Director: William Dutton.
E   An institute at the University of Oxford.

e-Research Centre
      see **Oxford e-Research Centre.**

e-SCIENCE CENTRES

Note: Several regional centres have been set up in the UK under the auspices of the National e-Science Centre, (qv). Each centre aims to stimulate and sustain the development of e-Science in its region and to contribute significantly to its development.

e-Science Centre [Belfast]
      see **Belfast e-Science Centre.**

e-Science Centre [Birmingham]
      see **Midlands e-Science Centre.**

e-Science Centre [Cambridge]
      see **Cambridge e-Science Centre.**

e-Science Centre [Didcot]
      see **CLRC e-Science Centre.**

e-Science Centre [Reading]
      see **Reading e-Science Centre.**

e-Science Centre [Southampton]
      see **Southampton Regional e-Science Centre.**

e-SCIENCE CENTRES of EXCELLENCE

Note: There are several e-Science Centres of Excellence which have been set up to augment the existing National and Regional **e-Science Centres** in the UK. Each centre provides additional expertise in e-Science applications and further resources for the e-Science Grid.

e-Science Centre of Excellence [Leicester]
      see **Leicester e-Science Centre of Excellence.**

e-Science Centre of Excellence [London]
      see **UCL e-Science Centre of Excellence.**

e-Science Centre of Excellence [York]
      see **White Rose Grid e-Science Centre of Excellence.**

e-Science Institute   (eSI)   2001

■   University of Edinburgh, 15 South College Street, Edinburgh, EH8 9AA.
      0131-650 9833   fax 0131-650 9819
      http://www.nesc.ac.uk/esi/
E   A research institute at the University of Edinburgh.
O   To focus on long-term and research-centred e-science topics
Note: A joint venture with the University of Glasgow which houses the National e-Science Centre (qv).

e-Science North West Centre   (ESNW)   2001
- Department of Computer Science, University of Manchester, Kilburn Building, Oxford Road, Manchester, M13 9PL.
  0161-275 0650
  http://www.esnw.ac.uk/
  Co-Director: Prof Carole Goble. Co-Director: Dr John Brooke.
- E A centre at the University of Manchester.

Note: See **e-Science Centres** for further information.

e-Science Research Institute
- University of Durham, Science Laboratories, South Road, Durham, DH1 3LE.
  0191-334 4297   fax 0191-334 4301
  http://www.dur.ac.uk/e-science/
  Director: Prof Malcolm Munro.
- E A research institute within the University of Durham.

Note: See **e-Science Centres** for further information.

e-SOCIAL SCIENCE CENTRES
Note: Several regional centres have been set up in the UK under the auspices of the National Centre for e-Social Science (qv).

e2v Centre for Electronic Imaging   (CEI)
- School of Engineering and Design, Brunel University, Uxbridge, Middlesex, UB8 3PH.
  01895 268000   fax 01895 269773
  http://dea.brunel.ac.uk/cei/
  Director: Prof Andrew Holland.
- E A research centre at Brunel University.
- ○ To conduct research into e2v technologies - the radio frequency and sensing technology that enables innovative medical and science, aerospace and defence, and industrial and commercial systems worldwide

Early Childhood Research Centre   (ECRC)
- School of Education, Froebel College, University of Roehampton, Roehampton Lane, London, SW15 5PJ.
  020 8392 3689   fax 020 8392 3322
  http://www.roehampton.ac.uk/researchcentres/ecrc/
  Director: Prof Kevin J Brehony.
- E A research centre at Roehampton University.
- ○ To conduct research in a wide variety of fields covering history, policy and practice across early childhood studies
- ● Froebel Archive for Childhood Studies

Earth and Biosphere Institute   (EBI)
- School of Earth and Environment, University of Leeds, Woodhouse Lane, Leeds, LS2 9JT.
  0113-343 5241
  http://www.earth.leeds.ac.uk/ebi/
- E A research institute at the University of Leeds.
- ○ To study the effects of biotic and environmental changes on a spectrum of time and space scales, from short term to geological, and from nano-scale to global

Earth, Energy and the Environment University Interdisciplinary Institute   (EEEI)
- School of Earth and Environment, University of Leeds, Leeds, LS2 9JT.
  0113-343 5222; 6461   fax 0113-343 5259; 6716
  http://www.eee.leeds.ac.uk/
  Contact: Prof Jane Francis.
- E A research centre at the University of Leeds.
- ○ To conduct high quality, focused research, teaching and training that will underpin advances in the efficient exploration, production, use, and environmental impact of existing resources; to increase the contribution to the development, engineering and monitoring of effective alternative energy systems

Note: Also known as the Institute for the Earth, Energy and the Environment.

Earth Science Centre   (ESC)
- School of Mathematics, Science and Technology, University of London, 20 Bedford Way, London, WC1H 0AL.
  020 7612 6451
  http://www.ioe.ac.uk/esc/
- E A research centre within the Institute of Education (qv) at the University of London.

Earthkind Humane Education Centre
Note: No longer in existence.

© CBD Research Ltd · Beckenham · Kent BR3 5JS · Tel 020 8650 7745 · Fax 020 8650 0768 · E-mail cbd@cbdresearch.com · www.cbdresearch.com

Earthquake Engineering Research Centre   (EERC)   1998

■   Faculty of Engineering, University of Bristol, Queen's Building, University Walk, Bristol, BS8 1TR.
    0117-928 7716   fax 0117-928 7783
    http://www.bristol.ac.uk/civilengineering/research/structures/eerc/
    Contact: Prof C A Taylor.

E   A department of the University of Bristol.

O   To carry out research into areas of structural dynamics, including dams, geotechnics and signal processing; to combine analytical techniques, laboratory experiments and measurements on structures, to reach a better understanding of the behaviour of structures and to improve methods of analysis and design

●   Conference facilities - Education and training

Earthwatch Institute (Europe)   1985

■   267 Banbury Road, Oxford, OX2 7HT.
    01865 318838   fax 01865 311383
    http://www.earthwatch.org/
    Executive Director: Nigel Winser.

E   A registered charity.

O   To conserve the diversity and integrity of life on earth to meet the needs of current and future generations

●   Education and training - Information service - Statistics

¶   Expedition Guide.

East Asia Institute   (EAI)

■   Faculty of Oriental Studies, University of Cambridge, Sidgwick Avenue, Cambridge, CB3 9DA.
    01223 335106
    http://www.eai.cam.ac.uk/
    Director: Prof D L McMullen.

E   An institute at the University of Cambridge.

O   To support integrated study of the languages, history, culture, social sciences and cultures of north-east Asia, comprising Japan, China, Korea, and Mongolia

East European Advice Centre   (EEAC)   1984

■   Room 209-210 - Palingswick House, 241 King Street, London, W6 0RE.
    020 8741 1288   fax 020 8741 8388
    http://www.eeac.org.uk/
    Co-ordinator: Magdalena Dykier.

E   A registered charity.

O   To relieve poverty and enhance education of East European immigrants living or working in the UK

●   Information service

East Midlands Eurocentre

■   Loughborough University, Ashby Road, Loughborough, Leicestershire, LE11 3TU.
    01509 222983; 222991   fax 01509 223917
    http://www.lboro.ac.uk/research/eurocentre/
    Director: Prof Michael Smith.

E   A Jean Monnet Centre of Excellence at Loughborough University.

O   To bring together the talents, activities and resources of those teaching and researching European Union studies in the East Midlands region

Eastern Cancer Registration and Information Centre   (ECRIC)

■   PO Box 193 - Level 5 Oncology, University of Cambridge, Hills Road, Cambridge, CB2 2QQ.
    01223 213625   fax 01223 213571
    http://www.ecric.org.uk/

E   A centre at the University of Cambridge.

O   To register all malignant tumours and some pre-cancerous lesions occurring in people resident in East Anglia at the time of diagnosis

Eastman Dental Institute
    see **UCL Eastman Dental Institute.**

Eccles Centre for American Studies   1991

■   British Library, 96 Euston Road, London, NW1 2DB.
    020 7412 7551; 7757   fax 020 7412 7792
    http://www.bl.uk/collections/americas/american.html
    Director: Prof Philip Davies, FRSA, AcSS.

E   An independently funded body within the British Library.

O   To promote the British Library's North American materials; to support American Studies in schools and universities

●   Conference facilities - Education and training - Exhibitions - Information service

¶   American Studies in the United Kingdom: Undergraduate and postgraduate courses. Guides to American Materials in the British Library.

eCentre   2003
■   Department of Information Systems and Multimedia, Maritime Greenwich Campus, University of Greenwich, Park Row, London, SE10 9LS.
        020 8331 8503
        http://www.cms.gre.ac.uk/research/centres/ecentre.asp
E   A centre at the University of Greenwich.

eCommerce Innovation Centre   (eCIC)
■   Cardiff Business Technology Centre, Cardiff University, Senghennydd Road, Cardiff, CF24 4AY.
        029 2064 7028   fax 029 2064 7029
        http://www.ecommerce.ac.uk/
        Director: Prof Paul Beynon-Davies.
E   A centre at Cardiff University.
O   To be involved in e-commerce, broadband developments, innovation, and consultancy

Economic Research Institute of Northern Ireland   (ERINI)   2004
■   Floral Buildings, 2-14 East Bridge Street, Belfast, BT1 3NQ.
        028 9072 7350   fax 028 9031 9003
        http://www.erini.ac.uk/
        Chairman: Prof John Beath.
E   A company limited by guarantee.
O   To provide, for the public benefit, good quality, independent economic research and analyses and advice, aimed at challenging and developing public policy making and strategic thinking on the issues facing Northern Ireland society

Economic and Social Research Council
        see **ESRC**

Economics Network   2000
■   University of Bristol, 8-10 Berkeley Square, Bristol, BS8 1HH.
        0117-928 7071   fax 0117-928 7112
        http://www.economicsnetwork.ac.uk/
E   A Government funded national centre within the University of Bristol.
O   To foster world-class education in economics
●   Education and training - Information service - Statistics
✕   LTSN Economics Subject Centre.
Note: One of the 24 Subject Centres of the Higher Education Academy, (qv).

Edinburgh Buddhist Centre
■   30 Melville Terrace, Edinburgh, EH9 1LP.
        0131-662 6699
        http://www.edinburghbuddhistcentre.org.uk/
E   An independent non-profit-distributing organisation and a registered charity.
O   To teach meditation and Buddhism
●   Education and training - The Centre provides meditation cushions and mats
Note: For other Buddhist centres see note under **Buddhist Centres**.

Edinburgh Centre for Bioinformatics   (ECB)
■   University of Edinburgh, 6-06 Appleton Tower, Crichton Street, Edinburgh, EH8 9LE.
        0131-651 3291
        http://www.bioinformatics.ed.ac.uk/
        Director: Prof Igor Goryanin. Contact: Jan Grant.
E   An interdisciplinary research centre at the University of Edinburgh.
O   To stimulate and support collaborative research in bioinformatics

Edinburgh Dental Institute   (EDI)
■   University of Edinburgh, Lauriston Building, Lauriston Place, Edinburgh, EH3 9HA.
        0131-536 4920
        http://www.epdi.org.uk/
        Clinical Director: Prof R J Ibbetson.
E   A research institute at the University of Edinburgh.
O   To serve the needs of patients by providing excellence in oral healthcare, teaching, training and research

Edinburgh Europa Institute   1968
■   School of Law, University of Edinburgh, Old College, South Bridge, Edinburgh, EH8 9YL.
        0131-650 2006
        http://www.law.ed.ac.uk/europa/
        Director: Prof Andrew Scott.
E   A research institute at the University of Edinburgh.

© CBD Research Ltd · Beckenham · Kent BR3 5JS · Tel 020 8650 7745 · Fax 020 8650 0768 · E-mail cbd@cbdresearch.com · www.cbdresearch.com

Edinburgh Parallel Computing Centre   (EPCC)   1990

- ■ School of Informatics, University of Edinburgh, James Clerk Maxwell Building, Mayfield Road, Edinburgh, EH9 3JZ.
     0131-650 5030   fax 0131-650 6555
     http://www.epcc.ed.ac.uk/
     Commercial Manager: Mark Parsons.
- E A research centre at the University of Edinburgh.
- ○ To be a leading European centre of expertise in advanced research, technology transfer and the provision of supercomputer services to universities

Edinburgh Virtual Environment Centre   (EdVEC)

- ■ University of Edinburgh, The King's Buildings, Edinburgh, EH9 3JZ.
     0131-650 4994   fax 0131-650 6552
     http://www.edvec.ed.ac.uk/
     Director: Roy Middleton.
- E A research centre at the University of Edinburgh.
- ○ To pursue research into and exploit the development and application of virtual reality and virtual environments in academia, industry and commerce

Education Research Centre   (ERC)

- ■ Faculty of Education and Sport, University of Brighton, Mayfield House, Falmer, Brighton, East Sussex, BN1 9PH.
     01273 643444   fax 01273 643463
     http://www.brighton.ac.uk/education/research/erc.htm

Education and Resources for Improving Childhood Continence   (ERIC)   1988

- ■ 34 Old School House, Britannia Road, Bristol, BS15 8DB.
     0117-960 3060   fax 0117-960 0401
     http://www.eric.org.uk/
     Director: Penny Dobson. Deputy Director: Beverley Leesan.
- E A registered charity.
- ○ To provide information and support, promote public awareness, stimulate new research and encourage best clinical practice in relation to childhood bedwetting, daytime wetting and soiling
- ● Education and training - Information service - Helpline Mon-Fri 1000-1600
- ¶ Wide range of publications.
- ✕ Enuresis Resource and Information Centre.

Education and Social Research Institute   (ESRI)

- ■ Faculty of Health, Social Care and Education, Manchester Metropolitan University, 799 Wilmslow Road, Didsbury, Manchester, M20 2RR.
     0161-247 2320   fax 0161-247 6353
     http://www.esri.mmu.ac.uk/
     Director: Prof Harry Torrance. Contact: Barbara Ashcroft.
- E A department of Manchester Metropolitan University.
- ○ To conduct applied educational research and evaluation in the UK

Educational Development Centre
     see **Centre for Educational and Academic Practices.**

Educational Initiative Centre   (EIC)

- ■ University of Westminster, 309 Regent Street, London, W1B 2UW.
     020 7911 5000
     http://www.wmin.ac.uk/page-4110
- E A department of the University of Westminster.
- ○ To encourage the development and evaluation of school-based initiatives by facilitating locally developed, university-wide applications of both skills and resources

Edward Grey Institute of Field Ornithology   (EGI)   1936

- ■ Department of Zoology, University of Oxford, South Parks Road, Oxford, OX1 3PS.
     01865 271275   fax 01865 271168
     http://egizoosrv.zoo.ox.ac.uk/egi/
     Director: Prof Ben Sheldon.
- E A research institute at the University of Oxford.
- ○ To conduct research in the behaviour, ecology, evolution and conservation of birds, with a strong emphasis on understanding organisms in their natural environments

Edward Jenner Institute for Vaccine Research   (EJIVR)   1995

- ■ Institute for Animal Health, Compton, Newbury, Berkshire, RG20 7NN.
     01635 577900   fax 01635 577901
     http://www.jenner.ac.uk/
- E An independent non-profit-making company and a registered charity based at the Institute for Animal Health (qv).
- ○ To conduct research on areas of immunology relevant to the development of all vaccines, including antigen presentation, immunological memory and autoimmunity; to work on specific diseases or targets where vaccines, or improved vaccines, are needed

Ehrenberg Centre for Research in Marketing   1993
- Faculty of Business, Computing and Information Management, London South Bank University, 103 Borough Road, London, SE1 0AA.
    020 7815 6162
    http://www.lsbu.ac.uk/bcim/research/ehrenberg/
    Head: John Scriven.
- E   A research centre at London South Bank University.
- O   To develop, publish and disseminate reliable marketing knowledge, based on well-grounded patterns and theory concerning consumer behaviour across many industries and countries

Note: Named after Prof Andrew Ehrenberg who founded the Centre in 1993.

Eighteenth Century Centre
    see **Warwick Eighteenth Century Centre.**

Elections Centre
    see **Local Government Chronicle Elections Centre.**

Electrical Drives Centre
    see **Nottingham University Electrical Drives Centre.**

Electrochemical and Materials Processing Centre   (EMPC)
- School of Chemical Engineering and Advanced Materials, University of Newcastle upon Tyne, Merz Court, Newcastle upon Tyne, NE1 7RU.
    0191-222 7266   fax 0191-222 5292
    http://www.ncl.ac.uk/ceam/empc/
- E   A research centre at the University of Newcastle upon Tyne.
- O   To conduct research into electrochemical systems, with a major focus on innovative technologies for energy generation and environmental applications

Electron Microscopy Centre
    see **Plymouth Electron Microscopy Centre.**

Electronic Publishing Innovation Centre   (EPICentre)
- Department of Information Science, Loughborough University, Ashby Road, Loughborough, Leicestershire, LE11 3TU.
    01509 223052   fax 01509 223053
    http://www.epicentre-research.org/
    Director: Dr Fytton Rowland. Administrator: Heather Rees.
- E   A research centre at Loughborough University.
- O   To investigate all areas of electronic publishing, from technical aspects and languages of document engineering right through to usability and usage studies of journals, e-books and websites

Electronic Systems Design Centre   (ESDC)   1994
- Department of Electronics, University of Kent, Canterbury, Kent, CT2 7NT.
    01227 823251   fax 01227 824066
    http://esd-centre.kent.ac.uk/
    Director: Peter Lee.
- E   A research centre at the University of Kent.

Electronics Design Centre   (EDC)
- Department of Electronics and Electrical Engineering, University of Glasgow, Rankine Building, Oakfield Avenue, Glasgow, G12 8LT.
    0141-330 5233; 5242
    http://www.elec.gla.ac.uk/centres/edc/
- E   A research centre at the University of Glasgow.
- O   To provide fundamental research into electronic design

Electronics Systems Design Centre   (ESDC)
- School of Engineering, Swansea University, Singleton Park, Swansea, SA2 8PP.
    01792 205678
    http://www.swan.ac.uk/research/centresandinstitutes/ElectronicsSystemDesignCentre/
- E   A research centre at Swansea University.
- O   To conduct research in semiconductor device modelling

Elm Farm Research Centre   (EFRC)   1980
- Hamstead Marshall, Newbury, Berkshire, RG20 0HR.
    01488 658298   fax 01488 658503
    http://www.efrc.com/
    Director: Lawrence Woodward.
- E   A research centre.
- O   To develop and support sustainable land-use, agriculture and food systems, primarily within local economies, which build on organic principles to ensure the health and well-being of soil, plant, animal, humans and their environment

© CBD Research Ltd · Beckenham · Kent BR3 5JS · Tel 020 8650 7745 · Fax 020 8650 0768 · E-mail cbd@cbdresearch.com · www.cbdresearch.com

Elphinstone Institute   (EI)

■   School of Education, MacRobert Building, King's College, University of Aberdeen, Aberdeen, AB24 5UA.
     01224 272996   fax 01224 272728
     http://www.abdn.ac.uk/elphinstone/
     Director: Dr Ian Russell.
E   A centre at the University of Aberdeen.
O   To study human traditions, especially the traditions of the North and the North-East of Scotland

Emerging Technologies Research Centre   (EMTERC)   1995

■   De Montfort University, Hawthorn Building, The Gateway, Leicester, LE1 9BH.
     0116-250 6158   fax 0116-250 6473
     http://www.eng.dmu.ac.uk/emterc/
E   A research centre and department of De Montfort University.
O   To carry out fundamental and applied research in microelectronics

Empeiria Centre

■   University of Gloucester Business School, University of Gloucester, The Park, Cheltenham, Gloucestershire, GL50 2RH.
     0870 721 0210
     http://www.glos.ac.uk/faculties/ugbs/research/empeiria.cfm
E   A centre at the University of Gloucestershire.
O   To provide learning based on observation and experience in the health and social care fields

Employee Share Ownership Centre   (ESOP Centre)   1988

■   2 Ridgmount Street, London, WC1E 7AA.
     020 7436 9936   fax 020 7580 0016
     http://www.mhcc.co.uk/esop/esop/
     Chairman: Malcolm Hurlston.
E   A non-profit subscription-based organisation.
O   To inform, lobby and research in the interest of broad based employee share ownership plans

Employment Research Institute   (ERI)

■   Napier University, Redwood House, 66 Spylaw Road, Edinburgh, EH10 5BR.
     0131-455 5104   fax 0131-455 5102
     http://www.napier.ac.uk/depts/eri/HOME.htm
     Director: Prof Ronald McQuaid.
E   A research institute at Napier University.
O   To carry out applied and theoretical research into the changing nature of work and employment, and their implications for
     organisations, individuals and the wider economy

Enabling Achievement within a Diverse Student Body CETL   2005

■   University of Wolverhampton, Wulfruna Street, Wolverhampton, WV1 1SB.
     01902 322361   fax 01902 518539
     http://www.wlv.ac.uk/cetl
     Contact: Alison Halstead.
E   A Centre for Excellence in Teaching and Learning (CETL) at the University of Wolverhampton.
Note: See **Centres for Excellence in Teaching and Learning** for more information.

Energy Centre for Sustainable Communities   (ECSC)   1982

■   Unit 327, 30 Great Guildford Street, London, SE1 0HS.
     020 7922 1662   fax 020 7928 8153
     http://www.ecsc.org.uk/
E   A registered charity.
O   To provide a wide range of services and projects to local and regional Governments to achieve the objectives of reducing energy
     consumption, fuel poverty and building sustainable futures

Energy Economics Centre
        see **Surrey Energy Economics Centre.**

Energy and Resources Research Institute   (ERRI)

■   School of Process, Environmental and Materials Engineering, University of Leeds, Houldsworth Building, Clarendon Road, Leeds,
     LS2 9JT.
     0113-343 2498   fax 0113-246 7310
     http://www.leeds.ac.uk/speme/erri/
     Director: Prof Paul Williams.
E   A research institute within the University of Leeds.
O   To conduct research into creating a cleaner, greener, sustainable future
●   Consultancy service

Energy Technology Centre   (ETC)   2005
- Sustainable Systems Department, Cranfield University, Building 61, Cranfield, Bedfordshire, MK43 0AL.
  01234 754253
  http://www.cranfield.ac.uk/sas/sustainablesystems/energytechnology/
  Director: J E Oakey.
- E A research centre at Cranfield University.
- O To offer specialist research, training and consultancy in wet and dry renewable energy, biomass conversion and energy from waste, process simulation, diving and underwater technology and offshore materials engineering

Engineering Centre for Excellence in Teaching and Learning   (engCETL)   2005
- Faculty of Engineering, Loughborough University, Ashby Road, Loughborough, Leicestershire, LE11 3TU.
  01509 227191
  http://www.engcetl.ac.uk/
  Director: Prof John Dickens.
- E A Centre for Excellence in Teaching and Learning (CETL) at Loughborough University.
- O To be a centre of excellence for research and development in, support for, and implementation of, industry-linked higher education in a wide range of engineering disciplines

Note: See **Centres for Excellence in Teaching and Learning** for further information.

Engineering Composites Research Centre   (ECRE)   1989
- Faculty of Engineering, University of Ulster, Shore Road, Newtownabbey, County Antrim, BT37 0QB.
  028 9036 8120   fax 028 9036 6864
  http://www.engj.ulst.ac.uk/~roy/r-institutes/index.php?id=76
- E A research centre at the University of Ulster.
- O To promote interdisciplinary research, in collaboration with industry, to develop composite materials and assess the interaction between the materials, processing and performance, leading to improved design concepts, more cost-effective processing techniques and new applications.

Engineering Design Centre [Cambridge]
> see **Cambridge Engineering Design Centre.**

Engineering Design Centre   (EDC)   1990
- School of Marine Science and Technology, University of Newcastle upon Tyne, Stephenson Building, Newcastle upon Tyne, NE1 7RU.
  0191-222 8555   fax 0191-261 6059
  http://www.edc.ncl.ac.uk/
  Administrator: Carol Lee.
- E A research centre at the University of Newcastle upon Tyne.
- O To specialise in the design, development and performance of systems for the production and operation of complex products, which are made on an engineer-to-order basis with high levels of customisation

Engineering Design Research Centre   (EDRC)
- School of Engineering, Coventry University, Priory Street, Coventry, CV1 5FB.
  024 7688 8363
  http://www.corporate.coventry.ac.uk/cms/jsp/polopoly.jsp?d=1001&a=876
  Contact: Mike Evatt.
- E A centre at Coventry University.
- O To conduct world class research into all aspects of engineering design

Engineering Dynamics Centre
- Engineering Systems Department, Cranfield University, Shrivenham, Swindon, Wiltshire, SN6 8LA.
  01793 785352   fax 01793 783192
  http://www.dcmt.cranfield.ac.uk/esd/edc
  Contact: Dr D J Purdy.
- E A research centre at Cranfield University.
- O To conduct brief assessments of equipment and detailed investigations in the fields of vibration and noise, flow-induced vibration, active control of dynamic systems, mitigation of vibration and noise, Structural integrity assessments, and weapon systems

Engineering IMRC
> see **Innovative Manufacturing Research Centre - Engineering.**

Engineering and Medicine Elastomers Research Centre   (EMER)
- Faculty of Computing, Engineering and Mathematical Sciences, Frenchay Campus, University of the West of England, Coldharbour Lane, Bristol, BS16 1QY.
  0117-344 2639   fax 0117-344 3800
  http://www.uwe.ac.uk/cems/research/centres/emer
  Director: Vince Coveney.
- E An interdisciplinary research centre at the University of the West of England.
- O To perform research to benefit society and industry and particular in health-related areas

Engineering and Physical Sciences Research Council
> see **EPSRC**

Engineering Structures Research Centre   (ESRC)   1982
- ■   Department of Engineering, Tait Building, City University, Northampton Square, London, EC1V 0HB.
     020 7040 0113   fax 020 7040 8101
     http://www.city.ac.uk/sems/research/esrc/
- E   A research centre at City University.
- ○   To provide a focus for research and teaching in structural engineering

Engineering Subject Centre   (ESC)   2000
- ■   Loughborough University, Loughborough, Leicestershire, LE11 3TU.
     01509 227170   fax 01509 227172
     http://www.engsc.ac.uk/
     Director: John Dickens. Manager: Carol Arlett.
- E   A department of Loughborough University.
- ○   To improve the student learning experience in partnership with the UK engineering community
- ●   Education and training
- ¶   'Translate' (newsletter).
- ✕   LTSN Engineering.
Note: One of the 24 Subject Centres of the Higher Education Academy, (qv).

English Institute of Sport   (EIS)
- ■   4th Floor - Byrom House, 21 Quay Street, Manchester, M3 3JD.
     0870 759 0400
     http://www.eis2win.co.uk/
     Director: Wilma Shakespear.
- E   A nationwide network of support services.
- ○   To foster the talents of England's elite athletes

English Language Centre   (ELC)   2001
- ■   School of Arts and Social Sciences, Northumbria University, 108 Squires Workshops, Newcastle upon Tyne, NE1 8ST.
     0191-227 4919   fax 0191-227 4439
     http://northumbria.ac.uk/sd/academic/sass/engl_lang/
- E   A research centre at Northumbria University.
- ○   To provide a focus for English language teaching, learning and research
Note: Many such centres exist in the UK at major educational institutions.

English Language Institute
    see **Centre for Language Studies.**

English Research Institute   (ERI)   2003
- ■   Faculty of Humanities, Law and Social Science, Manchester Metropolitan University, Geoffrey Manton Building, Rosamond Street West, Manchester, M15 6LL.
     0161-247 1762   fax 0161-247 6345
     http://www.eri.mmu.ac.uk/
     Director: Prof Berthold Schoene.
- E   A research institute at Manchester Metropolitan University.
- ○   To conduct teaching and research in various English language fields, with particular emphasis on postcolonial and critical theory, film and American studies, drama and creative writing, and literature and modernity

English Subject Centre   2000
- ■   Royal Holloway University, Egham, Surrey, TW20 0EX.
     01784 443221   fax 01784 470684
     http://www.english.heacademy.ac.uk/
- E   A Government funded national centre within Royal Holloway, University of London.
- ○   To foster world-class education in the English language
- ●   Education and training - Information service - Statistics
Note: One of the 24 Subject Centres of the Higher Education Academy, (qv).

English Wine Centre   (EWC)   1968
- ■   Alfriston, East Sussex, BN26 5QS.
     01323 870164   fax 01323 870005
     http://www.englishwine.co.uk/
- E   Established as a wholesale wine business.

Enhancing, Embedding and Integrating Employability CETL   (E3I)   2005
- ■   Faculty of Organisation and Management, City Campus, Sheffield Hallam University, Sheffield, S1 1WB.
     0114-225 3084; 4735   fax 0114-225 4755
     http://www.shu.ac.uk/cetl/e3i/
     Director: David Laughton.
- E   A Centre for Excellence in Teaching and Learning (CETL) at Sheffield Hallam University.
Note: See **Centres for Excellence in Teaching and Learning** for more information.

Entrepreneurship Centre [Cambridge]
    see **Cambridge Entrepreneurship Centre.**

Entrepreneurship Centre   2001
- ■   Tanaka Business School, South Kensington Campus, Imperial College London, Exhibition Road, London, SW7 2AZ.
      020 7594 9190   fax 020 7594 9189
      http://www3.imperial.ac.uk/entrepreneurship/
      Manager: Dr Tim Meldrum.
- E   A research centre at Imperial College London.
- ○   To conduct research and teaching on new venture creation in the technology sectors

Enuresis Resource and Information Centre
   see **Education and Resources for Improving Childhood Continence.**

Environment Centre
   see **Caledonian Environment Centre.**

Environment Institute [London]
   see **UCL Environment Institute.**

Environment Institute at York
   see **Stockholm Environment Institute at York.**

Environment Monitoring and Response Centre   (EMARC)   1999
- ■   Met Office - Fastnet 1, Fitzroy Road, Exeter, EX1 3PB.
      01392 886095   fax 01392 884549
      Manager: Stewart Wortley.
- ○   To provide weather and environment advice to emergency services and Government departments
- ●   Information service

Environment Research Institute
   see **Hull Environment Research Institute.**

Environmental Change Institute   (ECI)
- ■   School of Geography, University of Oxford, Dyson Perrins Building, South Parks Road, Oxford, OX1 3QY.
      01865 275848   fax 01865 275850
      http://www.eci.ox.ac.uk/
      Director: Prof Diana Liverman.
- E   An institute within the Oxford University Centre for the Environment (qv) at the University of Oxford.
- ○   To conduct research on climate, ecosystems, and low carbon uses of energy

Environmental Change Research Centre   (ECRC)
- ■   Department of Geography, University College London, Pearson Building, Gower Street, London, WC1E 6BT.
      020 7679 0575   fax 020 7679 0565
      http://www.ecrc.ucl.ac.uk/
      Contact: Dr Heather Binney.
- E   An interdisciplinary research centre at University College London.
- ○   To conduct research in aquatic ecosystem change and climate change on a range of time scales, past, present and future

Environmental Engineering Research Centre   (EERC)
- ■   School of Planning, Architecture and Civil Engineering, Queen's University, Belfast, David Keir Building, Stranmillis Road, Belfast, BT9 5AG.
      028 9097 4006
      http://www.qub.ac.uk/eerc/
      Director: Prof Bob Kalin.
- E   A research centre at Queen's University, Belfast.

Environmental Flow Research Centre   (EnFlo)   1993
- ■   School of Engineering, University of Surrey, Guildford, Surrey, GU2 7XH.
      01483 686292
      http://www.portal.surrey.ac.uk/eng/research/fluids/fluids_research/enflo
      Director: Prof Alan Robins.
- E   A research centre at the University of Surrey.
- ○   To conduct research on laboratory scale simulation of atmospheric flow and pollutant dispersion

Environmental Impact Assessment Centre   (EIA)   1988
- ■   School of Environment and Development, University of Manchester, Oxford Road, Manchester, M13 9PL.
      0161-275 6881   fax 0161-275 6893
      http://www.art.man.ac.uk/EIA/eiac.htm
      Contact: Carys E Jones.
- E   A research centre at the University of Manchester.
- ○   To specialise in environmental impact assessment (EIA) research, training and information

© CBD Research Ltd · Beckenham · Kent BR3 5JS · Tel 020 8650 7745 · Fax 020 8650 0768 · E-mail cbd@cbdresearch.com · www.cbdresearch.com

Environmental Information Centre
    see **Centre for Ecology and Hydrology.**

Environmental Radioactivity Research Centre   (ERRC)
■   Faculty of Science, University of Liverpool, 765 Brownlow Hill, Liverpool, L69 7ZX.
       0151-794 4020   fax 0151-794 4061
       http://www.liv.ac.uk/
       Director: Prof Peter G Appleby.
E   A research centre at the University of Liverpool.

Environmental Research Centre   (ERC)   1990
■   Science Laboratories, University of Durham, South Road, Durham, DH1 3LE.
       0191-374 2432   fax 0191-374 2456
       http://www.dur.ac.uk/ERC
       Director: Prof Brian Huntley.
E   A research centre at the University of Durham.
O   To undertake fundamental and applied research on the present, past and future environments of the Earth

Environmental Research Institute   (ERI)   1999
■   North Highland College, University of the Highlands and Islands (UHI) Institute, Castle Street, Thurso, Caithness, Sutherland,
       KW14 7JD.
       01847 889581   fax 01847 890014
       http://www.erionline.co.uk/
       Director: Dr Stuart W Gibb.
E   A research institute at the University of the Highlands and Islands (UHI) Institute.
O   To conduct research in various environmental fields, including climatic and environmental change, biogeochemical cycling,
       environmental sensitivity and risk, waste and remediation, innovation in natural products, and renewable energy and sustainable
       design

Environmental Science and Technology Research Centre
    see **Queen's University Environmental Science and Technology Research Centre.**

Environmental Sciences Research Centre   (ESRC)
■   Faculty of Science and Technology, Anglia Ruskin University, East Road, Cambridge, CB1 1PT.
       01223 363271   fax 01223 417712
       http://web.anglia.ac.uk/envsci/
       Director: Prof John Waterhouse.
E   A research centre at Anglia Ruskin University.

Environmental Systems Science Centre   (ESSC)   1995
■   University of Reading, Harry Pitt Building, 3 Earley Gate, Reading, Berkshire, RG6 6AL.
       0118-378 8741   fax 0118-378 6413
       http://www.nerc-essc.ac.uk/
       Director: Prof Robert Gurney.
E   A research centre of the Natural Environment Research Council at the University of Reading.
O   To research into new ways of handling spatial data, particularly remotely sensed data within computer models, in the
       environmental sciences

Environmental Technologies Centre for Industrial Collaboration   (ETCIC)
■   University of Hull, Cottingham Road, Hull, HU6 7RX.
       01482 466937   fax 01482 466884
       http://www.etcic.com/
E   A research centre at the University of Hull.

Environmental Technology Centre   (ETC)
■   School of Chemical Engineering and Analytical Science, PO Box 88, University of Manchester, Manchester, M60 1QD.
       0161-306 3980
       http://www.ceas.manchester.ac.uk/research/centres/etc/
       Director: Prof R F Griffiths.
E   A research centre at the University of Manchester.
O   To conduct research in a wide variety of areas of environmental technology, including industrial and environmental risk
       assessment, wastewater treatment and waste recycling, atmospheric dispersion, catalysis, recycling and development of cleaner
       processes, numerical modelling, rheology and colloid science, environmental applications of electrochemical technology, and
       clean synthesis of chemicals, zeolite membranes, and clean technology and process design for environmental performance

Environmental Training and Research Centre
    see **Northumbrian Environmental Training and Research Centre.**

Epidemiology Resource Centre
    see **MRC Epidemiology Resource Centre.**

EPSRC INNOVATIVE MANUFACTURING RESEARCH CENTRES
Note: There are several Innovative Manufacturing Centres in the UK. Each Centre is funded by the Engineering and Physical Sciences Research Council.

EPSRC NanoPhotonics Portfolio Centre
- School of Physics and Astronomy, University of Southampton, Highfield, Southampton, SO17 1BJ.
  023 8059 2083
  http://www.nanophotonics.org.uk/
  Group Leader: Prof N I Zheludev.
- E   A research centre at the University of Southampton.
- O   To support activities connected with nanoscale photonics

EPSRC National Centre for III-V Technologies   1979
- Department of Electronic and Electrical Engineering, University of Sheffield, Sir Frederick Mappin Building, Mappin Street, Sheffield, S1 3JD.
  0114-222 5355   fax 0114-222 5143
  http://www.sheffield.ac.uk/eee/research/nc35t
  Co-Director: Prof Peter Houston. Co-Director: Prof Maurice Skolnick.
- E   An Engineering and Physical Sciences Research Council centre at the University of Sheffield.
- O   To supply a wide range of well characterised, state-of-the-art III-V epitaxial layers and a comprehensive range of prototype device fabrication services

EPSRC National Mass Spectrometry Service Centre
- Swansea University, Singleton Park, Swansea, SA2 8PP.
  01792 295553   fax 01792 295554
  http://www.swan.ac.uk/nmssc/
  Director: Prof A G Brenton.
- E   A research centre at Swansea University.
- O   To produce high quality mass spectra using a variety of ionisation techniques
Note: Also known as the Institute of Mass Spectrometry.

Equality and Discrimination Centre   (EDC)
- Department of Educational and Professional Studies, University of Strathclyde, Sir Henry Wood Building, 76 Southbrae Drive, Glasgow, G13 1PP.
  0141-950 3365
  http://www.strath.ac.uk/edc/
  Contact: Jane Dobie.
- E   A research centre at the University of Strathclyde.

Ergonomics Information Analysis Centre   (EIAC)   1968
- School of Electronic, Electrical and Computer Engineering, University of Birmingham, Edgbaston, Birmingham, B15 2TT.
  0121-414 4239   fax 0121-414 3476
  http://www.eee.bham.ac.uk/eiac/
  Director: E D Megaw. Editor: Christine Stapleton.
- E   A department of the University of Birmingham.
- O   To disseminate information on ergonomics (human factors)
- ● Ergonomics abstracts (online database) - Preparation of specialised bibliographies - Enquiry service - Consultancy (various charges for all services)

Ergonomics and Safety Research Institute   (ESRI)   2002
- Faculty of Social Sciences and Humanities, Loughborough University, Holywell Building, Holywell Way, Loughborough, Leicestershire, LE11 3UZ.
  01509 226900   fax 01509 226960
  http://www.lboro.ac.uk/research/esri/
  Director: Prof Alastair G Gale.
- E   A research institute at Loughborough University.
- O   To apply research based knowledge to solve real world problems and the study of real world problems to advance understanding

Eric Bywaters Centre for Vascular Inflammation   (EBC)
- Faculty of Medicine, Hammersmith Campus, Imperial College London, Du Cane Road, London, W12 0NN.
  020 8383 3064   fax 020 8383 1640
  http://www1.imperial.ac.uk/medicine/about/institutes/ebc/
  Director: Prof Dorian O Haskard.
- E   A research centre at Imperial College London.
- O   To bring together researchers with interests in vascular inflammation, angiogenesis, and thrombosis
Note: Named after the late Prof Eric Bywaters.

Esperanto Centre   1976
- 140 Holland Park Avenue, London, W11 4UF.
  http://www.esperanto.org/
- E   A registered charity.

ESRC Centre for Analysis of Risk and Regulation   (CARR)
■ LSE, Houghton Street, London, WC2A 2AE.
  020 7955 6577   fax 020 7955 6578
  http://www.lse.ac.uk/collections/CARR/
  Administrator: Phil Lomas.
E An interdisciplinary research centre at the London School of Economics and Political Science.
○ To focus research on the organisational and institutional settings for risk management and regulatory practices

ESRC Centre for Business Relationships, Accountability, Sustainability and Society   (BRASS)   2001
■ Cardiff University, 55 Park Place, Cardiff, CF10 3AT.
  029 2087 6562   fax 029 2087 6061
  http://www.brass.cf.ac.uk/
  Director: Prof Ken Peattie.
E A centre at Cardiff University.
○ To understand and promote the vital issues of sustainability, accountability and social responsibility, through research in key business relationships

ESRC Centre for Business Research   (CBR)   1994
■ Judge Business School, University of Cambridge, Trumpington Street, Cambridge, CB2 1AG.
  01223 765320
  http://www.cbr.cam.ac.uk/
  Acting Director: Simon Deakin.
E A centre at the University of Cambridge.
○ To conduct research programmes in the fields of corporate governance, and enterprise and innovation

ESRC Centre for Economic Learning and Social Evolution   (ELSE)   1995
■ University College London, Drayton House, Gordon Street, London, WC1H 0AN.
  020 7679 5817   fax 020 7916 2774
  http://else.econ.ucl.ac.uk/
  Director: Prof Mark Armstrong.
E An interdisciplinary research centre at University College London.
○ To conduct research in those areas of human behaviour in which economics and psychology come together

ESRC Centre for Genomics in Society   (EGENIS)
■ University of Exeter, Byrne House, St German's Road, Exeter, EX4 4PJ.
  01392 269140   fax 01392 264676
  http://www.centres.ex.ac.uk/egenis/
  Director: Prof John Dupré.
E A research centre at the University of Exeter.
○ To study the meaning and social implications of contemporary genomic science

ESRC Centre for Neighbourhood Research
Note: Now in abeyance following the cessation of its ESRC funding in July 2006.

ESRC Centre for Organisation and Innovation   (COI)   1996
■ Department of Social Sciences, University of Sheffield, Sheffield, S10 2TN.
  0114-222 3271
  http://esrccoi.group.shef.ac.uk/
  Administrator: Mark Steele.
E A research centre within the Institute of Work Psychology (qv) at the University of Sheffield.
○ To conduct research into how work organisation affects employee well-being and performance, and how new technologies, techniques and management practices can be effectively applied

ESRC Centre for Research in Economic Development and International Trade   (CREDIT)   1988
■ School of Economics, University of Nottingham, University Park, Nottingham, NG7 2RD.
  0115-951 5250   fax 0115-951 4159
  http://www.nottingham.ac.uk/economics/credit/
  Director: Prof Oliver Morrissey.
E A research centre at the University of Nottingham.
○ To foster research in the areas of economic development and international trade and the dissemination of research findings
● Conference facilities

ESRC Centre for Research on Innovation and Competition   (CRIC)
■ School of Social Sciences, University of Manchester, Harold Hankins Building, Booth Street West, Manchester, M13 9QH.
  0161-275 7365   fax 0161-275 7361
  http://www.cric.ac.uk/cric/
  Executive Director: Prof Jeremy Howells.
E A research centre at the University of Manchester.
○ To conduct research on competition and the role that innovation plays in this area

ESRC Centre for Research on Socio-Cultural Change   (CRESC)   2004
NR   School of Social Sciences, University of Manchester, 178 Waterloo Place, Oxford Road, Manchester, M13 9PL.
         0161-275 8985   fax 0161-275 8986
         http://www.cresc.ac.uk/
         Convening Director: Prof Mike Savage.
E   A research centre at the University of Manchester.
O   To analyse socio-cultural change and its economic, social and political implications
Note: A joint venture with the Open University.

ESRC Centre for Research on Socio-Cultural Change   (CRESC)   2004
NR   Open University, Walton Hall, Milton Keynes, MK7 6AA.
         0870 333 4340
         http://www.cresc.ac.uk/
E   A research centre at the Open University.
Note: A joint venture with the University of Manchester (see above).

ESRC Centre on Skills, Knowledge and Organisational Performance and Organisational Performance   (SKOPE)   1998
NR   Department of Economics, University of Oxford, Manor Road, Oxford, OX1 3UQ.
         01865 271087   fax 01865 281488
         http://www.skope.ox.ac.uk/
         Administrator: Fiona Chavner.
E   A research centre at the University of Oxford.
O   To examine the links between the acquisition and use of skills and knowledge, product market strategies and performance
Note: A joint venture with the University of Cardiff.

ESRC Centre for Social and Economic Research on Innovation in Genomics
         see **Innogen - ESRC Centre for Social and Economic Research on Innovation in Genomics.**

ESRC Innogen Centre
         see **Innogen - ESRC Centre for Social and Economic Research on Innovation in Genomics.**

ESRC National Centre for e-Social Science   (NCeSS)   2004
■   School of Social Sciences, University of Manchester, Dover Street, Manchester, M13 9PL.
         0161-275 1383   fax 0161-275 1390
         http://www.ncess.ac.uk/
         Executive Director: Prof Peter Halfpenny.
E   A research centre at the University of Manchester.
O   To investigate and promote the use of e-science to benefit social science research

ESRC National Centre for Research Methods   (NCRM)
■   School of Social Sciences, University of Southampton, Highfield, Southampton, SO17 1BJ.
         023 8059 4539   fax 023 8059 8908
         http://www.ncrm.ac.uk/
         Administrator: Annabel Preston.
E   A hub-node network of research groups co-ordinated by the University of Southampton.
O   To be a focal point for research, training and capacity building activities, aimed at promoting a step change in the quality and range of methodological skills and techniques used by the UK social science community

ESRC Research Centre for the Analysis of Social Exclusion   (CASE)   1997
■   LSE, Houghton Street, London, WC2A 2AE.
         020 7955 6679
         http://sticerd.lse.ac.uk/case/
         Director: Prof John Hills. Deputy Director: Prof Anne Power.
E   A research centre within the Suntory and Toyota International Centres for Economics and Related Disciplines (qv) at the London School of Economics and Political Science.
O   To conduct research into the concept of social exclusion, its causes and methods of prevention, including analysis of the efficacy of social welfare institutions in preventing social exclusion and the factors of area decline and regeneration in contributing to it

ESRC Research Centre on Micro-Social Change   (MISOC)   2004
■   University of Essex, Wivenhoe Park, Colchester, Essex, CO4 3SQ.
         01206 872957   fax 01206 873151
         http://www.iser.essex.ac.uk/misoc/
E   A research centre within the Institute for Social and Economic Research (qv) at the University of Essex.

ESRC United Kingdom Centre for Evidence Based Policy and Practice   2000
■   School of Social Science and Public Policy, King's College London, Strand, London, WC2R 2LS.
         020 7836 5454
         http://www.evidencenetwork.org/
         Director: Charlotte Humphrey.
E   A research centre within King's College, London.
O   To provide a focal point for those who are interested in evidence based policy and practice (EBPP) to access useful information and resources

ESRC United Kingdom Longitudinal Studies Centre   (ULSC)   1999
■   University of Essex, Wivenhoe Park, Colchester, Essex, CO4 3SQ.
　　01206 872957   fax 01206 873151
　　http://www.iser.essex.ac.uk/ulsc/
E   A research centre within the Institute for Social and Economic Research (qv) at the University of Essex.
○   To promote the use of the UK's longitudinal data sets and to improve the practice of longitudinal research

Essex Biomedical Sciences Institute   (EBSI)
■   Department of Biological Sciences, University of Essex, Wivenhoe Park, Colchester, Essex, CO4 3SQ.
　　01206 872918
　　http://www.essex.ac.uk/bs/ebsi/
　　Director: Prof John D Norton.
E   A research institute at the University of Essex.
○   To promote and facilitate clinically relevant translational research activities in the biomedical sciences

Essex Finance Centre   (EFiC)   2003
■   Department of Accounting, Finance and Management, University of Essex, Wivenhoe Park, Colchester, Essex, CO4 3SQ.
　　01206 872364   fax 01206 873429
　　http://www.essex.ac.uk/afm/
　　Director: Prof Jerry Coakley.
E   A centre at the University of Essex.
○   To act as a focus for finance research activities

Essex Management Centre   (EMC)   1998
■   Department of Accounting, Finance and Management, University of Essex, Wivenhoe Park, Colchester, Essex, CO4 3SQ.
　　01206 872364   fax 01206 873429
　　http://www.essex.ac.uk/afm/
　　Contact: Prof George Cairns.
E   A centre at the University of Essex.
○   To bring together more effectively the range of expertise in management that exists at the University

Ethnic Minorities Law Centre   (EMLC)   1992
■   41 St Vincent Street, Glasgow, G1 2ER.
　　0141-204 2888   fax 0141-204 2006
　　http://www.emlc.org.uk/
　　Principal Solicitor: Rosie Sorrell.
E   A registered charity and a company limited by guarantee.
○   To meet unmet legal needs of members of ethnic minority communities
●   Education and training of solicitors and advice workers - Information service into legal problems affecting ethnic minorities - Provision of legal services
¶   Annual Report. Newsletter. (many other publications).

Ethnic Minority Studies Centre
　　see **Centre for Ethnic Minority Studies.**

Ethox Centre
■   Department of Public Health and Primary Care, Block 21 - Gibson Buidling, Radcliffe Infirmary, Oxford, OX2 6HE.
　　01865 287887   fax 01865 287884
　　http://www.ethox.org.uk
　　Director: Prof Michael Parker.
E   An institute at the University of Oxford.
○   To improve patient care through raising ethical understanding and ethical standards

EURO INFORMATION CENTRES (EICs)
　　http://www.euro-info.org.uk/
Note: There are 19 of these Centres thoughout the UK. They assist small and medium-sized enterprises to obtain information about business opportunities in the European Union.

Europa Institute
　　see **Edinburgh Europa Institute.**

Europe Japan Research Centre   (EJRC)   2001
■   School of Social Sciences and Law, Gipsy Lane Campus, Oxford Brookes University, Headington, Oxford, OX3 0BP.
　　01865 484901
　　http://ssl.brookes.ac.uk/jig/ejrc/
E   A research centre at Oxford Brookes University.

Europe-Japan Social Science Research Centre   1997

■   Faculty of Social Sciences, University of Glasgow, Adam Smith Building, 40 Bute Gardens, Glasgow, G12 8RT.
      0141-330 3701
      http://www.arts.gla.ac.uk/europejapan/
      Administrator: Yushin Toda.
E   A centre at the University of Glasgow.
○   To serve as a focus for, and to stimulate further, advanced academic exchange within the social sciences between Japan and
      Europe

Europe in the World Centre   (EWC)

NR   School of Politics and Communication Studies, University of Liverpool, Liverpool, L69 7ZT.
      0151-794 2904   fax 0151-794 3948
      http://www.liv.ac.uk/ewc/
      Contact: John Corner.
E   A research centre at the University of Liverpool.
○   To focus research on relationships between Europe and the rest of the world
Note: A Jean Monnet Centre of Excellence.

European Accounting Research Centre   (EARC)   1985

■   School of Business and Regional Development, University of Wales Bangor, Bangor, Gwynedd, LL57 2DG.
      01248 382180   fax 01248 364760
      http://sbard.bangor.ac.uk/
      Contact: Prof S J McLeay.
E   A research centre within the Centre for Banking and Finance (qv) at the University of Wales, Bangor.
○   To conduct research on the comparative and international aspects of accounting and finance

European Centre for Analysis in the Social Sciences   (ECASS)

■   University of Essex, Wivenhoe Park, Colchester, Essex, CO4 3SQ.
      01206 872957   fax 01206 873151
      http://www.iser.essex.ac.uk/
E   A research centre within the Institute for Social and Economic Research (qv) at the University of Essex.
○   To conduct and facilitate the empirical study of social and economic change by integrating longitudinal and cross-national
      European datasets

European Centre for Biodiversity and Conservation Research   (BIOCONS)

■   School of Earth and Environment, University of Leeds, Woodhouse Lane, Leeds, LS2 9JT.
      0113-343 5241
      http://www.earth.leeds.ac.uk/ebi/biocons.htm
E   A research centre within the Earth and Biosphere Institute (qv) at the University of Leeds.

European Centre on Health of Societies in Transition   (ECOHOST)   1997

■   London School of Hygiene and Tropical Medicine, University of London, Keppel Street, London, WC1E 7HT.
      020 7927 2833   fax 020 7612 7812
      http://www.lshtm.ac.uk/ecohost/
      Director: Prof Martin McKee.
E   A World Health Organisation (WHO) Collaborating Centre at the London School of Hygiene and Tropical Medicine, University of
      London.
○   To conduct research and analyse policy on health and health care in the transition countries of Eastern Europe and Russia
Note: ECOHOST is a World Health Organisation **WHO Collaborating Centre** for Health of Societies in Transition.

European Centre for Management Education   (ECME)

■   Manchester Business School, University of Manchester, Booth Street West, Manchester, M15 6PB.
      0161-275 6538   fax 0161-275 6587
      http://www.mbs.ac.uk/executive-education/customised/european-centre
      Contact: Jane Crombleholme.
E   A centre at the University of Manchester.
○   To offer a wide range of business and management training programmes for young managers and postgraduate students

European Centre for Medium-Range Weather Forecasts   (ECMWF)   1975

■   Shinfield Park, Reading, Berkshire, RG2 9AX.
      0118-949 9000   fax 0118-986 9450
      http://www.ecmwf.int/
      Director: D Marbouty. Head of Operations Department: W Zwieflhofer.
E   A statutory organisation set up under the auspices of COST (European Co-operation in Science and Technology) Committee for
      the EU, signed and ratified by 18 European Member States.
○   To develop numerical methods for medium-range and seasonal weather forecasting; to provide operational forecasts to the
      meteorological services of the member states and to make available computer resources to the meteorological services of
      member states; to provide operational forecasts to the meteorological services of member states
●   Education and training Collection and storage of appropriate meteorological data and provision of advanced training in
      numerical weather prediction (courses, seminars and workshops)
Note: The ECMWF is an international organisation.

European Centre for Occupational Health, Safety and the Environment   (ECOHSE)
- University of Glasgow, Adam Smith Building, 40 Bute Gardens, Glasgow, G12 8QQ.
  0141-330 4665
  http://www.gla.ac.uk/ecohse/
  Director: Dr Charles Woolfson.
- E   A research centre at the University of Glasgow.
- O   To stimulate advanced comparative academic research in the fields of industrial relations and social dialogue, corporate social responsibility, and workplace health, safety and the environment

European Centre for the Study of Migration and Social Care   (MASC)   2004
- School of Social Policy, Sociology and Social Research, University of Kent, Beverley Farm, Canterbury, Kent, CT2 7LZ.
  01227 827613   fax 01227 763674
  http://www.kent.ac.uk/masc/
  Director: Dr Charles Watters.
- E   A research centre within the Tizard Centre (qv) at the University of Kent.
- O   To conduct research and teaching in the fields of migration, social care and mental health

European Centre for the Study of Policing   (ECSP)   1996
- Faculty of Arts, Open University, Walton Hall, Milton Keynes, MK7 6AA.
  01908 652477   fax 01908 653750
  http://www.open.ac.uk/Arts/history/policing/
  Director: Prof Clive Emsley. Contact: Dr Paul Lawrence.
- E   A research centre within the International Centre for Comparative Criminological Research (qv) at the Open University.
- O   To promote and facilitate research into the history and practice of modern policing around the world (since c 1750), and to generate the exchange of ideas between academics and serving policemen

European Construction Institute   (ECI)   1990
- Loughborough University, Sir Frank Gibb Annexe, West Park, Loughborough, Leicestershire, LE11 3TU.
  01509 223526   fax 01509 260118
  http://www.eci-online.org/
- E   A research institute at Loughborough University.
- O   To bring together innovative clients, contractors, specialists and support organisations in Europe to develop and share knowledge aimed at improving the entire construction supply chain

European Documentation Centre   (EDC)
- Glasgow University Library, University of Glasgow, Glasgow, G12 8QE.
  0141-330 6704
  http://www.lib.gla.ac.uk/
  Head: Mrs H M Durndell.
- E   A centre at the University of Glasgow.
- O   To make available for inspection major documents issued by the European Union
Note: Many such centres exist in the UK, mostly housed within universities.

European Human Rights Advocacy Centre   (EHRAC)
- London Metropolitan University, Ladbroke House, 62-66 Highbury Grove, London, N5 2AD.
  020 7133 5111
  http://www.londonmet.ac.uk/research-units/hrsj/ehrac/
  Director: Philip Leach.
- E   A research centre within the Human Rights and Social Justice Research Institute (qv) at London Metropolitan University.
- O   To assist individuals, lawyers and non-governmental organisations within the Russian Federation to take human rights cases to the European Court of Human Rights

European Humanities Research Centre   (EHRC)
- New College, University of Oxford, Oxford, OX1 3BN.
  01865 271978   fax 01865 279590
  http://www.ehrc.ox.ac.uk/
  Director: Prof Catriona Kelly.
- E   A research centre at the University of Oxford.
- O   To further research in the humanities, especially culture, literature, history, and anthropology

European Information Centre   (EIC/LCCI   1990
- London Chamber of Commerce, 33 Queen Street, London, EC4R 1AP.
  020 7489 1992   fax 020 7203 1812
  http://www.londonchamber.co.uk/europe/
  Manager: Mette Lorentzen. European Information Officer: Paul Dowling.
- E   An independent non-profit-distributing organisation at the London Chamber of Commerce and Industry,
- O   To lead small and medium sized enterprises (SMEs) through a sequence of information, advice and action in winning business in the European market place
- ●   Information and advice on EU affairs, directives and regulations, structural funds, European grants and loans, public tenders, EU programmes, business contacts and international trade - Seminars

European Institute [Brighton]
   see **Sussex European Institute.**

European Institute   1991

■   LSE, Houghton Street, London, WC2A 2AE.
    020 7955 6780; 6839; 7537   fax 020 7955 7546
    http://www.lse.ac.uk/collections/europeanInstitute/
    Contact: Bob Millett.
E   A research institute at the London School of Economics and Political Science.
O   To be a leading international centre for the study of contemporary Europe beyond the border of the enlarged European Union

European Institute of Health and Medical Sciences   (EIHMS)

■   University of Surrey, Duke of Kent Building, Guildford, Surrey, GU2 7XH.
    01483 686700
    http://www.eihms.surrey.ac.uk
    Acting Head: Ken Gilbert.
E   A department of the University of Surrey.
O   To generate significant improvements in health care through high quality education, practice development and research to inform best practice

European Institute of Social Services   (EISS)

■   School of Social Policy, Sociology and Social Research, University of Kent, Keynes College, Canterbury, Kent, CT2 7NP.
    01227 823038   fax 01227 827246
    http://www.kent.ac.uk/eiss/
    Director: Linda Pizani Williams.
E   A department of the University of Kent.

European Institute for Urban Affairs   (EIUA)

■   Faculty of Technology and Environment, Liverpool John Moores University, 51 Rodney Street, Liverpool, L1 9AT.
    0151-231 5172   fax 0151-708 0650
    http://www.ljmu.ac.uk/eiua/
    Contact: Jean Parry.
E   A research institute within Liverpool John Moores University.
O   To specialise in areas of crucial concern to urban policy-makers throughout the world
●   Consultancy - Information service

European Law Institute
    see **Durham European Law Institute.**

European Policies Research Centre   (EPRC)   1978

■   Strathclyde Business School, University of Strathclyde, 40 George Street, Glasgow, G1 1QE.
    0141-548 3672   fax 0141-548 4898
    http://www.eprc.strath.ac.uk/
    Director: Prof Douglas Yuill.
E   An independent research centre at the University of Strathclyde.

European Research Centre [Keele]
    see **Keele European Research Centre.**

European Research Centre
    see **Centre for the Study of International Governance** which has replaced this centre.

European Research Institute   (ERI)   1994

■   Department of Social and Policy Sciences, University of Bath, Claverton Down, Bath, BA2 7AY.
    01225 386831   fax 01225 386381
    http://www.bath.ac.uk/eri/
    Director: Dr Theo Papadopoulos.
E   A research institute at the University of Bath.

European Research Institute   (ERI)   2001

■   University of Birmingham, Edgbaston, Birmingham, B15 2TT.
    0121-414 6928   fax 0121-414 8221
    http://www.eri.bham.ac.uk/
    Director: Prof Cillian Ryan.
E   A research institute at the University of Birmingham.
O   To act as a catalyst for research and postgraduate study in European studies

European Research Institute [Manchester]
    see **Manchester European Research Institute.**

European Social and Cultural Studies Centre
Note: No longer in existence.

© CBD Research Ltd · Beckenham · Kent BR3 5JS · Tel 020 8650 7745 · Fax 020 8650 0768 · E-mail cbd@cbdresearch.com · www.cbdresearch.com

European Studies Centre   1976

■ St Antony's College, University of Oxford, Oxford, OX2 6JF.
  01865 274470   fax 01865 274478
  Administrator: Ulli Parkinson.
E A research centre at the University of Oxford.
○ To conduct research and teaching into politics, economics, history, and international relations
● Conference facilities

European Studies Research Institute   (ESRI)   1992

■ Faculty of Arts, Media and Social Sciences, University of Salford, Salford, Manchester, M5 4WT.
  0161-295 5614   fax 0161-295 2818
  http://www.esri.salford.ac.uk/
  Director: Prof John Keiger.
E A department of the University of Salford.
○ To conduct research in contemporary European history and politics, European language and linguistics, European literary and cultural studies, and European policy studies

European Topic Centre on Water

Note: Is based in the Czech Republic and is therefore outside the scope of this directory.

European Work and Employment Research Centre   (EWERC)   1994

■ Manchester Business School, University of Manchester, Booth Street West, Manchester, M15 6PB.
  0161-275 2908   fax 0161-200 3622
  http://www.mbs.ac.uk/research/european-employment/
  Director: Dr Damian Grimshaw. Administrator: Mary O'Brien.
E A research centre at the University of Manchester.
○ To conduct research in management, labour economics, sociology, geography and industrial relations

Evaluation Institute

■ School of Humanities and Social Sciences, University of Glamorgan, Pontypridd, CF37 1GY.
  01443 483693
  http://www.glam.ac.uk/hassschool/Evaluation/
  Contact: Sarah Batterbury.
E A research institute within the University of Glamorgan.
○ To provide consultancy, research and training in evaluation studies
● Consultancy - Education and training

Exeter Biocatalysis Centre   (EBC)   2003

■ University of Exeter, The Henry Wellcome Building for Catalysis, Stocker Road, Exeter, EX4 4QD.
  01392 263468   fax 01392 263489
  http://www.centres.ex.ac.uk/biocatalysis/
  Contact: Prof Jenny Littlechild.
E A centre at the University of Exeter.
○ To study the structure, mechanism and commercial application of enzymes

Exeter Centre for Cognitive Neuroscience   (ECCN)

■ School of Psychology, University of Exeter, Washington Singer Laboratories, Perry Road, Exeter, EX4 4QG.
  01392 264626   fax 01392 264623
  http://psy.ex.ac.uk/eccn/
E A centre at the University of Exeter.

Exeter Centre for Hellenistic and Greco-Roman Culture

■ Department of Classics and Ancient History, University of Exeter, Amory Building, Rennes Drive, Exeter, EX4 4RJ.
  01392 264202   fax 01392 264195
  http://www.huss.ex.ac.uk/classics/research/hellenistic_centre.htm
E A centre at the University of Exeter.
○ To be an internationally recognised focus for the study of the history and culture of the post-classical Greek world (c 323 BC to c 200 AD), in all its variety

eXeter Centre for Research in Strategic Processes and Operations   (XSPO)

■ School of Business and Economics, University of Exeter, Xfi Building, Rennes Drive, Exeter, EX4 4ST.
  01392 263213
  http://www.centres.ex.ac.uk/xspo/
E A centre at the University of Exeter.
○ To focus research on investigating approaches for the design, analysis and management of business processes

Exeter Centre for the Study of Esotericism   (EXESESO)

■   School of Humanities and Social Sciences, University of Exeter, Amory Building, Rennes Drive, Exeter, EX4 4RJ.
      01392 264631   fax 01392 263305
      http://www.huss.ex.ac.uk/research/exeseso
      Director: Prof Nicholas Goodrick-Clarke.
E   A research centre at the University of Exeter.
○   To foster advanced research into historical and comparative aspects of the esoteric traditions from the Hellenistic period in late antiquity through the Renaissance and early modern period to the present

Exeter Manufacturing Enterprise Centre   (XMEC)   2002

■   The Queen's Drive, Exeter, EX4 4QJ.
      01392 661000
      http://www.projects.ex.ac.uk/xmec/
      Director: Prof David Zhang.
E   A centre at the University of Exeter.
○   To carry out advanced research in manufacturing technology, systems, and management - with particular current focus on agile / lean enterprise, dynamically integrated manufacturing systems, e-business and e-Manufacturing, virtual and distributed enterprise, supply chain modelling and integration, multi-agent systems, business systems modelling and simulation, rapid manufacturing, and agile quality and process control systems
×   Manufacturing Systems and Agility Group (University of Liverpool).

Expedition Advisory Centre
      see **Geography Outdoors.**

Experiential Learning in Environmental and Natural Sciences CETL   2005

■   University of Plymouth, Drake Circus, Plymouth, PL4 8AA.
      01752 233057
      http://www.plymouth.ac.uk/cetl/el
      Contact: Ruth Weaver.
E   A Centre for Excellence in Teaching and Learning (CETL) at the University of Plymouth.
Note: See **Centres for Excellence in Teaching and Learning** for more information.

Experimental Techniques Centre   (ETC)   1974

■   Brunel University, Uxbridge, Middlesex, UB8 3PH.
      01895 255793   fax 01895 812544
      http://www.brunel.ac.uk/about/acad/etc
      Director: Dr Robert Bulpett. Senior Experimental Officer: Dr Alan Reynolds.
E   A department of Brunel University.
○   To develop and extend expertise in electron microscopy and surface analytical techniques for teaching, research and commercial development; to promote a confidential professional consultancy service in fibre and particle sizing and indentification, failure analysis, materials specification, and environmental and biological analysis
●   Consultancy - Research support - Short courses in principles and application of techniques - Taught Masters courses - Commercial service (Mon-Fri 0845-1800) - Various equipment available

© CBD Research Ltd · Beckenham · Kent BR3 5JS · Tel 020 8650 7745 · Fax 020 8650 0768 · E-mail cbd@cbdresearch.com · www.cbdresearch.com

Facial Cosmetic Surgery Centre   (FCSC)
- ■ Fawkham Manor Hospital, Manor Lane, Fawkham, Longfield, Kent, DA3 8ND.
  01474 875636
- ○ To perform all kinds of facial cosmetic surgery including nasal reshaping, ear correction, eyelid surgery (blepharoplasty), face lift, brow lift, laser removal of thread veins, etc
- ● 24-hour resident medical officers

Facilities Management Graduate Centre   (FMGC)
- ■ Faculty of Organisation and Management, Sheffield Hallam University, 7 Science Park, Howard Street, Sheffield, S1 1WB.
  0114-225 3240   fax 0114-225 4038
  http://www.shu.ac.uk/research/fmgc/
  Head: Tim Davidson-Hague.
- E A research centre at Sheffield Hallam University.
- ○ To carry out academic, grant-aided and contract research, to deliver leading-edge education and training; to offer consultancy services in all aspects of facilities management

Families, Life Course and Generations Research Centre   (FLaG)   2005
- ■ University of Leeds, Beech Grove House, Leeds, LS2 9JT.
  0113-343 4874   fax 0113-343 4600
  http://www.leeds.ac.uk/family/
- E A research centre at the University of Leeds.
- ○ To provide a forum for researchers and research users interested in families and intergenerational relationships across childhood, youth, adulthood and older life
- × Centre for Family, Kinship and Childhood.

Family and Child Psychology Research Centre
Note: has closed.

Family Business Centre
  see **Caledonian Family Business Centre.**

Family Records Centre   (FRC)   1997
- ■ 1 Myddelton Street, London, EC1R 1UW.
  0845 603 7788   fax 01704 550013
  http://www.familyrecords.gov.uk/frc/
- E Part of a Government consortium of various national register offices, museums and libraries.
- ○ To help find Government records and other sources needed for family research

Farm Energy Centre   (FEC)   1967
- ■ Stoneleigh, Kenilworth, Warwickshire, CV8 2LS.
  024 7669 6512
  http://www.fecservices.co.uk/
- E An independent non-profit-distributing organisation.
- ○ To work with farmers, utilities, research institutes and manufacturers providing expertise on energy applications and energy efficiency

Farnborough Aerospace Centre
- ■ PO Box 87, Farnborough, Hampshire, GU14 6YU.
  01252 373232   fax 01252 383000
  http://www.baesystems.com/
- E A part of BAE Systems.

Fashion, Business and Technology Research Centre   (FBT)
- ■ Department of Clothing Design and Technology, Manchester Metropolitan University, Old Hall Lane, Manchester, M14 6HR.
  0161-247 2603   fax 0161-247 6872
  http://www.miriad.mmu.ac.uk/fbt/
  Contact: Dr Rose Otieno.
- E A research centre within the Manchester Institute for Research and Innovation in Art and Design (qv) at Manchester Metropolitan University.
- ○ To conduct research into various areas of clothing design and technology

Fashion Industry Research Centre   (FIRC)
- ■ Faculty of Art, Design and Architecture, Kingston University, Knights Park, Kingston-upon-Thames, Surrey, KT1 2QJ.
  020 8547 8062   fax 020 8547 8272
  http://www.kingston.ac.uk/design/research_centres.html
  Director: Anne Creigh-Tyte.
- E A research centre at Kingston University, London.
- ○ To focus research on professional practice in the contemporary, international fashion industry

Feline Advisory Bureau   (FAB)   1958
- ■   Taeselbury, High Street, Salisbury, Wiltshire, SP3 6LD.
     0870 742 2278   fax 01747 871873
     http://www.fabcats.org/
- E   A registered charity and membership organisation.
- ○   To promote the health and welfare of cats through improved feline knowledge, to help all care better for cats

Ferguson Centre for African and Asian Studies   (FCAS)   2002
- ■   Faculty of Arts, Open University, Walton Hall, Milton Keynes, MK7 6AA.
     01908 655244   fax 01908 653973
     http://www.open.ac.uk/Arts/ferguson-centre/
     Director: Suman Gupta. Secretary: Heather Scott.
- E   A research centre at the Open University.
- ○   To foster and develop research related to Africa and Asia
- Note: Named in honour of the founding Dean of the Faculty.

Fertility Centre at Life
      see **Newcastle Fertility Centre at Life.**

Field Studies Council Centres   (FSC)   1943
- ■   Montford Bridge, Preston Montford, Shrewsbury, Shropshire, SY4 1HW.
     0845 345 4071   fax 01743 852101
     http://www.field-studies-council.org/centres/
- E   An educational charity.
- ○   To promote better understanding of the environment
- ●   Residential and day courses for schools and colleges - Annual programme of special interest courses for adults and families
- Note: The FSC runs all its activities in its 17 through its national network of 17 centres - see website for details.

Finance Centre
      see **Essex Finance Centre.**

Finance Research Institute
      see **Warwick Finance Research Institute.**

Financial Econometrics Research Centre   (FERC)   1998
- ■   Warwick Business School, University of Warwick, Coventry, CV4 7AL.
     024 7652 4118   fax 024 7652 4167
     http://www.wbs.ac.uk/faculty/research/ferc.cfm
     Director: Prof Mark Salmon.
- E   A research centre at the University of Warwick.
- ○   To generate first class research in empirical finance, both in the development of statistical methods of financial econometrics and their application to financial markets

Financial Investigation Bureau
      see **ICC Financial Investigation Bureau.**

Financial Markets Group Research Centre   (FMC)
- ■   LSE, Houghton Street, London, WC2A 2AE.
     020 7955 7891   fax 020 7852 3580
     http://fmg.lse.ac.uk/
     Director: Prof D Webb.
- E   A research centre at the London School of Economics and Political Science.
- ○   To conduct high-quality investigation into the workings of the financial markets and their regulation

Financial Options Research Centre   (FORC)   1989
- ■   Warwick Business School, University of Warwick, Coventry, CV4 7AL.
     024 7652 4118   fax 024 7652 4167
     http://www.wbs.ac.uk/faculty/research/forc.cfm
     Director: Prof Mark Salmon.
- E   A research centre within the Warwick Finance Research Institute (qv) at the University of Warwick.
- ○   To undertake and disseminate applied research on options and related instruments, of direct relevance to the financial institutions which fund it

Financial Research Centre
      see **Oxford Financial Research Centre.**

Fish Conservation Centre (FCC) 1986

■ Gladshot, Haddington, Lothian, EH41 4NR.
  01620 823691   fax 01620 823691
  Consultant: Prof Peter S Maitland.
E A private venture.
O To conserve fish species through their sustainable use based on a full understanding of their geographic distribution, conservation status and ecological requirements
● Active conservation - Collation of information on species distribution - Publicity regarding the threats faced by rare species - Publication of studies
¶ Wide range of publications.

Flight Operations Research Centre of Excellence (FORCE)

■ Department of Human Factors, Cranfield University, Cranfield, Bedfordshire, MK43 0AL.
  01234 754606
  http://www.cranfield.ac.uk/soe/hf/force/
  Director: Captain Simon Wood.
E A research centre at Cranfield University.
O To provide independent research on key safety issues in aviation

Flood Hazard Research Centre (FHRC) 1970

■ School of Health and Social Sciences, Middlesex University, Queensway, Enfield, Middlesex, EN3 4SA.
  020 8411 5359   fax 020 8411 5403
  http://www.fhrc.mdx.ac.uk/
  Head of Centre: Prof Edmund Penning-Rowsell. Senior Research Fellow: Sue Tapsell.
E A department of Middlesex University.
O To undertake research and disseminate findings on environmental issues with particular reference to water management
● Conference facilities - Education and training - Information service - Library available by appointment

Flour Advisory Bureau Ltd (FAB) 1956

■ 21 Arlington Street, London, SW1A 1RN.
  020 7493 2521   fax 020 7493 6785
  http://www.fabflour.co.uk/
E An independent non-profit-distributing organisation.
O To be the central source of information on flour and bread in the UK; to encourage people to eat more bread as part of a healthy, balanced diet under the Bread of Life Campaign
● Information service

Fluid Dynamics Research Centre

■ School of Engineering, University of Warwick, Coventry, CV4 7AL.
  024 7652 3523
  http://www2.warwick.ac.uk/fac/sci/eng/cmd/research/fluid/
E A research centre at the University of Warwick.
O To conduct research into a wide range of interests in fluid dynamics and thermodynamics

Fluid Loading and Instrumentation Centre (FLIC)

■ School of the Built Environment, Heriot-Watt University, Riccarton, Edinburgh, EH14 4AS.
  0131-451 3866; 8062
  http://www.sbe.hw.ac.uk/research/flic/
E A research centre at Heriot-Watt University.

Fluids Research Centre (FRC)

■ School of Engineering, University of Surrey, Guildford, Surrey, GU2 7XH.
  01483 686292
  http://www.portal.surrey.ac.uk/eng/research/fluids/fluids_research
  Director: Prof Alan Robins.
E A research centre at the University of Surrey.
O To promote excellence in fluids science, technology and engineering

Food, Consumer Behaviour and Health Research Centre

■ Department of Psychology, University of Surrey, Guildford, Surrey, GU2 7XH.
  01483 689994   fax 01483 689553
  http://www.surrey.ac.uk/shs/fcbh.html
  Co-Director: Prof Richard Shepherd. Co-Director: Dr Monique Raats.
E A research centre at the University of Surrey.
O To conduct research in the need to translate basic biological knowledge on food safety, diet and health in order to facilitate the improvement of people's lives

Food Industry Centre

- Cardiff School of Health Sciences, Llandarff Campus, University of Wales Institute Cardiff, Western Avenue, Cardiff, CF5 2YB.
  029 2041 6409   fax 029 2041 6306
  http://www.uwic.ac.uk/sas/FRCU/fic.asp
  Director: David Lloyd.
- E   A research centre at the University of Wales Institute, Cardiff.
- O   To develop links between the School and the food processing sector

Food Innovation Research Centre   (FIRC)

- Sheffield Hallam University, Howard Street, Sheffield, S1 1WB.
  0114-225 3556   fax 0114-225 4038
  http://www.shu.ac.uk/research/firc/
  Business Development Manager: David M Johnson.
- E   A research centre at Sheffield Hallam University.
- O   To understand the requirements of the complete food supply chain, and provide it with appropriate services common to all levels, from retailer, through major groups, to small and medium-sized companies

Food Refrigeration and Process Engineering Research Centre   (FRPERC)   1991

- University of Bristol, Churchill Building, Langford, Bristol, BS40 5DU.
  0117-928 9239   fax 0117-928 9314
  http://www.frperc.bris.ac.uk/
  Director: Steve James.
- E   A research centre at the University of Bristol.
- O   To conduct research into food production and processing and the relationship of these to food quality, safety and the economics of food production

Food Research Centre   (FRC)   1993

- Faculty of Engineering, Science and the Built Environment, London South Bank University, 103 Borough Road, London, SE1 0AA.
  020 7815 7970
  Director: Prof Martin Chaplin.
- E   A research centre at London South Bank University.
- O   To focus on issues of importance to the food industry

Food Supply Chain Centre   (FSCC)

- University of Gloucester Business School, University of Gloucester, The Park, Cheltenham, Gloucestershire, GL50 2RH.
  0870 721 0210
  http://www.glos.ac.uk/faculties/ugbs/
- E   A research centre at the University of Gloucestershire.
- O   To focus on research, development and consultancy for firms in the food supply chain, and specialising in marketing and market research, logistics, warehouse and retail location, supply consolidation and replenishment

Food Technology Centre   (FTC)

- University of Teesside, Middlesbrough, TS1 3BA.
  01642 384624   fax 01642 384631
  http://www.foodtechnologycentre.com/
  Head: Dr Leo Guevara.
- E   A research centre at the University of Teesside.
- O   To offer training and technical assistance to food and drink companies

Football Development Centre

- Darlington College, Central Park, Haughton Road, Darlington, DL1 1DR.
  01325 503030   fax 01325 503000
  http://www.darlington.ac.uk/index.asp?id=78
- E   A centre at Darlington College.

Football Governance Research Centre   (FGRC)

- Faculty of Social Sciences, Birkbeck College London, Malet Street, London, WC1E 7HX.
  020 6731 6740
  http://www.football-research.org/
  Director: Prof Christine Oughton.
- E   A centre at Birkbeck, University of London.
- O   To focus research on governance and regulatory issues facing the football industry

Foreign Language Centre   (FLC)

- School of Modern Languages, University of Exeter, Queen's Building, The Queen's Drive, Exeter, EX4 4QH.
  01392 264306
  http://www.centres.ex.ac.uk/flc/
  Manager: Dr Marie Danielle Chamary.
- E   A centre at the University of Exeter.
- O   To provide credit-rated and non credit-rated Chinese, French, German, Italian and Spanish language courses

Note: Many of the UK universities have similar such centres.

Formulation Engineering Research Centre
- Department of Chemical Engineering, University of Birmingham, Edgbaston, Birmingham, B15 2TT.
  0121-414 5354   fax 0121-414 5377
  http://www.form-eng.bham.ac.uk/
  Head: Prof J P K Seville.
E   A research centre at the University of Birmingham.

Fort Bovisand Underwater Centre Ltd   (FBUC)   1970
- Plymouth, PL9 0AB.
  01752 408021   fax 01752 481952
  http://www.divingheritage.com/bovisand.htm
E   A profit-making business.
O   To conduct basic, advanced and specialist courses for the offshore and inshore diving industries

Foundation Direct CETL   2005
- University of Portsmouth, 6-8 Hampshire Terrace, Portsmouth, PO1 2QF.
  023 9284 3008   fax 023 9284 5894
  http://www.port.ac.uk/departments/studentsupport/foundationdirect/
  Director: Frank Lyons.
E   A Centre for Excellence in Teaching and Learning (CETL) at the University of Portsmouth.
Note: See **Centres for Excellence in Teaching and Learning** for more information.

Fraser of Allander Institute for Research in the Scottish Economy   (FAI)   1975
- Strathclyde Business School, University of Strathclyde, The Sir William Duncan Building, 130 Rottenrow, Glasgow, G4 0GE.
  0141-548 3958   fax 0141-548 5776
  http://www.fraser.strath.ac.uk/
  Policy Director: Prof Brian Ashcroft.
E   An independent economic research and policy institute at the University of Strathclyde.
O   To analyse regional economic issues in general and the operation of the Scottish economy in particular

Frognal Centre for Medical Studies
Note: Is the Postgraduate Centre of Queen Mary's Hospital, Sidcup.

Fuel and Energy Centre
   see **Nottingham Fuel and Energy Centre.**

Further Mathematics Centre
   see **Derbyshire Further Mathematics Centre.**

Future of Humanity Institute   (FHI)   2005
- Faculty of Philosophy, University of Oxford, Suite 8 - Littlegate House, 16-17 St Ebbe's Street, Oxford, OX1 1PT.
  01865 286279
  http://www.fhi.ox.ac.uk/
  Director: Dr Ian Goldin. Contact: Miriam Wood.
E   An interdisciplinary research institute at the University of Oxford.
O   To understand and evaluate humanity's long term prospects

Future Railway Research Centre   (FRRC)
- Department of Mechanical Engineering, University of Oxford, Exhibition Road, London, SW7 2AZ.
  020 7594 7000
  http://www3.imperial.ac.uk/merailways
  Director: Prof Rod A Smith.
E   A research centre at Imperial College London.
O   To conduct a variety of railway research, with particular emphasis on structural integrity, metal fatigue, and high speed trains

Ganolfan Troseddeg Gymharol a Chyfiawnder Troseddol
    see **Centre for Comparative Criminology and Criminal Justice.**

Garlic Information Centre
■   Saberdene House, Church Road, Catsfield, East Sussex, TN33 9DP.
      01424 892440   fax 01424 892988
      http://www.mistral.co.uk/garlic/
      Contact: Peter Josling.
○   To provide fully independent advice on the medicinal and culinary benefits of garlic and apple cider vinegar
●   Information on gingko bilboa, hypericum, saw palmetto, valerian, dandelion, bearberry, vitamins and minerals

Gatty Marine Research Institute
■   School of Biology, University of St Andrews, St Andrews, Fife, KY16 8LB.
      01334 463440
      http://medicine.st-and.ac.uk/
E   A research institute at the University of St Andrews.

Geddes Institute
■   School of Social Sciences, University of Dundee, 13 Perth Road, Dundee, DD1 4HN.
      01382 345236   fax 01382 204234
      http://www.trp.dundee.ac.uk/research/cpr.html
      Administrator: Anne Mather.
E   A research institute and department of the University of Dundee.
○   To extend and advance high quality research, and scholarly activity in Scotland, the UK and overseas in town and regional
      planning, community regeneration, conservation and design, environmental management and environmental justice,
      underpinning the delivery of distinctive undergraduate and postgraduate programmes

Gender Institute   1993
■   LSE, Houghton Street, London, WC2A 2AE.
      020 7955 7602   fax 020 7955 6408
      http://www.lse.ac.uk/collections/genderInstitute/
      Director: Dr Diane Perrons.
E   A research institute at the London School of Economics and Political Science.
○   To conduct gender research

Gender and Religion Research Centre
    see **Centre for Gender and Religions Research.**

Gender and Sexuality Research Centre   (GSRC)
■   Department of Sociology, Manchester Metropolitan University, Geoffrey Manton Building, Rosamond Street West, Manchester,
      M15 6LL.
      0161-247 2799
      http://www.icgc.mmu.ac.uk/research_centres/gsrc/
      Contact: Dr Kate Cook.
E   A research centre within the Institute of Culture, Gender and the City (qv) at Manchester Metropolitan University.

General Engineering Research Institute   (GERI)   2002
■   Faculty of Technology and Environment, Liverpool John Moores University, Room 114 - James Parsons Building, Byrom Street,
      Liverpool, L3 3AF.
      0151-231 2516   fax 0151-298 2447
      http://www.ljmu.ac.uk/geri/
      Co-Director: Prof David Burton. Co-Director: Prof Michael J Lalor.
E   A research institute within Liverpool John Moores University.
○   To conduct research in various specialised fields, including fringe pattern analysis, optics, precision measurement, computer vision,
      grinding processes in manufacturing, hardware design and manufacture, radio frequency and microwave technology, lasers,
      sensors, non-destructive testing, etc

Genetic Therapies Centre
■   Department of Chemistry, Imperial College London, Flowers Building, Armstrong Road, London, SW7 2AZ.
      020 7594 5869   fax 020 7594 5803
      http://www.gtc.ch.ic.ac.uk/
      Contact: Prof Andrew D Miller.
E   A research centre at Imperial College London.
○   To conduct research in synthetic non-viral vector systems for gene therapy, the engineering of delivery systems for therapeutic
      agents, the chemistry of stress and the proteomic code

Genetics Education - Networking of Innovation and Excellence CETL   (GENIE)
■   Department of Genetics, University of Leicester, Leicester, LE1 7RH.
      0116-252 3374
      http://www.le.ac.uk/cetl/genie.html
      Contact: Annette Cashmore.
E   A Centre for Excellence in Teaching and Learning (CETL) at the University of Leicester.
Note: See **Centres for Excellence in Teaching and Learning** for more information.

© CBD Research Ltd · Beckenham · Kent BR3 5JS · Tel 020 8650 7745 · Fax 020 8650 0768 · E-mail cbd@cbdresearch.com · www.cbdresearch.com

Genetics and Insurance Research Centre   (GIRC)   1999

■   Department of Actuarial Mathematics and Statistics, Heriot-Watt University, Riccarton, Edinburgh, EH14 4AS.
     0131-451 3209
     http://www.ma.hw.ac.uk/ams/girc/
     Director: Prof Angus Macdonald.
E   A research centre at Heriot-Watt University.
O   To develop mathematical models of single-gene disorders, and their effect on insurance and service costs; to develop methods of modelling multifactorial genetic conditions; to develop actuarial models of all kinds of personal insurance, incorporating genetic knowledge
●   To develop links and collaborations with geneticists, epidemiologists and health economists

Genome Centre   2001

■   Barts and the London, Queen Mary's School of Medicine and Dentistry, Queen Mary, University of London, John Vane Building, Charterhouse Square, London, EC1M 6BQ.
     020 7882 5776   fax 020 7882 5672
     http://www.smd.qmul.ac.uk/gc/
     Manager: Dr Charles Mein.
E   A research centre within the William Harvey Research Institute (qv) at Queen Mary, University of London.
O   To focus on a wide area of genetic and genomic research

Genome Damage and Stability Centre
   see **MRC Genome Damage and Stability Centre.**

Genomics Research Institute
   see **Bristol Genomics Research Institute.**

GeoData Institute

■   Faculty of Engineering, Science and Mathematics, University of Southampton, Highfield, Southampton, SO17 1BJ.
     023 8059 2719   fax 023 8059 2849
     http://www.geodata.soton.ac.uk/
E   A University-based consultancy group at the University of Southampton.
O   To specialise in environmental data management, analysis and processing

Geoenvironmental Research Centre   (GRC)   Canolfan Ymchwil Ddaearamgylcheddol

■   Cardiff School of Engineering, Cardiff University, Queen's Buildings - PO Box 925, Newport Road, Cardiff, CF24 3AA.
     029 2087 2004   fax 029 2087 4004
     http://www.grc.cf.ac.uk/
     Administrator: Pauline Townsend.
E   An integrated research centre within the Institute of Sustainability, Energy and Environmental Management (qv) at Cardiff University.
O   To conduct research and development solutions for a variety of land environment problems

Geography, Earth and Environmental Sciences Subject Centre   (GEES)   2000

■   University of Plymouth, Buckland House, Drake Circus, Plymouth, PL4 8AA.
     01752 233530   fax 01752 233534
     http://www.gees.ac.uk/
E   A Government funded national centre within the University of Plymouth.
O   To foster world-class education in geography, earth and the environmental sciences
●   Education and training - Information service - Statistics
×   LTSN Geography, Earth and Environmental Sciences Subject Centre.
Note: One of the 24 Subject Centres of the Higher Education Academy, (qv).

Geography Outdoors   1980

■   Royal Geographical Society, 1 Kensington Gore, London, SW7 2AR.
     020 7591 3000
     http://www.rgs.org/OurWork/Fieldwork+and+Expeditions/
E   A registered charity and part of the Royal Geographical Society.
O   To provide information, training and advice to anyone involved in expeditions, field research or outdoor learning in the UK and overseas
×   Expedition Advisory Centre.

George Ewart Evans Centre for Storytelling

■   School of Humanities and Social Sciences, University of Glamorgan, Pontypridd, CF37 1DL.
     01443 483312
     http://www.glam.ac.uk/hass/738
     Co-Director: Prof Mike Wilson. Co-Director: Prof Hamish Fyfe.
E   A research centre within the University of Glamorgan.
O   To promote, develop and research storytelling in all its forms
●   Conferences - Seminars

George Green Institute for Electromagnetics Research   (GGIER)   2003

- ■ School of Electrical and Electronic Engineering, University of Nottingham, University Park, Nottingham, NG7 2RD.
  0115-846 8296   fax 0115-951 5616
  http://www.nottingham.ac.uk/ggiemr/
  Director: Prof Christos Christopoulos.
- E A research institute at the University of Nottingham.
- ○ To conduct postgraduate teaching and research in all areas of electromagnetics and its applications

Geotechnical Engineering Research Centre   (GERC)   1980

- ■ Department of Engineering, City University, Tait Building, Northampton Square, London, EC1V 0HB.
  020 7040 0113
  http://www.city.ac.uk/sems/research/geotech/
- E A centre at City University.
- ○ To conduct geotechnical research involving physical modelling, laboratory testing and numerical analysis

German Historical Institute London   (GHIL)   1976

- ■ 17 Bloomsbury Square, London, WC1A 2NJ.
  020 7309 2050   fax 020 7309 2055
  http://www.ghil.ac.uk/
  Director: Prof Hagen Schulze. Deputy Director: Dr Benedikt Stuchtey.
- E Part of a foundation.
- ○ To conduct historical research
- ● Information service - Library
- ¶ Bulletin. Annual Lecture.

Gestalt Centre London   1980

- ■ 62 Paul Street, London, EC2A 4NA.
  020 7613 4480
  http://www.gestaltcentre.co.uk/
  Manager: Jacqueline Wearn.
- E A partnership and a training organisation.
- ○ To train people to become Gestalt psychotherapists; to run Gestalt therapy groups; to run post-graduate training with international leaders; to offer low cost therapy

Gibson Institute for Land, Food and Environment   1999

- ■ Queen's University, Belfast, David Keir Building, Stranmillis Road, Belfast, BT9 5AG.
  028 9097 5562   fax 028 9097 5457
  http://www.qub.ac.uk/sites/GibsonInstitute/
  Director: Dr Sally Shortall.
- E An institute at Queen's University, Belfast.
- ○ To ensure the sustainability of agriculture in Northern Ireland, especially the small farming sector

giCentre

- ■ Department of Information Science, City University, Northampton Square, London, EC1V 0HB.
  020 7040 8389   fax 020 7040 8584
  http://www.soi.city.ac.uk/organisation/is/research/giCentre/
- E A centre at City University.
- ○ To develop novel ways of understanding the world through digital geographical information; to achieve new insights about society and the environment, and to enable access to information in ways that are beneficial and effective

Gifted Children's Information Centre   (GCIC)   1978

- ■ Hampton Grange, 21 Hampton Lane, Solihull, West Midlands, B91 2QJ.
  0121-705 4547   fax 0121-705 4547
  Director: Dr Peter J Congdon.
- E A private venture.
- ○ To publish and disseminate information on the subject of children who are gifted, left-handed, handicapped or have specific learning difficulties such as dyslexia, AD/HD (Attention Deficit / Hyperactivity Disorder) and Asperger syndrome - the information is essentially practical in nature and is designed for teachers, parents and children
- ● Advice on running courses for gifted children - Independent psychological assessments and consultations - Supply of equipment for aiding left-handed people in writing, measuring and cutting
- ¶ Wide range of publications.

Gillette Rugby League Heritage Centre

- ■ The George Hotel, 1 St Georges Square, Huddersfield, HD1 1JA.
  01484 515444; 542458   fax 01484 435056
  http://www.rlheritage.co.uk/

Glaciology Centre
   see **Bristol Glaciology Centre.**

Glasgow Buddhist Centre

- ■ 329 Sauchiehall Street, Glasgow, G2 3HW.
  - 0141-333 0524
  - http://www.glasgowbuddhistcentre.com/
- E An independent non-profit-distributing organisation and a registered charity.
- ○ To teach meditation and Buddhism
- ● Education and training - The Centre provides meditation cushions and mats

Note: For other Buddhist centres see note under **Buddhist Centres**.

Glasgow Cardiovascular Research Centre
see **BHF Glasgow Cardiovascular Research Centre.**

Glasgow Centre for the Child and Society   (GCCS)   2004

- NR Glasgow School of Social Work, University of Strathclyde, Sir Henry Wood Building, 76 Southbrae Drive, Glasgow, G13 1PP.
  - 0141-950 3380   fax 0141-330 4856
  - http://www.gccs.gla.ac.uk/
  - Head: Prof Joan Orme.
- E A centre at the University of Strathclyde.
- ○ To conduct research, teaching, consultancy and policy advice primarily in the areas of child welfare, children's rights, child protection and young people and crime

Note: Jointly run with the University of Glasgow.

Glasgow Centre for Medieval and Renaissance Studies   (GCMRS)   1997

- ■ Department of History, University of Glasgow, 2-10 University Gardens, Glasgow, G12 8QQ.
  - 0141-330 4087; 4509   fax 0141-330 5000
  - http://www.gla.ac.uk/centres/mars
  - Head: Dr Kathryn Lowe.
- E An interdisciplinary research centre at the University of Glasgow.
- ○ To bring together scholars who are active in research on all aspects of the Middle Ages and the Renaissance

Glasgow Centre for Retailing   (GCR)   2001

- ■ Caledonian Business School, Glasgow Caledonian University, Cowcaddens Road, Glasgow, G4 0BA.
  - 0141-331 8238   fax 0141-331 8210
  - http://www.glasgowcentreforretailing.co.uk
  - Director: Prof Christopher M Moore.
- E A research centre at Glasgow Caledonian University.
- ○ To specialise in consumer research

Glasgow Centre for the Study of Violence   (GCSV)   2003

- ■ Department of Psychology, Glasgow Caledonian University, Cowcaddens Road, Glasgow, G4 0BA.
  - 0141-331 8969   fax 0141-331 3636
  - http://www.gcal.ac.uk/violence/
  - Co-Director: Roger Houchin. Co-Director: Dr David Shewin.
- E A research centre at Glasgow Caledonian University.
- ○ To research the causes of criminal violence, collaborating with a range of agencies that work with violent offenders

Glasgow Marine Technology Centre   (GMTC)

- ■ Department of Mechanical Engineering, University of Glasgow, James Watt Building, Glasgow, G12 8QQ.
  - 0141-339 0969   fax 0141-330 4015
  - http://www.eng.gla.ac.uk/marine/
  - Director: Prof Mike Cowling.
- E An interdisciplinary research centre at the University of Glasgow.
- ○ To work with industry and Government on a broad range of offshore and marine problems

Glaxo Neurological Centre
see **Mersey Neurological Trust, Glaxo Centre.**

Glenamara Centre for International Research in Arts and Society

- ■ School of Arts and Social Sciences, Northumbria University, Lipman Building, Newcastle City Campus, Newcastle upon Tyne, NE1 8ST.
  - 0191-227 4473
  - http://northumbria.ac.uk/sd/academic/sass/res_con/lordglen/
  - Contact: Prof Lynn Dobbs.
- E An interdisciplinary research centre at Northumbria University.
- ○ To conduct research in art history, criminology, English, fine art, history, linguistics, media, nation studies, performing arts, politics, public policy and administration and sociology

Global Network of World Health Organisation Collaborating Centres for Nursing and Midwifery Development
- School of Nursing, Midwifery and Community Health, Glasgow Caledonian University, 70 Cowcaddens Road, Glasgow, G4 0BA.
  0141-331 3459; 8310   fax 0141-331 8312
  http://www.whocc.gcal.ac.uk/
  Secretary: Prof Barbara A Parfitt.
- E   A collaborating centre at Glasgow Caledonian University.
- O   To maximise the contribution of nursing and midwifery in order to advance Health for All in partnership with the World Health Organisation and its member states, member centres, NGOs, and others interested in promoting the health of populations

Glycobiology Institute
   see **Oxford Glycobiology Institute.**

Glycobiology Training, Research and Infrastructure Centre   (GlycoTRIC)   2004
- Faculty of Life Sciences, South Kensington Campus, Imperial College London, Exhibition Road, London, SW7 2AZ.
  020 7594 5220   fax 020 7594 5207
  http://www3.imperial.ac.uk/glycotric
  Head: Prof Anne Bell.
- E   A research centre at Imperial College London.
- O   To facilitate glycobiology research at the interface between biochemistry and medicine

Graduate Centre for Medieval Studies   (GCMS)   1965
- Faculty of Arts and Humanities, Whiteknights, PO Box 218, University of Reading, Reading, Berkshire, RG6 6AA.
  0118-378 8148   fax 0118-378 6440
  http://www.reading.ac.uk/Study/Departments/medieval.asp
  Director: Dr Anne Lawrence-Mathers. Secretary: Mrs E Berry.
- E   A research centre at the University of Reading.
- O   To study medieval history at MA and PhD level
- ● Education and training

Graduate Institute of Management and Organisation Research   (GIMOR)
- University of East London Business School, Docklands Campus, University of East London, 4-6 University Way, London, E16 2RD.
  020 8223 2202
  http://www.uel.ac.uk/gimor
  Director: Prof Kazem Chaharbaghi.
- E   An institute at the University of East London.

Graduate Institute of Political and International Studies   (GIPIS)   1965
- Whiteknights, PO Box 217, University of Reading, Reading, Berkshire, RG6 6AH.
  0118-378 8378
  http://www.reading.ac.uk/GIPIS/
- E   An institute within the University of Reading.
- O   To be one of the leading multi-disciplinary centres of teaching and research in European and international studies
- ● Education and training

Granada Centre for Visual Anthropology   (GCVA)   1987
- School of Social Sciences, University of Manchester, Roscoe Building, Oxford Road, Manchester, M13 9PL.
  0161-275 4002
  http://www.socialsciences.man.ac.uk/visualanthropology/
  Director: Prof Paul Henley.
- E   A research centre at the University of Manchester.

Grantham Institute for Climate Change   2007
- South Kensington Campus, Imperial College London, Exhibition Road, London, SW7 2AZ.
  020 7594 5477   fax 020 7594 1418
  http://www3.imperial.ac.uk/climatechange
- E   A research centre at Imperial College London.

Great Britain - China Centre   1974
- 15 Belgrave Square, London, SW1X 8PS.
  020 7235 6696   fax 020 7245 6885
  http://www.gbcc.org.uk/
  Chairman: Peter Batey, OBE.
- E   A centre of excellence.
- O   To promote understanding between Britain and China, particularly in the areas of legal and judicial reform, and labour reform

Great Chapel Street Medical Centre
- 13 Great Chapel Street, London, W1V 7AL.
  020 7437 9360   fax 020 7734 1475
Note: A statutory organisation set up to provide primary clinical and psychiatric services to single homeless people in London.

Greater Glasgow Health Board Continence Resource Centre and Helpline for Scotland   (CRC)   1989
- Central Medical Block, Southern General Hospital, 1345 Govan Road, Glasgow, G51 4TF.
  0141-201 1861   fax 0141-201 2987
  Senior Clinical Nurse Specialist: Sister Mary Ballentyne. Medical Director & Consultant Urologist: Dr Ian Ramsay.
- O   To provide a self-referral advisory service for clients with bladder dysfunction throughout the Glasgow area
- ●   Exhibitions - Information service - Training courses - Clinics for continence and management advice - Carer groups
- ¶   Annual Report. Newsletter.

Green Chemistry Centre of Excellence
- Department of Chemistry, University of York, Heslington, York, YO10 5DD.
  01904 434550   fax 01904 432705
  http://www.york.ac.uk/res/gcg/
  Administrator: Dr Helen Coombs.
- E   A research centre at the University of York.
- O   To promote the development and implementation of green and sustainable chemistry and related technologies in new products and processes

Greenwich Maritime Institute   (GMI)   1998
- Old Royal Naval College, University of Greenwich, Park Row, London, SE10 9LS.
  020 8331 8000
  http://ils-web.gre.ac.uk/schools/gmi/
  Director: Prof Sarah Palmer.
- E   A free standing institute within the University of Greenwich.
- O   To offer postgraduate programmes in maritime management, policy and history

Greenwood Institute of Child Health   1993
- University of Leicester, Westcotes House, Westcotes Drive, Leicester, LE3 0QU.
  0116-225 2885   fax 0116-225 2881
  http://www.le.ac.uk/greenwood/
- E   An institute within the University of Leicester.
- O   To conduct, supervise and manage research in child mental health and associated areas

Grid Support Centre   (GSC)   2003
- Rutherford Appleton Laboratory, Chilton, Didcot, Oxfordshire, OX11 0QX.
  01235 446822   fax 01235 445945
  http://www.grid-support.ac.uk/
  Director: Dr Neil Geddes.
- E   A research centre led and co-ordinated by the Central Laboratory of the Research Councils (CCLRC)
- O   To provide coherent electronic access, for UK researchers, to all computational and data based resources and facilities required to carry out their research, independent of resource or researcher location
Note: A collaborative venture with the Universities of Edinburgh, Leeds and Manchester. See **e-Science Centres** for further information.

Griffith Institute   1937
- Sackler Library, University of Oxford, 1 St John Street, Oxford, OX1 2LG.
  01865 278097; 278099   fax 01865 278100
  http://www.ashmolean.museum/gri/
- E   A research institute at the University of Oxford.
- O   To specialise in Egyptology and Ancient Near Eastern studies

Grubb Institute of Behavioural Studies   (The Grubb)   1969
- Cloudesley Street, London, N1 0HU.
  020 7278 8061   fax 020 7278 0728
  http://www.grubb.org.uk/
  Executive Director: Bruce Irvine.
- E   A registered charity and a company limited by guarantee.
- O   To provide a space of peace and discernment where people, organisations and institutions become energised and equipped for action in the world
- ●   Conference facilities - Education and training - Library
- ¶   Many different publications.

Gulf Centre for Strategic Studies   (GCSS)   1986
- Third Floor, 46 Gray's Inn Road, London, WC1X 8LR.
  020 7430 1367   fax 020 7404 9025
  http://www.gcss.org.bh/
- E   An independent academic research centre.
- O   To carry out studies and research on the Gulf States and related Arab and international issues - political, military, security, social and economic

Gurdon Institute of Cancer and Developmental Biology
    see **Wellcome Trust/Cancer Research UK Gurdon Institute of Cancer and Developmental Biology.**

Hadley Centre for Climate Change   1990
- ■ Meteorological Office, Hadley Centre, Fitzroy Road, Exeter, EX1 3PB.
  0870 900 0100   fax 0870 900 5050
  http://www.metoffice.gov.uk/research/hadleycentre/index.html
- E A research centre within the Meteorological Office.
- O To understand physical, chemical and biological processes within the climate system and develop state-of-the-art climate models which represent them

Haemostasis and Thrombosis Centre
- ■ Department of Haematology, University of Liverpool, Liverpool, L69 3BX.
  0151-706 3390
  http://www.liv.ac.uk/haematology/
- E A department of the University of Liverpool.
- O To direct the management of patients with a variety of bleeding and thrombotic disorders

Hallam Centre for Community Justice   (HCCJ)
- ■ Sheffield Hallam University, The Lodge, Collegiate Crescent Campus, Sheffield, S10 2BP.
  0114-225 5725
  http://www.shu.ac.uk/research/hccj/
  Director: Prof Paul Senior.
- E A research centre at Sheffield Hallam University.
- O To deliver a service to various clients throughout the community and criminal justice sector in the areas of applied research, action research, evaluations, information exchange and consultancy, and continuing professional development

Hamilton Kerr Institute   (HKI)
- ■ University of Cambridge, Whittlesford, Cambridge, CB2 4NE.
  01223 832040   fax 01223 837595
  http://www.www-hki.fitzmuseum.cam.ac.uk/
  Director: Ian McClure.
- E A department of Fitzwilliam Museum at the University of Cambridge.
- O To undertake the conservation of easel paintings for public and publicly shown collections as well as the Museum

Hampstead Garden Suburb Institute   (HGSI)   1909
- ■ Central Square, London, NW11 7BN.
  020 8455 9951   fax 020 8201 8063
  http://www.hgsi.ac.uk/
  Principal & Chief Executive: Mrs Fay Naylor. Chief Administrative Officer: Bob Bissell.
- E A registered charity and a company limited by guarantee.
- O To promote educational opportunities for people of all ages and income levels and abilities in the Suburb and elsewhere; to provide cultural and community facilities for the locality
- ● Education and training

Hang Seng Centre for Cognitive Studies   1992
- ■ Department of Philosophy, University of Sheffield, Sheffield, S10 2TN.
  http://www.philosophy.dept.shef.ac.uk/hangseng/
  Co-Director: George Botterill. Co-Director: Stephen Laurence.
- E A research centre at the University of Sheffield.
- O To promote productive collaborative research in the area of cognitive studies - in particular between philosophy and psychology

Hannah Research Institute   (HRI)   1928
- ■ Hannah Research Park, Ayr, KA6 5HL.
  01292 674000   fax 01292 674003
  http://www.hri.sari.ac.uk/
- E Part of the Hannah Research Foundation, a charitable trust.
- O To generate and integrate new knowledge for the achievement of lifelong health and the prevention of lifestyle-related diseases in Scotland

Hatter Institute for Cardiovascular Studies
see **Centre for Cardiology and The Hatter Institute for Cardiovascular Studies.**

Hazard Research Centre
see **Benfield Hazard Research Centre.**

Health Communication Research Centre   (HCRC)   1998
- ■ Cardiff School of English, Communication and Philosophy, Cardiff University, Colum Drive, Cardiff, CF10 3EU.
  029 2087 4901
  http://www.cardiff.ac.uk/encap/hcrc/
  Director: Prof Srikant Sarangi. Contact: Dr Lucy Brookes-Howell.
- E A centre at Cardiff University.
- O To co-ordinate communication and discourse based research in the broad area of health and social care in Wales and beyond

Health Economics Research Centre   (HERC)   1996
■   Department of Public Health, Old Road Campus, University of Oxford, Headington, Oxford, OX3 7LF.
     01865 226679   fax 01865 226842
     http://www.herc.ox.ac.uk/
     Director: Prof Alastair Gray.
E   A centre at the University of Oxford.
○   To perform applied and methodological research in health economics

Health Economics Resource Centre   (HERC)   1996
■   Department of Economics and Related Studies, University of York, Heslington, York, YO10 5DD.
     01904 433788   fax 01904 433759
     http://www.york.ac.uk/res/herc/
E   A centre at the University of York.
○   To be the focus for health economics teaching and research

Health and Human Sciences Research Institute   (HHSRI)
■   University of Hertfordshire, College Lane, Hatfield, Hertfordshire, AL10 9AB.
     01707 285269   fax 01707 285995
     http://perseus.herts.ac.uk/uhinfo/research/hhsri/
E   A department of the University of Hertfordshire.
○   To offer a range of courses and degrees in health and human sciences

Health Policy Management Centre
     see **Cambridge University Health - Health Policy Management Centre.**

Health Protection Agency Centre for Emergency Preparedness and Response   (CEPR)
■   Health Protection Agency, Porton Down, Salisbury, Wiltshire, SP4 0JG.
     01980 612100
     http://www.hpa.org.uk/cepr/
E   A research centre within the Health Protection Agency.
○   To prepare for and co-ordinate responses to potential healthcare emergencies, including possible acts of deliberate release; to
     conduct basic and applied research into understanding infectious diseases

Health Protection Agency Centre for Infections   (CfI)
■   Health Protection Agency, 61 Colindale Avenue, London, NW9 5EQ.
     020 8200 4400   fax 020 8200 7868
     http://www.hpa.org.uk/cfi/
E   A research centre within the Health Protection Agency.
○   To carry out a broad spectrum of work relating to prevention of infectious disease, including infectious disease surveillance,
     providing specialist and reference microbiology and microbial epidemiology, co-ordinating the investigation and cause of
     national and uncommon outbreaks, helping advise Government on the risks posed by various infections and responding to
     international health alerts
Note: The Centre is a World Health Organisation **WHO Collaborating Centre** for Haemophilus Influenzae.

Health Protection Agency Centre for Radiation, Chemical and Environmental Hazards   (CRCE)
■   Health Protection Agency, Chilton, Didcot, Oxfordshire, OX11 0RQ.
     01235 831600   fax 01235 833891
     http://www.hpa.org.uk/crce/
E   A research centre within the Health Protection Agency.
○   To undertake research so as to advance knowledge about protection from the risks of ionising and non-ionising radiations
●   Laboratory and technical services - Information - Training courses
Note: The CRCE is a World Health Organisation **WHO Collaborating Centre** for Ionizing and Non-Ionizing Radiation Protection.

Health and Rehabilitation Sciences Research Institute   (HRSRI)   1989
■   Faculty of Life and Health Sciences, Coleraine Campus, University of Ulster, Cromore Road, Coleraine, County Londonderry,
     BT52 1SA.
     028 7032 4159   fax 028 7032 4956
     http://www.science.ulster.ac.uk/hrsri/
E   A research institute at the University of Ulster.
○   To conduct research into the critical evaluation of the therapeutic practices and procedures employed by therapists in clinical
     practice

Health Sciences and Practice Subject Centre   2000
■   Room 3/12 - Waterloo Bridge Wing, King's College, London, Franklin-Wilkins Building, 150 Stamford Street, London, SE1 9NN.
     020 7848 3141   fax 020 7848 3130
     http://www.health.heacademy.ac.uk/
E   A Government funded national centre within King's College, London.
○   To foster world-class education in health sciences and practice
●   Education and training - Information service - Statistics
Note: One of the 24 Subject Centres of the Higher Education Academy, (qv).

Health Sciences Research Institute   (HSRI)
■   Warwick Medical School, University of Warwick, Gibbet Hill Road, Coventry, CV4 7AL.
     024 7657 2950   fax 024 7652 8375
     http://www2.warwick.ac.uk/fac/med/research/hsri/
E   A research institute at the University of Warwick.
O   To conduct research within the major multi-disciplinary areas of diabetes and cardiovascular disease, emergency care and
     rehabilitation, emotional and social development, health decision making, public mental health, and self management and
     patient centred care
●   Education and training - Information service

Health Services Management Centre   (HSMC)   1972
■   University of Birmingham, Park House, 40 Edgbaston Park Road, Birmingham, B15 2RT.
     0121-414 7050   fax 0121-414 7051
     http://www.hsmc.bham.ac.uk/
     Contact: Susan Alleyne.
E   A centre at the University of Birmingham.
O   To specialise in development, education and research in health and social care services in the UK

Health Services Research Centre   (HSRC)   2002
■   Faculty of Health and Life Sciences, Coventry University, Priory Street, Coventry, CV1 5FB.
     024 7688 8718   fax 024 7688 3000
     http://www.corporate.coventry.ac.uk/?d=791
     Director: Prof Louise Wallace.
E   A centre at Coventry University.
O   To contribute to the evidence base for NHS policy, management and practice and at national and local levels; to contribute to the
     evidence base for comparative international health services research

Health and Social Policy Research Centre   (HSPRC)   1991
■   Faculty of Health, University of Brighton, Mayfield House, Falmer, Brighton, East Sussex, BN1 9PH.
     http://www.brighton.ac.uk/sass/
     Director: Prof Susan Balloch, BSc, MSc.
E   A centre at the University of Brighton.

Healthcare Workforce Research Centre   (HWRC)
■   University of Surrey, Duke of Kent Building, Guildford, Surrey, GU2 7XH.
     01483 684631   fax 01483 682541
     http://www.portal.surrey.ac.uk/hwrc
     Director: Prof Karen Bryan.
E   An interdisciplinary research centre within the European Institute of Health and Medical Sciences (qv) at the University of Surrey.
O   To conduct research so as to help organisations focus on changing workforce requirements to achieve health care reform

Hearing and Balance Centre
■   Faculty of Engineering, Science and Mathematics, University of Southampton, Southampton, SO17 1BJ.
     023 8059 2294   fax 023 8059 3190
     http://www.isvr.soton.ac.uk/audiology/HABC.htm
E   A part of the Institute of Sound and Vibration Research (qv) at the University of Southampton.
O   To conduct research into the assessment and management of hearing and balance disorders; to enable clinical provision for
     profoundly deaf children and adults as provided by the South of England Cochlear Implant Centre (qv); to provide teaching
     support for short courses and the MSc in Audiology
●   Consultancy - Teaching

Hearing and Speech Centre
        see **Nuffield Hearing and Speech Centre**.

Heart Institute
        see **Bristol Heart Institute**.

Heat Treatment Centre
        see **Wolfson Heat Treatment Centre**.

Hedge Fund Centre
        see **BNP Paribas Hedge Fund Centre**.

HEFCE Centres
        see **Centres for Excellence in Teaching and Learning**.

Helen Arkell Dyslexia Centre (HADC) 1971
- Frensham, Farnham, Surrey, GU10 3BW.
  01252 792400   fax 01292 795669
  http://www.arkellcentre.org.uk/
- E   A registered charity.
- O   To maximise the educational opportunities and qualities of life for dyslexics of all ages, by providing comprehensive services for individual dyslexics, training specialist teachers, helping schools and researching more effective methods of assessment and remedial teachings

Helen Bamber Centre for the Study of Rights and Conflict   2004
- Faculty of Arts and Social Sciences, Kingston University, Penrhyn Road, Kingston-upon-Thames, Surrey, KT1 2EE.
  020 8547 2000
  http://www.kingston.ac.uk/research/centres/Helen_Bamber
- E   A research centre at Kingston University, London.
- O   To provide a forum for serious and sustained and practical reflection on major abuses of, and threats to, human rights in the modern world, and the kinds of international conflicts that often generate them
- Note: Named after Helen Bamber, a veteran human rights campaigner.

Helen Hamlyn Research Centre   1999
- Royal College of Art, Kensington Gore, London, SW7 2EU.
  020 7590 4444   fax 020 7590 4500
  http://www.hhrc.rca.ac.uk/
  Co-Director: Jeremy Myerson. Co-Director: Roger Coleman.
- E   A research centre within the Royal College of Art.
- O   To research, develop and design items which will make life easier for older people

Helen Rollason Cancer Care Centre Laboratory
- Department of Advanced Practice and Research, Anglia Ruskin University, East Road, Cambridge, CB1 1PT.
  0845 271 3333
  http://www.anglia.ac.uk/ruskin/en/home/faculties/ihsc/departments/practice_research/helen_rollason_centre.html
- E   A research centre at Anglia Ruskin University.

Hellenic Institute   1993
- Department of History and Classics, Royal Holloway, University of London, Egham, Surrey, TW20 0EX.
  01784 443086; 443311; 443791   fax 01784 433032
  http://www.rhul.ac.uk/hellenic-institute/
  Director: Julian Chrysostomides.
- E   An interdisciplinary research institute at Royal Holloway, University of London.
- O   To conduct teaching and research into the study of the language, literature, history and culture of ancient Greece and Byzantium; to promote further the study of Hellenic tradition across across the centuries, from the archaic and classical Greece, through the Hellenistic and Roman times, to Byzantium, the post-Byzantium period and the modern world

Help Counselling Centre   1968
- 57 Portobello Road, London, W11 3DB.
  020 7221 9974
  Office Manager: Miriam Szopa.
- E   A private venture.
- O   To provide one to one counselling on personal life issues, including loss and bereavement, life changes, decision making, relationship difficulties, self esteem

Henry Martyn Centre for the Study of Mission and World Christianity   (HMC)   1897
- Westminster College, University of Cambridge, Cambridge, CB3 0AA.
  01223 741120
  http://www.martynmission.cam.ac.uk/
  Director: Brian Stanley, MA, PhD.
- E   A centre at the University of Cambridge.

Heriot-Watt Institute of Petroleum Engineering   (IPE)   2002
- Heriot-Watt University, Riccarton, Edinburgh, EH14 4AS.
  0131-451 3543; 3545   fax 0131-451 3127
  http://www.pet.hw.ac.uk/
  Head: Prof Patrick Corbett.
- E   A research institute at Heriot-Watt University.
- O   To enhance the intellectual and economic wealth of the nation and the petroleum engineering community by providing leadership, innovation and the highest level of quality in its work

Heritage Motor Centre
- Banbury Road, Gaydon, Warwickshire, CV35 0BJ.
  01926 641188   fax 01926 645103
  http://www.heritage-motor-centre.co.uk/
- E   A registered charity.
- O   To preserve the heritage of the British motor industry - the Centre is the largest purpose-built transport museum in the UK

Heythrop Institute for Religion, Ethics and Public Life   (HIREPL)   2003
- ■ Heythrop College, Kensington Square, London, W8 5HQ.
  020 7795 4244
  http://www.heythrop.ac.uk/hirepl/
  Contact: Moyra Tourlamain.
- E A research institute at Heythrop College.
- ○ To promote sustained cultural analysis and dialogue and to be both a resource and a stimulus in formulating Christian responses to the many complex questions that arise on topics ranging from 'the human person' to 'the common good'

High Voltage Research Centre
  see **National Grid High Voltage Research Centre.**

Higher Education Funding Council for England
  see **Centres for Excellence in Teaching and Learning.**

Higher Education Learning Partnerships CETL   (HELP)   2005
- ■ University of Plymouth, Drake Circus, Plymouth, PL4 8AA.
  01752 238440
  http://www.help-cetl.ac.uk/
  Contact: Mark Stone.
- E A Centre for Excellence in Teaching and Learning (CETL) at the University of Plymouth.
- Note: See **Centres for Excellence in Teaching and Learning** for more information.

Higher Education Research Centre   (HERC)
- ■ Faculty of Business, Law and the Built Environment, University of Salford, Crescent House, Salford, Manchester, M5 4WT.
  0161-295 5000
  http://www.edu.salford.ac.uk/her/
- E A research centre within the Informatics Research Institute (qv) at the University of Salford.
- ○ To promote scholarship in learning and teaching, and to support research into higher educational practice and organisation

Highlands and Islands Health Research Institute
  see **Centre for Rural Health Research and Policy.**

Hispanic Research Centre   (HRC)
- ■ School of Arts, University of Roehampton, Fincham Building - 114, Roehampton Lane, London, SW15 5PH.
  020 8392 3345; 3572   fax 020 8392 3146
  http://www.roehampton.ac.uk/researchcentres/hispanic/
  Contact: Dr Isabel Santaolalla. Contact: Dr Carrie Hamilton.
- E An interdisciplinary research centre at Roehampton University.
- ○ To conduct research in a wide variety of Hispanic texts, including film and television, dictionaries, translation, oral history, and autobiography, and covering much of Spain and its historical nationalities, as well as parts of Latin America, especially Cuba

Historical Institute
  see **Marc Fitch Historical Institute.**

History and Governance Research Institute   (HAGRI)
- ■ University of Wolverhampton, Wulfruna Street, Wolverhampton, WV1 1SB.
  01902 322145
  http://www.wlv.ac.uk/hagri
  Director: Prof Mark Phythian.
- E An interdisciplinary research institute at the University of Wolverhampton.

History Centre
  see **Raphael Samuel History Centre.**

Horder Centre for Arthritis   1966
- ■ St John's Road, Crowborough, East Sussex, TN6 1XP.
  01892 665577   fax 01892 662142
  http://www.hordercentre.co.uk/
- E A registered charity.
- ○ To admit arthritic patients for further treatment of their condition and rehabilitation

Hospitality, Leisure, Sport and Tourism Network   (HLST)   2000
- ■ Wheatley Campus, Oxford Brookes University, Wheatley, Oxford, OX33 1HX.
  01865 483861   fax 01865 485830
  http://www.hlst.heacademy.ac.uk/
- E A Government funded national centre within the Oxford Brookes University.
- ○ To foster world-class education in hospitality, leisure, sport and tourism
- ● Education and training - Information service - Statistics
- ✕ LTSN Hospitality and Leisure Studies Subject Centre.
- Note: One of the 24 Subject Centres of the Higher Education Academy, (qv).

© CBD Research Ltd · Beckenham · Kent BR3 5JS · Tel 020 8650 7745 · Fax 020 8650 0768 · E-mail cbd@cbdresearch.com · www.cbdresearch.com

Huck Centre for Management Research   2006
- University of Reading Business School, University of Reading, Reading, Berkshire, RG6 6AW.
  0118-378 8226
  http://www.reading.ac.uk/business/default.asp?id=106
  President: Dr Simon Booth.
- E   Jointly established with Royal Holloway, University of London the centre is part of the University of Reading.
- O   To promote management understanding, strategic planning, practical solutions for fine tuned operations, corrective action, and bottom-line profit performance in a humanitarian setting

Hugh and Catherine Stevenson Centre for Childhood Infectious Diseases and Immunology   2007
- Institute of Child Health, University College London, 30 Guilford Street, London, WC1N 1EH.
  020 7239 3082
  http://www.ich.ucl.ac.uk/website/ich/academicunits/Infectious_diseases_and_microbiology/Custom%20Menu_03
  Development Manager: Alison Woolley.
- E   A research centre within the Institute of Child Health (qv) at University College London.
- O   To help prevent, detect and treat serious infections in children.

Hull Centre for Management Development   (HCMD)
- Lincoln Business School, University of Lincoln, Brayford Pool, Lincoln, LN6 7TS.
  01522 882000
  http://www.lincoln.ac.uk/hcmd/
- E   A research centre at the University of Lincoln.
- O   To serve the needs for part-time management and professional development programmes
- ● Education and training

Hull Environment Research Institute   (HERI)   2004
- Department of Geography, University of Hull, Cottingham Road, Hull, HU6 7RX.
  01482 466341   fax 01482 466340
  http://www.hull.ac.uk/HERI
  Director: Prof Lynne Frostick.
- E   An institute within the University of Hull.
- O   To become a centre of excellence for research across the interdisciplinary span of environmental science

Hull International Fisheries Institute   (HIFI)   1989
- Faculty of Science and the Environment, University of Hull, Cottingham Road, Hull, HU6 7RX.
  01482 466421   fax 01482 470129
  http://www.hull.ac.uk/hifi/
  Director: Prof Ian Cowx. Deputy Director: Dr J Harvey.
- E   A department of the University of Hull.
- O   To conduct research, consultancy and teaching in fisheries and aquatic resources on an international basis
- ● Education and training
- ×   University of Hull International Fisheries Institute.

Human Communication Research Centre   (HCRC)   1989
- NR   University of Edinburgh, 2 Buccleuch Place, Edinburgh, EH8 9LW.
  0131-650 4665   fax 0131-650 4587
  http://www.hcrc.ed.ac.uk/
- E   An interdisciplinary research centre at the University of Edinburgh.
- O   To conduct research in a wide range of human communication including, computational linguistics, cognitive psychology, psycholinguistics, and many aspects of artificial intelligence
Note: A joint venture with the University of Glasgow.

Human Genome Mapping Project Resource Centre
Note: No longer in existence.

Human Nutrition Research Centre   (HNRC)   1994
- School of Clinical Medical Sciences, University of Newcastle upon Tyne, 4th Floor - William Leech Building, Framlington Place, Newcastle upon Tyne, NE2 4HH.
  0191-222 7149   fax 0191-222 0723
  http://medical.faculty.ncl.ac.uk/
- E   A research centre at the University of Newcastle upon Tyne.
- O   To undertake nutrition research from the molecular level to major human intervention trails

Human Performance Centre
- Academy of Sport, Physical Activity and Wellbeing, London South Bank University, 103 Borough Road, London, SE1 0AA.
  020 7815 7594   fax 020 7815 7859
  http://lsbu.ac.uk/sports/hpc.htm
  Business Development Manager: Pat Fox.
- E   A research centre within London South Bank University.
- O   To provide the highest quality support services in sports science, physical activity and wellbeing, in an efficient and effective manner, to clients and members of the public from a variety of backgrounds

Human Resource Research Centre (HRRC) 1984
- Cranfield School of Management, Cranfield University, Cranfield, Bedfordshire, MK43 0AL.
  01234 754415   fax 01234 751806
  http://www.som.cranfield.ac.uk/som/research/centres/hrc.asp
  Director: Prof Shaun Tyson.
- E   A research centre within the Cranfield Management Research Institute (qv) at Cranfield University.
- O   To assist organisations in evaluating the effectiveness and efficiency of their human resource policies

Human Resources Management Research Centre (HRMRC) 1991
- University of Gloucester Business School, University of Gloucester, The Park, Cheltenham, Gloucestershire, GL50 2RH.
  0870 721 0210
  http://www.glos.ac.uk/faculties/ugbs/research/hrmrc.cfm
- E   A centre at the University of Gloucestershire.
- O   To undertake consultancy, training and research in the general area of human resource management

Human Rights and Social Justice Research Institute (HRSJ) 2003
- London Metropolitan University, Ladbroke House, 62-66 Highbury Grove, London, N5 2AD.
  020 7133 5055   fax 020 7133 5101
  http://www.londonmet.ac.uk/research-units/hrsj/
  Contact: Philip Leach.
- E   An interdisciplinary research institute at London Metropolitan University.
- O   To facilitate international research, policy analysis, consultancy and teaching, in a way which substantiates the link between human rights and social justice

Human Rights Centre
- School of Law, Queen's University, Belfast, 27 University Square, Belfast, BT7 1NN.
  028 9097 3141   fax 028 9097 3376
  http://www.law.qub.ac.uk/schools/SchoolofLaw/Research/HumanRightsCentre/
  Director: Prof Colin Harvey.
- E   A research centre at Queen's University, Belfast.

Human Rights Centre 1982
- Department of Law, University of Essex, Wivenhoe Park, Colchester, Essex, CO4 3SQ.
  01206 872558   fax 01206 873627
  http://www2.essex.ac.uk/human_rights_centre/
  Director: Prof Kevin Boyle.
- E   A centre at the University of Essex.
- O   To conduct research and teaching on civil and political rights, as well as international humanitarian law, and the protection of human rights in situations of armed conflict

Human Rights Centre (HRC) 2001
- Department of Law, University of Durham, 50 North Bailey, Durham, DH1 3ET.
  0191-334 2800
  http://www.dur.ac.uk/hrc/
  Co-Director: Prof H M Fenwick. Co-Director: Prof I D Leigh.
- E   A centre at the University of Durham.
- O   To co-ordinate the research activities across the whole field of the law of human rights

Human Rights Law Centre (HRLC)
- School of Law, University of Nottingham, University Park, Nottingham, NG7 2RD.
  0115-951 5700; 5701   fax 0115-951 5696
  http://www.nottingham.ac.uk/law/hrlc/
  Co-Director: Prof David Harris. Co-Director: Prof Michael O'Flaherty.
- E   A research centre at the University of Nottingham.
- O   To be committed to the promotion and protection of human rights and the establishment and strengthening of the rule of law worldwide, by means of research, training, publications and capacity building

Humanities Advanced Technology and Information Institute (HATII) 1997
- Faculty of Arts, George Service House, University of Glasgow, 11 University Gardens, Glasgow, G12 8QQ.
  0141-330 5512
  http://www.hatii.arts.gla.ac.uk/
  Director: Prof Seamus Ross. Administrator: Elaine Wilson.
- E   A department of the University of Glasgow.
- O   To actively encourage the use of information and communication technology to enhance research and teaching in the arts and humanities

Humanities and Arts Research Centre (HARC) 2002
- Royal Holloway, University of London, Egham, Surrey, TW20 0EX.
  01784 443203   fax 01784 439855
  http://www.rhul.ac.uk/research/harc/
  Director: Prof Ahuvia Kahane.
- E   A department of Royal Holloway, University of London.
- O   To foster interdisciplinary initiatives in the arts and humanities

Humanities Research Centre   (HRC)

■ Main Arts Building, University of Wales, Bangor, College Road, Bangor, Gwynedd, LL57 2DG.
01248 382133   fax 01248 388483
http://www.bangor.ac.uk/hrc
E A research centre within the Welsh Institute for Social and Cultural Affairs (qv) at the University of Wales, Bangor.

Humanities Research Centre   (HRC)   1985

■ Faculty of Arts, Room H452 (Humanities), University of Warwick, Coventry, CV4 7AL.
024 7652 3401   fax 024 7657 2997
http://www2.warwick.ac.uk/fac/arts/hrc/
Director: Prof John King. Secretary: Sue Dibben.
E A department of the University of Warwick.
○ To promote comparative and interdisciplinary research in the Humanities through the development and administration of long-term collaborative research projects, the fostering and support of medium-term individual, or small-team, research projects, the administration of a Visiting Fellowships scheme for researchers from elsewhere in the UK and abroad, the development and extension of the University's links with institutions abroad engaged in research in the Humanities, and the dissemination of the findings of research carried out with the Centre's support
● Conference facilities - Lectures - Seminars and lectures
¶ HRC Newsletter.

Humanities Research Centre   (HRC)

■ City Campus, Sheffield Hallam University, Sheffield, S1 1WB.
0114-225 4364
http://www.shu.ac.uk/research/hrc/
Contact: Prof Chris Hopkins.
E A research centre within the Cultural, Communication and Computing Research Institute (qv) at Sheffield Hallam University.
○ To bring together the work of English, history and film studies; to support the strategy and development of the three humanities areas
Note: Also known as Centre for Humanities Research.

Humanities Research Institute [Leeds]
   see **Leeds Humanities Research Institute.**

Humanities Research Institute   (HRI)

■ University of Sheffield, 34 Gell Street, Sheffield, S3 7QW.
0114-222 9890   fax 0114-222 9894
http://www.shef.ac.uk/hri/
Director: Prof D G Shepherd.
E A research institute at the University of Sheffield.
○ To promote and champion the significance and excellence of arts and humanities research conducted at the University
● Information service

Hydroenvironmental Research Centre   (HRC)   1997

■ Cardiff School of Engineering, PO Box 925, University of Wales, Cardiff, Newport Road, Cardiff, CF24 0YF.
029 2087 4280
http://www.cardiff.ac.uk/schoolsanddivisions/academicschools/engin/hydroenv/aboutus.html
Leader: Prof R A Falconer.
E An integrated research centre within the Institute of Sustainability, Energy and Environmental Management (qv) at Cardiff University.
○ To undertake research into the development, refinement and application of hydro-environmental numerical models for predicting flow, water quality, sediment and contaminant transport processes in estuarine and inland waters, and water treatment and wastewater treatment works

Hyperbaric Medical Centre
   see **Diving Diseases Research Centre Ltd.**

ICC Commercial Crime Bureau
   see **ICC Financial Investigation Bureau.**

ICC Counterfeiting Intelligence Bureau   (ICC-CIB   1985

■   Maritime House, 1 Linton Road, Barking, Essex, IG11 8HG.
   020 8591 3000   fax 020 8594 2833
   http://www.icc-ccs.org/cib/overview.php
   Director: P Mukundan. Assistant Director: Peter Lowe.
E   A specialised division of the International Chamber of Commerce.
○   To investigate and seek to prevent counterfeiting of trademarked goods and trade dress, as well as patents, copyrights and
   industrial designs and models
●   Collection of information on counterfeiters - Investigations at international level of counterfeit products - Education

ICC Financial Investigation Bureau   (ICC-FIB   1994

■   Maritime House, 1 Linton Road, Barking, Essex, IG11 8HG.
   020 8591 3000   fax 020 8594 2833
   http://www.icc-ccs.org/fib/overview.php
   Director: P Mukundan. Assistant Director: Jon Merrett.
E   A specialised division of the International Chamber of Commerce.
○   To deal with frauds and malpractice in both the public and private sectors
✕   ICC Commercial Crime Bureau.

ICC International Maritime Bureau   (ICC-IMB   1981

■   Maritime House, 1 Linton Road, Barking, Essex, IG11 8HG.
   020 8591 3000   fax 020 8594 2833
   http://www.icc-ccs.org/imb/overview.php
   Director: P Mukundan. Assistant Director: M Howlett.
E   A specialised division of the International Chamber of Commerce.
○   To deal with frauds and suspect practices during transport, in port and on board ships; to provide advice on security

IDEA CETL   2005

■   University of Leeds, Leeds, LS2 9JT.
   0113-243 1751
   http://www.idea.leeds.ac.uk/
   Director: Chris Megone.
E   A Centre for Excellence in Teaching and Learning (CETL) at the University of Leeds.
Note: IDEAS = Inter-disciplinary Ethics Across Subject Disciplines. See **Centres for Excellence in Teaching and Learning** for more
   information.

Illicit Antiquities Research Centre   (IARC)   1996

■   University of Cambridge, Downing Street, Cambridge, CB2 3ER.
   01223 339291   fax 01223 333536
   http://www.mcdonald.cam.ac.uk/iarc/home.htm
   Research Director: Dr Neil Brodie.
E   A research centre within the McDonald Institute for Archaeological Research (qv) at the University of Cambridge.
○   To monitor and report upon the detrimental effects of the international trade in illicit antiquities (ie antiquities which have been
   stolen or clandestinely excavated and illegally exported)

Impact Assessment Research Centre   (IARC)   1999

■   School of Environment and Development, Harold Hankins Building, University of Manchester, Booth Street West, Manchester,
   M13 9QH.
   0161-275 2807   fax 0161-275 0423
   http://www.sed.manchester.ac.uk/research/iarc/
   Director: Prof Colin Kirkpatrick.
E   A research centre within the Institute for Development Policy and Management (qv) at the University of Manchester.
○   To specialise in the integrated assessment of the economic, social and environmental impacts on sustainable development of
   national, regional and international policies

Impact Centre
   see **Cranfield Impact Centre.**

Impact Research Centre   1985

■   Department of Engineering, University of Liverpool, Brownlow Hill, Liverpool, L69 3GH.
   0151-794 6801   fax 0151-794 4930
   http://www.liv.ac.uk/engdept/research/index.htm#impact
E   A research centre at the University of Liverpool.
○   To integrate several disciplines which contribute to the understanding of those problems involving the large dynamic loading
   responsive and failure of materials and structures which occur throughout the field of engineering

Imperial College Centre for Interfacial Science and Technology
- ■ Department of Chemistry, Flowers Building, Imperial College London, Armstrong Road, London, SW7 2AZ.
  020 7594 5797   fax 020 7594 5801
  http://www3.imperial.ac.uk/courses/azofdepartmentsandcentres/interfacialscienceandtechnology
  Co-ordinator: Dr John M Seddon.
- E An interdisciplinary research centre at Imperial College London.
- O To provide a focus for researchers on various types of interfaces

Inclusive Design Research Centre
   see **Surface: Inclusive Design Research Centre.**

Inclusivity in Contemporary Music Culture CETL   2005
- NR School of Arts and Cultures, Armstrong Building, University of Newcastle upon Tyne, Newcastle upon Tyne, NE1 7RU.
  0191-222 5336; 6736   fax 0191-222 5242
  http://www.ncl.ac.uk/sacs/
  Director: Dr Ian Biddle.
- E A Centre for Excellence in Teaching and Learning (CETL) at the University of Newcastle upon Tyne.
- Note: See International Centre for Music Studies for more information. A joint venture with the Universities of Durham, Northumbria, Sunderland, Teesside and the Open University.

Incredible Years Wales Centre
   see **Welsh Centre for Promoting the Incredible Years Programmes.**

India Centre
   see **Aditya V Birla India Centre.**

India and South Asia Business Centre   (ISABC)   2003
- ■ Leeds University Business School, Maurice Keyworth Building, University of Leeds, Leeds, LS2 9JT.
  0113-343 4492
  http://lubswww.leeds.ac.uk/isabc/
  Director: Dr Malcolm K Chapman.
- E A research centre within the University of Leeds.
- O To contribute to the increase in knowledge of understanding in international business and management in India and South Asia

Industrial Centre of Particle Science and Engineering   (ICPSE)
- ■ School of Process, Environmental and Materials Engineering, Houldsworth Building, University of Leeds, Clarendon Road, Leeds, LS2 9JT.
  0113-343 2379
  http://www.particletechnology.org
  Director: Simon Lawson. Administrator: Lorraine Bate.
- E A research centre within the Institute of Particle Science and Engineering (qv) at the University of Leeds.
- O To provide contract solutions for industrial needs in particle and colloid technology

Industrial Control Centre
- ■ Department of Electronic and Electrical Engineering, Royal College Building, University of Strathclyde, 204 George Street, Glasgow, G1 1XW.
  0141-548 2350
  http://www.icc.strath.ac.uk/
- E A research centre at the University of Strathclyde.

Industrial Process Tomography Centre   (IPT)
- ■ School of Chemical Engineering and Analytical Sciences, University of Manchester, Oxford Road, Manchester, M13 9PL.
  0161-306 6000
  http://www.tomography.manchester.ac.uk/
- E A virtual interdisciplinary research centre at the University of Manchester.

Industrial Psychology Research Centre   (IPRC)   1986
- ■ School of Psychology, William Guild Building, University of Aberdeen, Aberdeen, AB24 2UB.
  01224 273210   fax 01224 273211
  http://www.abdn.ac.uk/iprc/
  Director: Prof Rhona Flin.
- E A centre at the University of Aberdeen.

Inflammation Research Centre   (IRC)
- ■ School of Medicine and Dentistry, Whitla Medical Building, Queen's University, Belfast, 97 Lisburn Road, Belfast, BT9 7BL.
  028 9097 5778   fax 028 9033 0571
  http://www.ciir.qub.ac.uk/
- E A centre at Queen's University, Belfast.
- O To study various types of inflammation in the fields of arthritis, immunology, respiration, trauma, neurovirology and multiple sclerosis, and bacterial pathogenesis and genomics

Informatics Research Institute   (IRIS)

- Salford Business School, Maxwell Building, University of Salford, Salford, Manchester, M5 4WT.
  0161-295 5923
  http://www.iris.salford.ac.uk/
  Director: Prof Yacine Rezqui. Research Officer: Nathalie Audren Howarth.
- E   A department of the University of Salford.
- O   To pursue the vision of a sustainable knowledge society supported by novel information communication technology-enabled physical as well as virtual modes of socialisation, communication and collaboration across disparate geographical locations and time zones

Informatics Research Institute   (IRI)

- 2nd Floor - Devonshire Building, University of Newcastle upon Tyne, Newcastle upon Tyne, NE1 7RU.
  0191-246 4936   fax 0191-246 4905
  http://www.ncl.ac.uk/iri/
  Director: Michael Harrison.
- E   A research institute within the University of Newcastle upon Tyne.
- O   To bring together academics, from the full spectrum of engineering, mathematical, physical, life and social sciences, to conduct informatics research

Informatics and Technology Research Institute   (ITRI)

- Faculty of Computing, Engineering and Technology, Staffordshire University, Stoke-on-Trent, ST4 2DF.
  01782 294000
  http://www.fcet.staffs.ac.uk/research/res_institute.htm
- E   A research institute at Staffordshire University.

Information and Biomedical Engineering Research Centre   (IBEC)   1985

- Department of Engineering, Tait Building, City University, Northampton Square, London, EC1V 0HB.
  020 7040 0113
  http://www.city.ac.uk/sems/research/ibec/
  Co-Director: Dr P Liatsis. Co-Director: Dr P A Kyriacou.
- E   A centre at City University.
- O   To undertake theoretical and applied research in biomedical engineering, image analysis, intelligent systems, communications and networks

Information Centre about Asylum and Refugees in the UK   (ICAR)

- School of Social Sciences, City University, Northampton Square, London, EC1V 0HB.
  020 7040 4596
  http://www.icar.org.uk/
  Chairman: Lord Browne-Wilkinson.
- E   An independent information and research organisation at City University.
- O   To increase public understanding of asylum issues in the UK, and to improve policy and practice through applied research and policy evaluation

Information Integrity Research Centre
     see **Computer Security and Audit Centre.**

Information Research Institute   (TIRI)

- Department of Information and Communications, Geoffrey Manton Building, Manchester Metropolitan University, Rosamond Street West, Manchester, M15 6LL.
  0161-247 6144   fax 0161-247 6351
  http://www.tiri.mmu.ac.uk/
  Director: Prof Dick Hartley.
- E   A research institute at Manchester Metropolitan University.
- O   To focus on techniques and processes of acquiring, storing, transmitting and exploiting information

Information Systems, Organisation and Society Research Centre   (ISOS)

- Faculty of Business, Law and the Built Environment, Maxwell Building, University of Salford, Salford, Manchester, M5 4WT.
  0161-295 5262; 5278
  http://www.iris.salford.ac.uk/
  Director: Prof Alison Adam.
- E   A research centre within the Informatics Research Institute (qv) at the University of Salford.
- O   To bring together those interested in researching the social and organisational aspects of information systems

Information Systems Research Centre   (ISRC)   1993

- Cranfield School of Management, Cranfield University, Cranfield, Bedfordshire, MK43 0AL.
  01234 754498   fax 01234 752691
  http://www.som.cranfield.ac.uk/som/research/centres/isrc/
  Director: Prof Joe Peppard. Contact: Maggie Bridge.
- E   A research centre within the Cranfield Management Research Institute (qv) at Cranfield University.
- O   To research and study the rapidly developing area of information systems, and thus to understand how the new technology can be of maximum use to businesses

Information Technology Innovation Centre
    see **IT Innovation Centre.**

Information Technology Research Institute
Note: Closed in 2005.

Infrastructure Engineering and Management Research Centre
■   Department of Civil Engineering, University of Birmingham, Edgbaston, Birmingham, B15 2TT.
      0121 414 5067   fax 0121 414 3675
      http://www.iem.bham.ac.uk/
      Contact: Prof Chris Baker.
E   A research centre at the University of Birmingham.
○   The Centre has three research themes: Engineering computation (to bring together and create a common focus for those members
      of staff of Civil Engineering with an expertise or interest in computational work); Infrastructure engineering and management
      research (to explore all aspects of creating and maintaining railways, roads, bridges, cuttings and embankments, sewers, rivers
      and canals, pipelines, tunnels, buildings and other structures) and water engineering, wind engineering and environmental
      management (to cover all aspects of the interrelationship between engineering and the natural environment).

Ingeborg Bachmann Centre for Austrian Literature   2002
■   School of Advanced Study, Senate House, University of London, Malet Street, London, WC1E 7HU.
      020 7862 8959   fax 020 7862 8672
      http://igrs.sas.ac.uk/
      Contact: Dr Martin Liebscher.
E   A research centre within the Institute of Germanic and Romance Studies (qv) at the University of London.
○   To conduct research on Austrian culture and literature

Innogen - ESRC Centre for Social and Economic Research on Innovation in Genomics   (Innogen)   2002
NR   University of Edinburgh, Old Surgeons' Hall, High School Yards, Edinburgh, EH1 1LZ.
      0131-650 9113   fax 0131-651 4278
      http://www.innogen.ac.uk/
E   A research centre within the Institute for the Study of Science, Technology and Innovation (qv) at the University of Edinburgh.
○   To enable social scientists and the Economic and Social Research Council to take a leading role in policy, public and innovation-
      related debates on life science issues; to contribute to the shaping of the biotechnology trajectory along with other research
      councils, from a well informed, evidence-based position
Note: A joint venture with the Open University. Also known as ESRC Innogen Centre.

Innogen - ESRC Centre for Social and Economic Research on Innovation in Genomics   (Innogen)   2002
NR   Faculty of Technology, Open University, Walton Hall, Milton Keynes, MK7 6AA.
      01908 654782   fax 01908 654825
      http://www.innogen.ac.uk/
E   A research centre within the Centre for Technology Strategy (qv) at the Open University.
Note: A joint venture with the University of Edinburgh (see above).

Innovate - Centre for Creative Industries   (INNOVATE)
■   Unit 301 - Tamar Science Park, University of Plymouth, 1 Davy Road, Plymouth, PL6 8BX.
      01752 764486   fax 01752 764487
      http://www.innovatecentre.co.uk/
      Director: Martin Woolner.
E   A research centre at the University of Plymouth.
○   To foster productive and progressive research and commercialisation opportunities, ideas exchange and technology transfer

Innovation Centre
    see **William Lee Innovation Centre.**

Innovation Studies Centre   (ISC)   2003
■   Department of Civil and Environmental Engineering, Imperial College London, Exhibition Road, London, SW7 2AZ.
      020 7589 5111   fax 020 7594 6102
      http://www.imperial.ac.uk/innovationstudies/
E   A department of Imperial College London.

Innovative Construction Research Centre   (ICRC)   2002
NR   School of Construction Management and Engineering, Whiteknights, PO Box 219, University of Reading, Reading, Berkshire,
      RG6 6AW.
      0118-378 7181   fax 0118-931 3856
      http://www.icrc-reading.org/
      Director: Prof Stuart Green. Contact: Elizabeth Holloman.
E   An EPSRC Innovative Manufacturing Research Centre at the University of Reading.
○   To work collaboratively with leading players in the construction sector to encourage the development of a knowledge-based
      industry responsive to change
Note: One of the EPSRC funded centres in the UK - for further information see EPSRC Innovative Manufacturing Research Centres.

Innovative Electronics Manufacturing Research Centre   (IeMRC)
NR   Wolfson School of Mechanical and Manufacturing Engineering, Loughborough University, Loughborough, Leicestershire, LE11 3TU.
        01509 227614; 227688   fax 01509 227615
        http://www.lboro.ac.uk/research/iemrc/
        Industrial Director: Dr Maryin Goosey. Academic Director: Prof Paul Conway.
E   An EPSRC Innovative Manufacturing Research Centre at Loughborough University.
O   To be a centre of expertise through which UK industry can access and influence research in electronics manufacturing
Note: One of the EPSRC funded centres in the UK - for further information see EPSRC Innovative Manufacturing Research Centres. The IeMRC is a joint venture with the Universities at Bath, Brunel, Greenwich, Lancaster, Sheffield, and Strathclyde.

Innovative Manufacturing Centres
        see **EPSRC Innovative Manufacturing Research Centres**.

Innovative Manufacturing and Construction Research Centre
        see **Loughborough Innovative Manufacturing and Construction Research Centre.**

Innovative Manufacturing Research Centre [Cardiff]
        see **Cardiff University Innovative Manufacturing Research Centre.**

Innovative Manufacturing Research Centre [Cranfield]
        see **Cranfield Innovative Manufacturing Research Centre.**

Innovative Manufacturing Research Centre - Engineering IMRC   (IMRC)
NR   Faculty of Engineering and Design, University of Bath, Claverton Down, Bath, BA2 7AY.
        01225 384026; 386371; 388388   fax 01225 386928
        http://www.bath.ac.uk/eimrc/
        Director: Prof Chris McMahon.
E   An EPSRC Innovative Manufacturing Research Centre at the University of Bath.
O   To focus on world-leading research into the design & manufacture of machines, systems and processes
Note: One of the EPSRC funded centres in the UK - for further information see EPSRC Innovative Manufacturing Research Centres.

Innovative Manufacturing Research Centre (IMRC) for Bioprocessing   (IMRC)
NR   Department of Biochemical Engineering, University College London, Torrington Place, London, WC1E 7JE.
        020 7679 7031   fax 020 7209 0703
        http://www.ucl.ac.uk/biochemeng/industry/imrc.htm
        Director: Prof Mike Hoare.
E   An EPSRC Innovative Manufacturing Research Centre at University College London.
O   To focus on new ways of speeding the translation of discoveries in the life sciences to practical outcomes, especially advanced medicines
Note: One of the EPSRC funded centres in the UK - for further information see EPSRC Innovative Manufacturing Research Centres.

Innovative Manufacturing Research Centre - Management IMRC   (IMRC)
NR   School of Management, University of Bath, Claverton Down, Bath, BA2 7AY.
        01225 386473; 386689   fax 01225 386135
        http://www.bath.ac.uk/imrc/
        Co-Director: Prof Andrew Graves. Co-Director: Prof Christine Harland.
E   An EPSRC Innovative Manufacturing Research Centre at the University of Bath.
O   To focus on agility, lean manufacturing processes and supply networks
Note: One of the EPSRC funded centres in the UK - for further information see EPSRC Innovative Manufacturing Research Centres. IMRC = Innovative Manufacturing Research Centre.

InQbate The Centre of Excellence in Teaching and Learning in Creativity   (InQbate)   2005
NR   School of Science and Technology, University of Sussex, Falmer, Brighton, East Sussex, BN1 9QT.
        01273 678793
        http://www.sussex.ac.uk/cetl/
        Director: Prof Peter Childs.
E   A Centre for Excellence in Teaching and Learning (CETL) at the University of Sussex.
Note: A joint initiative with the University of Brighton. See **Centres for Excellence in Teaching and Learning** for more information.

Institut français   (IFRU)   1910
■   17 Queensberry Place, London, SW7 2DT.
        020 7073 1350   fax 020 7073 1355
        http://www.institut-francais.org.uk/
        Director: Olivier Chambard.
E   Established by the French Government.
O   To promote French language and culture

Institute for Accelerator Science
        see **John Adams Institute for Accelerator Science.**

© CBD Research Ltd · Beckenham · Kent BR3 5JS · Tel 020 8650 7745 · Fax 020 8650 0768 · E-mail cbd@cbdresearch.com · www.cbdresearch.com

Institute for Access Studies   (IAS)

- Brindley Building, Staffordshire University, Leek Road, Stoke-on-Trent, ST4 2DF.
  01782 295731   fax 01782 295752
  http://www.staffs.ac.uk/institutes/access/
  Director: Prof Peter Davies.
- E   A sub-group of the Institute for Education Policy Research (qv) at Staffordshire University.
- O   To focus on widening participation in post-compulsory education; to promote lifelong learning amongst non-traditional learners

Institute for Adaptive and Neural Computation   (ANC)

- School of Informatics, University of Edinburgh, Appleton Tower, Crichton Street, Edinburgh, EH8 9LE.
  0131-650 2690   fax 0131-651 1426
  http://www.inf.ed.ac.uk/research/ianc/
  Director:
- E   A research institute at the University of Edinburgh.
- O   To study brain processes and artificial learning systems, theoretically and empirically, drawing on the disciplines of neuroscience, cognitive science, computer science, computational science, mathematics and statistics

Institute of Advanced Legal Studies   (IALS)   1946

- School of Advanced Study, University of London, Charles Clore House, 17 Russell Square, London, WC1B 5DR.
  020 7862 5800   fax 020 7862 5850
  http://ials.sas.ac.uk/
  Director: Prof Avrom Sherr. Associate Director & Librarian: Jules Winterton.
- E   A department of the University of London.
- O   To promote and facilitate research and scholarship at an advanced level across the whole field of law; to disseminate the results of such research and scholarship; to provide a library facility, international in character and standing, to all those undertaking research in law
- ●   Conference facilities - Education and training - Information service - Library
- ¶   Annual Report. Amicus Cumae (newsletter).

Institute of Advanced Materials and Energy Systems

- Cardiff School of Engineering, Queen's Buildings, Cardiff University, Newport Road, Cardiff, CF24 3AA.
  029 2087 5951
  http://www.engin.cf.ac.uk/research/institute.asp?InstNo=6
  Leader: Prof David C Jiles.
- E   A research institute at Cardiff University.
- O   To carry out research within the broad themes of magnetic technology and sensors, and electrical energy systems and nano-technology

Institute of Advanced Musical Studies   (IAMS)

- Department of Music, King's College London, Strand, London, WC2R 2LS.
  020 7848 2384
  http://www.kcl.ac.uk/humanities/music/res/
  Director: Dr Daniel Chua.
- E   A research institute at King's College, London.

Institute for Advanced Studies in the Humanities   (IASH)   1969

- University of Edinburgh, Hope Park Square, Edinburgh, EH8 9NW.
  0131-650 4671   fax 0131-668 2252
  http://www.iash.ed.ac.uk/
  Director: Prof Susan Manning.
- E   A research institute at the University of Edinburgh.
- O   To promote interdisciplinary research in the humanities and social sciences

Institute for Advanced Studies in the Humanities [Kent]
   see **Kent Institute for Advanced Studies in the Humanities.**

Institute for Advanced Studies in Social and Management Sciences   (IAS)   2005

- Lancaster University, County South, Bailrigg, Lancaster, LA1 4YD.
  01524 510816   fax 01524 510857
  http://www.lancaster.ac.uk/ias/
  Director: Bob Jessop.
- E   A multidisciplinary research institute within Lancaster University.
- O   To conduct research in management, social sciences, the arts and humanities

Institute of Advanced Study   (IAS)   2006

- University of Durham, 77 Hallgarth Street, Durham, DH1 3AY.
  0191-334 2589   fax 0191-334 2501
  http://www.dur.ac.uk/ias/
  Executive Director: Prof Ash Amin.
- E   A think tank and part of the University of Durham.
- O   To examine themes of major intellectual, scientific, political and practical significance

Institute of Advanced Telecommunications (IAT) 2007
■ Swansea University, Singleton Park, Swansea, SA2 8PP.
01792 205678
http://www.swan.ac.uk/iat/
Contact: Prof Jaafar Elmirghani.
E A research institute at Swansea University.
Note: In process of formation.

Institute for the Advancement of University Learning
see **Oxford Learning Institute.**

Institute for Aeronautics
see **Sir Arthur Marshall Institute for Aeronautics.**

Institute of Ageing
see **Oxford Institute of Ageing.**

Institute for Ageing and Health (IAH) 1994
■ School of Neurology, Neurobiology and Psychiatry, Newcastle General Hospital, Newcastle upon Tyne, NE4 6BE.
0191-256 3014   fax 0191-256 3011
http://www.ncl.ac.uk/iah/
Co-Director: Prof Tom Kirkwood. Co-Director: Prof Jim Edwardson.
E A research institute within the Wolfson Research Centre (qv) at the University of Newcastle upon Tyne.
○ To bring together basic, clinical and social scientists in research on ageing, age-related disorders, and the health and welfare of older people

Institute of Agricultural Management (IAgrM) 1966
■ Farm Management Unit, University of Reading, Reading, Berkshire, RG6 6AR.
0118-378 6578   fax 0118-975 6467
http://www.rdg.ac.uk/iagrm/
Director: David Ansell.
E A registered charity, an independent non-profit distributing organisation and part of University of Reading.
○ To promote high standards in the practice and business of management in agriculture; to promote training, and to encourage the provision and attainment of professional qualifications in the principles and practice of management of agriculture
● Conferences - Education and training - Information service - Workshops and local discussion groups - The Institute also maintains a Register for those managing in agriculture

Institute of Agri-Food and Land Use
■ School of Biological Sciences, Queen's University, Belfast, 97 Lisburn Road, Belfast, BT9 7BL.
028 9097 5787   fax 028 9097 5877
http://www.qub.ac.uk/schools/Agri-FoodLandUse/Research/
Director: Prof Jenny Ames.
E A research institute at Queen's University, Belfast.

Institute of Alcohol Studies (IAS) 1982
■ Alliance House, 12 Caxton Street, London, SW1H 0QS.
020 7222 4001   fax 020 7799 2510
http://www.ias.org.uk/
Director: Derek Rutherford. Director: A McNeill.
E A registered charity.
○ To prevent alcohol abuse
● Information - Library
¶ Alcohol Alert (newsletter). The Globe (journal). Factsheets.

Institute for Animal Health (IAH) 1988
■ Compton Laboratory, Compton, Newbury, Berkshire, RG20 7NN.
01635 578411   fax 01635 577237
http://www.iah.bbsrc.ac.uk/
E An independent non-profit-distributing organisation and a registered charity.
○ To deliver high quality fundamental, strategic and applied science research into infectious animal disease; to advance veterinary and medical science, enhance the sustainability of livestock farming, improve animal welfare; to safeguard the supply and safety of food, and protect public health and the environment
● Education and training

Institute for Applied Cognitive Science (IACS)
■ Faculty of Science, University of Warwick, Coventry, CV4 7AL.
024 7652 3537
http://www2.warwick.ac.uk/fac/sci/psych/research/facilities/iacs/
Director: Prof Nick Chater.
E A research institute at the University of Warwick.

© CBD Research Ltd · Beckenham · Kent BR3 5JS · Tel 020 8650 7745 · Fax 020 8650 0768 · E-mail cbd@cbdresearch.com · www.cbdresearch.com

Institute of Applied Ethics   (IAE)

■ Faculty of Arts and Social Sciences, Room 278 - Wilberforce Building, University of Hull, Cottingham Road, Hull, HU6 7RX.
  01482 465184
  http://www.hull.ac.uk/IAE/
  Director: Dr Suzanne Uniacke.
E A research institute at the University of Hull.

Institute of Applied Health Sciences   (IAHS)   1999

■ School of Medical Sciences, Polwarth Building, University of Aberdeen, Aberdeen, AB25 2ZD.
  01224 552479   fax 01224 550925
  http://www.abdn.ac.uk/iahs/
  Director: Prof Phil Hannaford.
E A research institute at the University of Aberdeen.
○ To improve health and health care delivery through excellence in applied health sciences research

Institute for Applied Language Studies   (IALS)   1979

■ College of Humanities and Social Science, University of Edinburgh, 21 Hill Place, Edinburgh, EH8 9DP.
  0131-650 6200   fax 0131-667 5927
  http://www.ials.ed.ac.uk/
  Director: Eric H Glendinning.
E A self-funding unit at the University of Edinburgh.
○ To conduct English language teaching, modern language teaching, and teacher education and research

Institute of Applied Macroeconomics
   see **Julian Hodge Institute of Applied Macroeconomics.**

Institute for Applied Social Research   (IASR)

■ Luton Campus, University of Bedfordshire, Luton, Bedfordshire, LU1 3JU.
  01234 400400
  http://www.beds.ac.uk/research/iasr/
E A research institute at the University of Bedfordshire.
○ To generate high quality research that anticipates and informs policy, administration and practice in the areas of social work, social care, youth work, special education, occupational health, youth justice, and community safety

Institute of Applied Social Studies

■ School of Social Sciences, The Terrace Huts, Edgbaston, University of Birmingham, Birmingham, B15 2TT.
  0121-414 2676
  http://www.spsw.bham.ac.uk/
  Contact: Sue Abbey.
E A research institute at the University of Birmingham.
○ To conduct research and teaching in the fields of social policy, social care, and health and professional practice

Institute of Aquaculture   (IOA)

■ University of Stirling, Stirling, FK9 4LA.
  01786 467878   fax 01786 472133
  http://www.aquaculture.stir.ac.uk/
  Director: Prof R H Richards.
E A department of the University of Stirling.
○ To study and research all aspects of aquaculture
● Teaching

Institute of Arab and Islamic Studies   (IAIS)   1999

■ School of Humanities and Social Sciences, Stocker Road, University of Exeter, Exeter, EX4 4ND.
  01392 264036   fax 01392 264035
  http://www.huss.ex.ac.ukk/iais/
  Head: Prof Rasheed El-Enany. Contact: Catherine Bell.
E A department of the University of Exeter.
○ To focus research in Middle East politics, economics, social history and culture, Arabic literature, linguistics and historiography, Islamic theology and intellectual history, Sufism, Islam in the modern world, and Gulf studies

Institute of Arable Crops Research
   see **Rothamsted Research.**

Institute for Archaeo-Metallurgical Studies   (IAMS)

■ Faculty of Social and Historical Sciences, University College London, 31-34 Gordon Square, London, WC1H 0PY.
  020 7679 4918
  http://www.ucl.ac.uk/iams/
  Director: Prof Beno Rothenburg.
E A research institute within the UCL Institute of Archaeology (qv) at University College London.
○ To initiate and promote research into the origins and developments of metallurgy and its culture-historical significance, from its earliest, prehistoric beginnings to present times

Institute for Archaeological Research
　　see **McDonald Institute for Archaeological Research.**

Institute of Archaeology [London]
　　see **UCL Institute of Archaeology.**

Institute of Archaeology   1962
- School of Archaeology, University of Oxford, 36 Beaumont Street, Oxford, OX1 2PG.
　　01865 278240   fax 01865 278254
　　http://www.archinst.ox.ac.uk/
　　Director: Dr Gary Lock.
- E　A department of the University of Oxford.
- O　To offer a vibrant environment in which to conduct research in archaeology

Institute of Archaeology and Antiquity   (IAA)
- Arts Building, University of Birmingham, Edgbaston, Birmingham, B15 2TT.
　　0121-414 5497   fax 0121-414 3595
　　http://www.iaa.bham.ac.uk/
　　Director: Prof Ken Dowden.
- E　A department of the University of Birmingham.
- O　To conduct research into archaeology and antiquity arranged around six main research themes - the city, editing and interpreting courses, the individual in society, landscape and the environment, reception of the past, and warfare and catastrophe

Institute of Architecture   (IoA)
- School of the Built Environment, University of Nottingham, University Park, Nottingham, NG7 2RD.
　　0115-951 3134
　　http://www.nottingham.ac.uk/sbe/research/research_architecture.php
- E　An institute within the University of Nottingham.
- O　To organise and run a range of undergraduate and postgraduate courses in architecture

Institute for Archives
　　see **Borthwick Institute for Archives.**

Institute of Art and Design
　　see **Birmingham Institute of Art and Design.**

Institute for Art History   (IAH)   1998
- Department of History of Art, University of Glasgow, 8 University Gardens, Glasgow, G12 8QQ.
　　0141-330 5677   fax 0141-330 3513
　　http://www.iah.arts.gla.ac.uk/
　　Director: Prof Nick Pearce.
- E　An institute at the University of Glasgow.
- O　To provide a framework for art historical studies at the University, with related institutions in Glasgow and elsewhere

Institute for the Arts, Social Sciences and Humanities
　　see **Newcastle Institute for the Arts, Social Sciences and Humanities.**

Institute for Arts in Therapy and Education   (IATE)
- 2-18 Britannia Row, London, N1 8PA.
　　020 7704 2534   fax 020 7704 0171
　　http://www.artspsychotherapy.org/
　　Director: Margot Sutherland. Head of Studies: Dr Kenneth Pickering.
- E　An independent non-profit educational organisation and a company limited by guarantee.
- O　To advance integrated arts psychotherapy and related subjects
- ●　Conference facilities - Education and training

Institute of Asia-Pacific Studies   (IAPS)   1994
- School of Politics and International Relations, University of Nottingham, University Park, Nottingham, NG7 2RD.
　　0115-951 4862   fax 0115-951 4859
　　http://www.nottingham.ac.uk/iaps/
　　Chairman: Prof Chris Pierson. Deputy Director: Dr Pauline Eadie.
- E　A research institute at the University of Nottingham.
- O　To conduct research in a wide variety of Asia-Pacific topics

Institute of Astronomy   (IoA)   1823

■   The Observatories, University of Cambridge, Madingley Road, Cambridge, CB3 0HA.
   01223 337548   fax 01223 337523
   http://www.ast.cam.ac.uk/
   Director: Prof G P Efstathiou. Secretary: P M Aslin.
E   A department of the University of Cambridge.
○   To conduct research and teaching in all aspects of astronomy
●   Library - Education and training

Institute for Astronomy   (IfA)

■   School of Physics, Royal Observatory, University of Edinburgh, Blackford Hill, Edinburgh, EH9 3HJ.
   0131-668 8356   fax 0131-668 8416
   http://www.roe.ac.uk/ifa/
   Head: Prof James S Dunlop. Contact: Mrs E Gibson.
E   An institute within the University of Edinburgh.

Institute of Atmospheric and Environmental Science   (IAES)

■   Crew Building, The King's Buildings, University of Edinburgh, West Mains Road, Edinburgh, EH9 3JU.
   0131-650 6708   fax 0131-662 0478
   http://www.ed.ac.uk/
E   A department of the University of Edinburgh.
○   To carry out teaching and research in agriculture, ecology, environmental science, forestry, global environmental change, and
   resource economics
●   Conference facilities - Education and training - Exhibitions - Information service - Library - Recreational facilities - Statistics
✕   Institute of Ecology and Resource Management.

Institute for Atmospheric Science   (IAS)

■   School of Earth and Environment, University of Leeds, Leeds, LS2 9JT.
   0113-343 5222; 6461   fax 0113-343 5259; 6716
   http://www.see.leeds.ac.uk/research/ias/
   Director of Research: Prof Ken Carslaw.
E   A department of the University of Leeds.

Institute for Automotive and Manufacturing Advanced Practice   (AMAP)

■   School of Computing and Technology, Edinburgh Building, University of Sunderland, Chester Road, Sunderland, Tyne and Wear,
   SR1 3SD.
   0191-515 3888   fax 0191-515 3377
   http://www.amap.sunderland.ac.uk/
E   A research institute at the University of Sunderland.
○   To conduct research and provide solutions to manufacturers within niche areas of the automotive manufacturing sector

Institute for Aviation and the Environment   (IAE)

■   Department of Applied Mathematics and Theoretical Physics, University of Cambridge, Wilberforce Road, Cambridge, CB3 0WA.
   http://www.iae.damtp.cam.ac.uk/
   Director: Prof Peter Haynes.
E   An institute at the University of Cambridge.
○   To conduct research into the impact of aviation on the environment

Institute of Behavioural Neuroscience   (IBN)

■   Department of Psychology, University College London, 26 Bedford Way, London, WC1H 0AP.
   020 7679 5308
   http://www.ucl.ac.uk/ibn/
   Director: Dr K J Jeffery.
E   An interdisciplinary research institute at University College London.
○   To facilitate communication among researchers interested in how low-level neural processes collectively translate to high-level
   processes such as behaviour, thinking, emotion and consciousness

Institute of Behavioural Studies
      see **Grubb Institute of Behavioural Studies.**

Institute for Biocomplexity
      see **Liverpool Institute for Biocomplexity.**

Institute of Bioelectronic and Molecular Microsystems   (IBMM)

■   Schools of Electronic Engineering and Computer Science, University of Wales, Bangor, Dean Street, Bangor, Gwynedd, LL57 1UT.
   01248 382010   fax 01248 361429
   http://www.ibmm-microtech.co.uk/
   Commercial Manager: Mick Card.
E   A research institute at the University of Wales, Bangor.

Institute for Bioengineering
      see **Brunel Institute for Bioengineering.**

Institute of Biological Anthropology
Note: The activities of the Institute are suspended.

Institute of Biological Sciences   (IBS)
■   Edward Llwyd Building, University of Wales, Aberystwyth, Aberystwyth, Ceredigion, SY23 3DA.
     01970 622316   fax 01970 622350
     http://www.aber.ac.uk/biology/
     Director: Dr J D Fish.
E   A research institute within the Aberystwyth BioCentre (qv) at the University of Wales, Aberystwyth.
○   To conduct research in ecology and the environment

Institute of Biomedical and Biomolecular Sciences   (IBBS)
■   St Michael's Building, University of Portsmouth, White Swan Road, Portsmouth, PO1 2DT.
     023 9284 3379
     http://www.port.ac.uk/research/ibbs/
     Secretary: Mrs Claire Rutter.
E   A department of the University of Portsmouth.

Institute of Biomedical and Clinical Sciences Research
■   Faculty of Health, University of East Anglia, Norwich, NR4 7TJ.
     01603 456161   fax 01603 458553
     http://www1.uea.ac.uk/cm/home/schools/foh/res/bcsres

Institute of Biomedical Engineering   (IBE)
■   South Kensington Campus, Imperial College London, Exhibition Road, London, SW7 2AZ.
     020 7594 0701   fax 020 7594 0704
     http://www.imperial.ac.uk/biomedeng/
     Executive Director: Prof C Toumazou.
E   An interdisciplinary research institute at Imperial College London.
○   To create an international centre of excellence in biomedical engineering research

Institute of Biomedical and Life Sciences   (IBLS)   2000
■   Wolfson Building, University of Glasgow, Glasgow, G12 8QQ.
     0141-330 3524   fax 0141-330 4758
     http://www.gla.ac.uk/ibls/
     Dean: Prof Paul Hagan.
E   A faculty of the University of Glasgow.
○   To encourage research and teaching in the biological sciences
●   22 Honours Degree courses - Various Masters Courses

Institute for Biomedical Research
       see **Wolfson Institute for Biomedical Research.**

Institute for Biomolecular Research
       see **Krebs Institute for Biomolecular Research.**

Institute for Biophysical and Clinical Research into Human Movement   (IRM)
■   Manchester Metropolitan University, Hassall Road, Alsager, Cheshire, ST7 2HL.
     0161-247 5593; 5605   fax 0161-247 6375
     http://www.irm.mmu.ac.uk/
     Contact: Anthony Sargeant.
E   A research institute at Manchester Metropolitan University.
○   To develop a framework, based on empirical research, for understanding the constraints, limitations, control and execution of athletic, normal and disordered human movement throughout the life span

Institute for Biotechnological Law and Ethics
       see **Sheffield Institute for Biotechnological Law and Ethics.**

Institute of Biotechnology   1988
■   University of Cambridge, Tennis Court Road, Cambridge, CB2 1QT.
     01223 334160   fax 01223 334162
     http://www.biot.cam.ac.uk/administration/
E   A department of the University of Cambridge.
○   To conduct research into selected areas of biotechnology; to provide high quality training for graduates

© CBD Research Ltd · Beckenham · Kent BR3 5JS · Tel 020 8650 7745 · Fax 020 8650 0768 · E-mail cbd@cbdresearch.com · www.cbdresearch.com

Institute of Brain Chemistry and Human Nutrition   (IBCHN)   1989
- ■ Department of Health and Human Sciences, North Campus, London Metropolitan University, 166-220 Holloway Road, London, N7 8DB.
    020 7133 2446   fax 020 7133 2453
    http://www.north.londonmet.ac.uk/ibchn/
    Director: Prof Michael A Crawford.
- E A research institute at the London Metropolitan University.
- ○ To understand how environmental factors, particularly nutrients, influence human development and health

Institute of Building Technology   (IBT)
- ■ School of the Built Environment, University of Nottingham, University Park, Nottingham, NG7 2RD.
    0115-951 3134
    http://www.nottingham.ac.uk/sbe/research/berg_intro.php
- E A research institute at the University of Nottingham.
- ○ To carry out high-quality, strategic and applied research related to the environmental performance of building services

Institute for the Built and Human Environment
    see **Research Institute for the Built and Human Environment.**

Institute of Business and Law
- ■ Bournemouth Law School, Talbot Campus, Bournemouth University, Poole, Dorset, BH12 5BB.
    01202 965211   fax 01202 965261
    http://business.bournemouth.ac.uk/
- E A department of Bournemouth University.
- ○ To co-ordinate the various research activities within the School
Note: Encompasses the Centre for Accounting, Finance and Taxation, the Centre for Corporate Governance and Regulation, the Centre for Intellectual Property Policy and Management, and the Centre for Organisational Effectiveness.

Institute for Business and Management
    see **Research Institute for Business and Management.**

Institute of Byzantine Studies   2000
- ■ School of History and Anthropology, Queen's University, Belfast, 15 University Square, Belfast, BT7 1NN.
    028 9097 3238; 5247
    http://www.qub.ac.uk/schools/ByzantineStudies/
    Director: Prof Margaret Mullett.
- E A research institute at Queen's University, Belfast.
- ○ To examine the people, society and culture of the Byzantine Empire (AD330-1453)

Institute of Cancer   2003
- ■ Barts and the London, Queen Mary's School of Medicine and Dentistry, Queen Mary, University of London, Charterhouse Square, London, EC1M 6BQ.
    020 7014 0462   fax 020 7014 0461
    http://www.cancer.qmul.ac.uk/
    Director: Prof Nicholas Lemoine.
- E A department of Queen Mary, University of London.
- ○ To be a major international centre of excellence in both cancer research and clinical cancer care

Institute of Cancer and Developmental Biology
    see **Wellcome Trust/Cancer Research UK Gurdon Institute of Cancer and Developmental Biology.**

Institute of Cancer Genetics and Pharmacogenomics
    see **Brunel Institute of Cancer Genetics and Pharmacogenomics.**

Institute for Cancer Research [Glasgow]
    see **Beatson Institute for Cancer Research.**

Institute of Cancer Research   (ICR)   1909
- ■ University of London, 123 Old Brompton Road, London, SW7 3RP.
    020 7352 8133   fax 020 7370 5261
    http://www.icr.ac.uk/
    Chief Executive: Prof Peter Rigby. Secretary: Jonathan Kipling.
- E A registered charity and a not-for-profit company limited by guarantee at the University of London.
- ○ To relieve human suffering by pursuing excellence in the fight against cancer, so that people may live their lives free from the fear of cancer as a life threatening disease

Institute for Cancer Research [Manchester]
    see **Paterson Institute for Cancer Research.**

Institute for Cancer Studies [Birmingham]
    see **Cancer Research UK Institute for Cancer Studies.**

Institute of Cancer Studies [Liverpool]
see **Liverpool University Institute of Cancer Studies.**

Institute for Cancer Studies   (ICS)
- Division of Genomic Medicine, Medical School, University of Sheffield, Beech Hill Road, Sheffield, S10 2RX.
  0114-271 2237   fax 0114-271 3515
  Head: Prof Mark Meuth.
E   A research institute at the University of Sheffield.

Institute of Cancer Therapeutics   (ICT)
- School of Life Sciences, University of Bradford, Bradford, West Yorkshire, BD7 1DP.
  01274 233562   fax 01274 309742
  http://www.cancer.brad.ac.uk/
  Director: Prof Laurence H Patterson.
E   A research institute at the University of Bradford.
O   To conduct research in the development of new molecules, and to describe three broad stages of medicine development -
  discovery, pre-clinical evaluation, and clinical application

Institute for Capitalising on Creativity   (ICC)
- University of St Andrews, College Gate, North Street, St Andrews, Fife, KY16 9AJ.
  01334 462016   fax 01334 462554
  http://www.capitalisingoncreativity.ac.uk/
  Course Administrator: Barbara Porter.
E   An institute at the University of St Andrews.

Institute of Cardiovascular Research
see **Tayside Institute of Cardiovascular Research.**

Institute for Cardiovascular Studies
see **Centre for Cardiology and The Hatter Institute for Cardiovascular Studies.**

Institute for the Care of the Elderly
see **Research Institute for the Care of the Elderly.**

Institute of Cell Biology   (ICB)
- School of Biological Sciences, University of Edinburgh, The King's Buildings, Mayfield Road, Edinburgh, EH9 3JR.
  0131-650 5366   fax 0131-650 8650
  http://www.biology.ed.ac.uk/research/institutes/cell/
E   A research institute at the University of Edinburgh.
O   To be a world leading centre for cell and molecular biology

Institute for Cell and Molecular Biosciences   2004
- Faculty of Medical Sciences, Catherine Cookson Building, University of Newcastle upon Tyne, Framlington Place,
  Newcastle upon Tyne, NE2 4HH.
  0191-222 8126   fax 0191-222 7424
  http://www.ncl.ac.uk/camb/
  Director: Prof Jeffery Errington.
E   An institute within the University of Newcastle upon Tyne.
O   To conduct cellular and molecular biology with a post-genomic perspective

Institute of Cell and Molecular Science   (ICMS)   2003
- Barts and the London, Queen Mary's School of Medicine and Dentistry, Queen Mary, University of London, 4 Newark Street,
  London, E1 2AT.
  020 7882 2483   fax 020 7882 2200
  http://www.icms.qmul.ac.uk/
  Director: Prof Mike Curtis.
E   A department of Queen Mary, University of London.
O   To conduct world class biomedical research which integrates basic science, clinical research and translational research activity

Institute of Cell Signalling   (ICS)
- Queen's Medical Centre, University of Nottingham, Nottingham, NG7 2UH.
  0115-823 0083   fax 0115-823 0081
  http://www.nottingham.ac.uk/ics/
  Director: Prof Steve Hill.
E   A research institute at the University of Nottingham.
O   To utilise the advances being made in molecular genetics and cell biology; to study the regulation of cell signalling pathways in
  healthy and diseased human cells

Institute of Cellular Medicine   (ICM)

■ Faculty of Medical Sciences, University of Newcastle upon Tyne, Newcastle upon Tyne, NE2 4HH.
0191-222 6000
http://www.ncl.ac.uk/icm/
E A research institute at the University of Newcastle upon Tyne.

Institute of Central and East European Studies

Note: Is now the School of Slavonic, Central and East European Studies at the University of Glasgow.

Institute for Chemistry in Industry   (ICI)   1992

■ Department of Chemistry, University of Hull, Cottingham Road, Hull, HU6 7RX.
01482 465433
http://www.hull.ac.uk/ici/
Director: Prof Paul Fletcher.
E An institute at the University of Hull.
○ To maintain and develop strong links with the industrial and public services

Institute of Child Care Research   (ICCR)

■ School of Sociology, Social Policy and Social Work, Queen's University of Belfast, 5A Lennoxvale, Belfast, BT9 5BY.
028 9097 5401   fax 028 9068 7416
http://www.qub.ac.uk/ss/cccr/
Director: Dr Rosemary Kilpatrick.
E A centre at Queen's University, Belfast.
○ To play a key role in influencing the development of child care policy and practice in Northern Ireland

Institute of Child Health [Leicester]
see Greenwood Institute of Child Health.

Institute of Child Health   1969

■ Faculty of Medicine, University of Liverpool, Alder Hey, Eaton Road, Liverpool, L12 2AP.
0151-252 5439   fax 0151-252 5456
http://www.liv.ac.uk/childhealth/
E A department of the University of Liverpool.

Institute for Chinese Studies

■ Faculty of Oriental Studies, Clarendon Institute Building, University of Oxford, Walton Street, Oxford, OX1 2HG.
01865 280387   fax 01865 280435
http://www.orinst.ox.ac.uk/ea/chinese/
E A research centre within the Oriental Institute (qv) at the University of Oxford.

Institute for Citizenship   (IfC)   1992

■ 60 Queen Victoria Street, London, EC4N 4TW.
020 7844 5444   fax 020 7844 5541
http://www.citizen.org.uk/
E A registered charity and a company limited by guarantee.
○ To promote informed, active citizenship and greater participation in democracy and society

Institute of Classical Studies   (ICLS)   1953

■ School of Advanced Study, University of London, Senate House, Malet Street, London, WC1E 7HU.
020 7862 8700
http://icls.sas.ac.uk/
Director: Prof Michael Edwards.
E A department of the University of London.
○ To conduct research and postgraduate study in ancient Greek and Roman language and culture

Institute of Clinical Education   (ICE)

■ Warwick Medical School, University of Warwick, Gibbet Hill Road, Coventry, CV4 7AL.
024 7652 8101
http://www2.warwick.ac.uk/fac/med/about/ice/
Head: Prof Ed Peile, EdD, FRCP, FRCPCH, FRCGP.
E An institute within the University of Warwick.
○ To promote clinical service delivery, education and research
● Education and training

Institute of Clinical Research   (ICR)

■ Medical School, University of Nottingham, Queen's Medical Centre, Nottingham, NG7 2UH.
0115-823 0141   fax 0115-823 0142
http://www.nottingham.ac.uk/icr/
E A department of the University of Nottingham.
○ To conduct high quality, integrative, translational, and population based clinical research

Institute of Clinical Sciences   (ICS)

■   Faculty of Medicine and Health, The Worsley Building, University of Leeds, Clarendon Way, Leeds, LS2 9JT.
    0113-343 4361
    http://www.leeds.ac.uk/medhealth/
E   A department of the University of Leeds.

Institute for Coastal Science and Management
    see **Aberdeen Institute for Coastal Science and Management.**

Institute of Cognition and Culture   2004

■   School of History and Anthropology, Queen's University Belfast, 2-4 Fitzwilliam Street, Belfast, BT7 1NN.
    028 9097 1333   fax 028 9097 1332
    http://www.qub.ac.uk/schools/InstituteofCognitionCulture/
    Director: Prof Harvey Whitehouse.
E   A research institute at Queen's University, Belfast.

Institute of Cognitive Neuroscience   (ICN)

■   University College London, Alexandra House, 17 Queen Square, London, WC1N 3AR.
    020 7679 1177   fax 020 7813 2835
    http://www.icn.ucl.ac.uk/
    Director: Prof Jon Driver.
E   An interdisciplinary research institute at University College London.
○   To study how mental processes relate to the human brain, in health and disease, for adults and children

Institute for Colonial and Postcolonial Studies   (ICPS)   2005

■   Faculty of Arts, University of Leeds, Leeds, LS2 9JT.
    0113-343 3609   fax 0113-343 2759
    http://www.leeds.ac.uk/icps/
    Co-Director: Prof Graham Huggan. Co-Director: Prof Andrew Thompson.
E   A research institute and part of the Leeds Humanities Research Institute (qv) at the University of Leeds.
○   To re-assess colonial histories, in all their complexity and diversity, and to gauge their continuing impact upon our globalised world

Institute of Commonwealth Studies   (ICS)   1949

■   School of Advanced Study, University of London, 28 Russell Square, London, WC1B 5DS.
    020 7862 8844   fax 020 7862 8820
    http://commonwealth.sas.ac.uk/
    Director: Prof Richard Crook.
E   A postgraduate institute of the University of London.
○   To promote advanced study of the Commonwealth in the social sciences and humanities
●   Conference facilities - Education and training - Information service - Library

Institute for Communicating and Collaborative Systems   (ICCS)

■   School of Informatics, University of Edinburgh, 2 Buccleuch Place, Edinburgh, EH8 9LW.
    0131-650 4665   fax 0131-650 4587
    http://www.inf.ed.ac.uk/research/iccs/
    Co-Director: Prof Johanna Moore. Co-Director: Prof Mark Steedman.
E   A research institute at the University of Edinburgh.
○   To conduct basic research into the nature of communication among humans and between humans and machines using text, speech, and graphics, and the design of interactive dialog systems with applications, including information retrieval and presentation, education and instruction

Institute of Communication and Neuroscience
    see **MacKay Institute of Communication and Neuroscience.**

Institute for Communications and Signal Processing

■   Department of Electronic and Electrical Engineering, University of Strathclyde, Royal College Building, 204 George Street, Glasgow, G1 1XW.
    0141-548 2350
    http://www.eee.strath.ac.uk/
    Contact: Prof Jim M McDonald.
E   A research institute at the University of Strathclyde.

Institute of Communications Studies   (ICS)   1989

■   Faculty of Performance, Visual Arts and Communications, Level 3 - Houldsworth Building, Houldsworth Building, University of Leeds, Leeds, LS2 9JT.
    0113-343 7608   fax 0113-343 1117
    http://ics.leeds.ac.uk/
    Director: Dr Graham Roberts.
E   A department of the University of Leeds.
○   To conduct research and teaching in communications studies, broadcasting, new media, broadcast journalism, political communications, cinema, photography and television, visual culture, and international communications

© CBD Research Ltd · Beckenham · Kent BR3 5JS · Tel 020 8650 7745 · Fax 020 8650 0768 · E-mail cbd@cbdresearch.com · www.cbdresearch.com

Institute of Community Cohesion   (ICoCo)   2005

NR   10 Innovation Village, Coventry University Technology Park, Cheetah Way, Coventry, CV1 2TL.
     024 7679 5757
     http://www.coventry.ac.uk/icoco/
E   A research institute at Coventry University.
Note: A co-operative venture with de Montfort University, and the Universities of Leicester and Warwick.

Institute for Community and Primary Care Research

■   School of Health Studies, University of Bradford, 25 Trinity Road, Bradford, West Yorkshire, BD5 0BB.
     01274 236367   fax 01274 236302
     http://www.brad.ac.uk/health/research/pcg/
     Head: Prof Neil Small.
E   A department of the University of Bradford.

Institute for Competition Law and Economics
     see **Jevons Institute for Competition Law and Economics.**

Institute for Computational Cosmology   (ICC)   2002

■   Department of Physics, University of Durham, South Road, Durham, DH1 3LE.
     0191-334 3635   fax 0191-334 3645
     http://icc.dur.ac.uk/
     Director: Prof C S Frenk.
E   A research institute within the Ogden Centre for Fundamental Physics (qv) at the University of Durham.
○   To conduct research into the origin and evolution of the universe

Institute of Computational Mathematics
     see **Brunel Institute of Computational Mathematics.**

Institute for Computer Based Learning   (ICBL)

■   School of Mathematical and Computer Sciences, Earl Mountbatten Building, Heriot-Watt University, Riccarton, Edinburgh, EH14 4AS.
     0131-451 3280   fax 0131-451 3327
     http://www.icbl.hw.ac.uk/
     Director: Roger Rist.
E   A research centre at Heriot-Watt University.
○   To specialise in the design, description and evaluation of computer-based resources and their use in further and higher education

Institute for Computing Research   (ICR)

■   Faculty of Business, Computing and Information Management, London South Bank University, 103 Borough Road, London, SE1 0AA.
     020 7815 7413
     http://www.lsbu.ac.uk/bcimicr/
     Head: Prof Mark Josephs.
E   A research institute within London South Bank University.
○   To facilitate and consolidate high-quality research that addresses a range of computing-related topics and themes

Institute for Computing Systems Architecture   (ICSA)

■   School of Informatics, James Clerk Maxwell Building, University of Edinburgh, Mayfield Road, Edinburgh, EH9 3JZ.
     0131-650 5116   fax 0131-667 7209
     http://www.inf.ed.ac.uk/research/icsa/
     Director: Prof Nigel Topham.
E   A research institute at the University of Edinburgh.
○   To extend the understanding of the performance and scalability of existing computational systems; to improve the characteristics of current systems through innovations in algorithms, architectures, compilers, languages and protocols; to develop new and novel architectures and to develop new engineering methods by which future systems can be created and maintained

Institute for Connective Environmental Research
     see **Zuckerman Institute for Connective Environmental Research.**

Institute of Conservation and Ecology
     see **Durrell Institute of Conservation and Ecology.**

Institute for Consumer Affairs
     see **Research Institute for Consumer Affairs.**

Institute of Contemporary British History
     see **Centre for Contemporary British History.**

Institute of Contemporary Chinese Studies

Note: is now the School of Contemporary Chinese Studies at Nottingham University and is therefore outside the scope of this directory.

Institute of Continuing Education   (ICE)

- ■ Madingley Hall, University of Cambridge, Madingley, Cambridge, CB3 8AQ.
  01223 280280   fax 01223 280200
  http://www.cont-ed.cam.ac.uk/
  Director: Prof Dick Taylor.
- E An institute at the University of Cambridge.
- ○ To offer a large and flexible programme of part-time learning opportunities for adults

Institute of Cornish Studies   (ICS)   1970

- ■ Cornwall Campus, University of Exeter, Penryn, Cornwall, TR10 9EZ.
  01326 371807
  http://www.institutes.ex.ac.uk/ics/
  Director: Prof Philip Payton.
- E An institute at the University of Exeter.
- ○ To support and foster academic research on Cornwall, and to carry out research projects on Cornwall and its past

Institute for Corporate Learning   (IfCL)

- ■ Leeds University Business School, Maurice Keyworth Building, University of Leeds, Leeds, LS2 9JT.
  0113-384 6080   fax 0113-384 6081
  http://www.leeds.ac.uk/ifcl/
  Corporate Learning & Development Manager: Paula Burkinshaw.
- E A research institute within the University of Leeds.
- ○ To develop and expand the University's interface with the corporate sector with the formation of long-run partnership relationships in the fields of education and training
- ● Education and training

Institute of Cosmology and Gravitation   (ICG)

- ■ Faculty of Technology, University of Portsmouth, Mercantile House, Hampshire Terrace, Portsmouth, PO1 2EG.
  023 9284 5151   fax 023 9284 5626
  http://www.icg.port.ac.uk/
  Director: Prof Roy Maartens.
- E A department of the University of Portsmouth.
- ○ To conduct research in a wide range of topics, in the theoretical and mathematical aspects of relativistic astrophysics and cosmology, including structure formation in the universe, early universe and particle cosmology, relativistic cosmology, and relativistic astrophysics and gravitational waves

Institute for Creative Arts and Sciences
   see **Adelphi Research Institute for Creative Arts and Sciences.**

Institute of Creative Technologies   (IOCT)   2006

- ■ De Montfort University, Gateway House, 1 The Gateway, Leicester, LE1 9BH.
  0116-250 6146
  http://www.ioct.dmu.ac.uk/
  Director: Prof Andrew Hugill.
- E An institute at De Montfort University.
- ○ To undertake research work in emerging areas at the intersection of e-science, the digital arts, and the humanities

Institute of Crime Science
   see **UCL Jill Dando Institute of Crime Science.**

Institute of Criminal Justice   (ICJ)   1986

- ■ School of Law, University of Southampton, Highfield, Southampton, SO17 1BJ.
  023 8059 3421   fax 023 8059 3885
  http://www.law.soton.ac.uk/icj/
  Director: Dr Julia Fionda.
- E A research institute at the University of Southampton.

Institute of Criminal Justice Studies   (ICJS)   1992

- ■ Faculty of Humanities and Social Sciences, University of Portsmouth, Ravelin House, Museum Road, Portsmouth, PO1 2QQ.
  023 9284 3933   fax 023 9284 3939
  http://www.port.ac.uk/departments/academic/icjs/
  Director: Prof Les Johnston.
- E A department of the University of Portsmouth.
- ○ To conduct a wide variety of research in the fields of governance, accountability and regulation, international and comparative justice, criminal investigation and detection, risk, security and community safety, and equity, fairness and human rights

Institute for Criminal Policy Research   (ICPR)

■ School of Law, University College London, 26-29 Drury Lane, London, WC2B 5RL.
  020 7848 1742
  http://www.kcl.ac.uk/schools/law/research/icpr/
  Director: Mike Hough.
E A research institute at King's College, London.
○ To carry out research into crime and the criminal justice system, especially the quality and effectiveness of public services and resources (including police, probation and services for drug users)

Institute of Criminology   (IoC)   1959

■ Faculty of Law, University of Cambridge, Sidgwick Avenue, Cambridge, CB3 9DT.
  01223 335360   fax 01223 335356
  http://www.crim.cam.ac.uk/
  Director: Prof Friedrich Lösel.
E A department of the University of Cambridge.
○ To conduct research in a wide range of criminological fields
● Education and training - Library

Institute of Criminology and Criminal Justice   (ICCJ)

■ School of Law, Queen's University Belfast, 27 University Square, Belfast, BT7 1NN.
  028 9097 3873   fax 028 9097 3376
  http://www.law.qub.ac.uk/iccj/
  Director: Dr Kieran McEvoy.
E A research institute at Queen's University, Belfast.
○ To carry out high quality criminological and criminal justice research

Institute of Cultural Affairs   (ICA:UK)

■ PO Box 171, Manchester, M15 5BE.
  0845 450 0305
  http://www.ica-uk.org.uk/
  Administrator: Humey Saeed.
E The UK arm of a global network of organisations with the same name.
○ To conduct research and training in the human factor in world development

Institute for Cultural Analysis, Nottingham   (ICAn)

■ School of Arts and Humanities, Clifton Campus, Nottingham Trent University, Nottingham, NG11 8NS.
  0115-848 6330   fax 0115-848 6331
  http://www.ntu.ac.uk/research/school_research/hum/29479gp.html
  Contact: Prof John Tomlinson.
E A research institute at Nottingham Trent University.
○ To study culture in the context of globalisation in the 21st century

Institute for Cultural Research   (ICR)   1966

■ Faculty of Social Sciences, Lancaster University, Bowland Tower South, Lancaster, LA1 4YT.
  01524 592497   fax 01524 594273
  http://www.lancs.ac.uk/fss/cultres/
  Director: Prof Michael Dillon. Director of Graduate Studies: Dr Annette Kuhn.
E A department of Lancaster University.
○ To promote interdisciplinary research into the cultural values of modern societies; to encourage descriptive, explanatory and critical studies which draw upon the intellectual resources of the humanitarian and social sciences
● Conference facilities - Education and training

Institute of Culture, Gender and the City   (ICGC)

■ Faculty of Humanities, Law and Social Science, Geoffrey Manton Building, Manchester Metropolitan University, Rosamond Street West, Manchester, M15 6LL.
  0161-247 3027   fax 0161-247 6321
  http://www.icgc.mmu.ac.uk/
  Director: Dr Jon Binnie.
E A research institute at Manchester Metropolitan University.
○ To investigate cultural and social issues through understandings of space, place, power and difference

Institute of Dentistry   1995

■ Barts and the London, Queen Mary's School of Medicine and Dentistry, Queen Mary, University of London, Turner Street, London, E1 2AD.
  020 7377 7611   fax 020 7377 7612
  http://www.smd.qmul.ac.uk/dental/
  Director: Prof Paul Wright.
E A department of Queen Mary, University of London.
○ To conduct research into various fields of dentistry, with particular focus on microbiology and infectious diseases, biophysics and biomaterials, biometry and population studies, and cell and molecular biology

Institute of Dermatology
  see Saint John's Institute of Dermatology.

Institute for Development Policy and Management   (IDPM)   1958

■   School of Environment and Development, Harold Hankins Building, University of Manchester, Booth Street West, Manchester, M13 9QH.
       0161-275 2800   fax 0161-273 8829
       http://www.sed.manchester.ac.uk/idpm/
       Contact: Prof Anthony Bebbington.
E   A department of the University of Manchester.
O   To promote social and economic development, particularly in lower-income countries and for disadvantaged groups, by enhancing the capabilities of individuals and organisations through education, training, consultancy, research and policy analysis

Institute of Development Studies   (IDS)   1966

■   University of Sussex, Falmer, Brighton, East Sussex, BN1 9RE.
       01273 606261   fax 01273 621202
       http://www.ids.ac.uk/
E   A registered charity and part of the University of Sussex.
O   To be the world's leading organisation for research, teaching and communications on international development
●   Conference facilities - Information service - Library
¶   Annual Report. Bulletin. Catalogue. (many other publications available).

Institute for Developmental Potential   1982

■   49 West Street, Tavistock, Devon, PL19 8JZ.
       01822 614471   fax 01822 614471
       Director: R J Bennett.
E   A profit-making private venture.
O   The treatment of physical and emotional problems in adults and educational underachievement and behavioural problems in children The Institute has recently completed a 23 year research programme into the cause of anxiety / stress problems, physical difficulties, educational and behavioural problems in children
●   Education and training - Integration Therapy treatment (available in Plymouth and London)

Institute for Diet, Exercise and Lifestyle   (IDEAL)

■   West Medical Building, University of Glasgow, Glasgow, G12 8QQ.
       0141-330 2916   fax 0141-330 2915
       http://www.gla.ac.uk/ibls/NBS/reserexer.html
       Co-ordinator: Dr J Gill.
E   A research centre within the Institute of Biomedical and Life Sciences (qv) at the University of Glasgow.

Institute of Digital Art and Technology   (i-DAT)

■   School of Computing, Communications and Electronics, University of Plymouth, Portland Square, Drake Circus, Plymouth, PL4 8AA.
       01752 232560   fax 01752 232540
       http://www.i-dat.org/
       Director: Mike Phillips.
E   A centre at the University of Plymouth.
O   To define and establish new fields of practice and critical discourse in the context of emergent technologies and cultural forms, new scientific paradigms, and new media art

Institute for Drug Research
       see **Strathclyde Institute for Drug Research.**

Institute for the Earth, Energy and the Environment
       see **Earth, Energy and Environment University Interdisciplinary Institute.**

Institute of Ecology and Resource Management
       see **Institute of Atmospheric and Environmental Science.**

Institute of Education [Coventry]
       see **Warwick Institute of Education.**

Institute of Education   (IoE)   1902

■   University of London, 20 Bedford Way, London, WC1H 0AL.
       020 7612 6312   fax 020 7612 6177
       http://ioewebserver.ioe.ac.uk/
E   A college of the University of London.
O   To be a world class centre for research, teacher training, higher degrees and consultancy in education and education-related areas of social science

© CBD Research Ltd · Beckenham · Kent BR3 5JS · Tel 020 8650 7745 · Fax 020 8650 0768 · E-mail cbd@cbdresearch.com · www.cbdresearch.com

Institute of Education   (IoE)
■   Manchester Metropolitan University, 799 Wilmslow Road, Didsbury, Manchester, M20 2RR.
    0161-247 2026   fax 0161-247 6397
    http://www.ioe.mmu.ac.uk/
    Director: Prof Michael S Totterdell.
E   A department of Manchester Metropolitan University.
O   To be a leading UK centre for educational research and study, and to be the major provider of initial teacher education and
    training and continuing professional development in the North West

Institute of Education [Oxford]
    see **Westminster Institute of Education.**

Institute of Education
■   University of Reading, Bulmershe Court, Earley, Reading, Berkshire, RG6 1HY.
    0118-378 8811
    http://www.education.rdg.ac.uk/
E   An institute within the University of Reading.

Institute of Education   (IoE)
■   University of Stirling, Stirling, FK9 4LA.
    01786 467600; 467940   fax 01786 466131
    http://www.ioe.stir.ac.uk/
    Contact: Dorothy Christie.
E   A department of the University of Stirling.
O   To engage in research, teacher education and training, language teaching, as well as the continuing professional development of
    education practitioners, the training of new researchers, and research and consultancy services

Institute for Education Policy Research   (IEPR)   2001
■   Brindley Building, Staffordshire University, Leek Road, Stoke-on-Trent, ST4 2DF.
    01782 295731   fax 01782 295752
    http://www.staffs.ac.uk/schools/business/iepr/
    Director: Prof Nick Adnett.
E   A research institute within Staffordshire University.
O   To research, advise and report on various aspects of educational policy at national and international levels

Institute of Educational Technology   (IET)
■   Open University, Walton Hall, Milton Keynes, MK7 6AA.
    01908 274066
    http://iet.open.ac.uk/
    Director: Peter Knight.
E   A department of the Open University.
O   To provide advice on the use of information, communication and other modern technologies to support effective learning in higher
    education, particularly in distance learning and e-learning

Institute for Electromagnetics Research
    see **George Green Institute for Electromagnetics Research.**

Institute of Electronics, Communications and Information Technology   (ECIT)   2003
■   School of Electronics, Electrical Engineering and Computer Science, Queen's University Belfast, Northern Ireland Science Park,
    Queen's Road, Belfast, BT3 9DT.
    028 9097 1700   fax 028 9097 1702
    http://www.ecit.qub.ac.uk/
E   A research institute at Queen's University, Belfast.
O   To stimulate major opportunities for economic growth by pioneering future directions and innovation in key areas of advanced
    technology, through the integration of complementary research expertise in a world-leading facility

Institute for Emergent Infections of Humans
■   Zoology Department, University of Oxford, South Parks Road, Oxford, OX1 3PS.
    01865 271210   fax 01865 310447
    http://www.emdis.ox.ac.uk/
    Director: Prof Angela McLean.
E   A research institute within the University of Oxford.
O   To understand the underlying processes that drive the emergence and spread of novel human infectious diseases

Institute for Employee Relations
    see **Oxford Institute for Employee Relations.**

Institute for Employment Law   (IEL)
- ■   Aberdeen Business School, Management Building, Robert Gordon University, Garthdee Road, Aberdeen, AB10 7QE.
    01224 263408   fax 01224 263434
    http://www.rgu.ac.uk/abs/centres/page.cfm?pge=4868
    Senior Lecturer: Sam Middlemiss.
- E   A research institute at the Robert Gordon University.
- O   To promote and undertake collaborative research, with a view to publication, in the field of employment law

Institute for Employment Research
   see **Warwick Institute for Employment Research.**

Institute for Employment Studies   (IES)   1969
- ■   Mantell Building, University of Sussex, Falmer, Brighton, East Sussex, BN1 9RF.
    01273 686751   fax 01273 690430
    http://www.employment-studies.co.uk/
- E   A registered charity and an independent non-profit-distributing organisation based at the University of Sussex.
- O   To help bring about sustainable improvements in employment policy and human resource management, by increasing the understanding and improving the practice of key decision makers in policy bodies and employing organisations

Institute for Energy and Environment   (IEE)
- ■   Department of Electronic and Electrical Engineering, Royal College Building, University of Strathclydge, 204 George Street, Glasgow, G1 1XW.
    0141-548 2485   fax 0141-548 4872
    http://www.instee.strath.ac.uk/
    Head: Prof Scott J MacGregor.
- E   A research institute at the University of Strathclyde.
- O   To undertake basic, strategic and applied research in electrical power engineering

Institute for Energy Research and Policy   (IERP)   2005
- ■   University of Birmingham, Edgbaston, Birmingham, B15 2TT.
    0121-415 8216
    http://www.ierp.bham.ac.uk/
    Director: Prof Richard Green.
- E   A research institute at the University of Birmingham.
- O   To be recognised, nationally and internationally, for the quality of its pure and applied research in both technical and non-technical aspects of energy

Institute for Energy Studies
   see **Oxford Institute for Energy Studies.**

Institute of Energy and Sustainable Development   (IESD)
- ■   De Montfort University, Queen's Buildings, The Gateway, Leicester, LE1 9BH.
    0116-257 7962   fax 0116-257 7977
    http://www.iesd.dmu.ac.uk/
    Director: Prof Kevin Lomas.
- E   A research institute and department of De Montfort University.
- O   To focus research on the clean, efficient use of energy in the built environment and to develop ways in which greater use can be made of renewable energy in domestic buildings, industry and commerce

Institute of Energy Technologies
- ■   College of Physical Sciences, Fraser Noble Building, King's College, University of Aberdeen, Old Aberdeen, AB24 3UE.
    01224 272984   fax 01224 272818
    http://www.abdn.ac.uk/energy/
- E   A research institute at the University of Aberdeen.
- O   To conduct research in a wide variety of energy and energy-related fields, including chemistry, computer science, economics, energy efficiency, engineering, environmental science, petroleum geology, and renewables

Institute of Engineering Surveying and Space Geodesy   (IESSG)   1988
- ■   School of Civil Engineering, University of Nottingham, University Park, Nottingham, NG7 2RD.
    0115-951 3907   fax 0115-951 3898
    http://www.nottingham.ac.uk/civeng/research/research_iessg.php
    Director: Prof Terry Moore.
- E   A research institute at the University of Nottingham.
- O   To conduct research and teaching in the fields of traditional engineering surveying and geodesy, satellite systems, photogrammetry, remote sensing, sensor integration and geographical information systems

Institute for English Research
   see **Nottingham Institute for English Research.**

© CBD Research Ltd · Beckenham · Kent BR3 5JS · Tel 020 8650 7745 · Fax 020 8650 0768 · E-mail cbd@cbdresearch.com · www.cbdresearch.com

Institute of English Studies   (IES)   1999

- School of Advanced Study, University of London, Senate House, Malet Street, London, WC1E 7HU.
  020 7862 8675   fax 020 7862 8720
  http://ies.sas.ac.uk/
  Director: Prof Warwick Gould.
- E   A department of the University of London.
- O   To facilitate advanced study and research in English studies

Institute for Enterprise

- 2nd Floor - Old School Board, Leeds Metropolitan University, Calverley Street, Leeds, LS1 3ED.
  0113-283 1752; 2600
  http://www.leedsmet.ac.uk/enterprise/
  Contact: Alison Price.
- E   A Centre for Excellence in Teaching and Learning (CETL) at Leeds Metropolitan University.
- Note: See **Centres for Excellence in Teaching and Learning** for more information.

Institute for Enterprise and Innovation
   see **University of Nottingham Institute for Enterprise and Innovation**.

Institute for Entrepreneurship   (IfE)

- Faculty of Law, Arts and Social Sciences, University of Southampton, Highfield, Southampton, SO17 1BJ.
  023 8059 3076
  http://www.ife.soton.ac.uk/
- E   A research institute at the University of Southampton.

Institute for Entrepreneurship and Enterprise Development

- Lancaster University Management School, Lancaster University, Bailrigg, Lancaster, LA1 4YX.
  01524 594727   fax 01524 594743
  http://www.lums.lancs.ac.uk/Departments/Entrep/
  Contact: Emma Steel.
- E   A research institute within Lancaster University.
- O   To create an environment where entrepreneurial research, education and business support can flourish

Institute for the Environment

- Brunel University, Uxbridge, Middlesex, UB8 3PH.
  01895 266105   fax 01895 269761
  http://www.brunel.ac.uk/about/acad/ife
  Director: Prof John Dodson.
- E   A department of Brunel University.
- O   To conduct postgraduate studies in tackling environmental problems in collaboration with industry and the public sector

Institute of Environment and Health   (IEH)   2005

- Cranfield University, Silsoe, Bedfordshire, MK45 4DT.
  01525 863347   fax 01525 863344
  http://www.silsoe.cranfield.ac.uk/ieh/
  Director: Dr Paul T C Harrison. Academic Director: Prof Leonard S Ley.
- E   A department of Cranfield University.
- O   To assess and evaluate environmental pollution and human health impacts; to investigate disease conditions caused by environmental exposures, including occupational and dietary exposures; to evaluate the impact of human activities on the natural environment; to co-ordinate and manage research programmes
- ● Conference facilities - Education and training - Information service
- ¶ Annual Report.

Institute for the Environment, Physical Sciences and Applied Mathematics
   see **Research Institute for the Environment, Physical Sciences and Applied Mathematics**.

Institute for Environment and Sustainability Research   (IESR)   2002

- Mellor Building, Staffordshire University, College Road, Stoke-on-Trent, ST4 2DF.
  01782 294110
  http://www.staffs.ac.uk/schools/sciences/geography/links/IESR/
  Co-Director: Dr John Dover. Co-Director: Prof Geoff Pugh.
- E   A research institute at Staffordshire University.
- O   To develop and support existing research activity on environmental and sustainability topics, facilitate greater collaboration and cross-fertilisation and provide co-ordinated strategic direction
- Note: Also known as Institute for Environment, Sustainability and Regeneration.

Institute for Environmental History   (IEH)   1992
- ■   School of History, University of St Andrews, St Katharine's Lodge, The Scores, St Andrews, Fife, KY16 9AL.
    01334 463302   fax 01334 463025
    http://www.st-andrews.ac.uk/institutes/envhist/
    Director: Dr J F M Clark.
- E   A research institute at the University of St Andrews.
- O   To study the interaction between human beings and nature since the Ice Age, with particular reference to European and Scottish conditions

Institute of Environmental and Natural Sciences   1997
- ■   Faculty Office, Lancaster University, Lancaster, LA1 4YQ.
    01524 593836   fax 01524 843854
    http://bssv01.lancs.ac.uk/faculty/home.htm/
    Dean: Prof T McMillan.
- E   A department of Lancaster University.
- O   To encourage interdisciplinary teaching and research in the fields of environmental sciences, biological sciences, geography, and physics
- ●   Education and training - Statistics

Institute of Environmental Sustainability   (IES)
- ■   School of the Environment and Society, Swansea University, Singleton Park, Swansea, SA2 8PP.
    01792 295361
    http://www.swan.ac.uk/research/centresandinstitutes/InstituteofEnvironmentalSustainability/
    Director: Prof Mike Barnsley.
- E   An interdisciplinary research institute and department of Swansea University.
- O   To bring together biologists, geographers and development studies specialists working across a broad range of environmental research issues

Institute for Estuarine and Coastal Studies   (IECS)   1982
- ■   Faculty of Science and the Environment, University of Hull, Cottingham Road, Hull, HU6 7RX.
    01482 465667   fax 01482 465001
    http://www.hull.ac.uk/iecs/
    Director: Prof Mike Elliott.
- E   An institute within the University of Hull.
- O   To bring together people concerned with estuarine and coastal issues across a wide range of disciplines

Institute for Ethics and Communication in Health Care Practice
   see **Oxford Institute for Ethics and Communication in Health Care Practice.**

Institute of European and Comparative Law   (IECL)   1995
- ■   Faculty of Law, University of Oxford, St Cross Building, St Cross Road, Oxford, OX1 3UL.
    01865 281610   fax 01865 281611
    http://denning.law.ox.ac.uk/
    Director: Prof Mark Freedland, FBA.
- E   A research institute at the University of Oxford.
- O   To develop and further work in the fields of European and comparative law

Institute of European Cultural Identity Studies   (IECIS)   1998
- ■   School of Modern Languages, University of St Andrews, Buchanan Building, Union Street, St Andrews, Fife, KY16 9PH.
    01334 463646
    http://www.st-andrews.ac.uk/modlangs/modlangs/IECIS/
    Director: Prof Paul P D Gifford.
- E   A research institute at the University of St Andrews.
- O   To provide a focus and a forum for high-level teaching and research into cultural identity in all its aspects

Institute for European Environmental Policy   (IEEP)   1980
- ■   28 Queen Anne's Gate, London, SW1H 9AB.
    020 7799 2244   fax 020 7799 2600
    http://www.ieep.org.uk/
    Director: David Baldock.
- E   A company limited by guarantee, a registered charity and an independent non-profit-distributing organisation.
- O   To undertake research and consultancy work on the development, implementation and evaluation of environmental and environment-related policies in Europe

Institute for European Finance
   see **Centre for Banking and Finance.**

© CBD Research Ltd · Beckenham · Kent BR3 5JS · Tel 020 8650 7745 · Fax 020 8650 0768 · E-mail cbd@cbdresearch.com · www.cbdresearch.com

Institute of European Law   (IEL)   1989

■   School of Law, University of Birmingham, Edgbaston, Birmingham, B15 2TT.
    0121-414 6282   fax 0121-414 3585
    http://www.iel.bham.ac.uk/
    Director: Joerg Biermann.
E   A research institute at the University of Birmingham.
○   To provide an interdisciplinary centre for research on European law

Institute of European Public Law   (IEPL)   1992

■   Law School, University of Hull, Cottingham Road, Hull, HU6 7RX.
    01482 465917   fax 01482 466388
    http://www.hull.ac.uk/law/research/iepl/
    Director: Prof Patrick Birkinshaw. Secretary: Mrs Denise Townsend.
E   A research institute at the University of Hull.

Institute of Evolutionary Biology   (IEB)

■   School of Biological Sciences, University of Edinburgh, The King's Buildings, Mayfield Road, Edinburgh, EH9 3JR.
    0131-650 5560
    http://www.biology.ed.ac.uk/research/institutes/evolution/
    Head: Prof Andrew Leigh Brown.
E   An institute within the University of Edinburgh.
○   To study evolution in the broadest possible sense, from virtually every angle and using a great range of organisms and techniques

Institute of Family Therapy   (IFT)   1977

■   24-32 Stephenson Way, London, NW1 2HX.
    020 7391 9150   fax 020 7391 9169
    http://www.instituteoffamilytherapy.org.uk/
    Director: Dr Barbara McKay.
E   A registered charity and membership organisation.
○   To provide training courses in family therapy and systematic practice - from introductory to MSc and doctorate levels; to provide clinical services for families and couples; to provide mediation services and carry out research

Institute of Field Ornithology
   see **Edward Grey Institute of Field Ornithology.**

Institute of Film and Television Studies   (IFTS)   1998

■   School of American and Canadian Studies, University of Nottingham, University Park, Nottingham, NG7 2RD.
    0115-951 4261   fax 0115-951 4270
    http://www.nottingham.ac.uk/american/film/
    Director: Prof Roberta Pearson.
E   A research institute at the University of Nottingham.
○   To encourage research in a wide range of issues within the study of film, including production, marketing, distribution, exhibition, critical mediation, consumption, audience studies, political economy, theory, and textual analysis

Institute of Finance and Accounting   (IFA)   1973

■   London Business School, Sussex Place, Regent's Park, London, NW1 4SA.
    020 7262 5050
    http://www.london.edu/finance/
    Chairman: Prof James Dow.
E   A department of the London Business School.
○   To be an international centre of excellence in financial research and education, covering the fields of corporate financial management, capital markets, financial instruments, financial institutions and regulation, with strong emphasis on the practical applications of financial research and on close connections with business
●   Education and training - Statistics

Institute for Financial Management

Note: Is now Business and Management Education Ltd (www.mbs-worldwide.ac.uk).

Institute of Fine Arts
   see **Barber Institute of Fine Arts.**

Institute for Fiscal Studies   (IFS)

■   3rd Floor, 7 Ridgmount Street, London, WC1E 7AE.
    020 7291 4800   fax 020 7323 4780
    http://www.ifs.org.uk/
E   An independent research institute.
○   To provide top quality economic analysis independent of Government, political party or any other vested interest

Institute for Flexible Materials
   see **Research Institute for Flexible Materials.**

Institute for Folklore Studies in Britain and Canada   (IFSBAC)   1986
■ School of English, University of Sheffield, Sheffield, S10 2TN.
    0114-222 6296   fax 0114-222 6299
    http://www.shef.ac.uk/english/
    Director: Prof Paul S Smith. Director: Prof J C Beal.
E A collaborative venture between the Memorial University of Newfoundland and the University of Sheffield.
○ To promote the study of folklore in Britain and Canada, and to encourage and engage in research on all aspects of folklore and
    related disciplines which link the two nations in a common tradition; to encourage the promotion of new ventures and projects in
    folklore studies, with programmes in disciplines such as oral history, linguistics, anthropology, sociology, literature and Canadian
    studies; to foster the existing co-operation and scholarly endeavour between the two founding universities, and to extend these
    links to other academic institutions
● Education and training - Exhibitions - Information service - Library - To act as a clearing house for the exchange of information in
    folklore studies with special reference to their shared traditional heritage

Institute of Food, Active Living and Nutrition   (IFANC)   2003
■ Thoday Building, Normal Site, University of Wales Bangor, Bangor, Gwynedd, LL57 2UW.
    01248 383634   fax 01248 354997
    http://www.ifanc.bangor.ac.uk/
    Director: Prof Gareth Edwards Jones.
E An interdisciplinary research institute at the University of Wales, Bangor.
○ To improve policy relevant research and education in the areas of food, nutrition and active living, thereby assisting the
    improvement of public health in Wales

Institute of Food Research   (IFR)   1986
■ Norwich Research Park, Colney, Norwich, NR4 7UA.
    01603 255000   fax 01603 507723
    http://www.ifr.bbsrc.ac.uk/
    Director: David White. Deputy Director: Prof Mike Gasson.
E A registered charity and a not-for-profit company limited by guarantee.
○ To undertake international quality scientific research relevant to food and human health; to work in partnership with others to
    provide underpinning science for consumers, policy makers, the food industry and academia
● Training
¶ Brochure. Many different publications.

Institute for the Future of the Mind
■ Department of Pharmacology, University of Oxford, Mansfield Road, Oxford, OX1 3QT.
    01865 281528   fax 01865 271853
    http://www.futuremind.ox.ac.uk/
    Director: Baroness Susan Greenfield.
E An institute at the University of Oxford.
○ To determine ways of harnessing new technologies to maximise the potential of each individual and safeguard their individuality

Institute of Gastrointestinal Nursing
    see **Burdett Institute of Gastrointestinal Nursing.**

Institute of Genetics
■ Department of Genetics, Adrian Building, University of Leicester, University Road, Leicester, LE1 7RH.
    0116-252 3438   fax 0116-252 3378
    http://www.le.ac.uk/iog
    Chairman: Prof Ed Louis.
E An institute within the University of Leicester.
○ To promote interaction and collaboration between scientists carrying out genetic research

Institute of Genetics
■ Queen's Medical Centre, University of Nottingham, Nottingham, NG7 2UH.
    0115-823 0310   fax 0115-823 0313
    http://www.nottingham.ac.uk/genetics/
E A department of the University of Nottingham.
○ To conduct research into various aspects of genetics, including population and evolutionary genetics, human genetics, fungal
    biology and genetics, developmental genetics and gene control, and molecular microbiology and genome dynamics,

Institute of Genetics, Health and Therapeutics
    see **Leeds Institute of Genetics, Health and Therapeutics.**

Institute of Geography and Earth Sciences   (IGES)   1988
■ Llandinam Building, University of Wales, Aberystwyth, Aberystwyth, Ceredigion, SY23 2DB.
    01970 622596; 622606   fax 01970 622659
    http://www.aber.ac.uk/iges/
    Director: Prof Martin Jones. Secretary: Mrs Valerie Grant.
E A department of the University of Wales, Aberystwyth.
○ To conduct teaching and research into various fields of geography and earth sciences

   © CBD Research Ltd · Beckenham · Kent BR3 5JS · Tel 020 8650 7745 · Fax 020 8650 0768 · E-mail cbd@cbdresearch.com · www.cbdresearch.com

Institute of Geological Sciences   (IGS)

■   School of Earth and Environment, University of Leeds, Leeds, LS2 9JT.
       0113-343 5222; 6461   fax 0113-343 5259; 6716
       http://www.see.leeds.ac.uk/research/igs/
       Contact: Prof Jane Francis.
E   A department of the University of Leeds.

Institute of Geophysics and Tectonics   (IGT)

■   School of Earth and Environment, University of Leeds, Leeds, LS2 9JT.
       0113-343 5222; 6461   fax 0113-343 5259; 6716
       http://www.see.leeds.ac.uk/igt
       Contact: Prof Derek Fairhead.
E   A department of the University of Leeds.

Institute for German Studies   (IGS)   1994

■   University of Birmingham, Edgbaston, Birmingham, B15 2TT.
       0121-414 7185   fax 0121-414 7329
       http://www.igs.bham.ac.uk/
       Director: Prof Thomas Poguntke.
E   A research centre within the European Research Institute (qv) at the University of Birmingham.
O   To provide a unique research-led social-science based perspective on Germany, including politics, economics, international
       relations, history and culture of contemporary Germany

Institute of Germanic and Romance Studies   (IGRS)   2004

■   School of Advanced Study, University of London, Senate House, Malet Street, London, WC1E 7HU.
       020 7862 8677   fax 020 7862 8672
       http://igrs.sas.ac.uk/
       Administrator: Jane Lewin.
E   A department of the University of London.
O   To promote and facilitate the study of the cultures of German-speaking and Romance language countries across a range of
       disciplines in the humanities
✕   Institute of Germanic Studies. Institute of Romance Studies.

Institute of Germanic Studies
       see **Institute of Germanic and Romance Studies.**

Institute of Gerontology   (IOG)   1986

■   Franklin Wilkins Building, King's College London, 150 Stamford Street, London, SE1 9HN.
       020 7848 3035   fax 020 7848 3235
       http://www.kcl.ac.uk/acig/
       Director: Prof Simon Briggs. Deputy Director: Dr Jane Preston
E   A department of King's College, London.
O   To increase knowledge and understanding of ageing and old age
●   Education and training

Institute of Global Law   (IGL)   2000

■   Faculty of Laws, University College London, Bentham House, Endsleigh Gardens, London, WC1H 0EG.
       020 7679 1474; 1478   fax 020 7679 1502
       http://www.ucl.ac.uk/laws/global_law
       Director: Dr Jörg Fedtke. Administrator: Cinzia Polese.
E   A research institute at University College London.
O   To conduct research and teaching in law across national boundaries

Institute for Global Studies   (IGS)   1997

■   Department of Sociology, Manchester Metropolitan University, Geoffrey Manton Building, Rosamond Street West, Manchester,
       M15 6LL.
       0161-247 3034
       http://www.sociology.mmu.ac.uk/igs
       Contact: Liz Marr.
E   A research centre within the Institute of Culture, Gender and the City (qv) at Manchester Metropolitan University.
O   To conduct teaching and research in the growing transnational relations, exchanges, identities and interests emerging at the global
       level

Institute of Governance   (IoG)   2002

■   University of Edinburgh, Chisholm House, High School Yards, Edinburgh, EH1 1LZ.
       0131-650 8093
       http://www.institute-of-governance.org/
       Co-Director: Prof David McCrone. Co-Director: Prof Charlie Jeffery.
E   An institute within the University of Edinburgh.
O   To provide a range of expertise on issues of specific relevance to constitutional change and areas of policy related work

Institute of Governance and Public Management (IGPM) 2001

- Warwick Business School, University of Warwick, Coventry, CV4 7AL.
  024 7652 4505   fax 024 7652 4410
  http://www.wbs.ac.uk/faculty/igpm/
  Director: Prof Colin Crouch.
- E   An institute within the University of Warwick.
- O   To consolidate the Warwick Business School's research and teaching on governance, public policy and public management

Institute of Governance, Public Policy and Social Research

- School of Law, Queen's University Belfast, 63 University Road, Belfast, BT7 1NN.
  028 9097 2549   fax 028 9097 2551
  http://www.governance.qub.ac.uk/
  Director: Prof Sally Wheeler.
- E   An institute at Queen's University, Belfast.
- O   To conduct interdisciplinary research which brings together practitioners and researchers in the field of public policy and governance

Institute of Grassland and Environmental Research
  see **BBSRC Institute of Grassland and Environmental Research.**

Institute for Gravitational Research (IGR)

- Department of Physics and Astronomy, University of Glasgow, Kelvin Building, Glasgow, G12 8QQ.
  0141-330 3340   fax 0141-330 6833
  http://www.physics.gla.ac.uk/igr/
  Director: Prof James Hough.
- E   A department of the University of Glasgow.

Institute of Greece, Rome and the Classical Tradition
  see **Bristol Institute of Greece, Rome and the Classical Tradition.**

Institute of Grinding Technology (IGT) 1986

- Faculty of Computing, Engineering and Mathematical Sciences, Frenchay Campus, University of the West of England, Coldharbour Lane, Bristol, BS16 1QY.
  0117-328 2654
  http://www.uwe.ac.uk/cems/research/centres/amrc/igt.html
  Director: Dr Thomas Pearce.
- E   A research institute within the Aerospace Manufacturing Research Centre (qv) at the University of the West of England.
- O   To carry out research on abrasive processes; to transfer technology to industry through research and development projects, seminars and training programmes

Institute for Hazard and Risk Research (IHR²) 2006

- Department of Geography, University of Durham, South Road, Durham, DH1 3LE.
  0191-334 1800   fax 0191-334 1801
  http://www.dur.ac.uk/geography/research/researchclusters/?mode=centre&id=326
  Director: Prof Phil Macnaghten.
- E   A research centre within the University of Durham.
- O   To conduct research into risk, vulnerability, resilience and response in natural and social environments

Institute of Health 2001

- School of Health and Social Studies, University of Warwick, Coventry, CV4 7AL.
  024 7652 3164   fax 024 7657 4101
  http://www2.warwick.ac.uk/fac/cross_fac/healthatwarwick/
  Co-Director: Prof Gillian Hundt. Co-Director: Dr Hannah Bradby.
- E   An institute within the University of Warwick.
- O   To promote, support and develop social science research in health and social care

Institute of Health and Community Studies (IHCS) 1992

- University of Bournemouth, Royal London House, Christchurch Road, Bournemouth, Dorset, BH1 3LT.
  01202 962114   fax 01202 962131
  http://www.bournemouth.ac.uk/ihcs/
- E   A department of Bournemouth University.
- O   To embrace the spectrum of health and social care

Institute for Health Research (IHR) 1994

- Luton Campus, University of Bedfordshire, Luton, Bedfordshire, LU1 3JU.
  01582 743797   fax 01582 743918
  http://www.beds.ac.uk/research/ihr/
  Contact: Gurch Randhawa.
- E   A research institute at the University of Bedfordshire.
- O   To bring together researchers who are committed to real-world health research, providing information which can influence policy and practice

Institute for Health Research   (IHR)
- Faculty of Social Sciences, Lancaster University, Bowland Tower East, Lancaster, LA1 4YT.
  01524 592127   fax 01524 592401
  http://www.lancs.ac.uk/fass/ihr/
  Contact: Chris Jarvis.
- E   A research institute at Lancaster University.
- O   To conduct research in various aspects of health, including public health, mental health, learning disabilities, supportive and end of life care, clinical psychology, science, technology and medicine

Institute for Health Research   (IHR)   2001
- Faculty of Health and Sciences, Mellor Building, Staffordshire University, College Road, Stoke-on-Trent, ST4 2DF.
  01782 294648   fax 01782 294986
  http://www.staffs.ac.uk/schools/sciences/ihr/
  Director: Prof David White.
- E   A research institute at Staffordshire University.
- O   To draw together researchers and practitioners from nursing and midwifery, medicine, health policy, social care, psychology, sport science, and clinical and sports biomechanics

Institute for Health Research   (IHR)
- School of Health Science, Swansea University, Singleton Park, Swansea, SA2 8PP.
  01792 518531
  http://www.swan.ac.uk/health_science/Research/InstituteforHealthResearch/
- E   A research institute at Swansea University.
- O   To conduct research into various fields of health, including biosciences, health economics, philosophy of health care, research into health care practices, and the organisation of health care

Institute of Health Research and Development
  see **Wessex Institute of Health Research and Development.**

Institute for Health Research and Policy   (IHRP)   2003
- London Metropolitan University, Tower Building, 166-220 Holloway Road, London, N7 8DB.
  020 7133 2140   fax 020 7753 5402
  http://www.londonmet.ac.uk/about/institute-for-health-research-and-policy.cfm
  Director: Prof Chris Branford-White.
- E   A research institute at London Metropolitan University.
- O   To address major social, scientific, technological or health-policy related issues

Institute of Health Sciences   (IHS)   1993
- City University, Northampton Square, London, EC1V 0HB.
  020 7040 0231   fax 020 7040 8556
  http://www.city.ac.uk/ihs/
- E   A federal structure within City University.
- O   To co-ordinate and provide a focal point for areas of the University with an interest in clinical and health-related activity; to promote the University, exploring opportunities for new clinical and health-related ventures; to provide a link between the University and external agencies

Institute of Health Sciences   (IHS)
- Faculty of Medical and Human Sciences, University of Manchester, Williamson Building, Oxford Road, Manchester, M13 9PL.
  0161-275 7657   fax 0161-275 7600
  http://www.ihs.man.ac.uk/
- E   A research institute within the National Primary Care Research and Development Centre (qv) at the University of Manchester.
- O   To promote health sciences research and postgraduate education

Institute of Health Sciences
Note: is the Division of Public Health and Primary Health Care of the University of Oxford, and is therefore not within the scope of this Directory.

Institute of Health Sciences Education   (IHSE)   2005
- Barts and the London, Queen Mary's School of Medicine and Dentistry, Queen Mary, University of London, Abernethy Building, 2 Newark Street, London, E1 2AT.
  020 7882 2509   fax 020 7882 2552
  http://www.ihse.qmul.ac.uk/
  Lead: Prof Martin Underwood.
- E   A department of Queen Mary, University of London.
- O   To focus primarily on medical education

Institute of Health Sciences and Public Health Research
  see **Leeds Institute of Health Sciences.**

Institute for Health Sciences and Social Care Research
■ School of Health and Social Care, Centuria Building, University of Teesside, Middlesbrough, TS1 3BA.
   01642 342750
   http://www.tees.ac.uk/schools/soh/research.cfm
E A department of the University of Teesside.
○ To co-ordinate research activities in the fields of health sciences and social care

Institute of Health and Social Care   (IHSC)
■ Anglia Ruskin University, Bishop Hall Lane, Chelmsford, Essex, CM1 1SQ.
   0845 271 3333
   http://www.anglia.ac.uk/ruskin/en/home/faculties/ihsc.html
   Dean: Prof Mike Cook.
E A department of Anglia Ruskin University.
○ To be a major provider of education and research in the UK into nursing, midwifery, health visiting and social care

Institute for Health and Social Care Research   (IHSCR)
■ Faculty of Health and Social Care, University of Salford, Allerton Building, Salford, Manchester, M6 6PU.
   0161-295 2312; 7006
   http://www.ihscr.salford.ac.uk/
   Director: Prof Steven M Shardlow.
E A department of the University of Salford.
○ To provide a creative and dynamic environment for the conduct of research about real world issues across the health and social care spectrum

Institute for Health and Social Change
   see **Research Institute for Health and Social Change.**

Institute of Health and Social Science Research
■ University of East Anglia, Norwich, NR4 7TJ.
   01603 593681
   http://www1.uea.ac.uk/cm/home/schools/foh/res/hss
E A department of the University of East Anglia.

Institute of Health and Society   (IHS)
■ University of Newcastle upon Tyne, 21 Claremont Place, Newcastle upon Tyne, NE2 4AA.
   0191-222 7045
   http://www.ncl.ac.uk/ihs/
   Director: Prof Cam Donaldson.
E A research institute at the University of Newcastle upon Tyne.
○ To conduct research on population health, health services and health-related social science
Note: Centre for Health Services Research

Institute for Health Studies
   see **Tayside Institute for Health Studies.**

Institute in Healthcare Science
   see **Research Institute in Healthcare Science.**

Institute of Healthy Ageing   (IHA)
■ The Darwin Building, University College London, Gower Street, London, WC1E 6BT.
   020 7679 2000
   http://www.ucl.ac.uk/~ucbtdag/iha/
E A research institute at University College London.

Institute of Hearing Research
   see **MRC Institute of Hearing Research.**

Institute of Hepatology
   see **UCL Institute of Hepatology.**

Institute for High Performance Computing
   see **Microsoft Institute for High Performance Computing.**

Institute for Historical and Cultural Research   (IHCR)
■ School of Arts and Humanities, Oxford Brookes University, Oxford, OX3 0BP.
   01865 483665
   http://www.ah.brookes.ac.uk/ihcr/
   Director: Prof Elisabeth Jay.
E An institute within Oxford Brookes University.

Institute of Historical Research   (IHR)   1921

■   School of Advanced Study, University of London, Senate House, Malet Street, London, WC1E 7HU.
     020 7862 8758
     http://www.history.ac.uk/
     Director: Prof David Bates. Administrator: Elaine Walters.
E   A department of the University of London.
○   To offer a facility for information, meetings and other resources for historians from all over the world

Institute for the Historical Study of Language   (IHSL)   1998

■   Department of English Language, University of Glasgow, 12 University Gardens, Glasgow, G12 8QQ.
     0141-330 4150   fax 0141-330 3531
     http://www.arts.gla.ac.uk/sesll/EngLang/research/historical.html
     Convener: Dr Simon Horobin.
E   An institute at the University of Glasgow.
○   To promote and sustain research into the historical development of languages, particularly, but not exclusively, the English
     language

Institute of Human Genetics   (IHG)   2001

■   School of Clinical Medical Sciences, University of Newcastle upon Tyne, Central Parkway, Newcastle upon Tyne, NE1 3BZ.
     0191-241 8600; 8616   fax 0191-241 8666
     http://www.ncl.ac.uk/ihg/
     Head: Prof John Burn.
E   A research institute within the Centre for Life (qv) at the University of Newcastle upon Tyne.
○   To understand biological processes by investigating the structure of genes, how they vary and how they function

Institute of Human Genetics and Health   (IHGH)

■   Department of Medicine, University College London, Gower Street, London, WC1E 6BT.
     020 7679 4143
     http://www.gene.ucl.ac.uk/IHGH/
     Director: Prof N Wood.
E   An interdisciplinary research institute at University College London.

Institute for Human Health and Performance
       see **UCL Institute for Human Health and Performance.**

Institute of Human Relations
       see **Tavistock Institute of Human Relations.**

Institute of Human Sciences   (HIS)

■   The Pauling Centre, University of Oxford, 58A Banbury Road, Oxford, OX2 6QS.
     01865 274702   fax 01865 274699
     http://www.human-sciences.ox.ac.uk/
     Chairman: Prof David A Coleman. Course Administrator: Mrs Ros Odling-Smee.
E   A department of the University of Oxford.
○   To provide an inter-disciplinary undergraduate education in human sciences, covering several biological, social and cultural
     aspects Future objectives include the provision of research and fellowship opportunities to successful graduates by forming
     stronger links with other post-graduate facilities and the relevant industry
●   Conference facilities - Education and training - Exhibitions - Library - Meetings and conferences (evenings and holidays - by
     appointment only)
¶   Human Sciences Prospectus. Human Sciences Undergraduate Handbook.
Note: Also known as the Pauling Human Sciences Centre.

Institute for Human Sciences   (HIS)

■   Faculty of Arts, Media and Design, Staffordshire University, Mellor Building, College Road, Stoke-on-Trent, ST4 2DF.
     01782 294648
     http://www.staffs.ac.uk/research/institutes/humansci.php
     Contact: Prof David White.
E   An institute within the Centre for Health Psychology (qv) at Staffordshire University.
○   To provide training for health psychologists; to promote psychological research into illness and health and into health care delivery

Institute for Humanities [Keele]
       see **Research Institute for Humanities.**

Institute for the Humanities [London]
       see **Birkbeck Institute for the Humanities.**

Institute of Immunology and Infection Research   (3IR)   2004

■   School of Biological Sciences, University of Edinburgh, The King's Buildings, Mayfield Road, Edinburgh, EH9 3JR.
   0131-650 5511
   http://www.biology.ed.ac.uk/research/institutes/immunology/
   Director: Prof Rick Maizels.
E   An institute at the University of Edinburgh.
○   To conduct research into immunology and infection biology from the level of the molecule to that of the population

Institute for Indian Art and Culture   1972   Bharatiya Vidya Bhavan (BHAVAN)

■   4a Castletown Road, London, W14 9HQ.
   020 7381 3086   fax 020 7381 8758
   http://www.bhavan.net/
E   A registered charity and membership organisation.
○   To preserve, encourage and propagate the teaching and understanding of Indian art and culture as an integral part of the culture of the United Kingdom

Institute for Industrial Mathematics and System Engineering
   see **Smith Institute for Industrial Mathematics and System Engineering.**

Institute of Industrial Research   (IIR)

■   Faculty of Creative and Cultural Industries, Burnaby Building, University of Portsmouth, Burnaby Road, Portsmouth, PO1 3QL.
   023 9284 4448   fax 023 9284 4447
   http://www.port.ac.uk/research/iir/
   Director: Prof George Turnbull.
E   A department of the University of Portsmouth.
○   To conduct research into the use artificial intelligence techniques, which enable computational systems to adapt and learn by interacting with their environments

Institute of Infection, Immunity and Inflammation   (III)   1994

■   School of Molecular Medical Sciences, C Floor - West Block, University of Nottingham, Queen's Medical Centre, Nottingham, NG7 2UH.
   0115-823 1101   fax 0115-823 1102
   http://www.nottingham.ac.uk/iii/
   Contact: Emma Bradley.
E   A research institute within the Centre for Biomolecular Sciences (qv) at the University of Nottingham.
○   To conduct research in various areas of immunity, infection and inflammation, including gastrointestinal mucosal biology, allergy, molecular bacteriology and immunology, virology, ophthalmology, respiratory cell biology, biophysics and biochemistry of biomembranes

Institute in Information and Language Processing
   see **Research Institute in Information and Language Processing.**

Institute for Information Management
   see **Oxford Institute for Information Management.**

Institute of Information Systems and Integration Technology

■   Cardiff School of Engineering, Cardiff University, Queen's Buildings, Newport Road, Cardiff, CF24 3AA.
   029 2087 5917
   http://www.engin.cf.ac.uk/research/institute.asp?InstNo=7
   Leader: Prof Jonathon A Chambers.
E   A research institute at Cardiff University.
○   To co-ordinate research activities within the broad themes of microwave devices and applications, signal processing and information technology

Institute for Information Technology   (IIT)

■   Thames Valley University, Wellington Street, Slough, Berkshire, SL1 1YG.
   01753 697732   fax 01753 697750
   http://iit.tvu.ac.uk/
   Director: Dr Andy Smith.
E   A research institute at Thames Valley University.
○   To provide collaborative research, knowledge transfer, consultancy and training to support IT in the Thames Valley region

Institute of Information Technology Training
   see **Institute of IT Training.**

Institute for Infrastructure and Environment   (IIE)

■   School of Engineering and Electronics, University of Edinburgh, The King's Buildings, Mayfield Road, Edinburgh, EH9 3JR.
   0131-650 5719   fax 0131-650 6781
   http://www.see.ed.ac.uk/research/IIE/
E   A research institute at the University of Edinburgh.
○   To conduct research in civil and environmental engineering

Institute for Innovation and Enterprise   (IIE)
- University of Wolverhampton Business School, Telford Campus, Shifnal Road, Telford, Shropshire, TF2 9NT.
  01902 518960   fax 01902 323957
  http://www.wlv.ac.uk/default.aspx?page=8487
- E   An institute at the University of Wolverhampton.
- O   To give organisations and individuals the knowledge, skills and support they need to start new businesses, develop existing organisations and create innovation and enterprise

Institute for Innovation and Improvement
   see **NHS Institute for Innovation and Improvement.**

Institute of Innovation Research
   see **Manchester Institute of Innovation Research.**

Institute of Integrated Information Systems   (IIIS)
- School of Electronic and Electrical Engineering, University of Leeds, Woodhouse Lane, Leeds, LS2 9JT.
  0113-343 7105   fax 0113-343 2032
  http://www.eenweb.leeds.ac.uk/research/srw_institute_IIIS.php
  Director: Prof Garik Markarian.
- E   A research institute within the University of Leeds.
- O   To conduct research into all aspects of fixed, mobile and satellite communications, satellite navigation systems, radio wave propagation, signal processing, and coding and process tomography
- ●   Laboratory facilities

Institute of Integrative and Comparative Biology   (IICB)   2005
- Faculty of Biological Sciences, University of Leeds, Miall Building, Leeds, LS2 9JT.
  0113-343 2880
  http://www.fbs.leeds.ac.uk/institutes/iicb/
  Director: Prof Tim Benton.
- E   A research institute at the University of Leeds.
- O   To provide a stimulating environment in which to conduct world class research in genetics, through development, cellular biology, physiology, life history, and ecology to evolution
- ●   Education and training - Large laboratories

Institute of Intensive Care Medicine
   see **Centre for Intensive Care Medicine and Bloomsbury Institute of Intensive Care Medicine.**

Institute of International Business   (IIB)
- Lancashire Business School, University of Central Lancashire, Greenbank Building, Preston, PR1 2HE.
  01772 894531
  http://www.uclan.ac.uk/facs/lbs/research/institutes_and_centres/IIB/
  Director: Prof John Wilson.
- E   A research institute at the University of Central Lancashire.
- O   To promote research leadership in the business and academic communities on issues related to industrial corporate change at the international and global levels

Institute of International Development Studies
   see **David Livingstone Institute of International Development Studies.**

Institute for International Health and Development   (IIHD)   1993
- Faculty of Health and Social Sciences, Corstorphine Campus, University of Edinburgh, Clerwood Terrace, Edinburgh, EH12 8TS.
  0131-317 3491
  http://www.qmuc.ac.uk/cihs/
  Director: Prof Barbara McPake.
- E   A research centre at Queen Margaret University.
- O   To support international health development in low and middle-income countries
- ×   Centre for International Health Studies.

Institute for International Policy Analysis   (IfIPA)   1998
- Faculty of Humanities & Social Sciences, University of Bath, Claverton Down, Bath, BA2 7AY.
  01225 386033   fax 01225 383423
  http://www.bath.ac.uk/ifipa/
- E   A research institute at the University of Bath.

Institute for International Research in Glass   (IIRG)   1988
- School of Arts, Design, Media and Culture, University of Sunderland, Liberty Way, Sunderland, Tyne and Wear, SR6 0GL.
  0191-515 3697   fax 0191-515 2132
  http://www.sunderland.ac.uk/~as0kpe
  Chairman: Prof Flavia Swann.
- E   A research institute within the National Glass Centre (qv) at the University of Sunderland.
- O   To promote and facilitate research in glass at a national and international level, and to foster a wider public awareness of the artistic dimensions of studio art glass

Institute of International Shipping and Trade Law   (IISTL)   2000
- School of Law, Swansea University, Singleton Park, Swansea, SA2 8PP.
  01792 295831   fax 01792 295855
  http://www.swan.ac.uk/law/istl/
  Director: Prof D Rhidian Thomas.
- E   A research institute at Swansea University.
- O   To promote research and teaching in the fields of international shipping and trade law

Institute of International Visual Arts   (inIVA)   1994
- 6-8 Standard Place, Rivington Street, London, EC2A 3BE.
  020 7729 9616   fax 020 7729 9509
  http://www.iniva.org/
  Marketing Manager: Natasha Anderson.
- E   A non-profit-making charitable institution.
- O   To create exhibitions, publications, multimedia, education and research projects, designed to bring the work of artists from culturally-diverse backgrounds to the attention of the widest possible public

Institute of Irish and Scottish Studies
  see **Research Institute of Irish and Scottish Studies.**

Institute of Irish Studies   (IIS)   1965
- School of History and Anthropology, 53-67 University Road, Belfast, BT7 1NF.
  028 9097 3386   fax 028 9097 3388
  http://www.qub.ac.uk/iis/
  Director: Dr Dominic Bryan.
- E   A research institute at Queen's University, Belfast.

Institute of Irish Studies   (IIS)   1988
- Faculty of Arts, University of Liverpool, 1 Abercromby Square, Liverpool, L69 7WY.
  0151-794 3831   fax 0151-794 3836
  http://www.liv.ac.uk/irish/
  Director: Prof Marianne Elliott.
- E   A department of the University of Liverpool.
- O   To conduct teaching and research in Irish culture, history and politics; to promote understanding between the people of Britain and Ireland

Institute of IT Training   (IITT)
- Westwood House, Westwood Business Park, Coventry, CV4 8HS.
  0845 006 8858   fax 0845 006 8871
  http://www.iitt.org.uk/
  Chief Executive Officer: Colin Steed.
- E   A not-for-profit organisation loosely affiliated to the National Computing Centre (qv).
- O   To raise continuously the standards of professionalism within the IT training industry, and to establish benchmarks of excellence against which practitioners may be measured

Institute for Japanese-European Technology Studies   (JETS)   1989
- University of Edinburgh, Old Surgeons' Hall, High School Yards, Edinburgh, EH1 1LZ.
  0131-650 2468   fax 0131-650 2390
  http://www.jets.man.ed.ac.uk/
  Director: Prof Martin J Fransman.
- E   An institute within the Institute for the Study of Science, Technology and Innovation (qv) at the University of Edinburgh.
- O   To conduct policy-oriented research on science, technology, industry and business strategy in Japan and Europe

Institute of Japanese Studies
  see **Nissan Institute of Japanese Studies.**

Institute of Jewish Studies   (IJS)
- Department of Hebrew and Jewish Studies, University College London, Foster Court, Gower Street, London, WC1E 6BT.
  020 7679 3520   fax 020 7209 1026
  http://www.ucl.ac.uk/hebrew-jewish/ijs
- E   A research institute at University College London.
- O   To promote all aspects of Jewish scholarship and civilisation at the highest level of academic excellence

Institute of Judicial Administration   (IJA)   1968
- School of Law, University of Birmingham, Edgbaston, Birmingham, B15 2TT.
  0121-414 6282
  http://www.law.bham.ac.uk/ija.htm
  Director: Prof Stephen Shute.
- E   A research institute at the University of Birmingham.

Institute for Land, Food and Environment
  see **Gibson Institute for Land, Food and Environment.**

© CBD Research Ltd · Beckenham · Kent BR3 5JS · Tel 020 8650 7745 · Fax 020 8650 0768 · E-mail cbd@cbdresearch.com · www.cbdresearch.com

Institute of Language and Linguistic Studies
see **Saint Andrews University Institute of Language and Linguistic Studies.**

Institute of Language Research
see **Cambridge Institute of Language Research.**

Institute for Language, Speech and Hearing   (ILASH)   1994
■   University of Sheffield, Mappin Street, Sheffield, S1 3JD.
0114-222 2000
http://www.dcs.shef.ac.uk/research/ilash/
Director: Prof Yorick Wilks.
E   A research institute at the University of Sheffield.
○   To provide a focus and common resource for interdisciplinary research in language, speech and hearing

Institute of Laryngology and Otology   (ILO)   1946
■   Faculty of Biomedical Sciences, University College London, 332 Gray's Inn Road, London, WC1X 8EE.
020 7679 8909 020 7915 1514; 1592   fax 020 7837 9279
http://www.ilo.ucl.ac.uk/
Head: Prof Tony Wright.
E   A department of University College London.
○   To conduct research and run teaching courses in a wide variety of fields, including speech therapy, screening hearing, ENT surgery and audiological medicine, facial plastic surgery, and voice pathology
Note: Also known as the UCL Ear Institute.

Institute of Latin American Studies   (ILAS)   1965
■   School of Languages, Cultures and Area Studies, University of Liverpool, 88 Bedford Street South, Liverpool, L69 7WW.
0151-794 3079   fax 0151-794 3080
http://www.liv.ac.uk/ilas/
E   A department of the University of Liverpool.
○   To promote teaching and research on Latin America in the UK

Institute of Latin American Studies [London]
see **Institute for the Study of the Americas.**

Institute for Law, Politics and Justice
see **Research Institute for Law, Politics and Justice.**

Institute for Learning   (IfL)
■   University of Hull, Cottingham Road, Hull, HU6 7RX.
01482 466871   fax 01482 466135
http://www.hull.ac.uk/ifl/
E   A department of the University of Hull.
○   To be recognised as a research-based centre of excellence in learning and teaching, both nationally and internationally, whilst continuing to have a particular commitment to serving the educational needs of the local region

Institute for Learning and Research Technology   (ILRT)
■   University of Bristol, 8-10 Berkeley Square, Bristol, BS8 1HH.
0117-928 7193   fax 0117-928 7112
http://www.ilrt.bris.ac.uk/
Administrator: Frances Tyson.
E   A centre of excellence at the University of Bristol.
○   To pursue the development and use of technology-based methods in teaching, learning and research

Institute of Legal Practice
see **Bristol Institute of Legal Practice.**

Institute for Life Course Studies
see **Research Institute for Life Course Studies.**

Institute of Life Science   (ILS)   2007
■   Swansea University, Singleton Park, Swansea, SA2 8PP.
01792 205678
http://www.medicine.swan.ac.uk/ils_innovation3.html
E   A department of Swansea University.
○   To host various research activities and facilities, including medical visualisation, biomedical research, micro-technium, deep computing, public health, and clinical research

Institute of Lifelong Learning   (LILL)
■　University of Leicester, 128 Regent Road, Leicester, LE1 7PA.
　　0116-252 5911　fax 0116-252 5909
　　http://www.le.ac.uk/lifelonglearning/
E　An institute at the University of Leicester.

Institute for Lifelong Learning [London]
　　see **Birkbeck Institute for Lifelong Learning.**

Institute of Local Government Studies   (INLOGOV)
■　School of Public Policy, University of Birmingham, Edgbaston, Birmingham, B15 2TT.
　　0121-414 5008
　　http://www.inlogov.bham.ac.uk/
E　A research institute at the University of Birmingham.
○　To be a leading centre for the applied study of local and community governance

Institute of Machines and Structures
■　Cardiff School of Engineering, Cardiff University, Queen's Buildings, Newport Road, Cardiff, CF24 3AA.
　　029 2087 5694
　　http://www.engin.cf.ac.uk/research/institute.asp?InstNo=3
　　Leader: Prof John C Miles.
E　A research institute at Cardiff University.
○　To conduct research in the application of novel and leading-edge technologies to the larger scale aspects of engineering such as machines, including cars, aeroplanes or hydraulic power systems and structures such as dams, bridges and buildings

Institute for Manufacturing   (IfM)
NR　Department of Engineering, University of Cambridge, Mill Lane, Cambridge, CB2 1RX.
　　01223 766141　fax 01223 464217
　　http://www.ifm.eng.cam.ac.uk/
E　An EPSRC Innovative Manufacturing Research Centre at the University of Cambridge.
○　To provide industrial services, and conduct research, education and courses that aim to provide a clear understanding of the challenges that face manufacturing today
Note: Is one of the EPSRC funded centres in the UK - for further information see EPSRC Innovative Manufacturing Research Centres.

Institute of Marine Sciences   (IMS)
■　Faculty of Science, Ferry Road, Eastney, Portsmouth, PO4 9LY.
　　023 9284 5798　fax 023 9284 5800
　　http://www.port.ac.uk/departments/academic/ims/
　　Manager: Dr Gordon Watson.
E　A department of the University of Portsmouth.
○　To conduct research and teaching in marine sciences

Institute of Maritime Law   (IML)   1982
■　School of Law, Highfield, Southampton, SO17 1BJ.
　　023 8059 3449　fax 023 8059 3789
　　http://www.iml.soton.ac.uk/
　　Director: Prof Robert Grime.
E　An institute at the University of Southampton.
○　To be the leading UK centre for the study of maritime law, and for teaching, research and consultancy in the subject

Institute of Mass Spectrometry
　　see **EPSRC National Mass Spectrometry Service Centre.**

Institute for Materials Research   (IMR)
■　School of Process, Environmental and Materials Engineering, University of Manchester, Houldsworth Building, Clarendon Road, Leeds, LS2 9JT.
　　0113-343 2348　fax 0113-343 2384
　　http://www.materials.leeds.ac.uk/
　　Director: Prof A J Bell.
E　A research institute within the University of Leeds.
○　To undertake leading research and postgraduate training in materials science and engineering in selected fields (especially electronic and photonic materials, carbon, metallurgy, and characterisation modelling) for serving the future emerging needs of industry and society

© CBD Research Ltd · Beckenham · Kent BR3 5JS · Tel 020 8650 7745 · Fax 020 8650 0768 · E-mail cbd@cbdresearch.com · www.cbdresearch.com

Institute for Materials Research   (IMR)   1999
- Faculty of Science, Engineering and Environment, University of Salford, Newton Building, Salford, Manchester, M5 4WT.
  0161-295 5303   fax 0161-295 5147
  http://www.imr.salford.ac.uk/
  Contact: Dr Ian Morrison.
- E   A department of the University of Salford.
- O   To co-ordinate and support activities within the fields of materials research, specifically applied mathematics, atomic collisions in solids and ion-beam physics, chemical physics and biomaterials, chemistry and nanotechnology, magnetic materials and nanostructures,materials characterisation and modelling, photonics and nonlinear science, polymers, space and solar plasma physics, spray research, stress analysis, and surface engineering

Institute for Materials Technology
see **University of Nottingham Institute for Materials Technology.**

Institute of Mathematical and Physical Sciences   (IMPS)   2003
- University of Wales Aberystwyth, Penglais, Aberystwyth, Ceredigion, SY23 3BZ.
  01970 622802   fax 01970 622826
  http://www.aber.ac.uk/maps/en/
  Director: Prof Neville Greaves.
- E   A department of the University of Wales, Aberystwyth.
- O   To deliver world class research in mathematics and physical sciences, with particular emphasis on solar systems physics, materials physics, applied mathematics, and pure mathematics

Institute for Mathematical Sciences   (IMS)   2002
- Faculty of Life Sciences, Imperial College London, 53 Prince's Gate, South Kensington, London, SW7 2PG.
  020 7594 1746   fax 020 7594 0923
  http://www3.imperial.ac.uk/mathsinstitute/
  Director: Prof P Hall. Administrator: Eileen Boyce.
- E   A research institute at Imperial College London.
- O   To bring together researchers to tackle fundamental problems needing significant mathematical input

Institute for Mathematical Sciences [Cambridge]
see **Isaac Newton Institute for Mathematical Sciences.**

Institute for Mathematical Sciences [Edinburgh]
see **Maxwell Institute for Mathematical Sciences.**

Institute for Mathematical Sciences [Manchester]
see **Manchester Institute for Mathematical Sciences.**

Institute of Mathematical Sciences [University College London]
see **Lighthill Institute of Mathematical Sciences.**

Institute of Mathematics, Statistics and Actuarial Science   (IMS)
- University of Kent, Room E102 - Cornwallis Building, Canterbury, Kent, CT2 7NF.
  01227 827181   fax 01227 827932
  http://www.kent.ac.uk/ims/
- E   A department of the University of Kent.

Institute for Media, Art and Design
see **Research Institute for Media, Art and Design.**

Institute of Medical and Biological Engineering   (IMBE)
- School of Mechanical Engineering, University of Leeds, Woodhouse Lane, Leeds, LS2 9JT.
  0113-343 2080
  http://www.imbe.org.uk/
  Contact: Debra Baldwin.

Institute of Medical Engineering and Medical Physics
- Cardiff School of Engineering, Cardiff University, Queen's Buildings, Newport Road, Cardiff, CF24 3AA.
  029 2087 5907
  http://www.engin.cf.ac.uk/research/institute.asp?InstNo=5
  Leader: Prof Len D M Nokes.
- E   A research institute at Cardiff University.
- O   To conduct research involving the application of engineering principles to solve problems in medicine and health care

Institute of Medical Genetics, Cardiff University 2004

- Cardiff University, Heath Park, Cardiff, CF14 4XN.
  029 2074 4028   fax 029 2074 7603
  http://www.cardiff.ac.uk/medicine-genetics/medical_genetics/research/
  Head of Department: Prof Julian Sampson. Director, Wales Gene Park: Prof Nicholas Lench.
- E A department of Cardiff University.
- O To provide an environment in which molecular, cellular, mathematical and clinical geneticists (including those with medical, psychological and social science backgrounds) work together on the inherited bases of human disease and the consequences for individuals, families and society
- ● Education and training - Medical services by appointment Mon-Fri
- ¶ Wales Gene Park Annual Report.

Institute of Medical Law   (IML)   2004

- School of Law, University of Birmingham, Edgbaston, Birmingham, B15 2TT.
  0121-414 6286
  http://www.law.bham.ac.uk/iml/
  Administrator: Mrs Alison Wagstaff.
- E A research institute at the University of Birmingham.

Institute for Medical Research
     see **Cambridge Institute for Medical Research.**

Institute of Medical Sciences   (IMS)   1996

- School of Medical Sciences, University of Aberdeen, Polwarth Building, Aberdeen, AB25 2ZD.
  01224 555700   fax 01224 555844
  http://www.abdn.ac.uk/ims/
  Director: Prof Ian Booth.
- E A research institute at the University of Aberdeen.
- O To conduct cutting edge molecular and cell biology research in a variety of fields

Institute of Medical and Social Care Research   (IMSCaR)   1997

- University of Wales Bangor, Dean Street Building, Bangor, Gwynedd, LL57 1UT.
  01248 383002
  http://www.bangor.ac.uk/imscar/
  Head: Vanessa Burholt. Contact: Ann Pierce-Jones.
- E A department of the University of Wales, Bangor.
- O To enhance the health and welfare of the people of Wales, the UK and the rest of the world, through research and education in medicine, health issues and social care

Institute of Medicine and Health Sciences
     see **Kent Institute of Medicine and Health Sciences.**

Institute of Medicine, Law and Bioethics   (IMLAB)   1995

- NR Liverpool School of Law, University of Liverpool, Liverpool, L69 7ZS.
  0151-794 2882   fax 0151-794 2829
  http://www.imlab.ac.uk/
  Director: Samantha Halliday.
- E A research institute at the University of Liverpool.
- O To consolidate the Institute's national and international profile as an authoritative body on medico-legal and bioethical issues
- Note: A collaborative venture involving the Universities of Liverpool, Keele, Manchester, Lancaster and Central Lancashire.

Institute of Medieval Studies   (IMS)   2001

- School of Humanities, University of Wales Lampeter, College Street, Lampeter, Ceredigion, SA48 7ED.
  01570 424872   fax 01570 424872
  http://www.lamp.ac.uk/ims/
- E An institute at the University of Wales, Lampeter.
- O To promote scholarship and research in medieval studies

Institute for Medieval Studies   (IMS)   1967

- University of Leeds, Parkinson Building, Leeds, LS2 9JT.
  0113-343 3620   fax 0113-343 3616
  http://www.leeds.ac.uk/ims/
  Director: Richard Morris. Director of Studies: Dr M Swan.
- E A department of the University of Leeds.
- O To foster research in the field of medieval studies and in particular to facilitate the exchange of ideas and access to expertise across departments; to provide training for employment, particularly training in research skills and access to medieval language-learning for postgraduates working for higher degrees; to broaden the experience of research graduates in the medieval field in all disciplines through interdisciplinary seminars and conferences
- ● Conference facilities - Education and training - The International Medieval Congress is held each year in Leeds The University of Leeds library has extensive holdings in all areas of Medieval Studies Provision of study programmes in Medieval Studies, including a taught MA and interdisciplinary TLD.
- × Centre for Medieval Studies.

© CBD Research Ltd · Beckenham · Kent BR3 5JS · Tel 020 8650 7745 · Fax 020 8650 0768 · E-mail cbd@cbdresearch.com · www.cbdresearch.com

Institute for Medieval Studies (IMS) 1988
- ■ School of History, University of Nottingham, University Park, Nottingham, NG7 2RD.
  0115-951 5928   fax 0115-951 5948
  http://www.nottingham.ac.uk/medieval/
  Director: Dr Ross Balzaretti.
- E An interdisciplinary research institute at the University of Nottingham.
- O To conduct research in the cultures of the Middle Ages

Institute of Membrane and Systems Biology (IMSB) 2005
- ■ Faculty of Biological Sciences, University of Leeds, Garstang Building, Leeds, LS2 9JT.
  0113-343 3115
  http://www.fbs.leeds.ac.uk/institutes/imsb/
  Director: Prof David J Beech.
- E A research institute at the University of Leeds.
- O To provide an environment for modern research relating to animal and human health
- ● Education and training - Large laboratories

Institute for Microstructural and Mechanical Process Engineering   (IMMPETUS)
- ■ University of Sheffield, Mappin Street, Sheffield, S1 3JD.
  0114-222 6018   fax 0114-222 6015
  http://immpetus.shef.ac.uk/
  Director: Prof W M Rainforth.
- E A research institute at the University of Sheffield.
- O To provide scientific underpinning for the development of physically based models to be used in thermomechanical processing of metals

Institute of Microwaves and Photonics   (IMP)
- ■ School of Electronic and Electrical Engineering, University of Leeds, Woodhouse Lane, Leeds, LS2 9JT.
  0113-343 2070   fax 0113-343 7265
  http://www.engineering.leeds.ac.uk/imp/
  Director: Prof A G Davies.
- E A research institute within the University of Leeds.
- O To conduct research in the fields of generation, detection and exploitation, of radiation in the microwave and millimetre spectrum of the electromagnetic spectrum; to conduct research into the design, fabrication and measurement of electronic and photonic nanostructured devices
- ● Laboratory facilities

Institute of Middle East, Central Asia and the Caucasus Studies   (MECACS)
- ■ School of International Relations, University of St Andrews, St Andrews, Fife, KY16 9AL.
  01334 462861; 462938   fax 01334 462937
  http://www.st-andrews.ac.uk/mecacs/
- E An interdisciplinary research institute at the University of St Andrews.
- O To stimulate discourse, research and teaching on the region

Institute for Middle Eastern and Islamic Studies (IMEIS) 1962
- ■ School of Government and International Affairs, University of Durham, The Al-Qasimi Building, Elvet Hill Road, Durham, DH1 3TU.
  0191-334 5656   fax 0191-334 5661
  http://www.dur.ac.uk/sgia/imeis/
  Head: Prof Anoush Ehteshami.
- E A department of the University of Durham.
- O To encourage, through teaching and research, the growth of knowledge and understanding concerning the countries of the contemporary Middle East and Islamic world, and their peoples
- ● Library (over 200,000 publications)
- ✕ Centre for Middle Eastern and Islamic Studies.

Institute for Middle Eastern Studies   (IMES)
- ■ School of Politics and International Relations, University of Nottingham, University Park, Nottingham, NG7 2RD.
  0115-951 4862   fax 0115-951 4859
  http://www.nottingham.ac.uk/middleeast/
  Manager: Ian Nelson.
- E An interdisciplinary research institute at the University of Nottingham.

Institute of Molecular and Cellular Biology (IMCB) 2005
- ■ Faculty of Biological Sciences, University of Leeds, Manton Building, Leeds, LS2 9JT.
  0113-343 3115
  http://www.fbs.leeds.ac.uk/institutes/imcb/
  Director: Prof Steve Homans.
- E A research institute at the University of Leeds.
- O To provide a stimulating environment for world class research in molecular cell biology
- ● Education and training - Large laboratories

Institute of Molecular Medicine [Leeds]
> see **Leeds Institute of Molecular Medicine.**

Institute of Molecular Medicine [Oxford]
> see **Weatherall Institute of Molecular Medicine.**

Institute of Molecular Plant Sciences (IMPS)
■ School of Biological Sciences, University of Edinburgh, The King's Buildings, Mayfield Road, Edinburgh, EH9 3JH.
  0131-650 5318   fax 0131-650 5392
  http://www.biology.ed.ac.uk/research/institutes/plant/
  Director: Prof Andrew Hudson.
E An institute at the University of Edinburgh.
O To use genetics, biochemistry, cell biology and modelling to examine how plants develop, function and evolve

Institute of Motion Tracking and Research (IMAR)
■ Section of Orthpaedic and Trauma Surgery, Ninewells Hospital and Medical School, Dundee, DD1 9SY.
  01382 425746   fax 01382 496200
  http://www.dundee.ac.uk/orthopaedics/imar/welcome.htm
E A research institute at the University of Dundee.

Institute of Movement Neuroscience (IMN)
■ University College London, Queen Square, London, WC1N 3BG.
  020 7837 3611
  http://www.imn.ucl.ac.uk/
  Director: Prof John Rothwell.
E A research institute at University College London.
O To bring together researchers with a common interest in movement control

Institute of Multimedia and Network Systems
> see **Brunel Advanced Institute of Multimedia and Network Systems.**

Institute for Multiphase Flow
> see **BP Institute for Multiphase Flow.**

Institute for Musculoskeletal Research
> see **Sackler Institute for Musculoskeletal Research.**

Institute of Musical Research (IMR) 2006
■ School of Advanced Study, University of London, Senate House, Malet Street, London, WC1E 7HU.
  020 7664 4865   fax 020 7862 8657
  http://www.music.sas.ac.uk/
  Director: Prof Katharine Ellis. Administrator: Mrs Valerie James.
E A department of the University of London.
O To offer a meeting point for researchers and postgraduate students across the UK, and to act as a hub for collaborative work on a national and international scale

Institute for Name-Studies **(INS) 2002**
■ School of English Studies, University of Nottingham, University Park, Nottingham, NG7 2RD.
  0115-951 5900   fax 0115-951 5924
  http://www.nottingham.ac.uk/english/research/CENS/about.html
  Contact: Prof Thorlac Turville-Petre.
E A research institute at the University of Nottingham.
O To conduct research in English place-names
● Research projects: The Survey of English Place-Names and The Vocabulary of English Place-Names
     Centre for English Name-Studies.

Institute of Nanoscale Science and Technology (INSAT) 1999
■ University of Newcastle upon Tyne, Newcastle upon Tyne, NE1 7RU.
  0191-222 8665
  http://www.ncl.ac.uk/insat/
  Director: Prof Nick Wright.
E A research institute at the University of Newcastle upon Tyne.
O To conduct research on the pursuit of microsystems and nanotechnology development, especially on the nanoengineering of the interface between biological, physical and information paradigms

© CBD Research Ltd · Beckenham · Kent BR3 5JS · Tel 020 8650 7745 · Fax 020 8650 0768 · E-mail cbd@cbdresearch.com · www.cbdresearch.com

Institute of Nephrology   1967
- Cardiff School of Medicine, Cardiff University, Heath Park, Cardiff, CF14 4XN.
  http://www.cardiff.ac.uk/medicine/nephrology/
  Director: Prof John Williams.
- E   A research institute within the Cardiff Institute of Tissue Engineering and Repair (qv) at Cardiff University.
- O   To address important clinical problems, including the control of progression in diabetic renal disease, the control of inflammation, mechanisms of matrix expansion and cortical scarring, and investigation into the genetic basis of kidney disease

Institute for Neuro-Physiological Psychology   (INPP)   1975
- 1 Stanley Street, Chester, CH1 2LR.
  01244 311414   fax 01244 311414
  http://www.inpp.org.uk/
  Director: Sally Goddard Blythe.
- E   A company limited by guarantee.
- O   To assess and supervise remedial programmes for children with special learning difficulties; to train other professionals in methods developed at the Institute
- ●   Education and training - Information service
- ¶   Reflexes, Learning and Behaviour. The Well Balanced Child.

Institute of Neurological Sciences
- Southern General Hospital, 1345 Govan Road, Glasgow, G51 4TF.
  0141-201 1100   fax 0141-201 2999
  http://www.nhsgg.org.uk/

Institute of Neurological Studies
> see **Reta Lila Weston Institute of Neurological Studies.**

Institute of Neurology   (IoN)   1950
- Faculty of Biomedical Sciences, National Hospital for Neurology and Neurosurgery, Queen Square, London, WC1N 3BG.
  020 7837 3611   fax 020 7278 5069
  http://www.ion.ucl.ac.uk/
  Director: Prof Roger Lemon.
- E   A faculty of University College London.
- O   To provide teaching and research of the highest quality in neurology and the neurosciences, and professional training for clinical careers in neurology, neurosurgery, neuropsychiatry, neuroradiology, neuropathology, and clinical neurophysiology

Note: The Institute is a World Health Organisation WHO Collaborating Centre (qv) for Research and Training in Neurosciences.

Institute of Neuroscience   (IoN)   2004
- School of Neurology, Neurobiology and Psychiatry, University of Newcastle upon Tyne, Henry Wellcome Building for Neuroecology, Framlington Place, Newcastle upon Tyne, NE2 4HH.
  0191-222 6968
  http://www.ncl.ac.uk/ion/
  Director: Prof Anya Hurlbert.
- E   A research institute at the University of Newcastle upon Tyne.
- O   To draw together brain scientists for research in various fields of neuroscience

Institute of Neuroscience   2003
- School of Biomedical Sciences, E Floor - Medical School, University of Nottingham, Queen's Medical Centre, Nottingham, NG7 2UH.
  0115-823 0147
  http://www.nottingham.ac.uk/neuroscience/
  Administrator: Wendy Brennan.
- E   A research institute at the University of Nottingham.
- O   To promote and develop fundamental and clinical neuroscience

Institute of Neuroscience Research
> see **Neuroscience Research Institute.**

Institute of Nuclear Medicine   (INM)   1961
- The Middlesex Hospital, Mortimer Street, London, W1T 3AA.
  020 7380 9421
  http://www.ucl.ac.uk/nuclear-medicine/
- E   A research institute at University College London.

Institute of Nursing and Midwifery   (INAM)
- Faculty of Health, University of Brighton, Westlain House, Village Way, Brighton, East Sussex, BN1 9PH.
  01273 644013   fax 01273 644010
  http://www.brighton.ac.uk/inam/
- E   An institute at the University of Brighton.

Institute of Nursing and Midwifery

■ School of Health and Social Sciences, Middlesex University, Queensway, Enfield, Middlesex, EN3 4SA.
020 8411 6458
http://www.mdx.ac.uk/hssc/
Director: Dr Kay Caldwell.
E An institute at Middlesex University.

Institute of Nursing Research   (INR)

■ Faculty of Life and Health Sciences, Coleraine Campus, University of Ulster, Cromore Road, Coleraine, County Londonderry, BT52 1SA.
028 7032 4623
http://www.science.ulster.ac.uk/inr/
Director: Prof Kader Parahoo.
E A research institute at the University of Ulster.
O To facilitate, co-ordinate and to carry out nursing research in partnership with health providers, commissioners and other centres of excellence

Institute of Occupational and Environmental Medicine   (IOEM)   1982

■ University of Birmingham, Edgbaston, Birmingham, B15 2TT.
0121-414 6030   fax 0121-414 6217
http://www.pcpoh.bham.ac.uk/ioem/
Director: Prof Jouni Jaakkola.
E A research institute at the University of Birmingham.
O To develop and conduct research and teaching programmes in occupational and environmental medicine, epidemiology, ergonomics, toxicology, hygiene, and other related disciplines, in order to prevent health hazards in the workplace, and in the common environment, with an aim to create healthy general and working environments
Note: Institute of Occupational Health.

Institute for Occupational Ergonomics   (IOE)   1986

■ School of Mechanical Materials and Manufacturing Engineering, University of Nottingham, ITRC Building, University Park, Nottingham, NG7 2RD.
0115-951 4040   fax 0115-846 6771
http://www.virart.nottingham.ac.uk/ioe.htm
E An institute at the University of Nottingham.
O To offer clients advice, investigations and training in ergonomics

Institute of Occupational Health
see **Institute of Occupational and Environmental Medicine.**

Institute of Occupational Medicine   (IOM)   1969

■ University of Edinburgh, Riccarton, Edinburgh, EH14 4AP.
0870 850 5131   fax 0870 850 5132
http://www.iom-world.org/
Chief Executive: Dr Philip Woodhead.
E An independent registered charity and centre of scientific excellence.
O To benefit those at work and in the community by providing quality research, training and consultancy in health, hygiene and safety
Note: The Institute also has offices in Chesterfield, London and Stafford.

Institute of Ophthalmology

■ Faculty of Biomedical Sciences, University College London, 11-43 Bath Street, London, EC1V 9EL.
020 7608 6800
http://www.ucl.ac.uk/ioo/
Contact: Chris Hayden.
E A department of University College London.
O To further the understanding of the processes of vision and to develop new diagnostic and therapeutic strategies for the benefit of patients worldwide

Institute of Optometry   (IOO)   1922

■ 56-62 Newington Causeway, London, SE1 6DS.
020 7407 4183   fax 020 7403 8007
http://www.ioo.org.uk/
Chief Executive: Sir Patrick Cable-Alexander.
E A registered charity and a not-for-profit company limited by guarantee.
O To provide general optometric services, including specialist clinics; to conduct postgraduate education, particularly for optometrists
● Conference facilities - Education and training - Library

Institute for Orthodox Christian Studies (IOCS) 1999

■ Wesley House, University of Cambridge, Jesus Lane, Cambridge, CB5 8BJ.
  01223 741037   fax 01223 741370
  http://www.iocs.cam.ac.uk/
  Principal and Administrator: Prof David Frost, MA, PhD.
E An institute at the University of Cambridge.
○ To offer full-time and part-time courses in the Orthodox theological tradition

Institute of Orthopaedics 1971

■ Keele University, Oswestry, Shropshire, SY10 7AG.
  01691 404000   fax 01691 404050
  http://www.keele.ac.uk/depts/rjah/
  Director: Prof J B Richardson.
E A research institute with close links to Keele University.
○ To provide elective orthopaedic surgery and musculo-skeletal medical services

Institute of Orthopaedics and Musculo-Skeletal Science (IOMS) 1946

■ Faculty of Biomedical Sciences, Royal Free and University College Medical School, University College London, Brockley Hill,
  Stanmore, Middlesex, HA7 4LP.
  020 8909 5494
  http://www.ucl.ac.uk/orthopaedics/
  Director: Prof Allen Goodship.
E A department of University College London.
○ To be a world leading centre for innovative translational research in the restoration of pain free functional mobility and high
  quality independent living

Institute for Particle Physics Phenomenology (IPPP) 2002

■ Department of Physics, University of Durham, South Road, Durham, DH1 3LE.
  0191-334 3811   fax 0191-334 3658
  http://www.ippp.dur.ac.uk/
  Director: Prof E W Nigel Glover.
E A research institute within the Ogden Centre for Fundamental Physics (qv) at the University of Durham.
○ To foster world class research in particle phenomenology

Institute of Particle Science and Engineering (IPSE)

■ School of Process, Environmental and Materials Engineering, University of Leeds, Houldsworth Building, Clarendon Road, Leeds,
  LS2 9JT.
  0113-343 2406
  http://www.leeds.ac.uk/speme/ipse/
  Director: Prof Mojtaba Ghadiri.
E A research institute within the University of Leeds.
○ To undertake research in the engineering science of particulate processes and products by applying an integrated approach to
  their design and manufacture
● Information service - Seminars

Institute for Peace and Conflict Research
  see **Richardson Institute for Peace and Conflict Research.**

Institute of Perception, Action and Behaviour

■ School of Informatics, University of Edinburgh, Appleton Tower, Crichton Street, Edinburgh, EH8 9LE.
  0131-650 2690   fax 0131-651 1426
  http://www.inf.ed.ac.uk/research/ipab/
E An institute at the University of Edinburgh.
○ To link computational action, perception, representation, transformation and generation processes to real or virtual worlds

Institute of Performing Arts
  see **Liverpool Institute of Performing Arts.**

Institute of Petroleum Engineering
  see **Heriot-Watt Institute of Petroleum Engineering.**

Institute of Pharmaceutical Innovation (IPI)

■ School of Life Sciences, University of Bradford, Bradford, West Yorkshire, BD7 1DP.
  01274 236160
  http://www.ipi.ac.uk/
  Commercial Manager: Piers Lincoln.
E A department of the University of Bradford.
○ To conduct research in ways of accelerating drug development, and supporting bioscience businesses

Institute for Pharmaceutical Materials Science
  see **Pfizer Institute for Pharmaceutical Materials Science.**

Institute of Pharmaceutical Sciences and Experimental Therapeutics   (IPSET)
- University of Nottingham, University Park, Nottingham, NG7 2RD.
   0115-951 5059   fax 0115-846 6296
   http://www.nottingham.ac.uk/ipset/
   Secretary: Julie Woodhouse.
- E   A department of the University of Nottingham.
- O   To bring together researchers who have a research focus from molecules to man, with particular emphasis on the physical sciences and the life sciences

Institute of Pharmacy and Biomedical Sciences
   see **Strathclyde Institute of Pharmacy and Biomedical Sciences.**

Institute of Philosophy   (IP)   2005
- School of Advanced Study, University of London, Senate House, Malet Street, London, WC1E 7HU.
   020 7862 8683
   http://www.philosophy.sas.ac.uk/
   Director: Prof Tim Crane. Administrator: Dr Shahrar Ali.
- E   A department of the University of London.
- O   To promote and support philosophy of the highest quality in all its forms, both inside and outside the University

Institute for Philosophy and Public Policy   (IPPP)
- Faculty of Social Sciences, Furness College, Lancaster University, Lancaster, LA1 4YG.
   01524 592674   fax 01524 592503
   http://www.lancs.ac.uk/fass/ippp/
   Director: Prof David Archard.
- E   A research institute at Lancaster University.

Institute of Photonics   (IOP)   1996
- Faculty of Science, University of Strathclyde, Wolfson Centre, 106 Rottenrow, Glasgow, G4 0NW.
   0141-548 4120   fax 0141-552 1575
   http://www.photonics.ac.uk/
   Administrator: Lynda McLaughlin.
- E   A commercially-oriented research unit at the University of Strathclyde.
- O   To bridge the gap between academic research and industrial applications and development in the area of photonics

Institute for Policy and Practice   (IPP)
- University of Newcastle upon Tyne, 4th Floor - Claremont Bridge Building, Newcastle upon Tyne, NE1 7RU.
   0191-222 5037   fax 0191-232 9259
   http://www.ncl.ac.uk/ipp/
   Administrator: Mrs Barbara Cochrane.
- E   A department of the University of Newcastle upon Tyne.
- O   To facilitate the development of social science research of the highest quality which engages with policy and practice

Institute for Policy Studies in Education   (IPSE)
- Department of Education, North Campus, London Metropolitan University, 166-220 Holloway Road, London, N7 8DB.
   020 7133 4220   fax 020 7133 4219
   http://www.londonmet.ac.uk/research-units/ipse/
   Director: Prof Alistair Ross.
- E   A research institute at London Metropolitan University.
- O   To conduct research and analysis in educational policy, with a focus on education for social inclusion and social justice

Institute for Political and Economic Governance   (iPEG)
- School of Social Sciences, University of Manchester, Williamson Building, Oxford Road, Manchester, M13 9PL.
   0161-275 0792; 0798   fax 0161-275 0793
   http://www.ipeg.org.uk/
   Director: Prof Peter John.
- E   A research institute at the University of Manchester.
- O   To provide long-term understanding and strategy insights, and so contribute to the development of effective governance, appropriate to the needs of the economy and society, in the new century

Institute of Politics and International Studies
Note: Now the School of Politics and International Studies (POLIS) at the University of Leeds.

Institute of Polymer Technology and Materials Engineering   (IPTME)   1967

- ■ Faculty of Science, Loughborough University, Ashby Road, Loughborough, Leicestershire, LE11 3TU.
  01509 223331   fax 01509 223949
  http://www.lboro.ac.uk/departments/iptme/
  Head of Institute: Prof Jon Binner.
- E   A department of Loughborough University.
- O   To offer a range of undergraduate, graduate and research programmes based on the engineering application and use of materials which, when processed, are altered in structure and properties - all types of materials are covered, including ceramics, metals, polymers and their composites
- ● Conference facilities - Education and training - Wide range of equipment, particularly relating to characterisation and processing
- ¶ IPTME Biennial Report.

Institute of Popular Music   (IPM)   1988

- ■ School of Music, University of Liverpool, 80 Bedford Street South, Liverpool, L69 7WW.
  0151-794 3096   fax 0151-794 3141
  http://www.liv.ac.uk/ipm/
  Director: Dr Sara Cohen.
- E   A registered charity at the University of Liverpool.
- O   To further the academic study of popular music

Institute for Postgraduate Medicine and Primary Care   1999

- ■ Faculty of Life and Health Sciences, Coleraine Campus, University of Ulster, Cromore Road, Coleraine, County Londonderry, BT52 1SA.
  028 7032 4159   fax 028 7032 4956
  http://www.science.ulster.ac.uk/medicinehealth/
  Director: Prof Frank Dobbs.
- E   A research institute at the University of Ulster.

Institute of Power Systems
> see **Brunel Institute of Power Systems.**

Institute of Preventive Medicine [Bushey]
> see **Lister Institute of Preventive Medicine.**

Institute of Preventive Medicine [London]
> see **Wolfson Institute of Preventive Medicine.**

Institute for Primary Care Development

- ■ School of Health and Social Sciences, Middlesex University, Furnival Building, Archway Campus, London, N19 5LW.
  020 8411 6930   fax 020 8411 6942
  http://www.mdx.ac.uk/hssc/acstructure/primary.asp
  Director: Kate Brown.
- E   An institute at Middlesex University.

Institute of Primary Care and Public Health   (IPCPH)   2002

- ■ Faculty of Health and Social Care, London South Bank University, 103 Borough Road, London, SE1 0AA.
  020 7815 8000
  http://www.lsbu.ac.uk/health/research_groups.shtml#institute
- E   A research institute within London South Bank University.
- O   To act as a focus for work on health improvement undertaken within the University

Institute of Professional Legal Studies   (IPLS)   1977

- ■ Queen's University, Belfast, 10 Lennoxvale, Belfast, BT9 5BY.
  028 9097 5567   fax 028 9066 1192
  http://www.qub.ac.uk/ipls/
  Director: Mrs Anne Fenton.
- E   An institute at Queen's University, Belfast.
- O   To offer postgraduate courses in vocational training for trainee barristers and solicitors

Institute of Psychiatry   1923

- ■ King's College London, De Crespigny Park, London, SE5 8AF.
  020 7848 0483
  http://www.iop.kcl.ac.uk/
- E   A research institute at King's College, London.
Note: The Institute is a World Health Organisation WHO Collaborating Centre (qv) for Research and Training in Mental Health.

Institute of Psychobiological Research
> see **Sackler Institute of Psychobiological Research.**

Institute of Psychological Sciences   (IPS)

■   Faculty of Medicine and Health, University of Leeds, Leeds, LS2 9JT.
    0113-343 5724   fax 0113-343 5749
    http://www.psych.leeds.ac.uk/
    Director: Prof Martin Conway.
E   A research institute at the University of Leeds.

Institute for the Psychology of Elite Performance   (IPEP)

■   School of Sport, Health and Exercise Sciences, University of Wales Bangor, George Building, Normal Site, Bangor, Gwynedd,
    LL57 2PZ.
    01248 382756   fax 01248 371053
    http://www.shes.bangor.ac.uk/institute.php?catid=&subid=1276
    Co-Director: Prof Jeremy Jones. Co-Director: Prof Lew Hardy.
E   A research institute at the University of Wales, Bangor.
O   To pursue research which is focused on elite performance in sport, business, the performing arts and the armed services

Institute of Psychosynthesis   1973

■   65a Watford Way, London, NW4 3AQ.
    020 8202 4525   fax 020 8202 6166
    http://www.psychosynthesis.org/
E   A private company limited by guarantee.
O   To conduct research and training in psychosynthesis

Institute of Psychotherapy and Social Studies   (IPSS)   1978

■   PO Box 1955, London, N5 1YJ.
    020 7284 4762
    http://www.ipss-psychotherapy.org/
E   A membership organisation.
O   To provide training in individual psychotherapy

Institute of Public Health   (IPH)

■   School of Clinical Medicine, University of Cambridge, Robinson Way, Cambridge, CB2 2SR.
    01223 330300   fax 01223 330349
    http://www.iph.cam.ac.uk/
    Director: Dr Ron Zimmern.
E   An institute at the University of Cambridge.
O   To improve the health of the population by understanding of the cause and natural history of disease; to identify and evaluate new
    possibilities for both primary and secondary care intervention and prevention; to monitor on a population basis interventions as
    they are currently applied

Institute for Public Health Research and Policy
    see **Centre for Public Health Research.**

Institute for Public Policy and Management
    see **Research Institute for Public Policy and Management.**

Institute for Public Policy Research   (IPPR)   1988

■   30-32 Southampton Street, Covent Garden, London, WC2E 7RA.
    020 7470 6100   fax 020 7470 6111
    http://www.ippr.org.uk/
    Director: Nick Pearce.
E   An independent research institute.
O   To conduct research and inform policy debates with the aim of building a fairer, more democratic and environmentally sustainable
    world

Institute of Public Sector Accounting Research   (IPSAR)   1987

■   Management School and Economics, University of Edinburgh, William Robertson Building, 50 George Square, Edinburgh,
    EH8 9JY.
    0131-650 3900
    http://www.man.ed.ac.uk/research/centres/ipsar/
E   A research institute at the University of Edinburgh.
O   To identify, develop and promulgate principles for best accounting practice in the public sector

Institute of Pulmonary Pharmacology
    see **Sackler Institute of Pulmonary Pharmacology.**

© CBD Research Ltd · Beckenham · Kent BR3 5JS · Tel 020 8650 7745 · Fax 020 8650 0768 · E-mail cbd@cbdresearch.com · www.cbdresearch.com

Institute of Railway Studies and Transport History   (IRS&TH)   1995
- National Railway Museum, Leeman Road, York, YO26 4XJ.
  - 01904 621261   fax 01904 611112
  - http://www.york.ac.uk/inst/irs/
  - Contact: Prof Colin Divall.
- E   A research institute at the University of York.
- O   To study the history of transport and mobility

Institute for Rehabilitation
- School of Sport, Health and Exercise Sciences, University of Wales Bangor, George Building, Normal Site, Bangor, Gwynedd, LL57 2PZ.
  - 01248 382756   fax 01248 371053
  - http://www.shes.bangor.ac.uk/institute1.php?catid=&subid=985
- E   An institute at the University of Wales, Bangor.
- O   To oversee a number of multi-disciplinary research programmes in rehabilitation and proactive health promotion

Institute of Rehabilitation   1997
- University of Hull, 215 Anlaby Road, Hull, HU3 2PG.
  - 01482 675602   fax 01482 675636
  - http://www.hull.ac.uk/instrehab/
  - Director: Prof Leslie G Walker.
- E   An institute within the University of Hull.
- O   To perform nationally and internationally significant research

Institute for Religion, Ethics and Public Life
    see **Heythrop Institute for Religion, Ethics and Public Life.**

Institute of Reproductive and Developmental Biology   (IRDB)   2001
- Faculty of Medicine, Hammersmith Campus, Imperial College London, Du Cane Road, London, W12 0NN.
  - 020 7594 2176   fax 020 7594 2154
  - http://www1.imperial.ac.uk/medicine/about/divisions/sora/irdb/irdb/
  - Scientific Director: Prof Malcolm Parker.
- E   A research institute at Imperial College London.
- O   To conduct research in reproductive and developmental biology, with particular emphasis on gonandal development, uterine biology, stem cell biology, fetal and maternal medicine, cell signalling and gene expression

Institute for Research in Applicable Computing   (IRAC)
- Department of Computing and Information Systems, Luton Campus, University of Bedfordshire, Luton, Bedfordshire, LU1 3JU.
  - 01582 489230   fax 01582 489212
  - http://www.beds.ac.uk/research/irac/
  - Director: Prof Gordon Clapworthy.
- E   A research centre at the University of Bedfordshire.
- O   To develop novel applications of computer technology to solve real world problems; to provide innovative tools to enable users to employ computer technology more efficiently and more effectively

Institute of Research in Applied Natural Sciences
    see **Luton Institute of Research in Applied Natural Sciences.**

Institute for Research on Contemporary China   (IRCC)   2002
- University of Leeds, 14-20 Cromer Terrace, Leeds, LS2 9JT.
  - 0113-343 6749   fax 0113-343 6808
  - http://www.smlc.leeds.ac.uk/ircc/
  - Director: Dr Flemming Christiansen.
- E   An interdisciplinary research centre within the University of Leeds.
- O   To facilitate research and research co-operation on contemporary China

Institute for Research on the Environment and Sustainability   (IRES)
- Devonshire Building, University of Newcastle upon Tyne, Newcastle upon Tyne, NE1 7RU.
  - 0191-246 4949   fax 0191-246 4998
  - http://www.ncl.ac.uk/environment/
  - Administrator: Miss Anne Buckle.
- E   An interdisciplinary research institute at the University of Newcastle upon Tyne.
- O   To draw together researchers involved in various disciplines from some aspect of environmental research

Institute for Research in Health and Human Sciences
- Faculty of Health and Human Sciences, Thames Valley University, Westel House, 32-38 Uxbridge Road, London, W5 2BS.
  - 020 8280 5145; 5295   fax 020 8280 5143
  - http://www.health.tvu.ac.uk/research/index.asp
  - Director: Prof Norma Reid Birley.
- E   A research institute at Thames Valley University.

Institute for Research in the Humanities and Arts
see **Bristol Institute for Research in the Humanities and Arts.**

Institute for Research and Innovation in Art and Design
see **Manchester Institute for Research and Innovation in Art and Design.**

Institute for Research into Learning and Teaching in Higher Education   (IRLTHE)
- ■ School of Education, Jubilee Campus, University of Nottingham, Wollaton Road, Nottingham, NG8 1BB.
   0115-951 4498   fax 0115-951 4475
   http://www.nottingham.ac.uk/education/centres/irlthe/
   Director: Prof Roger Murphy.
- E A research institute at the University of Nottingham.
- ○ To conduct high quality academic research on learning and teaching in higher education

Institute for Research in the Scottish Economy
see **Fraser of Allander Institute for Research in the Scottish Economy.**

Institute for Research in the Social Sciences   (IRISS)   1982
- ■ Alcuin College, University of York, Heslington, York, YO10 5DD.
   01904 321290
   http://www.york.ac.uk/inst/iriss/
- E A research institute at the University of York.
- ○ A multi-disciplinary centre for research in the social sciences

Institute for Research in Visual Culture
see **Nottingham Institute for Research in Visual Culture.**

Institute for Retail Studies   (IRS)   1983
- ■ Department of Marketing, University of Stirling, Stirling, FK9 4LA.
   01786 467041
   http://www.irs.stir.ac.uk/
- E A research centre at the University of Stirling.
- ○ To provide a resource base for academic and industry-based researchers, management development services to professional management in the retail industry, academic and applied research for retail and distributive companies, and retail support for companies, local and national governments and research councils

Institute of Rheumatology
see **Kennedy Institute of Rheumatology.**

Institute of Romance Studies
see **Institute of Germanic and Romance Studies.**

Institute of Rural Health   (IRH)   1997
- ■ Gregynog, Newtown, Powys, SY16 3PW.
   01686 650800   fax 01686 650300
   http://www.irh.ac.uk/
   Chief Executive: Jane Randall-Smith. Education Manager: Ann Whale.
- E A registered charity and a company limited by guarantee.
- ○ To sustain and optimise the health and well-being of rural people and their communities
- ● Conference facilities - Education and training - Library - Policy analysis
- ¶ Newsletter. (wide range of other publications).

Institute of Rural Sciences   (IRS)
- ■ University of Wales Aberystwyth, Llanbadarn Fawr, Aberystwyth, Ceredigion, SY23 3AL.
   01970 621986   fax 01970 611264
   http://www.irs.aber.ac.uk/
   Research Director: Prof Jamie Newbold.
- E A department of the University of Wales, Aberystwyth.
- ○ To conduct research in rural development, animal science and environmental ecology

Institute of Russian and East European Studies
see **Nottingham Institute of Russian and East European Studies.**

Institute for Safety Risk and Reliability
see **Cranfield Institute for Safety Risk and Reliability.**

© CBD Research Ltd · Beckenham · Kent BR3 5JS · Tel 020 8650 7745 · Fax 020 8650 0768 · E-mail cbd@cbdresearch.com · www.cbdresearch.com

Institute of Safety in Technology and Research   (ISTR)
- ■ University of Birmingham, Edgbaston, Birmingham, B15 2TT.
  0121-414 3344
  http://www.istr.bham.ac.uk/
- E An institute at the University of Birmingham.

Institute of Satellite Navigation
- E A research institute within the Institute of Integrated Information Systems (qv) at the University of Leeds.
- O To conduct research in global navigation satellite systems
      see **CAA Institute of Satellite Navigation.**

Institute for Science and Civilisation
      see **James Martin Institute for Science and Civilisation.**

Institute for Science Education   (ISE)
- ■ School of Earth, Ocean and Environmental Sciences, University of Plymouth, Portland Square, Drake Circus, Plymouth, PL4 8AA.
  Contact: Dr David Harwood.
- E An institute within the University of Plymouth.

Institute for Science and Society   (ISS)
- ■ West Wing, Law and Social Sciences Building, University of Nottingham, University Park, Nottingham, NG7 2RD.
  0115-846 7173   fax 0115-846 6349
  http://www.nottingham.ac.uk/iss
  Director: Prof Robert Dingwall.
- E A school at the University of Nottingham.
- O To deliver internationally recognised research and research training on innovation and change in society, science, technology and medicine
Note: Institute for the Study of Genetics, Biorisks and Society

Institute for Science and Technology in Medicine   (ISTM)   2004
- ■ Keele University Medical School, Keele University, Hartshill Campus, Thornburrow Drive, Stoke-on-Trent, ST4 7QB.
  01782 554605
  http://www.keele.ac.uk/research/istm/
  Director: Prof Alicia El Haj.
- E A research institute at Keele University.
- O To focus research on science and technology in medicine in the fields of cell and tissue engineering and cell physiology, imaging and diagnostics, human disease and genomics, and applied entomology and parasitology

Institute for Small Business and Entrepreneurship   (ISBE)   1992
- ■ 2nd Floor, 3 Ripon Road, Harrogate, North Yorkshire, HG1 2SX.
  01423 500046   fax 01423 500046
  http://www.isbe.org.uk/
- E A registered charity.
- O To promote knowledge and expertise in small business and entrepreneurship

Institute of Social and Cultural Anthropology   (ISCA)   1990
- ■ University of Oxford, 51 Banbury Road, Oxford, OX2 6PE.
  01865 274670   fax 01865 274630
  http://www.isca.ox.ac.uk/
- E A department of the University of Oxford.
- O To conduct research in all fields of anthropology

Institute for Social, Cultural and Policy Research   (ISCPR)
- ■ Faculty of Arts, Media and Social Sciences, University of Salford, Salford, Manchester, M5 4WT.
  0161-295 5876
  http://www.iscpr.salford.ac.uk/
  Director: Prof Paul Bellaby.
- E A department of the University of Salford.
- O To build, sustain and enhance research activity at the University into social, cultural and policy questions of major real world significance

Institute for Social and Economic Research   (ISER)   1989
- ■ University of Essex, Wivenhoe Park, Colchester, Essex, CO4 3SQ.
  01206 872957   fax 01206 873151
  http://www.iser.essex.ac.uk/
  Director: Prof Stephen Jenkins.
- E A research institute at the University of Essex.
- O To specialise in the production and analysis of longitudinal data (evidence which tracks changes in the lives of the same individuals over time)

Institute for Social and Health Research   2004
- ■   University of Chester, Parkgate Road, Chester, CH1 4BJ.
         01244 513115
         http://www.chester.ac.uk/ishr/
         Contact: Prof Roger Ellis, OBE.
- E   A department of the University of Chester.

Institute of Social and Health Research   (ISHR)
- ■   School of Health and Social Sciences, Middlesex University, Queensway, Enfield, Middlesex, EN3 4SA.
- E   An institute at Middlesex University.
- ○   To promote and support high quality research and postgraduate education and training in social and health sciences
- ●   Education and training

Institute for Social Marketing   (ISM)
- ■   University of Stirling, Stirling, FK9 4LA.
         01786 467390   fax 01786 464745
         http://www.ism.stir.ac.uk/
         Director: Prof Gerard Hastings.
- E   A research institute at the University of Stirling.
- ○   To study social marketing theory and practice

Institute of Social Psychology   1964
- ■   Department of Sociology, LSE, Houghton Street, London, WC2A 2AE.
         020 7955 7712   fax 020 7955 7565
         http://www.lse.ac.uk/collections/socialPsychology/
         Head: Prof Patrick Humphreys.
- E   A research institute at the London School of Economics and Political Science.

Institute of Social Research   (ISR)
- ■   Department of Sociology, University of Surrey, Guildford, Surrey, GU2 7XH.
         01483 689365   fax 01483 689551
         http://www.soc.surrey.ac.uk/research/isr.htm
         Administrator: Agnes McGill.
- E   A research institute at the University of Surrey.

Institute of Social Work, Advice Work and Social Studies
- ■   Faculty of Health and Sciences, Staffordshire University, Brindley Building, Leek Road, Stoke-on-Trent, ST4 2DF.
         01782 294000
         http://www.staffs.ac.uk/schools/health/
         Head: Bernard Moss.
- E   A research institute at Staffordshire University.
              Institute of Social Work and Applied Social Studies

Institute of Social Work and Applied Social Studies
         see **Institute of Social Work, Advice Work and Social Studies.**

Institute of Society, Health and Ethics
         see **Cardiff Institute of Society, Health and Ethics.**

Institute for Socio-Technical Research and Innovation   (Chimera)
- ■   Ross Building - PP1, Adastral Park, Ipswich, Suffolk, IP5 3RE.
         01473 631182   fax 01473 614936
         http://www.essex.ac.uk/chimera/
         Business Co-ordinator: Alison Lealman.
- E   A research institute at the University of Essex.
- ○   To combine the social and technological sciences so as to generate insights into the personal and social use of information and communication technologies

Institute in Software Evolution
         see **Research Institute in Software Evolution.**

Institute of Sound Recording   (IoSR)
- ■   School of Arts, Communication and Humanities, University of Surrey, Guildford, Surrey, GU2 7XH.
         01483 686500   fax 01483 686501
         http://www.surrey.ac.uk/soundrec/
         Director: Prof Dave Fisher.
- E   A research institute at the University of Surrey.

Institute of Sound and Vibration Research   (ISVR)   1963

■ Faculty of Engineering, Science and Mathematics, University of Southampton, Highfield, Southampton, SO17 1BJ.
   023 8059 2294   fax 023 8059 3190
   http://www.isvr.soton.ac.uk/
   Director: S J Elliott.
E   A department of the University of Southampton.
○   To be the world's foremost teaching, research and consulting centre for the study of all aspects of sound and vibration; to be a centre for postgraduate and postdoctoral research with four interactive groups - fluid dynamics and acoustics, human sciences, signal processing control, and dynamics
●   Consultancy - Teaching Equipment includes - large anechoic room, reverberation rooms, subjective acoustics laboratories, engine noise and vibration test cells, wind tunnel, acoustic fatigue test facility, motion simulation laboratory, computing facilities for signal processing
Note: See also the Hearing and Balance Centre.

Institute for Spatial and Environmental Planning   (ISEP)

■ School of Planning, Architecture and Civil Engineering, David Keir Building, Stranmillis Road, Belfast, BT9 5AG.
   028 9097 4006
   http://www.qub.ac.uk/ep/isep/
   Director: Prof Joe Howe.
E   A research institute at Queen's University, Belfast.

Institute of Sport and Exercise   (ISE)

■ Dundee, DD1 4HN.
   01382 384122
   http://www.dundee.ac.uk/sportexercise/
E   A research institute at the University of Dundee.

Institute of Sport and Exercise Medicine   1958

■ Department of Surgery, University College London, 157 Waterloo Road, London, SE1 8US.
   020 7902 9000   fax 020 7928 0927
   http://www.ucl.ac.uk/surgery/ISM.htm
   Chairman: Sir David Money-Coutts, KCVO.
E   A research institute at University College London.
○   To advance medical knowledge and technique in the treatment of sports injuries
●   Lecture courses - Seminars - Study days

Institute for Sport and Exercise Sciences
   see **Research Institute for Sport and Exercise Sciences.**

Institute of Sport and Leisure Policy   (ISLP)   1990

■ School of Sport and Exercise Sciences, Loughborough University, Ashby Road, Loughborough, Leicestershire, LE11 3TU.
   01509 226365   fax 01509 226301
   http://www.lboro.ac.uk/departments/sses/institutes/salp
   Director: Dr Paul Downward.
E   A research institute at Loughborough University.
○   To focus on the theoretically informed analysis of sport and leisure policy

Institute for Stem Cell Biology
   see **Wellcome Trust Centre for Stem Cell Research and Institute for Stem Cell Biology.**

Institute of Stem Cell Biology and Regenerative Medicine
   see **North East England Stem Cell Institute.**

Institute for Stem Cell Research   **(ISCR)**

■ School of Biological Sciences, University of Edinburgh, The King's Buildings, West Mains Road, Edinburgh, EH9 3JQ.
   0131-650 5828   fax 0131-650 7773
   http://www.iscr.ed.ac.uk/
E   A Medical Research Council research institute at the University of Edinburgh.
○   To provide scientific foundations for the application of cell replacement therapies in treatment of human disease and injury
      See Medical Research Council Collaborative Centre for further information.
Note: Also known as the Centre for Stem Cell Research.

Institute of Structural and Molecular Biology   (ISMB)

■ School of Biological Sciences, University of Edinburgh, The King's Buildings, Mayfield Road, Edinburgh, EH9 3JR.
   0131-650 5366   fax 0131-650 8650
   http://www.biology.ed.ac.uk/research/institutes/structure/
   Head: Prof Graeme Reid.
E   An institute within the University of Edinburgh.
○   To study the structural nature and impact of biomolecules from details of their atomic structure, through their assembly into larger scale molecular machines, up to the study of the large scale effects of these molecular assemblies

Institute of Structural Molecular Biology (ISMB)   2003
NR   School of Crystallography, Birkbeck, University of London, Malet Street, Bloomsbury, London, WC1E 7HX.
    020 7631 6830   fax 020 7631 6803
    http://www.ismb.lon.ac.uk/
    Director: Prof Gabriel Waksman. Administrator: Tim Hoe.
E   A research institute at Birkbeck, University of London.
O   To provide a scientific environment conducive to world class research in the field of protein science
Note: A joint initiative with University College London.

Institute for Studies on Ageing
    see **Sheffield Institute for Studies on Ageing.**

Institute for the Study of the Americas   2004
■   School of Advanced Study, University of London, Senate House, Malet Street, London, WC1E 7HU.
    020 7862 8870   fax 020 7862 8886
    http://americas.sas.ac.uk/
E   A department of the University of London.
O   To promote, co-ordinate and provide a focus, in the University of London, for research and postgraduate teaching on the Americas - Canada, the USA, Latin America and the Caribbean
✕   Institute of Latin American Studies. Institute of United States Studies.

Institute for the Study of Children, Families and Social Issues   (ISCFSI)
■   Faculty of Science, Birkbeck, University of London, 7 Bedford Square, London, WC1B 3RA.
    020 7079 0823   fax 020 7323 4738
    http://www.iscfsi.bbk.ac.uk/
    Director: Prof Jay Belsky.
E   An institute at Birkbeck, University of London.
O   To undertake basic and applied research related to the development, functioning and well-being of children and families, and to address pressing social issues

Institute for the Study of Christianity and Sexuality   (ISCS)   1986
■   Oxford House, Derbyshire Street, London, E2 6HG.
    020 7739 1249   fax 020 7739 1249
    http://www.lgcm.org.uk/
    General Secretary: Rev Richard Kirker.
E   A registered charity.
O   To advance the Christian religion by promoting objective debate within the churches upon matters concerning human sexuality
●   Conference facilities - Counselling services - Education and training - Information service

Institute for the Study of Drug Dependence
    see **DrugScope.**

Institute for the Study of European Transformations   (ISET)   2002
■   London Metropolitan University, Tower Building, 166-220 Holloway Road, London, N7 8DB.
    020 7133 2927
    http://www.londonmet.ac.uk/research-units/iset/
E   An interdisciplinary research institute at London Metropolitan University.
O   To conduct research into European integration and enlargement, migrations and immigrations, citizenship, allegiances and identity, European global interactions, and cultural politics

Institute for the Study of Genetics, Biorisks and Society
    see **Institute for Science and Society.**

Institute for the Study of Japanese Arts and Cultures
    see **Sainsbury Institute for the Study of Japanese Arts and Cultures.**

Institute for the Study of Jewish / non-Jewish Relations
    see **Parkes Institute for the Study of Jewish / non-Jewish Relations.**

Institute for the Study of Language and Social Sciences   (ISLS)   1992
■   School of Languages and Social Sciences, Aston University, Aston Triangle, Birmingham, B4 7ET.
    0121-204 3000   fax 0121-204 3766
    http://www.aston.ac.uk/lss/research/centres/isls/
    Director of Postgraduate Programmes: Dr Christina Schaeffner. Director of Research: Prof Malcolm Coulthard.
E   A research institute at Aston University.
O   To encourage research which builds on a discourse-analytic approach that sees language as an activity embedded in social interaction; to interpret results of such analysis against the political, ideological, functional determination of communication
●   Conference facilities - Education and training

Institute for the Study of Political Parties   (ISPP)   1990
- ■   Department of Politics, University of Sheffield, Elmfield, Northumberland Road, Sheffield, S10 2TU.
      0114-222 1700   fax 0114-222 1717
      http://www.shef.ac.uk/politics/ispp
      Co-Director: Prof Patrick Seyd. Co-Director: Prof Paul Whiteley.
- E   A research institute at the University of Sheffield.
- O   To specialise in the study of political parties

Institute for the Study of Science, Technology and Innovation   (ISSTI)
- ■   College of Humanities and Social Science, University of Edinburgh, Old Surgeons' Hall, High School Yards, Edinburgh, EH1 1LZ.
      0131-650 6384; 6388 (mornings)   fax 0131-650 6399
      http://www.issti.ed.ac.uk/
      Director: Prof Robin Williams. Information Officer: Mrs Moyra Forrest.
- E   A department of the University of Edinburgh.
- O   An international organisation concerned with fundamental and policy-relevant academic research
- ●   Postgraduate supervision

Institute for the Study of Slavery   (ISOS)   1998
- ■   School of History, University of Nottingham, University Park, Nottingham, NG7 2RD.
      0115-951 5935   fax 0115-951 5948
      http://www.nottingham.ac.uk/isos/
      Co-Director: Prof Dick Geary. Co-Director: Prof Stephen Hodkinson.
- E   A research institute at the University of Nottingham.
- O   To pursue and develop research on slavery, in all parts of the globe and through all periods
- ×   International Centre for the History of Slavery.

Institute for the Study of Slavery and Emancipation
      see **Wilberforce Institute for the Study of Slavery and Emancipation.**

Institute of Surface Science Technology   (ISST)   1977
- ■   Faculty of Science, Loughborough University, Loughborough, Leicestershire, LE11 3TU.
      01509 223387   fax 01509 234225
      http://www.lboro.ac.uk/departments/iptme/lmcc/isst/
      Contact: Dr Gary Critchlow.
- E   A research institute within the Loughborough Materials Characterisation Centre (qv) at Loughborough University.
- O   To carry out research in the field of surfaces and related phenomena

Institute of Sustainability, Energy and Environmental Management   (ISEEM)
- ■   Cardiff School of Engineering, Cardiff University, PO Box 925, Newport Road, Cardiff, CF24 0YF.
      029 2087 4280
      http://www.engin.cf.ac.uk/research/institute.asp?InstNo=4
      Director: Prof R A Falconer.
- E   A research institute at Cardiff University.
- O   To conduct multi-disciplinary research in numerous areas connected with the environment

Institute for Sustainable Development
      see **Oxford Institute for Sustainable Development.**

Institute of Sustainable Energy Technology   (ISET)
- ■   School of the Built Environment, University of Nottingham, David Wilson Millennium Eco-House, University Park, Nottingham, NG7 2RD.
      0115-951 3134
      http://www.nottingham.ac.uk/sbe/institutes/institute_sustain_tech.php
- E   A research institute at the University of Nottingham.
- O   To conduct high quality research into renewable and/or sustainable technologies, attract funding from outside sources, run training programmes and short courses, and participate in network activities

Institute for Sustainable Water, Integrated Management and Ecosystem Research   (SWIMMER)   2006
- ■   University of Liverpool, Nicholson Building, Liverpool, L3 5QA.
      0151-795 4642
      http://www.liv.ac.uk/swimmer/
      Director: Prof Edward Maltby.
- E   A department of the University of Liverpool.
- O   To provide a focus for interdisciplinary water science research

Institute for System Level Integration   (iSLI)   1998

NR   Alba Centre, Alba Campus, Livingston, EH54 7EG.
       01506 469300   fax 01506 469301
       http://www.sli-institute.ac.uk/
       Director and Chief Executive: Tony Harker. Chairman: Ronald Dunn.
E   A research institute.
O   To support the development of electronics systems design worldwide and to encourage the exploration of new technologies
       through research; to produce highly skilled design engineers and researchers to meet the needs of the rapidly changing global
       semiconductor industry
Note: The iSLI is a collaborative academic venture with the Universities of Edinburgh, Glasgow, Heriot-Watt, and Strathclyde.

Institute in Systematic Theology
       see **Research Institute in Systematic Theology.**

Institute of Technology   (IoT)

■   London Business School, Sussex Place, Regent's Park, London, NW1 4SA.
       020 7000 7000   fax 020 7000 7001
       http://www.london.edu/instituteoftechnology.html
       Director: Prof Gerry George.
E   A research centre at the London Business School.
O   To provide independent, unbiased teaching, research and practice of technology management benefiting students, companies and
       the UK and European economies

Institute of Technology [Southampton]
       see **Wessex Institute of Technology.**

Institute of Theology

■   Queen's University, Belfast, University Square, Belfast, BT7 1NN.
       028 9097 5108   fax 028 9024 9864
       http://www.qub.ac.uk/ithe/
       Director: Dr J Lewis.
E   A school at Queen's University, Belfast.

Institute of Theology [Cambridge]
       see **Margaret Beaufort Institute of Theology.**

Institute for Theology, Imagination and the Arts   (ITIA)

■   School of Divinity, University of St Andrews, South Street, St Andrews, Fife, KY16 9JU.
       01334 462841   fax 01334 462852
       http://www.st-andrews.ac.uk/itia/
       Director: Prof Trevor Hart.
E   A research institute at the University of St Andrews.
O   To conduct teaching and research with the goal of advancing and enriching theological reflection through an engagement with the
       imagination and the arts

Institute of Theoretical, Applied and Computational Mechanics

■   Cardiff School of Engineering, Cardiff University, Queen's Buildings, Newport Road, Cardiff, CF24 3AA.
       029 2087 4934
       http://www.engin.cf.ac.uk/research/institute.asp?InstNo=2
       Leader: Prof Bhushan L Karihaloo.
E   A research institute at Cardiff University.
O   To conduct research in various fields of mechanics, including mechanics of materials, tribology and contact mechanics, and
       transcendental eigenproblems

Institute of Theoretical Geophysics   (ITG)

■   University of Cambridge, Wilberforce Road, Cambridge, CB3 0WA.
       01223 337094   fax 01223 765900
       http://www.esc.cam.ac.uk/new/v10/research/institutes/itg/body.html
       Contact: Doris Allen
E   An institute within the Centre for Mathematical Sciences (qv) at the University of Cambridge.
O   To conduct research in quantitative descriptions of processes fundamental to the Earth

Institute of Tissue Engineering and Repair
       see **Cardiff Institute of Tissue Engineering and Repair.**

Institute for Transatlantic, European and American Studies   (ITEAS)   2003

■   School of Humanities, University of Dundee, Tower Building, Nethergate, Dundee, DD1 4HN.
       01382 384588
       http://www.dundee.ac.uk/iteas/
       Director: Prof Alan Dobson.
E   A research institute at the University of Dundee.

     © CBD Research Ltd · Beckenham · Kent BR3 5JS · Tel 020 8650 7745 · Fax 020 8650 0768 · E-mail cbd@cbdresearch.com · www.cbdresearch.com

Institute for Transfusion Sciences
 see **Bristol Institute for Transfusion Sciences.**

Institute for Transport Studies   (ITS)   1966
■   University of Leeds, 36-40 University Road, Leeds, LS2 9JT.
     0113-343 5325; 5326   fax 0113-343 5334
     http://www.its.leeds.ac.uk/
     Director: Prof Oliver Carsten.
E   A department of the University of Leeds.
O   To advance the understanding of transport systems throughout the world, through teaching and research activities which develop
     the necessary skills and best practice in the planning, design, operation and use of transport systems
●   Education and training

Institute of Transport and Tourism   (ITT)
■   Lancashire Business School, University of Central Lancashire, Greenbank Building, Preston, PR1 2HE.
     01772 894531; 894912
     http://www.uclan.ac.uk/facs/lbs/research/institutes_and_centres/transport/
     Director: Prof Les Lumsdon.
E   A research institute at the University of Central Lancashire.
O   To advance knowledge about travel for leisure and tourism

Institute for Tribotechnology
 see **Jost Institute for Tribotechnology.**

Institute for Tropical Ecosystem Dynamics
 see **York Institute for Tropical Ecosystem Dynamics.**

Institute of Ulster-Scots Studies   2001
■   Faculty of Arts, University of Ulster, Room MI 021 - Magee Campus, Northland Road, Londonderry, BT48 7JL.
     028 7137 5612   fax 028 7137 5543
     http://www.arts.ulster.ac.uk/ulsterscots/
     Director: Prof John Wilson.
E   A research institute at the University of Ulster.
O   To explore the history, heritage and legacy of the Ulster-Scots people

Institute of United States Studies
 see **Institute for the Study of the Americas.**

Institute of Urban Planning   (IUP)   1967
■   School of the Built Environment, University of Nottingham, University Park, Nottingham, NG7 2RD.
     0115-951 3134
     http://www.nottingham.ac.uk/sbe/institutes/institute_urbanplanning.php
E   An institute within the University of Nottingham.
O   To organise and run a range of postgraduate courses in urban design

Institute of Urology   1951
■   Faculty of Biomedical Sciences, Royal Free and University College Medical School, University College London, 48 Riding House
     Street, London, W1W 7EY.
     020 7679 9381   fax 020 7637 7076
     http://www.ucl.ac.uk/uro-neph/
     Director: Prof A R Mundy.
E   A registered charity and specialist medical institute at University College London.
O   To be a major centre for clinical and laboratory based nephro-urological research

Institute for Vaccine Research
 see **Edward Jenner Institute for Vaccine Research.**

Institute for Volunteering Research   (IVR)
■   Regent's Wharf, 8 All Saints Street, London, N1 9RL.
     020 7520 8902   fax 020 7520 8910
     Director: Justin Davis Smith.
E   A registered charity.
O   To develop knowledge and understanding of volunteering, with particular relevance to policy and practice
¶   Voluntary Action Journal.

Institute of Water and Environment   (IWE)

- ■ Cranfield University, Silsoe, Bedfordshire, MK45 4DT.
  01525 863327   fax 01525 863344
  http://www.silsoe.cranfield.ac.uk/iwe/
  Administrator: Carolyn King.
- E A research institute at Cranfield University.
- ○ To provide practical and cost-effective solutions to the challenges of managing water for users, consumers and the environment within the context of sustainable natural resource use

Institute of Welsh Politics   Sefydliad Gwleidyddiaeth Cymru

- ■ Department of International Politics, University of Wales Aberystwyth, Adeilad Llandinam Building, Penglais, Aberystwyth, Ceredigion, SY23 3DB.
  01970 622336   fax 01970 622709
  http://www.aber.ac.uk/interpol/IWP/
  Director: Dr Richard Wyn Jones.
- E A research institute at the University of Wales, Aberystwyth.
- ○ To promote the academic study and analysis of all aspects of Welsh politics

Institute of Women's Health

- ■ 8 De Montfort Street, Leicester, LE1 7GA.
  0116-225 5100   fax 0116-225 5100
- E A registered charity.
- ○ To provide women with information on the menopause and osteoporosis
- ● Education and training

Institute for Women's Studies   1984

- ■ Lancaster University, County South, Bailrigg, Lancaster, LA1 4YD.
  01524 592680   fax 01524 592400
  http://www.lancs.ac.uk/fss/
  Director: Dr Gail Lewis.
- E A research institute at Lancaster University.
- ○ To conduct research and teaching in women's studies

Institute of Work, Health and Organisations   (I-WHO   1999

- ■ University of Nottingham, 8 William Lee Buildings, University Boulevard, Nottingham, NG7 2RQ.
  0115-846 7523   fax 0115-846 6625
  http://www.nottingham.ac.uk/iwho/
  Director: Prof Tom Cox.
- E A department of the University of Nottingham.
- ○ To be a world-class centre of excellence in research in applied psychology and related areas; to be a quality provider of postgraduate education and training in vocational areas of applied psychology and related subjects; to be active and influential in policy and related legal research and in policy development
- ● Education and training Collection, evaluation and dissemination of information on research, education, practice and policy in its core areas
- ¶ See website for publications list.
Note: The Institute is a World Health Organisation WHO Collaborating Centre (qv) for Occupational Health.

Institute of Work Psychology   (IWP)   1994

- ■ Department of Social Sciences, University of Sheffield, Sheffield, S10 2TN.
  0114-222 3271
  http://www.shef.ac.uk/iwp/
  Administrator: Mark Steele.
- E A research institute at the University of Sheffield.
- ○ To advance knowledge about the causes of individual, team and organizational effectiveness at work

Institute of Youth Sport   (IYS)   1998

- ■ School of Sport and Exercise Sciences, Loughborough University, Ashby Road, Loughborough, Leicestershire, LE11 3TU.
  01509 226302
  http://www.lboro.ac.uk/departments/sses/institutes/iys/
  Director: Dr Mary Nevill.
- E A research institute at Loughborough University.
- ○ To draw together people with an interest in the welfare, education, performance and development of young people participating (or being encouraged to participate) in sport and physical education

Institute of Zoology

- ■ Regent's Park, London, NW1 4RY.
  020 7722 3333   fax 020 7586 2870
  http://www.zoo.cam.ac.uk/ioz/
- E The research section of the Zoological Society of London

© CBD Research Ltd · Beckenham · Kent BR3 5JS · Tel 020 8650 7745 · Fax 020 8650 0768 · E-mail cbd@cbdresearch.com · www.cbdresearch.com

Institution of Occupational Safety and Health   (IOSH)   1945
- ■   The Grange, Highfield Drive, Wigston, Leicestershire, LE18 1NN.
     0116-257 3198   fax 0116-257 3101
     http://www.iosh.co.uk/
- E   A membership organisation.

Insurance Fraud Bureau   (IFB)   2006

0800 328 2550
http://www.insurancefraudbureau.org/
- ○   To co-ordinate direct action to optimise the disruption of organised and cross-industry insurance fraud

Integrated Earth System Sciences Institute   (IESSI)
- ■   Natural Resources' Department, Cranfield University, Silsoe, Bedfordshire, MK45 4DT.
     01525 863000
     http://www.cranfield.ac.uk/sas/naturalresources/iessi/
     Director: Prof Sue White.
- E   A research institute at Cranfield University.
- ○   To conduct research on the application of biophysical science to integrated land management

Integrated Protein Research Centre   (IPRC)
- ■   Department of Medical Biochemistry and Immunology, Cardiff University, Henry Wellcome Building, Heath Park, Cardiff, CF14 4XN.
     029 2074 4009
     http://iprc.cf.ac.uk/
     Contact: Ian Brewis.
- E   A research centre at Cardiff University.
- ○   To enable improvements in the quality of protein research

Integrated Waste Management Centre
   see **Centre for Resource Management & Efficiency.**

Intellectual Property Institute   (IPI)
- ■   36 Great Russell Street, London, WC1B 3QB.
     020 7436 3040   fax 020 7323 5312
     http://www.ip-institute.org.uk/
     Chairman: Ian Harvey. Director: Dr Paul Leonard.
- E   A registered charity and non-profit-making organisation.
- ○   To promote, through high quality independent research, awareness and understanding of intellectual property law and its contribution to economic and social welfare

Intellectual Property Research Centre
   see **Oxford Intellectual Property Research Centre.**

Intelligent Systems Research Centre   (ISRC)
- ■   Department of Computing, Communications Technology and Mathematics, City Campus, London Metropolitan University, 100 Minories, London, EC3N 1JY.
     020 7320 3109   fax 020 7320 1717
     http://www.londonmet.ac.uk/depts/cctm/research/intelligent-systems-research-centre.cfm
     Director: Dr Hassan Kazemian.
- E   A research centre at London Metropolitan University.

Intelligent Technologies Research Centre   (ITRC)   2005
- ■   School of Engineering, Science and Design, University of Glasgow, Cowcaddens Road, Glasgow, G4 0BA.
     0141-331 3826
     http://www.gcal.ac.uk/esd/research/centres_intelligent.html
     Contact: Dr Barry Beggs.
- E   A research centre at Glasgow Caledonian University.
- ○   To marry telecommunications and educational technology research

Interaction Centre
   see **UCL Interaction Centre.**

Interdisciplinary Centre for Astrobiology   (ICA)
- ■   Open University, Walton Hall, Milton Keynes, MK7 6AA.
     01908 659599
     http://ica.open.ac.uk/
     Director: Prof John Zarnecki.
- E   An interdisciplinary research centre at the Open University.
- ○   To study the origins of life in the Universe and the search for planets beyond the Earth that may support life even in the most primitive form

Interdisciplinary Centre for Child and Youth Focused Research   (ICCFYR)   2002
■   School of Health Sciences and Social Care, Brunel University, Uxbridge, Middlesex, UB8 3PH.
　　01895 268775
　　http://www.brunel.ac.uk/research/centres/iccfyr
　　Director: Prof Judith Harwin.
E　A research centre at Brunel University.
O　To bring together academics who have a shared interest in researching the lives of children and youth

Interdisciplinary Centre for Computer Music Research   (ICCMR)
■   School of Computing, Communications and Electronics, University of Plymouth, Portland Square, Drake Circus, Plymouth, PL4 8AA.
　　01752 232579
　　http://cmr.soc.plymouth.ac.uk/
　　Contact: Prof Eduardo R Miranda.
E　A research centre at the University of Plymouth.
O　To conduct research in the fields of computer-aided musical composition, generative music, software sound synthesis, interaction and control, robotics and music, auditory, neuroscience of music, brain-computer music interface, computational biomusicology, and the relationships between language, speech and music

Interdisciplinary Centre for Scientific Research in Music   (ICSRiM)
■   School of Computing and School of Music, University of Leeds, Leeds, LS2 9JT.
　　0113-343 2583   fax 0113-343 2586
　　http://www.leeds.ac.uk/icsrim/
　　Director: Dr Kia Ng.
E　A research centre within the University of Leeds.
O　To provide a venue for research in creative human-computer interactions, applications of music psychology, and analysis, synthesis and encoding of musical sound

Inter-Disciplinary Ethics Across Subject Disciplines [CETL]
　　see **IDEA CETL.**

Interdisciplinary Research Centre in Advanced Knowledge Technologies   (AKT)
NR　Department of Electronics and Computer Science, University of Southampton, Southampton, SO17 1BJ.
　　023 8059 3523
　　http://www.aktors.org/
　　Director: Prof Nigel Shadbolt. Contact: Susan D Davies.
E　An interdisciplinary research centre at the University of Southampton.
O　To develop and extend a range of technologies which provide integrated methods and services for the capture, modelling, publishing, reuse and management of knowledge
Note: A joint venture with the Open University and the Universities of Aberdeen, Edinburgh and Sheffield.

Interdisciplinary Research Centre on Ageing
　　see **Cambridge Interdisciplinary Research Centre on Ageing.**

Interdisciplinary Research Centre (IRC) in Biomedical Materials   1991
■   School of Science and Engineering, Queen Mary, University of London, Mile End Road, London, E1 4NS.
　　020 7882 5285   fax 020 8983 1799
　　http://www.materials.qmul.ac.uk/irc/
　　Director: Prof Pankaj Vadgama. Contact: Catherine Jones.
E　A department of Queen Mary, University of London.
O　To conduct research and development in biomedical materials, including the development of improved prostheses and implant materials with medical and dental applications

Interdisciplinary Research Centre in Dependability of Computer-Based Systems   (DIRC)   2000
NR　School of Computing Science, University of Newcastle upon Tyne, 8th Floor - Claremont Tower, Newcastle upon Tyne, NE1 7RU.
　　0191-222 7972; 8183
　　http://www.dirc.org.uk/
　　Director: Prof Cliff Jones.
E　An interdisciplinary research centre at the University of Newcastle upon Tyne.
O　To develop knowledge, methods and tools that contribute to our understanding of socio-technical system dependability and that support developers of dependable systems
Note: A joint venture with City University, Lancaster University and the Universities of Edinburgh and York.

Interdisciplinary Research Centre in Health   (IRCH)   2002
■   Coventry University, Priory Street, Coventry, CV1 5FB.
　　024 7688 7452
　　http://www.coventry.ac.uk/cms/jsp/polopoly.jsp?d=796
　　Director: Prof Julie Barlow.
E　An interdisciplinary research centre at Coventry University.
O　To raise awareness of the needs of people with long term health conditions and disability; to promote understanding of psychological and social issues experienced by people with long term health conditions and disability; to enhance the quality of life for people with long term health conditions and disability, and everyone involved in their care

Interdisciplinary Research Centre in Materials Processing (IRC Materials) 1989
- University of Birmingham, Edgbaston, Birmingham, B15 2TT.
  0121-414 3446   fax 0121-414 3441
  http://www.irc.bham.ac.uk/
  Head: Prof S Blackburn.
- E A research centre at the University of Birmingham.
- O To conduct research in the development of materials, of materials processing and of manufacturing technologies so that the properties of materials are fully exploited

Interdisciplinary Research Centre in Polymer Science and Technology (Polymer IRC) 1989
- Department of Physics and Astronomy, University of Leeds, Leeds, LS2 9JT.
  0113-343 3810   fax 0113-343 3846
  http://www.dur.ac.uk/irc.web/
  Director: Prof Tom McLeish
- E A research centre based at the University of Leeds.
- O To conduct research in all aspects of materials and polymer chemistry

Interdisciplinary Research Centre in Superconductivity 1988
- University of Cambridge, Madingley Road, Cambridge, CB3 0HE.
  01223 337076   fax 01223 337074
  http://www.phy.cam.ac.uk/research/sucon/
  Director: Prof A M Campbell.
- E A centre at the University of Cambridge.
- O To improve the understanding of new high temperature oxide superconductors, and to develop and realise their potential future applications

Interface Analysis Centre (IAC)
- University of Bristol, Oldbury House, 121 St Michael's Hill, Bristol, BS2 8BS.
  0117-331 1170
  http://www.iac.bris.ac.uk/
  Director: Prof G C Allen.
- E An interdisciplinary research centre at the University of Bristol.
- O To investigate the surfaces and interfaces in solid-state materials

Interface - The Centre for Interdisciplinary Practice 2001
- School of Education, University of Aberdeen, MacRobert Building, King's College, Aberdeen, AB24 5UA.
  01224 274676; 274682
  http://www.abdn.ac.uk/interface/
  Contact: Norma Hart.
- E A centre at the University of Aberdeen.
- O To support staff and agencies in the development of integrated provision for children, young people and their families

Interfaith Education Centre (IEC) 1986
- Listerhills Road, Bradford, West Yorkshire, BD7 1HD.
  01274 731674   fax 01274 731621
  http://www.educationbradford.com/
- E A Bradford local education authority resource centre.
- O To provide support for religious education and collective worship in Bradford schools

International Agriculture and Technology Centre (IATC)
- Corner of Avenue J and 10th Street, Stoneleigh Park, Kenilworth, Warwickshire, CV8 2LZ.
  0870 720 0275
  http://www.theiatc.org/
- E A joint initiative between Government and the Royal Agricultural Society of England.
- O To promote the capability of the UK agri-technology sector

International Arbitration and Mediation Centre
- 12 Bloomsbury Square, London, WC1A 2LP.
  020 7421 7444   fax 020 7404 4023
  http://www.arbitrators.org/
- E The headquarters of the Chartered Institute of Arbitrators.

International Automotive Research Centre (IARC) 1985
- University of Warwick, Coventry, CV4 7AL.
  024 7657 2574
  http://www.iarc.warwick.ac.uk/
  Programme Director: Dr Charles Carey. Senior Research Fellow: Alan Curtis.
- E A department of the University of Warwick.
- O To conduct research and development programmes (currently 20) to enhance manufacturing and design capabilities of West Midlands automotive suppliers
- ● Conference facilities - Education and training
- × Advanced Technology Centre.

International Biographical Centre   (IBC)   1960
- ■   St Thomas Place, Ely, Cambridgeshire, CB7 4EX.
     01353 646600
     http://www.internationalbiographicalcentre.com/
- E   A publisher of biographical reference books.

International Centre for Advanced Research in Identification Science   (ICARIS)
- ■   Department of Electronic and Electrical Engineering, University of Sheffield, Sir Frederick Mappin Building, Mappin Street, Sheffield, S1 3JD.
     0114-222 5414
     http://www.icaris.group.shef.ac.uk/
     Director: Prof Nigel Allinson.
- E   A research centre at the University of Sheffield.
- O   To lead international interdisciplinary research in human identification

International Centre against Censorship
     see **Article 19: International Centre against Censorship.**

International Centre for Archives and Records Management Research and User Studies   (ICARUS)   2005
- ■   School of Library, Archive and Information Studies, University College London, Henry Morley Building, Gower Street, London, WC1E 6BT.
     020 7679 7204   fax 020 7383 0557
     http://www.ucl.ac.uk/slais/research/icarus/
     Contact: Andrew Flinn.
- E   A research centre at University College London.
- O   To develop knowledge and understanding of the creation, management and use of records and their role in society; to map, monitor and evaluate significant changes in the archives and records domain using robust evidence-based methods

International Centre for Arts in Health Care
     see **Arts for Health Centre.**

International Centre for Biblical Interpretation
- ■   Department of Humanities, Francis Close Hall Campus, University of Gloucestershire, Swindon Road, Cheltenham, Gloucestershire, GL50 4AZ.
     0870 721 0210
     http://www.glos.ac.uk/faculties/ehs/humanities/projects/icbi/
- E   A research centre at the University of Gloucestershire.
- O   To promote scholarship that engages with the subject matter of the Bible in such a way as to advocate its continuing significance for life in church and society

International Centre for Brewing and Distilling   (ICBD)   1988
- ■   School of Life Sciences, University of Edinburgh, Riccarton, Edinburgh, EH14 4AS.
     0131-451 3184   fax 0131-449 7459
     http://www.bio.hw.ac.uk/icbd/icbd.htm
     Director: Prof Paul Hughes.
- E   A research centre at Heriot-Watt University.
- O   To offer services, expertise and facilities consistent with the standards required in the local, national, and international markets; to offer both Honours and Masters Degrees in brewing and distilling

International Centre for Chinese Heritage and Archaeology   (ICCHA)   2003
- ■   Faculty of Social and Historical Sciences, University College London, 31-34 Gordon Square, London, WC1H 0PY.
     020 7679 7495   fax 020 7383 2572
     http://www.ucl.ac.uk/archaeology/china-archaeology/
     Contact: Prof Peter Ucko.
- E   A research centre within the UCL Institute of Archaeology (qv).
- O   To develop specialist knowledge about China's past and safeguarding China's heritage

International Centre for Circulatory Health   (ICCH)
- ■   Faculty of Medicine, Imperial College London, 59 North Wharf Road, London, W2 1LA.
     020 7594 1100
     http://www.icch.org.uk/
- E   A research centre within the National Heart and Lung Institute (qv) at Imperial College London.
- O   To investigate the aetiology of cardiovascular disease and preventative strategies as they relate to different ethnic groups at various stages of the ecological transition

International Centre for Comparative Criminological Research   (ICCCR)   2003
- ■   Open University, Walton Hall, Milton Keynes, MK7 6AA.
     0870 333 4340
     http://www.open.ac.uk/icccr/
     Co-Director: Prof Clive Emsley. Co-Director: Prof John Muncie.
- E   An interdisciplinary research centre at the Open University.
- O   To unite practice-based criminological research and critical policy analysis with an awareness of historical and social context, with a particular emphasis on policing, community safety, prisons and penology

International Centre for Corporate Social Responsibility (ICCSR) 2002

■ Nottingham University Business School, Jubilee Campus, University of Nottingham, Wollaton Road, Nottingham, NG8 1BB.
  0115-846 6976   fax 0115-846 8074
  http://www.nottingham.ac.uk/business/
  Director: Prof Jeremy Moon.
E A research centre at the University of Nottingham.
○ To engage in mainstream teaching and research in the broad area of corporate social responsibility, including the attention of business to community involvement, socially responsible products and processes, and socially responsible employee relations

International Centre for Cultural and Heritage Studies (ICCHS)

■ School of Arts and Cultures, University of Newcastle upon Tyne, Bruce Building, Newcastle upon Tyne, NE1 7RU.
  0191-222 7419   fax 0191-222 5564
  http://www.ncl.ac.uk/sacs/research/icchs/
E A research centre at the University of Newcastle upon Tyne.
○ To be a leading academic centre for international research in museum, gallery and heritage studies, to provide excellent postgraduate teaching, and to contribute to the growth of the cultural sector both nationally and internationally and particularly in the North-East of England

International Centre for Digital Content (ICDC) 2000

■ Faculty of Media, Arts and Social Science, Liverpool John Moores University, 2nd Floor - Faraday House, 360 Edge Lane, Liverpool, L7 9NJ.
  0151-231 4777   fax 0151-231 4812
  http://www.icdc.org.uk/
E A research centre within Liverpool John Moores University.
○ To conduct research on projects involving new and emerging technology, including developing solutions for interactive TV, mobile, wireless, Bluetooth, and GPS for various markets
● Education and training - Information service

International Centre for East African Running Science (ICEARS)

■ West Medical Building, University of Glasgow, Glasgow, G12 8QQ.
  0141-330 3858
  http://www.icears.org/
  Director: Dr Yannis Pitsiladis.
E An international interdisciplinary research centre within the Institute of Biomedical and Life Sciences (qv) at the University of Glasgow.
○ To co-ordinate and facilitate excellence in research, training, education and sports science support in the context of elite East African running

International Centre for Education in Development (INCED)

■ School of Health and Social Studies, University of Warwick, Coventry, CV4 7AL.
  024 7652 3838   fax 024 7657 4415
  http://www2.warwick.ac.uk/fac/soc/shss/inced/
  Director: Dr Rosemary Preston.
E A research centre at the University of Warwick.

International Centre for English Language Studies (ICELS)

■ Headington Campus, Gipsy Lane Campus, Oxford Brookes University, Headington, Oxford, OX3 0BP.
  01865 483874   fax 01865 484377
  http://www.brookes.ac.uk/icels/
  Head: Mary Anne Ansell. Deputy Head: Richard Haill.
E Part of the Institute of Education at Oxford Brookes University.
○ To provide a comprehensive range of English language courses, for academic and work purposes, from one year foundation programmes to short summer school courses (All courses are accredited by the British Council and designed by qualified academic staff, who are specialists in English for academic purposes, and have trained, taught and researched overseas)
● Education and training

International Centre for the Environment (ICE)

■ School of Management, University of Bath, Claverton Down, Bath, BA2 7AY.
  01225 386156
  http://www.bath.ac.uk/ice/
  Director: Prof Geoff Hammond.
E A research centre at the University of Bath.
○ To promote leadership in environmental research and education

International Centre for Evidence-Based Oral Health (ICEBOH)

■ Department of Periodontology, University College London, 256 Gray's Inn Road, London, WC1X 8LD.
  020 7915 2340   fax 020 7915 1268
  http://www.eastman.ucl.ac.uk/iceboh
  Director: Dr Ian Needleman.
E A research centre within the UCL Eastman Dental Institute (qv) at University College London.
○ To develop the best evidence for prevention, diagnosis and treatment in oral healthcare

International Centre for Eye Health   (ICEH)   1980
- ■   Department of Infectious and Tropical Diseases, London School of Hygiene and Tropical Medicine, University of London, Keppel Street, London, WC1E 7HT.
     020 7636 8636
     http://www.iceh.org.uk/
     Director: Prof Allen Foster.
- E   A research centre at the London School of Hygiene and Tropical Medicine, University of London.
- O   To provide information and conduct research and teaching to empower local eye health workers to deliver quality eye care to people living in the poorest communities in the world, where blindness is ten times more common than in the developed world
- Note: The ICEH is a World Health Organisation WHO Collaborating Centre (qv) for Prevention of Blindness and Trachoma.

International Centre for Families in Business   (ICFB)
- ■   University of Gloucestershire, The Park, Cheltenham, Gloucestershire, GL50 2RH.
     01242 714109   fax 01242 714398
     http://www.icfib.com/
- E   A research centre within the Centre for Enterprise and Innovation (qv) at the University of Gloucestershire.
- O   To offer the family business a place for learning, education, support and advice

International Centre for Fine Art Research   (ICFAR)   2005
- ■   Central Saint Martins College of Art and Design, University of the Arts, Southampton Row, London, WC1B 4AP.
     020 7514 7000
     http://www.csm.arts.ac.uk/22025.htm
     Director: Prof Mark Nash.
- E   A research centre at the University of the Arts, London.

International Centre for Gender and Women's Studies   (ICGWS)   1993
- ■   Adam Smith Building, University of Glasgow, 40 Bute Gardens, Glasgow, G12 8RT.
     0141-330 5144   fax 0141-330 5071
     http://www.gla.ac.uk/centres/icgws/
     Convener: Prof Chris Corrin.
- E   A research centre at the University of Glasgow.
- O   To be a focus for international research on gender rights and other issues

International Centre for Higher Education Management   (ICHEM)   1994
- ■   School of Management, University of Bath, Claverton Down, Bath, BA2 7AY.
     01225 386213
     http://www.bath.ac.uk/ichem/
     Director: Prof Jeroen Huisman.
- E   A research centre at the University of Bath.
- O   To provide a focus for researchers into higher education management and policy

International Centre for the History of Slavery
   see **Institute for the Study of Slavery.**

International Centre for Intercultural Studies   (ICIS)
- ■   School of Culture, Language and Education, University of London, 20 Bedford Way, London, WC1H 0AL.
     020 7612 6000; 6722   fax 020 7612 6177
     http://www.ioewebserver.ioe.ac.uk/ioe/cms/get.asp?cid=6327
     Director: Prof Jaqdish S Gundara.
- E   A research centre within the Institute of Education (qv) at the University of London.
- O   To focus on the national and international study of intercultural educational issues

International Centre for Island Technology   (ICIT)   1989
- ■   Old Academy, Heriot-Watt University, Back Road, Stromness, Orkney, KW16 3AW.
     01856 850605   fax 01856 851349
     http://www.icit.org.uk/
     Director: Prof Jonathan Side.
- E   A research centre and specialist arm of the Heriot-Watt Institute of Petroleum Engineering (qv) at Heriot-Watt University.
- O   To carry out advanced research, postgraduate training and consultancy in marine resource management and related issues, with particular emphasis on renewable energy research, sustainable development, coastal zone management, environmental risk assessment, environmental economics, fisheries and marine bioresources, biodiversity, alternative energy, and waste disposal systems

International Centre for Life Trust
   see **Centre for Life.**

© CBD Research Ltd · Beckenham · Kent BR3 5JS · Tel 020 8650 7745 · Fax 020 8650 0768 · E-mail cbd@cbdresearch.com · www.cbdresearch.com

International Centre for Mathematical Sciences (ICMS) 1990

NR   Heriot-Watt University, 14 India Street, Edinburgh, EH3 6EZ.
      0131-220 1777   fax 0131-220 1053
      http://www.icms.org.uk/
      Scientific Director: Prof John Toland.

E   A research centre at Heriot-Watt University.

O   To create an environment in which mathematical sciences will develop in new directions; to encourage and exploit those areas of mathematics that are of relevance to other sciences, industry and commerce

Note: A joint undertaking with the University of Edinburgh.

International Centre for Music Studies (ICMuS)

■   School of Arts and Cultures, University of Newcastle upon Tyne, Armstrong Building, Newcastle upon Tyne, NE1 7RU.
      0191-222 5336; 6736   fax 0191-222 5242
      http://www.ncl.ac.uk/sacs/research/music/
      Contact: Dr Ian Biddle.

E   A research centre at the University of Newcastle upon Tyne.

O   To pursue and encourage work which recognises the reality of the contemporary musical world - a world in which familiarity, with a range of musical repertoires and skills, will increasingly be the key

Note: See **Centres for Excellence in Teaching and Learning** for further information.

International Centre for Nursing Ethics (ICNE) 1999

■   University of Surrey, Duke of Kent Building, Guildford, Surrey, GU2 7XH.
      01483 686030
      http://www.nursing-ethics.org/
      Director: Verena Tschudin.

E   A research centre within the European Institute of Health and Medical Sciences (qv) at the University of Surrey.

O   To focus research on issues of morality, professional ethics, the philosophy of care, cultural and religious values, law and accountability

International Centre for Participation Studies (ICPS) 2003

■   School of Social and International Studies, University of Bradford, Bradford, West Yorkshire, BD7 1DP.
      01274 236044
      http://www.bradford.ac.uk/acad/icps/
      Director: Prof Jenny Pearce.

E   A centre at the University of Bradford.

O   To conduct research and teaching about the relationship between participation and peace at the local, regional and international levels

International Centre for Planning Research (ICPR)

■   Cardiff School of City and Regional Planning, Cardiff University, Glamorgan Building, King Edward VII Avenue, Cardiff, CF10 3WA.
      029 2087 4956
      http://www.cf.ac.uk/cplan/icpr/
      Research Administrator: Shelagh Lloyd.

E   A research centre at Cardiff University.

O   To stimulate active engagement with international policy and practice

International Centre for Prison Studies (ICPS) 1997

■   School of Law, King's College London, 3rd Floor - 26-29 Drury Lane, London, WC2B 5RL.
      020 7848 1922   fax 020 7848 1901
      http://www.kcl.ac.uk/depsta/rel/icps/

E   A centre at King's College, London.

O   To assist Governments and other relevant agencies to develop appropriate policies on prisons and the use of imprisonment

International Centre for Protected Landscapes (ICPL) 1990

■   8E - Science Park, Aberystwyth, Ceredigion, SY23 3AH.
      01970 622620   fax 01970 622619
      http://www.protected-landscapes.org/
      Executive Director: Dr Liz Hughes.

E   A research and consultancy centre attached to the University of Wales, Aberystwyth.

O   To promote and facilitate approaches to conservation management that also support sustainable social and economic development

International Centre for Publishing Studies
     see **Oxford International Centre for Publishing Studies.**

International Centre for Research in Accelerator Science and Technology
     see **Cockcroft Institute: An International Centre for Research in Accelerator Science and Technology.**

International Centre for Research in Accounting   (ICRA)   1971
- Lancaster University Management School, Lancaster University, Bailrigg, Lancaster, LA1 4YX.
  01524 593976   fax 01524 594334
  http://www.lums.lancs.ac.uk/Departments/Accounting/Research/ICRA/
  Secretary: Freda Widders.
- E   A research centre at Lancaster University.

International Centre for Research in Music Education   (ICRME)   1976
- Department of Music Education, University of Reading, Bulmershe Court, Reading, Berkshire, RG6 1HY.
  0118-378 8843
  http://www.education.rdg.ac.uk/icrme/
  Director: Dr Gordon Cox. Director of MTPP Programme: Nils Franke.
- E   A research centre within the Institute of Education (qv) at the University of Reading.
- O   To provide full-time and part-time courses, ranging from BA to MA and PhD; to provide a general support service for all teachers of music, both specialist and non-specialist
- ●   Education and training

International Centre for Shipping, Trade and Finance   (ICSTF)   1983
- Cass Business School, City University, 106 Bunhill Row, London, EC1Y 8TZ.
  020 7040 0104
  http://www.cass.city.ac.uk/
  Contact: Dr Nikos Nomikos.
- E   A centre at City University.
- O   To develop postgraduate studies in shipping, trade and finance

International Centre for Sports History and Culture   (ICSHC)   1996
- Faculty of Humanities, De Montfort University, Clephan Building, The Gateway, Leicester, LE1 9BH.
  0116-250 6486
  http://www.dmu.ac.uk/sportshistory/
  Director: Prof Jeff Hill.
- E   A centre at De Montfort University.
- O   To study sports history

International Centre for the Study of Violence and Abuse   (ICVA)   1999
- School of Health, Natural and Social Sciences, University of Sunderland, Priestman Building, Green Terrace, Sunderland, Tyne and Wear, SR1 3PZ.
  0191-515 3218
  Director: Dr Catherine Donovan.
- E   A research centre at the University of Sunderland.
- O   To conduct national, cross-national and international research, into a wide variety of violence and abuse, and of the impacts of colonisation, imperialism and decolonisation on indigenous and minority groups

International Centre for System-on-Chip and Advanced Microwireless Integration   (SoCaM)   2005
- School of Electronics, Electrical Engineering and Computer Science, Queen's University Belfast, Northern Ireland Science Park, Queen's Road, Belfast, BT3 9DT.
  028 9097 1700   fax 028 9097 1702
  http://www.ecit.qub.ac.uk/
- E   A research centre within the Institute of Electronics, Communications and Information Technology (qv) at Queen's University, Belfast.

International Centre for Tourism and Hospitality Research   (ICTHR)
- School of Services Management, Bournemouth University, Dorset House, Fern Barrow, Poole, Dorset, BH12 5BB.
  01202 965163
  http://www.bournemouth.ac.uk/services-management/research/icthr.html
  Head: Prof John Fletcher.
- E   A centre at Bournemouth University.
- O   To undertake tourism research in countries on every continent

International Centre for Trade Union Rights   (ICTUR)   1987
- UCATT House, 177 Abbeville Road, London, SW4 9RL.
  020 7498 4700   fax 020 7498 0611
  http://www.ictur.org/
  President: Sharan Burrow. Director: Daniel Blackburn.
- E   An independent forum.
- O   To promote discussion and debate between trade unionists, labour lawyers and academics worldwide

International Centre for the Uplands - Cumbria   2004
- Unit 8 - Hackthorpe Hall Business Centre, Hackthorpe, Penrith, Cumbria, CA10 2HX.
  01931 711112   fax 01931 711116
  http://www.theuplandcentre.org.uk/
  Director: Ian Soane.
- E   An independent centre.
- O   To improve the quality of the environment, economy and society in the uplands

International Centre on Vibro-Impact Systems   (ICoVIS)
- Loughborough University, Loughborough, Leicestershire, LE11 3TU.
  01509 263171
  http://www.lboro.ac.uk/departments/mm/research/icovis
  Director: Prof V I Babitsky.
E   A research centre at Loughborough University.
O   To provide a forum for and build collaboration between academia and industry from different countries in the broad area of vibro-impact systems and processes

International Centre for Voice   (ICV)   2000
- Central School of Speech and Drama, Embassy Theatre, Eton Avenue, London, NW3 3HY.
  020 7722 8183
  http://www.cssd.ac.uk/pages/icv.html
E   A centre at the Central School of Speech and Drama.
O   To serve the professional development of teachers of voice and speech

International Centres for Economics and Related Disciplines
  see **Suntory and Toyota International Centres for Economics and Related Disciplines.**

International Chamber of Commerce Bureaux
  see **ICC**

International Child Abduction Centre
  see **Reunite, International Child Abduction Centre.**

International Development Centre   (IDC)   2001
- Faculty of Social Sciences, Open University, Pentz Building, Walton Hall, Milton Keynes, MK7 6AA.
  01908 653651
  http://www.open.ac.uk/idc/
E   A research centre at the Open University.
O   To develop a centre of excellence in international development research

International Development Centre [Oxford]
  see **Queen Elizabeth House International Development Centre.**

International Dispute Resolution Centre
  see **Centre for Effective Dispute Resolution**.

International Eating Disorders Centre   (IEDC)   1996
- 119-121 Wendover Road, Aylesbury, Buckinghamshire, HP21 9LW.
  01296 330557   fax 01296 339209
  http://www.eatingdisorderscentre.co.uk/
  Registered Nurse Manager: Lydia Myers. Unit Co-ordinator: Beryl Foy.
E   A private registered mental care home with nursing.
O   To provide adequate and appropriate inpatient, outpatient and day-care to persons of 16 years and over with eating disorders
●   Conference facilities - Information service - Recreational facilities - Statistics

International Fisheries Institute
  see **Hull International Fisheries Institute.**

International Football Institute   (IFI)   2003
- Lancashire Business School, University of Central Lancashire, Greenbank Building, Preston, PR1 2HE.
  01772 894531; 894622
  http://www.uclan.ac.uk/host/ifi/
  Director: Kevin Moore.
E   A research institute at the University of Central Lancashire.
O   To promote the study and development of football through research and higher education provision

International Fraud Prevention Research Centre   (IFPRC)
- Nottingham Business School, University of Nottingham, Burton Street, Nottingham, NG1 4BU.
  0115-848 2824
  http://www.ntu.ac.uk/nbs/spec/ifp
  Director: Dr Paul Barnes.
E   A research centre at Nottingham Trent University.
O   To conduct research in relation to the investigation, prevention, detection and regulation of financial fraud in the international arena

International Gender Studies Centre   (IGS)   1983
- ■   Department of International Development, University of Oxford, Queen Elizabeth House, Mansfield Road, Oxford, OX1 3TB.
  01865 273644
  http://users.ox.ac.uk/ccrw/
  Director: Maria Jaschok.
- ✕   Centre for Cross-Cultural Research on Women.

International Health and Medical Education Centre
   see **UCL Centre for International Health and Development.**

International Health Development Research Centre   (IHDRC)
- ■   Faculty of Health, University of Brighton, Mayfield House, Falmer, Brighton, East Sussex, BN1 9PH.
  http://www.brighton.ac.uk/health/ihdrc/
  Director: John Kenneth Davies.
- E   A centre at the University of Brighton.
- O   To provide a focus for research, development and consultancy, related to knowledge development and dissemination, in salutogenic and socio-ecological aspects of health

International Institute of Banking and Financial Services   (IIBFS)   1995
- ■   Leeds University Business School, University of Leeds, Maurice Keyworth Building, Leeds, LS2 9JT.
  0113-343 4359   fax 0113-343 4459
  http://www.casif.leeds.ac.uk/iibfs/
  Administrator: Michelle Dickson.
- E   A research institute within the University of Leeds.
- O   To focus on understanding how the three primary forces of strategic imperatives, technology and regulation interweave to define the future of the financial services industry

International Institute for Culture, Tourism and Development   (IICTD)
- ■   London Metropolitan University, Stapleton House, 277-281 Holloway Road, London, N7 8HN.
  020 7133 3035   fax 020 7133 3082
  http://www.londonmet.ac.uk/research-units/iictd/
- E   A research institute at London Metropolitan University.
- O   To conduct research in the cultural, tourism, development, hospitality and leisure industries

International Institute for Education Leadership   (IIEL)
- ■   University of Lincoln, Brayford Pool, Lincoln, LN6 7TS.
  01522 882000
  http://www.lincoln.ac.uk/mht/research-mh/iiel_default.htm
- E   A research centre at the University of Lincoln.
- ●   Education and training

International Institute for Society and Health
   see **UCL International Institute for Society and Health.**

International Language Centre
   see **Cheltenham International Language Centre.**

International Longevity Centre-UK   (ILC-UK)
- ■   22-26 Albert Embankment, London, SE1 7TJ.
  020 7735 7565
  http://www.ilcuk.org.uk/
  Chief Executive: Baroness Sally Greengross, OBE.
- E   A registered charity and limited company.
- O   To empower decision makers in Government, business, the professions and the media, to address the issues of longevity, our ageing populations and life-course planning

International Manufacturing Centre
- ■   Warwick Manufacturing Group, University of Warwick, Coventry, CV4 7AL.
  024 7652 4672   fax 024 7652 4307
  http://www2.warwick.ac.uk/study/postgraduate/courses/researchcentres/imc/
  Director: Prof Lord Kumar Bhattacharyya.
- E   A research centre at the University of Warwick.

International Maritime Bureau
   see **ICC International Maritime Bureau.**

International Marketing and Purchasing Centre   (IMP)
- ■   University of Bath School of Management, University of Bath, Claverton Down, Bath, BA2 7AY.
  01225 386473
  http://www.bath.ac.uk/imp
- E   A research centre at the University of Bath.

© CBD Research Ltd · Beckenham · Kent BR3 5JS · Tel 020 8650 7745 · Fax 020 8650 0768 · E-mail cbd@cbdresearch.com · www.cbdresearch.com

International Non-Governmental Organisation Training and Research Centre   (INTRAC)   1991
- ■   PO Box 563, Oxford, OX2 6RZ.
       01865 201851   fax 01865 201852
       http://www.intrac.org/
       Executive Director: Dr Brian Pratt. Research Director: Kasturi Sen.
- ○   To provide specially designed training, consultancy and research services to organisations involved in international development
       and relief; to improve NGO performance by exploring NGO policy issues and by strengthening NGO management and
       organisational effectiveness; to strengthen the organisational and management capacity of NGOs, analysing global NGO
       trends, and supporting the institutional development of the sector as a whole
- ●   Education and training - Library

International Pesticide Application Research Centre   (IPARC)   1955
- ■   Department of Biological Sciences, Imperial College London, Silwood Park, Ascot, Berkshire, SL5 7PY.
       020 7594 2248   fax 020 7594 2339
       http://www.iparc.org.uk/
       Director: Prof Denis J Wright.
- E   A department of Imperial College London.
- ○   To carry out research, evaluation and training on the application of both chemical and biological pesticides; to provide practical
       and cost-effective techniques to manage pests, while reducing the use of chemical pesticides and promoting the efficacy of
       natural processes and alternative biological agents

Note: IPARC is a World Health Organisation **WHO Collaborating Centre** for Testing of Insecticidal Application Equipment.

International Research Centre for Experimental Physics   (IRCEP)   2005
- ■   School of Mathematics and Physics, Queen's University, Belfast, Belfast, BT7 1NN.
       028 9097 3546; 3941   fax 028 9097 3110
       http://www.ircep.qub.ac.uk/
       Director: Prof W G Graham.
- E   A research centre at Queen's University, Belfast.
- ○   To bring together physicists whose research expertise lies mainly, but not exclusively, in experimental physics

International Rights Centre   (IRC)
- ■   London Book Fair, Earls Court Exhibition Centre, Warwick Road, London, SW5 9TA.
       020 8910 7899
       http://www.londonbookfair.co.uk/
- E   A special facility located within the annual London International Book Fair.
- ○   To offer professional facilities for private rights negotiations

International Schizophrenia Centre

Note: has closed.

International Seismological Centre   (ISC)   1964
- ■   Pipers Lane, Thatcham, Newbury, Berkshire, RG19 4NS.
       01635 861022   fax 01635 872351
       http://www.isc.ac.uk/
- E   An independent non-profit-distributing organisation and a membership body.
- ○   To collect, analyse and publish world earthquake data taken from 3,000 seismograph stations around the world

International Shakespeare Globe Centre   (ISGC)   1972
- ■   New Globe Walk, Southwark, London, SE1 9ED.
       020 7902 1406; 1492
       http://www.shakespeares-globe.org/
- E   A registered charity and a company limited by guarantee.

International Standard Serial Numbers UK Centre
       see **ISSN UK Centre.**

International Studies Centre
       see **Plymouth International Studies Centre.**

International Surfing Centre
- ■   Fistral Beach, Newquay, Cornwall, TR7 1HY.
       01637 850737; 876474
       http://www.nationalsurfingcentre.com/
- E   A surfing school run by the British Surfing Association.
- ○   To organise surfing courses at Fistral Beach

Note: Also known as the National Surfing Centre.

International Teledemocracy Centre   (ITC)
- ■ Merchiston Campus, Napier University, 10 Colinton Road, Edinburgh, EH10 5DT.
   0131-455 2545   fax 0131-455 2282
   http://itc.napier.ac.uk/
   Director: Prof Ann Macintosh.
- E A centre at Napier University.
- ○ To research and apply information and communication technologies to enhance and support the democratic decision-making processes
- ● Information service

Internet Institute
   see **Oxford Internet Institute.**

Ion Beam Centre
   see **Surrey Ion Beam Centre.**

IRC. . .
   see **Interdisciplinary Research Centre**.

Irish Linen Centre and Lisburn Museum
- ■ Market Square, Lisburn, County Antrim, BT28 1AG.
   028 9266 3377   fax 028 9267 2624
   http://www.lisburncity.gov.uk/irish-linen-centre-and-lisburn-museum/
- E A local authority managed museum.

Irish Studies Centre
- ■ Department of Humanities, Arts and Languages, London Metropolitan University, Tower Building, 166-220 Holloway Road, London, N7 8DB.
   020 7133 2927
   http://www.londonmet.ac.uk/irishstudiescentre/
- E A research centre within the Institute for the Study of European Transformations (qv) at London Metropolitan University.

Irish Women's Centre
   see **London Irish Women's Centre.**

Iron and Steel Statistics Bureau   (ISSB Ltd)   1967
- ■ 1 Carlton House Terrace, London, SW1Y 5DB.
   020 7343 3900   fax 020 7343 3901
   http://www.issb.co.uk/
- E A profit-making business.
- ○ To offer a wide range of publications and custom reports covering the UK, European and Global trade in steel and raw materials

Ironbridge Institute
- ■ Ironbridge Gorge Museum, Coalbrookdale, Telford, Shropshire, TF8 7DX.
   01952 432751   fax 01952 435937
   http://www.ironbridge.bham.ac.uk/
   Contact: Janice Fletcher.
- E An institute within the Institute of Archaeology and Antiquity (qv) at the University of Birmingham.
- ○ To provide top class courses in heritage management and industrial archaeology

Isaac Newton Institute for Mathematical Sciences   1992
- ■ University of Cambridge, 20 Clarkson Road, Cambridge, CB3 0EH.
   01223 335999   fax 01223 330508
   http://www.newton.cam.ac.uk/
   Director: Sir John Kingman.
- E A UK National Institute for Mathematical Sciences and part of the University of Cambridge.
- ○ To conduct research into all aspects of mathematical sciences
Note: Also known as the Newton Institute.

Islamic Cultural Centre and London Central Mosque   (ICC)   1974
- ■ 146 Park Road, London, NW7 8RG.
   020 7724 3363   fax 020 7724 0493
   http://www.iccuk.org/
   Director General: Dr Ahmed Dubayan. Deputy Director General: Anwar Mady.
- E A registered charity.
- ○ To teach and promote a proper understanding of Islam
- ● Conference facilities - Education - Library - Recreational facilities
- ¶ Islamic Quarterly (journal). Newsletter.

© CBD Research Ltd · Beckenham · Kent BR3 5JS · Tel 020 8650 7745 · Fax 020 8650 0768 · E-mail cbd@cbdresearch.com · www.cbdresearch.com

ISSN UK Centre

- The British Library, Boston Spa, Wetherby, West Yorkshire, LS23 7BQ.
  01937 546959   fax 01937 546562
  http://www.bl.uk/services/bibliographic/issn.html
- ○ To assign International Standard Serial Numbers to serials published in the UK

IT Innovation Centre

- School of Engineering and Computer Science, University of Southampton, 2 Venture Road, Chilworth Science Park, Southampton, SO16 7NP.
  023 8076 0834   fax 023 8076 0833
  http://www.it-innovation.soton.ac.uk/
- E   A research centre at the University of Southampton.
- ○   To conduct research focused on enabling the innovative application of information technology by industry and commerce
- ×   Parallel Applications Centre.

James Martin Institute for Science and Civilisation

■ Saïd Business School, University of Oxford, 1 Park End Street, Oxford, OX1 1HP.
01865 288859   fax 01865 288959
http://www.martininstitute.ox.ac.uk/
Director: Prof Steve Rayner. Executive Director: Sara Ward.
E   An institute at the University of Oxford.
○   To identify science and technology issues critical in shaping the future of world civilization

James Watt Nanofabrication Centre   (JWNC)

■ Department of Electronics and Electrical Engineering, University of Glasgow, Rankine Building, Oakfield Avenue, Glasgow, G12 8LT.
0141-330 5218   fax 0141-330 4907
http://www.jwnc.gla.ac.uk/
E   A research centre at the University of Glasgow.

Japan Research Centre   (JRC)

■ School of Oriental and African Studies, University of London, Thornhaugh Street, Russell Square, London, WC1H 0XG.
020 7898 4892; 4893   fax 020 7898 4489
http://www.soas.ac.uk/japan/
Manager: Jane Savory. Executive Officer: Sara Hamza.
E   An interdisciplinary research centre at the School of Oriental and African Studies, University of London.
○   To co-ordinate academic research and teaching within the School into aspects of Japanese culture, and to further the disciplines within the UK
●   Conferences - Education and training - Statistics

Japan Trade Centre
see **JETRO London (Japan Trade Centre).**

Japanese Studies Centre
see **Cardiff Japanese Studies Centre.**

JEAN MONNET CENTRES

Note: Jean Monnet Centres exist at many UK universities. The broad remit of each centre is to co-ordinate a wide range of teaching and research activities in the area of European politics.

JETRO London (Japan Trade Centre)   (JETRO)   1958

■ MidCity Place, 71 High Holborn, London, WC1V 6AL.
020 7421 8300
http://www.jetro.go.jp/uk/
E   A Japanese Government organisation.
○   To promote mutually beneficial trade and investment relations between Japan and other nations
●   Exhibitions - Seminars - Trade information service
Note: JETRO runs a total of 74 offices overseas and 38 offices in Japan.

Jevons Institute for Competition Law and Economics   2006

■ Faculty of Laws, University College London, Bentham House, Endsleigh Gardens, London, WC1H 0EG.
020 7679 1514   fax 020 7679 1442
http://www.ucl.ac.uk/laws/jevons/
Administrator: Lisa Penfold.
E   A research institute at University College London.
○   To conduct teaching, research and debate concerning the application of competition law and industry regulation to the marketplace

Jewish Education Bureau   (JEB)   1974

■ 8 Westcombe Avenue, Leeds, LS8 2BS.
0870 800 8532   fax 0870 800 8533
http://www.jewisheducationbureau.co.uk/
E   A private venture and an independent non-profit-distributing organisation.
○   To promote the study of Judaism as a world religion in British schools and colleges; to work, with educational organisations and faith communities, to eradicate prejudice and to work for harmony and understanding in multi-faith and multi-cultural Britain

Jill Dando Institute of Crime Science
see **UCL Jill Dando Institute of Crime Science.**

Joanna Briggs Institute   (JBI)   1995

■   School of Nursing and Academic Division of Midwifery, University of Nottingham, Queen's Medical Centre, Nottingham, NG7 2UH.
      0115-823 0814   fax 0115-823 1208
      http://www.nottingham.ac.uk/nursing/research/centres/jbi.php
      Director: Prof Veronica James.
E   A research centre at the University of Nottingham.
○   To work collaboratively with local health care providers to contribute to the development of the evidence base for nursing and midwifery

Jodrell Bank Science Centre   1967

■   University of Manchester, Macclesfield, Cheshire, SK11 9DL.
      01477 571339
      http://www.jb.man.ac.uk/
E   The astronomy research centre of the University of Manchester.
○   To educate and inform visitors on astronomy, particularly the research in radio astronomy carried out by the radio telescopes of the observatory at Jodrell Bank

John Adams Institute for Accelerator Science   (JAI)   2004

NR   Department of Physics, Royal Holloway, University of London, Egham, Surrey, TW20 0EX.
      01784 443448   fax 01784 472794
      http://www.adams-institute.ac.uk/
E   A research institute at Royal Holloway, University of London.
Note: Jointly hosted with the University of Oxford (see above).

John Adams Institute for Accelerator Science   (JAI)   2004

NR   Department of Physics, Clarendon Laboratory, University of Oxford, Parks Road, Oxford, OX1 3PU.
      01865 272200   fax 01865 272400
      http://www.physics.ox.ac.uk/
E   A research institute at the University of Oxford.
○   To provide expertise, research, development and training in accelerator techniques; to promote advanced accelerator applications in science and society
Note: Jointly hosted with Royal Holloway, University of London. Sir John Adams (1920-1984) was recognised as the leading expert in giant particle accelerators which

John Grieve Centre for Policing and Community Safety   2003

■   Department of Applied Social Sciences, North Campus, London Metropolitan University, 166-220 Holloway Road, London, N7 8DB.
      020 7133 5107
      http://www.londonmet.ac.uk/depts/dass/research/jgc/
E   A research centre at London Metropolitan University.
○   To provide an active contribution towards effective policing in the UK

John Innes Centre   (JIC)   1910

■   Norwich Research Park, Colney, Norwich, NR4 7UH.
      01603 450000   fax 01603 450045
      http://www.jic.bbsrc.ac.uk/
      Director: Prof C J Lamb.
E   A registered charity and a not-for-profit company limited by guarantee.
○   To carry out basic research into plant molecular biology, plant genetics, cell biology and microbial genetics
●   Conference facilities - Education and training - Exhibitions - Library

Joining Technology Research Centre   (JTRC)

■   School of Technology, Gipsy Lane Campus, Oxford Brookes University, Headington, Oxford, OX3 0BP.
      01865 483504   fax 01865 484179
      http://www.brookes.ac.uk/other/jtrc/
      Head: Prof A R Hutchinson.
E   A research centre at Oxford Brookes University.

Joint Centre for Mesoscale Meteorology   (JCMM)   2006

■   Department of Meteorology, PO Box 243, University of Reading, Earley Gate, Reading, Berkshire, RG2 2BB.
      0118-378 8315; 8954   fax 0118-378 8905
      http://www.met.rdg.ac.uk/Research/jcmm/jcmm.html
E   Part of the National Centre for Atmospheric Science (qv) and housed within the University of Reading.
○   To conduct research in mesoscale meteorology (small-scale weather systems).

Joint Centre for Scottish Housing Research   (JCSHR)   1990

■   School of Social Sciences, University of Dundee, 13 Perth Road, Dundee, DD1 4HN.
      01382 345236   fax 01382 204234
      http://www.trp.dundee.ac.uk/research/jcshr.html
E   A research centre within the Geddes Institute (qv) at the University of Dundee.
○   To facilitate inter-institutional and cross-disciplinary research on the Scottish housing market

Joint Centre for Urban Design   (JCUD)   1972
■   School of the Built Environment, Gipsy Lane Campus, Oxford Brookes University, Headington, Oxford, OX3 0BP.
01865 483200   fax 01865 483298
http://www.brookes.ac.uk/schools/be/jcud/
E   A research centre at Oxford Brookes University.
○   To promote an interdisciplinary approach to urban design, bringing together architecture, town planning, landscape architecture, estate management, traffic engineering, and other relevant disciplines
●   Education and training

Joint Terrorism Analysis Centre   (JTAC)   2003
■   Thames House, 11 Millbank, London, SW1P.
http://www.mi5.gov.uk/output/Page63.html
E   A centre within the MI5, the Security Service.
○   To analyse and assess all intelligence relating to international terrorism, at home and overseas

Jorvik Viking Centre   (JVC)   1984
■   Coppergate, York, YO1 1NT.
01904 643211   fax 01904 627097
http://www.vikingjorvik.com/
E   A registered charity.
○   To provide a centre for Viking history
●   Education and training - Exhibitions - Reproduction of the 1,000 year old Viking settlement of Jorvik, including street vendors and working craftsmen Open daily 0900-1730

Joseph Bell Centre for Forensic Statistics and Legal Reasoning   (CFSLR)   2001
NR   School of Law, Old College, University of Edinburgh, South Bridge, Edinburgh, EH8 9YL.
0131-650 9704   fax 0131-650 6317
http://www.cfslr.ed.ac.uk/
E   A research centre at the University of Edinburgh.
○   To research, develop, extend and apply techniques and technology that support the criminal justice system
Note: A joint venture with Glasgow Caledonian University.

Jost Institute for Tribotechnology   (JIT)   2002
■   Department of Technology, University of Central Lancashire, Computing and Technology Building, Preston, PR1 2HE.
01772 893312
http://www.uclan.ac.uk/facs/destech/tech/jost/
Director: Prof Ian Sherrington.
E   A research institute at the University of Central Lancashire.
○   To provide, within the area of tribotechnology, industrially relevant research, teaching and knowledge transfer
Note: Named after Dr Peter Jost who chaired a Department of Education and Science committee which introduced and defined the term tribology in 1966.

Joule Centre for Energy Research
NR   School of Mechanical, Aerospace and Civil Engineering, University of Manchester, The Pariser Building, Sackville Street, Manchester, M60 1QD.
0161-306 4626; 4656   fax 0161-306 3755
http://www.joulecentre.org/
Director: Prof Nick Jenkins. Administrator: Mrs Laura Mitchell.
E   A research centre at the University of Manchester.
○   To create an internationally-leading energy research centre in England's North-West which will significantly increase the region's research capacity and activity in key areas of new sustainable energy technologies, supporting science and technology, energy efficiency and integrated assessment of the energy system
Note: A collaborative project with 5 other Universities in the North West - Central Lancashire, Lancaster, Liverpool, Manchester Metropolitan, and Salford.

Jubilee Centre   1983
■   Jubilee House, 3 Hooper Street, Cambridge, CB1 2NZ.
01223 566319   fax 01223 566359
http://www.jubilee-centre.org/
E   An independent non-profit-distributing organisation and a registered charity
○   To encourage and equip Christians to shape society according to biblical principles

Judge Institute of Management Studies
Note: is now the Judge Business School of the University of Cambridge and is therefore no longer within the scope of this directory.

Julian Hodge Institute of Applied Macroeconomics   (JHIAMe)   1999
■   Cardiff Business School, Cardiff University, Aberconway Building, Colum Drive, Cardiff, CF10 3EU.
029 2087 5728   fax 029 2087 4419
http://www.cardiff.ac.uk/carbs/research/centres_units/jhiam.html
Director: Prof Patrick Minford.
E   A centre at Cardiff University.
○   To carry out research into the behaviour of the UK economy, and to study in particular its relationship with other economies of Europe

Justice and Violence Research Centre

■ School of Social Sciences and Cultural Studies, Arts C, University of Sussex, Falmer, Brighton, East Sussex, BN1 9SJ.
01273 606755
http://www.sussex.ac.uk/justice/

E An interdisciplinary research centre at the University of Sussex.

Keele Centre for Wave Dynamics   (KCWD)   2002

■   Department of Mathematics, Keele University, Keele, Staffordshire, ST5 5BG.
    01782 583270   fax 01782 584268
    http://www.keele.ac.uk/depts/ma/kcwd/
E   A centre at Keele University.
O   To promote research on wave activity

Keele European Research Centre   (KERC)

■   School of Politics, International Relations and Philosophy, Keele University, Keele, Staffordshire, ST5 5BG.
    01782 584316
    http://www.keele.ac.uk/depts/spire/research/kerc/kerc_home.htm
E   A research centre at Keele University.
O   To link together all those involved in research into various aspects of the politics of the remaking of Europe

Kelvin Nanocharacterisation Centre   (KNC)

■   University of Glasgow, Kelvin Building, Glasgow, G12 8QQ.
    0141-330 4707   fax 0141-330 4464
    http://www.knc.gla.ac.uk/
E   A department of the University of Glasgow.
O   To develop and use state-of-the-art imaging, diffraction and analytical techniques to characterise advanced functional and structural materials

Kelvin Research Centre
    see **Environmental Research Institute**.

Kennedy Institute of Rheumatology   (KIR)   1965

■   Faculty of Medicine, Imperial College London, ARC Building, 1 Apenlea Road, London, W6 8LH.
    020 8383 4444
    http://www1.imperial.ac.uk/medicine/about/divisions/kennedy/
    Head: Prof M Feldmann.
E   A research institute at Imperial College London.
O   To enable basic and clinical research to be undertaken into the aetiology of rheumatoid and osteorarthritis, and to develop preventative and therapeutic interventions

Kent Centre for European and Comparative Law   (KCECL)   2004

■   Kent Law School, Eliot College, University of Kent, Canterbury, Kent, CT2 7NS.
    01227 823445   fax 01227 827831
    http://www.kent.ac.uk/law/KCECL/
    Co-Director: Prof Geoffrey Samuel. Co-Director: Dr Harm Schepel.
E   A research centre at the University of Kent.
O   To provide a framework for the further development of the Law School's activities in the areas of European and comparative law, in research as in teaching

Kent Criminal Justice Centre   (KCJC)   1996

■   School of Social Policy, Sociology and Social Research, University of Kent, Cornwallis George Allen Wing, Canterbury, Kent, CT2 7NF.
    01227 823275   fax 01227 827038
    http://www.kent.ac.uk/kcjc/
    Director: Prof Chris Hale.
E   A research centre at the University of Kent.
O   To provide high quality research, policy development and education in the field of criminology and criminal justice

Kent Institute for Advanced Studies in the Humanities   (KIASH)

■   School of English, University of Kent, Rutherford College Extension, Canterbury, Kent, CT2 7NX.
    01227 764000
    http://www.kent.ac.uk/kiash/
    Chairman: Dr Elizabeth Cowie.
E   A research institute at the University of Kent.
O   To organise and co-ordinate a programme of research activity in all fields of the humanities and cognate areas of the social sciences

Kent Institute of Medicine and Health Sciences   (KIMHS)

■   Faculty of Science, Technology and Medical Studies, University of Kent, Canterbury, Kent, CT2 7PD.
    01227 827312   fax 01227 824054
    http://www.kent.ac.uk/kimhs/
    Dean: Prof Cornelius Katona.
E   A research institute at the University of Kent.
O   To attract the best clinicians into academic divisions providing the research and education to promote their clinical practice for the benefit of the patient

   © CBD Research Ltd · Beckenham · Kent BR3 5JS · Tel 020 8650 7745 · Fax 020 8650 0768 · E-mail cbd@cbdresearch.com · www.cbdresearch.com

Kent Technology Transfer Centre   (KTTC)

■   University of Kent, Canterbury, Kent, CT2 7PD.
    01227 764000   fax 01227 763424
    http://www.kent.ac.uk/departments/results.html?action=deptcard&deptid=197
E   An external agency based at the University of Kent.

Keswick Hall Centre for Research and Development in Religious Education   (KHREC)   1993

■   School of Education and Lifelong Learning, University of East Anglia, Norwich, NR4 7TJ.
    01603 592632
    http://www.uea.ac.uk/edu/
E   A centre at the University of East Anglia.
○   To research and develop religious education

Khalili Research Centre for the Art and Material Culture of the Middle East   (KRC)   2005

■   Faculty of Oriental Studies, University of Oxford, Clarendon Institute Building, Walton Street, Oxford, OX1 2HG.
    01865 278222   fax 01865 278190
    http://www.krc.ox.ac.uk/
    Contact: David Griffiths.
E   A research centre within the Oriental Institute (qv) at the University of Oxford.
○   To provide facilities for research in the field of Middle Eastern art and architecture

King's Centre for Military Health Research   (KCMHR)

■   King's College, London, Weston Education Centre, Cutcombe Road, London, SE5 9RJ.
    020 7848 5351   fax 020 7848 5397
    http://www.kcl.ac.uk/kcmhr/
    Director: Prof Simon Wessely.
E   A research centre within the Institute of Psychiatry (qv) at King's College, London.
○   To conduct research primarily on the effects of war on UK service personnel, concentrating on war and health, war and psychiatry, and personal issues and social policy

King's Centre for Risk Management   (KCRM)

■   School of Social Science and Public Policy, King's College, London, 138-142 Strand, London, WC2R 1HH.
    020 7848 2102   fax 020 7848 2748
    http://www.kcl.ac.uk/kcrm/
    Director: Prof Ragnar Löfstedt.
E   A research centre at King's College, London.
○   To conduct scientifically-based research in risk management in the environmental, technological, health, safety, food, business and terrorism contexts

King's Fund Centre   1897

■   11-13 Cavendish Square, London, W1M 0AN.
    020 7307 2400   fax 020 7307 2801
    http://www.kingsfund.org.uk/
    Chairman: Prof Sir Cyril Chantler.
E   A registered charity and non-profit-making organisation.
○   To support innovation in the National Health Service and other related organisations, and to encourage the spread of good ideas and practices; to work for better health in London and in the national and international context

Knowledge Media Institute   (KMi)   1995

■   Open University, Walton Hall, Milton Keynes, MK7 6AA.
    01908 653800   fax 01908 653169
    http://kmi.open.ac.uk/
    Director: Prof Enrico Motta.
E   A department of the Open University.
○   To conduct research and development in the various processes of generating, understanding and sharing knowledge using several media, as well as understanding how the use of different media shape these processes

Knowledge Transfer Partnerships Centres   (KTP Centres)

■   KTP Programme Office, Momenta, Didcot, OX11 0QJ.
    0870 190 2829
    http://www.ktponline.org.uk
Note: A Knowledge Transfer Partnership (KTP) involves at least one high-quality graduate working in a company for 1 to 3 years on a project central to the needs of the company, whilst drawing on knowledge and expertise from the University.

Krebs Institute for Biomolecular Research   1988

■   Firth Court, University of Sheffield, Western Bank, Sheffield, S10 2TN.
    0114-222 2000
    http://www.shef.ac.uk/krebs/
E   An inter-departmental research institute at the University of Sheffield.
○   To analyse the structure / function relationships in biological molecules
●   Education and training

Kroto Research Institute Nanoscience and Technology Centre
- ■   North Campus, University of Sheffield, Broad Lane, Sheffield, S3 7HQ.
      0114-222 7445
      http://www.shef.ac.uk/northcampus/
      Business Development Manager: George Rees.
- E   A research institute at the University of Sheffield.

Kurdish Cultural Centre Ltd   (KCC)   1985
- ■   14 Stannary Street, London, SE11 4AA.
      020 7735 0918   fax 020 7582 8894
      http://www.kcclondon.org/
      Manager: Julian Walker. Deputy Manager: Sarbest Kirkuky.
- E   A registered charity and a not-for-profit company limited by guarantee.
- ○   To relieve poverty and distress among Kurdish asylum seekers and refugees by providing information, assistance and advice on immigration, welfare rights, health, housing, integration and employment; to advance education and knowledge of the culture of the Kurdish peoples and preserve the heritage of the Kurdish nation
- ●   Advice service - Education and training - Information service - Library - Drop-in centre Mon-Fri 0930-1730
- ¶   Malband Cultural Newsletter. Panabiri Kurd Practical Advice (newsletter). Annual Report.

© CBD Research Ltd · Beckenham · Kent BR3 5JS · Tel 020 8650 7745 · Fax 020 8650 0768 · E-mail cbd@cbdresearch.com · www.cbdresearch.com

Laare-Studeyrys Manninagh
    see **Centre for Manx Studies.**

Labanotation Institute   (LI)

■   Department of Dance Studies, University of Surrey, Guildford, Surrey, GU2 7XH.
    01483 689317   fax 01483 686171
    http://www.surrey.ac.uk/dance/
E   An institute at the University of Surrey.
O   To promote and develop Labanotation (a system, named after Rudolf Laban (1879-1958) for recording the choreography of ballet and dance)

Lairdside Laser Engineering Centre   1988

■   Campbeltown Road, Birkenhead, Wirral, CH41 9HP
    0151-650 2305   fax 0151-650 2304
    http://www.llec.co.uk
    General Manager: Dr Martin Sharp
E   A research centre of the University of Liverpool.
O   To conduct research in laser materials processing

Lairdside Maritime Centre   2000

■   Faculty of Technology and Environment, Liverpool John Moores University, 3 Vanguard Way, Campbeltown Road, Birkenhead, Wirral, CH41 9HX.
    0151-647 0494; 0496   fax 0151-647 0498
    http://www.lairdside-maritime.com/
    Director: Philip M J Russ. Business Development Manager: Bert Kunze.
E   A research centre at Liverpool John Moores University.
O   To train mariners in ship handling; to operate and maintain the UK's most advanced 360-degree full mission ship-handling simulator

Lancashire Buddhist Centre

■   Richmond Chambers, Richmond Terrace, Blackburn, Lancashire, BB1 7AR.
    01245 889228
    http://www.geocities.com/fwboeastlancs/
E   An independent non-profit-distributing organisation and a registered charity.
O   To teach meditation and Buddhism
●   Education and training - The Centre provides meditation cushions and mats cushions and mats
Note: For other Buddhist centres see note under **Buddhist Centres**.

Lancaster Centre for e-Science

■   C Floor, Lancaster University, Bowland Tower South, Lancaster, LA1 4YT.
    01524 592175   fax 01524 594459
    http://e-science.lancs.ac.uk/
E   A research centre at Lancaster University.
Note: See **e-Science Centres of Excellence** for further information.

Lancaster Centre for Forecasting   (LCF)   1990

■   Lancaster University Management School, Lancaster University, Bailrigg, Lancaster, LA1 4YX.
    01524 594285
    http://www.lums.lancs.ac.uk/Research/Centres/forecasting/
E   A research centre at Lancaster University.

Lancaster China Management Centre   (LCMC)

■   Lancaster University Management School, Lancaster University, Bailrigg, Lancaster, LA1 4YX.
    01524 594059; 594206
    http://www.lums.lancs.ac.uk/Research/Centres/ChinaCentre/
    Director: Prof David Brown. Administrator: Susan Lucas.
E   A research centre at Lancaster University.

Lancaster Literacy Research Centre

■   Faculty of Social Sciences, Lancaster University, Lancaster, LA1 4YT.
    01524 510853   fax 01524 510855
    http://www.literacy.lancs.ac.uk/
    Director: Prof David Barton.
E   A research centre at the Lancaster University.

Lancaster University Engineering Design Centre

Note: No longer in existence.

Language Institute
    see **Sussex Language Institute.**

Language and Literacy Research Centre   (LLRC)

■ School of Psychology and Human Development, University of London, 25 Woburn Square, London, WC1H 0AA.
   020 7612 6271   fax 020 7612 6304
   http://ioewebserver.ioe.ac.uk/
   Director: Dr Rhona Stainthorp.
E   A research centre within the Institute of Education (qv) at the University of London.
○   To support theoretical and applied research in the areas of spoken and written language with the specific aim of developing an understanding of language acquisition, literacy development and the relationship between the two

Languages and Humanities Centre   (LHC)   1990

■ School of Literatures, Languages and Cultures, University of Edinburgh, Basement - David Hume Tower, George Square, Edinburgh, EH8 9JX.
   0131-650 3974   fax 0131-650 6538
   http://www.arts.ed.ac.uk/lhc/
   Head: Peter Glasgow.
E   A centre at the University of Edinburgh.

Languages Information Centre   1983   Canolfan Hysbysrwydd Ieithyddol

■ c/o Joseph Biddulph (Publisher), 32 Stryd Ebeneser, Pontypridd, CF37 5PB.
   01443 662559
   Director & Proprietor: Joseph Biddulph, BA(Hons).
E   A private venture.
○   To increase awareness and knowledge of the vernacular languages of Africa, and of minority and neglected languages and cultures worldwide; to enable enquirers to make overviews of the early Germanic and other languages of British Isles antiquity; to preserve and discuss heraldic sources
●   Information service - Library - Publication of source materials
¶   Moto Na Maji (A Guide to all the Languages of Africa). The Nubian Digest. Troglodyte (cultural magazine). (many other publications).

Languages of the Wider World CETL   2005

■ School of Oriental and African Studies, University of London, Room 443 Thornhaugh Street, Russell Square, London, WC1H 0XG.
   020 7898 4516
   http://www.lww-cetl.ac.uk/
   Contact: Itesh Sachdev.
E   A Centre for Excellence in Teaching and Learning (CETL) at the School of Oriental and African Studies, University of London.
Note: See **Centres for Excellence in Teaching and Learning** for more information.

Lansdown Centre for Electronic Arts   (LCEA)

■ School of Arts, Middlesex University, Cat Hill, Barnet, Hertfordshire, EN4 8HT.
   020 8411 5363
   http://www.cea.mdx.ac.uk/
   Head of Centre: Dr Stephen Boyd Davies.
E   A centre at Middlesex University.
○   To be the leading innovator in education concerning the understanding and application of computing to media and the arts
●   Education and training

Laser Engineering Centre
   see **Lairdside Laser Engineering Centre.**

Laser and Optical Systems Engineering Centre   (LOSEC)   1987

■ Department of Mechanical Engineering, University of Glasgow, James Watt (South) Building, Glasgow, G12 8QQ.
   0141-330 4972   fax 0141-330 4358
   http://www.mech.gla.ac.uk/Research/Losec/
   Contact: Dr Ian Watson.
E   A research centre at the University of Glasgow.
○   To conduct research in the fields of optical correlators, laser sterilisation, laser processing of magnetic materials, single crystal fibre sensors, fibre optic sensors, laser cleaning, laser welding of alloys, high PRF laser, and applications of speckle

Laser Processing Research Centre   (LPRC)   2000

■ School of Mechanical, Aerospace and Civil Engineering, University of Manchester, The Pariser Building, Sackville Street, Manchester, M60 1QD.
   0161-200 3816   fax 0161-299 3803
   http://www.mace.manchester.ac.uk/project/research/manufacturing/laser/
   Director: Prof Lin Li.
E   A research centre at the University of Manchester.
○   To carry out research in high power laser engineering particularly in novel material synthesis and modification, micro / nano engineering, rapid prototyping and manufacturing and technical innovations and novel applications of lasers for cutting, welding, drilling and surface engineering that are beyond the existing limits of manufacturing technology aiming at creating step changes in productivity, capability and quality as well as new scientific knowledge on laser processing

© CBD Research Ltd · Beckenham · Kent BR3 5JS · Tel 020 8650 7745 · Fax 020 8650 0768 · E-mail cbd@cbdresearch.com · www.cbdresearch.com

Latin America Bureau (LAB) 1977

- ■ 1 Amwell Street, London, EC1R 1UL.
  020 7278 2829   fax 020 7833 0715
  http://www.latinamericabureau.org/
- E A limited company.
- O To undertake research, education and publishing on Latin America and the Caribbean

Latin American Centre (LAC) 1964

- ■ School for Interdisciplinary Area Studies, St Antony's College, University of Oxford, Oxford, OX2 6JF.
  01865 274486   fax 01865 274489
  http://www.lac.ox.ac.uk/
  Director: Rosemary Thorp.
- E A research centre at the University of Oxford.
- O To further postgraduate work on Latin America; to encourage the development of Latin American studies

Lauterpacht Centre for International Law (LCIL) 1985

- ■ Faculty of Law, University of Cambridge, 5 Cranmer Road, Cambridge, CB3 9BL.
  01223 335358   fax 01223 300406
  http://lcil.law.cam.ac.uk/
  Director: Prof James Crawford, SC, FBA. Administrator: Anita Rutherford.
- E A centre at the University of Cambridge.
- O To be the leading centre in the UK in the field of international law

Law Centre [Derby]
  see **Derby Law Centre.**

Law Centre (NI)

- ■ 124 Donegall Street, Belfast, BT1 2GY.
  028 9024 4401   fax 028 9023 6340
  http://www.lawcentreni.org/
- E A referral organisation.

Lean Enterprise Research Centre (LERC) 1994

- ■ Aberconway Building, Cardiff University, Colum Drive, Cardiff, CF10 3EU.
  029 2087 4544   fax 029 2087 4556
  http://www.cf.ac.uk/carbs/research/centres_units/lerc.html
  Director: Prof Peter Hines.
- E A research centre within the Cardiff University Innovative Manufacturing Research Centre (qv) at Cardiff University.
- O To develop pioneering leading-edge lean thinking research tools and techiques; to help organisations achieve world class performance through the application of lean thinking principles and techniques

LearnHigher CETL

- ■ Liverpool Hope University, Hope Park, Liverpool, L16 9JD.
  0151-291 3289
  http://learnhigher.hope.ac.uk/
  Director: Jill Armstrong.
- E A Centre for Excellence in Teaching and Learning (CETL) at Liverpool Hope University College.
- Note: See **Centres for Excellence in Teaching and Learning** for more information.

Learning Institute
  see **Oxford Learning Institute.**

Learning Laboratories Centre for Excellence
  see **ArtsWork: Learning Laboratories Centre for Excellence.**

Learning Sciences Research Institute (LSRI) 2002

- ■ School of Education, Jubilee Campus, University of Nottingham, Wollaton Road, Nottingham, NG8 1BB.
  0115-846 7671   fax 0115-846 7931
  http://www.nottingham.ac.uk/lsri/
  Director: David Wood.
- E A research institute at the University of Nottingham.
- O To explore the cognitive, social and cultural aspects of learning and to design innovative technologies and environments for learners

Learning and Teaching Institute (LTI)

- ■ City Campus, Sheffield Hallam University, Howard Street, Sheffield, S1 1WB.
  0114-225 4754   fax 0114-225 4755
  http://www.shu.ac.uk/services/lti
  Head: Paul Helm.
- E An institute at Sheffield Hallam University.
- O To shape the development of quality, enhancement of learning, teaching and assessment at the University

Learning Technology Research Institute   (LTRI)
■ Department of Computing, Communications Technology and Mathematics, London Metropolitan University, 35 Kingsland Road, London, E2 8AA.
  020 7749 3754
  http://www.londonmet.ac.uk/ltri/
  Director: Tom Boyle.
E A research institute at London Metropolitan University.
O To focus research on the application of information and communication technologies to augment, support and transform learning, especially in the areas of learning objects and learning design, learning interaction and dialogue design, and designing for informal and lifelong learning

Learning Through Action Centre   (LTA)   1983
■ High Close School, Wiltshire Road, Wokingham, Berkshire, RG40 1TT.
  0870 770 7985   fax 0870 770 7987
  http://www.learning-through-action.org.uk/
  Chief Executive: Annette Cotterill.
E A registered charity and non-profit-making company limited by guarantee.
O To develop and deliver a wide range of interactive learning projects and workshops for children and young people (aged 4 to 19+) and for parents and other carers, particularly in the context of personal and social behaviour, health and citizenship issues

Leather Conservation Centre   1978
■ Boughton Green Road, Northampton, NN2 7AN.
  01604 719766   fax 01604 719649
  Director: I Beaumont.
E An independent non-profit-distributing organisation, a registered charity and a company limited by guarantee within the University of Northampton.
O To promote all aspects relating to the conservation and restoration of leather objects of historic cultural and artistic value
● Conservation - Education and training (Mon-Fri 0900-1700)

Leeds Buddhist Centre
■ 2-7 Woodhouse Square, Leeds, LS3 1AD.
  0113-278 3395
  http://www.leedsbuddhistcentre.org/index.html
E An independent non-profit-distributing organisation and a registered charity.
O To teach meditation and Buddhism
● Education and training - The Centre provides meditation cushions and mats
Note: For other Buddhist centres see note under **Buddhist Centres**.

Leeds Dental Institute   (LDI)
■ Faculty of Medicine and Health, University of Leeds, The Worsley Building, Clarendon Way, Leeds, LS2 9JT.
  0113-343 6172
  http://www.leeds.ac.uk/dental/
  Director: Dr Margaret Kellett.
E A research institute of the University of Leeds.
O To provide dental education for dental undergraduate and postgraduate students, students of dental hygiene, and therapy and dental auxiliary staff
● Education and training
Note: The Institute is a World Health Organisation WHO Collaborating Centre (qv) for Research and Development for Oral Health, Migration and Inequalities.

Leeds Humanities Research Institute   (LHRI)
■ University of Leeds, 29-31 Clarendon Place, Leeds, LS2 9JY.
  0113-343 5636
  http://www.leeds.ac.uk/lhri/
E A research institute at the University of Leeds.

Leeds Institute of Genetics, Health and Therapeutics   (LIGHT)   2004
■ Faculty of Medicine and Health, University of Leeds, The Worsley Building, Clarendon Way, Leeds, LS2 9JT.
  0113-343 4361
  http://www.leeds.ac.uk/medhealth/light/
  Acting Director: Prof Chris Wild.
E A research institute of the University of Leeds.
O To perform internationally competitive translational research into complex diseases (cardiovascular illness, diabetes, neurodegenerative diseases, and cancer)

Leeds Institute of Health Sciences   2004
■ Faculty of Medicine and Health, University of Leeds, 15 Hyde Terrace, Leeds, LS2 9JT.
  0113-343 2701   fax 0113-343 3719
  http://www.leeds.ac.uk/hsphr/
  Director: Prof Allan House.
E A research institute at the University of Leeds.
O To foster research in the psychological, social and cultural aspects of health and healthcare
✕ Institute of Health Sciences and Public Health Research

Leeds Institute of Molecular Medicine   (LIMM)

■   Faculty of Medicine and Health, University of Leeds, The Worsley Building, Clarendon Way, Leeds, LS2 9JT.
      0113-343 4361
      http://www.leeds.ac.uk/medhealth/limm/
      Director: Prof Terence Rabbitts.
E   A research institute at the University of Leeds.

Leeds Social Sciences Institute   (LSSI)   2006

■   Faculty of Education, Social Sciences and Law, University of Leeds, Beech Grove House, Leeds, LS2 9JT.
      0113-343 3912   fax 0113-343 7071
      http://www.leeds.ac.uk/socsci/
      Director: Prof Gill Valentine.
E   A research institute within the University of Leeds.
O   To develop interdisciplinary excellence in the social sciences

Leeds University Centre for African Studies   (LUCAS)

■   Faculty of Education, Social Sciences and Law, University of Leeds, Leeds, LS2 9JT.
      0113-343 7428
      http://www.leeds.ac.uk/lucas/
E   A research centre at the University of Leeds.
O   To promote studies relating to Africa
●   Information service - Conferences - Seminars - Annual lecture

Legal Research Institute   (LRI)

■   Faculty of Social Studies, University of Warwick, Coventry, CV4 7AL.
      024 7652 3157   fax 024 7652 4105
      http://www2.warwick.ac.uk/fac/soc/law/research/
      Director: Prof Istvan Pogany.
E   A research institute at the University of Warwick.
O   To research on the twin themes of law in context and the international character of law
●   Education and training

Lehman Brothers Centre for Women in Business

■   London Business School, Sussex Place, Regent's Park, London, NW1 4SA.
      020 7000 8941
      http://www.london.edu/womeninbusiness.html
      Academic Co-Leader: Prof Laura D Tyson. Academic Co-Leader: Prof Lynda Gratton.
E   A research centre at the London Business School.
O   To promote women at all stages of their careers; to assist organisations to attract, retain and develop the broadest talent pool

Leicester e-Science Centre of Excellence   2003

■   Department of Physics and Astronomy, University of Leicester, Leicester, LE1 7RH.
      0116-252 3575   fax 0116-252 2770
      http://www.e-science.le.ac.uk/
      Contact: Tony Linde.
E   A research centre at the University of Leicester.
Note: See **e-Science Centres of Excellence** for further information.

Leo Baeck College - Centre for Jewish Education   (LBC-CJE   1986

■   The Sternberg Centre, 80 East End Road, London, N3 2SY.
      020 8349 5600   fax 020 8349 5619
      http://www.lbc-cje.ac.uk/
      Vice-Principal: Rabbi Dr Michael Shire. Director: Dr Helena Miller.
E   A registered charity within the Sternberg Centre for Judaism (qv).
O   To bring about the development of life-long Jewish education in synagogues and schools; to encourage self-reliance, innovation and inspiration in the practice of Jewish education in individuals and communities
●   Academic study courses - Education and training Rabbis - Information service - Library
¶   Annual Review (many other publications).

Leonard Cheshire Centre of Conflict Recovery   (LCC)   1995

■   Department of Surgery, University College London, 4 Taviton Street, London, WC1H 0BT.
      020 7679 4517; 4518   fax 020 7813 2844
      http://www.ucl.ac.uk/lc-ccr/
      Director: Prof Colonel James Ryan.
E   A research centre at University College London.
O   To study the medical and social consequences of war and conflict; to support and improve the healthcare and rehabilitation of victims of victims of conflict; to provide training and international support to local medics and the wider medical community who are working in post-conflict countries

Leopardi Centre   1998
- Department of Italian Studies, University of Birmingham, Edgbaston, Birmingham, B15 2TT.
  0121-414 5996   fax 0121-414 3834
  http://www.leopardi.bham.ac.uk/
  Director: Dr Franco D'Intino.
- E   A centre at the University of Birmingham.
- O   To promote the study and knowledge of the Italian poet Giacomo Leopardi (1798-1837) and his European context; to act as a UK focus for research into the cultures of 18th and 19th century Italy

Lesbian Archive and Information Centre   (LAIC)   1984
- c/o Glasgow Women's Library, 109 Trongate, Glasgow, G1 5HD.
  0141-552 8345   fax 0141-552 8345
  http://www.womens-library.org.uk/laic/laic.html
- Library (the Centre contains the UK's largest collection of material about lesbian lives, histories and achievements)

Leslie and Elizabeth Alcock Centre for Historical Archaeology   2005
- Department of Archaeology, University of Glasgow, The Gregory Building, Lilybank Gardens, Glasgow, G12 8QQ.
  0141-330 5690   fax 0141-330 3544
  http://www.gla.ac.uk/archaeology/alcock/
  Chairman: Prof Christopher D Morris.
- E   A charitable trust at the University of Glasgow.
- O   To encourage research into the study of historical archaeology, with particular emphasis to the early middle ages of Scotland and the British Isles
- Substantial Alcock collection of books, papers, notes and photographs
Note: Also known by its shorter name of Alcock Centre for Historical Archaeology.

Leverhulme Centre for Human Evolutionary Studies   (LCHES)   2000
- University of Cambridge, The Henry Wellcome Building, Fitzwilliam Street, Cambridge, CB2 1QH.
  01223 764700   fax 01223 764710
  http://www.human-evol.cam.ac.uk/
  Administrator: Sara Harrop.
- E   A centre at the University of Cambridge.
- O   To promote research in human evolution and diversity

Leverhulme Centre for Research on Globalization and Economic Policy   (GEP)   2001
- School of Economics, University of Nottingham, University Park, Nottingham, NG7 2RD.
  0115-951 5469   fax 0115-951 5552
  http://www.nottingham.ac.uk/economics/leverhulme/
  Director: Prof David Greenaway.
- E   A research centre at the University of Nottingham.
- O   To conduct research around four programmes linked by the common theme of the economic analysis of globalisation - theory and methods, globalisation and labour markets, globalisation, productivity and technology, and China and the world economy

Liddell Hart Centre for Military Archives   1964
- King's College, London, Strand, London, WC2R 2LS.
  020 7836 5454
  http://www.kcl.ac.uk/iss/archives/about/lhcma.html
- E   A centre at King's College, London.
- O   A repository for research into modern defence policy in Britain - its strategy, planning and conduct

Life Bioscience Centre
- Times Square, Newcastle upon Tyne, NE1 4EP.
  0191-243 8210   fax 0191-243 8201
  http://www.life.org.uk/about/bioscience/
- E   A purpose-built centre within the Centre for Life (qv) at the University of Newcastle upon Tyne.

Lifeboat Support Centre
- West Quay Road, Poole, Dorset, BH15 1HZ.
  0845 122 6999   fax 0845 126 1999
  http://www.rnli.org.uk/
Note: A centre at the headquarters of the Royal National Lifeboat Institution.

Lifelong Learning Institute   (LLI)
- School of Education, University of Leeds, Leeds, LS2 9JT.
  0113-343 4545
  http://www.education.leeds.ac.uk/research/lifelong/
- E   A research institute within the University of Leeds.
- O   To enhance lifelong learning for individuals, organisations and communities in the UK and overseas

Lighthill Institute of Mathematical Sciences

- Department of Mathematics, University College London, De Morgan House, 57-58 Russell Square, London, WC1B 4HS.
  020 7863 0881
  http://www.ucl.ac.uk/lims/
  Director: Frank Smith.
- E   A research institute at University College London.
- O   To establish a critical mass of mathematicians, statisticians and mathematical scientists interested in collaborating through research and seminars

Limb Fitting Centre
   see **Dundee Limb Fitting Centre.**

Lime Centre   1990

- Long Barn, Morestead, Winchester, Hampshire, SO21 1LZ.
  01962 713636   fax 01962 715350
  http://www.thelimecentre.co.uk/
  Contact: D A Thompson. Contact: J A Stevenson.
- E   A private venture and a profit-making business.
- O   To spread the knowledge of working with traditional building materials to conserve old buildings and structures
- ●   Education and training - Information service

Linacre Centre for Healthcare Ethics   1977

- 60 Grove End Road, London, NW8 9NH.
  020 7289 3625   fax 020 7266 5424
  http://www.linacre.org/
- E   A registered charity and an independent non-profit-distributing organisation, the Centre was created under a charitable trust formed by the five Roman Catholic archbishops of England and Wales.
- O   To maintain and develop common moral values in the field of health care and with contributing to this task from within the Catholic moral tradition
- ●   Conferences - Courses - Lectures - Library - Publications - The public can contact the Centre at any time to discuss matters of medical ethics, or (by appointnent only) use the library
- ¶   Many different publications.

Lincoln Theological Institute for the Study of Religion and Society   (LTI)   1997

- School of Arts, Histories and Cultures, University of Manchester, Oxford Road, Manchester, M13 9PL.
  0161-275 3064; 8596
  http://www.arts.manchester.ac.uk/lti/
  Director: Dr Peter Scott.
- E   A research institute at the University of Manchester.
- O   To create a national and international centre of expertise in the theological study of religion and society; to promote theological research and study into a variety of ethical, pastoral, social and ecclesial issues

Link Centre for Deafened People   (LINK)   1972

- 19 Hartfield Road, Eastbourne, East Sussex, BN21 2AR.
  01323 638230   fax 01323 642968
  http://www.linkdp.org/
  Chief Executive: Dr Lorraine Gailey.
- E   A registered charity.
- O   To adjust to deafness in everyday living through rehabilitation and life-skills programmes; to train health care professionals in acquired deafness, and to conduct research into this type of deafness
- ●   Education and training
- ¶   Annual Report. Linked Up Magazine.

Lipids Research Centre

- Department of Chemistry, University of Hull, Cottingham Road, Hull, HU6 7RX.
  01482 465464; 465485
  http://www.hull.ac.uk/lipids/
  Director: Prof K Coupland.
- E   A part of the Centre for Organic and Biological Chemistry (qv) at the University of Hull.
- O   To develop research in lipids - strategic raw materials in the form of natural oils and fats, for the oleochemicals industry
- ×   Centre for Advanced Lipids Research.

Liquid Glass Centre   2000

- Stowford Manor, Wingfield, Trowbridge, Wiltshire, BA18 9LY.
  01225 768888
  http://www.liquidglasscentre.co.uk
  Contact: Kim Atherton.
- O   To provide the very best standard of tuition in glassmaking

Lister Institute of Preventive Medicine   (LIPM)   1891
- PO Box 1083, Bushey, Hertfordshire, WD23 9AG.
   01923 801886   fax 01923 801886
   http://www.lister-institute.org.uk/
- E   A registered charity.
- ○   To further understanding and progress in preventive medicine by promoting biomedical excellence in the UK through its support of the biological and biomedical sciences, and to ensure long-term public benefit through publication of the knowledge gained and, where appropriate, by encouraging its exploitation; to offer research prizes to selected young scientists each year, and so provide them with five years of flexible support, which gives them an opportunity to develop their research careers

Literacy Research Centre
   see **Lancaster Literacy Research Centre.**

LIVE Centre for Excellence in Lifelong and Independent Veterinary Education   (LIVE)   2005
- Royal Veterinary College, University of London, Hawkshead Lane, North Mymms, Hatfield, Hertfordshire, AL9 7TA.
   01707 666270; 666657
   http://www.live.ac.uk/
   Contact: Prof Stephen May.
- E   A Centre for Excellence in Teaching and Learning (CETL) at the Royal Veterinary College, University of London.
- Note: See **Centres for Excellence in Teaching and Learning** for more information.

Liverpool Centre for Medieval Studies   1963
- School of History, University of Liverpool, 9 Abercromby Square, Liverpool, L3 4FB.
   0151-794 2394   fax 0151-794 2366
   http://www.liv.ac.uk/history/cms/
   Head: Prof Michael Hughes.
- E   A research centre at the University of Liverpool.
- ○   To promote the study of the middle ages, broadly defined, throughout Merseyside and the North West

Liverpool Institute for Biocomplexity   (LIBC)   2006
- School of Biological Sciences, The Biosciences Building, University of Liverpool, Crown Street, Liverpool, L69 7ZB.
   0151-795 4510
   http://www.liv.ac.uk/biocomplexity/
   Director: Prof Andrew Cossins.
- E   A research institute at the University of Liverpool.

Liverpool Institute of Performing Arts   (LIPA)   1996
- Mount Street, Liverpool, L1 9HF.
   0151-330 3000   fax 0151-330 3131
   http://www.lipa.ac.uk/
- E   A registered charity and a company limited by guarantee.
- ○   To provide the best teaching and learning for people who want to pursue a lasting career in the arts and entertainment economy; to provide education and training through a variety of styles and courses aimed at different age groups

Liverpool University Centre for Archive Studies   (LUCAS)   1996
- School of History, University of Liverpool, 9 Abercromby Square, Liverpool, L69 7WZ.
   0151-794 2414   fax 0151-794 3153
   http://www.liv.ac.uk/lucas/
   Director: Caroline Williams.
- E   A department of the University of Liverpool.
- ○   To co-ordinate research, education and training in archives and records management studies

Liverpool University Institute of Cancer Studies   (LUICS)   2004
- Faculty of Medicine, University of Liverpool, Daulby Street, Liverpool, L69 3GA.
   0151-706 4175   fax 0151-706 5798
   http://www.liv.ac.uk/FacultyMedicine/luics
   Director: Prof John Neoptolemos.
- E   A department of the University of Liverpool.

Liverpool Wellcome Trust Centre for Research in Clinical Tropical Medicine
   see **Wellcome Trust Tropical Centre**

Lloyd's Register University Technology Centre   (LR UTC)
- School of Engineering Sciences, University Road, Highfield, Southampton, SO17 1BJ.
   023 8059 5000   fax 023 8059 3131
   http://www.soton.ac.uk/ses/research/centres.html
- E   A research centre at the University of Southampton.

Llysdinam Field Centre
   see **Wales Biomass Centre.**

   © CBD Research Ltd · Beckenham · Kent BR3 5JS · Tel 020 8650 7745 · Fax 020 8650 0768 · E-mail cbd@cbdresearch.com · www.cbdresearch.com

Local Government Centre (LGC)
- ■ Warwick Business School, Coventry, CV4 7AL.
  024 7652 4306
  http://www.wbs.ac.uk/faculty/research/lgc.cfm
- E A research centre at the University of Warwick.
- O To study issues that confront local authorities at the level of corporate and inter-agency policy making and management

Local Government Chronicle Elections Centre   1985
- ■ School of Law and Social Science, University of Plymouth, Drake Circus, Plymouth, PL4 8AA.
  01752 233207   fax 01752 232785
  http://www.plymouth.ac.uk/pages/view.asp?page=16182
  Contact: Dawn Cole.
- E A research centre at the University of Plymouth.
- O To compile, analyse and publish information relating to all aspects of electoral politics in Britain, with particular emphasis on local election results

Local Government Information Bureau
Note: Has become the European and International Unit of the Local Government Association and is therefore outside the scope of this directory.

Logistics Education Centre   (LEC)   1970
- ■ Building 243, Cranfield University, University Campus, Cranfield, Bedfordshire, MK43 0AL.
  01234 712618
  http://www.logisticseducation.co.uk/
- E A training centre at Cranfield University.
- O To provide courses in various types of logistics, including warehouse design, logistics management, outsourcing, e-fulfilment, supply chain strategy, cost and error reduction, and efficiency assessment
- × National Materials Handling Centre.

Logistics Institute
>   see **University of Hull Logistics Institute.**

Logistics Research Centre   (LRC)   1996
- ■ School of Management and Languages, Heriot-Watt University, Riccarton, Edinburgh, EH14 4AS.
  0131-451 3557   fax 0131-451 3498
  http://www.sml.hw.ac.uk/logistics/
  Director: Prof Alan McKinnon.
- E A research centre at Heriot-Watt University.
- O To conduct research on freight transport and logistics

Logos: Centre for the Study of Ancient Systems of Knowledge   2001
- ■ School of Classics, University of St Andrews, Swallowgate, Butts Wynd, St Andrews, Fife, KY16 9AL.
  01334 462608
  http://www.st-andrews.ac.uk/classics/logos
  Director: Prof Greg Woolf.
- E A research centre at the University of St Andrews.
- O To develop collaborative research projects into the systems of knowledge by which Greeks and Romans organised their understanding and description of the world

London BioScience Innovation Centre   (LBIC)
- ■ Royal Veterinary College, University of London, 2 Royal College Street, London, NW1 0NH.
  020 7691 1122   fax 020 7681 9129
  http://www.londonlifesciences.com/
  Manager: Bradley Hardiman.
- E A research centre at the Royal Veterinary College, University of London.
- O To provide a focus for life sciences activity

London Brass Rubbing Centre   1975
- ■ St Martin-in-the-Fields Church, Trafalgar Square, London, WC2N 4JJ.
  020 7766 1100   fax 020 7839 5163
  http://www2.stmartin-in-the-fields.org/page/visiting/brass.html
- E A profit-making business.
- O To make the craft of brass rubbing, with all its historical, educational, social, artistic and ecclesiastical aspects available to the widest possible public

London Buddhist Centre   (LBC)   1967
- ■ 51 Roman Road, London, E2 0HU.
  0845 458 4716   fax 020 8980 1960
  http://www.lbc.org.uk/
- E An independent non-profit-distributing organisation and a registered charity.
- O To teach meditation and Buddhism
- ● Education and training - The Centre provides meditation cushions and mats
Note: For other Buddhist centres see note under **Buddhist Centres.**

London Centre for Arts and Cultural Enterprise   (LCACE)
■ 2nd Floor - South Building, Somerset House, London, WC2R 1LA.
   020 7420 9444   fax 020 7420 9445
   http://www.lcace.org.uk/
   Director: Sally Taylor.
E   A university initiative.
○   To promote the exchange of knowledge and expertise with the capital's arts and cultural sectors
Note: A collaborative venture involving many prominent London universities and colleges.

London Centre for Clean Energy   (LCCE)   2006
■ Department of Materials, Queen Mary, University of London, Mile End Road, London, E1 4NS.
   020 7882 5569   fax 020 7882 5154
   http://www.materials.qmul.ac.uk/lcce/
   Director: Prof Z Xiao Guo.
E   A research centre at Queen Mary, University of London.
○   To focus research on renewable energy generation, energy storage and management

London Centre for Fashion Studies   1991
■ Bradley Close, White Lion Street, London, N1 9PF.
   020 7713 1991
   http://www.fashionstudies.com/
E   A private venture.
○   To provide professional skills training for sample machinists, designers, pattern cutters, graders and merchandisers
● Equipment includes industrial sewing machines, fusing press and computer aided design (CAD) Hours Mon-Fri 1000-1700 (term time) - Equipment includes industrial sewing machines, fusing press, Computer Aided Design (CAD).

London Centre for the History of Science, Medicine and Technology   1987
■ Faculty of Physical Sciences, South Kensington Campus, Imperial College, Exhibition Road, London, SW7 2AZ.
   020 7594 9360   fax 020 7594 9353
   http://www3.imperial.ac.uk/historyofscience/graduateprogramme/mscprogramme/thelondoncentre/
   Head: Prof Andrew Warwick.
E   A research centre at Imperial College London.
○   To run the MSc programme in the history of science, medicine and technology

London Centre for Leadership in Learning   (LCLL)   2005
■ University of London, 20 Bedford Way, London, WC1H 0AL.
   020 7911 5533   fax 020 7612 6618
   http://ioewebserver.ioe.ac.uk/
   Manager: Patti Gram.
E   A school within the Institute of Education (qv) at the University of London.
○   To make a major contribution to the development of London as a world-class city for education

London Centre for Marine Technology
■ Imperial College London, Prince Consort Road, London, SW7 2AZ.
   020 7589 5111
   http://www3.imperial.ac.uk/courses/azofdepartmentsandcentres/londoncentreformarinetechnology
E   A research centre at Imperial College London.
○   To conduct research in the general field of offshore technology

London Centre for Nanotechnology   (LCN)   2006
NR   Department of Chemistry, South Kensington Campus, University College London, Exhibition Road, London, SW7 2AZ.
   020 7594 5883   fax 020 7594 5801
   http://www.london-nano.ucl.ac.uk/
   Co-Director: Prof Gabriel Aeppli. Co-Director: Prof Tim Jones.
E   A research centre at Imperial College London.
○   To provide the nanoscience and nanotechnology needed to solve major problems in information processing, health care, energy and the environment
Note: A joint venture with University College London.

London Centre for Nanotechnology   (LCN)   2006
NR   Department of Physics and Astronomy, University College London, 17-19 Gordon Street, London, WC1H 0AH.
   020 7679 0055   fax 020 7679 0595
   http://www.london-nano.ucl.ac.uk/
E   A research centre at University College London.
Note: A joint venture with Imperial College London (see above).

London Centre for Paediatric Endocrinology and Metabolism   (LCPEM)   1994
■ Endocrinology Unit, Great Ormond Street Hospital, London, WC1N 3JH
   020 7405 9200   fax 020 7829 8885
   http://www.ich.ucl.ac.uk/gosh/clinicalservices/Endocrinology/Homepage
E   A research centre within the UCL Institute of Child Health (qv) at University College London.

London e-Science Centre   (LeSC)

■   Department of Computing, South Kensington Campus, Imperial College, Exhibition Road, London, SW7 2AZ.
     020 7594 8360
     http://www.lesc.imperial.ac.uk/
     Director: Prof John Darlington.
E   A research centre at Imperial College London.
Note: See **e-Science Centres** for further information.

London East Research Institute   (LERI)

■   School of Social Sciences, Media and Cultural Studies, Docklands Campus, University of East London, 4-6 University Way, London, E16 2RD.
     020 8223 7641
     http://www.uel.ac.uk/londoneast
     Administrator: Emma Roberts.
E   A research institute at the University of East London.
O   To provide a single point of access to high quality research, consultancy and information whenever there is a proposed social and cultural and planning initiative that will impact upon the Thames Gateway

London Environment Centre   (LEC)   1994

■   London Metropolitan University, 133 Whitechapel High Street, London, E1 7QA.
     020 7320 2236   fax 020 7320 2297
     http://www.londonenvironment.co.uk/
E   A research centre at London Metropolitan University.
O   To build close working relationships with businesses of all sizes and develop tailored strategies to help them understand and respond strategically to the evolving challenges of sustainable development

London European Research Centre

■   London Metropolitan University, Tower Building, 166-220 Holloway Road, London, N7 8DB.
     020 7133 2927
     http://www.londonmet.ac.uk/research-units/iset/research/lerc.cfm
E   A research centre within the Institute for the Study of European Transformations (qv) at London Metropolitan University.

London Fertility Centre

■   Cozens House, 112a Harley Street, London, W1G 7JH.
     020 7317 1076   fax 020 7224 3102
     http://www.lfc.org.uk/
E   A treatment centre.
O   To offer a broad scope of services for both males and females with infertility

London Food Centre   (LFC)   1998

■   Faculty of Engineering, Science and the Built Environment, London South Bank University, 103 Borough Road, London, SE1 0AA.
     020 7815 7988   fax 020 7815 7986
     http://www.londonfood.org.uk/
     Head: Alan Bent.
E   A research centre at London South Bank University.
O   To assist small and medium sized food businesses to expand and improve their profitability

London Geotechnical Centrifuge Centre   (LGCC)

■   Department of Engineering, City University, Tait Building, Northampton Square, London, EC1V 0HB.
     020 7040 0113
     http://www.city.ac.uk/sems/research/geotech/centrifuge.html
     Director: Prof R N Taylor.
E   A research centre within the Geotechnical Engineering Research Centre (qv) at City University.

London Hazards Centre   (LHC)   1984

■   Hampstead Town Hall Centre, 213 Haverstock Hill, London, NW3 4QP.
     020 7794 5999   fax 020 7794 4702
     http://www.lhc.org.uk/
E   A registered charity and a company limited by guarantee
O   To be a resource centre for Londoners fighting health and safety hazards in their workplace and community

London Irish Women's Centre   (LIWC)   1986

■   59 Stoke Newington Church Street, London, N16 0AR.
     020 7249 7318   fax 020 7923 9599
     Director: Tish Collins. Counselling Co-ordinator: Jennifer Trainor.
E   A registered charity.
O   To empower, inspire, mobilise and celebrate women of Irish birth and descent in London; to provide advice on housing, welfare, discrimination, domestic violence, debt and other issues
●   Counselling - Information service - Statistics
¶   Rights for Travellers. Roots and Realities. Annual Report. Irish Women and Mental Health.

London Mathematics Centre

- School of Mathematics, Science and Technology, University of London, 11 Woburn Square, London, WC1H 0AL.
  020 7612 6965   fax 020 7612 6792
  http://ioewebserver.ioe.ac.uk/
  Director: Teresa Smart.
- E   A research centre within the Institute of Education (qv) at the University of London.
- O   To provide innovative professional development for teachers of mathematics in London

London Metropolitan Polymer Centre   (LMPC)   2002

- North Campus, 166-220 Holloway Road, London, N7 8DB.
  020 7133 2248   fax 020 7133 2184
  http://www.londonmet.ac.uk/depts/polymers/
  Head: Dr Michael O'Brien.
- E   A research centre at London Metropolitan University.
- O   To conduct research, education, training and consultancy in polymer engineering, science and technology as these concern the needs of plastics, rubber and associated industries

London Middle East Institute   (LMEI)

- Thornhaugh Street, Russell Square, London, WC1H 0XG.
  020 7898 4442   fax 020 7898 4329
  http://www.lmei.soas.ac.uk/
- E   A research institute at the School of Oriental and African Studies, University of London.
- O   To provide training, research and consultancy related to the Middle East
- ×   Centre of Near and Middle Eastern Studies.

London Research Institute [Cancer Research UK]
     see **Cancer Research UK London Research Institute.**

London School of Economics...
     see **LSE**

London Shipping Law Centre   1993

- Faculty of Laws, Bentham House, Endsleigh Gardens, London, WC1H 0EG.
  020 7679 2000
  http://www.ucl.ac.uk/laws/
- E   An industry research forum at University College London.
- O   To conduct research and teaching in shipping law, interaction with the new generation of shipping, and the development of professional links

London Sport Institute

- School of Health and Social Sciences, Middlesex University, Highgate Hill, London, N19 5LW.
  020 8411 4690; 6707
  http://www.mdx.ac.uk/hssc/lsi/
  Director: Prof Chris Riddoch.
- E   An institute at Middlesex University.

London Underwriting Centre   (LUC)   1993

- 3 Minster Court, Mincing Lane, London, EC3R 7DD.
  020 7617 5000   fax 020 7617 5050
  http://www.luc.co.uk/
- E   A purpose-built international market building for the world's leading insurance and reinsurance companies.

Longitudinal Studies Centre [Colchester]
     see **ESRC United Kingdom Longitudinal Studies Centre.**

Longitudinal Studies Centre - Scotland   (LSCS)   2001

- School of Geography and Geosciences, University of St Andrews, St Andrews, Fife, KY16 9AL.
  01334 462397
  http://www.lscs.ac.uk/
  Director: Prof Paul Boyle.
- E   A research centre at the University of St Andrews.
- O   To establish and maintain the Scottish Longitudinal Study (SLS) - an initiative of the General Register Office for Scotland

© CBD Research Ltd · Beckenham · Kent BR3 5JS · Tel 020 8650 7745 · Fax 020 8650 0768 · E-mail cbd@cbdresearch.com · www.cbdresearch.com

Loughborough Innovative Manufacturing and Construction Research Centre   (LIMCRC)

NR   Wolfson School of Mechanical and Manufacturing Engineering, Loughborough University, Loughborough, Leicestershire, LE11 3TU.
     01509 227530   fax 01509 227549
     http://www.lboro.ac.uk/eng/esearch/imcrc/
     Contact: Prof Phill Dickens.

E   An EPSRC Innovative Manufacturing Research Centre at Loughborough University.

O   To focus research on manufacturing and construction around six key themes - advanced information and communication technologies, innovative production technologies, improving business processes, human factors, sports technology, and rapid manufacturing

Note: One of the EPSRC funded centres in the UK - for further information see EPSRC Innovative Manufacturing Research Centres.

Loughborough Materials Characterisation Centre   (LMCC)   2000

■   Faculty of Science, Loughborough University, Loughborough, Leicestershire, LE11 3TU.
     01509 223331   fax 01509 223949
     http://www.lboro.ac.uk/departments/iptme/services/lmcc.html
     Director: David Hall.

E   A research centre within the Institute of Polymer Technology and Materials Engineering (qv) at Loughborough University.

O   To support materials research in the IPTME

Loughborough Sleep Research Centre

■   Department of Human Sciences, Loughborough University, Loughborough, Leicestershire, LE11 3TU.
     01509 223091
     http://www.lboro.ac.uk/departments/hu/groups/sleep/
     Director: Prof Jim Horne.

E   A research centre at Loughborough University.

O   To conduct basic, applied and clinical research into sleepiness and daytime well-being

Loughborough University Banking Centre
     see **Banking Centre.**

Loughborough University Telecommunications and Computer-Human Interface Research Centre
Note: No longer in existence.

LSE Centre for Urban Research

■   St Clements Building, LSE, Houghton Street, London, WC2A 2AE.
     020 7955 7588
     http://www.lse.ac.uk/collections/urbanResearch/
     Director: Dr Andy C Pratt.

E   A research centre at the London School of Economics and Political Science.

O   To be the hub of debate and innovative research about contemporary urbanism in all parts of the world

LSE Environment: Centre for Environmental Policy and Governance   (CPEG)

■   Department of Geography and Environment, LSE, Houghton Street, London, WC2A 2AE.
     020 7955 7588   fax 020 7955 7412
     http://www.lse.ac.uk/collections/geographyAndEnvironment/CEPG/
     Director: Prof Yvonne Rydin.

E   A research centre at the London School of Economics and Political Science.

O   To develop a greater understanding about the management and governance of environmental policy problems, and contribute to improvements in such management and governance

●   Seminars - Workshops - Various public events

LSE London Centre for Urban and Metropolitan Research

■   Room PS300 - Portsmouth Street, LSE, Houghton Street, London, WC2A 2AE.
     020 7955 6522
     http://www.lse.ac.uk/LSELondon/
     Director: Tony Travers.

E   A research centre at the London School of Economics and Political Science.

O   To conduct research on the economic and social issues of the London region, as well as the problems and possibilities of other urban and metropolitan regions

LSE Mackinder Centre for the Study of Long Wave Events

■   LSE, Houghton Street, London, WC2A 2AE.
     020 7405 7686
     http://www.lse.ac.uk/collections/mackinderCentre
     Contact: Martin Kender.

E   An interdisciplinary research centre at the London School of Economics and Political Science.

O   To promote new approaches to and improved methods for research on geopolitical issues - long wave events - which pose some of the greatest challenges to the 21st century, such as the HIV/AIDS epidemic or global climate change

Note: The Centre is named after Sir Halford Mackinder, the second director of the LSE and founder of modern geo-politics.

LTSN Accountancy, Business and Management Subject Centre
     see **Business, Management, Accountancy and Finance Subject Centre.**

LTSN Art, Design and Communication Subject Centre
see **Art Design Media Subject Centre.**

LTSN Bioscience Subject Centre
see **Centre for Bioscience.**

LTSN Built Environment Subject Centre
see **Centre for Education in the Built Environment [Cardiff and Salford].**

LTSN Economics Subject Centre
see **Economics Network.**

LTSN Education Subject Centre
see **Subject Centre for Education.**

LTSN Engineering
see **Engineering Subject Centre.**

LTSN Geography, Earth and Environmental Sciences Subject Centre
see **Geography, Earth and Environmental Sciences Subject Centre.**

LTSN History, Archaeology and Classics Subject Centre
see **Subject Centre for History, Classics and Archaeology.**

LTSN Hospitality and Leisure Studies Subject Centre
see **Hospitality, Leisure, Sport and Tourism Network.**

LTSN Information and Computer Sciences Subject Centre
see **Subject Centre for Information and Computer Sciences [Loughborough and Ulster].**

LTSN Languages and Area Studies Subject Centre
see **Subject Centre for Languages, Linguistics and Area Studies.**

LTSN Law Subject Centre
see **United Kingdom Centre for Legal Education.**

LTSN Materials Subject Centre
see **United Kingdom Centre for Materials Education.**

LTSN Mathematics, Statistics and Operational Research Subject Centre
see **Mathematics, Statistics and Operational Research Subject Centre.**

LTSN Medicine Subject Centre
see **Subject Centre for Medicine, Dentistry and Veterinary Medicine.**

LTSN Performing Arts Subject Centre
see **PALATINE - Dance, Drama and Music.**

LTSN Philosophy and Theology Subject Centre
see **Subject Centre for Philosophical and Religious Studies.**

LTSN Physical Sciences Subject Centre
see **Physical Sciences Centre.**

LTSN Psychology Subject Centre
see **Psychology Network [Glasgow and York].**

LTSN Social Policy, Administration and Social Work Subject Centre
see **Subject Centre for Social Policy and Social Work.**

LTSN Sociology and Politics Subject Centre
see **Subject Network for Sociology, Anthropology, Politics.**

LTSN Subjects Allied to Medicine Subject Centre
see **Subject Centre for Medicine, Dentistry and Veterinary Medicine.**

© CBD Research Ltd · Beckenham · Kent BR3 5JS · Tel 020 8650 7745 · Fax 020 8650 0768 · E-mail cbd@cbdresearch.com · www.cbdresearch.com

Luton Institute of Research in Applied Natural Sciences   (LIRANS)
- ■ University of Bedfordshire, The Spires, 2 Adelaide Street, Luton, Bedfordshire, LU1 5DU.
  01582 743700   fax 01582 743701
  http://www.beds.ac.uk/research/lirans/
- E A research institute at the University of Bedfordshire.
- ○ To conduct research into cryobiology, environmental change and sensors

Macaulay Institute   1987
- Craigiebuckler, Aberdeen, AB15 8QH.
  01224 498200   fax 01224 311556
  http://www.macaulay.ac.uk/
- E   A research institute.
- O   To conduct research exploring the interactions between society's use of land and soil quality, understanding biodiversity, changing landscapes, climate change, water resources, and society and the countryside

MacKay Institute of Communication and Neuroscience   (CNS)   1998
- School of Life Sciences, Keele University, Keele, Staffordshire, ST5 5BG.
  01782 583057   fax 01782 583055
  http://www.keele.ac.uk/depts/co/cnshome.html
  Director: Dr Dave Furness.
- E   A research institute at Keele University.
- O   To foster research into normal and impaired sensory communication

Magnetic Resonance Centre
   see **Sir Peter Mansfield Magnetic Resonance Centre.**

Magnetic Resonance Research Centre   (MRRC)
- Department of Chemical Engineering, New Museums Site, University of Cambridge, Pembroke Street, Cambridge, CB2 3RA.
  01223 334762
  http://www.cheng.cam.ac.uk/research/groups/mri/html/mrrc.htm
- E   A centre at the University of Cambridge.
- O   To conduct experimental and theoretical studies of heterogeneous porous materials, in order to gain a better understanding of their structural and transport properties

Management Centre
   see **Sunley Management Centre.**

Management in Construction Research Centre
- Faculty of Business, Law and the Built Environment, University of Salford, Maxwell Building, Salford, Manchester, M5 4WT.
  0161-295 5357
  http://www.buhu.salford.ac.uk/mgtcon/
  Contact: Prof Keith Alexander.
- E   A research centre within the Research Institute for the Built and Human Environment (qv) at the University of Salford.
- O   To provide tailor-made research and information, training and education in the area of facilities management

Management and Enterprise Development Centre   (MEDC)
- UCE Birmingham Business School, Birmingham City University, Galton Building, Perry Barr, Birmingham, B42 2SU.
  0121-331 5200   fax 0121-331 6366
  http://www.bs.uce.ac.uk/Research/Research_Groups.aspx
  Director: Prof John Sparrow.
- E   A research centre at Birmingham City University.
- O   To conduct research in business development

Management IMRC
   see **Innovative Manufacturing Research Centre - Management IMRC.**

Management and Management Sciences Research Institute   (MaMS)   2004
- Salford Business School, University of Salford, Maxwell Building, Salford, Manchester, M5 4WT.
  0161-295 4369
  http://www.mams.salford.ac.uk/
  Director: Prof Khairy A H Kobbacy.
- E   A department of the University of Salford.
- O   To co-ordinate and support research activities within the fields of management and management sciences

Management Research Centre [London]   (MRC)
- Department of Management and Professional Development, North Campus, London Metropolitan University, 166-220 Holloway Road, London, N7 8DB.
  020 7133 1542
  http://www.londonmet.ac.uk/depts/mpd/research/mrc.cfm
  Director: Prof John Walton.
- E   A research centre at London Metropolitan University.
- O   To conduct research on key issues and developments in management, particularly in the context of significant change within organisations and their environments

Management Research Centre [Wolverhampton] (MRC) 1996
■ University of Wolverhampton Business School, Wulfruna Street, Wolverhampton, WV1 1SB.
  01902 321767
  http://www.wlv.ac.uk/Default.aspx?page=7525
  Director: Prof Les Worrall.
E A centre at the University of Wolverhampton.
○ To be a focus for applied management research and research-based consultancy

Management Research Institute
  see **Cranfield Management Research Institute.**

Management Studies Centre (MSC) 1992
■ Faculty of Engineering Sciences, University College London, Gower Street, London, WC1E 6BT.
  020 7679 6240   fax 020 7679 6238
  http://www.ucl.ac.uk/management-centre/
E A centre at University College London.
○ To provide management instruction in a wide range of degree courses

Manchester Buddhist Centre
■ 16-20 Turner Street, Manchester, M4 1DZ.
  0161-834 9232   fax 0870 134 7356
  http://www.manchesterbuddhistcentre.org.uk/
E An independent non-profit-distributing organisation and a registered charity.
○ To teach meditation and Buddhism
● Education and training - The Centre provides meditation cushions and mats
Note: For other Buddhist centres see note under **Buddhist Centres.**

Manchester Cancer Research Centre (MCRC) 2006
■ University of Manchester, Wilmslow Road, Withington, Manchester, M20 4BX.
  0161-446 3156   fax 0161-446 3109
  http://www.mcrc.manchester.ac.uk/
  Director: Prof Nic Jones.
E A research centre within the Paterson Institute for Cancer Research (qv) at the University of Manchester.
○ To help promote close interaction between those dedicated to basic research into the causes and progression of cancer, those who are dedicated to the translation of new knowledge into novel treatments and those who provide state-of-the-art patient care

Manchester Centre for Anglo-Saxon Studies (MCASS) 1984
■ School of Arts, Histories and Cultures, Humanities Lime Grove, University of Manchester, Oxford Road, Manchester, M13 9PL.
  0161-306 1240
  http://www.arts.manchester.ac.uk/mancass/
  Director: Dr Alexander Rumble.
E A research centre within the Centre for Interdisciplinary Research in the Arts (qv) at the University of Manchester.
○ To conduct research in the many aspects of pre-Conquest life and culture, including spelling, writing and inscriptions, costume and textiles, landscape, agriculture and place-names, Old English literature, historical texts and charters, fortifications and towns, and kingship and nationality
● Database of 11th century manuscripts and texts

Manchester Centre for Integrative Systems Biology (MCISB) 2006
■ University of Manchester, 131 Princess Street, Manchester, M1 7DN.
  0161-306 8917   fax 0161-306 8918
  http://www.mcisb.org/
  Director: Prof Douglas Kell.
E A research centre within the Manchester Interdisciplinary Biocentre (qv) at the University of Manchester.
○ To conduct multidisciplinary research combining theory, computer modelling and experiments in a systems approach across the life sciences and industry

Manchester Centre for Magnetic Resonance (MCMR) 1997
■ School of Chemistry, University of Manchester, Oxford Road, Manchester, M13 9PL.
  0161-275 4665   fax 0161-275 4598
  http://mch3w.ch.man.ac.uk/
  Contact: Prof G A Morris.
E A research centre at the University of Manchester.
○ To promote research in magnetic resonance and its applications in science and medicine

Manchester Centre for Mesoscience and Nanotechnology (CMN) 2003
■ School of Computer Science, Information Technology Building, University of Manchester, Oxford Road, Manchester, M13 9PL.
  0161-275 4552   fax 0161-275 4527
  http://www.cs.manchester.ac.uk/nanotechnology/
  Director: Prof A K Geim.
E An interdisciplinary research centre at the University of Manchester.
○ To create an easy-to-access-and-use, multidisciplinary workshop that allows researchers to fabricate, visualise and characterise structures and devices containing individual elements from a size of a few microns down to 10 nm

Manchester Centre for Music in Culture   (MC2)   2002
- School of Arts, Histories and Cultures, Humanities Lime Grove, University of Manchester, Oxford Road, Manchester, M13 9PL.
  0161-306 1240
  http://www.arts.manchester.ac.uk/mc2/
  Contact: Dr Penelope Gouk.
- E An interdisciplinary research centre within the Centre for Interdisciplinary Research in the Arts (qv) at the University of Manchester.
- O To bring together researchers with an interest in music and its relationship to culture

Manchester Centre for Nonlinear Dynamics   (MCND)
- School of Physics and Astronomy, University of Manchester, Oxford Road, Manchester, M13 9PL.
  0161-306 6000
  http://www.mcnd.man.ac.uk/
  Director: Prof Tom Mullin.
- E An interdisciplinary research centre at the University of Manchester.
- O To conduct research in the application of a combined approach of theoretical modelling, computation and detailed quantitative experimental investigations of nonlinear phenomena

Manchester Centre for Public Theology   (MCPT)
- School of Arts, Histories and Cultures, University of Manchester, Oxford Road, Manchester, M13 9PL.
  0161-306 1240
  http://www.arts.manchester.ac.uk/subjectareas/religionstheology/research/crpc/mcpt/
- E An interdisciplinary research institute within the Centre for Religion and Political Culture (qv) at the University of Manchester.
- O To contribute theological understanding and practice to the well-being to communities and individuals in contemporary society

Manchester Centre for Regional History   (MCRH)   1998
- Department of History and Economic History, Manchester Metropolitan University, Room 122 - Geoffrey Manton Building, Rosamond Street West, Manchester, M15 6LL.
  0161-247 6491; 6688
  http://www.mcrh.mmu.ac.uk/
  Director: Melanie Tebbutt. Administrator: Craig Horner.
- E A research centre within the Manchester European Research Institute (qv) at Manchester Metropolitan University.
- O To consolidate and expand existing expertise in the history of the Manchester region by promoting historical research on the North West of England

Manchester European Research Institute   (MERI)   2003
- Faculty of Humanities, Law and Social Science, Manchester Metropolitan University, Geoffrey Manton Building, Rosamond Street West, Manchester, M15 6LL.
  0161-247 3030
  http://www.meri.mmu.ac.uk/
  Director: Prof Clive Archer.
- E A research institute at Manchester Metropolitan University.
- O To aim at sustaining and enhancing research potential in areas focussing on European issues or involving Europe's relationship with the rest of the world, especially in the cultural, economic, legal, literary, political and social fields

Manchester Institute of Innovation Research   (IoIR)   2003
- Harold Hankins Building, University of Manchester, Booth Street West, Manchester, M13 9QH.
  0161-275 7365   fax 0161-275 7361
  http://les.man.ac.uk/
  Executive Director: Prof Jeremy Howells.
- E A research institute at the University of Manchester.

Manchester Institute for Mathematical Sciences   (MIMS)
- School of Mathematics, University of Manchester, Sackville Street, Manchester, M60 1QD.
  0161-306 3641   fax 0161-306 3669
  http://www.mims.manchester.ac.uk/
  Head: Prof Paul Glendinning.
- E An interdisciplinary research institute at the University of Manchester.
- O To organise core research activities in pure and applied mathematics, numerical analysis, probability and statistics, and mathematical logic

Manchester Institute for Research and Innovation in Art and Design   (MIRIAD)
- Faculty of Art and Design, Manchester Metropolitan University, Cavendish North Building, Cavendish Street, Manchester, M15 6BG.
  0161-247 1744   fax 0161-247 6839
  http://www.miriad.mmu.ac.uk/
  Director: Prof John Hyatt.
- E An institute at Manchester Metropolitan University.
- O To provide structures, processes and opportunities to extend, support, develop quality, and profile research, within the subject areas of art and design, architectural design, drama, dance, performance arts, and histories and theories of art and design; to provide postgraduate research awards, research, training and taught postgraduate programme opportunities, as well as professional practice, knowledge transfer, and enterprise and design

© CBD Research Ltd · Beckenham · Kent BR3 5JS · Tel 020 8650 7745 · Fax 020 8650 0768 · E-mail cbd@cbdresearch.com · www.cbdresearch.com

Manchester Interdisciplinary Biocentre (MIB) 2006

- University of Manchester, 131 Princess Street, Manchester, M1 7DN.
  0161-306 8917   fax 0161-306 8918
  http://www.mib.ac.uk/
  Director: John McCarthy.
- E   A department of the University of Manchester.
- ○   To explore specific areas of interdisciplinary quantitative bioscience at the highest level, in c 80 research groups

Manchester Poetry Centre 1969

- School of Languages, Linguistics and Cultures, University of Manchester, Oxford Road, Manchester, M13 9PL.
  0161-275 8311   fax 0161-275 3031
  http://www.llc.manchester.ac.uk/
- E   A centre at the University of Manchester.

Manchester Regional Economics Centre 2005

- School of Social Sciences, Williamson Building, University of Manchester, Oxford Road, Manchester, M13 9PL.
  0161-275 0792; 0798   fax 0161-275 0793
  http://www.ipeg.org.uk/mrec/
  Director: Prof Michael Artis.
- E   A research centre within the Institute for Political and Economic Governance (qv) at the University of Manchester.

Manchester Science Enterprise Centre (MSEC) 2002

- Faculty of Engineering and Physical Sciences, PO Box 88, University of Manchester, Sackville Street, Manchester, M60 1QD.
  0161-306 8484   fax 0161-306 8488
  http://www.msec.ac.uk/
  Director: Peter Winter.
- E   A research centre at the University of Manchester.
- ○   To empower people to exploit knowledge and ideas in science enterprise
Note: See United Kingdom Science Enterprise Centres for further information.

Manchester-Sheffield Centre for Dead Sea Scrolls Research

NR   School of Arts, Histories and Cultures, University of Manchester, Oxford Road, Manchester, M13 9PL.
  0161-275 3609   fax 0161-275 3264
  http://www.arts.manchester.ac.uk//subjectareas/religionstheology/research/centreforbiblicalstudies/
  Contact: Prof George J Brooke.
- E   A sub-unit of the Centre for Biblical Studies (qv) at the University of Manchester.
- ○   To conduct research in early Judaism
Note: A joint venture with the University of Sheffield.

Mannheim Centre for the Study of Criminology and Criminal Justice 1990

- Department of Social Policy, LSE, Houghton Street, London, WC2A 2AE.
  020 7955 7044
  http://www.lse.ac.uk/collections/mannheim/
  Director: Prof Tim Newburn. Administrator: Iman Heflin.
- E   A research centre at the London School of Economics and Political Science.
- ○   To provide a forum for criminology, including undergraduate and postgraduate courses and funded research
- ●   Conferences - Seminars - Various public events
Note: Usually known as the Mannheim Centre for Criminology. The Centre is named after Prof Hermann Mannheim (b1889) a noted criminologist.

Manufacturing Architecture Research Centre (MARC)

- Department of Architecture and Spatial Design, London Metropolitan University, Spring House, 40-44 Holloway Road, London, N7 8JL.
  020 7133 2711   fax 020 7133 2039
  http://www.londonmet.ac.uk/architecture/research/marc/
- E   A research centre at London Metropolitan University.
- ○   To study materials and manufacturing processes which directly inform the creation of high quality modern architecture

Manufacturing Centre
   see **Teesside Manufacturing Centre.**

Manufacturing Engineering Centre (MEC) 1996

- Aberconway Building, Cardiff University, Colum Drive, Cardiff, CF10 3EU.
  029 2087 9611
  http://www.mec.cf.ac.uk/
  Director: Prof Duc-Truong Pham.
- E   A research centre within the Cardiff University Innovative Manufacturing Research Centre (qv) at Cardiff University.
- ○   To conduct world-class research and development in all major areas of advanced manufacturing technology, and use the output to promote the introduction of knowledge based manufacturing to industry in Wales and the rest of the UK

Manufacturing Enterprise Centre
   see **Exeter Manufacturing Enterprise Centre.**

Manufacturing Science and Engineering Research Centre   (MSERC)

■ Department of Engineering, Ashton Building, University of Liverpool, Liverpool, L69 3GH.
0151-794 6801   fax 0151-794 4675
http://mserc.liv.ac.uk/
E A research centre at the University of Liverpool.
○ To conduct research in engineering, utilising the most modern and advanced methods known

Manufacturing Systems Centre

■ Manufacturing Department, Building 50, Cranfield University, Cranfield, Bedfordshire, MK43 0AL.
01234 750111
http://www.cranfield.ac.uk/sas/mem/manufacturingsystems/
Director: Prof Tim Baines.
E A research centre at Cranfield University.
○ To conduct research and teaching in manufacturing strategy, manufacturing system design and modelling, supply chain and manufacturing management, and informatics

Manufacturing Systems Integration Research Institute

■ Loughborough University, Loughborough, Leicestershire, LE11 3TU.
01509 263171
http://www.lboro.ac.uk/departments/mm/research/manufacturing-systems/
E A research institute within Loughborough University.
○ To conduct leading-edge research in systems engineering and change, business process modelling visualisation and analysis, human systems design and enactment, machine and software component design and implementation, workflow management, and internet-enabled distribution of design, engineering and monitoring services

Marc Fitch Historical Institute

■ University of Leicester, 5 Salisbury Road, Leicester, LE1 7QR.
0116-252 2762   fax 0116-252 5769
http://www.le.ac.uk/elh/
E An institute at the University of Leicester.
● Marc Fitch library (extensive collection of local history records)

Margaret Beaufort Institute of Theology   1994

■ University of Cambridge, 12 Grange Road, Cambridge, CB3 9DU.
01223 741039   fax 01223 741054
http://www.margaretbeaufort.cam.ac.uk/
Director of Studies: Fäinche Ryan.
E An institute at the University of Cambridge.
○ To provide a facility for women's studies in theology, spirituality and leadership for the lay ministry

Marine Biology and Ecology Research Centre   (MBERC)

■ School of Biological Sciences, University of Plymouth, Davy Building, Drake Circus, Plymouth, PL4 8AA.
01752 232967   fax 01752 232970
http://www.research.plymouth.ac.uk/mberc/
Contact: Dr Simon Rundle.
E A research centre at the University of Plymouth.
○ To conduct research in the areas of aquatic biodiversity and ecology, conservation biology and pollution, developmental plasticity and ecophysiology, behavioural ecology, and global climate change

Marine Centre
see **NAFC Marine Centre.**

Marine Institute

■ School of Earth, Ocean and Environmental Sciences, University of Plymouth, Portland Square, Drake Circus, Plymouth, PL4 8AA.
01752 233719   fax 01752 233039
http://www.research.plymouth.ac.uk/marine/
Director: Prof Laurence Mee.
E An institute within the University of Plymouth.
○ To help consolidate the ongoing University marine activities into a coherent programme

Marine Pollution Information Centre   (MARPIC)   1970

■ National Marine Biological Library, Citadel Hill, Plymouth, PL1 2PB.
01752 633266   fax 01752 633102
http://www.mba.ac.uk/nmbl/publications/mprt/information_centre.htm
Contact: Linda Noble.
E A centre at the National Marine Biological Library.
○ To collect, index and make available information about all types of marine and estuarine pollution

Marine Research Institute
see **Gatty Marine Research Institute.**

Marine Technology Centre
 see **Glasgow Marine Technology Centre.**

Maritime Historical Studies Centre   (MHSC)   1996
■   Department of History, University of Hull, Blaydes House, 6 High Street, Hull, HU1 1HA.
    01482 305110; 346311
    http://www.hull.ac.uk/mhsc/
    Administrator: Josephine Affleck.
E   A centre at the University of Hull.
○   To improve knowledge and understanding of the maritime dimensions of history

Maritime Institute
 see **Greenwich Maritime Institute.**

Martin Centre for Architectural and Urban Studies   1967
■   Department of Architecture, University of Cambridge, 6 Chaucer Road, Cambridge, CB2 2EB.
    01223 331700   fax 01223 331701
    http://www.arct.cam.ac.uk/ArchIntranet/Section.aspx?p=1&ix=2
E   A research centre at the University of Cambridge.
○   To undertake research and postgraduate teaching in the fields of environmental design, architectural computer-aided design,
    architectural acoustics, energy conservation, earthquake engineering and appropriate technology

Mary Ann Baxter Centre for Interdisciplinary Gender Research   2006
■   College of Arts and Social Sciences, University of Dundee, Nethergate, Dundee, DD1 4HN.
    01382 384177; 384180
E   A research centre at the University of Dundee.

Mary Seacole Centre for Nursing Practice   1998
■   Faculty of Health and Human Sciences, Thames Valley University, Westel House, 32-38 Uxbridge Road, London, W5 2BS.
    020 8231 2915
    http://www.maryseacole.com/
    Contact: Prof Elizabeth Anionwu.
E   A research centre at Thames Valley University.
○   To enable the integration of a multi-ethnic philosophy into the process of nursing and midwifery recruitment, education, practice,
    management and research
●   Information service

Mary Seacole Research Centre   (MSRC)
■   School of Nursing and Midwifery, Charles Frears Campus, De Montfort University, 266 London Road, Leicester, LE2 1RQ.
    0116-201 3906   fax 0116-201 3805
    http://www.dmu.ac.uk/faculties/hls/research/msrc/
    Director: Prof Mark R D Johnson.
E   A centre at De Montfort University.
○   To conduct research on care planning in a multi-ethnic NHS, employment opportunities, and career development of black and
    minority ethnic staff, and specific ethnic health care needs
Note: Mary Seacole was a nurse of Jamaican origin who cared for the sick and wounded of the army in the West Indies, Panama, and
    the Crimea

Mary Ward Centre   1890
■   42 Queen Square, London, WC1N 3AQ.
    020 7269 6000   fax 020 7269 6001
    http://www.marywardcentre.ac.uk/
    Chairman: Colin Hopkins.
E   A registered charity and a company limited by guarantee.
○   To provide educational opportunities for adults in both the local community and London

Massachusets Institute of Technology Institute
 see **Cambridge-MIT Institute.**

Materials Analysis and Research Services - Centre for Industrial Collaboration   (MARS CIC)
■   City Campus, Sheffield Hallam University, Sheffield, S1 1WB.
    0114-225 2017; 4078   fax 0114-225 3501
    http://www.shu.ac.uk/research/meri/mars/
    Commercial Manager: Dr Nick Farmilo.
E   A research centre within the Materials and Engineering Research Institute (qv) at Sheffield Hallam University.
○   To deliver analysis and consultancy services to any industry which has material-based needs

Materials And The Arts Research Centre   (MATAR)

- London College of Communication, University of the Arts, London, Elephant and Castle, London, SE1 6SB.
  020 7514 6500
  http://www.matar.co.uk/
  Director: Dr Andrew Manning.
- E   A research centre at the University of the Arts, London.
- O   To promote investigation of the chemical and physical properties of materials used by designers, art practitioners and commercial printers

Materials and Catalysis Centre
  see **Wolfson Materials and Catalysis Centre.**

Materials Characterisation Centre
  see **Loughborough Materials Characterisation Centre.**

Materials and Engineering Research Institute   (MERI)   1990

- City Campus, Sheffield Hallam University, Sheffield, S1 1WB.
  0114-225 3500   fax 0114-225 3501
  http://www.shu.ac.uk/research/meri/
  Director: Prof Roger Eccleston.
- E   A research institute at Sheffield Hallam University.
- O   To conduct research in, and provide consultancy on, a broad range of materials and engineering research

Materials Institute
  see **UniS Materials Institute.**

Materials Performance Centre   (MPC)

- School of Materials, PO Box 88, Sackville Street, Manchester, M60 1QD.
  0161-306 4848   fax 0161-306 4865
  http://www.materials.manchester.ac.uk/esearch/centres/materialsperformancecentre/
  Director: Prof Andrew Sherry.
- E   A research centre at the University of Manchester.
- O   To provide support on materials issues to the operating companies of British Nuclear Fuels Ltd and other external chemical and power industry companies

Materials Research Centre   (MRC)   2000

- Department of Mechanical Engineering, University of Bath, Claverton Down, Bath, BA2 7AY.
  01225 386708   fax 01225 386098
  http://www.bath.ac.uk/mrc/
  Director: Prof D P Almond.
- E   A centre at the University of Bath.
- O   To provide a stimulating informed environment for the pursuit of research in the field of materials science and engineering

Materials Research Centre

- School of Engineering, Swansea University, Singleton Park, Swansea, SA2 8PP.
  01792 205678
  http://www.swan.ac.uk/engineering/Research/MaterialsResearchCentre/
  Head: Prof W John Evans.
- E   A research centre at Swansea University.
- O   To conduct research and teaching in materials engineering, steel technology, and recycling technology

Materials Science Research Centre   (MSRC)

- Department of Metallurgy and Materials, University of Birmingham, Edgbaston, Birmingham, B15 2TT.
  0121-414 5168   fax 0121-414 5232
  http://www.mat-sci.bham.ac.uk/
  Head: Prof J S Abell.
- E   A research centre at the University of Birmingham.

Mathematical Institute

- University of Oxford, 24-29 St Giles', Oxford, OX1 3LB.
  01865 273525   fax 01865 273 583
  http://www.maths.ox.ac.uk/
  Administrator: Charlotte Rimmer.
- E   A department of the University of Oxford.
- O   To nurture a mathematical culture, by promoting a pervasive understanding of the mathematical way of thought and by supporting the study of mathematics for its own sake

Mathematics Education Centre   (MEC)   2002
- Loughborough University, Loughborough, Leicestershire, LE11 3TU.
  01509 227460
  http://mec.lboro.ac.uk/
  Head: Dr Tony Croft.
- E A centre at Loughborough University.
- ○ To oversee mathematics teaching to engineering undergraduates and provide a focus for those working in mathematics education

Mathematics Education Research Centre   (MERC)   1977
- Faculty of Social Studies, University of Warwick, Coventry, CV4 7AL.
  024 7652 3211   fax 024 7652 3237
  http://fcis1.wie.warwick.ac.uk/
  Director: Dr Eddie Gray.
- E A research centre within the Warwick Institute of Education (qv) at the University of Warwick.

Mathematics Institute
   see **Warwick Mathematics Institute.**

Mathematics Learning Support Centre   1996
- Loughborough, Leicestershire, LE11 3TU.
  01509 227460
  http://mec.lboro.ac.uk/
- E A research centre within the Mathematics Education Centre (qv) at Loughborough University.
- ○ To support students needing help with basic mathematics

Mathematics Research Centre   (MRC)   1968
- Faculty of Science, University of Warwick, Coventry, CV4 7AL.
  024 7652 8317   fax 024 7652 3548
  http://www.maths.warwick.ac.uk/mrc/
- E A research centre within the Warwick Mathematics Institute (qv) at the University of Warwick.

Mathematics Research Centre   (MRC)
- School of Mathematical Sciences, Queen Mary, University of London, Mile End Road, London, E1 4NS.
  020 7882 5440   fax 020 8981 9587
  http://www.maths.qmul.ac.uk/MRC
  Contact: Prof David K Arrowsmith.
- E A research centre at Queen Mary, University of London.
- ○ To promote and conduct mathematics research

Mathematics, Statistics and Operational Research Subject Centre   (MSOR Network)
- School of Mathematics, University of Birmingham, Edgbaston, Birmingham, B15 2TT.
  0121-414 7095   fax 0121-414 3389
  http://mathstore.ac.uk/
  Director & Head of School: Prof John Blake. Network Manager: M J Grove.
- E A Government funded national centre within the University of Birmingham.
- ○ To foster world-class education in the fields of mathematics, statistics and operational research
- ● Education and training - Information service - Statistics
- ✕ LTSN Mathematics, Statistics and Operational Research Subject Centre.
Note: One of 24 centres serving different disciplines which form the Subject Network of the Higher Education Academy, (qv).

Max Beloff Centre for the Study of Liberty   2005
- FREEPOST (MK 1534), University of Buckingham, Buckingham, MK18 1EG.
  01280 820263   fax 01280 822245
  http://www.buckingham.ac.uk/ubfoundation/beloff/
  Director: Dr Mary Welstead.
- E A centre at the University of Buckingham.
- ○ To create a forum where defenders of freedom can work and think together to create a critical but interdisciplinary mass in the study of liberty

Max Lock Centre
- School of Architecture and the Built Environment, University of Westminster, 35 Marylebone Road, London, NW1 5LS.
  020 7911 5000 ext 3131
  http://www.wmin.ac.uk/builtenv/maxlock
  Director: Michael Theis.
- E A research centre at the University of Westminster.
- ○ To conduct research on sustainable urban development, tools for managing rapid urbanisation, community asset management, research knowledge management, and implementation of the habitat agenda

Maxwell Institute for Mathematical Sciences
■ School of Mathematics, James Clerk Maxwell Building, University of Edinburgh, Mayfield Road, Edinburgh, EH9 3JZ.
   0131-650 5060   fax 0131-650 6553
   http://www.maxwell.ac.uk/
   Director: Prof Angus Macdonald.
E   A centre at the University of Edinburgh.
O   To be an internationally recognised and pre-eminent centre for research and for postgraduate training in the mathematical sciences
Note: The Institute is a joint venture with Heriot-Watt University.

McCoubrey Centre for International Law   2001
■ Law School, University of Hull, Cottingham Road, Hull, HU6 7RX.
   01482 465857   fax 01482 466388
   http://www.hull.ac.uk/law/research/mccoubrey/
   Director: Dr Richard Burchill.
E   A research centre at the University of Hull.

McDonald Institute for Archaeological Research   1990
■ Downing Street, Cambridge, CB2 3ER.
   01223 333538   fax 01223 333536
   http://www.mcdonald.cam.ac.uk/
   Director: Prof Graeme Barker.
E   A department of the University of Cambridge.
O   To provide support for researchers in many branches of archaeology, especially the archaeology of early human cognition

Measurement and Instrumentation Centre   (MIC)   1970
■ Department of Engineering, City University, Tait Building, Northampton Square, London, EC1V 0HB.
   020 7040 0113
   http://www.city.ac.uk/sems/research/mic
   Director: Prof K T V Grattan.
E   A centre at City University.
O   To develop measurement and instrumentation as a scientific discipline, and to promote it through education, research and interaction with industry; to conduct research in photonics modelling, fibre optic sensing systems, and fibre Bragg grating fabrication and applications

Mechatronics Research Centre   (MRC)
■ School of Engineering and Technology, De Montfort University, The Gateway, Leicester, LE1 9BH.
   0116-257 7456
   http://www.mrg.dmu.ac.uk/
E   A centre at De Montfort University.
O   To conduct high quality fundamental and applied research within the integrated disciplines of mechanical, electronic, and computing / software engineering that is innovative and relevant to the needs of UK and European society and industry

Media Research Institute
      see **Stirling Media Research Institute.**

Media Technology Research Centre   (MTRC)
■ Department of Computer Science, University of Bath, Claverton Down, Bath, BA2 7AY.
   01225 386811   fax 01225 383493
   http://www.bath.ac.uk/media/
   Director: Prof Philip Willis.
E   A research centre at the University of Bath.
O   To study computer technology for animation, graphics, image processing, music, rendering, and virtual reality

Medical Computing Centre
      see **Teesside Medical Computing Centre.**

Medical Polymers Research Institute   (MPRI)
■ School of Mechanical and Manufacturing Engineering, Queen's University, Belfast, Ashby Building, Stranmillis Road, Belfast, BT9 5AH.
   028 9097 4563   fax 028 9066 0631
   http://www.qub.ac.uk/mpri/
   Director: Prof John Orr.
E   An interdisciplinary research institute at Queen's University, Belfast.

Medical Research Council Collaborative Centre   (MRC CC)   1986
■ 20 Park Crescent, London, W1B 1AL.
   020 7636 5422   fax 020 7436 6179
   http://www.mrc.ac.uk/
E   A publicly funded organisation.
O   To support research across the entire spectrum of medical sciences
Note: Currently the MRC is overseeing 46 collaborative projects at various institutions. See also **MRC**

© CBD Research Ltd · Beckenham · Kent BR3 5JS · Tel 020 8650 7745 · Fax 020 8650 0768 · E-mail cbd@cbdresearch.com · www.cbdresearch.com

Medieval Research Centre (MRC) 1996
■ University of Leicester, University Road, Leicester, LE1 7RH.
   0116-252 2522
   http://www.le.ac.uk/arts/medieval/
E   A research centre at the University of Leicester.
○   To co-ordinate research in medieval subjects

Mental Health Knowledge Centre (MHKC)
■ King's College, London, DeCrespigny Park, London, SE5 8AF.
   020 7848 0252
   http://www.iop.kcl.ac.uk/departments/?locator=860&context=main
   Contact: Richard Hornsby.
E   A research centre within the Centre for Public Engagement in Mental Health Sciences (qv) at King's College, London.
○   To disseminate science-based fact about mental health to the media, health services, Government agencies, as well as to the
   public at large
Note: Also known as the Centre for Public Engagement in Mental Health Sciences.

Menzies Centre for Australian Studies (MCAS) 1982
■ The Australia Centre, Corner Strand and Melbourne Place, London, WC2B 4LG.
   020 7240 0220   fax 020 7240 8292
   http://www.kcl.ac.uk/menzies/
   Head of Centre: Prof Carl Bridge. Lecturer: Dr Ian Henderson.
E   A department of the 14 subscribing Australian universities and associated with King's College, London.
○   To promote a deeper understanding in Britain and Europe of Australia's culture and role in the world; to encourage Australian
   studies in European higher education
●   Education and training - Information service - Library - Access to the Australia House Collection in the University of London and the
   Institute of Commonwealth Studies
×   Sir Robert Menzies Centre for Australian Studies.

Mersey Neurological Trust, Glaxo Centre
■ Norton Street, Liverpool, L3 8LR.
   0151-298 2999   fax 0151-298 2333
   Manager: Maureen Kelly. Information Officer: Kathryn Topping.
E   Run by the Mersey Neurological Trust, and independent charitable trust.
○   To offer advice and information on all aspects of neurological disorder
●   Conference facilities - Education and training - Information service - Library and database
¶   Glance Newsletter.
×   Glaxo Neurological Centre.

Metal Joining Research Centre 1993
■ Sheffield Hallam University, Room 4005 - Sheaf Building, Howard Street, Sheffield, S1 1WB.
   0114-225 3099   fax 0114-225 3433
   http://www.shu.ac.uk/research/meri/
   Director: Dr Alan Smith.
E   A research centre within the Structural Materials and Integrity Research Centre (qv) at Sheffield Hallam University.
○   To conduct research on the development of new, sustainable protocols for existing joining techniques and manufacturing processes
Note: Also known as the Outukumpu Research Centre.

Metals Advisory Centre
   see **Sheffield University Metals Advisory Centre.**

Methodology Institute
■ LSE, Columbia House, Houghton Street, London, WC2A 2AE.
   020 7955 7639
   http://www.lse.ac.uk/collections/methodologyInstitute/
   Administrator: Victoria Grey-Edwards.
E   A research institute at the London School of Economics and Political Science.

Methods and Data Institute (M+Di
■ West Wing - Law and Social Sciences Building, University of Nottingham, University Park, Nottingham, NG7 2RD.
   0115-846 8150   fax 0115-846 8149
   http://www.nottingham.ac.uk/mdi/
   Director: Prof Cees van der Eijk.
E   A research institute at the University of Nottingham.
○   To support people engaged in social science research

Metrology Centre
   see **Mitutoyo Metrology Centre.**

Michael Barber Centre for Mass Spectrometry (MBCMS) 1990

■ School of Chemistry, University of Manchester, 131 Princess Street, Manchester, M1 7DN.
   0161-306 4532
   http://www.mbc.manchester.ac.uk/
   Director: Prof Simon Gaskell.
E   A research centre within the Manchester Interdisciplinary Biocentre (qv) at the University of Manchester.
O   To conduct research in the development of mass spectrometry and related analytical techniques, and their application to problems of biological performance
Note: The Centre is named after Professor Michael Barber who made significant contributions to the science of mass spectrometry.

Michael Palin Centre for Stammering Children 1993

■ Finsbury Health Centre, Pine Street, London, EC1R 0LP.
   020 7530 4238   fax 020 7833 3842
   http://www.stammeringcentre.org/
E   A registered charity.
O   To provide specialist help in speech therapy to children aged 2-18 years, who stammer

Microelectronics Industrial Centre (MIC)

■ School of Computing, Engineering and Information Sciences, Ellison Building, Northumbria University, Ellison Place, Newcastle upon Tyne, NE1 8ST.
   0191-227 4599   fax 0191-227 4599
   http://mic.unn.ac.uk/
   Director: Safwat Mansi.
E   A research centre at Northumbria University.
O   To help small and medium-sized enterprises in the North East that design, manufacture or use electronic equipment

Microelectronics Research Centre

■ Cavendish Laboratory, University of Cambridge, Madingley Road, Cambridge, CB3 0HE.
   01223 337200; 337556   fax 01223 337706
   http://www-mrc.phy.cam.ac.uk/
E   A centre at the University of Cambridge.
O   To undertake research on the physics of novel electronic quantum devices

Microsoft Institute for High Performance Computing 2005

■ School of Engineering Sciences, University Road, Highfield, Southampton, SO17 1BJ.
   023 8059 3116; 8353   fax 023 8059 4813
   http://www.soton.ac.uk/ses/research/mshpci/
   Co-Director: Prof Simon Cox. Co-Director: Dr Kenji Takeda.
E   A research centre at the University of Southampton.

MIcroSystems Engineering Centre (MISEC)

■ School of Mathematical and Computer Sciences, Heriot-Watt University, Earl Mountbatten Building, Riccarton, Edinburgh, EH14 4AS.
   0131-449 5111
   http://www.cee.hw.ac.uk/misec/
   Contact: Marc Desmulliez.
E   A research centre at Heriot-Watt University.
O   To provide facilities, infrastructure and a team environment to enable and facilitate cross-disciplinary interdepartmental research in microtechnology, with an emphasis on the integration of microwave electronics, microelectronics, optoelectronics and micromechanics

Microsystems and Nanotechnology Centre 1994

■ Materials Department, Building 70, Cranfield University, Cranfield, Bedfordshire, MK43 0AL.
   01234 750111   fax 01234 751346
   http://www.cranfield.ac.uk/sas/materials/nanotech/
   Head: Dr Robert Dorey. Contact: Mrs Enza Giaracini.
E   A research centre at Cranfield University.
O   To conduct research and teaching in many aspects of nanotechnology, from the development of new functional materials through to the prototyping of microelectromechanical system (MEMS) devices

Middle East Centre 1957

■ St Antony's College, University of Oxford, 62 Woodstock Road, Oxford, OX2 6JF.
   01865 284780   fax 01865 274529
   http://www.sant.ox.ac.uk/mec/
E   A research centre at the University of Oxford.

Middlesex University Translation Institute

■ School of Arts, Trent Park, Middlesex University, Bramley Road, London, N14 4YZ.
   http://www.mdx.ac.uk/research/centres/langtrans.asp
E   An institute at Middlesex University.
O   To promote translation teaching, research and practice
●   Education and training

Midlands Centre for Criminology and Criminal Justice   1990

■   Department of Social Sciences, Loughborough University, Brockington Building, Loughborough, Leicestershire, LE11 3TU.
    01509 228369
    http://www.lboro.ac.uk/departments/ss/centres/criminology/crime.html
    Director: Prof Graham Farrell.
E   A research centre at Loughborough University.
○   To be a focal point for crime-related research in a number of areas including crime prevention, policing, drug policy, and the criminal justice system

Midlands e-Science Centre   (MeSC)

■   School of Computer Science, University of Birmingham, Edgbaston, Birmingham, B15 2TT.
    0121-414 4773; 5100   fax 0121-414 3675
    http://www.cs.bham.ac.uk/
E   A research centre at the University of Birmingham.
Note: See **e-Science Centres of Excellence** for further information.

Mine Action and Disaster Management Centre
    see **Cranfield Mine Action and Disaster Management Centre.**

Mining and Mineral Centre
    see **Nottingham Mining and Mineral Centre.**

MIT Institute
    see **Cambridge-MIT Institute.**

Mitutoyo Metrology Centre

■   Aberconway Building, Cardiff University, Colum Drive, Cardiff, CF10 3EU.
    029 2087 9611
    http://www.mec.cf.ac.uk/
E   A research centre within the Manufacturing Engineering Centre (qv) at Cardiff University.

Mixed Media Grid [Research Centre]   (MiMeG)

NR Department of Computer Science, University of Bristol, Merchant Venturers Building, Woodland Road, Bristol, BS8 1UB.
    0117-954 5264   fax 0117-954 5208
    http://www.ncess.ac.uk/research/nodes/MiMeG/
    Contact: Dr Mike Fraser.
E   An interdisciplinary research centre at the University of Bristol.
○   To generate tools for social scientists to collaboratively analyse audio-visual qualitative data over the Grid
Note: A joint venture with King's College London, and a research node of the **ESRC National Centre for e-Social Science**.

Mobile Information and Network Technologies Research Centre   (MINT@K

■   Faculty of Computing, Information Systems and Mathematics, Kingston University, London, Penrhyn Road, Kingston-upon-Thames, Surrey, KT1 2EE.
    020 8547 2000; 7576   fax 020 8547 7971
    http://mint.kingston.ac.uk/
    Director: Prof Robert S H Istepanian.
E   A research centre at Kingston University, London.
○   To bring together clinicians, engineers and scientists, at the forefront of information and communication technologies, for medicines and solutions to perplexing health problems in the areas of bio-information systems and the application, of emerging mobile and network technologies, to health care systems

Mobile and Satellite Communications Research Centre   (MSCRC)

■   School of Engineering, Design and Technology, University of Bradford, Bradford, West Yorkshire, BD7 1DP.
    01274 234009; 234151   fax 01273 233727
    http://www.mscrc.net/
E   A research centre at the University of Bradford.

Mobile VCE
    see **Virtual Centre of Excellence in Mobile Personal Communications.**

Mobility Centre
    see **Queen Elizabeth's Foundation Mobility Centre.**

Modelling Research Centre   (MRC)

■   City Campus, Sheffield Hallam University, Sheffield, S1 1WB.
    0114-225 3500   fax 0114-225 3501
    http://www.shu.ac.uk/research/meri/
    Head: Prof Chris Care.
E   A constituent research centre within the Materials and Engineering Research Institute (qv) at Sheffield Hallam University.
○   To conduct research in, and provide consultancy on, the modelling of materials at molecular length scales through to the modelling of complete manufacturing systems

Modelling and Simulation for e-Social Science [Research Centre]   (MoSeS)   2005
NR   School of Geography, Woodhouse Lane, Leeds, LS2 9JT.
     0113-343 3300   fax 0113-343 3308
     http://www.ncess.ac.uk/research/nodes/MoSeS/
     Contact: Dr Mark Birkin.
E   A research centre at the University of Leeds.
O   To develop representation of the entire UK population as individuals and households, together with a package of modelling tools
     which allow specific social research and policy issues to be addressed
Note: A research node of the **ESRC National Centre for e-Social Science**.

Modern Interiors Research Centre   (MIRC)
■   Faculty of Art, Design and Architecture, Kingston University, London, Knights Park, Kingston-upon-Thames, Surrey, KT1 2QJ.
     020 8547 8062   fax 020 8547 8272
     http://www.kingston.ac.uk/design/mirc/
     Contact: Prof Penny Sparke.
E   A research centre at Kingston University, London.
O   To focus research on design history, architectural history, and visual, material and spatial culture of the design of interiors of the
     'modern period' (1870-1970)
Note: previously Centre for the Study of the Design of the Modern Interior

Modern Records Centre   1973
■   The Library, University of Warwick, Coventry, CV4 7AL.
     024 7652 4219   fax 024 7652 4211
     http://www2.warwick.ac.uk/services/library/mrc/
E   A department of the University of Warwick.
O   To collect and make available for research primary sources for British social, political and economic history, especially the records
     of trade unions, employers' and trade associations and the motor industry
●   Archive repository (Mon-Thur 0900-1900; Fri 0900-1600)

Moffat Centre for Travel and Tourism Business Development   (MC)   1998
■   Caledonian Business School, Health Building, Cowcaddens Road, Glasgow, G4 0BA.
     0141-331 8400   fax 0141-331 8411
     http://www.moffatcentre.com/
     Director: Prof John Lennon.
E   A centre at Glasgow Caledonian University.
O   To provide consultancy and contract research to the travel and tourism industry

Molecular Imaging Centre
     see **Wolfson Molecular Imaging Centre.**

Molecular Materials Centre   (MMC)   2001
NR   School of Chemical Engineering and Analytical Science, University of Manchester, PO Box 88, Manchester, M60 1QD.
     0161-306 3982
     http://www.ceas.manchester.ac.uk/research/centres/molecularmaterialscentre/
E   A research centre at the University of Manchester.
O   To define the science underlying molecular materials that are not only important to business, but to life itself
Note: A joint project with the University of Liverpool.

Molecular Organisation and Assembly in Cells Doctoral Training Centre   (MOAC)
■   Faculty of Science, University of Warwick, Gibbet Hill Road, Coventry, CV4 7AL.
     024 7657 4695
     http://www2.warwick.ac.uk/fac/sci/moac/
     Director: Alison Rodger.
E   A research centre within the Warwick Mathematics Institute (qv) at the University of Warwick.
O   To offer a range of MSc programmes at the interface between biology, chemistry, mathematics and physics
●   Education and training

Møller Centre for Continuing Education   1992
■   Storey's Way, Cambridge, CB3 0DE.
     01223 465500   fax 01223 465525
     http://www.mollercentre.co.uk/
     Sales and Marketing Manager: Mark Carberry.
E   A profit-making business.
O   To provide a premier all-year round residential conference and training facility
Note: See also Centres for Continuing Education.

Monkey World Ape Rescue Centre   1987
■   Longthorns, Wareham, Dorset, BH20 6HH.
     01929 462537   fax 01929 405414
     http://www.monkeyworld.co.uk/

© CBD Research Ltd · Beckenham · Kent BR3 5JS · Tel 020 8650 7745 · Fax 020 8650 0768 · E-mail cbd@cbdresearch.com · www.cbdresearch.com

Montessori Centre International   (MCI)   1970

■   18 Balderton Street, London, W1K 6TG.
    020 7493 0165   fax 020 7629 7808
    http://www.montessori.uk.com/
E   An independent teacher training college.
○   To provide training to all those who wish to work in childcare and early years settings using the Montessori method of education
Note: Named after Dr Maria Montessori (1870-1952), who set up the Centre as her London base.

Mood Disorders Centre

■   School of Psychology, Washington Singer Laboratories, University of Exeter, Perry Road, Exeter, EX4 4QG.
    01392 264645
    http://www.centres.ex.ac.uk/mood/
    Co-Ordinator: Sandra Kennell-Webb.
E   A centre at the University of Exeter.
○   To support research that contributes to our understanding of depression and the development of interventions for people with
    mood disorders

Moredun Research Institute   (MRI)   1920

■   Pentlands Science Park, Bushloan, Penicuik, Midlothian, EH26 0PZ.
    0131-445 5111
    http://www.mri.sari.ac.uk/
    Director: Prof Julie Fitzpatrick.
E   A registered charity and private company limited by guarantee.
○   To carry out basic and strategic research on diseases which undermine biological efficiency, impair animal welfare or threaten
    public health, with particular emphasis on sheep and other ruminants

Morgan Centre for the Study of Relationships and Personal Life   2005

■   School of Social Sciences, University of Manchester, Roscoe Building, Oxford Road, Manchester, M13 9PL.
    0161-275 0265
    http://www.socialsciences.manchester.ac.uk/morgancentre/
    Co-Director: Prof Carol Smart. Co-Director: Prof Jennifer Mason.
E   A research centre at the University of Manchester.
○   To conduct research in the fields of family life, contemporary relationships, parenting and partnering and childhood

Mortimer Market Centre   (MMC)

■   Mortimer Market, off Capper Street, London, WC1E 6JB.
    020 7530 5050-5053
    http://www.ucl.ac.uk/sexual-health/mmc.htm
E   A part of the Camden Primary Care Trust.
○   To treat patients with a very wide variety of genitourinary problems

Motor Insurance Repair Research Centre   (Thatcham MIRRC)   1969

■   Colthrop Lane, Thatcham, Newbury, Berkshire, RG19 4NP.
    01635 868855   fax 01635 871346
    http://www.thatcham.org/
    Chief Executive: Peter Roberts. Director of Communications: Lesley Upham.
E   An independent non-profit-distributing organisation.
○   To carry out research targeted at containing or reducing the cost of motor insurance claims, whilst maintaining safety and quality
    standards
●   Education and training - Information service
¶   Methods Manuals. Newsletters. Annual Report. Parts Guides.

Motor Insurers Bureau   (MIB)   1946

■   Linford Wood House, 6-12 Capital Drive, Milton Keynes, MK14 6XT.
    01908 830001   fax 01908 671681
    http://www.mib.org.uk/
E   A company limited by guarantee, and membership organisation comprising all UK Motor Insurers (who must be members, under
    the Road Traffic Act 1988).
○   To compensate the victims of negligent uninsured and untraced motorists
Note: The MIB also operates the Motor Insurers Information Centre which operates a national Motor Insurance Database -
    0870 241 6732.

Mountbatten Centre for International Studies   (MCIS)

■   School of Social Sciences, University of Southampton, Highfield, Southampton, SO17 1BJ.
    023 8059 2522   fax 023 8059 3533
    http://www.mcis.soton.ac.uk/
    Director: Prof John Simpson.
E   A research centre at the University of Southampton.
○   To explore trends in international security, particularly the global spread of weapons of mass destruction, and the different ways of
    controlling them

Mountjoy Research Centre   1986

■   University of Durham, Stockton Road, Durham, DH1 3UZ.
      0191-334 3208   fax 0191-334 1524
      http://www.dur.ac.uk/mountjoy.researchcentre/
      Contact: James Pettican.
E   A centre at the University of Durham.
○   To provide facilities for start-up and growing companies involved in advanced technology

Mouse Genome Centre   (MGC)

■   Medical Research Council, Harwell Site, Chilton, Didcot, Oxfordshire, OX11 0RD.
      01235 834393   fax 01235 834776
      http://www.mgu.har.mrc.ac.uk/
E   A research centre within the Mammalian Genetics Unit at the Medical Research Council.
○   To carry out research into synaptic plasticity; to explore why, where and how the brain alters levels of synaptic strength during
      normal activities (especially learning and memory) and in illnesses such as Alzheimer's Disease

MRC-Asthma UK Centre in Allergic Mechanisms of Asthma

■   School of Medicine, 5th Floor - Thomas Guy House, Guy's Hospital, London, SE1 9RT.
      020 7188 1943   fax 020 7403 8640
      http://www.asthma-allergy.ac.uk
E   A Medical Research Council research centre at King's College, London.
○   To advance understanding of allergic mechanisms at system, cellular and molecular levels; to develop a quality integrated
      environment for basic and clinical research training in allergy and asthma
Note: See **Medical Research Council Collaborative Centre** for further information.

MRC Biomedical NMR Centre   1980

■   The Ridgeway, Mill Hill, London, NW7 1AA.
      020 8959 3666   fax 020 8906 4477
      http://www.nmrcentre.mrc.ac.uk/
E   A Medical Research Council research centre within the National Institute for Medical Research (qv).
○   A multi-user facility for biomedical nuclear magnetic resonance (NMR)
Note: See **Medical Research Council Collaborative Centre** for further information.

MRC Centre for Behavioural and Clinical Neuroscience
      see **Behavioural and Clinical Neurosciences Institute.**

MRC Centre for Developmental Neurobiology   2000

■   4th Floor - New Hunt's House, Guy's Hospital Campus, London, SE1 1UL.
      020 7848 6520   fax 020 7848 6550
      http://www.kcl.ac.uk/depsta/biomedical/mrc/
      Director: Prof Andrew Lumsden.
E   A Medical Research Council research centre at King's College, London.
○   To understand the early events during brain development and, through this, to increase our knowledge of the mechanisms that
      lead to malformation and that limit to regenerative processes in the human nervous system
Note: See **Medical Research Council Collaborative Centre** for further information.

MRC Centre for Immune Regulation   1999

■   Division of Immunity and Infection, The Medical School, Edgbaston, Birmingham, B15 2TT.
      0121-414 3094
      http://www.mrcbcir.bham.ac.uk/
      Contact: Jackie Hawkins.
E   A Medical Research Council centre at the University of Birmingham.
○   To study the multiple facets of immune responses in the context of selected diseases
Note: See **Medical Research Council Collaborative Centre** for further information.

MRC Centre for Neurodegenerative Research   (CNR)   2006

■   Box PO37, De Crespigny Park, London, SE5 8AF.
      020 7848 0259; 0267   fax 020 7848 0017
      http://cnr.iop.kcl.ac.uk/
      Director: Prof Brian Anderton.
E   A Medical Research Council research centre within the Institute of Psychiatry (qv) at King's College, London.
○   To focus research on Alzheimer's disease and motor neurone disease
Note: See **Medical Research Council Collaborative Centre** for further information.

MRC Centre for Nutritional Epidemiology in Cancer Prevention and Survival   (CNC)   2006

■   Department of Public Health and Primary Care, Cambridge, CB1 8RN.
      01223 740151
      http://www.srl.cam.ac.uk/cnc/
      Director: Dr Sheila Bingham.
E   A Medical Research Council research centre at the University of Cambridge.
○   To conduct research into the impact of diet on cancer
Note: See **Medical Research Council Collaborative Centre** for further information.

© CBD Research Ltd · Beckenham · Kent BR3 5JS · Tel 020 8650 7745 · Fax 020 8650 0768 · E-mail cbd@cbdresearch.com · www.cbdresearch.com

MRC Centre for Protein Engineering (CPE) 1989
- ■ Hills Road, Cambridge, CB2 2QH.
  01223 402100   fax 01223 402140
  http://www.mrc-cpe.cam.ac.uk/
  Director: Prof A R Fersht, FRS. Contact: Paula Murphy.
- E   A Medical Research Council centre at the University of Cambridge.
- ○   To bring together groups with overlapping interests in protein structure and design
- Note: See **Medical Research Council Collaborative Centre** for further information.

MRC Centre for Stem Cell Biology and Medicine
- ■ Cambridge Stem Cell Initiative, Cambridge, CB2 2XY.
  01223 763366
  http://www.stemcells.cam.ac.uk/
- E   A Medical Research Council centre at the University of Cambridge.
- ○   To harness the basic knowledge of stem cell biology and medicine to the therapy of human diseases
- Note: See **Medical Research Council Collaborative Centre** for further information.

MRC Centre for Synaptic Plasticity
- ■ School of Medical Sciences, University Walk, Bristol, BS8 1TD.
  0117-928 7402   fax 0117-929 1687
  http://www.bristol.ac.uk/Depts/Synaptic/
- E   A Medical Research Council research centre at the University of Bristol.
- ○   To understand how, where and why the brain modifies synaptic strength during normal function, in particular during learning and memory, and in certain pathological states
- Note: See **Medical Research Council Collaborative Centre** for further information.

MRC Clinical Sciences Centre (CSC) 1994
- ■ Faculty of Medicine, Hammersmith Hospital Campus, Du Cane Road, London, W12 0NN.
  020 8383 8250   fax 020 8383 8337
  http://www.csc.mrc.ac.uk/
  Director: Chris Higgins.
- E   A Medical Research Council interdisciplinary research centre at Imperial College London.
- ○   To conduct research, training and undergraduate programmes in molecular and cell biology, genomics, and biological and clinical imaging with the aim of improving disease prevention, diagnosis and treatment
- Note: See **Medical Research Council Collaborative Centre** for further information.

MRC Epidemiology Resource Centre 2003
- ■ Faculty of Medicine, Health and Life Sciences, Southampton General Hospital, Tremona Road, Southampton, SO16 6YD.
  023 8077 7624   fax 023 8070 4021
  http://www.mrc.soton.ac.uk/
  Director: Prof Cyrus Cooper.
- E   A Medical Research Council centre at the University of Southampton.
- ○   To investigate occupational and environmental causes of disease within the UK
- Note: See **Medical Research Council Collaborative Centre** for further information.

MRC Genome Damage and Stability Centre 2001
- ■ Falmer, Brighton, East Sussex, BN1 9RR.
  01273 678123   fax 01273 678121
  http://www.sussex.ac.uk/gdsc/
- E   A Medical Research Council centre at the University of Sussex.
- ○   To understand the relationships between different pathways in the context of nuclear architecture and basic cellular processes
- Note: See **Medical Research Council Collaborative Centre** for further information.

MRC Institute of Hearing Research - Nottingham Clinical Section (IHR) 1978
- ■ Queen's Medical Centre, University Park, Nottingham, NG7 2RD.
  0115-922 3431   fax 0115-951 8503
  http://www.ihr.mrc.ac.uk/
- E   A Medical Research Council research centre at the University of Nottingham.
- Note: See **Medical Research Council Collaborative Centre** for further information.

MRC Institute of Hearing Research - Scottish Section (IHR) 1978
- ■ Glasgow Royal Infirmary, 16 Alexandra Parade, Glasgow, G31 2ER.
  0141-211 4695   fax 0141-552 8411
  http://www.ihr.mrc.ac.uk/scottish/
- E   A Medical Research Council research centre at the University of Glasgow.
- Note: See **Medical Research Council Collaborative Centre** for further information.

MRC Institute of Hearing Research - Southampton Section (IHR) 1978
- ■ Royal South Hampshire Hospital, Southampton, SO14 0YG.
  023 8063 7946   fax 023 8082 5611
  http://www.ihr.mrc.ac.uk/
- E   A Medical Research Council centre at the University of Southampton.
- Note: See **Medical Research Council Collaborative Centre** for further information.

MRC Resource Centre for Human Nutrition Research   (HNR)   1998
■   Elsie Widdowson Laboratory, Fulbourn Road, Cambridge, CB1 9NL.
     01223 426356   fax 01223 437515
     http://www.mrc-hnr.cam.ac.uk/
E   A Medical Research Council research centre at the University of Cambridge.
○   To conduct strategic and applied nutrition research in the fields of nutrition and bone health, nutrition and health, nutrition communications, micronutrients, nutritional epidemiology, and stable isotopes
Note: See **Medical Research Council Collaborative Centre** for further information.

MRC Social, Genetic and Developmental Psychiatry Centre
     see **Social, Genetic and Developmental Psychiatry Centre (MRC).**

MRC UCL Centre for Medical Molecular Virology
■   Department of Molecular Pathology and Clinical Biochemistry, University College London, 46 Cleveland Street, London, W1P 6DB.
     020 7504 9343   fax 020 7387 3310
     http://www.ucl.ac.uk/medicalschool/infection-immunity/mrc-centre/mrc-centre.htm
E   A Medical Research Council centre at University College London.
○   To develop a centre of excellence in viral pathogenesis and virally-mediated gene therapy
Note: See **Medical Research Council Collaborative Centre** for further information.

MRC-University of Edinburgh Centre for Inflammation Research
■   University of Edinburgh, 47 Little France Crescent, Edinburgh, EH16 4TJ.
     0131-242 9195   fax 0131-242 6578
     http://www.cir.med.ed.ac.uk/
     Administrator: Dr Sharon Hannah.
E   A Medical Research Council centre within the Queen's Medical Research Institute (qv) at the University of Edinburgh.
○   To promote the prevention, diagnosis and treatment of inflammatory diseases
Note: See **Medical Research Council Collaborative Centre** for further information.

Multi-Imaging Centre   (MIC)
■   Department of Anatomy, University of Cambridge, Anatomy Building, Cambridge, CB2 3DY.
     01223 333774
     http://www.bio.cam.ac.uk/dept/mic/
     Technical Director: Dr J N Skepper.
E   A facility and research centre at the University of Cambridge.
○   To conduct biological imaging by light, laser confocal, two-photon excitation microscopy and electron microscopy

Multidisciplinary Assessment of Technology Centre for Healthcare   (MATCH)
NR   Uxbridge, Middlesex, UB8 3PH.
     01895 266051   fax 01895 269727
     http://www.match.ac.uk/
     Programme Manager: David Lawes.
E   An EPSRC Innovative Manufacturing Research Centre at Brunel University.
○   To develop concepts of value to help unify the medical devices sector and catalyse a new consensus between the manufacturer, regulator and user communities
Note: A joint venture between the Universities of Birmingham, Brunel, King's College London, Nottingham and Ulster.

Multidisciplinary Nanotechnology Centre   (MNC)   2002
■   School of Engineering, Swansea University, Singleton Park, Swansea, SA2 8PP.
     01792 205678
     http://mnc.swan.ac.uk/
E   A research centre at Swansea University.
○   To develop projects that bridge traditional disciplines, to provide a step change in technology, especially in the fields of semiconductors, oxides, liquids, and organic and biological materials

Multiple Sclerosis Resource Centre   (MSRC)   1993
■   7 Peartree Business Centre, Peartree Road, Colchester, Essex, CO3 0JN.
     01206 505444; 0800 783 0518   fax 01206 505449
     http://www.msrc.co.uk/
E   A registered charity and a company limited by guarantee.
○   To inform, advise and educate people with MS so that they, their families and carers have a better understanding of the disease and ways to adapt to it and thus maintain the best possible quality of life

MUNDI Centre for Global Education   1989
■   School of Education, Jubilee Campus, Wollaton Road, Nottingham, NG8 1BB.
     0115-951 4485   fax 0115-951 4583
     http://www.mundi.org.uk/
E   A Development Education centre at the University of Nottingham.
Note: For further information see Development Education Centres.

Museum of Costume and Fashion Research Centre

■ Bennett Street, Bath, BA1 2QH.
  01225 477173   fax 01225 477743
  http://www.museumofcostume.co.uk/
E   A research centre.
O   To provide reference and study facilities in the history of dress to all members of the public, at both regional and national level

Museum Documentation Centre

Note: is now the Museum Studies Collection and is therefore outside the scope of this Directory.

Museums, Galleries and Collections Institute   (MGCI)   2003

■ School of Art History, University of St Andrews, 9 The Scores, St Andrews, Fife, KY16 9AR.
  01334 462356
  http://www-ah.st-andrews.ac.uk/mgci/
  Director: Prof Ian Carradice.
E   A department of the University of St Andrews.
O   To be a focus for training, consultancy and research on the history, theory and practice of museums

Music Research Centre   (MRC)

■ Department of Music, University of York, Heslington, York, YO10 5DD.
  01904 432446   fax 01904 432450
  http://music.york.ac.uk/mrc/
E   A research centre at the University of York.
O   To support creative research into the use and application of technology in music

Music, Technology and Innovation Research Centre   (MTI)   1999

■ Faculty of Humanities, De Montfort University, Clephan Building, The Gateway, Leicester, LE1 9BH.
  0116-257 7956
  http://www.mti.dmu.ac.uk/
  Director: Leigh Landy.
E   A centre at De Montfort University.
O   To conduct research in a continually evolving range of artistic creation and theory focused on innovative application of new
    technologies to music

Music Therapy Centre
    see **Nordoff-Robbins Music Therapy Centre.**

NAFC Marine Centre   1988
- Shetland School of Nautical Studies, University of the Highlands and Islands (UHI) Institute, Port Arthur, Scalloway, Shetland, ZE1 0UN.
  01595 772000   fax 01595 772001
  http://www.nafc.ac.uk/
- E   A research centre at the University of the Highlands and Islands (UHI) Institute.
- O   To provide high quality resources to support and enhance the development and sustainability of the marine industries
- Note: NAFC = North Atlantic Fisheries College.

Nanocharacterisation Centre
> see **Kelvin Nanocharacterisation Centre.**

Nanoelectronics Research Centre
- Department of Electronics and Electrical Engineering, University of Glasgow, Rankine Building, Oakfield Avenue, Glasgow, G12 8LT.
  0141-330 6670   fax 0141-330 4907
  http://www.elec.gla.ac.uk/content/nanoelectronics.html
- E   A research centre at the University of Glasgow.
- O   To understand and exploit the properties of devices with critical dimensions on the nanometre scale (10-9m)

Nanofabrication Centre
> see **James Watt Nanofabrication Centre.**

NanoPhotonics Portfolio Centre
> see **EPSRC NanoPhotonics Portfolio Centre.**

Nanoscience Centre   2003
- University of Cambridge, 11 J J Thomson Avenue, Cambridge, CB3 0FF.
  01223 760304   fax 01223 760306
  http://www.nanoscience.cam.ac.uk/
- E   A centre at the University of Cambridge.
- O   To provide a control focus for nanoscience research

Nanoscience and Technology Centre
> see **Kroto Research Institute Nanoscience and Technology Centre.**

Nanotec Northern Ireland
- NR   Queen's University Belfast, University Road, Belfast, BT7 1NN.
  028 9097 3572
  http://www.nanotecni.com/
  Co-Director: Dr Robert Bowman (Queen's University). Co-Director: Prof Jim Mclaughlin (University of Ulster).
- E   A research centre at Queen's University, Belfast.
- O   To conduct research in the design, fabrication, characterisation and commercial exploitation of nanotechnology processes
- Note: A joint venture with the University of Ulster.

Nanotechnology Centre for PVD Research   (NCPVD)
- City Campus, Sheffield Hallam University, Sheffield, S1 1WB.
  0114-225 2017   fax 0114-225 3501
  http://www.shu.ac.uk/research/meri/ncpvd/
  Head: Prof Papken Eh Hovsepian.
- E   A research centre within the Materials and Engineering Research Institute (qv) at Sheffield Hallam University.
- O   To conduct research in the processing, characterisation and use of advanced nanostructural materials
- Note: PVD = Physical Vapour Deposition.

Nanotechnology and Nanoscience Centre
> see **Nottingham Nanotechnology and Nanoscience Centre.**

National Advice Centre for Postgraduate Dental Education   (NACPDE)   1980
- Faculty of Dental Surgery, Royal College of Surgeons of England, 35-43 Lincoln's Inn Fields, London, WC2A 3PE.
  020 7869 6804   fax 020 7869 6816
  http://www.rcseng.ac.uk/fds/nacpde
- E   A registered charity.
- O   To provide mainly overseas and refugee dentists with information and advice on postgraduate dental education and training in the United Kingdom
- ● Advisory service - Information service (available Mon-Fri 1000-1600)

National Agricultural Centre   (NAC)   1963
- Stoneleigh Park, Kenilworth, Warwickshire, CV8 2LZ.
  024 7669 6969   fax 024 7669 6900
  http://www.stoneleigh-park.co.uk/
- E   The headquarters of the Royal Agricultural Society of England.

National Badminton Centre   (NBC)
- Milton Keynes, MK8 9LA.
  01908 268400   fax 01908 268412
  http://www.badmintonengland.co.uk/
- E   The headquarters of Badminton England.

National Birds of Prey Centre   (NBPC)   1967
- Newent, Gloucestershire, GL18 1JJ.
  0870 990 1992
  http://www.nbpc.co.uk/
- E   A profit-making business.
- O   To achieve the conservation of birds of prey through education, captive breeding, research and rehabilitation

National Bureau for Students with Disabilities
  see **Skill: National Bureau for Students with Disabilities.**

National Centre for Atmospheric Science   (NCAS)   2006
- Polaris House, North Star Avenue, Swindon, Wiltshire, SN2 1EU.
  01793 411609
  http://www.ncas.ac.uk/
  Director: Prof Stephen Mobbs.
- E   A Natural Environment Research Council collaborative research centre.
- O   To provide the UK with stable, long-term and broad national capability in atmospheric science research
- Note: NCAS is not based in one location - as a collaborative centre it is made up of various centres and facilities across many universities and institutions.

National Centre for Autism Studies   (NCAS)   2003
- Faculty of Education, University of Strathclyde, Sir Henry Wood Building, 76 Southbrae Drive, Glasgow, G13 1PP.
  0141-950 3071; 3234
  http://www.strath.ac.uk/autism-ncas/
  Contact: Prof Aline-Wendy Dunlop.
- E   A research centre at the University of Strathclyde.

National Centre for Biotechnology Education   (NCBE)   1985
- Science and Technology Centre, University of Reading, Earley Gate, Reading, Berkshire, RG6 6BZ.
  0118-987 3743   fax 0118-975 0140
  http://www.ncbe.reading.ac.uk/
  Co-Director: John Schollar. Co-Director: Dean Madden.
- E   A department of the University of Reading.
- O   To promote education in molecular biology and biotechnology
- ●   Education and training

National Centre for Bowling
- Hunters Avenue, Ayr, KA8 9AL.
  01292 294623
- O   To control and foster the level green game of bowls
- ●   Competitions

National Centre for Business and Sustainability
  see **Sustainability Northwest and National Centre for Business and Sustainability.**

National Centre for Carnival Arts
- University of Bedfordshire, Park Square, Luton, Bedfordshire, LU1 3JU.
  01234 400400
  http://www.beds.ac.uk/
- E   A centre at the University of Bedfordshire.
- Note: Due to be launched in 2008.

National Centre for Computer Animation   (NCCA)   1989
- Bournemouth Media School, Bournemouth University, Weymouth House, Talbot Campus, Poole, Dorset, BH12 5BB.
  01202 965360   fax 01202 965530
  http://ncca.bournemouth.ac.uk/
  Director: Prof Peter Comninos.
- E   A research centre at Bournemouth University.
- O   To conduct research and teaching in computer visualisation and animation

National Centre for e-Social Science
  see **ESRC National Centre for e-Social Science.**

National Centre for English Cultural Tradition   (NATCECT)   1964

■ School of English, University of Sheffield, 9 Shearwood Road, Sheffield, S10 2TD.
   0114-222 0196   fax 0114-222 6299
   http://www.shef.ac.uk/english/natcect/
   Director: Prof J C Beal. Deputy Director: Dr M H Jones.
E A research centre at the University of Sheffield.
○ To stimulate interest in all aspects of folklore, language and cultural tradition, especially, but not exclusively those of England; to act as a forum for research in these areas, and to engage in research and in teaching at undergraduate and postgraduate levels
● Archives (by appointment) - Library

National Centre for Environmental Toxicology   (NCET)   1995

■ Frankland Road, Blagrove, Swindon, Wiltshire, SN5 8YF.
   01793 865000; 865153   fax 01793 865001
   http://www.wrcplc.co.uk/default.aspx?item=19
   Director: Dr Paul Rumsby.
E A centre managed by WRc plc (qv).
○ To offer high quality data and expert advice concerning the risks posed to humans and wildlife by chemical contaminants and harmful microorganisms in the environment
Note: The NCET is a World Health Organisation WHO Collaborating Centre (qv) for Drinking Water and Water Pollution Control.

National Centre for Human Retrovirology   2006

■ Faculty of Medicine, St Mary's Campus, Norfolk Place, London, W2 1PG.
   020 7589 5111
E A centre at Imperial College London.
○ To treat people infected with Human T-cell Lymphotropic Virus (HTLV) - viruses that can cause leukaemia and a condition similar to multiple sclerosis

National Centre for III-V Technologies
   see **EPSRC National Centre for III-V Technologies.**

National Centre for Language and Literacy   (NCLL)   1974

■ University of Reading, Bulmershe Court, Earley, Reading, Berkshire, RG6 1HY.
   0118-378 8820   fax 0118-378 6801
   http://www.ncll.org.uk/
   Director: Prof Viv Edwards.
E A research centre within the Institute of Education (qv) at the University of Reading.
○ To support teachers, parents and governors in efforts to achieve greater literacy

National Centre for Languages
   see **CILT, The National Centre for Languages.**

National Centre for Macromolecular Hydrodynamics   (NCMH)   1987

■ School of Biosciences, Sutton Bonington Campus, University of Nottingham, Loughborough, Leicestershire, LE12 5RD.
   0115-951 6148   fax 0115-951 6142
   http://www.nottingham.ac.uk/ncmh/
   Director: Prof Stephen Harding.
E A research centre at the University of Nottingham.
○ To conduct research into the characterisation of the sizes, shapes and interactions of large macro-molecules of biomedical and industrial importance (proteins, polysaccharides, DNA, synthetic polymers etc}; in the environment many occur naturally in water or aqueous solution

National Centre for Ornithology

■ The Nunnery, Thetford, Norfolk, IP24 2PU.
   01842 750050   fax 01842 750030
   http://www.bto.org/
E The headquarters of the British Trust for Ornithology.

National Centre for Physical Activity and Health
   see **BHF National Centre for Physical Activity and Health.**

National Centre for Product Design and Development Research   (PDR)

■ Cardiff School of Health Sciences, Llandarff Campus, Western Avenue, Cardiff, CF5 2YB.
   029 2041 6725   fax 029 2041 6973
   http://www.pdronline.co.uk/
   Commercial Director: Jarred Evans.
E A research centre at the University of Wales Institute, Cardiff.
○ To provide practical, commercial solutions to industry through innovation, design engineering, prototyping, agile manufacture, market feasibility and support

National Centre for Project Management   (NCPM)

■ Middlesex University, College House, Bramley Road, London, N14 4YZ.
   020 8411 2299   fax 020 8411 5133
   http://www.cs.mdx.ac.uk/ncpm/
   Director: Prof Darren Dalcher.
E An interdisciplinary research centre at Middlesex University.
O To set the national agenda and establish project management as a major profession and discipline in the UK

National Centre for Public Policy   (NCPP)   1999

■ Swansea University, Singleton Park, Swansea, SA2 8PP.
   01792 295059
   http://www.swan.ac.uk/ncpp/
   Director: Prof Mike Sullivan.
E A research centre at Swansea University.
O To contribute to the development and reshaping of public policy in Wales, the UK and Europe

National Centre for the Replacement, Refinement and Reduction of Animals in Research   (NC3Rs)   2004

■ Medical Research Council, 20 Park Crescent, London, W1B 1AL.
   020 7670 5331   fax 020 7670 5178
   http://www.nc3rs.org.uk/
   Chief Executive: Dr Vicky Robinson.
E A research centre at the Medical Research Council.
O To replace, refine and reduce the use of animals in research

National Centre for Research in Children's Literature   (NCRCL)   1991

■ School of Arts, Froebel College, Roehampton University, Roehampton Lane, London, SW15 5PJ.
   020 8392 3008   fax 020 8392 3819
   http://www.ncrcl.ac.uk/
   Contact: Dr Gillian Lathey.
E A research centre at Roehampton University.
O To facilitate and support research exchange in the field of children's literature
● Children's Literature Collection - Froebel Archive for Childhood Studies

National Centre for Research Methods
   see **ESRC National Centre for Research Methods.**

National Centre for Social Research   (NCSR)   1969

■ 35 Northampton Square, London, EC1V 0AX.
   020 7250 1866   fax 020 7250 1524
   http://www.natcen.ac.uk/
   Director: Simon Anderson.
E An independent social research institute.
O To aim for a society better informed through high-quality social research

National Centre for Tactile Diagrams   (NCTD)

■ 58-72 John Bright Street, Birmingham, B1 1BN.
   0845 257 2587   fax 0845 257 2588
   http://www.nctd.org.uk/
   Contact: Dr Sarah Morley Wilkins.
E A part of the Royal National Institute for the Blind.
O To provide tactile diagrams, maps and pictures for blind and partially sighted people of all ages and in all walks of life

National Centre for Text Mining   (NaCTeM)

NR School of Informatics, University of Manchester, 131 Princess Street, Manchester, M1 7DN
   0161-306 8917   fax 0161-306 8918
   http://www.nactem.ac.uk/
   Director: Prof Jun'ichi Tsujii.
E A research centre within the Manchester Interdisciplinary Biocentre (qv) at the University of Manchester.
O To provide text mining services in response to the requirements of the UK academic community; to conduct research in text mining
Note: A joint venture with the University of Liverpool. See **e-Science Centres** for further information.

National Centre for Training and Education in Prosthetics and Orthotics   (NCTEPO)   1970

■ Curran Building, University of Strathclyde, 131 St James Road, Glasgow, G4 0LS.
   0141-551 3692   fax 0141-552 1283
   http://www.strath.ac.uk/prosthetics/
   Director: Mrs Sandra Sexton.
E A centre at the University of Strathclyde.
O To provide training and education to healthcare professionals and students of the rehabilitation professions
Note: The Centre is a World Health Organisation WHO Collaborating Centre (qv) for Research and Training in Prosthetics, Orthotics and
   Orthopaedic Technology.

National Centre of Tribology   (NCT)   1968

- 410 Whittle House, Birchwood Park, Warrington, Cheshire, WA3 6FW.
  01925 843410   fax 01925 843500
  http://www.esrtechnology.com/centres/nct.php
- E   A profit-making business.
- O   To provide a focus for expertise in tribology and its application in industry

National Centre for Vocational Qualifications   (NRP)

- Oriel House, Oriel Road, Cheltenham, Gloucestershire, GL50 1XP.
  0870 990 4088   fax 0870 990 1560
  http://www.naric.org.uk/
- E   An independent unit under the management of the National Recognition Information Centre for the United Kingdom (qv).
- O   To be a central information resource for UK skilled worker, trade and technician level qualifications

National Centre for Work Based Learning Partnerships   (NCWBLP)   1993

- Trent Park Campus, Middlesex University, Bramley Road, London, N14 4YZ.
  020 8411 6118   fax 020 8411 4551
  http://www.mdx.ac.uk/www/ncwblp/
  Director: Prof Jonathan Garnett.
- E   A Centre for Excellence in Teaching and Learning (CETL) at Middlesex University.
- O   To offer comprehensive programmes of work based learning and/or university-level learning in the workplace

Note: also known as Centre for Excellence in Teaching and Learning for Work Based Learning See **Centres for Excellence in Teaching and Learning** for further information.

National Centre for Writing   (NCfW)

- Faculty of Humanities and Social Sciences, University of Glamorgan, Pontypridd, CF37 1DL.
  01443 654450   fax 01443 654040
  http://www.glam.ac.uk/hassschool/
- E   A centre at the University of Glamorgan.

National Chemical Emergency Centre   (NCEC)   1973

- B329 Harwell, Didcot, Oxfordshire, OX11 0QJ.
  0870 190 6621   fax 0870 190 6614
  http://www.the-ncec.com/
- E   A statutory organisation which is also profit-making.
- O   To provide chemical hazard information services and a 24-hour emergency response advice service to the public emergency services as part of the nationwide CHEMSAFE Scheme (a voluntary scheme run by the Chemical Industries Association)

National Children's Bureau   (NCB)   1963

- 8 Wakley Street, London, EC1V 7QE.
  020 7843 6000   fax 020 7278 9512
  http://www.ncb.org.uk/
  Chief Executive: Paul Ennals. Director of Strategy & Communications: Sally Whitaker.
- E   A registered charity.
- O   To identify and promote the interests and well-being of all children and young people across every aspect of their lives; to encourage professionals and policy makers to see the needs of the whole child and emphasise the importance of multi-disciplinary, cross-agency partnerships; to identify, develop and promote good practice
- ● Conference facilities - Education and training - Exhibitions - Information service - Library - In-house specialist databases To undertake high quality research and disseminate information to professionals, policy makers, parents and children of any age

National Children's Centre   (NCC)   1974

- Brian Jackson House, New North Parade, Huddersfield, HD1 5JP.
  01484 519988   fax 01484 435150
  http://www.nccuk.org.uk/
- E   A registered charity.
- O   To provide practical services aimed at improving the lives of children, young people and families most in need and to work to influence national policy and delivery of services for children

National Collaborating Centre for Acute Care   (NCCAC)   2003

- 35-43 Lincoln's Inn Fields, London, WC2A 3PN.
  020 7405 3474
  http://www.nice.org.uk/page.aspx?o=202090
  Director: Dr Jennifer Hill.
- E   A centre established by the National Institute for Health and Clinical Excellence (qv).
- O   To develop acute care guidelines

National Collaborating Centre for Cancer   (NCCC)   2003

- 2nd Floor - Park House, Greyfriars Road, Cardiff, CF10 3AF.
  http://www.nice.org.uk/page.aspx?o=202067
  Manager: Dr Andrew Champion.
- E   A centre established by the National Institute for Health and Clinical Excellence (qv).
- O   To develop cancer care guidelines

© CBD Research Ltd · Beckenham · Kent BR3 5JS · Tel 020 8650 7745 · Fax 020 8650 0768 · E-mail cbd@cbdresearch.com · www.cbdresearch.com

National Collaborating Centre for Chronic Conditions   (NCCCC)   2003

- ■   11 St Andrews Place, London, NW1 4LE.
  020 7935 1174
  http://www.nice.org.uk/page.aspx?o=202075
  Manager: Jill Parnham.
- E   A centre established by the National Institute for Health and Clinical Excellence (qv).
- ○   To develop care guidelines for chronic conditions

National Collaborating Centre for Mental Health   (NCCMH)   2001

- ■   4th Floor - Standon House, 21 Mansell Street, London, E1 8AA.
  020 7977 6670
  http://www.nccmh.org.uk/page.aspx?o=202067
  Contact: Dr Catherine Pettinari.
- E   A centre established by the National Institute for Health and Clinical Excellence (qv).
- ○   To develop mental health guidelines

National Collaborating Centre for Nursing and Supportive Care   (NCCNSC)   2003

- ■   Radcliffe Infirmary, Woodstock Road, Oxford, OX2 6HE.
  http://www.nice.org.uk/page.aspx?o=202059
  Director: Ian Bullock.
- E   A centre established by the National Institute for Health and Clinical Excellence (qv).
- ○   To develop guidelines for nursing and supportive care

National Collaborating Centre for Primary Care   (NCCPC)   2003

- ■   14 Prince's Gate, London, SW7 1PU.
  020 7581 3232
  http://www.nice.org.uk/page.aspx?o=202051
  Chief Executive: Nancy Turnbull.
- E   A centre established by the National Institute for Health and Clinical Excellence (qv).
- ○   To develop guidelines for primary care

National Collaborating Centre for Women and Children's Health   (NCCWCH)   2003

- ■   27 Sussex Place, London, NW1 4RG.
  020 7772 6200
  http://www.nice.org.uk/page.aspx?o=202042
  Executive Lead: Andrea Sutcliffe.
- E   A centre established by the National Institute for Health and Clinical Excellence (qv).
- ○   To develop care guidelines for women and children's health

National Community Fire Safety Centre   (NCFSC)   1998

- ■   Office of the Deputy Prime Minister, Floor 4 - Allington Towers, Allington Street, London, SW1E 5EB.
  020 7944 5628
  Head of Centre: Ian Evans.
- E   A part of Government.
- ○   To lead the fight against fires, fire deaths and injuries in the home by concentrating on fire prevention, early warning and escaping from fire; to co-ordinate media campaigns on these subjects using television, radio and the whole spectrum of the press; to co-ordinate campaigns with all fire rescue services in England and Wales and provide them with resources and materials for fire prevention education
- ●   Information service
- ¶   Range of Fire Safety Leaflets / Materials.

National Computing Centre   (NCC)

- ■   Oxford House, Oxford Road, Manchester, M1 7ED.
  0161-241 2121   fax 0161-242 2499
  http://www.ncc.co.uk/
  Chairman: Prof Peter Ford. Chief Executive Officer: Michael Gough.
- E   A membership organisation.
- ○   To champion the effective deployment of information technology to maximise the competitiveness of members' businesses; to serve the corporate, vendor and Government communities

National Coordinating Centre for Health Technology Assessment   (NCCHTA)

- ■   Mailpoint 728 - Boldrewood, University of Southampton, Bassett Crescent East, Southampton, SO16 7PX.
  023 8059 5586   fax 023 8059 5639
  http://www.hta.nhsweb.nhs.uk/
  Director: James Raftery.
- E   A centre at the University of Southampton.
- ○   To manage, support and develop the NHS Health Technology Assessment programme

National e-Science Centre, Glasgow (NeSC)
- Kelvin Building, University of Glasgow, Glasgow, G12 8QQ.
  0141-330 8606   fax 0141-330 8625
  http://www.nesc.ac.uk/
- E   A centre at the University of Glasgow.
- O   To stimulate and sustain the development of e-Science in the UK, to contribute significantly to its international development; to ensure that its techniques are rapidly propagated to commerce and industry

Note: A joint venture with the University of Edinburgh which houses the e-Science Institute (qv).

National Energy Centre (NEC) 1999
- Davy Avenue, Knowl Hill, Milton Keynes, MK5 8NG.
  01908 354535; 354538   fax 01908 665577
  http://www.nef.org.uk/aboutus/thecentre.htm
  Contact: Kathy Wyatt.
- E   An independent educational charity based at the headquarters of the National Energy Foundation.
- O   To work for the more efficient, innovative and safe use of energy, and to increase the public awareness of energy in all its aspects

National Epilepsy Centre
  see **David Lewis National Epilepsy Centre.**

National Exhibition Centre (NEC)
- Birmingham, B40 1NT.
  0121-780 4141
  http://www.necgroup.co.uk/
- E   A commercial exhibition venue.

National Eye Research Centre (NERC) 1986
- Bristol Eye Hospital, Lower Maudlin Street, Bristol, BS1 2LX.
  0117-929 0024   fax 0117-925 1421
  http://www.nerc.co.uk/
- E   A registered charity.
- O   To fund research into the causes, treatments and prevention of diseases and disabilities of the eye and blindness

National Family and Parenting Institute (NFPI) 1999
- 430 Highgate Studios, 53-79 Highgate Road, London, NW5 1TL.
  020 7424 3460   fax 020 7485 3590
  http://www.nfpi.org/
- E   A registered charity.
- O   To research the concerns of families and the support available, and to trial new ways of providing support to families, bringing together organisations and knowledge, and influencing policy makers

National Fishing Heritage Centre (NFHC) 1992
- Alexandra Dock, Grimsby, Lincolnshire, DN31 1UZ.
  01472 323345   fax 01472 323555
- E   A local authority run centre.
- O   To tell the story of local fishermen, their boats and the waters in which they fished

National Flying Laboratory Centre (NFLC)
- School of Engineering, Cranfield University, Cranfield, Bedfordshire, MK43 0AL.
  01234 754071   fax 01234 750892
  http://www.cranfield.ac.uk/soe/nflc/
  Co-ordinator: Roger Bailey.
- E   A research centre at Cranfield University.
- O   To assist with the teaching of the postgraduate courses, and to provide self contained short courses for undergraduates from other universities requiring flying laboratories

National Gardening Centre 1969
- Bullsmoor Lane, Enfield, Middlesex, EN1 4RQ.
  0845 612 2122
  http://www.capel.ac.uk/gardens/index.html
- E   An independent non-profit distributing organisation and registered charity at Capel Manor College.
- O   To provide facilities for all who are interested in garden design, horticulture, landscaping, floristry, countryside, arboriculture, animal care, horse studies and management of the environment

National Glass Centre 1998
- Liberty Way, Sunderland, Tyne and Wear, SR6 0GL.
  0191-515 5555   fax 0191-515 5556
  http://www.nationalglasscentre.com/
  Chief Executive: Katherine Pearson.
- O   To develop and promote excellence in the art and industry of glass

© CBD Research Ltd · Beckenham · Kent BR3 5JS · Tel 020 8650 7745 · Fax 020 8650 0768 · E-mail cbd@cbdresearch.com · www.cbdresearch.com

National Grid High Voltage Research Centre
- ■ School of Electrical and Electronic Engineering, PO Box 88, University of Manchester, Manchester, M60 1QD.
  0161-306 4777   fax 0161-306 9341
  http://www.eee.manchester.ac.uk/research/groups/eeps/facilities/
- E A research centre at the University of Manchester.

National Health Service Institute for Innovation and Improvement
  see **NHS Institute for Innovation and Improvement.**

National Heart and Lung Institute   (NHLI)
- ■ Faculty of Medicine, Imperial College London, Dovehouse Street, London, SW3 6LY.
  020 7351 8188; 7589 5111
  http://www1.imperial.ac.uk/medicine/about/divisions/nhli/
  Head: Prof Anthony J Newman Taylor, CBE.
- E A research institute at Imperial College London.
- ○ To conduct research into all aspects of heart, lung and cardiovascular disease

National Hyperbaric Centre   (NHC)   1987
- ■ 123 Ashgrove Road West, Aberdeen, AB16 5FA.
  01224 698895   fax 01224 692222
  http://www.nationalhyperbariccentre.com
  Contact: Angela Ralph.
- E An independent company.
- ○ To offer a broad range of services connected with underwater intervention technology, including training, testing and trials, medical and diving emergency, consulting, equipment servicing, and research and development

National Indoor Athletics Centre
- ■ Sports Facilities Management, University of Wales Institute Cardiff, Cyncoed Road, Cardiff, CF23 6XD.
  029 2041 6777   fax 029 2041 6737
  http://www2.uwic.ac.uk/UWIC/schools/sport/SportsFacilities/Facilities/NationalIndoorAthleticsCentre.htm
- E A centre at the University of Wales Institute, Cardiff.

National Information Centre for Speech-Language Therapy   (NICeST)
- ■ Department of Human Communication Science, University College London, Remax House, 31/32 Alfred Place, London, WC1E 7DP.
  020 7679 4207   fax 020 7713 0861
  http://www.ucl.ac.uk/HCS/HCSlibrary/
  Contact: Stevie Russell.
- E An information centre and library at University College London.
- ○ To care for its stock of books, journals and videos covering all aspects of speech and language disorders, as well as linguistics, language acquisition, psychology, hearing, voice, special education and neurological disorders

National Institute for Biological Standards and Control   (NIBSC)
- ■ Blanche Lane, South Mimms, Potters Bar, Hertfordshire, EN6 3QG.
  01707 641000   fax 01707 641050
  http://www.nibsc.ac.uk/
- E The operations arm of the National Biological Standards Board, a non-departmental public body.
- ○ To safeguard and enhance public health through standardisation and control of biological products used in medicine; to provide independent testing of biological medicines for the UK market, in particular with vaccines for the UK children's vaccination programme
- Note: The Institute is a World Health Organisation WHO Collaborating Centre (qv) for International Laboratory for Biological Standards and the **WHO Collaborating Centre** for Reference and Research on Poliomyelitis.

National Institute for Careers Education and Counselling   (NICEC)   1972
- ■ Sheraton House, Castle Park, Cambridge, CB3 0AX.
  01223 460277   fax 01223 311708
  http://www.crac.org.uk/nicec/
- E An institute sponsored by the Careers Research and Advisory Centre (qv).
- ○ To develop theory, inform policy, and enhance practice in the broad fields of careers guidance and careers development

National Institute for Conductive Education   (NICE)   1986
- ■ Cannon Hill House, Russell Road, Birmingham, B13 8RD.
  0121-449 1569   fax 0121-449 1611
  http://www.conductive-education.org.uk/
  Director: David Wood.
- E A registered charity.
- ○ To train people in conductive education - a specialised teaching system which helps people with motor disorders such as cerebral palsy and Parkinson's disease to live more independently
- ● Education and training - Information service - Library

National Institute of Economic and Social Research   (NIESR)   1938

■   2 Dean Trench Street, Smith Square, London, SW1P 3HE.
      020 7222 7665   fax 020 7654 1900
      http://www.niesr.ac.uk/
      Director: Martin Weale. Secretary: Gill Clisham.
E   An independent non-profit-distributing organisation, the Institute is a registered charity and a company limited by guarantee.
O   To conduct economic and social research in macro-economic modelling of the world and UK economies, labour market
      productivity, international trade and investment, and European financial integration
●   Conference facilities - Education and training - Information service - Library - Statistics
¶   See website for list.

National Institute for Environmental eScience   (NIEeS)   2002

■   Department of Earth Sciences, University of Cambridge, Downing Street, Cambridge, CB2 3EQ.
      01223 333482; 711541   fax 01223 333450
      http://www.niees.ac.uk/
      Director: Dr Martin Dove.
E   A Natural Environment Research Council collaborative research institute at the University of Cambridge.
O   To promote and support the use of e-science and grid technologies within the UK environmental science community

National Institute for Excellence in Creative Industries   (NIECI)

■   University of Wales, Bangor, Bangor, Gwynedd, LL57 2DG.
      01248 383215
      http://www.bangor.ac.uk/creative_industries/
      Director: Prof Graeme Harper.
E   A school at the University of Wales, Bangor.
O   To conduct teaching, research and knowledge transfer in creative industries subjects
×   Centre for Advanced Development in the Creative Industries, Centre for Creative and Performing Arts.

National Institute for Health and Clinical Excellence   (NICE)   1999

■   MidCity Place, 71 High Holborn, London, WC1V 6NA.
      020 7067 5800   fax 020 7067 5801
      http://www.nice.org.uk/
E   An independent organisation.
O   To provide national guidance on the promotion of good health and the prevention and treatment of ill health, with guidance
      targeted on three areas of health - Public health, Health technologies, and Clinical practice
Note: NICE is a World Health Organisation WHO Collaborating Centre (qv) for Investment for Health and Health Promotion.

National Institute for Medical Research   (NIMR)   1913

■   Medical Research Centre, The Ridgeway, Mill Hill, London, NW7 1AA.
      020 8959 3666   fax 020 8906 4477
      http://www.nimr.mrc.ac.uk/
      Director: Sir John Skehel.
E   A research institute of the Medical Research Council.
O   To conduct fundamental research in sciences relevant to health
●   Library - Outreach to schools
¶   Research Opportunities. Mill Hill Essays.
Note: See **Medical Research Council Collaborative Centre** for further information. The NIMR is also a World Health Organisation
      WHO Collaborating Centre (qv) for Reference and Research on Influenza.

National Map Centre

■   22-24 Caxton Street, London, SW1H 0QU.
      020 7222 2466
      http://www.mapstore.co.uk/
E   A retailer of worldwide maps.

National Mass Spectrometry Service Centre
      see **EPSRC National Mass Spectrometry Service Centre.**

National Materials Handling Centre
      see **Logistics Education Centre.**

National Medical Laser Centre   (NMLC)   1986

■   Department of Surgery, University College London, Charles Bell House, 67-73 Riding House Street, London, W1P 7PN.
      020 7679 9060   fax 020 7813 2828
      http://www.ucl.ac.uk/surgery/nmlc/
      Director: Prof Stephen Bown.
E   A research centre at University College London.
O   To increase scientific understanding of how the interaction of laser light and biological tissues can improve treatment for a range of
      diseases

National Metals Technology Centre (NAMTEC) 2002
- ■ Swinden House, Moorgate Road, Rotherham, South Yorkshire, S60 3AR.
  01709 724990   fax 01709 724999
  http://www.namtec.co.uk/
- E An industry sponsored body.
- O To stimulate high technology innovation and research and development in metals technology so as to improve the competitiveness of the UK metals industry

National Monuments Record Centre (NMRC)
- ■ Kemble Drive, Churchward, Swindon, Wiltshire, SN2 2GZ.
  01793 414700
  http://www.english-heritage.org.uk/server/show/conWebDoc.4609
- E A part of English Heritage.
- O To preserve and care for a public archive, relating to the architecture and archaeology of England, containing over 12 million items, including maps, photographs and reports

NATIONAL NETWORK OF ASSESSMENT CENTRES

Note: A UK-wide network of specialist services that work together to facilitate access for disabled people to education, training, employment and personal development.

National Network of Assessment Centres Administration Centre
- ■ The Royal National College, College Road, Hereford, HR1 1EB.
  01432 376630   fax 01432 376630
  http://www.nnac.org
- E The administrative headquarters of the National Network of Assessment Centres (qv).

National Non-Destructive Testing Centre (NNDTC) 1967
- ■ 16 North Central 127, Milton Park, Abingdon, Oxfordshire, OX14 4SA.
  01235 213402   fax 01235 213401
  http://www.esrtechnology.com/centres/nndt.php
- E A business centre within ESR Technology (formerly AEA Technology).
- O To undertake contract research and development in all aspects of non-destructive testing

National Oceanography Centre (NOC) 1995
- ■ University of Southampton, Waterfront Campus, Southampton, SO14 3ZH.
  023 8059 6666
  http://www.noc.soton.ac.uk/
  Director: Prof E Hill.
- E A Natural Environment Research Council collaborative research centre and department of the University of Southampton.
- O To advance understanding of the oceanic environment and the process of environmental change in the ocean, and to predict future change
- ● Conference facilities - Education and training - Exhibitions - Information service - Library - Statistics The Centre also houses the premier UK department for teaching and research in oceanography
- × Southampton Oceanography Centre.

National Primary Care Research and Development Centre (NPCRDC) 1995
- NR School of Medicine, Williamson Building, Oxford Road, Manchester, M13 9PL.
  0161-275 7601   fax 0161-275 0611
  http://www.npcrdc.ac.uk/
  Director: Prof Martin Roland, CBE.
- E A research centre at the University of Manchester.
- O To undertake a programme of policy related research in primary care
Note: A collaborative venture with the University of York.

National Printing Skills Centre (NPSC) 1994
- ■ University of Leicester, Grafton Place, St John Street, Leicester, LE1 3WL.
  0116-251 2367   fax 0116-251 2368
  http://www.lec.ac.uk/npsc/
  Centre Manager: Carolyn Rees.
- E University of Leicester.
- O To deliver unique professional training in digital media (pre-press and multimedia), press and post-press
- ● Conference facilities - Education and training - State-of-the-art digital and conventional equipment
- ¶ Training Portfolio.

National Recognition Information Centre for the United Kingdom (UK NARIC) 1975
- ■ Oriel House, Oriel Road, Cheltenham, Gloucestershire, GL50 1XP.
  0870 990 4088   fax 0870 990 1560
  http://www.naric.org.uk/
- E A national agency of the Department for Education and Skills.
- O To provide a recognition service, and comparability information, on all international qualifications from 183 countries worldwide with those in the UK; to promote UK qualifications abroad through the promotion of recognition and acceptance of British awards

National Research and Development Centre for Adult Literacy and Numeracy   (NRDCALN)
- Bedford Group for Lifecourse and Statistical Studies, 20 Bedford Way, London, WC1H 0AL.
  020 7612 6476   fax 020 7612 6671
  http://www.nrdc.org.uk/
  Director: Ursula Howard.
- E   A research centre within the Institute of Education (qv) at the University of London.
- O   To conduct research into adult literacy, numeracy, ESOL and ICT; to help improve the quality of teaching and learning so that young people and adults can progress in life and work

National Resource Centre for Dance   (NRCD)   1982
- University of Surrey, Guildford, Surrey, GU2 7XH.
  01483 689316   fax 01483 689500
  http://www.surrey.ac.uk/nrcd/
  Manager: Helen Roberts. Archive and Research Officer: Christine Jones.
- E   A non-profit-distributing organisation with a voluntary membership and a department of the University of Surrey.
- O   To collect, organise and make accessible a wide range of materials related to dance and movement, predominantly theatre dance; to house archives of national and international importance donated by noted companies, organisations and individuals in the dance community; to preserve and catalogue the archive collections to international archival standards
- ●   Provision of support services to dance education via an annual programme of short courses, including a week long summer school and a publications programme to assist dance teachers, primarily those delivering the GCSE, AS and A-level Dance Information service for the dance profession and the public - Visits by appointment only
- ¶   Over 100 different publications - see website.

National Rural Enterprise Centre   (NREC)   1986
- Stoneleigh Park, Warwickshire, CV8 2RR.
  0845 130 0411   fax 0845 130 0433
- E   A registered charity and non-profit-making organisation.
- O   To promote a living and working countryside through development of businesses, skills and jobs in rural areas

National Safety Centre
- 70 Chancellors Road, London, W6 9RS.
  020 8741 1231   fax 020 8741 4555
  http://www.britishsafetycouncil.co.uk/
- E   The headquarters of the British Safety Council.

National Schoolwear Centres
Note: A national retail chain selling schoolwear.

National Science Learning Centre   (NSLC)
- NR   University of York, Heslington, York, YO10 5DD.
  01904 328300   fax 01904 328328
  http://www.sciencelearningcentres.org.uk/
  Director: Prof John Holman.
- E   A research centre at the University of York.
- O   To provide the highest quality continuing professional development for everyone involved in science education, at all levels
Note: There are 9 regional centres - these are listed under **Science Learning Centre**.

National Small Press Centre
- BM BOZO, London, WC1N 3XX.
  http://www.smallpress.org.uk/

National Soil Resources Institute   (NSRI)   2001
- Natural Resources' Department, Cranfield University, Silsoe, Bedfordshire, MK45 4DT.
  01525 863000
  http://www.silsoe.cranfield.ac.uk/nsri/
  Director: Prof Mark Kibblewhite.
- E   A research institute at Cranfield University.
- O   To focus on the long-term development of the sustainable management of soil and land resources both in the UK and around the world
Note: The NSRI is also based in York (01904 435220), Devon (01837 89188), and Newport, Wales (029 2046 6120).

National Space Centre   (NSC)   1997
- Exploration Drive, Leicester, LE4 5NS.
  0116-261 0261
  http://www.spacecentre.co.uk/
- E   A centre with links to the University of Leicester.

© CBD Research Ltd · Beckenham · Kent BR3 5JS · Tel 020 8650 7745 · Fax 020 8650 0768 · E-mail cbd@cbdresearch.com · www.cbdresearch.com

National Spinal Injuries Centre   (NSIC)   1944
- Stoke Mandeville Hospital, Aylesbury, Buckinghamshire, HP21 8AL.
  01296 315000   fax 01296 315268
  http://www.spinal.org.uk/
- E   An NHS organisation run by the Buckinghamshire Hospitals NHS Trust.
- O   To provide comprehensive care to adult patients with acute spinal cord injury and the lifelong complications of cord injury; to offer, in a dedicated paediatric unit, rehabilitation to children with spinal cord injury
- ● The Centre has 106 beds

National Star Centre for Disabled Youth   1967
- Ullenwood, Cheltenham, Gloucestershire, GL53 9QU.
  01242 527631   fax 01242 222234
  http://www.natstar.ac.uk/
- E   A registered charity and a company limited by guarantee.
- O   To serve students with physical disabilities and acquired brain injuries; to identify existing and potential abilities and their development in order to maximise the present and future quality of life for each student

National Stone Centre   (NSC)   1983
- Porter Lane, Wirksworth, Derby, DE4 4LS.
  01629 824833 (office); 825403 (shop)   fax 01629 824833
  http://www.nationalstonecentre.org.uk/
  Director: Ian A Thomas.
- E   A registered charity and a company limited by guarantee.
- O   To tell all aspects of the 'Story of Stone' in the UK; to provide technical, educational, advisory and consultancy services to industry, schools and the public; to provide retail, industrial, training and demonstration services relating to stone and quarrying; to act as the liaison point for the 10 regional aggregate working parties covering England and Wales
- ● Education and training - Exhibitions - Information service - Library - Recreational facilities - Sculpture park - Workshop facilities - Open 1000-1700 (summer) and 1000-1600 (winter)
- ¶ Directory of Educational Resources Relating to the Minerals Industry. Science of the Earth Primary Pack. Educational Use of Aggregates Sites. Educational Use of Geological Sites.

National Surfing Centre
see **International Surfing Centre.**

National Watersports Centre   1983
- Plas Menai, Caernarfon, Gwynedd, LL55 1UE.
  01248 670964   fax 01248 673939
  http://www.plasmenai.co.uk/
  Manager: Alan Williams. Chief Instructor: Jamie Johnson.
- E   Established as a national outdoors centre.
- O   To provide outdoor activity courses and training for all ages and abilities, including taster sessions, qualification courses and instructor training (including national squad training for sailing)
- ● Conference facilities - Education and training - Recreational facilities

National Wildflower Centre   (NWC)
- Court Hey Park, Roby Road, Liverpool, L16 3NA.
  0151-738 1913
  http://www.nwc.org.uk/
- E   A visitor attraction.
- ● Open from March to September each year

Nationwide Children's Research Centre   (NCRC)
- School of Human and Health Sciences, University of Huddersfield, Brian Jackson House, New North Parade, Huddersfield, HD1 5JP.
  01484 415461   fax 01484 435150
  http://www.hud.ac.uk/hhs/research/ncrc/
  Director: Martin Manby. Administrator: Jacqi Wesencraft.
- E   A research centre at the University of Huddersfield.
- O   To promote high quality research which will improve the quality of life of children and young people and their contribution to society, which will seek to meet their aspirations and to integrate their diverse needs for care, education, a stimulating and safe environment and positive health, and which will reflect their rights and capabilities to influence policy and service priorities within a multi cultural and multi faith society

Natural Death Centre   1991
- 12a Blackstock Mews, Blackstock Road, London, N4 2BT.
  0871 288 2098   fax 020 7354 3831
  http://www.naturaldeath.org.uk/
- E   A registered charity.
- O   To help to improve the quality of dying through supporting those dying at home and their carers, and to help people arrange inexpensive, family-organised, and environmentally-friendly funerals

Natural Environment Research Council
see **NERC.**

Natural Resources Institute   (NRI)   1990

- University of Greenwich, Central Avenue, Chatham Maritime, Kent, ME4 4TB.
  01634 880088   fax 01634 883386
  http://www.nri.org/
  Director: Dr Guy Poulter.
- E A free standing institute within the University of Greenwich.
- ○ To carry out research, development and training to promote efficient management and use of renewable natural resources in support of sustainable livelihoods
- ● Conference facilities - Education and training - Library - Consultancy in environmental and resources management

Natural Resources Management Institute   (NRMI)

- Natural Resources' Department, Cranfield University, Silsoe, Bedfordshire, MK45 4DT.
  01525 863000
  http://www.cranfield.ac.uk/sas/naturalresources/nrmi/
  Director: Prof Joe Morris.
- E A research institute at Cranfield University.
- ○ To use anthropology and environmental sociology to understand human behaviour towards natural resources and how institutions regulate relationships between people and their environment, including property rights and entitlements

NDE Centre
> see **UCL NDE Centre.**

NERC Centre for Population Biology   (CPB)   1989

- Faculty of Life Sciences, Silwood Park Campus, Imperial College London, Ascot, Berkshire, SL5 7PY.
  020 7594 2475   fax 01344 873173
  http://www3.imperial.ac.uk/cpb/about
  Director: Prof H Charles J Godfray.
- E A Natural Environment Research Council collaborative research centre at Imperial College London.
- ○ To study the fundamental ecological processes which link individuals, populations and whole communities of plants, animals and micro-organisms

Neuroimaging Centre
> see **York Neuroimaging Centre.**

Neurological Institute
> see **Burden Neurological Institute.**

Neuroscience Centre   2003

- Barts and the London, Queen Mary's School of Medicine and Dentistry, 4 Newark Street, London, E1 2AT.
  020 7882 2483   fax 020 7882 2200
  http://www.smd.qmul.ac.uk/neuro/
  Head: Prof John Priestley.
- E A research centre within the Institute of Cell and Molecular Science (qv) at Queen Mary, University of London.
- ○ To conduct research into various area of neuroscience, with particular emphasis on plasticity of primary afferents and spinal cord pathways, neurotrophic factors, traumatic injury, molecular genetics and cell biology of degenerative disorders, motor neurone disease, cellular and neurotransmitter changes underlying schizophrenia and depression, and strategies for regeneration and neuroprotection

Neuroscience Research Institute   (NRI)

- Oxford Road, Manchester, M13 9PL.
  0161-306 6000
  http://www.neuroscience.manchester.ac.uk/
- E A research institute at the University of Manchester.
- ○ To bring together researchers from different backgrounds spanning science, engineering and medicine to produce high-quality research in the area of neuroscience

Note: Also known as **Institute of Neuroscience Research**.

Neurosciences Institute

- College of Medicine, Dentistry & Nursing, Ninewells Hospital and Medical School, Dundee, DD1 9SY.
  01382 632161   fax 01382 667120
  http://www.dundee.ac.uk/pharmacology/
  Contact: Prof Mike Ashford.
- E A research centre at the University of Dundee.

New and Renewable Energy Centre   (NaREC)

- Eddie Ferguson House, Ridley Street, Blyth, Northumberland, NE24 3AG.
  01670 359555
  http://www.narec.co.uk/
  Chairman: Dr Alan Rutherford.
- E A centre of excellence set up by the Government Agency One North East.
- ○ To conduct programmes of research with industry and academia in the field of new and renewable energy

© CBD Research Ltd · Beckenham · Kent BR3 5JS · Tel 020 8650 7745 · Fax 020 8650 0768 · E-mail cbd@cbdresearch.com · www.cbdresearch.com

Newcastle Centre for Family Studies   (NCFS)   1985
- ■ School of Geography, Politics and Sociology, University of Newcastle upon Tyne, 18 Windsor Terrace, Newcastle upon Tyne, NE1 7RU.
     0191-222 7642   fax 0191-222 7871
     http://www.ncl.ac.uk/ncfs/
     Director: Prof Janet Walker.
- E   A research centre within the Institute for Policy and Practice (qv) at the University of Newcastle upon Tyne.
- O   To be a leading centre of excellence in undertaking and promoting research on family life and relationships, and to play a central and influential role in the development of family policy

Newcastle Centre for Railway Research   (NewRail)   2006
- ■ Faculty of Science, Agriculture and Engineering, Stephenson Building, University of Newcastle upon Tyne, Newcastle upon Tyne, NE1 7RU.
     0191-222 5821   fax 0191-222 5821
     http://www.ncl.ac.uk/newrail/
     Director: Prof Mark Robinson.
- E   A research centre at the University of Newcastle upon Tyne.
- O   To develop and maintain the highest international standards of excellence in rail-related research, with particular emphasis on materials, structure and design, wheel rail interfaces, freight and logistics, and rail systems

Newcastle Centre for Social and Business Informatics   (SBI)
- ■ University of Newcastle Business School, 4th Floor, University of Newcastle upon Tyne, Claremont Bridge, Newcastle upon Tyne, NE1 7RU.
     0191-222 6300   fax 0191-232 9259
     http://www.campus.ncl.ac.uk/unbs/sbi/
     Co-Director: James Cornford. Co-Director: Ian McLoughlin.
- E   A research centre at the University of Newcastle upon Tyne.
- O   To focus on the social, economic, managerial, organisational and cultural aspects of the design, development, deployment and use of information and communication technologies and their social consequences

Newcastle Fertility Centre at Life
- ■ Life Bioscience Centre, Times Square, Newcastle upon Tyne, NE1 4EP.
     0191-219 4740   fax 0191-219 4747
     http://www.nfc-life.com/
- E   An NHS-funded centre within the Centre for Life (qv) at the University of Newcastle upon Tyne.
- O   To offer, within purpose built facilities, a comprehensive service for the investigation and treatment of couples with infertility
- ● Specialist laboratories

Newcastle Institute for the Arts, Social Sciences and Humanities   (NIASSH)   2003
- ■ 7th Floor - Daysh Building, University of Newcastle upon Tyne, Newcastle upon Tyne, NE1 7RU.
     0191-222 8679
     http://www.ncl.ac.uk/niassh/
     Director: Prof Phil Powrie.
- E   A department of the University of Newcastle upon Tyne.
- O   To provide the highest possible regional, national and international profile for creative practice and research in the arts, humanities and social sciences

Newport Centre for Criminal and Community Justice   (NCCJ)
- ■ School of Social Studies, Allt-yr-yn Campus, PO Box 180, University of Wales, Newport, Newport, NP20 5XR.
     01633 432314   fax 01633 432530
     http://nccj.newport.ac.uk/
     Contact: Davinia Lawrence.
- E   A research centre at the University of Wales, Newport.
- O   To become one of the leading centres in the UK that provides teaching, research and consultancy in the application of theory and practice within the criminal and community justice system

Newton Institute
   see **Isaac Newton Institute for Mathematical Sciences.**

NHS Institute for Innovation and Improvement   2005
- ■ Coventry House, Coventry, CV4 7AL.
     0800 555 550
     http://www.institute.nhs.uk/
     Chairman: Dame Yve Buckland.
- E   An institute within the National Health Service.
- O   To improve health outcomes and raise the quality of delivery in the NHS

Nissan Institute of Japanese Studies   1981
- ■ University of Oxford, 27 Winchester Road, Oxford, OX2 6NA.
  01865 274570   fax 01865 274574
  Director: Dr Ann Waswo.
- E An institute at the University of Oxford.
- O To undertake teaching and research on modern Japan
- ● Conference facilities - Education and training - Library - Academic staff members also participate in a variety of activities, nationally and internationally, in relation to the study of modern Japan

Nomura Centre for Quantitative Finance   (NCQF)   2001
- ■ University of Oxford, 24-29 St Giles, Oxford, OX1 3LB.   fax 01865 270515
  http://www.maths.ox.ac.uk/
  Director: Dr Sam Howison.
- E A research centre within the Oxford Centre for Industrial and Applied Mathematics (qv) at the University of Oxford.
- O To promote research in mathematics and finance, with a special emphasis on approaches that combine practical relevance with mathematical interest

Non Destructive Evaluation Centre
   see **UCL NDE Centre.**

Norah Fry Research Centre   1988
- ■ Faculty of Social Sciences and Law, University of Bristol, 3 Priory Road, Bristol, BS8 1TX.
  0117-331 0987   fax 0117-331 0978
  http://www.bristol.ac.uk/norahfry/
  Director: Prof Linda Ward.
- E A department of the University of Bristol.
- O To research into the needs of people with learning and other disabilities

Nordic Policy Studies Centre   (NPSC)   1996
- ■ School of Social Science, College Office, University of Aberdeen, Powis Gate, Aberdeen, AB24 3UG.
  01224 272084   fax 01224 272082
  http://www.abdn.ac.uk/pir/department/research_centers.php#centre
  Director: Prof David Arter.
- E A research centre at the University of Aberdeen.

Nordoff-Robbins Music Therapy Centre   (NRMTC)   1977
- ■ 2 Lissenden Gardens, London, NW5 1PP.
  020 7267 4496   fax 020 7267 4369
  http://www.nordoff-robbins.org.uk/
- E A registered charity.
- O To give music therapy to handicapped children and adults

North Atlantic Fisheries College Marine Centre
   see **NAFC Marine Centre.**

North East England History Institute   (NEEHI)   1995
- ■ School of Arts and Humanities, Northumbria University, 5th Floor - Bolbec Hall, Westgate Road, Newcastle upon Tyne, NE1 1SE.
  0191-221 2477
  http://www.neehi.org.uk
  Director: Dr Bill Lancaster.
- E A research institute at Northumbria University.
- O To conduct research of the very highest quality into the history of north-east England, so that as much as possible of the region's history can be reliably established

North East England Stem Cell Institute   (NESCI)
- NR University of Newcastle upon Tyne, Life Bioscience Centre, Times Square, Newcastle upon Tyne, NE1 4EP.
  0191-241 8698   fax 0191-241 8799
  http://www.nesci.ac.uk
- E An interdisciplinary research institute within the Centre for Life (qv) at the University of Newcastle upon Tyne.
- O To convert stem cell research and technologies into cost-effective, ethically robust 21st century health solutions to help ameliorate degenerative diseases, the effects of ageing and serious injury
- ✕ Institute of Stem Cell Biology and Regenerative Medicine
- Note: A joint venture with the University of Durham and various other public bodies.

North East Regional e-Science Centre   (NEReSC)   2001
- ■ School of Computing Science, University of Newcastle upon Tyne, Devonshire Building, Claremont Road, Newcastle upon Tyne, NE1 7RU.
  0191-246 4926   fax 0191-222 8232
  http://www.neresc.ac.uk/
  Director: Prof Paul Watson.
- E A research centre at the University of Newcastle upon Tyne.
- Note: See **e-Science Centres** for further information.

© CBD Research Ltd · Beckenham · Kent BR3 5JS · Tel 020 8650 7745 · Fax 020 8650 0768 · E-mail cbd@cbdresearch.com · www.cbdresearch.com

North London Buddhist Centre

- ■ 72 Holloway Road, London, N7 8JG.
  020 7700 1177
  http://www.northlondonbuddhistcentre.com/
- E An independent non-profit-distributing organisation and a registered charity.
- ○ To teach meditation and Buddhism
- ● Education and training - The Centre provides meditation cushions and mats

Note: For other Buddhist centres see note under **Buddhist Centres**.

North West Cancer Research Fund Institute (NWCRF) 2003

- ■ School of Biological Sciences, University of Wales, Bangor, Brambell Building, Deiniol Road, Bangor, Gwynedd, LL57 2UW.
  01248 382604   fax 01248 370731
  http://www.nwcrfinstitute.co.uk/
  Director: Dr Thomas Caspari. Contact: Dr Sue Assinder.
- E A research institute at the University of Wales, Bangor.
- ○ To conduct research in molecular cancer

North West Centre for European Marketing
  see **Centre for Research in Marketing.**

North West Centre for Learning and Development Ltd (NWCLD) 1978

- ■ Unit 3 - Hyde Business Park, Pennyburn Industrial Estate, Derry, BT48 0LU.
  028 7128 6201   fax 028 7126 0303
  http://www.nwcld.org/
  Acting Manager: Marie Donashy.
- E An independent non-profit-distributing organisation.
- ○ To provide a wide range of services such as training, work placements, re-skilling, advice on training, career guidance, information, delivery and support services
- ● Education and training - The NWCLD operates 5 programmes covering Network engineering, Electronic engineering, Women into IT, Adult learner support and Essential skills learning for young people

North West Food Centre (NWFC)

- ■ Hollings Campus, Manchester Metropolitan University, Old Hall Lane, Manchester, M14 6HR.
  0161-247 2493   fax 0161-247 6391
  http://www.nwfoodcentre.com/
- E A centre at Manchester Metropolitan University.
- ○ To help food producers get their products to market

Northern Centre for the History of Medicine (NCHM)

- ■ Queen's Campus, University of Durham, University Boulevard, Thornaby, Stockton on Tees, TS17 6BH.
  0191-334 0701
  http://www.dur.ac.uk/nchm/
  Director: Prof Andreas-Holger Maehle.
- E A research centre within the Wolfson Research Institute (qv) at the University of Durham.
- ○ To provide a co-ordinated research programme (with the University of Newcastle upon Tyne), a Masters training programme in the history of medicine, a number of PhD projects, a series of workshops, seminars and conferences, as well as teaching initiatives within the medical curriculum, and public engagement activities

Northern Institute for Cancer Research (NICR) 1998

- ■ School of Clinical Medical Sciences, University of Newcastle upon Tyne, Paul O'Gorman Building, Framlington Place, Newcastle upon Tyne, NE2 4HH.
  0191-246 4300   fax 0191-246 4301
  http://www.ncl.ac.uk/nicr/
  Manager: Mrs Jill Hogg. Contact: Mrs Sandra Cartwright.
- E A research institute at the University of Newcastle upon Tyne.
- ○ To conduct cancer research in a wide variety of fields

Northern Ireland Bio-Engineering Centre (NIBEC) 1986

- ■ Jordanstown Campus, University of Ulster, Shore Road, Newtownabbey, County Antrim, BT37 0QB.
  028 9036 6329   fax 028 9036 6863
  http://www.engj.ulster.ac.uk/nibec/
- E A research centre at the University of Ulster.
- ○ To provide a vehicle for focusing appropriate skills in medicine, science, engineering and electronics onto the design and development of bio-engineering and devices systems with commercial potential

Northern Ireland Centre for Advanced Materials (NICAM)

- ■ Jordanstown Campus, University of Ulster, Shore Road, Newtownabbey, County Antrim, BT37 0QB.
  028 9036 8339   fax 028 9036 6863
  http://www.engj.ulster.ac.uk/nicam/
  Business Manager: Pauline McCann.
- E A research centre at the University of Ulster.
- ○ To contribute to wealth creation in Northern Ireland, by utilising the expertise in the universities in advanced functional materials and surface science

Northern Ireland Centre for Biodiversity and Conservation Biology   (Quercus)

■   School of Biological Sciences, Queen's University, Belfast, 97 Lisburn Road, Belfast, BT9 7BL.
     028 9097 2281   fax 028 9097 5877
     http://www.quercus.ac.uk/
     Manager: Dr Robbie McDonald.
E   A research centre at Queen's University, Belfast.

Northern Ireland Centre for Energy Research and Technology   (NICERT)

■   Coleraine Campus, University of Ulster, Cromore Road, Coleraine, County Londonderry, BT52 1SA.
     028 7032 4469   fax 028 7032 4900
     http://www.engj.ulster.ac.uk/NICERT/
E   A research centre at the University of Ulster.
O   To conduct research and provide consultancy on energy and the environment

Northern Ireland Centre for Entrepreneurship   (NICENT)

NR   Room 2B22, University of Ulster, Shore Road, Newtownabbey, County Antrim, BT37 0QB.
     028 9036 6011   fax 028 9036 6015
     http://nicent.ulster.ac.uk/
E   An institute at the University of Ulster.
O   To drive, support and promote entrepreneurship in science and technology subjects
Note: A joint venture with Queen's University, Belfast.

Northern Ireland Centre for European Co-operation

Note: has closed.

Northern Ireland Centre for Food and Health   (NICHE)

■   School of Biomedical Sciences, Coleraine Campus, University of Ulster, Cromore Road, Coleraine, County Londonderry,
     BT52 1SA.
     028 7032 3039   fax 028 7032 3023
     http://www.science.ulster.ac.uk/niche/
     Contact: Mrs Alison Deehan.
E   A research centre within the Biomedical Sciences Research Institute (qv) at the University of Ulster.
O   To elucidate the relationship between diet and common chronic diseases; to provide support and advice to industry for the
     development of new food products

Northern Ireland Centre for Health Informatics   (NICHI)

■   Coleraine Campus, University of Ulster, Cromore Road, Coleraine, County Londonderry, BT52 1SA.
     028 7032 4207   fax 028 7032 4287
     http://nichi.infm.ulst.ac.uk/
     Co-ordinator: Prof Mary Chambers.
E   A research centre at the University of Ulster.
O   To facilitate and enhance research and development and education and training within healthcare informatics in Northern Ireland

Northern Ireland Centre for Information on Language Teaching and Research   (NICILT)   1995

■   School of Education, Queen's University, Belfast, University of Ulster, 8 College Green, Belfast, BT7 1LN.
     028 9097 5955   fax 028 9032 6571
     http://www.qub.ac.uk/edu/nicilt/
     Director: Dr Eugene McKendry. Executive Officer: Wendy Phipps.
E   A partnership between CILT, The National Centre for Languages (qv) in London and Queen's University, Belfast.
O   To provide information and research, resources, publications and training for anyone with a language interest or concern
●   Conference facilities - Exhibitions - Information service - Library - Hours Mon-Fri (0930-1300, 1400-1700)
✕   Centre for Modern Language Teaching.

Northern Ireland Centre for Postgraduate Pharmaceutical Education   (NICPPET)

■   FREEPOST BEL3149, Belfast, BT9 7BR.
     028 9097 2005   fax 028 9097 2368
     http://www.nicppet.org/
O   To support, through education and training, a quality pharmaceutical service

Northern Ireland Centre for Trauma and Transformation   (NICTT)   2002

■   2 Retreat Close, Killyclogher Road, Omagh, County Tyrone, BT79 0HW.
     028 8225 1500
     http://www.nictt.org/
     Director: David Bolton.
E   A charitable trust.
O   To provide training and support developments in relation to cognitive therapy and psychological trauma related disorders

Northern Ireland Semiconductor Research Centre   (NISRC)

■   School of Electrical and Electronic Engineering, Queen's University, Belfast, Ashby Building, Stranmillis Road, Belfast, BT9 5AH.
     028 9097 5439   fax 028 9066 7023
     http://www.ee.qub.ac.uk/nisrc/
     Contact: Prof Harold Gamble.
E   A centre at Queen's University, Belfast.

Northern Ireland Technology Centre   (NITC)   1968

■   Queen's University, Belfast, Cloreen Park, Malone Road, Belfast, BT9 5HN.
028 9097 5433   fax 028 9097 4332
http://www.nitc.qub.ac.uk/
Director: Tom Edgar.
E   A department of Queen's University, Belfast.
○   To provide a technology transfer conduit between academia and engineering enterprise

Northern Refugee Centre   (NRC)   1983

■   Scotia Works, Leadmill Road, Sheffield, S1 4SE.
0114-241 2780   fax 0114-241 2744
http://www.nrcentre.org.uk/
Chief Executive: Jim Steinke. Advice Services Manager: John Donkersley.
E   A registered charity and a company limited by guarantee.
○   To promote the welfare of all refugees and asylum seekers within the Yorkshire and Humber region
●   Education and training - Information service

Northern Studies Centre   (NSC)   2001

■   School of Social Science, University of Aberdeen, Cruickshank Building, St Machar Drive, Aberdeen, AB24 3UU.
01224 272688   fax 01224 272703
http://www.abdn.ac.uk/northernstudies/
Contact: Dr Sarah Woodin.
E   A centre at the University of Aberdeen.
○   To bring together ecologists, social anthropologists and environmental scientists, actively involved in research in Scotland, the sub -
Arctic and the High Arctic

Northumbrian Environmental Training and Research Centre   (NETREC)   1996

■   School of Applied Sciences, Northumbria University, Ellison Building, Ellison Place, Newcastle upon Tyne, NE1 8ST.
0191-227 4668   fax 0191-227 3519
http://www.netrec.uk.com/
Manager: Dr Michael Deary.
E   A research centre at Northumbria University.
○   To offer consultancy and training in various areas, including environmental, chemical and microbial analysis, contaminated land,
air quality, and safety and chemical hazards
●   Consultancy - Education and training - Information service

Northwest Composites Centre   2006

NR   School of Materials, University of Manchester, Paper Science Building, Sackville Street, Manchester, M60 1QD.
0161-306 3612
http://www.futurecomposites.org.uk/
Director: Dr Richard Day.
E   A research centre at the University of Manchester.
○   To undertake applied research leading to the development of new, cost-effective, low energy, low cycle time composite processing
routes for making real components and demonstrators
Note: A collaborative project with the 3 other Universities in the North West - Bolton, Lancaster and Liverpool.

Norwegian Study Centre   (NSC)   1981

■   University of York, New Building, Main Street, York, YO10 5EA.
01904 433235   fax 01904 433236
http://www.york.ac.uk/inst/nsc/
Director: Dr Jon Orten.
E   A department of the University of York.
○   To provide intensive English language courses for higher education students from Norway, as well as undergraduate courses in co-
operation with the Department of English and Related Literature
●   Education and training

Norwich Buddhist Centre

■   14 Bank Street, Norwich, NR2 4SE.
01603 627034
http://www.norwichbuddhistcentre.com/
E   An independent non-profit-distributing organisation and a registered charity.
○   To teach meditation and Buddhism
●   Education and training - The Centre provides meditation cushions and mats
Note: For other Buddhist centres see note under **Buddhist Centres**.

Nottingham Arabidopsis Stock Centre   (NASC)   1991

■   School of Biosciences, Sutton Bonington Campus, Loughborough University, Loughborough, Leicestershire, LE12 5RD.
0115-951 3237   fax 0115-951 3297
http://arabidopsis.info/
Director: Dr Sean May.
E   A research centre at the University of Nottingham.
○   To provide seed and information resources to the International Arabidopsis Genome Programme and the wider research
community
Note: Arabidopsis is a small annual weed which offers many advantages for rapid genetic and molecular analysis.

Nottingham Centre for Geomechanics   (NCG)
■ School of Civil Engineering, Coates Building, University of Nottingham, University Park, Nottingham, NG7 2RD.
  0115-951 3951   fax 0115-951 3898
  http://www.nottingham.ac.uk/ncg/
  Director: Prof Hai-Sui Yu.
E A research centre at the University of Nottingham.
○ To draw together expertise from the worlds of civil and mining engineering, and mathematics to solve all forms of soil and rock-related, engineering design and construction problems

Nottingham Centre for Pavement Engineering
     see **Nottingham Transportation Engineering Centre.**

Nottingham Centre for the Study and Reduction of Hate Crimes, Bias and Prejudice
■ School of Social Sciences, Nottingham Trent University, Burton Street, Nottingham, NG1 4BU.
  0115-848 6807   fax 0115-848 6808
  http://www.ntu.ac.uk/soc/school_and_staff/criminology/12544gp.html
E A research centre at Nottingham Trent University.

Nottingham Fuel and Energy Centre   (NFEC)
■ School of Chemical, Environmental and Mining Engineering, Coates Building, University of Nottingham, University Park, Nottingham, NG7 2RD.
  0115-951 4166   fax 0115-951 4115
  http://www.fuelandenergy.info/
  Director of Research: Prof Colin Snape.
E A research centre at the University of Nottingham.
○ To conduct research into the new technologies and environmental controls shaping the future of fuel, including cleaner coal technology, advanced carbon materials, advanced microscopic, spectroscopic and pyrolysis techniques for coal, oil and pollutant characterization, multiphase flow and separation, energy and electrochemical technology, and paleoclimate and the earth's carbon cycle

Nottingham Innovative Manufacturing Research Centre   (NIMRC)
NR School of Mechanical Materials and Manufacturing Engineering, University of Nottingham, University Park, Nottingham, NG7 2RD.
  0115-951 5997
  http://www.nimrc.nottingham.ac.uk/
  Director: Prof Nabil Gindy. Project Manager: Mrs Janet Walters.
E An EPSRC Innovative Manufacturing Research Centre at the University of Nottingham.
○ To develop knowledge driven manufacturing to create high value products, new methods, materials, processes and systems to contribute to a sustainable future in the areas of advanced manufacturing technology, lightweight structures manufacturing, and responsive manufacturing enterprise
Note: One of the EPSRC funded centres in the UK - for further information see EPSRC Innovative Manufacturing Research Centres.

Nottingham Institute for English Research   (NifER)
■ School of Arts and Humanities, Nottingham Trent University, Clifton Lane, Nottingham, NG11 8NS.
  0115-848 3060
  http://www2.ntu.ac.uk/english/englishresearch/
  Director: Prof David Worrall.
E A research institute at Nottingham Trent University.
○ To promote and advance research, particularly recovery research into radical, working-class, labouring class, experimental and interrogative writing and texts, with particular reference to English literary traditions, colonial and post-colonial literary and cultural traditions, creative writing and experimentation and the limits of canonicity

Nottingham Institute for Enterprise and Innovation
     see **University of Nottingham Institute for Enterprise and Innovation**.

Nottingham Institute for Research in Visual Culture   (NIRVC)
■ Department of Art History, Lakeside Arts Centre, University of Nottingham, University Park, Nottingham, NG7 2RD.
  0115-951 3318   fax 0115-846 7778
  http://www.nottingham.ac.uk/nirv/
  Co-ordinator: Richard Wrigley.
E A research institute at the University of Nottingham.

Nottingham Institute of Russian and East European Studies   (NIREES)   1986
■ Department of Slavonic Studies, University of Nottingham, University Park, Nottingham, NG7 2RD.
  0115-951 5730; 5928   fax 0115-951 5249
  http://www.nottingham.ac.uk/nirees/
  Chairman: Dr Adam Swain. Secretary: Dr Nick Baron.
E A department of the University of Nottingham.
○ To encourage research into Russia and Eastern Europe

   © CBD Research Ltd · Beckenham · Kent BR3 5JS · Tel 020 8650 7745 · Fax 020 8650 0768 · E-mail cbd@cbdresearch.com · www.cbdresearch.com

Nottingham Mining and Mineral Centre   (NMMC)

- ■ School of Chemical, Environmental and Mining Engineering, University of Nottingham, University Park, Nottingham, NG7 2RD.
  0115-951 4086   fax 0115-951 4115
  http://www.nottingham.ac.uk/scheme/nmmc/
  Head: Prof Nick Miles.
- E A research centre at the University of Nottingham.
- O To conduct research into a wide variety of areas connected with the mining and extractive industries

Nottingham Nanotechnology and Nanoscience Centre   (NNNC)   2005

- ■ School of Chemistry, University of Nottingham, University Park, Nottingham, NG7 2RD.
  0115-951 3481
  http://www.nottingham.ac.uk/nano/
  Director: Prof Clive Roberts. Contact: Wendy Kirk.
- E A research centre at the University of Nottingham.

Nottingham Policy Centre   (NPC)   2004

- ■ School of Sociology and Social Policy, University of Nottingham, University Park, Nottingham, NG7 2RD.
  0115-951 5234   fax 0115-951 5232
  http://www.nottingham.ac.uk/npc/
  Director: Prof Bruce Stafford.
- E A research centre at the University of Nottingham.
- O To provide a core of research and teaching expertise in a variety of public policy areas

Nottingham Transportation Engineering Centre   (NTEC)

- ■ School of Civil Engineering, University of Nottingham, University Park, Nottingham, NG7 2RD.
  0115-951 3907
  http://www.nottingham.ac.uk/~evzncpe/frameindex.htm
  Director: Prof Andrew C Collop.
- E A research centre at the University of Nottingham.
- O To be an internationally renowned centre of excellence in pavement engineering, providing a focus for fundamental and applied research and technical service support for the pavement industry, with an emphasis in the areas of pavement design and performance prediction using mechanistic methods, rail track design, evaluation and materials, mechanical properties of bituminous and cement treatment materials, mechanical properties of sub-grade soils, granular and alternative materials, and sustainable pavements

Nottingham Trent Centre for Colonial and Postcolonial Studies   (CCPS)   2000

- ■ School of Arts and Humanities, Clifton Campus, Nottingham Trent University, Nottingham, NG11 8NS.
  0115-848 3202
  http://www2.ntu.ac.uk/english/ccps/
  Acting Director: Dr Alison Donnell.
- E A research centre within the Nottingham Institute for English Research (qv) at Nottingham Trent University.
- O To encourage, focus and develop investigations into current and ongoing issues in colonial and postcolonial writing and theory

Nottingham Trent Centre for Travel Writing Studies   (CTWS)   2003

- ■ School of Arts and Humanities, Clifton Lane, Nottingham Trent University, Nottingham, NG11 8NS.
  0115-848 3276
  http://www2.ntu.ac.uk/english/centrefortravelwriting/
  Director: Prof Tim Youngs.
- E A research centre within the Nottingham Institute for English Research (qv) at Nottingham Trent University.
- O To facilitate, promote and disseminate scholarly research on travel writing and its contexts, without restriction of period, locus, or type of travel writing

Nottingham University Electrical Drives Centre

- ■ University of Nottingham, University Park, Nottingham, NG7 2RD.
  0115-951 5626
  http://www.eee.nott.ac.uk/
  Technical Director: Dr K J Bradley.
- E A research centre at the University of Nottingham.
- O To offer a range of testing and consultancy services covering the principle types of motor drive - induction, synchronous, DC and SR

Nuclear Institute
  see **Dalton Nuclear Institute.**

Nuffield Centre for Community Care Studies
  see **Community Care Works.**

Nuffield Centre for International Health and Development   (NCIHD)   1981

■ Faculty of Medicine and Health, University of Leeds, 15 Hyde Terrace, Leeds, LS2 9JT.
    0113-343 4361
    http://www.leeds.ac.uk/hsphr/ihsphr_ihd/home
    Research Administrator: Anthonia James.
E A research centre within the Leeds Institute of Health Sciences (qv) at the University of Leeds.
○ To enhance understanding of the health system management processes and policies necessary for the promotion of health and
    equity in middle and low-income countries
Note: The Centre is a World Health Organisation WHO Collaborating Centre (qv) for Research and Development in Health Systems
    Strengthening.

Nuffield Hearing and Speech Centre   1963

■ Royal National Throat, Nose and Ear Hospital, Gray's Inn Road, London, WC1X 8DA.
    020 7915 1641   fax 020 7915 1641
    http://www.royalfree.nhs.uk/default.aspx?top_nav_id=1&sel_left_nav=25&tab_id=369
    Clinical Lead Consultant: Katherine Harrop-Griffith. Consultant: Deirdre Lucas.
○ To investigate children suffering from disorders of hearing, balance and speech and language
● Education and training - Information service - Medical investigation and management

Nursing, Health and Social Care Research Centre   (NHSCRC)

■ Cardiff School of Nursing and Midwifery Studies, 4th Floor - Eastgate House, Cardiff University, 35-43 Newport Road, Cardiff,
    CF24 0AB.
    029 2091 7800   fax 029 2091 7803
    http://www.cardiff.ac.uk/nursing/research
E A department of Cardiff University.
○ To focus research on the health and social care delivery system

Nursing and Midwifery Research Centre
    see **Caledonian Nursing and Midwifery Research Centre.**

© CBD Research Ltd · Beckenham · Kent BR3 5JS · Tel 020 8650 7745 · Fax 020 8650 0768 · E-mail cbd@cbdresearch.com · www.cbdresearch.com

Ocean Engineering Research Centre
see **Engineering Structures Research Centre.**

Ocean Systems Laboratory
■ Heriot-Watt University, Riccarton, Edinburgh, EH14 4AS.
0131-449 5111
http://www.ece.eps.hw.ac.uk/Research/oceans/
E A research centre at Heriot-Watt University.
○ To conduct research, development and exploitation of acoustic, robotic and video-imaging systems, with particular emphasis on signal processing, control, architecture and modelling

Ofcom Licensing Centre
■ PO Box 885, Bristol, BS99 5LG.
0117-925 8333; 0870 243 4433
http://www.ofcom.org.uk/licensing/olc/
○ To issue radio operating licences to individuals and ships
Note: Radio Licensing Centre.

Ogden Centre for Fundamental Physics   2002
■ Department of Physics, University of Durham, South Road, Durham, DH1 3LE.
0191-334 3520   fax 0191-334 5823
http://ogdencentre.dur.ac.uk/
E An institute at the University of Durham.
○ To encourage and promote the teaching and learning of science; contains the Institute for Computational Cosmology and the Institute for Particle Physics Phenomenology (qqv)

Oil Depletion Analysis Centre   (ODAC)
■ 162 Skene Street (2nd floor), Aberdeen, AB10 1PE.
01224 631697
http://www.odac-info.org/
Contact: Douglas Low
E An independent charity.
○ To raise international public awareness and promote better understanding of the world's oil-depletion problem.

Oil and Gas Centre   (OGC)
■ University Office, King's College, University of Aberdeen, Aberdeen, AB24 3FX.
01224 272484   fax 01224 272319
http://www.abdn.ac.uk/oilgas/
Company Development Manager: Dr Liz Rattray.
E A centre at the University of Aberdeen.
○ To develop solutions which will boost the sustainability and competitiveness of the energy sector

Olympic Medical Institute   (OMI)   2003
■ Northwick Park Hospital, Harrow, Middlesex, HA1 3UJ.
020 8423 7200   fax 020 8423 7201
http://www.olympics.org.uk/omi/
Director of Medical Services: Dr Richard Budgett.
E A partnership between the English Institute of Sport (qv) and the British Olympic Association.
○ To offer world class care to athletes in the form of residential rehabilitation, out-patient sports medicine and physiotherapy services, squad-based sports physiology, and research developments
✕ British Olympic Medical Centre.

One World Centre   (OWC)   1983
■ 189 Princes Street, Dundee, DD4 6DQ.
01382 454603
http://www.oneworldcentredundee.org.uk/
E A registered charity and a membership organisation.
○ To enable people to understand the links between their own lives and those of people throughout the world; to increase understanding of the economic, social, political and environmental forces which shape all our lives; to enable people to find ways to bring about change by acting locally to create a more just world

Open Centre   1977
■ 3rd Floor, 188 Old Street, London, EC1V 9FR.
020 7251 1504
http://www.opencentre.com/
Contact: Juliana Brown.
E A partnership.
○ To offer people an opportunity, in group work and in individual sessions, to increase their own awareness of themselves

Open Middleware Infrastructure Institute UK (OMII)

NR   Suite 6005 - Faraday Building, Highfield Campus, University of Southampton, Southampton, SO17 1BJ.
      023 8059 8862   fax 023 8059 8870
      http://www.omii.ac.uk
      Contact: Prof David De Roure.
E   A research institute at the University of Southampton.
○   To provide software and support to enable a sustained future for the UK e-science community and its international collaborators
Note: A joint venture with the Universities of Edinburgh and Manchester. See **e-Science Centres** for further information.

Open University Centre for Education in Medicine (OUCEM) 1991

■   Open University, Walton Hall, Milton Keynes, MK7 6AA.
      01908 274066
      http://iet.open.ac.uk/
E   A research centre within the Institute of Educational Technology (qv) at the Open University.

Operations Management Research Centre (OMRC)

■   Cranfield School of Management, Cranfield University, Cranfield, Bedfordshire, MK43 0AL.
      01234 751122   fax 01234 751806
      http://www.som.cranfield.ac.uk/som/research/centres/omrc.asp
      Contact: Dawn Gallyot.
E   A research centre within the Cranfield Management Research Institute (qv) at Cranfield University.
○   To determine best manufacturing performance, the relationship of complexity to performance, and the establishment of generic benchmarking standards
●   UK Best Factory Awards (database containing detailed descriptions and performance data of over 600 UK manufacturing plants across a wide spectrum of industries)

Ophthalmology and Vision Science Research Centre

■   Department of Ophthalmology, The Royal Group of Hospitals, Belfast, BT12 6BA.
      028 9034 6278
      http://www.qub.ac.uk/cm/oph
      Director: Prof Alan Stitt.
E   A research centre at Queen's University, Belfast.

Optoelectronics Research Centre (ORC)

■   University of Southampton, Highfield, Southampton, SO17 1BJ.
      023 8059 4521   fax 023 8059 3142
      http://www.orc.soton.ac.uk/
      Director: Prof David N Payne. Deputy Director: Prof David Richardson.
E   A department of the University of Southampton.
○   To conduct research in telecommunications, bio photonics, nano photonics, and optical sensing
●   Education and training
¶   (see website for publications).

Ordnance Test and Evaluation Centre
    see **Cranfield Ordnance Test and Evaluation Centre.**

Organic Centre Wales (OCW) 2000

■   University of Wales, Aberystwyth, Aberystwyth, Ceredigion, SY23 3AL.
      01970 622100; 622248   fax 01970 622238
      http://www.organic.aber.ac.uk/
      Manager: Neil Pearson.
E   A research centre within the Institute of Rural Sciences (qv) at the University of Wales, Aberystwyth.
○   To be the focal point in Wales for the dissemination of information on organic food and farming to producers and other interested parties

Organic Materials Innovation Centre (OMIC)

NR   School of Chemistry, University of Manchester, Oxford Road, Manchester, M13 9PL.
      0161-275 1314   fax 0161-275 4273
      http://www.omic.org.uk/
      Contact: Dr Mike Holmes.
E   A research centre at the University of Manchester.
○   To facilitate knowledge transfer in organic materials to businesses in the UK to help those businesses to innovate and grow
Note: A collaborative project with the 4 other Universities in the North West - Bolton, Liverpool, Liverpool John Moores, and Manchester Metropolitan.

Organic Semiconductor Centre (OSC)

■   School of Physics and Astronomy, University of St Andrews, North Haugh, St Andrews, Fife, KY16 9SS.
      01334 463103   fax 01334 463104
      http://www.st-andrews.ac.uk/~osc/
      Contact: Prof I D W Samuel.
E   An interdisciplinary research centre at the University of St Andrews.
○   To advance organic semiconductors towards applications in the semiconductor, electronics and optoelectronics industries

Organisation and Systems Design Centre
see **Brunel Organisation and Systems Design Centre.**

Oriental Institute
- Faculty of Oriental Studies, University of Oxford, Clarendon Institute Building, Pusey Lane, Oxford, OX1 2LE.
  01865 278200   fax 01865 278190
  http://www.orinst.ox.ac.uk/
- E   An institute at the University of Oxford.
- O   To conduct research on, and teaching in, the language, literature, social sciences, history, archaeology and art history of countries in Near East, Middle East, South and East Asia

Orkney Seal Rescue Centre   (OSR)   1988
- Dyke End, South Ronaldsway, Orkney, KW17 2TJ.
  01856 831463   fax 01856 831463
- E   A registered charity.
- O   To relieve the suffering and distress of seals, and to study and monitor seal behaviour and population in the interest and welfare of seals

Orthopaedic and Rehabilitation Technology Centre
see **Tayside Orthopaedic and Rehabilitation Technology Centre.**

Osteopathic Centre for Children   (OCC)   1991
- 15a Woodbridge Street, London, EC1R 0ND.
  020 7490 5510
  http://www.occ.uk.com/
- E   A registered charity.
- O   To provide treatment for all babies and children, regardless of the family's ability to pay; to train postgraduate osteopaths in paediatrics; to raise public awareness of the benefits of paediatric osteopathy for children; to research into effectiveness of paediatric osteopathy

Outukumpu Research Centre
see **Metal Joining Research Centre.**

Overseas Development Institute   (ODI)   1960
- 111 Westminster Bridge Road, London, SE1 7JD.
  020 7922 0300   fax 020 7922 0399
  http://www.odi.org.uk/
- E   An independent think tank.
- O   To conduct research and inform debate on international development and humanitarian issues

Oxford Centre for Advanced Materials and Composites   (OCAMAC)
- University of Oxford, Parks Road, Oxford, OX1 3PH.
  01865 283777   fax 01865 841943
  http://www.ocamac.ox.ac.uk/
  Director: Dr Richard Todd.
- E   A centre at the University of Oxford.
- O   To foster interdisciplinary research into the scientific and technological problem of processing, properties, design and fabrication associated with advanced materials

Oxford Centre for Buddhist Studies   (OCBS)
- Balliol College, University of Oxford, Oxford, OX1 3BJ.
  http://www.ocbs.org
  Contact: Prof Richard Gombrich.
- E   A research centre at the University of Oxford.

Oxford Centre for Cognitive Neuroscience
see **Oxford McDonnell Centre for Cognitive Neuroscience.**

Oxford Centre for Computational Finance
Note: has merged into the Mathematical and Computational Finance Group of the University of Oxford, and is therefore not within the scope of this directory.

Oxford Centre for Diabetes, Endocrinology and Metabolism   (OCDEM)
- The Churchill Hospital, Headington, Oxford, OX3 7LJ.
  01865 857300
  http://ocdem.customers.composite.net/
- E   A research centre.

Oxford Centre for Enablement   (OCE)   2002
- ■   Windmill Road, Headington, Oxford, OX3 7LD.
    01865 737325   fax 01865 737309
    http://www.noc.nhs.uk/ourservices/neurological_rehabilitation.aspx
    Contact: Dr Rachel Botell.
- E   A research centre.
- ○   To provide a full range of disability and rehabilitation services

Oxford Centre for Environmental Biotechnology   (OCEB)   1997
- ■   Department of Engineering, University of Oxford, 43 Banbury Road, Oxford, OX2 6PE.
    01865 274748   fax 01865 274752
    http://www.eng.ox.ac.uk/oceb/
    Director: Prof C J Knowles.
- E   A research centre at the University of Oxford.

Oxford Centre for Ethics and Communication in Health Care
    see **Ethox Centre.**

Oxford Centre for Ethics and Philosophy of Law   (CEPL)
- ■   Corpus Christi College, University of Oxford, Oxford, OX1 4JF.
    01865 276700
    http://www.univ.ox.ac.uk/cepl/
- E   A research centre at the University of Oxford.

Oxford Centre for Evidence-Based Medicine
    see **Centre for Evidence-Based Medicine.**

Oxford Centre for Functional Magnetic Resonance Imaging of the Brain   (FMRIB)
- ■   Department of Clinical Neurology, John Radcliffe Hospital, Headington, Oxford, OX3 9DU.
    01865 222729   fax 01865 222717
    http://www.fmrib.ox.ac.uk/
    Director: Prof Irene Tracey.
- E   A centre at the University of Oxford.
- ○   To conduct research into determining which parts of the brain are activated by different physical sensation or activity, such as sight, sound, or the movement of a subject's fingers

Oxford Centre for Hebrew and Jewish Studies   1972
- ■   University of Oxford, Yarnton Manor, Yarnton, Oxford, OX5 1PY.
    01865 377946   fax 01865 375079
    http://www.ochjs.ac.uk
    President: Peter Oppenheimer. Bursar: Peter Da Costa.
- E   A registered charity, a company limited by guarantee and an affiliated institution of the University of Oxford.
- ○   To promote teaching and research in Hebrew and Jewish studies; to conduct research into all aspects of Jewish tradition and civilisation to the highest standards of academic excellence
- ●   Conference facilities - Exhibitions - Library Courses for Masters Degree in Jewish Studies (University of Oxford) - Cottages for occupancy by visiting scholars and fellows

Oxford Centre for Higher Education Policy Studies   (OxCHEPS)
- ■   New College, University of Oxford, Oxford, OX1 3BN.
    01865 279536; 279550   fax 01865 279251
    http://oxcheps.new.ac.uk/
    Director: David Palfreyman.
- E   A research centre at the University of Oxford.
- ○   To carry out comparative research in higher education policy and management

Oxford Centre for Hindu Studies   (OCHS)   1997
- ■   University of Oxford, 15 Magdalen Street, Oxford, OX1 3AE.
    01865 304300   fax 01865 304301
    http://www.ochs.org.uk/
- E   A research centre at the University of Oxford.
- ○   To study Hindu culture and tradition

Oxford Centre for Industrial and Applied Mathematics   (OCIAM)
- ■   University of Oxford, 24-29 St Giles', Oxford, OX1 3LB.
    01865 280612   fax 01865 270515
    http://www.maths.ox.ac.uk/ociam
- E   A research centre within the Mathematical Institute (qv) at the University of Oxford.
- ○   To pursue collaborative research with industry and other disciplines, as well as basic research in applied mathematics

Oxford Centre for Islamic Studies (OCIS) 1985

■ University of Oxford, George Street, Oxford, OX1 2AR.
  01865 278743   fax 01865 278741
  http://www.oxcis.ac.uk/
E A research centre at the University of Oxford.

Oxford Centre for Maritime Archaeology (OCMA)

■ School of Archaeology, University of Oxford, 36 Beaumont Street, Oxford, OX1 2PG.
  01865 278240   fax 01865 278254
  http://www.ocma.ox.ac.uk/
  Contact: Jonathan Cole.
E A research centre within the Institute of Archaeology (qv) at the University of Oxford.

Oxford Centre for Mission Studies (OCMS) 1982

■ University of Oxford, PO Box 70, Oxford, OX2 6HB.
  01865 556071   fax 01865 510823
  http://www.ocms.ac.uk/
  Executive Director: Canon Dr V Samuel. Director of Academic Affairs: Dr B Farr.
E A registered charity, a company limited by guarantee and part of the University of Oxford.
O To continue being engaged in effective holistic mission especially amongst the poor and marginalised; to equip leaders, nurture scholars and enable institutions for ministry particularly in the two-thirds world churches
¶ Many publications available.

Oxford Centre for Molecular Sciences (OCMS) 1988

■ Department of Biochemistry, University of Oxford, South Parks Road, Oxford, OX1 3QU.
  01865 275345   fax 01865 275253
  http://www.ocms.ox.ac.uk/
  Director: Prof Iain Campbell, FRS.
E A centre at the University of Oxford.
O To conduct interdisciplinary research into the structure, function and reactivity of protein molecules
● Education and training - Information service

Oxford Centre for Population Research (OCPR)

■ Department of Social Policy and Social Work, Barnett House, University of Oxford, 32 Wellington Square, Oxford, OX1 2ER.
  01865 270345   fax 01865 270324
  http://www.apsoc.ox.ac.uk/Oxpop/
  Director: Prof David Coleman.
E A research centre at the University of Oxford.

Oxford Centre for Publishing Consultancy and Research

Note: is now Oxford Publishing and Digital Media and is therefore outside the scope of this Directory.

Oxford Centre for Science of the Mind (OXCSOM)

■ Department of Pharmacology, University of Oxford, Mansfield Road, Oxford, OX1 3QT.
  01865 280532   fax 01865 271853
  http://www.oxcsom.ox.ac.uk/
  Contact: Ruth Collier.
E An interdisciplinary research centre at the University of Oxford.
O To enrich understanding of the mind, beliefs and consciousness by encouraging cross-fertilization of between conventionally disparate disciplines

Oxford Centre for Staff and Learning Development (OCSLD) 1989

■ Wheatley Campus, Oxford Brookes University, Wheatley, Oxford, OX33 1HX.
  01865 485910   fax 01865 485937
  http://www.brookes.ac.uk/services/ocsld
E A centre at Oxford Brookes University.

Oxford Centre for Water Research (OCWR)

■ School of Geography, University of Oxford, Dyson Perrins Building, South Parks Road, Oxford, OX1 3QY.
  01865 285070   fax 01865 275885
  http://ocwr.ouce.ox.ac.uk/
E A research centre within the Oxford University Centre for the Environment (qv) at the University of Oxford.

Oxford e-Research Centre (OeRC)

■ University of Oxford, e-Science Laboratory Building, 13 Banbury Road, Oxford, OX2 6NN.
  01865 283678   fax 01865 273275
  http://www.oerc.ox.ac.uk/
  Co-Director: Dr Anne Trefethen. Co-Director: Prof Paul Jeffreys.
E A research centre at the University of Oxford.
  See **e-Science Centres** for further information.

Oxford Financial Research Centre (OFRC)

- Saïd Business School, University of Oxford, Wolfson Building, Parks Road, Oxford, OX1 3QD.
  01865 273838   fax 01865 273839
  http://www.finance.ox.ac.uk/
- E   A centre at the University of Oxford.
- O   To bring together researchers in finance working across the University

Oxford Forestry Institute

Note: Now incorporated into the Department of Plant Sciences of the University of Oxford.

Oxford Glycobiology Institute

- Department of Biochemistry, University of Oxford, South Parks Road, Oxford, OX1 3UQ.
  01865 275342   fax 01865 275216
  http://www.bioch.ox.ac.uk/glycob/
  Contact: Dr Mark Wormald.
- E   A department of the University of Oxford.

Oxford Institute of Ageing (OIA)

- University of Oxford, Manor Road Building, Manor Road, Oxford, OX1 3UQ.
  01865 286193   fax 01865 286191
  http://www.ageing.ox.ac.uk/
  Director: Dr Sarah Harper.
- E   An institute at the University of Oxford.
- O   To address ageing at the global, societal and individual level

Oxford Institute for Employee Relations (OXIFER) 1985

- Saïd Business School, University of Oxford, Egrove Park, Oxford, OX1 5NY.
  01865 422738   fax 01865 422501
  http://www.sbs.ox.ac.uk/oxifer
- E   A research centre at the University of Oxford.

Oxford Institute for Energy Studies (OIES) 1982

- 57 Woodstock Road, Oxford, OX2 6FA.
  01865 311377   fax 01865 310527
  http://www.oxfordenergy.org/
  Administrator: Kate Teasdale.
- E   A registered charity, a company limited by guarantee and a membership organisation.
- O   To conduct research encompassing the economics of petroleum, gas, coal, nuclear power, solar and renewable energy; to study the politics and sociology of energy, and the international relations of oil-producing and oil-consuming nations, including the economic development of oil-producing countries and the energy problems of other developing countries

Oxford Institute for Ethics and Communication in Health Care Practice
    see **Ethox Centre.**

Oxford Institute for Information Management (OXIIM)

- Saïd Business School, University of Oxford, 1 Park End Street, Oxford, OX1 1HP.
  01865 278804   fax 01865 288831
  http://www.sbs.ox.ac.uk/oxirm
- E   A research centre at the University of Oxford.

Oxford Institute for Retail Management (OXIRM) 1985

- Saïd Business School, University of Oxford, 1 Park End Street, Oxford, OX1 1HP.
  01865 278804   fax 01865 288831
  http://www.sbs.ox.ac.uk/oxiim
- E   A research centre at the University of Oxford.

Oxford Institute for Sustainable Development (OISD)

- School of the Built Environment, Gipsy Lane Campus, Oxford Brookes University, Headington, Oxford, OX3 0BP.
  01865 483213; 483401
  http://www.brookes.ac.uk/schools/be/oisd
- E   An institute within Oxford Brookes University.
- O   To raise the profile of research into sustainable development

Oxford Intellectual Property Research Centre (OIPRC) 1990

- St Peter's College, University of Oxford, New Inn Hall Street, Oxford, OX1 2DL.
  01865 278952   fax 01865 278855
  http://www.oiprc.ox.ac.uk/
  Director: Prof David Vaver.
- E   A centre at the University of Oxford.
- O   To facilitate and conduct advanced research into all aspects of intellectual property, particularly the proper role of intellectual property in the light of the new technologies

Oxford International Centre for Publishing Studies

■ School of Arts and Humanities, The Richard Hamilton Building, Oxford Brookes University, Oxford, OX3 0BP.
   01865 483665
   http://ah.brookes.ac.uk/publishing/
   Contact: Dr Jane Potter.
E A research centre at Oxford Brookes University.

Oxford Internet Institute   (OII)   2001

■ Social Sciences Division, University of Oxford, 1 St Giles, Oxford, OX1 3JS.
   01865 287210   fax 01865 287211
   http://www.oii.ox.ac.uk/
   Director: Prof William Dutton.
E A department of the University of Oxford.
O To be the world's leading independent centre of excellence in academic research on the impact of the Internet on society, and in informing policy and generating debate

Oxford Learning Institute   (OLI)   2000

■ University of Oxford, Littlegate House, 16-17 St Ebbe's Street, Oxford, OX1 1PT.
   01865 286809
   http://www.learning.ox.ac.uk/
E An institute at the University of Oxford.
O To support excellence in learning, teaching and research at the University
× Institute for the Advancement of University Learning.

Oxford McDonnell Centre for Cognitive Neuroscience   (CCN)   1990

■ University Laboratory of Physiology, University of Oxford, Parks Road, Oxford, OX1 3PT.
   01865 272497   fax 01865 272488
   http://www.cogneuro.ox.ac.uk/
E A centre at the University of Oxford.
O To support and promote interaction between research groups in aspects of basic and clinical neuroscience
Note: Also known as McDonnell Centre for Cognitive Neuroscience.

Oxford Uehiro Centre for Practical Ethics   2002

■ University of Oxford, Littlegate House, St Ebbe's Street, Oxford, OX1 1PT.
   01865 286888   fax 01865 286886
   http://www.practicalethics.ox.ac.uk/
   Director: Prof Julian Savulescu.
E A research centre at the University of Oxford.
O To conduct research in a broad range of practical ethics and moral philosophy

Oxford University Centre for Business Taxation   2005

■ Saïd Business School, University of Oxford, 1 Park End Street, Oxford, OX1 1HP.
   01865 278804   fax 01865 288831
   http://www.sbs.ox.ac.uk/tax
   Director: Michael Devereux.
E A research centre at the University of Oxford.

Oxford University Centre for the Environment   (OUCE)

■ School of Geography, University of Oxford, Dyson Perrins Building, South Parks Road, Oxford, OX1 3QY.
   01865 285070   fax 01865 275885
   http://www.ouce.ox.ac.uk/
   Director: Prof Gordon Clark.
E A centre at the University of Oxford.
O To be a world-class research and educational hub for the natural and social sciences

PACE Centre   1990
■   Paskin and Morris House, Coventon Road, Aylesbury, Buckinghamshire, HP19 3JL.
01296 392739
http://www.pacecentre.co.uk/
Director: Heather Last.
E   A registered charity and a company limited by guarantee.
○   To provide intensive learning programmes, tailored to the individual needs of children with motor impairments (aged 6 months to 12 years)
Note: PACE = Positive Achievement inspired by the principles of Conductive Education.

Pain Management Research Centre
■   University of Abertay Dundee, Bell Street, Dundee, DD1 1HG.
01382 308700   fax 01382 308749
http://www.health.abertay.ac.uk/
Director: Dr David McNaughton.
E   A research centre within the Tayside Institute for Health Studies (qv) at the University of Abertay, Dundee.
○   To specialise in the research and teaching of the management of chronic pain
Note: Also known as the Centre for Research in Pain Management.

Paisley Enterprise Research Centre   (PERC)   1995
■   Paisley Business School, University of Paisley, Paisley, PA1 2BE.
0141-848 3399   fax 0141-848 3618
http://www.paisley.ac.uk/business/perc/
Director: Prof David Deakins.
E   A research centre at the University of Paisley.
○   To produce high quality, policy-relevant applied research
Note: At the time of going to press, the University of Paisley was preparing to merge with Bell College to form the University of the West of Scotland.

PALATINE - Dance, Drama and Music   2000
■   The Great Hall, Lancaster University, Lancaster, LA1 4YW.
01524 592614   fax 01524 593071
http://www.lancs.ac.uk/palatine/
Contact: Barbara Hargreaves.
E   A Government funded national centre within Lancaster University.
○   To foster world-class education in the fields of dance, drama and music
●   Education and training - Information service - Statistics
✕   LTSN Performing Arts Subject Centre.
Note: One of the 24 Subject Centres of the Higher Education Academy, (qv).

Pan-European Institute   1997
■   University of Essex, Wivenhoe Park, Colchester, Essex, CO4 3SQ.
01203 873976   fax 01203 873965
http://www.essex.ac.uk/centres/pei/
Director: Alastair McAuley.
E   A research institute at the University of Essex.

Pankhurst Centre   1987
■   60-62 Nelson Street, Manchester, M13 9WP.
0161-273 5673   fax 0161-274 4979
E   The home of Emmeline Pankhurst and her family.
○   To provide a heritage area open to all and a women-only space where women can learn together, work on projects and socialise

PAPRI: Pension and Population Research Institute   (PAPRI)   1988
■   35 Canonbury Road, London, N1 2DG.
020 7354 5667   fax 020 7226 6601
Director of Research: Patrick Carroll.
E   A registered charity and an independent non-profit-distributing organisation.
○   To conduct research in pensions, demography, investment and insurance
●   Conference facilities - Education and training - Statistics - Publishing research findings

Parallel Applications Centre
see **IT Innovation Centre.**

Parallelism, Algorithms and Architectures Research Centre   (PÅRC
■   Department of Computer Science, Loughborough University, Loughborough, Leicestershire, LE11 3TU.
01509 222692   fax 01509 211586
http://parc.lboro.ac.uk/
Co-Director: Dr Helmut Bez. Co-Director: Dr Ondrej Sykora.
E   A research centre at Loughborough University.
○   To focus research on theoretical problems and computationally challenging tasks of practical interest in the areas of parallel algorithms, concurrency, vision and visualisation, coding and signal processing, future architectures of parallel computers, and fundamental theoretical research

Parkes Institute for the Study of Jewish / non-Jewish Relations   2000
- ■ School of Humanities, The James Parkes Building, University of Southampton, Highfield, Southampton, SO17 1BJ.
     023 8059 2261   fax 023 8059 3458
     http://www.parkes.soton.ac.uk/
     Contact: Prof Anthony Kushner.
- E A research institute at the University of Southampton.
- ○ To act as a regional, national and international research institute in Jewish / non-Jewish relations

Paterson Institute for Cancer Research   (PICR)
- ■ University of Manchester, Wilmslow Road, Withington, Manchester, M20 4BX.
     0161-446 3156   fax 0161-446 3109
     http://www.paterson.man.ac.uk/
     Director: Prof Nic Jones.
- E A department of the University of Manchester.
- ○ To support a wide variety of investigative research programmes spanning both basic and translational cancer research
- ● Various testing facilities including microarrays, confocal microscopy, bioinformatics, histology

Pauling Human Sciences Centre
   see **Institute of Human Sciences.**

Pedagogic Research and Scholarship Institute   (PRSI)   2006
- ■ University of Gloucestershire, The Park, Cheltenham, Gloucestershire, GL50 2RH.
     0870 721 0210
     http://www.glos.ac.uk/research/prsi.cfm
- E A research institute at the University of Gloucestershire.

Pension and Population Research Institute
   see **PAPRI: Pension and Population Research Institute.**

Pensions Institute
- ■ Cass Business School, City University, 106 Bunhill Row, London, EC1Y 8TZ.
     020 7040 0287
     http://www.pensions-institute.org/
     Director: David Blake.
- E A research institute at City University.
- ○ To undertake, or organise, high quality research in all fields related to pensions; to disseminate the results of that research to both the academic and practitioner community; to establish an international network of pension researchers from a variety of disciplines; to provide expert advice to the pensions industry and government

Performance Translation Centre   (PTC)   1997
- ■ Department of Drama and Music, University of Hull, Cottingham Road, Hull, HU7 6RX.
     01482 466210   fax 01482 466727
     Contact: Mrs Paula Lambert.
- E A centre at the University of Hull.
- ○ To provide a structure and focus for the study of questions relating to the translation of dramatic and performance material from English into another language, and from other languages into English; to promote performance translation as an area of research

Note: Also known as the Centre for Performance Translation and Dramaturgy.

Personalised Integrated Learning Support CETL   (PILS)   2005
- ■ Open University, Walton Hall, Milton Keynes, MK7 6AA.
     01908 659357
     http://cetl.open.ac.uk/pils/
     Director: Christina Lloyd.
- E A Centre for Excellence in Teaching and Learning (CETL) at the Open University.

Note: See **Centres for Excellence in Teaching and Learning** for more information.

Peter Harrison Centre for Disability Sport
- ■ School of Sport and Exercise Sciences, Loughborough University, Ashby Road, Loughborough, Leicestershire, LE11 3TU.
     01509 226386
     http://www.peterharrisoncentre.org.uk/
     Director: Ken Black.
- E A research centre at Loughborough University.
- ○ To generate and implement research and development projects in the area of disability sport and inclusive physical activity

Pfizer Institute for Pharmaceutical Materials Science
- ■ Department of Materials Science and Metallurgy, University of Cambridge, Pembroke Street, Cambridge, CB2 3QZ.
     01223 767060   fax 01223 767063
     http://www.msm.cam.ac.uk/pfizer/
- E An institute at the University of Cambridge.
- ○ To conduct research which encompasses all aspects of the structure, manufacture and behaviour of solid dosage forms, such as tablets, at all relevant scales of operation and use

PharmacoEconomics Research Centre   (PERC)   1992
- School of Management, University of St Andrews, The Gateway, North Haugh, St Andrews, Fife, KY16 9SS.
  01334 462810   fax 01334 462812
  http://www.st-andrews.ac.uk/management/index_perc.htm
  Director: Dr Manouche Tavakoli.
- E   A research centre at the University of St Andrews.
- O   To conduct research and provide expert advice and analyses on economic issues in the provision and utilisation of medicines and other health technologies

Note: A collaborative venture with the University of Dundee.

Philosophy Centre
- University of Oxford, 10 Merton Street, Oxford, OX1 4JJ.
  01865 276926   fax 01865 276932
  http://www.philosophy.ox.ac.uk/
  Contact: Prof Robert Merrihew Adams.
- E   A research centre at the University of Oxford.

Photography and the Archive Research Centre   (PARC)   2004
- London College of Communication, University of the Arts, London, Elephant and Castle, London, SE1 6SB.
  020 7514 6625; 6919   fax 020 7514 6535
  http://www.photographyresearchcentre.co.uk/
  Director: Val Williams.
- E   A research centre at the University of the Arts, London.
- O   To raise the profile and improve the quality of research work in photography in the UK

Photon Science Institute   (PSI)   2006
- Faculty of Engineering and Physical Sciences, Simon Building, University of Manchester, Oxford Road, Manchester, M13 9PL.
  0161-275 1000   fax 0161-275 1001
  http://www.psi.manchester.ac.uk/
  Director: Prof Klaus Müller-Dethlefs.
- E   A research centre at the University of Manchester.
- O   To provide a dynamic culture for the progression of new ideas in photon science

Note: The term photon science encompasses all areas where light is used in scientific endeavour - light for science.

Photonics Innovation Centre   (PIC)
- School of Physics and Astronomy, University of St Andrews, North Haugh, St Andrews, Fife, KY16 9SS.
  01334 463327; 467314
  http://www.st-andrews.ac.uk/pic/
  Technical Manager: Dr Cameron Rae. Business Development Manager: Donald Walker.
- E   A centre at the University of St Andrews.
- O   To offer a state-of-the-art facility for application orientated development of photonic and quasi-optical (mm-Wave) devices

Photophysics Research Centre
- Faculty of Engineering, Science and the Built Environment, London South Bank University, 103 Borough Road, London, SE1 0AA.
  020 7815 7564
  http://www.eeie.sbu.ac.uk/research/photo/
  Director: Prof Robert E Imhof.
- E   A research centre at London South Bank University.
- O   To conduct research in the use of optically generated thermal waves in condensed media for measurements ranging from thermal diffusity of engineering materials to properties of live human skin

Physical Sciences Centre   2000
- Department of Chemistry, University of Hull, Cottingham Road, Hull, HU6 7RX.
  http://www.physsci.heacademy.ac.uk/
- E   A Government funded national centre within the University of Hull.
- O   To foster world-class education in the physical sciences
- ●   Education and training - Information service - Statistics
- ×   LTSN Physical Sciences Subject Centre.

Note: One of the 24 Subject Centres of the Higher Education Academy, (qv).

Pig Disease Information Centre   (PDIC)   1996
- 4 New Close Farm Business Park, Bar Road, Lolworth, Cambridgeshire, CB3 8DS.
  01954 780695
  http://www.pighealth.com/
  Chief Executive Officer: Dr Mike Meredith.
- E   A limited company.

© CBD Research Ltd · Beckenham · Kent BR3 5JS · Tel 020 8650 7745 · Fax 020 8650 0768 · E-mail cbd@cbdresearch.com · www.cbdresearch.com

Pinter Centre for Research in Performance   (PCRP)   2003
- Drama Department, Goldsmiths, University of London, London, SE14 6NW.
  020 7919 7414   fax 020 7919 7413
  http://www.goldsmiths.ac.uk/departments/drama/pinter-centre/
  Contact: Gerald Lidstone.
- E   A research centre at Goldsmiths, University of London.
- O   To initiate and promote the development of new methodologies of practice and training in the performing arts

PLaCe
- Bristol School of Art, Media and Design, Bower Ashton Campus, University of the West of England, Kennel Lodge Road, Bristol, BS3 2JT.
  0117-328 4716   fax 0117-328 4745
  http://www.placeresearch.co.uk/
  Director: Prof Paul Gough.
- E   A research centre at the University of the West of England.
- O   To conduct research into issues of place, location and context

Place-Name Research Centre
- Department of Archives and Manuscripts, University of Wales Bangor, Bangor, Gwynedd, LL57 2DG.
  01248 383214
  http://www.bangor.ac.uk/PlaceNames/English
  Director: Prof Hywel Wyn Owen.
- E   A research centre at the University of Wales, Bangor.
- O   To promote place-name studies, with particular reference to Wales

Placement Learning in Health and Social Care CETL
> See **Centre for Excellence in Professional Placement Learning**

Planetary and Space Sciences Research Institute   (PSSRI)
- Faculty of Science, Open University, Walton Hall, Milton Keynes, MK7 6AA.
  01908 655808   fax 01908 858022
  http://pssri.open.ac.uk/
  Head: Dr Ian Wright. Chairman: Prof Colin T Pillinger.
- E   A research institute within the Centre for Earth, Planetary, Space and Astronomical Research (qv) at the Open University.
- O   To develop high sensitivity, high precision, stable isotope instrumentation and methodology for laboratory and space projects; to study the nature and effects of interplanetary dust and its hypervelocity impacts

Plymouth Electron Microscopy Centre
- Faculty of Science, University of Plymouth, Drake Circus, Plymouth, PL4 8AA.
  01752 233092
  http://www.plymouth.ac.uk/pages/view.asp?page=12257
  Manager: Dr Roy Moate.
- E   A research centre at the University of Plymouth.

Plymouth Environmental Research Centre
Note: No longer in existence.

Plymouth International Studies Centre   (PISC)   1997
- School of Geography, 9 Portland Villas, University of Plymouth, Drake Circus, Plymouth, PL4 8AA.
  01752 233204   fax 01752 233206
  http://www.research.plymouth.ac.uk/pisc/
  Director: Prof Richard Gibb.
- E   A research centre at the University of Plymouth.
- O   To enhance the research base for staff in various disciplines who are working in areas related to international studies

Poetry Centre
> see **Manchester Poetry Centre.**

Poetry Translation Centre   (PTC)   2004
- Faculty of Arts and Humanities, University of London, Thornhaugh Street, Russell Square, London, WC1H 0XG.
  020 7898 4367   fax 020 7898 4239
  http://www.poetrytranslation.soas.ac.uk/
- E   A research centre at the School of Oriental and African Studies, University of London.
- O   To translate contemporary poetry from non-European languages into English to the highest literary standards through a series of collaborations between leading international poets and poets based in the UK

Polar Research Institute
> see **Scott Polar Research Institute.**

Policy Centre
> see **Nottingham Policy Centre.**

Policy, Ethics and Life Sciences Research Centre   (PEALS)   1999

NR   School of Geography, Politics and Sociology, University of Newcastle upon Tyne, Life Bioscience Centre, Times Square, Newcastle upon Tyne, NE1 4EP.
       0191-241 8614   fax 0191-243 8233
       http://www.ncl.ac.uk/peals/
       Executive Director: Prof Erica Haimes.

E   A research centre within the Centre for Life (qv) at the University of Newcastle upon Tyne.

O   To research, inform and improve policy, professional practice and participation in the life sciences, with particular emphasis on the promotion of research and debate on the social and ethical aspects of genetics and other life sciences

Note: A joint venture with the University of Durham and the Centre for Life (qv).

Policy Research Institute   (PRI)   1987

■   Faculty of Business and Law, Leeds Metropolitan University, 22 Queen Square, Leeds, LS2 8AF.
       0113-283 1960   fax 0113-283 1961
       http://www.leedsmet.ac.uk/lbs/pri/
       Director: Steven Johnson.

E   A department of Leeds Metropolitan University.

O   To conduct high quality applied economic and social research

Policy Research Institute   (PRI)

■   University of Wolverhampton, Wolverhampton Science Park, Glaisher Drive, Wolverhampton, WV10 9RU.
       01902 824103   fax 01902 824005
       http://www.wlv.ac.uk/pri/
       Director: Prof Dee Cook.

E   A research institute at the University of Wolverhampton.

O   To provide social research in the areas of community justice and community safety, community consultation and empowerment, social capital and community networks, and social inclusion and exclusion

Policy Studies Institute   (PSI)   1998

■   50 Hanson Street, London, W1W 6UP.
       020 7911 7500   fax 020 7911 7501
       http://www.psi.org.uk/
       Director: Malcolm Rigg.

E   An independent subsidiary of the University of Westminster.

O   To undertake and publish research studies relevant to social, economic and social policy

Political Economy Research Centre   (PERC)   1993

■   Department of Politics, University of Sheffield, Elmfield Lodge, Northumberland Road, Sheffield, S10 2TY.
       0114-222 0660   fax 0114-222 1717
       http://www.shef.ac.uk/perc/
       Administrator: Sylvia McColm.

E   A research centre at the University of Sheffield.

O   To explore new approaches to politics and economics that jointly challenge our existing explanations of human behaviour

Polymer Centre
      see **Sheffield Polymer Centre.**

Polymer Processing Research Centre   (PPRC)

■   School of Mechanical and Manufacturing Engineering, Queen's University, Belfast, Ashby Building, Stranmillis Road, Belfast, BT9 5AH.
       028 9097 4700   fax 028 9066 0631
       http://www.qub.ac.uk/research-centres/PolymerProcessingResearchCentre/
       Director: Gerry McNally.

E   A centre at Queen's University, Belfast.

O   To provide the necessary technological infrastructure to support the activities of the plastics industry

Polymer Science Centre   (PSC)

■   J J Thomson Physical Laboratory, University of Reading, Reading, Berkshire, RG6 6AF.
       0118-378 8573   fax 0118-975 0203
       http://www.rdg.ac.uk/psc/

E   A research centre at the University of Reading.

O   To conduct research in the theory, design, synthesis, and physical study of organic and inorganic polymeric materials

Population Centre
      see **Sir David Owen Population Centre.**

Portsmouth Centre for Enterprise   2000

■ Faculty of Creative and Cultural Industries, University of Portsmouth, Floor 9 - Mercantile House, Hampshire Terrace, Portsmouth, PO1 2EG.
    023 9284 3543   fax 023 9284 5626
    http://www.port.ac.uk/departments/academic/enterprise/
    Manager: Tony Greatbatch.
E   A department of the University of Portsmouth.
○   To inspire students to learn and succeed in entrepreneurship through developing enterprise skills and experience

Positive Achievement inspired by the principles of Conductive Education Centre
    see **PACE Centre.**

Positron Imaging Centre   1984

■ School of Physics and Astronomy, University of Birmingham, Edgbaston, Birmingham, B15 2TT.
    0121-414 4564   fax 0121-414 4644
    http://www.np.ph.bham.ac.uk/pic/
    Contact: Dr D J Parker.
E   A centre at the University of Birmingham.
○   To study flow techniques using positron emitting radioactive tracers

Post-Adoption Centre   (PAC)   1986

■ 5 Torriano Mews, Torriano Avenue, London, NW5 2RZ.
    020 7284 0555 (office); 0870 777 2197 (advice line)   fax 0870 777 2167
    http://www.postadoptioncentre.org.uk/
    Fundraising Manager: Christine Billings. Training Manager: Maggie Rogers.
E   An independent non-profit-distributing organisation and an association with a voluntary subscribing membership.
○   To provide advice, support and information for anyone involved in adoption; to relieve mental distress, strengthen family relationships and inform and improve professional practice
●   Education and training - Information service - Counselling
¶   Annual Report. ImPACt (newsletter). Directory of Approved Counsellors. (many other publications).

Postgraduate Institute for Medicine and Dentistry

■ University of Newcastle upon Tyne, 10-12 Framlington Place, Newcastle upon Tyne, NE2 4AB.
    0191-222 6772   fax 0191-221 1049
    http://www.pimd.co.uk/
E   An institute within the University of Newcastle upon Tyne.
○   To train and assess medical and dental staff in the Northern Deanery
●   Education and training

Powertrain and Vehicle Research Centre   (PVRC)

■ Department of Mechanical Engineering, University of Bath, Claverton Down, Bath, BA2 7AY.
    01225 383870   fax 01225 386928
    http://www.bath.ac.uk/mech-eng/auto/
    Contact: Prof Gary Hawley.
E   A research centre at the University of Bath.
○   To conduct research in powertrain and vehicle systems

Practice-based Professional Learning CETL   (PBPL)   2005

■ Walton Hall, Milton Keynes, MK7 6AA.
    01908 653536
    http://cetl.open.ac.uk/pbpl/
    Director: Prof Peter Knight.
E   A Centre for Excellence in Teaching and Learning (CETL) within the Institute of Educational Technology (qv) at the Open University.
Note: See **Centres for Excellence in Teaching and Learning** for more information.

Praxis Centre - Centre for the Study of Information and Technology in Peace, Conflict Resolution and Human Rights

■ School of Applied Global Ethics, Leeds Metropolitan University, The Northern Terrace - Queen Square Court, Civic Quarter, Leeds, LS1 3HE.
    0113-283 2600; 3113   fax 0113-283 3114
    http://praxis.leedsmet.ac.uk/
E   A research centre at Leeds Metropolitan University.
○   To investigate all aspects of the effects of information technology in the context of peace and conflict studies

Precision Engineering Centre

■ Materials Department, Building 61, Cranfield University, Cranfield, Bedfordshire, MK43 0AL.
    01234 754086
    http://www.cranfield.ac.uk/sas/materials/precisionengineering/
    Contact: Prof P Shore.
E   A research centre at Cranfield University.
○   To conduct precision engineering using advanced techniques, including ultra-high precision diamond turning, micro-machining, precision grinding, superabrasive machining, machining process monitoring and modelling, and the Barkhausen noise technique

Primary Care Musculoskeletal Research Centre
- Keele University, Keele, Staffordshire, ST5 5BG.
  01782 583905   fax 01782 583911
  http://www.keele.ac.uk/research/pchs/pcmrc/
  Co-Director: Prof Peter Croft. Co-Director: Prof Elaine Hay.
- E   A research centre at Keele University.
- O   To conduct research into two main programmes, in the fields of epidemiology of pain and joint problems, and in intervention studies in musculoskeletal pain

Primary Care Training Centre Ltd   (PCTC)   1996
- Crow Trees, 27 Town Lane, Bradford, West Yorkshire, BD10 8NT.
  01274 617617   fax 01274 621621
  http://www.primarycaretraining.co,uk
  Clinical Director: Dr Paul Sheldon. Finance Director: Mark Sheldon.
- E   A profit-making business.
- O   To educate medical professionals and support staff in all aspects of primary care
- ● Conference facilities - Education and training

Prince of Wales International Centre for Research into Schizophrenia and Depression   (POWIC/SANE   1994
- Warneford Hospital, Oxford, OX3 7JX.
  01865 455918
  http://www.sane.org.uk/public_html/Research/Oxford.shtm
  Director: Prof Tim Crow.
- O   To study all types of mental illness

Prisons Research Centre
- University of Cambridge, Sidgwick Avenue, Cambridge, CB3 9DT.
  01223 335364   fax 01223 335356
  http://www.crim.cam.ac.uk/research/prc/
  Director: Dr Alison Liebling. Administrator: Ann Phillips.
- E   A research centre within the Institute of Criminology (qv) at the University of Cambridge.

Private Equity Institute   (PEI)
- London Business School, Sussex Place, Regent's Park, London, NW1 4SA.
  020 7262 5050   fax 020 7724 6573
  http://www.london.edu/privateequityinstitute.html
  Executive Director: Senia Rapisarda.
- E   A research centre at the London Business School.
- O   To advance the understanding of private equity and venture capital by conducting objective, reliable research and providing a forum for disseminating accurate, meaningful information and current trends and challenges, sharing insights and solutions

Private Equity and Venture Capital Research Centre   (PERC)
- Cass Business School, City University, 106 Bunhill Row, London, EC1Y 8TZ.
  020 7040 8774
  http://www.cass.city.ac.uk/perc/
  Director: Prof Robert Cressy.
- E   A centre at City University.
- O   To conduct research to investigate the structure, functioning and performance of private equity firms and their investee companies, especially (but not exclusively) within the European Community

Product and Knowledge Research Centre   (PKRC)
- Psalter Lane Campus, Sheffield Hallam University, Sheffield, S11 8UZ.
  0114-225 2669
  http://www.shu.ac.uk/research/c3ri/pk.html
- E   A research centre within the Cultural, Communication and Computing Research Institute (qv) at Sheffield Hallam University.

Progressive Supranuclear Palsy Research Centre
> see **Sara Koe PSP Research Centre.**

Promethean Centre of Excellence
- Manchester Metropolitan University, 799 Wilmslow Road, Didsbury, Manchester, M20 2RR.
  0161-247 2007; 2371   fax 0161-247 6377
  http://www.ioe.mmu.ac.uk/promethean/
  Director: Maureen Haldane.
- E   A research centre within the Institute of Education (qv) at Manchester Metropolitan University.
- O   To demonstrate and promote the highest quality of learning, teaching and training at all levels through the innovation, development and effective use of learning technologies

PSP Research Centre
> see **Sara Koe PSP Research Centre.**

Psychological Therapies Research Centre   (PTRC)   1995
■   Faculty of Medicine and Health, University of Leeds, 17 Blenheim Terrace, Leeds, LS2 9JT.
    0113-343 5699
    http://www.psych.leeds.ac.uk/ptrc/
    Director: Prof Michael Barkham.
E   A research centre within the Institute of Psychological Sciences (qv) at the University of Leeds.

Psychology Network   2000
■   Department of Psychology, University of York, Heslington, York, YO10 5DD.
    01904 433154   fax 01904 433181
    http://www.psychology.heacademy.ac.uk/
E   A Government funded national centre within the University of York.
○   To foster world-class education in psychology
●   Education and training - Information service - Statistics
✕   LTSN Psychology Subject Centre.
Note: One of the 24 Subject Centres of the Higher Education Academy, (qv).

Psychotherapy Centre   (TPC)   1958
■   67 Upper Berkeley Street, London, W1H 7QX.
    020 7723 6173
    http://www.the-psychotherapy-centre.com/
E   A private venture.

Publishing Training Centre at Book House   (PTC)   1979
■   45 East Hill, Wandsworth, London, SW18 2QZ.
    020 8874 2718   fax 020 8870 8985
    http://www.train4publishing.co.uk/
    Chief Executive: John Whitley.
E   A registered charity and an independent non-profit-making organisation.
○   To provide effective and high quality training for publishers in the UK and overseas

Pulp and Paper Information Centre
Note: is the Confederaton of Paper Industries and is therefore outside the scope of this Directory.

Puppet Centre Trust   (PCT)   1974
■   Battersea Arts Centre, Lavender Hill, London, SW11 5TN.
    020 7228 8335
    http://www.puppetcentre.org.uk
    Chairman: Prof Anthony Dean. Managing Director: Barry Smith.
E   A registered charity and a company limited by guarantee.
○   To support artists using puppetry; to encourage the use of puppetry within a variety of other performing arts and disciplines; to
    advocate the art form
●   Education and training - Library - Commissions - Bursaries
¶   Alive and Kicking (annual). Animations (journal).

Quaker International Centre
Note: The Centre closed in 2004.

Quality Centre
■ School of Engineering and Science, University of Paisley, Paisley, PA1 2BE.
  0141-848 3669   fax 0141-848 3663
  http://www.paisley.ac.uk/es/consultancy.asp
E A department of the University of Paisley.
○ To provide education, training, research and consultancy on quality management, technology and engineering
Note: At the time of going to press, the University of Paisley was preparing to merge with Bell College to form the University of the West of Scotland.

Quality in Education Centre   (QIE)
■ Department of Educational and Professional Studies, Sir Henry Wood Building, University of Strathclyde, 76 Southbrae Drive, Glasgow, G13 1PP.
  0141-950 3186   fax 0141-950 3172
  http://www.strath.ac.uk/qie/
  Director: Summer Kenesson.
E A research centre at the University of Strathclyde.
○ To improve the quality of education

Queen Elizabeth House International Development Centre   1954
■ Department of International Development, Queen Elizabeth House, University of Oxford, Mansfield Road, Oxford, OX1 3TB.
  01865 281800   fax 01865 281801
E A centre at the University of Oxford.

Queen Elizabeth's Foundation Mobility Centre   (QEF Mobility Centre)   1981
■ Damson Way, Fountain Drive, Carshalton, Surrey, SM5 4NR.
  020 8770 1151   fax 020 8770 1211
  http://www.qefd.org/mobilitycentre/
  Centre Manager: Sue Vernon. Operations Manager: Sal Grier.
E A registered charity.
○ To provide information, assessment and training on all aspects of outdoor mobility for disabled and elderly people
● Conference facilities - Education and training - Exhibitions - Information service - Overnight accommodation rental
¶ Annual Report. Mobility Centre Leaflets. Bungalow Accommodation Leaflets.
✕ Banstead Mobility Centre.

Queen Victoria Hospital Blond McIndoe Research Foundation   1960
■ Queen Victoria Hospital, Holtye Road, East Grinstead, West Sussex, RH19 3DZ.
  01342 414295   fax 01342 414550
  http://www.blondmcindoe.com/
  Operations Director: Heather Shearer. Head of Research: Dr Elizabeth James Phd
E A registered charity and a company limited by guarantee.
○ To protect and preserve public health by the promotion and carrying out of research into tissue regeneration, replacement and reconstruction, wound healing, burns and plastic surgery; to advance the education of scientists, doctors and other health professionals; to advance the education of the public
● Statistics
¶ Annual Report.
Note: Generally known as the Blond McIndoe Centre.

Queen's Medical Centre
Note: is now the Queen's Campus Hospital and therefore no longer within the scope of this directory.

Queen's Medical Research Institute
■ University of Edinburgh, 47 Little France Crescent, Edinburgh, EH16 4TJ.
  0131-242 9515   fax 0131-242 6578
  http://www.mvm.ed.ac.uk/LittleFrance/RI
E A research institute at the University of Edinburgh.

Queen's University Environmental Science and Technology Research Centre   (QUESTOR)   1989
■ David Keir Building, Queen's University Belfast, Stranmillis Road, Belfast, BT9 5AG.
  028 9097 5577   fax 028 9066 1462
  http://questor.qub.ac.uk/
  Director: Dr Wilson McGarel.
E A centre at Queen's University, Belfast.
○ To carry out a broad spectrum of research and development projects on environmental issues

Queen's University Ionic Liquid Laboratories (QUILL Centre) 1999
- ■ David Keir Building, Queen's University Belfast, Stranmillis Road, Belfast, BT9 5AG.
   028 9097 5577   fax 028 9066 1462
   http://quill.qub.ac.uk/
   Co-Director: Prof Jim Swandall, OBE. Co-Director: Prof Ken Seddon.
- E A centre at Queen's University, Belfast.
- ○ To provide training in industrial applications of ionic liquids for sustainable chemistry

QUILL Centre
   see **Queen's University Ionic Liquid Laboratories.**

Quoile Countryside Centre   1988
- ■ 5 Quay Road, Downpatrick, County Down, BT30 7JB.
   028 4461 5520   fax 028 4461 3280
   Regional Manager: Dr Shaun D'Accy-Burt.
- E A statutory organisation.
- ○ To provide information about the Quoile Pondage and many other nature reserves in the area
- ● Education and training - Information service

R S Thomas Study Centre   2000   Canolfan Astudiaeth R S Thomas
- Department of English, University of Wales, Bangor, Bangor, Gwynedd, LL57 2DG.
  01248 382102; 382240
  http://www.bangor.ac.uk/rsthomas/
  Contact: Jason Walford-Davies. Contact: Dr Tony Brown.
- E   A research centre at the University of Wales, Bangor.
- O   To study the work of the poet Ronald Stuart Thomas

Radio Advertising Bureau   (RAB)   1992
- RadioCentre, 77 Shaftesbury Avenue, London, W1D 5DU.
  020 7306 2500
  http://www.rab.co.uk/
  Strategic Solutions Director: Peter Cory.
- E   Funded by commercial radio stations.
- O   To advise national advertisers and advertising agencies on commercial radio advertising campaigns; to run training courses free of charge for national advertisers and their agencies; to conduct research on advertisement awareness, sales, response, brand building, radio's multiplier effect, radio listening, and measuring radio's effect

Radio Licensing Centre
   see **Ofcom Licensing Centre.**

Rail Research UK   (RRUK)
- School of Engineering, University of Birmingham, Gisbert Kapp, Prittchatts Road, Birmingham, B15 2TT.
  0121-414 5063   fax 0121-414 3145
  http://portal.railresearch.org.uk/RRUK/default.aspx
- E   A research centre at the University of Birmingham.
- O   To support the UK railway industry by providing a focal point for university-based world class research
Note: A collaborative venture with eight other UK universities.

Railway Centre
   see **Didcot Railway Centre.**

Rainbow Centre   1985
- 27 Lilymead Avenue, Bristol, BS4 2BY.
  0117-985 3343; 3354
  http://www.rainbowcentre.org.uk/
- E   A registered charity.
- O   To provide a haven of peace for children and their families who are suffering from the effects of bereavement, cancer and life-threatening illness

Rainbow Resource Centre
   see **Sumac Centre.**

Random Systems Research Centre
   see **Brunel University Random Systems Research Centre.**

Raphael Samuel History Centre   1995
- School of Social Sciences, Media and Cultural Studies, Docklands Campus, University of East London, 4-6 University Way, London, E16 2RD.
  020 8223 2756; 7692
  http://www.uel.ac.uk/smcs/research/raphael-samuel.htm
  Co-Director: Prof Barbara Taylor. Co-Director: Dr John Marriott.
- E   A research centre at the University of East London.

Rapid Design and Manufacture Centre
Note: No longer in existence.

Raptor Centre   1977
- Ivy Cottage, Groombridge, Royal Tunbridge Wells, Kent, TN3 9QG.
  01892 861175
  http://www.raptorcentre.co.uk/
- E   A charitable organisation.
- O   A conservation centre for birds of prey

Ravenscroft Centre
Note: No longer in existence.

Raymond Williams Centre for Recovery Research   (RW)   1995
- School of Arts and Humanities, Nottingham Trent University, Clifton Lane, Nottingham, NG11 8NS.
   0115-848 3060
   http://english.ntu.ac.uk/raymondwilliamscentre/
   Contact: Roberta Davari-Zanjani.
- E   A research centre within the Nottingham Institute for English Research (qv) at Nottingham Trent University.
- O   To bring together individual researchers with a collective interest in resistance, radical writing and publishing, recovery research and cultural theory
Note: Raymond Williams (1921-1988), cultural historian, critic, theorist and commentator.

RCN Development Centre
- Faculty of Health and Social Care, London South Bank University, 103 Borough Road, London, SE1 0AA.
   020 7815 8000   fax 020 7815 8099
   http://www.lsbu.ac.uk/health/cn_dev.shtml
   Contact: Susan McLaren.
- E   A research centre at London South Bank University.
- O   To develop and deliver leading edge nursing programmes, underpinned by innovative research and practice development

REACH (National Advice Centre for Children with Reading Difficulties)
Note: No longer in existence.

Reading e-Science Centre   (ReSC)   2003
- Department of Computer Science, University of Reading, Harry Pitt Builidng, 3 Earley Gates, Reading, Berkshire, RG6 6AL.
   0118-931 8615   fax 0118-975 1994
   http://www.resc.rdg.ac.uk/
   Co-Director: Prof Keith Haines. Co-Director: Prof Rachel Harrison.
- E   A research centre at the University of Reading.
Note: See **e-Science Centres of Excellence** for further information.

Red Centre for Herring Research
- 15 Wickham Road Beckenham Kent, BR3 5JS.
Note: This is a control entry.

Reformation Studies Institute
   see **Saint Andrews Reformation Studies Institute.**

Refugee Research Centre   (RRC)
- School of Social Sciences, Media and Cultural Studies, Docklands Campus, University of East London, 4-6 University Way, London, E16 2RD.
   020 8223 7690
   http://www.uel.ac.uk/ssmcs/research/rrc/
   Contact: Phil Marfleet.
- E   A research centre at the University of East London.
- O   To study forced migration at the local, national and global levels

Refugee Studies Centre   (RSC)   1982
- Department of International Development, University of Oxford, Queen Elizabeth House, Mansfield Road, Oxford, OX1 3TB.
   01865 270722   fax 01865 270721
   http://www.rsc.ox.ac.uk/
   Director: Prof Roger Zetter.
- E   A centre at the University of Oxford.
- O   To carry out multidisciplinary research into the causes and consequences of forced migration, with an emphasis on understanding the experiences of those affected

Regeneration Institute
- Cardiff School of City and Regional Planning, Cardiff University, Glamorgan Building, King Edward VII Avenue, Cardiff, CF10 3WA.
   029 2087 6412   fax 029 2087 4846
   http://www.cf.ac.uk/cplan/ri
   Director: Dr Robert Smith.
- E   A centre at Cardiff University.
- O   To act as a vehicle for research in area-based regeneration, embracing academic and policy-related research at both local and international levels

Regional Centre for Manufacturing Industry   (RCMI)   1998
- Faculty of Technology, University of Portsmouth, Portland Building, Portland Street, Portsmouth, PO1 3AH.
   023 9284 2011   fax 023 9284 2584
   http://www.port.ac.uk/departments/faculties/facultyoftechnology/southeastknowledgeexchange/partnerspecialisms/
- E   A centre at the University of Portsmouth.
- O   To deliver services in design and manufacturing innovation

Regional Economics Centre
   see **Manchester Regional Economics Centre.**

Regional Sports Performance Centre   (RSPC)
- Faculty of Health and Sciences, Staffordshire University, Mellor Building, College Road, Stoke-on-Trent, ST4 2DF.
  01782 294648
  http://www.staffs.ac.uk/schools/sciences/ihr/rspc/
- E   A research centre within the Institute for Health Research (qv) at Staffordshire University.
- O   To help athletes maximise their potential, by providing sport science support services to teams and individual athletes

Rehabilitation Resource Centre   (RRC)   1984
- St Bartholomew School of Nursing and Midwifery, City University, 20 Bartholomew Close, London, EC1A 7QN.
  020 7040 5783
  http://www.city.ac.uk/sonm/rrc/
- E   A centre at City University.
- O   To improve the employment and training opportunities of people with disabilities

Reinvention Centre for Undergraduate Research   2005
- The Learning Grid, University of Warwick, University House, Coventry, CV4 8UW.
  024 7657 4953
  http://www2.warwick.ac.uk/fac/soc/sociology/research/cetl/
  Director: Dr Mike Neary.
- E   A Centre for Excellence in Teaching and Learning (CETL) at the University of Warwick.
- Note: See **Centres for Excellence in Teaching and Learning** for more information.

Religious Education Centre in York
   see **David Hope RE Centre in York.**

Research Centre for Advancing Innovation and Management   (AIM)
- Faculty of Business, Computing and Law, University of Derby, Kedleston Road, Derby, DE22 1GB.
  01332 591896   fax 01332 597741
  http://dbs.derby.ac.uk/
  Contact: Bill Murphy.
- E   A research centre at the University of Derby.
- O   To fulfil the research aim of the Faculty of Business, Computing and Law

Research Centre for American Studies   (RCAS)
- Department of American Studies, King's College London, Strand, London, WC2R 2LS.
  020 7848 2551
  http://www.kcl.ac.uk/humanities/
  Director: Dr Alan Marshall.
- E   A research centre at King's College, London.

Research Centre in Applied Sciences   (RCAS)   2005
- School of Applied Sciences, City Campus South, University of Wolverhampton, Wulfruna Street, Wolverhampton, WV1 1SB.
  01902 322667   fax 01902 322714
  http://www.wlv.ac.uk/Default.aspx?page=8860
- E   A research institute at the University of Wolverhampton.
- O   To encourage, support and manage research into the applied sciences

Research Centre for Clinical Kinaesiology   1999
- Cardiff School of Healthcare Studies, Cardiff University, Heath Park, Cardiff, CF14 4XN.
  029 2074 2907
  http://www.cardiff.ac.uk/healthcarestudies/Research
- E   A centre at Cardiff University.
- O   To analyse movement in order to measure particular characteristics such as walking, jogging, sit-to-standing and standing balance

Research Centre for Education and Professional Practice   1998
- School of Education, University of Derby, Kedleston Road, Derby, DE22 1GB.
  01332 591703
  http://www.derby.ac.uk/research/research-centre-for-education-and-professional-practice
  Contact: Prof Marie-Parker Jenkins.
- E   A centre at the University of Derby.
- O   To provide an organisational framework for research in issues of policy and practice

Research Centre for the Education of the Visually Handicapped
   see **Visual Impairment Centre for Teaching and Research.**

© CBD Research Ltd · Beckenham · Kent BR3 5JS · Tel 020 8650 7745 · Fax 020 8650 0768 · E-mail cbd@cbdresearch.com · www.cbdresearch.com

Research Centre for English and Applied Linguistics   (RCEAL)
- University of Cambridge, 9 West Road, Cambridge, CB3 9DP.
  01223 767397   fax 01223 767398
  http://www.rceal.cam.ac.uk/
  Director: Prof John Hawkins.
- E   A centre at the University of Cambridge.
- ○   To conduct and promote research in English and applied linguistics

Research Centre for Environmental History
   see **AHRC Research Centre for Environmental History.**

Research Centre for Evacuee and War Child Studies   (ResCEW)   2004
- Bulmershe Court, University of Reading, Earley, Reading, Berkshire, RG6 1HY.
  0118-378 5824
  http://www.extra.rdg.ac.uk/evacueesarchive/
  Director: Dr Martin Parsons. Contact: Sue Coffey.
- E   A research centre within the Institute of Education (qv) at the University of Reading.
- ○   To conduct research and teaching into evacuees and war children

Research Centre for the Evolution of Cultural Diversity
   see **AHRC Research Centre for the Evolution of Cultural Diversity.**

Research Centre in Evolutionary Anthropology and Palaeoecology   (RCEAP)
- School of Biological and Earth Sciences, James Parsons Building, Liverpool John Moores University, Byrom Street, Liverpool, L3 3AF.
  0151-231 2488   fax 0151-207 3224
  http://www.ljmu.ac.uk/rceap/
  Contact: Dr Filippo Aureli.
- E   A research centre at Liverpool John Moores University.
- ○   To study humanness within a biological and evolutionary framework, and the interaction of organisms with their physical and biotic environments in the past

Research Centre for Future Communications
- Faculty of Performance, Visual Arts and Communications, Level 6 - Worsley Medical and Dental Building, University of Leeds, Leeds, LS2 9JT.
  0113-343 5805   fax 0113-343 5808
  http://ics.leeds.ac.uk/
  Director: Michael Svennevig.
- E   A research centre within the Institute of Communications Studies (qv) at the University of Leeds.

Research Centre for German and Austrian Exile Studies   1995
- School of Advanced Study, University of London, Senate House, Malet Street, London, WC1E 7HU.
  020 7862 8677
  http://igrs.sas.ac.uk/
- E   A research centre within the Institute of Germanic and Romance Studies (qv) at the University of London.
- ○   To focus research on the history of those German-speaking emigrés from Austria, Germany, Czechoslovakia, Hungary, Poland and other European countries, who found refuge in Great Britain, mainly in the 1930s and 1940s but also during earlier times
- ●   Exile archive

Research Centre for the History and Analysis of Recorded Music
   see **AHRC Research Centre for the History and Analysis of Recorded Music.**

Research Centre for the Holocaust and 20th-Century History   1998
- Department of German, Royal Holloway University of London, Egham, Surrey, TW20 0EX.
  01784 443201   fax 01784 470180
  http://www.rhul.ac.uk/german/
  Director: Prof Peter Longerich.
- E   A research centre at Royal Holloway, University of London.

Research Centre for Illuminated Manuscripts   (RCIM)
- Somerset House, Strand, London, WC2R 0RN.
  020 7848 2777
  http://www.courtauld.ac.uk/research/rcims/rcims.html
- E   A research centre within the Courtauld Institute of Art (qv) at the University of London.

Research Centre for Late Antique and Byzantine Studies
- Whiteknights, PO Box 216, University of Reading, Reading, Berkshire, RG6 6AA.
  0118-931 8148
  http://www.rdg.ac.uk/byzantinestudies/
  Director: Dr Ken Dark.
- E   A research centre at the University of Reading.

Research Centre for the Learning Society   (RCLS)   2000
- ■   School of Education and Lifelong Learning, St Luke's Campus, University of Exeter, Heavitree Road, Exeter, EX1 2LU.
  01392 264939
  http://www.education.ex.ac.uk/pages.php?id=152
  Co-Director: Prof William Richardson. Co-Director: Prof Gert Biesta.
- E   A centre at the University of Exeter.
- O   To evaluate through independent research, the coherence and effectiveness of policies and programmes designed to bring about the learning society

Research Centre for Literature and Cultural History   1998
- ■   School of Media, Critical and Creative Arts, Dean Walters Building, Liverpool John Moores University, St James Road, Liverpool, L1 7BR.
  0151-231 5196   fax 0151-231 5049
  http://www.ljmu.ac.uk/mcc/englishresearch/
  Contact: Amanda Greening.
- E   A research centre within Liverpool John Moores University.
- O   To foster interdisciplinary research into the perspective methodologies of cultural historians and literary critics

Research Centre in Modern and Contemporary Poetry   1998
- ■   School of Arts and Humanities, Oxford Brookes University, Oxford, OX3 0BP.
  01865 483665
  http://ah.brookes.ac.uk/english/poetry/
  Contact: Dr Rachel Brown.
- E   A research centre at Oxford Brookes University.
- O   To involve academics and poets in the discussion of central themes and ideas relating to British, Irish, American and post-colonial poetry (in English) across the twentieth and into the twenty-first century

Research Centre in Non-destructive Evaluation   (RCNDE)
- NR   Department of Mechanical Engineering, Imperial College London, Exhibition Road, London, SW7 2AZ.
  020 7594 7216   fax 020 7584 1560
  http://www.rcnde.ac.uk/
  Director: Chris Scruby.
- E   A research centre at Imperial College London.
- Note: A collaborative venture with the University of Strathclyde.

Research Centre for Organisational Excellence   (COrE)
- ■   Faculty of Business, Law and the Built Environment, University of Salford, Salford, Manchester, M5 4WT.
  0161-295 2479; 5750   fax 0161-295 3821
  http://www.mams.salford.ac.uk/mams/pages/page_main.php?s=5
  Director: Dr John Davies.
- E   A research centre within the Management and Management Sciences Research Institute (qv) at the University of Salford.
- O   To focus on understanding and developing the concepts and practice of organisational excellence, in all types of organisation, including commercial businesses, charities and public sector enterprises

Research Centre for the Philosophy of Logic, Language, Mathematics and Mind
   see **AHRC Research Centre for the Philosophy of Logic, Language, Mathematics and Mind.**

Research Centre for Social Sciences   (RCSS)   1984
- ■   Old Surgeons' Hall, University of Edinburgh, High School Yards, Edinburgh, EH1 1LZ.
  0131-650 6387
  http://www.issti.ed.ac.uk/centres/researchcentre/1
  Director: Prof Robin Williams.
- E   A research centre within the Institute for the Study of Science, Technology and Innovation (qv) at the University of Edinburgh.
- O   To promote and host multidisciplinary socio-economic research on technology, innovation and society

Research Centre in Sport, Exercise and Performance
- ■   School of Sport, Performing Arts and Leisure, Walsall Campus, University of Wolverhampton, Gorway Road, Walsall, West Midlands, WS1 3BD.
  01902 322898   fax 01902 322894
  http://www.wlv.ac.uk/Default.aspx?page=11831
- E   A research centre at the University of Wolverhampton.

Research Centre for Studies in Intellectual Property and Technology Law
   see **AHRC Research Centre for Studies in Intellectual Property and Technology Law.**

Research Centre for Therapeutic Education   (RCTE)
- ■   School of Human and Life Sciences, Whitelands College, Roehampton University, Holybourne Avenue, London, SW15 4JD.
  020 8392 3500   fax 020 8392 3531
  http://www.roehampton.ac.uk/research/rcte
- E   A research centre at Roehampton University.
- O   To conduct research in therapeutic education as a cultural practice influenced by European philosophy, with particular emphasis given to the relational aspects of professional work, health, learning and communication

Research Centre for Transcultural Studies in Health   (RCTSH)

■ School of Health and Social Sciences, Middlesex University, Furnival Building, 10 Highgate Hill, London, N19 3UA.
020 8411 3214   fax 020 8411 6106
http://www.mdx.ac.uk/www/rctsh/
E A centre at Middlesex University.
○ To enable the development of health professionals and health services to deliver culturally competent care, that ultimately ensures high quality care for all

Research Centre for the Vocational Training of Musicians   (RCVTM)

■ Royal Northern College of Music, 124 Oxford Road, Manchester, M13 9RD.
0161-907 5200   fax 0161-273 7611
E A research centre at the Royal Northern College of Music.
○ To support the work of the Centre for Excellence in Dynamic Career Building for Tomorrow's Musician (qv)

Research Institute for the Built and Human Environment   (BuHu)

■ Faculty of Business, Law and the Built Environment, Maxwell Building, University of Salford, Salford, Manchester, M5 4WT.
0161-295 4600   fax 0161-295 5011
http://www.buhu.salford.ac.uk/
Director: Prof Mustafa Alshawi.
E A department of the University of Salford.
○ To deliver a built environment that is manageable, sustainable, accessible, maintainable, environmental friendly, comfortable to live in, and economically viable

Research Institute for Business and Management   (RIBM)

■ Manchester Metropolitan University Business School, Aytoun Building, Aytoun Street, Manchester, M1 3GH.
0161-247 2838; 3953   fax 0161-236 6975
http://www.ribm.mmu.ac.uk/
Director: Prof Gillian Wright.
E A department of Manchester Metropolitan University.
○ To be the focus for the strategic development of research in management domains across the University

Research Institute for the Care of the Elderly   (RICE)   1985

■ St Martin's Hospital, Midford Road, Combe Down, Bath, BA2 5RP.
01225 835866   fax 01225 840395
http://www.rice.org.uk/
Director: Prof R W Jones.
E A registered charity and a company limited by guarantee at the University of Bath.
○ To promote and advance medical knowledge with particular reference to the care of the elderly; to undertake related research, and to run Memory Clinics for the National Health Service
● Education and training - Information service - Carers courses - Self-referral memory clinics by appointment

Research Institute for Consumer Affairs
see **Ricability (Research Institute for Consumer Affairs).**

Research Institute for Enhancing Learning

Note: Closed on 1 August 2006.

Research Institute for the Environment, Physical Sciences and Applied Mathematics   (EPSAM)

■ Keele University, Keele, Staffordshire, ST5 5BG.
01782 584116
http://www.keele.ac.uk/research/epsam/
Director: Prof Peter Styles.
E A research institute at Keele University.

Research Institute for Flexible Materials   (RIFlex)   1999

■ School of Textiles and Design, Heriot-Watt University, Netherdale, Galashiels, TD1 3HF.
01896 892135; 892136
http://www.hw.ac.uk/sbc/RIFleX/
Director: Prof George K Stylios.
E A research centre at Heriot-Watt University.
○ To conduct research into various kinds of flexible materials

Research Institute for Health and Social Change   (RIHSC)

■ Faculty of Health, Social Care and Education, Elizabeth Gaskell Campus, Manchester Metropolitan University, Hathersage Road, Manchester, M13 0JA.
0161-247 2774   fax 0161-247 6842
http://www.rihsc.mmu.ac.uk/
Director: Prof Carolyn Kagan. Administrator: David Brown.
E A department of Manchester Metropolitan University.
○ To conduct research in developments in clinical intervention, professional practice development and evaluation, processes and experiences of social exclusion, policy development and social change, and critical theoretical social research

Research Institute in Healthcare Science   (RIHS)

■ School of Applied Sciences, University of Wolverhampton, Wulfruna Street, Wolverhampton, WV1 1SB.
  01902 321129   fax 01902 322714
  http://www.wlv.ac.uk/Default.aspx?page=7105
  Director: Prof John L Darling.
E A research institute at the University of Wolverhampton.
○ To support interdisciplinary research for the development and promotion of healthcare science research activities

Research Institute for Humanities

■ Chancellor's Building, Keele University, Keele, Staffordshire, ST5 5BG.

Research Institute in Information and Language Processing   (RIILP)

■ University of Wolverhampton, Wulfruna Street, Wolverhampton, WV1 1SB.
  01902 321470
  http://www.wlv.ac.uk/Default.aspx?page=7108
E A research institute at the University of Wolverhampton.
○ To bring together research teams that explore the potential of advanced computing technologies for 'understanding' human language and social sciences

Research Institute of Irish and Scottish Studies   (RIISS)   1999

■ Humanity Manse, University of Aberdeen, 19 College Bounds, Aberdeen, AB24 3UG.
  01224 273683   fax 01224 273677
  http://www.abdn.ac.uk/riiss/
  Director: Prof Cairns Craig.
E A research institute at the University of Aberdeen.
○ To offer taught masters and doctoral programmes of the highest quality in the history, literature and culture of Ireland and Scotland; to carry out research in these disciplines

Research Institute for Law, Politics and Justice

■ Keele University, Chancellor's Building, Keele, Staffordshire, ST5 5BG.
  01782 584336
  http://www.keele.ac.uk/research/lpj
  Director: Dr Barry Godfrey.
E A research institute at Keele University.
○ To explore diverse methodologies and interdisciplinary approaches to legal analysis
● Education and training

Research Institute for Life Course Studies

■ Keele University, Keele, Staffordshire, ST5 5BG.
  01782 583355
  http://www.keele.ac.uk/research/lcs
  Director: Prof Miriam Bernard.
E A research institute at Keele University.
○ To support and promote research and enterprise on a range of health and social concerns across the life course, from childhood to old age

Research Institute for Media, Art and Design   (RIMAD)   2005

■ Luton Campus, University of Bedfordshire, Luton, Bedfordshire, LU1 3JU.
  01234 400400
  http://www.beds.ac.uk/research/rimad/
  Director: Prof Alexis Weedon.
E A research institute at the University of Bedfordshire.
○ To support research initiatives in media, art and design
● Workshops

Research Institute for Public Policy and Management

■ School of Economics and Management Studies, Darwin Building, Keele University, Keele, Staffordshire, ST5 5BG.
  01782 583193
  http://www.keele.ac.uk/research/ppm
  Director: Prof Steve Cropper.
E A research institute at Keele University.
○ To research into questions of public policy, in the regulation and governance of institutions, and in managerial and organisational practices

© CBD Research Ltd · Beckenham · Kent BR3 5JS · Tel 020 8650 7745 · Fax 020 8650 0768 · E-mail cbd@cbdresearch.com · www.cbdresearch.com

Research Institute in Software Evolution   (RISE)

■ Department of Computer Science, University of Durham, South Road, Durham, DH1 3LE.
  0191-334 1744
  http://www.dur.ac.uk/RISE
  Contact: Prof Malcolm Munro. Contact: Prof David Budgen.
E A department of the University of Durham.
O To carry out research in the aspects of software maintenance with special reference to software maintenance and evolving software systems
● Education and training
✕ Centre for Software Maintenance.

Research Institute for Sport and Exercise Sciences   (RISES)   1997

■ Henry Cotton Campus, Liverpool John Moores University, 15-21 Webster Street, Liverpool, L3 2ET.
  0151-231 4323   fax 0151-231 4353
  http://www.ljmu.ac.uk/sportandexercisesciences/rises/
  Director: Prof Thomas Reilly.
E A research institute within Liverpool John Moores University.
O To provide a focus for research in sport and exercise sciences, including studies at cellular level, to whole-body responses to exercise (from elite athletes to novices at physical activity)

Research Institute in Systematic Theology   (RIST)   1988

■ School of Humanities, King's College London, Strand, London, WC2R 2LS.
  020 7836 5454
  http://www.kcl.ac.uk/ip/moiralangston/Resinst.html
E A research institute at King's College, London.
O To provide a framework within which postgraduate theological research can be pursued

Research Unit in Humanities Computing
    see **Centre for Computing in the Humanities.**

Resilience Centre
    see **Cranfield Resilience Centre.**

Resource Centre for Comparative Genomics
    see **Cambridge Resource Centre for Comparative Genomics.**

Resource Centre for Randomised Trials

■ University of Oxford, Old Road, Headington, Oxford, OX3 7LF.
  01865 227100   fax 01865 227047
  http://www.rcrt.ox.ac.uk/
E A research centre within the Institute for Health Sciences (qv) at the University of Oxford.

Resource and Research Centre in Textiles
    see **Constance Howard Resource and Research Centre in Textiles.**

Respiratory Support and Sleep Centre   (RSSC)   1992

■ Papworth Hospital, Papworth Everard, Cambridge, CB3 8RE.
  01480 830541   fax 01480 831315
  http://www.papworthpeople.com/services.asp?section=services&nav=rssc
E A research centre within Papworth Hospital.
O To develop and provide services for patients with respiratory failure, sleep disorders and latent conditions; to conduct research to further the understanding of these conditions, and to improve the method of treatment

Reta Lila Weston Institute of Neurological Studies   (RLWI)   1977

■ Faculty of Biomedical Sciences, University College London, 1 Wakefield Street, London, WC1N 1PJ.
  020 7679 4246   fax 020 7679 4236
  http://www.ucl.ac.uk/rlweston-inst/
  Director: Prof Andrew Lees.
E A department of University College London.
O To further knowledge about stroke and neurodegenerative disorders

Retail Centre

■ Manchester Business School, University of Manchester, Booth Street West, Manchester, M15 6PB.
  0161-275 2917; 6481
  http://www.mbs.ac.uk/executive-education/customised/retail-centre.htm
  Director: Prof Nitin Sanghavi. Administrator: Janine May.
E A centre at the University of Manchester.
O To provide retail executive education in Europe

Reunite, International Child Abduction Centre   1986

- ■ PO Box 7124, Leicester, LE1 7XX.
   0116-255 5345; 6234   fax 0116-255 6370
   http://www.reunite.org.uk/
   Director: Denise Carter, OBE. Chief Administrator: Alison Shalaby.
- E A registered charity.
- ○ To provide a telephone advice line offering practical advice and information on the issue of parental child abduction and international custody disputes; to campaign for improved legislation on international parental child abduction
- ● Conference facilities - Education and training - Information service - Liaison with Government - Meetings - Statistics - Self help support groups - Professional legal network

Ricability (Research Institute for Consumer Affairs)   (RICA)   1961

- ■ 30 Angel Gate, London, EC1V 2PT.
   020 7427 2460   fax 020 7427 2468
   http://www.ricability.org.uk/
   Director: David Yelding. Company Secretary: Andrew Day.
- E A registered charity and a company limited by guarantee.
- ○ To carry out research and produce information on products and services for older and disabled consumers
- ● Office open Mon-Fri (0900-1700)

Richard Attenborough Centre for Disability and the Arts   (RAC)   1997

- ■ PO Box 138, University of Leicester, University Road, Leicester, LE1 9HN.
   0116-252 2455   fax 0116-252 5165
   http://www.le.ac.uk/racentre/
   Director: Louisa Milburn.
- E A research centre at the University of Leicester.
- ○ To focus on people with disabilities and other members of the public who have previously found access to art education difficult

Richard Burton Centre for Film and Popular Culture   2006

- ■ Swansea University, Singleton Park, Swansea, SA2 8PP.
   01792 205678
   http://www.swan.ac.uk/research/centresandinstitutes/RichardBurtonCentre/
   Chairman: Dr Hywel Francis.
- E A centre at Swansea University.
- ○ To house and care for the papers, diaries, photographs and books belonging to the film and theatre actor Richard Burton (1925 - 1984),

Richard Wells Research Centre   1995

- ■ Faculty of Health and Human Sciences, Thames Valley University, Westel House, 32-38 Uxbridge Road, London, W5 2BS.
   020 8280 5145   fax 020 8280 5143
   http://www.richardwellsresearch.com/richardwells/
   Director: Prof Robert Pratt. Administrator: Meg Morse.
- E A research centre at Thames Valley University.
- ○ To develop research and educational initiatives within the field of caring for patients with HIV disease

Richardson Institute for Peace and Conflict Research   1959

- ■ Department of Politics and International Relations, Lancaster University, Lancaster, LA1 4YD.
   01524 594262   fax 01524 594238
   http://www.lancs.ac.uk/depts/richinst/
   Director: Dr Feargal Cochrane.
- E A registered charity and a department of Lancaster University.
- ○ To research into the causes of conflict and establishment of peace
- ● Education and training

Risk Institute   (RI)

- ■ Cass Business School, City University, 106 Bunhill Row, London, EC1Y 8TZ.
   020 7040 5222
   http://www.cass.city.ac.uk/ri
- E A research institute at City University.

RNCM Centre for Young Musicians

- ■ Royal Northern College of Music, 124 Oxford Road, Manchester, M13 9RD.
   0161-907 5200; 5205   fax 0161-273 7611
   http://www.rncm.ac.uk/content/view/16/135/
   Director: Geoffrey Reed.
- E A centre within the Centre for Excellence in Dynamic Career Building for Tomorrow's Musician at Royal Northern College of Music.

© CBD Research Ltd · Beckenham · Kent BR3 5JS · Tel 020 8650 7745 · Fax 020 8650 0768 · E-mail cbd@cbdresearch.com · www.cbdresearch.com

Robens Centre for Health Ergonomics (Robens CHE) 1978
■ Duke of Kent Building, University of Surrey, Guildford, Surrey, GU2 7XH.
  01483 689213 fax 01483 689395
  http://www.surreyergonomics.org.uk/
E A research centre within the European Institute of Health and Medical Sciences (qv) at the University of Surrey.
O To conduct research, teaching and application of ergonomics - the science of designing systems to match human capabilities with the aim of optimising productivity while preserving health and reducing accidents and errors

Robens Centre for Occupational Health and Safety (Robens COHS) 1984
■ Duke of Kent Building, University of Surrey, Guildford, Surrey, GU2 7XH.
  01483 686690 fax 01483 686691
  http://www.rcohs.com/
E A research centre within the European Institute of Health and Medical Sciences (qv) at the University of Surrey.
O To provide a wide range of occupational health services in the South East of England

Robens Centre for Public and Environmental Health (Robens CPEH) 1997
■ Duke of Kent Building, University of Surrey, Guildford, Surrey, GU2 7XH.
  01483 689209 fax 01483 689971
  http://www.rcpeh.com/
E A research centre within the European Institute of Health and Medical Sciences (qv) at the University of Surrey.
O To increase understanding of the ways in which water exerts an impact on human health
Note: The Centre is a World Health Organisation WHO Collaborating Centre (qv) for the Protection of Water Quality and Human Health.

Robert Clark Centre for Technological Education (RCC) 1987
■ Department of Educational Studies, University of Glasgow, 11 Eldon Street, Glasgow, G3 6NH.
  0141-330 3097; 4976
  http://www.gla.ac.uk/rcc/
  Director: Dr Jane Magill.
E A centre at the University of Glasgow.
O To conduct teaching and research in technological education

Robert Hill Institute (RHI)
■ Department of Animal and Plant Sciences, University of Sheffield, Western Bank, Sheffield, S10 2TN.
  0114-222 2000 fax 0114-222 0002
  http://www.shef.ac.uk/rhi/
E A research institute at the University of Sheffield.
O To consolidate and enhance research into photosynthesis, in plants and micro-organisms, from molecular and cellular aspects to ecophysiology and global change
Note: Also known as the Centre for Photosynthesis Research.

Robertson Centre for Biostatistics (RCB)
■ Department of Statistics, University of Glasgow, 15 University Gardens, Glasgow, G12 8QQ.
  0141-330 5024 fax 0141-330 4814
  http://www.rcb.gla.ac.uk/
  Director: Prof Ian Ford.
E A research centre at the University of Glasgow.
O To carry out research in biostatistical methodology, to encourage its application to practical problems and to participate in research initiatives addressing major medical and biological issues

Roehampton Social Research Centre (RSRC) 2004
■ School of Business and Social Sciences, Southlands College, Roehampton University, 80 Roehampton Lane, London, SW15 5SL.
  020 8392 3604
  http://www.roehampton.ac.uk/research/researchcentres/socialcentre.html
  Director: Stephen Driver. Contact: Linda Wilson.
E A research centre at Roehampton University.
O To carry out social research for a variety of clients in the public, voluntary and community sectors

ROLLS-ROYCE UNIVERSITY TECHNOLOGY CENTRES
  http://www.rolls-royce.com/education/utc/uk/
Note: Rolls-Royce plc works to support and develop research with a number of universities (in the UK and worldwide) where the universities can benefit from prime access to Rolls-Royce's capability bases and information networks. These partnerships create a cross-cultural working environment for the company and university staff in areas of basic science, applied research, staff training, and technology transfer

Roseland Institute 1991
■ Gorran, St Austell, Cornwall, PL26 6NT.
  01726 843501 fax 01726 843501
  Director: Dr James Whetter.
E A private venture.
O To be a centre for Cornish studies
● Library (A L Rowse Memorial Room) with 2,500 of his books - Cataloguing collection of 20,000 Cornish and other works
¶ The Cornish Banner (journal).

Roslin Institute   (RI)   1993

■   University of Edinburgh, Roslin BioCentre, Roslin, Midlothian, EH25 9PS.
     0131-527 4200   fax 0131-440 0434
     http://www.roslin.ac.uk/
E   An institute at the University of Edinburgh.
O   To conduct studies relating to animal genetics and development, particularly the genetics and genomics of farm animal species and their application in animal breeding and conservation, biotechnology and biomedicine, and in basic biology

Rothamsted Centre for Bioenergy and Climate Change

■   Rothamsted, Harpenden, Hertfordshire, AL5 2JQ.
     01582 763133   fax 01582 760981
     http://www.rothamsted.ac.uk/Research/Centres/index.php?Centre=BCC
     Director: Angela Karp.
E   A research centre within Rothamsted Research (qv).
O   To understand and predict the impacts of climate change on biotic and abiotic components of agro-ecosystems and provide land-based solutions for mitigation and adaptation through carbon-neutral renewable bioenergy crops and sustainable management strategies that retain ecosystem services and reduce greenhouse gas emissions.

Rothamsted Centre for Crop Genetic Improvement

■   Rothamsted, Harpenden, Hertfordshire, AL5 2JQ.
     01582 763133   fax 01582 760981
     http://www.rothamsted.ac.uk/Research/Centres/index.php?Centre=CGI
     Director: Peter Shewry.
E   A research centre within Rothamsted Research (qv).
O   To elucidate the genetic, biochemical and molecular mechanisms controlling resource use efficiency, performance, yield and end-use quality of the major UK arable food and non-food crops and thereby influence sustainability of production and value for producers, processors and consumers.

Rothamsted Centre for Mathematical and Computational Biology

■   Rothamsted, Harpenden, Hertfordshire, AL5 2JQ.
     01582 763133   fax 01582 760981
     http://www.rothamsted.ac.uk/Research/Centres/index.php?Centre=MCB
     Director: Chris Rawlings.
E   A research centre within Rothamsted Research (qv).
O   To develop and apply predictive models of biological systems and their interactions with the environment at multiple biological scales and to create novel methods for the integration, analysis and interpretation of highly variable and complex datasets to be used in integrative biology research.

Rothamsted Centre for Sustainable Pest and Disease Management

■   Rothamsted, Harpenden, Hertfordshire, AL5 2JQ.
     01582 763133   fax 01582 760981
     http://www.rothamsted.ac.uk/Research/Centres/index.php?Centre=PDM
     Director: John Pickett.
E   A research centre within Rothamsted Research (qv).
O   To provide the scientific base for novel and improved approaches to pest and disease management that are sustainable and to transfer these technologies into wide commercial practice.

Rothamsted Centre for Sustainable Soils and Ecosystem Functions

■   Rothamsted, Harpenden, Hertfordshire, AL5 2JQ.
     01582 763133   fax 01582 760981
     http://www.rothamsted.ac.uk/Research/Centres/index.php?Centre=SEF
     Director: Brian Kerry.
E   A research centre within Rothamsted Research (qv).
O   To predict and mitigate (or should this be manipulate?) processes affecting ecosystem productivity and resilience by understanding biotic and abiotic interactions within and between soil and above-ground ecosystems at scales from the molecular to the community level

Rothamsted Research   1903

■   Rothamsted, Harpenden, Hertfordshire, AL5 2JQ.
     01582 763133   fax 01582 760981
     http://www.rothamsted.ac.uk/
E   A research institute.
O   A centre of excellence for science in support of sustainable land management and its environmental impact.
Note: Institute of Arable Crops Research

Rothermere American Institute   (RAI)   2001

■   University of Oxford, 1A South Parks Road, Oxford, OX1 3TG.
     01865 282710   fax 01865 282720
     http://www.rai.ox.ac.uk/
     Director: Dr Paul Giles.
E   An institute at the University of Oxford.
O   An international centre dedicated to the interdisciplinary and comparative study of the United States

Rowett Research Institute   (RRI)   1913
- ■   Greenburn Road, Bucksburn, Aberdeen, AB2 9SB.
  01224 712751   fax 01224 715349
  Director: Prof Peter Morgan.
- E   A registered charity and a company limited by guarantee.
- ○   To undertake research into human and animal nutrition and related biological sciences
- ●   Education and training - Library

Royal Bank of Scotland Centre for Community Arts Research and Practice
- ■   Corstorphine Campus, Queen Margaret University, Clerwood Terrace, Edinburgh, EH12 8TS.
- E   A centre in process of formation within Queen Margaret University, Edinburgh.

Royal Bank of Scotland Centre for the Older Person's Agenda   2004
- ■   Corstorphine Campus, Queen Margaret University, Clerwood Terrace, Edinburgh, EH12 8TS.
  0131-317 3770
  http://www.qmuc.ac.uk/opa/
  Director: Maureen O'Neill, BA.
- E   A research centre at Queen Margaret University, Edinburgh.
- ○   To provide multi-professional multi-disciplinary expertise, dedicated to enhancing the quality of life of older people through research, practice development and education
- ●   Education and training - Information service

Royal College of Nursing Development Centre
   see **RCN Development Centre.**

Royal Free Centre for Biomedical Science
- ■   University College London, Royal Free and University College Medical School, Rowland Hill Street, London, NW3 2PF.
  020 7433 2801; 2821   fax 020 7433 2803
  http://www.ucl.ac.uk/medicalschool/departments/biomedical-science/
  Scientific Director: Prof M B Pepys. Executive Director: Dr J J Hsuan.
- E   A research centre at University College London.
- ○   To enhance, facilitate and promote the work of leading biomedical researchers

Royal Highland Centre Limited
- ■   Ingliston, Edinburgh, EH28 8NF.
  0131-335 6200   fax 0131-333 5236
  http://www.royalhighlandcentre.co.uk
- ○   To host shows and exhibitions
- ●   Exhibitions

Royal Holloway Institute for Environmental Research
Note: Closed in 2005.

Royal Literary and Scientific Institution
   see **Bath Royal Literary and Scientific Institution.**

Royal Northern College of Music
   see **RNCM Centre for Young Musicians.**

Royal Statistical Society Centre for Statistical Education   (RSS Centre)   1995
- ■   School of Computing and Informatics, Clifton Campus, Nottingham Trent University, Clifton Lane, Nottingham, NG11 8NS.
  0115-848 8301
  http://www.rsscse.org.uk/
  Director: Prof Neville Davies.
- E   A research centre at Nottingham Trent University.
- ○   To improve education and understanding of statistics

Rugby League Heritage Centre
   see **Gillette Rugby League Heritage Centre.**

Rural History Centre
Note: Now the Museum of English Rural Life (merl.org.uk).

Saad Centre for Clinical Skills Education   2006

■   City University, Northampton Square, London, EC1V 0HB.
      020 7040 5060   fax 020 7040 5070
      http://www.city.ac.uk/radiography/
E   A research centre at City University.

Sackler Institute for Musculoskeletal Research   2001

■   Division of Medicine, University College London, Rayne Building, 5 University Street, London, WC1E 6JF.
      020 7679 6169   fax 020 7679 6219
      http://www.ucl.ac.uk/medicine/bmc/
      Contact: Prof Michael Horton.
E   A research institute within the Bone and Mineral Centre (qv) at University College London.

Sackler Institute of Psychobiological Research

■   Department of Psychological Medicine, University of Glasgow, Glasgow, G12 8QQ.
      0141-211 3926
      http://www.gla.ac.uk/centres/sackler/
      Chairman: Prof Colin Espie.
E   A research institute at the University of Glasgow.
O   To improve understanding of emotional disorders; to develop and validate novel biological measurement techniques; to
      understand the biological underpinnings of recovery

Sackler Institute of Pulmonary Pharmacology   1993

■   School of Biomedical and Health Sciences, King's College London, Strand, London, WC2R 2LS.
      020 7836 5454
      http://www.kcl.ac.uk/schools/biohealth/research/pharmsci/groups/sackler
      Contact: Prof Clive Page.
E   A research institute at King's College, London.

Safety and Accident Investigation Centre
      see **Cranfield Safety and Accident Investigation Centre.**

Safety Systems Research Centre   (SSRC)

■   Department of Civil Engineering, University of Bristol, Queen's Building, University Walk, Bristol, BS8 1TR.
      0117-331 5081   fax 0117-928 7783
      http://www.cen.bris.ac.uk/civil/ssrc/index/
      Contact: Prof John May.
E   An interdisciplinary research centre at the University of Bristol.
O   To carry out research into the design, operation and maintenance of safe and reliable computer-based systems for use in industry

Sainsbury Centre for Mental Health   (SCMH)   1985

■   134-138 Borough High Street, London, SE1 1LB.
      020 7827 8300   fax 020 7403 9482
      http://www.scmh.org.uk/
      Chief Executive Officer: Angela Greatley.
E   A registered charity.
O   To improve the quality of life for people with severe mental health problems by influencing policy and improving practice in health,
      social care and related services
●   Education and training

Sainsbury Centre for Visual Arts   (SCVA)   1978

■   University of East Anglia, Norwich, NR4 7TJ.
      01603 593199
      http://www.scva.org.uk/
E   A department of the University of East Anglia.
O   To provide educational resources and to encourage awareness and accessibility of art to all

Sainsbury Institute for the Study of Japanese Arts and Cultures   1999

NR   School of Oriental and African Studies, University of London, Thornhaugh Street, Russell Square, London, WC1H 0XG.
      020 7898 4453   fax 020 7898 4699
      http://www.soas.ac.uk/centres/centreinfo.cfm?navid=22
      Contact: Dr Timon Screech.
E   An independent research institute at the School of Oriental and African Studies, University of London.
O   To promote the study of the material and visual cultures of the Japanese archipelago, and in doing so to act as a catalyst for
      international research in the field
Note: A joint venture with the University of East Anglia.

Saint Andrews Centre for Advanced Materials   (StACAM)

■   University of St Andrews, Purdie Building, St Andrews, Fife, KY16 9ST.
      01334 463817   fax 01334 463808
      http://ch-www.st-andrews.ac.uk/staff/rem/stacam/stacam.html
      Director: Prof John Irvine.
E   A research centre at the University of St Andrews.

© CBD Research Ltd · Beckenham · Kent BR3 5JS · Tel 020 8650 7745 · Fax 020 8650 0768 · E-mail cbd@cbdresearch.com · www.cbdresearch.com

Saint Andrews Reformation Studies Institute   1993

■ School of History, University of St Andrews, St John's House, 69 South Street, St Andrews, Fife, KY16 9AL.
   01334 462909   fax 01334 463334
   http://www.st-andrews.ac.uk/reformation/
   Founding Director: Prof Andrew Pettegree.
E A department of the University of St Andrews.
O To conduct research and teaching in Reformation and early modern British and European history
● Education and training
¶ St Andrews Studies.

Saint Andrews Scottish Studies Centre   (SASSC) 1993

■ School of English, University of St Andrews, Castle House, The Poetry House, St Andrews, Fife, KY16 9AL.
   01334 462666   fax 01334 462655
   http://www.st-andrews.ac.uk/sassi/
   Director: Prof Douglas Dunn.
E An interdisciplinary research centre at the University of St Andrews.
O To provide a focus for research on Scotland's past, present and future

Saint Andrews University Institute of Language and Linguistic Studies   (SAILLS)

■ School of Modern Languages, University of St Andrews, Buchanan Building, Union Street, St Andrews, Fife, KY16 9PH.
   01334 476161
   http://www.st-andrews.ac.uk/modlangs/SAILLS/
E A department of the University of St Andrews.
O To promote the academic study of natural language

Saint John's House Centre for Advanced Historical Research

■ School of History, University of St Andrews, University of St Andrews, South Street, St Andrews, Fife, KY16 9AL.
   01334 462900
   http://www.st-andrews.ac.uk/academic/history/about.shtml
E A department of the University of St Andrews.

Saint John's Institute of Dermatology

■ School of Medicine, St Thomas' Hospital, Lambeth Palace Road, London, SE1 7EH.
   020 7188 6255   fax 020 7928 1428
   http://www.kcl.ac.uk/depsta/
E A department of King's College, London.
O To conduct collaborative research to increase understanding of normal and diseased skin

Salford Centre for Nursing, Midwifery and Collaborative Research   (SCNMCR)

■ Faculty of Health and Social Care, Allerton Building, University of Salford, Salford, Manchester, M6 6PU.
   0161-295 2768
   http://www.ihscr.salford.ac.uk/SCNMCR/
   Director: Prof Martin Johnson. Administrator: Wendy Moran.
E A research centre within the Institute for Health and Social Care Research (qv) at the University of Salford.
O To develop nursing and midwifery practice and education through collaborative research, and to undertake research and
   scholarship of national and international standing

Salford Centre for Research and Innovation in the Built and Human Environment   (SCRI)   2002

NR Maxwell Building, University of Salford, Salford, Manchester, M5 4WT.
   0161-295 5176   fax 0161-295 5011
   http://www.buhu.salford.ac.uk/scri/
   Director: Prof Ghassan Aouad.
E An EPSRC Innovative Manufacturing Research Centre within the Research Institute for the Built and Human Environment (qv) at the
   University of Salford.
O To fulfill its overall vision of a built environment, which enables the delivery of an effective healthcare service, including prevention
Note: One of the EPSRC funded centres in the UK - for further information see EPSRC Innovative Manufacturing Research Centres.

Salford Centre for Social Work Research   (SCSWR)

■ Faculty of Health and Social Care, Allerton Building, University of Salford, Salford, Manchester, M6 6PU.
   0161-295 2082; 2768
   http://www.ihscr.salford.ac.uk/SCSWR/
   Director: Stephen Myers. Administrator: Wendy Moran.
E A research centre within the Institute for Health and Social Care Research (qv) at the University of Salford.
O To provide and promote high quality research that explores the interactive links between social work practice, policy and theory

Salisbury Centre   (Salisbury Centre)   1973
- 2 Salisbury Road, Edinburgh, EH16 5AB.
  0131-667 5438
  http://www.salisburycentre.org/
  Co Manager: Ian Heslop. Co Manager: Val Duncan.
- E   A registered charity and an independent non-profit-distributing organisation.
- O   To provide a valuable resource to anyone who would like to improve the quality of their life by becoming more internally conscious and aware The inter-connectedness of body, mind and spirit (as symbolised in the time of the Celts) is the foundation of the centre's work and belief that healings arise naturally from this recognition
- ● Education and training - Library

Salters' Institute   1918
- Salters' Hall, Fore Street, London, EC2Y 5DE.
  020 7628 5962
  http://www.salters.co.uk/
- E   A registered charity.
- O   To support chemistry teaching, and to encourage young people to pursue careers in the UK chemical industries

Sanger Centre
  see **Wellcome Trust Sanger Institute.**

Sara Koe PSP Research Centre
- Faculty of Biomedical Sciences, University College London, 1 Wakefield Street, London, WC1N 1PJ.
  020 7837 3611   fax 020 7278 5069
  http://www.ion.ucl.ac.uk/research/mol_neurosci/molneuro-themes-psp.html
  Contact: Mrs Susan Stoneham.
- E   A research centre within the Institute of Neurology (qv) at University College London.
- O   To conduct research in progressive supranuclear palsy (PSP)

Satake Centre for Grain Process Engineering
- School of Chemical Engineering and Analytical Science, PO Box 88, University of Manchester, Sackville Street, Manchester, M60 1QD.
  0161-306 4379
  http://www.ceas.manchester.ac.uk/research/centres/satakecentre/
  Director: Prof Colin Webb.
- E   A research centre at the University of Manchester.
- O   To provide a focus for post-graduate research and teaching relevant to the grain processing industries, all of which share common challenges
Note: Satake Corporation of Japan, a cereal milling engineers, provided an initial donation for the creation of the Centre.

SATRA Technology Centre   (SATRA)   1919
- SATRA House, Rockingham Road, Kettering, Northamptonshire, NN16 9JH.
  01536 410000   fax 01536 410626
  http://www.satra.co.uk/
- E   An industrial research organisation with a worldwide membership of 1,500 companies in 70 countries.
- O   To offer a wide range of testing, research, training and consultancy services so as to benefit member firms who are manufacturers, retailers and repairers and suppliers of materials in the footwear, clothing, safety products, leather goods and furniture industries

Scarborough Centre for Coastal Studies   (SCCS)
- Faculty of Science and the Environment, University of Hull, Scarborough Campus, Filey Road, Scarborough, North Yorkshire, YO11 3AZ.
  01723 362392
  http://www.coastal-studies.org/
- E   A department of the University of Hull.
- O   To conduct research into all aspects of coastal environments, both nationally and internationally

Scarman Centre for the Study of Public Order
Note: Now the Department of Criminology at the University of Leicester.

School Improvement and Leadership Centre   (SILC)   2005
- University of Reading, Bulmershe Court, Earley, Reading, Berkshire, RG6 1HY.
  0118-378 8811
  http://www.education.rdg.ac.uk/silc/
  Director: Prof Brian Fidler.
- E   A research centre within the Institute of Education (qv) at the University of Reading.
- O   To support schools and local education authorities as they strive to strengthen their improvement, efforts and leadership skills

Science Centre
- Department of Health and Human Sciences, North Campus, 166-220 Holloway Road, London Metropolitan University, London, N7 8DB.
  020 7133 4545   fax 020 7133 2844
  http://www.londonmet.ac.uk/depts/hhs/
- E   A research centre at London Metropolitan University.

Science Enterprise Centres
  see **United Kingdom Science Enterprise Centres.**

Science Learning Centre East of England
NR   University of Hertfordshire, Bayfordbury, Hertfordshire, SG13 8LD.
        01992 503498   fax 01992 537805
        http://www.sciencelearningcentres.org.uk/
        Director: Alison Redmore.
E   A centre at the University of Hertfordshire.
Note: One of the nine regional science learning centres headed by theNational Science Learning Centre (qv).

Science Learning Centre East Midlands
NR   School of Education, University of Leicester, 21 University Road, Leicester, LE1 7RF.
        0116-252 3771   fax 0116-252 5772
        http://www.sciencelearningcentres.org.uk/
        Director: Dr Tina Jarvis.
E   A centre at the University of Leicester.
Note: One of the nine regional science learning centres headed by theNational Science Learning Centre (qv).

Science Learning Centre London
NR   School of Mathematics, Science and Technology, University of London, 20 Bedford Way, London, WC1H 0AL.
        020 7612 6664   fax 020 7612 6792
        http://www.sciencelearningcentres.org.uk/
        Director: Angela Hall.
E   A research centre within the Institute of Education (qv) at the University of London.
Note: One of the nine regional science learning centres headed by theNational Science Learning Centre (qv).

Science Learning Centre North East
NR   University of Durham, Front Street, Pity Me, Durham, DH1 5BZ.
        0191-370 6200   fax 0191-374 1806
        http://www.sciencelearningcentres.org.uk/
        Director: Dr Sally Preston.
E   A centre at the University of Durham.
Note: One of the nine regional science learning centres headed by theNational Science Learning Centre (qv).

Science Learning Centre North West
NR   Manchester Metropolitan University, 799 Wilmslow Road, Manchester, M20 2RR.
        0161-247 2944
        http://www.sciencelearningcentres.org.uk/
        Director: Amanda Smith.
E   A research centre within the Institute of Education (qv) at Manchester Metropolitan University.
Note: One of the nine regional science learning centres headed by theNational Science Learning Centre (qv).

Science Learning Centre South East
NR   University of Southampton, Level 3 - The Graham Hills Building 29, Highfield, Southampton, SO17 1BJ.
        023 8059 8810   fax 023 8059 8811
        http://www.sciencelearningcentres.org.uk/
        Director: Dr Marcus Grace.
E   A centre at the University of Southampton.
Note: One of the nine regional science learning centres headed by theNational Science Learning Centre (qv).

Science Learning Centre South West
NR   At-Bristol, Harbourside, Bristol, BS1 5DB
        0845 345 3344   fax 0117-915 7202
        http://www.sciencelearningcentres.org.uk/
        Director: Bryan Berry.
E   A centre at the University of Bristol.
Note: One of the nine regional science learning centres headed by theNational Science Learning Centre (qv). A joint venture with the
        University of Plymouth.

Science Learning Centre West Midlands
NR   Keele University, Keele, Staffordshire, ST5 5BG.
        01782 584429   fax 01782 584430
        http://www.sciencelearningcentres.org.uk/
        Director: Christina Whittaker.
E   A centre at Keele University.
Note: One of the nine regional science learning centres headed by theNational Science Learning Centre (qv).

Science Learning Centre Yorkshire and the Humber
NR   Sheffield Hallam University, Howard Street, Sheffield, S1 1WB.
     0114-225 4891   fax 0114-225 4872
     http://www.sciencelearningcentres.org.uk/
     Director: John Wardle.
E   A centre at Sheffield Hallam University.
Note: One of the nine regional science learning centres headed by theNational Science Learning Centre (qv).

Science Research and Investment Fund
    see **SRIF Centre for Virtual Organisation Technology Enabling Research.**

Science Studies Centre   (SSC)   1974
■   Faculty of Humanities & Social Sciences, University of Bath, Claverton Down, Bath, BA2 7AY.
     01225 383939   fax 01225 386113
     http://www.bath.ac.uk/ssc/
     Director: Prof David Gooding, BA, MA, DPhil.
E   A centre at the University of Bath.
○   To further research and teaching in the history, philosophy and social studies of science and technology, with particular reference to innovation and cultural change, science communication, and the public understanding of science

Science and Technology Research Institute   (STRI)   1997
■   University of Hertfordshire, College Lane, Hatfield, Hertfordshire, AL10 9AB.
     01707 286083   fax 01707 284185
     http://perseus.herts.ac.uk/
E   A department of the University of Hertfordshire.
○   To offer a range of courses and degrees in the science and technology fields

Scientific Analysis and Visualisation Centre   (SAVIC)
■   Faculty of Computing, Information Systems and Mathematics, Kingston University London, Penrhyn Road, Kingston-upon-Thames, Surrey, KT1 2EE.
     020 8547 2000
     http://cism.kingston.ac.uk/
     Contact: Dr David Wertheim.
E   A research centre at Kingston University, London.
○   To develop and apply methods for analysis of different types of image and signal data such as photographs, microscope images, medical images from different imaging modalities, and physiological signals, and used in investigations in the fields of medicine, biology, earth sciences, and engineering

Scotch Whisky Heritage Centre   1987
■   354 Castlehill, The Royal Mile, Edinburgh, EH1 2NE.
     0131-220 0441   fax 0131-220 6288
     http://www.whisky-heritage.co.uk/
E   A profit-making business.
○   To promote the enjoyment of Scotch whisky by providing a world-class visitor attraction, giving visitors from all over the world an excellent appreciation of Scotch whisky in an entertaining and informative way

Scott Polar Research Institute   (SPRI)   1920
■   School of Physical Sciences, University of Cambridge, Lensfield Road, Cambridge, CB2 1ER.
     01223 336540   fax 01223 336549
     http://www.spri.cam.ac.uk/
     Director: Prof Julian Dowdeswell.
E   A department of the University of Cambridge.
○   To research into the Arctic and the Antarctic Past and present research areas include remote sensing, sea ice and polar oceanography, glacier hydrology, polar ecology and management, polar history and humanities, and polar biology
●   Library and archives - Museum - Picture library

Scottish Biotechnology Training Centre   (SBTC)
■   Bell College, Almada Street, Hamilton, ML3 0JB.
     01698 894431   fax 01698 894404
     http://www.bell.ac.uk/bdia/scottish_biotechnology.htm
E   A research centre at Bell College.
Note: At the time of going to press, Bell College was preparing to merge with the University of Paisley to form the University of the West of Scotland.

Scottish Book Centre
■   137 Dundee Street, Edinburgh, EH11 1BG.
     0131-228 6866   fax 0131-228 3220
     http://www.scottishbooks.org/
E   A part of Publishing Scotland.
●   Information service

Scottish Centre for Carbon Storage   (SCCS)
- School of Geosciences, University of Edinburgh, The King's Buildings, West Mains Road, Edinburgh, EH9 3JW.
  0131-651 3400
  http://www.geos.ed.ac.uk/
- E   A research centre at the University of Edinburgh.

Scottish Centre for Children with Motor Impairments   (SCCMI)   1990
- 1 Craighalbert Way, Cumbernauld, Glasgow, G68 0LS.
  01236 456100   fax 01236 736889
  http://www.craighalbert.org.uk/
- E   A registered charity and a company limited by guarantee.
- O   To teach self-help skills to children under the age of 7 years who have cerebral palsy, using a combination of conductive education and Scottish early education practice

Note: Also known as the Craighalbert Centre.

Scottish Centre for Crime and Justice Research   (SCCJR)
- Department of Sociology, Anthropology and Applied Social Sciences, University of Glasgow, Adam Smith Building, 40 Bute Gardens, Glasgow, G12 8RT.
  0141-330 2514   fax 0141-330 3547
  http://www.ccjr.ac.uk/
  Contact: Prof Harvie Ferguson.
- E   A research centre at the University of Glasgow.

Scottish Centre for Enterprise and Ethnic Business Research   (SCEEBR)   2005
- Corstophine Campus, Queen Margaret University, Edinburgh, Clerwood Terrace, Edinburgh, EH12 8TS.
  0131-317 3000
  http://www.qmuc.ac.uk/sceebr/
- E   A research centre at Queen Margaret University.
- O   To promote socially relevant research, training and access in business and management, with particular reference to the key business issues within ethnic minority groups in Scotland

Scottish Centre for Facilities Management   (SCFM)
- School of the Built Environment, Merchiston Campus, Napier University, 10 Colinton Road, Edinburgh, EH10 5DT.
  0131-455 2642   fax 0131-455 2239
  http://www.sbe.napier.ac.uk/scfm
  Contact: Prof Brian Sloan.
- E   A research centre at Napier University.

Scottish Centre for Financial Education   (SCFE)
- The Optima, 58 Robertson Street, Glasgow, G2 8DU.
  0870 010 0297   fax 0870 010 0298
  http://www.ltscotland.org.uk/financialeducation/
- E   An independent centre within Learning and Teaching Scotland.
- O   To help teachers, schools and education authorities to provide a high standard of financial education to meet the needs of all their learners

Scottish Centre for Genomic Technology and Informatics
Note: has been replaced by the Division of Pathway Medicine at the University of Edinburgh and is therefore no longer within the scope of this directory.

Scottish Centre for Healthy Working Lives   2004
- Princes Gate, Castle Street, Hamilton, ML3 6BU.
  0800 019 2211
  http://www.healthscotland.org.uk/hwl
- E   An initiative of the Scottish Executive.

Scottish Centre for Himalayan Research   (SCHR)
- School of Social Science, University of Aberdeen, King's College, Aberdeen, AB24 3UJ.
  01224 272274   fax 01224 273750
  http://www.abdn.ac.uk/schr/
- E   A research centre at the University of Aberdeen.

Scottish Centre for Information on Language Teaching   (SCILT)   1992
- University of Stirling, Stirling, FK9 4LA.
  01786 467600; 467940
  http://www.scilt.stir.ac.uk/
- E   A research centre within the Institute of Education (qv) at the University of Stirling.
- O   To conduct research in teaching, learning, policy and use of languages; to develop networks of professionals in Scotland and the European arena to provide support and facilitate information exchange

Scottish Centre for International Law (SCIL)

■ School of Law, Old College, University of Edinburgh, South Bridge, Edinburgh, EH8 9YL.
     0131-650 2006   fax 0131-650 6317
     http://www.law.ed.ac.uk/scil
E   A research centre at the University of Edinburgh.

Scottish Centre for Journalism Studies (SCJS) 1990

NR Faculty of Law, Arts and Social Sciences, Crawfurd Building, University of Strathclyde, 76 Southbrae Drive, Glasgow, G13 1PP.
     0141-950 3281   fax 0141-950 3676
     http://www.strath.ac.uk/scjs/
     Director: Dr Martin Montgomery.
E   A centre at the University of Strathclyde.
○   To train journalists to the highest standards
Note: A collaborative venture with Glasgow Caledonian University.

Scottish Centre for Nonviolence 2003

■ 1 Kirk Street, Dunblane, FK15 0AJ.
     01786 824730
     http://www.nonviolence-scotland.org.uk/
E   An independent campaigning group.

Scottish Centre for Occupational Safety and Health (SCOSH)

■ Graham Hills Building, University of Strathclyde, 40 George Street, Glasgow, G1 1QE.
     0141-548 2392   fax 0141-553 1270
     http://www.cll.strath.ac.uk/cpd/scosh.htm
E   A part of the Centre for Lifelong Learning (qv) at the University of Strathclyde.

Scottish Centre for Police Studies 2003

■ Bell College, Almada Street, Hamilton, ML3 0JB.
     01698 283100
     http://www.bell.ac.uk/bdia/police.htm
E   A research centre at Bell College.
○   To be a focus for research activities in policing
Note: At the time of going to press, Bell College was preparing to merge with the University of Paisley to form the University of the West of Scotland.

Scottish Centre for Pollen Studies (SCPS) 1987

■ School of Life Sciences, Merchiston Campus, Napier University, Colinton Road, Edinburgh, EH10 5DT.
     01875 320444 (home)   fax 0131-455 2291
E   A research centre at Napier University.
○   To provide a daily, seasonal, pollen count for sufferers of hay fever (seasonal rhinitis) and potential asthma sufferers; to undertake research involving pollen in animal faeces as environmental indicators of habitat and foraging
●   Information service - Aerobiological sampling for particular pollens, such as ferns and fungi
¶   Annual Report.

Scottish Centre for Public Policy (SCPP)

■ 20 Forth Street, Edinburgh, EH1 3LH.
     0131-477 8219

Scottish Centre for Regeneration (SCR) 2003

■ Festival Business Centre, 150 Brand Street, Glasgow, G51 1DH.
     0141-419 1690
     http://www.scr.communitiesscotland.gov.uk/
     Director: Craig Mclaren.
E   A Government organisation and part of Communities Scotland.
○   To contribute to the Scottish Executive's aim of closing the opportunity gap, by building skills and expertise and sharing knowledge in regeneration

Scottish Centre for Research into On-line Learning and Assessment (SCROLLA) 2001

■ University of Edinburgh, Paterson's Land, Holyrood Road, Edinburgh, EH8 8AQ.
     0131-651 6545
     http://www.scrolla.ac.uk/
     Contact: Prof Cliff Beevers.
E   A research centre at the University of Edinburgh.

Scottish Centre for Research on Social Justice (SCRSJ) 2002

■ Department of Urban Studies, University of Glasgow, 29 Bute Gardens, Glasgow, G12 8RS.
     0141-330 2094   fax 0141-330 2095
     http://www.scrsj.ac.uk/
     Director: Kenneth Gibb.
E   A research centre at the University of Glasgow.
○   To promote better understanding, and more informed debate, about the nature of social justice in Scotland, particularly in relation to public policy

Scottish Centre for Social Research   (ScotCen)   2004

- 5 Leamington Terrace, Edinburgh, EH10 4JW.
  0131-228 2167   fax 0131-228 8250
  http://www.natcen.ac.uk/scotland/
  Director: Simon Anderson.
- E   A research centre within the National Centre for Social Research (qv).

Scottish Centre for Stopping Smoking and Health

- 69 Buchanan Street, Glasgow, G1 3HL.
  0800 071 7969
  http://www.weightlossclinicsscotland.co.uk/
- E   A hypnotherapy centre.

Scottish Centre for Studies in School Administration   (SCSSA)   1972

- Faculty of Education, University of Edinburgh, Holyrood Road, Edinburgh, EH8 8AQ.
  0131-651 6265   fax 0131-651 6264
  http://www.scssa.ed.ac.uk/
- E   A research centre at the University of Edinburgh.

Scottish Centre for Sustainable Community Development   (SCSCD)

- Department of Educational and Professional Studies, Sir Henry Wood Building, University of Strathclyde, 76 Southbrae Drive, Glasgow, G13 1PP.
  0141-950 3601   fax 0141-950 3374
  http://www.strath.ac.uk/Departments/CommunEdu/research/scscdcadispa.html
  Director: Dr Geoff Fagan.
- E   A research centre at the University of Strathclyde.
- O   To help small rural communities develop their own solutions to the challenges posed by sustainable development and to meet locally identified community needs within the definition of sustainability

Scottish Centre of Tourism   (SCoT)

- Aberdeen Business School, Robert Gordon University, Garthdee II, Garthdee Road, Aberdeen, AB10 7QG.
  01224 263036   fax 01224 263038
  http://www.gu.ac.uk/abs/centres/page.cfm?pge=5611
  Director: Andrew Martin.
- E   A research centre at the Robert Gordon University.
- O   To undertake consultancy, research, tourism development education, human resource development, and to provide impartial expertise and comment on tourism issues of regional and national importance

Scottish Centre for War Studies   (SCWS)   1996

- Department of History, University of Glasgow, 2 University Gardens, Glasgow, G12 8QQ.
  0141-330 8581   fax 0141-330 5000
  http://www.history.arts.gla.ac.uk/Warstud/
  Director: Dr Phillips O'Brien.
- E   A research centre at the University of Glasgow.
- O   To promote research in, and understanding of, war in all its aspects

Scottish Centre for Work Based Learning   (SCWBL)

- Glasgow Caledonian University, Cowcaddens Road, Glasgow, G4 0BA.
  0141-273 1277   fax 0141-331 8835
  http://www.gcal.ac.uk/scwbl/
  Head: Vince Mills.
- E   A centre at Glasgow Caledonian University.
- O   To conduct research into the practical and theoretical aspects of work based learning, continuous professional development and lifelong learning
- ✕   Caledonian Centre for Engineering Education.

Scottish Child Law Centre   (SCLC)   1988

- 54 East Crosscauseway, Edinburgh, EH8 9HD.
  0131-667 6333   fax 0131-662 1713
  http://www.sclc.org.uk/
- E   A registered charity, an independent non-profit-distributing organisation and a company limited by guarantee.
- O   To promote knowledge and use of Scots law and children's rights for the benefit of children and young people in Scotland; to provide a free telephone advice service giving information on all aspects of Scots law relating to young children and young people; to consult and advise both local and central government
- ●   Education and training - Information service - Advice line 0800 328 8970 (Mon-Fri 0930-1600)
- ¶   Many different publications.

Scottish Community Development Centre   (SCDC)
■   Suite 329 - Baltic Chambers, 50 Wellington Street, Glasgow, G2 6HJ.
        0141-248 1924   fax 0141-248 4938
        http://www.scdc.org.uk/
        Co-Director: Dr Alan Barr. Co-Director: Stuart Hashagen.
E   A partnership between the Community Development Foundation and the University of Glasgow.
O   To support community groups, achieve effective community participation, research issues and disseminate lessons

Scottish Council for Research on Education
        see **SCRE Centre.**

Scottish Crop Research Institute   (SCRI)   1981
■   University of Edinburgh, Invergowrie, Dundee, DD2 5DA.
        01382 562731   fax 01382 562426
        http://www.scri.ac.uk
        Director: Prof P J Gregory. Company Secretary: Dr N Hattersley.
E   A registered charity and a company limited by guarantee at the University of Edinburgh.
O   To be Scotland's leading institute for research on plants and their interactions with the environment, particularly in managed
        ecosystems; to deliver innovative products, knowledge and services that enrich the life of the community and address the public
        demands for sustainability and high quality and healthy food
●   Exhibitions - Information service - Library - Statistics - Diagnostic services
¶   Annual Report. Occasional publications.

Scottish Deer Centre   1988
■   Bow-of-Fife, By Cupar, Fife, KY15 4NQ.
        01337 810391   fax 01337 810477
        http://www.foreverscotland.com/mini_sites/deer_centre/
E   A visitor centre and profit-making venture.

Scottish Development Education Centre   (Scotdec)   1984
■   Courtyard Rooms, Simon Laurie House, Holyrood Campus, Edinburgh, EH8 8AQ.
        0131-557 6087   fax 0131-557 1499
        http://www.scotdec.org.uk/
E   A registered charity and a company limited by guarantee.
O   To work, with teachers and others responsible for education, to promote global citizenship in schools and to ensure that there is a
        global dimension throughout Scottish education

Scottish Fish Immunology Research Centre   (SFIRC)   2003
■   Zoology Building, University of Aberdeen, Tillydrone Avenue, Aberdeen, AB24 2TZ.
        01224 272857   fax 01224 272396
        http://www.abdn.ac.uk/sfirc/
        Director: Prof Chris Secombes. Research Manager: Dr Jun Zou.
E   A research centre at the University of Aberdeen.
O   To conduct research and training in fish immune discovery

Scottish Gliding Centre   1934
■   Portmoak Airfield, Scotlandwell, Kinross, Fife, KY13 9JJ.
        01592 850543
E   The trading name of the Scottish Gliding Union Ltd.
O   To provide and promote gliding activities
●   Training of glider pilots - Trial flights

Scottish Human Rights Centre
Note: has closed.

Scottish Informatics, Mathematics, Biology and Statistics Centre   (SIMBIOS)
NR   School of Engineering and Physical Science, University of Dundee, Dundee, DD1 4HN.
        01382 308640
        http://www.simbios.ac.uk/
        Chairman: Prof John Palfreyman.
E   A research centre at the University of Dundee.
O   To bring together scientists with diverse backgrounds, to undertake research in the mathematical and computational modelling of
        biomedical / environmental problems with an aim of using the results to provide a deeper insight into the underlying biological
        processes, which in turn will have a direct impact upon the quality of life of the Scottish public
Note: A joint venture with the University of Abertay, Dundee.

Scottish Institute for Enterprise   (SIE)
NR   The King's Buildings, University of Edinburgh, Mayfield Road, Edinburgh, EH9 3JL.
        0131-472 4756   fax 0131-662 4678
        http://www.sie.ed.ac.uk/
        Training Manager: Dr Donna Murray.
E   An institute at the University of Edinburgh.
O   To provide training and support in entrepreneurship and business skills
Note: The SIE is a project involving all 13 Scottish Universities.

Scottish Institute for Excellence in Social Work Education   (SIESWE)   2003
■   School of Education, Social Work and Community Education, Gardyne Road Campus, University of Dundee, Dundee, DD5 1NY.
        01382 464980   fax 01382 464469
        http://www.sieswe.org/
E   A research institute at the University of Dundee.
Note: A collaborative venture with eight other Scottish Universities.

Scottish Institute of Human Relations   (SIHR)   1971
■   172 Leith Walk, Edinburgh, EH6 5EA.
        0131-454 3240   fax 0131-454 3241
        http://www.sihr.org.uk/
        Executive Director: Amanda Cornish.
E   A registered charity and a company limited by guarantee.
O   To offer services and courses in translating psychoanalytic, psychodynamic and systematic ideas into practical tools for
        professionals in the health service, voluntary and faith organisations, and education and social services

Scottish Institute for Maritime Studies
Note: Closed in 2002.

Scottish Institute for Northern Renaissance Studies   (SINRS)
■   Department of English Studies, University of Stirling, Stirling, FK9 4LA.
        01786 473171
        http://www.english.stir.ac.uk/
E   A research institute at the University of Stirling.

Scottish Institute for Research in Investment and Finance   (SIRIF)   1999
■   Strathclyde Business School, University of Strathclyde, Curran Building, 100 Cathedral Street, Glasgow, G4 0LN.
        0141-548 3261   fax 0141-552 3547
        http://www.strath.ac.uk/
E   A research institute at the University of Strathclyde.

Scottish Institute for Residential Child Care   (SIRCC)
NR   Glasgow School of Social Work, University of Strathclyde, 5th Floor - Sir Henry Wood Building, 76 Southbrae Drive, Glasgow,
        G13 1PP.
        0141-950 3683   fax 0141-950 3681
        http://www.sircc.strath.ac.uk/
        Director: Jennifer Davidson.
E   An institute at the University of Strathclyde.
O   To ensure that residential child care staff throughout Scotland have access to the skills and knowledge they require to meet the
        needs of the children and young people in their care
Note: A joint venture with the Robert Gordon University and various other organisations.

Scottish Institute for Sustainable Technology   (SISTech)
■   Heriot-Watt University, James Nasmyth Building, Riccarton, Edinburgh, EH14 4AS.
        0131-451 8162   fax 0131-451 8150
        http://www.sistech.co.uk/
        Executive Director: Paul Jowitt.
E   A research institute at Heriot-Watt University.
O   To research, promote and foster best practice for sustainable technology development within the community

Scottish Institute for Wood Technology   (SIWT)   1992
■   University of Abertay Dundee, Bell Street, Dundee, DD1 1HG.
        01382 308231
        http://scieng.abertay.ac.uk/siwt/
        Research Director: Dr Allan Bruce.
E   A research institute at the University of Abertay, Dundee.
O   To carry out research into forest products technology; to support the Scottish forest products industry
●   Consultancy - Information service - Product testing and development - Building conservation - Timber survey service

Scottish International Tourism Industries Research Centre   (SITI)
- ■ School of Business and Enterprise, Queen Margaret University, Corstophine Campus, Clerwood Terrace, Edinburgh, EH12 8TS.
  - 0131-317 3596
  - http://www.qmuc.ac.uk/siti/
  - Director: Prof Andy Frew.
- E A research centre at Queen Margaret University.

Scottish Manufacturing Institute   (SMI)
- NR Heriot-Watt University, Riccarton, Edinburgh, EH14 4AS.
  - 0131-451 3041
  - http://www.smi.hw.ac.uk/
  - Director: Prof Julian Jones. Administrator: David J Nisbet.
- E An EPSRC Innovative Manufacturing Research Centre at Heriot-Watt University.
- ○ To capture research technology for for the benefit of the global manufacturing industry; to deliver innovative manufacturing technology solutions for high value, low volume, highly customised, and high IP content products
- ● Three research groups - digital tools, microsystems, and photonics

Note: One of the EPSRC funded centres in the UK - for further information see EPSRC Innovative Manufacturing Research Centres.

Scottish Mask and Puppet Centre   (SMPC)   1985
- ■ 8-10 Balcarres Avenue, Kelvindale, Glasgow, G12 0QF.
  - 0141-339 6185   fax 0141-357 4484
  - http://www.scottishmaskandpuppetcentre.co.uk/
  - Chairman: Dr Edward Argent.
- E A registered charity and membership organisation.
- ○ To act as a central information and advisory point for mask and puppet work in Scotland; to raise the profile of puppet theatre and mask theatre within the mainstream of cultural provision within Scotland

Scottish Music Information Centre Ltd   (SMIC)   1968
- ■ 1 Bowmont Gardens, Glasgow, G12 9LR.
  - 0141-334 6393   fax 0141-337 1161
  - http://www.scottishmusiccentre.com/
  - Managing Director: Gill Maxwell. Information Manager: Alasdair Pettinger.
- E A registered charity.
- ○ To document, preserve and promote Scottish music of all types and all periods, making it available to all worldwide
- ● Information service - Library - Open Mon-Fri 0930-1730

Scottish National Sports Centre
> see **SportScotland National Centre**

Scottish Offshore Materials Centre   (SOMC)   1999
- ■ Department of Engineering, University of Aberdeen, Meston Building, Meston Walk, Old Aberdeen, AB24 3UE.
  - 01224 272795
  - http://www.abdn.ac.uk/somc/
  - Contact: Robin Henderson.
- E A research centre at the University of Aberdeen.
- ○ To provide advice, testing, analysis and research support for any metals, polymers, cements, ceramics or rock encountered by the industry

Scottish Polymer Development Centre   (SPDC)   1997
- ■ Bell College, Almada Street, Hamilton, ML3 0JB.
  - 01698 894428   fax 01698 894428
  - http://www.bell.ac.uk/bdia/scottish_polymer.htm
  - Co-ordinator: Kenny Cameron.
- E A research centre at the Bell College.
- ○ To develop the competitiveness of the plastics industry in Scotland by providing a supply of suitably qualified and trained personnel in design, development and processing in polymers
- ● Education and training - Information service

Note: At the time of going to press, Bell College was preparing to merge with the University of Paisley to form the University of the West of Scotland.

Scottish Schools Equipment Research Centre   (SSERC)   1968
- ■ South Pitreavie Business Park, Dunfermline, Fife, KY11 8UB.
  - 01383 626070   fax 01383 842793
  - http://www.sserc.org.uk/
- E A company limited by guarantee.
- ○ To provide advice, information, consultancy and training on educational equipment and facilities for use in science and technology

Scottish Sensory Centre (SSC) 1992

■ Moray House School of Education, University of Edinburgh, Holyrood Road, Edinburgh, EH8 8AQ.
0131-651 6501   fax 0131-651 6502
Co-ordinator: Marianna Buultjens.
E   A research centre at the University of Edinburgh.
○   To promote and support new developments for education for children and young people who are visually impaired or deaf; to work in collaboration with teachers, parents' groups and voluntary organisations
●   Collection of resources and materials - Conferences - Dissemination of information - Help with discussions about equipment and other resources (telephone Mon-Fri 0930-1600)

Scottish Storytelling Centre 1992

■ 43-45 High Street, Edinburgh, EH1 1SR.
0131-556 9579   fax 0131-557 5224
http://www.scottishstorytellingcentre.co.uk/
Contact: Dr Donald Smith.
E   A registered charity and an independent membership organisation.
○   To encourage and support the telling and sharing of stories across all ages and all sectors of society

Scottish Studies Centre
    see **Saint Andrews Scottish Studies Centre.**

Scottish Universities Environmental Research Centre (SUERC)

■ Scottish Enterprise Technology Park, University of Glasgow, Rankine Avenue, East Kilbride, Glasgow, G75 0QF.
01355 223332   fax 01355 229898
http://www.gla.ac.uk/acad/suerc/
Director: Prof A E Fallick, FRSE, FRSA, FMin Soc.
E   A centre at the University of Glasgow.
○   To provide to universities of the Scottish consortium collaborative access to expensive equipment and specialist expertise

Scottish Water Ski Centre (SWSC) 1992

■ Town Loch, Townhill Country Park, Dunfermline, Fife, KY12 0HT.
01383 620123   fax 01383 620122
http://www.waterskiscotland.co.uk/
E   The headquarters of WaterskiScotland, the governing body for the sport in Scotland.

Scottish Wool Centre 1992

■ Off the Main Street, Aberfoyle, Stirling, FK8 3UQ.
01877 382850
http://www.foreverscotland.com/mini_sites/wool_centre/
E   A private venture and profit-making business set up as a visitor centre.

SCRE Centre 1928

■ Department of Adult and Continuing Education, University of Glasgow, St Andrew's Building, 11 Eldon Street, Glasgow, G3 6NH.
0141-330 3490   fax 0141-330 3491
http://www.scre.ac.uk/
Director: Paul Brna.
E   A centre at the University of Glasgow.
○   To conduct educational research of the highest quality and to support the research outcomes through the dissemination of findings
Note: SCRE = Scottish Council for Research on Education.

Screen Media Research Centre (SMRC)

■ School of Arts, Brunel University, Uxbridge, Middlesex, UB8 3PH.
01895 274000
http://www.brunel.ac.uk/about/acad/sa/artresearch/smrc/
E   A centre at Brunel University.
○   To conduct research in a broad range of screen media, including cult media and transgression, the politics of representation and cultural identity, dominant and alternative cinemas, videogames and digital media, and spectacle, documentary and the real
●   Cult Film Archive (approx 3,000 titles)

Seafarers International Research Centre (SIRC) 1995

■ Cardiff School of Social Sciences, Cardiff University, 52 Park Place, Cardiff, CF10 3AT.
029 2087 4620   fax 029 2087 4619
http://www.sirc.cf.ac.uk/
Director: Dr Helen Sampson.
E   A centre at Cardiff University.
○   To conduct research on seafarers, with particular emphasis on issues of occupational health and safety

Seal Rescue Centre
    see **Orkney Seal Rescue Centre.**

Security Studies Institute   (SSI)
- ■   Department of Defence Management and Security, Cranfield University, Shrivenham, Swindon, Wiltshire, SN6 8LA.
      01793 785474   fax 01793 785459
      http://www.dcmt.cranfield.ac.uk/ddmsa/ssi/
      Co-Director: Prof Richard Holmes. Co-Director: Prof Christopher Bellamy.
- E   A research institute at Cranfield University.
- O   To conduct research, teaching and consultancy in a wide range of defence-related subjects, including defence policy and military history

Sefydliad Cerddoriaeth Cymru
    see **Welsh Music Institute.**

Sefydliad Gwleidyddiaeth Cymru
    see **Institute of Welsh Politics.**

Self Realisation Meditation Healing Centre   1989
- ■   Laurel Lane, Queen Camel, Somerset, BA22 7NU.
      01935 850266   fax 01935 850234
      Co-ordinator: Christie Casley.
- E   A registered charity.
- O   To establish residential and educational centres throughout the world to practice, promote and teach alternative holistic methods of healing, counselling and meditation
- ●   Education and training - Exhibitions - Information service - Clinics (by appointment) for guidance, healing and progressive counselling - Lecturing in hospitals, schools and communities on all aspects of self-development

Sesame Institute UK   (Sesame)   1964
- ■   Christchurch, 27 Blackfriars Road, London, SE1 8NY.
      020 7633 9690
      http://www.sesame-institute.org/
      Chairman: Rebecca Mackeoris.
- E   A registered charity.
- O   To research and train students in the use of drama and movement in therapy; to provide professional membership, supervision, support and a networking community for sesame practitioners
- ●   Education and training - Information service

Shakespeare Centre   1964
- ■   Henley Street, Stratford-upon-Avon, Warwickshire, CV37 6QW.
      01789 204016
      http://www.shakespeare.org.uk/
- E   An independent non-profit-distributing organisation.
- O   To provide a base and facilities for the Shakespeare Birthplace Trust to carry out its objectives, which are to promote in every part of the world an appreciation and study of the plays and other works of William Shakespeare and the general advancement of Shakespearean knowledge

Shakespeare Institute   1951
- ■   Mason Croft, Church Street, Stratford-upon-Avon, Warwickshire, CV37 6HP.
      0121-414 9500
      http://www.shakespeare.bham.ac.uk/
      Director: Prof Kate McLuskie.
- E   A department of the University of Birmingham.
- O   To conduct research and teaching of the life and works of William Shakespeare

Sheep Centre
- ■   Malvern, Worcestershire, WR13 6PH.
      01684 892661   fax 01684 892663
      http://www.nationalsheep.org.uk/
- E   Part of the National Sheep Association.
- O   To breed, manage and promote sheep as a species and as an industry

Sheffield Centre for Advanced Magnetic Materials and Devices   (SCAMMD)
- ■   Department of Engineering Materials, University of Sheffield, Sir Robert Hadfield Building, Mappin Street, Sheffield, S1 3JD.
      0114-222 5467; 5941   fax 0114-222 5943
      http://www.sheffield.ac.uk/materials/research/centres/magnetics
      Director: Prof M R J Gibbs.
- E   A research centre at the University of Sheffield.
- O   To provide a focus for research innovation and for the exploitation of a wide range of magnetic materials and devices

Sheffield Centre for Aegean Archaeology   (SCAA)   1995
- ■   Department of Archaeology, University of Sheffield, Northgate House, West Street, Sheffield, S4 1ET.
      0114-222 5103   fax 0114-272 2563
      http://www.shef.ac.uk/archaeology/research/aegean/
- E   A research centre at the University of Sheffield.
- O   To stimulate and promote inter-disciplinary research in the archaeology of the Aegean

Sheffield Centre for Dead Sea Scrolls Research University of Sheffield,
   see **Manchester-Sheffield Centre for Dead Sea Scrolls Research**.

Sheffield Centre for Geographic Information and Spatial Analysis
Note: The work of this Centre is being carried forward by the Informatics Collaboratory of the Social Sciences at the University of
   Sheffield, which is not within the scope of this Directory.

Sheffield Centre for International Drylands Research   (SCIDR)   1995
■   Department of Geography, University of Sheffield, Winter Street, Sheffield, S10 2TN.
     0114-222 7900   fax 0114-279 7912
     http://www.shef.ac.uk/scidr/
     Director: Dr Mark D Bateman.
E   A research centre at the University of Sheffield.
O   To conduct research into the past, present and future of dryland environments and peoples

Sheffield Institute for Biotechnological Law and Ethics   (SIBLE)   1994
■   University of Sheffield, Sheffield, S10 1DF.
     0114-222 2000   fax 0114-222 6886
     http://www.sible.group.shef.ac.uk/
E   An inter-faculty institute of the University of Sheffield.
O   To be an inter-disciplinary forum for the discussion of ethical and legal issues raised by developments in biotechnology

Sheffield Institute for Studies on Ageing   (SISA)
■   University of Sheffield, Elmfield, Northumberland Road, Sheffield, S10 2TU.
     0114-222 6270   fax 0114-222 6230
     http://www.shef.ac.uk/sisa/
     Director: Prof Stuart Parker.
E   A research institute within the University of Sheffield.
O   To support research into human ageing
●   Seminars - Workshops

Sheffield Polymer Centre
■   University of Sheffield, Dainton Building, Brook Hill, Sheffield, S3 7HF.
     0114-222 9537
     http://www.polymer.group.shef.ac.uk/
     Director: Prof Anthony Ryan. Manager: Dr Malcolm Butler.
E   A research centre at the University of Sheffield.
O   To conduct research into every aspect of polymer science
●   Seminars

Sheffield University Metals Advisory Centre   (SUMAC)   1980
■   Department of Engineering Materials, University of Sheffield, Mappin Street, Sheffield, S1 3JD.
     0114-282 5491
     http://www.sumac.group.shef.ac.uk/
E   A research centre at the University of Sheffield.
O   To provide metallurgical expertise to industry, insurers, the legal profession, research organisations and the public
●   SUMAC is an accredited testing house under the National Testing Laboratory Accreditation Scheme, and has gained Ministry of
     Defence Quality Assurance Directorate approval 05-32 status Services include melting and casting, hot and cold working,
     chemical analysis, optical metallography, scanning electron microscopy with analysis, transmission electron microscopy with
     analysis, mechanical testing, failure investigations, general metallurgical investigations, weld procedure tests, general structural
     and machinery

Sheffield University Waste Incineration Centre   (SUWIC)
■   Department of Chemical and Process Engineering, University of Sheffield, Mappin Street, Sheffield, S1 3JD.
     0114-222 7500   fax 0114-222 7501
     http://www.suwic.group.shef.ac.uk/
     Director: Prof V N Sharifi.
E   A research centre at the University of Sheffield.

Sheffield Vascular Institute   (SVI)   1995
■   University of Sheffield, Western Bank, Sheffield, S10 2TN.
     http://www.shef.ac.uk/svi/
E   A research institute at the University of Sheffield.
O   To offer a full range of clinical services relating to vascular disease, including research into the causes, diagnosis and treatment of
     the disease

Ship Stability Research Centre   (SSRC)   1997
NR   Department of Naval Architecture and Marine Engineering, University of Strathclyde, 8th Floor - Colville Building,
      48 North Portland Street, Glasgow, G1 1XM.
         0141-548 4092   fax 0141-552 2879
         http://www.na-me.ac.uk/index_2.htm
         Head: Prof Dracos Vassalos.
E   A research centre at the University of Strathclyde.
○   To combine effectively national and European research efforts, targeting safety as a life-cycle issue for all safety-critical ship types
Note: A joint venture with the University of Glasgow.

Shipwreck and Coastal Heritage Centre   1986
■   Rock-a-Nore Road, Hastings, East Sussex, TN34 3DW.
         01424 437452   fax 01424 437452
         http://www.shipwreck-heritage.org.uk/
         Manager: Yasmin Ornsby.
E   Part of the Nautical Museum Trust, a registered charity.
○   To illustrate the history of ships and seafaring in North-West Europe, primarily from archaeological remains which have been
         rescued and preserved

Siemens Automation and Drives Centre
■   Aberconway Building, Cardiff University, Colum Drive, Cardiff, CF10 3EU.
         029 2087 9611
         http://www.mec.cf.ac.uk/
E   A research centre within the Manufacturing Engineering Centre (qv) at Cardiff University.

Silwood Centre for Pest Management   (SCPM)   1982
■   Imperial College London, Silwood Park, Ascot, Berkshire, SL5 7PY.
         020 7594 2316   fax 020 7594 2339
         http://www3.imperial.ac.uk/lifesciences/research/ecologyandevolution/pestmanagement
         Contact: Dr Simon Leather.
E   A research centre at Imperial College London.

Sir Arthur Marshall Institute for Aeronautics   (SAMIA)
■   Department of Engineering, University of Cambridge, Mill Lane, Cambridge, CB2 1RX.
         01223 766401
         http://www.samia.org.uk/
         Contact: Prof W N Dawes.
E   An interdisciplinary research institute at the University of Cambridge.
○   To support teaching and research in the field of aeronautics

Sir David Owen Population Centre   (DOC)   1972
■   School of Economics and Management Studies, Darwin Building, Keele University, Keele, Staffordshire, ST5 5BG.
         01782 593192   fax 01782 711737
         http://www.keele.ac.uk/depts/hm/units/david%20owen.htm
E   A research centre within the Centre for Health Planning and Management (qv) at Keele University.

Sir George Cayley Research Centre
■   Harrow School of Computing Science, University of Westminster, Watford Road, Harrow, Middlesex, HA1 3TP.
         020 7911 5917
         http://www.wmin.ac.uk/hscs/page-4
         Director: Prof Vladimir Getov.
E   A research centre at the University of Westminster.
○   The research arm of the Harrow School of Computer Science

Sir Geraint Evans Wales Heart Research Institute   (WHRI)   1999
■   Cardiff School of Medicine, Cardiff University, Heath Park, Cardiff, CF14 4XN.
         029 2074 7747
         http://www.cardiff.ac.uk/medicine/whri
         Chairman: Prof Tony Lai.
E   A research institute at Cardiff University.
○   To conduct collaborative research into all aspects of cardiovascular medicine, including cardiology, diagnostic radiology,
         pharmacology, medical biochemistry, and medical microbiology

Sir James Black Centre
■   College of Life Sciences, University of Dundee, Dow Street, Dundee, DD1 5EH.
         01382 388377   fax 01382 223778
         http://www.lifesci.dundee.ac.uk/
         Contact: Alison Nicoll.
E   A centre at the University of Dundee.

Sir Leon Bagrit Centre   1991

- ■ Department of Bioengineering, Imperial College London, South Kensington Campus, London, SW7 2AZ.
  020 7594 5179   fax 020 7584 6897
  http://www3.imperial.ac.uk/bioengineering
- E A department of Imperial College London.
- Note: A building dedicated to a very wide variety of bioengineering research.

Sir Norman Chester Centre for Football Research
  see **Centre for the Sociology of Sport.**

Sir Peter Mansfield Magnetic Resonance Centre   1991

- ■ University of Nottingham, University Park, Nottingham, NG7 2RD.
  0115-951 4747   fax 0115-951 5166
  http://www.magres.nottingham.ac.uk/
  Chairman: Prof Peter Morris.
- E A department of the University of Nottingham.
- ○ To develop new techniques for magnetic resonance imaging and spectroscopy and their application to biomedical and other systems
- ● Education and training - Equipment includes Whole body MRI/S systems (3 0 T and 7 0 T), NMR microscope (11 7 T) and NMR spectrometers (11 7 T and 4 7 T)

Sir Robert Menzies Centre for Australian Studies
  see **Menzies Centre for Australian Studies.**

Sir William Dale Centre for Legislative Studies   (CLS)   1997

- ■ School of Advanced Study, University of London, Charles Clore House, 17 Russell Square, London, WC1B 5DR.
  020 7862 5861   fax 020 7862 5855
  http://ials.sas.ac.uk/
  Director: Richard Nzerem. Academic Director: Dr Helen Xanthaki.
- E A research centre within the Institute of Advanced Legal Studies (qv) at the University of London.
- ○ To specialise in teaching and research in the field of legislative drafting and law reform

SITA Centre for Sustainable Wastes Management

- ■ School of Environmental Sciences, University of Northampton, Boughton Green Road, Northampton, NN2 7AL.
  01604 735500
  http://www2.northampton.ac.uk
  Co-Director: Dr Margaret Bates. Co-Director: Dr Nigel Freestone.
- E A research centre at the University of Northampton.
- ○ To introduce techniques and policies, in the UK, that will dramatically alter practices for effective waste management
- ● Information service

Sivananda Yoga Vedanta Centre   1970

- ■ 51 Felsham Road, London, SW15 1AZ.
  020 8780 0160   fax 020 8780 0128
  http://www.sivananda.org/london/
- E A non-profit, non-sectarian organisation.
- ○ To propagate the teaching of yoga in order to help individuals achieve health, happiness and inner peace
- ● Courses in Hatha Yoga, meditation, Yoga in pregnancy, Teacher training - Daily 'drop in' yoga classes - Retreats - Pensioners' class - Satsang (group meditation) - Vegetarian cooking workshops - Library (members only)
- ¶ Sivananda Book of Meditation.

Skill: National Bureau for Students with Disabilities   (SKILL)   1975

- ■ Chapter House, 18-20 Crucifix Lane, London, SE1 3JW.
  020 7450 0620   fax 020 7450 0650
  http://www.skill.org.uk/
- E A registered charity and a company limited by guarantee.
- ○ To promote opportunities for young people and adults with any kind of disability in post-16 education, training and employment
- Note: Skill also has offices in Northern Ireland, Scotland and Wales.

Skin Research Centre   (SRC)   1990

- ■ Faculty of Biological Sciences, University of Leeds, Garstang Building, Leeds, LS2 9JT.
  0113-343 5615
  http://www.leeds.ac.uk/src/
- E A research centre within the Institute of Molecular and Cellular Biology (qv) at the University of Leeds.
- ○ To be a leading research centre concerned with skin and dermatology

Skoll Centre for Social Entrepreneurship

- ■ Saïd Business School, University of Oxford, 1 Park End Street, Oxford, OX1 1HP.
  01865 288838
  http://www.sbs.ox.ac.uk/skoll/
  Director: Rowena Young.
- E A research centre at the University of Oxford.

Skye Environmental Centre Ltd   (SEC)   1985

- Harapool, Broadford, Isle of Skye, IV49 9AQ.
  01471 822487   fax 01471 822487
  http://www.otter.org/sec.html
- E   A registered charity and a company limited by guarantee.
- O   To carry out various types of ecological and environmental work

Slade Centre for Electronic Media in Fine Art   (SCEMFA)   1995

- Slade School of Fine Art, University College London, Gower Street, London, WC1E 6BT.
  020 7679 2313   fax 020 7679 7801
  http://www.scemfa.org/
  Head: Susan Collins.
- E   A department of University College London.
- O   To focus on electronic media and fine art

Sleep Research Centre [Loughborough]
   see **Loughborough Sleep Research Centre.**

Sleep Research Centre [Surrey]
   see **Surrey Sleep Research Centre.**

Small Business Bureau Ltd   (SBB)   1976

- Curzon House, Church Road, Windlesham, Surrey, GU20 6BH.
  01276 452010   fax 01276 451602
  Chairman: Dr Marilyn Orcharton. Managing Director: Alan M Cleverly.
- E   A limited company.
- O   To be the representative body for smaller businesses (those with up to 50 employees)
- ● Liaison with government ministers and MPs and MEPs - Contact with like-minded people in business and politics - Conferences and seminars - Business information service
Note: The Bureau incorporates the Women into Business network and also has a Westminster-based secretariat.

Small Business Research Centre   (SBRC)

- Kingston Business School, Kingston University London, Kingston Hill, Kingston-upon-Thames, Surrey, KT1 7LB.
  020 8547 2000
  http://business.kingston.ac.uk/
- E   A research centre at Kingston University, London.
- O   To use rigorous approaches to investigating small firms and entrepreneurship

Smart Card Centre   (SCC)   2002

- Information Security Group, Royal Holloway University of London, Egham, Surrey, TW20 0EX.
  01784 443101   fax 01784 430766
  http://www.scc.rhul.ac.uk/
  Contact: Dr Keith Mayes. Contact: Dr Konstantinos Markantonakis.
- E   A research centre at Royal Holloway, University of London.
- O   To create a worldwide centre of excellence for training and research in the field of Smart Cards, applications and related technologies

Smith Institute for Industrial Mathematics and System Engineering   1997

- PO Box 183, Guildford, Surrey, GU2 7GG.
  01483 579108   fax 01483 568710
  http://www.smithinst.co.uk/
  Director: Dr Robert Leese.
- E   A not-for-profit company limited by guarantee.
- O   To help companies gain a competitive advantage, through the application of mathematical modelling and analysis, for their products, processes and operations

Smooth Muscle Research Centre

Note: Note: is now based at the Dundalk Institute of Technology, Dublin Road, Dundalk, Co. Louth, Republic of Ireland, and is therefore no longer within the scope of this Directory.

Social Care Institute for Excellence   (SCIE)

- Goldings House, 2 Hay's Lane, London, SE1 2HB.
  020 7089 6840; 6917   fax 020 7089 6841
  http://www.scie.org.uk/
  Contact: Annie Goss.
- O   To collect and synthesise up-to-date knowledge about what works in social care

© CBD Research Ltd · Beckenham · Kent BR3 5JS · Tel 020 8650 7745 · Fax 020 8650 0768 · E-mail cbd@cbdresearch.com · www.cbdresearch.com

Social Contexts of Pathways in Crime Centre   (SCoPiC)
■   University of Cambridge, Sidgwick Avenue, Cambridge, CB3 9DT.
      01223 335378
      http://www.scopic.ac.uk/
      Director: Prof Per-Olof Wikström.
E   A research centre within the Institute of Criminology (qv) at the University of Cambridge.
O   To achieve a better understanding of how young people become involved in crime

Social Dimensions of Health Institute   (SDHI)   2003
NR   College of Arts & Social Sciences, University of Dundee, Airlie Place, Dundee, DD1 4HJ.
      01382 388661   fax 01382 388533
      http://www.sdhi.ac.uk/
      Director: Prof Paul Boyle.
E   A research institute at the University of Dundee.
O   To bring together social scientists, medical researchers and practitioners, nurses, midwives, allied health professionals, doctors and paramedics to tackle widespread public and political concern with health issues
Note: A joint initiative with the University of St Andrews.

Social Economy Evaluation Bureau   (SEEB)
■   UCE Birmingham Business School, Galton Building, Birmingham City University, Perry Barr, Birmingham, B42 2SU.
      0121-331 5200   fax 0121-331 6366
      http://www.bs.uce.ac.uk/
      Contact: Phil Rose.
E   A resource centre within the Management and Enterprise Development Centre (qv) at Birmingham City University.
O   To provide social economy organisations with information, research services and expertise

Social Enterprise Institute   (SEI)
■   School of Management and Languages, Heriot-Watt University, Riccarton, Edinburgh, EH14 4AS.
      0131-451 3858   fax 0131-451 3296
      http://www.som.hw.ac.uk/socialenterprise/
      Director: Declan Jones.
E   An institute at Heriot-Watt University.
O   To provide research, training, business planning, education and consultancy practice for the social or 'not-for-profit' economy in Scotland

Social and Environmental Art Research Centre   (SEA)
■   School of Art, Manchester Metropolitan University, Cavendish North Building, Cavendish Street, Manchester, M15 6BG.
      0161-247 1714
      http://www.miriad.mmu.ac.uk/sea/
      Leader: Prof Margaret Harrison.
E   An interdisciplinary research centre within the Manchester Institute for Research and Innovation in Art and Design (qv) at Manchester Metropolitan University.
O   To conduct research in various areas of social and environmental art, with particular emphasis on the effectiveness of creativity, culture and the arts on health and economic outcomes

Social Futures Institute   (SFI)
■   School of Social Sciences and Law, University of Teesside, Middlesbrough, TS1 3BA.
      01642 342321
      http://www.tees.ac.uk/depts/
      Director: Dr Tony Chapman.
E   A department of the University of Teesside.
O   To conduct research with an ongoing commitment to the future of the Tees Valley and the North East of England's social and economic regeneration

Social, Genetic and Developmental Psychiatry Centre   1994
■   PO Box 80, King's College London, DeCrespigny Park, London, SE5 8AF.
      020 7848 5341   fax 020 7848 0866
      http://www.iop.kcl.ac.uk/
      Manager: Melissa Cooper.
E   A Medical Research Council research centre within the Institute of Psychiatry (qv) at King's College, London.
O   To undertake research on the interplay between genetic, environmental and maturational factors, and their roles in the causal processes underlying the origins and course of multifactorial mental disorders
Note: See **Medical Research Council Collaborative Centre** for further information.

Social Policy Research Centre   (SPRC)   1990
■   School of Health and Social Sciences, Roberts Building, Middlesex University, Queensway, Enfield, Middlesex, EN3 4SA.
      020 8411 4772
      http://www.mdx.ac.uk/hssc/
      Director: Dr Betsy Thom. Research Administrator: Veena Meetoo.
E   A research centre within the Institute of Social and Health Research (qv) at Middlesex University.
O   To conduct research in the areas of ethnicity, migration and human rights, health and well-being, drug and alcohol policy, and urban policy, regeneration and communities

Social and Policy Research Institute   (SPRI)

■   School of Policy Studies, Jordanstown Campus, University of Ulster, Shore Road, Newtownabbey, County Antrim, BT37 0QB.
   028 9036 6159
   http://www.socsci.ulster.ac.uk/
   Director: Prof Bob Osborne.
E   A research institute at the University of Ulster.

Social Psychology European Research Institute   (SPERI)   1993

■   Department of Psychology, University of Surrey, Guildford, Surrey, GU2 7XH.
   01483 686902   fax 01483 689553
   http://www.psy.surrey.ac.uk/
   Contact: Dr Evanthia Lyons.
E   A research institute at the University of Surrey.
O   To conduct research in social psychology, with special emphasis on self and identity processes, and upon risk perception, communication and management

Social Research Centre
   see **Roehampton Social Research Centre.**

Social Research Methodology Centre   (SRMC)   2001

■   Department of Sociology, Social Sciences Building, City University, Northampton Square, London, EC1V 0HB.
   020 7040 5060   fax 020 7040 5070
   http://www.city.ac.uk/sociology/
E   A centre at City University.
O   To provide a forum for research training and methodological research within City University and the wider social research community

Social Sciences, Arts and Humanities Research Institute   (SSAHRI)

■   University of Hertfordshire, College Lane, Hatfield, Hertfordshire, AL10 9AB.
   01707 284000   fax 01707 284115
   http://perseus.herts.ac.uk/
E   A department of the University of Hertfordshire.
O   To offer a range of courses and degrees in the arts, humanities and social sciences

Social Sciences Institute
   see **Leeds Social Sciences Institute.**

Social Theory Centre   (STC)   1997

■   Faculty of Social Studies, University of Warwick, Coventry, CV4 7AL.
   024 7652 3114
   http://www2.warwick.ac.uk/fac/soc/sociology/theory/
E   A research centre at the University of Warwick.
O   To promote and develop social theory
●   Conferences - Seminars

Social Work Research Centre   (SWRC)   1986

■   Department of Applied Social Science, University of Stirling, Stirling, FK9 4LA.
   01786 467724   fax 01786 466319
   http://www.dass.stir.ac.uk/
   Director: Prof Gill McIvor. Senior Research Fellow: Moira Walker.
E   A department of the University of Stirling.
O   To research and evaluate the effectiveness of social work
●   Conferences - Seminars - Workshops

Sociology Research Centre   (SRC)

■   Faculty of Arts, Media and Social Sciences, University of Salford, Salford, Manchester, M5 4WT.
   0161-295 5876
   http://www.iscpr.salford.ac.uk/
   Director: Prof Paul Bellaby.
E   A research centre within the Institute for Social, Cultural and Policy Research (qv) at the University of Salford.
O   To conduct research in sociology

Soil Survey and Land Research Centre   (SSLRC)   1939

■   Natural Resources' Department, Cranfield University, Silsoe, Bedfordshire, MK45 4DT.
   01525 863000
   http://www.silsoe.cranfield.ac.uk/nsri/
E   A research centre within the National Soil Resources Institute (qv) at Cranfield University.
O   To conduct research, carry out consultancy, and offer a range of scientific services, to individuals and organisations, who have a requirement for land and soil resource assessment, evaluation and advice

   © CBD Research Ltd · Beckenham · Kent BR3 5JS · Tel 020 8650 7745 · Fax 020 8650 0768 · E-mail cbd@cbdresearch.com · www.cbdresearch.com

SOLSTICE Centre   (SOLSTICE)   2005
- ■   LINC Building, Edge Hill College of Higher Education, Edge Hill, Ormskirk, Lancashire, L39 4QP.
  01695 584744
  http://www.edgehill.ac.uk/
  Contact: Mark Schofield.
- E   A Centre for Excellence in Teaching and Learning (CETL) at Edge Hill College of Higher Education.
- Note: SOLSTICE = Supported Online Learning for Students using Technology for Information and Communication in their Education.
  See **Centres for Excellence in Teaching and Learning** for more information.

Sonic Arts Research Centre   (SARC)   2004
- ■   School of Music and Sonic Arts, Queen's University of Belfast, Belfast, BT7 1NN.
  028 9097 4829
  http://www.sarc.qub.ac.uk/
  Director: Prof Michael Alcorn.
- E   A centre at Queen's University, Belfast.
- O   To conduct research in music technology in the areas of musical composition, signal processing, internet technology, and digital hardware

Sorby Centre for Electron Microscopy and Microanalysis
- ■   Department of Engineering Materials, Sir Robert Hadfield Building, University of Sheffield, Mappin Street, Sheffield, S1 3JD.
  0114-222 5467; 5941   fax 0114-222 5943
  http://www.shef.ac.uk/materials/research/centres/sorby/
  Manager: Dr G Möbus.
- E   A research centre at the University of Sheffield.
- O   To use advanced transmission and scanning electron microscopy to investigate the microstructure and chemistry of materials

South Bank Centre   (SBC)   1986
- ■   Royal Festival Hall, Belvedere Road, London, SE1 8XX.
  0870 380 4300   fax 0870 163 3898
  http://www.rfh.org.uk/
- E   A registered charity and an independent non-profit-making organisation.
- O   To promote the arts

South of England Cochlear Implant Centre   (SOECIC)   1990
- ■   University of Southampton, Highfield, Southampton, SO17 1BJ.
  023 8059 3604   fax 023 8059 4981
  http://www.soton.ac.uk/
- E   A centre at the University of Southampton.

Southampton Oceanography Centre
   see **National Oceanography Centre**

Southampton Regional e-Science Centre   (SeSC)
- ■   School of Engineering Science, University of Southampton, Highfield, Southampton, SO17 1BJ.
  023 8059 8353   fax 023 8059 4813
  http://www.e-science.soton.ac.uk/
  Director: Prof A J Keane. Centre Manager: Trevor Cooper-Chadwick.
- E   A research centre at the University of Southampton.
- Note: See **e-Science Centres** for further information.

Southampton Statistical Sciences Research Institute   (S³RI)   2003
- ■   Faculty of Engineering, Science and Mathematics, Building 39, University of Southampton, Highfield, Southampton, SO17 1BJ.
  023 8059 3216   fax 023 8059 5763
  http://www.s3ri.soton.ac.uk/
  Director: Prof Susan Lewis.
- E   A research centre at the University of Southampton.
- O   To support and co-ordinate the research activities of statisticians and demographers

Southampton University Microelectronics Centre
Note: Now Innos Ltd (www.innos.co.uk).

Sowerby Centre for Health Informatics   (SCHIN)   1993
- ■   University of Newcastle upon Tyne, Bede House, All Saints Business Centre, Newcastle upon Tyne, NE1 2ES.
  0191-243 6100   fax 0191-243 6101
  http://www.schin.co.uk/
- E   A research centre within the University of Newcastle upon Tyne.
- O   To enhance health care across a broad range of health informatics disciplines

Space Centre
   see **Surrey Space Centre.**

Space Research Centre
>see **Cranfield Space Research Centre.**

Space Science Centre

■ School of Science and Technology, Pevensey II Building, University of Sussex, Falmer, Brighton, East Sussex, BN1 9QH.
01273 678557   fax 01273 873124
http://www.sussex.ac.uk/space-science/
Head: Prof Paul Gough.
E   A research centre at the University of Sussex.

Space Structures Research Centre   (SSRC)

■ School of Engineering, University of Surrey, Guildford, Surrey, GU2 7XH.
01483 686600
http://www.surrey.ac.uk/eng/
E   A research centre within the Centre for Materials, Surfaces and Structural Systems (qv) at the University of Surrey.
O   To conduct research in structural systems that involve three dimensions

Spatial Literacy in Teaching CETL   (SPLINT)

■ Department of Geography, University of Leicester, Leicester, LE1 7RH.
0116-223 1320; 252 3823
http://www.geog.le.ac.uk/
Contact: Dr Nicholas Tate.
E   A Centre for Excellence in Teaching and Learning (CETL) at the University of Leicester.
Note: See **Centres for Excellence in Teaching and Learning** for more information.

Speech Science Research Centre   (SSRC)

■ Corstorphine Campus, Queen Margaret University, Clerwood Terrace, Edinburgh, EH12 8TS.
0131-317 3000
http://www.qmuc.ac.uk/ssrc/
Director: Prof William J Hardcastle.
E   A research centre at Queen Margaret University.
O   To promote both pure and applied research into speech and non-verbal communication in normal speakers and in those with a variety of speech and language disorders

Sport Industry Research Centre   (SIRC)

■ Faculty of Health and Well Being, Unit 1 - Science Park, City Campus, Sheffield Hallam University, Sheffield, S1 1WB.
0114-225 3972   fax 0114-225 4488
http://www.shu.ac.uk/research/sirc/
Co-Director: Simon Shibli. Co-Director: Peter Taylor.
E   A research centre at Sheffield Hallam University.
O   To provide bespoke consultancy services in the areas of economic analysis, strategic planning, analysis and reporting, market forecasting, tailored professional training, and performance measurement (including statistical data collection)

Sport Institute
>see **London Sport Institute.**

Sport Performance Assessment and Rehabilitation Centre   (SPARC)   1998

■ School of Human and Life Sciences, Whitelands College, Roehampton University, Holybourne Avenue, London, SW15 4JD.
020 8392 3541
http://www.roehampton.ac.uk/sparc/
Contact: Jon Harrison.
E   A research centre within the Centre for Scientific and Cultural Research in Sport (qv) at Roehampton University.
O   To offer a number of support services accessible to all standards of sports performer, as well as to individuals interested in exercise;
●   supports physiology, sports psychology, biomechanics, sports massage, physiotherapy, podiatry, pilates, and sports nutrition

Sports and Exercise Research Centre   (SERC)

■ Academy of Sport, Physical Activity and Wellbeing, London South Bank University, 103 Borough Road, London, SE1 0AA.
020 7915 7959   fax 020 7815 7454
http://www.lsbu.ac.uk/sports/
Contact: Dr Jo Bowtell.
E   A research centre within London South Bank University.

© CBD Research Ltd · Beckenham · Kent BR3 5JS · Tel 020 8650 7745 · Fax 020 8650 0768 · E-mail cbd@cbdresearch.com · www.cbdresearch.com

SportScotland National Centre, Cumbrae

- ■ Isle of Cumbrae, Ayrshire, KA28 0HQ.
  01475 530757   fax 01475 530013
  http://www.nationalcentrecumbrae.org.uk/
- E   A statutory organisation.
- O   To improve the standards of participation in water sports in Scotland; to place emphasis on the training of instructors and coaches, National Squad training and the promotion of courses which increase the safety of the sport
- ● National Squad training (November-March) - Courses for the public based on the Royal Yachting Association syllabus (summer) - The Centre has a full range of modern dinghies, keelboats, two cruisers/yachts, sea kayaks, windsurfers and rescue craft - Workshop and store of equipment
- ✕   Scottish National Sports Centre, Cumbrae.

SportScotland National Centre, Inverclyde

- ■ Burnside Road, Largs, Ayrshire, KA30 8RW.
  0845 126 0664   fax 01475 674720
  http://www.nationalcentreinverclyde.org.uk/
- E   A statutory organisation.
- O   To provide a residential resource for the training of coaches, instructors and leaders in a wide range of indoor and outdoor sports
- ● Wide range of indoor and outdoor facilities - Sports science laboratory and fitness training - Fully-equipped audio-visual conference and seminar facilities - Purpose-built golf practice facility
- ✕   Scottish National Sports Centre, Inverclyde.

SRIF Centre for Virtual Organisation Technology Enabling Research   (VOTER)

- ■ School of Computing and Mathematical Sciences, Glasgow Caledonian University, Cowcaddens Road, Glasgow, G4 0BA.
  0141-331 3000   fax 0141-331 3005
  http://www.gcal.ac.uk/cms/
  Director: Prof Huaglory Tianfield.
- E   A research centre at Glasgow Caledonian University.
- O   To undertake funded projects relating to new technologies enabling virtual organisations, with particular emphasis on Multi-Agent Systems (MAS), Computer Supported Collaborative Work (CSCW), Software Systems Engineering (SSE), Human Computer Interaction (HCI), and Knowledge Management (KM)

Note: SRIF is the Science Research Investment Fund of the UK Office of Science and Technology.

St . . .
    see **Saint**

Staffordshire University Centre for Professional Management
    see **Ashley Centre for Professional Management.**

Stamp Bureau
    see **Crown Agents Stamp Bureau.**

Stanley Burton Centre for Holocaust Studies   1990

- ■ Department of History, University of Leicester, University Road, Leicester, LE1 7RH.
  0116-252 2802   fax 0116-252 3986
  http://www.le.ac.uk/hi/centres/burton/
  Co-Director: Dr Chris Szejnmann. Co-Director: Martin Davies.
- E   An autonomous centre at the University of Leicester.
- O   To promote study and research into the Holocaust, at University level and amongst members of the public, both in Leicester and elsewhere
- ● Conference facilities - Education and training - Exhibitions - Information service - Library

Statistics, Operational Research and Mathematics Research Centre   (STORM)

- ■ Department of Computing, Communications Technology and Mathematics, North Campus, London Metropolitan University, 166-220 Holloway Road, London, N7 8DB.
  020 7753 3251   fax 020 7753 7061
  http://www.londonmet.ac.uk/depts/research/storm/
- E   A research centre at London Metropolitan University.
- O   To conduct academic research in generalised linear models, generalised additive models for location, scale and shape, queuing theory and reliability, combinatorial optimisation, operator, banach and C algebras, algebraic topology, homotopy and category theory

Statistical Sciences Research Institute
    see **Southampton Statistical Sciences Research Institute.**

Statistical Services Centre   (SSC)   1983

- ■ Harry Pitt Building, PO Box 240, University of Reading, Whiteknights Road, Reading, Berkshire, RG6 6FN.
  0118-378 8025   fax 0118-975 3169
  http://www.reading.ac.uk/ssc/
  Director: Eleanor Allan.
- E   A centre at the University of Reading.
- O   To offer training and advisory services in statistics and data management

---

Steel Can Recycling Information Bureau   (SCRIB)
- ■   Trostre Works, Llanelli, Camarthenshire, SA14 9SD.
       01554 712632   fax 01554 712571
       http://www.scrib.org/
- E   A sponsored organisation.
- ○   To raise awareness of the importance of recycling steel by providing information on steel packaging recycling to the general public, local authorities and the public sector

Sternberg Centre for Judaism   1981
- ■   80 East End Road, London, N3 2SY.
       020 8349 1143; 5600   fax 020 8343 2162; 5619
       http://www.jewishmuseum.org.uk/
- E   Home of the Jewish Museum.

Stirling Centre for Economic Methodology   (SCEME)   2003
- ■   Department of Economics, University of Stirling, Stirling, FK9 4LA.
       01786 467483; 467485
       http://www.economics.stir.ac.uk/
       Contact: Prof David Bell.
- E   A research centre at the University of Stirling.

Stirling Centre of Poetry   (SCOP)
- ■   Department of English Studies, University of Stirling, Stirling, FK9 4LA.
       01786 473171
       http://www.english.stir.ac.uk/
- E   A research centre at the University of Stirling.

Stirling Centre for Scottish Studies   (SCSS)
- ■   University of Stirling, Stirling, FK9 4LA.
       01786 467041
       http://www.stir.ac.uk/
- E   An interdisciplinary research centre at the University of Stirling.
- ○   To conduct research into Scottish culture and society, past and present

Stirling Media Research Institute   (SMRI)   1994
- ■   Department of Film and Media Studies, University of Stirling, Stirling, FK9 4LA.
       01786 467041
       http://www.stir.ac.uk/
- E   A research institute at the University of Stirling.
- ○   To conduct specialist research in media and national / cultural identities, screen analysis and mediated language, political communication and the sociology of journalism, promotional culture and public relations, cultural, creative and leisure industries, and media management and media policy

Stockholm Environment Institute at York   (SEI-Y   1989
- ■   University of York, Heslington, York, YO10 5DD.
       01904 432897
       http://www.york.ac.uk/inst/sei/
- E   An independent research organisation at the University of York.
- ○   To conduct research, consultancy and training which focuses on the links between the ecological, social and economic systems at global, regional and national and local levels

Strategic Management Centre
       see **Ashridge Strategic Management Centre.**

Strathclyde Centre for Disability Research   (SCDR)
- ■   Department of Sociology, Anthropology and Applied Social Sciences, Adam Smith Building, University of Strathclyde, 40 Bute Gardens, Glasgow, G12 8RT.
       0141-330 4545   fax 0141-330 3919
       http://www.gla.ac.uk/centres/disabilityresearch/
       Director: Prof Nick Watson.
- E   A research centre at the University of Glasgow.
- ○   To provide an academic base for research and teaching in social aspects of disability, with particular emphasis on the education, training, employment, health and legal needs of disabled people

Strathclyde Centre for European Economies in Transition   (SCEET)
- ■   Graham Hills Building, University of Strathclyde, 50 George Street, Glasgow, G1 1BA.
       0141-548 3851; 4843   fax 0141-548 4592
       http://www.strath.ac.uk/sceet/
       Kenneth N Bernard.
- E   A research centre at the University of Strathclyde.

Strathclyde Centre in Gender Studies   (SCIGS)

■   Department of History, McCance Building, University of Strathclyde, 16 Richmond Street, Glasgow, G1 1XQ.
      0141-548 2206   fax 0141-552 8509
      http://www.strath.ac.uk/departments/
      Director: Prof Eileen Yeo.
E   A research centre at the University of Strathclyde.

Strathclyde Institute for Drug Research   (SIDR)   1988

■   University of Strathclyde, 27 Taylor Street, Glasgow, G4 0NR.
      0141-553 4155   fax 0141-552 8376
      http://www.strath.ac.uk/departments/sidr/
      Director: Prof Alan Harvey. Business Development Manager: Anne Muir.
E   A department of the University of Strathclyde.
O   To facilitate collaboration and interaction between scientists of Strathclyde University and industry; to promote drug research work
      carried out at Strathclyde University; to license out intellectual property rights, held by the University, in the area of drug design;
      to license out an extensive library of natural product extracts for screening purposes
●   Conference facilities - Education and training - Information service

Strathclyde Institute of Pharmacy and Biomedical Sciences   (SIPBS)   2006

■   Faculty of Science, The John Arbuthnott Building, University of Strathclyde, 27 Taylor Street, Glasgow, G4 0NR.
      0141-548 2125   fax 0141-552 2562
      http://www.strath.ac.uk/sipbs/
E   A department of the University of Strathclyde.

Stroke Association Rehabilitation Research Centre   2004

■   Faculty of Medicine, Health and Life Sciences, Southampton General Hospital, Tremona Road, Southampton, SO16 6YD.
      023 8079 4575   fax 023 8079 4340
      http://www.stroke.soton.ac.uk/
      Contact: Prof Ann Ashburn.
E   A research centre at the University of Southampton.
O   To focus on investigating and understanding which rehabilitation interventions are most effective for patients with stroke

Structural Materials and Integrity Research Centre   (SMIRC)

■   City Campus, Sheffield Hallam University, Sheffield, S1 1WB.
      0114-225 3500   fax 0114-225 3501
      http://www.shu.ac.uk/research/meri/
      Head: Prof Robert Akid.
E   A constituent research centre within the Materials and Engineering Research Institute (qv) at Sheffield Hallam University.
O   To conduct research on the characterisation / behaviour of structural and functional materials so as to enable the predication of
      component / structure lifetimes

Structures Research Centre
      see **Engineering Structures Research Centre.**

Subject Centre for Dance, Drama and Music
      see **PALATINE - Dance, Drama and Music.**

Subject Centre for Education   (ESCalate)   2000

■   Graduate School of Education, University of Bristol, 35 Berkeley Square, Bristol, BS8 1JA.
      0117-331 4291   fax 0117-925 1537
      http://escalate.ac.uk/
      Director: Dr Tony Brown. Administrator: Mrs Liz Hankinson.
E   A Government funded national centre within the University of Bristol.
O   To foster world-class education in higher education, continuing and adult education, teacher education and lifelong learning
●   Education and training - Information service - Statistics
×   LTSN Education Subject Centre.
Note: One of the 24 Subject Centres of the Higher Education Academy, (qv).

Subject Centre for History, Classics and Archaeology   (HCA)   2000

■   Department of History, University of Glasgow, 1 University Gardens, Glasgow, G12 8QQ.
      0141-330 4942   fax 0141-330 5518
      http://www.hca.heacademy.ac.uk
      Director: Dr Colin Brooks. Administrator: Marion Cochrane.
E   A Government funded national centre within the University of Glasgow.
O   To foster world-class education in the fields of history, classics and archaeology
●   Education and training - Information service - Statistics
×   LTSN History, Archaeology and Classics Subject Centre.
Note: One of the 24 Subject Centres of the Higher Education Academy, (qv).

Subject Centre for Information and Computer Sciences   (ICS)   2000
■   Research School of Informatics, Loughborough University, Hollywell Park, Loughborough, Leicestershire, LE11 3TU.
    01509 635708
    http://www.ics.heacademy.ac.uk/
E   A Government funded national centre within Loughborough University.
○   To foster world-class education in information science
●   Education and training - Information service - Statistics
✕   LTSN Information and Computer Sciences Subject Centre.
Note: One of the 24 Subject Centres of the Higher Education Academy, (qv).

Subject Centre for Information and Computer Sciences   (ICS)   2000
■   Faculty of Engineering, University of Ulster, Shore Road, Newtownabbey, County Antrim, BT37 0QB.
    028 9036 8020   fax 028 9036 8206
    http://www.ics.heacademy.ac.uk/
E   A Government funded national centre within the University of Ulster.
○   To foster world-class education in computer science
●   Education and training - Information service - Statistics
✕   LTSN Information and Computer Sciences Subject Centre.
Note: One of the 24 Subject Centres of the Higher Education Academy, (qv).

Subject Centre for Languages, Linguistics and Area Studies   (LLAS)   2000
■   School of Humanities, University of Southampton, Highfield, Southampton, SO17 1BJ.
    023 8059 4814   fax 023 8059 4815
    http://www.llas.soton.ac.uk/
    Director: Prof Michael Kelly.
E   A Government funded national centre within the University of Southampton.
○   To foster world-class education in languages, linguistics and area studies
●   Education and training - Information service - Statistics
✕   LTSN Languages and Area Studies Subject Centre.
Note: One of the 24 Subject Centres of the Higher Education Academy, (qv).

Subject Centre for Medicine, Dentistry and Veterinary Medicine   (MEDEV)   2000
■   Faculty of Medical Sciences, University of Newcastle upon Tyne, Newcastle upon Tyne, NE2 4HH.
    0191-222 5888
    http://www.medev.ac.uk
E   A Government funded national centre within the University of Newcastle upon Tyne.
○   To foster world-class education in the fields of dentistry, medicine and veterinary medicine
●   Education and training - Information service - Statistics
✕   LTSN Medicine Subject Centre and LTSN Subjects Allied to Medicine Subject Centre.
Note: One of the 24 Subject Centres of the Higher Education Academy, (qv).

Subject Centre for Philosophical and Religious Studies   (SC for PRS)   2000
■   School of Theology and Religious Studies, University of Leeds, Leeds, LS2 9JT.
    0113-343 4184   fax 0113-343 3654
    http://www.prs.heacademy.ac.uk/
    Director: George MacDonald Ross. Manager: Dr Simon Smith.
E   A Government funded national centre within the University of Leeds.
○   To foster world-class studies in philosophy and religion
●   Education and training - Information service - Statistics
✕   LTSN Philosophy and Theology Subject Centre.
Note: One of the 24 Subject Centres of the Higher Education Academy, (qv).

Subject Centre for Social Policy and Social Work   2000
■   School of Humanities, University of Southampton, Highfield, Southampton, SO17 1BJ.
    023 8059 2925   fax 023 8059 2779
    http://www.soton.ac.uk/
    Contact: Jacqueline Rafferty.
E   A Government funded national centre within the University of Southampton.
○   To foster world-class education in the fields of social policy and social work
●   Education and training - Information service - Statistics
✕   LTSN Social Policy, Administration and Social Work Subject Centre.
Note: One of the 24 Subject Centres of the Higher Education Academy, (qv).

SUBJECT CENTRES OF THE HIGHER EDUCATION ACADEMY
Note: A nationwide network of 24 centres involved in different disciplines, each of which engages in a wide variety of activities to support academics, departments and institutions.

Subject Network for Sociology, Anthropology, Politics   (C-SAP   2000

- ■ Nuffield Building, University of Birmingham, Edgbaston, Birmingham, B15 2TT.
  0121-414 7919   fax 0121-414 7920
  http://www.c-sap.bham.ac.uk/
- E   A Government funded national centre within the University of Birmingham.
- ○   To foster world-class education in anthropology, politics and sociology
- ●   Education and training - Information service - Statistics
- ✕   LTSN Sociology and Politics Subject Centre.

Note: One of the 24 Subject Centres of the Higher Education Academy, (qv). Also known as Centre for Learning and Teaching Sociology, Anthropology and Politics.

Sue Ryder Care Centre for Palliative and End of Life Studies   2005

- ■ School of Nursing and Academic Division of Midwifery, Queen's Medical Centre, University of Nottingham, Nottingham, NG7 2UH.
  0115-823 1202
  http://www.nottingham.ac.uk/nursing/
  Contact: Prof Jane Seymour.
- E   A research centre at the University of Nottingham.
- ○   To produce high quality research and conceptual analyses to inform palliative and end of life care, particularly in chronic and advanced illness beyond cancer

Sugar Bureau   1964

- ■ Duncan House, Dolphin Square, London, SW1V 3PW.
  020 7828 9465   fax 020 7821 5393
  http://www.sugar-bureau.co.uk/
- E   The trade association for the UK sugar industry.

Sumac Centre   1984

- ■ 245 Gladstone Street, Nottingham, NG7 6HX.
  0845 458 9595
  http://www.veggies.org.uk/
- E   A secondary co-operative with limited liability.
- ○   To provide resources for local groups and individuals campaigning for human and animal rights on environmental issues, and for peace and co-operation worldwide
- ●   Education and training - Exhibitions - Information service - Library
- ✕   Rainbow Resource Centre.

Summer Institute of Linguistics

Note: No longer in existence.

Sunley Management Centre   (SMC)   1981

- ■ Northampton Business School, University of Northampton, Boughton Green Road, Northampton, NN2 7AL.
  01604 719531   fax 01604 777201
  http://www.sunley-northampton.co.uk/
- E   A registered charity at the University of Northampton.
- ○   To provide the broadest possible range of management training programmes

Suntory and Toyota International Centres for Economics and Related Disciplines   (STICERD)   1978

- ■ LSE, Houghton Street, London, WC2A 2AE.
  020 7405 7686; 7955 6679   fax 020 7955 6951
  http://sticerd.lse.ac.uk/
  Director: Prof Tim Besley. Centre Manager: Jane Dickson.
- E   A department of the London School of Economics and Political Science.
- ○   To further research in the fields of economics and related disciplines
- ●   Conferences - Seminars

Supply Chain Research Centre   (SCRC)

- ■ Cranfield School of Management, Cranfield University, Cranfield, Bedfordshire, MK43 0AL.
  01234 754180   fax 01234 751712
  http://www.som.cranfield.ac.uk/som/
  Director: Prof Alan Harrison. Project Manager: Lynne Hudston.
- E   A research centre within the Cranfield Management Research Institute (qv) at Cranfield University.
- ○   To conduct research in logistics and supply chain management

Supported Online Learning for Students using Technology for Information and Communication in their Education [Centre]
   see **SOLSTICE Centre.**

Surface: Inclusive Design Research Centre

- ■ Faculty of Business, Law and the Built Environment, Maxwell Building, University of Salford, Salford, Manchester, M5 4WT.
  0161-295 4600   fax 0161 295 5011
  http://www.surface.salford.ac.uk/
- E   A centre within the Research Institute for the Built and Human Environment (qv) at the University of Salford.

Surface Science and Engineering Centre
- Materials Department, Building 61, Cranfield University, Cranfield, Bedfordshire, MK43 0AL.
  01234 754039
  http://www.cranfield.ac.uk/sas/
  Contact: Prof J R Nicholls.
- E   A research centre at Cranfield University.

Surface Science Research Centre   (SSRC)   1989
- Faculty of Science, University of Liverpool, Liverpool, L69 3BX.
  0151-794 3870   fax 0151-794 3870
  http://www.ssci.liv.ac.uk/
  Director: Prof Rasmita Raval.
- E   A research centre at the University of Liverpool.
- O   To achieve nanoscale control, design and assembly of function

Surrey Centre for Excellence in Professional Training and Education   (SCEPTrE)   2005
- AC Building, University of Surrey, Guildford, Surrey, GU2 7XH.
  01483 684920
  http://www.surrey.ac.uk/sceptre/
  Director: Prof Norman Jackson.
- E   A Centre for Excellence in Teaching and Learning (CETL) at the University of Surrey.
- Note: See **Centres for Excellence in Teaching and Learning** for more information.

Surrey Centre for International Economic Studies   (SCIES)   1992
- Department of Economics, University of Surrey, Guildford, Surrey, GU2 7XH.
  01483 689380   fax 01483 689548
  http://www.econ.surrey.ac.uk/
  Director: Graham Bird.
- E   A research centre at the University of Surrey.
- O   To conduct research in international economics and to provide a framework for raising research funding

Surrey Centre for Research in Ion Beam Applications University of Surrey,
     see **Surrey Ion Beam Centre.**

Surrey Energy Economics Centre   (SEEC)   1980
- Department of Economics, University of Surrey, Guildford, Surrey, GU2 7XH.
  01483 686956   fax 01483 689548
  http://www.econ.surrey.ac.uk/
  Director: Prof Lester C Hunt.
- E   A department of the University of Surrey.
- O   To conduct research across the whole spectrum of energy economics

Surrey Ion Beam Centre   (IBC)
- School of Electronics and Physical Sciences, University of Surrey, Guildford, Surrey, GU2 7XH.
  01483 686090   fax 01483 686091
  http://www.ee.surrey.ac.uk/IBC
  Director: Prof R P Webb.
- E   A research centre at the University of Surrey.
- O   To promote research in the field of ion beam applications for the UK and industrial communities
- Note: Also known as the Surrey Centre for Research in Ion Beam Applications.

Surrey Sleep Research Centre   (SSRC)
- School of Biomedical and Molecular Sciences, University of Surrey, Egerton Road, Guildford, Surrey, GU2 7XP.
  01483 682502   fax 01483 682501
  http://www.surrey.ac.uk/sbms/
  Director: Dr Derk-Jan Dijk.
- E   A research centre at the University of Surrey.

Surrey Space Centre   (SSC)
- Department of Electronic Engineering, University of Surrey, Guildford, Surrey, GU2 7XH.
  01483 689278   fax 01483 689503
  http://www.ee.surrey.ac.uk/
  Director: Prof Sir Martin Sweeting, OBE.
- E   A research centre at the University of Surrey.
- O   To underpin the technical development of the small satellite industry

Sussex Astronomy Centre
- Department of Physics and Astronomy, Pevensey II Building, University of Sussex, Falmer, Brighton, East Sussex, BN1 9QH.
  01273 678557   fax 01273 873124
  http://astronomy.sussex.ac.uk/
  Director: Prof Andrew R Liddle.
- E   A research centre at the University of Sussex.
- O   To conduct research and surveys in a very wide range of space projects

Sussex Centre for Advanced Microscopy

■ School of Life Sciences, John Maynard Smith Building, University of Sussex, Falmer, Brighton, East Sussex, BN1 9QG.
   01273 877585   fax 01273 678433
   http://www.lifesci.sussex.ac.uk/
   Contact: Dr Julian R Thorpe.
E   A research centre at the University of Sussex.

Sussex Centre for Intellectual History   (CIH)

■ School of Humanities, Arts A 36, University of Sussex, Falmer, Brighton, East Sussex, BN1 9QN.
   01273 872725
   http://www.sussex.ac.uk/cih/
   Director: Prof Knud Haakonssen.
E   A research centre at the University of Sussex.

Sussex Centre for Migration Research   (SCMR)

■ Department of Cultural Studies, University of Sussex, Falmer, Brighton, East Sussex, BN1 9SJ.
   01273 873394   fax 01273 620662
   http://www.sussex.ac.uk/migration/
   Contact: Prof Richard Black.
E   An interdisciplinary research centre within the Centre for Culture, Development and the Environment (qv) at the University of Sussex.
O   To further understanding of migration, population movements and the policies that affect migrants

Sussex Centre for Neuroscience

■ Department of Biology and Environmental Science, University of Sussex, Falmer, Brighton, East Sussex, BN1 9QG.
   01273 678511
   http://www.sussex.ac.uk/biology/
E   A research centre at the University of Sussex.

Sussex Centre for Research into Alcohol, Alcoholism and Drug Addiction   (SCRAADA)

■ School of Life Sciences, University of Sussex, Falmer, Brighton, East Sussex, BN1 9QG.
   01273 678879
   http://www.biols.susx.ac.uk/
   Co-Director: Prof Theodora Duka. Co-Director: Prof Dai Stephens.
E   A research centre at the University of Sussex.

Sussex Centre for Research in the History of Art   1999

■ Department of Art History, University of Sussex, Falmer, Brighton, East Sussex, BN1 9QN.
   01273 873525
   http://www.sussex.ac.uk/arthistory/
E   A research centre at the University of Sussex.

Sussex European Institute   (SEI)   1998

■ Department of Contemporary European Studies, University of Sussex, Falmer, Brighton, East Sussex, BN1 9RG.
   01273 678578   fax 01273 678571
   http://www.sussex.ac.uk/sei/
   Head: Prof Jorg Monar.
E   A Jean Monnet Centre of Excellence (qv) and a department of the University of Sussex.

Sussex Institute   (SI)

■ Ground Floor - Essex House, University of Sussex, Falmer, Brighton, East Sussex, BN1 9QQ.
   01273 877888   fax 01273 877534
   http://www.sussex.ac.uk/si/
E   A part of the University of Sussex.
O   The SI consists of the Centre for Continuing Education, and the Schools of Law, Social work and social care, and Education

Sussex Language Institute

■ School of Humanities, University of Sussex, Falmer, Brighton, East Sussex, BN1 9SH.
   01273 872575; 873234   fax 01273 678476
   http://www.sussex.ac.uk/languages/
   Director: Mrs Sue Sheerin.
E   A department of the University of Sussex.
O   To offer courses in the English language and a variety of modern languages

Sustainability Centre in Glasgow   (SCG)   2004

- School of the Built and Natural Environment, Glasgow Caledonian University, 3rd Floor - Drummond House, 1 Hill Street, Glasgow, G3 6RN.
  - 0141-273 1366
  - http://www.sustainabilitycentre.org/
  - Administrator: Marianne Halforty.
- E   A research centre at Glasgow Caledonian University.
- O   To conduct research in sustainability spanning the areas of autonomous housing, urban regeneration, environmental and social justice, construction processes, knowledge mapping and sustainable procurement, the re-use of re-cycled products, modelling and measuring sustainability, sustainable resource use, and skilling the workforce in sustainability solutions

Sustainability Northwest and National Centre for Business and Sustainability   (SNW and NCBS)   1995

- Fourways House, 57 Hilton Street, Manchester, M1 2EJ.
  - 0161-247 7800   fax 0161-247 7870
  - http://www.snw.org.uk/
  - Chief Executive: Erik Bichard.
- E   A registered charity.
- O   To offer practical, focused and sustainable solutions to a range of businesses and organisations The Centre operates in four main areas - Developing global sustainable strategies, Providing applied environmental consultancy to larger organisations, Assisting small companies through subsidised programmes, and Advising companies on social rseponsibility and social auditing
- ●   Consultancy - Education and training
- ×   Co-operative Bank plc National Centre of Business and Ecology.

Sustainability Research Institute   (SRI)

- School of Earth and Environment, University of Leeds, Leeds, LS2 9JT.
  - 0113-343 5222; 6461   fax 0113-343 5259; 6716
  - http://www.see.leeds.ac.uk/
  - Director: Prof Andy Gouldson.
- E   A department of the University of Leeds.

Sustainable Cities Research Institute   (SCRI)   1999

- 6 North Street East, Newcastle upon Tyne, NE1 8ST.
  - 0191-227 3500   fax 0191-227 3066
  - http://www.sustainable-cities.org.uk/
- E   A research institute at Northumbria University.
- O   To develop and promote sustainable approaches to urban living

Sustainable Design Research Centre   (SDRC)   2001

- Faculty of Art, Design and Architecture, Kingston University London, Knights Park, Kingston-upon-Thames, Surrey, KT1 2QJ.
  - 020 8547 7410; 8062   fax 020 8547 7148
  - http://www.kingston.ac.uk/design/
  - Director: Anne Chick.
- E   A research centre at Kingston University, London.
- O   To undertake research projects and knowledge transfer activities that connect design and designers with issues of sustainability

Sustainable Design Research Centre   (SDRC)

- School of Design, Engineering and Computing, Bournemouth University, Fern Barrow, Poole, Dorset, BH12 5BB.
  - 01202 503765   fax 01202 503751
  - http://dec.bournemouth.ac.uk/
  - Director: Dr Mark Hadfield.
- E   A centre at Bournemouth University.
- O   To research into the integration of sustainable development with traditional design issues, with particular emphasis on tribology and waste minimisation in relation to sustainable design

Sustainable Development Research Centre   (SDRC)

- The Enterprise Park, Forres, Morayshire, IV36 2AB.
  - 01309 678111   fax 01309 678114
  - http://www.sustainableresearch.com/
  - Chief Executive: Dr Stephen Tinsley.
- E   A research centre at the University of the Highlands and Islands (UHI) Institute.
- O   To undertake applied research in the areas of corporate social responsibility, social enterprise management and environmental management

Sustainable Environment Research Centre   (SERC)

- School of Applied Sciences, University of Glamorgan, Pontypridd, CF37 1DL.
  - 01443 480480
  - http://www.glam.ac.uk/sapsschool/research/serc/
- E   A research centre within the University of Glamorgan.
- O   To produce high quality scientific research in sustainable environmental technologies

Sustainable Technology Research Centre   (STRC)
- Faculty of Engineering, Kingston University London, Friars Avenue, Roehampton Vale, London, SW15 3DW.
  020 8547 7704   fax 020 8547 7887
  http://engineering.kingston.ac.uk/
  Director: Dr Mukesh Limbachiya.
- E   A research centre at Kingston University, London.
- ○   To conduct research in the fields of concrete and masonry, geotechnics, sustainable energy systems, hydraulics, and remote sensing to find effective sustainable solutions in land use, building design and construction, re-cycling waste materials, efficient energy use and distribution, water resources, and remote sensing monitoring

Sustainable Transport Research Centre   (STRC)
- Faculty of Engineering, Science and the Built Environment, London South Bank University, 103 Borough Road, London, SE1 0AA.
  020 7815 7682
  http://www.lsbu.ac.uk/esbe/
  Head: Dr Deborah Andrews.
- E   A research centre at London South Bank University.

Suzy Lamplugh Trust Research Institute   (SLTRI)   1999
- School of Technology, University of Glamorgan, Pontypridd, CF37 1DL.
  01443 483625   fax 01443 482169
  http://www.glam.ac.uk/
- E   A research institute within the University of Glamorgan.
- ○   To pursue research that can usefully be applied to enhancing knowledge of personal safety issues

Systems Biology Centre
  see **Warwick Systems Biology Centre.**

Systems Engineering Innovation Centre   (SEIC)   2003
- Sir Denis Rooke Building, Holywell Park, Loughborough University, Loughborough, Leicestershire, LE11 3TU.
  01509 635200   fax 01509 635231
  http://seic.lboro.ac.uk/
- E   A research centre at Loughborough University.
- ○   To encourage collaborative research on the latest innovations in products, processes and services

Tagore Centre UK   1985
- Alexandra Park Library, Alexandra Park Road, London, N22 4UJ.
  020 8444 6751   fax 020 8909 2933
  http://www.tagorecentre.org.uk/
  Chairman: Amalendu Biswas. Executive Director: Kalyan Kundu.
- E   A registered charity.
- O   To develop awareness and interest in the work and life of artist Rabindranath Tagore (1861-1941)
- Note: The Centre also has a contact point at the Mitchell Library, Glasgow - (0141-572 7138).

Tavistock Institute of Human Relations   1947
- Tavistock House, 30 Tabernacle Street, London, EC2A 4UE.
  020 7417 0407   fax 020 7417 0566
  http://www.tavinstitute.org/
  Director: Phil Swann.
- E   A registered charity.
- O   To contribute to human well-being and development by advancing the theory, methodology and evaluation of change within and between groups, communities, organisations and the wider society

Tax Research Institute
   see **University of Nottingham Tax Research Institute.**

Tayside Institute of Cardiovascular Research   (TICR)
- College of Medicine, Dentistry & Nursing, Ninewells Hospital and Medical School, Dundee, DD1 9SY.
  01382 660111
  http://www.ticrappeal.com/
  Chairman: Shobna Vasishta.
- E   A research institute in process of formation at the University of Dundee.
- O   To bring together a team of specialists in vascular biology, cardiac disease, nutrition, epidemiology and fundamental laboratory science to enable detection and intervention of heart-related diseases at an earlier stage
- Note: The contact details are for the TICR fundraising appeal.

Tayside Institute for Health Studies
- School of Social and Health Studies, University of Abertay Dundee, Bell Street, Dundee, DD1 1HG.
  01382 308700   fax 01382 308749
  http://www.abertay.ac.uk/schools/shs/
- E   A research institute at the University of Abertay, Dundee.
- O   To conduct research, education, training and consultancy in health care

Tayside Orthopaedic and Rehabilitation Technology Centre   (TORT Centre)
- Section of Orthpaedic and Trauma Surgery, Ninewells Hospital and Medical School, Dundee, DD1 9SY.
  01382 425746   fax 01382 496200
  http://www.dundee.ac.uk/orthopaedics/
- E   A modern purpose built unit and part of the University of Dundee.
- O   To conduct training in orthopaedics and to host the Dundee Limb Fitting Centre (qv)

Teacher and Leadership Research Centre   (TLRC)
- School of Education, Jubilee Campus, University of Nottingham, Wollaton Road, Nottingham, NG8 1BB.
  0115-951 4473   fax 0115-951 4435
  http://www.nottingham.ac.uk/education/
  Director: Prof Christopher Day.
- E   A research centre at the University of Nottingham.
- O   To focus research on understanding and contributing to the further development and effectiveness of teachers, schools and school leaders within changing and challenging social and policy agendas
- ×   Centre for Research on Teacher and School Development.

Teaching Excellence and Mentoring of Postgraduates using Statistics   (TEMPUS)   2005
- Department of Mathematics and Statistics, Fylde College, Lancaster University, Lancaster, LA1 4YF.
  01524 593560   fax 01524 592681
  http://cetl.maths.lancs.ac.uk/
  Director: Prof Amanda Chetwynd.
- E   A Centre for Excellence in Teaching and Learning (CETL) at Lancaster University.
- Note: See **Centres for Excellence in Teaching and Learning** for more information.

Teaching and Learning Technology Centre   (TLTC)
- North Campus, London Metropolitan University, 166-220 Holloway Road, London, N7 8DB.
  020 7133 2984
  http://www.londonmet.ac.uk/tltc/
  Administrator: Nicole Ereira.
- E   A centre at the London Metropolitan University.
- O   To promote and support the effective use of learning technologies in teaching and learning

Technium CAST
   see **Centre for Advanced Software Technology.**

© CBD Research Ltd · Beckenham · Kent BR3 5JS · Tel 020 8650 7745 · Fax 020 8650 0768 · E-mail cbd@cbdresearch.com · www.cbdresearch.com

Technology and Engineering Innovation Centre   (TEIC)   2003
- Jordanstown Campus, University of Ulster, Shore Road, Newtownabbey, County Antrim, BT37 0QB.
   028 9036 6178; 6305   fax 028 9036 8229
   http://www.engj.ulster.ac.uk/
- E   A research centre at University of Ulster.

Technology Innovation Centre   (TIC)
- Birmingham City University, Millennium Point, Curzon Street, Birmingham, B4 7XG.
   0121-331 5400   fax 0121-331 5401
   http://www.tic-online.com/
- E   A faculty of Birmingham City University.
- O   To support individuals, organisations and communities in developing their understanding and capabilities within a rapidly developing technology-based society, providing cutting-edge resources and specialised knowledge to meet the demands of the 21st century

Technology Transfer Centre
   see **Kent Technology Transfer Centre.**

Teesside Centre for Nanotechnology and Microfabrication   (TCNM)   2004
- School of Science and Technology, University of Teesside, Borough Road, Middlesbrough, TS1 3BA.
   01642 342455   fax 01642 342401
   http://www.tees.ac.uk/researchcentres/tcnm/
- E   A research centre at the University of Teesside.
- O   To undertake research, innovation and enterprise activities in nanotechnology and microfabrication in the North East

Teesside Manufacturing Centre   (TMC)
- School of Science and Technology, University of Teesside, Borough Road, Middlesbrough, TS1 3BA.
   01642 342481   fax 01642 342424
   http://www.tees.ac.uk/schools/sst/
- E   A research centre at the University of Teesside.
- O   To offer an integration service in design, manufacturing and business process improvement

Teesside Medical Computing Centre
- School of Computing, University of Teesside, Middlesbrough, TS1 3BA.
   01642 342645
   http://www.tees.ac.uk/schools/scm/
   Contact: Derek Simpson.
- E   A research centre at the University of Teesside.
- O   To conduct research in the application of computerised technology to improving patient care and processing medical information

Television Centre
   see **BBC Television Centre.**

Tennyson Research Centre   1964
- Lincoln Central Library, Free School Lane, Lincoln, LN2 1EZ.
   01522 510800   fax 01522 575011
   Research Officer: Grace Timmins.
- E   A department of the Lincolnshire County Library Service.
- O   To house the Tennyson family archives consisting of letters, proofs, manuscripts, family papers and illustrations relating to the poet Alfred, Lord Tennyson (1809-1892) and his family; to provide research facilities for visiting students
- ● Library (by written application) - Exhibitions (at the Usher Gallery, Lincoln)

Tenovus Centre for Cancer Research   (TCCR)   Canolfan Ymchwil Canser Tenovus
- Welsh School of Pharmacy, Redwood Building, Cardiff University, King Edward VII Avenue, Cardiff, CF10 3XF.
   029 2087 5226   fax 029 2087 5152
   http://www.cardiff.ac.uk/phrmy/
   Director: Prof Robert I Nicholson.
- E   A research centre at Cardiff University.
- O   To focus on cancer of the breast and prostate

Textile Conservation Centre   (TCC)   1975
- Faculty of Law, Arts and Social Sciences, Winchester School of Art, University of Southampton, Park Avenue, Winchester, Hampshire, SO23 8DL.
   023 8059 6900
   http://www.wsa.soton.ac.uk/
   Contact: Mrs Nell Hoare.
- E   A research centre at the University of Southampton.
- O   To be a leading international centre for the education of textile conservators and for research into textile conservation
- ● Education and training

Theological Institute for the Study of Religion and Society
   see **Lincoln Theological Institute for the Study of Religion and Society.**

Theory, Culture and Society Centre   (TCS Centre)   1996
- ■ School of Arts and Humanities, Nottingham Trent University, Clifton Lane, Nottingham, NG11 8NS.
  0115-848 6330   fax 0115-848 6331
  http://tcs.ntu.ac.uk/
  Director: Mike Featherstone.
- E A research centre within the Institute for Cultural Analysis, Nottingham (qv) at Nottingham Trent University.
- O To conduct research around technological culture, globalization, postcolonial issues, critical theory, and global knowledge

Therapeutics and Toxicology Centre   (TTC)
- ■ Department of Pharmacology, Therapeutics and Toxicology, UWCM Academic Centre, Llandough Hospital, Cardiff, CF64 2XX.
  029 2071 6944   fax 029 2070 3454
  http://www.cardiff.ac.uk/medicine/
- E A research centre at Cardiff University.
- O To provide advice to health professionals, individuals and Government agencies on the acute and chronic toxicity of drugs, chemicals and naturally occurring agents

Thermo-Fluid Mechanics Research Centre   (TFMRC)   1977
- ■ Department of Engineering and Design, University of Sussex, Falmer, Brighton, East Sussex, BN1 9QT.
  01273 678407
  http://www.sussex.ac.uk/units/tfmrc/
  Director: Prof Alan B Turner.
- E A research centre at the University of Sussex.
- O To conduct research in the fields of fluid mechanics, heat transfer and engine component design

Thermo-Fluid Systems University Technology Centre   (TFS UTC)   2003
- ■ School of Engineering, University of Surrey, Guildford, Surrey, GU2 7XH.
  01483 686292
  http://www.surrey.ac.uk/eng/research/fluids/UTC/
  Director: Prof John W Chew.
- E A research centre at the University of Surrey.
- O To conduct research which is focused on turbomachinery internal fluid and thermal systems

Thin Film Centre   (TFC)
- ■ School of Engineering and Science, University of Paisley, Paisley, PA1 2BE.
  0141-848 3601   fax 0141-848 3616
  http://www.paisley.ac.uk/physics/es/tfc/
  Director: Prof F Placido.
- E A research centre at the University of Paisley.
- O To conduct research and development of thin film properties and applications
Note: At the time of going to press, the University of Paisley was preparing to merge with Bell College to form the University of the West of Scotland.

3rd Generation Proteomics Centre   (3GP)
- NR School of Chemistry, University of Manchester, Oxford Road, Manchester, M13 9PL.
  0161-306 9260   fax 0161-275 4598
  http://www.postgenomeconsortium.com/3gp/
- E A research centre at the University of Manchester.
- O To support supramolecular structural studies and proteome analysis
Note: A collaborative project with 2 other Universities in the North West - Liverpool and Salford.

Thoroughbred Rehabilitation Centre   (TRC)   1991
- ■ Whinney Hill, Aughton Road, Halton, Lancashire, LA2 6PQ.
  http://www.thoroughbredrehabilitationcentre.co.uk/
  Founder & Director: Carrie Humble Deputy Director: Penny Phillips.
- E A registered charity and a company limited by guarantee.
- O To care, rehabilitate and rehome thoroughbred ex-racehorses, and to protect them from suffering and cruelty
- ● Animal welfare
- ¶ Newsletter.

Thrombosis Research Institute   (TRI)   1990
- ■ Emmanuel Kay Building, Manresa Road, London, SW3 6LR.
  020 7351 8300   fax 020 7351 8324
  http://www.tri-london.ac.uk/
  Director: Prof Vijay Kakkar.
- E A research institute.
- O To provide excellence in thrombosis research, education and patient care, by seeking a deeper understanding of the molecular pathogenesis of disorders of coagulation, in order to develop new strategies to prevent and treat thrombosis

© CBD Research Ltd · Beckenham · Kent BR3 5JS · Tel 020 8650 7745 · Fax 020 8650 0768 · E-mail cbd@cbdresearch.com · www.cbdresearch.com

Tizard Centre

- University of Kent, Beverley Farm, Canterbury, Kent, CT2 7LZ.
  01227 827373   fax 01227 763674
  http://www.kent.ac.uk/tizard/
  Director: Prof J Mansell.
- E   A department of the University of Kent.
- ○   To research, teach and consult on matters relating to quality of life for people with learning disabilities and/or mental health problems
- ●   Consultancy - Education and training

Tom Connors Cancer Research Centre

- School of Life Sciences, University of Bradford, Bradford, West Yorkshire, BD7 1DP.
  01274 233226   fax 01274 233234
  http://www.bradford.ac.uk/acad/lifesci/
- E   A research centre within the Institute of Cancer Therapeutics (qv) at the University of Bradford.

Tom Hopkinson Centre for Media Research

- Cardiff School of Journalism, Media and Cultural Studies, The Bute Building, King Edward VII Avenue, Cardiff University, Cardiff, CF10 3NB.
  029 2087 4000
  http://www.cardiff.ac.uk/
- E   A research centre at Cardiff University.

Tourism Research Centre
see **Crichton Tourism Research Centre.**

Tourism and Travel Research Institute
see **Christel DeHaan Tourism and Travel Research Institute.**

Townsend Centre for International Poverty Research

- School for Policy Studies, University of Bristol, 8 Priory Road, Bristol, BS8 1TZ.
  0117-954 6755   fax 0117-954 6756
  http://www.bristol.ac.uk/poverty/
  Contact: Dr Dave Gordon.
- E   A multidisciplinary research centre at the University of Bristol.
- ○   To promote research-based initiatives with the aim of producing practical policies and solutions for the alleviation and eventual ending of world poverty

trAce Online Writing Centre   1995

- School of Media, Art and Design, Luton Campus, University of Bedfordshire, Luton, Bedfordshire, LU1 3JU.
  01582 489230   fax 01582 489212
  http://www.beds.ac.uk/departments/mediaartdesign/trace
- E   A centre at the University of Bedfordshire.

Trafford Centre for Graduate Medical Education and Research   (TCMR)   1973

- University of Sussex, Falmer, Brighton, East Sussex, BN1 9RY.
  01273 678446
  http://www.sussex.ac.uk/tcmr/
  Contact: Dr Lynne Mayne.
- E   A department of the University of Sussex.

Trans-Cultural Research Centre
see **Centre for Business in Society.**

Transitional Justice Institute   (TJI)

- Jordanstown Campus, University of Ulster, Shore Road, Newtownabbey, County Antrim, BT37 0QB.
  028 9036 6202   fax 028 9036 8962
  http://www.transitionaljustice.ulster.ac.uk/
  Director: Prof Christine Bell.
- E   An institute within the University of Ulster.
- ○   To examine how law and legal institutions assist (or not) the move from conflict to peace

Translation Institute
see **Middlesex University Translation Institute.**

Transnational Art, Identity and Nation Research Centre   (TrAIN)
■   Central Saint Martins College of Art and Design, University of the Arts London, Southampton Row, London, WC1B 4AP.
020 7514 7000
http://www.csm.arts.ac.uk/
Director: Prof Toshio Watanabe.
E   A research centre at the University of the Arts, London.
○   To conduct research in transnational issues in art and design, on both a local and global level

Transport Research and Consultancy   (TRaC)   1990
■   Department of Business and Service Sector Management, Ladbroke House, London Metropolitan University, 62-66 Highbury Grove, London, N5 2AD.
020 7133 5105   fax 020 7133 5123
http://www.londonmet.ac.uk/
Director: Steve Shaw.
E   A research centre within the Cities Institute (qv) at London Metropolitan University.
○   To work with transport providers and users to develop sustainable practices that enhance access and mobility, and improve people's quality of life

Transport Research Institute   (Tri)   1996
■   Sighthill Campus, Napier University, Edinburgh, EH11 4BN.
0131-455 3200   fax 0131-455 3201
http://www.tri.napier.ac.uk/
Contact: Debbie McEwan.
E   A research institute at Napier University.
○   To develop, in Scotland, a worldwide reputation for research and work in transport and related issues

Transport Research Institute - Northern Ireland Centre   (TRi-NIC
■   Department of Environmental Planning, David Keir Building, Queen's University Belfast, Stranmillis Road, Belfast, BT9 5AG.
028 9027 4755   fax 028 9068 7652
http://www.qub.ac.uk/ep/
Director: Prof Austin Smyth.
E   A centre at Queen's University, Belfast.

Transport and Road Assessment Centre   (TRAC)
■   University of Ulster, Jordanstown, Newtownabbey, County Antrim, BT37 0QB.
028 9036 8706   fax 028 9036 8707
http://www.engj.ulster.ac.uk/
Director: Prof Alan Woodside.
E   A research centre at the University of Ulster.
○   To conduct research in highways, logistics, transport planning and policy

Transport Technology Ergonomics Centre   (TTEC)
■   Faculty of Social Sciences and Humanities, Loughborough University, Holywell Building, Holywell Park, Loughborough, Leicestershire, LE11 3TU.
01509 226900   fax 01509 226960
http://www.lboro.ac.uk/research/esri/
E   A research centre within the Ergonomics and Safety Research Institute (qv) at Loughborough University.

Travel Law Centre   1991
■   School of Law, DX 65174, University of Newcastle upon Tyne, Newcastle upon Tyne, NE1 8ST.
0191-243 7587   fax 0191-243 7506
http://northumbria.ac.uk/sd/
Director: Prof David Grant.
E   A research centre at Northumbria University.
○   To publish, undertake research and consultancy and promote courses and conferences on travel law
¶   International Travel Law Journal.

Treaty Centre   1983
■   School of Law, University of Nottingham, University Park, Nottingham, NG7 2RD.
0115-951 5700   fax 0115-951 5696
http://www.nottingham.ac.uk/law/
E   A research centre at the University of Nottingham.
○   To conduct research into the law of treaties and the practice of treaty-making

Trent Institute for Health Services Research
Note: Is now the Trent Research and Development Support Unit at the Queen's Medical Centre.

© CBD Research Ltd · Beckenham · Kent BR3 5JS · Tel 020 8650 7745 · Fax 020 8650 0768 · E-mail cbd@cbdresearch.com · www.cbdresearch.com

Tyndall Centre for Climate Change Research   (TYN)
NR   School of Environmental Sciences, University of East Anglia, Norwich, NR4 7TJ.
         01603 593900   fax 01603 593901
         http://www.tyndall.ac.uk/
         Director: Prof Mike Hulme.
E   A Natural Environment Research Council collaborative research centre within the Zuckerman Institute for Connective Environmental
         Research (qv) at the University of East Anglia.
○   To bring together scientists, economists, engineers and social scientists, who together are working to develop sustainable responses
         to climate change through trans-disciplinary research and dialogue, (on both a national and international level) - not just within
         the research community, but also with business leaders, policy advisors, the media and the public in general
Note: Norwich is the headquarters of the Tyndall Centre - it has five regional offices at the Universities of Brighton, Manchester,
         Newcastle upon Tyne, Oxford, and Southampton.

UCE Birmingham Institute of Art and Design
   see **Birmingham Institute of Art and Design.**

UCL Cancer Trials Centre
   see **Cancer Research UK and UCL Cancer Trials Centre.**

UCL Centre for Anaesthesia   1998
■   Department of Surgery, Great Ormond Street Hospital for Children, University College London, 30 Guilford Street, London,
      WC1N 1EH.
         020 7905 2382   fax 020 7829 8634
         http://www.ucl.ac.uk/anaesthesia/
         Director: Prof: Michael Mythen. Administrator: Pippa Moss.
E   A department of University College London.
O   To be at the forefont of expertise in anaesthesia, critical care and pain management

UCL Centre for BioScience and Society   (CBaS)
■   University College London, Gower Street, London, WC1E 6BT.
         020 7679 1328
         http://www.ucl.ac.uk/cbas/
         Contact: Dr Brian Balmer.
E   A research centre at University College London.
O   To promote multidisciplinary inquiry into a broad range of social issues linked to the contemporary life sciences

UCL Centre for Cosmic Chemistry and Physics   (CCCP)
■   Department of Physics and Astronomy, University College London, Gower Street, London, WC1E 6BT.
         020 7679 1785
         http://www.chem.ucl.ac.uk/
         Co-Director: Prof D E Williams. Co-Director: Prof D A Williams.
E   A research centre at University College London.
O   To apply research to fundamental chemical processes which are believed to occur throughout the universe

UCL Centre for European Studies   (CES)
■   Faculty of Social and Historical Sciences, University College London, Gower Street, London, WC1E 6BT.
         020 7679 2000
         http://www.ucl.ac.uk/ces/
         Contact: Dr Mark Hewitson.
E   A department of University College London.
O   To study Europe in its entirety
Note: See also Jean Monnet Centres.

UCL Centre for Human Communication   (CHC)
■   Department of Phonetics and Linguistics, University College London, Gower Street, London, WC1E 6BT.
         020 7679 7172   fax 020 7383 4108
         http://www.chc.ucl.ac.uk/
         Co-Director: Prof Peter Howell. Co-Director: Prof Moira Yip.
E   A department of University College London.
O   To encourage and facilitate research on human language and communication

UCL Centre for International Health and Development   (CIHD)
■   University College London, 30 Guilford Street, London, WC1N 1EH.
         020 7242 9789   fax 020 7831 0488
         http://www.ich.ucl.ac.uk/
         Head: Prof Andrew Tomkins, OBE.
E   An interdisciplinary research centre within the UCL Institute of Child Health (qv) at University College London.
O   To conduct research and teaching on health and development in a global context
Note: International Health and Medical Education Centre.

UCL Centre for Medical Molecular Virology
   see **MRC UCL Centre for Medical Molecular Virology.**

UCL Centre for Neuroimaging Techniques   1997
■   University College London, 12 Queen Square, London, WC1N 3BG.
         020 7833 7472
         Director: Prof Robert Turner.
E   An interdisciplinary research centre at University College London
O   To promote an awareness of research on brain anatomy, function, physiology and pathology using a variety of non-invasive
         imaging techniques, including MRI, PET, MEG, TMS, EIT, NIRS, radioisotope scanning, EEG and microscopy

            © CBD Research Ltd · Beckenham · Kent BR3 5JS · Tel 020 8650 7745 · Fax 020 8650 0768 · E-mail cbd@cbdresearch.com · www.cbdresearch.com

UCL Centre for Publishing

■ School of Library, Archive and Information Studie, Henry Morley Building, University College London, Gower Street, London, WC1E 6BT.
  020 7679 2000; 2477   fax 020 7383 0557
  http://www.publishing.ucl.ac.uk/
  Director: Prof David Nicholas.
E   A centre at University College London.
O   To conduct teaching programs in publishing at both degree and postgraduate levels
Note: The Centre's research is carried out by the Centre for Information Behaviour and the Evaluation of Research (qv).

UCL Centre for Research on Ageing   (CRA)

■ Department of Biology, The Darwin Building, University College London, Gower Street, London, WC1E 6BT.
  020 7679 4381
  http://www.ucl.ac.uk/biology/
E   A research centre at University College London.
O   To conduct research dedicated to understanding the mechanisms that underlie ageing and the processes that act against it, with special research emphasis given to the manner in which ageing gives rise to diseases of ageing, and to thereby identify therapeutic targets for intervention

UCL Centre for Security and Crime Science   (CS^2)

■ Faculty of Engineering Sciences, 2nd Floor - Brook House, University College London, 2-16 Torrington Place, London, WC1E 7HN.
  020 7679 0818   fax 020 7679 0828
  http://www.ucl.ac.uk/jdi/
E   An interdisciplinary research centre within the UCL Jill Dando Institute of Crime Science (qv) at University College London.
O   To bring together innovative thought and research to deliver solutions to crime and security issues that will benefit society, industry and Government

UCL Centre for Sustainable Heritage   (CSH)   2001

■ The Bartlett, Faculty of the Built Environment, Torrington Place Site, University College London, Gower Street, London, WC1E 6BT.
  020 7679 1665
  http://www.ucl.ac.uk/sustainableheritage/
  Director: Prof May Cassar.
E   A department of University College London.
O   To realise the aim of filling the gap between disciplines responsible for the physical protection of the movable and immovable heritage, through participation in collaborative environmental, scientific and technological research, teaching, advice and consultancy

UCL Centre for Systems Engineering   (UCLse)

■ University College London, Gower Street, London, WC1E 6BT.
  020 7679 4908   fax 020 7679 4911
  http://www.mssl.ucl.ac.uk/
  Director: Prof Alan Smith. Administrator: Marion Andrew.
E   An interdisciplinary research centre at University College London.
O   To advance the state-of-the-art in systems engineering

UCL e-Science Centre of Excellence

■ University College London, Gower Street, London, WC1E 6BT.
  020 7679 7394
  http://www.ucl.ac.uk/research-computing/
  Co-ordinating Manager: Clare Gryce.
E   A research centre at University College London.
Note: See **e-Science Centres of Excellence** for further information.

UCL Ear Institute

see **Institute of Laryngology and Otology.**

UCL Eastman Dental Institute

■ Faculty of Biomedical Sciences, University College London, 256 Gray's Inn Road, London, WC1X 8LD.
  020 7915 1038
  http://www.eastman.ucl.ac.uk/
  Contact: Geoff Dunk.
E   A department of University College London.
O   To advance orofacial health care sciences, so as to benefit society by research, scholarship, and education of the highest international standard
Note: The Institute is a World Health Organisation WHO Collaborating Centre (qv) for Research, Education and Service in Oral Health.

UCL Environment Institute   2003

■ Faculty of Social and Historical Sciences, Pearson Building, University College London, Gower Street, London, WC1E 6BT.
020 7679 0534
http://www.ucl.ac.uk/environment-institute/
E A department of University College London.
O To understand how the environment functions, how human activities impact on it and how environmental policies can be effectively implemented
Note: Continuing the initiatives of the Bloomsbury Institute of the Natural Environment.

UCL Institute of Archaeology

■ Faculty of Social and Historical Sciences, University College London, 31-34 Gordon Square, London, WC1H 0PY.
020 7679 7495   fax 020 7383 2572
http://www.ucl.ac.uk/archaeology/
Director: Prof Stephen Shennan.
E A research institute at University College London.
O To be internationally pre-eminent in the study, and comparative analysis, of world archaeology

UCL Institute of Child Health   (ICH)

■ Faculty of Biomedical Sciences, University College London, 30 Guilford Street, London, WC1N 1EH.
020 7242 9789   fax 020 7831 0488
http://www.ich.ucl.ac.uk/
E A department of University College London.
O To conduct research in various fields related to child health, including biochemical and nutritional sciences, cancer, cardiorespiratory sciences, genes, development and disease, infection and immunity, neurosciences and mental health, and population health sciences

UCL Institute of Hepatology   1996

■ Department of Medicine, University College London, 69-75 Chenies Mews, London, WC1E 6HX.
020 7679 6510   fax 020 7380 0405
http://www.ucl.ac.uk/medicine/hepatology/
Director: Prof Roger Williams, CBE.
E A registered charity and a department of University College London.
O To conduct research in autoimmune liver disease including the virological and immunological mechanisms involved in HBU and HCU chronic hepatitis, the metabolic derangements in cirrhosis, new approaches to prevention of alcoholic mediated liver injury, and the treatment of acute liver failure including extra-corporeal liver support devices. Current research programmes encompass both laboratory-based work as well as clinical projects
● Annual postgraduate teaching course for specialist registrars in training - Weekly sessions for X-ray and histopathology interpretation
¶ Annual Report. Various Reports (on website).
Note: Now incorporates the former Centre for Hepatology.

UCL Institute for Human Health and Performance   (IHHP)

■ Department of Medicine, Ground Floor - Charterhouse Building, University College London, Highgate Hill, London, N19 5LW.
020 7288 3891
http://www.ucl.ac.uk/medicine/
Director: Dr Hugh Montgomery.
E A department of University College London.
O To study the mechanisms which regulate health in all its aspects and human physical performance

UCL Interaction Centre   (UCLIC)

■ 4th Floor - Remax House, University College London, 31-32 Alfred Place, London, WC1E 7DP.
020 7679 5248   fax 020 7679 5295
http://www.uclic.ucl.ac.uk/
Director: Prof Ann Blandford.
E An interdisciplinary research centre at University College London.
O To conduct research in a broad range of phenomena related to human-computer interaction

UCL International Institute for Society and Health   (IISH)   2005

■ University College London, Gower Street, London, WC1E 6BT.
020 7679 8249
http://www.ucl.ac.uk/iish/
Chairman: Prof Sir Michael Marmot.
E An institute at the University College London.
O To take action on the social determinants of health; to provide solutions to global health problems; to improve the health and well being of all, especially the poorest

UCL Jill Dando Institute of Crime Science   (JDI)

■ Faculty of Engineering Sciences, 2nd Floor - Brook House, University College London, 2-16 Torrington Place, London, WC1E 7HN.
020 7679 0818   fax 020 7679 0828
http://www.ucl.ac.uk/jdi/
Director: Prof Gloria Laycock.
E A department of University College London.
O To reduce crime through teaching, research, public policy analysis and by the dissemination of evidence-based information on crime reduction

© CBD Research Ltd · Beckenham · Kent BR3 5JS · Tel 020 8650 7745 · Fax 020 8650 0768 · E-mail cbd@cbdresearch.com · www.cbdresearch.com

UCL NDE Centre   1985
- Department of Mechanical Engineering, University College London, Torrington Place, London, WC1E 7JE.
  020 7679 3928; 7178
  http://www.mecheng.ucl.ac.uk/
  Manager: Dr Feargal P Brennan.
- E   A research centre at University College London.
- O   To provide an integrated approach for structural integrity and defect assessment

Uehiro Centre for Practical Ethics
   see **Oxford Uehiro Centre for Practical Ethics.**

UHI Centre for History   2005
- North Highland College, University of the Highlands and Islands (UHI) Institute, Ross House, Grange Road, Dornoch, Sutherland, IV25 3LE.
  01847 889388; 01862 811855   fax 01862 811853
  http://www.nhcscotland.com/www/uhihistory/
  Director: Prof James Hunter. Contact: Stephen Mackay.
- E   A research centre at the University of the Highlands and Islands (UHI) Institute.
- O   To develop a research portolio in history

UHI Decommissioning and Environmental Remediation Centre   (DERC)
- North Highland College, University of the Highlands and Islands (UHI) Institute, Thurso, Caithness, Sutherland, KW14 1EE.
  01847 889586
  http://www.derc.uhi.ac.uk/
- E   A research centre at the University of the Highlands and Islands (UHI) Institute.
- O   To conduct research and consultancy on the decommisioning of nuclear facilities and their environmental remediation

UK
   see **United Kingdom.**

Ukraine Centre
Note: Has been disbanded.

Underwater Centre (Fort William) Ltd   1994
- An-aird, Fort William, Inverness-shire, PH33 6AN.
  01397 703786   fax 01397 704969
  http://www.theunderwatercentre.com/
  Operational Manager: Allan Brown. Administration Manager: John Reed.
- E   A profit-making business.
- O   To provide and maintain the highest standard in Health and Safety Executive (HSE) courses and commercial diver training, as well as remotely operated vehicle training, and leisure diving facilities
- ●   Conference facilities - Education and training - Recreational facilities - The Centre also has a wide range of equipment such as decompression chamber, diving equipment, 3 barges, private pier, wet bell, NDT station

Underwater Centre [Plymouth]
   see **Fort Bovisand Underwater Centre Ltd.**

UNESCO Centre for Comparative Education Research   (UCCER)
- School of Education, Jubilee Campus, University of Nottingham, Wollaton Road, Nottingham, NG8 1BB.
  0115-951 3717   fax 0115-951 4397
  http://www.nottingham.ac.uk/education/
  Director: Prof John Morgan.
- E   A research centre at the University of Nottingham.
- O   To promote research, scholarship, post-graduate education and advanced training in comparative and international education policy, management and finance, with particular emphasis on the comparative policy analysis of post-school education

UNESCO Centre in Education for Pluralism, Human Rights and Democracy   2000
- Coleraine Campus, University of Ulster, Cromore Road, Coleraine, County Londonderry, BT52 1SA.
  028 7032 3593   fax 028 7032 3021
  http://www.ulster.ac.uk/unesco/
- E   A research centre at the University of Ulster.

UNESCO Centre for Water Law, Policy and Science
- Postgraduate School of Management and Policy, University of Dundee, Dundee, DD1 4HN.
  01382 384451   fax 01382 388671
  http://www.dundee.ac.uk/iwlri/
- E   A centre at the University of Dundee.
- O   To conduct research into water law on the basis that all citizens, especially the most disadvantaged, have an equitable and sustainable access to water

Unilever Centre for Molecular Science Informatics

■ University Chemical Laboratory, University of Cambridge, Lensfield Road, Cambridge, CB2 1EW.
01223 336432
http://www.msm.cam.ac.uk/

E A research centre within the Pfizer Institute for Pharmaceutical Materials Science (qv) at the University of Cambridge.

UniS Materials Institute   (UMI)

■ School of Biomedical and Molecular Sciences, University of Surrey, Guildford, Surrey, GU2 7XH.
01483 689617   fax 01483 686291
http://www.umi.surrey.ac.uk/
Director: Prof John Watts.

E A research institute at the University of Surrey.
O To conduct research addressing pure and applied aspects of polymers, metals, particles, coatings and dispersions

United Kingdom Astronomy Technology Centre   (UK ATC)   1996

■ Royal Observatory Edinburgh, Blackford Hill, Edinburgh, EH9 3HJ.
0131-668 8100   fax 0131-668 8264
http://www.roe.ac.uk/ukatc/
Director: Prof Ian Robson. Director of Technology Development: Colin Cunningham.

E An independent non-profit-distributing organisation.
O To support the mission and strategic aims of the Particle Physics and Astronomy Research Council; to help keep the UK at the forefront of world astronomy by providing a UK focus for the design, production and promotion of state of the art astronomical technology
● Education and training - Information service - Library - Fully equipped instrumentation laboratory - Public observings - Talks - Special events (details 0131-668 8404 or website)

United Kingdom Centre for the Advancement of Interprofessional Education   (CAIPE)   1987

■ Hamilton House, Mabledon Place, London, WC1H 9BB.
020 7554 8539
http://www.caipe.org.uk/

E An independent charity and a membership organisation.
O To promote and develop interprofessional education

United Kingdom Centre for Economic and Environmental Development   (UK CEED)   1984

■ 48 Broadway, Peterborough, PE1 1SB.
01733 311644   fax 01733 808168
http://www.ukceed.org/
Chairman: John C L Cox, CBE.

E A registered charity and a company limited by guarantee.
O To promote the business case for sustainable development policies and actions; to undertake a broad range of research, demonstration projects, engagement and education activities with its partners in the UK and Europe

United Kingdom Centre for Events Management   (UKCEM)   2000

■ Leslie Silver International Faculty, Leeds Metropolitan University, Civic Quarter, Calverley Street, Leeds, LS1 3HE.
0113-283 3464   fax 0113-283 3111
http://www.leedsmet.ac.uk/lsif/

E A research centre at Leeds Metropolitan University.
O To provide education in events management

United Kingdom Centre for Evidence Based Policy and Practice
see **ESRC United Kingdom Centre for Evidence Based Policy and Practice.**

United Kingdom Centre of Excellence in Biocatalysis, Biotransformation and Biomanufacturing

■ School of Chemical Engineering and Analytical Sciences, University of Manchester, Oxford Road, Manchester, M13 9PL.
0161-275 8256
http://www.knowledgehorizons.manchester.ac.uk/

E A research centre at the University of Manchester.

United Kingdom Centre for Legal Education   (UKCLE)   2000

■ Coventry, CV4 7AL.
024 7652 3117   fax 024 7652 3290
http://www.ukcle.ac.uk/

E A Government funded national centre within the University of Warwick.
O To foster world-class education in law
● Education and training - Information service - Statistics
× LTSN Law Subject Centre.
Note: One of the 24 Subject Centres of the Higher Education Academy, (qv).

United Kingdom Centre for Materials Education   2000

■   Department of Engineering, University of Liverpool, Victoria Building, Liverpool, L69 3GH.
        0151-794 5364   fax 0151-794 4466
        http://www.materials.ac.uk/
E   A Government funded national centre within the University of Liverpool.
○   To foster world-class education in materials science
●   Education and training - Information service - Statistics
✕   LTSN Materials Subject Centre.
Note: One of the 24 Subject Centres of the Higher Education Academy, (qv).

United Kingdom Centre for Tissue Engineering   (UKCTE)   2001

NR   Department of Clinical Engineering, University of Liverpool, Liverpool, L69 3GA.
        0151-706 4913   fax 0151-706 5803
        http://www.ukcte.org/
        Director: Prof D F Williams.
E   A research centre at the University of Liverpool.
○   To extend the base of scientific knowledge that underpins tissue engineering and to translate this knowledge to the development of
        commercial products and clinical treatments for healing injured and diseased tissues
Note: A joint initiative with the University of Manchester.

United Kingdom Centre for Tissue Engineering   (UKCTE)   2001

NR   Faculty of Life Sciences, Michael Smith Building, University of Manchester, Oxford Road, Manchester, M13 9PT.
        0161-275 5777   fax 0161-275 5082
        http://www.ukcte.org/
        Contact: Miss Sarah Farrar.
E   A research centre at the University of Manchester.
Note: A joint initiative with the University of Liverpool (see above).

United Kingdom Longitudinal Studies Centre
        see **ESRC United Kingdom Longitudinal Studies Centre.**

United Kingdom National Europass Centre   (UK NEC)

■   Oriel House, Oriel Road, Cheltenham, Gloucestershire, GL50 1XP.
        0870 990 4088   fax 0870 990 1560
        http://www.naric.org.uk/
E   An independent unit under the management of the National Recognition Information Centre for the United Kingdom (qv).
○   To provide information and guidance on the Europass initiative and the comprising five documents, which record qualifications
        and skills in an understandable manner, to enable the holder to change jobs and move around Europe more easily

United Kingdom Science Enterprise Centres   (UKSEC)   2000

■   PO Box 88, Sackville Street, Manchester, M60 1QD.
        0161-306 8484   fax 0161-306 8488
        http://www.enterprise.ac.uk/
Note: An initiative which started in 2000, UKSEC is a network of over 90 higher education institutions. Each institution is committed to
        maximising entrepreneurial potential and capability.

United Kingdom Sports Institute   (UKSI)   1999

■   40 Bernard Street, London, WC1N 1ST.
        020 7211 5100   fax 020 7211 5246
        http://www.uksport.gov.uk/
        Chairman: Sue Campbell.
E   A Government organisation.
○   To work in partnership with the home country sports councils and other agencies to lead sport in the UK to world class success
Note: The UKSI runs a network of centres throughout the UK.

United Kingdom Wolf Centre   (UKWCT)   1995

■   Butlers Farm, Beenham, Reading, Berkshire, RG7 5NT.
        0118-971 3330
E   A part of the UK Wolf Conservation Trust.
○   To care for wolves

United States Studies Centre
        see **American (United States) Studies Centre.**

University of Central England, Birmingham Institute of Art and Design
        see **Birmingham Institute of Art and Design.**

UNIVERSITY CENTRES of CRICKETING EXCELLENCE Scheme

        http://www.lords.org/
Note: The Scheme was established by the England and Wales Cricket Board to ensure that the best young cricketers are encouraged to
        go into further education by providing them with the best possible opportunities to develop their cricket at university. There are
        currently six centres based at Cambridge, Cardiff, Durham, Leeds, Loughborough, and Oxford.

University College London...
    see **UCL**

University of Edinburgh Centre for Inflammation Research
    see **MRC-University of Edinburgh Centre for Inflammation Research.**

University of Hull International Fisheries Institute
    see **Hull International Fisheries Institute.**

University of Hull Logistics Institute
■   University of Hull Business School, University of Hull, Cottingham Road, Hull, HU6 7RX.
        01482 463010
        http://www.hull.ac.uk/hubs/
        Director: Prof John Mangan.
E   An institute at the University of Hull.
○   To provide a range of business support services, research, education and facilities to add value to industry through efficiences and innovations in the management of supply chains

University of London Centre for Transport Studies
        The co-ordinating name of the **Centre for Transport Studies** at Imperial College and University College London.

University of Manchester Aerospace Research Institute   (UMARI)
■   School of Mechanical, Aerospace and Civil Engineering, PO Box 88, University of Manchester, Sackville Street, Manchester, M60 1QD.
        0161-306 9200   fax 0161-306 3755
        http://www.mace.manchester.ac.uk/
E   A research institute at the University of Manchester.
○   To conduct research in the delivery of greener, faster, safer and more extensive travel

University of Manchester Institute of Science and Technology
Note: No longer in existence.

University of Nottingham Institute for Enterprise and Innovation   (UNIEI)   2000
■   Nottingham University Business School, University of Nottingham, Jubilee Campus, Wollaton Road, Nottingham, NG8 1BB.
        0115-846 6602; 951 5505   fax 0115-846 6667
        http://www.nottingham.ac.uk/business/
        Director: Prof Alistair Bruce.
E   A Government funded Science Enterprise Centre (qv) at the University of Nottingham.
○   To be a centre of excellence in the development of enterprise, entrepreneurial skills, innovation, and the commercialisation of research

University of Nottingham Institute for Materials Technology   (UNIMAT)
■   School of Mechanical Materials and Manufacturing Engineering, University of Nottingham, University Park, Nottingham, NG7 2RD.
        0115-846 8468   fax 0115-951 3633
        http://www.nottingham.ac.uk/unimat/
E   A research centre at the University of Nottingham.
○   To specialise in developing novel materials, as well as associated techniques, for synthesis, processing, analysis or testing

University of Nottingham Tax Research Institute   (TRI)   2004
■   Nottingham University Business School, University of Nottingham, Jubilee Campus, Wollaton Road, Nottingham, NG8 1BB.
        0115-846 6602
        http://www.nottingham.ac.uk/business/
E   A research institute at the University of Nottingham.
○   To conduct rigorous policy and practice research in taxation, with particular emphasis on the behavioural effects of taxation, tax regulation and administration, and micro-modelling of tax policy

University of Oxford Centre for Competition Law and Policy   (CCLP)
■   Faculty of Law, University of Oxford, St Cross Building, St Cross Road, Oxford, OX1 3UL.
        01865 281610   fax 01865 281611
        http://www.competition-law.ac.uk/
        Director: Dr Ariel Ezrachi.
E   A research centre within the Institute of European and Comparative Law (qv) at the University of Oxford.

University of Oxford Centre for Criminological Research
    see **Centre for Criminology.**

University of Oxford Centre for Suicide Research   1998
- ■ Department of Psychiatry, Warneford Hospital, Oxford, OX3 7JX.
     01865 226451   fax 01865 793101
     http://www.psychiatry.ox.ac.uk/
     Director: Prof Keith Hawton.
- E A research centre at the University of Oxford.

University of Stirling Centre for English Language Teaching   (CELT)   1981
- ■ University of Stirling, Airthrey Castle, Stirling, FK9 4LA.
     01786 467934   fax 01786 466131
     http://www.celt.stir.ac.uk/
     Head: Prof Richard Johnstone.
- E A research centre within the Institute of Education (qv) at the University of Stirling.
- ○ To teach English to non-native speakers; to provide undergraduate and postgraduate degree courses in English as a Foreign Language (EFL); to train both native and non-native speakers of English to be teachers of EFL
- ● Education and training PhD studies in language education

University Technology Centres
     see **Rolls-Royce University Technology Centres.**

UnumProvident Centre for Psychosocial and Disability Research
- ■ Cardiff University, 51a Park Place, Cardiff, CF10 3AT.
     029 2087 0316   fax 029 2087 0196
     http://www.cf.ac.uk/psych/
     Director: Prof Mansel Aylward. Administrator: Louise Morris.
- E A centre at Cardiff University.
- ○ To extend knowledge and understanding of the psychosocial, social, economic and cultural factors that influence health, illness and disease, recovery, rehabilitation and reintegration into rewarding work

Urban Renaissance Institute   (URI)   2005
- ■ University of Greenwich, Central Avenue, Chatham Maritime, Kent, ME4 4TB.
     020 8331 9156
     http://ils-web.gre.ac.uk/uri/
     Director: Louise Thomas.
- E A free standing institute within the University of Greenwich.
- ○ To enable professionals and local people to build more sustainable communities

Urban Water Technology Centre   (UWTC)   1993
- ■ School of Contemporary Sciences, Level 5 - Kidd Building, University of Abertay Dundee, Bell Street, Dundee, DD1 1HG.
     01382 308170   fax 01382 308117
     http://www.uwtc.tay.ac.uk/
     Head: Prof Chris Jefferies.
- E A research centre at the University of Abertay, Dundee.
- ○ To provide a service to the water industry and various other related clients (eg consulting engineers), in three main areas - research, academic and consultancy; to undertake research into wastewater technology in terms of control, monitoring, treatment and optimum management systems for surface waters, industrial wastes and sanitary sewage
- ● Conference facilities - Consultancy - Education and training - Exhibitions - Information service - Postgraduate courses in water and environmental management

Vasari Centre for Digital Art History   2002

- School of History of Art, Film and Visual Media, Birkbeck University of London, Malet Street, Bloomsbury, London, WC1E 7HX.
  020 7631 6861
  http://www.bbk.ac.uk/
- E   A research centre within the Birkbeck Institute for the Humanities (qv) at Birkbeck, University of London.

Vascular Institute
   see **Sheffield Vascular Institute.**

Vauxhall Centre for the Study of Crime

- Luton Campus, University of Bedfordshire, Luton, Bedfordshire, LU1 3JU.
  01234 400400
  http://www.beds.ac.uk/research/iasr/
  Director: Prof John Pitts.
- E   A research centre within the Institute for Applied Social Research (qv) at the University of Bedfordshire.
- O   To conduct research into youth crime and victimization, policing, the operation of the youth justice and community safety services, and the analysis of policy and practice in these fields

Vehicle Safety Research Centre   (VSRC)   1982

- Faculty of Social Sciences and Humanities, Loughborough University, Holywell Building, Holywell Park, Loughborough, Leicestershire, LE11 3TU.
  01509 226900   fax 01509 226960
  http://www.lboro.ac.uk/research/esri/
  Head: Prof Pete Thomas.
- E   A research centre within the Ergonomics and Safety Research Institute (qv) at Loughborough University.
- O   To investigate the causes of road accidents and injuries; to conduct research into the improvement of road and vehicle safety

Vehicle Technology Research Centre   (VTRC)

- Department of Mechanical Engineering, University of Birmingham, Edgbaston, Birmingham, B15 2TT.
  0121-414 4161   fax 0121-414 3958
  http://www.eng.bham.ac.uk/
  Head: Prof Miroslaw Lech Wyszynski.
- E   A research centre at the University of Birmingham.
- O   To conduct research into producing low emission and fuel thrifty vehicles

Verification Research, Training and Information Centre   (VERTIC)   1986

- Development House, 56-64 Leonard Street, London, EC2A 4JX.
  020 7065 0880   fax 020 7065 0890
  http://www.vertic.org/
  Executive Director: Michael Crowley. Administrator: Ben Handley.
- E   A registered charity.
- O   To promote effective and efficient verification of international agreements within three programmes - arms control and disarmament, peace agreements and the environment
- ●   Education and training
- ¶   Verification Yearbook. Trust and Verify (newsletter).

Veterinary Clinical Skills Centre   2004

- Hawkshead Campus, Royal Veterinary College, University of London, North Mymms, Hatfield, Hertfordshire, AL9 7TA.
  01707 666333
  http://www.rvc.ac.uk/
- E   A research centre at the Royal Veterinary College, University of London.

Veterinary Surveillance Centre   2003

- Hawkshead Campus, Royal Veterinary College, University of London, North Mymms, Hatfield, Hertfordshire, AL9 7TA.
  01707 666333
  http://www.rvc.ac.uk/
- E   A research centre at the Royal Veterinary College, University of London.

Veterinary Surveillance Centre

- Department of Veterinary Pathology, University of Liverpool, Leahurst, Neston, South Wirral, CH64 7TE.
  0151-794 6120
- E   A research centre at the University of Liverpool.

Vibration University Technology Centre   (VUTC)   1990

- Department of Mechanical Engineering, South Kensington Campus, Imperial College London, Exhibition Road, London, SW7 2AZ.
  020 7594 7078   fax 020 7584 1560
  http://www3.imperial.ac.uk/vutc
  Director: Prof Mehmet Imregun.
- E   A research centre at Imperial College London.
- O   To provide a focus for the prosecution of vibration research which is of direct relevance to the aerospace and power generation industries

Victorian Studies Centre 1966

■ Department of English, University of Leicester, University Road, Leicester, LE1 7RH.
  0116-252 3943   fax 0116-252 2065
  http://www.leicester.ac.uk/
  Director: Prof Joanne Shattock.
E A department of the University of Leicester.
○ To promote interdisciplinary research and postgraduate teaching on Victorian literature and culture
● Postgraduate taught MA course - Advice and information on Victorian matters (Mon-Fri 0900-1300)

Viking Centre
  see **Jorvik Viking Centre.**

Vinogradoff Institute 1982

■ Faculty of Laws, University College London, Bentham House, Endsleigh Gardens, London, WC1H 0EG.
  020 7679 4556
  http://www.ucl.ac.uk/laws/
  Director: Prof William E Butler.
E A research institute at University College London.
○ To co-ordinate research and teaching concerning Russian and the other CIS (Commonwealth of Independent States) legal systems

Virion Centre
  see **Wohl Virion Centre.**

Virtual Centre of Excellence in Mobile Personal Communications   (Mobile VCE)   1996

■ Grove House, Lutyens Close, Basingstoke, Hampshire, RG24 8AG.
  01256 316590   fax 01256 316589
  http://www.mobilevce.com/
  Director: Walter Tuttlebee. Administration Manager: Jenny Johnson.
E A collaborative venture between mobile communication companies and seven UK universities.
○ To conduct industrially-led, long term, research in mobile and personal communications
Note: Is commonly referred to as Mobile VCE.

Virtual Engineering Centre   (VEC)

■ School of Mechanical and Manufacturing Engineering, Queen's University Belfast, Cloreen Park, Malone Road, Belfast, BT9 5HN.
  028 9097 4131
  http://www.ee.qub.ac.uk/
  Research Director: Prof G W Irwin.
E A research centre within the Northern Ireland Technology Centre (qv) at Queen's University, Belfast.
○ To bring together expertise on virtual reality, engineering computation, physical modelling and CAD technologies

Virtual Environment Centre
  see **Edinburgh Virtual Environment Centre.**

Virtual Reality Centre for the Built Environment
  see **VR Centre for the Built Environment.**

Virtual Reality Centre at Teesside

■ University of Teesside, Borough Road, Middlesbrough, TS1 3BA.
  01642 384324
  http://vr.tees.ac.uk/
E A research centre at the University of Teesside.

Visual Art Practice Research Centre

■ Sir John Cass Department of Art, Media and Design, London Metropolitan University, 41 Commercial Road, London, E1 1LA.
  020 7133 4200
  http://www.londonmet.ac.uk/jcamd/
  Director: Chris Smith.
E An interdisciplinary research centre at London Metropolitan University.
○ To provide a focus for studio-centred research that encourages enquiry into the visual arts, design and architecture

Visual Culture Research Centre

■ School of Art, Cavendish North Building, Manchester Metropolitan University, Cavendish Street, Manchester, M15 6BG.
  0161-247 1928
  http://www.miriad.mmu.ac.uk/visualculture/
  Leader: Dr Jim Aulich.
E A research centre within the Manchester Institute for Research and Innovation in Art and Design (qv) at Manchester Metropolitan University.
● There are three research groups - Archives, Collections and Objects Research Network (ACORN), Images, Narratives and Cultures Research Group, and Location, Memory and the Visual Research Group

Visual Impairment Centre for Teaching and Research   (VICTAR)   2001
- ■ School of Education, University of Birmingham, Edgbaston, Birmingham, B15 2TT.
    0121-414 4866   fax 0121-414 4865
    http://www.education.bham.ac.uk/
- E   A research centre at the University of Birmingham.
- ○   To undertake social and educational research in the field of visual impairment
- ✕   Research Centre for the Education of the Visually Handicapped.

Visual and Information Design Research Centre   (VIDe)
- ■ Coventry University, Priory Street, Coventry, CV1 5FB.
    024 7688 8521
    http://corporate.coventry.ac.uk/cms/jsp/polopoly.jsp?d=134&a=789
    Director: Andree Woodcock.
- E   A research centre within the Coventry University Design Institute (qv) at Coventry University.
- ○   To contribute to an improvement in the competitiveness of European manufacturing and commerce, especially in the automobile and aerospace industries, through the development of improved methods and techniques for design and information access

Visual LearningLab CETL   2004
- ■ School of Education, Dearing Building, University of Nottingham, Wollaton Road, Nottingham, NG8 1BB.
    0115-846 7201
    http://www.visuallearninglab.ac.uk/
    Director: Prof Roger Murphy.
- E   A Centre for Excellence in Teaching and Learning (CETL) within the Institute for Research into Learning and Teaching in Higher Education (qv) at the University of Nottingham.
- Note: See **Centres for Excellence in Teaching and Learning** for more information.

Visual Research Centre   (VRC)
- ■ Duncan of Jordanstone College of Art and Design, University of Dundee, 152 Nethergate, Dundee, DD1 4DY.
    01382 388064; 388070   fax 01382 388105
    http://www.vrc.dundee.ac.uk/
    Contact: Jane Cumberlidge.
- E   A department of the University of Dundee.
- ○   To conduct practice-led research in the visual arts

Volapük Centre   (ZbVp)   1979
- ■ 155 Leighton Avenue, Leigh-on-Sea, Essex, SS9 1PX.
    01702 714538
    Director: Brian R Bishop, BA, DMS, DBEA. Vice-President: Jean-Claude Caraco.
- E   An independent non-profit-distributing organisation and an association with a voluntary subscribing membership.
- ○   To conserve the Volapük language, literature, publications and artefacts - Volapük is a universal language invented in 1879 by Johann Schleyer
- ●   Document Research - Information service - Publications

Voluntary Sector Research Centre   (VSRC)   1998
- ■ Caledonian Business School, Glasgow Caledonian University, Cowcaddens Road, Glasgow, G4 0BA.
    0141-331 3872   fax 0141-331 8526
    http://www.gcal.ac.uk/vsrc/
    Director: Dr Rona S Beattie.
- E   A research centre at Glasgow Caledonian University.
- ○   To provide high quality professional research designed to meet the needs of the voluntary sector community

VR Centre for the Built Environment   (VRC)   1997
- NR   The Bartlett School of Architecture, Torrington Place Site, University College London, Gower Street, London, WC1E 6BT.
    020 7679 1987   fax 020 7916 1887
    http://www.vr.ucl.ac.uk/
    Director: Prof Alan Penn.
- E   An interdisciplinary research centre at University College London.
- ○   To bring the full range of computer graphics, interaction and digital data to the virtual building that currently drives the design-development-operation cycle
- Note: A collaborative initiative involving various othe research centres and Imperial College. Also known as the Virtual Reality Centre.

© CBD Research Ltd · Beckenham · Kent BR3 5JS · Tel 020 8650 7745 · Fax 020 8650 0768 · E-mail cbd@cbdresearch.com · www.cbdresearch.com

Wales Biomass Centre   (WBC)   1992
- Cardiff School of Biosciences, Cardiff University, Newbridge-on-Wye, Llandrindod Wells, Powys, LD1 6NB.
  01597 860308; 860373
  http://www.walesbiomass.org/
  Project Manager: Dr Simone Lowthe-Thomas. Site Manager: Dr Robert Luxton.
- E   A centre at Cardiff University.
- O   To undertake energy crop research at the Llysdinam Field Centre

Wales Centre for Behaviour Analysis   (WCBA)   2004
- School of Psychology, University of Wales Bangor, Adeilad Brigantia, Bangor, Gwynedd, LL57 2AS.
  01248 382211
  http://www.psychology.bangor.ac.uk/research/su/behavioural.php?catid=&subid=3679
  Director: Prof C Fergus Lowe.
- E   A research centre at the University of Wales, Bangor.

Wales Centre for Evidence Based Care   (WCEBC)
- Cardiff School of Nursing and Midwifery Studies, Cardiff University, 4th Floor - Eastgate House, 35-43 Newport Road, Cardiff, CF24 0AB.
  029 2091 7800   fax 029 2091 7803
  http://www.cardiff.ac.uk/nursing/
- E   A collaborating centre of the Joanna Briggs Institute (Australia) within the Nursing, Health and Social Care Research Centre (qv) at Cardiff University.
- O   To develop the science of implementation and promote evidence-based practice, through the development and evaluation of internationally excellent systems, for evidence appraisal, translation, utilisation and continuing professional development, and through programmatic primary research

Wales Centre for Health   (WCH)   2003   Canolfan Iechyd Cymru
- 14 Cathedral Road, Cardiff, CF11 9LJ.
  029 2022 7744   fax 029 2022 6749
  http://www.wales.nhs.uk/
  Chairman: Prof Mansel Aylward.
- E   A Welsh Assembly Sponsored Public Body.
- O   To lead improvements in the Welsh nation's health

Wales Centre for Intergenerational Practice   (CCIP)   2004   Canolfan Ymarfer Rhwng Cenedlaethau
- University of Glamorgan, 6 Forest Grove, Pontypridd, CF37 1DL.
  01443 482372   fax 01443 483799
  http://www.ccip.org.uk/
- E   A research centre at the University of Glamorgan.
- Note: Also known as Cymru Centre for Intergenerational Practice.

Wales Centre for Mental Health Service Development   2003
- School of Psychology, University of Wales Bangor, Adeilad Brigantia, Bangor, Gwynedd, LL57 2AS.
  01248 382211
  http://www.psychology.bangor.ac.uk/research/su/wcmhs.php?catid=&subid=3671
- E   A research centre at the University of Wales, Bangor.

Wales Centre for Podiatric Studies
- Cardiff School of Health Sciences, Llandarff Campus, University of Wales Institute Cardiff, Western Avenue, Cardiff, CF5 2YB.
  029 2041 6865   fax 029 2041 7191
  http://www2.uwic.ac.uk/UWIC/schools/HealthSciences/SchoolStructure/DeptHealthPsychology/podiatry/
  Head: Paul Frowen.
- E   A centre at the University of Wales Institute, Cardiff.
- O   To conduct teaching courses and programmes in podiatry

Wales Heart Research Institute
  see **Sir Geraint Evans Wales Heart Research Institute.**

Wales Institute for Research into Co-operatives   (WIRC)
- Cardiff School of Management, University of Wales Institute Cardiff, Colchester Avenue, Cardiff, CF23 9XR.
  029 2041 6315   fax 029 2041 6940
  http://www2.uwic.ac.uk/uwic/schools/business/research/wirc.htm
- E   A research institute at the University of Wales Institute, Cardiff.

Wales Millennium Centre
- Bute Place, Cardiff, CF10 5AL.

Wales Quality Centre   1988
- Treforest Estate, Pontypridd, CF37 5XD.
  01443 841192   fax 01443 841457
  http://www.walesqualitycentre.org.uk/
  Chief Executive: Vincent Kane. Operations Director: Alan Jones.
- ○ To promote a world class private and public sector

Wales Transport Research Centre   (WTRC)   2001
- School of Technology, University of Glamorgan, Treforest, Pontypridd, CF37 1DL.
  01443 482123
  http://www.glam.ac.uk/sot/1452
  Director: Prof Stuart Cole.
- E   A research institute within the University of Glamorgan.
- ○ To develop, in Wales, an independent, analytical research facility for transport

Wales Waste and Resources Research Centre   (WWRReC)   2006   Canolfan Ymchwil Cymru er Gwastraff ac Adnoddau
- Cardiff School of Engineering, Cardiff University, Queen's Buildings, Newport Road, Cardiff, CF24 3AA.
  029 2087 4004
  http://www.wwrrec.cf.ac.uk/
  Contact: Dr Robert W Francis.
- E   A centre at Cardiff University.
- ○ To further develop and co-ordinate the research base for the management of waste and resources

Walks of Life Heritage Centre   1997
- 33 Lincoln Road, Newark, Nottinghamshire, NG22 0HR.
  01777 870427
  Owner & Curator: Dorothy Harrison.
- E   A private venture.
- ○ To preserve, maintain and show a collection of hand-pushed vehicles ie vehicles which rely totally on human muscle power for their movement
- ● Exhibitions

Walton Centre for Neurology and Neurosurgery
- Lower Lane, Liverpool, L9 7LJ.
  0151-529 5484   fax 0151-529 5485
  http://www.thewaltoncentre.nhs.uk/
  Contact: Mrs T Jones.
- E   A research centre.

Warburg Institute   1921
- School of Advanced Study, University of London, Woburn Square, London, WC1H 0AB.
  020 7862 8949   fax 020 7862 8955
  http://warburg.sas.ac.uk/
  Director: Prof Charles Hope.
- E   A department of the University of London.
- ○ To further the study of the classical tradition - those elements of European thought, literature, art and institutions which derive from the ancient world
- ● Archive - Library - Photographic collection
Note: The Institute stems from the personal library of the Hamburg scholar Aby Warburg (1866-1929).

Warwick Centre for the Study of Sport in Society   (WCSSS)   1993
- Department of Sociology, University of Warwick, Coventry, CV4 7AL.
  024 7652 3065
  http://www2.warwick.ac.uk/fac/soc/sociology/sport/
  Director: Dr Andrew Parker.
- E   A research centre at the University of Warwick.
- ○ To foster study and debate on sport

Warwick Eighteenth Century Centre
- Department of History, University of Warwick, Coventry, CV4 7AL.
  024 7652 3523
  http://www2.warwick.ac.uk/fac/arts/history/ecc/
  Director: Prof Maxine Berg.
- E   A research centre at the University of Warwick.
- ○ To run major research projects and to provide a forum for academic staff and postgraduate students in the humanities
- ● Education and training - Information service - Seminars

© CBD Research Ltd · Beckenham · Kent BR3 5JS · Tel 020 8650 7745 · Fax 020 8650 0768 · E-mail cbd@cbdresearch.com · www.cbdresearch.com

Warwick Finance Research Institute (WFRI)

- Warwick Business School, University of Warwick, Coventry, CV4 7AL.
  024 7652 4118   fax 024 7652 4167
  http://www.wbs.ac.uk/
  Director: Prof Mark Salmon.
- E   A research centre at the University of Warwick.
- O   To co-ordinate and stimulate research in the area of finance

Warwick Innovative Manufacturing Research Centre (WIMRC)

- NR Faculty of Science, University of Warwick, Coventry, CV4 7AL.
  024 7657 2696
  http://www2.warwick.ac.uk/fac/sci/wimrc/
  Director: Dr Ken Young. Research Manager: Dr Nick Mallinson.
- E   An EPSRC Innovative Manufacturing Research Centre within the International Manufacturing Centre (qv) at the University of Warwick.
- O   To focus research on the traditional areas of manufacturing and in emerging sectors, including photonics, medical technology and knowledge-based systems; to conduct research on the integration of engineering and management science to deliver novel, competitive and relevant research outputs

Note: One of the EPSRC funded centres in the UK - for further information see EPSRC Innovative Manufacturing Research Centres.

Warwick Institute of Education (WIE)

- University of Warwick, Coventry, CV4 7AL.
  024 7652 3801   fax 024 7652 4609
  http://www2.warwick.ac.uk/fac/soc/wie/
  Director: Prof Alma Harris.
- E   A research institute at the University of Warwick.
- O   To be a leading contributor to the creation of learning societies in the three key areas of childhood, policy and pedagogy
- ●   Education and training

Warwick Institute for Employment Research (IER) 1981

- Faculty of Social Studies, University of Warwick, Coventry, CV4 7AL.
  024 7652 3514   fax 024 7652 4241
  http://www2.warwick.ac.uk/fac/soc/ier/
  Director: Prof Robert Lindley. Administrator: Margaret Birch.
- E   An autonomous research institute of the University of Warwick.
- O   To research into all aspects of labour market processes and evaluation of labour market programmes
- ●   Conference facilities - Education and training - Statistics
- ¶   Bulletin.

Warwick Mathematics Institute (WMI)

- Faculty of Science, University of Warwick, Coventry, CV4 7AL.
  024 7652 4661   fax 024 7652 4182
  http://www2.warwick.ac.uk/fac/sci/maths/
  Head: Prof Colin Sparrow.
- E   A department of the University of Warwick.
- O   To conduct research and teaching in a very wide variety of mathematics fields

Warwick Systems Biology Centre 2006

- Faculty of Science, Coventry House, University of Warwick, Coventry, CV4 7AL.
  024 7652 3184; 3599   fax 024 7652 3701
  http://www2.warwick.ac.uk/fac/sci/systemsbiology/
  Co-Director: Prof David Rand. Co-Director: Prof Liz Wellington.
- E   A research centre at the University of Warwick.

Waste Incineration Centre
  see **Sheffield University Waste Incineration Centre.**

Water Engineering and Development Centre (WEDC) 1971

- Department of Civil and Building Engineering, Loughborough University, Ashby Road, Loughborough, Leicestershire, LE11 3TU.
  01509 222884; 263171   fax 01509 223981
  http://wedc.lboro.ac.uk/
  Director: Ian Smout.
- E   A research centre at Loughborough University.
- O   To improve the health and well-being of people living in rural areas and urban communities

Weather Centre
  see **BBC Weather Centre.**

Weatherall Institute of Molecular Medicine   1989
■   John Radcliffe Hospital, Headington, Oxford, OX3 9DS.
      01865 222443   fax 01865 222737
      http://www.imm.ox.ac.uk/
      Administrator: Lynne Hughson.
E   A department of the University of Oxford.
○   To foster research in molecular and cell biology with direct application to the study of human disease

Welding Engineering Research Centre   (WERC)
■   Materials Department, Cranfield University, Building 61, Cranfield, Bedfordshire, MK43 0AL.
      01234 754086
      http://www.cranfield.ac.uk/sas/welding/research.htm
E   A research centre at Cranfield University.
○   To provide basic, strategic and applied research and related postgraduate training in welding engineering

Wellcome Centre for Clinical Tropical Medicine   1995
■   Faculty of Medicine, St Mary's Campus, Imperial College London, Norfolk Place, London, W2 1PG.
      020 7594 3891; 3914   fax 020 7594 3894
      http://www1.imperial.ac.uk/medicine/about/institutes/tropical/
      Director: Prof Geoff Pasvol. Administrator: Nicolette Davies.
E   A research centre within the Wright Fleming Institute (qv) at Imperial College London.
○   To conduct research in clinical tropical medicine to treat various tropical diseases, especially HIV, malaria and tuberculosis

Wellcome Centre for Molecular Parasitology   (WCMP)   1987
■   University of Glasgow, 120 University Place, Glasgow, G12 8TA.
      0141-330 2684   fax 0141-330 5422
      http://www.gla.ac.uk/centres/wcmp/
      Director: Prof Dave Barry.
E   A research centre within the Institute of the Biomedical and Life Sciences (qv) at the University of Glasgow.
○   To conduct research in molecular parasitology, with particular emphasis on African trypanosomes (microscopic parasites that cause human sleeping sickness and the wasting disease nagana in domestic animals)

Wellcome Trust Biocentre
■   College of Life Sciences, University of Dundee, Dow Street, Dundee, DD1 5EH.
      01382 388377   fax 01382 223778
      http://www.dundee.ac.uk/biocentre/SLSBOVWellcome.htm
      Contact: Alison Nicoll.
E   A research centre at the University of Dundee.

Wellcome Trust/Cancer Research UK Gurdon Institute of Cancer and Developmental Biology   1989
■   University of Cambridge, Tennis Court Road, Cambridge, CB2 1QN.
      01223 334088   fax 01223 334089
      http://www.gurdon.cam.ac.uk/
E   An institute at the University of Cambridge.
○   To support research into the complementary areas of cancer and developmental biology

Wellcome Trust Centre for Cell Biology   (WTCCB)   2001
■   School of Biological Sciences, The King's Buildings, University of Edinburgh, Mayfield Road, Edinburgh, EH9 3JR.
      0131-650 5668   fax 0131-650 5379
      http://www.wcb.ed.ac.uk/
      Director: Prof Adrian Bird.
E   A research centre within the Institute of Cell Biology (qv) at the University of Edinburgh.
○   To perform cutting-edge research into cellular and molecular biology

Wellcome Trust Centre for Cell-Matrix Research   (WTCCMR)   1995
■   Faculty of Life Sciences, Michael Smith Building, University of Manchester, Oxford Road, Manchester, M13 9PT.
      0161-275 1516
      http://www.wtccmr.manchester.ac.uk/
      Contact: Dr Linda Green.
E   A research centre at the University of Manchester.

Wellcome Trust Centre for Human Genetics   (WTCHG)   1994
■   University of Oxford, Roosevelt Drive, Oxford, OX3 7BN.
      01865 287500   fax 01865 287501
      http://www.well.ox.ac.uk/
      Director: Prof Anthony Monaco.
E   A department of the University of Oxford.
○   To undertake research into the genetic basis of common diseases

Wellcome Trust Centre for Stem Cell Research and Institute for Stem Cell Biology   (ISCB)
- ■   School of the Biological Sciences, University of Cambridge, Tennis Court Road, Cambridge, CB2 1QT.
  01223 333605   fax 01223 333345
  http://www.cscr.cam.ac.uk/
  Administrator: Lynn Kennedy.
- E   A centre at the University of Cambridge.
- ○   To bring together leading investigators with interests in stem cells and affiliated disciplines

Wellcome Trust Sanger Institute   1993
- ■   Wellcome Trust Research Campus, Hinxton, Cambridge, CB10 1SA.
  01223 834244
  http://www.sanger.ac.uk/
- E   A registered charity and a company limited by guarantee.
- ○   To further the knowledge of genomes, particularly through large scale sequencing and analysis
- ✕   Sanger Centre.

Wellcome Trust Tropical Centre   1994
- ■   Faculty of Medicine, University of Liverpool, Pembroke Place, Liverpool, L3 5QA.
  0151-708 9393   fax 0151-705 3370
  http://www.liv.ac.uk/lstm/
- E   A research centre at the University of Liverpool.
- ○   To facilitate significant scientific advances in tropical medicine
Note: Also known as the Liverpool Wellcome Trust Centre for Research in Clinical Tropical Medicine.

Welsh Centre for International Affairs   (WCIA)   1973   Canolfan Gymreig Materion Rhyngwladol
- ■   Temple of Peace, Cathays Park, Cardiff, CF10 3AP.
  029 2022 8549   fax 029 2064 0333
  http://www.wcia.org.uk/
  Director: Stephen Thomas. Administrative Officer: Sue Coles.
- E   A registered charity and membership organisation.
- ○   To raise awareness of global issues in Wales; to campaign to promote world peace, human rights and international understanding; to provide a key point of contact in Wales for international bodies and institutions

Welsh Centre for Learning Disabilities   (WCLD)   1975
- ■   Cardiff School of Medicine, Cardiff University, Heath Park, Cardiff, CF14 4YS.
  029 2068 7204   fax 029 2068 7100
  http://www.cardiff.ac.uk/dentistry/medicine/psychological_medicine/research/welsh_centre_learning_disabilities/
  Administrator: Rosy Allcott.
- E   A centre at Cardiff University.
- ○   To bring together a range of expertise in clinical practice, research, teaching and service development associated with many aspects of the lives of people with learning disabilities

Welsh Centre for Post-Graduate Pharmaceutical Education   (WCPPE)
- ■   Welsh School of Pharmacy, Cardiff University, 8 North Road, Cardiff, CF10 3DY.
  029 2087 4784   fax 029 2087 4540
  http://www.cardiff.ac.uk/phrmy/
  Director: Dr David J Temple.
- E   A centre at Cardiff University.
- ○   To provide an all-embracing continuing professional development service to all pharmacists and their support staff in Wales

Welsh Centre for Printing and Coating   (WCPC)   1995
- ■   School of Engineering, Swansea University, Singleton Park, Swansea, SA2 8PP.
  01792 295091   fax 01792 295816
  http://www.swan.ac.uk/printing/
  Director: Prof D T Gethin. Director: Dr T C Claypole.
- E   A research centre within the Multidisciplinary Nanotechnology Centre (qv) at Swansea University.
- ○   To be a centre of excellence for research and education for the printing and coating industries including graphical and industrial applications, digital, flexo, offset, pad, screen, gravure, along with single and multiroll coating
- ●   Education and training - Technology transfer and networking activities - Discussions of interest over a wide range of industry sectors

Welsh Centre for Promoting the Incredible Years Programmes   2003
- ■   School of Psychology, 8th Floor - Alun Roberts Building, University of Wales Bangor, Bangor, Gwynedd, LL57 2UW.
  01248 383758
  http://www.incredibleyearswales.co.uk/
  Director: Dr Judy Hutchings.
- E   A centre at the University of Wales, Bangor.
- ○   To maintain an active programme of child and teacher classroom management programmes
Note: Also known as the Incredible Years Wales Centre.

Welsh Centre for Research into Lifelong Learning
- Department of Adult Continuing Education, Swansea University, Singleton Park, Swansea, SA2 8PP.
    01792 295657; 295786
    http://www.swan.ac.uk/research/centresandinstitutes/Lifelonglearning/
E   A research centre at Swansea University.
○   To conduct research in lifelong learning

Welsh Centre for Tourism Research   (WCTR)
- Welsh School of Hospitality, Tourism and Leisure Management, University of Wales Institute Cardiff, Colchester Avenue, Cardiff, CF23 9XR.
    029 2041 6315; 6425   fax 029 2041 6930
    http://www.uwic.ac.uk/shtl/
    Director: Dr Annette Pritchard.
E   A research centre at the University of Wales Institute, Cardiff.

Welsh e-Science Centre   (WeSC)   2005   Canolfan e-Wyddoniaeth Cymru
- Cardiff School of Computer Science, Cardiff University, Queen's Buildings, 5 The Parade, Cardiff, CF24 3AA.
    029 2087 4812   fax 029 2087 4598
    http://www.wesc.ac.uk/
    Director: Prof David W Walker.
E   A centre at Cardiff University.
Note: See **e-Science Centres** for further information.

Welsh Economy Labour Market Evaluation and Research Centre   (WELMERC)   2002
- Department of Economics, James Callaghan Building, Swansea University, Singleton Park, Swansea, SA2 8PP.
    01792 205678   fax 01792 295157
    http://www.swan.ac.uk/welmerc/
    Director: Prof Peter Sloane.
E   A research centre at Swansea University.
○   To provide evidence-based economics policy advice

Welsh Enterprise Institute   (WEI)
- Glamorgan Business School, University of Glamorgan, Treforest, Pontypridd, CF37 1DL.
    01443 482818   fax 01443 483560
    http://www.glam.ac.uk/bus/1233
    Director: Prof David Brooksbank.
E   A research institute within the University of Glamorgan.
○   To provide a centre of expertise in the areas of entrepreneurship, innovation and small business management

Welsh Governance Centre   (WGC)   1999   Canolfan Llywodraethiant Cymru
- Cardiff School of European Studies, Cardiff University, PO Box 908, Cardiff, CF10 3YQ.
    029 2087 4885
    http://www.cf.ac.uk/euros/welsh-governance/
    Contact: Lisa Chivers.
E   A centre at Cardiff University.
○   To study the nature of the 'new' UK state and the impact and extent of outside influence on the UK, its central Government and the devolved administration in Cardiff

Welsh Hawking Centre   (WHC)   1980
- Weycock Road, Barry, Vale of Glamorgan, CF62 3AA.
    01446 734687   fax 01446 739620
    Owner: C J Griffiths. Owner: N Griffiths.
E   A private venture.
●   Daily flying displays of birds of prey - Children's animal park

Welsh Hearing Institute   (WHI)   1978   Athrofa Clyw Cymru
- Department of Neurology, Ophthalmology and Audiological Medicine, University Hospital of Wales, Heath Park, Cardiff, CF14 4XW.
    029 2074 7747
E   An NHS research institute at Cardiff University.
○   To undertake research in audiological medicine; to provide services for people with hearing and balance disorders and tinnitus

Welsh Institute for Competitive Advantage   (WICA)
- Glamorgan Business School, University of Glamorgan, Treforest, Pontypridd, CF37 1DL.
    01443 482818
    http://wica.research.glam.ac.uk/
    Contact: Jane Boggan.
E   A research institute within the University of Glamorgan.

© CBD Research Ltd · Beckenham · Kent BR3 5JS · Tel 020 8650 7745 · Fax 020 8650 0768 · E-mail cbd@cbdresearch.com · www.cbdresearch.com

Welsh Institute for Minimal Access Therapy   (WIMAT)   1994
- School of Postgraduate Medical and Dental Education, Cardiff University, Heath Park, Cardiff, CF14 4XN.
  029 2074 3927   fax 029 2075 4966
  http://www.cardiff.ac.uk/pgmde/wimat/
- E   An institute at Cardiff University.
- O   To provide a wide range of postgraduate education and training in medical and surgical specialties, including laparoscopy

Welsh Institute for Research in Economics and Development   (WIRED)
- Cardiff Business School, Cardiff University, Colum Drive, Cardiff, CF10 3EU.
  http://www.cardiff.ac.uk/carbs/research/centres_units/wired.html
  Director: Prof James Foreman-Beck.
- E   A research institute at Cardiff University.
- O   To promote, through research, a deeper understanding of the interaction of economic and social forces that affect well-being

Welsh Institute for Social and Cultural Affairs   (WISCA)
- Main Arts Building, University of Wales Bangor, College Road, Bangor, Gwynedd, LL57 2DG.
  01248 382133   fax 01248 388483
  http://www.bangor.ac.uk/wisca/
  Director: Prof Duncan Tanner. Administrator: Mrs Stephanie Dolben.
- E   A research institute at the University of Wales, Bangor.
- O   To conduct research and teaching in a variety of fields, including bilingualism, language policy and education, heritage developments, law and crime, rural housing and other rural issues, regional economic issues, and contemporary politics

Welsh Institute of Sport   1972   Athrofa Chwaraeon Cymru
- Sophia Gardens, Cardiff, CF11 9SW.
  0845 045 0902   fax 029 2030 0599
  http://www.welsh-institute-sport.co.uk/
- E   A non-departmental body.
- O   To develop sport and physical activity in Wales by providing opportunities for everyone to participate and enjoy the benefits of sport, whatever their background or ability

Welsh Language Teaching Centre   (WLTC)   Canolfan Dysgu Cymraeg
- School of Welsh, Humanities Building, Cardiff University, Colum Drive, Cardiff, CF10 3EU.
  029 2087 4710   fax 029 2087 4708
  http://www.cardiff.ac.uk/cymraeg/
  Director: Ifor Gruffydd.
- E   A centre at Cardiff University.
- O   To teach a variety of courses in Welsh for beginners up to 'A' level standard

Welsh Music Information Centre   (WMIC)   1993   Canolfan Hysbysrwydd Cerddoriaeth Cymru (CHCC)
- Ty Cerdd, Wales Millennium Centre, Bute Place, Cardiff, CF10 5AL.
  029 2063 5640   fax 029 2063 5641
  http://www.wmic.org/
  Director: Keith Griffin. Manager: Ruth Leggett.
- E   A registered charity.
- O   To support, promote and provide an information resource on the Music of Wales
- ●   Education and training - Information service - Library - Open Mon-Fri 0930-1700
- ¶   Composers of Wales (series of 4 monographs).

Welsh Music Institute   (WMI)   1994   Sefydliad Cerddoriaeth Cymru
- School of Music, University of Wales Bangor, Bangor, Gwynedd, LL57 2DG.
  01248 382181   fax 01248 383895
  http://www.bangor.ac.uk/music//WMI/WMI.html
  Contact: Mrs Helen Roberts.
- E   An institute at the University of Wales, Bangor.
- O   To bring together music at Bangor, including the Archive of Traditional Welsh Music, Electroacoustic Wales, and Studio Cantor

Welsh National Centre for Religious Education   1979   Canolfan Genedlaethol Addysg Grefyddol
- Department of Theology and Religious Studies, University of Wales Bangor, Normal Site, Bangor, Gwynedd, LL57 2PZ.
  01248 382956   fax 01248 383954
  http://www.bangor.ac.uk/rs/pt/wncre/
  Director: Prof Leslie J Francis, PhD, ScD, DD. Secretary: Mrs Susan Thomas.
- E   Part of St Mary's Trust and based within the University of Wales, Bangor.
- O   To provide a religious education resources centre and a development education centre; to prepare curriculum materials for religious and world development education; to undertake religious education research
- ●   Resources Centre (open Mon-Fri 0900-1700) has books, audio-visual aids and equipment, posters and teaching packs available for hire To offer church education, in-service education and training for religious education teachers and clergy

Welsh School of Pharmacy Centre for Socioeconomic Research   (CSER)   1999
- ■   Welsh School of Pharmacy, Cardiff University, Redwood Building, King Edward VII Avenue, Cardiff, CF10 3XF.
     029 2087 6017   fax 029 2087 4535
     http://www.cardiff.ac.uk/phrmy/
     Director: Prof Sam Salek.
- E   A research centre at Cardiff University.
- ○   To be a leading centre for health-related quality of life and economic outcomes research

Wessex Institute of Health Research and Development   (WIHRD)
- ■   School of Medicine, Mailpoint 728, University of Southampton, Boldrewood, Southampton, SO16 7PX.
     023 8059 5591   fax 023 8059 5639
     http://www.wihrd.soton.ac.uk/
- E   A research institute within the University of Southampton.
- ○   To support the national and international prosecution of the highest possible quality of health technology assessment (HTA) and HTA-related research, in order to inform and improve the provision of health care

Wessex Institute of Technology   (WIT)   1986
- ■   Ashurst Lodge, Ashurst, Southampton, SO40 7AA.
     023 8029 3223   fax 023 8029 2853
     http://www.wessex.ac.uk/
     Principal: Prof C A Brebbia.
- E   An educational organisation with charitable status.
- ○   To develop a series of knowledge transfer mechanisms, particularly directed towards the exchange of information between academics and professional users, within industry

West London Buddhist Centre
- ■   94 Westbourne Park Villas, London, W2 5EB.
     0845 458 5461
     http://www.westlondonbuddhistcentre.com/
- E   An independent non-profit-distributing organisation and a registered charity.
- ○   To teach meditation and Buddhism
- ●   Education and training - The Centre provides meditation cushions and mats
Note: For other Buddhist centres see note under **Buddhist Centres**.

Westlakes Research Institute
Note: is now Survey and Statistical Computing, and is therefore outside the scope of this Directory.

Westminster Institute of Education   (WIE)
- ■   Harcourt Hill Campus, Oxford Brookes University, Oxford, OX2 9AT.
     01865 488600
     http://www.brookes.ac.uk/schools/education/
- E   An institute within Oxford Brookes University.
- ○   To focus research on human development, learning and education

Wetland Archaeology and Environments Research Centre   (WAERC)   2000
- ■   Department of Geography, University of Hull, Cottingham Road, Hull, HU6 7RX.
     01482 465554   fax 01482 466340
     http://www.hull.ac.uk/wetlands/
     Director: Dr Malcolm C Lillie.
- E   A centre at the University of Hull.
- ○   To provide a range of commercial services to support archaeological and environmental studies of past environments, regionally, nationally and internationally, principally, but not exclusively, in wetland contexts

Whalley Centre for Transport Studies   (CTS)   1979
- ■   Aldwych House, Box 71, Clitheroe, Lancashire, BB7 9GF.
     01254 248177   fax 01254 240858
- E   A private venture.
- ○   To provide transport management training
- ●   Education and training

White Rose Centre for Excellence in the Teaching and Learning of Enterprise   (CETLE)   2005
- ■   Department of Mechanical Engineering, University of Sheffield, 65 Wilkinson Street, Sheffield, S10 2GJ.
     0114-222 4045; 7748
     http://www.wrce.org.uk/
     Director: Prof John R Yates.
- E   A Centre for Excellence in Teaching and Learning (CETL) at the University of Sheffield.
Note: See **Centres for Excellence in Teaching and Learning** for more information.

White Rose Grid e-Science Centre of Excellence   (WRG)
NR   University of York, York Science Park, York, YO10 5DG.
         01904 435353   fax 01904 435350
         http://www.wrgrid.org.uk/
E   A research centre at the University of York.
Note: A joint venture with the Universities of Leeds and Sheffield. See **e-Science Centres of Excellence** for further information.

WHO COLLABORATING CENTRES
Note: Many centres, institutes and other organisations in the UK collaborate with the World Health Organisation (WHO), the United
         Nations specialized agency for health based in Geneva, Switzerland. Each UK institution provides WHO with research
         information etc which can benefit other organisations in other countries worldwide.

WHO Collaborating Centre for the Characterization of Rabies and Rabies-related Viruses
■   Department of Virology, New Haw, Addlestone, Weybridge, Surrey, KT15 3NB.
         01932 357840   fax 01932 357239
         http://www.defra.gov.uk/
         Contact: Dr Anthony R Fooks.
E   A World Health Organisation (WHO) Collaborating Centre at the Veterinary Laboratories Agency.

WHO Collaborating Centre for Child Care and Protection
       see **Centre for Forensic and Family Psychology.**

WHO Collaborating Centre for Community Control of Hereditary Disorders
       see **Centre for Health Informatics and Multiprofessional Education.**

WHO Collaborating Centre for Diphtheria and Streptococcal Infections
■   Respiratory and Systemic Infection Laboratory, 61 Colindale Avenue, London, NW9 5HT.
         020 8200 4400   fax 020 8205 6528
         http://www.hpa.org.uk/
         Contact: Dr Androulla Efstratiou.
E   A World Health Organisation (WHO) Collaborating Centre at the Health Protection Agency.

WHO Collaborating Centre for Drinking Water and Water Pollution Control
       see **National Centre for Environmental Toxicology.**

WHO Collaborating Centre for Groundwater Quality Assessment and Protection
■   Maclean Building, Crowmarsh Gifford, Wallingford, Oxfordshire, OX10 8BB.
         01491 838800   fax 01491 692345
         http://www.bgs.ac.uk/
         Contact: Dr Denis W Peach.
E   A World Health Organisation (WHO) Collaborating Centre at the British Geological Survey.

WHO Collaborating Centre for Haemophilus Influenzae
       see **Health Protection Agency Centre for Infections.**

WHO Collaborating Centre for Health Policy and Pharmaceutical Economics
■   LSE, Houghton Street, London, WC2A 2AE.
         020 7955 7540   fax 020 7955 6803
         http://www.lse.ac.uk/
         Contact: Prof Elias Mossialos.
E   A World Health Organisation (WHO) Collaborating Centre at the London School of Economics and Political Science.

WHO Collaborating Centre for Health Promotion and Public Health Development
■   Woodburn House, Canaan Lane, Edinburgh, EH10 4SC.
         0131-536 5500   fax 0131-536 5501
         http://www.nhs.uk/
         Contact: Graham Robertson.
E   A World Health Organisation (WHO) Collaborating Centre within NHS Health Scotland.

WHO Collaborating Centre for Health of Societies in Transition
       see **European Centre on Health of Societies in Transition.**

WHO Collaborating Centre for Healthy Cities and Urban Policy
■   Faculty of the Built Environment, Frenchay Campus, University of the West of England, Coldharbour Lane, Bristol, BS16 1QY.
         0117-328 3000
         http://www.built-environment.uwe.ac.uk/
E   A research centre at the University of the West of England.
O   To undertake research and provide advice in the field of healthy urban planning

WHO Collaborating Centre for Identification and Characterization of Schistosome Strains and their Snail Intermediate Hosts
- Department of Zoology, Wolfson Wellcome Biomedical Laboratories, Natural History Museum, Cromwell Road, London, SW7 5BD.
  020 7942 5152; 5181   fax 020 7942 5518
  http://www.nhm.ac.uk/
  Contact: Dr David Rollinson.
- E   A World Health Organisation (WHO) Collaborating Centre at the Natural History Museum.

WHO Collaborating Centre for Immunohaematology
  see **Bristol Institute for Transfusion Sciences.**

WHO Collaborating Centre for International Laboratory for Biological Standards
  see **National Institute for Biological Standards and Control.**

WHO Collaborating Centre for Investment for Health and Health Promotion
  see **National Institute for Health and Clinical Excellence.**

WHO Collaborating Centre for Ionizing and Non-Ionizing Radiation Protection
  see **Health Protection Agency Centre for Radiation, Chemical and Environmental Hazards.**

WHO Collaborating Centre for Laboratory and Diagnostic Support
- Sexually Transmitted and Bloodborne Virus Laboratory, 61 Colindale Avenue, London, NW9 5HT.
  020 8200 4400
  http://www.hpa.org.uk/
  Contact: Dr John Parry.
- E   A World Health Organisation (WHO) Collaborating Centre at the Health Protection Agency.

WHO Collaborating Centre for Metabolic Bone Diseases
- Department of Human Metabolism and Clinical Biochemistry, University of Sheffield Medical School, Beech Hill Road, Sheffield, S10 2RX.
  0114-285 1109   fax 0114-285 1813
  http://www.shef.ac.uk/
  Contact: Dr John A Kanis.
- E   A World Health Organisation (WHO) Collaborating Centre at the University of Sheffield.

WHO Collaborating Centre for Midwifery
- Royal College of Midwives, 15 Mansfield Street, London, W1G 9NH.
  020 7312 3443   fax 020 7312 3442
  http://www.rcm.org.uk/
  Contact: Dame Karlene Davis.
- E   A World Health Organisation (WHO) Collaborating Centre at the Royal College of Midwives.

WHO Collaborating Centre for Nursing and Midwifery Education, Research and Practice
- School of Nursing, Midwifery and Community Health, Glasgow Caledonian University, 70 Cowcaddens Road, Glasgow, G4 0BA.
  0141-331 3459   fax 0141-331 8312
  http://www.gcal.ac.uk/
  Contact: Prof Barbara A Parfitt.
- E   A World Health Organisation (WHO) Collaborating Centre at Glasgow Caledonian University.

WHO Collaborating Centre for Nutrition and Oral Health
- Department of Child Dental Health, Dental School, University of Newcastle upon Tyne, Framlington Place, Newcastle upon Tyne, NE2 4BW.
  0191-222 7863   fax 0191-222 5928
  http://www.ncl.ac.uk/dental/
  Contact: Dr Paula J Moynihan.
- E   A World Health Organisation (WHO) Collaborating Centre at the University of Newcastle upon Tyne.

WHO Collaborating Centre for Occupational Health
  see **Institute of Work, Health and Organisations.**

WHO Collaborating Centre for Occupational Health and Safety Research
- Harpur Hill, Buxton, Derbyshire, SK17 9JN.
  01298 218000; 218400   fax 01298 218405
  http://www.hsl.gov.uk/
  Contact: Eddie Morland.
- E   A World Health Organisation (WHO) Collaborating Centre at the Health and Safety Laboratory.

WHO Collaborating Centre for Occupational Medicine
  see **Institute of Occupational Medicine.**

© CBD Research Ltd · Beckenham · Kent BR3 5JS · Tel 020 8650 7745 · Fax 020 8650 0768 · E-mail cbd@cbdresearch.com · www.cbdresearch.com

WHO Collaborating Centre for Policy and Practice Development in Women's Health and Gender Mainstreaming
- Department of Public Health, Dalian House, 350 St Vincent Street, Glasgow, G3 8YU.
  0141-201 4444   fax 0141-201 4949
  Contact: Sue Laughlin.
- E A World Health Organisation (WHO) Collaborating Centre.

WHO Collaborating Centre for Policy Research on Social Determinants of Health
- Faculty of Medicine, University of Liverpool, Liverpool, L69 3GB.
  0151-794 5576   fax 0151-794 5588
  http://www.liv.ac.uk/PublicHealth
  Contact: Prof Margaret Whitehead.
- E A World Health Organisation (WHO) Collaborating Centre at the University of Liverpool.

WHO Collaborating Centre for Prevention of Blindness and Trachoma
  see **International Centre for Eye Health.**

WHO Collaborating Centre for Prevention and Control of Sexually Transmitted Infections (STI)
- Clinical Research Unit, London School of Hygiene and Tropical Medicine, University of London, Keppel Street, London, WC1E 7HT.
  020 7927 2297   fax 020 7637 4314
  http://www.lshtm.ac.uk/
  Contact: Prof David Mabey.
- E A World Health Organisation (WHO) Collaborating Centre at the London School of Hygiene and Tropical Medicine, University of London.

WHO Collaborating Centre for the Prevention of Deafness and Hearing Impairment
- Liverpool School of Tropical Medicine, University of Liverpool, Pembroke Place, Liverpool, L3 5QA.
  0151-708 9393   fax 0151-707 1709
  http://www.liv.ac.uk/
  Contact: Dr Ian J MacKenzie.
- E A World Health Organisation (WHO) Collaborating Centre at the University of Liverpool.

WHO Collaborating Centre for Promoting Health in Prisons
- Department of Health, Wellington House, 133-155 Waterloo Road, London, SE1 8UG.
  020 7972 3925   fax 020 7972 4881
  http://www.hipp-europe.org/
  Contact: John Boyington.
- E A World Health Organisation (WHO) Collaborating Centre.

WHO Collaborating Centre for the Protection of Water Quality and Human Health
  see **Robens Centre for Public and Environmental Health.**

WHO Collaborating Centre for Public Health Issues on Congenital Anomalies and Technology Transfer
- Unit of Dental and Oral Health, University of Dundee Dental School, Park Place, Dundee, DD1 4HR.
  01382 425761   fax 01382 206321
  http://www.dundee.ac.uk/
  Contact: Dr Peter A Mossey.
- E A World Health Organisation (WHO) Collaborating Centre at the University of Dundee.

WHO Collaborating Centre for Public Health Issues on Congenital Anomalies and Technology Transfer (Treatment and Management of Craniofacial Anomalies)
- Orthodontic Unit, University of Manchester, Oxford Road, Manchester, M13 9PL.
  0161-275 6620   fax 0161-275 6794
  http://www.man.ac.uk/
  Contact: Prof William Christie Shaw.
- E A World Health Organisation (WHO) Collaborating Centre at the University of Manchester.

WHO Collaborating Centre for the Public Health Management of Chemical Incidents
- Chemical Hazards and Poison Division, University of Wales Institute Cardiff, Colchester Avenue, Penylan, Cardiff, CF23 9XR.
  029 2041 6852   fax 029 2041 6803
  http://www.uwic.ac.uk/
  Contact: Prof Gary Coleman.
- E A World Health Organisation (WHO) Collaborating Centre within the Health Protection Agency at the University of Wales Institute, Cardiff.

WHO Collaborating Centre for Quality Assessment in Haematology
- Watford General Hospital, PO Box 14, Watford, WD18 0FJ.
  01923 217878   fax 01923 217879
  http://www.ukneqas.org.uk/
  Contact: Dr Keith Hyde.
- E A World Health Organisation (WHO) Collaborating Centre within the United Kingdom National External Quality Assessment Scheme for General Haematology.

WHO Collaborating Centre for Reference and Research on Brucellosis
- Department of Statutory and Exotic Bacteria, New Haw, Addlestone, Weybridge, Surrey, KT15 3NB.
  01932 357610   fax 01932 357216
  http://www.defra.gov.uk/
  Contact: Dr J A Stack.
- E   A World Health Organisation (WHO) Collaborating Centre at the Veterinary Laboratories Agency.

WHO Collaborating Centre for Reference and Research on Hospital Infections
- PHLS Laboratory of Hospital Infection, 61 Colindale Avenue, London, NW9 5HT.
  020 8200 4400   fax 020 8200 7449
  http://www.hpa.org.uk/
  Contact: Dr Barry D Cookson.
- E   A World Health Organisation (WHO) Collaborating Centre within the Health Protection Agency.

WHO Collaborating Centre for Reference and Research on Influenza
  see **National Institute for Medical Research.**

WHO Collaborating Centre for Reference and Research on Poliomyelitis
  see **National Institute for Biological Standards and Control.**

WHO Collaborating Centre for Reference, Research and Training in Travel Medicine
  see **Academic Centre for Travel Medicine and Vaccines.**

WHO Collaborating Centre for Research and Development in Health Systems Strengthening
  see **Nuffield Centre for International Health and Development.**

WHO Collaborating Centre for Research and Development for Oral Health, Migration and Inequalities
  see **Leeds Dental Institute.**

WHO Collaborating Centre for Research, Education and Service in Oral Health
  see **UCL Eastman Dental Institute.**

WHO Collaborating Centre for Research on Oral Health in Deprived Communities
- Department of Clinical Dental Sciences, University of Liverpool, Pembroke Place, Liverpool, L3 2PS.
  0151-706 5070   fax 0151-706 5250
  http://www.liv.ac.uk/dental/research/public_health.htm
  Contact: Prof Cynthia Pine.
- E   A World Health Organisation (WHO) Collaborating Centre at the University of Liverpool.

WHO Collaborating Centre for Research and Reference Services in Clinical Chemistry
- Wolfson EQA Laboratory, PO Box 3909, Queen Elizabeth Medical Centre, Birmingham, B15 2UE.
  0121-414 7300   fax 0121-414 1179
  Contact: Dr David G Bullock.
- E   A World Health Organisation (WHO) Collaborating Centre at the Queen Elizabeth Medical Centre, Birmingham.

WHO Collaborating Centre for Research and Training in Injury and Violence Prevention
- London School of Hygiene & Tropical Medicine, University of London, 49-51 Bedford Square, London, WC1B 3DP.
  020 7299 4738   fax 020 7299 4663
  http://www.lshtm.ac.uk/
  Contact: Dr Ian Roberts.
- E   A World Health Organisation (WHO) Collaborating Centre at the London School of Hygiene and Tropical Medicine, University of London.

WHO Collaborating Centre for Research & Training in Mental Health
- PO Box 35, King's College London, DeCrespigny Park, London, SE5 8AF.
  020 7848 0383; 0668   fax 020 7848 0669
  http://www.iop.kcl.ac.uk/departments/?locator=430
  Director: Prof Rachel Jenkins.
- E   A research centre within the Institute of Psychiatry (qv) at King's College, London.
- O   To provide support to national and international Governmental organisations, NGOs, mental health professionals and general health care workers on research and dissemination, teaching and training, policy development and implementation

WHO Collaborating Centre for Research and Training in Neurosciences
  see **Institute of Neurology.**

WHO Collaborating Centre for Research and Training in Prosthetics, Orthotics and Orthopaedic Technology
  see **National Centre for Training and Education in Prosthetics and Orthotics.**

WHO Collaborating Centre for Strengthening Poisons Centres Programmes in South-East Asia
- Medical Toxicology Unit, Guy's and St Thomas' Hospital Trust, Avonley Road, London, SE14 5ER.
  020 7771 5370   fax 020 7771 5306
  Contact: Dr Glys Volans.
- E   A World Health Organisation (WHO) Collaborating Centre.

WHO Collaborating Centre for the Surveillance of Congenital Anomalies
- EUROCAT Central Registry, University of Ulster, Shore Road, Newtownabbey, County Antrim, BT37 0QB.
  028 9036 6639   fax 028 9036 8341
  http://www.eurocat.ulster.ac.uk/
  Contact: Prof Helen Dolk.
- E   A World Health Organisation (WHO) Collaborating Centre at the University of Ulster.

WHO Collaborating Centre for Testing of Insecticidal Application Equipment
  see **International Pesticide Application Research Centre.**

WHO Collaborating Centre for Training, Evaluation and Research in Diabetes
- School of Clinical Medical Sciences, Medical School, University of Newcastle upon Tyne, Framlington Place, Newcastle upon Tyne, NE2 4HH.
  0191-222 7020   fax 0191-222 0723
  http://medical.faculty.ncl.ac.uk/
  Contact: Prof Philip Home. Contact: Dr Nigel Unwin.
- E   A World Health Organisation (WHO) Collaborating Centre at the University of Newcastle upon Tyne.

WHO Collaborating Centre for Training and Research in Communications and Information Technology in Health Promotion and Disease Prevention
- 18 Ormeau Avenue, Belfast, BT2 8HS.
  028 9031 1611   fax 028 9031 1711
  http://www.healthpromotionagency.org.uk/AboutHPA/who.htm
  Director: Dr Brian Gaffney.
- E   A World Health Organisation (WHO) Collaborating Centre at the Health Promotion Agency for Northern Ireland.

Wilberforce Institute for the Study of Slavery and Emancipation   (WISE)   2006
- Faculty of Arts and Social Sciences, University of Hull, Oriel Chambers, 27 High Street, Hull, HU1 1NE.
  01482 305176
  http://www.hull.ac.uk/wise/
  Contact: Heidi Lovell.
- E   A research institute at the University of Hull.

Wildfowl and Wetland Trust Centres   (WWT)   1946
- Slimbridge, Gloucestershire, GL2 7BT.
  01453 891900   fax 01453 890827
  http://www.wwt.org.uk/
- E   A registered charity.
- O   A specialist conservation charity and a world leader in the conservation of ducks, geese, swans and flamingos and the wetlands they inhabit
Note: The Trust runs nine different wetland centres throughout the UK and its website has up-to-date information on each.

William Harvey Research Institute   (WHRI)   1986
- Barts and the London, Queen Mary's School of Medicine and Dentistry, John Vane Building, Charterhouse Square, London, EC1M 6BQ.
  020 7882 5776   fax 020 7882 5672
  http://www.whri.qmul.ac.uk/
  Director: Prof Mark Caulfield.
- E   A department of Queen Mary, University of London.
- O   To provide a world-class environment for the prosecution of leading edge research into cardiovascular, inflammatory and endocrine diseases

William Lee Innovation Centre   (WLIC)   2002
- School of Materials, PO Box 88, University of Manchester, Sackville Street, Manchester, M60 1QD.
  0161-306 5747   fax 0161-306 5748
  http://www.wlic.ac.uk/
  Head: Dr Tilak Dias.
- E   A research centre at the University of Manchester.
- O   To conduct fundamental, applied and industry-funded research into fibre assemblies involving smart and intelligent knitted materials

Williamson Research Centre for Molecular Environmental Science   (WRC)   2001

■ Department of Earth Sciences, University of Manchester, Oxford Road, Manchester, M13 9PL.
  0161-275 3804   fax 0161-275 3947
  http://www.wrc.man.ac.uk/
  Director: Prof David Vaughan.
E An interdisciplinary research centre at the University of Manchester.
O To promote research in molecular environmental science, which is essential for an understanding of our environment and the effect of human behaviour upon environmental systems

Wohl Virion Centre   1999

■ Department of Immunology and Molecular Pathology, Windeyer Building, University College London, 46 Cleveland Street, London, W1T 4JF.
  020 7679 9556
  http://www.ucl.ac.uk/medicalschool/infection-immunity/departments/departments.htm
  Director: Prof Robin Weiss.
E A research centre at University College London.
O To conduct research in retroviruses, including HIV, human retrovirus 5 and Kaposi's sarcoma-associated herpes virus; to exploit bioinformatics and genomics technologies to search for novel pathogens, and to investigate host-pathogen interactions
Note: Named after the Maurice Wohl Charitable Foundation, which made the Centre possible through financial support.

Wolfson Brain Imaging Centre   (WBIC)

■ PO Box 65, Addenbrooke's Hospital, Cambridge, CB2 2QQ.
  01223 331823   fax 01223 331826
  http://www.wbic.cam.ac.uk/
  Director: Prof John Pickard.
E A centre at the University of Cambridge.
O To conduct research in imaging function in the injured human brain using positron emission tomography and magnetic resonance

Wolfson Centre for Age-Related Diseases   (CARD)   2006

■ The Wolfson Wing - Hodgkin Building, Guy's Campus, King's College London, London, SE1 1UL.
  020 7836 5454
  http://www.kcl.ac.uk/kis/schools/biohealth/research/wolfson/
  Director: Prof Pat Doherty.
E A research centre within King's College, London.
O To conduct research into reaching a better understanding of the factors impinging on the nervous system with advancing years

Wolfson Centre for Bulk Solids Handling Technology   1973

■ Medway School of Engineering, Duncan Building, University of Greenwich, Central Avenue, Chatham Maritime, Kent, ME4 4TB.
  020 8331 8646   fax 020 8331 8647
  http://www.wolfsoncentre.com/
  Director: Prof A R Reed.
E A research centre at the University of Greenwich.
O To solve various types of bulk solids materials handling problems

Wolfson Centre for Carbon and Silicon-Based Electronics

■ Department of Electrical Engineering and Electronics, University of Liverpool, Brownlow Hill, Liverpool, L69 3GJ.
  0151-794 4539   fax 0151-794 4540
  http://www.liv.ac.uk/eee/
E A research centre at the University of Liverpool.

Wolfson Centre for Magnetics Technology   1969

■ Cardiff School of Engineering, Cardiff University, Queen's Buildings, Newport Road, Cardiff, CF24 3AA.
  029 2087 6729   fax 029 2087 6729
  http://www.cardiff.ac.uk/schoolsanddivisions/academicschools/engin/wolfson/
  Director: Prof David C Jiles.
E A research centre within the Institute of Advanced Materials and Energy Systems (qv) at Cardiff University.
O To conduct research and provide consultancy, short courses, services and information on general aspects, properties and applications of soft magnetic materials and associated products and systems
● Conference facilities - Education and training - Exhibitions - Information service - Library - Statistics

Wolfson Centre for Materials Processing   (WCMP)   1987

■ Brunel University, Uxbridge, Middlesex, UB8 3PH.
  01895 265628   fax 01895 269737
  http://www.brunel.ac.uk/about/acad/wolfson
  Director: Prof Jack Silver.
E A centre at Brunel University.
O To conduct research in the synthesis and morphological control of small inorganic micrometer size particles as well as nanometer size particles
Note: Also known as the Centre for Materials.

© CBD Research Ltd · Beckenham · Kent BR3 5JS · Tel 020 8650 7745 · Fax 020 8650 0768 · E-mail cbd@cbdresearch.com · www.cbdresearch.com

Wolfson Centre for Rational Design of Molecular Diagnostics
■ School of Pharmacy and Pharmaceutical Sciences, Coupland III Building, University of Manchester, Coupland Street, Manchester, M13 9PL.
   0161-275 2411
   http://www.pharmacy.manchester.ac.uk/aboutus/pioneeringcentres/wolfson/
   Director: Prof Ken Douglas.
E A research centre at the University of Manchester.

Wolfson Centre for Translational Research
■ Postgraduate Medical School, University of Surrey, Daphne Jackson Road, Manor Park, Guildford, Surrey, GU2 7WG.
   01483 688500
   http://www.portal.surrey.ac.uk/
E A research centre at the University of Surrey.

Wolfson Digestive Diseases Centre
■ C Floor - South Block, University Hospital, Nottingham, NG7 2UH.
   0115-823 1034
   http://www.nottingham.ac.uk/wddc/
   Director: Prof John Atherton.
E A research centre within the Institute of Clinical Research (qv) at the University of Nottingham.
O To conduct international quality research relating to gastrointestinal and liver disease, including fundamental science, translational research, clinical trials, and population studies

Wolfson Heat Treatment Centre   (WHTC)   1973
■ Federation House, 10 Vyse Street, Birmingham, B18 6LT.
   0121-237 1122   fax 0121-237 1124
   http://www.sea.org.uk/whtc/
E A centre operating within the Surface Engineering Association.
O To be British industry's focal point for information, advice and education on the processing aspects of metal heat treatment

Wolfson Institute for Biomedical Research   (WIBR)
■ Faculty of Biomedical Sciences, The Cruciform Building, University College London, Gower Street, London, WC1E 6BT.
   020 7679 6697
   http://www.ucl.ac.uk/wibr/
   Director: Salvador Moncada.
E A research institute at University College London.
O To pursue excellence in biomedical research in the post-genomic era

Wolfson Institute of Preventive Medicine   (WIPM)   1991
■ Barts and the London, Queen Mary's School of Medicine and Dentistry, Queen Mary, University of London, Charterhouse Square, London, EC1M 6BQ.
   020 7882 6190; 6263   fax 020 7882 6270
   http://www.wolfson.qmul.ac.uk/index.html
   Director: Prof Nicholas Wald, FRS.
E A department of Queen Mary, University of London.
O To research into preventive medicine, especially for the prevention of cancer, heart disease, Down's Syndrome and spina bifida, by screening techniques and epidemiology; to teach medical students, both undergraduate and postgraduate
● Education and training - Statistics - Antenatal screening for Down's Syndrome (appointment only)
¶ Antenatal and Neonatal Screening. The Epidemiological Approach. Various undergraduate and graduate prospectuses.

Wolfson Materials and Catalysis Centre   (WMCC)   2000
■ School of Chemical Sciences and Pharmacy, University of East Anglia, Norwich, NR4 7TJ.
   01603 592044
   http://www.uea.ac.uk/che/wmcc/
   Co-Director: Prof Manfred Bochmann. Co-Director: Prof Michael J Cook.
E A centre at the University of East Anglia.
O To bring a multi-disciplinary approach to molecular-level research in catalysis and materials chemistry

Wolfson Molecular Imaging Centre   (MIC)   2004
■ School of Medicine, University of Manchester, 27 Palatine Road, Manchester, M20 3LJ.
   0161-275 0000
   http://www.manchestermolecularimaging.com/
   Director: Prof Karl Herholz.
E A research centre at the University of Manchester.
O To be recognised as a world leading centre in the use of positron emission tomography (PET) for research in cancer patients, and as an internationally competitive centre for PET based research in brain disorders

Wolfson Research Centre
■ Newcastle General Hospital, Newcastle upon Tyne, NE4 6BE.
   0191-256 3206
   http://www.ncl.ac.uk/
E A research centre at the University of Newcastle upon Tyne.

Wolfson Research Institute   2001
- School for Health, Queen's Campus, University of Durham, University Boulevard, Stockton on Tees, TS17 6BH.
  0191-334 0012   fax 0191-334 0075
  http://www.dur.ac.uk/wolfson.institute/
  Director: Prof Ray Hudson.
- E   A research institute within the University of Durham.
- O   To develop and reinforce existing research strengths in medicine, health and the well-being of people and places

Women's Alcohol Centre
   see **ARP Women's Alcohol Centre.**

Women's Holiday Centre Ltd   1980
- The Old Vicarage, Horton-in-Ribblesdale, North Yorkshire, BD24 0HD.
  01729 860207
  Joint Co-ordinator: Catriona Yule. Joint Co-ordinator: Sue Walmsley.
- E   A registered charity.
- O   To provide self-catering holidays for women and children on low incomes
- ●   Themed weekends - Many facilities

Women's Studies Centre
   see **Centre for Women's Studies.**

Wordsworth Centre   1987
- Department of English, Bowland College, Lancaster University, Lancaster, LA1 4YT.
  01524 592451   fax 01524 594247
  http://www.lancs.ac.uk/depts/english/research/wordsworth.htm
  Co-Director: Simon Bainbridge. Co-Director: Sally Bushell.
- E   A research centre at Lancaster University.
- O   To promote interest in Wordsworth and the Lake District at an undergraduate, postgraduate and wider level; to explore questions about poetry and landscape, poetry and conservation; to connect romanticism to the present day; to promote links between the University and the Wordsworth Trust
- ●   Conference facilities - Education and training - Exhibitions - Library
- ¶   Napoleon and English Romanticism. British Poetry and the Napoleonic Wars. Wordsworth: A poet's history.

Work and Employment Research Centre   (WERC)   1997
- School of Management, University of Bath, Claverton Down, Bath, BA2 7AY.
  01225 386473
  http://www.bath.ac.uk/werc/
  Director: Prof John Purcell.
- E   A research centre at the University of Bath.
- O   To develop research in key areas of contemporary practice in the world of work and employment

Work Institute
- Nottingham Business School, Nottingham Trent University, Burton Street, Nottingham, NG1 4BU.
  0115-848 4488
  http://www.ntu.ac.uk/nbs/
- E   A research institute at Nottingham Trent University.

Working Lives Research Institute   (WRLI)   2003
- Department of Education, London Metropolitan University, 31 Jewry Street, London, EC3N 2EY.
  020 7320 3042
  http://www.workinglives.org/
- E   A research institute at London Metropolitan University.
- O   To conduct academic and applied research into all aspects of working lives, with particular emphasis on equality and social justice, and working for and in partnership with trade unions

World Bureau of Metal Statistics   (WBMS)   1947
- 27a High Street, Ware, Hertfordshire, SG12 9BA.
  01920 461274   fax 01920 464258
  http://www.world-bureau.com/
- E   An independent non-profit-distributing organisation.
- O   To collect and collate data on world metals for the benefit of the many and varied users of metal statistics
- ¶   World Metal Statistics Bulletin.

World Conservation Monitoring Centre   (WCMC)   1988
- 219 Huntingdon Road, Cambridge, CB3 0DL.
  01223 277314   fax 01223 277136
  http://www.unep-wcmc.org/
- E   Part of the United Nations Environment Programme.
- O   To be an internationally recognised centre of excellence for the synthesis, analysis and dissemination of global biodiversity knowledge, providing authoritative, strategic and timely information for conventions, countries, organizations and companies to use in the development and implementation of their policies and decisions

© CBD Research Ltd · Beckenham · Kent BR3 5JS · Tel 020 8650 7745 · Fax 020 8650 0768 · E-mail cbd@cbdresearch.com · www.cbdresearch.com

World Data Centre for Glaciology, Cambridge   (WDCGC)   1957
- ■   School of Physical Sciences, University of Cambridge, Lensfield Road, Cambridge, CB2 1ER.
      01223 336565   fax 01223 336549
      http://wdcgc.spri.cam.ac.uk/
      Manager: Rick Frolich.
- E   A research centre within the Scott Polar Research Institute (qv) at the University of Cambridge.
- O   To be Europe's primary resource and referral centre for published information on all aspects of snow and ice research

World Education Centre   (WEC)
- NR   Department of Theology and Religious Studies, Normal Site, University of Wales Bangor, Bangor, Gwynedd, LL57 2PZ.
      01248 383728
      http://www.bangor.ac.uk/addysgbyd/eng/
      Director: Prof Leslie J Francis.
- E   A centre at the University of Wales, Bangor.
- O   To explore the links between our lives and those of people throughout the world

World Health Organisation Collaborating Centres
    see **WHO Collaborating Centres.**
Note: See also **Global Network of WHO Collaborating Centres for Nursing and Midwifery Development.**

World Jersey Cattle Bureau   (WJCB)   1951
- ■   Royal Jersey Showground, Trinity, Jersey, JE3 5JP.
      01534 862327   fax 01534 865619
      http://www.worldjerseycattle.com/
- E   A membership organisation.
- O   To promote the Jersey breed of dairy cattle, and improve their profitability

World Poverty Institute
    see **Brooks World Poverty Institute.**

Worm Research Centre   (WRC)   2000
- ■   Phoenix Farm, Asselby, Goole, East Yorkshire, DN14 7HF.
      01757 630456   fax 01757 638879
      http://www.wormresearchcentre.co.uk/
      Director: Steve Ross-Smith.
- E   A research centre with links to the Open University.

WRc plc   1989
- ■   Frankland Road, Blagrove, Swindon, Wiltshire, SN5 8YF.
      01793 865000   fax 01793 865001
      http://www.wrcplc.co.uk/
      Chief Executive Officer: Ron Chapman.
- E   A profit-making-business.
- O   To conduct research and development in water, wastewater and the environment, and to provide innovative and practical solutions to customers operating in these areas

Wright Fleming Institute
- ■   Faculty of Medicine, St Mary's Campus, Imperial College London, Norfolk Place, London, W2 1PG.
      020 7594 3611; 3730   fax 020 7706 0094
      http://www1.imperial.ac.uk/medicine/about/institutes/wfi/
      Chairman: Prof Charles Bangham.
- E   A research institute at Imperial College London.
- O   To bring together groups studying virus and bacterial infections in relation to human disease

Write Now CETL
- ■   Tower Building T6-01, London Metropolitan University, 166-220 Holloway Road, London, N7 8DB.
      020 7133 4200
      Contact: James Elander.
- E   A Centre for Excellence in Teaching and Learning (CETL) at London Metropolitan University.
- Note: See **Centres for Excellence in Teaching and Learning** for more information.

Writers Bureau   1988
- ■   Sevendale House, 7 Dale Street, Manchester, M1 1JB.
      0845 345 5995
      http://www.writersbureau.com/
      Principal: E H Metcalfe.
- E   A profit-making business.
- O   To provide correspondence courses on creative writing

Wu Shu Kwan Chinese Boxing Centre   1967

■   PO Box 766, Wembley, Middlesex, HA0 3ZP.
       020 8749 8537   fax 020 8749 8537

E   A martial arts organisation limited by guarantee.

○   To teach Wu Shu Kwan Chinese Boxing as a martial art for fitness and self-defence

●   Education and training

© CBD Research Ltd · Beckenham · Kent BR3 5JS · Tel 020 8650 7745 · Fax 020 8650 0768 · E-mail cbd@cbdresearch.com · www.cbdresearch.com

Xfi Centre for Finance and Investment   (Xfi)

- School of Business and Economics, Xfi Building, University of Exeter, Rennes Drive, Exeter, EX4 4ST.
  01392 263463   fax 01392 262475
  http://www.xfi.ex.ac.uk/
  Director: Prof Ian Tonks.
- E   A department of the University of Exeter.
- ○   To be an internationally recognised centre for excellence in financial market research

York Centre for Complex Systems Analysis   (YCCSA)
- Department of Biology (Area 17), PO Box 373, University of York, York, YO10 5YW.
  01904 328396
  http://www.yccsa.york.ac.uk
- E   A research centre at the University of York.

York Electronics Centre
Note: Has closed.

York Institute for Tropical Ecosystem Dynamics   (KITE)
- Environment Department, University of York, Heslington, York, YO10 5DD.
  01904 434061   fax 01904 432998
  http://www.york.ac.uk/res/kite/
  Co-ordinator: Dr Rob Marchant.
- E   A research institute at the University of York.
- O   To conduct research in tropical ecosystem dynamics, in the areas of biogeography, modelling, palaeoecology, and phylogeography

York Neuroimaging Centre   (YNiC)   2005
- Department of Psychology, York Science Park, University of York, Heslington, York, YO10 5DG.
  01904 435346   fax 01904 435356
  http://www.ynic.york.ac.uk/
  Director: Prof Gary Green.
- E   A research centre at the University of York.
- O   To conduct research in the chemistry, physiology and psychology of human brain function

York Religious Education Centre
   see **David Hope RE Centre in York.**

Yorkshire Centre for Health Informatics   (YCHI)   2004
- Faculty of Medicine and Health, University of Leeds, 24 Hyde Terrace, Leeds, LS2 9LN.
  0113-343 4961
  http://www.ychi.leeds.ac.uk/
  Director: Dr Susan Clamp.
- E   A research centre within the Leeds Institute of Health Sciences (qv) at the University of Leeds.
- O   To be a focus for health informatics activity, developing partnerships with NHS organisations, industry and other academic disciplines

© CBD Research Ltd · Beckenham · Kent BR3 5JS · Tel 020 8650 7745 · Fax 020 8650 0768 · E-mail cbd@cbdresearch.com · www.cbdresearch.com

Zinc Information Centre
- Broadway House, Calthorpe Road, Birmingham, B15 1TN.
  0121-456 1103
- E A part of the Non-Ferrous Alliance.
- O To provide information on all aspects of zinc

Zuckerman Institute for Connective Environmental Research   (ZICER)   2003
- School of Environmental Sciences, University of East Anglia, Norwich, NR4 7TJ.
  01603 592542   fax 01603 591327
  http://www.uea.ac.uk/zicer/
- E A centre at the University of East Anglia.
- O To bring together, in an interdisciplinary institute, a range of social and natural scientists who are dedicated to the study of the environment; together with the ways and means for sustainability, using nature's wealth in order to protect and enhance people's livelihoods

Centres, Bureaux and Research Institutes

a directory of UK concentrations of effort, information and expertise

published by CBD Research Ltd
Chancery House, 15 Wickham Road, Beckenham, Kent, BR3 5JS
Tel: 020 8650 7745 Fax: 020 8650 0768 E-mail: cbd@cbdresearch.com

Free Entry Questionnaire

1. **Name** of organisation as stated in articles or constitution.

2. **Abbreviation** (if any) by which your organisation is generally known.

3. **Year** of establishment.

4. **Address**.

5. **Telephone**.

6. **Fax**.

7. **Email**.

7a. **Website**.

8. **Names** and **positions** of senior staff.

9. **Constitution**: please tick if your organisation is any of the following:

- ❏ An independent non-profit distributing organisation
- ❏ A registered charity
- ❏ A department of a university or professional body
- ❏ A statutory organisation
- ❏ An association with a voluntary subscribing membership

- ❏ A private venture
- ❏ A profit making business or consortium
- ❏ A company limited by guarantee
- ❏ Other - please give details

10. **Branches** – please state number only.

11. **Membership**: please indicate the number of members that belong to your organisation - individual / corporate / organisations / clubs etc.

12. **How is your organisation financed**? e.g. Government grant, subscriptions, donations, etc.

13. **Names of sponsoring organisations.**

_____

_____

14. **Objectives or purposes of your organisation.**

_____

_____

_____

_____

15. **Activities**: please tick the following boxes appropriate to the activities of your organisation.

❏ Research   ❏ Exhibitions
❏ Conference facilities   ❏ Statistics
❏ Recreational facilities   ❏ Information service
❏ Library   ❏ Other (please describe)
❏ Education and training

Services: if your organisation provides a service to the public, please state days and hours available, whether by appointment only, etc.

_____

Equipment: please describe any special installed equipment indicative of the scope of your service or activities, indicating any available for use by other organisations.

_____

16. **Publications**: please give details of any regular publications including Annual Reports, Yearbooks, Directories etc, and of any important non-recurring works:

Title	Frequency	Publication date	Price

Specimen copies and / or a publications list will be much appreciated.

17. Would you like to receive details of **Centres, Bureaux and Research Institutes**? YES / NO

Signature

_____

Designation or function   Date

_____

THANK YOU

Please reply to: **CBD Research Ltd, Chancery House, 15 Wickham Road, Beckenham, Kent, BR3 5JS.**
Telephone: 020 8650 7745   **Fax:** 020 8650 0768
Email:cbd@cbdresearch.com   _Established 1961._

ABBREVIATIONS INDEX

3CL — Centre Corporate & Commercial Law
3GP — 3rd Generation Proteomics Centre
3IR — Institute Immunology & Infection Research
4CJ — Centre Comparative Criminology & Criminal Justice
4CMR — Cambridge Centre Climate Change Mitigation Research
4E CETL — Centre Excellence Teaching & Learning Clinical & Communication Skills

A

ABC — Aberystwyth BioCentre
Active Birth Centre
Advanced Biotechnology Centre
Audit Bureau Circulations Ltd
ABRC — Asia Business Research Centre
ABS — American Bureau Shipping
ACBE — Advanced Centre Biochemical Engineering
ACBMC — Anglo-Chinese Business & Management Centre
ACC — Applied Criminology Centre
ACCRC — Advanced Composites & Coatings Research Centre
ACDMH — Academic Centre Defence Mental Health
ACE — Abertay Centre Environment
Advisory Centre Education
ACERO — Aberdeen Centre Energy Regulation & Obesity
ACES — Aberdeen Centre Environmental Sustainability
ACHR — Aston Centre Human Resource
ACID — Advanced Centre Drawing
ACLE — Aston Centre Leadership Excellence
ACM — Advanced Concrete & Masonry Centre
ACMC — Advanced Composites Manufacturing Centre
ACRC — Advanced Computing Research Centre
ACREF — Aston Centre Research Experimental Finance
ACSMB — Astbury Centre Structural Molecular Biology
ACTR — Aberdeen Centre Trauma Research
ACVAR — Aston Centre Voluntary Action Research
ADI — Academic Development Institute
ADM-HEA — Art Design Media Subject Centre
ADMEC — Advanced Design & Manufacturing Engineering Centre
ADRC — Alzheimer's Disease Research Centre
Art & Design Research Centre [Salford]
Art & Design Research Centre [Sheffield Hallam]
ADSIP — Applied Digital Signal & Image Processing Research Centre
AEC — Automotive Engineering Centre
AEM — Centre Advanced Engineering Methods
AERC — Applied Educational Research Centre
Applied Electromagnetics Research Centre
Applied Engineering Research Centre
AFC — Anna Freud Centre
Africa Centre — Africa Centre Peace & Conflict Studies
AGSC — Access Grid Support Centre
AHI — Aviation Health Institute
AIAI — Artificial Intelligence Applications Institute
AIC — Asbestos Information Centre Ltd
AICSM — Aberdeen Institute Coastal Science & Management

AIM — Advanced Institute Management Research
Research Centre Advancing Innovation and Management
AIMS — AIMS Centre (Applied & Integrated Medical Sciences)
AIRC — Alternative Investments Research Centre
AKT — Interdisciplinary Research Centre Advanced Knowledge Technologies
ALiC — Active Learning Computing: Centre Excellence Teaching & Learning
ALPS — Assessment & Learning Practice Settings CETL
AMA — Art & Media Arts Research Centre
AMAP — Institute Automotive & Manufacturing Advanced Practice
AMBRC — Advanced Materials & Biomaterials Research Centre
AMC — Address Management Centre
Advanced Materials Centre
AMRC — Advanced Manufacturing Research Centre
Aerospace Manufacturing Research Centre
AMRI — Advanced Materials Research Institute
AMTRI — Advanced Manufacturing Technology Research Institute (CBRI)
ANC — Institute Adaptive & Neural Computation
ANI — Autonomic Neuroscience Institute
APB — Arson Prevention Bureau
AQMRC — Air Quality Management Resource Centre
ARC — Acoustics Research Centre
Actuarial Research Centre
Aerospace Research Centre
Antibody Resource Centre
Antimicrobial Research Centre
Arthur Rank Centre
Autism Research Centre
Arché — AHRC Research Centre Philosophy Logic, Language, Mathematics & Mind
ARCHS — Applied Research Centre Human Security
ARI — Advanced Research Institute
Astrophysics Research Institute
ARICAS — Adelphi Research Institute Creative Arts & Sciences
ARRC — Acupuncture Research Resource Centre
Alcuin Research Resource Centre
Article 19 — Article 19: International Centre against Censorship
ASC — Asian Studies Centre
Centre African Studies [Cambridge]
ASCent — Automation Systems Centre
ASI — Adam Smith Institute
ASKe — Assessment Standards Knowledge exchange CETL
ASMC — Ashridge Strategic Management Centre
Aspire — Advancing Skills Professionals Rural Economy CETL
ASTeC — Accelerator Science & Technology Centre
ATC — Aquaculture Technology Centre
ATI — Advanced Technology Institute
AVRC — Applied Vision Research Centre

B

B&BC — Brain & Body Centre
BACC — Broadcast Advertising Clearance Centre
BACE — Brunel Able Children's Education Centre

BADC	British Atmospheric Data Centre
BARC	Biological Anthropology Research Centre
BAS	Bureau Analysed Samples Ltd
BBPC	Basil Bunting Poetry Centre
	Behavioural Biology Research Centre
	Biomaterials & Biomechanics Research Centre
	Bristol Biogeochemistry Research Centre
BCAST	Brunel Centre Advanced Solidification Technology
BCB	Bloomsbury Centre Bioinformatics
BCCW	Brunel Centre Contemporary Writing
BCDE	Brunel Centre Democratic Evaluation
BCHW	Bedford Centre History Women
BCID	Bradford Centre International Development
BCISS	Brunel Centre Intelligence & Security Studies
BCLT	British Centre Literary Translation
BCMM	Brunel Centre Manufacturing Metrology
BCNI	Behavioural & Clinical Neurosciences Institute
	Blind Centre Northern Ireland
BCPT	Brunel Centre Packaging Technology
BCSB	Bloomsbury Centre Structural Biology
BDRC	Bradford Disarmament Research Centre
BEIC	Built Environment Innovation Centre
BeSC	Belfast e-Science Centre
BEWC	Britain-Russia Centre & British East-West Centre
BFP	Bureau Freelance Photographers
BGRI	Bristol Genomics Research Institute
BHFGCRC	BHF Glasgow Cardiovascular Research Centre
BHFNC	BHF National Centre Physical Activity & Health
BHI	Bristol Heart Institute
BHRC	Benfield Hazard Research Centre
BIAD	Birmingham Institute Art & Design
BIB	Brunel Institute Bioengineering
BIBIC	British Institute Brain Injured Children
BICGP	Brunel Institute Cancer Genetics & Pharmacogenomics
BICOM	Brunel Institute Computational Mathematics
BIGN	Burdett Institute Gastrointestinal Nursing
BIH	British Institute Homeopathy
BIHR	British Institute Human Rights
BIICL	British Institute International & Comparative Law
BIJS	British Institute Jazz Studies
BILL	Birkbeck Institute Lifelong Learning
BILP	Bristol Institute Legal Practice
BIME	Bath Institute Medical Engineering
BIOCONS	European Centre Biodiversity & Conservation Research
BIOPoM	Centre Business Information, Organisation & Process Management
BIPS	Brunel Institute Power Systems
BIRD	Centre Brain Injury Rehabilitation & Development
BIRTHA	Bristol Institute Research Humanities & Arts
BLAC	British Light Aviation Centre
BLDSC	British Library Document Supply Centre
BLU	Blended Learning Unit CETL
BMAF	Business, Management, Accountancy & Finance Subject Centre
BMC	Bone & Mineral Centre
BMIC	British Music Information Centre
BMRC	Biomedical Research Centre
BMRI	Business & Management Research Institute
BMSRC	Biomolecular Sciences Research Centre
BNSC	British National Space Centre
BOSdc	Brunel Organisation & Systems Design Centre
BPRI	British Polarographic Research Institute

BRAINS	Brunel Advanced Institute Multimedia and Network Systems
BRASS	ESRC Centre Business Relationships, Accountability, Sustainability & Society
BRaVE	Centre Research Beliefs, Rights & Values Education
BRC	Bioinformatics Research Centre
	Biological Records Centre
	Biomedical Research Centre
	Cambridge Centre Brain Repair
BRCA	Breakthrough Breast Cancer Research Centre
BRI	Biomedical Sciences Research Institute
BRICMAR	Bristol Centre Management Accounting Research
BRLSI	Bath Royal Literary & Scientific Institution
BSERC	Biomedical Science Enterprise & Research Centre
BTRC	Biomedical Textiles Research Centre
	Business Travel Research Centre
BuHu	Research Institute Built & Human Environment
BURSt	Brunel University Random Systems Research Centre
BWPI	Brooks World Poverty Institute

C

C-CoDE	Centre Coastal Dynamics & Engineering
C-FAR	Centre Child-focused Anthropological Research
C-Mar	Centre Marine Resources & Mariculture
C-SAP	Subject Network Sociology, Anthropology, Politics
C-SAPH	Centre Spatial Analysis Public Health
C2M2	Cardiff Centre Multidisciplinary Microtechnology
C3RI	Cultural, Communication & Computing Research Institute
C3S	Centre Complex Cooperative Systems
C4C	C4C: Collaborating Creativity CETL
C4PM	Centre Project Management
CAAA	Centre Applied Archaeological Analyses
CAAPP	Centre Amyloidosis & Acute Phase Proteins
CAB	Centre Applied Bioethics
	Centre Artists' Books
	Citizens Advice Bureaux
CABI	CAB International
CABS	Centre Ageing & Biographical Studies
CAC	Centre Applied Catalysis
	Communication Aid Centre
CACS	Centre Applied Childhood Studies
CADRE	Centre Ancient Drama & its Reception
	Centre Art & Design & Research Experimentation
CAE	Centre Accessible Environments
	Centre Applied Ethics
CAEC	Community Audit & Evaluation Centre
CAEE	Cranfield Centre Agricultural & Environmental Engineering
CAEP	Centre Applied Entomology & Parasitology
CAER	Centre Agri-Environmental Research
CAERT	Centre Automotive Engineering Research & Technology
CAF	Childhood & Families Research & Development Centre
CAFA	Centre Archaeological & Forensic Analysis
CAFM	Centre Applied Formal Methods
CAFT	Centre Accounting, Finance & Taxation
CAGCR	Centre Anglo-German Cultural Relations
CAHHM	Centre Arts & Humanities Health & Medicine
CAHO	Centre Archaeology Human Origins
CAHPR	Centre Allied Health Professions Research
	Centre Applied Human Resource Research

CAIM	Centre Automotive Industries Management	CASCAID	Centre Analysis Supply Chain Innovation & Dynamics
CAIPE	United Kingdom Centre Advancement Interprofessional Education	CASCM	Centre Advanced Studies Christian Ministry
CAIR	Centre Applied Interaction Research	CASE	Centre Aviation, Space & Extreme Environment Medicine
	Centre Automotive Industry Research		ESRC Research Centre Analysis Social Exclusion
CAIS	Centre Advanced Instrumentation Systems		
	Centre Archive & Information Studies	CASIF	Centre Advanced Studies Finance
CAJ	Centre Advanced Joining	CASIM	Centre Accelerator Science, Imaging and Medicine
CAL	Centre Active Lifestyles		
	Centre Arts & Learning	CASIS	Centre Advanced Software & Intelligent Systems
CALL Centre	Communication Aids Language & Learning		
CALR	Centre Applied Language Research	CASIX	Centre Observation Air-Sea Interactions & Fluxes
CALS	Centre Applied Language Studies [Reading]		
	Centre Applied Language Studies [Swansea]	CASKE	Centre Anthropological Study Knowledge & Ethics
	Centre Applied Laser Spectroscopy		
CALT	Centre Advancement Learning & Teaching	CASM	Centre Applied Simulation Modelling
CAM	Centre Automotive Management	CASN	Centre Advanced Studies Nursing
CAMA	Centre Antiquity & Middle Ages	CASP	Centre Analysis Social Policy
CAMH	Centre Ageing & Mental Health		Centre Applied Social Psychology
CAMHS	Centre Ageing & Mental Health Sciences	CASPIE	Centre Advanced Surface, Particle & Interface Engineering
CAMQD	Centre Atomic & Molecular Quantum Dynamics		
		CASSM	Centre Applied Statistics & Systems Modelling
CAMR	Centre Advanced Management Research	CASW	Centre Australian Studies Wales
CAMRI	Communication & Media Research Institute	CAT	Centre Alternative Technology
CAMS	Centre Applied Medical Statistics	CATE	Centre Aviation, Transport & Environment
CAO	Centre Applied Oceanography	CATR	Centre Applied Theatre Research
CAOH	Centre Adult Oral Health	CATS	Centre Analysis Time Series
CAP	Centre Academic & Professional Development	CAW	Centre Academic Writing
		CAWMS	Centre Advanced Welsh Music Studies
	Centre Psychology & Learning Context	CAWP	Centre Advancement Women Politics
CAPG	Centre Adult & Paediatric Gastroenterology	CAZS-NR	CAZS Natural Resources
CAPHC	Centre Applied Psychology, Health & Culture	CBA	Centre Battlefield Archaeology
CAPLITS	Centre Academic & Professional Literacies	CBaS	UCL Centre BioScience & Society
CAPR	Centre Applied Psychological Research	CBC	Centre Bioactive Chemistry
CAPS	Centre Asia-Pacific Studies		Chemical Biology Centre [Birkbeck, London]
	Centre Astrophysics & Planetary Science		Chemical Biology Centre [Gloucester]
CAR	Centre Allergy Research		Cranfield Biotechnology Centre
	Centre Appearance Research	CBCB	Centre Biochemistry & Cell Biology
	Centre Astrophysics Research	CBCD	Centre Brain & Cognitive Development
	Centre Auditory Research	CBE	Centre Biomedical Engineering
CARD	Wolfson Centre Age-Related Diseases		Centre Built Environment [Scotland]
CARE	Centre Advanced Research English	CBEM	Centre Biomolecular Electron Microscopy
	Centre Applied Research Economics	CBER	Centre Built Environment Research
	Centre Applied Research Education	CBF	Centre Banking & Finance
CARES	Centre Addiction Research & Education Scotland	CBG	Centre British Government
		CBH	Centre Business History
			Centre Business History Scotland
CARET	Centre Applied Research Educational Technologies	CBHR	Centre Broadcasting History Research
		CBI	Centre BioMedical Informatics
CARIS	Centre Applied Research Information Systems	CBJ	Centre Broadcasting & Journalism
CARISMA	Centre Analysis Risk & Optimisation Modelling Applications	CBLAS	Centre Brazilian & Latin America Studies
		CBME	Centre Biomedical Engineering
CARM	Centre Advanced & Renewable Materials	CBMS	Centre Biomolecular Sciences
CARPP	Centre Action Research Professional Practice	CBNT	Centre Biomimetic & Natural Technologies
CARR	ESRC Centre Analysis Risk & Regulation	CBO&MGS	Centre Byzantine, Ottoman & Modern Greek Studies
CARTE	Centre Arts Research Technology & Education		
CARTS	Centre Advanced Religious & Theological Studies	CBOS	Centre Business Organisations & Society
		CBP	Centre Business Performance
CAS	Andrew Hook Centre American Studies	CBPE	Centre Business & Professional Ethics
	Centre Academic Surgery	CBPP	Centre Black Professional Practice
	Centre Adaptive Systems	CBR	Centre Biosciences Research
	Centre African Studies [Coventry]		Centre Business Research
	Centre African Studies [Edinburgh]		ESRC Centre Business Research
	Centre African Studies [School of Oriental & African Studies, London]	CBRAIDD	Centre Behavioural Research, Analysis, & Intervention Developmental Disabilities
	Centre Agricultural Strategy		
	Centre American Studies	CBRC	Cardiovascular Biology Research Centre
	Centre Amerindian Studies	CBS	Centre Biblical Studies
	Centre Animal Sciences		Centre Brazilian Studies
	Centre Atmospheric Science		Centre Buddhist Studies
	Centre Austrian Studies	CBT	Centre Business Transformation
CASA	Centre Advanced Spatial Analysis	CBTE	Centre Biomaterials & Tissue Engineering
	Centre Advanced Studies Architecture	CCAB	Cardiff Centre Astrobiology
CASAS	Centre Applied South Asian Studies	CCAH	Centre Child & Adolescent Health
CASB	Crown Agents Stamp Bureau		

CCARM	Cranfield Centre Advanced Research Marketing		Centre Competitiveness & Innovation
CCAWI	Centre Clinical & Academic Workforce Innovation		Centre Computational Intelligence
			Centre Constructions & Identity
CCBB	Centre Cellular Basis Behaviour		Centre Creative Industries
CCBD	Centre Chinese Business Development		Centre Creative Industry
CCBH	Centre Contemporary British History		Centre Creativity & Innovation
CCBI	Cambridge Computational Biology Institute		Centre Crime Informatics
CCBP	Chiron Centre Ltd	CCIB	Centre Cell & Integrative Biology
CCBS	Centre Central Banking Studies	CCID	Centre Christianity & Interreligious Dialogue
	Centre Cross Border Studies		Centre Comparative Infectious Diseases
CCC	Centre Carbohydrate Chemistry	CCIG	Centre Citizenship, Identities & Governance
	Centre Cement & Concrete	CCIP	Wales Centre Intergenerational Practice
	Centre Creative Communities	CCIPS	Centre Collaborative Intervention Public Sector
	Common Cold & Nasal Research Centre	CCIR	Centre Communication Interface Research
CCCAC	Centre Contemporary Central Asia & Caucasus		Centre Construction Innovation & Research
CCCB	Centre Cell & Chromosome Biology	CCJC	Centre Criminal Justice & Criminology
CCCC	Centre Cognition, Computation & Culture	CCJEP	Centre Criminal Justice Economics & Psychology
CCCD	Centre Study Comparative Change & Development	CCJPR	Centre Criminal Justice Policy & Research
CCCI	Centre Cross Curricular Initiatives	CCJS	Centre Crime & Justice Studies
CCCJ	Centre Criminology & Criminal Justice		Centre Criminal Justice Studies
CCCLS	Centre Contemporary Civil Law Studies	CCL	Centre Commercial Law
CCCMH	Centre Citizenship & Community Mental Health	CCLCJ	Centre Criminal Law & Criminal Justice
		CCLL	Centre Community & Lifelong Learning
CCCN	Centre Cognitive & Computational Neuroscience	CCLM	Centre Construction Law & Management
CCCP	UCL Centre Cosmic Chemistry & Physics	CCLP	Centre Corporate Law & Practice
CCCS	Centre Contemporary Chinese Studies		University Oxford Centre Competition Law & Policy
	Centre Cross-Cultural Studies	CCLR	Centre Contaminated Land Remediation
CCCT	Centre Critical & Cultural Theory	CCLS	Centre Commercial Law Studies [London Business School]
CCDC	Cambridge Crystallographic Data Centre		Centre Commercial Law Studies [Swansea]
CCE	Centre Cell Engineering at Glasgow		Centre Comparative Labour Studies
	Centre Charity Effectiveness	CCM	Centre Cold Matter
	Centre Commonwealth Education		Centre Contemporary Ministry
	Centre Creative Empowerment		Centre Contemporary Music
CCEC	Civil & Computational Engineering Centre		Communication, Cultural & Media Studies Research Centre
CCEES	Centre Central & Eastern European Studies		
CCEIB	Centre Communication & Ethics International Business	CCMC	Centre Contemporary Music Cultures
		CCMD	Centre Cell & Molecular Dynamics
CCELS	Cardiff Centre Ethics, Law & Society		Centre Clinical Management Development
CCEPP	Cambridge Centre Economic & Public Policy	CCMGH	Cardiff Centre Modern German History
CCER	Cranfield Centre Ecological Restoration	CCMP	Centre Contemporary Music Practice
CCES	Centre Contemporary European Studies	CCMR	Centre Coastal & Marine Research
CCESD	Centre Comparative European Survey Data	CCMS	Centre Career Management Skills
CCFEA	Centre Computational Finance & Economic Agents	CCN	Oxford McDonnell Centre Cognitive Neuroscience
CCFN	Centre Contemporary Fiction and Narrative	CCNi	Centre Cognitive Neuroimaging
CCFR	Centre Child & Family Research	CCNI	Centre Cognition & Neuroimaging
CCG	Centre Comparative Genomics	CCNR	Centre Computational Neuroscience & Robotics
	Centre Corporate Governance [Cambridge]		
	Centre Corporate Governance [London Business School]	CCO	Clatterbridge Centre Oncology
		CCORR	Cranfield Centre Competition & Regulation Research
CCGIM	Cranfield Centre Geographical Information Management		
		CCP	Cambridge Centre Proteomics
CCGL	Centre Contemporary German Literature		Centre Citizen Participation
CCGR	Centre Corporate Governance and Regulation		Centre Competition Policy
			Centre Crisis Psychology
CCGS	Cambridge Centre Gender Studies	CCPF	Cranfield Centre Precision Farming
CCGV	Centre Computer Graphics & Visualisation	CCPR	Centre Cultural Policy Research
CCH	Centre Computing Humanities	CCPS	Centre Capital Punishment Studies
CCHIM	Centre Complementary Healthcare & Integrated Medicine		Centre Clinical & Population Studies
			Centre Cultural Policy Studies
CCHPR	Cambridge Centre Housing & Planning Research		Nottingham Trent Centre Colonial & Postcolonial Studies
CCHR	Centre Comparative Housing Research	CCR	Centre Cardiovascular Research
CCHRE	Centre Citizenship & Human Rights Education		Centre Child Research
			Centre Communications Research
CCHSR	Centre Clinical & Health Services Research		Centre Community Research
CCHW	Centre Cultural History War		Centre Conflict Resolution
CCI	Central Cities Institute		Centre Cutaneous Research
	Centre Cancer Imaging		University Oxford Centre Criminological Research
	Centre Cell Imaging		

CCRC	Cancer Care Research Centre	CDM	Centre Digital Music
	Communication & Computing Research Centre	CDMA	Centre Dynamic Macroeconomic Analysis
		CDMM	Centre Diabetes & Metabolic Medicine
	Crime & Conflict Research Centre	CDMR	Centre Drug Misuse Research
CCRCB	Centre Cancer Research & Cell Biology	CDOS	Centre Clinical & Diagnostic Oral Sciences
CCRE	Crichton Centre Rural Enterprise	CDPR	Centre Development Policy & Research
CCRGS	Cardiff Centre Research Genetics & Society	CDR	Centre Dance Research
CCRM	Centre Cultural Resource Management		Centre Decision Research
CCRP	Centre Competition & Regulatory Policy	CDRC	Colour Design Research Centre
CCRS	Centre City & Regional Studies	CDS	Centre Defence Studies
CCRSS	Chester Centre Research Sport Society		Centre Democracy Studies
CCS	Centre Canadian Studies		Centre Democratization Studies
	Centre Caribbean Studies [Warwick]		Centre Development Studies [Bath]
	Centre Catalan Studies		Centre Development Studies [Glasgow]
	Centre Chemical Sciences		Centre Development Studies [Leeds]
	Centre Child Studies		Centre Development Studies [Swansea]
	Centre Chinese Studies [Lampeter]		Centre Disability Studies
	Centre Chinese Studies [Manchester]		Centre Dutch Studies
	Centre Chinese Studies [School of Oriental & African Studies, London]	CDSP	Centre Digital Signal Processing
		CDSPR	Centre Digital Signal Processing Research
	Centre Civil Society	CDTS	Centre Dental Technology Studies
	Centre Combined Studies	CDW	Child Development & Well-Being Interdisciplinary Research Centre
	Centre Commonwealth Studies		
	Centre Computational Science	CDWP	Centre Diversity & Work Psychology
	Centre Counselling Studies	CEA	Centre Environmental Archaeology
	Centre Cultural Studies	CEA@Cass	Centre Econometric Analysis
CCSE	Centre Citizenship Studies Education	CEABuR	Centre Europe-Asia Business Research
CCSIR	Centre Computer Science & Informatics Research	CeAL	Centre Active Learning Geography, Environment & Related Disciplines
CCSLS	Centre Criminology & Socio-Legal Studies	CEAL	Centre East Asian Law
CCSM	Centre Clinical Science & Measurement	CEAMP	Centre Environmental Assessment, Management & Policy
	Centre Crowd & Safety Management		
CCSR	Cathie Marsh Centre Census & Survey Research	CEAP	Centre Educational and Academic Practices
		CEAS	Centre East Anglian Studies
	Centre Communication Systems Research		Centre East Asian Studies
	Centre Computing & Social Responsibility	CEASR	Centre Engineering & Applied Sciences Research
	Chester Centre Stress Research		
CCSS	Centre Church School Studies	CEB	Centre Economic Botany
	Centre Comparative Social Surveys	CEB	Centre Epidemiology & Biostatics
	Cranfield Centre Sports Surfaces	CEBARD	Centre Economic & Behavioural Analysis Risk & Decision
CCST	Cranfield Centre Supramolecular Technology		
CCSV	Centre Concurrent Systems & Very Large Scale Integration	CEBC	Centre Evidence-Based Conservation
		CEBCH	Centre Evidence-Based Child Health
CCT	Centre Corrosion Technology	CEBD	Centre Evidence-Based Dentistry
CCUS	Centre Conservation & Urban Studies	CeBE	Centre Built Environment
CCVA	Centre Contemporary Visual Arts	CEBE	Centre Economics & Business Education
CCW	Centre Contemporary Writing		Centre Education Built Environment [Cardiff]
	Centre Creative Writing		Centre Education Built Environment [Salford]
	Community Care Works	CEBM	Centre Evidence-Based Medicine
CCWAS	Cardiff Centre Welsh American Studies	CEBMH	Centre Evidence-Based Mental Health
CCWT	Centre Clean Water Technologies	CEBN	Centre Evidence-Based Nursing
CCY	Centre Children & Youth	CEC	Caledonian Environment Centre
CDAC	Centre Design against Crime	CECD	AHRC Research Centre Evolution Cultural Diversity
CDAM	Centre Discrete & Applicable Mathematics		
CDAS	Centre Death & Society	CeCeps	Centre Critical Education Policy Studies
CDBG	Centre Developmental & Biomedical Genetics	CECQR	Centre Environmental Change & Quaternary Research
CDC	Chemical Dependency Centre	CECS	Centre Eighteenth Century Studies [Belfast]
CDDA	Centre Data Digitisation & Analysis		Centre Eighteenth Century Studies [York]
CDE	Centre Culture, Development & Environment		Centre Study Environmental Change & Sustainability
	Centre Defence Economics		
	Centre Director Education	CED	Centre Educational Development
	Culture, Development & Environment Centre	CEDAR	Centre Dairy Research
CDEI	Centre Diversity, Equity & Inclusion		Centre Developing Areas Research
CDELL	Centre Developing & Evaluating Lifelong Learning		Centre Educational Development, Appraisal & Research
CDG	Centre Democracy & Governance	CEDaR	Centre Environmental Data & Recording
	Centre Democratic Governance	CEDC	Computational Engineering and Design Centre
Cdi	Centre Digital Imaging		
CDI	Centre Design Innovation		Cambridge Engineering Design Centre
CDISS	Centre Defence & International Security Studies	CeDEx	Centre Decision Research & Experimental Economics
CDLR	Centre Digital Library Research	CEDI	Centre Economic Development & Institutions
CDLT	Centre Development Learning & Teaching	CeDIS	Centre Diplomatic & International Studies

CEDM	Centre Educational Development & Materials			Centre Enhancement Learning & Teaching [Robert Gordon]
CEDR	Centre Effective Dispute Resolution			University Stirling Centre English Language Teaching
CEE	Centre Ecology & Evolution			
	Centre Economics Education		CELTE	Centre English Language Teacher Education
	Centre Energy & Environment [City]		CELTS	Centre Leisure & Tourism Studies
	Centre Energy & Environment [Exeter]			Centre Leisure, Tourism & Society
	Centre Equity Education		CEM	Centre Electron Microscopy
CEEBL	Centre Excellence Enquiry-Based Learning			Centre Enterprise Management
CEEC	Centre Ecology, Evolution & Conservation			Centre Entrepreneurial Management
CEEDR	Centre Enterprise & Economic Development Research			Centre Environmental Management
				Curriculum Evaluation & Management Centre
CEEE	Centre Enterprise, Ethics & Environment			
CEEES	Centre Enterprise, European & Extension Services		CeMaC	Centre Research Midwifery & Childbirth
			CeMAP	Centre Media, Arts & Performance
CEER	Centre Education & Employment Research		CEMH	Centre Economics Mental Health
CEESR	Centre Earth and Environmental Science Research		CEMI	Centre Enterprise & Management Innovation
			CeMoRe	Centre Mobilities Research
CEF	Centre Environmental Forensics		CEMP	Centre Excellence Media Practice
CEFAS	Centre Environment, Fisheries & Aquaculture Science		CEMPR	Centre Early Music Performance Research
			CEMRC	Central European Music Research Centre
CeFiMS	Centre Financial & Management Studies		CEMS	Centre Early Modern Studies [Aberdeen]
CEFM	Centre Education & Finance Management			Centre Early Modern Studies [Sussex]
CEFR	Centre Economics & Finance Research			Centre Ethnic Minority Studies [Royal Holloway, London]
CEGF	Centre Environmental & Geophysical Flows			
CEGG	Centre Evolution, Genes & Genomics			Centre Ethnic Minority Studies [School of Oriental & African Studies, London]
CeGS	Centre Guidance Studies			
CEH	Centre Ecology & Hydrology		CEMT	Centre Environmental Management & Technology
	Centre Economics Health			
CEHE	Centre Environmental Health Engineering		CENCS	Centre European Nineteenth-Century Studies
CEHRE	Centre Equality & Human Rights Education		CENDEP	Centre Development & Emergency Practice
CEHS	Centre Environment & Human Settlements		CENMAC	Centre Micro-Assisted Communication
CEHSR	Centre Epidemiology & Health Service Research		CENS	Centre Environmental Studies
			CENS	Centre Exercise & Nutrition Science
CEI	Centre Education & Industry		CenTACat	Centre Theory & Application Catalysis
	Centre Educational Innovation		CENTICA	Centre Tourism Islands & Coastal Areas
	Centre Enterprise & Innovation		CENTIVE	Centre New Technologies, Innovation & Entrepreneurship
	Centre Environmental Informatics			
	Centre Environmental Initiatives		CeNTRAL	CLIO Centre Narratives & Transformative Learning
	Centre European Integration			
	e2v Centre Electronic Imaging		CeNTRE	Centre New Technologies Research Education
CEIC	Centre Study Education an International Context			
			CentreCATH	Centre Cultural Analysis, Theory & History
CEIMH	Centre Excellence Interdisciplinary Mental Health		CentreLGS	AHRC Research Centre Law, Gender & Sexuality
CEIR	Centre Editorial & Intertextual Research		CENTRIM	Centre Research Innovation Management
CEISR	Centre European & International Studies Research		CEOP	Child Exploitation & Online Protection Centre
			CEOS	Centre Electron Optical Studies
CEL	Centre Educational Leadership		CEP	Centre Economic Performance
	Centre Election Law			Centre Environment & Planning
	Centre Environmental Law			Centre Environmental Policy
	Centre European Law		CEPA	Centre Excellence Performance Arts
	Centre Executive Learning		CEPAR	Centre European Protected Areas Research
CELC	Centre English Language & Communication		CEPE	Centre Electrical Power Engineering
	Centre European Languages & Cultures			Centre Electronic Product Engineering
	Centre European Literatures & Cultures		CEPL	Oxford Centre Ethics & Philosophy Law
CeLD	Centre eLearning Development		CEPLW	Centre Excellence Professional Learning from Workplace
CELE	Centre English Language Education			
CELH	Centre English Local History		CEPM	Centre Environmental & Preventive Medicine
CELL	AHRC Centre Editing Lives & Letters		CEPMLP	Centre Energy, Petroleum & Mineral Law & Policy
CELM	Centre Educational Leadership & Management			
			CEPMMA	Centre Performance Measurement & Management
CELMR	Centre European Labour Market Research			
CELP	Centre Ecology, Law & Policy		CEPPA	Centre Ethics, Philosophy & Public Affairs
CELPD	Centre Education, Leadership & Professional Development		CEPPCG	Centre Ethics Public Policy & Corporate Governance
CELS	Centre Effective Learning Science		CEPR	Centre Economic Policy Research
	Centre English Language Studies			Centre Education Psychology Research
	Centre European Legal Studies [Cambridge]			Health Protection Agency Centre Emergency Preparedness & Response
	Centre European Legal Studies [Exeter]			
	Centre Excellence Life Sciences		CEPSAR	Centre Earth, Planetary, Space & Astronomical Research
CELT	Centre Enhancement Learning & Teaching [Hertfordshire]			
			CEPSI	Centre European Politics, Security & Integration
	Centre Enhancement Learning & Teaching [Lancaster]			

 © CBD Research Ltd · Beckenham · Kent BR3 5JS · Tel 020 8650 7745 · Fax 020 8650 0768 · E-mail cbd@cbdresearch.com · www.cbdresearch.com

CEQM	Centre Enterprise, Quality & Management
CER	Centre Education Research
	Centre Entrepreneurship Research [Edinburgh]
	Centre Entrepreneurship Research [Essex]
	Centre Environmental Research
	Centre Extremophile Research
CERA	Centre Economic Research Ageing
CeRAeBEM	Centre Research Business, Economics & Management
CeRAHP	Centre Research Allied Health Professions
CERC	Control Engineering Research Centre
Cercia	Centre Excellence Research Computational Intelligence & Applications
CeReGo	Centre Regulatory Governance
CeREPP	Centre Research Education Policy & Professionalism
CeReS	Centre Research Service
CERF	Cambridge Endowment Research Finance
CERI	Centre Economic Research & Intelligence
	Centre Enterprise Research & Innovation
CERLIM	Centre Research Library & Information Management
CERM	Centre Environmental Resource Management
CERMARK	Centre Research Marketing
CERPD	Centre Economic Renewable Power Delivery [Glasgow]
	Centre Economic Renewable Power Delivery [Strathclyde]
CERS	Centre Ethnicity & Racism Studies
CERT	Centre Economic Reform & Transformation
	Centre Environmental Research & Training
CERTE	Centre European, Regional & Transport Economics
CES	Centre Educational Sociology
	Centre Educational Studies
	Centre Electronic Systems
	Centre Emblem Studies
	Centre Environment & Society
	Centre Environmental Sciences
	Centre Environmental Strategy
	Centre European Studies [Bradford]
	Centre European Studies [Exeter]
	UCL Centre European Studies
CESA	Centre Environmental & Spatial Analysis
CESAGen	Centre Economic & Social Aspects Genomics [Cardiff]
	Centre Economic & Social Aspects Genomics [Lancaster]
CeSC	Cambridge e-Science Centre
CESEM	Centre Environmental Scanning Electron Microscopy
CESHI	Centre Environmental Studies Hospitality Industries
CESMB	Centre Environment & Safety Management Business
CeSNER	Centre Special Needs Education & Research
CESR	Centre Environmental Systems Research
	Centre Event & Sport Research
CESSA	Centre Environmental & Social Study Aging
CETH	Centre Employability Through Humanities
CETIS	Centre Educational Technology Interoperability Standards
CETL-AURS	Centre Excellence Teaching & Learning Applied Undergraduate Research Skills
CETL:IPPS	Centre Excellence Inter Professional Learning Public Sector
CETL4HealthNE	Centre Excellence Healthcare Professional Education
CETLD	Centre Excellence Teaching & Learning through Design
CETLE	White Rose Centre Excellence Teaching & Learning Enterprise

CETLs	CENTRES EXCELLENCE TEACHING & LEARNING
CETT	Centre Excellence Training Theatre
CEUS	Centre European Union Studies
CEWM	Centre Environmental & Waste Management
CfAI	Centre Advanced Instrumentation
CfAM	Centre Advanced Microscopy
CFAP	Centre Fine Art & Philosophy
CFAR	Centre Fine Art Research
CFAS	Centre Formative Assessment Studies
CFAs	Centre Assessment Solutions
CfB	Centre Biophotonics
CfBE	Centre Business Excellence
CFC	Centre Coaching
CFD	Centre Computational Fluid Dynamics
CfDPR	Centre Diversity Policy Research
CfDR	Centre Design Research
CfE	Centre Employability
	Centre Environment
	Centre Europe
	Charles P Skene Centre Entrepreneurship
CFE	Centre Enterprise
CfEL	Centre Entrepreneurial Learning
CFEM	Centre Festival & Event Management
CFERA	Centre Future & Emerging Technologies - Research & Applications
CFFC	Centre Forensic Computing
CFFP	Centre Forensic & Family Psychology
CFFS	Centre Finance & Financial Services
CFHC	Centre French History & Culture
CFI	Centre Forensic Investigation [Glasgow Caledonian]
	Centre Forensic Investigation [Teesside]
CfI	Health Protection Agency Centre Infections
CfIG	Centre International Governance
CfLG	Centre Local Governance
CFLM	Centre Forensic & Legal Medicine
CFM	Centre Financial Management
CFMR	Centre Financial Markets Research
CforC	Centre Competitiveness
CfP	Centre Psychiatry
CFPM	Centre Policy Modelling
CFPR	Centre Fine Print Research
CfPS	Centre Public Scrutiny
CFR	Centre Family Research
	Centre Financial Research
	Centre Foodservice Research
CFRC	Crime Fictions Research Centre
	Centre Financial Regulation & Crime
CfRI	Centre Rural Innovation
CFS	Centre Film Studies [Queen Mary, London]
	Centre Film Studies [St Andrews]
	Centre Forensic Science
CFSA	Centre Fusion, Space & Astrophysics
CfSD	Centre Sustainable Design
	Centre Sustainable Development
CFSLR	Joseph Bell Centre Forensic Statistics & Legal Reasoning
CfT	Centre Toxicology
CfTP	Centre Transport Policy
CGBCR	Centre Growth & Business Cycle Research
CGCM	Centre Government & Charity Management
CGES	Centre Global Energy Studies
CGJS	Centre German-Jewish Studies
CGMR	Centre Media: Globalisation: Risk
CGP	Centre General Practice
	Centre Gerontological Practice
CGPE	Centre Global Political Economy
CGR	Centre Gender Research
	Centre Glass Research
	Centre Globalisation Research
CGS	Centre Gender Studies [Kent]
	Centre Gender Studies [Sheffield]

	Centre Gender Studies [School of Oriental & African Studies, London]	CHSR	Centre Health & Social Research
			Centre Health Sciences Research
	Centre Gender Studies [Sussex]	CHSS	Centre Health Services Studies
	Centre Geospatial Science	CHST	Centre Human Service Technology
CGWS	Centre Gender & Women's Studies	CHSTM	Centre History Science, Technology & Medicine
CHAD	Centre Healthcare Architecture & Design		
CHAI	Centre Healthcare Associated Infections	CHWB	Centre History Wales and its Borderlands
CHAIR	Centre Health & International Relations	CI	Cities Institute
CHARM	AHRC Research Centre History & Analysis Recorded Music	CI-CD	Centre Intercultural Development
		CIAD	Centre Interactive Assessment Development
CHaRM	Centre Hazard & Risk Management	CIAM	Centre Industrial Automation & Manufacture
CHaSCI	Centre Health & Social Care Informatics	CIB	Centre International Briefing
CHASE	Centre Health & Social Evaluation		Centre International Business, Research & Development
CHC	UCL Centre Human Communication		
CHCR	Centre Housing & Community Research		Charities Information Bureau
CHDW	Centre Study Human Development & Well-Being	CIBAM	Centre International Business & Management
		CIBER	Centre Information Behaviour & Evaluation Research
CHE	Centre Health Economics		
	Centre Human Ecology	CIBH	Centre International Business History
CHEBS	Centre Bayesian Statistics Health Economics	CIBI	Centre International Business & Innovation
CHEC	City Health Economics Centre	CIBP	Centre International Borders Research
CHER	Centre Health, Exercise & Rehabilitation		Centre International Business Policy
CHERC	Children's Health & Exercise Research Centre	CIBS	Centre International Business & Strategy
CHERI	Centre Higher Education Research & Information		Centre International Business Studies
		CIBSH	Centre Industrial Bulk Solids Handling
CHERRY	Centre Historical Economics & Related Research at York	CIBUL	Centre International Business, University Leeds
CHES	Centre Higher Education Studies	CIC	Cranfield Impact Centre
CHFE	Centre High Frequency Engineering	CICE	Centre Innovative & Collaborative Engineering
CHG	Centre Human Genetics		
CHI	Centre Health Informatics [City]	CICM	Centre International Capital Markets
CHILL	Centre Health Improvement & Leadership Lincoln		Centre Ion Conducting Membranes
		CICR	Centre International Communications Research
CHIME	Centre Health Informatics & Multiprofessional Education		
		CICS	Centre International Co-operation and Security
Chimera	Institute Socio-Technical Research & Innovation		
		CICT	Centre International Courts & Tribunals
CHIRAL	Centre Health Information, Research & Evaluation	CID	Centre Infectious Disease [Durham]
			Centre Infectious Disease [Queen Mary, London]
CHM	Centre Health Management		
	Centre History Medicine [Birmingham]	CIDE	Centre Infectious Disease Epidemiology
	Centre History Medicine [Glasgow]	CIDRA	Centre Interdisciplinary Research Arts
	Centre History Medicine [Newcastle upon Tyne]	CIDS	Centre Integrated Diagnostic Systems
		CIE	Centre International Education
	Centre History Medicine [Warwick]		Centre Integral Excellence
CHMD	Centre History Medicine & Disease	CIEC	Chemical Industry Education Centre
CHMR	Centre Hospitality Management & Retailing	CIEL	Centre International Exchange & Languages
CHMS	Centre History Mathematical Sciences	CIER	Centre Informatics Education Research
CHO	Centre Heuristic Optimisation		Centre International Education & Research
CHoSTM	Centre History Science, Technology & Medicine	CIES	Centre Intelligent Environmental Systems
			Centre International & European Studies
CHP	Centre Health Psychology [Queen Margaret]	CIF	Centre Empirical Finance
	Centre Health Psychology [Staffordshire]	CIFC	Centre Interfirm Comparison
	Centre Housing Policy	CIFLS	Centre International Family Law Studies
	Centre Human Palaeoecology	CIGMR	Centre Integrated Genomic Medical Research
	Clinical & Health Psychology Research Centre	CIGS	Centre Interdisciplinary Gender Studies
CHPM	Centre Health Planning & Management	CIH	Sussex Centre Intellectual History
CHPR	Centre Health Promotion Research	CIHCR	Centre Integrated Health Care Research
CHPSM	Centre Health & Public Services Management	CIHD	UCL Centre International Health & Development
CHPT	Centre History Political Thought		
	Centre History Philosophical Theology	CIHMR	Centre International Hospitality Management Research
CHRC	Centre Human Rights Conflict		
CHRE	Centre Health Research & Evaluation	CIHR	Centre Integrated Healthcare Research
CHRONO	Chrono Centre Climate, Environment, & Chronology	CIHT	Centre Innovation Healthcare Technology
		CIIS	Centre Interactive Intelligent Systems
CHRPD	Centre Health Research and Practice Development	CIISS	Centre Intelligence & International Security Studies
CHS	Centre Health Sciences	CILASS	Centre Inquiry-based Learning Arts & Social Sciences
	Centre Hellenic Studies [King's College London]		
		CILC	Centre International Law & Colonialism
	Centre Hellenic Studies [Reading]		Cheltenham International Language Centre
CHSCI	Centre Health & Social Care Improvement	CILMS	Centre International Labour Market Studies
CHSCR	Centre Health & Social Care Research	CILP	Centre Insolvency Law & Policy
CHSE	Centre Health, Safety & Environment	CILR	Cambridge Institute Language Research

CIM	Centre Information Management		Centre Interdisciplinary Studies Higher Education
	Centre Infrastructure Management	CISR	Centre Interactive Systems Research
	Centre Interactive Media	CISRR	Cranfield Institute Safety Risk & Reliability
	Centre Interfaces & Materials	CIT	Centre Internet Technologies
CIMA	Centre International Media Analysis	CITAdel	Centre Innovation and Technical Applications
CIMEL	Centre Islamic & Middle East Law	CITER	Cardiff Institute Tissue Engineering & Repair
CIMM	Centre Industrial Mathematical Modelling	CITLL	Centre Information Technology Language Learning
CIMMS	Centre Innovative Manufacture & Machine Vision Systems	CITM	Centre International Transport Management
CIMR	Cambridge Institute Medical Research	City Lit	City Literary Institute
	Centre Interdisciplinary Mathematical Research	CJCR	Centre Study Jewish-Christian Relations
CIMS	Centre Imperial & Maritime Studies	CJRC	Criminal Justice Research Centre
	Centre Intelligent Monitoring Systems	CJS	Centre Jewish Studies [Leeds]
CIMT	Centre Innovation Mathematics Teaching		Centre Jewish Studies [School of Oriental & African Studies, London]
Cimtech	Centre Information Management & Technology		Centre Journalism Studies
CINA	Centre Interactive Network Arts	CJSC	Cardiff Japanese Studies Centre
CIOD	Centre Individual & Organisational Development	CJSW	Criminal Justice Social Work Development Centre Scotland
CIOS	Centre Integrated Optoelectronic Systems	CKM	Centre Knowledge Management
CIP	Centre Images Practice	CKS	Centre Korean Studies
	Centre Institutional Performance	CLA	Centre Late Antiquity
	Centre Intergenerational Practice	CLACS	Centre Latin American Cultural Studies [King's College London]
	Centre International Politics		
	Centre Irish Politics		Centre Latin American Cultural Studies [Manchester]
CIPCS	Centre Imperial & Post-Colonial Studies	CLAMS	Centre Late Antique & Medieval Studies
CIPeL	Centre Inter-Professional e-Learning Health & Social Care	CLAR	Centre Latin American Research
		CLARC	Centre Late Antique Religion & Culture
CIPIL	Centre Intellectual Property & Information Law	CLARe	Centre Language Assessment Research
		CLARRC	Contaminated Land Assessment & Remediation Research Centre
CIPL	Centre International & Public Law		
CIPP	Centre Inter-professional Practice	CLAS	Centre Latin American Studies [Cambridge]
CIPPM	Centre Intellectual Property Policy & Management		Centre Latin American Studies [Essex]
			Centre Latin American Studies [Exeter]
CIPS	Centre Information Policy Studies	CLASSIC	Climate & Land-Surface Systems Interaction Centre
CIQM	Centre Information Quality Management		
CIR	Centre Institutional Research	CLBS	Centre Land-Based Studies
CIRCA	Cambridge Interdisciplinary Research Centre Ageing	CLC	Centre Law & Conflict
		CLCR	Centre Language & Communication Research
	Centre Interdisciplinary Research Computational Algebra		
		CLD	Centre Learning Development
CIRCAh	Cultural Informatics Research Centre Arts & Humanities		Centre Local Democracy
		CLE	Centre Law & Environment
CIRCLE	Centre International Research Creativity & Learning Education	CLEMANCE	Clean Environment Management Centre
		CLEME	Centre Languages, English & Media Education
CIREA	Centre Innovation Raising Educational Achievement		
		CLEO	Centre Learning & Enterprise Organisations
CIRSE	Centre Innovation & Research Science Education	CLES	Centre Local Economic Strategies
			Centre Local Enterprise & Skills
CIS	Centre Institutional Studies	CLGE	Centre Law & Governance Europe
	Centre Intercultural Studies [Glasgow]	CLH	Centre Local History [Essex]
	Centre Intercultural Studies [University College London]		Centre Local History [Nottingham]
		CLHR	Centre Life History Research
	Centre International Studies [Cambridge]	CLHS	Centre Local History Studies
	Centre International Studies [Leeds]	CLIC	Centre Learning, Innovation & Collaboration
	Centre International Studies [London School of Economics]	ClinBio	Clinical Biosciences Institute
		CLIP	Creative Learning Practice Centre Excellence Teaching & Learning
	Centre International Studies [Oxford]		
	Centre Iranian Studies	CLLC	Centre Leadership, Learning & Change
	Centre Islamic Studies	CLMS	Centre Labour Market Studies
	Centre Italian Studies	CLOC	Centre Leadership & Organisational Change
CISA	Centre Intelligent Systems & their Applications	CLP	Centre Legal Practice
CISBIC	Centre Integrative Systems Biology at Imperial College	CLPE	Centre Literacy Primary Education
		CLPI	Centre Leadership & Practice Innovation
CISBM	Centre Integrated Systems Biology & Medicines	CLR	Centre Law & Religion
			Centre Legal Research [Middlesex]
CISC	Community Information Systems Centre		Centre Legal Research [Nottingham Trent]
CISD	Centre International Studies & Diplomacy		Centre Legal Research [West of England]
CISE	Centre Interactive Systems Engineering		Centre Leisure Retailing
CISEMT	Centre International Studies Education, Management & Training		Centre Linguistic Research
			Centre Literacy Research
CISHE	Cardiff Institute Society, Health & Ethics	CLRC	Computer Learning Research Centre

© CBD Research Ltd · Beckenham · Kent BR3 5JS · Tel 020 8650 7745 · Fax 020 8650 0768 · E-mail cbd@cbdresearch.com · www.cbdresearch.com

CLRCeSC	CLRC e-Science Centre		Centre Media Research
CLREA	Centre Local & Regional Economic Analysis		Centre Materials Research
CLRGR	Centre Local & Regional Government Research	CMRC	Credit Management Research Centre
		CMRI	Centre Magnetic Resonance Investigations
CLRPS	Centre Legal Research & Policy Studies		Cranfield Management Research Institute
CLS	Centre Language Studies [City]	CMRP	Centre Mindfulness Research & Practice
	Centre Language Studies [Surrey]	CMRS	Centre Medieval & Renaissance Studies
	Centre Language Study	CMS	Centre Manx Studies
	Centre Leadership Studies		Centre Materials Science
	Centre Lebanese Studies		Centre Mathematical Science
	Centre Legislative Studies		Centre Mathematical Sciences
	Centre Life Sciences		Centre Medieval Studies [Bangor]
	Centre Longitudinal Studies		Centre Medieval Studies [Bristol]
	Sir William Dale Centre Legislative Studies		Centre Medieval Studies [Exeter]
CLT	Centre Learning & Teaching		Centre Medieval Studies [York]
CLTA	Centre Landscape & Townscape Archaeology		Centre Mediterranean Studies [Exeter]
CLTR	Centre Learning & Teaching Research		Centre Mediterranean Studies [Leeds]
CLTRHE	Centre Learning, Teaching & Research Higher Education		Centre Migration Studies at Ulster-American Folk Park
CLUWRR	Centre Land Use & Water Resources Research		Centre Ministry Studies
			Centre Modernist Studies
CLWR	Centre Learning and Workforce Research		Centre Mountain Studies
CM	Centre Marketing	CMSB	Centre Metalloprotein Spectroscopy & Biology
CMA	Centre Maritime Archaeology		
CMA&DMC	Cranfield Mine Action & Disaster Management Centre	CMSE	Centre Materials Science & Engineering [Cranfield]
CMALS	Centre Mathematics Applied to Life Sciences		Centre Materials Science & Engineering [Edinburgh]
CMB	Centre Molecular Biosciences	CMSR	Centre Materials Science Research
	Centre Mathematical Biology [Bath]	CMT	Centre Music Technology [Glasgow]
	Centre Mathematical Biology [Oxford]		Centre Music Technology [Kent]
CMBB	Centre Marine Biodiversity & Biotechnology		Centre Music Theatre
CMBOR	Centre Management Buy-Out Research	CMuR	Centre Management under Regulation
CMBR	Centre Management & Business Research	CNAHPR	Centre Nursing & Allied Health Professionals Research
CMC	Centre Management Creativity		
CMCA	Centre Marine & Coastal Archaeology	CNAP	Centre Novel Agricultural Products
CMCR	Centre Mass Communication Research	CNC	Centre Novel Computing
	Centre Mobile Communications Research		MRC Centre Nutritional Epidemiology Cancer Prevention & Survival
CMCW	Centre Modern & Contemporary Wales		
CMD	Centre Molecular Design	CNDA	Centre Nonlinear Dynamics & its Applications
CMDD	Centre Molecular Drug Design		
CME	Centre MicroEnterprise	CNE	Centre Neuroscience Education
	Centre Medical Education [Dundee]	CNEM	Centre New & Emerging Markets
	Centre Medical Education [Lancaster]	CNM	Centre Nanoporous Materials
	Centre Medical Education [Queen Mary, London]		Centre Nanostructured Media
			Centre Nonlinear Mechanics
CMEIS	Centre Middle Eastern & Islamic Studies	CNMPA	Centre Numerical Modelling & Process Analysis
CMET	Centre Medical Engineering & Technology		
CMFS	Centre Media & Film Studies	CNMR	Centre New Media Research
CMH	Centre Men's Health		Centre Nursing & Midwifery Research
	Centre Marine Hydrodynamics	CNPVSM	Centre Nonprofit & Voluntary Section Management
	Centre Metropolitan History		
	Centre Medical History	CNR	Centre Narrative Research
CMHE	Centre Medical & Healthcare Education		Centre Neuroscience Research
CMHS	Centre Maritime Historical Studies		MRC Centre Neurodegenerative Research
CMI	Cambridge-MIT Institute	CNRP	Centre Nuclear & Radiation Physics
CMLD	Centre Management Learning & Development	CNS	Centre Community Neurological Studies
			Centre Nanoscale Science
CMLE	Centre Medical Law & Ethics		Centre Nordic Studies
CMLS	Centre Medico-Legal Studies		MacKay Institute Communication & Neuroscience
CMM	Centre Mathematical Medicine		
	Centre Medical Microbiology	CNTR	Centre Networking & Telecommunications Research
CMMFA	Centre Mathematical Modelling & Flow Analysis		
		CNWRS	Centre North-West Regional Studies
CMMI	Centre Molecular Microbiology & Infection	COB	Centre Orthopaedic Biomechanics
CMMS	Centre Mechatronics & Manufacturing Systems	COBC	Centre Organic & Biological Chemistry
		COE	Centre Organisational Effectiveness
CMN	Manchester Centre Mesoscience & Nanotechnology	COERC	Comparative Organisation & Equality Research Centre
CMO	Centre Molecular Oncology	COGD	Centre Oral Growth & Development
	Centre Medical Oncology	COGS	Centre Ombudsman & Governance Studies
CMPO	Centre Market & Public Organisation		Centre Research Cognitive Science
CMPS	Centre Manuscript & Print Studies	COHS	Centre Occupational Health & Safety
CMR	Centre Materials Research	COI	ESRC Centre Organisation & Innovation
	CMR International		

© CBD Research Ltd · Beckenham · Kent BR3 5JS · Tel 020 8650 7745 · Fax 020 8650 0768 · E-mail cbd@cbdresearch.com · www.cbdresearch.com

COJS	Centre Jaina Studies	CPLS	Centre Professional Legal Studies
COLMSCT	Centre Open Learning Mathematics, Science, Computing & Technology	CPM	Ashley Centre Professional Management
		CPMH	Centre Port & Maritime History
COMET	Centre Observation & Modelling Earthquakes & Tectonics	CPMSD	Centre Protein & Membrane Structure & Dynamics
COMPAS	Centre Migration, Policy & Society	CPNSS	Centre Philosophy Natural & Social Science
COMPH	Centre Multimedia Performance History	CPOD	Centre Professional & Organisation Development
CoMPLEX	Centre Mathematics & Physics Life Sciences & Experimental Biology	CPOM	Centre Polar Observation & Modelling
CoPS	Centre Planning Studies	CPP	Centre Particle Physics
	Complex Product Systems Innovation Centre		Centre Plasma Physics
CORA	Centre Osmosis Research & Applications		Centre Public Policy
CORAS	Centre Operational Research & Applied Statistics	CPPM	Centre Photonics & Photonic Materials
			Centre Public Policy & Management [Glasgow Caledonian]
CORE	Centre Outcomes Research and Effectiveness		Centre Public Policy & Management [Manchester]
COrE	Research Centre Organisational Excellence		
CORMSIS	Centre Operational Research, Management Science & Information Systems		Centre Public Policy and Management [Robert Gordon]
			Centre Public Policy & Management [St Andrews]
COS&R	Centre Olympic Studies & Research		
CoSIC	Coffee Science Information Centre	CPPR	Centre Public Policy Regions
COST	Centre Ordnance Science & Technology		Centre Public Policy Research
COT	Centre Organisational Transformation	CPR	Centre Pain Research
COTEC	Cranfield Ordnance Test & Evaluation Centre		Centre Performance Research
CPA	Centre Performance Analysis		Centre Property Research
	Centre Policy Ageing	CPRC	Chronic Poverty Research Centre
	Centre Professional Accounting & Financial Services		Construction & Property Research Centre
			Contemporary Poetics Research Centre
	Centre Psychological Astrology	CPRS	Centre Peace & Reconciliation Studies
CPACT	Centre Process Analytics & Control Technology	CPS	Centre Performance Science
			Centre Performance Sport
CPaRA	Centre Practice as Research Arts		Centre Philosophical Studies
CPB	NERC Centre Population Biology		Centre Plant Sciences
CPC	Centre Parallel Computing		Centre Policy Studies
	Centre Primary Care		Centre Population Sciences
CPCA	Contextual, Public & Commemorative Art Research Centre		Centre Psychosocial Studies
		CPSA	Centre Planetary Science & Astrobiology
CPCR	Centre Public Communication Research	CPSE	Centre Policy Studies Education
CPCS	Centre Parent & Child Support		Centre Process Systems Engineering
	Centre Peace & Conflict Studies	CPSM	Centre Public Services Management
	Centre Pentecostal & Charismatic Studies	CPSO	Centre Public Services Organisations
CPD	Centre Practice Development	CPT	Centre Particle Theory
	Centre Professional Development		Centre Polymer Therapeutics
	Centre Professional Development Art & Design		Centre Precision Technologies
		CPTI	Centre Political Theory & Ideologies
CPDE	Centre Parties & Democracy Europe	CQC	Centre Quantum Computation [Cambridge]
CPDM	Centre Phosphors & Display Materials		Centre Quantum Computation [Oxford]
CPDS	Centre Political & Diplomatic Studies	CQeSS	Collaboratory Quantitative e-Social Science [Research Centre]
CPE	Centre Performance Enhancement		
	Centre Pipeline Engineering	CQF	Centre Quantitative Finance
	Centre Policy Evaluation	CQGSC	Centre Quality Global Supply Chain
	Centre Professional Ethics	CQIS	Centre Quality, Innovation & Support
	MRC Centre Protein Engineering	CQR	Centre Qualitative Research
CPEG	LSE Environment: Centre Environmental Policy & Governance		Centre Quaternary Research
		CR	Centre Rheumatology
CPERM	Centre Performance Evaluation & Resource Management	CRA	Centre Research Architecture
			Centre Robotics & Automation
CPESP	Centre Physical Education & Sport Pedagogy		UCL Centre Research Ageing
CPH	Centre Public Health	CRAAG	Centre Research Accounting, Accountability & Governance
CPH	Centre Performance History, incorporating Museum Instruments		
		CRAC	Careers Research & Advisory Centre
CPHCS	Centre Primary Health Care Studies	CRADALL	Centre Research & Development Adult & Lifelong Learning
CPHR	Centre Public Health Research [Brunel]		
	Centre Public Health Research [Chester]	CRAG	Centre Research Ageing & Gender
	Centre Public Health Research [Salford]	CRaG	Cullen Centre Risk & Governance
	Centre Public Health Research [West of England]	CRAL	Centre Research Applied Linguistics
		CRAMSS	Centre Research Analytical, Materials & Sensor Science
CPI	Caucasus Policy Institute		
	Centre Process Integration	CRASSH	Centre Research Arts, Social Sciences, & Humanities
	China Policy Institute		
CPIMT	Centre Process Integration & Membrane Technology	CRB	Centre Religion & Biosciences
			Criminal Records Bureau
CPL	Centre Public Law	CRBP	Centre Regional Business Productivity
CPLA	Centre Promoting Learner Autonomy		
CPLIS	Centre Public Library & Information Society		

CRC	Centre Regulation & Competition
	Centre Research Computing
	Children's Research Centre
	Cities Research Centre
	Clinical Research Centre Health Professions
	Communications Research Centre [Cardiff]
	Communications Research Centre [Loughborough]
	Cranfield Resilience Centre
	Greater Glasgow Health Board Continence Resource Centre & Helpline Scotland
CRCE	Centre Research Post-Communist Economies
	Health Protection Agency Centre Radiation, Chemical & Environmental Hazards
CRCEES	Centre Russian, Central & East European Studies
CRCF	Centre Research Child & Family
CRCG	Centre Research Corporate Governance
CRCL	Centre Research Communication & Language
CRD	Centre Reviews & Dissemination
CRD	Centre Research & Development
CRDCE	Centre Research & Development Catholic Education
CRDHB	Centre Research Drugs and Health Behaviour
CRE	Centre Rehabilitation Engineering
	Centre Research Education
	Centre Research & Evaluation
	Centre Rural Economy
CRE+E	Centre Research Energy & Environment
CREA	Centre Research Evolutionary Anthropology
CREAC	Centre Research Electronic Art & Communication
CREAM	Centre Research Environmental Appraisal & Management
	Centre Research Marketing
	Centre Service Management
CReAM	Centre Research & Analysis Migration
CREAM	Centre Research & Education Art & Media
CREATE	Centre Research, Education & Training Energy
CreaTE	Centre Research Tertiary Education
CRED	Centre Regional Economic Development
	Centre Research Education & Democracy
	Centre Research Equality & Diversity
CREDE	Centre Research Equity & Diversity Education
CREDIT	ESRC Centre Research Economic Development & International Trade
	Centre Research Distributed Technologies
CREE	Centre Research Ecology & Environment
	Centre Research Education & Environment
	Centre Research Emerging Economies
CREECS	Centre Russian & East European Cultural Studies
CREEM	Centre Research Ecological and Environmental Modelling
CREES	Centre Russian & East European Studies
CREET	Centre Research Education & Educational Technology
CREFMI	Centre Research European Financial Markets & Institutions
CREFSA	Centre Research Economics & Finance Southern Africa
CREH	Centre Research Environment & Health [Aberystwyth]
	Centre Research Environment & Health [Cardiff]
	Centre Research Environment & Health [Lampeter]
CREID	Centre Research Education Inclusion & Diversity
CREL	Centre Reproduction and Early Life
CRELH	Centre Research English & Local History

CRELLA	Centre Research English Language Learning & Assessment
CReME	Centre Research Management Expatriation
CREME	Centre Research Ethnic Minority Entrepreneurship
CREMS	Centre Reformation & Early Modern Studies
	Centre Renaissance and Early Modern Studies [Queen Mary, London]
	Centre Renaissance & Early Modern Studies [York]
CREOLE	CLIO Centre Research Language & Education
CRER	Centre Real Estate Research
CRER	Centre Research Ethnic Relations
CRERS	Centre Research East Roman Studies
CRERT	Centre Research Excellence Religion & Theology
CRES	Centre Research Employment Studies
	Centre Research Environmental Sciences
	Centre Russian & Eurasian Studies
CRESC	ESRC Centre Research Socio-Cultural Change [Manchester]
	ESRC Centre Research Socio-Cultural Change [Open]
CRESR	Centre Regional Economic & Social Research
CRESS	Centre Research Social Simulation
CREST	Centre Research European Studies
	Centre Renewable Energy Systems Technology
CREW	Centre Research Emotion Work
	Centre Research English Literature & Language Wales
CRFAC	Centre Research Film & Audiovisual Cultures
CRFES	Centre Research Fire & Explosion Studies
CRFR	Centre Research Families & Relationships
CRH	Centre Rural Health Research & Policy
CRHaM	Centre Research Health & Medicine
CRHE	Centre Research Higher Education
CRHF	Centre Rail Human Factors
CRHPR	Centre Rehabilitation & Human Performance Research
CRHR	Centre Research Human Rights
CRHSC	Centre Research Health & Social Care
CRI	Cancer Research UK Cambridge Research Institute
	Carnegie Research Institute
	Centre Study Regulated Industries
CRiB	Centre Research Biomedicine
CRIB	Centre Research Infant Behaviour
CRIC	ESRC Centre Research Innovation & Competition
CRICEI	Centre Research Cognition, Emotion & Interaction
CRICP	Centre Research & Implementation Clinical Practice
CRIE	Centre Research Institutional Economics
CRIEFF	Centre Research Industry, Enterprise, Finance & Firm
CRiFA	Centre Research Finance & Accounting
CRIL	Centre Research Interactive Learning
CRILE	Centre Research Language Education
CRinCH	Centre Research Childhood
CRIPACC	Centre Research Primary & Community Care
CRIPS	Centre Research Plant Science
CRIPSAT	Centre Research Primary Science & Technology
CRIS	Centre Research Sustainability
	Centre Risk & Insurance Studies
	Centre Study Religion, Ideas & Society
CRISE	Centre Research Inequality, Human Security & Ethnicity
CRiSM	Centre Research Statistical Methodology
CRiSP	Centre Recovery Severe Psychosis

© CBD Research Ltd · Beckenham · Kent BR3 5JS · Tel 020 8650 7745 · Fax 020 8650 0768 · E-mail cbd@cbdresearch.com · www.cbdresearch.com

CRiSPS	Centre Research Strategic Purchasing & Supply	CSAR	Centre Sustainable Aquaculture Research
CRISSPI	Centre Research Six Sigma & Process Improvement	CSAS	Centre South Asian Studies [Coventry]
			Centre South Asian Studies [Edinburgh]
CRISTAL	Cardiovascular Research Institute at Leeds		Centre South Asian Studies [School of Oriental & African Studies, London]
CRKT	Centre Research & Knowledge Transfer	CSAT	Centre Sociocultural & Activity Theory Research
CRL	Centre Reading & Language		
CRLHR	Centre Regional & Local Historical Research	CSB	Centre Structural Biology
CRLL	Centre Research Lifelong Learning		Centre Systems Biology
CRM	Centre Regenerative Medicine	CSBE	Centre Systems Biology at Edinburgh
	Centre Research Marketing [Aberystwyth]	CSBR	Centre Study Byron & Romanticism
	Centre Research Marketing [Salford]	CSC	Caribbean Studies Centre
	Centre Research Marketing [Westminster]		Catchment Science Centre
	Centre Russian Music		Centre Scientific Computing
CRM&E	Centre Resource Management & Efficiency		Centre Sustainable Consumption
CRMDE	Centre Research Medical & Dental Education		Centre Systems & Control
CRMEP	Centre Research Modern European Philosophy		Clinical Skills Centre [Dundee]
			Clinical Skills Centre [Robert Gordon]
CRMP	Centre Reputation Management through People		Crafts Study Centre
			MRC Clinical Sciences Centre
CRMSHP	Centre Research Medical Sociology & Health Policy	CSCB	Centre Stem Cell Biology
		CSCC	Centre Study Christian Church
CRNME	Centre Research Nursing & Midwifery Education	CSCE	Centre Study Central Europe
		CSCFL	Centre Study Child, Family & Law
CROLMS	Centre Research Leather & Materials Science	CSCM	Centre Supply Chain Management
CROMT	Centre Research Opera & Music Theatre	CSCR	Centre Study Cities & Regions
CRONEM	Centre Research Nationalism, Ethnicity & Multiculturalism		Centre Supply Chain Research
			Chelsea School Research Centre
CRPC	Centre Religion & Political Culture	CSCRS	Centre Scientific & Cultural Research Sport
CRPF	Centre Regional Public Finance	CSCS	Centre Study Comprehensive Schools
CRPH	Centre Research Polish History		Centre Study Composition Screen
CRPL	Centre Research Philosophy & Literature	CSCY	Centre Study Childhood & Youth
CRQ	Centre Research Quality	CSCYM	Centre Study Children, Youth & Media
CRR	Centre Radiochemistry Research	CSD	Centre Studies Democratization
	Centre Research Rehabilitation		Centre Study Democracy
	Centre Research Romanticism	CSDI	AHRC Centre Study Domestic Interior
	Centre Respiratory Research	CSE	Centre Science Education [Glasgow]
	Centre Retail Research		Centre Science Education [Sheffield Hallam]
	Centre Risk Research		Centre Study Evolution
	Centre Rural Research		Centre Study Expertise
CRRE	Centre Research Religious Experience		Centre Systems Engineering
CRREN	Centre Research Racism, Ethnicity & Nationalism	CSEAR	Centre Social & Environmental Accounting Research
		CSEAS	Centre South East Asian Studies
CRRS	Centre Research Renaissance Studies	CSEC	Centre Science Extreme Conditions
CRS	Centre Renaissance Studies		Centre Study Environmental Change
	Centre Romantic Studies		Centre Study Ethnic Conflict
	Centre Russian Studies	CSEE	Centre Sound & Experimental Environments
	Centre Study Renaissance	CSEES	Centre South-East European Studies
CRSCEES	Centre Russian, Soviet & Central and Eastern European Studies	CSEG	Centre Study European Governance
		CSEL	Centre Scientific Enterprise
CRSEM	Centre Remote Sensing & Environmental Monitoring	CSEM	Centre Sports & Exercise Medicine
			Centre Study Emotion & Motivation
CRSI	Centre Research Self & Identity	CSEP	Centre Social Ethics & Policy
CRSIS	Centre Research Socially Inclusive Services	CSER	Centre Social Evaluation Research
CRSP	Centre Research Social Policy		Centre Sport & Exercise Research
CRSPS	Centre Research Social & Political Sciences		Welsh School Pharmacy Centre Socioeconomic Research
CRUCiBLE	CRUCiBLE: Centre Rights, Understanding & Citizenship Based Learning through Experience	CSERGE	Centre Social & Economic Research Global Environment
		CServ	Centre Service Research
CS2	UCL Centre Security & Crime Science	CSES	Centre Sport & Exercise Science
CSA	Centre System Analysis		Centre Sports & Exercise Science
CSAC	Centre Social Anthropology & Computing	CSESCE	Centre Study Economic & Social Change Europe
	Computer Security & Audit Centre		
CSAD	Centre Study Ancient Documents	CSET	Centre Study Education & Training
CSAE	Centre Structural & Architectural Engineering		Centre Study Educational Technologies
	Centre Study African Economies	CSF	Centre Sustainable Futures
CSAIC	Cranfield Safety & Accident Investigation Centre	CSFI	Centre Study Financial Innovation
		CSG	Centre Social Gerontology
CSALT	Centre Studies Advanced Learning Technology		Centre Study Gambling
		CSGE	Centre Study Global Ethics
CSAOS	Centre Space, Atmospheric & Oceanic Science	CSGEU	Centre Study Governance European Union
CSAPP	Centre Study Anomalous Psychological Processes	CSGG	Centre Study Global Governance

CSGP	Centre Study Group Processes	CSSERC	Communications & Software Systems Engineering Research Centre
CSGR	Centre Study Globalisation & Regionalisation	CSSGJ	Centre Study Social & Global Justice
CSGS	Centre Scottish & Gaelic Studies	CSSME	Centre Studies Science & Mathematics Education
CSH	UCL Centre Sustainable Heritage		
CSHE	Centre Study Higher Education	CSSPM	Centre Study Social & Political Movements
CSHHH	Centre Social History Health & Healthcare [Glasgow Caledonian]	CSSTM	Centre Study Socialist Theory & Movement
		CST	Centre Sustainable Technologies
	Centre Social History Health & Healthcare [Strathclyde]	CSTO	Centre Study Technology & Organisations
		CSTPV	Centre Study Terrorism & Political Violence
CSHI	Centre Study Health & Illness	CSTR	Centre Speech Technology Research
CSHR	Centre Sexual Health Research	CSVCR	Centre Studies Visual Culture Religion
	Centre Study Human Rights	CSWR	Centre Social Work Research [London]
	Centre Study Human Relations	CTAC	Control Theory & Applications Centre
CSHRL	Centre Study Human Rights Law [Glasgow]	CTB	Centre Tumour Biology
	Centre Study Human Rights Law [Strathclyde]	CTC	Cancer Research UK & UCL Cancer Trials Centre
CSHS	Centre Sheltered Housing Studies		
CSI	Centre Social Inclusion		Centre Theatre & Community
	Centre Study Islam		Constructive Teaching Centre
CSI-UK	Centre Study Islam UK	CTCCS	Centre Translation & Comparative Cultural Studies
CSIE	Centre Studies Inclusive Education		
CSIG	Centre Study International Governance	CTCD	Centre Terrestrial Carbon Dynamics
CSIP	Centre Sensory Impaired People	CTCE	Centre Tourism & Cultural Change
CSIR	Centre Studies Implicit Religion	CTCFL	Centre Teaching Chinese as a Foreign Language
CSISP	Centre Study Invention & Social Process		
CSJ	Centre Social Justice	CTCR	Centre Tobacco Control Research
CSJR	Centre Study Japanese Religions	CTE	Centre Timber Engineering
CSLP	Centre Stakeholder Learning Partnerships	CTERC	China & Transitional Economics Research Centre
CSLPE	Centre Study Law & Policy Europe		
CSM	Centre Study Migration	Cti	Castings Technology International
	Centre Systems and Modelling	CTI	Cultural Theory Institute
CSME	Centre Small & Medium Sized Enterprises	CTIS	Centre Translation & Intercultural Studies
	Centre Study Mathematics Education	CTISS	Centre Translating & Interpreting Studies Scotland
CSMSC	Centre Study Medieval Society & Culture		
CSPD	Centre Sustainable Power Distribution	CTL	Centre Tax Law
CSPE	Centre Study Perceptual Experience	CTM	Centre Technology Management
CSPP	Centre Study Policy & Practice Health and Social Care	CTMM	Centre Theoretical Modelling Medicine
		CTO	Centre Translational Oncology
	Centre Study Public Policy	CTP	Centre Transpersonal Psychology
CSPR	Centre Social & Policy Research	CTPAM	Centre Technology, Production & Ancient Materials
CSPRD	Centre Social Policy Research & Development		
CSpREE	Centre Spatial & Real Estate Economics	CTR	Centre Telecommunications Research
CSPSJ	Centre Study Poverty Social Justice	CTR	Centre Transcultural Research
CSPT	Centre Software Process Technologies	CTRC	Crichton Tourism Research Centre
CSPW	Centre Study Propaganda	CTRC	Centre Theology, Religion & Culture
CSR	Centre Sentencing Research	CTRE	Centre Theatre Research Europe
	Centre Social Research	CTS	Centre Taiwan Studies
	Centre Software Reliability [City]		Centre Technology Strategy
	Centre Software Reliability [Newcastle upon Tyne]		Centre Textual Scholarship
			Centre Theatre Studies
CSRC	Complexity Science Research Centre		Centre Thermal Studies
	Crisis States Research Centre		Centre Translation Studies
CSRE	Centre Study Race & Ethnicity		Centre Transport & Society
CSRHHC	Centre Social Research Health & Health Care		Centre Transport Studies [Imperial College London]
CSRI	Clinical Sciences Research Institute		
CSRM	Centre Studies Rural Ministry		Centre Transport Studies [University College London]
CSRP	Centre Study Religion & Politics		
CSRS	Centre Study Retailing Scotland		Whalley Centre Transport Studies
CSRV	Centre Study Radicalisation & Contemporary Political Violence	CTUS	Centre Trade Union Studies
		CTWS	Nottingham Trent Centre Travel Writing Studies
CSS	Centre Science Studies		
	Centre Scottish Studies	CUBE	Centre Urban Built Environment
	Centre Screen Studies [Glasgow]	CUBIC	Cranfield University Business Incubation Centre
	Centre Screen Studies [Manchester]		
	Centre Security Studies	CUBRIC	Cardiff University Brain & Repair Imaging Centre
	Centre Sports Studies		
	Centre Strategic Studies [Anglia Ruskin]	CUC	Centre Urban Culture
	Centre Suburban Studies	CUCR	Centre Urban & Community Research
	Centre Surgical Science	CUDEM	Centre Urban Development & Environmental Management
	Centre Syrian Studies		
CSSC	Centre Study Sexuality & Culture	CUE	Centre Ultrasonic Engineering
CSSD	Centre Study Sexual Dissidence		Centre Urban Education
	Centre Studies Security & Diplomacy	CUH	Cambridge University Health - Health Policy & Management Centre
CSSE	Centre Stakeholding & Sustainable Enterprise		
	Centre Systems & Software Engineering		

© CBD Research Ltd · Beckenham · Kent BR3 5JS · Tel 020 8650 7745 · Fax 020 8650 0768 · E-mail cbd@cbdresearch.com · www.cbdresearch.com

	Centre Urban History
CUHTec	Centre Usable Home Technology
CUIMRC	Cardiff University Innovative Manufacturing Research Centre
CUPS	Centre Urban Policy Studies
CURDS	Centre Urban & Regional Development Studies
CURE	Centre Urban & Regional Ecology
CURG	Centre Study Urban & Regional Governance
CURS	Centre Urban & Regional Studies
CVA	Centre Visual Anthropology
CVAS	Centre Voluntary Action Studies
CVC	Centre Video Communications
CVE	Centre Virtual Environments
CVS	Centre Veterinary Science
	Centre Victorian Studies [Chester]
	Centre Victorian Studies [Exeter]
	Centre Vision Sciences & Vascular Biology
	Centre Visual Studies [Oxford]
	Centre Visual Studies [Sussex]
CVSSP	Centre Vision, Speech & Signal Processing
CVVC	Centre Vision & Visual Cognition
CWA	Centre Creative Writing & Arts
CWAL	Centre Work & Learning
CWAS	Centre West African Studies
CWCT	Centre Window and Cladding Technology
CWEH	Centre World Environmental History
CWH	Centre Workplace Health
CWIND	Centre Wireless Network Design
CWiPP	Centre Well-being Public Policy
CWLA	Centre Welsh Legal Affairs
CWLR	Centre Working Life Research
CWLS	Centre Welsh Language Services
CWM	Centre Waste Management
CWPD	Centre Water Policy & Development
CWS	Centre Water Science
	Centre Water Systems
	Centre Whistler Studies
	Centre Women's Studies
CWSC	Cold War Studies Centre
CYM	Centre Young Musicians
CYWS	Centre Youth Work Studies

D

DAC	Defence Animal Centre
DARC	Data Assimilation Research Centre
DARM	Centre Decision Management & Risk Management
DBC	David K E Bruce Centre American Studies
DBC	Dugald Baird Centre Research Women's Health
DCAL	Deafness, Cognition & Language Research Centre
DCAPS	Durham Centre Advanced Photography Studies
DCC	Digital Curation Centre
DCC	Drug Control Centre
DCRE	Durham Centre Renewable Energy
DDC	Disaster & Development Centre
DDMI	David Davies Memorial Institute
DDP	Drama, Dance & Performing Arts Research Centre
DDRC	Digestive Disease Research Centre
	Diving Diseases Research Centre Ltd
DEC	Decision Engineering Centre
	Design Enterprise Centre
DELI	Durham European Law Institute
DERC	UHI Decommissioning & Environmental Remediation Centre
DESTIN	Development Studies Institute
DICE	Durrell Institute Conservation & Ecology

DIRC	Digital Imaging Research Centre
	Interdisciplinary Research Centre Dependability Computer-Based Systems
DLDCN	Centre Developmental Language Disorders & Cognitive Neuroscience
DLIIDS	David Livingstone Institute International Development Studies
DMC	Disaster Management Centre
DMRC	Digital Media Research Centre
DOC	Sir David Owen Population Centre
DPIC	Digital & Photographic Imaging Centre
DRC	Design Research Centre
	Development Research Centre Migration, Globalisation & Poverty
	Dictionary Research Centre
DSDC	Dementia Services Development Centre
	Dementia Services Development Centre Wales
DTC	Doctoral Training Centre Medical Devices
	Dyslexia Teaching Centre
DWRC	Digital World Research Centre

E

E3I	Enhancing, Embedding & Integrating Employability CETL
EAI	East Asia Institute
EARC	European Accounting Research Centre
EBC	Eric Bywaters Centre Vascular Inflammation
	Exeter Biocatalysis Centre
EBI	Earth & Biosphere Institute
EBSI	Essex Biomedical Sciences Institute
ECASS	European Centre Analysis Social Sciences
ECB	Edinburgh Centre Bioinformatics
ECCN	Exeter Centre Cognitive Neuroscience
ECI	Environmental Change Institute
ECI	European Construction Institute
eCIC	eCommerce Innovation Centre
ECIT	Institute Electronics, Communications & Information Technology
ECME	European Centre Management Education
ECMWF	European Centre Medium-Range Weather Forecasts
ECOHOST	European Centre Health Societies Transition
ECOHSE	European Centre Occupational Health, Safety & Environment
ECRC	Early Childhood Research Centre
	Environmental Change Research Centre
ECRE	Engineering Composites Research Centre
ECRIC	Eastern Cancer Registration & Information Centre
ECSC	Energy Centre Sustainable Communities
ECSP	European Centre Study Policing
EDC	Electronics Design Centre
	Engineering Design Centre
	Equality & Discrimination Centre
	European Documentation Centre
EDI	Edinburgh Dental Institute
EDRC	Engineering Design Research Centre
EdVEC	Edinburgh Virtual Environment Centre
EEAC	East European Advice Centre
EEEI	Earth, Energy & Environment University Interdisciplinary Institute
EERC	Earthquake Engineering Research Centre
	Environmental Engineering Research Centre
EFiC	Essex Finance Centre
EFRC	Elm Farm Research Centre
EGENIS	ESRC Centre Genomics Society
EGI	Edward Grey Institute Field Ornithology
EHRAC	European Human Rights Advocacy Centre
EHRC	European Humanities Research Centre
EI	Elphinstone Institute

EIA	Environmental Impact Assessment Centre
EIAC	Ergonomics Information Analysis Centre
EIC	Educational Initiative Centre
EIC/LCCI	European Information Centre
EICs	EURO INFORMATION CENTRES
EIHMS	European Institute Health & Medical Sciences
EIS	English Institute Sport
EISS	European Institute Social Services
EIUA	European Institute Urban Affairs
EJIVR	Edward Jenner Institute Vaccine Research
EJRC	Europe Japan Research Centre
ELC	English Language Centre
ELSE	ESRC Centre Economic Learning & Social Evolution
EMARC	Environment Monitoring & Response Centre
EMC	Essex Management Centre
EMER	Engineering & Medicine Elastomers Research Centre
EMLC	Ethnic Minorities Law Centre
EMPC	Electrochemical & Materials Processing Centre
EMTERC	Emerging Technologies Research Centre
EnFlo	Environmental Flow Research Centre
engCETL	Engineering Centre Excellence Teaching & Learning
EPCC	Edinburgh Parallel Computing Centre
EPICentre	Electronic Publishing Innovation Centre
EPPI-Centre	Centre Evidence-informed Policy & Practice Education
EPRC	European Policies Research Centre
EPSAM	Research Institute Environment, Physical Sciences & Applied Mathematics
ERC	Education Research Centre
	Environmental Research Centre
ERI	Employment Research Institute
	English Research Institute
	Environmental Research Institute
	European Research Institute [Bath]
	European Research Institute [Birmingham]
ERIC	Education & Resources Improving Childhood Continence
ERINI	Economic Research Institute Northern Ireland
ERRC	Environmental Radioactivity Research Centre
ERRI	Energy & Resources Research Institute
ESC	Earth Science Centre
	Engineering Subject Centre
ESCalate	Subject Centre Education
ESDC	Electronic Systems Design Centre
	Electronics Systems Design Centre
eSI	e-Science Institute
ESNW	e-Science North West Centre
ESOP Centre	Employee Share Ownership Centre
ESRC	Engineering Structures Research Centre
	Environmental Sciences Research Centre
ESRI	Education & Social Research Institute
	Ergonomics & Safety Research Institute
	European Studies Research Institute
ESSC	Environmental Systems Science Centre
ETC	Energy Technology Centre
	Environmental Technology Centre
	Experimental Techniques Centre
ETCIC	Environmental Technologies Centre Industrial Collaboration
EurPolCom	Centre European Political Communications
EWC	English Wine Centre
	Europe World Centre
EWERC	European Work & Employment Research Centre
EXEC	Centre Experimental Economics
EXESESO	Exeter Centre Study Esotericism
ExPERT Centre	Centre Excellence Professional Development Through Use Relevant Technologies

F

FAB	Feline Advisory Bureau
	Flour Advisory Bureau Ltd
FAI	Fraser Allander Institute Research Scottish Economy
FBT	Fashion, Business & Technology Research Centre
FBUC	Fort Bovisand Underwater Centre Ltd
FCAS	Ferguson Centre African & Asian Studies
FCC	Fish Conservation Centre
FCSC	Facial Cosmetic Surgery Centre
FEC	Farm Energy Centre
FERC	Financial Econometrics Research Centre
FGRC	Football Governance Research Centre
FHI	Future Humanity Institute
FHRC	Flood Hazard Research Centre
FIRC	Fashion Industry Research Centre
FIRC	Food Innovation Research Centre
FLaG	Families, Life Course & Generations Research Centre
FLC	Foreign Language Centre
FLIC	Fluid Loading & Instrumentation Centre
FMC	Financial Markets Group Research Centre
FMGC	Facilities Management Graduate Centre
FMRIB	Oxford Centre Functional Magnetic Resonance Imaging Brain
FORC	Financial Options Research Centre
FORCE	Flight Operations Research Centre Excellence
FRC	Family Records Centre
	Fluids Research Centre
	Food Research Centre
French Centre	Centre Charles Péguy
FRPERC	Food Refrigeration & Process Engineering Research Centre
FRRC	Future Railway Research Centre
FSC	Field Studies Council Centres
FSCC	Food Supply Chain Centre
FTC	Food Technology Centre

G

GCCS	Glasgow Centre Child & Society
GCIC	Gifted Children's Information Centre
GCMRS	Glasgow Centre Medieval & Renaissance Studies
GCMS	Graduate Centre Medieval Studies
GCR	Glasgow Centre Retailing
GCSS	Gulf Centre Strategic Studies
GCSV	Glasgow Centre Study Violence
GCVA	Granada Centre Visual Anthropology
GEES	Geography, Earth & Environmental Sciences Subject Centre
GENCAS	Centre Research Gender Culture & Society
GENIE	Genetics Education - Networking Innovation & Excellence CETL
GEP	Leverhulme Centre Research Globalization & Economic Policy
GERC	Geotechnical Engineering Research Centre
GERI	General Engineering Research Institute
GES	CLIO Centre Globalisation, Education & Societies
GGIER	George Green Institute Electromagnetics Research
GHIL	German Historical Institute London
GIMOR	Graduate Institute Management & Organisation Research
GIPIS	Graduate Institute Political & International Studies
GIRC	Genetics & Insurance Research Centre

GIS	Centre Geo-Information Studies
GlycoTRIC	Glycobiology Training, Research & Infrastructure Centre
GMI	Greenwich Maritime Institute
GMTC	Glasgow Marine Technology Centre
GRC	Geoenvironmental Research Centre
GRR	Centre Gender & Religions Research
GSC	Grid Support Centre
GSRC	Gender & Sexuality Research Centre

H

HADC	Helen Arkell Dyslexia Centre
HAGRI	History & Governance Research Institute
HARC	Humanities & Arts Research Centre
HATII	Humanities Advanced Technology & Information Institute
HCA	Subject Centre History, Classics & Archaeology
HCCJ	Hallam Centre Community Justice
HCMD	Hull Centre Management Development
HCRC	Health Communication Research Centre
	Human Communication Research Centre
HECH	Centre Research & Scholarship History, Education & Cultural Heritage
HELM	Aston Business School Research Centre Higher Education Learning & Management
HELP	Higher Education Learning Partnerships CETL
HERC	Health Economics Research Centre
	Health Economics Resource Centre
	Higher Education Research Centre
HERI	Hull Environment Research Institute
HGSI	Hampstead Garden Suburb Institute
HHSRI	Health & Human Sciences Research Institute
HIFI	Hull International Fisheries Institute
HIREPL	Heythrop Institute Religion, Ethics & Public Life
HIS	Institute Human Sciences
HIS	Institute Human Sciences
HKI	Hamilton Kerr Institute
HLST	Hospitality, Leisure, Sport & Tourism Network
HMC	Henry Martyn Centre Study Mission & World Christianity
HNR	MRC Resource Centre Human Nutrition Research
HNRC	Human Nutrition Research Centre
HRC	Hispanic Research Centre
	Human Rights Centre
	Humanities Research Centre [Bangor]
	Humanities Research Centre [Sheffield Hallam]
	Humanities Research Centre [Warwick]
	Hydroenvironmental Research Centre
HRI	Hannah Research Institute
	Humanities Research Institute
HRLC	Human Rights Law Centre
HRMRC	Human Resources Management Research Centre
HRRC	Human Resource Research Centre
HRSJ	Human Rights & Social Justice Research Institute
HRSRI	Health & Rehabilitation Sciences Research Institute
HSC	Centre Health & Social Care Research
HSMC	Health Services Management Centre
HSPRC	Health & Social Policy Research Centre
HSRC	Health Services Research Centre
HSRI	Health Sciences Research Institute
HWRC	Healthcare Workforce Research Centre

I

i-DAT	Institute Digital Art & Technology
I-WHO	Institute Work, Health & Organisations
IAA	Institute Archaeology & Antiquity
IAC	Interface Analysis Centre
IACS	Institute Applied Cognitive Science
IAE	Institute Applied Ethics
	Institute Aviation and Environment
IAES	Institute Atmospheric & Environmental Science
IAgrM	Institute Agricultural Management
IAH	Institute Ageing & Health
	Institute Animal Health
	Institute Art History
IAHS	Institute Applied Health Sciences
IAIS	Institute Arab & Islamic Studies
IALS	Institute Applied Language Studies
IALS	Institute Advanced Legal Studies
IAMS	Institute Archaeo-Metallurgical Studies
	Institute Advanced Musical Studies
IAPS	Institute Asia-Pacific Studies
IARC	International Automotive Research Centre
	Impact Assessment Research Centre
	Illicit Antiquities Research Centre
IAS	Institute Access Studies
	Institute Advanced Studies Social & Management Sciences
	Institute Advanced Study
	Institute Alcohol Studies
	Institute Atmospheric Science
IASH	Institute Advanced Studies Humanities
IASR	Institute Applied Social Research
IAT	Institute Advanced Telecommunications
IATC	International Agriculture & Technology Centre
IATE	Institute Arts Therapy & Education
IBBS	Institute Biomedical & Biomolecular Sciences
IBC	International Biographical Centre
	Surrey Ion Beam Centre
IBCHN	Institute Brain Chemistry & Human Nutrition
IBE	Institute Biomedical Engineering
IBEC	Information & Biomedical Engineering Research Centre
IBLS	Institute Biomedical & Life Sciences
IBMM	Institute Bioelectronic & Molecular Microsystems
IBN	Institute Behavioural Neuroscience
IBS	Institute Biological Sciences
IBT	Institute Building Technology
ICA	Interdisciplinary Centre Astrobiology
ICA:UK	Institute Cultural Affairs
ICAn	Institute Cultural Analysis, Nottingham
ICAR	Information Centre about Asylum & Refugees UK
ICARIS	International Centre Advanced Research Identification Science
ICARUS	International Centre Archives & Records Management Research and User Studies
ICB	Institute Cell Biology
ICBD	International Centre Brewing & Distilling
ICBL	Institute Computer Based Learning
ICC	Institute Capitalising Creativity
	Institute Computational Cosmology
	Islamic Cultural Centre & London Central Mosque
ICC-CIB	ICC Counterfeiting Intelligence Bureau
ICC-FIB	ICC Financial Investigation Bureau
ICC-IMB	ICC International Maritime Bureau
ICCCR	International Centre Comparative Criminological Research

ICCFYR	Interdisciplinary Centre Child & Youth Focused Research	
ICCH	International Centre Circulatory Health	
ICCHA	International Centre Chinese Heritage & Archaeology	
ICCHS	International Centre Cultural & Heritage Studies	
ICCJ	Institute Criminology & Criminal Justice	
ICCMR	Interdisciplinary Centre Computer Music Research	
ICCR	Institute Child Care Research	
ICCS	Institute Communicating & Collaborative Systems	
ICCSR	International Centre Corporate Social Responsibility	
ICDC	International Centre Digital Content	
ICE	Institute Clinical Education	
	Institute Continuing Education	
	International Centre Environment	
ICEARS	International Centre East African Running Science	
ICEBOH	International Centre Evidence-Based Oral Health	
ICEH	International Centre Eye Health	
ICELS	International Centre English Language Studies	
ICFAR	International Centre Fine Art Research	
ICFB	International Centre Families Business	
ICG	Institute Cosmology & Gravitation	
ICGC	Institute Culture, Gender & City	
ICGWS	International Centre Gender & Women's Studies	
ICH	UCL Institute Child Health	
ICHEM	International Centre Higher Education Management	
ICI	Institute Chemistry Industry	
ICIS	International Centre Intercultural Studies	
ICIT	International Centre Island Technology	
ICJ	Institute Criminal Justice	
ICJS	Institute Criminal Justice Studies	
ICLS	Institute Classical Studies	
ICM	Institute Cellular Medicine	
ICMS	Institute Cell & Molecular Science	
	International Centre Mathematical Sciences	
ICMuS	International Centre Music Studies	
ICN	Institute Cognitive Neuroscience	
ICNE	International Centre Nursing Ethics	
ICoCo	Institute Community Cohesion	
ICON	Centre Industrial & Commercial Optoelectronics	
ICoVIS	International Centre Vibro-Impact Systems	
ICPL	International Centre Protected Landscapes	
ICPR	Institute Criminal Policy Research	
	International Centre Planning Research	
ICPS	Institute Colonial & Postcolonial Studies	
	International Centre Participation Studies	
	International Centre Prison Studies	
ICPSE	Industrial Centre Particle Science & Engineering	
ICR	Institute Cancer Research	
	Institute Clinical Research	
	Institute Computing Research	
	Institute Cultural Research	
ICRA	International Centre Research Accounting	
ICRC	Innovative Construction Research Centre	
ICRME	International Centre Research Music Education	
ICS	CLIO Centre International & Comparative Studies	
	Institute Cancer Studies	
	Institute Cell Signalling	
	Institute Clinical Sciences	
	Institute Commonwealth Studies	
	Institute Communications Studies	

	Institute Cornish Studies	
	Subject Centre Information & Computer Sciences [Loughborough]	
	Subject Centre Information & Computer Sciences [Ulster]	
ICSA	International Centre Security Analysis	
	Institute Computing Systems Architecture	
ICSHC	International Centre Sports History & Culture	
ICSRiM	Interdisciplinary Centre Scientific Research Music	
ICSTF	International Centre Shipping, Trade & Finance	
ICT	Institute Cancer Therapeutics	
ICTHR	International Centre Tourism & Hospitality Research	
ICTUR	International Centre Trade Union Rights	
ICV	International Centre Voice	
ICVA	International Centre Study Violence and Abuse	
IDC	International Development Centre	
IDEAL	Institute Diet, Exercise & Lifestyle	
IDPM	Institute Development Policy & Management	
IDS	Institute Development Studies	
IEB	Institute Evolutionary Biology	
IEC	Interfaith Education Centre	
IECIS	Institute European Cultural Identity Studies	
IECL	Institute European & Comparative Law	
IECS	Institute Estuarine & Coastal Studies	
IEDC	International Eating Disorders Centre	
IEE	Institute Energy & Environment	
IEEP	Institute European Environmental Policy	
IEH	Institute Environment & Health	
	Institute Environmental History	
IEL	Institute Employment Law	
	Institute European Law	
IeMRC	Innovative Electronics Manufacturing Research Centre	
IEPL	Institute European Public Law	
IEPR	Institute Education Policy Research	
IER	Warwick Institute Employment Research	
IERP	Institute Energy Research & Policy	
IES	Institute Employment Studies	
	Institute English Studies	
	Institute Environmental Sustainability	
IESD	Institute Energy & Sustainable Development	
IESR	Institute Environment & Sustainability Research	
IESSG	Institute Engineering Surveying & Space Geodesy	
IESSI	Integrated Earth System Sciences Institute	
IET	Institute Educational Technology	
IFA	Institute Finance & Accounting	
IfA	Institute Astronomy	
IFANC	Institute Food, Active Living & Nutrition	
IFB	Insurance Fraud Bureau	
IfC	Institute Citizenship	
IfCL	Institute Corporate Learning	
IfE	Institute Entrepreneurship	
IFI	International Football Institute	
IfIPA	Institute International Policy Analysis	
IfL	Institute Learning	
IfM	Institute Manufacturing	
IFPRC	International Fraud Prevention Research Centre	
IFR	Institute Food Research	
IFRU	Institut français	
IFS	Institute Fiscal Studies	
IFSBAC	Institute Folklore Studies Britain & Canada	
IFT	Institute Family Therapy	
IFTS	Institute Film & Television Studies	
IGER	BBSRC Institute Grassland & Environmental Research	
IGES	Institute Geography & Earth Sciences	
IGL	Institute Global Law	

© CBD Research Ltd · Beckenham · Kent BR3 5JS · Tel 020 8650 7745 · Fax 020 8650 0768 · E-mail cbd@cbdresearch.com · www.cbdresearch.com

IGPM	Institute Governance & Public Management		Institute Maritime Law
IGR	Institute Gravitational Research	IMLAB	Institute Medicine, Law & Bioethics
IGRS	Institute Germanic & Romance Studies	IMMPETUS	Institute Microstructural & Mechanical Process Engineering
IGS	Institute Geological Sciences		
	Institute German Studies	IMN	Institute Movement Neuroscience
	Institute Global Studies	IMP	Institute Microwaves & Photonics
	International Gender Studies Centre		International Marketing & Purchasing Centre
IGT	Institute Geophysics & Tectonics	IMPS	Institute Mathematical & Physical Sciences
	Institute Grinding Technology		Institute Molecular Plant Sciences
IHA	Institute Healthy Ageing	IMR	Institute Materials Research [Manchester]
IHCR	Institute Historical and Cultural Research		Institute Materials Research [Salford]
IHCS	Institute Health & Community Studies		Institute Musical Research
IHDRC	International Health Development Research Centre	IMRC	Cranfield Innovative Manufacturing Research Centre
IHG	Institute Human Genetics		Innovative Manufacturing Research Centre - Engineering IMRC
IHGH	Institute Human Genetics & Health		
IHHP	UCL Institute Human Health & Performance		Innovative Manufacturing Research Centre - Management IMRC
IHR	Institute Health Research [Bedfordshire]		
	Institute Health Research [Lancaster]		Innovative Manufacturing Research Centre (IMRC) Bioprocessing
	Institute Health Research [Staffordshire]		
	Institute Health Research [Swansea]	IMS	Institute Marine Sciences
	Institute Historical Research		Institute Mathematical Sciences
	MRC Institute Hearing Research - Nottingham Clinical Section		Institute Mathematics, Statistics & Actuarial Science
	MRC Institute Hearing Research - Scottish Section		Institute Medical Sciences
			Institute Medieval Studies [Lampeter]
			Institute Medieval Studies [Leeds]
	MRC Institute Hearing Research - Southampton Section		Institute Medieval Studies [Nottingham]
IHR2	Institute Hazard & Risk Research	IMSB	Institute Membrane & Systems Biology
IHRP	Institute Health Research & Policy	IMSCaR	Institute Medical & Social Care Research
IHS	Institute Health Sciences [City]	INAM	Institute Nursing & Midwifery [Brighton]
	Institute Health Sciences [Manchester]	INCED	International Centre Education Development
	Institute Health & Society	inIVA	Institute International Visual Arts
IHSC	Institute Health & Social Care	INLOGOV	Institute Local Government Studies
IHSCR	Institute Health & Social Care Research	INM	Institute Nuclear Medicine
IHSE	Institute Health Sciences Education	Innogen	Innogen - ESRC Centre Social & Economic Research Innovation Genomics [Edinburgh]
IHSL	Institute Historical Study Language		
IIB	Institute International Business		Innogen - ESRC Centre Social & Economic Research Innovation Genomics [Open]
IIBFS	International Institute Banking & Financial Services		
		INNOVATE	Innovate - Centre Creative Industries
IICB	Institute Integrative & Comparative Biology	INPP	Institute Neuro-Physiological Psychology
IICTD	International Institute Culture, Tourism & Development	InQbate	InQbate Centre Excellence Teaching & Learning Creativity
IIE	Institute Infrastructure & Environment	INR	Institute Nursing Research
	Institute Innovation & Enterprise	INS	Institute Name-Studies
IIEL	International Institute Education Leadership	INSAT	Institute Nanoscale Science & Technology
IIHD	Institute International Health and Development	INTRAC	International Non-Governmental Organisation Training & Research Centre
III	Institute Infection, Immunity & Inflammation	IoA	Institute Architecture
IIIS	Institute Integrated Information Systems		Institute Astronomy
IIR	Institute Industrial Research	IOA	Institute Aquaculture
IIRG	Institute International Research Glass	IoC	Institute Criminology
IIS	Institute Irish Studies [Belfast]	IOCS	Institute Orthodox Christian Studies
IIS	Institute Irish Studies [Liverpool]	IOCT	Institute Creative Technologies
IISH	UCL International Institute Society & Health	IoE	Institute Education [London]
IISTL	Institute International Shipping & Trade Law		Institute Education [Manchester Metropolitan]
IIT	Institute Information Technology		Institute Education [Stirling]
IITT	Institute IT Training	IOE	Institute Occupational Ergonomics
IJA	Institute Judicial Administration	IOEM	Institute Occupational & Environmental Medicine
IJS	Institute Jewish Studies		
IKD	Centre Innovation, Knowledge & Development	IoG	Institute Governance
		IOG	Institute Gerontology
ILAS	Institute Latin American Studies	IoIR	Manchester Institute Innovation Research
ILASH	Institute Language, Speech & Hearing	IOM	Institute Occupational Medicine
ILC-UK	International Longevity Centre-UK	IOMS	Institute Orthopaedics & Musculo-Skeletal Science
ILO	Institute Laryngology & Otology		
ILRT	Institute Learning & Research Technology	IoN	Institute Neurology
ILS	Institute Life Science		Institute Neuroscience
IMAR	Institute Motion Tracking & Research	IOO	Institute Optometry
IMBE	Institute Medical & Biological Engineering	IOP	Institute Photonics
IMCB	Institute Molecular & Cellular Biology	IOSH	Institution Occupational Safety & Health
IMEIS	Institute Middle Eastern & Islamic Studies	IoSR	Institute Sound Recording
IMES	Institute Middle Eastern Studies	IoT	Institute Technology
IML	Institute Medical Law	IP	Institute Philosophy

IPARC	International Pesticide Application Research Centre
IPCPH	Institute Primary Care and Public Health
IPE	Heriot-Watt Institute Petroleum Engineering
iPEG	Institute Political & Economic Governance
IPEP	Institute Psychology Elite Performance
IPH	Institute Public Health
IPI	Institute Pharmaceutical Innovation
	Intellectual Property Institute
IPLS	Institute Professional Legal Studies
IPM	Institute Popular Music
IPP	Institute Policy & Practice
IPPP	Institute Particle Physics Phenomenology
	Institute Philosophy & Public Policy
IPPR	Institute Public Policy Research
IPRC	Industrial Psychology Research Centre
	Integrated Protein Research Centre
IPS	Institute Psychological Sciences
IPSAR	Institute Public Sector Accounting Research
IPSE	Institute Particle Science & Engineering
	Institute Policy Studies Education
IPSET	Institute Pharmaceutical Sciences & Experimental Therapeutics
IPSS	Institute Psychotherapy & Social Studies
IPT	Industrial Process Tomography Centre
IPTME	Institute Polymer Technology & Materials Engineering
IRAC	Institute Research Applicable Computing
IRC	Inflammation Research Centre
	International Rights Centre
IRC Materials	Interdisciplinary Research Centre Materials Processing
IRCC	Institute Research Contemporary China
IRCEP	International Research Centre Experimental Physics
IRCH	Interdisciplinary Research Centre Health
IRDB	Institute Reproductive & Developmental Biology
IRES	Institute Research Environment & Sustainability
IRH	Institute Rural Health
IRI	Informatics Research Institute
IRIS	Informatics Research Institute
IRISS	Institute Research Social Sciences
IRLTHE	Institute Research Learning & Teaching Higher Education
IRM	Institute Biophysical & Clinical Research Human Movement
IRS	Institute Retail Studies
IRS	Institute Rural Sciences
IRS&TH	Institute Railway Studies & Transport History
ISABC	India & South Asia Business Centre
ISBE	Institute Small Business & Entrepreneurship
ISC	Innovation Studies Centre
	International Seismological Centre
ISCA	Institute Social & Cultural Anthropology
ISCB	Wellcome Trust Centre Stem Cell Research & Institute Stem Cell Biology
ISCFSI	Institute Study Children, Families & Social Issues
ISCPR	Institute Social, Cultural & Policy Research
ISCR	Institute Stem Cell Research
ISCS	Institute Study Christianity and Sexuality
ISE	Institute Science Education
	Institute Sport & Exercise
ISEEM	Institute Sustainability, Energy & Environmental Management
ISEP	Institute Spatial & Environmental Planning
ISER	Institute Social & Economic Research
ISET	Institute Study European Transformations
	Institute Sustainable Energy Technology
ISGC	International Shakespeare Globe Centre
ISHR	Institute Social & Health Research
iSLI	Institute System Level Integration

ISLP	Institute Sport & Leisure Policy
ISLS	Institute Study Language & Social Sciences
ISM	Institute Social Marketing
ISMB	Institute Structural & Molecular Biology
	Institute Structural Molecular Biology
ISN	CAA Institute Satellite Navigation
ISOS	Information Systems, Organisation & Society Research Centre
	Institute Study Slavery
ISPP	Institute Study Political Parties
ISR	Institute Social Research
ISRC	Information Systems Research Centre
	Intelligent Systems Research Centre
ISS	Institute Science & Society
ISSB Ltd	Iron & Steel Statistics Bureau
ISST	Institute Surface Science Technology
ISSTI	Institute Study Science, Technology & Innovation
ISTM	Institute Science & Technology Medicine
ISTR	Institute Safety Technology & Research
ISVR	Institute Sound & Vibration Research
ITC	International Teledemocracy Centre
ITEAS	Institute Transatlantic, European & American Studies
ITG	Institute Theoretical Geophysics
ITIA	Institute Theology, Imagination & Arts
ITRC	Intelligent Technologies Research Centre
ITRI	Informatics & Technology Research Institute
ITS	Institute Transport Studies
ITT	Institute Transport & Tourism
IUP	Institute Urban Planning
IVR	Institute Volunteering Research
IWE	Institute Water & Environment
IWP	Institute Work Psychology
IYS	Institute Youth Sport

J

JAI	John Adams Institute Accelerator Science [Oxford]
	John Adams Institute Accelerator Science [Royal Holloway, London]
JBI	Joanna Briggs Institute
JCMM	Joint Centre Mesoscale Meteorology
JCSHR	Joint Centre Scottish Housing Research
JCUD	Joint Centre Urban Design
JDI	UCL Jill Dando Institute Crime Science
JEB	Jewish Education Bureau
JETRO	JETRO London (Japan Trade Centre)
JETS	Institute Japanese-European Technology Studies
JHIAMe	Julian Hodge Institute Applied Macroeconomics
JIC	John Innes Centre
JIT	Jost Institute Tribotechnology
JRC	Japan Research Centre
JTAC	Joint Terrorism Analysis Centre
JTRC	Joining Technology Research Centre
JVC	Jorvik Viking Centre
JWNC	James Watt Nanofabrication Centre

K

KCC	Kurdish Cultural Centre Ltd
KCECL	Kent Centre European & Comparative Law
KCJC	Kent Criminal Justice Centre
KCMHR	King's Centre Military Health Research
KCRM	King's Centre Risk Management
KCWD	Keele Centre Wave Dynamics
KERC	Keele European Research Centre

© CBD Research Ltd · Beckenham · Kent BR3 5JS · Tel 020 8650 7745 · Fax 020 8650 0768 · E-mail cbd@cbdresearch.com · www.cbdresearch.com

KES	Centre Study Knowledge, Expertise & Science
KHREC	Keswick Hall Centre Research & Development Religious Education
KIASH	Kent Institute Advanced Studies Humanities
KIMHS	Kent Institute Medicine & Health Sciences
KIR	Kennedy Institute Rheumatology
KITE	York Institute Tropical Ecosystem Dynamics
KMi	Knowledge Media Institute
KNC	Kelvin Nanocharacterisation Centre
KNOSSOS	Centre Research Knowledge Science & Society
KRC	Khalili Research Centre Art & Material Culture Middle East
KTP Centres	Knowledge Transfer Partnerships Centres
KTTC	Kent Technology Transfer Centre

L

L-KIT	CLIO Centre Learning, Knowing & Interactive Technologies
LAB	Latin America Bureau
LAC	Latin American Centre
LAIC	Lesbian Archive and Information Centre
LBC	London Buddhist Centre
LBC-CJE	Leo Baeck College - Centre Jewish Education
LBIC	London BioScience Innovation Centre
LCACE	London Centre Arts & Cultural Enterprise
LCC	Leonard Cheshire Centre Conflict Recovery
LCCE	London Centre Clean Energy
LCEA	Lansdown Centre Electronic Arts
LCF	Lancaster Centre Forecasting
LCHES	Leverhulme Centre Human Evolutionary Studies
LCIL	Lauterpacht Centre International Law
LCLL	London Centre Leadership Learning
LCMC	Lancaster China Management Centre
LCN	London Centre Nanotechnology
LCPEM	London Centre Paediatric Endocrinology & Metabolism
LDC	Centre Language, Discourse & Communication
LDI	Leeds Dental Institute
LEC	Logistics Education Centre
	London Environment Centre
LERC	Lean Enterprise Research Centre
LERI	London East Research Institute
LeSC	London e-Science Centre
LFC	London Food Centre
LGC	Local Government Centre
LGCC	London Geotechnical Centrifuge Centre
LHC	Languages & Humanities Centre
	London Hazards Centre
LHRI	Leeds Humanities Research Institute
LI	Labanotation Institute
LIBC	Liverpool Institute Biocomplexity
LIGHT	Leeds Institute Genetics, Health & Therapeutics
LILL	Institute Lifelong Learning [Leicester]
LIMCRC	Loughborough Innovative Manufacturing & Construction Research Centre
LIMM	Leeds Institute Molecular Medicine
LINK	Link Centre Deafened People
LIPA	Liverpool Institute Performing Arts
LIPM	Lister Institute Preventive Medicine
LIRANS	Luton Institute Research Applied Natural Sciences
LIVE	LIVE Centre Excellence Lifelong & Independent Veterinary Education
LIWC	London Irish Women's Centre
LLAS	Subject Centre Languages, Linguistics & Area Studies
LLI	Lifelong Learning Institute

LLRC	Language & Literacy Research Centre
LMCC	Loughborough Materials Characterisation Centre
LMEI	London Middle East Institute
LMPC	London Metropolitan Polymer Centre
LOSEC	Laser & Optical Systems Engineering Centre
LPRC	Laser Processing Research Centre
LR UTC	Lloyd's Register University Technology Centre
LRC	Logistics Research Centre
LRI	Cancer Research UK London Research Institute
	Legal Research Institute
LSCS	Longitudinal Studies Centre - Scotland
LSRI	Learning Sciences Research Institute
LSSI	Leeds Social Sciences Institute
LTA	Learning Through Action Centre
LTI	Learning & Teaching Institute
	Lincoln Theological Institute Study Religion & Society
LTRI	Learning Technology Research Institute
LUBC	Banking Centre
LUC	London Underwriting Centre
LUCAS	Leeds University Centre African Studies
	Liverpool University Centre Archive Studies
LUICS	Liverpool University Institute Cancer Studies

M

M+Di	Methods & Data Institute
MaMS	Management & Management Sciences Research Institute
MARC	Manufacturing Architecture Research Centre
MARPIC	Marine Pollution Information Centre
MARS CIC	Materials Analysis and Research Services - Centre Industrial Collaboration
MASC	European Centre Study Migration & Social Care
MaSSS	Centre Materials, Surfaces & Structural Systems
MATAR	Materials & Arts Research Centre
MATCH	Multidisciplinary Assessment Technology Centre Healthcare
MBCMS	Michael Barber Centre Mass Spectrometry
MBERC	Marine Biology & Ecology Research Centre
MC	Moffat Centre Travel & Tourism Business Development
MC2	Manchester Centre Music Culture
MCAS	Menzies Centre Australian Studies
MCASS	Manchester Centre Anglo-Saxon Studies
MCI	Montessori Centre International
MCIS	Mountbatten Centre International Studies
MCISB	Manchester Centre Integrative Systems Biology
MCMR	Manchester Centre Magnetic Resonance
MCND	Manchester Centre Nonlinear Dynamics
MCPT	Manchester Centre Public Theology
MCRC	Manchester Cancer Research Centre
MCRH	Manchester Centre Regional History
MEC	Manufacturing Engineering Centre
	Mathematics Education Centre
MECACS	Institute Middle East, Central Asia & Caucasus Studies
MEDC	Management and Enterprise Development Centre
MEDEV	Subject Centre Medicine, Dentistry & Veterinary Medicine
MedIC	Centre Medical Image Computing
MERC	Mathematics Education Research Centre
MERI	Manchester European Research Institute
	Materials & Engineering Research Institute
MeSC	Midlands e-Science Centre
MGC	Mouse Genome Centre

MGCI	Museums, Galleries & Collections Institute
MHKC	Mental Health Knowledge Centre
MHSC	Maritime Historical Studies Centre
MIB	Manchester Interdisciplinary Biocentre
	Motor Insurers Bureau
MIC	Measurement and Instrumentation Centre
	Microelectronics Industrial Centre
	Multi-Imaging Centre
	Wolfson Molecular Imaging Centre
MiMeG	Mixed Media Grid [Research Centre]
MIMS	Manchester Institute Mathematical Sciences
MINT@K	Mobile Information & Network Technologies Research Centre
MIRC	Modern Interiors Research Centre
MIRIAD	Manchester Institute Research & Innovation Art & Design
MISEC	MIcroSystems Engineering Centre
MISOC	ESRC Research Centre Micro-Social Change
MMC	Molecular Materials Centre
	Mortimer Market Centre
MNC	Multidisciplinary Nanotechnology Centre
MOAC	Molecular Organisation & Assembly Cells Doctoral Training Centre
Mobile VCE	Virtual Centre Excellence Mobile Personal Communications
MoSeS	Modelling & Simulation e-Social Science [Research Centre]
MPC	Materials Performance Centre
MPRI	Medical Polymers Research Institute
MRC	Management Research Centre [London]
	Management Research Centre [Wolverhampton]
	Materials Research Centre
	Mathematics Research Centre [Queen Mary, London]
	Mathematics Research Centre [Warwick]
	Mechatronics Research Centre
	Medieval Research Centre
	Modelling Research Centre
	Music Research Centre
MRC CC	Medical Research Council Collaborative Centre
MRI	Moredun Research Institute
MRRC	Magnetic Resonance Research Centre
MSC	Management Studies Centre
MSCRC	Mobile & Satellite Communications Research Centre
MSEC	Manchester Science Enterprise Centre
MSERC	Manufacturing Science & Engineering Research Centre
MSOR Network	Mathematics, Statistics & Operational Research Subject Centre
MSRC	Mary Seacole Research Centre
	Materials Science Research Centre
	Multiple Sclerosis Resource Centre
MTI	Music, Technology & Innovation Research Centre
MTRC	Media Technology Research Centre
MUCJS	Centre Jewish Studies

N

NAC	National Agricultural Centre
NACPDE	National Advice Centre Postgraduate Dental Education
NaCTeM	National Centre Text Mining
NAMTEC	National Metals Technology Centre
NaREC	New & Renewable Energy Centre
NASC	Nottingham Arabidopsis Stock Centre
NATCECT	National Centre English Cultural Tradition
NBC	National Badminton Centre
NBPC	National Birds Prey Centre

NC3Rs	National Centre Replacement, Refinement & Reduction Animals Research
NCAS	National Centre Atmospheric Science
NCAS	National Centre Autism Studies
NCB	National Children's Bureau
NCBE	National Centre Biotechnology Education
NCC	National Children's Centre
	National Computing Centre
NCCA	National Centre Computer Animation
NCCAC	National Collaborating Centre Acute Care
NCCC	National Collaborating Centre Cancer
NCCCC	National Collaborating Centre Chronic Conditions
NCCHTA	National Coordinating Centre Health Technology Assessment
NCCJ	Newport Centre Criminal & Community Justice
NCCMH	National Collaborating Centre Mental Health
NCCNSC	National Collaborating Centre Nursing & Supportive Care
NCCPC	National Collaborating Centre Primary Care
NCCWCH	National Collaborating Centre Women and Children's Health
NCEC	National Chemical Emergency Centre
NCeSS	ESRC National Centre e-Social Science
NCET	National Centre Environmental Toxicology
NCFS	Newcastle Centre Family Studies
NCFSC	National Community Fire Safety Centre
NCfW	National Centre Writing
NCG	Nottingham Centre Geomechanics
NCHM	Northern Centre History Medicine
NCIHD	Nuffield Centre International Health & Development
NCLL	National Centre Language and Literacy
NCMH	National Centre Macromolecular Hydrodynamics
NCPM	National Centre Project Management
NCPP	National Centre Public Policy
NCPVD	Nanotechnology Centre PVD Research
NCQF	Nomura Centre Quantitative Finance
NCRC	Nationwide Children's Research Centre
NCRCL	National Centre Research Children's Literature
NCRM	ESRC National Centre Research Methods
NCSR	National Centre Social Research
NCT	National Centre Tribology
NCTD	National Centre Tactile Diagrams
NCTEPO	National Centre Training & Education Prosthetics & Orthotics
NCWBLP	National Centre Work Based Learning Partnerships
NEC	National Energy Centre
	National Exhibition Centre
NEEHI	North East England History Institute
NERC	National Eye Research Centre
NEReSC	North East Regional e-Science Centre
NeSC	National e-Science Centre, Glasgow
NESCI	North East England Stem Cell Institute
NETREC	Northumbrian Environmental Training & Research Centre
NewRail	Newcastle Centre Railway Research
NFEC	Nottingham Fuel & Energy Centre
NFHC	National Fishing Heritage Centre
NFLC	National Flying Laboratory Centre
NFPI	National Family & Parenting Institute
NHC	National Hyperbaric Centre
NHLI	National Heart & Lung Institute
NHSCRC	Nursing, Health & Social Care Research Centre
NIASSH	Newcastle Institute Arts, Social Sciences & Humanities
NIBEC	Northern Ireland Bio-Engineering Centre
NIBSC	National Institute Biological Standards & Control

NICAM	Northern Ireland Centre Advanced Materials
NICE	National Institute Conductive Education
	National Institute Health & Clinical Excellence
NICEC	National Institute Careers Education & Counselling
NICENT	Northern Ireland Centre Entrepreneurship
NICERT	Northern Ireland Centre Energy Research & Technology
NICeST	National Information Centre Speech-Language Therapy
NICHE	Northern Ireland Centre Food & Health
NICHI	Northern Ireland Centre Health Informatics
NICILT	Northern Ireland Centre Information Language Teaching & Research
NICPPET	Northern Ireland Centre Postgraduate Pharmaceutical Education
NICR	Northern Institute Cancer Research
NICTT	Northern Ireland Centre Trauma & Transformation
NIECI	National Institute Excellence Creative Industries
NIEeS	National Institute Environmental eScience
NIESR	National Institute Economic & Social Research
NifER	Nottingham Institute English Research
NIMR	National Institute Medical Research
NIMRC	Nottingham Innovative Manufacturing Research Centre
NIREES	Nottingham Institute Russian & East European Studies
NIRVC	Nottingham Institute Research Visual Culture
NISRC	Northern Ireland Semiconductor Research Centre
NITC	Northern Ireland Technology Centre
NMLC	National Medical Laser Centre
NMMC	Nottingham Mining & Mineral Centre
NMRC	National Monuments Record Centre
NNDTC	National Non-Destructive Testing Centre
NNNC	Nottingham Nanotechnology & Nanoscience Centre
NOC	National Oceanography Centre
NPC	Nottingham Policy Centre
NPCRDC	National Primary Care Research & Development Centre
NPSC	National Printing Skills Centre
NPSC	Nordic Policy Studies Centre
NRC	Northern Refugee Centre
NRCD	National Resource Centre Dance
NRDCALN	National Research & Development Centre Adult Literacy & Numeracy
NREC	National Rural Enterprise Centre
NRI	Natural Resources Institute
	Neuroscience Research Institute
NRMI	Natural Resources Management Institute
NRMTC	Nordoff-Robbins Music Therapy Centre
NRP	National Centre Vocational Qualifications
NSC	National Space Centre
	National Stone Centre
	Northern Studies Centre
	Norwegian Study Centre
NSIC	National Spinal Injuries Centre
NSLC	National Science Learning Centre
NSRI	National Soil Resources Institute
NTEC	Nottingham Transportation Engineering Centre
NWC	National Wildflower Centre
NWCLD	North West Centre Learning & Development Ltd
NWCRF	North West Cancer Research Fund Institute
NWFC	North West Food Centre

O

OCAMAC	Oxford Centre Advanced Materials & Composites
OCBS	Oxford Centre Buddhist Studies
OCC	Osteopathic Centre Children
OCDEM	Oxford Centre Diabetes, Endocrinology & Metabolism
OCE	Oxford Centre Enablement
OCEB	Oxford Centre Environmental Biotechnology
OCHS	Oxford Centre Hindu Studies
OCIAM	Oxford Centre Industrial & Applied Mathematics
OCIS	Oxford Centre Islamic Studies
OCMA	Oxford Centre Maritime Archaeology
OCMS	Oxford Centre Mission Studies
	Oxford Centre Molecular Sciences
OCPR	Oxford Centre Population Research
OCSLD	Oxford Centre Staff & Learning Development
OCW	Organic Centre Wales
OCWR	Oxford Centre Water Research
ODAC	Oil Depletion Analysis Centre
ODI	Overseas Development Institute
OeRC	Oxford e-Research Centre
OFRC	Oxford Financial Research Centre
OGC	Oil & Gas Centre
OIA	Oxford Institute Ageing
OIES	Oxford Institute Energy Studies
OII	Oxford Internet Institute
OIPRC	Oxford Intellectual Property Research Centre
OISD	Oxford Institute Sustainable Development
OLI	Oxford Learning Institute
OMI	Olympic Medical Institute
OMIC	Organic Materials Innovation Centre
OMII	Open Middleware Infrastructure Institute UK
OMRC	Operations Management Research Centre
ORC	Optoelectronics Research Centre
OSC	Organic Semiconductor Centre
OSR	Orkney Seal Rescue Centre
OUCE	Oxford University Centre Environment
OUCEM	Open University Centre Education Medicine
OWC	One World Centre
OxCHEPS	Oxford Centre Higher Education Policy Studies
OXCSOM	Oxford Centre Science Mind
OXIFER	Oxford Institute Employee Relations
OXIIM	Oxford Institute Information Management
OXIRM	Oxford Institute Retail Management

P

PAC	Post-Adoption Centre
PAPRI	PAPRI: Pension & Population Research Institute
PARC	Photography & Archive Research Centre
PARC	Parallelism, Algorithms & Architectures Research Centre
PBPL	Practice-based Professional Learning CETL
PCRP	Pinter Centre Research Performance
PCT	Puppet Centre Trust
PCTC	Primary Care Training Centre Ltd
PDC	Central London Professional Development Centre
PDIC	Pig Disease Information Centre
PDR	National Centre Product Design & Development Research
PEAK	Centre Professional Ethics
PEALS	Policy, Ethics & Life Sciences Research Centre
PEI	Private Equity Institute
PEM	Centre Physical Electronics & Materials

PEQT	Centre Physical Electronics & Quantum Technology
PERC	Paisley Enterprise Research Centre
	PharmacoEconomics Research Centre
	Political Economy Research Centre
	Private Equity & Venture Capital Research Centre
PIC	Photonics Innovation Centre
PICR	Paterson Institute Cancer Research
PILS	Personalised Integrated Learning Support CETL
PISC	Plymouth International Studies Centre
PKRC	Product & Knowledge Research Centre
Polymer IRC	Interdisciplinary Research Centre Polymer Science & Technology
POWIC/SANE	Prince Wales International Centre Research Schizophrenia & Depression
PPRC	Polymer Processing Research Centre
PQSW	Centre Post Qualifying Social Work
PRI	Policy Research Institute [Leeds Metropolitan]
	Policy Research Institute [Wolverhampton]
PRISE	Centre Process & Information Systems Engineering
PRSI	Pedagogic Research & Scholarship Institute
PS	Centre Publishing Studies
PSC	Polymer Science Centre
PSI	Policy Studies Institute
	Photon Science Institute
PSM	Centre Public Services Management (Nottingham)
PSSRI	Planetary & Space Sciences Research Institute
PTC	Poetry Translation Centre
	Performance Translation Centre
	Publishing Training Centre at Book House
PTMC	Centre Power Transmission & Motion Control
PTRC	Psychological Therapies Research Centre
PVRC	Powertrain & Vehicle Research Centre

Q

QEF Mobility Centre	Queen Elizabeth's Foundation Mobility Centre
QIC	Quaker International Centre
QIE	Quality Education Centre
Quercus	Northern Ireland Centre Biodiversity & Conservation Biology
QUESTOR	Queen's University Environmental Science & Technology Research Centre
QUILL Centre	Queen's University Ionic Liquid Laboratories

R

RAB	Radio Advertising Bureau
RAC	Richard Attenborough Centre Disability & Arts
RAI	Rothermere American Institute
RCAS	Research Centre Applied Sciences
	Research Centre American Studies
RCB	Robertson Centre Biostatistics
RCC	Robert Clark Centre Technological Education
RCEAL	Research Centre English & Applied Linguistics
RCEAP	Research Centre Evolutionary Anthropology & Palaeoecology
RCIM	Research Centre Illuminated Manuscripts
RCLS	Research Centre Learning Society
RCMI	Regional Centre Manufacturing Industry
RCNDE	Research Centre Non-destructive Evaluation
RCSS	Research Centre Social Sciences
RCTE	Research Centre Therapeutic Education
RCTSH	Research Centre Transcultural Studies Health

RCVTM	Research Centre Vocational Training Musicians
ReSC	Reading e-Science Centre
ResCen	Centre Research Creation Performing Arts
ResCEW	Research Centre Evacuee & War Child Studies
RHI	Robert Hill Institute
RI	Roslin Institute
	Risk Institute
RIBM	Research Institute Business & Management
RICA	Ricability (Research Institute Consumer Affairs)
RICE	Research Institute Care Elderly
RICH	Centre Research Indoor Climate & Health
RIEL	Research Institute Enhancing Learning
RIFlex	Research Institute Flexible Materials
RIHS	Research Institute Healthcare Science
RIHSC	Research Institute Health & Social Change
RIILP	Research Institute Information & Language Processing
RIISS	Research Institute Irish and Scottish Studies
RIMAD	Research Institute Media, Art & Design
RISE	Research Institute Software Evolution
RISES	Research Institute Sport & Exercise Sciences
RIST	Research Institute Systematic Theology
RLWI	Reta Lila Weston Institute Neurological Studies
Robens CHE	Robens Centre Health Ergonomics
Robens COHS	Robens Centre Occupational Health & Safety
Robens CPEH	Robens Centre Public & Environmental Health
RRC	Refugee Research Centre
	Rehabilitation Resource Centre
RRI	Rowett Research Institute
RRUK	Rail Research UK
RSC	Refugee Studies Centre
RSPC	Regional Sports Performance Centre
RSRC	Roehampton Social Research Centre
RSS Centre	Royal Statistical Society Centre Statistical Education
RSSC	Respiratory Support & Sleep Centre
RW	Raymond Williams Centre Recovery Research

S

S3RI	Southampton Statistical Sciences Research Institute
SAILLS	Saint Andrews University Institute Language & Linguistic Studies
Salisbury Centre	Salisbury Centre
SAMIA	Sir Arthur Marshall Institute Aeronautics
SARC	Sonic Arts Research Centre
SASSC	Saint Andrews Scottish Studies Centre
SATRA	SATRA Technology Centre
SAVIC	Scientific Analysis & Visualisation Centre
SBB	Small Business Bureau Ltd
SBC	South Bank Centre
SBI	Newcastle Centre Social & Business Informatics
SBRC	Small Business Research Centre
SBTC	Scottish Biotechnology Training Centre
SC PRS	Subject Centre Philosophical & Religious Studies
SCAA	Sheffield Centre Aegean Archaeology
SCAMMD	Sheffield Centre Advanced Magnetic Materials & Devices
SCC	Smart Card Centre
SCCJR	Scottish Centre Crime & Justice Research
SCCMI	Scottish Centre Children with Motor Impairments
SCCS	Scottish Centre Carbon Storage
	Scarborough Centre Coastal Studies
SCDC	Scottish Community Development Centre

 © CBD Research Ltd · Beckenham · Kent BR3 5JS · Tel 020 8650 7745 · Fax 020 8650 0768 · E-mail cbd@cbdresearch.com · www.cbdresearch.com

SCDR	Strathclyde Centre Disability Research	SFI	Social Futures Institute
SCEEBR	Scottish Centre Enterprise & Ethnic Business Research	SFIRC	Scottish Fish Immunology Research Centre
		SI	Sussex Institute
SCEET	Strathclyde Centre European Economies Transition	SIBLE	Sheffield Institute Biotechnological Law & Ethics
SCEME	Stirling Centre Economic Methodology	SIDR	Strathclyde Institute Drug Research
SCEMFA	Slade Centre Electronic Media Fine Art	SIE	Scottish Institute Enterprise
SCEPTrE	Surrey Centre Excellence Professional Training & Education	SIESWE	Scottish Institute Excellence Social Work Education
SCFE	Scottish Centre Financial Education	SIHR	Scottish Institute Human Relations
SCFM	Scottish Centre Facilities Management	SILC	School Improvement & Leadership Centre
SCG	Sustainability Centre Glasgow	SIMBIOS	Scottish Informatics, Mathematics, Biology & Statistics Centre
SCHIN	Sowerby Centre Health Informatics		
SCHR	Scottish Centre Himalayan Research	SINRS	Scottish Institute Northern Renaissance Studies
SciCOMM	Centre Science Communication		
SCIDR	Sheffield Centre International Drylands Research	SIPBS	Strathclyde Institute Pharmacy & Biomedical Sciences
SCIE	Social Care Institute Excellence	SIRC	Seafarers International Research Centre
SCIES	Surrey Centre International Economic Studies		Sport Industry Research Centre
SCIGS	Strathclyde Centre Gender Studies	SIRCC	Scottish Institute Residential Child Care
SCIL	Scottish Centre International Law	SIRIF	Scottish Institute Research Investment & Finance
SCILT	Scottish Centre Information Language Teaching		
		SISA	Sheffield Institute Studies Ageing
SCJS	Scottish Centre Journalism Studies	SISTech	Scottish Institute Sustainable Technology
SCLC	Scottish Child Law Centre	SITI	Scottish International Tourism Industries Research Centre
SCMH	Sainsbury Centre Mental Health		
SCMR	Sussex Centre Migration Research	SIWT	Scottish Institute Wood Technology
SCNMCR	Salford Centre Nursing, Midwifery & Collaborative Research	SKILL	Skill: National Bureau Students with Disabilities
SCOP	Stirling Centre Poetry	SKOPE	ESRC Centre Skills, Knowledge & Organisational Performance
SCoPiC	Social Contexts Pathways Crime Centre		
SCOSH	Scottish Centre Occupational Safety & Health	SLTRI	Suzy Lamplugh Trust Research Institute
SCoT	Scottish Centre Tourism	SMC	Sunley Management Centre
ScotCen	Scottish Centre Social Research	SMI	Scottish Manufacturing Institute
Scotdec	Scottish Development Education Centre	SMIC	Scottish Music Information Centre Ltd
SCPM	Silwood Centre Pest Management	SMIRC	Structural Materials & Integrity Research Centre
SCPP	Scottish Centre Public Policy		
SCPS	Scottish Centre Pollen Studies	SMPC	Scottish Mask & Puppet Centre
SCR	Scottish Centre Regeneration	SMRC	Screen Media Research Centre
SCRAADA	Sussex Centre Research Alcohol, Alcoholism & Drug Addiction	SMRI	Stirling Media Research Institute
		SNW & NCBS	Sustainability Northwest & National Centre Business & Sustainability
SCRC	Supply Chain Research Centre		
SCRI	Salford Centre Research & Innovation Built & Human Environment	SoCaM	International Centre System-on-Chip & Advanced Microwireless Integration
	Scottish Crop Research Institute	SOECIC	South England Cochlear Implant Centre
	Sustainable Cities Research Institute	SOLAR	Centre Social & Organisational Learning as Action Research
SCRIB	Steel Can Recycling Information Bureau		
SCROLLA	Scottish Centre Research On-line Learning & Assessment	SOLSTICE	SOLSTICE Centre
		SOMC	Scottish Offshore Materials Centre
SCRSJ	Scottish Centre Research Social Justice	SOMS	Centre Self-Organising Molecular Systems
SCSCD	Scottish Centre Sustainable Community Development	SPARC	Sport Performance Assessment & Rehabilitation Centre
SCSS	Stirling Centre Scottish Studies	SPDC	Scottish Polymer Development Centre
SCSSA	Scottish Centre Studies School Administration	SPERI	Social Psychology European Research Institute
SCSWR	Salford Centre Social Work Research		
SCVA	Sainsbury Centre Visual Arts	SpiNSN	Centre Signal Processing Neuroimaging & Systems Neuroscience
SCWBL	Scottish Centre Work Based Learning		
SCWS	Scottish Centre War Studies	SPLINT	Spatial Literacy Teaching CETL
SDHI	Social Dimensions Health Institute	SPRC	Social Policy Research Centre
SDRC	Sustainable Design Research Centre	SPRI	Scott Polar Research Institute
	Sustainable Development Research Centre		Social & Policy Research Institute
	Sustainable Design Research Centre	SRC	Sociology Research Centre
SEA	Social & Environmental Art Research Centre		Skin Research Centre
SEC	Skye Environmental Centre Ltd	SRI	Sustainability Research Institute
SEEB	Social Economy Evaluation Bureau	SRMC	Social Research Methodology Centre
SEEC	Surrey Energy Economics Centre	SSAHRI	Social Sciences, Arts & Humanities Research Institute
SEI	Sussex European Institute		
	Social Enterprise Institute	SSC	Surrey Space Centre
SEI-Y	Stockholm Environment Institute at York		Statistical Services Centre
SEIC	Systems Engineering Innovation Centre		Scottish Sensory Centre
SERC	Sustainable Environment Research Centre		Science Studies Centre
	Sports & Exercise Research Centre	SSERC	Scottish Schools Equipment Research Centre
Sesame	Sesame Institute UK	SSI	Security Studies Institute
SeSC	Southampton e-Science Centre	SSLRC	Soil Survey & Land Research Centre

SSRC	Surface Science Research Centre
	Ship Stability Research Centre
	Speech Science Research Centre
	Safety Systems Research Centre
	Surrey Sleep Research Centre
	Space Structures Research Centre
StACAM	Saint Andrews Centre Advanced Materials
STC	Social Theory Centre
STICERD	Suntory & Toyota International Centres Economics & Related Disciplines
STORM	Statistics, Operational Research & Mathematics Research Centre
STRC	Sustainable Technology Research Centre
	Sustainable Transport Research Centre
STRI	Science & Technology Research Institute
SUERC	Scottish Universities Environmental Research Centre
SUMAC	Sheffield University Metals Advisory Centre
SURF	Centre Sustainable Urban & Regional Futures
SURGE	Applied Research Centre Sustainable Regeneration
SUWIC	Sheffield University Waste Incineration Centre
SVI	Sheffield Vascular Institute
SWELL	Centre Study Safety & Well-Being
SWIMMER	Institute Sustainable Water, Integrated Management & Ecosystem Research
SWRC	Social Work Research Centre
SWSC	Scottish Water Ski Centre

T

TBIC	Basement Information Centre
TCC	Textile Conservation Centre
TCCR	Tenovus Centre Cancer Research
TCGA	Centre Genetic Anthropology
TCMR	Trafford Centre Graduate Medical Education & Research
TCNM	Teesside Centre Nanotechnology & Microfabrication
TCRS	Centre Rehabilitation Sciences
TCS Centre	Theory, Culture and Society Centre
Technium CAST	Centre Advanced Software Technology
TEIC	Technology & Engineering Innovation Centre
TEMPUS	Teaching Excellence & Mentoring Postgraduates using Statistics
TFC	Thin Film Centre
TFMRC	Thermo-Fluid Mechanics Research Centre
TFS UTC	Thermo-Fluid Systems University Technology Centre
Thatcham MIRRC	Motor Insurance Repair Research Centre
The Grubb	Grubb Institute Behavioural Studies
TIC	Technology Innovation Centre
TICR	Tayside Institute Cardiovascular Research
TIRI	Information Research Institute
TJI	Transitional Justice Institute
TLA	Centre Teaching, Learning & Assessment
TLRC	Teacher & Leadership Research Centre
TLTC	Teaching & Learning Technology Centre
TMC	Teesside Manufacturing Centre
TNS	Centre Transnational Studies
TORT Centre	Tayside Orthopaedic & Rehabilitation Technology Centre
TPC	Psychotherapy Centre
TRaC	Transport Research & Consultancy
TRAC	Transport & Road Assessment Centre
TrAIN	Transnational Art, Identity & Nation Research Centre
TRAM	Centre Translation Research & Multilingualism
TRC	Thoroughbred Rehabilitation Centre
TRI	University Nottingham Tax Research Institute
	Thrombosis Research Institute

Tri	Transport Research Institute
TRi-NIC	Transport Research Institute - Northern Ireland Centre
TTC	Therapeutics & Toxicology Centre
TTEC	Transport Technology Ergonomics Centre
TTRI	Christel DeHaan Tourism & Travel Research Institute
TYN	Tyndall Centre Climate Change Research

U

UCCE	UNIVERSITY CENTRES CRICKETING EXCELLENCE Scheme
UCCER	UNESCO Centre Comparative Education Research
UCLIC	UCL Interaction Centre
UCLse	UCL Centre Systems Engineering
UK ATC	United Kingdom Astronomy Technology Centre
UK CEED	United Kingdom Centre Economic & Environmental Development
UK NARIC	National Recognition Information Centre United Kingdom
UK NEC	United Kingdom National Europass Centre
UKCEM	United Kingdom Centre Events Management
UKCLE	United Kingdom Centre Legal Education
UKCTE	United Kingdom Centre Tissue Engineering [Liverpool]
	United Kingdom Centre Tissue Engineering [Manchester]
UKSEC	United Kingdom Science Enterprise Centres
UKSI	United Kingdom Sports Institute
UKWCT	United Kingdom Wolf Centre
ULCTS	University London Centre Transport Studies
ULSC	ESRC United Kingdom Longitudinal Studies Centre
UMARI	University Manchester Aerospace Research Institute
UMI	UniS Materials Institute
UNIEI	University Nottingham Institute Enterprise and Innovation
UNIMAT	University Nottingham Institute Materials Technology
URI	Urban Renaissance Institute
UWTC	Urban Water Technology Centre

V

VEC	Virtual Engineering Centre
VERTIC	Verification Research, Training & Information Centre
VICTAR	Visual Impairment Centre Teaching & Research
VIDe	Visual & Information Design Research Centre
VOTER	SRIF Centre Virtual Organisation Technology Enabling Research
VRC	VR Centre Built Environment
VRC	Visual Research Centre
VSRC	Voluntary Sector Research Centre
	Vehicle Safety Research Centre
VTRC	Vehicle Technology Research Centre
VUTC	Vibration University Technology Centre

W

WAC	ARP Women's Alcohol Centre
WAERC	Wetland Archaeology & Environments Research Centre

WBC	Wales Biomass Centre
WBIC	Wolfson Brain Imaging Centre
WBL	Centre Research Wider Benefits Learning
WBMS	World Bureau Metal Statistics
WCBA	Wales Centre Behaviour Analysis
WCEBC	Wales Centre Evidence Based Care
WCH	Wales Centre Health
WCIA	Welsh Centre International Affairs
WCLD	Welsh Centre Learning Disabilities
WCMC	World Conservation Monitoring Centre
WCMP	Wellcome Centre Molecular Parasitology
	Wolfson Centre Materials Processing
WCPC	Welsh Centre Printing & Coating
WCPPE	Welsh Centre Post-Graduate Pharmaceutical Education
WCSSS	Warwick Centre Study Sport Society
WCTR	Welsh Centre Tourism Research
WDCGC	World Data Centre Glaciology, Cambridge
WEC	World Education Centre
WEDC	Water Engineering & Development Centre
WEI	Welsh Enterprise Institute
WELMERC	Welsh Economy Labour Market Evaluation & Research Centre
WERC	Work & Employment Research Centre
	Welding Engineering Research Centre
WeSC	Welsh e-Science Centre
WFRI	Warwick Finance Research Institute
WGC	Welsh Governance Centre
WHC	Welsh Hawking Centre
WHI	Welsh Hearing Institute
WHRI	William Harvey Research Institute
	Sir Geraint Evans Wales Heart Research Institute
WHTC	Wolfson Heat Treatment Centre
WIBR	Wolfson Institute Biomedical Research
WICA	Welsh Institute Competitive Advantage
WIE	Warwick Institute Education
	Westminster Institute Education
WIHRD	Wessex Institute Health Research & Development
WIMAT	Welsh Institute Minimal Access Therapy
WIMRC	Warwick Innovative Manufacturing Research Centre
WIPM	Wolfson Institute Preventive Medicine
WIRC	Wales Institute Research Co-operatives
WIRED	Welsh Institute Research Economics & Development
WISCA	Welsh Institute Social and Cultural Affairs
WISE	Wilberforce Institute Study Slavery & Emancipation

WIT	Wessex Institute Technology
WJCB	World Jersey Cattle Bureau
WLE Centre	Centre Excellence Work-Based Learning Education Professionals
WLIC	William Lee Innovation Centre
WLTC	Welsh Language Teaching Centre
WMCC	Wolfson Materials & Catalysis Centre
WMI	Warwick Mathematics Institute
	Welsh Music Institute
WMIC	Welsh Music Information Centre
WML	Centre Working Memory & Learning
WRC	Worm Research Centre
WRC	Williamson Research Centre Molecular Environmental Science
WRG	White Rose Grid e-Science Centre Excellence
WRLI	Working Lives Research Institute
WSC	Centre Women's Studies
WTCCB	Wellcome Trust Centre Cell Biology
WTCCMR	Wellcome Trust Centre Cell-Matrix Research
WTCHG	Wellcome Trust Centre Human Genetics
WTRC	Wales Transport Research Centre
WWRReC	Wales Waste & Resources Research Centre
WWT	Wildfowl & Wetland Trust Centres

X

Xfi	Xfi Centre Finance & Investment
XMEC	Exeter Manufacturing Enterprise Centre
XSPO	eXeter Centre Research Strategic Processes & Operations

Y

YCCSA	York Centre Complex Systems Analysis
YCHI	Yorkshire Centre Health Informatics
YNiC	York Neuroimaging Centre

Z

ZbVp	Volapük Centre
ZICER	Zuckerman Institute Connective Environmental Research

SPONSORS & UNIVERSITIES INDEX

Symbols used in this index are: > = see   >+ = see also

A

ABERDEEN, UNIVERSITY OF
Aberdeen Centre Environmental Sustainability
Aberdeen Institute Coastal Science & Management
AHRC Centre Irish & Scottish Studies
Centre Advanced Studies Nursing
Centre Austrian Studies
Centre Early Modern Studies
Centre Entrepreneurship
Centre European Labour Market Research
Centre Gender Studies
Centre Linguistic Research
Centre Novel
Centre Property Law
Centre Property Research
Centre Regional Public Finance
Centre Rural Health Research & Policy
Centre Scottish Studies
Centre Spirituality, Health & Disability
Centre Study Civil Law Tradition
Centre Study Public Policy
Clinical Skills Centre
Dugald Baird Centre Research Women's Health
Elphinstone Institute
Industrial Psychology Research Centre
Institute Applied Health Sciences
Institute Energy Technologies
Institute Medical Sciences
Interface - Centre Interdisciplinary Practice
Nordic Policy Studies Centre
Northern Studies Centre
Oil & Gas Centre
Research Institute Irish & Scottish Studies
Scottish Centre Himalayan Research
Scottish Fish Immunology Research Centre
Scottish Offshore Materials Centre

ABERTAY, DUNDEE, UNIVERSITY OF
Abertay Centre Environment
Pain Management Research Centre
Scottish Institute Wood Technology
Tayside Institute Health Studies
Urban Water Technology Centre

ANGLIA RUSKIN UNIVERSITY
Centre Business Transformation
Centre Communication & Ethics International Business
Centre International Business, Research & Development
Centre Research Health & Social Care
Centre Strategic Studies
Environmental Sciences Research Centre
Helen Rollason Cancer Care Centre Laboratory
Institute Health & Social Care

ARTS, UNIVERSITY OF THE, LONDON
Centre Design against Crime
Centre Drawing
Centre Fashion, Body & Material Cultures
Centre Interactive Network Arts
Creative Learning Practice Centre Excellence Teaching & Learning
International Centre Fine Art Research
Materials & Arts Research Centre
Photography & Archive Research Centre
Transnational Art, Identity & Nation Research Centre

ASTON UNIVERSITY
Aston Business School Research Centre Higher Education Learning & Management
Aston Centre Human Resource
Aston Centre Leadership Excellence
Aston Centre Research Experimental Finance
Aston Centre Voluntary Action Research
Centre English Language & Communication
Centre Performance Measurement & Management
Centre Research Social & Political Sciences
Institute Study Language & Social Sciences

B

BANK OF ENGLAND
Centre Central Banking Studies

BATH, UNIVERSITY OF
Applied Electromagnetics Research Centre
Centre Action Research Professional Practice
Centre Advanced Studies Architecture
Centre Analysis Social Policy
Centre Biomimetic & Natural Technologies
Centre Business Organisations & Society
Centre Death & Society
Centre Development Studies
Centre Electron Optical Studies
Centre Extremophile Research
Centre Information Management
Centre Mathematical Biology
Centre Nonlinear Mechanics
Centre Orthopaedic Biomechanics
Centre Photonics & Photonic Materials
Centre Power Transmission & Motion Control
Centre Regenerative Medicine
Centre Research Education & Environment
Centre Research Strategic Purchasing & Supply
Centre Sociocultural & Activity Theory Research
Centre Space, Atmospheric & Oceanic Science
Centre Structural & Architectural Engineering
Centre Study Education an International Context
Centre Study Regulated Industries
Centre Sustainable Power Distribution
Centre Window & Cladding Technology
Centre Women's Studies
European Research Institute
Innovative Manufacturing Research Centre - Engineering IMRC
Innovative Manufacturing Research Centre - Management IMRC
Institute International Policy Analysis
International Centre Environment
International Centre Higher Education Management
International Marketing & Purchasing Centre
Materials Research Centre
Media Technology Research Centre
Powertrain & Vehicle Research Centre
Research Institute Care Elderly
Science Studies Centre
Work & Employment Research Centre

BATH SPA UNIVERSITY
ArtsWork: Learning Laboratories Centre Excellence

BEDFORDSHIRE, UNIVERSITY OF
Business & Management Research Institute
Centre Computer Graphics & Visualisation

Centre International Media Analysis
Centre Research Distributed Technologies
Centre Research English Language Learning & Assessment
Centre Wireless Network Design
Institute Applied Social Research
Institute Health Research
Institute Research Applicable Computing
Luton Institute Research Applied Natural Sciences
National Centre Carnival Arts
Research Institute Media, Art & Design
trAce Online Writing Centre
Vauxhall Centre Study Crime

BELL COLLEGE
Centre Environmental Management & Technology
Scottish Biotechnology Training Centre
Scottish Centre Police Studies
Scottish Polymer Development Centre

BETH JOHNSON FOUNDATION
Centre Intergenerational Practice

BIRKBECK, UNIVERSITY OF LONDON
AHRB Centre British Film & Television Studies
Biophysics Centre
Birkbeck Institute Humanities
Birkbeck Institute Lifelong Learning
Bloomsbury Centre Bioinformatics
Bloomsbury Centre Structural Biology
Centre Brain & Cognitive Development
Centre Canadian Studies
Centre Crime Informatics
Centre European Protected Areas Research
Centre Nineteenth-Century Studies
Centre Planetary Science & Astrobiology
Centre Protein & Membrane Structure & Dynamics
Centre Psychosocial Studies
Chemical Biology Centre
Contemporary Poetics Research Centre
Football Governance Research Centre
Institute Structural Molecular Biology
Institute Study Children, Families & Social Issues
Vasari Centre Digital Art History

BIRMINGHAM, UNIVERSITY OF
Castings Centre
Centre Advanced Research English
Centre Applied Gerontology
Centre Business Strategy & Procurement
Centre Byzantine, Ottoman & Modern Greek Studies
Centre Corporate Governance Research
Centre Corpus Research
Centre Early Music Performance Research
Centre Electron Microscopy
Centre English Language Studies
Centre Environmental Research & Training
Centre European Languages & Cultures
Centre Evidence-Based Conservation
Centre Excellence Interdisciplinary Mental Health
Centre Excellence Research Computational Intelligence &
    Applications
Centre First World War Studies
Centre Forensic & Family Psychology
Centre History Medicine
Centre International Education & Research
Centre Learning, Innovation & Collaboration
Centre Modern Languages
Centre Ornithology
Centre Reformation & Early Modern Studies
Centre Research Brand Marketing
Centre Research Medical & Dental Education
Centre Russian & East European Studies
Centre Studies Security & Diplomacy
Centre Study Global Ethics
Centre Urban & Regional Studies
Centre West African Studies
Dictionary Research Centre
Ergonomics Information Analysis Centre

European Research Institute
Formulation Engineering Research Centre
Health Services Management Centre
Infrastructure Engineering & Management Research Centre
Institute Applied Social Studies
Institute Archaeology & Antiquity
Institute Energy Research & Policy
Institute European Law
Institute German Studies
Institute Judicial Administration
Institute Local Government Studies
Institute Medical Law
Institute Occupational & Environmental Medicine
Institute Safety Technology & Research
Interdisciplinary Research Centre Materials Processing
Ironbridge Institute
Leopardi Centre
Materials Science Research Centre
Mathematics, Statistics & Operational Research Subject
    Centre
Midlands e-Science Centre
MRC Centre Immune Regulation
Positron Imaging Centre
Rail Research UK
Shakespeare Institute
Subject Network Sociology, Anthropology, Politics
Vehicle Technology Research Centre
Visual Impairment Centre Teaching & Research

BIRMINGHAM CITY UNIVERSITY
Birmingham Institute Art & Design
Bournville Centre Visual Arts
Centre Community Mental Health
Centre Composition & Performance Using Technology
Centre Criminal Justice Policy & Research
Centre Design Innovation
Centre Fine Art Research
Centre Research Quality
Centre Stakeholder Learning Partnerships
Management & Enterprise Development Centre
Social Economy Evaluation Bureau
Technology Innovation Centre

BOLTON, UNIVERSITY OF
Centre Educational Technology Interoperability Standards

BOURNEMOUTH UNIVERSITY
Centre Accounting, Finance & Taxation
Centre Broadcasting History Research
Centre Conservation Ecology
Centre Corporate Governance & Regulation
Centre Cultural Resource Management
Centre Environmental Archaeology
Centre Environmental Forensics
Centre Event & Sport Research
Centre Excellence Applied Research Mental Health
Centre Excellence Media Practice
Centre Foodservice Research
Centre General Practice
Centre Geomorphology
Centre Intellectual Property Policy & Management
Centre Land-Based Studies
Centre Landscape & Townscape Archaeology
Centre Marine & Coastal Archaeology
Centre Organisational Effectiveness
Centre Post Qualifying Social Work
Centre Practice Development
Centre Public Communication Research
Centre Qualitative Research
Centre Research & Knowledge Transfer
Centre Technology, Production & Ancient Materials
Institute Business & Law
Institute Health & Community Studies
International Centre Tourism & Hospitality Research
National Centre Computer Animation
Sustainable Design Research Centre

© CBD Research Ltd · Beckenham · Kent BR3 5JS · Tel 020 8650 7745 · Fax 020 8650 0768 · E-mail cbd@cbdresearch.com · www.cbdresearch.com

BRADFORD, UNIVERSITY OF

Africa Centre Peace & Conflict Studies
Biological Anthropology Research Centre
Bradford Centre International Development
Bradford Disarmament Research Centre
Centre Citizenship & Community Mental Health
Centre Conflict Resolution
Centre European Studies
Centre Inclusion & Diversity
Centre International Co-operation & Security
Institute Cancer Therapeutics
Institute Community & Primary Care Research
Institute Pharmaceutical Innovation
International Centre Participation Studies
Mobile & Satellite Communications Research Centre
Tom Connors Cancer Research Centre

BRIGHTON, UNIVERSITY OF

Art Design Media Subject Centre
Centre Contemporary Visual Arts
Centre Excellence Teaching & Learning through Design
Centre Learning & Teaching
Centre Nursing & Midwifery Research
Centre Research & Development
Centre Research Innovation Management
Chelsea School Research Centre
Clinical Research Centre Health Professions
Health & Social Policy Research Centre
Institute Nursing & Midwifery
International Health Development Research Centre

BRISTOL, UNIVERSITY OF

Advanced Computing Research Centre
AIMS Centre (Applied & Integrated Medical Sciences)
Behavioural Biology Research Centre
Bristol Biogeochemistry Research Centre
Bristol ChemLabS Centre Excellence Teaching & Learning
    (Bristol Chemical Laboratory Sciences)
Bristol Glaciology Centre
Bristol Heart Institute
Bristol Institute Greece, Rome & Classical Tradition
Bristol Institute Research Humanities & Arts
Burden Neurological Institute
Centre Buddhist Studies
Centre Chemometrics
Centre Child & Adolescent Health
Centre Christianity & Culture
Centre Communications Research
Centre e-Research
Centre East Asian Studies
Centre Environmental & Geophysical Flows
Centre Market & Public Organisation
Centre Medieval Studies
Centre Romantic Studies
Centre Russian & East European Cultural Studies
Centre Study Colonial & Postcolonial Societies
Centre Study Ethnicity & Citizenship
Centre Study Poverty Social Justice
CLIO Centre Globalisation, Education & Societies
CLIO Centre International & Comparative Studies
CLIO Centre Learning, Knowing & Interactive Technologies
CLIO Centre Narratives & Transformative Learning
CLIO Centre Research Language & Education
COGNIT Research Centre
Earthquake Engineering Research Centre
Economics Network
Food Refrigeration & Process Engineering Research Centre
Institute Learning & Research Technology
Interface Analysis Centre
Mixed Media Grid [Research Centre]
MRC Centre Synaptic Plasticity
Norah Fry Research Centre
Safety Systems Research Centre
Science Learning Centre South West
Subject Centre Education
Townsend Centre International Poverty Research

BRITISH GEOLOGICAL SURVEY

WHO Collaborating Centre Groundwater Quality
    Assessment & Protection

BRUNEL UNIVERSITY

Brunel Able Children's Education Centre
Brunel Advanced Institute Multimedia & Network Systems
Brunel Centre Advanced Solidification Technology
Brunel Centre Contemporary Writing
Brunel Centre Democratic Evaluation
Brunel Centre Intelligence & Security Studies
Brunel Centre Manufacturing Metrology
Brunel Centre Packaging Technology
Brunel Institute Bioengineering
Brunel Institute Cancer Genetics & Pharmacogenomics
Brunel Institute Computational Mathematics
Brunel Institute Power Systems
Brunel Organisation & Systems Design Centre
Brunel University Random Systems Research Centre
Centre American, Trans-Atlantic & Caribbean History
Centre Analysis Risk & Optimisation Modelling Applications
Centre Applied Simulation Modelling
Centre Black Professional Practice
Centre Cell & Chromosome Biology
Centre Child-focused Anthropological Research
Centre Citizen Participation
Centre Cognition & Neuroimaging
Centre Contemporary Music Practice
Centre Economic Development & Institutions
Centre Epidemiology & Health Service Research
Centre International & Public Law
Centre Media: Globalisation: Risk
Centre Phosphors & Display Materials
Centre Public Health Research
Centre Research Emotion Work
Centre Research Infant Behaviour
Centre Research Marketing
Centre Research Rehabilitation
Centre Study Expertise
Centre Study Health & Illness
Centre Youth Work Studies
Diamond-like Carbon Coating Centre
e2v Centre Electronic Imaging
Experimental Techniques Centre
Institute Environment
Interdisciplinary Centre Child & Youth Focused Research
Multidisciplinary Assessment Technology Centre Healthcare
Screen Media Research Centre
Wolfson Centre Materials Processing

BUCKINGHAM, UNIVERSITY OF

Centre Business Society
Centre Education & Employment Research
Centre Multi-Cultural Studies Law & Family
Centre Service Management
Max Beloff Centre Study Liberty

BUCKINGHAMSHIRE CHILTERNS UNIVERSITY COLLEGE

Centre Crowd & Safety Management

C

CAMBRIDGE, UNIVERSITY OF

Autism Research Centre
Babraham Institute
Behavioural & Clinical Neurosciences Institute
BP Institute Multiphase Flow
Cambridge Centre Brain Repair
Cambridge Centre Climate Change Mitigation Research
Cambridge Centre Economic & Public Policy
Cambridge Centre Gender Studies
Cambridge Centre Housing & Planning Research
Cambridge Centre Proteomics
Cambridge Computational Biology Institute
Cambridge Crystallographic Data Centre

Cambridge e-Science Centre
Cambridge & East Anglia Centre Structural Biology
Cambridge Endowment Research Finance
Cambridge Engineering Design Centre
Cambridge Entrepreneurship Centre
Cambridge Institute Language Research
Cambridge Institute Medical Research
Cambridge Interdisciplinary Research Centre Ageing
Cambridge-MIT Institute
Cambridge Resource Centre Comparative Genomics
Cambridge University Health - Health Policy & Management
    Centre
Cancer Research UK Cambridge Research Institute
Centre Advanced Religious & Theological Studies
Centre African Studies
Centre Applied Medical Statistics
Centre Applied Research Educational Technologies
Centre Atmospheric Science
Centre Commonwealth Education
Centre Competitiveness & Innovation
Centre Corporate & Commercial Law
Centre Corporate Governance
Centre Entrepreneurial Learning
Centre European Legal Studies
Centre Family Research
Centre Financial Research
Centre Intellectual Property & Information Law
Centre International Business & Management
Centre International Studies
Centre Latin American Studies
Centre Mathematical Sciences
Centre Middle Eastern & Islamic Studies
Centre Neuroscience Education
Centre Penal Theory & Penal Ethics
Centre Public Law
Centre Quantum Computation
Centre Research Arts, Social Sciences, & Humanities
Centre South Asian Studies
Centre Speech, Language & Brain
Centre Study Jewish-Christian Relations
Centre Tax Law
Centre Technology Management
Centre Veterinary Science
Churchill Archives Centre
East Asia Institute
Eastern Cancer Registration & Information Centre
ESRC Centre Business Research
Hamilton Kerr Institute
Henry Martyn Centre Study Mission & World Christianity
Illicit Antiquities Research Centre
Institute Astronomy
Institute Aviation & Environment
Institute Biotechnology
Institute Continuing Education
Institute Criminology
Institute Manufacturing
Institute Orthodox Christian Studies
Institute Public Health
Institute Theoretical Geophysics
Interdisciplinary Research Centre Superconductivity
Isaac Newton Institute Mathematical Sciences
Lauterpacht Centre International Law
Leverhulme Centre Human Evolutionary Studies
Magnetic Resonance Research Centre
Margaret Beaufort Institute Theology
Martin Centre Architectural & Urban Studies
McDonald Institute Archaeological Research
Microelectronics Research Centre
MRC Centre Nutritional Epidemiology Cancer Prevention &
    Survival
MRC Centre Protein Engineering
MRC Centre Stem Cell Biology & Medicine
MRC Resource Centre Human Nutrition Research
Multi-Imaging Centre

Nanoscience Centre
National Institute Environmental eScience
Pfizer Institute Pharmaceutical Materials Science
Prisons Research Centre
Research Centre English & Applied Linguistics
Scott Polar Research Institute
Sir Arthur Marshall Institute Aeronautics
Social Contexts Pathways Crime Centre
Unilever Centre Molecular Science Informatics
Wellcome Trust/Cancer Research UK Gurdon Institute
    Cancer & Developmental Biology
Wellcome Trust Centre Stem Cell Research & Institute Stem
    Cell Biology
Wolfson Brain Imaging Centre
World Data Centre Glaciology, Cambridge

CAPEL MANOR COLLEGE
National Gardening Centre

CARDIFF UNIVERSITY
Biomaterials & Biomechanics Research Centre
Cardiff Centre Astrobiology
Cardiff Centre Ethics, Law & Society
Cardiff Centre History Crusades
Cardiff Centre Modern German History
Cardiff Centre Multidisciplinary Microtechnology
Cardiff Centre Research Genetics & Society
Cardiff Centre Welsh American Studies
Cardiff Institute Society, Health & Ethics
Cardiff Institute Tissue Engineering & Repair
Cardiff Japanese Studies Centre
Cardiff University Brain & Repair Imaging Centre
Cardiff University Innovative Manufacturing Research Centre
Central European Music Research Centre
Centre Applied Ethics
Centre Automotive Industry Research
Centre Contemporary Civil Law Studies
Centre Critical & Cultural Theory
Centre Digital Signal Processing
Centre Economic & Social Aspects Genomics
Centre Editorial & Intertextual Research
Centre Education Built Environment
Centre Health Sciences Research
Centre High Frequency Engineering
Centre International Family Law Studies
Centre Journalism Studies
Centre Language & Communication Research
Centre Late Antique Religion & Culture
Centre Law & Religion
Centre Local & Regional Government Research
Centre Medico-Legal Studies
Centre Polymer Therapeutics
Centre Research Energy, Waste & Environment
Centre Research Environment & Health
Centre Study Islam UK
Centre Study Knowledge, Expertise & Science
Centre Study Medieval Society & Culture
Collingwood & British Idealism Centre
Common Cold & Nasal Research Centre
Communications Research Centre
eCommerce Innovation Centre
ESRC Centre Business Relationships, Accountability,
    Sustainability & Society
Geoenvironmental Research Centre
Health Communication Research Centre
Hydroenvironmental Research Centre
Institute Advanced Materials & Energy Systems
Institute Information Systems & Integration Technology
Institute Machines & Structures
Institute Medical Engineering & Medical Physics
Institute Medical Genetics, Cardiff University
Institute Nephrology
Institute Sustainability, Energy & Environmental Management
Institute Theoretical, Applied & Computational Mechanics
Integrated Protein Research Centre
International Centre Planning Research

© CBD Research Ltd · Beckenham · Kent BR3 5JS · Tel 020 8650 7745 · Fax 020 8650 0768 · E-mail cbd@cbdresearch.com · www.cbdresearch.com

Julian Hodge Institute Applied Macroeconomics
Lean Enterprise Research Centre
Manufacturing Engineering Centre
Mitutoyo Metrology Centre
Nursing, Health & Social Care Research Centre
Regeneration Institute
Research Centre Clinical Kinaesiology
Seafarers International Research Centre
Siemens Automation & Drives Centre
Sir Geraint Evans Wales Heart Research Institute
Tenovus Centre Cancer Research
Therapeutics & Toxicology Centre
Tom Hopkinson Centre Media Research
UnumProvident Centre Psychosocial & Disability Research
Wales Biomass Centre
Wales Centre Evidence Based Care
Wales Waste & Resources Research Centre
Welsh Centre Learning Disabilities
Welsh Centre Post-Graduate Pharmaceutical Education
Welsh e-Science Centre
Welsh Governance Centre
Welsh Hearing Institute
Welsh Institute Minimal Access Therapy
Welsh Institute Research Economics & Development
Welsh Language Teaching Centre
Welsh School Pharmacy Centre Socioeconomic Research
Wolfson Centre Magnetics Technology

CENTRAL ENGLAND,UNIVERSITY OF, BIRMINGHAM >

BIRMINGHAM CITY UNIVERSITY

CENTRAL LANCASHIRE, UNIVERSITY OF
Applied Digital Signal & Image Processing Research Centre
Centre Astrophysics
Centre Contemporary Art
Centre Employability
Centre Employability Through Humanities
Centre Materials Science
Centre Professional Ethics
Centre Regional Economic Development
Centre Research Fire & Explosion Studies
Centre Waste Management
Institute International Business
Institute Transport & Tourism
International Football Institute
Jost Institute Tribotechnology

CENTRAL SCHOOL OF SPEECH AND DRAMA
Centre Excellence Training Theatre
International Centre Voice

CHESTER, UNIVERSITY OF
Centre Exercise & Nutrition Science
Centre Practice as Research Arts
Centre Public Health Research
Centre Religion & Biosciences
Centre Science Communication
Centre Study Religion & Popular Culture
Centre Victorian Studies
Chester Centre Research Sport Society
Chester Centre Stress Research
Institute Social & Health Research

CITY UNIVERSITY
Applied Vision Research Centre
Centre Allied Health Professions Research
Actuarial Research Centre
Alternative Investments Research Centre
Centre Aeronautics
Centre Career & Skills Development
Centre Charity Effectiveness
Centre Comparative Social Surveys
Centre Competition & Regulatory Policy
Centre Econometric Analysis
Centre Educational & Academic Practices
Centre Energy & Environment
Centre Financial Regulation & Crime
Centre Gender Research
Centre Health Informatics [City]

Centre Human Computer Interaction Design
Centre Information Policy Studies
Centre Interactive Systems Research
Centre Intercultural Music
Centre International Communications & Society
Centre International Politics
Centre Language Studies
Centre Leadership, Learning & Change
Centre Mathematical Science
Centre New Technologies, Innovation & Entrepreneurship
Centre Research Corporate Governance
Centre Research Education
Centre Research European Financial Markets & Institutions
Centre Risk Management, Reliability & Maintenance
Centre Software Reliability
Centre Study Human Development & Well-Being
Centre Study Race & Ethnicity
Centre Systems & Modelling
City Health Economics Centre
Compass Centre
Control Engineering Research Centre
Engineering Structures Research Centre
Geotechnical Engineering Research Centre
giCentre
Information & Biomedical Engineering Research Centre
Information Centre about Asylum & Refugees UK
Institute Health Sciences
International Centre Shipping, Trade & Finance
London Geotechnical Centrifuge Centre
Measurement & Instrumentation Centre
Pensions Institute
Private Equity & Venture Capital Research Centre
Rehabilitation Resource Centre
Risk Institute
Saad Centre Clinical Skills Education
Social Research Methodology Centre

COMMUNITIES SCOTLAND
Scottish Centre Regeneration

COVENTRY UNIVERSITY
Applied Research Centre Human Security
Applied Research Centre Sustainable Regeneration
Centre Academic Writing
Centre Advanced Joining
Centre African Studies
Centre Excellence Transport & Product Design
Centre Information Technology Language Learning
Centre Inter-Professional e-Learning Health & Social Care
Centre International & European Studies
Centre Media, Arts & Performance
Centre Peace & Reconciliation Studies
Centre Sonochemistry
Centre South Asian Studies
Centre Study Higher Education
Control Theory & Applications Centre
Coventry University Design Institute
Criminal Justice Research Centre
Engineering Design Research Centre
Health Services Research Centre
Institute Community Cohesion
Interdisciplinary Research Centre Health
Visual & Information Design Research Centre

CRANFIELD UNIVERSITY
Aircraft Design Centre
Bettany Centre Entrepreneurial Performance & Economics
Business Travel Research Centre
Centre Advanced Engineering Methods
Centre Air Transport Remoter Regions
Centre Applied Laser Spectroscopy
Centre Archaeological & Forensic Analysis
Centre Business Performance
Centre Executive Learning
Centre Forensic Computing
Centre Grid Computing
Centre Innovative Products & Services

Centre Managing Security Transitional Societies
Centre Materials Science & Engineering
Centre Ordnance Science & Technology
Centre Organisational Transformation
Centre Research Management Expatriation
Centre Resource Management & Efficiency
Centre Systems Engineering
Centre Water Science
Centre Women Business Leaders
Complex Systems Management Centre
Composites Centre
Cranfield BioMedical Centre
Cranfield Biotechnology Centre
Cranfield Centre Advanced Research Marketing
Cranfield Centre Agricultural & Environmental Engineering
Cranfield Centre Bioinformatics
Cranfield Centre Competition & Regulation Research
Cranfield Centre EcoChemistry
Cranfield Centre Ecological Restoration
Cranfield Centre Geographical Information Management
Cranfield Centre Precision Farming
Cranfield Centre Sports Surfaces
Cranfield Centre Supramolecular Technology
Cranfield Impact Centre
Cranfield Innovative Manufacturing Research Centre
Cranfield Institute Safety Risk & Reliability
Cranfield Management Research Institute
Cranfield Mine Action & Disaster Management Centre
Cranfield Ordnance Test & Evaluation Centre
Cranfield Resilience Centre
Cranfield Safety & Accident Investigation Centre
Cranfield Space Research Centre
Cranfield University Business Incubation Centre
Decision Engineering Centre
Disaster Management Centre
Doughty Centre Corporate Responsibility
Energy Technology Centre
Engineering Dynamics Centre
Flight Operations Research Centre Excellence
Human Resource Research Centre
Information Systems Research Centre
Institute Environment & Health
Institute Water & Environment
Integrated Earth System Sciences Institute
Logistics Education Centre
Manufacturing Systems Centre
Microsystems & Nanotechnology Centre
National Flying Laboratory Centre
National Soil Resources Institute
Natural Resources Management Institute
Operations Management Research Centre
Precision Engineering Centre
Security Studies Institute
Soil Survey & Land Research Centre
Supply Chain Research Centre
Surface Science & Engineering Centre
Welding Engineering Research Centre

CREATIVE ARTS, UNIVERSITY COLLEGE FOR THE
Centre Sustainable Design
Crafts Study Centre

D

DARLINGTON COLLEGE
Football Development Centre
DE MONTFORT UNIVERSITY
Centre Comparative Housing Research
Centre Computational Intelligence
Centre Computing & Social Responsibility
Centre Excellence Performance Arts
Centre Interactive Media
Centre Manufacturing

Centre Research Ethnic Minority Entrepreneurship
Centre Social Action
Centre Social Care Studies
Centre Textual Scholarship
Emerging Technologies Research Centre
Institute Creative Technologies
Institute Energy & Sustainable Development
International Centre Sports History & Culture
Mary Seacole Research Centre
Mechatronics Research Centre
Music, Technology & Innovation Research Centre
DERBY, UNIVERSITY OF
Centre Educational Development & Materials
Centre Entrepreneurial Management
Centre Guidance Studies
Centre Interactive Assessment Development
Centre Psychological Research Human Behaviour
Community Regeneration Research Centre
Derbyshire Further Mathematics Centre
Research Centre Advancing Innovation & Management
Research Centre Education & Professional Practice
DUNDEE, UNIVERSITY OF
Advanced Materials Centre
Alzheimer's Disease Research Centre
Biomedical Research Centre
Centre Addiction Research & Education Scotland
Centre Archive & Information Studies
Centre Artists' Books
Centre Conservation & Urban Studies
Centre Digital Imaging
Centre Energy, Petroleum & Mineral Law & Policy
Centre Enterprise Management
Centre Forensic & Legal Medicine
Centre Medical Education
Centre Professional Development Art & Design
Centre Remote Sensing & Environmental Monitoring
Clinical Skills Centre
Dundee Limb Fitting Centre
Geddes Institute
Institute Motion Tracking & Research
Institute Sport & Exercise
Institute Transatlantic, European & American Studies
Joint Centre Scottish Housing Research
Mary Ann Baxter Centre Interdisciplinary Gender Research
Neurosciences Institute
Scottish Informatics, Mathematics, Biology & Statistics Centre
Scottish Institute Excellence Social Work Education
Sir James Black Centre
Social Dimensions Health Institute
Tayside Institute Cardiovascular Research
Tayside Orthopaedic & Rehabilitation Technology Centre
UNESCO Centre Water Law, Policy & Science
Visual Research Centre
Wellcome Trust Biocentre
WHO Collaborating Centre Public Health Issues Congenital Anomalies & Technology Transfer
DURHAM, UNIVERSITY OF
Active Learning Computing: Centre Excellence Teaching & Learning
Basil Bunting Poetry Centre
Centre Advanced Instrumentation
Centre Arts & Humanities Health & Medicine
Centre Bioactive Chemistry
Centre Biomedical Engineering
Centre Clinical Management Development
Centre Communications Systems
Centre Contemporary Chinese Studies
Centre Contemporary Music
Centre Criminal Law & Criminal Justice
Centre Electronic Systems
Centre History Medicine & Disease
Centre History Political Thought
Centre Industrial Automation & Manufacture
Centre Infectious Disease

© CBD Research Ltd · Beckenham · Kent BR3 5JS · Tel 020 8650 7745 · Fax 020 8650 0768 · E-mail cbd@cbdresearch.com · www.cbdresearch.com

Centre Integrated Health Care Research
Centre Iranian Studies
Centre Learning, Teaching & Research Higher Education
Centre Medieval & Renaissance Studies
Centre Molecular & Nanoscale Electronics
Centre Particle Theory
Centre Public Policy & Health
Centre Stem Cell Biology & Regenerative Medicine
Centre Study Cities & Regions
Centre Vision & Visual Cognition
Curriculum Evaluation & Management Centre
Durham Centre Advanced Photography Studies
Durham Centre Renewable Energy
Durham Centre Roman Cultural Studies
Durham European Law Institute
e-Science Research Institute
Environmental Research Centre
Human Rights Centre
Institute Advanced Study
Institute Computational Cosmology
Institute Hazard & Risk Research
Institute Middle Eastern & Islamic Studies
Institute Particle Physics Phenomenology
Mountjoy Research Centre
Northern Centre History Medicine
Ogden Centre Fundamental Physics
Research Institute Software Evolution
Science Learning Centre North East
Wolfson Research Institute

E

EAST ANGLIA, UNIVERSITY OF
Arthur Miller Centre American Studies
British Centre Literary Translation
Centre Applied Research Education
Centre Carbohydrate Chemistry
Centre Competition Policy
Centre Counselling Studies
Centre East Anglian Studies
Centre Ecology, Evolution & Conservation
Centre Economic & Behavioural Analysis Risk & Decision
Centre Inter-professional Practice
Centre Interdisciplinary Mathematical Research
Centre Metalloprotein Spectroscopy & Biology
Centre Research Child & Family
Centre Research European Studies
Centre Social & Economic Research Global Environment
Institute Health & Social Science Research
Keswick Hall Centre Research & Development Religious
    Education
Sainsbury Centre Visual Arts
Tyndall Centre Climate Change Research
Wolfson Materials & Catalysis Centre
Zuckerman Institute Connective Environmental Research

EAST LONDON, UNIVERSITY OF
Centre Geo-Information Studies
Centre Human Rights Conflict
Centre Institutional Studies
Centre Narrative Research
Centre Social Work Research [London]
Continuum - Centre Widening Participation Policy Studies
Graduate Institute Management & Organisation Research
London East Research Institute
Raphael Samuel History Centre
Refugee Research Centre

EDGE HILL COLLEGE OF HIGHER EDUCATION
Centre Learning & Teaching Research
SOLSTICE Centre

EDINBURGH, UNIVERSITY OF
Institute Applied Language Studies

AHRC Research Centre Studies Intellectual Property &
    Technology Law
Artificial Intelligence Applications Institute
Centre African Studies
Centre Canadian Studies
Centre Communication Interface Research
Centre Educational Sociology
Centre Entrepreneurship Research
Centre Financial Markets Research
Centre Intelligent Systems & their Applications
Centre Law & Society
Centre Materials Science & Engineering
Centre Neuroscience Research
Centre Research Education Inclusion & Diversity
Centre Research Families & Relationships
Centre Science at Extreme Conditions
Centre South Asian Studies
Centre Speech Technology Research
Centre Study Environmental Change & Sustainability
Centre Systems Biology at Edinburgh
Centre Teaching, Learning & Assessment
Communication Aids Language & Learning
Contaminated Land Assessment & Remediation Research
    Centre
Criminal Justice Social Work Development Centre Scotland
Digital Curation Centre
e-Science Institute
Edinburgh Centre Bioinformatics
Edinburgh Dental Institute
Edinburgh Europa Institute
Edinburgh Parallel Computing Centre
Edinburgh Virtual Environment Centre
Human Communication Research Centre
Innogen - ESRC Centre Social & Economic Research
    Innovation Genomics
Institute Adaptive & Neural Computation
Institute Advanced Studies Humanities
Institute Astronomy
Institute Atmospheric & Environmental Science
Institute Cell Biology
Institute Communicating & Collaborative Systems
Institute Computing Systems Architecture
Institute Evolutionary Biology
Institute Governance
Institute Immunology & Infection Research
Institute Infrastructure & Environment
Institute Japanese-European Technology Studies
Institute Molecular Plant Sciences
Institute Perception, Action & Behaviour
Institute Public Sector Accounting Research
Institute Stem Cell Research
Institute Structural & Molecular Biology
Institute Study Science, Technology & Innovation
Joseph Bell Centre Forensic Statistics & Legal Reasoning
Languages & Humanities Centre
Maxwell Institute Mathematical Sciences
MRC-University Edinburgh Centre Inflammation Research
Queen's Medical Research Institute
Research Centre Social Sciences
Roslin Institute
Scottish Centre Carbon Storage
Scottish Centre International Law
Scottish Centre Research On-line Learning & Assessment
Scottish Centre Studies School Administration
Scottish Crop Research Institute
Scottish Institute Enterprise
Scottish Sensory Centre
Wellcome Trust Centre Cell Biology

ESSEX, UNIVERSITY OF
AHRC Research Centre Studies Surrealism & its Legacies
American (United States) Studies Centre
Centre Audio Research & Engineering
Centre Cognitive Science
Centre Computational Finance & Economic Agents

Centre Cultural & Social History
Centre Entrepreneurship Research
Centre Environment & Society
Centre Film Studies
Centre Latin American Studies
Centre Local History
Centre Local & Regional History
Centre Network Research
Centre Psychoanalytic Studies
Centre Social Responsibility Accounting & Management
Centre Sports & Exercise Science
Centre Systems Biology
Centre Theatre Studies
Centre Theoretical Studies Humanities & Social Sciences
Children's Legal Centre
Digital Lifestyles Centre
ESRC Research Centre Micro-Social Change
ESRC United Kingdom Longitudinal Studies Centre
Essex Biomedical Sciences Institute
Essex Finance Centre
Essex Management Centre
European Centre Analysis Social Sciences
Human Rights Centre
Institute Social & Economic Research
Institute Socio-Technical Research & Innovation
Pan-European Institute

EXETER, UNIVERSITY OF
Bill Douglas Centre History Cinema & Popular Culture
Centre Bioinformatics & Medical Informatics Training
Centre Business History
Centre Creative Writing & Arts
Centre Energy & Environment
Centre European Legal Studies
Centre European Nineteenth-Century Studies
Centre European Studies
Centre Geophysical & Astrophysical Fluid Dynamics
Centre Intermedia
Centre Latin American Studies
Centre Leadership Studies
Centre Maritime Historical Studies
Centre Medical History
Centre Medieval Studies
Centre Mediterranean Studies
Centre Regulatory Governance
Centre Research Film Studies
Centre Rural Research
Centre Service Research
Centre Study Christian Church
Centre Study War, State & Society
Centre Victorian Studies
Centre Water Systems
Children's Health & Exercise Research Centre
ESRC Centre Genomics Society
Exeter Biocatalysis Centre
Exeter Centre Cognitive Neuroscience
Exeter Centre Hellenistic & Greco-Roman Culture
eXeter Centre Research Strategic Processes & Operations
Exeter Centre Study Esotericism
Exeter Manufacturing Enterprise Centre
Foreign Language Centre
Institute Arab & Islamic Studies
Institute Cornish Studies
Mood Disorders Centre
Research Centre Learning Society
Xfi Centre Finance & Investment

G

GLAMORGAN, UNIVERSITY OF
Centre Border Studies
Centre Criminology
Centre Electronic Product Engineering

Centre Modern & Contemporary Wales
Evaluation Institute
George Ewart Evans Centre Storytelling
National Centre Writing
Sustainable Environment Research Centre
Suzy Lamplugh Trust Research Institute
Wales Centre Intergenerational Practice
Wales Transport Research Centre
Welsh Enterprise Institute
Welsh Institute Competitive Advantage

GLASGOW, UNIVERSITY OF
Andrew Hook Centre American Studies
Beatson Institute Cancer Research
BHF Glasgow Cardiovascular Research Centre
Bioinformatics Research Centre
Centre Advanced Studies Christian Ministry
Centre Battlefield Archaeology
Centre Business History Scotland
Centre Cell Engineering at Glasgow
Centre Cognitive Neuroimaging
Centre Cultural Policy Research
Centre Development Studies
Centre Drug Misuse Research
Centre Economic Renewable Power Delivery
Centre Emblem Studies
Centre History Medicine
Centre Integrated Diagnostic Systems
Centre Intercultural Studies
Centre Inter-Faith Studies
Centre Latin American Research
Centre Mathematics Applied to Life Sciences
Centre Music Technology
Centre Oncology & Applied Pharmacology
Centre Philosophy & Religion
Centre Public Policy Regions
Centre Rehabilitation Engineering
Centre Reputation Management through People
Centre Research & Development Adult & Lifelong Learning
Centre Research Higher Education
Centre Research Racism, Ethnicity & Nationalism
Centre Russian, Central & East European Studies
Centre Science Education
Centre Scottish & Gaelic Studies
Centre Screen Studies
Centre Study Human Rights Law
Centre Study Islam
Centre Study Literature, Theology & Arts
Centre Study Perceptual Experience
Centre Study Socialist Theory & Movement
Centre Supply Chain Management
Centre Systems & Control
Centre Whistler Studies
Community Care Works
Crichton Centre Research Health & Social Issues
Crichton Tourism Research Centre
Electronics Design Centre
European Centre Occupational Health, Safety & Environment
European Documentation Centre
Europe-Japan Social Science Research Centre
Glasgow Centre Medieval & Renaissance Studies
Glasgow Marine Technology Centre
Humanities Advanced Technology & Information Institute
Institute Art History
Institute Biomedical & Life Sciences
Institute Diet, Exercise & Lifestyle
Institute Gravitational Research
Institute Historical Study Language
International Centre East African Running Science
International Centre Gender & Women's Studies
James Watt Nanofabrication Centre
Kelvin Nanocharacterisation Centre
Laser & Optical Systems Engineering Centre
Leslie & Elizabeth Alcock Centre Historical Archaeology

© CBD Research Ltd · Beckenham · Kent BR3 5JS · Tel 020 8650 7745 · Fax 020 8650 0768 · E-mail cbd@cbdresearch.com · www.cbdresearch.com

MRC Institute Hearing Research - Scottish Section
Nanoelectronics Research Centre
National e-Science Centre, Glasgow
Robert Clark Centre Technological Education
Robertson Centre Biostatistics
Sackler Institute Psychobiological Research
Scottish Centre Crime & Justice Research
Scottish Centre Research Social Justice
Scottish Centre War Studies
Scottish Community Development Centre
Scottish Universities Environmental Research Centre
SCRE Centre
Strathclyde Centre Disability Research
Subject Centre History, Classics & Archaeology
Wellcome Centre Molecular Parasitology

GLASGOW CALEDONIAN UNIVERSITY
Adjudication Reporting Centre
Caledonian Environment Centre
Caledonian Family Business Centre
Caledonian Nursing & Midwifery Research Centre
Centre Built Environment [Scotland]
Centre Creative Industries
Centre Ethics Public Policy & Corporate Governance
Centre Forensic Investigation
Centre Gerontological Practice
Centre Industrial Bulk Solids Handling
Centre Innovation Healthcare Technology
Centre Political Song
Centre Public Policy & Management
Centre Research Indoor Climate & Health
Centre Research Lifelong Learning
Centre Research Six Sigma & Process Improvement
Centre Social History Health & Healthcare
Clinical Research Centre
Cullen Centre Risk & Governance
Glasgow Centre Retailing
Glasgow Centre Study Violence
Global Network World Health Organisation Collaborating
    Centres Nursing & Midwifery Development
Intelligent Technologies Research Centre
Moffat Centre Travel & Tourism Business Development
Scottish Centre Work Based Learning
SRIF Centre Virtual Organisation Technology Enabling
    Research
Sustainability Centre Glasgow
Voluntary Sector Research Centre
WHO Collaborating Centre Nursing & Midwifery Education,
    Research & Practice

GLOUCESTERSHIRE, UNIVERSITY OF
Centre Active Learning Geography, Environment & Related
    Disciplines
Centre Enterprise & Innovation
Centre Environmental Change & Quaternary Research
Centre Financial Management
Centre Research Service
Cheltenham International Language Centre
Empeiria Centre
Food Supply Chain Centre
Human Resources Management Research Centre
International Centre Biblical Interpretation
International Centre Families Business
Pedagogic Research & Scholarship Institute

GOLDSMITHS, UNIVERSITY OF LONDON
Centre Arts & Learning
Centre Caribbean Studies
Centre Cognition, Computation & Culture
Centre Contemporary Music Cultures
Centre Cultural Studies
Centre Research Architecture
Centre Russian Music
Centre Study Invention & Social Process
Centre Urban & Community Research
Centre Visual Anthropology
Constance Howard Resource & Research Centre Textiles

Pinter Centre Research Performance
GREENWICH, UNIVERSITY OF
Centre Applied Statistics & Systems Modelling
Centre Biosciences Research
Centre Contaminated Land Remediation
Centre Entrepreneurship
Centre Health Research & Evaluation
Centre Numerical Modelling & Process Analysis
Centre Research Computer Science
Computer Security & Audit Centre
eCentre
Greenwich Maritime Institute
Natural Resources Institute
Urban Renaissance Institute
Wolfson Centre Bulk Solids Handling Technology

H

HARPER ADAMS UNIVERSITY COLLEGE
Advancing Skills Professionals Rural Economy CETL
Centre Rural Innovation
HEALTH AND SAFETY LABORATORY
WHO Collaborating Centre Occupational Health & Safety
    Research
HEALTH PROMOTION AGENCY FOR NORTHERN IRELAND
Health Protection Agency Centre Emergency Preparedness &
    Response
Health Protection Agency Centre Infections
Health Protection Agency Centre Radiation, Chemical &
    Environmental Hazards
WHO Collaborating Centre Diphtheria & Streptococcal
    Infections
WHO Collaborating Centre Laboratory & Diagnostic
    Support
WHO Collaborating Centre Reference & Research Hospital
    Infections
WHO Collaborating Centre Training & Research
    Communications & Information Technology Health
    Promotion & Disease Prevention
HERIOT-WATT UNIVERSITY
Biomedical Textiles Research Centre
Centre Economic Reform & Transformation
Centre Environment & Human Settlements
Centre Environmental Resource Management
Centre Environmental Scanning Electron Microscopy
Centre Integrated Optoelectronic Systems
Centre Marine Biodiversity & Biotechnology
Centre Occupational Health & Safety
Centre Research Socially Inclusive Services
Centre Theoretical Modelling Medicine
Centre Translating & Interpreting Studies Scotland
Fluid Loading & Instrumentation Centre
Genetics & Insurance Research Centre
Heriot-Watt Institute Petroleum Engineering
Institute Computer Based Learning
International Centre Brewing & Distilling
International Centre Island Technology
International Centre Mathematical Sciences
Logistics Research Centre
MIcroSystems Engineering Centre
Ocean Systems Laboratory
Research Institute Flexible Materials
Scottish Institute Sustainable Technology
Scottish Manufacturing Institute
Social Enterprise Institute
HERTFORDSHIRE, UNIVERSITY OF
Automotive Engineering Centre
Biodeterioration Centre
Blended Learning Unit CETL
Centre Astrophysics Research
Centre Community Research
Centre Computer Science & Informatics Research

Centre Engineering & Applied Sciences Research
Centre Enhancement Learning & Teaching
Centre Information Management & Technology
Centre Research Electronic Art & Communication
Centre Research Employment Studies
Centre Research Finance & Accounting
Centre Research Institutional Economics
Centre Research Primary & Community Care
Complexity & Management Centre
Health & Human Sciences Research Institute
Science Learning Centre East England
Science & Technology Research Institute
Social Sciences, Arts & Humanities Research Institute

HEYTHROP COLLEGE
Centre Christianity & Interreligious Dialogue
Heythrop Institute Religion, Ethics & Public Life

HIGHLANDS AND ISLANDS, UNIVERSITY OF THE (UHI) INSTITUTE
Agronomy Institute
Centre Mountain Studies
Centre Nordic Studies
Environmental Research Institute
NAFC Marine Centre
Sustainable Development Research Centre
UHI Centre History
UHI Decommissioning & Environmental Remediation Centre

HUDDERSFIELD, UNIVERSITY OF
Applied Criminology Centre
Biomolecular Sciences Research Centre
Centre Applied Catalysis
Centre Applied Childhood Studies
Centre Applied Psychological Research
Centre Constructions & Identity
Centre Democracy & Governance
Centre Enterprise, Ethics & Environment
Centre Health & Social Care Research
Centre Precision Technologies
Centre Thermal Studies
Nationwide Children's Research Centre

HULL, UNIVERSITY OF
Centre City & Regional Studies
Centre Criminology & Criminal Justice
Centre Democratic Governance
Centre Educational Studies
Centre European Union Studies
Centre Learning Development
Centre Legislative Studies
Centre Magnetic Resonance Investigations
Centre Medical Engineering & Technology
Centre Organic & Biological Chemistry
Centre Renaissance Studies
Centre Research Social Inclusion & Social Justice
Centre Security Studies
Centre Study Comparative Change & Development
Clinical Biosciences Institute
Clinical Neuroscience Centre
Design Enterprise Centre
Environmental Technologies Centre Industrial Collaboration
Hull Environment Research Institute
Hull International Fisheries Institute
Institute Applied Ethics
Institute Chemistry Industry
Institute Estuarine & Coastal Studies
Institute European Public Law
Institute Learning
Institute Rehabilitation
Lipids Research Centre
Maritime Historical Studies Centre
McCoubrey Centre International Law
Performance Translation Centre
Physical Sciences Centre
Scarborough Centre Coastal Studies
University Hull Logistics Institute
Wetland Archaeology & Environments Research Centre

Wilberforce Institute Study Slavery & Emancipation

I

IMPERIAL COLLEGE, LONDON
Advanced Biotechnology Centre
Built Environment Innovation Centre
Centre Bioinformatics
Centre Biomolecular Electron Microscopy
Centre Cold Matter
Centre Environmental Policy
Centre Fusion Studies & Plasma Engineering
Centre Health Management
Centre History Science, Technology & Medicine
Centre Integrative Systems Biology at Imperial College
Centre Ion Conducting Membranes
Centre Molecular Microbiology & Infection
Centre Process Systems Engineering
Centre Professional Development
Centre Quantitative Finance
Centre Structural Biology
Centre Transport Studies
Chemical Biology Centre
Composites Centre
Entrepreneurship Centre
Eric Bywaters Centre Vascular Inflammation
Future Railway Research Centre
Genetic Therapies Centre
Glycobiology Training, Research & Infrastructure Centre
Grantham Institute Climate Change
Imperial College Centre Interfacial Science & Technology
Innovation Studies Centre
Institute Biomedical Engineering
Institute Mathematical Sciences
Institute Reproductive & Developmental Biology
International Centre Circulatory Health
International Pesticide Application Research Centre
Kennedy Institute Rheumatology
London Centre History Science, Medicine & Technology
London Centre Marine Technology
London Centre Nanotechnology
London e-Science Centre
MRC Clinical Sciences Centre
National Centre Human Retrovirology
National Heart & Lung Institute
NERC Centre Population Biology
Research Centre Non-destructive Evaluation
Silwood Centre Pest Management
Sir Leon Bagrit Centre
Vibration University Technology Centre
Wellcome Centre Clinical Tropical Medicine
Wright Fleming Institute

INSTITUTE OF ACTUARIES
Continuous Mortality Investigation Bureau

INSTITUTE FOR ANIMAL HEALTH
Edward Jenner Institute Vaccine Research

K

KEELE UNIVERSITY
Centre Applied Entomology & Parasitology
Centre Criminological Research
Centre Health Planning & Management
Centre International Exchange & Languages
Centre Law, Ethics & Society
Centre Politics & International Studies
Centre Professional Ethics
Centre Social Gerontology
Centre Successful Schools
David K E Bruce Centre American Studies

© CBD Research Ltd · Beckenham · Kent BR3 5JS · Tel 020 8650 7745 · Fax 020 8650 0768 · E-mail cbd@cbdresearch.com · www.cbdresearch.com

Institute Orthopaedics
Institute Science & Technology Medicine
Keele Centre Wave Dynamics
Keele European Research Centre
MacKay Institute Communication & Neuroscience
Primary Care Musculoskeletal Research Centre
Research Institute Environment, Physical Sciences & Applied
    Mathematics
Research Institute Law, Politics & Justice
Research Institute Life Course Studies
Research Institute Public Policy & Management
Science Learning Centre West Midlands
Sir David Owen Population Centre

KENT, UNIVERSITY OF
AHRC Research Centre Law, Gender & Sexuality
Anglo-Chinese Business & Management Centre
Canterbury Centre Medieval & Tudor Studies
Centre American Studies
Centre Astrophysics & Planetary Science
Centre BioMedical Informatics
Centre Colonial & Postcolonial Studies
Centre Creative Writing
Centre European, Regional & Transport Economics
Centre Gender, Sexuality & Writing
Centre Health Services Studies
Centre Heuristic Optimisation
Centre History Science, Technology & Medicine
Centre Modern Poetry
Centre Music Technology
Centre Regional Business Productivity
Centre Research Health Behaviour
Centre Social Anthropology & Computing
Centre Sports Studies
Centre Study Group Processes
Centre Study Propaganda
Centre Study Social & Political Movements
Centre Supply Chain Research
Centre Tourism Islands & Coastal Areas
Centre Work & Learning
Durrell Institute Conservation & Ecology
Electronic Systems Design Centre
European Centre Study Migration & Social Care
European Institute Social Services
Institute Mathematics, Statistics & Actuarial Science
Kent Centre European & Comparative Law
Kent Criminal Justice Centre
Kent Institute Advanced Studies Humanities
Kent Institute Medicine & Health Sciences
Kent Technology Transfer Centre
Tizard Centre

KING'S COLLEGE, LONDON
Academic Centre Defence Mental Health
Australia Centre
British Institute Human Rights
Burdett Institute Gastrointestinal Nursing
Caucasus Policy Institute
Centre Anxiety Disorders & Trauma
Centre Bioactivity Screening Natural Products
Centre British Constitutional Law & History
Centre Cell & Integrative Biology
Centre Cellular Basis Behaviour
Centre Computing Humanities
Centre Construction Law & Management
Centre Crime & Justice Studies
Centre Defence Studies
Centre Digital Signal Processing Research
Centre Economics Mental Health
Centre Environmental Assessment, Management & Policy
Centre European Law
Centre Hellenic Studies
Centre History Philosophical Theology
Centre Language, Discourse & Communication
Centre Late Antique & Medieval Studies
Centre Latin American Cultural Studies

Centre Mechatronics & Manufacturing Systems
Centre Medical Law & Ethics
Centre Parent & Child Support
Centre Philosophical Studies
Centre Public Policy Research
Centre Recovery Severe Psychosis
Centre Telecommunications Research
Centre Theology, Religion & Culture
Drug Control Centre
ESRC United Kingdom Centre Evidence Based Policy &
    Practice
Health Sciences & Practice Subject Centre
Institute Advanced Musical Studies
Institute Criminal Policy Research
Institute Gerontology
Institute Psychiatry
International Centre Prison Studies
King's Centre Military Health Research
King's Centre Risk Management
Liddell Hart Centre Military Archives
Mental Health Knowledge Centre
Menzies Centre Australian Studies
MRC-Asthma UK Centre Allergic Mechanisms Asthma
MRC Centre Developmental Neurobiology
MRC Centre Neurodegenerative Research
Research Centre American Studies
Research Institute Systematic Theology
Sackler Institute Pulmonary Pharmacology
Saint John's Institute Dermatology
Social, Genetic & Developmental Psychiatry Centre
WHO Collaborating Centre Research & Training Mental
    Health
Wolfson Centre Age-Related Diseases

KINGSTON UNIVERSITY, LONDON
Aerospace Research Centre
Applied Engineering Research Centre
Asia Business Research Centre
Business-to-Business Marketing Research Centre
Centre Applied Research Information Systems
Centre Contemporary Visual & Material Culture
Centre Earth & Environmental Science Research
Centre Economic Research & Intelligence
Centre Insolvency Law & Policy
Centre International Business Policy
Centre Iris Murdoch Studies
Centre Local History Studies
Centre Stakeholding & Sustainable Enterprise
Centre Suburban Studies
Centre Working Life Research
Colour Design Research Centre
Digital Imaging Research Centre
Fashion Industry Research Centre
Helen Bamber Centre Study Rights & Conflict
Mobile Information & Network Technologies Research
    Centre
Modern Interiors Research Centre
Scientific Analysis & Visualisation Centre
Small Business Research Centre
Sustainable Design Research Centre
Sustainable Technology Research Centre

L

LANCASTER UNIVERSITY
Centre Study Education & Training
Centre Collaborative Intervention Public Sector
Centre Study Environmental Change
Institute Cultural Research
Centre Applied Statistics
Centre Economic & Social Aspects Genomics
Centre Enhancement Learning & Teaching
Centre Language Social Life

Centre Medical Education
Centre Mobilities Research
Centre North-West Regional Studies
Centre Research Language Education
Centre Science Studies
Centre Studies Advanced Learning Technology
Centre Study Technology & Organisations
Collaboratory Quantitative e-Social Science [Research
    Centre]
Institute Advanced Studies Social & Management Sciences
Institute Entrepreneurship & Enterprise Development
Institute Environmental & Natural Sciences
Institute Health Research
Institute Philosophy & Public Policy
Institute Women's Studies
International Centre Research Accounting
Lancaster Centre e-Science
Lancaster Centre Forecasting
Lancaster China Management Centre
Lancaster Literacy Research Centre
PALATINE - Dance, Drama & Music
Richardson Institute Peace & Conflict Research
Teaching Excellence & Mentoring Postgraduates using
    Statistics
Wordsworth Centre

LEARNING AND TEACHING SCOTLAND
Scottish Centre Financial Education

LEEDS, UNIVERSITY OF
Antimicrobial Research Centre
Assessment & Learning Practice Settings CETL
Astbury Centre Structural Molecular Biology
CAA Institute Satellite Navigation
Cardiovascular Research Institute at Leeds
Centre Advanced Studies Finance
Centre Animal Sciences
Centre Bioscience
Centre British Government
Centre Business Law & Practice
Centre Business & Professional Ethics
Centre Canadian Studies
Centre Chinese Business Development
Centre Citizenship & Human Rights Education
Centre Computational Fluid Dynamics
Centre Criminal Justice Studies
Centre Cultural Analysis, Theory & History
Centre Decision Research
Centre Democratization Studies
Centre Development Studies
Centre Disability Studies
Centre Epidemiology & Biostatics
Centre Ethnicity & Racism Studies
Centre European Political Communications
Centre Health & Social Care
Centre Heritage Research
Centre Interdisciplinary Gender Studies
Centre International Business, University Leeds
Centre International Communications Research
Centre International Governance
Centre International Studies
Centre Jewish Studies
Centre Mediterranean Studies
Centre Plant Sciences
Centre Policy Studies Education
Centre Self-Organising Molecular Systems
Centre Studies Science & Mathematics Education
Centre Study Governance European Union
Centre Study Law & Policy Europe
Centre Translation Studies
Centre Water Policy & Development
Centre World Cinemas
Credit Management Research Centre
Earth & Biosphere Institute
Earth, Energy & Environment University Interdisciplinary
    Institute

Energy & Resources Research Institute
European Centre Biodiversity & Conservation Research
Families, Life Course & Generations Research Centre
IDEA CETL
India & South Asia Business Centre
Industrial Centre Particle Science & Engineering
Institute Atmospheric Science
Institute Clinical Sciences
Institute Colonial & Postcolonial Studies
Institute Communications Studies
Institute Corporate Learning
Institute Geological Sciences
Institute Geophysics & Tectonics
Institute Integrated Information Systems
Institute Integrative & Comparative Biology
Institute Materials Research
Institute Medieval Studies
Institute Membrane & Systems Biology
Institute Microwaves & Photonics
Institute Molecular & Cellular Biology
Institute Particle Science & Engineering
Institute Psychological Sciences
Institute Research Contemporary China
Institute Satellite Navigation
Institute Transport Studies
Interdisciplinary Centre Scientific Research Music
Interdisciplinary Research Centre Polymer Science &
    Technology
International Institute Banking & Financial Services
Leeds Dental Institute
Leeds Humanities Research Institute
Leeds Institute Genetics, Health & Therapeutics
Leeds Institute Health Sciences
Leeds Institute Molecular Medicine
Leeds Social Sciences Institute
Leeds University Centre African Studies
Lifelong Learning Institute
Modelling & Simulation e-Social Science [Research Centre]
Nuffield Centre International Health & Development
Psychological Therapies Research Centre
Research Centre Future Communications
Skin Research Centre
Subject Centre Philosophical & Religious Studies
Sustainability Research Institute
Yorkshire Centre Health Informatics

LEEDS METROPOLITAN UNIVERSITY
Carnegie National Sports Development Centre
Carnegie Research Institute
Centre Active Lifestyles
Centre Applied Psychology, Health & Culture
Centre Built Environment
Centre Community Neurological Studies
Centre Director Education
Centre Diversity, Equity & Inclusion
Centre Eating, Food & Health
Centre Education, Leadership & Professional Development
Centre Health Promotion Research
Centre Hospitality Management & Retailing
Centre Men's Health
Centre Pain Research
Centre Performance Sport
Centre Physical Education & Sport Pedagogy
Centre Project Management
Centre Research Childhood
Centre Tourism & Cultural Change
Centre Urban Development & Environmental Management
Institute Enterprise
Policy Research Institute
Praxis Centre - Centre Study Information & Technology
    Peace, Conflict Resolution & Human Rights
United Kingdom Centre Events Management

LEICESTER, UNIVERSITY OF
Advanced Microscopy Centre
Centre Applied Psychology

© CBD Research Ltd · Beckenham · Kent BR3 5JS · Tel 020 8650 7745 · Fax 020 8650 0768 · E-mail cbd@cbdresearch.com · www.cbdresearch.com

Centre Child Protection Studies
Centre Citizenship Studies Education
Centre Diplomatic & International Studies
Centre Educational Leadership & Management
Centre English Local History
Centre Innovation Raising Educational Achievement
Centre Labour Market Studies
Centre Mass Communication Research
Centre Quebec Studies
Centre Sociology Sport
Centre Study Country House
Centre Urban History
Genetics Education - Networking Innovation & Excellence
    CETL
Greenwood Institute Child Health
Institute Genetics
Institute Lifelong Learning
Leicester e-Science Centre Excellence
Marc Fitch Historical Institute
Medieval Research Centre
National Printing Skills Centre
National Space Centre
Richard Attenborough Centre Disability & Arts
Science Learning Centre East Midlands
Spatial Literacy Teaching CETL
Stanley Burton Centre Holocaust Studies
Victorian Studies Centre

LINCOLN, UNIVERSITY OF
Centre Clinical & Academic Workforce Innovation
Centre Health Improvement & Leadership Lincoln
Centre Management & Business Research
Hull Centre Management Development
International Institute Education Leadership

LIVERPOOL, UNIVERSITY OF
Centre Accelerator Science, Imaging & Medicine
Centre BioArray Innovation
Centre Cell Imaging
Centre Central & Eastern European Studies
Centre Comparative Infectious Diseases
Centre Excellence Teaching & Learning Developing
    Professionalism Medical Students
Centre Intelligent Monitoring Systems
Centre Manx Studies
Centre Nanoscale Science
Centre Port & Maritime History
Centre Research Primary Science & Technology
Centre Study Child, Family & Law
e-Business Research Centre
Environmental Radioactivity Research Centre
Europe World Centre
Haemostasis & Thrombosis Centre
Impact Research Centre
Institute Child Health
Institute Irish Studies
Institute Latin American Studies
Institute Medicine, Law & Bioethics
Institute Popular Music
Institute Sustainable Water, Integrated Management &
    Ecosystem Research
Lairdside Laser Engineering Centre
Liverpool Centre Medieval Studies
Liverpool Institute Biocomplexity
Liverpool University Centre Archive Studies
Liverpool University Institute Cancer Studies
Manufacturing Science & Engineering Research Centre
Surface Science Research Centre
United Kingdom Centre Materials Education
United Kingdom Centre Tissue Engineering
Veterinary Surveillance Centre
Wellcome Trust Tropical Centre
WHO Collaborating Centre Policy Research Social
    Determinants Health
WHO Collaborating Centre Prevention Deafness & Hearing
    Impairment

WHO Collaborating Centre Research Oral Health Deprived
    Communities
Wolfson Centre Carbon & Silicon-Based Electronics

LIVERPOOL HOPE UNIVERSITY COLLEGE
LearnHigher CETL

LIVERPOOL JOHN MOORES UNIVERSITY
Astrophysics Research Institute
Centre Excellence Leadership & Professional Learning
Centre Health & Social Care Informatics
Centre Public Health
Centre Writing
European Institute Urban Affairs
General Engineering Research Institute
International Centre Digital Content
Lairdside Maritime Centre
Research Centre Evolutionary Anthropology &
    Palaeoecology
Research Centre Literature & Cultural History
Research Institute Sport & Exercise Sciences

LONDON, UNIVERSITY OF
Breakthrough Breast Cancer Research Centre
Cancer Research UK Centre Cancer Therapeutics
Cancer Research UK Centre Cell & Molecular Biology
Centre Academic & Professional Literacies
Centre Behavioural Medicine
Centre Contemporary British History
Centre Corporate Law & Practice
Centre Critical Education Policy Studies
Centre Equality & Human Rights Education
Centre Evidence-informed Policy & Practice Education
Centre Excellence Work-Based Learning Education
    Professionals
Centre Higher Education Studies
Centre Longitudinal Studies
Centre Manuscript & Print Studies
Centre Metropolitan History
Centre Research & Development Catholic Education
Centre Research Wider Benefits Learning
Centre Study Children, Youth & Media
Courtauld Institute Art
Earth Science Centre
Ingeborg Bachmann Centre Austrian Literature
Institute Advanced Legal Studies
Institute Cancer Research
Institute Classical Studies
Institute Commonwealth Studies
Institute Education
Institute English Studies
Institute Germanic & Romance Studies
Institute Historical Research
Institute Musical Research
Institute Philosophy
Institute Study Americas
International Centre Intercultural Studies
Language & Literacy Research Centre
London Centre Leadership Learning
London Mathematics Centre
National Research & Development Centre Adult Literacy &
    Numeracy
Research Centre German & Austrian Exile Studies
Research Centre Illuminated Manuscripts
Science Learning Centre London
Sir William Dale Centre Legislative Studies
Warburg Institute

LONDON BUSINESS SCHOOL
Aditya V Birla India Centre
Advanced Institute Management Research
BNP Paribas Hedge Fund Centre
Centre Corporate Governance
Centre Marketing
Centre New & Emerging Markets
Centre Scientific Enterprise
Institute Finance & Accounting
Institute Technology

Lehman Brothers Centre Women Business
Private Equity Institute

LONDON CHAMBER OF COMMERCE AND INDUSTRY
European Information Centre

LONDON METROPOLITAN UNIVERSITY
Caribbean Studies Centre
Centre Comparative European Survey Data
Centre Environmental & Social Study Aging
Centre Ethnicity & Gender
Centre Excellence Teaching & Learning Reusable Learning
    Objects
Centre Housing & Community Research
Centre International Capital Markets
Centre International Transport Management
Centre Leisure & Tourism Studies
Centre MicroEnterprise
Centre Primary Health & Social Care
Centre Research Marketing
Centre Social Evaluation Research
Centre Trade Union Studies
Centre Transcultural Research
Cities Institute
Communications & Software Systems Engineering Research
    Centre
Comparative Organisation & Equality Research Centre
European Human Rights Advocacy Centre
Human Rights & Social Justice Research Institute
Institute Brain Chemistry & Human Nutrition
Institute Health Research & Policy
Institute Policy Studies Education
Institute Study European Transformations
Intelligent Systems Research Centre
International Institute Culture, Tourism & Development
Irish Studies Centre
John Grieve Centre Policing & Community Safety
Learning Technology Research Institute
London Environment Centre
London European Research Centre
London Metropolitan Polymer Centre
Management Research Centre [London]
Manufacturing Architecture Research Centre
Science Centre
Statistics, Operational Research & Mathematics Research
    Centre
Teaching & Learning Technology Centre
Transport Research & Consultancy
Visual Art Practice Research Centre
Working Lives Research Institute
Write Now CETL

**LONDON SCHOOL OF ECONOMICS AND POLITICAL
SCIENCE**
Asia Research Centre
BIOS Centre
Cañada Blanch Centre Contemporary Spanish Studies
Centre Analysis Time Series
Centre Civil Society
Centre Discrete & Applicable Mathematics
Centre Economic Performance
Centre Economics Education
Centre International Studies
Centre Philosophy Natural & Social Science
Centre Research Economics & Finance Southern Africa
Centre Study Global Governance
Centre Study Human Rights
Cold War Studies Centre
Crisis States Research Centre
Development Studies Institute
ESRC Centre Analysis Risk & Regulation
ESRC Research Centre Analysis Social Exclusion
European Institute
Financial Markets Group Research Centre
Gender Institute
Institute Social Psychology
LSE Centre Urban Research

LSE Environment: Centre Environmental Policy &
    Governance
LSE London Centre Urban & Metropolitan Research
LSE Mackinder Centre Study Long Wave Events
Mannheim Centre Study Criminology & Criminal Justice
Methodology Institute
Suntory & Toyota International Centres Economics & Related
    Disciplines
WHO Collaborating Centre Health Policy & Pharmaceutical
    Economics

**LONDON SCHOOL OF HYGIENE AND TROPICAL
MEDICINE, UNIVERSITY OF LONDON**
Centre Research Drugs & Health Behaviour
Centre Spatial Analysis Public Health
European Centre Health Societies Transition
International Centre Eye Health
WHO Collaborating Centre Prevention & Control Sexually
    Transmitted Infections (STI)
WHO Collaborating Centre Research & Training Injury &
    Violence Prevention

LONDON SOUTH BANK UNIVERSITY
Central London Professional Development Centre
Centre Accounting, Finance & Governance
Centre Applied Formal Methods
Centre Concurrent Systems & Very Large Scale Integration
Centre Cross Curricular Initiatives
Centre e-Security
Centre Energy Studies
Centre Government & Charity Management
Centre Information Management & E-Business
Centre Interactive Systems Engineering
Centre International Business Studies
Centre Knowledge Transfer
Centre Leadership & Practice Innovation
Centre Physical Electronics & Materials
Centre Research Allied Health Professions
Centre Sustainable Energy Systems
Centre Systems & Software Engineering
Ehrenberg Centre Research Marketing
Food Research Centre
Human Performance Centre
Institute Computing Research
Institute Primary Care & Public Health
London Food Centre
Photophysics Research Centre
RCN Development Centre
Sustainable Transport Research Centre
Sports & Exercise Research Centre

LOUGHBOROUGH UNIVERSITY
Applied Vision Research Centre
Banking Centre
BHF National Centre Physical Activity & Health
Centre Automotive Management
Centre Child & Family Research
Centre Environmental Studies
Centre Hazard & Risk Management
Centre Innovative & Collaborative Engineering
Centre Mobile Communications Research
Centre Nonlinear Mathematics & Applications
Centre Olympic Studies & Research
Centre Renewable Energy Systems Technology
Centre Research Social Policy
Centre Study International Governance
Communications Research Centre
East Midlands Eurocentre
Electronic Publishing Innovation Centre
Engineering Centre Excellence Teaching & Learning
Engineering Subject Centre
Ergonomics & Safety Research Institute
European Construction Institute
Innovative Electronics Manufacturing Research Centre
Institute Polymer Technology & Materials Engineering
Institute Sport & Leisure Policy
Institute Surface Science Technology

© CBD Research Ltd · Beckenham · Kent BR3 5JS · Tel 020 8650 7745 · Fax 020 8650 0768 · E-mail cbd@cbdresearch.com · www.cbdresearch.com

Institute Youth Sport
International Centre Vibro-Impact Systems
Loughborough Innovative Manufacturing & Construction
    Research Centre
Loughborough Materials Characterisation Centre
Loughborough Sleep Research Centre
Manufacturing Systems Integration Research Institute
Mathematics Education Centre
Mathematics Learning Support Centre
Midlands Centre Criminology & Criminal Justice
Parallelism, Algorithms & Architectures Research Centre
Peter Harrison Centre Disability Sport
Subject Centre Information & Computer Sciences
Systems Engineering Innovation Centre
Transport Technology Ergonomics Centre
Vehicle Safety Research Centre
Water Engineering & Development Centre

M

MANCHESTER, UNIVERSITY OF
3rd Generation Proteomics Centre
Access Grid Support Centre
AHRC Research Centre Studies Surrealism & its Legacies
Alan Turing Institute
Brooks World Poverty Institute
Cathie Marsh Centre Census & Survey Research
Centre Applied South Asian Studies
Centre Applied Theatre Research
Centre Assessment Solutions
Centre Biblical Studies
Centre Business Research
Centre Chinese Business & Management Studies
Centre Chinese Studies
Centre Combined Studies
Centre Criminology & Socio-Legal Studies
Centre Cultural History War
Centre Diversity & Work Psychology
Centre Educational Leadership
Centre Equity Education
Centre Excellence Enquiry-Based Learning
Centre Formative Assessment Studies
Centre Growth & Business Cycle Research
Centre Integrated Genomic Medical Research
Centre Interdisciplinary Research Arts
Centre Jewish Studies
Centre Late Antiquity
Centre Latin American Cultural Studies
Centre Local Governance
Centre Museology
Centre Nanoporous Materials
Centre Novel Computing
Centre Process Integration
Centre Public Policy & Management
Centre Radiochemistry Research
Centre Regulation & Competition
Centre Religion & Political Culture
Centre Russian & Eurasian Studies
Centre Screen Studies
Centre Social Ethics & Policy
Centre Study Sexuality & Culture
Centre Translation & Intercultural Studies
Centre Urban & Regional Ecology
Chronic Poverty Research Centre
Confucius Institute
Corrosion & Protection Centre
Cultural Theory Institute
Dalton Nuclear Institute
Environmental Impact Assessment Centre
Environmental Technology Centre
e-Science North West Centre
ESRC Centre Research Innovation & Competition

ESRC Centre Research Socio-Cultural Change
ESRC National Centre e-Social Science
European Centre Management Education
European Work & Employment Research Centre
Granada Centre Visual Anthropology
Impact Assessment Research Centre
Industrial Process Tomography Centre
Institute Development Policy & Management
Institute Health Sciences
Institute Political & Economic Governance
Jodrell Bank Science Centre
Joule Centre Energy Research
Laser Processing Research Centre
Lincoln Theological Institute Study Religion & Society
Manchester Cancer Research Centre
Manchester Centre Anglo-Saxon Studies
Manchester Centre Integrative Systems Biology
Manchester Centre Magnetic Resonance
Manchester Centre Mesoscience & Nanotechnology
Manchester Centre Music Culture
Manchester Centre Nonlinear Dynamics
Manchester Centre Public Theology
Manchester Institute Innovation Research
Manchester Institute Mathematical Sciences
Manchester Interdisciplinary Biocentre
Manchester Poetry Centre
Manchester Regional Economics Centre
Manchester Science Enterprise Centre
Manchester-Sheffield Centre Dead Sea Scrolls Research
Materials Performance Centre
Michael Barber Centre Mass Spectrometry
Molecular Materials Centre
Morgan Centre Study Relationships & Personal Life
National Centre Text Mining
National Grid High Voltage Research Centre
National Primary Care Research & Development Centre
Neuroscience Research Institute
Northwest Composites Centre
Organic Materials Innovation Centre
Paterson Institute Cancer Research
Photon Science Institute
Retail Centre
Satake Centre Grain Process Engineering
United Kingdom Centre Excellence Biocatalysis,
    Biotransformation & Biomanufacturing
United Kingdom Centre Tissue Engineering
University Manchester Aerospace Research Institute
Wellcome Trust Centre Cell-Matrix Research
WHO Collaborating Centre Public Health Issues Congenital
    Anomalies & Technology Transfer (Treatment &
    Management Craniofacial Anomalies)
William Lee Innovation Centre
Williamson Research Centre Molecular Environmental
    Science
Wolfson Centre Rational Design Molecular Diagnostics
Wolfson Molecular Imaging Centre

MANCHESTER METROPOLITAN UNIVERSITY
Arts Health Centre
Art & Media Arts Research Centre
Automation Systems Centre
Centre Aviation, Transport & Environment
Centre Dental Technology Studies
Centre Enterprise
Centre European Integration
Centre European Literatures & Cultures
Centre International Business & Innovation
Centre Materials Science Research
Centre Mathematical Modelling & Flow Analysis
Centre Policy Modelling
Centre Professional Accounting & Financial Services
Centre Quality, Innovation & Support
Centre Research Library & Information Management
Centre Urban Education
Community Audit & Evaluation Centre

Craft & Design Research Centre
Crime Fictions Research Centre
Dalton Research Institute
Drama, Dance & Performing Arts Research Centre
Education & Social Research Institute
English Research Institute
Fashion, Business & Technology Research Centre
Gender & Sexuality Research Centre
Information Research Institute
Institute Biophysical & Clinical Research Human Movement
Institute Culture, Gender & City
Institute Education
Institute Global Studies
Manchester Centre Regional History
Manchester European Research Institute
Manchester Institute Research & Innovation Art & Design
North West Food Centre
Promethean Centre Excellence
Research Institute Business & Management
Research Institute Health & Social Change
Science Learning Centre North West
Social & Environmental Art Research Centre
Visual Culture Research Centre

MEDICAL RESEARCH COUNCIL
Mouse Genome Centre
National Centre Replacement, Refinement & Reduction Animals Research

MI5, THE SECURITY SERVICE
Joint Terrorism Analysis Centre

MIDDLESEX UNIVERSITY
Centre Advanced Management Research
Centre Applied Research Economics
Centre Brazilian & Latin America Studies
Centre Decision Management & Risk Management
Centre Enterprise & Economic Development Research
Centre Environment & Safety Management Business
Centre Legal Research
Centre Psychoanalysis
Centre Research Creation Performing Arts
Centre Research Modern European Philosophy
Centre Research Translation
Crime & Conflict Research Centre
Flood Hazard Research Centre
Institute Nursing & Midwifery
Institute Primary Care Development
Institute Social & Health Research
Lansdown Centre Electronic Arts
London Sport Institute
Middlesex University Translation Institute
National Centre Project Management
National Centre Work Based Learning Partnerships
Research Centre Transcultural Studies Health
Social Policy Research Centre

MORLEY COLLEGE, LONDON
Centre Young Musicians

N

NAPIER UNIVERSITY
Centre Business Languages
Centre Entrepreneurship
Centre Festival & Event Management
Centre Mathematics & Statistics
Centre Timber Engineering
Employment Research Institute
International Teledemocracy Centre
Scottish Centre Facilities Management
Scottish Centre Pollen Studies
Transport Research Institute

NATIONAL BLOOD SERVICE
Bristol Institute Transfusion Sciences

NATIONAL HEALTH SERVICE
NHS Institute Innovation & Improvement
NATIONAL MARINE BIOLOGICAL LIBRARY
Marine Pollution Information Centre
NATIONAL MARITIME MUSEUM
Centre Imperial & Maritime Studies
NATIONAL SCHOOL OF GOVERNMENT
Centre Strategic Leadership
NATURAL HISTORY MUSEUM
WHO Collaborating Centre Identification & Characterization Schistosome Strains & their Snail Intermediate Hosts
NEWCASTLE UPON TYNE, UNIVERSITY OF
BALTIC Centre Contemporary Art
Centre Excellence Healthcare Professional Education
Centre Excellence Life Sciences
Centre Gender & Women's Studies
Centre History Medicine
Centre Land Use & Water Resources Research
Centre Life
Centre Pipeline Engineering
Centre Research Environmental Appraisal & Management
Centre Research Knowledge Science & Society
Centre Rural Economy
Centre Software Reliability
Centre Urban & Regional Development Studies
Electrochemical & Materials Processing Centre
Engineering Design Centre
Human Nutrition Research Centre
Inclusivity Contemporary Music Culture CETL
Informatics Research Institute
Institute Ageing & Health
Institute Cell & Molecular Biosciences
Institute Cellular Medicine
Institute Health & Society
Institute Human Genetics
Institute Nanoscale Science & Technology
Institute Neuroscience
Institute Policy & Practice
Institute Research Environment & Sustainability
Interdisciplinary Research Centre Dependability Computer-Based Systems
International Centre Cultural & Heritage Studies
International Centre Music Studies
Life Bioscience Centre
Newcastle Centre Family Studies
Newcastle Centre Railway Research
Newcastle Centre Social & Business Informatics
Newcastle Fertility Centre at Life
Newcastle Institute Arts, Social Sciences & Humanities
North East England Stem Cell Institute
North East Regional e-Science Centre
Northern Institute Cancer Research
Policy, Ethics & Life Sciences Research Centre
Postgraduate Institute Medicine & Dentistry
Sowerby Centre Health Informatics
Subject Centre Medicine, Dentistry & Veterinary Medicine
WHO Collaborating Centre Nutrition & Oral Health
WHO Collaborating Centre Training, Evaluation & Research Diabetes
Wolfson Research Centre
NHS ESTATES
Centre Healthcare Architecture & Design
NHS HEALTH SCOTLAND
WHO Collaborating Centre Health Promotion & Public Health Development
NORTHAMPTON, UNIVERSITY OF
Centre Children & Youth
Centre Contemporary Fiction & Narrative
Centre Learning & Enterprise Organisations
Centre Practice-led Research Arts
Centre Research Leather & Materials Science
Centre Special Needs Education & Research
Centre Study Anomalous Psychological Processes
Centre Study Comprehensive Schools

China & Transitional Economics Research Centre
Leather Conservation Centre
SITA Centre Sustainable Wastes Management
Sunley Management Centre

NORTHUMBRIA UNIVERSITY
Advanced Materials Research Institute
Biomolecular & Biomedical Research Centre
Centre Business Excellence
Centre Design Research
Centre Environmental & Spatial Analysis
Centre Excellence Teaching & Learning Assessment Learning
Centre Public Policy
Disaster & Development Centre
English Language Centre
Glenamara Centre International Research Arts & Society
Microelectronics Industrial Centre
North East England History Institute
Northumbrian Environmental Training & Research Centre
Sustainable Cities Research Institute
Travel Law Centre

NOTTINGHAM, UNIVERSITY OF
Bookham Centre Excellence Optoelectronic Simulation
Brain & Body Centre
Centre Ancient Drama & its Reception
Centre Applied Bioethics
Centre Biochemistry & Cell Biology
Centre Biomolecular Sciences
Centre Clean Water Technologies
Centre Decision Research & Experimental Economics
Centre Developing & Evaluating Lifelong Learning
Centre English Language Education
Centre Environment
Centre Environmental Law
Centre Environmental Management
Centre Europe-Asia Business Research
Centre Geospatial Science
Centre Healthcare Associated Infections
Centre Industrial Mathematical Modelling
Centre Integrated Systems Biology & Medicines
Centre Integrative Learning
Centre Literacy Research
Centre Local History
Centre Management Buy-Out Research
Centre Mathematical Medicine
Centre Policy Evaluation
Centre Population Sciences
Centre Quality Global Supply Chain
Centre Rail Human Factors
Centre Reproduction & Early Life
Centre Research Applied Linguistics
Centre Research Equity & Diversity Education
Centre Research Medical Sociology & Health Policy
Centre Respiratory Research
Centre Risk & Insurance Studies
Centre Social Research Health & Health Care
Centre Social Work
Centre Study Byron & Romanticism
Centre Study European Governance
Centre Study Human Relations
Centre Study Mathematics Education
Centre Study Post-Conflict Cultures
Centre Study Social & Global Justice
Centre Study Viking Age
Centre Urban Culture
China Policy Institute
Christel DeHaan Tourism & Travel Research Institute
D H Lawrence Research Centre
ESRC Centre Research Economic Development & International Trade
George Green Institute Electromagnetics Research
Human Rights Law Centre
Institute Architecture
Institute Asia-Pacific Studies
Institute Building Technology

Institute Cell Signalling
Institute Clinical Research
Institute Engineering Surveying & Space Geodesy
Institute Film & Television Studies
Institute Genetics
Institute Infection, Immunity & Inflammation
Institute Medieval Studies
Institute Middle Eastern Studies
Institute Name-Studies
Institute Neuroscience
Institute Occupational Ergonomics
Institute Pharmaceutical Sciences & Experimental Therapeutics
Institute Research Learning & Teaching Higher Education
Institute Science & Society
Institute Study Slavery
Institute Sustainable Energy Technology
Institute Urban Planning
Institute Work, Health & Organisations
International Centre Corporate Social Responsibility
Joanna Briggs Institute
Learning Sciences Research Institute
Leverhulme Centre Research Globalization & Economic Policy
Methods & Data Institute
MRC Institute Hearing Research - Nottingham Clinical Section
MUNDI Centre Global Education
National Centre Macromolecular Hydrodynamics
Nottingham Arabidopsis Stock Centre
Nottingham Centre Geomechanics
Nottingham Fuel & Energy Centre
Nottingham Innovative Manufacturing Research Centre
Nottingham Institute Research Visual Culture
Nottingham Institute Russian & East European Studies
Nottingham Mining & Mineral Centre
Nottingham Nanotechnology & Nanoscience Centre
Nottingham Policy Centre
Nottingham Transportation Engineering Centre
Nottingham University Electrical Drives Centre
Sir Peter Mansfield Magnetic Resonance Centre
Sue Ryder Care Centre Palliative & End Life Studies
Teacher & Leadership Research Centre
Treaty Centre
UNESCO Centre Comparative Education Research
University Nottingham Institute Enterprise & Innovation
University Nottingham Institute Materials Technology
University Nottingham Tax Research Institute
Visual LearningLab CETL
Wolfson Digestive Diseases Centre

NOTTINGHAM TRENT UNIVERSITY
Advanced Design & Manufacturing Engineering Centre
Centre Asia-Pacific Studies
Centre Automotive Industries Management
Centre Broadcasting & Journalism
Centre Effective Learning Science
Centre Growing Businesses
Centre Legal Research
Centre Leisure Retailing
Centre Public Services Management (Nottingham)
Centre Trauma, Resilience & Growth
Institute Cultural Analysis, Nottingham
International Fraud Prevention Research Centre
Nottingham Centre Study & Reduction Hate Crimes, Bias & Prejudice
Nottingham Institute English Research
Nottingham Trent Centre Colonial & Postcolonial Studies
Nottingham Trent Centre Travel Writing Studies
Raymond Williams Centre Recovery Research
Royal Statistical Society Centre Statistical Education
Theory, Culture & Society Centre
Work Institute

O

OPEN UNIVERSITY
Centre Ageing & Biographical Studies
Centre Analysis Supply Chain Innovation & Dynamics
Centre Citizenship, Identities & Governance
Centre Earth, Planetary, Space & Astronomical Research
Centre Educational Development
Centre Higher Education Research & Information
Centre History Mathematical Sciences
Centre Informatics Education Research
Centre Innovation, Knowledge & Development
Centre Institutional Research
Centre Open Learning Mathematics, Science, Computing & Technology
Centre Research Computing
Centre Research Education & Educational Technology
Centre Study Educational Technologies
Centre Technology Strategy
Charles Booth Centre Study History Social Investigation
Children's Research Centre
Complexity Science Research Centre
ESRC Centre Research Socio-Cultural Change
European Centre Study Policing
Ferguson Centre African & Asian Studies
Innogen - ESRC Centre Social & Economic Research Innovation Genomics
Institute Educational Technology
Interdisciplinary Centre Astrobiology
International Centre Comparative Criminological Research
International Development Centre
Knowledge Media Institute
Open University Centre Education Medicine
Personalised Integrated Learning Support CETL
Planetary & Space Sciences Research Institute
Practice-based Professional Learning CETL
Worm Research Centre

OXFORD, UNIVERSITY OF
Asian Studies Centre
Centre Brazilian Studies
Centre Criminology
Centre Evidence-Based Dentistry
Centre Evidence-Based Medicine
Centre Evidence-Based Mental Health
Centre Excellence Preparing Academic Practice
Centre International Studies
Centre Linguistics & Philology
Centre Mathematical Biology
Centre Migration, Policy & Society
Centre Observation & Modelling Earthquakes & Tectonics
Centre Quantum Computation
Centre Research Inequality, Human Security & Ethnicity
Centre Socio-Legal Studies
Centre Study African Economies
Centre Study Ancient Documents
Centre Teaching Chinese as a Foreign Language
Centre Visual Studies
Clifford Chance Centre Management Professional Service Firms
e-Horizons Institute
Edward Grey Institute Field Ornithology
Environmental Change Institute
ESRC Centre Skills, Knowledge & Organisational Performance & Organisational Performance
Ethox Centre
European Humanities Research Centre
European Studies Centre
Future Humanity Institute
Griffith Institute
Health Economics Research Centre
Institute Archaeology
Institute Chinese Studies

Institute Emergent Infections Humans
Institute European & Comparative Law
Institute Future Mind
Institute Human Sciences
Institute Social & Cultural Anthropology
James Martin Institute Science & Civilisation
John Adams Institute Accelerator Science
Khalili Research Centre Art & Material Culture Middle East
Latin American Centre
Mathematical Institute
Middle East Centre
Nissan Institute Japanese Studies
Nomura Centre Quantitative Finance
Oriental Institute
Oxford Centre Advanced Materials & Composites
Oxford Centre Buddhist Studies
Oxford Centre Environmental Biotechnology
Oxford Centre Ethics & Philosophy Law
Oxford Centre Functional Magnetic Resonance Imaging Brain
Oxford Centre Hebrew & Jewish Studies
Oxford Centre Higher Education Policy Studies
Oxford Centre Hindu Studies
Oxford Centre Industrial & Applied Mathematics
Oxford Centre Islamic Studies
Oxford Centre Maritime Archaeology
Oxford Centre Mission Studies
Oxford Centre Molecular Sciences
Oxford Centre Population Research
Oxford Centre Science Mind
Oxford Centre Water Research
Oxford e-Research Centre
Oxford Financial Research Centre
Oxford Glycobiology Institute
Oxford Institute Ageing
Oxford Institute Employee Relations
Oxford Institute Information Management
Oxford Institute Retail Management
Oxford Intellectual Property Research Centre
Oxford Internet Institute
Oxford Learning Institute
Oxford McDonnell Centre Cognitive Neuroscience
Oxford Uehiro Centre Practical Ethics
Oxford University Centre Business Taxation
Oxford University Centre Environment
Philosophy Centre
Queen Elizabeth House International Development Centre
Refugee Studies Centre
Resource Centre Randomised Trials
Rothermere American Institute
Skoll Centre Social Entrepreneurship
University Oxford Centre Competition Law & Policy
University Oxford Centre Suicide Research
Weatherall Institute Molecular Medicine
Wellcome Trust Centre Human Genetics

OXFORD BROOKES UNIVERSITY
Assessment Standards Knowledge exchange CETL
Business, Management, Accountancy & Finance Subject Centre
Centre Applied Human Resource Research
Centre Democracy Studies
Centre Development & Emergency Practice
Centre Diversity Policy Research
Centre Environmental Studies Hospitality Industries
Centre Health, Medicine & Society
Centre Legal Research & Policy Studies
Centre Proteins & Peptides
Europe Japan Research Centre
Hospitality, Leisure, Sport & Tourism Network
Institute Historical & Cultural Research
International Centre English Language Studies
Joining Technology Research Centre
Joint Centre Urban Design
Oxford Centre Staff & Learning Development

© CBD Research Ltd · Beckenham · Kent BR3 5JS · Tel 020 8650 7745 · Fax 020 8650 0768 · E-mail cbd@cbdresearch.com · www.cbdresearch.com

Oxford Institute Sustainable Development
Oxford International Centre Publishing Studies
Research Centre Modern & Contemporary Poetry
Westminster Institute Education

P

PAISLEY, UNIVERSITY OF
Advanced Concrete & Masonry Centre
Centre Contemporary European Studies
Centre Environmental & Waste Management
Centre Particle Characterisation & Analysis
Crichton Centre Rural Enterprise
Paisley Enterprise Research Centre
Quality Centre
Thin Film Centre

PLYMOUTH, UNIVERSITY OF
Advanced Composites Manufacturing Centre
Centre Chemical Sciences
Centre Coastal Dynamics & Engineering
Centre Excellence Professional Placement Learning
Centre Innovation Mathematics Teaching
Centre Interactive Intelligent Systems
Centre Legal Practice
Centre Observation Air-Sea Interactions & Fluxes
Centre Sustainable Futures
Centre Theoretical & Computational Neuroscience
Centre Thinking & Language
Experiential Learning Environmental & Natural Sciences
    CETL
Geography, Earth & Environmental Sciences Subject Centre
Higher Education Learning Partnerships CETL
Innovate - Centre Creative Industries
Institute Digital Art & Technology
Institute Science Education
Interdisciplinary Centre Computer Music Research
Local Government Chronicle Elections Centre
Marine Biology & Ecology Research Centre
Marine Institute
Plymouth Electron Microscopy Centre
Plymouth International Studies Centre

PORTSMOUTH, UNIVERSITY OF
Centre Creative Empowerment
Centre Enterprise Research & Innovation
Centre European & International Studies Research
Centre Excellence Professional Development Through Use
    Relevant Technologies
Centre Fine Art & Philosophy
Centre Images Practice
Centre Local & Regional Economic Analysis
Centre Molecular Design
Centre Music Theatre
Centre New Media Research
Centre Performance Enhancement
Centre Sound & Experimental Environments
Centre Theatre & Community
Foundation Direct CETL
Institute Biomedical & Biomolecular Sciences
Institute Cosmology & Gravitation
Institute Criminal Justice Studies
Institute Industrial Research
Institute Marine Sciences
Portsmouth Centre Enterprise
Regional Centre Manufacturing Industry

Q

QUEEN ELIZABETH MEDICAL CENTRE, BIRMINGHAM
WHO Collaborating Centre Research & Reference Services
    Clinical Chemistry

QUEEN MARGARET UNIVERSITY
Centre Health Psychology
Centre Integrated Healthcare Research
Institute International Health & Development
Royal Bank Scotland Centre Community Arts Research &
    Practice
Royal Bank Scotland Centre Older Person's Agenda
Scottish Centre Enterprise & Ethnic Business Research
Scottish International Tourism Industries Research Centre
Speech Science Research Centre

QUEEN MARY, UNIVERSITY OF LONDON
Centre General Practice & Primary Care
AHRC Centre Editing Lives & Letters
Centre Academic Surgery
Centre Adult Oral Health
Centre Adult & Paediatric Gastroenterology
Centre Anglo-German Cultural Relations
Centre Cancer Imaging
Centre Catalan Studies
Centre Cell
Centre Child Health
Centre Clinical & Diagnostic Oral Sciences
Centre Commercial Law Studies
Centre Cutaneous Research
Centre Diabetes & Metabolic Medicine
Centre Digital Music
Centre Environmental & Preventive Medicine
Centre Excellence Teaching & Learning Clinical &
    Communication Skills
Centre Film Studies
Centre Globalisation Research
Centre Haematology
Centre Health Sciences
Centre Infectious Disease
Centre Life Sciences
Centre Materials Research
Centre Medical Education
Centre Medical Oncology
Centre Micromorphology
Centre Molecular Oncology
Centre Oral Growth & Development
Centre Professionals Complementary to Dentistry
Centre Psychiatry
Centre Renaissance & Early Modern Studies
Centre Research Equality & Diversity
Centre Sports & Exercise Medicine
Centre Statistics
Centre Study Migration
Centre Surgical Science
Centre Translational Oncology
Centre Tumour Biology
Digestive Disease Research Centre
Digital & Photographic Imaging Centre
Dr Williams's Centre Dissenting Studies
Genome Centre
Institute Cancer
Institute Cell & Molecular Science
Institute Dentistry
Institute Health Sciences Education
Interdisciplinary Research Centre (IRC) Biomedical Materials
London Centre Clean Energy
Mathematics Research Centre
Neuroscience Centre
William Harvey Research Institute
Wolfson Institute Preventive Medicine

QUEEN'S UNIVERSITY, BELFAST
AHRB Centre Byzantine Cultural History
Belfast e-Science Centre
Canine Behaviour Centre
Centre Advancement Women Politics
Centre Atomic & Molecular Quantum Dynamics
Centre Built Environment Research
Centre Canadian Studies
Centre Cancer Research & Cell Biology

Centre Cardiovascular Research
Centre Clinical & Population Studies
Centre Creative Industry
Centre Cross Border Studies
Centre Data Digitisation & Analysis
Centre Eighteenth Century Studies
Centre International Borders Research
Centre Irish Politics
Centre Marine Resources & Mariculture
Centre Nanostructured Media
Centre Plasma Physics
Centre Social Research
Centre Study Ethnic Conflict
Centre Theory & Application Catalysis
Centre Vision Sciences & Vascular Biology
Chrono Centre Climate, Environment, & Chronology
Environmental Engineering Research Centre
Gibson Institute Land, Food & Environment
Human Rights Centre
Inflammation Research Centre
Institute Agri-Food & Land Use
Institute Byzantine Studies
Institute Child Care Research
Institute Cognition & Culture
Institute Criminology & Criminal Justice
Institute Electronics, Communications & Information
    Technology
Institute Governance, Public Policy & Social Research
Institute Irish Studies
Institute Professional Legal Studies
Institute Spatial & Environmental Planning
Institute Theology
International Centre System-on-Chip & Advanced
    Microwireless Integration
International Research Centre Experimental Physics
Medical Polymers Research Institute
Nanotec Northern Ireland
Northern Ireland Centre Biodiversity & Conservation Biology
Northern Ireland Centre Information Language Teaching &
    Research
Northern Ireland Semiconductor Research Centre
Northern Ireland Technology Centre
Ophthalmology & Vision Science Research Centre
Polymer Processing Research Centre
Queen's University Environmental Science & Technology
    Research Centre
Queen's University Ionic Liquid Laboratories
Sonic Arts Research Centre
Transport Research Institute - Northern Ireland Centre
Virtual Engineering Centre

R

READING, UNIVERSITY OF
Centre Advanced Microscopy
Centre Agri-Environmental Research
Centre Agricultural Strategy
Centre Applied Language Studies
Centre Biomimetics
Centre Career Management Skills
Centre Dairy Research
Centre Euro-Asian Studies
Centre Euro-Mediterranean Studies
Centre Excellence Teaching & Learning Applied
    Undergraduate Research Skills
Centre Hellenic Studies
Centre Institutional Performance
Centre International Business History
Centre International Business & Strategy
Centre International Security Studies & Non-proliferation
Centre International Studies Education, Management &
    Training

Centre Languages, English & Media Education
Centre Ombudsman & Governance Studies
Centre Planning Studies
Centre Real Estate Research
Centre Spatial & Real Estate Economics
Centre Strategic Studies [Reading]
Centre Stress Research
Centre Study Global Change & Governance
Data Assimilation Research Centre
Environmental Systems Science Centre
Graduate Centre Medieval Studies
Graduate Institute Political & International Studies
Huck Centre Management Research
Innovative Construction Research Centre
Institute Agricultural Management
Institute Education
International Centre Research Music Education
Joint Centre Mesoscale Meteorology
National Centre Biotechnology Education
National Centre Language & Literacy
Polymer Science Centre
Reading e-Science Centre
Research Centre Evacuee & War Child Studies
Research Centre Late Antique & Byzantine Studies
School Improvement & Leadership Centre
Statistical Services Centre

ROBERT GORDON UNIVERSITY
Aberdeen Centre Energy Regulation & Obesity
Aberdeen Centre Trauma Research
Advanced Materials & Biomaterials Research Centre
Centre Enhancement Learning & Teaching
Centre International Labour Market Studies
Centre Knowledge Management
Centre Process Integration & Membrane Technology
Centre Public Policy & Management
Centre Research Energy & Environment
Centre Transport Policy
Centre Video Communications
Charles P Skene Centre Entrepreneurship
Clinical Skills Centre
Institute Employment Law
Scottish Centre Tourism

ROEHAMPTON UNIVERSITY
AHRC Research Centre Cross-Cultural Music & Dance
    Performance
Centre Dance Research
Centre International Research Creativity & Learning
    Education
Centre Language Assessment Research
Centre Nonprofit & Voluntary Section Management
Centre Research Beliefs, Rights & Values Education
Centre Research Cognition, Emotion & Interaction
Centre Research Ecology & Environment
Centre Research Education Policy & Professionalism
Centre Research English & Local History
Centre Research Evolutionary Anthropology
Centre Research Film & Audiovisual Cultures
Centre Research Human Rights
Centre Research Postcolonial & Transcultural Studies
Centre Research Renaissance Studies
Centre Research Romanticism
Centre Scientific & Cultural Research Sport
Centre Theatre Research Europe
Clinical & Health Psychology Research Centre
CRUCiBLE: Centre Rights, Understanding & Citizenship
    Based Learning through Experience
Early Childhood Research Centre
Hispanic Research Centre
National Centre Research Children's Literature
Research Centre Therapeutic Education
Roehampton Social Research Centre
Sport Performance Assessment & Rehabilitation Centre

ROTHAMSTED RESEARCH
Rothamsted Centre Bioenergy & Climate Change

© CBD Research Ltd · Beckenham · Kent BR3 5JS · Tel 020 8650 7745 · Fax 020 8650 0768 · E-mail cbd@cbdresearch.com · www.cbdresearch.com

Rothamsted Centre Crop Genetic Improvement
Rothamsted Centre Mathematical & Computational Biology
Rothamsted Centre Sustainable Pest & Disease Management
Rothamsted Centre Sustainable Soils & Ecosystem Functions

ROYAL COLLEGE OF ART
AHRC Centre Study Domestic Interior
Helen Hamlyn Research Centre

ROYAL COLLEGE OF MIDWIVES
WHO Collaborating Centre Midwifery

ROYAL COLLEGE OF MUSIC
Centre Performance History, incorporating Museum
    Instruments
Centre Performance Science
Centre Study Composition Screen

ROYAL GEOGRAPHICAL SOCIETY
Geography Outdoors

ROYAL HOLLOWAY, UNIVERSITY OF LONDON
AHRC Research Centre History & Analysis Recorded Music
Bedford Centre History Women
Centre Developing Areas Research
Centre Ethnic Minority Studies
Centre Multimedia Performance History
Centre Particle Physics
Centre Public Services Organisations
Centre Quaternary Research
Centre Research Sustainability
Centre Victorian Studies
Computer Learning Research Centre
English Subject Centre
Hellenic Institute
Humanities & Arts Research Centre
John Adams Institute Accelerator Science
Research Centre Holocaust & 20th-Century History
Smart Card Centre

ROYAL NATIONAL INSTITUTE FOR THE BLIND
National Centre Tactile Diagrams

ROYAL NORTHERN COLLEGE OF MUSIC
Centre Excellence Dynamic Career Building Tomorrow's
    Musician
Research Centre Vocational Training Musicians
RNCM Centre Young Musicians

ROYAL VETERINARY COLLEGE, UNIVERSITY OF LONDON
Centre Human Performance
LIVE Centre Excellence Lifelong & Independent Veterinary
    Education
London BioScience Innovation Centre
Veterinary Clinical Skills Centre
Veterinary Surveillance Centre

S

ST ANDREWS, UNIVERSITY OF
AHRC Research Centre Philosophy Logic, Language,
    Mathematics & Mind
Centre Amerindian Studies
Centre Anthropological Study Knowledge & Ethics
Centre Biomolecular Sciences
Centre Dynamic Macroeconomic Analysis
Centre Ethics, Philosophy & Public Affairs
Centre Evolution, Genes & Genomics
Centre Film Studies
Centre French History & Culture
Centre Interdisciplinary Research Computational Algebra
Centre Peace & Conflict Studies
Centre Public Policy & Management
Centre Research Ecological & Environmental Modelling
Centre Research Industry, Enterprise, Finance & Firm
Centre Russian, Soviet & Central & Eastern European Studies
Centre Social & Environmental Accounting Research
Centre Social Learning & Cognitive Evolution
Centre Study Religion & Politics
Centre Study Terrorism & Political Violence

Centre Syrian Studies
Gatty Marine Research Institute
Institute Capitalising Creativity
Institute Environmental History
Institute European Cultural Identity Studies
Institute Middle East, Central Asia & Caucasus Studies
Institute Theology, Imagination & Arts
Logos: Centre Study Ancient Systems Knowledge
Longitudinal Studies Centre - Scotland
Museums, Galleries & Collections Institute
Organic Semiconductor Centre
PharmacoEconomics Research Centre
Photonics Innovation Centre
Saint Andrews Centre Advanced Materials
Saint Andrews Reformation Studies Institute
Saint Andrews Scottish Studies Centre
Saint Andrews University Institute Language & Linguistic
    Studies
Saint John's House Centre Advanced Historical Research

ST GEORGE'S, UNIVERSITY OF LONDON
Cardiovascular Biology Research Centre
Centre Clinical Neuroscience
Centre Medical & Healthcare Education

ST MARTIN'S COLLEGE
Centre Creativity & Innovation
Centre Development Learning & Teaching
Centre Health Research & Practice Development
Centre Research Excellence Religion & Theology
Centre Research & Scholarship History, Education & Cultural
    Heritage

SALFORD, UNIVERSITY OF
Acoustics Research Centre
Adelphi Research Institute Creative Arts & Sciences
Applied Informatics Research Centre
Art & Design Research Centre
Biomedical Sciences Research Institute
Centre Biophysics
Centre Contemporary History & Politics
Centre Economics & Finance Research
Centre Education Built Environment
Centre Environmental Systems Research
Centre IT Construction
Centre Language & Culture
Centre Molecular Drug Design
Centre Networking & Telecommunications Research
Centre Operational Research & Applied Statistics
Centre Public Health Research
Centre Rehabilitation & Human Performance Research
Centre Research Marketing
Centre Robotics & Automation
Centre Study Gambling
Centre Sustainable Urban & Regional Futures
Centre Urban Quality
Centre Virtual Environments
Communication, Cultural & Media Studies Research Centre
European Studies Research Institute
Higher Education Research Centre
Informatics Research Institute
Information Systems, Organisation & Society Research
    Centre
Institute Health & Social Care Research
Institute Materials Research
Institute Social, Cultural & Policy Research
Management Construction Research Centre
Management & Management Sciences Research Institute
Research Centre Organisational Excellence
Research Institute Built & Human Environment
Salford Centre Nursing, Midwifery & Collaborative Research
Salford Centre Research & Innovation Built & Human
    Environment
Salford Centre Social Work Research
Sociology Research Centre
Surface: Inclusive Design Research Centre

SCHOOL OF ORIENTAL AND AFRICAN STUDIES, UNIVERSITY OF LONDON

AHRC Research Centre Cross-Cultural Music & Dance Performance
Centre African Studies
Centre Buddhist Studies
Centre Chinese Studies
Centre Contemporary Central Asia & Caucasus
Centre Development Policy & Research
Centre East Asian Law
Centre Ethnic Minority Studies
Centre Financial & Management Studies
Centre Gender & Religions Research
Centre Gender Studies
Centre History Culture & Medicine
Centre International Law & Colonialism
Centre International Studies & Diplomacy
Centre Islamic & Middle East Law
Centre Islamic Studies
Centre Jaina Studies
Centre Jewish Studies
Centre Korean Studies
Centre Law & Conflict
Centre Media & Film Studies
Centre South Asian Studies
Centre South East Asian Studies
Centre Study Japanese Religions
Centre Taiwan Studies
Japan Research Centre
Languages Wider World CETL
London Middle East Institute
Poetry Translation Centre
Sainsbury Institute Study Japanese Arts & Cultures

SHEFFIELD, UNIVERSITY OF

Advanced Manufacturing Research Centre
Antibody Resource Centre
Bakhtin Centre
Catchment Science Centre
Centre Bayesian Statistics Health Economics
Centre Biomaterials & Tissue Engineering
Centre Cement & Concrete
Centre Criminological Research
Centre Developmental & Biomedical Genetics
Centre Dutch Studies
Centre Gender Studies
Centre Glass Research
Centre Inquiry-based Learning Arts & Social Sciences
Centre Nineteenth-Century Studies
Centre Political Theory & Ideologies
Centre Pregnancy Nutrition
Centre Public Library & Information Society
Centre Research Freemasonry
Centre Signal Processing Neuroimaging & Systems Neuroscience
Centre Stem Cell Biology
Centre Study Bible Modern World
Centre Study Childhood & Youth
Centre Terrestrial Carbon Dynamics
Centre Well-being Public Policy
Centre Workplace Health
EPSRC National Centre III-V Technologies
ESRC Centre Organisation & Innovation
Hang Seng Centre Cognitive Studies
Humanities Research Institute
Institute Cancer Studies
Institute Folklore Studies Britain & Canada
Institute Language, Speech & Hearing
Institute Microstructural & Mechanical Process Engineering
Institute Study Political Parties
Institute Work Psychology
International Centre Advanced Research Identification Science
Krebs Institute Biomolecular Research
Kroto Research Institute Nanoscience & Technology Centre

National Centre English Cultural Tradition
Political Economy Research Centre
Robert Hill Institute
Sheffield Centre Advanced Magnetic Materials & Devices
Sheffield Centre Aegean Archaeology
Sheffield Centre International Drylands Research
Sheffield Institute Biotechnological Law & Ethics
Sheffield Institute Studies Ageing
Sheffield Polymer Centre
Sheffield University Metals Advisory Centre
Sheffield University Waste Incineration Centre
Sheffield Vascular Institute
Sorby Centre Electron Microscopy & Microanalysis
White Rose Centre Excellence Teaching & Learning Enterprise
WHO Collaborating Centre Metabolic Bone Diseases

SHEFFIELD HALLAM UNIVERSITY

Advanced Composites & Coatings Research Centre
Art & Design Research Centre
Biomedical Research Centre
Centre Corrosion Technology
Centre Education Research
Centre Electronic Devices & Materials
Centre Health & Social Care Research
Centre Individual & Organisational Development
Centre Infrastructure Management
Centre Integral Excellence
Centre International Hospitality Management Research
Centre Professional & Organisation Development
Centre Promoting Learner Autonomy
Centre Regional Economic & Social Research
Centre Research & Evaluation
Centre Science Education
Centre Social Inclusion
Centre Sport & Exercise Science
Centre Sustainable Consumption
Communication & Computing Research Centre
Communication, Media & Communities Research Centre
Cultural, Communication & Computing Research Institute
Enhancing, Embedding & Integrating Employability CETL
Facilities Management Graduate Centre
Food Innovation Research Centre
Hallam Centre Community Justice
Humanities Research Centre
Learning & Teaching Institute
Materials Analysis & Research Services - Centre Industrial Collaboration
Materials & Engineering Research Institute
Metal Joining Research Centre
Modelling Research Centre
Nanotechnology Centre PVD Research
Product & Knowledge Research Centre
Science Learning Centre Yorkshire & Humber
Sport Industry Research Centre
Structural Materials & Integrity Research Centre

SOUTHAMPTON, UNIVERSITY OF

AHRC Research Centre Textile Conservation & Textile Studies
Centre AIDS Research
Centre Antiquity & Middle Ages
Centre Applied Archaeological Analyses
Centre Applied Language Research
Centre Archaeology Human Origins
Centre Behavioural Research, Analysis, & Intervention Developmental Disabilities
Centre Contemporary Art Research
Centre Contemporary Writing
Centre Environmental Sciences
Centre Excellence Inter Professional Learning Public Sector
Centre Human Service Technology
Centre Imperial & Post-Colonial Studies
Centre Language Study
Centre Maritime Archaeology
Centre Operational Research, Management Science & Information Systems

Centre Philosophy & Value
Centre Research Accounting, Accountability & Governance
Centre Research Self & Identity
Centre Rhetoric & Cultural Poetics
Centre Risk Research
Centre Sexual Health Research
Centre Study Emotion & Motivation
Centre Transnational Studies
Computational Engineering & Design Centre
EPSRC NanoPhotonics Portfolio Centre
ESRC National Centre Research Methods
GeoData Institute
Hearing & Balance Centre
Institute Criminal Justice
Institute Entrepreneurship
Institute Maritime Law
Institute Sound & Vibration Research
Interdisciplinary Research Centre Advanced Knowledge
	Technologies
IT Innovation Centre
Lloyd's Register University Technology Centre
Microsoft Institute High Performance Computing
Mountbatten Centre International Studies
MRC Epidemiology Resource Centre
MRC Institute Hearing Research - Southampton Section
National Coordinating Centre Health Technology
	Assessment
National Oceanography Centre
Open Middleware Infrastructure Institute UK
Optoelectronics Research Centre
Parkes Institute Study Jewish / non-Jewish Relations
Science Learning Centre South East
South England Cochlear Implant Centre
Southampton e-Science Centre
Southampton Statistical Sciences Research Institute
Stroke Association Rehabilitation Research Centre
Subject Centre Languages, Linguistics & Area Studies
Subject Centre Social Policy & Social Work
Textile Conservation Centre
Wessex Institute Health Research & Development

STAFFORDSHIRE UNIVERSITY
Academic Development Institute
Advanced Research Institute
Ashley Centre Professional Management
Centre Ageing & Mental Health
Centre Art, Design & Philosophy
Centre Economics & Business Education
Centre Education Psychology Research
Centre Health Psychology
Centre Intelligent Environmental Systems
Centre Local Enterprise & Skills
Centre Primary Care
Centre Rehabilitation Robotics
Centre Research Business, Economics & Management
Centre Research Emerging Economies
Centre Sport & Exercise Research
Informatics & Technology Research Institute
Institute Access Studies
Institute Education Policy Research
Institute Environment & Sustainability Research
Institute Health Research
Institute Human Sciences
Institute Social Work, Advice Work & Social Studies
Regional Sports Performance Centre

STIRLING, UNIVERSITY OF
AHRC Research Centre Environmental History
Aquaculture Technology Centre
Cancer Care Research Centre
Centre Cognitive & Computational Neuroscience
Centre Commonwealth Studies
Centre eLearning Development
Centre Entrepreneurship
Centre Publishing Studies
Centre Research Communication & Language

Centre Research Polish History
Centre Study Retailing Scotland
Centre Tobacco Control Research
Dementia Services Development Centre
Institute Aquaculture
Institute Education
Institute Retail Studies
Institute Social Marketing
Scottish Centre Information Language Teaching
Scottish Institute Northern Renaissance Studies
Social Work Research Centre
Stirling Centre Economic Methodology
Stirling Centre Poetry
Stirling Centre Scottish Studies
Stirling Media Research Institute
University Stirling Centre English Language Teaching

STRATHCLYDE, UNIVERSITY OF
Applied Educational Research Centre
Centre Applied Social Psychology
Centre Biophotonics
Centre Digital Library Research
Centre Economic Renewable Power Delivery
Centre Educational Support
Centre Electrical Power Engineering
Centre Forensic Science
Centre Marine Hydrodynamics
Centre Process Analytics & Control Technology
Centre Professional Legal Studies
Centre Research Interactive Learning
Centre Sentencing Research
Centre Social History Health & Healthcare
Centre Study Human Rights Law
Centre Ultrasonic Engineering
Centre Youth Work Studies
Childhood & Families Research & Development Centre
Doctoral Training Centre Medical Devices
Equality & Discrimination Centre
European Policies Research Centre
Fraser Allander Institute Research Scottish Economy
Glasgow Centre Child & Society
Industrial Control Centre
Institute Communications & Signal Processing
Institute Energy & Environment
Institute Photonics
National Centre Autism Studies
National Centre Training & Education Prosthetics &
	Orthotics
Quality Education Centre
Scottish Centre Journalism Studies
Scottish Centre Occupational Safety & Health
Scottish Centre Sustainable Community Development
Scottish Institute Research Investment & Finance
Scottish Institute Residential Child Care
Ship Stability Research Centre
Strathclyde Centre European Economies Transition
Strathclyde Centre Gender Studies
Strathclyde Institute Drug Research
Strathclyde Institute Pharmacy & Biomedical Sciences

SUNDERLAND, UNIVERSITY OF
Centre Adaptive Systems
Centre Environmental Informatics
Centre Internet Technologies
Centre Research Media & Cultural Studies
Control Systems Centre
Institute Automotive & Manufacturing Advanced Practice
Institute International Research Glass
International Centre Study Violence & Abuse

SURREY, UNIVERSITY OF
Advanced Technology Institute
AHRC Research Centre Cross-Cultural Music & Dance
	Performance
Centre Advanced Surface, Particle & Interface Engineering
Centre Biomedical Engineering
Centre Chronobiology

Centre Clinical Science & Measurement
Centre Communication Systems Research
Centre Election Law
Centre Environmental Health Engineering
Centre Environmental Strategy
Centre Language Studies
Centre Management Learning & Development
Centre Materials, Surfaces & Structural Systems
Centre Nuclear & Radiation Physics
Centre Osmosis Research & Applications
Centre Process & Information Systems Engineering
Centre Research Ageing & Gender
Centre Research Nationalism, Ethnicity & Multiculturalism
Centre Research Nursing & Midwifery Education
Centre Research Social Simulation
Centre Toxicology
Centre Translation Studies
Centre Vision, Speech & Signal Processing
Digital World Research Centre
Environmental Flow Research Centre
European Institute Health & Medical Sciences
Fluids Research Centre
Food, Consumer Behaviour & Health Research Centre
Healthcare Workforce Research Centre
Institute Social Research
Institute Sound Recording
International Centre Nursing Ethics
Labanotation Institute
National Resource Centre Dance
Robens Centre Health Ergonomics
Robens Centre Occupational Health & Safety
Robens Centre Public & Environmental Health
Social Psychology European Research Institute
Space Structures Research Centre
Surrey Centre Excellence Professional Training & Education
Surrey Centre International Economic Studies
Surrey Energy Economics Centre
Surrey Ion Beam Centre
Surrey Sleep Research Centre
Surrey Space Centre
Thermo-Fluid Systems University Technology Centre
UniS Materials Institute
Wolfson Centre Translational Research

SUSSEX, UNIVERSITY OF
Centre Automotive Systems, Dynamics & Control
Centre Colonial & Postcolonial Studies
Centre Computational Neuroscience & Robotics
Centre Critical Social Theory
Centre Culture, Development & Environment
Centre Early Modern Studies
Centre Educational Innovation
Centre Environmental Research
Centre Gender Studies
Centre German-Jewish Studies
Centre Global Political Economy
Centre International Education
Centre Life History Research
Centre Modernist Studies
Centre Parties & Democracy Europe
Centre Physical Electronics & Quantum Technology
Centre Research Cognitive Science
Centre Research Health & Medicine
Centre Research Opera & Music Theatre
Centre South Asian Studies
Centre Study Evolution
Centre Study Sexual Dissidence
Centre Visual Studies
Centre VLSI & Computer Graphics
Centre World Environmental History
Complex Product Systems Innovation Centre
Culture, Development & Environment Centre
Cunliffe Centre Study Constitutionalism & National Identity
Development Research Centre Migration, Globalisation & Poverty

InQbate Centre Excellence Teaching & Learning Creativity
Institute Development Studies
Institute Employment Studies
Justice & Violence Research Centre
MRC Genome Damage & Stability Centre
Space Science Centre
Sussex Astronomy Centre
Sussex Centre Advanced Microscopy
Sussex Centre Intellectual History
Sussex Centre Migration Research
Sussex Centre Neuroscience
Sussex Centre Research Alcohol, Alcoholism & Drug Addiction
Sussex Centre Research History Art
Sussex European Institute
Sussex Institute
Sussex Language Institute
Thermo-Fluid Mechanics Research Centre
Trafford Centre Graduate Medical Education & Research

SWANSEA UNIVERSITY
Callaghan Centre Study Conflict
Centre Applied Language Studies
Centre Child Research
Centre Commercial Law Studies
Centre Complex Fluids Processing
Centre Contemporary German Literature
Centre Criminal Justice & Criminology
Centre Development Studies
Centre Excellence Product Lifecycle Management
Centre Health Information, Research & Evaluation
Centre History Wales & its Borderlands
Centre Research English Literature & Language Wales
Centre Research Gender Culture & Society
Centre Sustainable Aquaculture Research
Centre Translation Research & Multilingualism
Centre Urban Theory
Civil & Computational Engineering Centre
Climate & Land-Surface Systems Interaction Centre
Electronics Systems Design Centre
EPSRC National Mass Spectrometry Service Centre
Institute Advanced Telecommunications
Institute Environmental Sustainability
Institute Health Research
Institute International Shipping & Trade Law
Institute Life Science
Materials Research Centre
Multidisciplinary Nanotechnology Centre
National Centre Public Policy
Richard Burton Centre Film & Popular Culture
Welsh Centre Printing & Coating
Welsh Centre Research Lifelong Learning
Welsh Economy Labour Market Evaluation & Research Centre

T

TEESSIDE, UNIVERSITY OF
Centre Applied Science
Centre Construction Innovation & Research
Centre Entrepreneurship & Small & Medium-sized Enterprise (SME) Development
Centre Food, Physical Activity & Obesity
Centre Forensic Investigation
Centre Health & Social Evaluation
Centre Leadership & Organisational Change
Centre Public Services Management
Centre Regional & Local Historical Research
Centre Rehabilitation Sciences
Centre Social & Policy Research
Clean Environment Management Centre
Food Technology Centre
Institute Health Sciences & Social Care Research

Social Futures Institute
Teesside Centre Nanotechnology & Microfabrication
Teesside Manufacturing Centre
Teesside Medical Computing Centre
Virtual Reality Centre at Teesside

THAMES VALLEY UNIVERSITY

Acupuncture Research Resource Centre
Centre Complementary Healthcare & Integrated Medicine
Centre Internationalisation & Usability
Centre Research & Implementation Clinical Practice
Centre Research Midwifery & Childbirth
Centre Research Tertiary Education
Centre Study Policy & Practice Health & Social Care
Criminal Justice Centre
Institute Information Technology
Institute Research Health & Human Sciences
Mary Seacole Centre Nursing Practice
Richard Wells Research Centre

U

ULSTER, UNIVERSITY OF

Biomedical Sciences Research Institute
Business & Management Research Institute
Centre Coastal & Marine Research
Centre Functional Genomics
Centre Media Research
Centre Molecular Biosciences
Centre Software Process Technologies
Centre Sustainable Technologies
Centre Voluntary Action Studies
Computer Science Research Institute
Engineering Composites Research Centre
Health & Rehabilitation Sciences Research Institute
Institute Nursing Research
Institute Postgraduate Medicine & Primary Care
Institute Ulster-Scots Studies
Northern Ireland Bio-Engineering Centre
Northern Ireland Centre Advanced Materials
Northern Ireland Centre Energy Research & Technology
Northern Ireland Centre Entrepreneurship
Northern Ireland Centre Food & Health
Northern Ireland Centre Health Informatics
Social & Policy Research Institute
Subject Centre Information & Computer Sciences
Technology & Engineering Innovation Centre
Transitional Justice Institute
Transport & Road Assessment Centre
UNESCO Centre Education Pluralism, Human Rights & Democracy
WHO Collaborating Centre Surveillance Congenital Anomalies

ULSTER-AMERICAN FOLK PARK

Centre Migration Studies at Ulster-American Folk Park

UNITED KINGDOM NATIONAL EXTERNAL QUALITY ASSESSMENT SCHEME FOR GENERAL HAEMATOLOGY

WHO Collaborating Centre Quality Assessment Haematology

UNIVERSITY COLLEGE LONDON

Centre Ageing & Mental Health Sciences
Centre Ageing Population Studies
Centre Infectious Disease Epidemiology
Centre Sexual Health & HIV Research
UCL Centre Neuroimaging Techniques
Academic Centre Travel Medicine & Vaccines
Advanced Centre Biochemical Engineering
AHRC Research Centre Evolution Cultural Diversity
Aspire Centre Disability Sciences
Autonomic Neuroscience Institute
Benfield Hazard Research Centre
Bone & Mineral Centre

Cancer Research UK & UCL Cancer Trials Centre
Centre Academic Clinical Orthopaedics
Centre Advanced Instrumentation Systems
Centre Advanced Spatial Analysis
Centre Advancement Learning & Teaching
Centre Allergy Research
Centre Amyloidosis & Acute Phase Proteins
Centre Applied Interaction Research
Centre Auditory Research
Centre Aviation, Space & Extreme Environment Medicine
Centre Behavioural & Social Sciences Medicine
Centre Bio-Medical Engineering
Centre Cardiology & Hatter Institute Cardiovascular Studies
Centre Cardiology Young
Centre Cardiovascular Biology & Medicine
Centre Cardiovascular Genetics
Centre Cell & Molecular Dynamics
Centre Clinical Infection (Bloomsbury)
Centre Clinical Infection (Hampstead)
Centre Clinical Pharmacology & Therapeutics
Centre Clinical Science & Technology
Centre CO2 Technology
Centre Commercial Law
Centre Comparative Genomics
Centre Computational Science
Centre Developmental Language Disorders & Cognitive Neuroscience
Centre Diabetes & Endocrinology
Centre Ecology & Evolution
Centre Empirical Legal Research
Centre Enterprise & Management Innovation
Centre European Politics, Security & Integration
Centre Evidence-Based Child Health
Centre Gastroenterology & Nutrition
Centre Genetic Anthropology
Centre Health Informatics & Multiprofessional Education
Centre Human Genetics
Centre Human Molecular Genetics
Centre Immunodeficiency
Centre Infectious Diseases & International Health
Centre Information Behaviour & Evaluation Research
Centre Intensive Care Medicine & Bloomsbury Institute Intensive Care Medicine
Centre Intercultural Studies
Centre Interdisciplinary Studies Higher Education
Centre International Courts & Tribunals
Centre Israeli Studies
Centre Italian Studies
Centre Law & Environment
Centre Law European Union
Centre Law & Governance Europe
Centre Materials Research
Centre Mathematics & Physics Life Sciences & Experimental Biology
Centre Medical Image Computing
Centre Medical Microbiology
Centre Molecular Cell Biology
Centre Molecular Medicine
Centre Nephrology
Centre Neuroendocrinology
Centre Nonlinear Dynamics & its Applications
Centre Nursing & Allied Health Professionals Research
Centre Outcomes Research & Effectiveness
Centre Paediatric & Adolescent Rheumatology
Centre Paediatric Epidemiology & Biostatistics
Centre Perinatal Brain Research
Centre Polar Observation & Modelling
Centre Research & Analysis Migration
Centre Respiratory Research
Centre Rheumatology
Centre Rheumatology & Connective Tissue Disease
Centre Russian Studies
Centre South-East European Studies
Centre Study Central Europe

Centre Study Economic & Social Change Europe
Centre Tissue Regeneration Science
Centre Transport Studies
Centre Virology
Cultural Informatics Research Centre Arts & Humanities
Deafness, Cognition & Language Research Centre
Design Research Centre
Environmental Change Research Centre
ESRC Centre Economic Learning & Social Evolution
Hugh & Catherine Stevenson Centre Childhood Infectious
        Diseases & Immunology
Innovative Manufacturing Research Centre (IMRC)
        Bioprocessing
Institute Archaeo-Metallurgical Studies
Institute Behavioural Neuroscience
Institute Cognitive Neuroscience
Institute Global Law
Institute Healthy Ageing
Institute Human Genetics & Health
Institute Jewish Studies
Institute Laryngology & Otology
Institute Movement Neuroscience
Institute Neurology
Institute Nuclear Medicine
Institute Ophthalmology
Institute Orthopaedics & Musculo-Skeletal Science
Institute Sport & Exercise Medicine
Institute Urology
International Centre Archives & Records Management
        Research & User Studies
International Centre Chinese Heritage & Archaeology
International Centre Evidence-Based Oral Health
Jevons Institute Competition Law & Economics
Leonard Cheshire Centre Conflict Recovery
Lighthill Institute Mathematical Sciences
London Centre Nanotechnology
London Centre Paediatric Endocrinology & Metabolism
London Shipping Law Centre
Management Studies Centre
MRC UCL Centre Medical Molecular Virology
National Information Centre Speech-Language Therapy
National Medical Laser Centre
Reta Lila Weston Institute Neurological Studies
Royal Free Centre Biomedical Science
Sackler Institute Musculoskeletal Research
Sara Koe PSP Research Centre
Slade Centre Electronic Media Fine Art
UCL Centre Anaesthesia
UCL Centre BioScience & Society
UCL Centre Cosmic Chemistry & Physics
UCL Centre European Studies
UCL Centre Human Communication
UCL Centre International Health & Development
UCL Centre Publishing
UCL Centre Research Ageing
UCL Centre Security & Crime Science
UCL Centre Sustainable Heritage
UCL Centre Systems Engineering
UCL e-Science Centre Excellence
UCL Eastman Dental Institute
UCL Environment Institute
UCL Institute Archaeology
UCL Institute Child Health
UCL Institute Hepatology
UCL Institute Human Health & Performance
UCL Interaction Centre
UCL International Institute Society & Health
UCL Jill Dando Institute Crime Science
UCL NDE Centre
Vinogradoff Institute
VR Centre Built Environment
Wohl Virion Centre
Wolfson Institute Biomedical Research

UNIVERSITY OF WALES INSTITUTE, CARDIFF
Biomedical Science Enterprise & Research Centre
Centre Ceramics Studies, Cardiff
Centre Dental Technology
Centre Health, Safety & Environment
Centre Performance Analysis
Food Industry Centre
National Centre Product Design & Development Research
National Indoor Athletics Centre
Wales Centre Podiatric Studies
Wales Institute Research Co-operatives
Welsh Centre Tourism Research
WHO Collaborating Centre Public Health Management
        Chemical Incidents

W

WALES, UNIVERSITY OF , ABERYSTWYTH
Aberystwyth BioCentre
BBSRC Institute Grassland & Environmental Research
Centre Advanced Software & Intelligent Systems
Centre Educational Studies
Centre Empirical Finance
Centre Glaciology
Centre Health & International Relations
Centre Intelligence & International Security Studies
Centre Performance Research
Centre Research Environment & Health
Centre Research Marketing
Centre Studies Visual Culture Religion
Centre Study Radicalisation & Contemporary Political
        Violence
Centre Welsh Language Services
Centre Welsh Legal Affairs
Centre Widening Participation & Social Inclusion
David Davies Memorial Institute
Institute Biological Sciences
Institute Geography & Earth Sciences
Institute Mathematical & Physical Sciences
Institute Rural Sciences
Institute Welsh Politics
International Centre Protected Landscapes
Organic Centre Wales
WALES, UNIVERSITY OF, BANGOR
BC
CAZS Natural Resources
Centre Advanced & Renewable Materials
Centre Advanced Software Technology
Centre Advanced Study Religion Wales
Centre Advanced Welsh Music Studies
Centre Applied Oceanography
Centre Banking & Finance
Centre Church School Studies
Centre Comparative Criminology & Criminal Justice
Centre Economics Health
Centre Health, Exercise & Rehabilitation
Centre Industrial & Commercial Optoelectronics
Centre Media Sound
Centre Medieval Studies
Centre Mindfulness Research & Practice
Centre Ministry Studies
Centre Pentecostal & Charismatic Studies
Centre Podcasting Research
Centre Social Policy Research & Development
Centre Standardisation Welsh Terminology
Centre Studies Implicit Religion
Centre Studies Rural Ministry
Dementia Services Development Centre Wales
European Accounting Research Centre
Humanities Research Centre
Institute Bioelectronic & Molecular Microsystems
Institute Food, Active Living & Nutrition

© CBD Research Ltd · Beckenham · Kent BR3 5JS · Tel 020 8650 7745 · Fax 020 8650 0768 · E-mail cbd@cbdresearch.com · www.cbdresearch.com

Institute Medical & Social Care Research
Institute Psychology Elite Performance
Institute Rehabilitation
National Institute Excellence Creative Industries
North West Cancer Research Fund Institute
Place-Name Research Centre
R S Thomas Study Centre
Wales Centre Behaviour Analysis
Wales Centre Mental Health Service Development
Welsh Centre Promoting Incredible Years Programmes
Welsh Institute Social & Cultural Affairs
Welsh Music Institute
Welsh National Centre Religious Education
World Education Centre

WALES, UNIVERSITY OF,LAMPETER
Bible & Visual Imagination Research Centre
Centre Australian Studies Wales
Centre Chinese Studies
Centre Comparative Study Modern British & European
    Religious History
Centre Contemporary Approaches to Bible
Centre Contemporary & Pastoral Theology
Centre Enterprise, European & Extension Services
Centre Research Environment & Health
Centre Research Religious Experience
Centre Study Liturgy & Architecture
Centre Study Religion Celtic Societies
Institute Medieval Studies

WALES, UNIVERSITY OF, NEWPORT
Centre Community & Lifelong Learning
Centre Enterprise, Quality & Management
Centre Photographic Research
Newport Centre Criminal & Community Justice

WARWICK, UNIVERSITY OF
Centre Academic & Professional Development
Centre Caribbean Studies
Centre Comparative Labour Studies
Centre Cultural Policy Studies
Centre Education & Industry
Centre Educational Development, Appraisal & Research
Centre English Language Teacher Education
Centre Fusion, Space & Astrophysics
Centre History Medicine
Centre Interfaces & Materials
Centre Management under Regulation
Centre New Technologies Research Education
Centre Primary Health Care Studies
Centre Research East Roman Studies
Centre Research Ethnic Relations
Centre Research Philosophy & Literature
Centre Research Statistical Methodology
Centre Scientific Computing
Centre Small & Medium Sized Enterprises
Centre Studies Democratization
Centre Study Globalisation & Regionalisation
Centre Study Renaissance
Centre Study Safety & Well-Being
Centre Study Women & Gender
Centre Translation & Comparative Cultural Studies
Clinical Sciences Research Institute
Financial Econometrics Research Centre
Financial Options Research Centre
Fluid Dynamics Research Centre
Health Sciences Research Institute
Humanities Research Centre
Institute Applied Cognitive Science
Institute Clinical Education
Institute Governance & Public Management
Institute Health
International Automotive Research Centre
International Centre Education Development
International Manufacturing Centre
Legal Research Institute
Local Government Centre

Mathematics Education Research Centre
Mathematics Research Centre
Modern Records Centre
Molecular Organisation & Assembly Cells Doctoral Training
    Centre
Reinvention Centre Undergraduate Research
Social Theory Centre
United Kingdom Centre Legal Education
Warwick Centre Study Sport Society
Warwick Eighteenth Century Centre
Warwick Finance Research Institute
Warwick Innovative Manufacturing Research Centre
Warwick Institute Education
Warwick Institute Employment Research
Warwick Mathematics Institute
Warwick Systems Biology Centre

WEST OF ENGLAND, UNIVERSITY OF THE
Advanced Centre Drawing
Aerospace Manufacturing Research Centre
Air Quality Management Resource Centre
Bristol Centre Management Accounting Research
Bristol Genomics Research Institute
Bristol Institute Legal Practice
Centre Appearance Research
Centre Clinical & Health Services Research
Centre Complex Cooperative Systems
Centre Environment & Planning
Centre Fine Print Research
Centre Innovative Manufacture & Machine Vision Systems
Centre Learning & Workforce Research
Centre Legal Research
Centre Leisure, Tourism & Society
Centre Local Democracy
Centre Psycho-Social Studies
Centre Public Health Research
Centre Research Analytical, Materials & Sensor Science
Centre Research Biomedicine
Centre Research Education & Democracy
Centre Research Environmental Sciences
Centre Research Plant Science
Centre Social & Organisational Learning as Action Research
Centre Studies Inclusive Education
Centre Transport & Society
Cities Research Centre
Community Information Systems Centre
Construction & Property Research Centre
Contextual, Public & Commemorative Art Research Centre
Digital Media Research Centre
Engineering & Medicine Elastomers Research Centre
Institute Grinding Technology
PLaCe
WHO Collaborating Centre Healthy Cities & Urban Policy

WESTMINSTER, UNIVERSITY OF
Central Cities Institute
Centre Arts Research Technology & Education
Centre Business Information, Organisation & Process
    Management
Centre Capital Punishment Studies
Centre Employment Research
Centre Excellence Professional Learning from Workplace
Centre Finance & Financial Services
Centre Parallel Computing
Centre Research Delivery Legal Services
Centre Research & Education Art & Media
Centre Research Marketing
Centre Study Democracy
Centre Study Law, Society & Popular Culture
Centre Study Urban & Regional Governance
Centre Sustainable Development
Centre System Analysis
Centre Tourism
China Media Centre
Communication & Media Research Institute
Educational Initiative Centre

Max Lock Centre
Policy Studies Institute
Sir George Cayley Research Centre

WOLVERHAMPTON, UNIVERSITY OF
Centre Art & Design & Research Experimentation
Centre Health & Social Care Improvement
Enabling Achievement within a Diverse Student Body CETL
History & Governance Research Institute
Institute Innovation & Enterprise
Management Research Centre
Policy Research Institute
Research Centre Applied Sciences
Research Centre Sport, Exercise & Performance
Research Institute Healthcare Science
Research Institute Information & Language Processing

Y

YORK, UNIVERSITY OF
Alcuin Research Resource Centre
Borthwick Institute Archives
Centre Criminal Justice Economics & Psychology
Centre Defence Economics
Centre Ecology, Law & Policy
Centre Eighteenth Century Studies
Centre Evidence-Based Nursing
Centre Experimental Economics
Centre Health Economics
Centre Health & Public Services Management
Centre Historical Economics & Related Research at York
Centre Housing Policy
Centre Human Palaeoecology
Centre Innovation & Research Science Education

Centre Language Learning Research
Centre Medieval Studies
Centre Novel Agricultural Products
Centre Performance Evaluation & Resource Management
Centre Reading & Language
Centre Renaissance & Early Modern Studies
Centre Research Equity & Impact Education
Centre Reviews & Dissemination
Centre Usable Home Technology
Centre Women's Studies
Centre Working Memory & Learning
Chemical Industry Education Centre
Child Development & Well-Being Interdisciplinary Research Centre
Green Chemistry Centre Excellence
Health Economics Resource Centre
Institute Railway Studies & Transport History
Institute Research Social Sciences
Music Research Centre
National Science Learning Centre
Norwegian Study Centre
Psychology Network
Stockholm Environment Institute at York
White Rose Grid e-Science Centre Excellence
York Centre Complex Systems Analysis
York Institute Tropical Ecosystem Dynamics
York Neuroimaging Centre

VETERINARY LABORATORIES AGENCY
WHO Collaborating Centre Characterization Rabies & Rabies-related Viruses
WHO Collaborating Centre Reference & Research Brucellosis

YORK ST JOHN UNIVERSITY COLLEGE
C4C: Collaborating Creativity CETL
David Hope RE Centre York

SUBJECT INDEX

Symbols used in this index are: > = see   >+ = see also

A

Abduction
  Reunite, International Child Abduction Centre
Abrasive processes
  Institute Grinding Technology
Abuse (physical or sexual)
  Glasgow Centre Study Violence
  International Centre Study Violence & Abuse
  Justice & Violence Research Centre
  Scottish Centre Nonviolence
  WHO Collaborating Centre Research & Training Injury &
      Violence Prevention
Academic development
  Academic Development Institute
Accelerator science & technology
  Centre Accelerator Science, Imaging & Medicine
  Cockcroft Institute
  John Adams Institute Accelerator Science [Oxford]
  John Adams Institute Accelerator Science [Royal Holloway,
      London]
Accountancy
  Bristol Centre Management Accounting Research
  Business, Management, Accountancy & Finance Subject
      Centre
  Centre Accounting, Finance & Governance
  Centre Accounting, Finance & Taxation
  Centre Advanced Studies Finance
  Centre Professional Accounting & Financial Services
  Centre Research Accounting, Accountability & Governance
  Centre Research Finance & Accounting
  Centre Social & Environmental Accounting Research
  Centre Social Responsibility Accounting & Management
  European Accounting Research Centre
  Institute Finance & Accounting
  Institute Public Sector Accounting Research
  International Centre Research Accounting
Acoustics > Sound & vibration research
Acquired immune deficiency syndrome > AIDS (disease)
Acting & actors > Theatre & theatre studies
Activism
  Centre Study Social & Political Movements
  Sumac Centre
Actuarial practice
  Actuarial Research Centre
  Institute Mathematics, Statistics & Actuarial Science
Acupuncture
  Acumedic Centre Chinese Medicine
  Acupuncture Research Resource Centre
  Centre Complementary Care
Acute care
  National Collaborating Centre Acute Care
Addiction > Alcohol, drug & other addictions
Adolescents > Youth & young people
Adoption
  Post-Adoption Centre
Adult & continuing education > Education: adult & continuing
Advanced study
  Institute Advanced Study
Advertising > Media
Advice centres & bureaux
  Citizens Advice Bureaux
Aeronautical engineering > Aviation
Aerospace > Aviation

Africa
  Africa Centre
  Centre African Studies [Cambridge]
  Centre African Studies [Coventry]
  Centre African Studies [Edinburgh]
  Centre African Studies [School of Oriental & African Studies,
      London]
  Centre Commonwealth Studies
  Centre Research Economics & Finance Southern Africa
  Centre Study African Economies
  Centre West African Studies
  Ferguson Centre African & Asian Studies
  Leeds University Centre African Studies
Ageing > Gerontology
Agriculture
  Aberystwyth BioCentre
  CAB International
  Centre Agricultural Strategy
  Centre Agri-Environmental Research
  Centre Land Use & Water Resources Research
  Centre Land-Based Studies
  Centre Novel Agricultural Products
  Cranfield Centre Agricultural & Environmental Engineering
  Cranfield Centre Precision Farming
  Institute Agricultural Management
  Institute Agri-Food & Land Use
  Institute Atmospheric & Environmental Science
  International Agriculture & Technology Centre
  National Agricultural Centre
  Scottish Crop Research Institute
  >+ Organic research & production
Agriculture: sustainable
  Rothamsted Centre Bioenergy & Climate Change
  Rothamsted Centre Crop Genetic Improvement
  Rothamsted Centre for Sustainable Soils and Ecosystem
      Functions
  Rothamsted Research
AIDS (disease)
  Centre AIDS Reagents
  Centre AIDS Research
  Richard Wells Research Centre
  Wohl Virion Centre
Air quality
  Air Quality Management Resource Centre
  Biodeterioration Centre
  Environmental Flow Research Centre
  Institute Atmospheric Science
  Institute Public Health
  >+ Pollution & pollution control
Air travel > Aviation
Aircraft > Aviation
Alcohol, drug & other addictions
  Centre Addiction Research & Education Scotland
  Centre Drug Misuse Research
  Centre Research Drugs & Health Behaviour
  Chemical Dependency Centre
  Drug Control Centre
  DrugScope
  Institute Alcohol Studies
  Scottish Centre Stopping Smoking & Health
  Sussex Centre Research Alcohol, Alcoholism & Drug
      Addiction
Alexander technique
  Bloomsbury Alexander Centre
  Constructive Teaching Centre

Algebra
  Centre Interdisciplinary Research Computational Algebra
  >+ Mathematics
Allergy
  Centre Allergy Research
Alternative technology
  Centre Alternative Technology
Alzheimer's disease
  Alzheimer's Disease Research Centre
  MRC Centre Neurodegenerative Research
America
  Andrew Hook Centre American Studies
  Arthur Miller Centre American Studies
  Cardiff Centre Welsh American Studies
  Centre American Studies
  Centre American, Trans-Atlantic & Caribbean History
  Centre Amerindian Studies
  Centre Migration Studies Ulster-American Folk Park
  David K E Bruce Centre American Studies
  Eccles Centre American Studies
  Institute Study Americas
  Institute Transatlantic, European & American Studies
  Research Centre American Studies
  Rothermere American Institute
  >+ Latin America; United States of America
Amerindians
  Centre Amerindian Studies
Anaesthesia
  UCL Centre Anaesthesia
Analytical chemistry > Chemical analysis & measurement
Ancient documents & manuscripts
  Centre Manuscript & Print Studies
  Centre Study Ancient Documents
  Research Centre Illuminated Manuscripts
Anglo-German relations
  Centre Anglo-German Cultural Relations
  >+ Germany & German people
Anglo-Saxon era
  Manchester Centre Anglo-Saxon Studies
  >+ Medieval studies
Animals > headings below; Specific animals; Zoology
Animals: behaviour
  Centre Social Learning & Cognitive Evolution
Animals: breeding
  Roslin Institute
Animals: health > Veterinary science
Animals: training
  Defence Animal Centre
Animals: welfare
  British Wildlife Rescue Centre
  CAB International
  National Centre Replacement, Refinement & Reduction
    Animals Research
  Sumac Centre
  Wildlife Rescue Centre Ltd
Anorexia > Eating disorders
Anthropology
  Biological Anthropology Research Centre
  Centre Genetic Anthropology
  Centre Amerindian Studies
  Centre Medical Anthropology
  Centre Research Evolutionary Anthropology
  Centre Social Anthropology & Computing
  Centre Visual Anthropology [Goldsmiths, London]
  Granada Centre Visual Anthropology
  Institute Social & Cultural Anthropology
  Research Centre Evolutionary Anthropology &
    Palaeoecology
  Subject Network Sociology, Anthropology, Politics
  Sussex European Institute
Antibodies
  Antibody Resource Centre
  >+ Biology & biological research

Antiquities: illicit
  Illicit Antiquities Research Centre
Anxiety disorders
  Centre Anxiety Disorders & Trauma
Apes
  Monkey World Ape Rescue Centre
Apparel > Fashion & costume
Appearance research > Disfigurement
Aquaculture
  Aquaculture Technology Centre
  Institute Aquaculture
  >+ Fish & fishing
Arab interests & studies
  Institute Arab & Islamic Studies
  >+ Middle East
Arabidopsis
  Nottingham Arabidopsis Stock Centre
Arbitration & mediation
  Centre Effective Dispute Resolution
  International Arbitration & Mediation Centre
Archaeology
  Centre Applied Archaeological Analyses
  Centre Archaeological & Forensic Analysis
  Centre Archaeology Human Origins
  Centre Battlefield Archaeology
  Centre Environmental Archaeology
  Centre Landscape & Townscape Archaeology
  Institute Archaeology & Antiquity
  Institute Archaeology [Oxford]
  Institute Archaeo-Metallurgical Studies
  Ironbridge Institute
  Leslie & Elizabeth Alcock Centre Historical Archaeology
  McDonald Institute Archaeological Research
  Sheffield Centre Aegean Archaeology
  Subject Centre History, Classics & Archaeology
  UCL Institute Archaeology
Architecture
  Centre Advanced Studies Architecture
  Centre Research Architecture
  Centre Study Liturgy & Architecture
  Institute Architecture
  Manufacturing Architecture Research Centre
  Martin Centre Architectural & Urban Studies
  Visual Art Practice Research Centre
Architecture: history
  Courtauld Institute Art
Archives & records
  AHRC Centre Editing Lives & Letters
  Family Records Centre
  International Centre Archives & Records Management
    Research & User Studies
  Liddell Hart Centre Military Archives
  Liverpool University Centre Archive Studies
  Modern Records Centre
Arid zones
  CAZS Natural Resources
Arms trade & control
  Verification Research, Training & Information Centre
Arson
  Arson Prevention Bureau
Art
  Advanced Research Institute
  ArtsWork: Learning Laboratories Centre Excellence
  Barber Institute Fine Arts
  Bath Royal Literary & Scientific Institution
  Bournville Centre Visual Arts
  Bristol Institute Research Humanities & Arts
  Centre Art, Design & Philosophy
  Centre Arts & Humanities Health & Medicine
  Centre Fine Art & Philosophy
  Centre Fine Art Research
  Centre Interactive Network Arts
  Centre Interdisciplinary Research Arts
  Centre Practice as Research Arts

© CBD Research Ltd · Beckenham · Kent BR3 5JS · Tel 020 8650 7745 · Fax 020 8650 0768 · E-mail cbd@cbdresearch.com · www.cbdresearch.com

Centre Practice-led Research Arts
Centre Research Electronic Art & Communication
Centre Study Literature, Theology & Arts
Centre Visual Studies [Oxford]
Centre Visual Studies [Sussex]
Cultural Informatics Research Centre Arts & Humanities
Cultural, Communication & Computing Research Institute
Humanities & Arts Research Centre
Humanities Advanced Technology & Information Institute
Institute International Visual Arts
London Centre Arts & Cultural Enterprise
Manchester Institute Research & Innovation Art & Design
Richard Attenborough Centre Disability & Arts
Sainsbury Centre Visual Arts
Social & Environmental Art Research Centre
Sussex Centre Research History Art
Transnational Art, Identity & Nation Research Centre
Visual Art Practice Research Centre
Visual Research Centre
Wales Millennium Centre
>+ specific subject

Art: conservation
Hamilton Kerr Institute

Art: contemporary
BALTIC Centre Contemporary Art
Centre Contemporary Art [Central Lancashire]
Centre Contemporary Art Research
Centre Contemporary Visual Arts
PLaCe

Art: education & research
Centre Artists' Books
Centre Arts & Learning
Centre Arts Research Technology & Education
Centre Research & Education Art & Media
Crafts Study Centre
International Centre Fine Art Research
Materials & Arts Research Centre

Art: electronic
Lansdown Centre Electronic Arts

Art: history
Courtauld Institute Art
Glenamara Centre International Research Arts & Society
Institute Art History
Vasari Centre Digital Art History

Art: research
Royal Bank Scotland Centre Community Arts Research & Practice

Arthritis & rheumatism
Arthritis Research Centre
Centre Paediatric & Adolescent Rheumatology
Horder Centre Arthritis
Inflammation Research Centre
Kennedy Institute Rheumatology

Artificial intelligence
Artificial Intelligence Applications Institute
Centre Advanced Software & Intelligent Systems
Centre Intelligent Environmental Systems

Artificial limbs > Prosthetics & orthotics

Asbestos
Asbestos Information Centre Ltd

Asia
Asia Research Centre
Asian Studies Centre
Centre Applied South Asian Studies
Centre Asia-Pacific Studies
Centre Contemporary Central Asia & Caucasus
Centre East Asian Studies
Centre Euro-Asian Studies
Centre South Asian Studies [Cambridge]
Centre South Asian Studies [Coventry]
Centre South Asian Studies [Edinburgh]
Centre South Asian Studies [School of Oriental & African Studies, London]
Centre South Asian Studies [Sussex]

Centre South East Asian Studies
East Asia Institute
Ferguson Centre African & Asian Studies
Institute Asia-Pacific Studies

Asperger syndrome
Gifted Children's Information Centre

Assessment
Centre Assessment Solutions
Centre Excellence Teaching & Learning Assessment Learning
Centre Formative Assessment Studies

Asthma
MRC-Asthma UK Centre Allergic Mechanisms Asthma

Astrobiology
Cardiff Centre Astrobiology
Interdisciplinary Centre Astrobiology

Astrology
Centre Psychological Astrology

Astronomy
Astrophysics Research Institute
Centre Astrophysics
Centre Astrophysics & Planetary Science
Centre Astrophysics Research
Centre Planetary Science & Astrobiology
Institute Astronomy [Cambridge]
Institute Astronomy [Edinburgh]
Institute Cosmology & Gravitation
Jodrell Bank Science Centre
Sussex Astronomy Centre
UK Astronomy Technology Centre

Asylum > Immigrants & refugees

Athletics
National Indoor Athletics Centre
>+ Sports: technology & science

Atmosphere > Air quality; Meteorology

Atomic science > Nuclear science & engineering

Audio engineering
Centre Audio Research & Engineering

Audiology > Hearing

Auditing > Accountancy

Australia & Australian people
Australia Centre
Centre Commonwealth Studies
Menzies Centre Australian Studies

Austria & Austrian people
Centre Austrian Studies
Ingeborg Bachmann Centre Austrian Literature

Autism
Autism Research Centre
National Centre Autism Studies

Automation & robotics
Automation Systems Centre
Centre Industrial Automation & Manufacture
Centre Robotics & Automation
Control Engineering Research Centre
Northern Ireland Technology Centre
Siemens Automation & Drives Centre
>+ Control engineering & systems

Automotive industry > Motor industry

Auxiliary languages
Esperanto Centre
Volapük Centre

Aviation
Aerospace Manufacturing Research Centre
Aerospace Research Centre
Aircraft Design Centre
British Light Aviation Centre
Centre Aeronautics
Centre Aviation, Transport & Environment
Farnborough Aerospace Centre
Flight Operations Research Centre Excellence
Scottish Gliding Centre
Sir Arthur Marshall Institute Aeronautics
University Manchester Aerospace Research Institute

Aviation: environment
    Institute Aviation & Environment
Aviation: medicine
    Aviation Health Institute
    Centre Aviation, Space & Extreme Environment Medicine

B

Babies > Children headings
Badminton
    National Badminton Centre
Bakhtin (Mikhail)
    Bakhtin Centre
Balance
    Institute Sound & Vibration Research
    Hearing & Balance Centre
Ballet > Dancing
Bangladesh & Bangladeshi people
    Centre South Asian Studies [Cambridge]
    Centre South Asian Studies [Coventry]
    Centre South Asian Studies [Edinburgh]
    Centre South Asian Studies [School of Oriental & African
        Studies, London]
    Centre South Asian Studies [Sussex]
Banking
    Banking Centre
    Centre Banking & Finance
    Centre Central Banking Studies
    International Institute Banking & Financial Services
Basements
    Basement Information Centre
Bedwetting > Incontinence
Behaviour studies
    Centre Behavioural Research, Analysis, & Intervention
        Developmental Disabilities
    Centre Research Drugs & Health Behaviour
    Grubb Institute Behavioural Studies
    Learning Through Action Centre
    Wales Centre Behaviour Analysis
    >+ Cognitive science
Betting > Gambling
Bible (The)
    Bible & Visual Imagination Research Centre
    Centre Biblical Studies
    Centre Contemporary Approaches to Bible
    Centre Study Bible Modern World
    International Centre Biblical Interpretation
Bibliography > Books; Literature
Biocatalysis
    Exeter Biocatalysis Centre
Biochemistry
    Advanced Centre Biochemical Engineering
    Brunel Institute Bioengineering
    Centre Biochemistry & Cell Biology
    >+ Biotechnology & bioscience
Biocomposites
    BC
Biodiversity
    Centre Sustainable Futures
    European Centre Biodiversity & Conservation Research
Bioenergy
    Rothamsted Centre for Bioenergy and Climate Change
    >+ Biotechnology & bioscience
Bioengineering > Biotechnology & bioscience
Bioethics
    Centre Applied Bioethics
Biographical research
    Centre Ageing & Biographical Studies
    International Biographical Centre
Bioinformatics
    Bioinformatics Research Centre
    Bloomsbury Centre Bioinformatics

Centre Bioinformatics [Imperial College London]Centre
    Bioinformatics & Medical Informatics Training
Cranfield Centre Bioinformatics
Edinburgh Centre Bioinformatics
Biological sensors > Sensors
Biology & biological research
    Aberystwyth BioCentre
    Behavioural Biology Research Centre
    Biological Records Centre
    Centre Carbohydrate Chemistry
    Centre Cell & Chromosome Biology
    Centre Cell & Integrative Biology
    Centre Life Sciences
    Centre Metalloprotein Spectroscopy & Biology
    Institute Biological Sciences
    Institute Environmental & Natural Sciences
    Institute Evolutionary Biology
    Institute Integrative & Comparative Biology
    Institute Reproductive & Developmental Biology
    Multi-Imaging Centre
    National Institute Biological Standards & Control
    Northern Ireland Centre Biodiversity & Conservation Biology
    Wellcome Trust/Cancer Research UK Gurdon Institute
        Cancer & Developmental Biology
    >+ Plants & plant fibres
Biology: computational & mathematical
    Cambridge Computational Biology Institute
    Centre Bioinformatics & Medical Informatics Training
    Centre Mathematical Biology [Bath]
    Centre Mathematical Biology [Oxford]
    Centre Mathematics & Physics Life Sciences & Experimental
        Biology
    Rothamsted Centre Mathematical & Computational Biology
    Scottish Informatics, Mathematics, Biology & Statistics Centre
Biology: structural
    Bloomsbury Centre Structural Biology
    Cambridge & East Anglia Centre Structural Biology
    Centre Structural Biology [Imperial College, London]
Biology: systems
    Centre Integrated Systems Biology & Medicines
    Centre Integrative Systems Biology Imperial College
    Centre Systems Biology Edinburgh
    Centre Systems Biology [Essex]
    COGNIT Research Centre
    Institute Membrane & Systems Biology
    Manchester Centre Integrative Systems Biology
    Warwick Systems Biology Centre
Biomedical research
    Babraham Institute
    Biomedical Research Centre [Dundee]
    Biomedical Research Centre [Sheffield Hallam]
    Biomedical Science Enterprise & Research Centre
    Biomedical Sciences Research Institute [Salford]
    Biomedical Sciences Research Institute [Ulster]
    Centre Bio-Medical Engineering [University College London]
    Centre Biomedical Engineering [Durham]
    Centre Biomedical Engineering [Surrey]
    Centre BioMedical Informatics
    Centre Mathematical Medicine
    Centre Research Biomedicine
    Cranfield BioMedical Centre
    Essex Biomedical Sciences Institute
    Information & Biomedical Engineering Research Centre
    Institute Biomedical & Biomolecular Sciences
    Institute Life Science
    Interdisciplinary Research Centre Biomedical Materials
    Magnetic Resonance Centre
    Magnetic Resonance Research Centre
    Royal Free Centre Biomedical Science
    Strathclyde Institute Pharmacy & Biomedical Sciences
    Wellcome Trust Biocentre
Biomimetics
    Centre Biomimetics

© CBD Research Ltd · Beckenham · Kent BR3 5JS · Tel 020 8650 7745 · Fax 020 8650 0768 · E-mail cbd@cbdresearch.com · www.cbdresearch.com

Centre Biomimetics & Natural Technologies
Biomolecular science
  Babraham Institute
Biomolecular science
  Biomedical Research Centre [Dundee]
  Biomedical Research Centre [Sheffield Hallam]
  Biomolecular & Biomedical Research Centre
  Biomolecular Sciences Research Centre
  Centre Biomolecular Electron Microscopy
  Centre Biomolecular Sciences [Nottingham]
  Centre Biomolecular Sciences [Saint Andrews]
  Institute Biomedical & Biomolecular Sciences
  Institute Biomedical & Life Sciences
  Institute Biomedical Engineering
  Krebs Institute Biomolecular Research
  National Centre Macromolecular Hydrodynamics
  Oxford Centre Molecular Sciences
  Roslin Institute
Biophysics
  Centre Biophysics
Bioscience > Biotechnology & bioscience
Biotechnology & bioscience
  Aberystwyth BioCentre
  Advanced Biotechnology Centre
  Babraham Institute
  Biomaterials & Biomechanics Research Centre
  Biophysics Centre
  BIOS Centre
  Brunel Institute Bioengineering
  Centre Bioactivity Screening Natural Products
  Centre Bioscience
  Centre Biosciences Research
  Centre for Complex Fluids Processing
  Centre Marine Biology & Biotechnology
  Clinical Biosciences Institute
  Cranfield Biotechnology Centre
  Institute Bioelectronic & Molecular Microsystems
  Institute Biotechnology
  Institute Medical & Biological Engineering
  Integrated Earth System Sciences Institute
  Life Bioscience Centre
  Liverpool Institute Biocomplexity
  London BioScience Innovation Centre
  Manchester Interdisciplinary Biocentre
  National Centre Biotechnology Education
  Northern Ireland Bio-Engineering Centre
  Oxford Centre Environmental Biotechnology
  Oxford Centre Molecular Sciences
  Scottish Biotechnology Training Centre
  Sheffield Institute Biotechnological Law & Ethics
  UCL Centre BioScience & Society
  UK Centre Excellence Biocatalysis, Biotransformation &
    Biomanufacturing
Birds > Ornithology; specific types of bird
Birth & birth control
  Active Birth Centre
  Brandon Centre Counselling & Psychotherapy Young People
  Brook Advisory Centres
  >+ Midwifery; Pregnancy
Birthmarks > Disfigurement
Bisexuality > Homosexuality
Bladder dysfunction > Incontinence
Blind & partially sighted
  Blind Centre Northern Ireland
  National Centre Tactile Diagrams
  Scottish Sensory Centre
  >+ Sight & vision
Blood > Haematology; Haemophilia & haemostasis;
  Thrombosis; Transfusion science
Body psychotherapy
  Chiron Centre Ltd
  >+ Psychotherapy & psychoanalysis
Bones & bone disease
  Centre Academic Clinical Orthopaedics

Centre Orthopaedic Biomechanics
Charles Salt Centre Human Metabolism
Institute Orthopaedics
Institute Orthopaedics & Musculo-Skeletal Science
Sackler Institute Musculoskeletal Research
WHO Collaborating Centre Metabolic Bone Diseases
Books
  British Library Document Supply Centre
  Centre Editorial & Intertextual Research
  Centre Novel
  Centre Publishing Studies
  Centre Textual Scholarship
  Scottish Book Centre
  >+ Literature
Botany > Plants & plant fibres
Bowling
  National Centre Bowling
Boxing
  Wu Shu Kwan Chinese Boxing Centre
Braille
  Blind Centre Northern Ireland
  >+ Blind & partially sighted
Brain damage / brain research
  Brain & Body Centre
  British Institute Brain Injured Children
  Cambridge Centre Brain Repair
  Cardiff University Brain & Repair Imaging Centre
  Centre Brain & Cognitive Development
  Centre Brain Injury Rehabilitation & Development
  Centre Perinatal Brain Research
  Institute Adaptive & Neural Computation
  Insitute Future Mind
  MRC Centre Synaptic Plasticity
  UCL Centre Neuroimaging Techniques
  Wolfson Brain Imaging Centre
  Wolfson Molecular Imaging Centre
  York Neuroimaging Centre
Brands: corporate
  Centre Research Brand Marketing
Brass rubbing
  London Brass Rubbing Centre
Brazil & Brazilian people
  Centre Brazilian & Latin America Studies
  Centre Brazilian Studies
Brewing & distilling
  International Centre Brewing & Distilling
  >+ Whisky; Wines
Bricks
  Bursledon Brickworks Conservation Centre
Britain > Great Britain
British Broadcasting Corporation
  BBC Television Centre
  BBC Weather Centre
  >+ Radio; Television
British Empire > Colonial research
Broadcasting
  Centre Broadcasting & Journalism
  Centre Broadcasting History Research
Brucellosis
  WHO Collaborating Centre Reference & Research
    Brucellosis
Buddhism
  Birmingham Buddhist Centre
  Brighton Buddhist Centre
  Bristol Buddhist Centre
  Cambridge Buddhist Centre
  Centre Buddhist Studies [Bristol]
  Centre Buddhist Studies [School of Oriental & African
    Studies, London]
  Croydon Buddhist Centre
  Edinburgh Buddhist Centre
  Glasgow Buddhist Centre
  Lancashire Buddhist Centre
  Leeds Buddhist Centre

London Buddhist Centre
Manchester Buddhist Centre
North London Buddhist Centre
Norwich Buddhist Centre
Oxford Centre Buddhist Studies
West London Buddhist Centre
Building & construction
Adjudication Reporting Centre
Building Centre
Centre Construction Law & Management
Construction & Property Research Centre
European Construction Institute
Institute Building Technology
Management Construction Research Centre
Building & construction: information technology
Centre IT Construction
Building & construction law > Law: construction
Buildings: conservation > Historic buildings & conservation
Buildings: historic > Historic buildings & conservation
Built environment
Built Environment Innovation Centre
Centre Built Environment [Leeds Metropolitan]
Centre Built Environment [Scotland]
Centre Built Environment Research
Centre Education Built Environment [Cardiff]
Centre Education Built Environment [Salford]
Centre Environment & Planning
Centre Management Systems Built & Human Environment
Centre Urban Built Environment
Research Institute Built & Human Environment
VR Centre Built Environment
Bulimia nervosa > Eating disorders
Bulk solids > Materials management / handling
Bunting (Basil)
Basil Bunting Poetry Centre
Burma > Myanmar & Burmese people
Burton (Richard)
Richard Burton Centre Film & Popular Culture
Business > headings below; e-Business; Management headings
Business: assessment
Centre Interfirm Comparison
Business: development
Centre Business Excellence
Centre Business Performance
Centre Business Strategy & Procurement
Centre Business Transformation
Centre Enterprise & Economic Development Research
Centre Enterprise & Innovation
Centre Enterprise & Management Innovation
Centre Enterprise & Regional Development
Centre Enterprise [Manchester Metropolitan]
Centre Enterprise Research & Innovation
Centre Entrepreneurship & SME Development
Centre Entrepreneurship [Aberdeen]
Centre Entrepreneurship [Greenwich]
Centre Entrepreneurship [Napier]
Centre Entrepreneurship [Stirling]
Centre Growing Businesses
Centre Growth & Business Cycle Research
Centre Institutional Performance
Centre International Business & Innovation
Centre International Business, Research & Development
Centre Learning & Enterprise Organisations
Centre Local Enterprise & Skills
Centre New Technologies, Innovation & Entrepreneurship
Centre Regional Business Productivity
Centre Scientific Enterprise
Centre Tomorrow's Company
Cranfield University Business Incubation Centre
ESRC Centre Business Relationships, Accountability, Sustainability & Society
eXeter Centre Research Strategic Processes & Operations
Institute Enterprise
Institute Entrepreneurship

Institute Entrepreneurship & Enterprise Development
Institute Innovation & Enterprise
Institute Small Business & Entrepreneurship
Lean Enterprise Research Centre
Mountjoy Research Centre
National Rural Enterprise Centre
Northern Ireland Centre Entrepreneurship
Portsmouth Centre Enterprise
Scottish Institute Enterprise
Skoll Centre Social Entrepreneurship
Social Futures Institute
University Nottingham Institute Enterprise & Innovation
Welsh Enterprise Institute
Work Institute
Business: education
Business, Management, Accountancy & Finance Subject Centre
Centre Economics & Business Education
Centre Entrepreneurial Learning
Centre Executive Learning
Institute Corporate Learning
Scottish Institute Enterprise
Social Enterprise Institute
Business: ethics
Centre Communication & Ethics International Business
>+ Corporate responsibility
Business: Europe
European Information Centre
Business: family
Caledonian Family Business Centre
Business: history
Centre Business History
Centre Business History Scotland
Business: informatics
Newcastle Centre Social & Business Informatics
Business: international
Centre Communication & Ethics International Business
Centre International Briefing
Centre International Business & Innovation
Centre International Business & Management
Centre International Business & Strategy
Centre International Business History
Centre International Business Policy
Centre International Business Studies
Centre International Business, Research & Development
Centre International Business, University Leeds
Institute International Business
Institute Japanese-European Technology Studies
Business: languages
Centre Business Languages
Business: research
Asia Business Research Centre
Aston Centre Human Resource
Cambridge Entrepreneurship Centre
Cambridge-MIT Institute
Centre Business Organisations & Society
Centre Business Research [Manchester]
Centre Business Society
Centre Entrepreneurship Research [Edinburgh]
Centre Entrepreneurship Research [Essex]
Centre Europe-Asia Business Research
Centre Heuristic Optimisation
Centre Management & Business Research
Centre Policy Modelling
Charles P Skene Centre Entrepreneurship
ESRC Centre Business Research
Paisley Enterprise Research Centre
Scottish Centre Enterprise & Ethnic Business Research
Welsh Institute Competitive Advantage
Work Institute
Business: small & medium
Centre MicroEnterprise
Institute Small Business & Entrepreneurship
International Centre Families Business

Small Business Bureau Ltd
Small Business Research Centre
Welsh Enterprise Institute
Byzantine studies
AHRB Centre Byzantine Cultural History
Centre Byzantine, Ottoman & Modern Greek Studies
Centre Hellenic Studies [King's College London]
Centre Hellenic Studies [Reading]
Hellenic Institute
Institute Byzantine Studies
Research Centre Late Antique & Byzantine Studies

C

Cambodia > Laos & Laotian people
Canada & Canadian people
Centre Canadian Studies [Belfast]
Centre Canadian Studies [Edinburgh]
Centre Canadian Studies [Leeds]
Centre Canadian Studies [Birkbeck, London]
Centre Quebec Studies
>+ America
Cancer
Beatson Institute Cancer Research
Biomedic Centre
Breakthrough Breast Cancer Research Centre
Bristol Cancer Help Centre
Brunel Institute Cancer Genetics & Pharmacogenomics
Cancer Care Research Centre
Cancer Research UK & UCL Cancer Trials Centre
Cancer Research UK Cambridge Research Institute
Cancer Research UK Centre Cancer Therapeutics
Cancer Research UK Centre Cell & Molecular Biology
Cancer Research UK Institute Cancer Studies
Cancer Research UK London Research Institute
Centre Cancer Imaging
Centre Cancer Research & Cell Biology
Centre Magnetic Resonance Investigations
Centre Surgical Science
Centre Tumour Biology
Chemical Biology Centre [Birkbeck, London]
Chemical Biology Centre [Imperial College London]
Clatterbridge Centre Oncology
Eastern Cancer Registration & Information Centre
Helen Rollason Cancer Care Centre Laboratory
Institute Cancer
Institute Cancer Research [Queen Mary, London]
Institute Cancer Studies [Sheffield]
Institute Cancer Therapeutics
Liverpool University Institute Cancer Studies
Manchester Cancer Research Centre
MRC Centre Nutritional Epidemiology Cancer Prevention &
Survival
National Collaborating Centre Cancer
North West Cancer Research Fund Institute
Northern Institute Cancer Research
Paterson Institute Cancer Research
Sir James Black Centre
Tenovus Centre Cancer Research
Tom Connors Cancer Research Centre
Wellcome Trust/Cancer Research UK Gurdon Institute
Cancer & Developmental Biology
Wolfson Molecular Imaging Centre
Canoes & canoeing
National Watersports Centre
Capital punishment
Centre Capital Punishment Studies
Carbon
Centre Terrestrial Carbon Dynamics
Diamond-like Carbon Coating Centre
Scottish Centre Carbon Storage

Carbon dioxide
Centre CO2 Technology
Cardiology
Centre Cardiology & Hatter Institute Cardiovascular Studies
Centre Cardiology Young
Sir Geraint Evans Wales Heart Research Institute
Cardiothoracic research
National Heart & Lung Institute
Sir Leon Bagrit Centre
BHF Glasgow Cardiovascular Research Centre
Bristol Heart Institute
Cardiovascular Biology Research Centre
Cardiovascular Research Institute Leeds
Centre Cardiology & Hatter Institute Cardiovascular Studies
Centre Cardiovascular Biology & Medicine
Centre Cardiovascular Genetics
Centre Cardiovascular Research
International Centre Circulatory Health
Sir Geraint Evans Wales Heart Research Institute
Tayside Institute Cardiovascular Research
Care homes (training)
Centre Sheltered Housing Studies
Careers
Careers Research & Advisory Centre
Centre Career & Skills Development
National Institute Careers Education & Counselling
Salters' Institute
Cargo: hazardous
Seafarers International Research Centre
Caribbean
Caribbean Studies Centre
Centre Caribbean Studies [Goldsmiths, London]
Centre Caribbean Studies [Warwick]
Centre American, Trans-Atlantic & Caribbean History
Centre Commonwealth Studies
Latin America Bureau
Latin American Centre
Carnivals
National Centre Carnival Arts
Cars > Motor headings
Cartography > Maps
Casting (metal)
Castings Centre
Castings Technology International
>+ Metals & metallurgy
Catalan region > Spain & Spanish people
Catalysis
Centre Applied Catalysis
Centre Materials Science
Centre Theory & Application Catalysis
Exeter Biocatalysis Centre
Surface Science Research Centre
Catering > Hotel & catering industry
Catholic > Roman Catholic Church
Cats
Feline Advisory Bureau
Cattle
World Jersey Cattle Bureau
Caucasus region
Caucasus Policy Institute
Centre Contemporary Central Asia & Caucasus
Cell engineering & research
Babraham Institute
Centre Biochemistry & Cell Biology
Centre Cell & Chromosome Biology
Centre Cell & Integrative Biology
Centre Cell & Molecular Dynamics
Centre Cell Engineering Glasgow
Centre Cell Imaging
Centre Cellular Basis Behaviour
Centre Regenerative Medicine
Centre Stem Cell Biology
Centre Stem Cell Biology & Developmental Genetics
Centre Stem Cell Biology & Regenerative Medicine

Institute Cell & Molecular Biosciences
Institute Cell & Molecular Science
Institute Cell Biology
Institute Cell Signalling
Institute Cellular Medicine
Institute Medical Sciences [Aberdeen]
Institute Molecular & Cellular Biology
Institute Stem Cell Biology & Regenerative Medicine
Institute Stem Cell Research
MRC Centre Stem Cell Biology & Medicine
MRC Clinical Sciences Centre
North East England Stem Cell Institute
Roslin Institute
Weatherall Institute Molecular Medicine
Wellcome Trust Centre Cell Biology
Wellcome Trust Centre Cell-Matrix Research
Wellcome Trust Centre Stem Cell Research & Institute Stem
    Cell Biology

Celtic studies
    Centre Advanced Welsh & Celtic Studies
    >+ Cornwall & Cornish people; Wales & Welsh people
Cement & concrete
    Advanced Concrete & Masonry Centre
    Centre Cement & Concrete
    Concrete Centre
Censorship
    Article 19: International Centre against Censorship
Census records
    Family Records Centre
Central Europe > Russia, Central & Eastern Europe
Centrifuge testing
    London Geotechnical Centrifuge Centre
Ceramics
    Centre Ceramics Studies, Cardiff
    Wolfson Centre Materials Processing
Cerebral palsy
    Bobath Centre Children with Cerebral Palsy
    PACE Centre
    Scottish Centre Children with Motor Impairments
Certificates (birth etc)
    Family Records Centre
Charities
    Centre Charity Effectiveness
    Centre Government & Charity Management
    Charities Information Bureau
    >+ Volunteers / voluntary organisations
Chemical analysis & measurement
    Bureau Analysed Samples Ltd
    Centre Chemometrics
Chemical industry
    Chemical Industry Education Centre
    National Chemical Emergency Centre
    Salters' Institute
Chemical physics
    Centre Chemical Physics
Chemical sensors > Sensors
Chemistry
    Centre Bioactive Chemistry
    Centre Carbohydrate Chemistry
    Centre Chemical Sciences
    Institute Chemistry Industry
    WHO Collaborating Centre Research & Reference Services
        Clinical Chemistry
Childbirth > Birth & birth control
Children: disabled
    British Institute Brain Injured Children
    Centre Micro-Assisted Communication
    Centre Studies Inclusive Education
    Gifted Children's Information Centre
    Nordoff-Robbins Music Therapy Centre
    PACE Centre
    Scottish Sensory Centre
    >+ Cerebral palsy; Disabled people; Special needs
        research

Children: gifted
    Brunel Able Children's Education Centre
    Gifted Children's Information Centre
Children: health
    Centre Child & Family Research
    Centre Child Health
    Centre Child Research
    Centre Child Studies
    Centre Child-focused Anthropological Research
    Centre Child-Related Studies
    Centre Clinical & Health Services Research
    Centre Evidence-Based Child Health
    Centre Research Infant Behaviour
    Education & Resources Improving Childhood Continence
    Greenwood Institute Child Health
    Hugh & Catherine Stevenson Centre Childhood Infectious
        Diseases & Immunology
    Institute Child Health [Liverpool]
    London Centre Paediatric Endocrinology & Metabolism
    Osteopathic Centre Children
    UCL Institute Child Health
Children: welfare
    Centre Applied Childhood Studies
    Centre Child Protection Studies
    Centre Fun & Families
    Centre Research Child & Family
    Centre Research Childhood
    Centre Research Equity & Diversity Education
    Child Development & Well-Being Interdisciplinary Research
        Centre
    Child Exploitation Online Protection Centre
    Childhood & Families Research & Development Centre
    Children's Research Centre
    Criminal Records Bureau
    Families, Life Course & Generations Research Centre
    Glasgow Centre Child & Society
    Institute Child Care Research
    Institute Developmental Potential
    Institute Study Children, Families & Social Issues
    Interface - Centre Interdisciplinary Practice
    Morgan Centre Study Relationships & Personal Life
    National Children's Bureau
    National Children's Centre
    Nationwide Children's Research Centre
    Reunite, International Child Abduction Centre
    Scottish Institute Residential Child Care
    Wales International Centre Childhood Studies
    >+ Law: family
China & Chinese people
    Anglo-Chinese Business & Management Centre
    Centre Chinese Business Development
    Centre Chinese Business & Management
    Centre Chinese Studies [Lampeter]
    Centre Chinese Studies [SOAS, London]
    Centre Chinese Studies [Manchester]
    Centre Contemporary Chinese Studies
    Centre Teaching Chinese as Foreign Language
    China & Transitional Economics Research Centre
    China Business Centre
    China Media Centre
    China Policy Institute
    East Asia Institute
    Great Britain - China Centre
    Institute Chinese Studies
    Institute Contemporary Chinese Studies
    Institute Research Contemporary China
    International Centre Chinese Heritage & Archaeology
    Lancaster Centre Management China
Chinese medicine
    Acumedic Centre Chinese Medicine
Chiropody
    Clinical Research Centre Health Professions
    Wales Centre Podiatric Studies

Christian activities & religion
    Arthur Rank Resource Centre
    Centre Advanced Studies Christian Ministry
    Centre Christianity & Culture
    Centre Christianity & Interreligious Dialogue
    Centre Study Christian Church
    Centre Study Jewish-Christian Relations
    Centre Theology, Religion & Culture
    Henry Martyn Centre Study Mission & World Christianity
    Institute Orthodox Christian Studies
    Institute Study Christianity & Sexuality
    Jubilee Centre
    Oxford Centre Mission Studies
    >+ individual churches & denominations
Chronic illness
    National Collaborating Centre Chronic Conditions
Chronobiology
    Centre Chronobiology
Chronology
    Chrono Centre Climate, Environment, & Chronology
Church of England
    Centre Contemporary Ministry
    >+ Christian activities & religion
Churchill (Winston Spencer)
    Churchill Archives Centre
Cinema
    Bill Douglas Centre History Cinema & Popular Culture
    Centre Advanced Development Creative Industries [Bangor]
    Centre World Cinemas
    >+ Films & film studies
Circuit design
    Centre Concurrent Systems & Very Large Scale Integration
Cities
    Cities Institute
    Cities Research Centre
    Sustainable Cities Research Institute
    >+ Planning: town & country; Regional & urban studies
Citizenship
    Bristol Institute Greece, Rome & Classical Tradition
    Centre Citizenship & Community Mental Health
    Centre Citizenship & Human Rights Education
    Centre Citizenship Studies Education
    Centre Citizenship, Identities & Governance
    Centre Study Ethnicity & Citizenship
    CRUCiBLE: Centre Rights, Understanding & Citizenship
        Based Learning through Experience
    Institute Citizenship
    Scottish Development Education Centre
City centres
    Central Cities Institute
Civil engineering
    Infrastructure Engineering & Management Research Centre
    Institute Infrastructure & Environment
    Nottingham Centre Infrastructure
Civil rights > Human rights
Cladding
    Centre Window & Cladding Technology
Classical studies
    Bristol Institute Greece, Rome & Classical Tradition
    Institute Classical Studies
    Subject Centre History, Classics & Archaeology
    Warburg Institute
Clean air > Air quality
Clergy > Christian activities & religion
Climate change
    Cambridge Centre Climate Change Mitigation Research
    Environmental Change Institute
    Environmental Change Research Centre
    Hadley Centre Climate Change
    Rothamsted Centre Bioenergy & Climate Change
    Tyndall Centre Climate Change Research
    >+ Meteorology
Clinical education
    Institute Clinical Education

    Saad Centre Clinical Skills Education
Clinical effectiveness
    Centre Outcomes Research & Effectiveness
Clinical management
    Centre Clinical Management Development
Clinical practice
    Centre Research & Implementation Clinical Practice
Clinical research
    Institute Life Science
Clinical sciences & skills
    Centre Clinical Science & Measurement
    Centre Clinical Science & Technology
    Centre Excellence Teaching & Learning Clinical &
        Communication Skills
    Clinical Sciences Research Institute
    Clinical Skills Centre [Aberdeen]
    Clinical Skills Centre [Robert Gordon]
    Clinical Skills Centre [Dundee]
    Institute Clinical Research
    Institute Clinical Science [Belfast]
    Institute Clinical Sciences [Leeds]
Clothing > Fashion & costume
Coaches: sports > Sports: coaching
Coastal studies
    Aberdeen Institute Coastal Science & Management
    Centre Coastal & Marine Research
    Centre Coastal Dynamics & Engineering
    Centre Marine & Coastal Archaeology
    GeoData Institute
    Institute Estuarine & Coastal Studies
    International Centre Island Technology
    Scarborough Centre Coastal Studies
Coatings & coated products
    Advanced Composites & Coatings Research Centre
    Welsh Centre Printing & Coating
    >+ Surface engineering & science
Coffee
    Coffee Science Information Centre
Cognitive science
    Centre Brain & Cognitive Development
    Centre Cognition & Neuroimaging
    Centre Cognition, Computation & Culture
    Centre Cognitive & Computational Neuroscience
    Centre Cognitive Behaviour Therapy
    Centre Cognitive Neuroimaging
    Centre Cognitive Science
    Centre Rational-Emotive Behaviour Therapy
    Centre Recovery Severe Psychosis
    Centre Research Cognition, Emotion & Interaction
    Centre Research Cognitive Science
    Centre Social Learning & Cognitive Evolution
    Centre Working Memory & Learning
    Exeter Centre Cognitive Neuroscience
    Hang Seng Centre Cognitive Studies
    Human Communication Research Centre
    Institute Cognition & Culture
    >+ Psychotherapy & psychoanalysis
Cold War
    Cold War Studies Centre
Colds (common)
    Common Cold & Nasal Research Centre
Collingwood (R G)
    Collingwood & British Idealism Centre
Colonial research
    Centre Colonial & Postcolonial Studies [Kent]
    Centre Colonial & Postcolonial Studies [Sussex]
    Centre Imperial & Maritime Studies
    Centre Research Postcolonial & Transcultural Studies
    Centre Study Britain & Empire
    Centre Study Colonial & Postcolonial Societies
    Centre Translation & Comparative Cultural Studies
    Institute Colonial & Postcolonial Studies
    Nottingham Trent Centre Colonial & Postcolonial Studies

Colour
    Colour Design Research Centre
Combustion engineering
    Thermo-Fluid Mechanics Research Centre
    Thermo-Fluid Systems University Technology Centre
Commerce > Business headings
Common Market > European Union
Commonwealth affairs
    Centre Commonwealth Education
    Centre Commonwealth Studies
    Commonwealth Institute
    Commonwealth Resource Centre
    Institute Commonwealth Studies
Communicable diseases
    Centre Clinical Infection (Bloomsbury)
    Centre Clinical Infection (Hampstead)
    Centre Comparative Infectious Diseases
    Centre Infectious Disease [Durham]
    Centre Infectious Disease [Queen Mary, London]
    Centre Infectious Disease Epidemiology
    Centre Infectious Diseases & International Health
    Health Protection Agency Centre Infections
    Hugh & Catherine Stevenson Centre Childhood Infectious
        Diseases & Immunology
    Institute Emergent Infections Humans
    Wright Fleming Institute
Communication: aids
    Centre Micro-Assisted Communication
    Communication Aid Centre
    Communication Aids Language & Learning
Communication: human
    Centre Intercultural Development
    Centre Language Social Life
    Human Communication Research Centre
    Institute Communicating & Collaborative Systems
    >+ Language teaching & research; Linguistics
Communications
    Centre Telecommunications Research
    Centre Video Communications
    Communication & Computing Research Centre
    Communications Research Centre [Cardiff]
    Communications Research Centre [Loughborough]
    Institute Communications Studies
    Institute Communications & Signal Processing
    Research Centre Future Communications
    Stirling Media Research Institute
    >+ Media
Communities
    Bayswater Institute
    Centre Creative Communities
    Scottish Community Development Centre
Community care policy & practice
    Community Care Works
Community development
    Centre Active Learning Geography, Environment & Related
        Disciplines
Community justice
    Hallam Centre Community Justice
Community regeneration
    Community Regeneration Research Centre
Community research
    Centre Community Research
    Community Information Systems Centre
    Institute Community Cohesion
Company directors > Directors (company); Management
    headings
Complementary medicine
    Centre Complementary Care
    Centre Complementary Healthcare & Integrated Medicine
    Dr Edward Bach Centre
    Self Realisation Meditation Healing Centre
    >+ specific form
Complex systems
    Centre Complex Cooperative Systems

York Centre Complex Systems Analysis
Composites & composite materials
    Advanced Composites Manufacturing Centre
    BC
    Centre Composite Materials
    Composites Centre [Cranfield]
    Composites Centre [Imperial College London]
    Engineering Composites Research Centre
    Northwest Composites Centre
    Oxford Centre Advanced Materials & Composites
    Wolfson Centre Materials Processing
Comprehensive education > Education: secondary
Computer-aided design (CAD)
    Martin Centre Architectural & Urban Studies
    >+ Design
Computers for disabled people
    Ability Net
Computers: application
    Advanced Computing Research Centre
    Centre Adaptive Systems
    Centre Advanced Software Technology
    Centre Applied Formal Methods
    Centre Composition & Performance Using Technology
    Centre Computational Intelligence
    Centre Computational Science
    Centre Computer Graphics & Visualisation
    Centre Computer Science & Informatics Research
    Centre Computing & Social Responsibility
    Centre Excellence Research Computational Intelligence &
        Applications
    Centre Grid Computing
    Centre Interactive Assessment Development
    Centre Novel Computing
    Centre Research Computer Science
    Centre Research Computing
    Centre Social Anthropology & Computing
    Centre VLSI & Computer Graphics
    Communication & Computing Research Centre
    Computational Engineering & Design Centre
    Computer Learning Research Centre
    Computer Science Research Institute
    Dalton Research Institute
    Digital Lifestyles Centre
    Grid Support Centre
    Institute Computing Research
    Institute Computing Systems Architecture
    Institute Perception, Action & Behaviour
    Institute Research Applicable Computing
    Interdisciplinary Research Centre Dependability Computer-
        Based Systems
    Microsoft Institute High Performance Computing
    National Centre Computer Animation
    National Computing Centre
    Safety Systems Research Centre
    Sir George Cayley Research Centre
    Teesside Medical Computing Centre
    UCL Interaction Centre
    >+ e-Research; e-Science; Information management;
        Networks; Parallel applications; Software
Computers: security
    Computer Security & Audit Centre
    Computer Security Research Centre
Computers: training
    Active Learning Computing: Centre Excellence Teaching &
        Learning
    Institute Computer Based Learning
Concrete > Cement & concrete
Conductive education
    British Institute Brain Injured Children
Conductive education
    National Institute Conductive Education
Conductivity > Superconductivity
Conferences & conventions
    Cromarty Training Centre

© CBD Research Ltd · Beckenham · Kent BR3 5JS · Tel 020 8650 7745 · Fax 020 8650 0768 · E-mail cbd@cbdresearch.com · www.cbdresearch.com

Conflict analysis
    Africa Centre Peace & Conflict Studies
    Callaghan Centre Study Conflict
    Centre Conflict Resolution
    Centre Peace & Conflict Studies
    Centre Peace & Reconciliation Studies
    Centre Study Post-Conflict Cultures
    Crime & Conflict Research Centre
    Leonard Cheshire Centre Conflict Recovery
    Praxis Centre - Centre Study Information & Technology
        Peace, Conflict Resolution & Human Rights
    Richardson Institute Peace & Conflict Research
    Transitional Justice Institute
    >+ Peace studies; War studies
Conservation of historic buildings > Historic buildings &
    conservation
Conservation: nature
    Centre Conservation Ecology
    Centre Conservation Science
    Centre Ecology, Evolution & Conservation
    Centre European Protected Areas Research
    Centre Evidence-Based Conservation
    Durrell Institute Conservation & Ecology
    Earthwatch Institute (Europe)
    European Centre Biodiversity & Conservation Research
    International Centre Protected Landscapes
    World Conservation Monitoring Centre
Constitutionalism
    Cunliffe Centre Study Constitutionalism & National Identity
Construction > Building & construction
Consumer affairs & protection
    Centre Sustainable Consumption
    Ricability (Research Institute Consumer Affairs)
Contamination > Pollution & pollution control
Contemporary art
    BALTIC Centre Contemporary Art
    Centre Contemporary Art
    Centre Contemporary Art Research
    Centre Contemporary Visual Arts
    >+ Art headings
Continence > Incontinence
Continuing education > Education: adult & continuing
Contraception > Birth & birth control
Control engineering & systems
    Centre Industrial Automation & Manufacture
    Centre Process Analytics & Control Technology
    Centre System Analysis
    Centre Systems & Control
    Centre Systems & Modellingz
    Control Systems Centre
    Control Theory & Applications Centre
    >+ Automation & robotics
Conventions > Conferences & conventions
Conversation analysis
    Centre Applied Interaction Research
Co-operatives
    Wales Institute Research Co-operatives
Cornwall & Cornish people
    Institute Cornish Studies
    Roseland Institute
Coronary diseases > Cardio- headings
Corporate governance
    Centre Corporate Governance [Cambridge]
    Centre Corporate Governance [London Business School]
    Centre Corporate Governance & Regulation
    Centre Corporate Governance Research
    Centre Research Corporate Governance
Corporate responsibility
    Centre Action Research Professional Practice
    Centre Study Corporate Responsibility
    Doughty Centre Corporate Responsibility
    International Centre Corporate Social Responsibility
Corpus research
    Centre Corpus Research

Corrosion
    Centre Corrosion Technology
    Corrosion & Protection Centre
Cosmetic surgery
    Facial Cosmetic Surgery Centre
Cosmic research
    UCL Centre Cosmic Chemistry & Physics
Cosmology
    Institute Computational Cosmology
    Institute Cosmology & Gravitation
Costume > Fashion & costume
Counselling
    Brandon Centre Counselling & Psychotherapy Young People
    Centre Counselling Studies
    Help Counselling Centre
    Institute Psychosynthesis
    >+ Psychotherapy & psychoanalysis
Counterfeiting
    ICC Counterfeiting Intelligence Bureau
Country houses > Historic buildings & conservation
Courts
    Centre International Courts & Tribunals
Crafts & craftsmanship
    Craft & Design Research Centre
    Crafts Study Centre
    >+ Art
Crash testing > Impact research
Creative industries & technologies
    C4C: Collaborating Creativity CETL
    Centre Advanced Development Creative Industries [Bangor]
    Centre Advanced Development Creative Industries
        [Portsmouth]
    Centre Creative Industries
    Centre Creative Industry
    Centre Leadership Creativity
    Creative Learning Practice Centre Excellence Teaching &
        Learning
    Innovate - Centre Creative Industries
    Institute Capitalising Creativity
    Institute Creative Technologies
    National Institute Excellence Creative Industries
    >+ specific type eg Media
Creativity > Innovation
Credit management
    Credit Management Research Centre
Crime protection & prevention > Criminology & criminal justice
Crime writing > Literature
Criminal law > Law: criminal
Criminology & criminal justice
    Applied Criminology Centre
    Centre Comparative Criminology & Criminal Justice
    Centre Crime & Justice Studies
    Centre Crime Informatics
    Centre Criminal Justice & Criminology
    Centre Criminal Justice Economics & Psychology
    Centre Criminal Justice Policy & Research
    Centre Criminal Justice Studies
    Centre Criminal Law & Criminal Justice
    Centre Criminological Research [Keele]
    Centre Criminological Research [Sheffield]
    Centre Criminology [Glamorgan]
    Centre Criminology [Oxford]
    Centre Criminology & Criminal Justice [Hull]
    Centre Criminology & Socio-Legal Studies
    Centre Law & Society
    Centre Sentencing Research
    Crime & Conflict Research Centre
    Criminal Justice Centre [Thames Valley]
    Criminal Justice Research Centre
    Criminal Justice Social Work Development Centre Scotland
    Glenamara Centre International Research Arts & Society
    Institute Criminal Justice
    Institute Criminal Justice Studies
    Institute Criminal Policy Research

Institute Criminology
Institute Criminology & Criminal Justice
International Centre Comparative Criminological Research
Kent Criminal Justice Centre
Mannheim Centre Study Criminology & Criminal Justice
Midlands Centre Criminology & Criminal Justice
Newport Centre Criminal & Community Justice
Nottingham Centre Study & Reduction Hate Crimes
Scottish Centre Crime & Justice Research
Social Contexts Pathways Crime Centre
UCL Jill Dando Institute Crime Science
Vauxhall Centre Study Crime
>+ Prisons

Crisis psychology > Trauma

Critical theory
Centre Critical & Cultural Theory

Crop research
Agronomy Institute
Institute Arable Crops Research
Rothamsted Centre Bioenergy & Climate Change
Scottish Crop Research Institute
Wales Biomass Centre

Crusades (The)
Cardiff Centre History Crusades

Crystallography
Cambridge Crystallographic Data Centre
Centre Materials Science
Oxford Centre Molecular Sciences

Cults
Cult Information Centre

Cultural studies
AHRC Centre Cultural Analysis, Theory & History
AHRC Research Centre Evolution Cultural Diversity
Centre Comparative Study Culture, Development & Environment
Centre Contemporary Visual & Material Culture
Centre Critical & Cultural Theory
Centre Cross-Cultural Studies
Centre Cultural Analysis, Theory & History
Centre Cultural Environment
Centre Cultural Policy Research
Centre Cultural & Social History
Centre Cultural Studies
Centre History Culture & Medicine
Centre Research & Scholarship History, Education & Cultural Heritage
Centre Translation & Comparative Cultural Studies
Cultural Theory Institute
Institute Cultural Affairs
Institute Cultural Analysis, Nottingham
Institute Cultural Research
Institute Culture, Gender & City
International Centre Cultural & Heritage Studies
Literary & Cultural Studies Research Centre
London Centre Arts & Cultural Enterprise
National Centre English Cultural Tradition
Nottingham Institute Research Visual Culture
Research Centre Literature & Cultural History
Theory, Culture & Society Centre
Visual Culture Research Centre
>+ Intercultural studies

Cultural studies: European
Centre European Literatures & Cultures
Centre French History & Culture

Cultural studies: Japanese
Sainsbury Institute Study Japanese Arts & Cultures

Curtain walling
Centre Window & Cladding Technology

Dairying
Centre Dairy Research
Dancing
AHRC Research Centre Cross-Cultural Music & Dance Performance [Roehampton]
AHRC Research Centre Cross-Cultural Music & Dance Performance [School of Oriental & African Studies, London]
AHRC Research Centre Cross-Cultural Music & Dance Performance [Surrey]
Centre Dance Research
Centre Excellence Performance Arts
Centre Research Creation Performing Arts
Drama, Dance & Performing Arts Research Centre
Labanotation Institute
National Resource Centre Dance
PALATINE - Dance, Drama & Music
Data analysis
Centre Comparative European Survey Data
Centre Data Digitisation & Analysis
Centre Longitudinal Studies
Data Assimilation Research Centre
European Centre Analysis Social Sciences
Data storage
Digital Curation Centre
Databases > Information management
Deafness
Centre Auditory Research
Centre Deaf Studies, Language & Cognition
Institute Sound & Vibration Research
Link Centre Deafened People
Scottish Sensory Centre
WHO Collaborating Centre Prevention Deafness & Hearing Impairment
>+ Communication: aids; Hearing
Death
Centre Death & Society
Continuous Mortality Investigation Bureau
Natural Death Centre
Decision management & research
Centre Decision Management & Risk Management
Centre Decision Research
Decommissioning (nuclear) > Nuclear science & engineering
UHI Decommissioning & Environmental Remediation Centre
>+ Nuclear science & engineering
Deer
Deer Study & Resource Centre
Deer
Scottish Deer Centre
Defence
Centre Defence & International Security Studies
Defence
Centre Defence Economics
Defence
Centre Defence Studies
Dementia
Dementia Services Development Centre [Stirling]
Dementia Services Development Centre Wales
>+ Mental health
Democracy & democratization
Brunel Centre Democratic Evaluation
Centre Citizen Participation
Centre Democracy & Governance
Centre Democracy Studies
Centre Democratic Governance
Centre Democratization Studies
Centre Development Studies [Bath]
Centre Development Studies [Glasgow]
Centre Development Studies [Leeds]
Centre Development Studies [Swansea]

© CBD Research Ltd · Beckenham · Kent BR3 5JS · Tel 020 8650 7745 · Fax 020 8650 0768 · E-mail cbd@cbdresearch.com · www.cbdresearch.com

Centre Local Democracy
Centre Parties & Democracy Europe
Centre Political & Diplomatic Studies
Centre Research Education & Democracy
Centre Studies Democratization
Centre Study Democracy
Institute Citizenship
International Teledemocracy Centre
UNESCO Centre Education Pluralism, Human Rights & Democracy
Demography > Population studies
Denmark & Danish people
Danish Cultural Institute
Dentistry
Centre Adult Oral Health
Centre Clinical & Diagnostic Oral Sciences
Centre Dental Technology
Centre Dental Technology Studies
Centre Evidence-based Dentistry
Centre Oral Growth & Development
Centre Professionals Complementary Dentistry
Centre Research Medical & Dental Education
Edinburgh Dental Institute
Institute Dentistry
International Centre Evidence-Based Oral Health
Leeds Dental Institute
National Advice Centre Postgraduate Dental Education
Postgraduate Institute Medicine & Dentistry
Subject Centre Medicine, Dentistry & Veterinary Medicine
UCL Eastman Dental Institute
Depressive illness
Mood Disorders Centre
Prince Wales International Centre Research Schizophrenia & Depression
>+ Mental health
Dermatology
Centre Cutaneous Research
Saint John's Institute Dermatology
Skin Research Centre
Desalination > Osmosis
Design
Advanced Design & Manufacturing Engineering Centre
Advanced Research Institute
AHRC Centre Study Domestic Interior
Art & Design Research Centre [Salford]
Art & Design Research Centre [Sheffield Hallam]
Art Design Media Subject Centre
Brunel Organisation & Systems Design Centre
Centre Art & Design & Research Experimentation
Centre Art, Design & Philosophy
Centre Design against Crime
Centre Design Innovation
Centre Design Research
Centre Excellence Teaching & Learning through Design
Centre Human Computer Interaction Design
Centre Professional Development Art & Design
Centre Research Electronic Art & Communication
Centre Study Design Modern Interior
Centre Sustainable Design
Coventry University Design Institute
Decision Engineering Centre
Design Enterprise Centre
Design Research Centre
Joint Centre Urban Design
Manchester Institute Research & Innovation Art & Design
Martin Centre Architectural & Urban Studies
Modern Interiors Research Centre
National Centre Product Design & Development Research
Research Institute Media, Art & Design
Sustainable Design Research Centre [Bournemouth]
Sustainable Design Research Centre [Kingston]
Transnational Art, Identity & Nation Research Centre
University Central England Birmingham Institute Art & Design

Visual & Information Design Research Centre
Visual Art Practice Research Centre
Developing countries & Third World
Bradford Centre International Development
Centre Developing Areas Research
Centre Development Policy & Research
Centre Development Studies [Bath]
Centre Development Studies [Glasgow]
Centre Development Studies [Leeds]
Centre Development Studies [Swansea]
Centre Economic Reform & Transformation
Centre Study Comparative Change & Development
Culture, Development & Environment Centre
David Livingstone Institute International Development Studies
Development Research Centre
Development Studies Institute
Institute Development Policy & Management
Institute Development Studies
Institute International Health & Development
International Development Centre [Milton Keynes]
Natural Resources Institute
Natural Resources Management Institute
One World Centre
Overseas Development Institute
Sir David Owen Population Centre
Water Engineering & Development Centre
Development studies > Developing countries & Third World
Diabetes
Centre Diabetes & Endocrinology
Centre Diabetes & Metabolic Medicine
Oxford Centre Diabetes, Endocrinology & Metabolism
Sir James Black Centre
WHO Collaborating Centre Training, Evaluation & Research Diabetes
Diagnostics
Centre Integrated Diagnostic Systems
Cranfield Biotechnology Centre
WHO Collaborating Centre Laboratory & Diagnostic Support
Dictionaries > Lexicography
Diet > Food headings; Nutrition
Digestive diseases
Digestive Disease Research Centre
Wolfson Digestive Diseases Centre
Digital technology / imaging
Digital World Research Centre
Institute Digital Art & Technology
International Centre Digital Content
>+ Imaging & image analysis
Diphtheria
WHO Collaborating Centre Diphtheria & Streptococcal Infections
Diplomacy
Centre Political & Diplomatic Studies
Directors (company)
Centre Director Education
>+ Management headings
Disabled people
Ability Net
Douglas Bader Centre
National Star Centre Disabled Youth
Richard Attenborough Centre Disability & Arts
Skill: National Bureau Students with Disabilities
>+ Children: disabled; Sports: disabled & handicapped
Disabled people: equipment
Bath Institute Medical Engineering
Brunel Institute Bioengineering
National Network Assessment Centres Administration Centre
Disabled people: mobility
Queen Elizabeth's Foundation Mobility Centre
Disabled people: research
Aspire Centre Disability Sciences

Centre Behavioural Research, Analysis, & Intervention
   Developmental Disabilities
Centre Disability Studies
Centre Research & Policy Disability
Norah Fry Research Centre
Strathclyde Centre Disability Research
UnumProvident Centre Psychosocial & Disability Research

Disarmament
   Bradford Disarmament Research Centre
   Centre Defence Economics

Disasters & disaster relief > Emergency planning & control

Discrimination
   Centre Diversity Policy Research
   Centre Diversity, Equity & Inclusion
   Centre Research Equality & Diversity
   Centre Social Action
   Comparative Organisation & Equality Research Centre
   Equality & Discrimination Centre
   International Centre Intercultural Studies
   Working Lives Research Institute
   >+ Ethnicity & ethnic minorities

Disease
   Biomedical Research Centre [Dundee]
   Biomedical Research Centre [Sheffield Hallam]
   >+ Communicable diseases; Health headings; Veterinary
      science

Disfigurement
   Centre Appearance Research

Dispute resolution
   Centre Effective Dispute Resolution

Dissenting studies
   Dr Williams's Centre Dissenting Studies

Distilling > Brewing & distilling; Whisky

Distributed technologies
   Centre Research Distributed Technologies

Diversity
   Centre Creative Communities

Diving (training & techniques)
   Diving Diseases Research Centre Ltd
   Fort Bovisand Underwater Centre Ltd
   International Centre Island Technology
   National Hyperbaric Centre
   Underwater Centre (Fort William) Ltd

DNA (Deoxyribo-nucleic acid) > Biomolecular science; Genetics /
genomics

Document management > Information management

Dogs
   Canine Behaviour Centre [Belfast]
   Canine Behaviour Centre [Greenhead]

Drama > Theatre & theatre studies

Drama: therapy
   Sesame Institute UK

Drawing
   Advanced Centre Drawing
   Centre Drawing
   >+ Art

Driving for the disabled > Disabled people: mobility

Drugs > Alcohol, drug & other addictions; Pharmaceuticals &
   pharmacology

Dry stone walling
   National Stone Centre

Drylands
   Sheffield Centre International Drylands Research

Dutch life > Netherlands & Dutch people

Dyslexia
   Dyslexia Teaching Centre
   Gifted Children's Information Centre
   Helen Arkell Dyslexia Centre

E

Eagles
   National Birds Prey Centre
   Raptor Centre
   >+ Ornithology

Early modern period
   Centre Early Modern Studies [Aberdeen]
   Centre Early Modern Studies [Sussex]
   Centre Reformation & Early Modern Studies
   Centre Renaissance & Early Modern Studies [Queen Mary,
      London]
   Centre Renaissance & Early Modern Studies [York]

Earth science
   Earth & Biosphere Institute
   Earth Science Centre
   >+ Environment headings

Earth structure & resources
   Institute Engineering Surveying & Space Geodesy

Earthquake studies
   Centre Observation & Modelling Earthquakes & Tectonics
   Earthquake Engineering Research Centre
   Institute Geophysics & Tectonics
   International Seismological Centre
   Martin Centre Architectural & Urban Studies

East Anglia
   Centre East Anglian Studies

East Asia > Asia

Eastern Europe > Russia, Central & Eastern Europe

Eating disorders
   Centre Eating, Food & Health
   International Eating Disorders Centre

e-Business
   Centre Information Management & E-Business
   e-Business Research Centre
   eCommerce Innovation Centre

Ecology
   CEH Banchory
   CEH Bangor
   CEH Dorset
   CEH Edinburgh
   CEH Lancaster
   CEH Monks Wood
   CEH Oxford
   CEH Wallingford
   Centre Conservation Ecology
   Centre Ecology & Evolution
   Centre Ecology & Hydrology
   Centre Ecology, Evolution & Conservation
   Centre Ecology, Law & Policy
   Centre Human Ecology
   Centre Research Ecological & Environmental Modelling
   Centre Research Ecology & Environment
   Centre Sustainable Futures
   Centre Urban & Regional Ecology
   Durrell Institute Conservation & Ecology
   Institute Atmospheric & Environmental Science
   Rothamsted Centre for Bioenergy and Climate Change
   Rothamsted Centre for Sustainable Soils and Ecosystem
      Functions
   >+ Environment headings

Econometrics
   Centre Advanced Studies Finance
   Centre Econometric Analysis
   Financial Econometrics Research Centre
   >+ Finance

Economics
   Bettany Centre Entrepreneurial Performance & Economics
   Centre Applied Research Economics
   Centre Computational Finance & Economic Agents
   Centre Decision Research & Experimental Economics
   Centre Economic Development & Institutions

© CBD Research Ltd · Beckenham · Kent BR3 5JS · Tel 020 8650 7745 · Fax 020 8650 0768 · E-mail cbd@cbdresearch.com · www.cbdresearch.com

Centre Economic Research & Intelligence
Centre Economics & Finance Research
Centre Enterprise & Economic Development Research
Centre Experimental Economics
Centre Historical Economics & Related Research York
Centre Research Business, Economics & Management
Centre Research Industry, Enterprise, Finance & Firm
Centre Research Institutional Economics
Centre Spatial & Real Estate Economics
Economic Research Institute Northern Ireland
Economics Network
Institute Social & Economic Research
Jevons Institute Competition Law & Economics
Lancaster Centre Forecasting
Leverhulme Centre Research Globalization & Economic
    Policy
Stirling Centre Economic Methodology
Suntory & Toyota International Centres Economics & Related
    Disciplines
UK Centre Economic & Environmental Development
Welsh Institute Research Economics & Development
>+ Finance
Economics: education
    Centre Economics & Business Education
    Centre Economics Education
Economics: environmental
    Surrey Energy Economics Centre
Economics: health
    Centre Health Economics
    City Health Economics Centre
    Health Economics Research Centre [Oxford]
    Health Economics Research Centre [York]
Economics: international
    Centre Economic Reform & Transformation
    Centre European Studies [Bradford]
    Centre European Studies [Exeter]
    ESRC Centre Research Economic Development &
        International Trade
    National Institute Economic & Social Research
    Strathclyde Centre European Economies Transition
    Surrey Centre International Economic Studies
Economics: local & regional
    Centre Local & Regional Economic Analysis
    Applied Research Centre Sustainable Regeneration
    Centre Local Economic Strategies
    Centre Regional Economic & Social Research
    Centre Regional Economic Development
    Manchester Regional Economics Centre
Economics: macroeconomics
    Centre Dynamic Macroeconomic Analysis
    Julian Hodge Institute Applied Macroeconomics
Economics: policy
    Adam Smith Institute
    Cambridge Centre Economic & Public Policy
    Centre Economic Performance
    Centre Economic Policy Research
    Policy Studies Institute
    Political Economy Research Centre
Economics: psychology
    Centre Economic & Behavioural Analysis Risk & Decision
    ESRC Centre Economic Learning & Social Evolution
Education
    Applied Educational Research Centre
    Blended Learning Unit CETL
    Centre Applied Research Education
    Centre Combined Studies
    Centre Education & Employment Research
    Centre Education Research
    Centre Educational Development
    Centre Educational Development & Materials
    Centre Educational Innovation
    Centre Educational Studies [Aberystwyth]
    Centre Educational Studies [Hull]
    Centre Innovation Raising Educational Achievement

Centre International Research Creativity & Learning
    Education
Centre International Studies Education, Management &
    Training
Centre Research & Evaluation
Centre Research & Scholarship History, Education & Cultural
    Heritage
Centre Research Beliefs, Rights & Values Education
Centre Research Education
Centre Research Equity & Impact Education
Centre Research Wider Benefits Learning
Centre Study Education & Training
City & Guilds London Institute
Curriculum Evaluation & Management Centre
Education Research Centre
Educational Initiative Centre
Learning & Teaching Institute
Research Centre Education & Professional Practice
SCRE Centre
Sussex Institute
UNESCO Centre Comparative Education Research
Warwick Institute Education
Westminster Institute Education
World Education Centre
>+ Schools; specific subject
Education: adult & continuing
    Birkbeck Institute Lifelong Learning
    Centre Community & Lifelong Learning
    Centre Developing & Evaluating Lifelong Learning
    Centre Excellence Professional Learning Workplace
    Centre Excellence Work Based Learning
    Centre Excellence Work-Based Learning Education
        Professionals
    Centre Guidance Studies
    Centre International Studies Education, Management &
        Training
    Centre Research & Development Adult & Lifelong Learning
    Centre Research Lifelong Learning [Glasgow Caledonian]
    Centre Research Lifelong Learning [Stirling]
    Centre Study Education & Training
    Centre Work & Learning
    City Literary Institute
    Continuum - Centre Widening Participation Policy Studies
    Hampstead Garden Suburb Institute
    Institute Access Studies
    Institute Continuing Education
    Institute Lifelong Learning [Leicester]
    Lifelong Learning Institute
    Møller Centre Continuing Education
    Mary Ward Centre
    National Centre Work Based Learning Partnerships
    Practice-based Professional Learning CETL
    Scottish Centre Work Based Learning
    Subject Centre Education
    Surrey Centre Excellence Professional Training & Education
    Sussex Institute
    UK Centre Advancement Interprofessional Education
    Welsh Centre Research Lifelong Learning
Education: equipment
    Centre Applied Research Educational Technologies
    Scottish Schools Equipment Research Centre
Education: financing
    Centre Educational Research
    Centre Educational Support
Education: higher
    Aston Business School Research Centre in Higher Education
        Learning and Management
    Centre Educational Sociology
    Centre Excellence Teaching & Learning Applied
        Undergraduate Research Skills
    Centre Higher Education Research & Information
    Centre Higher Education Studies
    Centre Interdisciplinary Studies Higher Education
    Centre Postgraduate Studies & Research Ltd

Centre Research Higher Education
Centre Research Tertiary Education
Centre Study Education & Training
Centre Study Higher Education
Higher Education Learning Partnerships CETL
Higher Education Research Centre
Institute Education [London]
Institute Education [Manchester Metropolitan]
Institute Education [Reading]
Institute Education [Stirling]
LearnHigher CETL
Oxford Centre Higher Education Policy Studies
Oxford Centre Staff & Learning Development
Subject Centre Education
Education: inclusion
Centre for Educational Development, Appraisal and
Research
Centre for Equality and Human Rights in Education
Centre Research Education Inclusion & Diversity
Centre Studies Inclusive Education
Education: international
Centre International Education
Centre International Education & Research
Centre Study Education International Context
Education: leadership
International Institute Education Leadership
London Centre Leadership Learning
Education: management
Aston Business School Research Centre Higher Education
Learning & Management
Centre Education & Finance Management
Centre Education, Leadership & Professional Development
Centre Educational Leadership
Centre Educational Leadership & Management
Education: policy
Centre Critical Education Policy Studies
Centre for Educational Development, Appraisal and
Research
Centre Educational Research
Centre Equity Education
Centre Evidence-informed Policy & Practice Education
Centre Institutional Studies
Centre Policy Studies Education
Centre Research Education Policy & Professionalism
Institute Education Policy Research
Institute Policy Studies Education
Oxford Centre Higher Education Policy Studies
Education: pre-school
Early Childhood Research Centre
Montessori Centre International
Education: primary
Centre Research Primary Science & Technology
Education: secondary
Centre Educational Sociology
Centre Study Comprehensive Schools
Education: State system
Advisory Centre Education
Education: technology of
Centre New Technologies Research Education
Centre Studies Advanced Learning Technology
Centre Study Educational Technologies
Institute Educational Technology
Institute Learning & Research Technology
Intelligent Technologies Research Centre
Learning Technology Research Institute
Teaching & Learning Technology Centre
Egypt & Egyptian people
Griffith Institute
Eighteenth century
Centre Eighteenth Century Studies [Belfast]
Centre Eighteenth Century Studies [York]
Warwick Eighteenth Century Centre
Elastomers > Rubber
Elderly people > Gerontology; Older people

e-Learning
Centre eLearning Development
Elections
Cathie Marsh Centre Census & Survey Research
Centre Election Law
Local Government Chronicle Elections Centre
>+ Political studies
Electrical engineering
Centre Electrical Power Engineering
Institute Energy & Environment
Interdisciplinary Research Centre Superconductivity
Nottingham University Electrical Drives Centre
Electricity
National Grid High Voltage Research Centre
Electrochemistry
Electrochemical & Materials Processing Centre
Electromagnetics > Magnetics & electromagnetics
Electron optics
Bookham Centre Excellence Optoelectronic Simulation
Centre Electron Optical Studies
Centre Industrial & Commercial Optoelectronics
Centre Integrated Optoelectronic Systems
Optoelectronics Research Centre
Electronic art > Art: electronic
Electronic imaging
e2v Centre Electronic Imaging
Electronic industry & engineering
Centre Advanced Electronically Controlled Drives
Centre Electronic Devices & Materials
Centre Electronic Product Engineering
Centre Electronic Systems
Centre Molecular & Nanoscale Electronics
Centre Physical Electronics & Materials
Centre Physical Electronics & Quantum Technology
Electronic Systems Design Centre
Electronics Design Centre
Electronics Systems Design Centre
Innovative Electronics Manufacturing Research Centre
Institute Electronics, Communications & Information
Technology
Institute System Level Integration
Interdisciplinary Research Centre Superconductivity
International Centre Research System-on-Chip & Advanced
Microwireless Integration
Microelectronics Industrial Centre
Microelectronics Research Centre
MIcroSystems Engineering Centre
Nanoelectronics Research Centre
Northern Ireland Semiconductor Research Centre
Wolfson Centre Carbon & Silicon-Based Electronics
Electronic publishing > Publishing
Emblems
Centre Emblem Studies
Emergency planning & control
Centre Development & Emergency Practice
Cranfield Mine Action & Disaster Management Centre
Cranfield Resilience Centre
Disaster & Development Centre
Disaster Management Centre
Health Protection Agency Centre Emergency Preparedness &
Response
National Chemical Emergency Centre
>+ Hazards & risks
Emerging markets
Centre Emerging Markets
Centre New & Emerging Markets
Centre Research Emerging Economies
Emerging technologies
Centre Future & Emerging Technologies - Research &
Applications
Emerging Technologies Research Centre
Emigration > Immigrants & refugees
Emotion & emotion work studies
Centre Research Cognition, Emotion & Interaction

© CBD Research Ltd · Beckenham · Kent BR3 5JS · Tel 020 8650 7745 · Fax 020 8650 0768 · E-mail cbd@cbdresearch.com · www.cbdresearch.com

Centre Research Emotion Work
Centre Study Emotion & Motivation
Sackler Institute Psychobiological Research
Empire (The) > Colonial research
Employment
Centre Comparative Labour Studies
Centre Education & Employment Research
Centre Educational Sociology
Centre Employability
Centre Employability Through Humanities
Centre Employment Research
Centre European Labour Market Research
Centre International Labour Market Studies
Centre Labour Market Studies
Centre Research Employment Studies
Centre Working Life Research
Comparative Organisation & Equality Research Centre
Employment Research Institute
European Work & Employment Research Centre
Institute Employment Studies
North West Centre Learning & Development Ltd
Oxford Institute Employee Relations
Warwick Institute for Employment Research
Welsh Economy Labour Market Evaluation & Research
    Centre
Work & Employment Research Centre
Working Lives Research Institute
Endocrinology
Behavioural Neuroendocrinology Research Centre
Centre Diabetes & Endocrinology
London Centre Paediatric Endocrinology & Metabolism
Oxford Centre Diabetes, Endocrinology & Metabolism
Tenovus Centre Cancer Research
Energy
Advanced Technology Institute
Centre Energy, Petroleum & Mineral Law & Policy
Centre Renewable Energy Systems Technology
Centre Research, Education & Training Energy
Energy & Resources Research Institute
Institute Energy Research & Policy
Joule Centre Energy Research
Northern Ireland Centre Energy Research & Technology
Oxford Institute Energy Studies
Thermo-Fluid Mechanics Research Centre
Thermo-Fluid Systems University Technology Centre
>+ Solar energy
Energy economics
Surrey Energy Economics Centre
Energy efficiency
Centre Economic Renewable Power Delivery [Glasgow]
Centre Economic Renewable Power Delivery [Strathclyde]
Centre Energy & Environment [City]
Centre Energy & Environment [Exeter]
Centre Energy Studies
Centre Research Energy & Environment
Centre Sustainable Energy Systems
Durham Centre Renewable Energy
Energy Centre Sustainable Communities
Energy Technology Centre
Farm Energy Centre
Institute Energy Technologies
Institute Sustainability, Energy & Environmental Management
Institute Sustainable Energy Technology
London Centre Clean Energy
Martin Centre Architectural & Urban Studies
National Energy Centre
New & Renewable Energy Centre
Nottingham Fuel & Energy Centre
Engineering
Applied Engineering Research Centre
Cambridge Engineering Design Centre
Centre Advanced Engineering Methods
Centre High Frequency Engineering
Centre Innovative & Collaborative Engineering

Centre Systems Engineering [Cranfield]
Computational Engineering & Design Centre
Dalton Research Institute
Engineering Centre Excellence Teaching & Learning
Engineering Design Centre [Newcastle]
Engineering Design Research Centre
Engineering Subject Centre
Environmental Engineering Research Centre
Formulation Engineering Research Centre
General Engineering Research Institute
Institute Machines & Structures
Science & Technology Research Institute
Wessex Institute Technology
Engineering computation
Infrastructure Engineering & Management Research Centre
>+ specific area of engineering
England & English people
Britain Visitor Centre
Institute English Studies
Institute Name-Studies
National Centre English Cultural Tradition
English as a foreign language
Centre English Language Teacher Education
English Language Centre
International Centre English Language Studies
Norwegian Study Centre
University Stirling Centre English Language Teaching
English language
Centre Advanced Research English
Centre English Language & Communication
Centre English Language Education
Centre English Language Studies
Centre English Language Teacher Education & Applied
    Linguistics
Centre Research English Language Learning & Assessment
Centre Research English Literature & Language Wales
English Research Institute
English Subject Centre
Glenamara Centre International Research Arts & Society
Institute English Studies
Nottingham Institute English Research
Research Centre English & Applied Linguistics
Enterprise > Business headings
Entomology
Centre Applied Entomology & Parasitology
Entrepreneurship > Business headings
Enuresis > Incontinence
Environment
Abertay Centre Environment
Bloomsbury Institute Natural Environment
CAB International
Caledonian Environment Centre
Centre Accessible Environments
Centre Active Learning Geography, Environment & Related
    Disciplines
Centre Aviation, Transport & Environment
Centre Enterprise, Ethics & Environment
Centre Environment & Human Settlements
Centre Environment & Safety Management Business
Centre Environment & Society
Centre Environment, Fisheries & Aquaculture Science
Centre Environmental Assessment, Management & Policy
Centre Environmental Policy
Centre Environmental Sciences
Centre Environmental Strategy
Centre Research Ecological & Environmental Modelling
Centre Research Ecology & Environment
Centre Research Environmental Sciences
Centre Social & Economic Research Global Environment
Centre Study Environmental Change
Chrono Centre Climate, Environment, & Chronology
Dalton Research Institute
Earth & Biosphere Institute

Earth, Energy & Environment University Interdisciplinary
      Institute
   Geddes Institute
   Gibson Institute Land, Food & Environment
   Institute Environment
   Institute Environmental & Natural Sciences
   International Centre Environment
   Oxford University Centre Environment
   >+ Ecology
Environment: awareness & education
   Centre Environmental Initiatives
   Centre Research Education & Environment
   Geography, Earth & Environmental Sciences Subject Centre
   London Environment Centre
   Northumbrian Environmental Training & Research Centre
Environment: economics > Economics: environmental
Environment: engineering
   Cranfield Centre Agricultural & Environmental Engineering
   Institute Infrastructure & Environment
Environment: health
   Centre Research Environment & Health [Aberystwyth]
   Centre Research Environment & Health [Cardiff]
   Centre Research Environment & Health [Crewe]
   Centre Research Environment & Health [Lampeter]
   Centre Research Environment & Health [Leeds]
   Institute Occupational Medicine
   Robens Centre Public & Environmental Health
   WHO Collaborating Centre Healthy Cities & Urban Policy
Environment: history
   AHRC Research Centre Environmental History
   Centre Research Environmental History
   Centre World Environmental History
   Institute Environmental History
Environment: indoor
   Centre Research Indoor Climate & Health
Environment: informatics
   Centre Environmental Informatics
Environment: management
   Centre Environment & Planning
   Centre Environmental Management & Technology
   Centre Environmental Management [Nottingham]
   Centre Environmental Resource Management
   Centre Evidence-Based Conservation
   Centre Management Systems Built & Human Environment
   Centre Research Environmental Appraisal & Management
   Clean Environment Management Centre
   Institute Sustainability, Energy & Environmental Management
Environment: monitoring
   Environment Monitoring & Response Centre
   Institute Environment & Health
Environment: research
   Aberdeen Centre Environmental Sustainability
   BBSRC Institute Grassland & Environmental Research
   Centre Agri-Environmental Research
   Centre Comparative Study Culture, Development &
      Environment
   Centre Cultural Resource Management
   Centre Earth & Environmental Science Research
   Centre Energy & Environment [City]
   Centre Energy & Environment [Exeter]
   Centre Environment [Nottingham]
   Centre Environmental & Spatial Analysis
   Centre Environmental Data & Recording
   Centre Environmental Research
   Centre Environmental Research & Training
   Centre Environmental Studies
   Centre Environmental Studies Hospitality Industries
   Centre Infrastructure Management
   Centre Research Energy & Environment
   Centre Study Environmental Change & Sustainability
   Cranfield Centre EcoChemistry
   Environmental Change Institute
   Environmental Change Research Centre
   Environmental Impact Assessment Centre

Environmental Research Centre
Environmental Research Institute
Environmental Sciences Research Centre
Environmental Systems Science Centre
Environmental Technologies Centre Industrial Collaboration
Environmental Technology Centre
Hull Environment Research Institute
Hydroenvironmental Research Centre
Institute Atmospheric & Environmental Science
Institute Aviation & Environment
Institute Biological Sciences
Institute Environment & Sustainability Research
Institute Environmental Sustainability
Institute European Environmental Policy
Institute Research Environment & Sustainability
National Institute Environmental eScience
Northumbrian Environmental Training & Research Centre
Queen's University Environmental Science & Technology
      Research Centre
Research Institute Built & Human Environment
Stockholm Environment Institute York
UCL Environment Institute
UK Centre Economic & Environmental Development
WRc Plc
Enzymes > Biocatalysis
Epidemiology
   Centre Epidemiology & Biostatics
   Centre Epidemiology & Health Service Research
   Health Protection Agency Centre for Infections
   MRC Epidemiology Resource Centre
   WHO Collaborating Centre Surveillance Congenital
      Anomalies
Epilepsy
   Chalfont Centre Epilepsy
   David Lewis National Epilepsy Centre
Epistemology
   Centre Anthropological Study Knowledge & Ethics
Equal opportunities > Discrimination
e-Research
   Centre e-Research
   eCentre
   Oxford e-Research Centre
Ergonomics
   Ergonomics & Safety Research Institute
   Ergonomics Information Analysis Centre
   Institute Occupational Ergonomics
   Robens Centre Health Ergonomics
Erosion
   Centre Land Use & Water Resources Research
e-Science
   Belfast e-Science Centre
   Cambridge e-Science Centre
   Centre Medical Image Computing
   CLRC e-Science Centre
   eCentre
   e-Horizons Institute
   e-Science Institute
   e-Science North West Centre
   e-Science Research Institute
   Lancaster Centre e-Science
   Leicester e-Science Centre Excellence
   London e-Science Centre
   Midlands e-Science Centre
   National e-Science Centre, Glasgow
   North East Regional e-Science Centre
   Open Middleware Infrastructure Institute UK
   Reading e-Science Centre
   Southampton e-Science Centre
   UCL e-Science Centre Excellence
   Welsh e-Science Centre
   White Rose Grid e-Science Centre Excellence
e-Security
   Centre e-Security
   >+ Computers: security

e-Social sciences > Social sciences
Esotericism
    Exeter Centre Study Esotericism
Esperanto
    Esperanto Centre
Essex > East Anglia
Estuarine studies
    Centre Ecology & Hydrology
    Institute Estuarine & Coastal Studies
Ethics
    Cardiff Institute Society, Health & Ethics
    Centre Applied Ethics
    Centre Business Organisations & Society
    Centre Communication & Ethics International Business
    Centre Ethics Public Policy & Corporate Governance
    Centre Ethics, Philosophy & Public Affairs
    Centre Social Ethics & Policy
    Centre Social Responsibility Accounting & Management
    Centre Study Global Ethics
    Institute Applied Ethics
    Oxford Uehiro Centre Practical Ethics
    Policy, Ethics & Life Sciences Research Centre
    >+ Medical ethics; Professional ethics
Ethnicity & ethnic minorities
    Centre Black Professional Practice
    Centre Ethnic Minority Studies [Royal Holloway, London]
    Centre Ethnic Minority Studies [School of Oriental & African
        Studies, London]
    Centre Ethnicity & Gender
    Centre Ethnicity & Racism Studies
    Centre Research Ethnic Minority Entrepreneurship
    Centre Research Inequality, Human Security & Ethnicity
    Centre Research Nationalism, Ethnicity & Multiculturalism
    Centre Research Racism, Ethnicity & Nationalism
    Centre Study Ethnic Conflict
    Centre Study Ethnicity & Citizenship
    Centre Study Race & Ethnicity
    Ethnic Minorities Law Centre
    Scottish Centre Enterprise & Ethnic Business Research
    >+ Immigrants & refugees
Europass
    UK National Europass Centre
Europe
    Centre Contemporary European Studies
    Centre Euro-Asian Studies
    Centre Euro-Mediterranean Studies
    Centre Europe
    Centre European & International Studies Research
    Centre European Integration
    Centre European Political Communications
    Centre European Studies [Bradford]
    Centre European Studies [Exeter]
    Centre European Studies Research
    Centre International & European Studies
    Centre Research European Studies
    Centre South-East European Studies
    Centre Study Economic & Social Change Europe
    Centre Study European Governance
    Edinburgh Europa Institute
    Europe World Centre
    European Institute [London School of Economics & Political
        Science]
    European Policies Research Centre
    European Research Institute [Bath]
    European Research Institute [Birmingham]
    European Studies Centre
    European Studies Research Institute
    Institute European Cultural Identity Studies
    Institute Study European Transformations
    Keele European Research Centre
    London European Research Centre
    Manchester European Research Institute
    Pan-European Institute
    Sussex European Institute

    UCL Centre European Studies
    >+ European Union
Europe: business > Business: Europe
European data & documentation
    Centre Comparative European Survey Data
    European Documentation Centre
European Union
    Centre European Union Studies
    Centre Law European Union
    Centre Legislative Studies
    Centre Public Law
    Centre Study Governance European Union
    East Midlands Eurocentre
    Local Government Information Bureau
Evacuees
    Research Centre Evacuee & War Child Studies
    Research Centre German & Austrian Exile Studies
Evaluation studies
    Centre Evaluation Studies
    Evaluation Institute
Events management
    UK Centre Events Management
    >+ Exhibition venues
Evidence-based policy & research
    ESRC UK Centre Evidence Based Policy & Practice
    >+ specific subject
Evolutionary studies
    Centre Ecology & Evolution
    Centre Ecology, Evolution & Conservation
    Centre Evolution, Genes & Genomics
    Centre Study Evolution
    Leverhulme Centre Human Evolutionary Studies
Exercise science > Physical education & activity
Exhibition venues
    National Exhibition Centre
    Royal Highland Centre Limited
Exiles > Evacuees
Experimental physics
    International Research Centre Experimental Physics
Expertise
    Centre Study Expertise
Explosions
    Centre Research Fire & Explosion Studies
Explosives
    Centre Ordnance Science & Technology
    Cranfield Ordnance Test & Evaluation Centre
Extremophile research
    Centre Extremophile Research
Eyes > Blind & partially sighted; Sight & vision

F

Facial disfigurement > Disfigurement
Facial surgery > Cosmetic surgery
Facilities management
    Facilities Management Graduate Centre
    Scottish Centre Facilities Management
Failure analysis
    Experimental Techniques Centre
    Sheffield University Metals Advisory Centre
Falconry
    National Birds Prey Centre
    Raptor Centre
    >+ Ornithology
Family businesses
    Caledonian Family Business Centre
    >+ Business headings
Family history
    Family Records Centre
Family law > Law: family
Family life
    Centre Family Research

Centre Research Child & Family
Families, Life Course & Generations Research Centre
Morgan Centre Study Relationships & Personal Life
National Family & Parenting Institute
Newcastle Centre Family Studies
Family planning > Birth & birth control
Family therapy
Centre Fun & Families
Centre Research Families & Relationships
Childhood & Families Research & Development Centre
Institute Family Therapy
Institute Study Children, Families & Social Issues
Interface - Centre Interdisciplinary Practice
Farming
Centre Sustainable Futures
Farm Energy Centre
>+ Agriculture
Fashion & costume
Centre Fashion, Body & Material Cultures
Fashion Industry Research Centre
Fashion, Business & Technology Research Centre
London Centre Fashion Studies
SATRA Technology Centre
Fats > Lipids
Felines
Feline Advisory Bureau
Fertility treatment
London Fertility Centre
Newcastle Fertility Centre Life
Festivals
Centre Festival & Event Management
Fiction > Literature
Field studies
Field Studies Council Centres
Films & film studies
Centre Film Studies [Essex]
Centre Film Studies [Queen Mary, London]
Centre Film Studies [St Andrews]
Centre Research Film & Audiovisual Cultures
Centre Research Film Studies
Centre Screen Studies [Glasgow]
Centre Screen Studies [Manchester]
Institute Film & Television Studies
>+ Cinema
Finance
Aston Centre Research Experimental Finance
Business, Management, Accountancy & Finance Subject
Centre
Cambridge Endowment Research Finance
Centre Accounting, Finance & Governance
Centre Accounting, Finance & Taxation
Centre Advanced Studies Finance
Centre Banking & Finance
Centre Economics & Finance Research
Centre Empirical Finance
Centre Finance & Financial Services
Centre Financial & Management Studies
Centre Financial Management
Centre Financial Regulation & Crime
Centre Financial Research
Centre Regional Public Finance
Centre Research Finance & Accounting
Centre Study Financial Innovation
Essex Finance Centre
Finance & Trade Policy Research Centre
Financial Options Research Centre
Institute Finance & Accounting
International Institute Banking & Financial Services
Oxford Centre Computational Finance
Oxford Financial Research Centre
Scottish Centre Financial Education
Scottish Institute Research Investment & Finance
Warwick Finance Research Institute
Xfi Centre Finance & Investment

>+ Accountancy; Econometrics; Economics headings
Finance: markets
Centre Financial Markets Research
Centre International Capital Markets
Centre Research European Financial Markets & Institutions
Financial Markets Group Research Centre
Finance: quantitative
Centre Quantitative Finance [Imperial College London]
Nomura Centre Quantitative Finance
Fine arts
Barber Institute Fine Arts
Centre Fine Art & Philosophy
Centre Fine Art Research
>+ Art headings
Fire protection & prevention
Arson Prevention Bureau
National Community Fire Safety Centre
Fire research
Centre Research Fire & Explosion Studies
Fiscal studies
Institute Fiscal Studies
Fish & fishing
Centre Applied Entomology & Parasitology
Centre Environment, Fisheries & Aquaculture Science
Fish Conservation Centre
Hull International Fisheries Institute
National Fishing Heritage Centre
Scottish Fish Immunology Research Centre
>+ Aquaculture
Floods
Flood Hazard Research Centre
Flour
Flour Advisory Bureau Ltd
Flowers
National Wildflower Centre
>+ Plants & plant fibres
Fluids, fluidics & fluid mechanics
BP Institute Multiphase Flow
Centre Complex Fluids Processing
Centre Computational Fluid Dynamics
Centre Geophysical & Astrophysical Fluid Dynamics
Centre Power Transmission & Motion Control
Fluid Loading & Instrumentation Centre
Fluids Research Centre
Thermo-Fluid Mechanics Research Centre
Thermo-Fluid Systems University Technology Centre
>+ Hydraulics & hydrodynamics
Foetal health > Pregnancy
Folk life & lore
Institute Folklore Studies Britain & Canada
National Centre English Cultural Tradition
>+ Cultural studies
Food > headings below; specific types of food
Food: hygiene & safety
Centre Eating, Food & Health
Centre Foodservice Research
Northern Ireland Centre Food & Health
Food: industry
Centre Agricultural Strategy
Food Industry Centre
Food Supply Chain Centre
Food, Consumer Behaviour & Health Research Centre
Food: research
Centre for Complex Fluids Processing
Food Innovation Research Centre
Food Refrigeration & Process Engineering Research Centre
Food Research Centre
Food Technology Centre
Food, Consumer Behaviour & Health Research Centre
Gibson Institute Land, Food & Environment
Institute Food Research
London Food Centre
North West Food Centre

Football (Association)
    Football Development Centre
    Football Governance Research Centre
    International Football Institute
Footwear
    SATRA Technology Centre
Forensic science
    Centre Archaeological & Forensic Analysis
    Centre Environmental Forensics
    Centre Forensic & Family Psychology
    Centre Forensic & Legal Medicine
    Centre Forensic Computing
    Centre Forensic Investigation [Glasgow Caledonian]
    Centre Forensic Investigation [Teesside]
    Centre Forensic Science
    Centre Haematology
    International Centre Advanced Research Identification
        Science
Forestry
    CAB International
Forestry
    Institute Atmospheric & Environmental Science
Forgery > Counterfeiting
France & French people
    Centre Charles Péguy
    Centre Mediterranean Studies [Exeter]
    Centre Mediterranean Studies [Leeds]
    Institut français
Franchises
    International Franchise Research Centre
Fraud
    Centre Financial Regulation & Crime
    Centre Fraud Risk Management
    ICC Counterfeiting Intelligence Bureau
    ICC Financial Investigation Bureau
    ICC International Maritime Bureau
    International Fraud Prevention Research Centre
Freedom of the individual > Human rights
Freemasonry
    Canonbury Masonic Research Centre
    Centre Research Freemasonry
Fruit
    Scottish Crop Research Institute
Fuel > Energy
Fund management
    BNP Paribas Hedge Fund Centre
    >+ Finance
Fundamental physics
    Ogden Centre Fundamental Physics
Fundraising
    Charities Information Bureau
Furniture
    British Regional Furniture Study Centre
    SATRA Technology Centre
Further education > Education: adult & continuing
Fusion
    Centre Fusion Studies & Plasma Engineering
Future studies
    Centre Future Studies
    Future Humanity Institute

G

Gambling
    Centre Study Gambling
Gardens & gardening
    National Gardening Centre
    >+ Flowers
Garlic
    Garlic Information Centre
Gas & gas turbines
    Oil & Gas Centre

Gastroenterology
    Centre Adult & Paediatric Gastroenterology
    Centre Gastroenterology & Nutrition
Gay people > Homosexuality
Gender studies & research
    AHRC Research Centre Law, Gender & Sexuality
    Cambridge Centre Gender Studies
    Centre Critical & Cultural Theory
    Centre Ethnicity & Gender
    Centre Gender & Religions Research
    Centre Gender Research
    Centre Gender, Sexuality & Writing
    Centre Gender Studies [Aberdeen]
    Centre Gender Studies [Sheffield]
    Centre Gender Studies [School of Oriental & African Studies,
        London]
    Centre Gender Studies [Sussex]
    Centre Gender & Women's Studies
    Centre Interdisciplinary Gender Studies
    Centre Equality & Human Rights Education
    Centre Research Ageing & Gender
    Centre Research Gender Culture & Society
    Centre Study Women & Gender
    Gender & Sexuality Research Centre
    Gender Institute
    Institute Culture, Gender & City
    International Centre Gender & Women's Studies
    International Gender Studies Centre
    Mary Ann Baxter Centre Interdisciplinary Gender Research
    Strathclyde Centre Gender Studies
    WHO Collaborating Centre Policy & Practice Development
        Women's Health & Gender Mainstreaming
    >+ Women: studies & research
Genealogy
    Family Records Centre
General practice
    Centre General Practice
    >+ Medical headings
Genes > Genetics / genomics
Genetics / genomics
    Babraham Institute
    Bioinformatics Research Centre
    Biomedical Research Centre [Dundee]
    Biomedical Research Centre [Sheffield Hallam]
    Bristol Genomics Research Institute
    Brunel Institute Cancer Genetics & Pharmacogenomics
    Cambridge Resource Centre Comparative Genomics
    Cardiff Centre Research Genetics & Society
    Centre Cardiovascular Genetics
    Centre Comparative Genomics [University College London]
    Centre Developmental & Biomedical Genetics
    Centre Economic & Social Aspects Genomics [Cardiff]
    Centre Economic & Social Aspects Genomics [Lancaster]
    Centre Evolution, Genes & Genomics
    Centre Functional Genomics
    Centre Human Genetics [University College London]
    Centre Human Molecular Genetics
    Centre Medical Genetics & Policy
    Centre Stem Cell Biology & Developmental Genetics
    Centre Stem Cell Biology & Regenerative Medicine
    ESRC Centre Genomics Society
    Genetic Therapies Centre
    Genetics & Insurance Research Centre
    Genetics Education - Networking Innovation & Excellence
        CETL
    Genome Centre
    Inflammation Research Centre
    Innogen - ESRC Centre Social & Economic Research
        Innovation Genomics [Edinburgh]
    Innogen - ESRC Centre Social & Economic Research
        Innovation Genomics [Open University]
    Institute Biological Sciences
    Institute Cell & Molecular Biosciences
    Institute Cell & Molecular Science

Institute Genetics [Leicester]
Institute Genetics [Nottingham]
Institute Human Genetics
Institute Human Genetics & Health
Institute Medical Genetics, Cardiff University
Institute Study Genetics, Biorisks & Society
Leeds Institute Genetics, Health & Therapeutics
Mouse Genome Centre
MRC Clinical Sciences Centre
MRC Genome Damage & Stability Centre
Scottish Centre Genomic Technology & Informatics
Wellcome Trust Centre Human Genetics
Wellcome Trust Sanger Institute
Geodesy
Institute Engineering Surveying & Space Geodesy
Geography
Centre Active Learning Geography, Environment & Related
Disciplines
Cranfield Centre Geographical Information Management
Geography Outdoors
Geography, Earth & Environmental Sciences Subject Centre
giCentre
Institute Environmental & Natural Sciences
Institute Geography & Earth Sciences
Geo-information studies
Centre Geo-Information Studies
Geology & geomechanics
Centre Environmental & Geophysical Flows
Centre Quaternary Research
Institute Geological Sciences
National Stone Centre
Nottingham Centre Geomechanics
Geophysics
Centre Environmental & Geophysical Flows
Institute Geophysics & Tectonics
Institute Theoretical Geophysics
Geosciences
Geotechnical Engineering Research Centre
Institute Environmental & Natural Sciences
>+ specific sciences
Geospatial science
Centre Geospatial Science
Geriatrics > Gerontology
Germany & German people
Cardiff Centre Modern German History
German Historical Institute London
Institute German Studies
Institute Germanic & Romance Studies
Gerontology
Cambridge Interdisciplinary Research Centre Ageing
Centre Ageing & Biographical Studies
Centre Applied Gerontology
Centre Economic Research Ageing
Centre Gerontological Practice
Centre Social Gerontology
Institute Ageing & Health
Institute Gerontology
International Longevity Centre-UK
Oxford Institute Ageing
Sheffield Institute Studies Ageing
UCL Centre Research Ageing
Wolfson Centre Age-Related Diseases
>+ Older people
Gestalt therapy
Gestalt Centre London
>+ Psychotherapy & psychoanalysis
Gifted children > Children: gifted
Glaciology
Bristol Glaciology Centre
Centre Glaciology
World Data Centre Glaciology, Cambridge
Glass & glazing
Centre Glass Research
Centre Window & Cladding Technology

Institute International Research Glass
Liquid Glass Centre
National Glass Centre
Gliding
Scottish Gliding Centre
Global warming > Climate change; Meteorology
Globalisation & global issues
Centre Globalisation Research
Centre Media: Globalisation: Risk
Centre Study Globalisation & Regionalisation
MUNDI Centre Global Education
>+ International headings
Glycobiology
Glycobiology Training, Research & Infrastructure Centre
Glycobiology
Oxford Glycobiology Institute
Governance / government
Centre British Government
Centre Strategic Leadership
History & Governance Research Institute
Institute Governance
Institute Governance & Public Management
Welsh Governance Centre
Government scrutiny
Centre Public Scrutiny
Gravity
Institute Gravitational Research
Great Britain
Britain Visitor Centre
Centre Contemporary British History
Centre English Language & British Studies
Centre Study Britain & Empire
Centre Translation & Comparative Cultural Studies
>+ individual countries
Greece & Greek people
Centre Byzantine, Ottoman & Modern Greek Studies
Centre Hellenic Studies [Reading]
Centre Hellenic Studies [School of Oriental & African
Studies, London]
Centre Mediterranean Studies [Exeter]
Centre Mediterranean Studies [Leeds]
Hellenic Institute
Logos: Centre Study Ancient Systems Knowledge
>+ Classical studies
Green chemistry
Green Chemistry Centre Excellence
Grinding technology
Institute Grinding Technology
Gulf (The)
Gulf Centre Strategic Studies
Institute Arab & Islamic Studies
>+ Middle East
Gynaecology > Women: health

H

Haematology
Centre Haematology
WHO Collaborating Centre Quality Assessment
Haematology
Haemophilia & haemostasis
Haemostasis & Thrombosis Centre
Handicapped people > Disabled people
Harbours > Ports & harbours
Hate crimes > Criminology & criminal justice
Hawks > Raptors
Hay fever
Common Cold & Nasal Research Centre
Scottish Centre Pollen Studies
Hazardous cargoes > Marine safety & security
Hazardous waste
Brunel Institute Bioengineering

© CBD Research Ltd · Beckenham · Kent BR3 5JS · Tel 020 8650 7745 · Fax 020 8650 0768 · E-mail cbd@cbdresearch.com · www.cbdresearch.com

>+ Waste management
Hazards & risks
    Benfield Hazard Research Centre
    Centre Hazard & Risk Management
    Flood Hazard Research Centre
    Health Protection Agency Centre Radiation, Chemical &
        Environmental Hazards
    Institute Hazard & Risk Research
Healing
    Salisbury Centre
Health & safety > Occupational health & safety
Health care
    Centre Excellence Healthcare Professional Education
    Centre Excellence Life Sciences
    Centre Health Improvement & Leadership Lincoln
    Centre Health Sciences
    Centre Innovation Healthcare Technology
    Centre Inter-Professional e-Learning Health & Social Care
    Centre Inter-professional Practice
    Centre Practice Development
    Centre Professional & Organisation Development
    Centre Reviews & Dissemination
    Centre Social History Health & Healthcare [Glasgow
        Caledonian]
    Centre Social History Health & Healthcare [Strathclyde]
    Centre Social Research Health & Health Care
    Clinical Research Centre
    Empeiria Centre
    European Centre Health Societies Transition
    European Institute Health & Medical Sciences
    Great Chapel Street Medical Centre
    Health Communication Research Centre
    Institute Child Health [Liverpool]
    Institute Health & Community Studies
    Institute Health & Social Care
    Institute Health & Social Care Research
    Institute Health Sciences & Social Care Research
    Institute Health Sciences [City]
    Institute Health Sciences [Manchester]
    Institute Health Sciences Education
    Kent Institute Medicine & Health Sciences
    King's Fund Centre
    Leeds Institute Health Sciences
    Multidisciplinary Assessment Technology Centre Healthcare
    Nuffield Centre International Health & Development
    Oxford Centre Enablement
    Queen's Medical Centre
    Research Institute Healthcare Science
    Salford Centre Research & Innovation
    Wales Centre Evidence Based Care
    WHO Collaborating Centre Promoting Health Prisons
    WHO Collaborating Centre Training & Research
        Communications & Information Technology Health
        Promotion & Disease Prevention
    >+ Public health
Health economics > Economics: health
Health care: ethics > Medical ethics
Health informatics
    Centre Health Informatics & Multiprofessional Education
    Centre Health Information, Research & Evaluation
    Northern Ireland Centre Health Informatics
    Sowerby Centre Health Informatics
    Yorkshire Centre Health Informatics
Health: politics
    Centre Health & International Relations
Health: public > Public health
Health research
    Brunel Institute Bioengineering
    Centre Allied Health Professions Research
    Centre Health & International Relations
    Centre Health Care Research
    Centre Health Information, Research & Evaluation
    Centre Health Management
    Centre Health Promotion Research

Centre Health Research & Evaluation
Centre Health Research & Practice Development
Centre Health Sciences Research
Centre Health Services Research
Centre Health Services Studies
Centre Inclusion & Diversity
Centre Integrated Health Care Research
Centre Integrated Healthcare Research
Centre Research Health & Medicine
Centre Research Health Behaviour
Centre Study Health & Illness
Centre Workplace Health
Health & Human Sciences Research Institute
Health Sciences & Practice Subject Centre
Health Sciences Research Institute
Institute Applied Health Sciences
Institute Health [Norwich]
Institute Health Research [Lancaster]
Institute Health Research [Bedfordshire]
Institute Health Research [Staffordshire]
Institute Health Research [Swansea]
Institute Health Sciences & Public Health Research
Institute Health Sciences & Social Care Research
Institute Health Sciences [City]
Institute Health Sciences [Manchester]
Institute Human Sciences [Oxford]
Institute Human Sciences [Staffordshire]
Institute Research Health & Human Sciences
Interdisciplinary Research Centre Health
International Health Development Research Centre
Leeds Institute Genetics, Health & Therapeutics
Leeds Institute Health Sciences
National Coordinating Centre Health Technology
    Assessment
Oxford Centre Enablement
Research Institute Life Course Studies
Scottish Centre Healthy Working Lives
Tayside Institute Health Studies
UCL Centre International Health & Development
UCL Institute Human Health & Performance
Wessex Institute Health Research & Development
Wolfson Research Centre
Wolfson Research Institute
>+ Medical research
Health research: arts
    Arts Health Centre
    Centre Arts & Humanities Health & Medicine
Health research: aviation
    Aviation Health Institute
Health research: environment
    Centre Research Environment & Health [Aberystwyth]
    Centre Research Environment & Health [Cardiff]
    Centre Research Environment & Health [Crewe]
    Centre Research Environment & Health [Lampeter]
    Centre Research Environment & Health [Leeds]
Health research: men
    Centre Men's Health
Health research: military
    King's Centre Military Health Research
Health research: policy
    Cambridge University Health - Health Policy Management
        Centre
    Institute Health Research & Policy
Health research: social
    Alcuin Research Resource Centre
    Cardiff Institute Society, Health & Ethics
    Centre Health & Social Care Research [Huddersfield]
    Centre Health & Social Care Research [Sheffield Hallam]
    Centre Health & Social Evaluation
    Centre Health & Social Research
    Centre Health, Medicine & Society
    Crichton Centre Research Health & Social Issues
    Institute Health Sciences & Social Care Research
    Institute Social & Health Research [Chester]

Institute Social & Health Research [Middlesex]
Research Institute Health & Social Change
UCL International Institute Society & Health
Welsh School Pharmacy Centre Socioeconomic Research
>+ Public health
Health services
Centre Clinical & Health Services Research
Centre Health Planning & Management
Centre Health & Public Services Management
Centre Health Services Research
Centre Research Allied Health Professions
Health Services Management Centre
Health Services Research Centre
Institute Health & Society
National Coordinating Centre Health Technology
Assessment
Nuffield Centre International Health & Development
Research Centre Transcultural Studies Health
Wales Centre Health
>+ National Health Service
Health: children > Children: health
Hearing
Centre Auditory Research
Hearing & Balance Centre
MRC Institute Hearing Research - Nottingham Clinical
Section
MRC Institute Hearing Research - Scottish Section
MRC Institute Hearing Research - Southampton Section
Nuffield Hearing & Speech Centre
South England Cochlear Implant Centre
Welsh Hearing Institute
>+ Deafness
Heart > Cardio- headings
Heat treatment & transfer
Thermo-Fluid Mechanics Research Centre
Thermo-Fluid Systems University Technology Centre
Wolfson Heat Treatment Centre
Hebrew studies
Oxford Centre Hebrew & Jewish Studies
>+ Jewish interests
Hellenic studies
Centre Hellenic Studies [Reading]
Centre Hellenic Studies [School of Oriental & African
Studies, London]
Exeter Centre Hellenistic & Greco-Roman Culture
Hellenic Institute
>+ Greece & Greek people
Helminthology
Centre Applied Entomology & Parasitology
Hepatology
UCL Institute Hepatology
Herbs & herbal medicine
Acumedic Centre Chinese Medicine
Garlic Information Centre
Heritage research
Centre Heritage Research
>+ Historic buildings & conservation
Hernias
British Hernia Centre
Higher education > Education: higher
Himalayas
Centre South Asian Studies [Cambridge]
Centre South Asian Studies [Coventry]
Centre South Asian Studies [Edinburgh]
Centre South Asian Studies [School of Oriental & African
Studies, London]
Centre South Asian Studies [Sussex]
Scottish Centre Himalayan Research
>+ Asia
Hinduism
Oxford Centre Hindu Studies
Historic buildings & conservation
Centre Active Learning Geography, Environment & Related
Disciplines

Centre Study Country House
Ironbridge Institute
Lime Centre
National Monuments Record Centre
UCL Centre Sustainable Heritage
Historical research & study
Borthwick Institute Archives
Centre Contemporary British History
Institute Historical & Cultural Research
Institute Historical Research
Marc Fitch Historical Institute
Raphael Samuel History Centre
Saint John's House Centre Advanced Historical Research
Subject Centre History, Classics & Archaeology
UHI Centre History
>+ specific era & type
History
Centre Research & Scholarship History, Education & Cultural
Heritage
Churchill Archives Centre
Glenamara Centre International Research Arts & Society
Sussex Centre Intellectual History
HIV positive > AIDS (disease)
Holidays > Tourism & travel
Holocaust
Research Centre Holocaust & 20th-Century History
Stanley Burton Centre Holocaust Studies
Homeopathy
British Institute Homeopathy
Homosexuality
Centre Study Sexual Dissidence
Institute Study Christianity & Sexuality
Lesbian Archive & Information Centre
Hong Kong
Centre South Asian Studies [Cambridge]
Centre South Asian Studies [Coventry]
Centre South Asian Studies [Edinburgh]
Centre South Asian Studies [School of Oriental & African
Studies, London]
Centre South Asian Studies [Sussex]
Hormone replacement therapy
Charles Salt Centre Human Metabolism
Horoscopes > Astrology
Horses & ponies
Thoroughbred Rehabilitation Centre
Horticulture > Gardens & gardening
Hospital infections
WHO Collaborating Centre Reference & Research Hospital
Infections
Hospitality industry > Hotel & catering industry
Hotel & catering industry
Centre Environmental Studies Hospitality Industries
Centre Hospitality Management & Retailing
Centre International Hospitality Management Research
Hospitality, Leisure, Sport & Tourism Network
Housing
Centre Comparative Housing Research
Centre Housing & Community Research
Centre Housing Policy
Joint Centre Scottish Housing Research
HRT > Hormone replacement therapy
Human behaviour
Centre Social Learning & Cognitive Evolution
Human development
Centre Study Human Development & Well-Being
Human movement > Movement (human)
Human relations
Centre Research Communications & Subjectivity
Centre Study Human Relations
Scottish Institute Human Relations
Tavistock Institute Human Relations
Human resources
Human Resource Research Centre
Human Resources Management Research Centre

Human rights
    Article 19: International Centre against Censorship
    British Institute Human Rights
    Centre Equality & Human Rights Education
    Centre Human Rights Conflict
    Centre Research Human Rights
    Centre Study Human Rights
    Centre Study Human Rights Law [Glasgow]
    Centre Study Human Rights Law [Strathclyde]
    European Human Rights Advocacy Centre
    Helen Bamber Centre Study Rights & Conflict
    Human Rights & Social Justice Research Institute
    Human Rights Centre [Belfast]
    Human Rights Centre [Essex]
    Human Rights Centre [Durham]
    Human Rights Law Centre
    Humanities Research Centre [Bangor]
    Humanities Research Centre [Sheffield Hallam]
    Humanities Research Institute [Sheffield]
    Institute Advanced Studies Humanities [Edinburgh]
    Max Beloff Centre Study Liberty
    Sumac Centre
Human sciences
    Centre Human Sciences
    Health & Human Sciences Research Institute
Human services
    Centre Human Service Technology
Humanities
    Birkbeck Institute Humanities
    Bristol Institute Research Humanities & Arts
    Centre Arts & Humanities Health & Medicine
    Centre Computing Humanities
    Centre Employability Through Humanities
    Centre Theoretical Studies Humanities & Social Sciences
    Cultural Informatics Research Centre Arts & Humanities
    Culture, Communications & Computing Research Institute
    European Humanities Research Centre
    Humanities & Arts Research Centre
    Humanities Advanced Technology & Information Institute
    Kent Institute Advanced Studies Humanities
    Leeds Humanities Research Institute
    Research Institute Humanities
Hydraulics & hydrodynamics
    Centre Land Use & Water Resources Research
    National Centre Macromolecular Hydrodynamics
Hydrology
    CEH Banchory
    CEH Bangor
    CEH Dorset
    CEH Edinburgh
    CEH Lancaster
    CEH Monks Wood
    CEH Oxford
    CEH Wallingford
    Centre Ecology & Hydrology
Hydromechanics > Hydraulics & hydrodynamics
Hyper / hypobaric research > Diving (training & techniques)

I

Iberia > Portugal & Portuguese people; Spain & Spanish people
Ice
    Fluid Loading & Instrumentation Centre
    >+ Glaciology
ICT > Information systems & technology
Idealism
    Collingwood & British Idealism Centre
Identification science > Forensic science
Identity > Individual identity
Illicit trading > specific object traded eg Antiquities
Imaging & image analysis
    Applied Digital Signal & Image Processing Research Centre

Centre Accelerator Science, Imaging & Medicine
Centre Digital Imaging
Centre Images Practice
Centre Information Management & Technology
Centre Magnetic Resonance Investigations
Centre Medical Image Computing
Centre Video Communications
Digital Imaging Research Centre
Information & Biomedical Engineering Research Centre
Kelvin Nanocharacterisation Centre
Magnetic Resonance Centre
Magnetic Resonance Research Centre
Multi-Imaging Centre
Positron Imaging Centre
Sir Peter Mansfield Magnetic Resonance Centre
Immigrants & refugees
    East European Advice Centre
    Information Centre about Asylum & Refugees UK
    International Centre Intercultural Studies
    Northern Refugee Centre
    Refugee Research Centre
    Refugee Studies Centre
    >+ Ethnicity & ethnic minorities
Immunisation
    Health Protection Agency Centre for Infections
Immunological sensors > Sensors
Immunology
    Babraham Institute
    Hugh & Catherine Stevenson Centre Childhood Infectious
        Diseases & Immunology
    Inflammation Research Centre
    Institute Immunology & Infection Research
    Institute Infection, Immunity & Inflammation
    MRC Centre Immune Regulation
    Windeyer Institute Medical Sciences
Impact research
    Cranfield Impact Centre
    Impact Research Centre
    International Centre Vibro-Impact Systems
    Motor Insurance Repair Research Centre
Imperial studies > Colonial research
Incontinence
    Education & Resources Improving Childhood Continence
    Greater Glasgow Health Board Continence Resource Centre
        & Helpline Scotland
    >+ Urinary problems
India & Indian people
    Aditya V Birla India Centre
    Centre South Asian Studies [Cambridge]
    Centre South Asian Studies [Coventry]
    Centre South Asian Studies [Edinburgh]
    Centre South Asian Studies [School of Oriental & African
        Studies, London]
    Centre South Asian Studies [Sussex]
    India & South Asia Business Centre
    Institute Indian Art & Culture
    Tagore Centre UK
Individual freedom > Human rights
Individual identity
    Institute Future Mind
    Centre Research Self & Identity
Indonesia & Indonesian people
    Centre South Asian Studies [Cambridge]
    Centre South Asian Studies [Coventry]
    Centre South Asian Studies [Edinburgh]
    Centre South Asian Studies [School of Oriental & African
        Studies, London]
    Centre South Asian Studies [Sussex]
Indoor environment > Environment: indoor
Industrial archaeology > Archaeology
Industrial law > Law: commercial
Industrial processes
    Centre Process & Information Systems Engineering

Industrial relations
    Centre Labour Market Studies
    European Work & Employment Research Centre
    >+ Employment
Industrial safety > Occupational health & safety
Industry
    Centre Advanced Industry
    Centre Study Regulated Industries
    Industrial Control Centre
    Institute Industrial Research
Infants > Children
Infectious diseases > Communicable diseases
Infertility > Fertility treatment
Inflammation > specific types eg Arthritis & rheumatism
Inflammatory diseases
    MRC-University Edinburgh Centre Inflammation Research
Informatics
    Applied Informatics Research Centre
    Centre Computer Science & Informatics Research
    >+ specific types
Information management
    Centre Applied Research Information Systems
    Centre Archive & Information Studies
    Centre Business Information, Organisation & Process
        Management
    Centre Informatics Education Research
    Centre Information Behaviour & Evaluation Research
    Centre Information Management
    Centre Information Management & E-Business
    Centre Information Management & Technology
    Centre Information Quality Management
    Centre Research Library & Information Management
    Information Research Institute
    Institute Information Systems & Integration Technology
    Institute Integrated Information Systems
    Mobile Information & Network Technologies Research
        Centre
    Oxford Institute Information Management
    Research Institute Information & Language Processing
    Subject Centre Information & Computer Sciences
        [Loughborough]
    Subject Centre Information & Computer Sciences [Ulster]
    >+ Computers: security; e-Business
Information policy
    Centre Information Policy Studies
Information systems & technology
    Centre Advanced Software & Intelligent Systems
    Centre Advanced Software Technology
    Centre Complex Cooperative Systems
    Centre Computing & Social Responsibility
    Centre Information Management & Technology
    Centre Interactive Systems Engineering
    Centre Interactive Systems Research
    Centre IT Construction
    Centre New Technologies Research in Education
    Informatics & Technology Research Institute
    Informatics Research Institute [Newcastle]
    Informatics Research Institute [Salford]
    Information Systems Research Centre
    Information Systems, Organisation & Society Research
        Centre
    Institute Information Technology
    Institute IT Training
    Institute Socio-Technical Research & Innovation
    IT Innovation Centre
    Wireless Information Technology Research Centre
    >+ Computer headings
Infrastructure engineering > Civil engineering
Innovation
    Cardiff University Innovative Manufacturing Research Centre
    Centre Clinical & Academic Workforce Innovation
    Centre Competitiveness & Innovation
    Centre Creativity & Innovation
    Centre Creativity Research

    Centre Enterprise & Innovation
    Centre Enterprise Research & Innovation
    Centre Innovation, Knowledge & Development
    Centre International Business & Innovation
    Centre Leadership & Practice Innovation
    Centre Leadership Creativity
    Centre New Technologies, Innovation & Entrepreneurship
    Centre Research Innovation Management
    Complex Product Systems Innovation Centre
    Complex Systems Management Centre
    ESRC Centre Organisation & Innovation
    ESRC Centre Research Innovation & Competition
    Innovation Studies Centre
    Institute Innovation & Enterprise
    Manchester Institute Innovation Research
    University Nottingham Institute Enterprise & Innovation
    Warwick Innovative Manufacturing Research Centre
    Welsh Enterprise Institute
    >+ Invention; specific fields
Insects > Entomology
Institutional studies
    Centre Institutional Studies
>+ Education: policy; Public policy
Instrumentation
    Centre Advanced Instrumentation
    Centre Advanced Instrumentation Systems
    Fluid Loading & Instrumentation Centre
    Measurement & Instrumentation Centre
Insurance
    Centre Decision Management & Risk Management
    Centre Risk & Insurance Studies
    Continuous Mortality Investigation Bureau
    Genetics & Insurance Research Centre
    King's Centre Risk Management
    London Underwriting Centre
    PAPRI: Pension & Population Research Institute
Insurance: motor > Motor insurance
Intellectual property > Trade marks / intellectual property
Intelligent systems
    Centre Intelligent Systems & Applications
    Centre Interactive Intelligent Systems
    Intelligent Systems Research Centre
Intensive care medicine
    Centre Intensive Care Medicine & Bloomsbury Instititue
        Intensive Care Medicine
Intercultural studies
    Centre Intercultural Studies [Glasgow]
    Centre Intercultural Studies [University College London]
>+ Cultural studies
Intergenerational practice
    Centre Intergenerational Practice
    Wales Centre Intergenerational Practice
Interior design > Design
Intermedia
    Centre Intermedia
    >+ Media
International affairs
    Centre International Communications & Society
    Centre International Communications Research
    Centre International Governance
    Centre Study Global Change & Governance
    Centre Study Global Governance
    CLIO Centre Globalisation, Education & Societies
    CLIO Centre International & Comparative Studies
    Institute International Policy Analysis
    Social & Policy Research Institute
    Welsh Centre International Affairs
    >+ Developing countries & Third World; Peace studies
International business > Business: international
International development > Developing countries & Third World
International law > Law: international
International studies
    Centre Diplomatic & International Studies
    Centre European & International Studies Research

Centre International & European Studies
Centre International Borders Research
Centre International Studies & Diplomacy
Centre International Studies [Cambridge]
Centre International Studies [Leeds]
Centre International Studies [London School of Economics &
    Political Science]
Centre International Studies [Oxford]
Centre Politics & International Studies
David Davies Memorial Institute
Graduate Institute Political & International Studies
Institute Global Studies
Mountbatten Centre International Studies
Plymouth International Studies Centre

Internet
    Centre Internet Technologies

Internet
    Oxford Internet Institute

Invention
    Centre Study Invention & Social Process
    >+ Innovation

Investment
    Alternative Investments Research Centre
    BNP Paribas Hedge Fund Centre
    PAPRI: Pension & Population Research Institute
    Private Equity & Venture Capital Research Centre
    Private Equity Institute
    Scottish Institute Research Investment & Finance
    Xfi Centre Finance & Investment

Ion beams
    Surrey Ion Beam Centre

Ion conducting membranes > Membranes

Ionic liquid research
    Queen's University Ionic Liquid Laboratories

Iran & Iranian people
    Centre Iranian Studies

Ireland & Irish people
    AHRC Centre Irish & Scottish Studies
    Centre Cross Border Studies
    Centre Irish Politics
    Institute Irish Studies [Belfast]
    Institute Irish Studies [Liverpool]
    Irish Studies Centre
    Research Institute Irish & Scottish Studies

Iron & steel
    Iron & Steel Statistics Bureau
    Steel Can Recycling Information Bureau

Islam & Islamic studies
    Centre Islamic & Middle East Law
    Centre Islamic Studies [School of Oriental & African Studies,
        London]
    Centre Middle Eastern & Islamic Studies [Cambridge]
    Centre Study Islam [Glasgow]
    Centre Study Islam UK [Cardiff]
    Institute Arab & Islamic Studies
    Institute Middle Eastern & Islamic Studies
    Institute Middle Eastern Studies
    Islamic Cultural Centre & London Central Mosque
    Oxford Centre Islamic Studies

Island technology
    International Centre Island Technology

Isle of Man > Manx studies

Israel & Jewish people > Jewish interests

IT > Information systems & technology

Italy & Italian people
    Centre Italian Studies
    Centre Mediterranean Studies [Exeter]
    Centre Mediterranean Studies [Leeds]
    Leopardi Centre
    >+ Classical studies

J

Jaina
    Centre Jaina Studies
Japan & Japanese people
    Cardiff Japanese Studies Centre
    Centre Study Japanese Religions
    Europe Japan Research Centre
    Europe-Japan Social Science Research Centre
    Institute Japanese-European Technology Studies
    Japan Research Centre
    JETRO London (Japan Trade Centre)
    Nissan Institute Japanese Studies
    Sainsbury Institute Study Japanese Arts & Cultures
Jazz & blues > Music: jazz & blues
Jewish interests
    Centre German-Jewish Studies
    Centre Israeli Studies
    Centre Jewish Studies [Leeds]
    Centre Jewish Studies [Manchester]
    Centre Jewish Studies [School of Oriental & African Studies,
        London]
    Institute Jewish Studies
    Jewish Education Bureau
    Leo Baeck College - Centre Jewish Education
    Manchester-Sheffield Centre Dead Sea Scrolls Research
    Oxford Centre Hebrew & Jewish Studies
    Parkes Institute Study Jewish / non-Jewish Relations
    Sternberg Centre Judaism
Jobs > Careers; Employment
Joining technology
    Joining Technology Research Centre
Journalism
    Centre Broadcasting & Journalism
    Centre Journalism Studies
    Scottish Centre Journalism Studies
Judaism > Jewish interests
Judicial administration
    Institute Judicial Administration

K

Kidney structure & disease > Urology & nephrology
Kinaesiology
    Research Centre Clinical Kinaesiology
    >+ Movement (human)
Knitted materials
    William Lee Innovation Centre
Knowledge management & transfer
    Assessment Standards Knowledge exchange CETL
    Centre Knowledge Management
    Centre Knowledge Transfer
    Centre Management Knowledge & Strategic Change
    Centre Research & Knowledge Transfer
    Interdisciplinary Research Centre Advanced Knowledge
        Technologies
    Knowledge Transfer Partnerships Centres
Korea & Korean people
    Centre Korean Studies
Kurdish peoples
    Kurdish Cultural Centre Ltd

L

Laban dance & notation
    Centre Dance Research
    Drama, Dance & Performing Arts Research Centre
    Labanotation Institute

>+ Dancing
Laboratories
    National Flying Laboratory Centre
    WHO Collaborating Centre Laboratory & Diagnostic
       Support
Labour
    Centre Comparative Labour Studies
Labour market > Employment
Labour relations > Employment; Industrial relations
Land usage
    Centre Land Use & Water Resources Research
    Contaminated Land Assessment & Remediation Research
       Centre
    Cranfield Centre Ecological Restoration
    Geoenvironmental Research Centre
    Gibson Institute Land, Food & Environment
    Institute Agri-Food & Land Use
    Macaulay Institute
    Soil Survey & Land Research Centre
Landscape
    Centre Active Learning Geography, Environment & Related
       Disciplines
    Centre Geomorphology
    International Centre Protected Landscapes
Language teaching & research
    AHRC Research Centre Philosophy Logic, Language,
       Mathematics & Mind
    Cambridge Institute Language Research
    Centre Applied Language Research
    Centre Applied Language Studies [Reading]
    Centre Applied Language Studies [Swansea]
    Centre Deaf Studies, Language & Cognition
    Centre Educational Studies [Aberystwyth]
    Centre European Languages & Cultures
    Centre Information Technology Language Learning
    Centre Interlanguage Studies
    Centre International Exchange & Languages
    Centre Language & Communication Research
    Centre Language & Culture
    Centre Language Assessment Research
    Centre Language Learning Research
    Centre Language Studies [City]
    Centre Language Studies [Surrey]
    Centre Language Study
    Centre Language, Discourse & Communication
    Centre Languages, English & Media Education
    Centre Modern Languages
    Centre Reading & Language
    Centre Research Communication & Language
    Centre Research Language Education
    Centre Research Second & Foreign Language Pedagogy
    Centre Speech, Language & Brain
    Centre Thinking & Language
    Centre Transcultural Research
    Cheltenham International Language Centre
    CILT, National Centre Languages
    CLIO Centre Research Language & Education
    Communication Aids Language & Learning
    Compass Centre
    Deafness, Cognition & Language Research Centre
    Foreign Language Centre
    Institute Applied Language Studies
    Institute Historical Study Language
    Institute Language, Speech & Hearing
    Institute Study Language & Social Sciences
    Language & Literacy Research Centre
    Languages & Humanities Centre
    Languages Information Centre
    Languages Wider World CETL
    National Centre Language & Literacy
    Northern Ireland Centre Information Language Teaching &
       Research
    Praxis: Centre Study Literary Discourse
    Research Institute Information & Language Processing

    Saint Andrews University Institute Language & Linguistic
       Studies
    Scottish Centre Information Language Teaching
    Subject Centre Languages, Linguistics & Area Studies
    Sussex Language Institute
    Welsh Language Teaching Centre
    >+ Linguistics; specific language or country
Laos & Laotian people
    Centre South Asian Studies [Cambridge]
    Centre South Asian Studies [Coventry]
    Centre South Asian Studies [Edinburgh]
    Centre South Asian Studies [School of Oriental & African
       Studies, London]
    Centre South Asian Studies [Sussex]
Laryngology
    Institute Laryngology & Otology
Lasers
    Centre Advanced Joining
    Centre Cold Matter
    Laser Engineering Centre
    Laser Processing Research Centre
    National Medical Laser Centre
Latin America
    Centre Brazilian & Latin America Studies
    Centre Brazilian Studies
    Centre Latin American Cultural Studies [Kings College
       London]
    Centre Latin American Cultural Studies [Manchester]
    Centre Latin American Research
    Centre Latin American Studies [Cambridge]
    Centre Latin American Studies [Essex]
    Centre Latin American Studies [Exeter]
    Institute Latin American Studies
    Latin America Bureau
    Latin American Centre
    >+ America
Law
    AHRC Research Centre Law, Gender & Sexuality
    Bristol Institute Legal Practice
    Centre British Constitutional Law & History
    Centre Ecology, Law & Policy
    Centre Intellectual Property & Information Law
    Centre Law & Conflict
    Centre Law Reform
    Centre Legal Practice
    Centre Legal Research [West of England]
    Centre Legal Research [Middlesex]
    Centre Legal Research [Nottingham Trent]
    Centre Legal Research & Policy Studies
    Centre Multi-Cultural Studies Law & Family
    Centre Professional Legal Studies
    Centre Research Delivery Legal Services
    Centre Social-Legal Studies
    Centre Study Law, Society & Popular Culture
    Ethnic Minorities Law Centre
    Institute Advanced Legal Studies
    Institute Global Law
    Institute Professional Legal Studies
    Kent Centre European & Comparative Law
    Legal Research Institute
    Vinogradoff Institute
Law: advice
    Law Centre (NI)
Law: children > Law: family
Law: civil
    Centre Contemporary Civil Law Studies
    Centre Study Civil Law Tradition
Law: commercial
    Centre Business Law & Practice
    Centre Commercial Law
    Centre Commercial Law Studies [Queen Mary, London]
    Centre Commercial Law Studies [Swansea]
    Centre Corporate & Commercial Law
    Centre Corporate Law & Practice

© CBD Research Ltd · Beckenham · Kent BR3 5JS · Tel 020 8650 7745 · Fax 020 8650 0768 · E-mail cbd@cbdresearch.com · www.cbdresearch.com

Centre Energy, Petroleum & Mineral Law & Policy
Centre Insolvency Law & Policy
Centre Legal Information Management & Business
Commercial Law Centre
Institute Business & Law
Jevons Institute Competition Law & Economics
University Oxford Centre Competition Law & Policy
Law: comparative
British Institute International & Comparative Law
Law: construction
Centre Construction Innovation & Research
Centre Construction Law & Management
Law: criminal
Centre Criminal Law & Criminal Justice
Centre Criminology & Socio-Legal Studies
Centre Law & Society
Law: East Asian
Centre East Asian Law
Law: education
Sussex Institute
United Kingdom Centre Legal Education
Law: employment
Institute Employment Law
Law: environment
Centre Environmental Law
Centre Law & Environment
Law: ethics
Cardiff Centre Ethics, Law & Society
Centre Law Ethics & Society
Oxford Centre Ethics & Philosophy Law
Law: European
Centre European Law
Centre European Legal Studies [Cambridge]
Centre European Legal Studies [Exeter]
Centre European Studies [Bradford]
Centre European Studies [Exeter]
Centre Law & Governance Europe
Centre Law European Union
Centre Study Law & Policy Europe
Durham European Law Institute
Institute European & Comparative Law
Institute European Law
Institute European Public Law
Kent Centre European & Comparative Law
Law: family
Centre International Family Law Studies
Centre Multi-Cultural Studies Law & Family
Centre Study Child, Family & Law
Children's Legal Centre
Scottish Child Law Centre
Law: forensics
Joseph Bell Centre Forensic Statistics & Legal Reasoning
Law: human rights
Centre Study Human Rights Law [Glasgow]
Centre Study Human Rights Law [Strathclyde]
Human Rights Law Centre
Law: international
British Institute International & Comparative Law
Centre International & Public Law
Centre International Law & Colonialism
Lauterpacht Centre International Law
Legal Research Institute
McCoubrey Centre International Law
Scottish Centre International Law
Law: Islamic & Middle Eastern
Centre Islamic & Middle East Law
Law: marine
Institute International Shipping & Trade Law
Institute Maritime Law
Institute Medicine, Law & Bioethics
London Shipping Law Centre
Law: medical
Centre Forensic & Legal Medicine
Centre Medical Law & Ethics

Centre Medico-Legal Studies
Institute Medical Law
Law: property
Centre Property Law
Law: public
Centre Election Law
Centre International & Public Law
Centre Public Law
Research Institute Law, Politics & Justice
Law: religion
Centre Law & Religion
Law: socio-legal > Socio-legal studies
Law: tax
Centre Tax Law
Law: technology
AHRC Research Centre Studies Intellectual Property & Technology Law
Sheffield Institute Biotechnological Law & Ethics
Law: travel
Travel Law Centre
Law: Wales
Centre Welsh Legal Affairs
Law: water
UNESCO Centre Water Law, Policy & Science
Lawrence (D H)
D H Lawrence Research Centre
Leadership
Aston Centre Leadership Excellence
Centre Executive Learning
Centre Leadership & Practice Innovation
Centre Leadership Studies
Centre Leadership, Learning & Change
>+ specific areas eg Education
Learning & teaching
Assessment & Learning Practice Settings CETL
Capital Centre (Creativity & Performance Teaching & Learning)
Centre Advancement Learning & Teaching
Centre Development Learning & Teaching
Centre Enhancement Learning & Teaching [Hertfordshire]
Centre Enhancement Learning & Teaching [Lancaster]
Centre Enhancement Learning & Teaching [Robert Gordon]
Centre Excellence Enquiry-Based Learning
Centre Excellence Leadership & Professional Learning
Centre Excellence Preparing Academic Practice
Centre Excellence Professional Development Through Use Relevant Technologies
Centre Excellence Teaching & Learning Assessment Learning
Centre Excellence Teaching & Learning Reusable Learning Objects
Centre Integrative Learning
Centre Learning & Teaching
Centre Learning & Teaching Research
Centre Learning & Workforce Research
Centre Learning Development
Centre Learning Organisations
Centre Learning, Teaching & Research Higher Education
Centre Promoting Learner Autonomy
Centre Research Interactive Learning
Centre Stakeholder Learning Partnerships
Centre Teaching, Learning & Assessment
CLIO Centre Learning, Knowing & Interactive Technologies
Enhancing, Embedding & Integrating Employability CETL
Foundation Direct CETL
IDEA CETL
InQbate Centre Excellence Teaching & Learning Creativity
Institute Learning
Institute Research Learning & Teaching Higher Education
Learning & Teaching Institute
Learning Through Action Centre
Oxford Learning Institute
Personalised Integrated Learning Support CETL
Physical Sciences Centre
Promethean Centre Excellence

Reinvention Centre Undergraduate Research
Research Centre Learning Society
Scottish Centre Research On-line Learning & Assessment
SOLSTICE Centre
Visual LearningLab CETL
White Rose Centre Excellence Teaching & Learning Enterprise
>+ Education headings; Teachers & teacher training
Learning disabilities
Welsh Centre Learning Disabilities
Leather
Centre Research Leather & Materials Science
Leather Conservation Centre
SATRA Technology Centre
Lebanon & Lebanese people
Centre Lebanese Studies
Left-handedness
Gifted Children's Information Centre
Legal > Law headings
Legislative studies
Sir William Dale Centre Legislative Studies
Leisure & recreation
Carnegie Research Institute
Centre Leisure & Tourism Studies
Centre Leisure, Tourism & Society
Hospitality, Leisure, Sport & Tourism Network
Institute Sport & Leisure Policy
Leopardi (Giacomo)
Leopardi Centre
Lesbians > Homosexuality
Letters
AHRC Centre Editing Lives & Letters
Lexicography
Dictionary Research Centre
Liberty > Human rights
Libraries
Centre Digital Library Research
Centre Public Library & Information Society
Centre Research Library & Information Management
>+ Books
Life history
Centre Life History Research
Life sciences > individual science
Lifeboats > Marine safety & security
Lifelong learning > Education: Adult & continuing
Lighting
Centre Phosphors & Display Materials
Lime
Lime Centre
Linen > Textiles
Linguistics
Centre English Language Studies
Centre English Language Teacher Education & Applied Linguistics
Centre Language Social Life
Centre Linguistic Research
Centre Linguistics & Philology
Centre Research Applied Linguistics
Glenamara Centre International Research Arts & Society
Literary & Linguistic Computing Centre
Research Centre English & Applied Linguistics
Subject Centre Languages, Linguistics & Area Studies
>+ Language teaching & research
Lipids
Lipids Research Centre
Literacy
Centre Academic & Professional Literacies
Centre Literacy Primary Education
Centre Literacy Research
Lancaster Literacy Research Centre
Language & Literacy Research Centre
National Centre Language & Literacy
National Research & Development Centre Adult Literacy & Numeracy

Spatial Literacy Teaching CETL
Literature
Basil Bunting Poetry Centre
Bath Royal Literary & Scientific Institution
Centre Commonwealth Studies
Centre Contemporary Fiction & Narrative
Centre Contemporary German Literature
Centre Editorial & Intertextual Research
Centre Editorial & Intertextual Research
Centre Modern Poetry
Centre Research Philosophy & Literature
Centre Study Literature, Theology & Arts
Centre Textual Scholarship
Crime Fictions Research Centre
Ingeborg Bachmann Centre Austrian Literature
Literary & Cultural Studies Research Centre
Manchester Poetry Centre
Poetry Translation Centre
Praxis: Centre Study Literary Discourse
Raymond Williams Centre Recovery Research
Research Centre Modern & Contemporary Poetry
Stirling Centre Poetry
Wordsworth Centre
>+ specific authors
Literature: children's
National Centre Research Children's Literature
Liturgy
Centre Study Liturgy & Architecture
Liver structure & disease > Hepatology
Local government
Centre Local & Regional Government Research
Centre Local Governance
Institute Local Government Studies
Local Government Information Bureau
Local history
Centre English Local History
Centre Local History [Essex]
Centre Local History [Nottingham]
Centre Local History Studies
Centre Regional & Local Historical Research
Centre Research English & Local History
>+ specific region
Logistics
Centre Analysis Supply Chain Innovation & Dynamics
Centre Supply Chain Management
Centre Supply Chain Research
Logistics Education Centre
Logistics Research Centre
Supply Chain Research Centre
University Hull Logistics Institute
Long wave events
LSE Mackinder Centre Study Long Wave Events
Longevity > Gerontology
Longitudinal research
Centre Longitudinal Studies
ESRC Research Centre Micro-Social Change
ESRC UK Longitudinal Studies Centre
European Centre Analysis Social Sciences
Institute Social & Economic Research
Longitudinal Studies Centre - Scotland
Lungs > Cardiothoracic research

M

Macroeconomics > Economics: macroeconomics
Magazines > Periodicals
Magic
Centre Magic Arts
Magnetic resonance imaging > Imaging & image analysis
Magnetics & electromagnetics
Applied Electromagnetics Research Centre
Centre Magnetic Resonance Investigations

 © CBD Research Ltd · Beckenham · Kent BR3 5JS · Tel 020 8650 7745 · Fax 020 8650 0768 · E-mail cbd@cbdresearch.com · www.cbdresearch.com

Centre Materials Science
George Green Institute Electromagnetics Research
Magnetic Resonance Centre
Magnetic Resonance Research Centre
Manchester Centre Magnetic Resonance
Oxford Centre Functional Magnetic Resonance Imaging Brain
Sheffield Centre Advanced Magnetic Materials & Devices
Wolfson Centre Magnetics Technology
Malaysia & Malay people
    Centre South Asian Studies [Cambridge]
    Centre South Asian Studies [Coventry]
    Centre South Asian Studies [Edinburgh]
    Centre South Asian Studies [School of Oriental & African Studies, London]
    Centre South Asian Studies [Sussex]
Malt & malt products
    International Centre Brewing & Distilling
    >+ Whisky
Malta & Maltese people
    Centre Mediterranean Studies [Exeter]
    Centre Mediterranean Studies [Leeds]
Management
    Advanced Institute Management Research
    Ashley Centre Professional Management
    Ashridge Strategic Management Centre
    Business & Management Research Institute [Bedfordshire]
    Business & Management Research Institute [Ulster]
    Business, Management, Accountancy & Finance Subject Centre
    Centre Advanced Management Research
    Centre Career Management Skills
    Centre Enterprise & Management Innovation
    Centre Enterprise Management
    Centre Enterprise, Quality & Management
    Centre Entrepreneurial Management
    Centre Financial & Management Studies
    Centre International Business & Management
    Centre Management & Business Research
    Centre Reputation Management through People
    Centre Research Management Expatriation
    Centre Social Responsibility Accounting & Management
    Centre Strategic Studies [Anglia Ruskin]
    Centre Strategic Studies [Reading]
    Clifford Chance Centre Management Professional Service Firms
    Cranfield Management Research Institute
    Essex Management Centre
    European Work & Employment Research Centre
    Graduate Institute Management & Organisation Research
    Grubb Institute Behavioural Studies
    Huck Centre Management Research
    Hull Centre Management Development
    Innovative Manufacturing Research Centre - Management IMRC
    Institute Advanced Studies Social & Management Sciences
    Institute Governance & Public Management
    International Centre Higher Education Management
    Lancaster Centre Management China
    Management Construction Research Centre
    Management & Enterprise Development Centre
    Management & Management Sciences Research Institute
    Management Research Centre [London Metropolitan]
    Management Research Centre [Wolverhampton]
    Management Studies Centre
    Professional & Management Development Centre
    Research Centre Advancing Innovation & Management
    Research Institute Business & Management
    Research Institute Public Policy & Management
    >+ Business headings
Management buy-outs
    Centre Management Buy-Out Research
Management education & training
    Centre Director Education

Centre Management Creativity
Centre Management Learning & Development
Centre Research Six Sigma & Process Improvement
European Centre Management Education
Judge Institute Management Studies
Sunley Management Centre
Manufacturing technology
    Advanced Manufacturing Research Centre
    Advanced Manufacturing Technology Research Institute
    Brunel Centre Manufacturing Metrology
    Cardiff University Innovative Manufacturing Research Centre
    Centre Design Innovation
    Centre Design Research
    Centre Industrial Automation & Manufacture
    Centre Innovative Manufacture & Machine Vision Systems
    Centre Manufacturing
    Centre Mechatronics & Manufacturing Systems
    Control Engineering Research Centre
    Cranfield Innovative Manufacturing Research Centre
    Exeter Manufacturing Enterprise Centre
    Innovative Electronics Manufacturing Research Centre
    Innovative Manufacturing Research Centre - Engineering IMRC
    Innovative Manufacturing Research Centre - Management IMRC
    Innovative Manufacturing Research Centre (IMRC) Bioprocessing
    Institute Manufacturing
    International Manufacturing Centre
    Manufacturing Engineering Centre
    Manufacturing Science & Engineering Research Centre
    Manufacturing Systems Centre
    Manufacturing Systems Integration Research Institute
    Modelling Research Centre
    Northern Ireland Technology Centre
    Nottingham Innovative Manufacturing Research Centre
    Operations Management Research Centre
    Regional Centre Manufacturing Industry
    Scottish Manufacturing Institute
    Teesside Manufacturing Centre
    Warwick Innovative Manufacturing Research Centre
Manx studies
    Centre Manx Studies
Maps
    National Map Centre
    National Monuments Record Centre
Marine archaeology & history
    Centre Imperial & Maritime Studies
    Centre Marine & Coastal Archaeology
    Centre Maritime Archaeology [Southampton]
    Centre Maritime Historical Studies
    Centre Port & Maritime History
    Maritime Historical Studies Centre
    Oxford Centre Maritime Archaeology
    Shipwreck & Coastal Heritage Centre
Marine law > Law: marine
Marine research & technology
    Centre Coastal & Marine Research
    Centre Marine Biology & Biotechnology
    Centre Marine Hydrodynamics
    Centre Marine Resources & Mariculture
    Gatty Marine Research Institute
    Glasgow Marine Technology Centre
    Greenwich Maritime Institute
    Institute Marine Sciences
    International Centre Island Technology
    Lairdside Maritime Centre
    London Centre Marine Technology
    Marine Biology & Ecology Research Centre
    Marine Institute
    Marine Pollution Information Centre
    Marine Structures Research Centre
    NAFC Marine Centre
    Ocean Systems Laboratory

Ship Stability Research Centre
Marine safety & security
    Lifeboat Support Centre
    Seafarers International Research Centre
Maritime > Marine headings
Marketing
    Business-to-Business Marketing Research Centre
    Centre Marketing
    Centre Research Marketing [Aberystwyth]
    Centre Research Marketing [Brunel]
    Centre Research Marketing [London Metropolitan]
    Centre Research Marketing [Westminster]
    Centre Research Marketing [Salford]
    Cranfield Centre Advanced Research Marketing
    Ehrenberg Centre Research Marketing
    Institute Social Marketing
    International Marketing & Purchasing Centre
Marriage & marital studies
    Newcastle Centre Family Studies
    Tavistock Institute Human Relations
Masks
    Scottish Mask & Puppet Centre
Mass spectrometry > Spectrometry & mass spectrometry
Massage
    Chiron Centre Ltd
    Centre Contemporary Visual & Material Culture
Material culture
    Centre Fashion, the Body & Material Cultures
> Cultural studies
Materials management / handling
    Centre Industrial Bulk Solids Handling
    Wolfson Centre Bulk Solids Handling Technology
Materials science & technology
    Advanced Materials & Biomaterials Research Centre
    Advanced Materials Centre
    Advanced Materials Research Institute
    Centre Advanced & Renewable Materials
    Centre Interfaces & Materials
    Centre Materials Research [University College London]
    Centre Materials Research [Queen Mary, London]
    Centre Materials Science
    Centre Materials Science & Engineering [Edinburgh]
    Centre Materials Science Research
    Centre Materials, Surfaces & Structural Systems
    Centre Nanoporous Materials
    Centre Research Analytical, Materials & Sensor Science
    Centre Research Leather & Materials Science
    Dalton Research Institute
    Experimental Techniques Centre
    Institute Advanced Materials & Energy Systems
    Institute Materials Research [Leeds]
    Institute Materials Research [Salford]
    Institute Polymer Technology & Materials Engineering
    Interdisciplinary Research Centre Materials Processing
    Loughborough Materials Characterisation Centre
    Materials & Arts Research Centre
    Materials & Engineering Research Institute
    Materials Analysis & Research Services - Centre Industrial
        Collaboration
    Materials Performance Centre
    Materials Research Centre [Bath]
    Materials Research Centre [Swansea]
    Materials Science Research Centre
    Modelling Research Centre
    Molecular Materials Centre
    Northern Ireland Centre Advanced Materials
    Oxford Centre Advanced Materials & Composites
    Research Institute Flexible Materials
    Saint Andrews Centre Advanced Materials
    Sheffield Centre Advanced Magnetic Materials & Devices
    UK Centre Materials Education
    UniS Materials Institute
    University Nottingham Institute Materials Technology
    Wolfson Centre Materials Processing

Wolfson Materials & Catalysis Centre
    >+ Composites & composite materials; specific materials
Maternity > Birth & birth control; Child headings; Family
    headings; Pregnancy
Mathematics
    AHRC Research Centre Philosophy Logic, Language,
        Mathematics & Mind
    Alan Turing Institute
    Brunel Institute Computational Mathematics
    Centre Discrete & Applicable Mathematics
    Centre History Mathematical Sciences
    Centre Industrial Mathematical Modelling
    Centre Innovation Mathematics Teaching
    Centre Interdisciplinary Mathematical Research
    Centre Interdisciplinary Research Computational Algebra
    Centre Mathematical Modelling & Flow Analysis
    Centre Mathematical Science
    Centre Mathematical Sciences
    Centre Mathematics & Physics Life Sciences & Experimental
        Biology
    Centre Mathematics & Statistics
    Centre Mathematics Applied Life Sciences
    Centre Nonlinear Mathematics & Applications
    Centre Open Learning Mathematics, Science, Computing &
        Technology
    Centre Studies Science & Mathematics Education
    Centre Study Mathematics Education
    Centre Theoretical Modelling Medicine
    Derbyshire Further Mathematics Centre
    Institute Mathematical & Physical Sciences
    Institute Mathematical Sciences [Imperial College, London]
    Institute Mathematics, Statistics & Actuarial Science
    International Centre Mathematical Sciences
    Isaac Newton Institute Mathematical Sciences
    Lighthill Institute Mathematical Sciences
    London Mathematics Centre
    Manchester Institute Mathematical Sciences
    Mathematical Institute
    Mathematics Education Centre
    Mathematics Learning Support Centre
    Mathematics Research Centre [Queen Mary, London]
    Mathematics Research Centre [Warwick]
    Mathematics, Statistics & Operational Research Subject
        Centre
    Maxwell Institute Mathematical Sciences
    Oxford Centre Industrial & Applied Mathematics
    Research Institute Environment, Physical Sciences & Applied
        Mathematics
    Scottish Informatics, Mathematics, Biology & Statistics Centre
    Smith Institute Industrial Mathematics & System Engineering
    Statistics, Operational Research & Mathematics Research
        Centre
    Warwick Mathematics Institute
Maxillofacial surgery
    Centre Clinical & Diagnostic Oral Sciences
Measurement > Metrology
Mechanical engineering
    Centre Mechatronics & Manufacturing Systems
    Civil & Computational Engineering Centre
    Institute Theoretical, Applied & Computational Mechanics
Mechatronics
    Centre Mechatronics & Manufacturing Systems
Mechatronics
    Mechatronics Research Centre
Media
    Art & Media Arts Research Centre
    Art Design Media Subject Centre
    Broadcast Advertising Clearance Centre
    Brunel Advanced Institute Multimedia & Network Systems
    Centre Creative & Performing Arts
    Centre Creative Media Research
    Centre Excellence Media Practice
    Centre Interactive Media
    Centre Intermedia

© CBD Research Ltd · Beckenham · Kent BR3 5JS · Tel 020 8650 7745 · Fax 020 8650 0768 · E-mail cbd@cbdresearch.com · www.cbdresearch.com

Centre International Media Analysis
Centre Languages, English & Media Education
Centre Mass Communication Research
Centre Media & Communications Research
Centre Media & Film Studies
Centre Media: Globalisation: Risk
Centre Media Research [Portsmouth]
Centre Media Research [Ulster]
Centre Media Sound
Centre Media, Arts & Performance
Centre New Media Research
Centre Research & Education Art & Media
Centre Research Media & Cultural Studies
Communication & Media Research Institute
Communication, Cultural & Media Studies Research Centre
Communication, Media & Communities Research Centre
Glenamara Centre International Research Arts & Society
Knowledge Media Institute
Media Technology Research Centre
Mixed Media Grid [Research Centre]
Music, Media & Performing Arts Research Centre
Screen Media Research Centre
Slade Centre Electronic Media Fine Art
Stirling Media Research Institute
Tom Hopkinson Centre Media Research
Centre Advanced Development Creative Industries [Bangor]
Centre Advanced Development Creative Industries [Portsmouth]
Mediation > Arbitration & mediation
Medical apparatus & appliances > Medical technology
Medical education
Centre Bioinformatics & Medical Informatics Training
Centre Cell
Centre Excellence Teaching & Learning Developing Professionalism Medical Students
Centre Medical & Healthcare Education
Centre Medical Education [Dundee]
Centre Medical Education [Lancaster]
Centre Medical Education [Queen Mary, London]
Centre Primary Health & Social Care
Open University Centre Education Medicine
Postgraduate Institute Medicine & Dentistry
Queen's Medical Centre
Trafford Centre Graduate Medical Education & Research
Welsh Centre Pharmacy Postgraduate Education
Welsh Institute Minimal Access Therapy
Medical engineering
Institute Medical & Biological Engineering
Institute Medical Engineering & Medical Physics
Medical ethics
Centre Human Science & Medical Ethics
Centre Medical Law & Ethics
Ethox Centre
Linacre Centre Health Care Ethics
Medical history
Centre Medical History
Medical law > Law: medical
Medical physics
Institute Medical Engineering & Medical Physics
Medical research
AIMS Centre (Applied & Integrated Medical Sciences)
Cambridge Institute Medical Research
Centre Evidence-Based Medicine
Centre Integrated Genomic Medical Research
Centre Mathematical Medicine
Institute Medical & Social Care Research
Medical Research Council Collaborative Centre
National Institute Medical Research
Queen's Medical Research Institute
Sir Leon Bagrit Centre
Trafford Centre Graduate Medical Education & Research
William Harvey Research Institute
>+ Health research
Medical sensors > Sensors

Medical technology
Bath Institute Medical Engineering
Centre Measurement & Information Medicine
Centre Medical Engineering & Technology
Doctoral Training Centre Medical Devices
Teesside Medical Computing Centre
Medical trials
Resource Centre Randomised Trials
Medicine & sport > Sports: medicine & therapy
Medicine > Pharmaceuticals & pharmacology; specific type
Medicine: alternative > Complementary medicine; specific type
Medicine: Chinese > Chinese medicine
Medicine: complementary > Complementary medicine
Medicine: herbal > Herbs & herbal medicine
Medicine: history of
Centre History Medicine & Disease
Centre History Medicine [Birmingham]
Centre History Medicine [Glasgow]
Centre History Medicine [Newcastle]
Centre History Medicine [Warwick]
Centre History Science, Technology & Medicine
Northern Centre History Medicine
Medicine: preventive > Preventive medicine
Medieval studies
Canterbury Centre Medieval & Tudor Studies
Centre Antiquity & Middle Ages
Centre Late Antique & Medieval Studies
Centre Medieval & Renaissance Studies [Durham]
Centre Medieval Studies [Bangor]
Centre Medieval Studies [Bristol]
Centre Medieval Studies [Exeter]
Centre Medieval Studies [York]
Centre Study Medieval Society & Culture
Glasgow Centre Medieval & Renaissance Studies
Graduate Centre Medieval Studies
Institute Medieval Studies [Lampeter]
Institute Medieval Studies [Leeds]
Institute Medieval Studies [Nottingham]
Liverpool Centre Medieval Studies
Medieval Research Centre
>+ Anglo-Saxon era
Meditation
Birmingham Buddhist Centre
Brighton Buddhist Centre
Bristol Buddhist Centre
Cambridge Buddhist Centre
Croydon Buddhist Centre
Edinburgh Buddhist Centre
Glasgow Buddhist Centre
Lancashire Buddhist Centre
Leeds Buddhist Centre
London Buddhist Centre
Manchester Buddhist Centre
North London Buddhist Centre
Norwich Buddhist Centre
Self Realisation Meditation Healing Centre
West London Buddhist Centre
Mediterranean studies
Centre Euro-Mediterranean Studies
Centre Late Antiquity
Centre Mediterranean Studies [Exeter]
Centre Mediterranean Studies [Leeds]
Membranes
Centre Complex Fluids Processing
Centre Ion Conducting Membranes
Institute Membrane & Systems Biology
Memory > Cognitive science
Men's health
Centre Men's Health
Mental health
Academic Centre Defence Mental Health
Centre Ageing & Mental Health
Centre Ageing & Mental Health Sciences
Centre Citizenship & Community Mental Health

Centre Community Mental Health
Centre Economics Mental Health
Centre Evidence-Based Mental Health
Centre Excellence Applied Research Mental Health
Centre Excellence Interdisciplinary Mental Health
Centre Nursing & Allied Health Professionals Research
Centre Public Engagement Mental Health Sciences
Dementia Services Development Centre [Stirling]
Mental Health Knowledge Centre
Mood Disorders Centre
National Collaborating Centre Mental Health
Sainsbury Centre Mental Health
Social, Genetic & Developmental Psychiatry Centre
Tizard Centre
Wales Centre for Mental Health Service Development
WHO Collaborating Centre Research & Training Mental Health
WHO Collaborating Centre & Section Mental Health Policy
Metabolic medicine
Centre Diabetes & Metabolic Medicine
Metals & metallurgy
Brunel Centre Advanced Solidification Technology
Castings Centre
Castings Technology International
Institute Archaeo-Metallurgical Studies
Metal Joining Research Centre
National Metals Technology Centre
Sheffield University Metals Advisory Centre
Wolfson Heat Treatment Centre
World Bureau Metal Statistics
Meteorology
BBC Weather Centre
Bristol Biogeochemistry Research Centre
Bristol Glaciology Centre
Centre Analysis Time Series
Centre Atmospheric Science
Centre Global Atmospheric Modelling
Centre Observation Air-Sea Interactions & Fluxes
Chrono Centre Climate, Environment, & Chronology
Climate & Land-Surface Systems Interaction Centre
European Centre Medium-Range Weather Forecasts
Institute Atmospheric Science
Joint Centre Mesoscale Meteorology
National Centre Atmospheric Science
Methodology
Centre Research Statistical Methodology
Methodology Institute
Social Research Methodology Centre
Stirling Centre Economic Methodology
Metrology
Brunel Centre Manufacturing Metrology
Fluid Loading & Instrumentation Centre
Measurement & Instrumentation Centre
Mitutoyo Metrology Centre
Metropolitan history
Centre Metropolitan History
Mexico > Latin America
Microanalysis > Microscopy
Microbiology
Antimicrobial Research Centre
Centre Ecology & Hydrology
Centre Molecular Microbiology & Infection
Institute Biological Sciences
>+ Biology & biological research
Microelectronics
Emerging Technologies Research Centre
Microelectronics Industrial Centre
Microelectronics Research Centre
Microsystems and Nanotechnology Centre
Microfabrication > Nanoscience & nanotechology
Microscopy
Advanced Microscopy Centre
Centre Advanced Microscopy [Reading]
Centre Electron Microscopy

Centre Environmental Scanning Electron Microscopy
Experimental Techniques Centre
Institute Polymer Technology & Materials Engineering
Plymouth Electron Microscopy Centre
Sheffield University Metals Advisory Centre
Sorby Centre Electron Microscopy & Microanalysis
Sussex Centre Advanced Microscopy
Microwaves
MIcroSystems Engineering Centre
Middle Ages > Medieval studies
Middle East
Centre International Studies & Diplomacy
Centre International Studies [Cambridge]
Centre International Studies [Leeds]
Centre International Studies [London School of Economics & Political Science]
Centre International Studies [Oxford]
Centre Islamic & Middle East Law
Centre Islamic Studies [School of Oriental & African Studies, London]
Centre Middle Eastern & Islamic Studies [Cambridge]
Gulf Centre Strategic Studies
Institute Arab & Islamic Studies
Institute Middle East, Central Asia & Caucasus Studies
Institute Middle Eastern & Islamic Studies
Institute Middle Eastern Studies
Khalili Research Centre Art & Material Culture Middle East
London Middle East Institute
Middle East Centre
>+ individual countries
Midwifery
Caledonian Nursing & Midwifery Research Centre
Centre Advanced Studies Nursing
Centre Nursing & Midwifery Research
Centre Research Midwifery & Childbirth
Centre Research Nursing & Midwifery Education
Global Network World Health Organisation Collaborating Centres Nursing & Midwifery Development
Institute Nursing & Midwifery [Brighton]
Institute Nursing & Midwifery [Middlesex]
Institute Nursing Research
Joanna Briggs Institute
Salford Centre Nursing, Midwifery & Collaborative Research
WHO Collaborating Centre Midwifery
WHO Collaborating Centre Nursing & Midwifery Education, Research & Practice
Migration
Centre Migration, Policy & Society
Centre Research & Analysis Migration
Centre Study Migration
Sussex Centre Migration Research
Military history
Churchill Archives Centre
Liddell Hart Centre Military Archives
Milk
Hannah Research Institute
Minerals
Bone & Mineral Centre
Centre Energy, Petroleum & Mineral Law & Policy
Nottingham Mining & Mineral Centre
Minorities > Ethnicity & ethnic minorities; Immigrants & refugees
Missionary organisations > Christian activities & religion
Mobile communications > Telecommunications
Mobilities research
Centre Mobilities Research
Mobility aids > Disabled people: mobility
Modern languages > Language teaching & research
Modernism
Centre Modernist Studies
Molecular biology
Astbury Centre Structural Molecular Biology
Cancer Research UK Centre Cell & Molecular Biology
Centre Molecular Cell Biology
Institute Medical Sciences [Aberdeen]

© CBD Research Ltd · Beckenham · Kent BR3 5JS · Tel 020 8650 7745 · Fax 020 8650 0768 · E-mail cbd@cbdresearch.com · www.cbdresearch.com

Institute Molecular & Cellular Biology
Institute Structural & Molecular Biology [Edinburgh]
Institute Structural Molecular Biology [Birkbeck, London]
Weatherall Institute Molecular Medicine
Molecular science
    Centre Cell & Molecular Dynamics
    Centre Molecular Biosciences
    Centre Molecular Design
    Centre Molecular Drug Design
    Centre Molecular Medicine
    Centre Molecular Microbiology & Infection
    Centre Molecular & Nanoscale Electronics
    Centre Molecular Oncology
    Centre Self-Organising Molecular Systems
    Institute Bioelectronic & Molecular Microsystems
    Leeds Institute Molecular Medicine
    Molecular Materials Centre
    Molecular Organisation & Assembly Cells (MOAC) Doctoral
        Training Centre
    MRC UCL Centre Medical Molecular Virology
    Unilever Centre Molecular Science Informatics
    Williamson Research Centre Molecular Environmental
        Science
    Wolfson Centre Rational Design Molecular Diagnostics
    Wolfson Molecular Imaging Centre
    >+ Biomolecular science
Monitoring systems > Sensors
Monkeys
    Monkey World Ape Rescue Centre
Montessori education
    Montessori Centre International
Monuments
    National Monuments Record Centre
Mood disorders > Mental health
Morphology
    Centre Micromorphology
Mortality studies
    Continuous Mortality Investigation Bureau
Mothers > Birth & birth control; Child headings; Family
    headings; Pregnancy
Motion control
    Centre Power Transmission & Motion Control
    >+ Fluids, fluidics & fluid mechanics
Motion research
    Institute Motion Tracking & Research
Motor disorders
    National Institute Conductive Education
    PACE Centre
    Scottish Centre Children with Motor Impairments
Motor drives
    Nottingham University Electrical Drives Centre
Motor heritage
    Heritage Motor Centre
Motor industry
    Automotive Engineering Centre
    Centre Automotive Industries Management
    Centre Automotive Industry Research
    Centre Automotive Management
    Centre Automotive Systems, Dynamics & Control
    Institute Automotive & Manufacturing Advanced Practice
    International Automotive Research Centre
    Vehicle Technology Research Centre
Motor insurance
    Motor Insurance Repair Research Centre
    Motor Insurers Bureau
Motor neurone disease
    MRC Centre Neurodegenerative Research
Mountains
    Centre Mountain Studies
Movement (human)
    Institute Biophysical & Clinical Research Human Movement
    Research Centre Clinical Kinaesiology
Movements
    Centre Study Social & Political Movements

Movements
    Centre Study Socialist Theory & Movement
Multiple sclerosis
    Inflammation Research Centre
    Multiple Sclerosis Resource Centre
Munitions testing
    Cranfield Ordnance Test & Evaluation Centre
Murdoch (Iris)
    Centre Iris Murdoch Studies
Musculo-skeletal science > Bones & bone disease
Museums
    Centre Museology
    Irish Linen Centre & Lisburn Museum
    Museum Costume & Fashion Research Centre
    Museum Documentation Centre
    Museums, Galleries & Collections Institute
Music
    AHRC Research Centre Cross-Cultural Music & Dance
        Performance [Roehampton]
    AHRC Research Centre Cross-Cultural Music & Dance
        Performance [School of Oriental & African Studies,
        London]
    AHRC Research Centre Cross-Cultural Music & Dance
        Performance [Surrey]
    AHRC Research Centre History & Analysis Recorded Music
    Barber Institute Fine Arts
    British Music Information Centre
    Central European Music Research Centre
    Centre Creative & Performing Arts
    Centre Intercultural Music
    Centre Music Theatre
    Centre Performance History
    Centre Research Creation Performing Arts
    Centre Research Opera & Music Theatre
    Centre Study Composition Screen
    Centre Study Music Performance
    Institute Advanced Musical Studies
    Institute Musical Research
    Manchester Centre Music Culture
    Music, Media & Performing Arts Research Centre
    PALATINE - Dance, Drama & Music
    Scottish Music Information Centre Ltd
    South Bank Centre
Music: contemporary
    Centre Contemporary Music
    Centre Contemporary Music Cultures
    Centre Contemporary Music Practice
    Inclusivity Contemporary Music Culture CETL
    International Centre Music Studies
Music: early
    Centre Early Music Performance Research
Music: education & teaching
    Centre Excellence Dynamic Career Building Tomorrow's
        Musician
    Centre Young Musicians [Morley Collge, London]
    International Centre Research Music Education
    Liverpool Institute Performing Arts
    Research Centre Vocational Training Musicians
    RNCM Centre Young Musicians
Music: jazz & blues
    British Institute Jazz Studies
Music: popular
    Institute Popular Music
Music: Russian
    Centre Russian Music
Music: science & technology
    Centre Composition & Performance Using Technology
    Centre Digital Music
    Centre Music Technology [Glsagow]
    Centre Music Technology [Kent]
    Interdisciplinary Centre Computer Music Research
    Interdisciplinary Centre Scientific Research Music
    Music Research Centre
    Music, Technology & Innovation Research Centre

Sonic Arts Research Centre
Music: Welsh
    Centre Advanced Welsh Music Studies
    Welsh Music Institute
Music: therapy
    Nordoff-Robbins Music Therapy Centre
Muslims > Islam & Islamic studies
Myanmar & Burmese people
    Centre South Asian Studies [Cambridge]
    Centre South Asian Studies [Coventry]
    Centre South Asian Studies [Edinburgh]
    Centre South Asian Studies [School of Oriental & African
       Studies, London]
    Centre South Asian Studies [Sussex]

N

Nanoporous materials
    Centre Nanoporous Materials
Nanoscience & nanotechnology
    Centre Molecular & Nanoscale Electronics
    Centre Nanoscale Science
    Centre Nanostructured Media
    Institute Nanoscale Science & Technology
    James Watt Nanofabrication Centre
    Kelvin Nanocharacterisation Centre
    London Centre Nanotechnology [Imperial College London]
    London Centre Nanotechnology [University College London]
    Manchester Centre Mesoscience & Nanotechnology
    Microsystems & Nanotechnology Centre
    Multidisciplinary Nanotechnology Centre
    Nanoscience Centre
    Nanotec Northern Ireland
    Nanotechnology Centre PVD Research
    Teesside Centre Nanotechnology & Microfabrication
    Nottingham Nanotechnology & Nanoscience Centre
National Health Service
    King's Fund Centre
    NHS Institute Innovation & Improvement
National identity
    Cunliffe Centre Study Constitutionalism & National Identity
Native Americans
    Centre Amerindian Studies
Natural history
    Quoile Countryside Centre
Natural sciences
    Centre Philosophy Natural & Social Science
    Experiential Learning Environmental & Natural Sciences
       CETL
    Institute Environmental & Natural Sciences
    Luton Institute Research Applied Natural Sciences
    >+ Geosciences
Nature study > Natural history
Nephrology & urology
    Centre Nephrology
    Institute Nephrology
    Institute Urology
Netherlands & Dutch people
    Centre Dutch Studies
Networks
    Brunel Advanced Institute Multimedia & Network Systems
    Centre Network Research
    Centre Networking & Telecommunications Research
    Centre Telecommunications Research
    Virtual Centre Excellence Mobile Personal Communications
Neurobiology
    MRC Centre Developmental Neurobiology
Neurodegeneration > Motor neurone disease
Neurology & neuroscience
    Autonomic Neuroscience Institute
    Babraham Institute
    Behavioural & Clinical Neurosciences Institute

    Burden Neurological Institute
    Centre Clinical Neuroscience
    Centre Cognitive & Computational Neuroscience
    Centre Community Neurological Studies
    Centre Computational Neuroscience & Robotics
    Centre Developmental Language Disorders & Cognitive
       Neuroscience
    Centre Neuroendocrinology
    Centre Neuroscience Education
    Centre Neuroscience Research
    Centre Signal Processing Neuroimaging & Systems
       Neuroscience
    Centre Theoretical & Computational Neuroscience
    Clinical Neuroscience Centre
    Exeter Centre Cognitive Neuroscience
    Inflammation Research Centre
    Institute Behavioural Neuroscience
    Institute Cognitive Neuroscience
    Institute Movement Neuroscience
    Institute Neurological Sciences
    Institute Neurology
    Institute Neuroscience [Newcastle]
    Institute Neuroscience [Nottingham]
    MacKay Institute Communication & Neuroscience
    Mersey Neurological Trust, Glaxo Centre
    Neuroscience Centre
    Neuroscience Research Institute
    Neurosciences Institute
    Oxford McDonnell Centre Cognitive Neuroscience
    Reta Lila Weston Institute Neurological Studies
    Sir Leon Bagrit Centre
    Sussex Centre Neuroscience
    Walton Centre Neurology & Neurosurgery
New Zealand
    Centre Commonwealth Studies
Newspapers
    Audit Bureau Circulations Ltd
Nineteenth century studies
    Centre European Nineteenth-Century Studies
    Centre Nineteenth-Century Studies [Birkbeck, London]
    Centre Nineteenth-Century Studies [Sheffield]
    >+ Historical research & study
Noise > Sound & vibration research
Non-destructive testing
    Advanced Composites Manufacturing Centre
    National Non-Destructive Testing Centre
    Research Centre Non-destructive Evaluation
Non-governmental organisations
    International Non-Governmental Organisation Training &
       Research Centre
Nonlinear applications
    Centre Nonlinear Dynamics & Applications
    Centre Nonlinear Mathematics & Applications
    Centre Nonlinear Mechanics
    Manchester Centre Nonlinear Dynamics
Nordic studies
    Centre Nordic Studies
    Nordic Policy Studies Centre
    >+ Viking history
Norfolk > East Anglia
North West England
    Centre North-West Regional Studies
Northern Ireland
    Centre Competitiveness
    Institute Ulster-Scots Studies
Novels > Books
Nuclear science & engineering
    Centre Atomic & Molecular Quantum Dynamics
    Centre Cold Matter
    Centre Nuclear & Radiation Physics
    Centre Radiochemistry Research
    Dalton Nuclear Institute
    Institute Nuclear Medicine
    MRC Biomedical NMR Centre

© CBD Research Ltd · Beckenham · Kent BR3 5JS · Tel 020 8650 7745 · Fax 020 8650 0768 · E-mail cbd@cbdresearch.com · www.cbdresearch.com

UHI Decommissioning & Environmental Remediation Centre

Numeracy
National Research & Development Centre Adult Literacy & Numeracy
>+ Mathematics

Numerical modelling
Centre Numerical Modelling & Process Analysis

Nurseries & nursery schools > Education: pre-school

Nursing
Burdett Institute Gastrointestinal Nursing
Caledonian Nursing & Midwifery Research Centre
Centre Advanced Studies Nursing
Centre Evidence-Based Nursing
Centre Nursing & Allied Health Professionals Research
Centre Nursing & Midwifery Research
Centre Primary Care
Centre Primary Health & Social Care
Centre Research Nursing & Midwifery Education
Global Network World Health Organisation Collaborating Centres Nursing & Midwifery Development
Institute Nursing & Midwifery [Brighton]
Institute Nursing & Midwifery [Middlesex]
Institute Nursing Research
International Centre Nursing Ethics
Joanna Briggs Institute
Mary Seacole Centre Nursing Practice
Mary Seacole Research Centre
National Collaborating Centre Nursing & Supportive Care
National Collaborating Centre Primary Care
Nursing, Health & Social Care Research Centre
RCN Development Centre
Salford Centre Nursing, Midwifery & Collaborative Research
WHO Collaborating Centre Nursing & Midwifery Education, Research & Practice

Nutrition
Biomedic Centre
Centre Exercise & Nutrition Science
Centre Gastroenterology & Nutrition
Centre Pregnancy Nutrition
Human Nutrition Research Centre
Institute Brain Chemistry & Human Nutrition
Institute Diet, Exercise & Lifestyle
MRC Centre Nutritional Epidemiology Cancer Prevention & Survival
MRC Resource Centre Human Nutrition Research
Rowett Research Institute
WHO Collaborating Centre Nutrition & Oral Health
>+ Food headings

O

Obesity
Aberdeen Centre Energy Regulation & Obesity
Centre Food, Physical Activity & Obesity

Obstetrics > Birth & birth control; Midwifery; Pregnancy

Occupational health & safety
Centre Occupational Health & Safety [Heriot-Watt]
Centre Working Life Research
Centre Workplace Health
European Centre Occupational Health, Safety & Environment
Healthcare Workforce Research Centre
Institute Occupational & Environmental Medicine
Institute Occupational Ergonomics
Institute Occupational Health
Institute Occupational Medicine
Institute Work, Health & Organisations
Institution Occupational Safety & Health
London Hazards Centre
Robens Centre Occupational Health & Safety
Scottish Centre Occupational Safety & Health

WHO Collaborating Centre Occupational Health & Safety Research

Occupational therapy
Clinical Research Centre Health Professions

Ocean engineering > Offshore & ocean engineering

Oceanography
Bristol Glaciology Centre
Centre Applied Oceanography
Centre Observation Air-Sea Interactions & Fluxes
Centre Space, Atmospheric & Oceanic Science
National Oceanography Centre, Southampton
>+ Marine headings

Offshore & ocean engineering
Fluid Loading & Instrumentation Centre
London Centre Marine Technology
Ocean Systems Laboratory
Scottish Offshore Materials Centre
>+ Marine headings

Oil
Centre Global Energy Studies
Oil Depletion Analysis Centre
Oil & Gas Centre
>+ Lipids

Older people
Centre Ageing Population Studies
Centre Applied Gerontology
Centre Environmental & Social Study Aging
Centre Policy Ageing
Helen Hamlyn Research Centre
Institute Healthy Ageing
Research Institute Care & Elderly
Royal Bank Scotland Centre Older Person's Agenda
>+ Gerontology

Olympic sports
Centre Olympic Studies & Research

Ombudsman schemes
Centre Ombudsman & Governance Studies

Oncology
Centre Medical Oncology
Centre Molecular Oncology
Centre Oncology & Applied Pharmacology
Centre Translational Oncology
Clatterbridge Centre Oncology
>+ Cancer

Operational research
Centre Operational Research & Applied Statistics
Centre Operational Research, Management Science & Information Systems
Mathematics, Statistics & Operational Research Subject Centre
Statistics, Operational Research & Mathematics Research Centre

Ophthalmology > Sight & vision

Optics
Centre Electron Optical Studies
Centre Photonics & Photonic Materials
Laser & Optical Systems Engineering Centre

Optoelectronics
Bookham Centre Excellence Optoelectronic Simulation
Centre Industrial & Commercial Optoelectronics
Centre Integrated Optoelectronic Systems
Optoelectronics Research Centre

Optometry > Sight & vision

Oral health > Dentistry

Ordnance
Centre Ordnance Science & Technology

Ordnance
Cranfield Ordnance Test & Evaluation Centre

Organic research & production
Centre Organic & Biological Chemistry
Elm Farm Research Centre
Organic Centre Wales
Organic Materials Innovation Centre
Organic Semiconductor Centre

Organisational research
    Centre Applied Human Resource Research
    Centre Individual & Organisational Development
    Centre Integral Excellence
    Centre Leadership & Organisational Change
    Centre Organisational Effectiveness
    Centre Organisational Transformation
    Centre Service Management
    Centre Social & Organisational Learning as Action Research
    Complexity & Management Centre
    ESRC Centre Skills, Knowledge & Organisational
        Performance
    Research Centre Organisational Excellence
    >+ Volunteers / voluntary organisations
Oriental studies
    Oriental Institute
    >+ specific countries
Ornithology
    Centre Ornithology
    Edward Grey Institute Field Ornithology
    National Centre Ornithology
    >+ specific types of bird
Orthopaedics > Bones & bone disease
Orthotics > Prosthetics & orthotics
Osmosis
    Centre Osmosis Research & Applications
Osteopathy
    Osteopathic Centre Children
Osteoporosis
    Charles Salt Centre Human Metabolism
Otology
    Institute Laryngology & Otology
Otters
    Skye Environmental Centre Ltd
Ottoman Empire
    Centre Byzantine, Ottoman & Modern Greek Studies
Outdoor sports > Sports
Overseas development > Developing countries & Third World;
    International headings
Owls
    National Birds Prey Centre
    >+ Ornithology

P

Pacific region
    Centre Asia-Pacific Studies
    Institute Asia-Pacific Studies
Packaging technology
    Brunel Centre Packaging Technology
Paediatrics > Children: health
Paget's disease
    Charles Salt Centre Human Metabolism
Pain research
    Centre Pain Research
    Pain Management Research Centre
Pakistan & Pakistani people
    Centre South Asian Studies [Cambridge]
    Centre South Asian Studies [Coventry]
    Centre South Asian Studies [Edinburgh]
    Centre South Asian Studies [School of Oriental & African
        Studies, London]
    Centre South Asian Studies [Sussex]
Palaeoecology
    Centre Human Palaeoecology
    Research Centre Evolutionary Anthropology &
        Palaeoecology
Palliative care
    Sue Ryder Care Centre Palliative & End Life Studies
Palsy
    Sara Koe PSP Research Centre

Paper & paper products
    Centre Materials Research [Queen Mary, London]
    Centre Materials Research [University College London]
Parallel applications
    Centre Parallel Computing
    Edinburgh Parallel Computing Centre
    Parallelism, Algorithms & Architectures Research Centre
    >+ Computer headings
Parasitology
    Centre Applied Entomology & Parasitology
Parasitology
    Wellcome Centre Molecular Parasitology
Parents
    Centre Parent & Child Support
    National Family & Parenting Institute
    Newcastle Centre Family Studies
    >+ Family headings
Partially sighted > Blind & partially sighted
Particle physics
    Centre Advanced Surface, Particle & Interface Engineering
    Centre Particle Characterisation & Analysis
    Centre Particle Physics
    Centre Particle Theory
    Industrial Centre Particle Science & Engineering
    Institute Particle Physics Phenomenology
    Institute Particle Science & Engineering
Pathogens
    Wohl Virion Centre
Pavements & pavement engineering
    Nottingham Transportation Engineering Centre
Peace studies
    Africa Centre Peace & Conflict Studies
    Centre Conflict Resolution
    Centre Peace & Conflict Studies
    Centre Peace & Reconciliation Studies
    International Centre Participation Studies
    Praxis Centre - Centre Study Information & Technology
        Peace, Conflict Resolution & Human Rights
    Richardson Institute Peace & Conflict Research
    Transitional Justice Institute
    >+ Conflict analysis; War studies
Pedagogy > Teachers & teacher training
Penal studies > Prisons
Pensions
    PAPRI: Pension & Population Research Institute
    Pensions Institute
Peptides
    Centre Proteins & Peptides
    Oxford Centre Molecular Sciences
    Strathclyde Institute Drug Research
Perceptual experience
    Centre Study Perceptual Experience
Performance analysis & research
    Centre Performance Analysis
    Centre Performance Evaluation & Resource Management
    Centre Performance History
    Centre Performance Measurement & Management
    Centre Performance Science
Performing arts > Dancing; Music; Theatre & theatre studies
Periodicals
    Audit Bureau Circulations Ltd
    ISSN UK Centre
Personal development
    Institute Development Policy & Management
    Institute Developmental Potential
    Open Centre
Personal safety
    Suzy Lamplugh Trust Research Institute
Personnel management
    Centre Intercultural Development
Pesticides & pest management
    CAB International
    International Pesticide Application Research Centre

   © CBD Research Ltd · Beckenham · Kent BR3 5JS · Tel 020 8650 7745 · Fax 020 8650 0768 · E-mail cbd@cbdresearch.com · www.cbdresearch.com

Rothamsted Centre for Sustainable Pest and Disease Management
    Scottish Crop Research Institute
    Silwood Centre Pest Management
Petroleum
    Centre Energy, Petroleum & Mineral Law & Policy
    Heriot-Watt Institute Petroleum Engineering
Pharmaceuticals & pharmacology
    Centre Clinical Pharmacology & Therapeutics
    Centre Materials Research [Queen Mary, London]
    Centre Materials Research [University College London]
    Centre Oncology & Applied Pharmacology
    CMR International
    Institute Pharmaceutical Innovation
    Institute Pharmaceutical Sciences & Experimental Therapeutics
    National Institute Health & Clinical Excellence
    Northern Ireland Centre Postgraduate Pharmaceutical Education
    Pfizer Institute Pharmaceutical Materials Science
    PharmacoEconomics Research Centre
    Sackler Institute Pulmonary Pharmacology
    Strathclyde Institute Drug Research
    Strathclyde Institute Pharmacy & Biomedical Sciences
    Welsh Centre for Post-Graduate Pharmaceutical Education
    WHO Collaborating Centre Health Policy & Pharmaceutical Economics
Pharmacology > Pharmaceuticals & pharmacology
Philately & postal history
    Crown Agents Stamp Bureau
Philippines & Philippino people
    Centre South Asian Studies [Cambridge]
    Centre South Asian Studies [Coventry]
    Centre South Asian Studies [Edinburgh]
    Centre South Asian Studies [School of Oriental & African Studies, London]
    Centre South Asian Studies [Sussex]
Philosophy
    AHRC Research Centre Philosophy Logic, Language, Mathematics & Mind
    Bakhtin Centre
    Centre Art, Design & Philosophy
    Centre Ethics, Philosophy & Public Affairs
    Centre Fine Art & Philosophy
    Centre History Philosophical Theology
    Centre Philosophical Studies
    Centre Philosophy & Religion
    Centre Philosophy & Value
    Centre Philosophy Natural & Social Science
    Centre Research Modern European Philosophy
    Centre Research Philosophy & Literature
    Confucius Institute
    Institute Philosophy
    Institute Philosophy & Public Policy
    Oxford Centre Ethics & Philosophy Law
    Philosophy Centre
    Subject Centre Philosophical & Religious Studies
Photography
    Bureau Freelance Photographers
    Centre Photographic Research
    Digital & Photographic Imaging Centre
    Durham Centre Advanced Photography Studies
    Photography & Archive Research Centre
Photonics & photon science
    Centre Biophotonics
    Centre Photonics & Photonic Materials
    EPSRC NanoPhotonics Portfolio Centre
    Institute Microwaves & Photonics
    Institute Photonics
    Photon Science Institute
    Photonics Innovation Centre
Photophysics
    Photophysics Research Centre

Photosynthesis
    Robert Hill Institute
Physical abuse > Abuse (physical or sexual)
Physical education & activity
    BHF National Centre Physical Activity & Health
    Centre Food, Physical Activity & Obesity
    Centre Physical Education & Sport Pedagogy
    Chelsea School Research Centre
    Children's Health & Exercise Research Centre
    Human Performance Centre
    >+ Sports headings
Physics > specific area of physics
Physiotherapy
    Clinical Research Centre Health Professions
Pigs
    Pig Disease Information Centre
Pipes & pipelines
    Centre Pipeline Engineering
Place names
    Institute Name-Studies
    Place-Name Research Centre
Placement learning
    Centre Excellence Professional Placement Learning
Planetary science & planets > Astronomy
Planning: town & country
    Cambridge Centre Housing & Planning Research
    Centre Planning Studies
    Geddes Institute
    Institute Spatial & Environmental Planning
    Institute Urban Planning
    International Centre Planning Research
Plants & plant fibres
    BC
    Centre Economic Botany
    Centre Plant Sciences
    Centre Research Plant Science
    Institute Molecular Plant Sciences
    John Innes Centre
    Nottingham Arabidopsis Stock Centre
    Robert Hill Institute
Plasma physics
    Centre Plasma Physics
Pleistocene period
    Centre Quaternary Research
Podcast research
    Centre Podcasting Research
Podiatry > Chiropody
Poetry
    Basil Bunting Poetry Centre
    Centre Modern Poetry
    Centre Rhetoric & Cultural Poetics
    Contemporary Poetics Research Centre
    Manchester Poetry Centre
    Poetry Translation Centre
    R S Thomas Study Centre
    Research Centre Modern & Contemporary Poetry
    Stirling Centre Poetry
    Tennyson Research Centre
    Wordsworth Centre
    >+ Literature
Poison > Toxicology
Poland & Polish people
    Centre Research Polish History
Polarography & polarology
    British Polarographic Research Institute
    Centre Polar Observation & Modelling
    Scott Polar Research Institute
Police
    Centre Public Services
    Centre Public Services Management [Nottingham Trent]
    Centre Public Services Management [Teesside]
    Centre Public Services Organisations
    European Centre Study Policing
    Institute Criminal Justice

Institute Criminal Justice Studies
Scottish Centre Police Studies
Political studies
    Centre Contemporary History & Politics
    Centre Critical Social Theory
    Centre History Political Thought
    Centre Legislative Studies
    Centre Political & Diplomatic Studies
    Centre Political Song
    Centre Political Theory & Ideologies
    Centre Religion & Political Culture
    Centre Research Social & Political Sciences
    Centre Study Religion & Politics
    Centre Study Social & Political Movements
    Centre Study Socialist Theory & Movement
    Institute Electoral Research
    Institute Political & Economic Governance
    Institute Study Political Parties
    Local Government Chronicle Elections Centre
    Political Economy Research Centre
    Research Institute Law, Politics & Justice
    Subject Network Sociology, Anthropology, Politics
Political studies: democracy & participation
    Brunel Centre Democratic Evaluation
    Centre Citizen Participation
    Centre Democracy & Governance
    Centre Democracy Studies
    Centre Democratic Governance
    Centre Democratization Studies
    Centre Local Democracy
    Centre Studies Democratization
    Centre Study Democracy
    UNESCO Centre Education Pluralism, Human Rights &
        Democracy
Political studies: European
    Centre European Political Communications
    Centre Parties & Democracy Europe
    Centre Study European Governance
    Keele European Research Centre
Political studies: health
    Centre Health & International Relations
Political studies: international
    Centre Global Political Economy
    Centre International Politics
    Centre Politics & International Studies
    Crisis States Research Centre
    Centre Study International Governance
    Glenamara Centre International Research Arts & Society
    Graduate Institute Political & International Studies
Political studies: Irish
    Centre Irish Politics
Political studies: Welsh
    Institute Welsh Politics
Political studies: women
    Centre Advancement Women Politics
Political studies: violence
    Centre Study Radicalisation & Contemporary Political
        Violence
    Centre Study Terrorism & Political Violence
Pollen
    Scottish Centre Pollen Studies
Pollution & pollution control
    Centre Contaminated Land Remediation
    Centre Energy & Environment [City]
    Centre Energy & Environment [Exeter]
    Centre Environmental Health Engineering
    Contaminated Land Assessment & Remediation Research
        Centre
    Institute Environment & Health
    International Pesticide Application Research Centre
    Marine Pollution Information Centre
    >+ Air quality
Polymers
    BC

Centre Interfaces & Materials
Centre Materials Research [Queen Mary, London]
Centre Materials Research [University College London]
Centre Polymer Therapeutics
Cranfield Centre Supramolecular Technology
Institute Polymer Technology & Materials Engineering
Interdisciplinary Research Centre Materials Processing
Interdisciplinary Research Centre Polymer Science &
    Technology [Durham]
Interdisciplinary Research Centre Polymer Science &
    Technology [Leeds]
London Metropolitan Polymer Centre
Materials Research Centre [Bath]
Materials Research Centre [Swansea]
Medical Polymers Research Institute
Polymer Processing Research Centre
Polymer Science Centre
Scottish Polymer Development Centre
Sheffield Polymer Centre
Wolfson Centre Materials Processing
Ponies > Horses & ponies
Popular music > Music: popular
Population studies
    Centre Ageing Population Studies
    Centre Clinical & Population Studies
    Centre Population Sciences
    NERC Centre Population Biology
    Oxford Centre Population Research
    PAPRI: Pension & Population Research Institute
    Sir David Owen Population Centre
Ports & harbours
    Centre Port & Maritime History
Portugal & Portuguese people
    Keele European Research Centre
Postal history > Philately & postal history
Postcodes
    Address Management Centre
Post-colonial era > Colonial research
Post-Communist countries
    Centre Research Post-Communist Economies
    >+ Russia, Central & Eastern Europe
Postgraduate studies > Education: higher
Postmodernity
    Centre Critical & Cultural Theory
Potatoes
    Scottish Crop Research Institute
Poverty
    Brooks World Poverty Institute
    Centre Development Policy & Research
    Centre Study Poverty Social Justice
    Chronic Poverty Research Centre
    Development Research Centre Migration, Globalisation &
        Poverty
    Townsend Centre International Poverty Research
    >+ Developing countries & Third World
Power systems & transmission
    Brunel Institute Power Systems
    Centre Electrical Power Engineering
    Centre Power Transmission & Motion Control
Powertrains
    Powertrain & Vehicle Research Centre
Precision engineering
    Precision Engineering Centre
Precision technology
    Centre Precision Technologies
Pregnancy
    Centre Pregnancy Nutrition
    Centre Reproduction & Early Life
Pre-school education > Education: pre-school
Preventive medicine
    Centre Environmental & Preventive Medicine
    Lister Institute Preventive Medicine
    Wolfson Institute Preventive Medicine

© CBD Research Ltd · Beckenham · Kent BR3 5JS · Tel 020 8650 7745 · Fax 020 8650 0768 · E-mail cbd@cbdresearch.com · www.cbdresearch.com

Primary care
  Centre General Practice & Primary Care
  Centre Nursing & Allied Health Professionals Research
  Centre Nursing & Midwifery Research
  Centre Primary Care
  Centre Primary Health & Social Care
  Centre Research Primary & Community Care
  Centre Research Primary Care
  Institute Community & Primary Care Research
  Institute Postgraduate Medicine & Primary Care
  Institute Primary Care & Development
  Institute Primary Care & Public Health
  National Collaborating Centre Primary Care
  National Primary Care Research & Development Centre
  Primary Care Musculoskeletal Research Centre
  Primary Care Training Centre Ltd
Primary education > Education: primary
Printing
  National Printing Skills Centre
  National Small Press Centre
  Welsh Centre Printing & Coating
  >+ Publishing
Printing: history
  Centre Manuscript & Print Studies
Prisons
  Centre Penal Theory & Penal Ethics
  Centre Sentencing Research
  International Centre Prison Studies
  Prisons Research Centre
Private equity > Investment
Problem-focused therapy
  Centre Problem-Focused Training & Therapy
Process engineering
  Centre Process Analytics & Control Technology
  Centre Process Integration
  Centre Process Integration & Membrane Technology
  Centre Process Systems Engineering
  Food Refrigeration & Process Engineering Research Centre
  Institute Microstructural & Mechanical Process Engineering
  Satake Centre Grain Process Engineering
Professional development
  Centre Professional Development
Professional ethics
  Centre Business & Professional Ethics
  Centre Human Science & Medical Ethics
  Centre Professional Ethics [Central Lancashire]
  Centre Professional Ethics [Keele]
  >+ specific professions
Progressive supranuclear palsy
  Sara Koe PSP Centre
Project management
  Centre Project Management
  National Centre Project Management
Propaganda
  Centre Study Propaganda
Property development & management
  Centre Construction Innovation & Research
  Centre Management Construction
  Centre Property Research
  Centre Real Estate Research
  Construction & Property Research Centre
  European Construction Institute
  Loughborough Innovative Manufacturing & Construction
    Research Centre
Prosthetics & orthotics
  Dundee Limb Fitting Centre
  Interdisciplinary Research Centre Biomedical Materials
  National Centre Training & Education Prosthetics &
    Orthotics
Protein / proteomics
  3rd Generation Proteomics Centre
  Biomedical Research Centre [Sheffield Hallam]
  Cambridge Centre Proteomics
  Centre Amyloidosis & Acute Phase Proteins

  Centre Metalloprotein Spectroscopy & Biology
  Centre Protein & Membrane Structure & Dynamics
  Centre Proteins & Peptides
  Cranfield Biotechnology Centre
  Integrated Protein Research Centre
  MRC Centre Protein Engineering
  Oxford Centre Molecular Sciences
Protest > Activism
Protestants > Christian activities & religion
Psychiatry
  Centre Psychiatry
  Institute Psychiatry
  Social, Genetic & Developmental Psychiatry Centre
Psychoanalysis > Psychotherapy & psychoanalysis
Psychology
  Centre Applied Psychological Research
  Centre Applied Psychology [Leicester]
  Centre Applied Social Psychology
  Centre Criminal Justice Economics & Psychology
  Centre Crisis Psychology
  Centre Diversity & Work Psychology
  Centre Education Psychology Research
  Centre Forensic & Family Psychology
  Centre Psychological Astrology
  Centre Psychological Research Human Behaviour
  Centre Study Anomalous Psychological Processes
  Centre Study Group Processes
  CLIO Centre Applied Psychology
  Industrial Psychology Research Centre
  Institute Human Sciences [Staffordshire]
  Institute Neuro-Physiological Psychology
  Institute Psychological Sciences
  Institute Social Psychology
  Institute Work Psychology
  Institute Work, Health & Organisations
  Psychological Therapies Research Centre
  Psychology Network [York]
  Social Psychology European Research Institute
  Wales Centre Behaviour Analysis
Psychology: health
  Centre Applied Psychology, Health & Culture
  Centre Health Psychology [Queen Margaret]
  Centre Health Psychology [Staffordshire]
  Centre Research Health Behaviour
  Clinical & Health Psychology Research Centre
Psychology: transpersonal
  Centre Transpersonal Psychology
Psychosis > Cognitive science
Psychosocial studies
  Centre Psycho-Social Studies [University of the West of
    England]
  Centre Psychosocial Studies [Birkbeck, London]
Psychotherapy & psychoanalysis
  Centre Cognitive Behaviour Therapy
  Centre Psychoanalysis
  Centre Rational-Emotive Behaviour Therapy
  Chiron Centre Ltd
  Gestalt Centre London
  Help Counselling Centre
  Psychotherapy Centre
Psychotherapy & psychoanalysis: studies & training
  Centre Psychoanalytic Studies
  Institute Psychosynthesis
  Institute Psychotherapy & Social Studies
Psychotherapy & psychoanalysis: young people
  Anna Freud Centre
  Brandon Centre Counselling & Psychotherapy Young People
Public affairs
  Centre Ethics, Philosophy & Public Affairs
  Centre Public Scrutiny
Public communication
  Centre Public Communication Research
Public health
  Centre Active Lifestyles

Centre Public Health
Centre Public Health Research [Brunel]
Centre Public Health Research [Chester]
Centre Public Health Research [Salford]
Centre Public Health Research [West of England]
Centre Spatial Analysis Public Health
Institute Health & Society
Queen Victoria Hospital Blond McIndoe Research
    Foundation
Social Dimensions Health Institute
WHO Collaborating Centre Health Promotion & Public
    Health Development
WHO Collaborating Centre Public Health Issues Congenital
    Anomalies & Technology Transfer
WHO Collaborating Centre Public Health Issues Congenital
    Anomalies & Technology Transfer (Treatment &
    Management Craniofacial Anomalies)
WHO Collaborating Centre Public Health Management
    Chemical Incidents
>+ Communicable diseases; Health care

Public policy
Cambridge Centre Economic & Public Policy
Centre Ethics Public Policy & Corporate Governance
Centre Institutional Studies
Centre Policy Evaluation
Centre Public Policy
Centre Public Policy & Health
Centre Public Policy & Management [Glasgow Caledonian]
Centre Public Policy & Management [Manchester]
Centre Public Policy & Management [Robert Gordon]
Centre Public Policy & Management [St Andrews]
Centre Public Policy Regions [Glasgow]
Centre Public Policy Regions [Strathclyde]
Centre Public Policy Research
Centre Study Public Policy
Centre Well-being Public Policy
Institute Governance & Public Management
Institute Governance, Public Policy & Social Research
Institute Philosophy & Public Policy
Institute Public Policy Research
International Policy Institute
National Centre Public Policy
Nottingham Policy Centre
Research Institute Public Policy & Management
Scottish Centre Public Policy
Scottish Centre Research Social Justice
Social & Policy Research Institute

Public relations
Centre Public Relations Studies

Public sector
Centre Collaborative Intervention Public Sector
Centre Excellence Inter Professional Learning Public Sector
Centre Health & Public Services Management
Centre Market & Public Organisation
Centre Public Services
Centre Public Services Management [Nottingham Trent]
Centre Public Services Management [Teesside]
Centre Public Services Organisations
Community Audit & Evaluation Centre
Institute Public Sector Accounting Research

Publishing
Centre Advanced Development Creative Industries [Bangor]
Centre Advanced Development Creative Industries
    [Portsmouth]
Centre Publishing Studies
Electronic Publishing Innovation Centre
International Rights Centre
National Small Press Centre
Oxford International Centre Publishing Studies
Publishing Training Centre Book House
UCL Centre Publishing

Puppetry
Puppet Centre Trust
Scottish Mask & Puppet Centre

Purchasing & supply
Centre Research Strategic Purchasing & Supply
International Marketing & Purchasing Centre

Q

Qualifications
National Centre Vocational Qualifications
National Recognition Information Centre UK
Qualitative data & research
Centre Qualitative Research
Quality assurance & management
Centre Enterprise, Quality & Management
Centre Information Quality Management
Centre Quality Global Supply Chain
Centre Quality, Innovation & Support
Centre Research Quality
Quality Centre
Quality Education Centre
Wales Quality Centre
Quantum technology & theory
Centre Atomic & Molecular Quantum Dynamics
Centre Particle Theory
Centre Physical Electronics & Quantum Technology
Centre Quantum Computation [Cambridge]
Centre Quantum Computation [Oxford]
Quarries
National Stone Centre
Quaternary research
Centre Environmental Change & Quaternary Research
Centre Quaternary Research
Quebec > Canada & Canadian people

R

Racism > Discrimination
Radiation physics
Centre Nuclear & Radiation Physics
Environmental Radioactivity Research Centre
Radical writing
Raymond Williams Centre Recovery Research
>+ Literature
Radio
Centre Communication Systems Research
Centre Communications Research
Centre Communications Systems
Ofcom Licensing Centre
Radio Advertising Bureau
Virtual Centre Excellence Mobile Personal Communications
Radiometric dating
Environmental Radioactivity Research Centre
Radiotherapy
Clatterbridge Centre Oncology
>+ Cancer
Railways
Centre Rail Human Factors
Didcot Railway Centre
Future Railway Research Centre
Institute Railway Studies & Transport History
Newcastle Centre Railway Research
Rail Research UK
Random systems
Brunel University Random Systems Research Centre
Rape > Abuse (physical or sexual)
Raptors
National Birds Prey Centre
Raptor Centre
Welsh Hawking Centre
>+ Ornithology
Reading > Literacy

© CBD Research Ltd · Beckenham · Kent BR3 5JS · Tel 020 8650 7745 · Fax 020 8650 0768 · E-mail cbd@cbdresearch.com · www.cbdresearch.com

Real estate > Property development & management
Recovery research
    Raymond Williams Centre Recovery Research
    >+ Literature
Recreation > Leisure & recreation
Rectal disorders
    Centre Academic Surgery
Recycling
    Centre Energy & Environment [City]
    Centre Energy & Environment [Exeter]
    Centre Excellence Product Lifecycle Management
    Centre Infrastructure Management
    Steel Can Recycling Information Bureau
    Saint Andrews Reformation Studies Institute
Reformation studies
    Centre Reformation & Early Modern Studies
Refrigeration
    Centre Air Conditioning & Refrigeration
    Food Refrigeration & Process Engineering Research Centre
Refugees & immigrants > Immigrants & refugees
Regeneration
    Applied Research Centre Sustainable Regeneration
    Regeneration Institute
    Scottish Centre Regeneration
    Social Futures Institute
Regional & urban studies
    Centre City & Regional Studies
    Centre Conservation & Urban Studies
    Centre Local & Regional History
    Centre North-West Regional Studies
    Centre Regional & Local Historical Research
    Centre Regional Economic & Social Research
    Centre Study Cities & Regions
    Centre Study Globalisation & Regionalisation
    Centre Study Urban & Regional Governance
    Centre Suburban Studies
    Centre Urban & Community Research
    Centre Urban & Regional Development Studies
    Centre Urban & Regional Studies [Birmingham]
    Centre Urban & Regional Studies [Cambridge]
    Centre Urban Culture
    Centre Urban Development & Environmental Management
    Centre Urban Education
    Centre Urban History
    Centre Urban Policy Studies
    Centre Urban Theory
    European Institute Urban Affairs
    Geographic Virtual Urban Environments [Research Centre]
    Joint Centre Urban Design
    London East Research Institute
    LSE London Centre Urban & Metropolitan Research
    Manchester Centre Regional History
    Martin Centre Architectural & Urban Studies
    North East England History Institute
    Northern Studies Centre
    Urban Renaissance Institute
Regional development
    Centre Enterprise & Regional Development
Regulated industries
    Centre Competition Policy
    Centre Competition & Regulatory Policy
    Centre Corporate Governance & Regulation
    Centre Management Regulation
    Centre Regulation & Competition
    Centre Regulatory Governance
    Centre Regulatory Studies
    Centre Study Regulated Industries
    Cranfield Centre Competition & Regulation Research
    >+ Industry
Rehabilitation
    Centre Brain Injury Rehabilitation & Development
    Centre Clinical & Health Services Research
    Centre Health, Exercise & Rehabilitation
    Centre Rehabilitation & Human Performance Research

Centre Rehabilitation Engineering
Centre Rehabilitation Robotics
Centre Rehabilitation Sciences
Centre Research Rehabilitation
Douglas Bader Centre
Health & Rehabilitation Sciences Research Institute
Institute Rehabilitation [Hull]
Rehabilitation Resource Centre
Sport Performance Assessment & Rehabilitation Centre
Stroke Association Rehabilitation Research Centre
Tayside Orthopaedic & Rehabilitation Technology Centre
Relationship research
    Morgan Centre Study Relationships & Personal Life
Religion
    Centre Advanced Religious & Theological Studies
    Centre Advanced Study Religion Wales
    Centre Comparative Study Modern British & European
        Religious History
    Centre Contemporary & Pastoral Theology
    Centre Gender & Religions Research
    Centre Inter-Faith Studies
    Centre Late Antique Religion & Culture
    Centre Law & Religion
    Centre Ministry Studies
    Centre Pentecostal & Charismatic Studies
    Centre Philosophy & Religion
    Centre Religion & Biosciences
    Centre Religion & Political Culture
    Centre Research Excellence Religion & Theology
    Centre Studies Implicit Religion
    Centre Studies Visual Culture Religion
    Centre Study Literature, Theology & Arts
    Centre Study Religion & Politics
    Centre Study Religion & Popular Culture
    Centre Study Religion Celtic Societies
    Centre Theology, Religion & Culture
    Cult Information Centre
    Heythrop Institute Religion, Ethics & Public Life
    Institute Theology [Belfast]
    Institute Theology, Imagination & Arts
    Interfaith Education Centre
    Lincoln Theological Institute Study Religion & Society
    Manchester Centre Public Theology
    Margaret Beaufort Institute Theology
    Research Institute Systematic Theology
    Subject Centre Philosophical & Religious Studies
    >+ individual church / form of religion
Religious education
    BFSS National Religious Education Centre
    Centre Research & Evaluation
    Centre Research Beliefs, Rights & Values Education
    David Hope RE Centre York
    Keswick Hall Centre Research & Development Religious
        Education
    Welsh National Centre Religious Education
Religious experience
    Centre Research Religious Experience
Remote sensing
    Centre Developing Areas Research
    Centre Remote Sensing & Environmental Monitoring
    Institute Engineering Surveying & Space Geodesy
    World Data Centre Glaciology, Cambridge
Renaissance studies
    Centre Medieval & Renaissance Studies [Durham]
    Centre Renaissance & Early Modern Studies [Queen Mary,
        London]
    Centre Renaissance & Early Modern Studies [York]
    Centre Renaissance Studies
    Centre Research Renaissance Studies
    Glasgow Centre Medieval & Renaissance Studies
    Scottish Institute Northern Renaissance Studies
Renewable energy > Energy efficiency
Reproduction (human) > Fertility treatment; Population studies

Respiration
Centre Respiratory Research [Nottingham]
Centre Respiratory Research [University College London]
Inflammation Research Centre
Respiratory Support & Sleep Centre
Sir Leon Bagrit Centre
Retailing
Centre Hospitality Management & Retailing
Centre Leisure Retailing
Centre Retail Research
Centre Study Retailing Scotland
Glasgow Centre Retailing
Institute Retail Studies
Oxford Institute Retail Management
Retail Centre
Retroviruses
Wohl Virion Centre
Rheumatic diseases > Arthritis & rheumatism
Rights of the individual > Human rights
Risk management (insurance) > Insurance
Risk modelling
Centre Analysis Risk & Optimisation Modelling Applications
Risk research
Centre Risk & Insurance Studies
Centre Risk Management, Reliability & Maintenance
Centre Risk Research
Cullen Centre Risk & Governance
ESRC Centre Analysis Risk & Regulation
Risk Institute
>+ Hazards & risks
Rivers
Centre Land Use & Water Resources Research
Rivers
GeoData Institute
>+ Water
Robotics > Automation & robotics
Roman Catholic Church
Centre Research & Development Catholic Education
Linacre Centre Health Care Ethics
Roman studies
Centre Research East Roman Studies
Durham Centre Roman Cultural Studies
Exeter Centre Hellenistic & Greco-Roman Culture
Logos: Centre Study Ancient Systems Knowledge
>+ Classical studies; Italy & Italian people
Romance languages & period
Institute Germanic & Romance Studies
Romanticism
Centre Research Romanticism
Centre Romantic Studies
Centre Study Byron & Romanticism
Rubber
Centre Materials Research [Queen Mary, London]
Centre Materials Research [University College London]
Engineering & Medicine Elastomers Research Centre
Rugby League
Gillette Rugby League Heritage Centre
Ruminants
BBSRC Institute Grassland & Environmental Research
>+ Cattle; Sheep
Running
International Centre East African Running Science
>+Sports: technology & science
Rural interests & studies
Advancing Skills Professionals Rural Economy CETL
Arthur Rank Resource Centre
Centre Agricultural Strategy
Centre Rural Economy
Centre Rural Health Research & Policy
Centre Rural Innovation
Centre Rural Research
Centre Studies Rural Ministry
Crichton Centre Rural Enterprise
Institute Rural Health

Institute Rural Sciences
Macaulay Institute
National Rural Enterprise Centre
Russia, Central & Eastern Europe
Britain-Russia Centre & British East-West Centre
Centre Central & Eastern European Studies
Centre Economic Reform & Transformation
Centre International Studies & Diplomacy
Centre International Studies [Cambridge]
Centre International Studies [Leeds]
Centre International Studies [London School of Economics & Political Science]
Centre International Studies [Oxford]
Centre Russian & East European Cultural Studies
Centre Russian & East European Studies
Centre Russian & Eurasian Studies
Centre Russian, Central & East European Studies [Glasgow]
Centre Russian, Soviet & Central & Eastern European Studies
Centre Study Central Europe
Centre Study Public Policy
East European Advice Centre
Nottingham Institute Russian & East European Studies
Pan-European Institute
Vinogradoff Institute
>+ individual countries
Russian music
Centre Russian Music

S

Safety
Centre Crowd & Safety Management
Centre Environment & Safety Management Business
Centre Health, Safety & Environment
Centre Occupational Health & Safety [Heriot-Watt]
Cranfield Institute Safety Risk & Reliability
Cranfield Safety & Accident Investigation Centre
Ergonomics & Safety Research Institute
European Centre Occupational Health, Safety & Environment
Institute Safety Technology & Research
John Grieve Centre Policing & Community Safety
National Community Fire Safety Centre
National Safety Centre
Safety Systems Research Centre
Vehicle Safety Research Centre
WHO Collaborating Centre Occupational Health & Safety Research
>+ Occupational health & safety
Sailing
National Watersports Centre
Satellites
Centre Communication Systems Research
Institute Satellite Navigation
Mobile & Satellite Communications Research Centre
Sayers (Dorothy L)
Dorothy L Sayers Centre
Schizophrenia
International Schizophrenia Centre
Prince Wales International Centre Research Schizophrenia & Depression
Schools
Centre Church School Studies
Centre Study Comprehensive Schools
Centre Successful Schools
School Improvement & Leadership Centre
Scottish Centre Studies School Administration
Scottish Schools Equipment Research Centre
>+ Education headings
Science
Adelphi Research Institute Creative Arts & Sciences
Bath Royal Literary & Scientific Institution

© CBD Research Ltd · Beckenham · Kent BR3 5JS · Tel 020 8650 7745 · Fax 020 8650 0768 · E-mail cbd@cbdresearch.com · www.cbdresearch.com

Catchment Science Centre
Centre Applied Science
Centre Life
Centre Research Knowledge Science & Society
Centre Science Communication
Centre Science Extreme Conditions
Complexity Science Research Centre
Imperial College Centre Interfacial Science & Technology
Institute Science & Technology Medicine
Institute Study Science, Technology & Innovation
James Martin Institute Science & Civilisation
Jodrell Bank Science Centre
Oxford Centre Science Mind
Research Centre Applied Sciences
Science & Technology Research Institute
Science Centre
Scientific Analysis & Visualisation Centre
>+ e-Science; specific sciences
Science: applied research
Centre Engineering & Applied Sciences Research
Science: business development
Babraham Institute
Centre Scientific Enterprise
Manchester Science Enterprise Centre
UK Science Enterprise Centres
Science: education
Bristol ChemLabS Centre Excellence Teaching & Learning
Centre Effective Learning Science
Centre Innovation & Research Science Education
Centre Open Learning Mathematics, Science, Computing & Technology
Centre Research Primary Science & Technology
Centre Science Education [Glasgow]
Centre Science Education [Sheffield Hallam]
Centre Studies Science & Mathematics Education
Institute Science Education
Learning Sciences Research Institute
National Science Learning Centre
Science Learning Centre East England
Science Learning Centre East Midlands
Science Learning Centre London
Science Learning Centre North East
Science Learning Centre North West
Science Learning Centre South East
Science Learning Centre South West
Science Learning Centre West Midlands
Science Learning Centre Yorkshire & Humber
Science Studies Centre
Science: history of
Centre History Science, Technology & Medicine
Centre History Technology, Science & Society
Centre Science Studies
London Centre History Science, Medicine & Technology
Scotland & Scottish people
AHRC Centre Irish & Scottish Studies
Britain Visitor Centre
Centre Scottish & Gaelic Studies
Centre Scottish Studies [Aberdeen]
Elphinstone Institute
Fraser Allander Institute Research Scottish Economy
Institute Environmental History
Institute Ulster-Scots Studies
Research Institute Irish & Scottish Studies
Saint Andrews Scottish Studies Centre
Skye Environmental Centre Ltd
Stirling Centre Scottish Studies
Scottish Reformation
Saint Andrews Reformation Studies Institute
Screen > Films & film studies; Television
Seals (mammals)
Orkney Seal Rescue Centre
Security
Applied Research Centre Human Security
Brunel Centre Intelligence & Security Studies

Centre Defence & International Security Studies
Centre Intelligence & International Security Studies
Centre International Co-operation & Security
Centre International Security Studies & Non-proliferation
Centre Managing Security Transitional Societies
Centre Research Inequality, Human Security & Ethnicity
Centre Security Studies
Centre Studies Security & Dipolomacy
Security Studies Institute
UCL Centre Security & Crime Science
Seismology > Earthquake studies
Semiconductors > Electronic industry & engineering
Sensors
Centre Chemometrics
Centre Intelligent Monitoring Systems
Centre Materials Science
Centre Research Analytical, Materials & Sensor Science
Cranfield Biotechnology Centre
Institute Sensors, Systems & Control
Interdisciplinary Research Centre Superconductivity
Wolfson Centre Magnetics Technology
Sensory research (human)
Centre Sensory Impaired People
Sentencing > Prisons
Service & service provision
Centre Research Service
Centre Service Research
Sewage & effluents > Waste management
Sex education & sexuality research
AHRC Research Centre Law, Gender & Sexuality
Centre Gender, Sexuality & Writing
Centre Sexual Health & HIV Research
Centre Sexual Health Research
Centre Study Sexual Dissidence
Centre Study Sexuality & Culture
Gender & Sexuality Research Centre
Gender Institute
Institute Study Christianity & Sexuality
WHO Collaborating Centre Prevention & Control Sexually Transmitted Infections (STI)
Sexual abuse > Abuse (physical or sexual)
Sexual dissidence
Centre Study Sexual Dissidence
Shakespeare (William)
International Shakespeare Globe Centre
Shakespeare Centre
Shakespeare Institute
Share ownership (employee)
Employee Share Ownership Centre
Sheep
Sheep Centre
Sheltered housing
Centre Sheltered Housing Studies
Ships & shipping
American Bureau Shipping
Bureau Veritas
Institute International Shipping & Trade Law
International Centre Shipping, Trade & Finance
London Shipping Law Centre
Ship Stability Research Centre
>+ Marine headings
Shipwrecks
Shipwreck & Coastal Heritage Centre
Shows > Exhibition venues
Sight & vision
Applied Vision Research Centre [City]
Applied Vision Research Centre [Loughborough]
Centre Vision & Visual Cognition
Centre Vision Sciences & Vascular Biology
Centre Vision, Speech & Signal Processing
Institute Ophthalmology
Institute Optometry
International Centre Eye Health
National Eye Research Centre

Ophthalmology & Vision Science Research Centre
Visual Impairment Centre Teaching & Research
Signal processing
Centre Digital Signal Processing
Centre Digital Signal Processing Research
Institute Communications & Signal Processing
Simulation modelling
Centre Applied Simulation Modelling
Singapore
Centre South Asian Studies [Cambridge]
Centre South Asian Studies [Coventry]
Centre South Asian Studies [Edinburgh]
Centre South Asian Studies [School of Oriental & African
Studies, London]
Centre South Asian Studies [Sussex]
Singing
Liverpool Institute Performing Arts
Skin > Dermatology; Disfigurement
Slavery
Institute Study Slavery
Wilberforce Institute Study Slavery & Emancipation
Sleep
Loughborough Sleep Research Centre
Respiratory Support & Sleep Centre
Surrey Sleep Research Centre
Small business > Business: small & medium
Small presses > Printing
Smart cards
Smart Card Centre
Smoking > Alcohol, drug & other addictions
Snow > Glaciology
Social care > Social work & services
Social exclusion
Centre Social & Policy Research
ESRC Research Centre Analysis Social Exclusion
Social inclusion & justice
Centre Research Social Inclusion & Social Justice
Centre Research Socially Inclusive Services
Centre Social Inclusion
Applied Research Centre Sustainable Regeneration
Centre Social Justice [London]
Centre Study Social & Global Justice
Centre Widening Participation & Social Inclusion
Social informatics
Newcastle Centre Social & Business Informatics
Social movements
Centre Study Social & Political Movements
Social policy
Centre Analysis Social Policy
Centre Policy Studies
Centre Research Social Policy
Centre Social Policy Research & Development
Centre Social Research
Health & Social Policy Research Centre
Policy Research Institute [Leeds Metropolitan]
Policy Research Institute [Wolverhampton]
Policy Studies Institute
Social Policy Research Centre
Subject Centre Social Policy & Social Work
>+ Public policy
Social sciences
Alcuin Research Resource Centre
Centre Behavioural & Social Sciences Medicine
Centre Comparative Research Social Welfare
Centre Critical Social Theory
Centre Environmental & Social Study Aging
Centre Health & Social Research
Centre Inquiry-based Learning Arts & Social Sciences
Centre Language Social Life
Centre Narrative Research
Centre Philosophy Natural & Social Science
Centre Regional Economic & Social Research
Centre Research Arts, Social Sciences, & Humanities
Centre Research Social & Political Sciences

Centre Social Research
Centre Theoretical Studies Humanities & Social Sciences
Charles Booth Centre Study History Social Investigation
Crichton Centre Research Health & Social Issues
Education & Social Research Institute
Empeiria Centre
European Centre Analysis Social Sciences
Europe-Japan Social Science Research Centre
Health Communication Research Centre
Institute Applied Social Research
Institute Applied Social Studies
Institute Governance, Public Policy & Social Research
Institute Health & Society
Institute Policy & Practice
Institute Psychotherapy & Social Studies
Institute Research Social Sciences
Institute Social & Health Research [Chester]
Institute Social & Health Research [Middlesex]
Institute Social Research
Institute Social Work & Applied Social Studies
Institute Social, Cultural & Policy Research
Institute Study Language & Social Sciences
Leeds Social Sciences Institute
National Centre Social Research
National Institute Economic & Social Research
Newcastle Institute Arts, Social Sciences & Humanities
Research Centre Social Sciences
Research Institute Health & Social Change
Roehampton Social Research Centre
Scottish Centre Social Research
Social & Policy Research Institute
Social Economy Evaluation Bureau
Social Sciences, Arts & Humanities Research Institute
>+ Psychosocial studies
Social sciences: e-social science
Collaboratory Quantitative e-Social Science [Research
Centre]
ESRC Centre e-Social Science
ESRC National Centre e-Social Science
Modelling & Simulation e-Social Science [Research Centre]
Oxford e-Social Science [Research Centre]
Social sciences: research methods
ESRC National Centre Research Methods
Methods & Data Institute
Social Research Methodology Centre
Social simulation
Centre Research Social Simulation
Centre Excellence Professional Placement Learning
Social work & services
Centre Health & Social Care
Centre Health & Social Care Improvement
Centre Health & Social Care Informatics
Centre Health & Social Care Research [Huddersfield]
Centre Health & Social Care Research [Sheffield Hallam]
Centre Inter-Professional e-Learning Health & Social Care
Centre Post Qualifying Social Work
Centre Primary Health & Social Care
Centre Professional & Organisation Development
Centre Research Health & Social Care
Centre Reviews & Dissemination
Centre Social Care Studies
Centre Social Work
Centre Social Work Research [East London]
Centre Study Policy & Practice Health & Social Care
Criminal Justice Social Work Development Centre Scotland
European Centre Study Migration & Social Care
European Institute Social Services
Institute Health & Community Studies
Institute Health & Social Care
Institute Health & Social Care Research
Institute Health Sciences & Social Care Research
Institute Medical & Social Care Research
Institute Social Work & Applied Social Studies
Nursing, Health & Social Care Research Centre

© CBD Research Ltd · Beckenham · Kent BR3 5JS · Tel 020 8650 7745 · Fax 020 8650 0768 · E-mail cbd@cbdresearch.com · www.cbdresearch.com

Portsmouth Institute Medicine, Health & Social Care
Salford Centre Social Work Research
Scottish Institute Excellence Social Work Education
Social Care Institute Excellence
Social Work Research Centre
Subject Centre Social Policy & Social Work

Socio-cultural studies
Centre Sociocultural & Activity Theory Research
ESRC Centre Research Socio-Cultural Change [Manchester]
ESRC Centre Research Socio-Cultural Change [Open University]

Socio-legal studies
Centre Criminology & Socio-Legal Studies
Centre Socio-Legal Studies

Sociology
Centre Constructions & Identity
Centre Educational Sociology
Centre Human Ecology
Centre Regional Economic & Social Research
Centre Research Medical Sociology & Health Policy
Centre Social Evaluation Research
Centre Social Research
Centre Sociology Sport
Centre Study Knowledge, Expertise & Science
Centre Urban & Community Research
European Work & Employment Research Centre
Glenamara Centre International Research Arts & Society
Institute Social & Economic Research
Sociology Research Centre
Subject Network Sociology, Anthropology, Politics
Sussex Institute
>+ Cultural studies; Human relations

Software
Centre Advanced Development Creative Industries [Bangor]
Centre Advanced Development Creative Industries [Portsmouth]
Centre Advanced Software & Intelligent Systems
Centre Advanced Software Technology
Centre Human Service Technology
Centre Internationalisation & Usability
Centre Research Computer Science
Centre Software Process Technologies
Centre Software Reliability [City]
Centre Software Reliability [Newcastle]
Centre Systems & Software Engineering
Communications & Software Systems Engineering Research Centre
Research Institute Software Evolution
Wessex Institute Technology
>+ Computer headings

Soil
Centre Land Use & Water Resources Research
Centre Micromorphology
Geotechnical Engineering Research Centre
Institute Biological Sciences
National Soil Resources Institute
Rothamsted Centre for Sustainable Soils and Ecosystem Functions
Soil Survey & Land Research Centre

Solar energy
Centre Alternative Technology

Solid-state materials
Interface Analysis Centre

Sonic arts
Sonic Arts Research Centre

Sound & vibration research
Acoustics Research Centre
Centre Energy & Environment [Exeter]
Centre Energy & Environment [City]
Centre Sonochemistry
Centre Sound & Experimental Environments
Engineering Dynamics Centre
Institute Sound & Vibration Research
International Centre Vibro-Impact Systems

Martin Centre Architectural & Urban Studies
Vibration University Technology Centre

Sound recording
Institute Sound Recording

South & South-East Asia > Asia

Southern Africa
Centre Research Economics & Finance Southern Africa
>+ Africa

Soviet Union > Russia, Central & Eastern Europe

Space research & technology
British National Space Centre
Brunel Institute Bioengineering
Centre Earth, Planetary, Space & Astronomical Research
Centre Fusion, Space & Astrophysics
Centre Space, Atmospheric & Oceanic Science
Cranfield Space Research Centre
Institute Engineering Surveying & Space Geodesy
National Space Centre
Planetary & Space Sciences Research Institute
Space Science Centre
Surrey Space Centre

Spain & Spanish people
Cañada Blanch Centre Contemporary Spanish Studies
Centre Catalan Studies
Centre Mediterranean Studies [Exeter]
Centre Mediterranean Studies [Leeds]
Hispanic Research Centre
Keele European Research Centre

Spatial analysis
Centre Advanced Spatial Analysis
Centre Environmental & Spatial Analysis
Institute Spatial & Environmental Planning
Sheffield Centre Geographic Information & Spatial Analysis

Special needs research
Centre Educational Development, Appraisal & Research
Centre Special Needs Education & Research
>+ Children: disabled; Disabled people

Spectrometry & mass spectrometry
EPSRC National Mass Spectrometry Service Centre
Michael Barber Centre Mass Spectrometry
Oxford Centre Molecular Sciences

Spectrophotometry
Scottish Institute Wood Technology

Spectroscopy
Bureau Analysed Samples Ltd
Centre Applied Laser Spectroscopy
Centre Magnetic Resonance Investigations
Centre Metalloprotein Spectroscopy & Biology
Experimental Techniques Centre
Magnetic Resonance Centre
Magnetic Resonance Research Centre
Sir Peter Mansfield Magnetic Resonance Centre

Speech, speech recognition & therapy
Centre Communication Interface Research
Centre Speech Technology Research
Centre Speech, Language & Brain
Centre Vision, Speech & Signal Processing
Communication Aid Centre
Communication Aids Language & Learning
Compass Centre
Human Communication Research Centre
Institute Language, Speech & Hearing
Institute Laryngology & Otology
International Centre Voice
National Information Centre Speech-Language Therapy
Nuffield Hearing & Speech Centre
Speech Science Research Centre

Spine & spinal injury
Centre Spinal Disorders
Centre Spinal Studies
National Spinal Injuries Centre

Spirituality
Centre Spirituality, Health & Disability

Sports
Carnegie National Sports Development Centre
Carnegie Research Institute
Centre Event & Sport Research
Centre Performance Enhancememt
Centre Performance Sport
Centre Scientific & Cultural Research Sport
Centre Sociology Sport
Centre Sport & Exercise Research
Centre Sport & Exercise Science
Centre Sports & Exercise Science
Centre Sports Science & History
Centre Sports Studies
Chester Centre Research Sport Society
English Institute Sport
Hospitality, Leisure, Sport & Tourism Network
Institute Sport & Exercise
Institute Sport & Leisure Policy
Institute Youth Sport
International Centre Sports History & Culture
London Sport Institute
National Watersports Centre
Regional Sports Performance Centre
Research Centre Sport, Exercise & Performance
Research Institute Sport & Exercise Sciences
Sport Industry Research Centre
Sports & Exercise Research Centre
UK Sports Institute
Warwick Centre Study Sport Society
Welsh Institute Sport
>+ specific sport
Sports: coaching
Centre Coaching
Chelsea School Research Centre
SportScotland National Centre, Cumbrae
SportScotland National Centre, Inverclyde
Sports: disabled & handicapped
Peter Harrison Centre Disability Sport
Sports: drug control
Drug Control Centre
Sports: medicine & therapy
Centre Physical Education & Sport Pedagogy
Centre Sports & Exercise Medicine
Human Performance Centre
Institute Sport & Exercise Medicine
Olympic Medical Institute
Sport Performance Assessment & Rehabilitation Centre
Sports: technology & science
Centre Human Performance
Cranfield Centre Sports Surfaces
International Centre East African Running Science
Sri Lanka & Sri Lankan people
Centre South Asian Studies [Cambridge]
Centre South Asian Studies [Coventry]
Centre South Asian Studies [Edinburgh]
Centre South Asian Studies [School of Oriental & African
Studies, London]
Centre South Asian Studies [Sussex]
Stammering
Michael Palin Centre Stammering Children
>+ Speech, speech recognition & therapy
Stamps > Philately & postal history
Stars > Astronomy
Statistics
Centre Applied Medical Statistics
Centre Applied Statistics
Centre Applied Statistics & Systems Modelling
Centre Bayesian Statistics & Health Economics
Centre Mathematics & Statistics
Centre Operational Research & Applied Statistics
Centre Paediatric Epidemiology & Biostatistics
Centre Research Statistical Methodology
Centre Statistics
Institute Mathematics, Statistics & Actuarial Science

Iron & Steel Statistics Bureau
Joseph Bell Centre Forensic Statistics & Legal Reasoning
Mathematics, Statistics & Operational Research Subject
Centre
Robertson Centre Biostatistics
Royal Statistical Society Centre Statistical Education
Scottish Informatics, Mathematics, Biology & Statistics Centre
Southampton Statistical Sciences Research Institute
Statistical Services Centre
Statistics, Operational Research & Mathematics Research
Centre
Teaching Excellence & Mentoring Postgraduates using
Statistics
World Bureau Metal Statistics
Steel > Iron & steel
Stem cell research > Cell engineering & research
Stocks & shares
Centre Financial Markets Research
Centre Research European Financial Markets & Institutions
Employee Share Ownership Centre
Stone
National Stone Centre
Storytelling
George Ewart Evans Centre Storytelling
Scottish Storytelling Centre
Strategic studies
Gulf Centre Strategic Studies
Stress (human)
Centre Stress Management
Centre Stress Research [Reading]
Chester Centre Stress Research
Stress analysis > Non-destructive testing
Structural engineering & materials
Centre Structural & Architectural Engineering
Engineering Structures Research Centre
Innovative Construction Research Centre
Loughborough Innovative Manufacturing & Construction
Research Centre
Space Structures Research Centre
Structural Materials & Integrity Research Centre
UCL NDE Centre
Students
Enabling Achievement within Diverse Student Body CETL
Skill: National Bureau Students with Disabilities
>+ Education headings
Suffolk > East Anglia
Sufism
Institute Arab & Islamic Studies
>+ Islam & Islamic studies
Sugar
Sugar Bureau
Suicide research
University Oxford Centre Suicide Research
Superconductivity
Interdisciplinary Research Centre Superconductivity
Supply > Purchasing & supply
Supply chain management > Logistics; Process engineering
Surface coatings > Coatings & coated products
Surface engineering & science
Centre Advanced Surface, Particle & Interface Engineering
Centre BioArray Innovation
Centre Materials, Surfaces & Structural Systems
Cranfield Centre Sports Surfaces
Experimental Techniques Centre
Institute Surface Science Technology
Materials Research Centre [Bath]
Materials Research Centre [Swansea]
Surface Science & Engineering Centre
Surface Science Research Centre
Surfing
International Surfing Centre
>+ Watersports
Surrealism
AHRC Research Centre Studies Surrealism & Legacies [Essex]

 © CBD Research Ltd · Beckenham · Kent BR3 5JS · Tel 020 8650 7745 · Fax 020 8650 0768 · E-mail cbd@cbdresearch.com · www.cbdresearch.com

AHRC Research Centre Studies Surrealism & Legacies [Manchester]

Surveying
Institute Engineering Surveying & Space Geodesy
Soil Survey & Land Research Centre

Surveys
Cathie Marsh Centre Census & Survey Research
Centre Comparative European Survey Data
Centre Comparative Social Surveys

Sustainable agriculture > Agriculture: sustainable

Sustainable technology
CAB International
Centre Alternative Technology
Centre Developing Areas Research
Centre Environmental Initiatives
Centre Environmental Research
Centre Environmental Research & Training
Centre Environmental Systems Research
Centre Excellence Teaching & Learning Education Sustainable Development
Centre Research Education & Environment
Centre Research Sustainability
Centre Stakeholding & Sustainable Enterprise
Centre Study Environmental Change & Sustainability
Centre Sustainable Aquaculture Research
Centre Sustainable Design
Centre Sustainable Development
Centre Sustainable Energy Systems
Centre Sustainable Futures
Centre Sustainable Power Distribution
Centre Sustainable Technologies
Centre Sustainable Urban & Regional Futures
Durrell Institute Conservation & Ecology
Earthwatch Institute (Europe)
Energy Centre Sustainable Communities
Environmental Research Centre
Environmental Research Institute
ESRC Centre Business Relationships, Accountability, Sustainability & Society
Impact Assessment Research Centre
Institute Energy & Sustainable Development
Institute Environment & Sustainability Research
Institute Environmental Sustainability
Institute Sustainability, Energy & Environmental Management
Institute Sustainable Energy Technology
Institute Sustainable Water, Integrated Management & Ecosystem Research
Macaulay Institute
Max Lock Centre
Natural Resources Institute
Natural Resources Management Institute
Oxford Institute Sustainable Development
Rothamsted Centre Bioenergy & Climate Change
Scottish Centre Sustainable Community Development
Scottish Institute Sustainable Technology
Scottish Universities Environmental Research Centre
SITA Centre Sustainable Wastes Management
Sustainability Centre Glasgow
Sustainability Northwest & National Centre Business & Sustainability
Sustainability Research Institute
Sustainable Cities Research Institute
Sustainable Design Research Centre [Bournemouth]
Sustainable Design Research Centre [Kingston]
Sustainable Development Research Centre
Sustainable Environment Research Centre
Sustainable Technology Research Centre
Sustainable Transport Research Centre
Zuckerman Institute Connective Environmental Research

Syria & Syrian people
Centre Syrian Studies

System analysis > Control engineering & systems

Systems engineering
Systems Engineering Innovation Centre

UCL Centre Systems Engineering

T

Tagore (Rabindranath)
Tagore Centre UK

Taiwan & Taiwanese people
Centre Taiwan Studies

Taxation
Centre Accounting, Finance & Taxation
Centre Tax Law
Oxford University Centre Business Taxation
University Nottingham Tax Research Institute
>+ Fiscal studies

Teachers & teacher training
Central London Professional Development Centre
Centre British Teachers
Centre Creative Empowerment
Centre English Language Teacher Education
Centre English Language Teacher Education & Applied Linguistics
Centre Research Second & Foreign Language Pedagogy
Centre Educational & Academic Practices
Oxford Centre Staff & Learning Development
Pedagogic Research & Scholarship Institute
Subject Centre Education
Teacher & Leadership Research Centre
Welsh Centre Promoting Incredible Years Programmes

Technology
Accelerator Science & Technology Centre
Advanced Manufacturing Technology Research Institute
Advanced Technology Institute
Cardiff Centre Multidisciplinary Microtechnology
Centre New Technologies, Innovation & Entrepreneurship
Centre Research Primary Science & Technology
Centre Scientific Enterprise
Centre Study Technology & Organisations
Centre Technology Management
Centre Technology Strategy
Centre Technology, Production & Ancient Materials
Centre Usable Home Technology
Entrepreneurship Centre [Imperial College London]
EPSRC National Centre III-V Technologies
Imperial College Centre Interfacial Science & Technology
Institute Japanese-European Technology Studies
Institute Study Science, Technology & Innovation
Institute Technology [London Business School]
Kent Technology Transfer Centre
Kroto Research Institute Nanoscience & Technology Centre
Lloyd's Register University Technology Centre
Music, Technology & Innovation Research Centre
Northern Ireland Technology Centre
Praxis Centre - Centre Study Information & Technology Peace, Conflict Resolution & Human Rights
Science & Technology Research Institute
Science Studies Centre
SRIF Centre Virtual Organisation Technology Enabling Research
Technology & Engineering Innovation Centre
Technology Innovation Centre
Wessex Institute Technology

Technology: education
Centre Educational Technology & Distance Learning
Centre Educational Technology Interoperability Standards
Centre Open Learning Mathematics, Science, Computing & Technology
Centre Research Education & Educational Technology
Centre Studies Advanced Learning Technology
Institute Educational Technology
Institute Learning & Research Technology
Learning Technology Research Institute
Robert Clark Centre Technological Education

Teaching & Learning Technology Centre
Technology: history of
  Centre History Science, Technology & Medicine
  Centre History Technology, Science & Society
  London Centre History Science, Medicine & Technology
Tectonics > Earthquake studies
Telecommunications
  Centre Communication Systems Research
  Centre Communications Research
  Centre Communications Systems
  Centre Mass Communication Research
  Centre Mobile Communications Research
  Centre Networking & Telecommunications Research
  Centre Telecommunications Research
  Centre Wireless Network Design
  Institute Advanced Telecommunications
  Intelligent Technologies Research Centre
  Virtual Centre Excellence Mobile Personal Communications
Television
  AHRB Centre British Film & Television Studies
  BBC Television Centre
  Broadcast Advertising Clearance Centre
  Centre Screen Studies [Glasgow]
  Centre Screen Studies [Manchester]
  Institute Film & Television Studies
Tennyson (Alfred, Lord)
  Tennyson Research Centre
Terrorism
  Centre Human Rights Conflict
  Centre Study Terrorism & Political Violence
  Crime & Conflict Research Centre
Testing, non-destructive > Non-destructive testing
Text mining
  National Centre Text Mining
Textiles
  AHRC Research Centre Textile Conservation & Textile Studies
  Biomedical Textiles Research Centre
  Constance Howard Resource & Research Centre Textiles
  Irish Linen Centre & Lisburn Museum
  Textile Conservation Centre
Textual studies > Books; Literature
Thailand & Thai people
  Centre South Asian Studies [Cambridge]
  Centre South Asian Studies [Coventry]
  Centre South Asian Studies [Edinburgh]
  Centre South Asian Studies [School of Oriental & African Studies, London]
  Centre South Asian Studies [Sussex]
Theatre & theatre studies
  Actors Centre
  Centre Ancient Drama & Reception
  Centre Applied Theatre Research
  Centre Creative & Performing Arts
  Centre Excellence Performance Arts
  Centre Excellence Training Theatre
  Centre Multimedia Performance History
  Centre Music Theatre
  Centre Performance History
  Centre Performance Research
  Centre Research Creation Performing Arts
  Centre Research Opera & Music Theatre
  Centre Theatre & Community
  Centre Theatre Research Europe
  Centre Theatre Studies
  Glenamara Centre International Research Arts & Society
  International Shakespeare Globe Centre
  Liverpool Institute Performing Arts
  PALATINE - Dance, Drama & Music
  Performance Translation Centre
  Pinter Centre Research Performance
  Richard Burton Centre Film & Popular Culture
  South Bank Centre
Theology > Religion

Therapeutics
  Centre Clinical Pharmacology & Therapeutics
  Leeds Institute Genetics, Health & Therapeutics
  Research Centre Therapeutic Education
Therapy > specific types of therapy
Thermal studies
  Centre Thermal Studies
Thermodynamics
  Thermo-Fluid Mechanics Research Centre
  Thermo-Fluid Systems University Technology Centre
Thin films
  Thin Film Centre
Third World > Developing countries & Third World
Thomas (R S)
  R S Thomas Study Centre
Thoracic research > Cardiothoracic research
Thrombosis
  Centre Surgical Science
  Eric Bywaters Centre Vascular Inflammation
  Haemostasis & Thrombosis Centre
  Thrombosis Research Institute
Timber > Wood technology
Tissue research
  Cardiff Institute Tissue Engineering & Repair
  Centre Biomaterials & Tissue Engineering
  Centre Regenerative Medicine
  Centre Rheumatology & Connective Tissue Disease
  Centre Tissue Regeneration Science
  Sir Leon Bagrit Centre
  United Kingdom Centre Tissue Engineering [Liverpool]
  United Kingdom Centre Tissue Engineering [Manchester]
Tobacco
  Centre Tobacco Control Research
  >+ Alcohol, drug & other addictions
Tomography
  Industrial Process Tomography Centre
Tourism & travel
  Academic Centre Travel Medicine & Vaccines
  Britain Visitor Centre
  Business Travel Research Centre
  Centre Leisure & Tourism Studies
  Centre Leisure, Tourism & Society
  Centre Tourism
  Centre Tourism & Cultural Change
  Centre Tourism Islands & Coastal Areas
  Christel DeHaan Tourism & Travel Research Institute
  Crichton Tourism Research Centre
  Hospitality, Leisure, Sport & Tourism Network
  Institute Transport & Tourism
  International Centre Tourism & Hospitality Research
  International Institute Culture, Tourism & Development
  Moffat Centre Travel & Tourism Business Development
  Nottingham Trent Centre Travel Writing Studies
  Scottish Centre Tourism
  Scottish International Tourism Industries Research Centre
  Travel Law Centre
  Welsh Centre Tourism Research
Town & country planning > Planning: town & country
Toxicology
  Centre Toxicology
  National Centre Environmental Toxicology
  Therapeutics & Toxicology Centre
  WHO Collaborating Centre Strengthening Poisons Centres Programmes South-East Asia
Trade marks / intellectual property
  AHRC Research Centre Studies Intellectual Property & Technology Law
  Centre Intellectual Property & Information Law
  Centre Intellectual Property Creative Industries
  Centre Intellectual Property Policy & Management
  ICC Counterfeiting Intelligence Bureau
  Intellectual Property Institute
  Oxford Intellectual Property Research Centre
  Centre Trade Union Studies

© CBD Research Ltd · Beckenham · Kent BR3 5JS · Tel 020 8650 7745 · Fax 020 8650 0768 · E-mail cbd@cbdresearch.com · www.cbdresearch.com

Trade unions
>   International Centre Trade Union Rights
Transfusion science
>   Bristol Institute Transfusion Sciences
Translation
>   British Centre Literary Translation
>   Centre Research Translation
>   Centre Translating & Interpreting Studies Scotland
>   Centre Translation & Comparative Cultural Studies
>   Centre Translation & Intercultural Studies
>   Centre Translation Research & Multilingualism
>   Centre Translation Studies [Leeds]
>   Centre Translation Studies [Surrey]
>   Middlesex University Translation Institute
>   Poetry Translation Centre
Translational research
>   Wolfson Centre Translational Research
Transnational studies
>   Centre Transnational Studies
Transpersonal psychology
>   Centre Transpersonal Psychology
>   >+ Psychology
Transport & transportation
>   Centre Air Transport Remoter Regions
>   Centre Aviation, Transport & Environment
>   Centre European, Regional & Transport Economics
>   Centre Excellence Transport & Product Design
>   Centre International Transport Management
>   Centre Transport & Society
>   Centre Transport Policy
>   Centre Transport Studies [Imperial College London]
>   Centre Transport Studies [University College London]
>   Institute Railway Studies & Transport History
>   Institute Transport & Tourism
>   Institute Transport Studies
>   Sustainable Transport Research Centre
>   Transport & Road Assessment Centre
>   Transport Research & Consultancy
>   Transport Research Institute - NI Centre
>   Transport Research Institute [Napier]
>   Transport Technology Ergonomics Centre
>   Wales Transport Research Centre
>   Whalley Centre Transport Studies
Trauma
>   Aberdeen Centre Trauma Research
>   Centre Anxiety Disorders & Trauma
>   Centre Crisis Psychology
>   Centre Trauma, Resilience & Growth
>   Inflammation Research Centre
>   Northern Ireland Centre Trauma & Transformation
Travel > Tourism & travel
Treaties
>   Treaty Centre
Tribology
>   Centre Materials Science
>   National Centre Tribology
Tribotechnology
>   Jost Institute Tribotechnology
Tribunals
>   Centre International Courts & Tribunals
Tropical diseases
>   Sir James Black Centre
Tropical ecosystems
>   York Institute Tropical Ecosystem Dynamics
Tropical medicine
>   Wellcome Trust Tropical Centre
Tumours > Cancer
Turbines
>   Fluid Loading & Instrumentation Centre
Turkey & Turkish people
>   AHRB Centre Byzantine Cultural History
>   Centre Byzantine, Ottoman & Modern Greek Studies
>   Centre Mediterranean Studies [Exeter]
>   Centre Mediterranean Studies [Leeds]

Twentieth century history
>   Research Centre Holocaust & 20th-Century History

U

Ulster & Ulster people
>   Institute Ulster-Scots Studies
Ultrasonics
>   Centre Ultrasonic Engineering
Underwriters > Insurance
Unemployment > Employment
United Kingdom > Great Britain; individual countries
United States of America
>   American (United States) Studies Centre
>   >+ America
Universe (The) > Cosmology
Uplands
>   International Centre Uplands - Cumbria
Urban development
>   Max Lock Centre
Urban studies > Regional & urban studies
Urinary problems
>   Mortimer Market Centre
Urology > Urology & nephrology
>   Institute Nephrology
USA > United States of America

V

Vaccines
>   Academic Centre Travel Medicine & Vaccines
>   Edward Jenner Institute Vaccine Research
>   Health Protection Agency Centre for Infections
Vascular research
>   Sheffield Vascular Institute
>   >+ Thrombosis
Vehicles
>   Powertrain & Vehicle Research Centre
Vehicles
>   Walks Life Heritage Centre
>   >+ Motor industry
Venture capital > Investment
Verification technology
>   Verification Research, Training & Information Centre
Veterinary science
>   Centre Animal Sciences
>   Centre Veterinary Science
>   Institute Animal Health
>   LIVE Centre Excellence Lifelong & Independent Veterinary
>   Education
>   Moredun Research Institute
>   Pig Disease Information Centre
>   Subject Centre Medicine, Dentistry & Veterinary Medicine
>   Veterinary Clinical Skills Centre
>   Veterinary Surveillance Centre [Liverpool]
>   Veterinary Surveillance Centre [Royal Veterinary College]
Vibration > Sound & vibration research
Victorian studies
>   Centre Victorian Art & Architecture
>   Centre Victorian Studies [Chester]
>   Centre Victorian Studies [Exeter]
>   Victorian Studies Centre
Vietnam & Vietnamese people
>   Centre South Asian Studies [Cambridge]
>   Centre South Asian Studies [Coventry]
>   Centre South Asian Studies [Edinburgh]
>   Centre South Asian Studies [School of Oriental & African
>   Studies, London]
>   Centre South Asian Studies [Sussex]

Viking history
    Centre Study Viking Age
    Jorvik Viking Centre
Violence > Abuse (physical or sexual)
Virology
    Centre Virology
    MRC UCL Centre Medical Molecular Virology
    National Centre Human Retrovirology
Virtual engineering
    Virtual Engineering Centre
Virtual environments
    Centre Virtual Environments
    Edinburgh Virtual Environment Centre
Virtual learning
    Access Grid Support Centre
Virtual reality
    Virtual Reality Centre Teesside
Viruses (animal & human)
    Centre Ecology & Hydrology
    WHO Collaborating Centre Characterization Rabies &
        Rabies-related Viruses
    WHO Collaborating Centre Virus Reference & Research
        (Special Pathogens)
Viruses (computer) > Computers: security
Vision > Sight & vision
Visual arts > Art
Visual culture > Cultural studies
Voice > Speech, speech recognition & therapy
Volapük
    Volapük Centre
Volunteers / voluntary organisations
    Aston Centre Voluntary Action Research
    Centre Civil Society
    Centre Nonprofit & Voluntary Section Management
    Centre Voluntary Action Studies
    Charities Information Bureau
    Institute Volunteering Research
    Voluntary Sector Research Centre

W

Wales & Welsh people
    Britain Visitor Centre
    Cardiff Centre Welsh American Studies
    Centre Advanced Welsh & Celtic Studies
    Centre Border Studies
    Centre History Wales & Borderlands
    Centre Modern & Contemporary Wales
    Centre Standardisation Welsh Terminology
    Centre Welsh Language Services
    Welsh Institute Social & Cultural Affairs
War child studies > Evacuees
War studies
    Centre Cultural History War
    Centre First World War Studies
    Centre Study War, State & Society
    Crisis States Research Centre
    Scottish Centre War Studies
    >+ Conflict analysis
Waste management
    Centre Environmental & Waste Management
    Centre Environmental Health Engineering
    Centre Research Energy, Waste & Environment
    Centre Resource Management & Efficiency
    Centre Waste Management
    Integrated Waste Management Centre
    Sheffield University Waste Incineration Centre
    SITA Centre Sustainable Wastes Management
    Urban Water Technology Centre
    Wales Waste & Resources Research Centre
    Water Engineering & Development Centre
    WRc Plc

Water
    Biodeterioration Centre
    Centre Clean Water Technologies
    Centre Energy & Environment [City]
    Centre Energy & Environment [Exeter]
    Centre Environmental Health Engineering
    Centre Land Use & Water Resources Research
    Centre Water Policy & Development
    Centre Water Science
    Centre Water Systems
    European Topic Centre Water
    Flood Hazard Research Centre
    Institute Sustainable Water, Integrated Management &
        Ecosystem Research
    Institute Water & Environment
    Oxford Centre Water Research
    UNESCO Centre Water Law, Policy & Science
    Urban Water Technology Centre
    WHO Collaborating Centre Groundwater Quality
        Assessment & Protection
    WRc Plc
Water: engineering
    Infrastructure Engineering & Management Research Centre
    Water Engineering & Development Centre
    >+ Hydraulics & hydromechanics; Hydrology
Waterfowl > Wildfowl & waterfowl
Watersports
    International Surfing Centre
    National Watersports Centre
    Scottish Water Ski Centre
Waves
    Keele Centre Wave Dynamics
Weapons & weapons testing
    Centre for Ordnance Science and Technology
    Cranfield Ordnance Test & Evaluation Centre
Weather > Meteorology
Welding
    Centre Advanced Joining
    Welding Engineering Research Centre
    Welding Institute
West Africa
    Centre West African Studies
    >+ Africa
Wetlands
    Wetland Archaeology & Environments Research Centre
Wetlands
    Wildfowl & Wetland Trust Centres
Wheelchairs > Disabled people: mobility
Whisky
    Scotch Whisky Heritage Centre
Whistler (James McNeill)
    Centre Whistler Studies
Wild flowers
    National Wildflower Centre
Wildfowl & waterfowl
    Wildfowl & Wetland Trust Centres
    >+ specific forms of wildlife
Wind engineering
    Infrastructure Engineering & Management Research Centre
Wind tunnel testing
    Centre Aeronautics
    Institute Sound & Vibration Research
    Martin Centre Architectural & Urban Studies
Windows
    Centre Window & Cladding Technology
Wines
    English Wine Centre
Wireless > Telecommunications
Wolves
    UK Wolf Centre
Women: health
    ARP Women's Alcohol Centre
    Charles Salt Centre Human Metabolism
    Dugald Baird Centre Research Women's Health

© CBD Research Ltd · Beckenham · Kent BR3 5JS · Tel 020 8650 7745 · Fax 020 8650 0768 · E-mail cbd@cbdresearch.com · www.cbdresearch.com

Institute Women's Health
National Collaborating Centre Women & Children's Health
WHO Collaborating Centre Policy & Practice Development
        Women's Health & Gender Mainstreaming
Women: studies & research
Bedford Centre History Women
Centre Advancement Women Politics
Centre Gender & Women's Studies
Centre Study Women & Gender
Centre Women Business Leaders
Centre Women's Studies [Bath]
Centre Women's Studies [York]
Institute Women's Studies
International Centre Gender & Women's Studies
Lehman Brothers Centre Women Business
>+ Gender studies & research
Women's organisations
London Irish Women's Centre
Pankhurst Centre
Women's Holiday Centre Ltd
Wood technology
Centre Timber Engineering
Scottish Institute Wood Technology
Wool & wool products
Scottish Wool Centre
>+ Textiles
Work placements
Centre Excellence Professional Placement Learning
World affairs > Globalisation & global issues; International
        headings
Worms
Worm Research Centre
Writing & writers
Brunel Centre Contemporary Writing
Centre Academic Writing
Centre Contemporary Writing [Southampton]
Centre Creative Writing
Centre Creative Writing & Arts
Centre Gender, Sexuality & Writing
Centre Writing
Institute International Visual Arts
National Centre Writing
Nottingham Trent Centre Travel Writing Studies
trAce Online Writing Centre
Write Now CETL

Writers Bureau

X

X-rays: applications
Centre Electron Optical Studies
Oxford Centre Molecular Sciences

Y

Yoga
Sivananda Yoga Vedanta Centre
Youth & young people
Brandon Centre Counselling & Psychotherapy Young People
Centre Applied Childhood Studies
Centre Child & Adolescent Health
Centre Children & Youth
Centre Study Childhood & Youth
Centre Study Children, Youth & Media
Centre Youth Work Studies [Brunel]
Centre Youth Work Studies [Strathclyde]
Institute Youth Sport
Interdisciplinary Centre Child & Youth Focused Research
Interface - Centre Interdisciplinary Practice
National Children's Bureau
National Children's Centre
>+ Children headings
Youth & young people: development
Centre Cross Curricular Initiatives
National Star Centre Disabled Youth

Z

Zinc
Zinc Information Centre
Zoology
Institute Zoology